Global Narratives on the Teaching Profession:

Are Teaching Jobs Going to be Extinct?

Natela Doghonadze
https://orcid.org/0000-0001-7333-8692
International Black Sea University, Georgia

Thomas C. De Bello
SUNY Buffalo State University, USA

IGI Global
Scientific Publishing
Publishing Tomorrow's Research Today

Vice President of Editorial — Melissa Wagner
Director of Acquisitions — Mikaela Felty
Director of Book Development — Jocelynn Hessler
Production Manager — Mike Brehm
Cover Design — Jose Rosado

Published in the United States of America by
IGI Global Scientific Publishing
701 East Chocolate Avenue
Hershey, PA, 17033, USA
Tel: 717-533-8845 | Fax: 717-533-7115
Website: https://www.igi-global.com E-mail: cust@igi-global.com

Library of Congress Cataloging-in-Publication Data

Names: Doghonadze, Natela, 1954- editor | De Bello, Thomas, 1943- editor
Title: Global narratives on the teaching profession : are teaching jobs going to be extinct? / edited by Natela Doghonadze, Thomas De Bello.
Description: Hershey, PA : IGI Global Scientific Publishing, [2027] | Includes bibliographical references and index. | Summary: "This book aims to draw attention to the teaching profession, its joys, crucial necessity, and great challenges"-- Provided by publisher.
Identifiers: LCCN 2026005959 (print) | LCCN 2026005960 (ebook) | ISBN 9798337389837 hardcover | ISBN 9798337389844 paperback | ISBN 9798337389851 ebook
Subjects: LCSH: Teaching | Teachers | Educational change | LCGFT: Cross-cultural studies | Interviews
Classification: LCC LB1025.3 .G564 2026 (print) | LCC LB1025.3 (ebook)
LC record available at https://lccn.loc.gov/2026005959
LC ebook record available at https://lccn.loc.gov/2026005960

British Cataloguing in Publication Data
A Cataloguing in Publication record for this book is available from the British Library.

Editorial Advisory Board

Table of Contents

Section 3

Detailed Table of Contents

Chapter 1 describes the challenges faced by educators, the impact of socio-political changes on education systems, and how the prestige of teaching jobs is changing. The level of knowledge and skills in many countries remains low. The reasons include pedagogical and socio-economic factors. Education cannot instantly make socioeconomic inequality, scarcity of resources, increased migration, violence, lack of cultural tolerance, and military conflicts disappear, but it can gradually contribute to struggling these challenges. Economic crises have a negative impact on the education system and the quality of education. Limited budget resources are a challenge for educators' salaries and educational resources. The third sub-chapter summarises previous publications of the authors dealing with popularity of teaching jobs. Teachers are one of the most numerous professions in the world. They greatly impact the future of educational institutions' leavers. Without them, there might not be any other professions. However, not many school leavers choose education majors worldwide.

The roots of education in the USA date back to its colonial past and early years, establishing traditions like co-educational classrooms, a ten-month school year, and local control via school boards. The Founding Fathers considered education essential for democracy and civic responsibility, creating a framework for funding public education through local taxes and promoting standardized curricula. As states evolved, so did teacher education. American pluralism offered diverse learning opportunities but also led to ongoing issues. The roles of women and the education of African Americans, Hispanics, and Native Americans have transformed over time. Challenges in meeting the needs of a diverse society and individuals with disabilities remain, but educators' dedication and commitment continue to be the system's strength. This section includes three teacher narratives.

This chapter provides an overview of the Canadian education system, including both K–12 and post-secondary education. It outlines the structure and functioning of educational systems across Canada's provinces and territories, as well as the federal government's responsibilities. The chapter examines licensing requirements within Canadian education and the stringency of professional certification processes. In addition, it explores the future of teaching, particularly in relation to the growing influence of artificial intelligence. The chapter further highlights Canada's standing as one of the world's most educated nations, with an internationally respected education system. The discussion concludes with reflective accounts from Canadian teachers.

This chapter examines education and the teaching profession in Brazil, situating them within historical, social, and political contexts. It outlines the structure of the Brazilian education system and key reforms in teacher education, highlighting persistent inequalities, professional challenges, and policy tensions. Drawing on legislation, international assessments, and the authors' professional experiences, the chapter discusses teaching in Brazil as a field marked by both recognition and resistance.

This chapter presents an overview of education in Colombia by situating current systems, policies, and practices within their historical, legal, and socio-economic context. It traces the development of education from pre-colonial community-based learning and Catholic-influenced formal schooling to the contemporary framework established by the 1991 Constitution and the General Education Law of 1994. The chapter describes the structure of the school system, teacher education pathways, assessment and accountability mechanisms, and recent reform initiatives, while identifying ongoing challenges related to inequality and uneven implementation. It concludes with personal narratives from three educators, illustrating diverse professional pathways and providing practical insight into how national policies related to areas such as bilingual education, assessment, school climate, and technology integration are enacted in school contexts.

also explores the growth of private and international schools and their implications for educational equity. Central to the analysis is teacher education and the teaching profession, highlighting enrollment trends, employability, and labor-market dynamics. Using a sociological and human capital perspective, the chapter offers insights into how education in Kurdistan reflects broader processes of state-building, social stratification, and workforce development.

This chapter centers on the lived experiences of three educators—Laila Addasi, Omar Wardere, and Sara Al-Essa—whose professional journeys offer a rich, practice-based perspective on teaching in Kuwait. Through their narratives, the chapter explores themes of career progression, cross-cultural engagement, instructional practice, and leadership within diverse school settings. Their stories highlight the personal and professional dimensions of teaching, including challenges, growth opportunities, and the evolving expectations placed on educators. While grounded in the broader context of Kuwait's education system and its ongoing reforms, the primary focus remains on how these developments are experienced in practice. Together, these accounts provide valuable insight into the realities of education in Kuwait, emphasizing the human element behind policy and reform.

Social stability, economic expansion, and national progress are all fundamentally influenced by education. The State of Qatar has made education a key pillar in line with Qatar National Vision 2030. Over the past 20 years, the system has evolved from mostly conventional models to one that is benchmarked globally. The following aspects are examined in this essay: the historical transition from informal learning to formal government schooling paths into the teaching profession, including academic credentials and regulatory obligations; the structure and stages of the current education system; the income and employment benefits of educators and professors; significant national accomplishments; and a professional perspective based on lived experience. Overall, the analysis portrays Qatar's educational system as a quickly evolving model that seeks to strike a compromise between cultural and linguistic preservation and global competitiveness.

South Korea is widely recognized as a high-performing education system, noted for strong student achievement, near-universal access to schooling, and high results in international assessments. At the

Section 3

The teaching profession stands at a pivotal crossroads, profoundly shaped by rapid technological advancements, shifting societal expectations, and unprecedented global interconnectedness. As we stand in early 2026, the reverberations of AI proliferation, post-pandemic recovery, and climate imperatives continue to redefine educational landscapes worldwide. This comprehensive chapter embarks on an expansive exploration of teaching's evolution—from its ancient origins as communal knowledge-sharing rituals to its anticipated future trajectories as a hybrid, human-AI symbiotic endeavor. By meticulously tracing historical patterns and projecting forward with evidence-based foresight, the analysis identifies pivotal drivers of change, including artificial intelligence's role in hyper-personalized learning ecosystems, sustainability imperatives that embed ecological stewardship into curricula, and the inexorable rise of data-driven pedagogies that prioritize learner agency over rote memorization.

This chapter examines the evolving role of teachers in an era shaped by artificial intelligence, declining professional prestige, and increasing labor precarity. Drawing on nearly two decades of adjunct faculty experience in an urban community college, it integrates reflective practitioner scholarship with recent research (2023–2025) on educational technology, labor conditions, and equity-driven pedagogy. The chapter argues that technological expansion intensifies rather than diminishes the need for teachers as relational, ethical, and interpretive professionals. Findings highlight teaching as a critical institutional infrastructure, particularly in access-oriented institutions serving historically marginalized students. The chapter concludes with implications for policy, faculty development, and the ethical integration of artificial intelligence in education.

Evolutionary changes in the teaching profession have been experienced in tandem with the technological changes and the increasing institutional expectation thus increasing the need of both affective and material support. The educators work in various capacities using limited resources and this creates stress and poses great challenges. Affective support, which takes the form of encouragement by leadership, coworker interaction and official reward, enhances well-being and motivation. Instructional effectiveness is improved by material support which includes infrastructure, digital equipment, professional growth, and fair remuneration. Leadership plays an important role in the development of trust and engagement, and a collaborative culture strengthens professional growth. The combination of emotional and material assistance determines the environment of sustainability that promotes the performance of teachers and enhances the general quality of education.

This chapter aims to foreground the value-based and moral dimensions of the teaching profession at a time when teaching is increasingly framed as a function that can be replaced by digital platforms and artificial intelligence (AI). This chapter challenges that reductionist view by arguing that teachers play a fundamentally irreplaceable role as carriers and mediators of values. The study involves 22 practising teachers working in public secondary schools in Türkiye. It adopts a qualitative, narrative-based research design with a qualitative narrative inquiry based on written narrative elicitation. The primary aim is to explore how teachers construct their professional identities and articulate values education within contemporary debates on technology and artificial intelligence (AI). Drawing on teachers' own narratives, the chapter seeks to demonstrate that teaching is not merely a cognitive activity but a deeply human, relational, and ethical practice through which core values such as responsibility, justice, respect, patience, and empathy are enacted and transmitted.

The rapid growth of automation and artificial intelligence (AI) is transforming educational systems, pedagogical practices, and teacher professional identity worldwide. Increasing public and political discourse regarding the potential replacement of human teachers by intelligent machines has intensified concerns about the declining attractiveness, status, and sustainability of the teaching profession. This chapter critically examines the assumption that AI can replace human teaching by advancing a human-centered perspective that positions teachers as essential to learning, socialization, and moral development. Drawing on a systematic narrative review of interdisciplinary research, the chapter analyzes how AI is reshaping instructional design, assessment, feedback, and classroom interaction while highlighting its limitations in addressing the cognitive, emotional, ethical, and sociocultural dimensions of teaching. It also discusses implications for professional development and policy reform, advocating collaborative human–AI models to support equitable and transformative education.

This chapter examines the rise of algorithmic pedagogy and its implications for teaching, knowledge, and democratic education, with a specific focus on the Indian educational context. It analyses how data-driven systems increasingly shape curricular decisions, assessment practices, and instructional strategies, positioning algorithms as influential pedagogical actors. Drawing on sociotechnical theory, critical pedagogy, and empirical evidence from India and global contexts, the chapter evaluates both the benefits and risks of algorithmic interventions, including personalization, efficiency, bias, surveillance, and epistemic injustice. The discussion highlights how linguistic diversity, social inequality, and governance structures in India intensify these dynamics. The chapter concludes by advancing principles for human-centered educational AI that prioritize pedagogical primacy, teacher autonomy, equity, transparency, and democratic governance, arguing that reclaiming pedagogy is essential to ensuring ethical and inclusive educational transformation.

Society and education are changing significantly due to increased global migration and diversity in student populations. Educational systems must accommodate these diverse learners, making cross-cultural collaboration crucial for fostering productive societies. Institutions must commit to inclusive education that addresses the needs of pluralistic societies. Technological advancements add complexity, as varying cultural values influence the ethical implications of technologies like artificial intelligence in education. Schools must promote technological literacy, ensure access to digital resources, and prepare students for a tech-driven workforce while addressing the digital divide faced by marginalized communities. To adapt, teachers will need greater cultural competency and professional development, and schools should focus on attracting a diverse staff and engaging communities to ensure equal access for all learners.

Preface

The book is dedicated to the problem of declining popularity of the teaching profession in the world. Although in some countries the problem is not so acute, in the majority of countries it constitutes a great challenge: the number of students keeps increasing, while the number of qualified teachers is going down, and so is the quality of education.

The editors and contributing authors of this book wanted to address education policy makers, the whole society with a request to review their attitude towards the profession. To some people nowadays it seems that it is an outdated profession, as AI and the internet can substitute teachers. To others teaching is a hard occupation demanding all time and energy but not offering any benefits. But practice has so far revealed that teachers are greatly needed – if not for transferring knowledge (this function still remains relevant!), then for communication, social skills development, empathy and support that no machine, even as sophisticated as AI, can provide.

CHAPTERS OVERVIEW

The book includes some theoretical chapters (overviews and researches) on teaching the goal of which is providing a deeper insight into this noble profession. It also includes more practical materials – descriptions of various countries' education systems accompanied by teacher voices from those countries telling their individual experiences of becoming a teacher, learning to understand the profession, to survive in it, to fulfil the mission of educators – developing young generations as humans adaptable to social life.

We made our conclusions – that teachers are even more needed in technocratic world than before and that they need support – financial, emotional, organizational – to be able to fulfil their mission. We hope that out book can help both education policy makers and ordinary people realize the great need in teachers and the necessity to support them.

From The Editors

How did I [Natela Doghonadze] come to decide to compile this book? First, I was very worried about what is happening in education in my country and the whole world. I was always happy about my choice of profession: for almost 50 years, I was enjoying learning and sharing my knowledge, I was relishing being with young people and feeling young, I was adoring developing as a teacher and as a person. I was happy to feel needed and to be able to help those who needed me, but not so much in the recent decade. Under the slogan of providing high standards, too much wrongly understood 'standardisation' (instead of high quality, everybody has to be the same) has taken place, well-written reports and answers to commissions have substituted the live process, students' shining eyes, rapport between teachers and students, creativity, etc. If there was a time when students were powerless figures (which was absolutely wrong), nowadays, teachers have become powerless figures (they depend too much on students', parents', and administration's assessments). Teachers used to be authorities for young children's parents; now, hiding behind the wonderful word "democracy," criticizing teachers has become a fad. Teaching has always been difficult – plenty of knowledge required, on the subject taught and beyond, pedagogy and psychology, a lot of skills including the use of technologies which are becoming more and more complex at a lightning speed; and so little support from the administration and government, such low salaries compared to those working in business or showbiz! But the creativity, constant development, the relationships, the achievements of your students – and it was worth it. Today, teachers have almost no time to ponder the best way to hold the next class, to read up, etc., so much time is taken by reading and then following tons of instructions, writing all sorts of reports, etc. And all this for a miserable salary! I'm afraid bureaucracy has won in the battle with creativity. I would be happy to admit that I exaggerate, but I believe I am not. Due to the difficulty of the job and the low pay, not so many people have always wanted to become teachers, but nowadays it is becoming a real problem.

These thoughts brought me to research the popularity of teaching jobs in several countries. I addressed those colleagues who would want to participate in the project through Academia and Research Gate, and some people responded. But then I realised the topic was too big for one article – so we wrote and published four, from students', parents', and teachers' viewpoints. And then I realised that the topic is too huge to be squeezed into a couple of articles. So we decided it would become a book.

The draft title said: "SOS – are teaching jobs going to be extinct?" The publishing house moved the accent to the global character of the book, which is fine, however, the dramatic intonation was lost. Why did we have "SOS" is the title? Unless society cares about teachers, who will care about society? Enthusiastic teachers (schoolteachers and university academic staff) serve people, but without support, their enthusiasm may fade away.

We very much want policy-makers, educators, students, mass media, and all people to read different scientific analyses and reviews in this book, and to experience individual teachers' stories.

Thanks to answering a call for stories about fathers' roles in education, I [Thomas C. De Bello] was introduced to the outstanding researcher, Natela Doghonadze, and I also got to know her as an exceptional educator who shared my passion for teaching. Over the course of preparing four research papers, we exchanged our interest in the job of teaching and the motivations of teachers, which ultimately led to the work now presented to you.

I have been involved in teacher education for a good part of my professional life, both in the United States and through my affiliation with SUNY Buffalo State's International Graduate Programs for Educators. That program's original director, Carolyn Brunner, a globalist, was influenced by my mentor, Dr Rita Dunn, of St. John's University, NYC. Today, under the guidance of its director, Brandon Kawa, the program has expanded to include schools in 37 different countries on five continents. Working as an adjunct professor in that program on and off for nearly as many years has fostered my interest and contributed to my experience in international education.

In the US, I worked in graduate programs that often included students who wanted to transition into teaching careers. Some had unrealistic notions of what life in the classroom was like. I would first encourage them to find experiences with children – anything from volunteering at a Scout program, religious education, sports teams, tutoring, etc., anything that would give them regular contact with students. I'd say, "You have to really like being with kids or this isn't for you!"

In my own life, I found this to be true, first with elementary school students in the Philippines, then with junior high school students in the USA, and eventually with graduate students. Seeing them learn and grow, both academically and as individuals, brings its own satisfaction. I noticed that teachers who loved teaching often told funny stories about their students and the things they said or did. Later, as a principal, I realized something else: I liked the company of teachers! The quirky humor they found in their everyday lives with kids is something I could relate to. In my experience, teachers worldwide share a great deal in common, despite cultural and societal differences. Not everything is always perfect, but it is in how teachers vent their frustrations that their commitment can be measured. Conscientious teachers put effort and thought into their work with students. It is disheartening when that is undervalued and underappreciated by society.

I hope that this book not only shares information about what teaching is and where it may be heading, but also, by relating teachers' experiences through personal stories, that it also celebrates teachers everywhere. Through that, I believe we can foster a more realistic appreciation of the role of teachers and the services they provide, not only to their students, but to the communities in which they serve.

Natela Doghonadze
International Black Sea University, Georgia

Thomas C. De Bello
SUNY Buffalo State University, USA

Acknowledgement

A special thank you to our (former) students, colleagues, and friends who have enriched our experience over the years and graciously contributed to this effort in various ways. Your commitment and excellence have been inspiring to us and will also inspire others.

We would also like to thank the people who helped us to find such a fantastic group of authors and contributors.

After 48 years in education, I [Natela Doghonadze] have exchanged a few jobs, as I loved what I did and the people I worked with. I thank my Alma Mater, my beloved Tbilisi I. Chavchavadze State Pedagogical Institute of Foreign Languages (now part of Ilia State University), for the knowledge and the first experience of teaching I gained there. I am grateful to the Georgian Technical University, where I gained expertise in teaching technical and business English, organized foreign language teaching at Master's department, and carried out my research for my Doctor of Science dissertation. And – my longest experience where I believe I finally developed into who I am today, a connoiseur in Education at international level – the International Black Sea University where I have worked for almost 30 years.

And, of course, my thanks go to my family, who have always supported me in my educational and research efforts.

After 36 years in public education, I [Thomas C. De Bello] retired, and in 2003 I began an adventure teaching in Buffalo State University's International Graduate Program for Educators (IGPE), an incredible program inspired by Carolyn Brunner and now directed by Brian Kawa. Today, that program offers an accredited master's degree approved by the State University of New York, available in 37 countries across 5 continents. I will forever be grateful for the opportunity that the program has provided its students and its teachers like me to learn and grow as educators.

Finally, I offer my deepest thanks to my family, whose encouragement, patience, and unwavering support sustained me throughout this process and throughout my career. I am grateful to my aunt, my children, and my grandchildren for their constant encouragement. I owe special recognition to my three educator-children, who have graciously endured my countless stories and anecdotes over the years. I always love hearing about their school experiences.

Most of all, I thank my wife, Pat. Throughout our marriage, she has continually encouraged me to venture beyond my comfort zone while so often assuming additional responsibilities at home to make those pursuits possible. As a school social worker, Pat has had more than enough opportunities to practice her professional skills with me. She has always been my greatest source of support, my most trusted advisor, and my first - and most thoughtful - critic. For her steadfast love, wisdom, and encouragement, I will remain forever grateful.

Natela Doghonadze
International Black Sea University, Georgia

Thomas C. De Bello
State University of New York at Buffalo State, USA

Introduction

1. OVERVIEW OF THE BOOK'S PURPOSE AND THEMES

The book's purpose is to draw public attention to the problem of the decreasing numbers of people who want to be employed as teachers. We want once again to remind people that without teachers there can be no other professions, as who can educate lawyers, doctors, computer specialists and businessmen (the professions so popular today) if not teachers?!

The book's structure includes an Introduction, a chapter overviewing the global context of education nowadays, a huge chapter *Teacher Voices*, including authors from all continents (15 countries and one autonomy), then several theoretical chapters (literature reviews and research dealing with the status of teachers and teaching, as well as the future of the professions, especially in the light of so noisily proclaimed opposition of Artificial Intelligence and teaching profession).

The chapter *Teacher Voices* aims to, first, create a better ground for the understanding of what is happening in the relevant country (description of the country's education system and teacher education), and then to present teachers' career stories – how and why they became teachers, what advantages and challenges they see in their jobs, what experiences, both positive and negative, brought them to their teaching philosophies. The content analysis of the teacher stories revealed that teachers are thinking over the following themes: family, teachers' and environment impact on choosing their profession, features of effective and poor teaching, insights of what teaching and education is, the advantages and challenges of the teaching jobs, the reasons to become a teacher, the components and the role of professional development, what sort of support teachers need, and, most importantly, what teacher mission is. Interestingly, the following theoretical chapters are also built around these topics, therefore, researchers' and teachers' view on the processes in contemporary education are close to each other.

The following eleven chapters by authors from India, US, Nigeria, Türkiye, and Bangladesh present literature analysis and research of the future perspectives of education.

Future perspectives of the teaching profession. Akhilesh Pandey, Rahul Bharadwaj, Himanshu Sharma, & Sudhanshu Bhushan

This chapter advances the argument that the future of the teaching profession lies in its evolution from a content-delivery function to an adaptive role. The human elements of education - empathy, trust, and interpersonal connection – are gaining even a greater significance. In turn, teachers as primary agents of change and ethical anchors need support (funding, professional and emotional support). If treated adequately, the teaching profession can evolve into a resilient, adaptive, and strategically positioned force capable of addressing the challenges of an increasingly complex and uncertain world.

Teaching on the margins, leading at the center: An urban community college adjunct's reflection on the enduring necessity of teachers in an AI Age. Marvin Espinoza

The teaching profession nowadays is experiencing a pronounced erosion of social prestige, material support, and institutional authority. This decline is occurring at a moment of intensifying demand. The chapter argues that in reality technological expansion intensifies rather than diminishes the need for teachers as relational, ethical, and interpretive professionals. The deskilling of teaching labor occurs not only through technology but also through institutional choices about implementation. This chapter contends that AI does not diminish teaching but redefines the forms of expertise required.

Emotional and material support needed by teachers. Velmurugan, R., Sudarvel, J., Bhuvaneswari, R., & Senthil Kumar S.

Contemporary educators work using limited resources, which creates stress. The support structures in essence play a crucial role in strengthening the teacher resilience, teacher satisfaction, and overall quality of education. Emotional support would temporarily counterbalance the lack of material resources; but persistent material deprivation would wear out the spirit and undermine the performance of emotional support. The support mechanisms include considerate leadership and strong collegial bonds, accessible workloads as well as all the classroom materials.

Teaching values in the age of artificial intelligence - A narrative-discursive study of teachers as irreplaceable moral agents. Ruhan Güçlü & Vildan İnci Kavak

This chapter aims to foreground the value-based and moral dimensions of the teaching profession at a time when teaching is increasingly framed as a function that can be replaced by digital platforms and artificial intelligence. This article challenges views of teaching that focus mainly on technical efficiency by emphasising teachers' roles as carriers and mediators of values. Teaching is a moral activity in which values are reflected through everyday pedagogical choices. Values serve as a foundation for community coexistence and interpersonal relationships.

Rethinking the future of the teaching profession in the age of automation and artificial intelligence. Md. Ashrafuzzaman

The chapter critically questions the arguments on teacher replacement by AI, developing a humanistic approach to intelligent technologies as pedagogical and not professional replacements. It discusses the way AI is transforming the method of instruction, the system of assessment, and the nature of the teacher, as well as the natural constraints of the automation process in relation to the social and ethical needs of education that cannot be fulfilled. It offers Human-centered AI as an outcome, which focuses on the design of intelligent systems that grow the human capabilities without violating ethical values, transparency, accountability, and inclusivity.

Moving beyond the 'Teaching jobs are going to get extinct in the age of generative AI' Narrative: Making teachers 'non-substitutable'. Ashraf Alam

The chapter is heavy with sophisticated terminology and not easy to read, however, very important for the book. It states that the teacher extinction narrative operates as a high-velocity social claim engineered by platform logics that privilege salience, virality, and performative certainty over institutional complexity. While discussing teaching jobs' prestige, it is treated as a multidimensional composite of dignity, authority, autonomy, remuneration justice, role clarity, and socially conferred trust, rather than as a sentimental reputation index.

The pedagogical soul: Why machines can't replace teachers. Sneh Lata

The notion of a pedagogical soul captures those elements of teaching that resist codification: moral responsibility, empathy, contextual understanding, and interpretive sensitivity. Machine-based learning environments, despite their adaptability, cannot replicate the subtle cues and empathic responses that constitute classroom life. The central argument of this chapter is that the irreplaceability of teachers lies not in their mastery of information but in their moral and relational capacities.

Reframing the Teacher's Mission in a Changing World: Evolving Roles, Responsibilities, and Professional Purpose? Andi Asrifan & Dewi Furwana

The accelerated technological growth has created a lot of debate on the need in teachers in the future. Some publications contained speculations that AI will soon substitute teachers and that teaching can be reduced to the transfer of information and acquisition of skills. The chapter rejects the idea, arguing that cultural tools, historical contexts and social interaction are the mediating factors in cognition. Teaching involves an awareness of the emotional conditions, cultural affiliations, social identities, lived in learners' experiences. The chapter recommends applying Human-centered AI (HCAI), which focuses on intelligent systems growing the human capabilities without violating ethical values, transparency, accountability, and inclusivity. Teachers need to apply these systems.

Algorithmic pedagogy: When data decides what teachers teach. Kusum Lata

Teaching, once grounded primarily in professional judgment, disciplinary expertise, and contextual understanding of learners, is increasingly shaped by algorithmic systems that recommend content, sequence lessons, predict student performance, and evaluate instructional effectiveness. This shift marks the emergence of what can be described as algorithmic pedagogy, a condition in which data-driven systems do not merely support teaching but actively participate in determining what teachers teach, how they teach, and how learning is valued.

Future direction in education. Thomas C. De Bello

The chapter states that inclusive, collaborative, and equitable education systems are needed for a sustainable future. Despite the obvious progress in education, millions of children are still excluded from it. So popular emphasis on competition can stimulate people to learn, however, eventually, it is collaboration (especially, cross-cultural collaboration) that needs to be stressed to achieve real results. Combined (including, international) efforts in adequate teacher training and professional development together with financial support can produce more efficient education in the future.

The authors of these chapters look at the topic from different angles, however, they are unanimous in their belief that technologies, in particular AI, are effective tools for making education more individualised, efficient, motivated, engaging, for permitting to better understand student needs, their strengths and weaknesses, to assess them more objectively. On the other hand, the authors believe that teacher role and responsibility in technologically-based society is even greater than before, as decision based on relationships, trust, ethics, and empathy are more important than those based on 'pure' objectivity.

The book ends in conclusion.

2. IS TEACHING A PROFESSION OR AN OCCUPATION?

Initially, I wanted to avoid this topic in the current book. However, I realise that this is indispensable. I had been already for 30 years in the profession when I first read in an American publication that teaching is not a profession, but an occupation, craft, or even artistic endeavour (Rowan, 1994; Huberman, 1993; Gage, 1978). In my country, as well as in many countries to the east, with thousands of years' tradition in education, it has never been viewed like this, it was not just a profession, but a respected profession at that time.

In the US this view is historically explained:

1. The first settlers had to survive in the new lands, but those who went north were religious and wanted people to be able to read the Bible. So anybody who could read could teach children to read, the Bible, first of all.
2. The majority of school teachers in the past were women, as women were treated as 'lower class' humans than men, teaching was an occupation of a lower level – hard, less paid, and less respected (teachers were often treated like servants; female teachers of that time in some states were not permitted to get married and have children, as that would distract them from the service).

3. The fact that a person of a relevant profession (a physicist, a chemist, a historian, etc.) could after half-a-year 30-60 credits become a teacher.

Nowadays, teachers are required heaps (sorry for a non-academic word!) of knowledge and skills: subject content, pedagogy, psychology, methods of teaching the particular subject, presentation, communication, technological skills, etc. In some countries teaching is equally (if not more) popular among men as (than) women. The majority of those who today become teachers undergo a minimum of three-year bachelor training (the teaching-related subjects are normally entangled with the course that they are going to teach).

Greenwood (1957) defined that professions (compared to occupations) are characterised by systematic theory, authority, community sanction, ethical codes and a culture. Probably, in the past, teaching lacked theoretical studies – today, there are so many that it is difficult to catch up and study all of them. In an occupation, he explains, there are customers, and they are always right. In the profession, there are clients. Clients are listened to, however, there are professional experts whose opinion matters more. If we understand the difference between occupations and professions like that today, probably professions no longer exist, because today market rules all sorts of relationships. Nowadays, to become a teacher, an academic degree is normally not sufficient, certification and/or licensure is mostly required. Code of ethics is a relatively new topic in teaching, however, an unwritten code has always existed. Professional culture is also developing within schools, universities, and teacher unions and other organisations.

In a more contemporary publication, Ingersoll and Collins (2018) define professions as having the following characteristics: credential and licensing levels, induction and mentoring programs for beginners, professional development support, opportunities, and participation, specialisation, authority over decision-making, compensation levels, prestige and social standing. Induction and mentoring programs for beginner teachers are becoming a standard at schools and even universities. Professional development support exists, however, it often is of formal character (not like that in other professions?). Teachers are educated according to their specialisations (primary school teacher, math teacher, etc.). In further chapters you will see that shared/distributed educational leadership is becoming more and more popular worldwide. Therefore, prestige (which greatly depends on how the society treats the profession, not so much on the profession itself) is nowadays the major barrier for acknowledging teaching as a profession, not just an occupation.

One of the goals of the current book is to demonstrate how unfair it is to view teaching as a 'B-list' job (Garon, 2013): "The irony is that the same people who feel very comfortable with the idea that teaching isn't a job for smart people, who cavalierly advise top graduates to pursue more lofty aspirations, will then decry teachers for not doing their jobs well enough, or myopically assert that under-qualified, ill-prepared teachers are responsible for the problems in education today". August et al. (2010) study states that in South Korea, Finland, and Singapore – countries where teaching profession is respected and supported - 100% of graduates at education programs are from the top 30% of higher education graduates. Meanwhile, in the US, according to Davis and Smith, (1996) teachers are in the middle of *occupations* list according to prestige (in the end, if we view only professions): 63 (in 1972) to 66 (in 1989) points out of the possible 100 points (compare with physicians who rate 82/86 and police who rank 48/60). And nowadays many countries where teachers used to be respected follow the American path.

Rowan (1994) mentioned that "teaching is a complex form of work that requires high levels of formal knowledge for successful performance" (p.4). Many practitioners and researchers would share his opinion. Teachers need to make hundreds of decisions daily. Most of them do not directly save or ruin students' lives like doctors' decisions do, however, eventually, they have a commensurable impact on people's lives and countries' development. The respect towards teachers and the prestige of their profession has a great impact on the quality of their teaching and, eventually, on the quality of life (Alemu, 2024; Bozkurt & Aktaş, 2022; Stromquist, 2018).

3. TEACHERS' IDENTITIES

The concept of teacher identity is controversial (Vazquez et al., 2024). On the one hand, teacher identity is a personal characteristic acquired in the process of work. On the other hand, it is a social construct, depending on the social context. Teacher identity may be perceived differently by students, their parents, other teachers, and administration. The study by

Vazquez et al. (2024) analysed teacher identity from the viewpoint of pre-service teachers, their beliefs, expectations, and practices. Unfortunately, many teachers getting a degree in education do not view teaching as their vocation. And, vice versa, some people who do not initially see themselves as (future) teachers, often become dedicated educators. Teacher identity includes the quality of obtained education, teaching style developed with observing others teach and later years of practice. One of the problems pre-service teachers come across is that they are taught by university professors who do not interact with school. The development of teaching identity has a 'dialogical and polyphonic' (Vazquez et al., 2024, p. 5) character. Professional excellence involves moral, ethical, academic, personal, and social aspects. Fairness, empathy, subject knowledge, ability to transfer that knowledge, and, especially important, relationships with students are needed to become a good teacher.

The below quotation exceeds the normally permitted length of quotations in the APA style, however, I find it so important that I did not try to abridge it:

> … narrowly instrumental, mechanical vision of learning that not only devalues teachers, but also reduces students to mere receptacles for productivity-enhancing skills and knowledge. But if it is accepted that any education system should be characterized by certain core values and transformative goals, including inclusion, social justice and the promotion of human agency and dignity, then it follows that teachers play a vital role in enacting and modelling these values. Valuing autonomy, dignity and agency in our students entails valuing the same qualities in our teachers. (Avalos et al., 2022, p. 666).

The popular today statements that it is possible to make education cheaper at the expense of using more technologies and reducing the number of teachers, according to Avalos et al. (2022) – and I completely agree with them – can bring to dehumanizing of the educational process. Teacher identity has an impact on student identities – an impact which any perfect technologies cannot have. The motives for entering teaching may be intrinsic or circumstances-based, however, teacher education and further practice are very important. "The quality of preparation programmes is key to transforming an initial, often naïve, enthusiasm into a professional identity founded upon assured handling of learning needs and student diversity" (Avalos et al., 2022, p. 704). Those teachers who develop the commitment to remain in the profession strengthen their Teacher identities. A teacher needs to comply with the official standards, but at the same time they need to have their own judgment and be involved in reflection over their work. The authors underline the need of the subject, pedagogical, psychological and general education level of teachers. Unfortunately, a teacher is often expected to be rather obedient and hardworking than able of making informed choices. Teachers experience larger stress than in many other professions, correspondingly, they should not be overloaded and have enough leisure time to restore their energy and psychological balance. Otherwise, stressed teachers can pour their dissatisfaction on their students whose knowledge and wellbeing will suffer.

According to Niemi et al. (2018), teacher autonomy is one of the crucial features of the teaching profession. Teachers spend most time in the classroom, facing their students alone. This is why they need to be able to make decisions independently. Of course, teachers are not fully independent, they have to follow school regulations and national curricula (where applicable), however, they have a high degree of autonomy, which varies depending on the country and the school they work in. In Finland, for instance, teachers have the freedom to design the syllabus, choose educational materials and teaching and assessment method. For innovations and reforms not to be top-down, teacher and school autonomy should be supported. The decentralisation of the education system does not guarantee teacher autonomy. For example, the fact that in the USA there is not one federal law regulating education, and school districts have much power, teacher voice is sometimes not heard, due to too much control from school administration or district power. In Finland and Estonia, it is emphasized that teachers are "creative designers of learning environments" (Niemi et al., p. 147). Teachers' initiatives need to be supported by their schools, however, they need long-term assessments, to see whether the suggested innovations are productive.

Ezer et al. (2010) mention that teacher education is expected to train quality teachers, but reality is not always like this. No humans are perfect, neither are teachers. Even if/when teacher education system were perfect, it would hardly be possible to receive teachers with all needed knowledge, skills, values, and personal features. Somebody will always be stronger in one respect and weaker in another. "The professionalising approach advocates creating standards in teaching and in curriculum planning" (Ezer et al., 2010, p.392). It means there are minimum requirements that are expected to be satisfied. Being a reflective practitioner is one of such requirements. Teachers are expected to be able both to 'translate' knowledge and 'transfer' it. In the first case, they have to provide direct teaching of readymade knowledge that their students have to memorise. In the second case, teachers serve as facilitators, people who co-create knowledge with their students – via learning-by-doing, teacher-student and student-student dialogue, providing materials for discovery learning, constructive feedback including the ways for improvement, etc. Although the second way is eventually more productive, it is time-consuming, and its efficiency largely depends on student mental development level and motivation, therefore teachers need to combine the two approaches. If a teacher does not analyse his/her teaching and seek for new ways to teach, his/her teaching, effective today, tomorrow may become boring and ineffective. "Quality teaching transcends teaching skills, and is manifested in a complex of components such as abilities, beliefs and perceptions, motivation and commitment, as well as the teacher's own personality" (Ezer et al., 2010, p. 394). According to the questionnaire conducted by Ezer and colleagues (2010) with 97 student teachers in their fourth year in a Bachelor of Education program in an Israeli college, a good teacher's intrinsic motivation and positive attitude towards their job should prevail over their extrinsic motivation and negative or indifferent attitude. According to their study, delivering knowledge by the importance of teacher roles is rated only in the fifth place (29.9% of the respondents), preceded by (in the given order) delivering universal values (80.4%), developing students' personal abilities (52.1%), forming socially appropriate behaviour (48.9%), and ensuring educational and social change (33.9%).

According to Dusaban and Olana (2025), there are certain behaviours expected of a teacher. Service should rather be their goal than personal gain. "Teachers who demonstrate values such as kindness, concern, and a willingness to sacrifice for their students might help their students develop their personalities. A healthy learning atmosphere is created when teachers show genuine interest in their students, stimulate innovation, and recognize and respect" (Dusaban & Olana, 2025, p. 807). Showing compassion and offering help in the classroom, sharing knowledge with colleagues, and promoting innovation is expected from good teachers. Teacher punctuality, responsibility, and organization will enable them to develop the same features in their students. Surprisingly, however, according to their survey with 160 Filipino teachers, the statistical significance of the positive correlation of teacher overall attitude towards their job and their performance was found insignificant, while teacher professional development and teacher attitude towards students with special needs were found statistically significantly positively correlated with teacher performance.

Editora (2023) claims that there has always been a paradox of the teaching profession: on the one hand, the profession has been needed to ensure the 'perpetuation of knowledge through generations' (p. 2), on the other hand, there has never been substantial support and respect from the state. Under these conditions, teachers need to be great enthusiasts of their profession and the social responsibilities they have. A conclusion is made that 'the teaching identity has to do with social changes' (p. 2).

Soundararajan et al. (2022) enumerate the following teacher roles: classroom manager, facilitator, evaluator, and guide and councilor. They should possess the following personal competencies: the ability to develop a positive self-concept, emotional stability, self-motivation, and a wide reading interest. Teachers have to be knowledgeable, aware of learner diversity, they should be good planners, have strong communication skills, and the ability to collaborate. Their communication with students, parents, colleagues, and administration should be respectful and polite, they should be honest and open. Teachers are continuous learners, imaginative and adaptable. Contemporary teachers have to regularly update their technological knowledge and skills.

Teacher identity develops over years. It greatly depends on what kind of a student the future teacher was, according to Felicetti (2011). Those experiences may enrich or inhibit the teacher's professional behaviour in the future. Teacher autonomy is emphasised by the author, explaining it as the ability to understand the educational and social context and, based on it, enhance his/her own and his/her students' knowledge. "The identity and the know-how of the teacher are related to the way in which he develops his classroom activities, in other words, through the different ways in which he can contribute to the development of the teaching and learning process" (Felicetti, 2011, p.3). "Being a teacher means being capable of programming one's own program of professional development. It means being open to learning as a whole, being an investigator in the whole of the teaching profession, to know how to adapt the content of the discipline to the needs of the job market" (ibid, p.3). The unity of theoretical views and the practice formed during years eventually constitutes teacher identity.

"The teaching profession is more than a job; it is often described as a calling. It requires dedication, empathy, and a commitment to lifelong learning" (Mondal & Panda, 2025, p. 289). If pre-service teachers are educated in positive attitude towards the teaching profession, they have more chances to develop this attitude themselves and to perform more efficiently. The factors that can ensure a positive attitude towards teaching include a positive institutional environment, friendly and supportive teaching-learning culture, evidence-based teaching, and mentorship. A negative attitude towards teaching can make teachers – and their teaching go sour or trigger them to leave (Issan et al., 2011). Teacher isolation often becomes a reason for the negative attitude towards the teaching profession, this is why administration and teacher support is so important. The educational institution working conditions – sufficient equipment and educational resources, induction/orientation programs for beginner teachers and newcomers, and peer support – contribute to the positive attitude towards the teaching profession. Among the personal characteristics of effective teachers are belief in self-efficacy, readiness for cooperation, and enthusiasm are named as typical teacher identities by Issan et al. (2011).

Daulay et al. (2023) claim that to prove teachers' professionalism, in more and more countries, besides the diploma of education, teacher certification is applied, which measures a teacher's performance, training, guiding, and fostering during a certain period. To serve students' positive role model, the teacher needs to observe the official standards and the code of ethics. Teacher dignity is especially stressed in the article. Teachers must be disciplined and committed to their profession, their communication skills should be on a high level. Teacher promotion should be based on their professional development, including their professional writing and participation in teacher conferences and training. The scientific basis of teaching has to be based on pedagogy, educational psychology, methods of teaching a particular subject, and sociology. While the scientific basis is mostly studied at university/college, in-service trainings should not only contribute to practical skills but also explain the theoretical basis of the efficiency of innovative practices.

According to Bademcioğlu et al. (2014), keeping up-to-date with professional innovations is an important feature of teacher identity, as teaching techniques and methods are changing, especially nowadays they are changing fast under the impact of technologies and the corresponding governmental requirements. The fact that teachers are nor only dedicated to their profession but also enjoy teaching and the relationships with students positively impacts their students' motivation and engagement. Students feeling harmoniously at school will easily adjust to societal requirements.

Ünsal et al. (2017) state that the status of teaching jobs tends to decline, especially in European countries. It is related to socio-cultural and economic contexts: teachers' job security, salary and working conditions, opportunities of professional development, autonomy, and quality of education. Empathy with students, sense of humour, patience, objectivity were named by the interviewees in Ünsal et al.'s (2017) study as typical of a good teacher's identity.

To sum up, autonomy, friendliness, openness, dignity, agency, prevailing intrinsic job motivation, reflectivity, care and empathy, enthusiasm, deep, wide, and strong knowledge, emotional stability, patience, optimism, sense of humour, and communicability are the features typical of teachers. The roles in the classroom and beyond it that teachers are expected to fulfil are classroom manager, facilitator, evaluator, and guide and councilor. And the typical behaviours include planning, translating and transferring knowledge, self-observation, reflection, constant professional growth, respectful and polite communication, adaptation to the new circumstances and requirements. School teachers can develop their identity not only through taking lectures but also by observing and communicating with school teachers, while university lecturers will develop their professional identities not only via lectures on higher school pedagogy but also via observing and communicating with university professors.

4. THE IMPORTANCE OF TEACHERS IN SHAPING THE FUTURE OF THE WORLD

It is a trite truth that children are our future, however, it is necessary to start with it. Parents, teachers, and doctors are the main people, all in their ways, in making the future of humankind possible. "The teacher role is of guides and facilitators, not mere providers of knowledge" (Jan, 2017, p. 53). Efficient and beloved teachers are role models, supporters, and inspirers for the young, thus forming the face of the future generations.

Malala Yousafzai is a Pakistani female education activist who was shot in her head by the Taliban for fighting for girls' right for education. She survived and in 2014 received the Noble Prize for Peace. In her speech to the United Nations Youth Assembly she stated: "One child, one teacher, one pen, and one book can change the world" (Speakola, 2013). The great role that teachers play in changing the world as a better place is undeniable.

According to Eacute and Esteve (2000), in the last two decades of the 20th century a very important change occurred: not only primary education became compulsory in the majority of countries in the world but also a record number of children started attending secondary school. This wonderful achievement brought in both an increased level of the world's population educated and the issue of the quality of that education. This is a responsibility of teachers and other educators. From the education of the elite an important step has been made to the mass education and the next logical step is to provide that the education obtained at schools and further is a quality one, which arms young people with relevant knowledge, skills, and values to be employed, to care about their families, eventually, to be happy. The role – and the responsibility – of teachers has immensely grown. Not only more teachers are needed than ever before but also their qualification should be at least average (single star teachers have always be around). To teach in socially, ethnically, and culturally diverse classes with a variety of intelligence types and learning styles, psychological and disciplinary problems brought from home and neighbourhood is much more difficult than it used to be in the past. To teach well, having motivated and – at least more or less – disciplined students are needed. Here so much depends on the parents first of all and of course the immediate environment a child grows in. If neither parents not the environment contribute to students' motivation, the difficulty of teachers' job doubles. Eacute and Esteve (2000) compare contemporary teachers having to work in politically and technologically fast-changing society to a cast of actors who discover in the middle of a play that the scenery has changed. Subject knowledge, cognitive and social-emotional skills, classroom management, fighting with distractions, creating safe and friendly environment, diversifying teaching and assessment methods, designing learning materials (including electronic) to compensate for textbooks' deficiencies – this is an incomplete list of what teachers have to care for. To say nothing of overload. Very often nowadays teachers have to readjust and relearn to be able to teach well. Numerous, growing like an avalanche challenges often lead to teacher burnout. Without the support coming from families, neighbourhood, governmental and non-governmentl educational organisations, mass-media, government and the whole society, it is too difficult for teachers to keep up. Many quit under the pressure, others are not able anymore to teach to the maximum of their abilities. Unfortunately, very often, instead of support, what teachers get is 'prejudgement' (Cole, 1985, as cited by Eacute & Esteve, 2000, p.203).

To provide good teaching, efficient curricula of teacher education are needed. Strong programs are needed to train really qualified teachers who then need relevant environment and support to teach well. Unfortunately, the 2011 of the US Department of Education report states that only 23% of all teachers, and only 14% of teachers in high-poverty schools, come from the top third of college graduates. Best graduates have to be attracted to teach at schools, however, the taken measures do not seem sufficient.

Aubusson and Schuck (2012) claim that the fact that in certain countries the level of student knowledge is less than desired causes teacher qualification doubts, which is only partially true, as there are also other factors that impact student knowledge: family socio-economic status, school equipment, situation in the country, peer impact, etc. However, teachers are those who are mainly blamed, which does not seem fair. There are some challenges to curricula improvement: "lack of data to tell teacher preparation programs how they are doing; the inability to attract the best students; inadequate preparation for the hard realities of the classroom; and a need to address critical shortages in certain subject areas such as maths or science" (US Department of Education, 2011 as cited in Aubusson & Schuck, 2012, p. 4). On the other hand, Redecker et al. (2011 as cited by Aubusson & Schuck, 2012, p. 5) indicate that the factors that will impact education in the future include demography, globalisation, immigration, technology and the labour market.

And, finally, a painful question for teachers. Robots will replace human teachers by 2027 - this was the prediction made by Sir Anthony Seldon in September 2017 (Houser, 2017). There is much talk today that the AI has the potential to replace teachers and learners (why learn – AI will do the job for you?!). Chan and Tsi (2023) conducted research with 384 undergraduate and graduate students and 144 teachers in Hong Kong universities and came to conclusion that "AI is better equipped than human educators to deliver standardized content and assessments, and can work tirelessly without fatigue or bias. However, … AI lacks the empathy and emotional intelligence necessary for effective teaching and learning" (p.2). AI does not have the pedagogical skills such as encouraging curiosity and open-mindedness needed for efficient teaching and learning, it cannot remove conflicts and make informed decisions. It does not foster creativity and teamwork, it only creates conditions for them which may be misused by students. Only sensation lovers without sufficient teaching and learning experience can announce the end of the teaching profession. Not only undergraduate, but also doctorate students regularly express the idea that they would not be able to do research without their lecturers' and supervisors' support (Almusaed & Almssad, 2020; Malunda et al., 2021).

So let us refer back to our original quote, "the teacher's role is one of guides and facilitators, not mere providers of knowledge." It seems then that we are at a turning point. What happens when teachers are poorly prepared, hindering their role as providers of knowledge? What happens if society undervalues the teachers' role as guides and facilitators? Can AI ever replace human interaction? Who will be there to speak about the importance of education for young women? Who will be there to guide and facilitate those students with special needs? If AI replaces teachers, will members of society be engineered by the creators of AI programs? This book's purpose is to look at teachers today in different cultures, in other places of the world, teachers with a variety of backgrounds, skills, and opinions. We hope to show that by examining the diversity of the teaching profession, readers can reach their conclusions about these and other serious questions facing education today.

5. THE ROLE OF TEACHERS IN EDUCATIONAL SYSTEMS

> "Teachers are often considered the backbone of schools; without them there would be no school. Thus, understanding teachers' roles is key to understanding the educational system" (Ingersoll & Collins, 2018, p. 199).
>
> "The quality of an education system cannot exceed the quality of its teachers" (Auguste et al., p. 5).

Administration, teachers, and students have always been the most important figures in education. Administration, because they were decision-makers, teachers, because they provided knowledge and student assessment, and students, because it all happened for them. Although schooling was about teaching and learning, and teachers and students had to be the central figures, the only decision-makers were administrators. Things changed in the 1980s with the democratization of society and the development of stakeholder theory (Freeman, 1984). All individuals or groups who were interested and impacted by the results of the educational process were named education stakeholders. Students, their parents, teachers, administrators, education policymakers, employers, and researchers in the field of education, non-governmental organisations dealing with education, even the wider society that gets the final product of education are nowadays viewed as stakeholders. To be a stakeholder, one has to be actively involved in decision-making and strategic planning, as well as develop relationships of mutual trust with other stakeholders (Khadija, 2022).

The government establishes the educational standards and is responsible for the quality control through the mechanisms of accreditation and authorization, it finances the public schools and (partially) universities. School administrators set the goals, mission, and vision, develop the strategies for implementing them. However, teachers' role is the most important one, as only they interact directly with students, deliver curriculum and syllabi content, create fruitful classroom environment, present the materials, organize the activities, provide constructive feedback, choose the approaches and the teaching methods, etc. They know their students – their learning styles, strengths and weaknesses – and adjust the syllabi to the students' needs and possibilities. Teachers communicate with support staff, administration, and parents. Teachers do not teach only their subject content – they teach how to learn and they develop moral values of their students (Swargiary, 2024).

According to Darling-Hammond (2010), all aspects of educational reform depend on teacher qualification. The more knowledgeable teachers are, the better they are aware of pedagogical and their field innovations and the more efficiently can they apply them in practice. This can be achieved through an effective system of professional development. Not only international experts and university professors but also teachers themselves have to be actively involved in gaining new knowledge and sharing it with colleagues, involving colleagues in the implementation of innovations. Teacher resistance often becomes a barrier to implementing educational reforms. Systematic teacher information about successful practices of their colleagues and research findings should be brought to teachers to enable/motivate them to use the new approaches in their everyday practice.

Teacher values have a great impact on their desire to get acquainted with novel practices. As Akın Sabuncu and Ok (2021) mention, national educational culture is often the reason for teacher resistance to innovation. It is essential to be aware of specific constraints in various cultural contexts such as collectivist oriental culture vs. individualist western culture, to support teacher development. In some cultures, the attitude towards the newest educational technologies is very positive, therefore, not much effort is needed to persuade teachers to use them in classroom management, teaching, and assessment, while in other cultures, much persuasion is needed to involve teachers in computer-assisted and mobile-assisted teaching, to say nothing about artificial intelligence. On the other hand, other educational systems may resist the development of learner autonomy and critical thinking, due to centuries-old traditions. In the Akın Sabuncu and Ok (2021) study, collaboration and group work was positively perceived both by teachers and their students, correspondingly, this turned out the most effective way to help teachers carry out their mission.

Teachers, especially primary school teachers, are parent substitutes (*in loco parentis* is the legal term when the teacher has to represent the student's interests in cases when parents are unavailable) in the classroom, during breaks, and out-of-school events like excursions, competitions, etc. Spending much time with students, the teacher ensures students' socialization, takes measures to solve conflicts, etc. Being an educated and experienced person, a teacher can often provide better advice than less competent parents, so students, when they feel a teacher's positive attitude, often address him/her to help with issues not directly related with educational issues. Teachers share both professional and life knowledge with their students. Enthusiastic and knowledgeable teachers often become their students' role models.

Although teamwork among teachers is growingly enhanced nowadays, there still are schools and universities where each teacher/lecturer is by him/herself. They plan and conduct their classes alone, not wanting to share their professional secrets, and struggle on their own with the arising disciplinary and instructional challenges, not getting any support. Little (1990) emphasizes the importance of being a member of 'masterful group' versus 'masterful teacher'. A lonely, even very qualified and enthusiastic teacher can do little to help students learn better, the whole environment would drag his efforts back and decrease the results. This is especially true for novice teachers. Short-term, survival-oriented inductions have revealed not to be sufficient. Long-term mentorship relationships between beginner and experienced teachers are more fruitful. This is not about master-teacher formal positions, which sometimes are gained and then the person in the position does not provide real support to colleagues, but about the intrinsic motivating of teacher-leaders to refine the work of their colleagues and eventually make their students happier. Teachers should be "colleagues not merely in name but also with regard to the core ideas, principles and practices of their work" (Little, 1990, p. 176). However, it is of critical importance that teachers are not overloaded by curricular and extracurricular duties to have sufficient time to develop relationships between one another.

Teachers as educational leaders is an important topic. If we want education to really progress, teachers have to inspire their students' desire to learn, more informed and experienced teachers should share their knowledge and experiences. Contemporary education administrators/managers no longer can effectively deal with an avalanche of requirements towards school, consequently, they have to delegate/distribute/share some of their responsibilities to/with teachers. Teacher-leaders initiate some practices and events on school and beyond-school levels. Peer assessment of each other's practices (the assessor is chosen by the teacher, so they are friendly and provide constructive feedback that does not impact teacher position or salary) helps teachers learn from each other by seeing the real classroom and not through official reports. Bennett (2008) mentions that educators tend to oppose 'they' (the Ministry of Education, national examination boards, and local authorities) to 'us' (teachers who have to comply with 'their' decisions). Distributed/shared leadership changes the 'top-down' requirements into collectively made decisions which teachers more eagerly fulfil. Although distributed/shared is mainly based on teamwork, it does not exclude individual teacher leadership, either. "In teacher-centered education, teachers used to be not simply leaders, but even dictators. However, in the contemporary student-centered educational paradigm, teachers are viewed 'in the shadow' – as facilitators, mediators (among administration, parents, students, course book and curriculum), efficient and friendly environment creators, stage managers, etc." (Doghonadze, 2020, p.148)."

Unfortunately, "policies at the local, state, and national levels are initiated, implemented, revised, and abolished continuously with little or no input from teachers" (Watkins, 2022, p. 1), legislation changes mostly occur based on policy decision-makers personal or political views (Black, 2020; Strauss, 2018). Teachers only via administrators or teacher organisations have a chance to indirectly be involved in the policymaking process, this is why their voice is seldom heard. "Teacher organizations such as the National Education Association or the American Federation of Teachers tend to focus on conditions of employment and not policy reform" (Watkins, 2022, p.8). This is one of the reasons why teachers so often resist reform – they do not feel that it is *their* reform and that it is going to help them or their students, to improve the education system. "Teachers are often skeptical or dissatisfied with reform but feel powerless and unimportant in the creation of policy and reform" (Watkins, 2022, p.14). "Teachers may be more likely to accept reforms they perceive as fitting with their preexisting beliefs and do not require them to significantly change what they do in their classroom" (Watkins, 2022, p.15).

To improve education systems, research plays an immense role. Innovations in teaching and learning methods and strategies, materials, educational technologies, classroom management can be suggested to wider application only after their empirical assessment. Although here researchers are the central figures, their cooperation with teachers plays a pivotal role. Experiments may be planned by researchers, but it is teachers who have to conduct them. The better teachers are informed, the more reliable are the experimentation results (Krainer, 2014).

To sum up: all educational stakeholders have an important role in education systems, however, teachers' role is special: teachers conduct classes, motivate students, provide feedback to them, report to administration and parents, look for new ways for efficient teaching and assessment, support each other, initiate events, etc. They are the face of the given school, eventually, they (of course, with their students) are the face of the educational system.

REFERENCES

Akın Sabuncu, S., & Ok, A. (2021). Essential qualities for elementary teachers of the 21st century: Voices of key stakeholders. *Elementary Education Online*, *20*(1), 523–552. DOI: 10.17051/ilkonline.2021.01.045

Alemu, A. (2024). Challenges and prospects: Understanding teachers' attitudes towards the teaching profession in Ethiopia. *Social Sciences & Humanities Open*, *10*, 100933. DOI: 10.1016/j.ssaho.2024.100933

Almusaed, A., & Almssad, A. (2020). *The role of the supervisor on developing PhD students' skills. International Conference on Social, and Education Science*. International Society for Technology, Education, and Science., Retrieved from https://files.eric.ed.gov/fulltext/ED626403.pdf

Auguste, B., Kihn, P., & Miller, M. (2010). *Closing the talent gap: Attracting and retaining top-third graduates to careers in teaching. An international and market research-based perspective.* McKinsey & Co. Retrieved from https://www.mckinsey.com/~/media/mckinsey/industries/public%20and%20social%20sector/our%20insights/closing%20the%20teaching%20talent%20gap/closing-the-teaching-talent-gap.pdf

Avalos, B., Gupta, L., LaDousa, C., Vickers, E. A., Ogunniran, M. O., & Chakraborty, A. (2022). The teaching profession in context: issues for policy and practice around the world. In A.K., Duraiappah, N.M. van Atteveldt, G. Borst, S. Bugden, O. Ergas, T. Gilead, L. Gupta, J. Mercier, K. Pugh, N.C. Singh, & and Vickers, E.A. (Eds.). *Reimagining education: The international science and evidence-based education assessment* (pp. 664-712). UNESCO MGIEP. DOI: 10.56383/PVBF4652

Bademcioğlu, M., Karataş, H., & Alcı, B. (2014). The investigation of teacher candidates' attitudes towards teaching profession. *International Journal of Educational Research*, *5*(2), 16–29.

Bennett, N. (2008). Distributed leadership and IT. In Voogt, J., & Knezek, G. (Eds.), *International handbook of information technology in primary and secondary education.* Springer., DOI: 10.1007/978-0-387-73315-9_35

Black, D. W. (2020). *Schoolhouse burning: Public education and the assault on American democracy.* Public Affairs, Hachette Book Group.

Bozkurt, B., & Aktaş, H. İ. (2022). The examination of teachers' perceptions relating to job satisfaction: A mixed-method study. *International Journal of Psychology and Educational Studies*, *9*, 841–855. DOI: 10.52380/ijpes.2022.9.4.704

Chan, C. K. Y., & Tsi, L. H. (2023). The AI revolution in education: will AI replace or assist teachers in higher education? *arXiv preprint* arXiv:2305.01185. Retrieved from https://arxiv.org/pdf/2305.01185

Cole, M. (1985). *A crisis of identity: Teachers in times of political and economical changes. Coloquio Internacional sobre Función Docente y Salud Mental*. Universidad de Salamanca.

Darling-Hammond, L. (2010). *Evaluating teacher effectiveness: How teacher performance assessments can measure and improve teaching*. Retrieved from https://edpolicy.stanford.edu/sites/default/files/publications/evaluatingteachereffectiveness_0.pdf

Daulai, R. F., Irawan, R., Nurhalizah, S., Murtadho, W., & Siahaan, A. (2023). Basic concepts of the teaching professionalism in elementary education institutions. *Jurnal Basicedu*, *7*(2), 1171–117. DOI: 10.31004/basicedu.v7i2.4826

Davis, J., & Smith, T. (1996). *General social surveys, 1972–1996: Cumulative codebook*. National Opinion Research Center.

Doghonadze, N. (2020). Teachers as educational leaders. In *International Research Conference on Education, English Language Teaching and Literature (IRCEELT) Proceedings*, pp.147-155. Tbilisi, International Black Sea University.

Dusaban, A. O., & Olana, S. S. (2025). Teachers' attitude towards their job and their work performance. *Psychology and Education*, *48*(5), 807–817. DOI: 10.70838/pemj.480509

Eacute, J., & Esteve, M. (2000). The transformation of the teachers' role at the end of the twentieth century: New challenges for the future. *Educational Review*, *52*(2), 197–207. DOI: 10.1080/713664040

Editora, A. (2023). The school and the appreciation of the teaching identity. *Arts, Linguistics, Literature, and Language*, *3*(6), 2–6. Advance online publication. DOI: 10.22533/at.ed.929362330085

Ezer, H., Gilat, I., & Sagee, R. (2010). Perception of teacher education and professional identity among novice teachers.

Felicetti, V. L. (2011). Teacher education: From education to teacher substance and practice. *Research in Higher Education*, *13*, 1–8.

Freeman, R. E. (1984). *Strategic management. A stakeholder approach*. Pitman.

Garon, I. (2013). Why do people view teaching as a 'B-list' job? Retrieved from https://www.theguardian.com/commentisfree/2013/sep/05/education-us-teacher-shortages

Greenwood, E. (1957). Attributes of a profession. *Social Work*, *2*(3), 45–55.

Houser, K. (2017, December 12). *The solution to our education crisis might be AI*. Futurism. Retrieved from https://futurism.com/ai-teachers-education-crisis

Ingersoll, R. M., & Collins, J. G. (2018). The status of teaching as a profession. In Ballantine, J. H., Spade, J. Z., & Stuber, J. M. (Eds.), *Schools and society: A sociological approach to education* (6th ed., pp. 199–213). SAGE.

Issan, S.A.Y., Al-Nabhani, H.Z., Kazem, A.M., &Al-Ani, W.T. (2011). Omani teachers' attitudes towards teaching as a profession.

Jan, H. (2017). Teacher of 21st century: Characteristics and development. *Research on Humanities and Social Sciences*, *7*(9), 50–54.

Khadija, H. (2022). Stakeholders in education. *The Annals of the University of Oradea. Economic Sciences*, *31*(1), 425–435.

Krainer, K. (2014). Teachers as stakeholders in mathematics education research. *The Montana Math Enthusiast*, *11*(1), 49–60. DOI: 10.54870/1551-3440.1291

Little, J. W. (1990). Teachers as colleagues. In Lieberman, A. (Ed.), *Schools as collaborative cultures* (pp. 165–194). The Falmer Press, Taylor and Francis.

Malunda, P. N., Atwebembeire, J., & Ssentamu, P. N. (2021). Research supervision as an antecedent to graduate student progression in the public higher institutions of learning in Uganda. *International Journal of Learning*. *Teaching and Educational Research*, *20*(5), 73–95.

Mondal, S., & Panda, R. (2025). Attitude of student teachers towards teaching profession. [IJOMR]. *Indian Journal of Multidisciplinary Research*, *2*(1), 288–295. DOI: 10.70798/IJOMR/020040033

Niemi, H., Toom, A., Kallioniemi, A., & Lavonen, J. (2018). The teaching profession amid changes in the educational ecosystems. In Niemi, H., Toom, A., Kallioniemi, A., & Lavonen, J. (Eds.), *The teacher's role in the changing globalizing world: Resources and challenges related to the professional work of teaching* (pp. 141–149). Brill Sense. DOI: 10.1163/9789004372573_010

Redecker, C., Leis, M., Leendertse, M., Punie, Y., Gijsbers, G., Kirshner, P., Stoyanov, S., & Hoogveld, B. (2011). *The future of learning: Preparing for change*. Publications Office of the European Union.

Rowan, B. (1994). Comparing teachers' work with work in other occupations: Notes on the professional status of teaching. *Educational Researcher*, *23*(6), 4–17. DOI: 10.3102/0013189X023006004

Soundararajan, M., Prabakaram, B., Padminidevi, K. R., & Saravanakumar, A. (2022). *Teacher professionalism and teacher education*. KAAV. DOI: 10.52458/9789391842598.2022.tb

Speakola. (2013). *Malala Yousafzai: 'One child, one teacher, one pen and one book can change the world', UN Youth Assembly – 2013.* Retrieved from https://speakola.com/ideas/malala-yousafzai-un-youth-assembly-2013

Strauss, V. (2018, February 12). *What happens when legislators don't ask teachers how education laws affect real kids in actual classrooms.* The Washington Post. https://www.washingtonpost.com/news/answer-sheet/wp/2018/02/12/what-happens-when-legislators-dont-ask-teachers-how-education-laws-affect-real-kids-in-actual-classrooms/classrooms/

Stromquist, N. P. (2018). *The global status of teachers and the teaching profession.* Education International Research. Retrieved from https://ei-ie-al.org/sites/default/files/docs/2018_ei_research_statusofteachers_eng_final.pdf

Swargiary, K. (2024). *The role of stakeholders in education: Government, school leaders, teachers, staff, parents, community, and society towards students.* EdTech Research Association.

United States Department of Education. (2011). *Our future, our teachers: The Obama administration's plan for teacher education. Reform and Improvement.* Retrieved from https://www.ed.gov/media/document/our-future-our-teachers-accesiblepdf-54971.pdf

Ünsal, S., Ağçam, R., & Korkmaz, F. (2017). Exploring teaching profession from a sociological perspective: Evidence from Turkey. *Universal Journal of Educational Research*, *5*(5), 874–880. DOI: 10.13189/ujer.2017.050519

Vazquez, A. B., Perez, L. D., Pacheco, L. C., & Flores, I. R. (2024). Becoming a secondary school teacher: Keys to a meaningful professional identity. *Teaching and Teacher Education*, *148*, 104697. Advance online publication. DOI: 10.1016/j.tate.2024.104697

Watkins, N. A. (2022). The role of teachers in educational policymaking. *Literature Reviews in Education and Human Services*, *1*(1), 1–23.

Section 1

Chapter 1
The Global Context of Education

Natela Doghonadze
http://orcid.org/0000-0001-7333-8692
International Black Sea University, Georgia

ABSTRACT

Chapter 1 describes the challenges faced by educators, the impact of socio-political changes on education systems, and how the prestige of teaching jobs is changing. The level of knowledge and skills in many countries remains low. The reasons include pedagogical and socio-economic factors. Education cannot instantly make socioeconomic inequality, scarcity of resources, increased migration, violence, lack of cultural tolerance, and military conflicts disappear, but it can gradually contribute to struggling these challenges. Economic crises have a negative impact on the education system and the quality of education. Limited budget resources are a challenge for educators' salaries and educational resources. The third sub-chapter summarises previous publications of the authors dealing with popularity of teaching jobs. Teachers are one of the most numerous professions in the world. They greatly impact the future of educational institutions' leavers. Without them, there might not be any other professions. However, not many school leavers choose education majors worldwide.

2.1. DISCUSSION OF THE CHALLENGES FACED BY EDUCATORS WORLDWIDE

The chapter is going to analyse and sum up the publications mentioning numerous challenges that contemporary education faces: increasing the level of education in those countries that lag behind those countries which have achieved better learning outcomes, solving the problem of increasing the number of teachers without decreasing their qualification level, etc. On the one hand, to provide quality education, peace is a prerequisite condition, on the other hand, if educators are supported to carry out their mission, there will be greater opportunities to achieve peace. Dealing with issues of globalisation and integration of technologies into education are simultaneously a rich soil for improving education and a threat, if applied unethically and thoughtlessly.

Pedagogical and socio-economic challenges

In 1993, UNESCO established a Commission on Education for the Twenty-first Century. The Commission, headed by Jacques Delors, aimed to develop a document that would enable education in the 21st century to help make society a happier place. "Its image of a successful education system is one built on four pillars: learning to know, learning to do, learning to be, and learning to live together" (Carneiro & Draxler, 2008, p. 149). While 'learning to know' has been the goal of education for a long time, still, the level of knowledge and skills in many countries remains lower than desirable. The reasons include both pedagogical (number and qualification of teachers, teaching and learning methods and strategies) and socio-economic (wars and conflicts, poverty, prejudices, material base of educational institutions, and the system as a whole) factors. 'Learning to do' deals with the pragmatics of education: how school and university graduates can apply

DOI: 10.4018/979-8-3373-8983-7.ch001

the obtained knowledge and skills in real life, can be employed, maintain the jobs and build successful careers, simply be happy. 'Learning to be' emphasises self-actualisation: realising their potential and achieving their dreams. The most problematic component of the education of the 21st century is 'learning to live together', beginning with building harmonious relations in the classroom, devoid of bullying, full of mutual respect and support, through culturally-sensitive environment in which diversity is viewed as a benefit and not as a challenge, to peaceful cohabitation between and within countries. Of course, it would be idealistic to believe that all these tasks can be fully fulfilled, however, "the Commission does not see education as a miracle cure or a magic formula opening the door to a world in which all ideals will be attained, but as one of the principal means available to foster a deeper and more harmonious form of human development and thereby to reduce poverty, exclusion, ignorance, oppression and war" (Delors et al., 1996, p.11). Inequality, scarcity of resources, increased migration, violence, lack of cultural tolerance, and military conflicts remain to be challenges to fulfilling the functions of education. While educational institutions are doing relatively well developing democracy and humanism, it is difficult to say so of the society (Carneiro & Draxler, 2008). In connection with massive migration, two views on 'learning to live together' develop: one, that the local community should be more tolerant to the traditions of migrants (such as Muslim girls wearing scarfs to schools and universities), the other, that the migrants should comply with the local norm. Both parties have their arguments, and the golden middle is difficult to find. The educational system have to do its best so that to benefit from both the 'importing' and 'exporting' societies (Carneiro & Draxler, 2008, p. 153). The Delors (1996) report recommends to teach/study history objectively, especially avoiding emotions of hate, trying to see both the advantages and the disadvantages of relationships between the neighbouring countries. The mosaic of views and not one-sided 'normative' interpretation of events is suggested.

Democratic management of educational institutions and inclusive admissions are other levers that have to ameliorate the society. "Learning to live together must be, including through images, a way to decode the reality of the other, to understand the real and perceived images that dominate her or his life, in order to find a meeting point" (Carneiro & Draxler, 2008, p. 155). Mass media have a great role in it, which, unfortunately, is not always positive. Schools have to select mass media materials that lead to better understanding each other and not to incitement of hatred.

Young people who live in an environment of hatred may develop disciplinary and aggression problems at school which mirror society outside the school building. Cooperation/collaboration skills and teamwork should and can be developed at school through relevant activities. Dichotomous (black-and-white) views on social problems should be avoided, especially while teaching at high school and university. Cultural sensitivity has to be developed in teachers and students. Students should have an opportunity to participate in "out-of-school experiences (exchange, volunteerism, peer teaching) that contribute to learning together" (Carneiro & Draxler, 2008, p. 160).

Challenges dealing with globalisation

"In 21st century, we live in an interconnected world where globalization, Information Communication Technology and knowledge explosion have shrunk the world into a global village" (Malik, 2018, p. 9). Schools are often unable to keep pace with technological and socio-economic developments. Due to it, they tend to produce graduates without skills needed in contemporary life. The internet provides plenty of information, but teachers (and students) often lack understanding about how to turn this information into practically applicable knowledge. Lecture and textbook-based, one-size-fits-all education is no longer appropriate. The volume of knowledge/information has increased so much that to learn everything, even within a narrow specialty, is impossible. That is why teachers' task, after providing some basic knowledge is rather to teach students how to learn than to provide to them heaps of information. "The modern global economy doesn't pay you for what you know because internet knows everything. The world economy pays you for what you can do with what you know" (Malik, 2018, p. 12). "Literacy and numeracy, ICT skills, learning to learn, evaluating and problem solving, interpersonal and civic competencies, entrepreneurship, cultural awareness, flexibility, adaptability, working independently, critical thinking and self-directed learning are some of the crucial skills are the required attributes of 21st century workforce" (Malik, 2018, p. 11). While literacy, numeracy, and ICT skills are taught within certain subjects, other skills need to be taught within all subjects, which often causes teacher resistance, due to overload, lack of corresponding knowledge, skills, and training, and conservative views on teaching. Besides, students lack opportunities to practice what they learn at school outside its walls.

Malik (2018) mentions commercialisation of higher education (including teacher education) as one of the challenges to providing quality education. Admission policies based on meritocracy seem effective for training qualified teachers. However, socially privileged groups have a better chance of being admitted, while problems dealing with equity, including gender and minorities, often do not enable the admission of enthusiastic candidates who would be able to contribute to the improvement of education quality.

With all social-economic problems and waves of migration (that often entail mutual misunderstanding and aggression) increasing, juvenile delinquency is on the rise. This concerns school, through the need to increase safety, on the one hand, and the need to teach students human values, on the other.

Challenges dealing with continuous reforms

Since the 1980s, the Global Education Reforms Movement (GERM), started by the US, UK, and Australia, has been spreading all over the world. Standards-based education must provide quality education wherever a person learns. However, it is not devoid of challenges. It often imposes principles and requirements typical for the Western world, without considering local traditions, which impedes the implication of reforms, and even causes conflicts. Focusing on core subjects may ignore literature and art as being 'useless', which brings about the technocratisation and dehumanisation of education (Doghonadze, 2016). Finnish education, instead of hunting for scores, offers to substitute subject-based education by topic/phenomenon teaching. Time will show whether after this innovation they will remain among nations leading in school education, however, I personally would express doubts dealing with less systematic approach in this case (haven't educators tried to advertise it under the name of project-based teaching, which eventually turned out an effective additional tool but a failed approach to curriculum building?).

One of the greatest challenges of providing quality education is the quality of teacher education and further professional development. Besides, teachers should be typically paid for their work to enable them to work at their best, rather than having to combine several jobs to earn enough money.

Masters (2015) identifies five main challenges education policy makers face today:

1) Improving the status of teachers – via creating/sharing their positive images through mass media, creating better conditions for their work (e.g., decreasing the workload and the number of students in class), and, of course, better salaries.
2) Reducing the socio-economic differences among students.
3) Improving the curriculum which provides links between subjects and integrates 'life skills'.
4) Personalising teaching and learning methods.
5) Timely identifying students at risk and providing support to them.

Mass media has a great impact on people's perception of things (Gurung & Chauhan, 2025), being the main source of information nowadays. Of course, people's opinions of teaching jobs are not limited by teachers' public image created by television, newspapers, and the internet. They are also formed based on personal experience and information obtained from family, friends, and acquaintances. That being said, it is difficult to underestimate the emotional impact of mass media and the speed with which it gets its message out.

While speaking about raising teacher salaries, it is important to realise that salary is important not *per se*, but in comparison of the costs of living. Raising it is crucial in countries where teachers' salaries do not enable them to survive, where they have to combine jobs to make enough money, leaving insufficient time to grow professionally. There are countries like Canada where teacher salaries are not the central issue of improving the quality of education, however, they matter, as teacher status and attitude towards teachers in society greatly depends on it. Salaries are also essential for teachers' self-respect and job satisfaction: when teachers' efforts are much more than their pay, it may cause dropout, burnout and a lack of self-respect.

In his later publication (Masters, 2023), he mentions two challenges of school reform: better preparing school graduates for their future and ensuring that every student learns as successfully as possible. The amount of curriculum content has to be reduced, according to him, in order to provide deeper understanding (critical and creative thinking, solving non-routine problems) and opportunities to apply knowledge. Promoting social and emotional skills have to be integrated into the curriculum. Personalised learning is needed, especially for underachievers. This problem can be solved only by applying modern technologies. Whole-person of holistic learning must be applied, taking into consideration students' strengths and weaknesses, their learning style. Probably, contemporary education system expects too much of a teacher. Specialists (and/or special computer programs) should help teachers define the most effective ways of teaching underachieving students. To provide learning as development, curricula should make learning systematic, linking knowledge of different subjects with each other. A good teacher and student support system is needed to provide quality teaching.

According to Salmi (2001), many universities refuse to update their policies. He even brings a shocking example of Bob Jones University in South Carolina where interracial dating is still prohibited. Salmi names three significant challenges to higher education in the 21st century: economic globalisation, the increasing role of knowledge as the basis of professional growth, and technological revolution, which entail both opportunities and threats.

Economic globalisation includes both opportunities (e.g., to study across the globe) and problems (e.g., crises tend to become global, as the COVID pandemic revealed). Degrees of international recognition are especially valued. Branches of internationally recognised universities are opened worldwide. All this increases competition and requires local universities to offer high-quality education at a cost-effective price. At the same time, cooperation between universities, both domestic and cross-border, also helps universities survive (Salmi, 2001).

Knowledge is becoming as (if not more) important as material resources; therefore, education is getting more and more commercialised. This brings about the issue of adequate financing of higher education. Multidisciplinarity is a new higher education feature, which requires to develop specialties at the intersection of traditional fields. The university that fall behind this trend may lose their popularity (Salmi, 2001).

Challenges dealing with the incorporation of new technologies

Due to technological revolution, knowledge can be disseminated through technologies, but how to judge what information available on the internet is reliable? Among the advantages of technology application in higher education is the opportunity to apply new knowledge to real-life situations. Continuing education (often done online) is becoming a necessity, but the issue is how to incorporate it into the system of higher education. In Finland, for example, more people study at university part-time, to compensate for some lacking knowledge of innovations, or to get a new specialty, than students who came to universities from the school bench. As higher education is no longer only for young people, so, teaching methods more appropriate for adults are gaining importance. Online classes, for example, should be not only synchronous (which enables some direct communication between lecturers and students) but also asynchronous (considering the busy schedules of older, usually employed, students) (Salmi, 2001).

The quality of wireless internet connectivity is becoming crucial for providing up-to-date education, as many universities are substituting on-paper libraries by virtual ones. In general, online education is viewed as a more cost-effective one; however, its quality so far raises many questions, such as the possibility of students' socialisation, developing values side by side with knowledge, and establishing teacher-student rapport. Students cannot benefit from immersion into a different culture through studies abroad if they occur online (Salmi, 2001). Kalyani (2024) enumerates the following possible challenges associated with technology application: inappropriate content of materials, disconnected youth lacking social-emotional development, cyberbullying, cheating, distraction, overdependence on technology, unequal access, technical difficulties, lack of hands-on learning, and inadequate teacher training.

Salmi (2001) expresses concern about the stability of education in ever-changing reality of the 21st century. He believes it will be difficult to provide balance between 'high tech' and 'high touch'. He views as problematic the control of national educational authorities over the work of branches of international higher education institutions. Intellectual property rights of online educational materials are an additional challenge.

Scott (2000) emphasises that it is incorrect to use 'globalisation' and 'internationalisation' of higher education as synonyms. He claims that globalisation implies cooperation, while internationalisation is a kind of neocolonialism, where

Western education is viewed as exemplary, while the rest is underestimated. Only after 1945 and, more so, the 1960s have the universities "came to be embraced within a wider democratic movement aimed at expanding educational opportunity" (Scott, 2000, p. 5). He characterises universities of the past with nostalgy as "a relatively autonomous space protected from the transgressions of politics or the market" (Scott, 2000, p. 7). The universities of today, he states, are losing more and more autonomy due to standardisation and viewing universities as factories. Due to democratic processes, university students and graduates are no longer representative of the elite; successful universities have developed tight links with business (he mentions them as 'corporate universities'), other universities are destined to decline.

Like many other authors, Judijanto et al. (2024) mention three factors of challenges in the 21st-century education: "technological advancements, globalization, and a rapidly evolving socio-economic landscape" (p. 298). Technology is only then stimulating education, when it is pedagogically appropriate. Virtual classrooms and online courses make education available 24/7 available, they break through classroom walls and open the possibilities of real-life application of the knowledge gained in class. However, research is needed how to minimise the possible harmful effects like game addiction, distraction, etc. Issues of equality and equity dealing with access to technologies play a huge role in the progress of education, especially in poorer countries. Student zero-percent or low-percent credit is offered as one of outcomes for helping young people from various social groups to enter into higher education.

Globalisation adds interconnectedness and diversity to educational environments. Still, it entails risks of cultural shock and even conflicts, as well as cyberbullying, if teachers (and parents) are not aware of methods to deal with them. Application of new technologies, project-based, interactive, and experiential learning requires higher qualifications from teachers, especially those who received their professional education before all these innovations. Without regularly reviewed teacher training and development, technologies and globalisation are rather a threat than an advantage. Healthcare crises, climatic changes, and military conflicts demand that education urgently brings up young people caring about the future of humanity, not only their personal goals (Judijanto et al., 2024). Applying innovations is more and more often required from educators, which often causes their resistance and irritation. Information about successful teaching and other ways of persuasion are needed to stimulate teachers not to lag behind the new trends. Legal considerations are particularly important in this context, especially in relation to AI and academic honesty (Judijanto et al., 2024).

Challenges inherited from the previous generations of teachers and students

Besides the challenges specific to the 21st century, there are the challenges of education that have not lost their significance: student discipline and lack of motivation, teacher qualification, overload and burnout, etc. Ispas and Ispas (2023) claim that discipline, including "rule adherence, respect for peers and objects, accountability, cooperation, and self-regulation" (p.5) is essential not only for teaching/learning environment but also in life, as discipline and organisation are valued at workplaces as well. Classroom discipline greatly depends on teachers: positive classroom environment, effective classroom planning and management, their rapport with students, application of innovative teaching methods, etc. However, the social impact (socio-economic status of children's families, stability in society, and socially widespread values) is an important factor as well.

Gregory et al. (2021) state that out-of-class and out-of-school suspensions as the methods of discipline establishment do not work, instead, they reinforce marginalisation and institutionalised racism. School-Wide Positive Behavioral Interventions and Supports (SWPBIS), Social–Emotional Learning (SEL), and Restorative Practices (RP) are actively applied to solve disciplinary and aggression problems at school.

> SWPBIS is based on a three-tiered public health approach, and suggests that a focus on systems (e.g., a school leadership team, teams for more intensive student support), data-based decision making (e.g., tracking the frequency, type, and location of office referrals and suspensions to support decision making), evidence-supported practices (behavioral, social–emotional, restorative, and trauma-informed), and monitoring outcomes (reduced disciplinary issues and improved school climate) will lead schools to sustainable and successful reform. (Gregory et al., 2021, p. 22)

The state of children's health (e.g., lack of iodine in water slows down their mental development) also impacts misbehaviour and academic achievement. Ertesvåg and Havik (2021) investigated students' proactive (i.e., not provoked by another person's behaviour) aggressiveness and their mental health issues. Among them are students who are highly motivated to gain social power by humiliating the powerless, including both students and teachers. Teachers in such cases need emotional and professional (psychologists') support to be able to work with such students. Support may also come from other students if the teacher has managed to build positive relationships with the class.

Student lack of motivation depends on their previous educational experience: if it was interesting, engaging, and successful, students normally further maintain motivation. However, if it was not positive, students are often prejudiced and do not easily react to teacher's efforts to motivate them. Zhang et al. (2022) emphasise that previous learning experiences have an impact on their expectations of learning outcomes. According to expectancy-value theory, learning motivation depends on whether students expect the study to be successful and the knowledge and outcomes to be valuable (Wigfield & Eccles, 2000). Although student motivation, like their discipline, also depends on social factors, teacher is much more powerful in influencing students' motivation via the content, activities, teaching and assessment methods.

Teacher qualification is critical for providing the knowledge and skills required by society. However, it is not always adequate. While in some countries teachers do not have the required degrees (Casian et al., 2021), in other, more developed countries, researchers (Smith, 2021) discuss the need to review the competency of teachers that stand behind the formal degree, especially, if it was obtained a long time ago. Teacher overload and burnout have a negative impact on the quality of their work. Lagawid (2024) enumerates the following factors that cause teacher overload: administrative responsibilities, class size, lesson planning, student assessments, extracurricular duties, broad curriculum requirements, insufficient time for professional development, and lack of support. Fatima et al. (2024) have found that those teachers who are not overloaded are more enthusiastic about their profession than those who are overloaded.

One more problem of schools in many countries is teacher average age. "Across OECD countries, the average age of secondary school teachers has increased by one month every year in the last decade" (OECD, 2014). Italy, Portugal, Bulgaria, Estonia, Lithuania, and Georgia are among the countries where this problem was especially acute in 2018 (OECD, 2018). The average age of school teachers was more than 50 in Czech Republic (53%), Estonia (51%), Greece (65%), Italy (61%), Lithuania (60%), Bulgaria (50%) in 2021 (OECD, 2023). Teachers working at schools are becoming older, as young people prefer to work elsewhere. Providing pensions that enable older teachers to retire, on the one hand, and creating a support and motivation system for novice teachers, on the other, is the task of the government and school administration. Teachers' age by itself is not a problem. Experienced teachers may be behind in using some contemporary technologies, but their capacity to solve problems and make decisions has increased with age, their knowledge of the subject, methods of teaching, and students' psychology have grown. The problem is that, if the trend continues, in a decade or so, countries will be experiencing a shortage of teachers, especially good ones.

The last, but not the least challenge - relationships with parents. There are two categories of parents: first, who avoid having any contact with school and believe (especially, if their children attend private schools) that their children's education is completely the responsibility of school, and second, who are actively involved in school life but are exercising too much pressure over the content and methods of education. The first category claims they are too busy and have no time to participate in school events. However, this challenge can be easily solved through contemporary technologies, organising teacher-parents meetings, both individual and group, online. Furthermore, teachers are willing to offer asynchronous communication to parents with busy schedules, providing them with information about the school and their children. Of course, much depends on teachers' ability to communicate with parents using simple vocabulary comprehensible for parents. Again, if in the past communicating parents whose native language was not the same that the education language of their children was a problem, nowadays, both teachers and parents can use online translation programs to be able to understand each other. Therefore, the problem is rather persuading parents that communication between school and them is in interests of them and their child. Some parents avoid group meeting as they are afraid of judgement (Hannon & O'Donnell, 2022). The second category may be aggressive and even take cases to court. Dealing with them requires delicacy of school administration and the effort to understand teacher motivation, to support their right for free speech (of course, when teachers observe educational ethics). In many cases, school administration prefers to support parents' claims in order to avoid social conflicts, even if the quality of education (especially students' ability to think critically) suffers as a result. Eckes and Russo (2021) mention that, although educators have been granted free speech rights by the First Amendment to the US Constitution, parents may be required to change the curriculum based on their social, political, or religious views. Due to it, American classics like *Tom Sawyer or The Catcher in the Rye* may be removed from the curriculum. If taken to court, such cases may be solved in favour of the teacher only if they can prove that the book/topic/idea is taught for purely educational reasons, not meaning any offence. However, courts often prefer to leave the decision to school boards.

To sum up,

- The challenges that teachers are experiencing nowadays are connected with the rapid changes in society as well as constantly ongoing education reform. On the one hand, the education system has to catch up and reflect the changes going on in society, on the other hand, it creates a very challenging situation for teachers not giving them enough time to be adjusted to some changes when new and new changes arise. It is especially difficult to tackle the arising challenges without a decent support from the state, the society and the educational institution they work in.
- Learning to know, to do, to be, and to live together are the goals of the education system worldwide. Teachers need to apply innovative methods of teaching and instruct students on how they can gain knowledge. While in the past teachers were mostly responsible for subject knowledge, nowadays they are also accountable for developing in their students skills that will enable them to be employed and to work efficiently. They must teach their students to engage in continuous learning, so both teachers and students must understand how learning occurs and what strategies are needed to solve educational and life problems.
- In democratic societies, education has to be student-centered, which implies knowing students' learning styles, their objective and subjective needs, strengths and weaknesses in order to help them learn to their maximum capacities. To learn efficiently, students need first of all self-observe and find out who they are and what they want. As teachers are often more qualified than parents in these respects, they need to help students in their self-assessment and self-study.
- Globalisation brings about both opportunities of various cultures benefitting from their knowledge and approaches and great threats through the interpersonal as well as international conflicts. Teaching to live together – in the classroom and in the world – is more crucial than providing students with subject knowledge. It is unrealistic to expect of educators to solve these problems, but without education the perspective of a more or less harmonious society would be too remote if possible at all.
- Disciplinary and aggression problems are getting more tense in educational institutions, solving these problems at least on the scale of one's classroom is a great step towards making societal problems less acute.
- ICT, similarly to globalisation, may contribute to improvement of education or to its deteriorisation. More visual, flexible, fast, patient, providing easy to understand and memorise materials are the features of technologies that are of great help to teachers and students. On the other hand, if completely let to be applied without any control, it may bring to cyberbullying, game addiction, and lack of motivation to study (why study, Google knows everything! – but can we understand and assess the materials that the internet offers us, without qualified guidance?). It is not by chance that Einstein warned people against a generation of idiots in the society where everything is done by machines (Government technology, 2025). Technologies have to be used to develop creativity and problem-solving skills, not to solve the problems instead of people.
- The grown numbers of people receiving education require methods that enable them to learn well, on the other hand, there is a great challenge of providing quality education to them, due to limited financial resources and to teacher qualification which is not always as high as it should be. University graduates who study well usually enter better paid and less overloaded professions. Governments need more effective approaches to teacher education and teacher support to attract best graduates to work at schools.
- Teacher education and development should provide, side by side with subject knowledge, pedagogical, psychological, social, and even financial issues. If the society wants teachers to contribute to its amelioration, society, in turn, should care more about teachers – work on improving their public image, provide them with a doable load that enables them to work on their professional growth, to be creative, and to realise individual approach to each student. Rewarding best teachers will eventually return in numerous benefits to society.
- One of the challenges schools face is the declining number of young people entering the workforce at schools. In some countries, schools risk experiencing a severe shortage of teachers within a decade.

- Relationships between schools and parents need to be harmonised. Parents must realise that teachers alone cannot provide the necessary knowledge, skills, and values to students. Schools and parents must support each other to better care for children and the future of the country they live in.

2.2. THE IMPACT OF SOCIO-POLITICAL CHANGES ON EDUCATION SYSTEMS

Gunawaradana and Karunarathna (2022) describe the impact of socio-political changes on the education system in the following way. After WWII, the concept of 'universal education' evolved, which means the right of any citizen of any country to get primary/elementary education. By the late 1960s, the majority of colonised countries gained independence, and education was regarded as one of the major public priorities. While economic growth stimulated the development of the education system, economic crises have a negative impact on it. Limited budget resources are a challenge for educators' salaries and educational resources (books, photocopies, technologies, internet availability, etc.). Young (2014) mentioned, for example, that during the economic recession in Greece, where most English-speaking educational programs are carried out by private educational institutions, the staff suffered from salary delays due to the delays in payment of study fees. According to Bamigboye et al. (2016), in Nigeria, the education system almost completely depends on governmental expenditure; not only did teacher salary decrease during the crisis but also so did the reputation of the teachers' profession, which had always before the crisis been very much respected. The best school graduates stopped choosing the profession, which, in turn, affected the quality of education negatively. Hungry students from poor families could not concentrate in class and often missed classes to help their parents make some money for living. In Indonesia, parents from poor families had to choose whether to let at least the elder children to complete their education in order to be able to support their families in the future or to keep their younger children in schools (Nambissan, 2010 as referred to in Gunawaradana & Karunarathna, 2022).

Both the COVID-19 pandemic and the economic crisis in Sri Lanka in the beginning of 2022 resulted in deprivation or loss of learning opportunities due to the school closure. Socioeconomically disadvantaged groups especially suffered from it – children's nutrition did not provide normal conditions for education. Online learning was problematic, too, as it increased parents' expenditures on their children's education. The crisis struck teachers as well (Leanage & Saito, 2023).

According to the International Telecommunication Union (2019), "93% of the world's population lives in areas with internet access, only 53% of them have the means to utilize it". A large number of students in India, for example, were unable to apply digital learning; students' physical and mental health was impacted (Dayal & Prabitha, 2023). According to the 130 online interviews conducted by Dayal and Prabitha (2023), only 22.1% of the respondents agreed that online education was fulfilling its purpose, while 30.6% were satisfied with the quality of online assessment. Almost half (44.6%) of the respondents would not like to continue learning online after the pandemic was over. "Substantial deficiencies in the education domain, which were already there, have not only become more prominent but have also been intensified within the COVID-19 crisis" (Dayal & Prabitha, 2023). These results, however, do not reject using online learning, on the contrary, they underline that better conditions for online learning should be created in developing countries. Online exams require better invigilation. The benefits of online learning should be combined with the advantages of face-to-face classes (of course, when feasible.

"Once an elite establishment that excluded individuals based on gender, religion, race/ethnicity, and social class, U.S. higher education has transformed itself over and over to fulfill its role as a primary gateway to the middle-class and an important provider of opportunities to historically oppressed members of society" (Smith, 2013, p. 154). In such developed countries as the USA, higher education also suffered from crises. Although about 80% of higher education institutions are not private, they employ various funding schemes which may become vulnerable during crises (Smith, 2013). Post-secondary education institutions are free of high levels of government control and have long protected its independence. However, in the circumstances of economic crises, it may become a challenge. While at least 37 states had to cut assistance to public colleges and universities by 2010, private higher educational institutions also had to reduce the expenditure due to decreased endowments. In crisis, enrollments in the free state universities increased, which might be viewed as a positive change for them, however, in conditions of reduced state assistance, this lead to the decrease in the quality of tuition. The Obama administration tried to compensate the economic downturn by providing a seven-billion-dollars assistance to public higher education and twenty billion for research, however, it could not help those higher education institutions where the financial problems turned out to be deep, due to the diversity of legislations in states and districts. To maintain their high reputation in an increasingly competitive world, according to Smith (2013), the decentralisation of the educational system creates many barriers.

Education and socio-political changes are interrelated concepts. Education can have a significant impact on the society and, vice-versa, social changes cause certain changes in education. Public education has always served the interests of the state. "The changes of the higher education systems, governments and finances are embedded in the political transformations, and aim to meet the needs of the political processes" (Kozma, 2008). The Bologna Process, for instance, which became possible only in conditions of globalisation, has reflected the development of the European Union, the desire to make European diplomas readable and legally accepted for/among European countries, at the same time one of its major goals had been to increase the respect of European education. It has exhibited the possibilities of free market: teacher, student, and graduate mobility, and possibilities to develop and carry out joint research and study projects. It has stimulated education reform, especially in East European countries and has contributed to democratic changes in education and the society.

According to Gadzhimuradova (2022), in ancient Greece, there were two approaches to the understanding the relations between society and education. One approach, Socratic, states that knowledge is acquired just for the love of truth. This approach probably influences the society, via developing knowledgeable population, but is not influenced by the latter. The other approach - that of Sophists - requires that learners develop their communication and public speaking skills, enabling them to become full members of society. In this approach, both society and the education impact each other: the society tends to develop individuals that match its demands and the outstanding individuals become politicians and can impact the development of society. In the process of development, society and education have been tightly linked. According to the mathematician and philosopher Rene Descartes, doubt provides progress of thought, education, and, therefore, the society, while Immanuel Kant insisted that only through education a person can realise his potential, to make public and private use of his knowledge, and Georg Wilhelm Hegel underscored that education develop continuously with society. Contemporary education is based on the socio-cultural approach to educational philosophy (Gadzhimuradova, 2022).

"Globalization, the rapid development of the post-industrial and informational society, natural and climatic changes, intercultural societies and the human capital required in its formation sharply marked the need to identify new ideological foundations and guidelines in the world educational system, in order to train people to answer properly to all these challenges " (Gadzhimuradova, 2022, p, 84). The globalisation and the consequent export of Western education to other countries serve the development of democratic societies. On the other hand, just introducing Western curricula/content and student-centered teaching style, without creating proper conditions of good teaching (normal class size, well-equipped educational institutions, adequate funding) cannot yield the desirable results. Besides, the active migration characteristic of today's world requires the existing education systems to adjust to develop a qualified group of migrants, as the Global Talent Competitiveness Index (GTCI, 2025) report revealed a growing gap of qualification levels in developed and developing countries. This emphasises the need to develop quality education across the globe, not only in developed countries. Online education is of great help in this process.

Zalli (2024) emphasised that globalisation encourages the exchange of ideas, growth of democratic values, and improves cultural understanding in education (however, it may lead to cultural conflicts, unless education underscores its benefits). It makes technological advances faster across the globe. "Multicultural curricula encompass educational approaches that embrace diversity and inclusivity within the learning environment. These programs are designed to go beyond traditional educational frameworks by incorporating a wide range of perspectives, experiences, and cultural content" (Zalli, 2024, p.59). With all the benefits to education, globalisation is linked with challenges as well: the inequality divide between the developed and developing nations, "Profit-driven motives in education, sometimes overshadow genuine learning.... The turning of knowledge into a commodity, especially by linking university work with community, business, and government priorities, has caused conflicts between more practical disciplines like science and technology and the more theoretical ones like arts and humanities " (Zalli, 2024, p. 61).

Nowadays, OECD countries' policies prefer those migrants who possess high-level of academic degrees and skills – these migrants more easily become green card holders. However, university ratings play a great role in defining whether the diploma does provide the knowledge and skills that are needed by employers (Niraula & Valentin, 2019). If the qualifications of high-skilled migrant workers, especially from Asia and Africa, mismatch the skill level of the jobs that they are offered, and their pay is low, 'deskilling' may occur. Guo (2015 as referred to by Niraula and Valentin, 2019), for instance, mentions that in Canada, a proclaimed multicultural/immigrant society, immigrants are often are often not only gendered and classed but also racialised, which becomes the reason of social tensions. Niraula and Valentin (2019) stress that Nordic countries view that inviting many international students to their universities can partially reduce the existing problems, as many of them eventually become high-skilled migrants. On the other hand, this attitude becomes the reason of 'brain drain' from developing countries.

Niraula and Valentin (2019) research describes Danish migration policy. In 2007, at the time of economic boom and shortage of high-skilled workers in certain sectors, Denmark allowed non-EU citizens with a minimum bachelor's degree equivalent to Danish standards to get work permits for an initial period of three years, with possibilities for further extension of maximum five years. However, 43 percent of the 5,800 green card holders were hired for low-skilled work. Most of them were from India, Iran, Pakistan, Bangladesh, Nepal, and China. They were not only low-paid but also low-status population. As a result, the process of getting a green card was reformed in 2015. The duration of stay was limited to five years, and the extension was possible only if they earned DKK 323,198 (approximately 44,000 Euro) during the preceding 12 months.

Although the majority of the skilled workers experiencing deskilling come from the so-called 'Global South' (countries with a relatively low level of economic development, situated to the south of most developed countries), some cases are different. Przybyszewska (2021) studied why many Polish high-skilled employees choose to work in Norway, taking low-skilled jobs. They are overrepresented in the construction industry and cleaning services, and underrepresented in managerial and academic jobs in Norway, compared to the locals. Due to the saturation of the Polish labour market with qualified specialists, some Poles, especially men, begin to underestimate their higher education diplomas obtained at home. "Working below one's level of competence, aside from being a loss at the macro-level, is also disadvantageous for individuals, who may suffer from psychological and social distress" (Moussaoui & Agoub, 2011 p. 102 as referenced in Przybyszewska (2021, p. 36). One of the reasons why they experience deskilling is the perception of 'otherness' by local employers. They take the jobs most of Norwegians do not want to take. Among the reasons many Polish migrants cannot get high-skilled jobs in Norway is lack of knowledge of the Norwegian language before the arrival to Norway. They are unaware of the agencies that would help them to have their diplomas recognised. The decision to migrate is often taken spontaneously, which means they arrive to the country unprepared. The 'temporary' low-skilled work often remains constant for years. Reskilling may help as long as they do not try to occupy jobs higher than locals. "Racialisation includes not only the personal quality of non-Norwegianness but also related attributes, like for instance, a lack of professional experience from Norway" (Przybyszewska (2021, p. 45). 'Polishness' and, more widely, 'East Europeanness' often becomes stigmatising for migrants seeking for jobs corresponding to their qualification.

2.3. PRESTIGE/POPULARITY OF TEACHING JOBS (A CASE OF AZERBAIJAN, GEORGIA, IRAQ, AND THE US/CANADA)

Introduction

The prestige of a profession/occupation in the chapter is understood as a social status/standing of a profession/occupation, including how people judge about a profession/job, possibility to be employed, the necessity of the job for others, the difficulty of obtaining the profession, and renumeration. (Pomeroy, 2008). The Britannica Dictionary (n.d., a), defines prestige as "the respect and admiration that someone or something gets for being successful or important", while it defines popularity as "the state of being liked, enjoyed, accepted, or done by a large number of people: the quality or state of being popular." Although the two terms are close, a prestigious/respected profession, however, may not be a popular choice, due to the difficulty of entering the profession (much time needed to learn, sophisticated and abundant content, high requirements to the quality of the job and its cost/efficiency outcomes may frighten away rather extrinsically than intrinsically motivated young people).

As mentioned in my foreword, together with four colleagues, I undertook three studies on the popularity/prestige of teaching jobs reflected in four publications:

Doghonadze, N., & De Bello, T. C. (2024). Why do young people not want to teach any more? Proceedings of international research conference on education, English language and literature teaching (IRCEELT) (pp. 6-10).
Doghonadze, N., De Bello, T. C., Aliyev, A., Halawachi, H., & Ulker, V. (2023). Student views on the popularity/ prestige of teaching jobs (A case of Georgia, Azerbaijan, Iraq, and the USA/Canada). Professional Studies: Theory and Practice, 28(1), 4–13. doi:10.56131/pstp.2024.28.1.240
Doghonadze, N., De Bello, T. C., Aliyev, A., Halawachi, H., & Ulker, V. (2025a). Do parents view teaching as a prestigious career for their children? Addaiyan Journal of Arts, Humanities and Social Sciences, 7(2), 07-19.
Doghonadze, N., De Bello, T. C., Aliyev, A., Ulker, V., & Halawachi, H. (2025b). Teachers' perceptions of their profession's prestige. Journal of Education in Black Sea Countries, 10(2), 25–52.

Initially, we wanted to include them in the book, but then, thinking about the need to get permissions from publishers, and the need to include more information on the topic, I decided that it would be better to write a summary of the studies. Whoever is interested in more details, can read those publications – they are in open access. This summary also contains analysis of some more publications on the topic. Initially, the three articles had to bear the same title with the difference of who were the subjects of the study – students, their parents, or teachers. However, the journals believed that this is self-plagiarism (the arguments that it was a cycle of articles – parts of the same study – did not work), so we had to keep similar but less 'unethical' titles). Besides, we discussed whether to mention 'teaching jobs' and 'teaching profession', but I, as the initiator of the study, believed that it is the job (and not the profession) that is catastrophically declining in popularity, this is why we kept the collocation I preferred.

All previous introductions agreed on some issues -

- "Although it seems logical that the two professional spheres: health and education - are the most valuable for society, as health workers care for people's lives, while teachers are responsible for their future, the situation is not like this in reality" (Doghonadze et al., 2023, p. 4). Not many school leavers choose education majors worldwide. Numerous ratings do not include school teachers or university lecturers in the winning list.
- Teachers not only serve the knowledge-based society by transferring knowledge and skills between generations, "according to Kraft and Lyon (2024), this is one of the most numerous professions: "teachers also collectively shape the democratic ideals, social cohesion, and economic competitiveness of the nation as a whole" (Kraft & Lyon, 2024 p. 2 as cited in Doghonadze et al., 25b, p. 25).
- There is an obvious "conflict between the obvious importance of teacher status for the country / the world (Cameron, 2003) and the lack of desire of young people (supported by their parents) to work in the sphere of education" (Doghonadze et al., 2025a, p.9).
- Teaching is often viewed in mass media as a dying profession, claiming that robots and AI will soon substitute teachers, as they do not require salary increases, never get tired or irritated, and do what they are programmed to do. Teachers' role has to be reinterpreted in the new reality where technology occupies a leading role.
- Parents have a great impact on their children's choice of employment, and they want their children to have well-paid, not exceedingly difficult/tiring, low-stress, and safe jobs, so they (even those who are teachers themselves) seldom recommend their children to work in education.

- Best university graduates seldom decide to teach at school and even at university.

Literature review

The current literature review does not reiterate the sources analysed in the previous publications.

Runcheva et al. (2022) enumerates the reasons why it may be good to be a teacher:

- Understanding the importance of the profession: they provide knowledge and skills necessary for all professions.
- Passion for teaching and expertise in both the subject and the teaching are the strong intrinsic motives of those who choose the profession, as extrinsic motives (especially salary and status in the society) are unable to motivate them.
- While in school, especially primary school, the majority of teachers are female, due to their inborn natural motherly feelings, on higher levels the number of male teachers increases, however, is still not too high.
- Family tradition of teaching is seldom followed, mostly the decision is self-initiated.

Madalińska-Michalak (2019) states that education should constitute the task of the state: "the quality of the school and the pupil's educational results largely depend on the quality of the teacher's work, while the quality of the teacher's work depends on the quality of their education" (p. 29), therefore, teachers should be treated as 'specific assets in education', otherwise, educational system will be caught in a trap: lower entrance requirements to teaching programs, lower education level of teachers, and, eventually, lower level of school graduates. The society puts great legal demands on teachers and has great expectations of teachers' work outcomes, however, governments and media insufficiently contribute to their status improvement and better work conditions. Lifelong learning has become compulsory for teachers to be efficient educators of the 21st century. "Teachers are expected to fully understand what they teach, who they teach it to and how they teach, and how their work impacts their pupils' development and learning" (ibid, p. 32).

The quality of teachers' work and the society views on teaching are mutually dependent. While negative view on teaching decreases teachers' motivation, poor teaching, in turn, decreases the society view on teaching. According to Fauziah et al. (2021), "teachers are engine and oil in the whole educational process; and once the teacher is internally or externally impacted, the whole teaching system will be also affected" (p. 546). Their research in Korea revealed that the perception by the society of teachers' profession includes the following components: ability, code of ethics, autonomy and subject knowledge. To increase the perception of the teachers' profession, teacher education and development need to be optimised, teachers' responsibility should be based on the code of ethics, awareness campaigns of the importance and difficulty of the teaching profession should be conducted, and teacher payment should be increased.

Valuing teachers' work is important for increasing the motivation and quality of teaching (Kan, 2015). The study by Meirkulova and Gelişli (2022) in Turkey and Kazakhstan revealed that teachers' status has become lower. They enumerate such factors of teacher's profession social status as teacher salaries, parents' willingness to let their children become teachers, the image of teachers that media are creating, and the trust towards the education system in the country. Two thirds of the respondent teachers in their study mentioned teaching was not their ideal job, and only one third confirmed that it was. In Kan's research in Turkey, those pre-service teachers who were asked the reasons of their choice of profession named that it was intrinsically motivating for them and it enabled them to be useful for the community. Other reasons were love for children, the noble nature of the profession, and the desire to improve the negative image of teachers in society. The need of students' fair treatment was emphasised in the research. Therefore, for raising teachers' profession's prestige, society has to create better conditions for teacher work: for their effective education and development, school material base, and payment. On the other hand, teachers need to work better to increase their image in society. Another study in Turkey, by Kilkan et al. (2013), stated that teacher's profession used to be a sacred one (as initially, education was often carried out by church), however, its status has changed with time, and people started looking at it more pragmatically. More than half of the respondents of the study chose the profession because they believe it corresponds to their abilities, however, many respondents mentioned that they chose the profession because their level of knowledge was acceptable to be admitted. The study revealed no difference between gender and social class motivation to become teachers and some difference between those who have relatives in teaching profession and those who do not have them in favour of those who have relatives. This reveals that teachers in Turkey are mostly satisfied with their jobs and do not experience big problems in connection with their profession's prestige or popularity. Some studies in the country (Bademcioglu, 2014), however, found that female teachers have a more positive attitudes towards the teaching profession.

Drelinga et al. (2017) state that there are four times less people in Latvia who want to become teachers than there were in the end of the 20th century, while the number of students is constantly growing. One of the reasons of the decreasing numbers of admitted to pedagogical departments students are the demands towards teacher competency which are growing, they include knowledge of the subject, pedagogy, psychology, and information technology, management and communicative skills, social-emotional skills, cooperative skills, etc. However, not all teacher education programs include all these in their curricula. Besides the competence, a positive attitude towards one's job is essential.

Taneri et al. (2014) and Bademcioglu et al. (2014) also support the importance of teacher's positive attitude towards their profession. Taneri et al. (2014), researchers from Turkey and Ireland, emphasise that universities alone should not be responsible for teacher education if teachers' profession prestige is to go up. There should be a national system of standards – requirements what knowledge, skills, and competences teachers should possess. Teacher candidates, participants of their research, expressed certain worry about the future of the profession. The Turkish respondents claimed that the profession requires sacrifice, while not many young people nowadays are ready to sacrifice. Nowadays, "teaching is seen as a warranty of having a job with long holidays" (Taneri et al., 2014, p.541). However, their Irish counterparts did not see the need for sacrifice in the profession, and they are not worried about the future of the profession if the financial benefits will be satisfactory. Bademcioglu et al. (2014) emphasise that teachers' negative attitude towards their profession has a crucial impact on the quality of their teaching. It also decreases their students' motivation to learn.

Moreno et al. (2023) mention that teaching is increasingly demanding and emotionally draining. Despite the importance of the profession, it is not named among the priorities in most countries. In Philippines, most of the respondents from the graduating class students chose professions of doctors, nurses, accountants, and business people. Even many pre-service students, who – logically – seem to have chosen the profession, state that teaching was not their first choice and they chose it as it was easier to be admitted than to many other departments or they could not afford their dream jobs. Teachers in Philippines are expected to be "a pinnacle of morals, an irrefutable source of knowledge, and an infallible advisor in times of challenges and difficulties" (Moreno et al., 2023, p. 3116) – such high demands and pressure for high expectations may make the profession too responsible and, consequently, stressful. Stress and burnout often become the reasons of young teachers quitting from the profession (Bademcioglu et al., 2014).

Issan et al. (2013) stress that teachers' attitude towards their profession has an impact on their performance and commitment to their responsibilities. Some of them quit due to their negative attitude, others continue working with a low quality. Many novice teachers in Oman are disappointed by disciplinary problems and lack of parental involvement. If not supported by more experienced teachers who can help them overcome these problems, they may experience burnout and eventually quit. Unfortunately, there are some teachers who choose the job because of economic hardships and lack of employment choices. Majority of these teachers cannot become enthusiastic about their jobs and fulfil them without caring about their students' learning outcomes. In developing countries the negative attitude towards teaching profession may be connected to poor working conditions, especially the material (including technical) resources that the school where they work possess.

According to Hayrutyunyan (2022), contemporary education system "emphasizes autonomous, self-evaluating, self-analyzing, and self-improving educational domains where educational consciousness will get its clear definition in the new culture of education" (p. 127). She writes about the paradox of the teaching profession: on the one hand, this is one of the most massive and demanded professions, on the other hand, the demands from the teacher's qualification and personality are very high. Due to this not many people entering the profession can satisfy these demands. The stress experienced by teachers nowadays is higher than ever. At the same time, teacher support, even if it exists, cannot catch up with the stress levels. The steps of reform (at least, in Armenia) are often contradictory and a new minister of education usually does not continue the measures offered by his predecessor, which causes disappointment both of society and teachers. Young people in her research have a negative view on teachers' job, as they see teachers as not respected by students, parents, and in general society, receiving low salary, not as exiting and promising than many new-born professions, depending too much on Ministry standards and administration demands. Those who still choose to become teachers feeling that this is their vocation view teachers as good psychologists, students' friend, equality and equity provider, and student-centered. They believe that a sense of humour is crucial for a teacher to win students hearts and survive/succeed in their jobs. Pedagogical innovations should be research-based and brought to teachers as able to improve both teaching and learning.

Method

All three studies applied online questionnaires as research tools. The choice of a survey as the research method was related to the possibility to reach many people in relatively short time. The method is objective and enables measurement, it is anonymous, which helps respondents to express their opinions openly. Compared to experiment, its results are less reliable and cannot lead to cause/result conclusions, however, they are good when descriptive research is needed. The limitations of this type of research include possible misunderstanding of the questions (and due to it, irrelevant answers given) and the status of the respondent (which may not coincide with the real one) (Taherdoost, 2022). The way to overcome these limitations triangulation should be applied. Collecting the results of the survey from several countries and analyzing them took much time, the publications were voluminous, therefore, at the moment, the researchers did not view interviews as a feasible approach at the moment. This book which includes teachers' stories about teacher roles, their roads to profession, and achievements they gain and challenges they come across partially compensated this limitation. This is why as a summary of chapter three I offer systematic content analysis of the teacher stories. Another way to compensate the limitations of the survey as the research method is looking at the issue under study from all interested parties point of view. This is exactly what was done in the three researches – students', their parents', and teachers views on teachers' jobs popularity/prestige was studied. The questionnaire items were developed based on literature analyses in the articles. Besides the questions dealing with demographic information, the majority of questions were in a 5-point Likert scale (1 totally disagree to 5 completely agree), some were in multiple choice or open-ended questions. The questionnaire was assessed by all authors and three more experts in the field. The necessary amendments were done. The reliability was assessed by test-retest procedure fulfilled by respondents who did not take part in the further research. The consistency of the questionnaire in all three studies was found .8 and above.

Sample

Sampling was done by convenience and snowball approaches. The questionnaire in Google Forms was placed on the authors' social media, with the request to share and/or fill it in. To increase the representativeness of the survey data, despite its being conducted through a non-random selection method, the researchers utilised a combination of stratified and cluster sampling approaches. The collected demographic data included information on gender, age distribution, living areas (urban, suburban, and rural), geographical distribution, and school/university involvement. This breakdown helps in understanding the diversity within the sample, which is crucial for representativeness. Stratification involves dividing the population into subgroups (or strata) that share similar characteristics (age groups, school/university students, living areas), while the cluster approach involves the geographical distribution of the respondents. This approach allows to ensure that each subgroup is represented in the sample. Thus, despite its non-probability character, the sample can still provide valuable insights. The researchers wanted to see whether the situation is different in developed countries, particularly in North America. We did our best to involve the US respondents, but it turned out to be difficult due to the red tape involved in the process and a lack of their interest in the research, due to this, they added Canadian respondents to them. Each of the questionnaire was online for 3 months but a limited number of respondents from five countries was collected – 657 from the first study, 336 from the second study, and 383 from the third study.

Results

The first (students' views) study obtained the answers to the following questions:

1. "I would like to become a teacher" – the lowest assessment from the US/Canada (M=2.4 on a 5-point Likert scale), with also low assessment from Georgia (M=2.58) and Azerbaijan (M=2.85). The only country where the result was reasonably positive was Iraq (M=3.64).

2. The following reasons why teachers choose the profession were given: although the chosen reasons differ, intrinsic motivation in both Georgia and Azerbaijan are rated higher than extrinsic motives. In Iraq and the USA/Canada, three leaders among the answers also include intrinsic motives and only one) extrinsic. "I love teaching" is the leader for Azerbaijan, "I love sharing my knowledge and skills" is the leader for Georgia and Iraq, and "I love sharing knowledge and skills/I like helping other to learn/this job is prestigious" are the three leaders for the US and Canada. Those students who chose the negative answers to their desire to take up teaching jobs named the following leading reasons: "It's not an interesting job" (Azerbaijan, Georgia, US/Canada) and "It's a difficult job" (Iraq).
3. Teachers' subject knowledge was more or less confirmed by the students: from M=3.52 (Azerbaijan) to 4.02 (US/Canada).
4. Teachers were more or less positively assessed as motivators: from M=3.27 in Georgia to M=3.82 in Iraq.
5. They were more or less recognised as contributors to their students' success: from 3.57 in Azerbaijan to 3.99 in Iraq.
6. However, they more or less supported Bernard Shaw's disrespectful saying about teachers (Who can do, do, who cannot, teach): from M=2.87 in Georgia to 3.38 in the US/Canada. Of course, this result can be ascribed to their healthy sense of humour, however, this reveals the fact that they may laugh at their teachers, which is not very pleasant.
7. Thanks God, the view that teachers are losers was not supported: from 1.77 in Georgia to 2.16 in the US/Canada. It can be summed up that the students view their teachers reasonably positively.
8. The rating of the factors that impacted the students' rating of their attitude towards teachers was as follows: teachers (graded as the first factor in all countries, which indicated that students are first of all paying attention to their own experiences), family (rated as second also in all countries), books and movies and mass media, and (the least important factor) peers.

The second (parents' views) study obtained the answers to the following questions:

1. The attitude of parents who are teachers, have some teachers in the family or neither are teachers nor have teachers in the family in different countries turned out to be different. In Azerbaijan, for example, the least desire that their children become teachers was expressed by parents who are teachers (M=2.8), and the most desire, however also not high, was expressed by those parents who are not teachers and have no teacher relatives. In Georgia, vice versa, the lowest result came from parents who are neither teachers nor related to teachers (M=2.5 and M=2.9), while the most positive answers come from teacher-parents who belonged to a dynasty of teachers (M= 3.3) (two or more generations of teachers in the family). It looks like Georgian teachers have had better experiences and like their profession more than Azerbaijani ones. On the whole, Georgian parents' attitude towards the possibility of their children becoming teachers is more positive. In Iraq, all parents look relatively positively on the perspective of their children becoming teachers ($2.9<M<3.3$). The answers from US/Canadian parents are a little higher ($2.9<M<3.5$). On the whole, no clear relation between being a teacher (or related to the profession) and the desire of their children to choose the profession was noticed. The general position on the issue is from neutral in Georgia (M=2.94) to reasonably positive in the US/Canada (M=3.26).
2. Those parents who do not mind if their children become teachers give various reasons to why they think so. The leader-reason in all countries is "It is a noble and socially important profession," however, then comes "It has advantages such as annual summer vacation, relatively short work day, flexible timetable, etc." Parents are thinking of both their children doing something important and having a comfortable life. Those parents who said they wouldn't like their children to become teachers gave two main reasons: "It's a low-paid job" and "It's a stressful job".
3. Although parents are not too eager that their children become teachers, they recognise that teaching is a very important profession ($4.24<M<4.65$), which reveals that parents are thinking about their children first and then about the country/humanity.
4. What mostly predetermined parents' opinion about the teaching jobs is their own experience and teachers whom they met.

The third (teachers' views) study obtained the answers to the following questions:

1. The views on prestige/popularity of teachers' jobs differ in the participant countries. The views of the Azerbaijani teachers are contradictory. On the one hand, they do not want their children to be teachers (M=2.85) and believe that the best teachers are seldom shown on TV, given awards, etc. (M=1.90). On the other hand, their attitude towards teaching jobs is reasonably positive: almost all of them have 'role model' teachers (M=4.27) and think that teachers are respected in society (M=3.1). The Iraqi teachers' views are also contradictory: low for consent for their children to become teachers (M=2.81) and teachers being awarded and shown positively on the media (M=2.13), but relatively high for respect towards teachers (M=3.12) and having a role model teacher (M=3.13). The views of Georgian teachers are quite negative (M=2.65 to 2.85). However, they do believe there are teachers in the country who can serve as role models (M=4.36). In the US/Canada, the general attitude is more or less positive (3.22<M<4.25), however, they also mention the absence of awards and positive teacher images shown on media (M=2.44).
2. The lowest interest/career aspirations were revealed for the Azerbaijani teachers (2.99<M<3.94), while the highest for the US/Canadian teachers (<3.32M<3.46). In all countries, many of them were not thinking of becoming school teachers (2.47<M<3.36), and relatively many were thinking about a university career (2.97<M<3.52).
3. The views on teachers' jobs security are the lowest in Georgia (1.90<M<2.81) and the highest in Azerbaijan (3.00<M<3.91). Only 'sort of' tenure exists in Georgia and Iraq, while the risks are assessed as high in the US/Canada (most probably, school and university shootings are meant) and Georgia (most probably, retaining one's job is meant).
4. Teacher autonomy is mostly assessed highly (3.11<M<4.09), however, the Iraqi teachers mention that academic freedom is limited (M=2.76) and school/university administration, parents and students interfere in the academic work (2.76<M<2.58), and the American/Canadian teachers are neither happy with the interference of school/university administration/parents/students.
5. Only Iraqi teachers mention that they feel quite happy with their profession (M=3.27), the answers of teachers from other countries are quite negative (below 3.00). However, burnout and stress is quite low (1.69<M<2.45).
6. Society trust towards teachers is high enough (3.49<M<4.0), except Iraq (2.00<M<3.00). However, relatively many parents who can afford it hire private tutors to prepare their children for admission to university (1.89<M<2.86).
7. Family life balance with work commitment is rather negative in all countries (2.03<M<3.03), only American/Canadian teachers are more or less satisfied with it (3.15<M<4.00).
8. The majority of teachers in all countries are interested in increasing their salary, being recognised by their students, and professional awards, they are proud of their students' achievements (3.23<M<4.27). Only Azerbaijani teachers expressed a reasonable desire to become administrators (M=3.23), others are more interested in other characteristics (mentioned above) of professional development (2.82<M<3.00).
9. Only the US/Canadian teachers are to some degree satisfied with their salary and believe that it can provide their decent lives (M=3.36), all others are not (2.09<M<2.91). Not a great, but a tangible part of teachers from all countries involved in the research believe that they deserve a higher salary (1.47<M<2.31).
10. Teachers in countries other than the US/Canada are little to reasonably satisfied with the support they receive (2.06<M<3.68), in the US/Canada satisfaction is higher (2.71<M<3.76), however, this level also leaves much to be desired.
11. Teachers are reasonably satisfied with the friendly atmosphere (3.25<M<3.82) and physical conditions (3.11<M<3.67) and only the US/Canadian and Georgian teachers are reasonably satisfied with how schools are equipped (M=3.67), others are not (2.33<M<2.81). Teachers in all countries are to some degree suffering from overload (2.22<M<2.55), however, some teachers from Georgia have to combine jobs to earn enough (M=2.26).
12. Teachers in all countries are reasonably satisfied with student discipline (3.15<M<3.71), however, the US/Canadian teachers are dissatisfied with student motivation (M=2.67) (in other countries satisfaction with student motivation is reasonable: 3.01<M<3.16).
13. Teachers in Azerbaijan and Iraq mention that parents are not enough involved in parents/school relationships (2.72<M<2.89), in other countries the situation is better (3.00<M<3.15). Parents' pressure on education content and methods is tolerable but tangible (2.93<M<3.00). Parent pressure requiring to give higher grades to their children is relatively high in Azerbaijan (3.28) and Iraq (3.30), and not so high in Georgia (2.97) and the US/Canada (2.74).

14. Teachers in Georgia (M=3.08) are less loyal to their job than in other countries ($2.43<M<2.69$), they are ready to change their work for becoming researchers, administrators, or totally quit from education. Teachers in Azerbaijan (M=2.69) and the US/Canada (M=2.96) do not think that teachers' profession has been positively reflected in media, books, movies, on television, etc. In other countries media reflection of teachers was assessed moderately positively ($3.13<M<3.24$).
15. Love for teaching and for sharing their knowledge and skills was the leading reason for Azerbaijani teachers to choose their profession, for Georgian teachers it was similarly love for sharing their knowledge and skills and love for children and young people. For Iraqi teachers it was love for sharing their knowledge and skills, and for the US/Canadian teachers it was love of sharing their knowledge and skills. It is easy to see how similar their intrinsic motives are.

DISCUSSION

The finding of the current researches that few people choose teaching as their job is supported by studies from Latvia (Drelinga et al., 2017), Kazakhstan and Turkey (Meirkulova & Gelişli (2022), and Philippines (Moreno et al., 2023). Gorard et al. (2022), based on European Commission (2018), state that "more than half of the countries in Europe, and almost all school districts in the US, have apparently reported chronic challenges in recruiting and retaining teachers. Parents, even those who are teachers and even hereditary teachers, often do not recommend their children to become teachers. This is in agreement with Tillman (2015), Christensen et al. (2022) and Mutluer and Yüksel (2019).

The viewpoint that teaching is noble and socially important, love for teaching and young people, as well as sharing one's knowledge and skills named as the main motives to become teachers are shared by numerous study results (Haddad et al., 2024; Mustafayev & Kazimi, 2023; Siostrom et al. (2023); Vulley, 2021; Wilson, 2024). At the same time, such extrinsic motives as annual summer vacation, relatively short work day, and flexible timetable was also in line with many studies (See et al., 2022; Straksiene et al., 2024; Whiteford et al., 2021).

However, what was more important for our studies was to understand why people do not want to become teachers or quit from the jobs, as this would enable us to give recommendations how to improve teacher training and development as well to attract people to the teaching jobs. Difficulties dealing with monotony (same topics for years), overload, stress and burnout, lack of support and security, parents', administration's and even students' pressure, lack of student discipline and motivation, and, last, but not least, low pay are the reasons names in our studies shared by some other studies (Amitai & Van Houtte, 2022; Forson et al., 2021; Schmitt & DeCourcy, 2022). Based on these reasons, a significant part of the respondents in the current studies characterise teaching as neither prestigious, not popular. This is in agreement with numerous studies, such as Kraft and Lyon (2024), Keturakyte (2021), and Bocskor (2022).

Teachers' subject knowledge and qualification, including their ability to motivate students and their contribution of their students' success, were found reasonably relevant in the study. The assessment of teacher qualification, of course, varies from country to country, for example, low in Rwanda (Casian et al., 2021) and high in Finland, Estonia, Japan, Singapore, and China (Tonga et al., 2019). The attitude towards teachers was impacted by personal experience, family, books, movies and mass media, and peers. This finding is in line with Mustafayev's and Kazimi's (2023) and Siostrom et al.'s (2023) studies.

The level of teacher autonomy was defined as high in all three current studies. Although, on the whole, teachers are trusted, parents often prefer to hire private tutors for their children's preparation for university admission. This is supported by Liu and Bray (2020), Kobakhidze (2014), and Heineman (2011).

CONCLUSIONS AND IMPLICATIONS

To sum up the most important findings of all three studies,

1. Teachers are first of all needed to develop the knowledge and skills of the young generation, which are the major resources in the knowledge-based economy. But their function in society is much greater: they teach students how to learn (as continuous learning nowadays is indispensable for any profession), they help form values and become citizens who will contribute to the development of their countries and humanity on the whole. Teachers' mission has to be brought to teacher-trainees and the society on the whole.
2. Clear state policies should exist about requirements from and care for teachers. Caring for the future of the country entails caring for children, youngsters, their parents and teachers. Teacher standards should be high but realistic, they should not ignore national educational traditions and experiences. Teacher assessment should not humiliate teachers but be of formative nature: information of assessment results should be first of all available to teachers themselves, to realise their weaker sides and to grow professionally; only if the assessment is repeatedly negative, administrative measures may be thought of. Education reform should be smooth, neither too fast nor lagging behind theoretical progress, it should be based on research results and not on the political will of the Minister of Education or the ruling party. Educational research should involve all stakeholders (students, parents, teachers, administrators, and policy-makers) to benefit both individual learners and the whole society.
3. Taking into consideration how important teachers' jobs are and the growing number of students, the number of people who want themselves or their children to become teachers is insufficient nowadays. Therefore, to attract more people to the teaching jobs, they should be attractive. Consequently, measures to increase teaching profession's prestige are needed, such as improvement of teacher training and development programs, their closer connection with the needs of practice at schools and universities, and teacher material and moral support. Novice teachers need special support. Positive teacher images should be created by television, social media, movies, and books. More events like 'Teacher of the Year' should be conducted to celebrate teachers' efficient and enthusiastic work. Teachers should be required to continuously work on their qualification, at the same time, conditions for it should be provided such as on-site free-of-charge training sessions.
4. Contemporary technologies should help teachers fulfil their jobs, they should not be viewed (and advertised) as rivals and even substitutes for teachers. There are things that technologies do faster and more easily that humans (teachers), however, there are things such as compassion, tolerance, kindness, moral support, that cannot be provided by technologies. IT companies, while advertising educational technologies, have to be more thoughtful and support both learners and teachers instead of thinking only about their own income.
5. Teacher knowledge of pedagogy, teaching and learning methods, and student psychology is not less important than teachers' attitudes towards their work – only those teachers who love to share their knowledge and skills with students and colleagues, who enjoy the communication in the process of teaching can really benefit students' learning outcomes and, what is especially important, graduates' wellbeing.
6. Teacher job promotion and salary increase have to be fair and based on achievements and satisfaction of their students, not necessarily on their administrative positions. The possibilities of professional growth should be equitable, regardless of teachers' ethnicity, race, religion, gender, etc. Loyalty to the profession in general and to the school/university where the teacher works should be recognised and supported. A teacher who has worked at the given school for decades should be heard no less than a newcomer with diplomas and certificates. Professional growth in education does not necessarily include steps from teacher assistant to the chair, then to the dean, rector, and minister, but it always includes the increased knowledge and understanding of the subject, learners, and educational process.
7. High schools and especially tertiary education institutions should from time to time put learners in teaching roles – to get the experiences, to understand the profession's difficulties and pleasures, and, possibly, to start thinking of becoming a teacher.
8. Young people should be taught by the family to respect teachers (at least, dedicated ones) and to observe normal class discipline.
9. A real teacher is not just an occupation or a profession, it is a way of life, a way of thinking. Teachers travel, meet friends, go to theatres and concerts, watch movies and read books and always enrich their pedagogically-useful 'luggage'. It's a day-and night, 24/7/365 profession. However, teachers should not be overloaded by classes and extracurricular responsibilities, as they need the time to grow as humans and as professionals, to read books, to ponder on problems, to attend events, etc.

REFERENCES

Amitai, A., & Van Houtte, M. (2022). Being pushed out of the career: Former teachers' reasons for leaving the profession. *Teaching and Teacher Education, 110*, 103540. Advance online publication. DOI: 10.1016/j.tate.2021.103540

Bademcioglu, M., Karatas, H., & Alci, B. (2014). The investigation of teacher candidates' attitudes towards teaching profession. *International Journal of Educational Research, 5*(2), 16–29.

Bocskor, A. (2022). Reputational status dynamics from a mixed methods perspective: Coolness and popularity in a Hungarian primary school sample. *Youth & Society, 54*(6), 1051–1076. DOI: 10.1177/0044118X211012815

Carneiro, R., & Draxler, A. (2008). Education for the 21st century: Lessons and challenges. *European Journal of Education, 43*(2), 149–160. DOI: 10.1111/j.1465-3435.2008.00348.x

Casian, M., Mugo, L., & Claire, M. M. (2021). Impact of teacher's qualification on students' academic performance in public secondary schools in Rwanda. *Journal of Education, 4*(2), 75–88.

Casian, M., Mugo, L., & Claire, M. M. (2021). Impact of teachers' qualification on students' academic performance in public secondary schools in Rwanda. *Journal of Education, 4*(2), 75–88.

Christensen, S., Davies, R. S., Larsen, R. A. A., Harris, S., Hanks, J., & Bowles, B. (2022). Parental perceptions of the teaching profession: Factors that predict parental encouragement of students to enter the teaching profession. *Education Sciences, 12*(11), 734. Advance online publication. DOI: 10.3390/educsci12110734

Dayal, S., & Pratibha, . (2023). Roadblocks in education amidst global crisis - A study based in India. *PLoS One, 18*(10), e0292465. DOI: 10.1371/journal.pone.0292465

Delors, J., Al Mufti, I., Amagi, I., Carneiro, R., Chung, F., Geremek, B., Gorham, W., Kornhauser, A., Manley, M., & Nanzhao, Z. (1996). *Learning: The treasure within.* UNESCO.

Doghonadze, N. (2016). Slow education movement as a student-centered approach. *Proceedings of International Research Conference on Education, English Language and Literature Teaching (IRCEELT)*, pp. 65-73.

Drelinga, E., Zariņa, S., Iliško, D., & Silova, L. (2017). Societal perceptions about being a good teacher in Latvia. Society, integration, education. Proceedings of the International Scientific Conference, I. May 26th -27th. Pp. 130-142. doi:10.17770/sie2017vol1.2392

European Commission/EACEA/Eurydice. (2018). Teaching careers in Europe: Access, progression and support. Eurydice Report. Publications Office of the European Union.

Eckes, S., & Russo, C. J. (2021). Teacher speech inside and outside of classrooms in the United States: Understanding the first amendment. *Laws, 10*(4), 88. Advance online publication. DOI: 10.3390/laws10040088

Ertesvåg, S. K., & Havik, T. (2021). Students' proactive aggressiveness, mental health problems and perceived classroom interaction. *Scandinavian Journal of Educational Research, 65*(1), 1–20. DOI: 10.1080/00313831.2019.1650822

Fatima, T., Bilal, A. R., Waqas, M., & Imran, M. K. (2024). Keeping up with this workload is difficult: The ramifications of work overload on career resilience. *Kybernetes, 53*(1), 188–215. DOI: 10.1108/K-01-2022-0063

Fauziah, A., Kim, M., Aye, M., Hakizimana, V., & Hur, J. (2021). Impact of the society's perception on teachers' professionalism. [EduLearn]. *Journal of Education and Learning, 15*(4), 545–552. DOI: 10.11591/edulearn.v15i4.20292

Forson, J. A., Ofosu-Dwamena, E., Opoku, R. A., & Adjavon, S. E. (2021). Employee motivation and job performance: A study of basic school teachers in Ghana. *Future Business Journal, 7*(1), 30. Advance online publication. DOI: 10.1186/s43093-021-00077-6

Gadzhimuradova, G. I. (2022). Philosophy of education in the context of new socio-political trends and migration of citizens. *ANNALS of the University of Bucharest. Philosophy Series, 61*(2), 79–90.

Gorard, S., See, B. H., & Morris, R. (2022). How to get more people into teaching? Comparing undergraduates' and teacher trainees' motivation and perceptions of a teaching career. *Education Sciences, 12*(11), 767. Advance online publication. DOI: 10.3390/educsci12110767

Government technology. (2025). Quote: Einstein on technology and humanity. Retrieved from https://www.govtech.com/em/emergency-blogs/disaster-zone/quote-einstein-on-technology-and-humanity-032513.html

Gregory, A., Osher, D., Bear, G. G., Jagers, R. J., & Sprague, J. R. (2021). Good intentions are not enough: Centering equity in school discipline reform. *School Psychology Review, 50*(2-3), 1–16. DOI: 10.1080/2372966X.2020.1861911

Gunawaradana, A. A., & Karunarathna, J. B. (2022). A review of the effect of economic crisis on education. In *Proceedings of international research symposium 'Towards a resilient future – opportunities and innovations, University of Vocational Technology'*, Sri Lamka (pp. 261-268).

Gurung, A., & Chauhan, D. D. (2025). Role of media in shaping public opinion. [JOIREM]. *Journal Publication of International Research for Engineering and Management, 5*(05), 1–6.

Haddad, B., McKim, A., Traini, H., Goodwin, C., & Gama-Romo, B. (2024). To those concerned with teacher retention: A collective thought experiment. *Journal of Agricultural Education, 65*(3), 129–150. DOI: 10.5032/jae.v65i3.2604

Hannon, L., & O'Donnell, G. M. (2022). Teachers, parents, and family-school partnerships: Emotions, experiences, and advocacy. *Journal of Education for Teaching, 48*(2), 241–255. DOI: 10.1080/02607476.2021.1989981

Hayrutyunyan, M. (2022). Perception of teacher's profession: Looking back and ahead. *Wisdom, 3*(23), 126–132. DOI: 10.24234/wisdom.v23i3.908

International Telecommunication Union. (2019). *Connecting the world and beyond.* Retrieved from https://www.itu.int/en/ITU-D/Statistics/Pages/stat/default.aspx

Ispas, C., & Ispas, A. (2023). Challenges and solutions of discipline in contemporary classroom education. Educatia 21 Journal, 26, 5-17. DOI: 10.24193/ed21.2023.26.01

Issan, S. A. Y., Al-Nabhani, H. Z., Kazem, A. M., & Al-Ani, W. T. (2013). Omani teachers' attitudes towards teaching as a profession. [IJPE]. *Indian Journal of Psychology and Education, 1*(1), 25–40.

Judijanto, L., Triolita, N., Machfiroh, R., & Yunanto, M.K., & Siminto. (2024). Navigating the landscape of higher education in the 21st century: Challenges, innovations, and future perspectives. [INJOTEL]. *International Journal of Teaching and Learning, 2*(1), 297–312.

Kalyani (2024). The role of technology in education: Enhancing learning outcomes and 21st century skills. (2024). International Journal of Scientific Research in Modern Science and Technology, 3(4), 05-10. DOI: 10.59828/ijsrmst.v3i4.199

Kan, A. U. (2015). Prospective teachers' perceptions of teaching profession. *Contemporary Educational Researches Journal, 5*(1), 12–16.

Keturakyte, J. (2021). *The prestige of teaching profession in the EU.* Master's thesis. Brussels Warmoesberg University.

Kilkan, B., Keçe, M., Çepni, E., & Kilinç, A. Ç. (2013). Prospective teachers' reasons for choosing teaching as a profession. *Kastamonu Eğitim Dergisi, 22*(1), 69–80.

Kobakhidze, M. N. (2014). Corruption risks of private tutoring: Case of Georgia. *Asia Pacific Journal of Education, 34*(4), 455–475. DOI: 10.1080/02188791.2014.963506

Kozma, T. (2008). Political transformations and higher education reforms. *European Education, 40*(2), 29–45. DOI: 10.2753/EUE1056-4934400202

Kraft, M. A., & Lyon, M. A. (2024). *The rise and fall of the teaching profession: Prestige, interest, preparation, and satisfaction over the last half-century. Working paper 32386.* National Bureau of Economic Research. Retrieved from https://www.nber.org/system/files/working_papers/w32386/w32386.pdf

Lagawid, E. L. (2024). Overloading in elementary school teachers: A review. *Cognizance Journal, 4*(11), 289–299. DOI: 10.47760/cognizance.2024.v04i11.016

Leanage, K., & Saito, E. (2023). Concerns about the impact of crisis on children in Sri Lanka. *Management in Education, 1-4*, 08920206231153291. Advance online publication. DOI: 0.1177/08920206231153291

Liu, J., & Bray, M. (2020). Accountability and (mis) trust in education systems: Private supplementary tutoring and the ineffectiveness of regulation in Myanmar. *European Journal of Education, 55*(3), 361–375. DOI: 10.1111/ejed.12409

Madalińska-Michalak, J. (2019). Shaping the future of teaching profession. *Labor et Educatio, 7*, 29–42. DOI: 10.4467/25439561LE.19.002.11519

Malik, R. S. (2018). Educational challenges in 21st century and sustainable development. *Journal of Sustainable Development Education and Research, 2*(1), 9–20. DOI: 10.17509/jsder.v2i1.12266

Masters, G. (2015, August 10). 'Big five' challenges in school education. Teacher Columnist. Retrieved from https://research.acer.edu.au/columnists/10/

Masters, G. (2023). Reform challenges in school education. ACER. Retrieved from https://research.acer.edu.au/cgi/viewcontent.cgi?article=1043&context=tll_misc

Meirkulova, A., & Gelişli, Y. (2022). The social status of the teaching profession: Teachers' views in Turkey and Kazakhstan. [Hacettepe University Journal of Education]. *Hacettepe University Journal of Education, 37*(2), 424–439. DOI: 10.16986/HUJE.2022074923

Moreno, N., Cruz, S. J., & Meneses, J. (2023). The making of teaching profession as a first choice. *Diversitas Journal, 8*(3), 3105–3122. DOI: 10.48017/dj.v8i3.2696

Mustafayev, A., & Kazimi, P. (2023). Motivation and nature of choosıng the teaching profession. *Akademik Tarih ve DüşünceDergisi/Academic Journal of History and Idea, 10*(5), 1824-1830. https://doi.org/DOI: 10.46868/atdd.2023

Mutluer, Ö., & Yüksel, S. (2019). The social status of teaching profession: A phenomenological study. *Journal of Teacher Education and Educators, 8*, 183–203.

Nambissan, G. B. (2010). The global economic crisis, poverty, and education: A perspective from India. *Journal of Education Policy, 25*(6), 729–737. DOI: 10.1080/02680939.2010.508180

Niraula, A., & Valentin, K. (2019). Mobile Brains and the Question of 'Deskilling': High Skilled South Asian Migrants in Denmark. *Nordic Journal of Migration Research, 9*(1), 19–35. DOI: 10.2478/njmr-2019-0008

OECD. (2014). How old are the teachers? Retrieved from https://www.oecd.org/en/publications/2014/03/how-old-are-the-teachers_g17a246b.html

OECD. (2018). Teachers and educators. Retrieved from https://www.oecd.org/en/topics/policy-issues/teachers-and-educators.html#:~:text=Teacher%20age,age%20of%20their%20teachers%20increase

OECD. (2023). Education at a glance 2023. Retrieved from https://www.oecd.org/en/publications/education-at-a-glance-2023_e13bef63-en/full-report/what-is-the-profile-of-vocational-teachers-and-what-is-the-student-vocational-teacher-ratio_c954dca2.html

Pomeroy, E. A. (2008). *Occupational prestige of Canadian professions in the new economy*. Doctoral dissertation. University of Waterloo. Retrieved from https://central.bac-lac.gc.ca/.item?id=TC-OWTU-4154&op=pdf&app=Library&oclc_number=1032979510

Portulans Institute. (2025). *The Global Talent Competitiveness Index 2025 ranks a total of 135 countries, collectively representing over 97% of the global GDP and 93% of the world's population.* Retrieved from https://www.globaltalentcompetitivenessindex.org/countries/

Przybyszewska, A. (2021). Downward professional mobility among Poles working and living in Norway. *Nordic Journal of Migration Research, 11*(1), 35–49. DOI: 10.33134/njmr.377

Runcheva, J., Sivevska, D., & Petrovska, S. (2022).Why is it good to be a part of the teaching profession? *Zbornik Odseka za pedagogiju* [In Macedonian: Proceedings of the Department of Pedagogy]. DOI: 10.19090/zop.2022.31.23-36

Salmi, J. (2001). Tertiary education in the 21st century: Challenges and opportunities. *Higher Education Management, 13*(2), 105–130.

Schmitt, J., & DeCourcy, K. (2022). *The pandemic has exacerbated a long-standing national shortage of teachers. Economic Policy Institute.* Retrieved from https://files.eric.ed.gov/fulltext/ED626637.pdf

Scott, P. (2000). Globalisation and higher education: Challenges for the 21st century. *Journal of Studies in International Education, 4*(1), 3–10. DOI: 10.1177/102831530000400102

See, B. H., Munthe, E., Ross, S. A., Hitt, L., & El Soufi, N. (2022). Who becomes a teacher and why? *Review of Education, 10*(3), e3377. DOI: 10.1002/rev3.3377

Siostrom, E., Mills, R., & Bourke, T. (2023). A scoping review of factors that influence career changers' motivations and decisions when considering teaching. *Teachers and Teaching, 29*(7–8), 850–869. DOI: 10.1080/13540602.2023.2208051

Smith, K. (2021). Educating teachers for the future school-the challenge of bridging between perceptions of quality teaching and policy decisions: Reflections from Norway. *European Journal of Teacher Education, 44*(3), 383–398. DOI: 10.1080/02619768.2021.1901077

Smith, M. S. (2013). The global economic crisis: Effects on US higher education. *Procedia: Social and Behavioral Sciences, 77*, 153–158. DOI: 10.1016/j.sbspro.2013.03.071

Straksiene, D., Kaffemaniene, I., Karveliene, R., & Bilbokaite, R. (2024). Motivation to become a teacher. In *ICERI2024 Proceedings* (pp. 2643-2652). IATED. DOI: 10.21125/iceri.2024.0697

Taherdoost, H. (2022). What are different research approaches? Comprehensive review of qualitative, quantitative, and mixed method research, their applications, types, and limitations. *Journal of Management Science & Engineering Research, 5*(1), 53–63. DOI: 10.30564/jmser.v5i1.4538

Taneri, P. O., Nayir, K. F., & McNamara, G. (2014). Teacher candidates' attitudes towards the teaching profession. *Turkish Studies - International Periodical for the Languages. Literature and History of Turkish or Turkic, 9*(11), 529–545.

The Britannica dictionary (n.d., a). *Prestige.* Retrieved from https://www.britannica.com/dictionary/prestige

The Britannica dictionary (n.d., b). *Popularity.* Retrieved from https://www.britannica.com/dictionary/popularity

Tillman, K. (2015). *Parental influence on college students' career aspirations* (Honors College Thesis 86). Georgia Southern University. Retrieved from https://digitalcommons.georgiasouthern.edu/cgi/viewcontent.cgi?article=1092&context=honors-theses

Tonga, F. E., Eryiğit, S., Yalçın, F. A., & Erden, T. F. (2019). Professional development of teachers in PISA achiever countries: Finland, Estonia, Japan, Singapore and China. *Professional Development in Education*. Advance online publication. DOI: 10.1080/19415257.20

Vulley, D. K. (2021). Factors influencing teacher job satisfaction and commitment at senior high schools in the Greater Accra Region, Ghana. *European Journal of Education Studies*, *8*(3), 46–64.

Whiteford, C., Kelly, N., & Dawes, L. (2021). Why become a teacher? Exploring motivations for becoming science and mathematics teachers in Australia. *The Australian Journal of Teacher Education*, *46*(3), 1–19. DOI: 10.14221/ajte.2021v46n3.1

Wigfield, A., & Eccles, J. S. (2000). Expectancy–value theory of achievement motivation. *Contemporary Educational Psychology*, *25*(1), 68–81. DOI: 10.1006/ceps.1999.1015

Wilson, K. (2024). *An examination of the level of participation in labor unions by social workers with a comparative analysis to teachers and nurses*. Doctoral dissertation. Yeshiva University.

Young, S. (2014). The impact of the economic crisis on English Language Teaching in Greece: A case study of a language school. MRes: Educational and Social Research. The University of London, Institute of Education.

Zalli, E. (2024). Globalization and education: exploring the exchange of ideas, values, and traditions in promoting cultural understanding and global citizenship. *Interdisciplinary Journal of Research and Development, 11*(1 S1), 55-55. DOI: 10.56345/ijrdv11n1s109

Zhang, J., Sun, G., Xu, L., Khan, I., Lv, W., & Philbin, S. P. (2022). The moderating effect of learning experience on learning motivation and learning outcomes of international students. *Frontiers in Psychology*, *13*, 913982. DOI: 10.3389/fpsyg.2022.913982

Section 2
Teacher Voices Across the Globe

While other chapters in this book are of more theoretical and/or research character, the chapter Teacher Voices is rather practical. It in short describes the systems of education and teacher training across 15 countries practically from all corners of the world, to provide the background for teacher stories - three stories per country. These stories are so different and at the same time so similar, as all teachers love their profession and believe it may change with time but will always remain indispensable, as we, teachers, do not just transfer subject content knowledge to our students, we communicate with our students, emapathise with them, support them, build up relations with them, and prepare them for life in society - things that no technology can do. The Chapter aims to create a better ground for the understanding of what is happening in each particular country and then to present various teachers' careers – how and why they became teachers, what advantages and challenges they see in their jobs, how they understand their profession, what mission they believe their profession has, what experiences brought them to their views on teaching and what they expect in the future. Although practical, it eventually supports the theoretical ideas expressed in other chapters, which makes both types of chapters in the book valid and their results trustworthy.

Chapter 2
Teachers' Voices From the USA

Thomas C. De Bello
http://orcid.org/0009-0007-4235-1174
Three Village CSD, USA (Retired)

Reginald O. York
University of North Carolina at Wilmington, USA

Richard J. Guez
Three Village CSD, USA

ABSTRACT

The roots of education in the USA date back to its colonial past and early years, establishing traditions like co-educational classrooms, a ten-month school year, and local control via school boards. The Founding Fathers considered education essential for democracy and civic responsibility, creating a framework for funding public education through local taxes and promoting standardized curricula. As states evolved, so did teacher education. American pluralism offered diverse learning opportunities but also led to ongoing issues. The roles of women and the education of African Americans, Hispanics, and Native Americans have transformed over time. Challenges in meeting the needs of a diverse society and individuals with disabilities remain, but educators' dedication and commitment continue to be the system's strength. This section includes three teacher narratives.

HISTORICAL ROOTS OF EDUCATION IN THE USA AND THEIR IMPLICATIONS TODAY

Thomas C. De Bello

American education is as sprawling and nearly as diverse as the geography of the country it is bound to. Elementary and secondary public schools in the United States enrolled 49.5 million students in grades pre-kindergarten through grade 12 (Soldner, 2025). That staggering number represents populations larger than many nations, including our nearest neighbor, Canada. Additionally, there are 3.3 million public school teachers in the United States, compared to 691,000 doctors and 728,000 attorneys. Four percent of all civilian workers are teachers (Goldstein, 2014). Put into that perspective, encapsulating a brief history of United States education becomes a daunting task, but one I will endeavor to undertake to provide context for the personal stories of educators that follow.

History of Ten-Month Schedule

American education had its roots in the nation's colonial past. While not as old as other ancient societies, Americans are inheritors of world history and culture. Colonists from England settled in what became the eastern states of the country. They brought with them diverse skills and knowledge, along with a sense of survival. Early education took place in

DOI: 10.4018/979-8-3373-8983-7.ch002

the home, but later became community-based. Farm work involved whole families, so schools, where they existed, were closed throughout the harvest season. Two persistent traditions that shape education in the United States to this day are local control of schools and a ten-month school year. While over 70% of US schools are in non-agricultural communities, only 4% of the nation's schools have opted for some version of K-12 year-round education. It is fair to observe that traditions run deep in American education (National Center for Education Statistics [NCES], 2018). This anomaly raises fundamental issues, such as determining schools' financial status (NCES, a, 2025). Thus, keeping track of school finances nationwide is akin to other complex problems in American education and is not a simple task.

At this point, you might be tempted to think that there are advantages to standardization. Why not have year-round schooling and be done with it? Wouldn't students achieve more academically if they didn't have that 2-month lag time between grades? It is interesting to note that research supporting year-round schooling based on academic improvement has not been conclusive. Huffman's study (2013) supported the notion of greater motivation to teach and indicated a positive impact on student achievement. However, one post-COVID mega-study, which also claimed modest improvement over traditional ten-month education, drew criticism based on the quality of the studies included in the analysis (Aloe et al., 2020). Proponents of year-round schooling anticipate that scheduling learning over the entire school year with shorter breaks in-between will produce more effective learning over time and additionally promote the attraction and retention of teachers. However, opponents of year-round schooling cite many non-academic reasons for keeping the status quo, including childcare, student and teacher summer employment, sports scheduling, and a lack of air conditioning. Such issues, while ancillary to academic concerns, have substantial economic, social, and cultural implications that seem to outweigh academic concerns. Thus, the debate rooted in a historical necessity that no longer exists continues to influence and shape education today.

Founding Fathers' view of education

As inheritors of the English language, history, and culture, Massachusetts Bay Colony settlers in 1642 set the earliest laws for education in what would become the United States. Those laws required that all children be taught to read, and have an understanding of the principles of religion, and understand the laws that govern society. By 1647, Massachusetts law required all communities with populations of over 100 families to support a public grammar school! Other colonies in the Northeast followed the suit. Thus, from the nation's earliest days, education was considered to be local and a public interest. The republic, under the Articles of Confederation, was a loose organization of the thirteen newly formed states that governed the country from 1781 to 1789. The Constitution replaced the Articles, along with its first ten amendments, known as the Bill of Rights. Amendment 10 of the Bill of Rights granted states authority over anything not explicitly delegated to the federal government, including education. It would not be until 1868, with the adoption of the 14th Amendment, that the federal government would find a place in education. But that's getting ahead of the story.

Neem, in *Democracy's Schools: The Rise of Public Education in America* (2017), discusses in great detail the evolution of public education during the transition from English colonies. He states that the nation's founders viewed education from two distinct perspectives. "To some, the real risk to the republic lay in the people, who were ignorant, selfish, and easily swayed. Schools were needed to make them fit for a free society. To others, like Thomas Jefferson, the real risk to freedom came from the leaders. Elites, Jefferson believed, tended to corrupt governments by using political power to serve themselves...Freedom had to be protected not from the people but from their rulers" (Neem, 2017, p.7). These two perspectives played a role in American education, since both promoted the importance of education in a fledgling republic, and ironically linked education and political perspectives in a way that continues to challenge the country today.

The Common School Movement and its legacy

In the years following the Revolution, schools in America were truly locally structured. As Neem points out, Americans, especially in the Northeast, were committed to organizing, funding, and building schools within their communities. Thus, schools were funded through local taxes, overseen by locally elected boards, and remained so even when state governments became involved (Neem, 2017). Often, schools reflected Calvinist beliefs about morality and virtue while supporting democratic principles. Schools in the southern states were similarly organized, though less common. It was not until Horace Mann, considered the "father of the Common School Movement," emerged in Massachusetts in the 1830s that a model for statewide educational systems began to spread to other states, laying the groundwork for modern public education. Among the reforms Mann's Common School Movement sought to implement were a systemized statewide curriculum and school financing through local property taxes. Schools used texts like Noah Webster's *Blue Backed Speller* and later McGuffey *Readers* to teach reading, writing, and spelling. Readings offered moral guidance and supported democratic and Christian values, as well as promoting literacy. Additionally, Mann was opposed to physical punishment, preferring positive reinforcement.

While schools served as avenues of acculturation for new immigrants, immigrants also left their mark on public education. German immigrants introduced kindergartens and the gymnasium, which influenced Mann, who advocated the Prussian model of schooling. That model included the technique of age grading, that is, assigning students to different grades based on age and progressing them through school accordingly. Some students progressed to the next grade and completed all the courses secondary education had to offer. They graduated and were given a certificate of completion. In that manner, "The property of this commonwealth is pledged for the education of all its youth to save them from poverty and vice, and prepare them for the adequate performance of their social and civil duties" (Dedham Museum & Archive, 2025). Mann's confidence in the brain's plasticity and his belief that social influences fundamentally shaped human beings ultimately reinforced Mann's egalitarianism: if brains were malleable, then education mattered even more, both for individuals and for society. Thus, universally accepted, commonplace practices today became part of the fabric of American education, thanks to this innovator (Neem, 2017).

From their earliest days, American schools were, for the most part, organized as coeducational institutions. According to the Ohio School Commissioner (1856) and Barney (1851), Ohio's superintendent of common schools, in defending coeducational buildings, argued that boys and girls were both endowed with the faculties "of memory, of reason, of conscience, of imagination, and of will" and that schools must ensure that "all these powers are to be developed." While separation of the sexes did exist in some schools, it became commonplace for American schools to educate boys and girls in the same classrooms. But the same could not be said of racial divides at this time in America's past.

Early models of teacher education and implications for perceptions of teachers today

But how would these new schools be staffed? How could communities afford teachers? The answer came once again, inspired by Horace Mann and made possible by a donation of land: the first normal schools opened in Massachusetts. Such institutions differed from colleges in that they focused solely on teacher education. Lexington (in 1839) and Framingham (in 1859) became normal schools. Some normal schools were for women only, but most were co-educational. Even so, most students were women (History, 1860). By the end of the 1860s, there were 35 Normal schools in 16 states. The idea had caught on! Christine Ogren in her monumental work, *The American State Normal School*, reports that "despite the persistence of in the late nineteenth and early twentieth centuries of teacher education in other types of institutions, the state normal schools were a dominant force in teacher education throughout this period" (Ogren, 2005, p.57). Ogren further reports that in 1914 there were 119,000 students enrolled in normal schools across the nation, a staggering 102,700 in state normal schools! (p.58). Focusing primarily on pedagogy, but expanding their curricula as they developed, they provided teachers for the growing nation's public schools. So, who were typical normal school students? Ogden tells us that the 1890s football cheer at Geneseo, New York, was, "We came to the gridiron fresh from the verdant farms" (ibid, p.69), reflecting the backgrounds of most of the students attracted to normal schools. Teaching became an alternative to farming. In my own family, my wife's great-uncle, John Hand, left the family farm in Pennsylvania, armed with a state normal school diploma, and became a teacher in Binghamton, NY, in the early years of the 20th century. He abandoned teaching when Thomas J. Watson offered him a more lucrative position at his International Business Machines (IBM) company in nearby Endicott. In that little piece of family history is a nugget of the story of teaching in America.

About 103,800 openings for kindergarten and elementary school teachers are projected each year, on average, over the coming decade (US Bureau of Labor Statistics, October 2025). Is the US able to meet these demands? Becoming a teacher in America usually requires earning a Bachelor's degree from an accredited college or university with an education program. These programs often include a supervised student-teaching component and lead to state certification. Requirements differ by state; for example, New York State mandates that graduates pass a certification exam, undergo a background security check, and, after five years of teaching, obtain a Master's degree to retain their position. In addition to maintaining certification, teachers in New York must complete ongoing education requirements throughout their careers. Although alternative certification pathways exist in New York, once certified and hired, the additional requirements still apply. Every state is different, but all require a bachelor's degree. Arizona law allows people to start teaching while still in college, provided they are supervised by a full-time educator and complete their bachelor's degree for full certification. In Florida, military veterans without a bachelor's degree may be eligible for a five-year teaching certificate. This diversity is a legacy of local control of education.

The American university system

The American university system can be traced back to the colonial period in US history. Harvard was founded in 1636, and like other colleges, it was initially established to train clergy and promote religious education. The earliest American institutions were primarily modeled after English universities, emphasizing classical education, theology, and the liberal arts. The American Revolution of 1776 brought changes to higher education, not only in name but in substance. Frederick Rudolph (2021) cites the name change of one of New York's most prestigious institutions, from King's College to Columbia. Along with that change came the curricular additions of economics, French, and natural history. In 1795, the University of North Carolina instituted courses in chemistry, agriculture, languages, and mechanical arts. It appears that a combination of the European Enlightenment's influence and the needs of a growing new society was reflected in the courses of study (Rudolph, 2021).

In the succeeding decades, as the nation developed, more disciplines were added based on the growing country's needs, and adaptations were made to accommodate those changes. In 1876, Johns Hopkins University was founded as a hybrid of English and German models, setting the pace for other American colleges and universities. It drew from the British model, which emphasized undergraduate education, and the German model, with its emphasis on advanced research. Like the country itself, "it was much less rigid and hierarchical than the German system and was more democratic in its organization and structure" (Cole, 2011, p. 28).

The rise of fascism in Europe in the 1930s, WWII, and the spread of communism in the post-war years brought many European scientists and educators to the United States. That "intellectual migration", as Cole (2011) refers to it, had a substantial influence on American education. The National Research Foundation is a government-endowed, independent organization that subsidizes fundamental research in science and engineering, including pure science and STEM education. That idea evolved into the National Science Foundation, which was established in 1950 and remains active today. American universities cultivated a strong belief in competition and, until recently, enjoyed a high level of autonomy from the state.

During the twentieth century, Normal Schools throughout the country transitioned into state teachers' colleges. That move often broadened the offerings and standardized the curriculum. Wendy Paterson, Dean of the School of Education at SUNY Buffalo State, when writing about the school's history and transition from a Normal School, put it this way, "Buffalo State was founded in 1871 as the Buffalo Normal School. It changed its name more often than it changed its building" (Paterson, 2021). Those name changes reflected the changing function of the institution within a larger state system. At about the same time, this process was repeated in nearly every state, as Normal Schools became incorporated into regional state-wide systems of education. At about the same time, in private universities, departments of education were expanding into schools of education. Stanford University's Labaree puts it this way," Teacher education, it turned out, was going to be carried out within a university, under the leadership of professors in a school or college of education located there. By this time, the former Normal Schools had evolved into universities. Once they achieved this status, they naturally imitated the structure of existing universities by setting up education schools and then assigning them the work that had once constituted the Normal Schools' entire mission, preparing teachers" (2008, p. 296).

John Dewey

Hundreds of doctoral dissertations have been written about John Dewey and his influence on philosophy, education, and social theory. His impact on education, particularly in the United States, has been both profound and significant. In

Democracy and Education, originally published in 1916, John Dewey states, "…it is the office of the school environment to balance the various elements in the social environment, and to see to it that each individual gets an opportunity to escape from the limitations of the social group in which he was born, and to come into living contact with a broader environment" (Dewey 2015, p.45). For over a century, his words have influenced policymakers, curriculum planners, and instructional designers. Like Horace Mann, Dewey saw schools as places where democracy's values could be fostered, and indeed, schools could repair the problems of modern society. They envisioned nothing less than fundamental change in mind, culture, and morality (Cohen, 1998).

Through what is often referred to as progressive education, the focus is on practical relevance, rather than traditional education's emphasis on memorization and mental discipline. Learning by doing is a cornerstone of Dewey's philosophy, facilitating understanding and meaning in a natural and psychologically relevant manner. Equally significant to the progressive approach is the sociological component, which promotes social responsibility and democratic principles within the educational process and context (Hopkins, 2017). Hopkins points out that an important feature of progressive education is that students are to perceive knowledge naturally, with teachers serving more as facilitators in the process of scientific discovery.

The legacy of Dewey's progressive education is evident in various ways today. Many schools emphasize collaborative learning, student voice, and fostering critical thinking skills, aligning with his vision of active, participatory citizenship. Instructional techniques that promote critical thinking, problem-solving, and interdisciplinary approaches align with Dewey's vision, as do efforts to make education more equitable and culturally responsive, especially in diverse and multicultural settings.

It is interesting to note that towards those ends, school districts across the nation have adopted programs of Social-Emotional Learning, a contemporary approach rooted in Dewey's philosophy (Brackett et al., 2011). For example, Dr. Mark Secaur, Superintendent of the Smithtown Central School District in New York State, wrote the following in a District Position Paper: "The inclusion of social emotional learning practices within the Smithtown Central School District is meant to increase the opportunity for students to strengthen their belief in themselves, enhance academic performance, and manage potential anxieties in a healthy manner. These acquired skills will likely increase college, career, and civic readiness. Additionally, students have the opportunity to benefit from improved attitudes about others, their school, and their academic achievement" (2022).

Women in Education: A Tough Road to Equality

Women dominated the field, especially the elementary schools, providing comparatively cheap labor that met the needs of an ever-expanding school system. The idea that women teachers should remain unmarried was prevalent at certain times, especially during the 19th and early 20th centuries. In fact, some policies and attitudes suggested that marriage could distract women from their teaching duties or undermine their authority and moral standing. Teaching was sometimes viewed as incompatible with marriage due to concerns about propriety, professional autonomy, and potential conflicts between marital and professional roles. This continued well into the 1950s. "Legal economic discrimination against college-educated, middle-class women, especially teachers, in the early twentieth century, is important in understanding why married women's entrance into the professions was protracted. Legal and social hostility combined with economic discrimination discouraged college-educated women from blending family and career" (Thomas, 2010, p.56).

Historically, women were often encouraged to pursue teaching because it was considered a suitable and respectable profession for them, but gender-based pay disparities indeed played a role. Of course, many women chose teaching out of genuine interest and a desire to serve their communities. During World War II, women took over factory jobs traditionally considered "men's work." After the war, they largely returned to traditional occupations, but with a different perspective. Many of the gender rules had been overturned by the wartime experience. But local traditions remained. My aunt, Gloria Damian Marrese, despite attaining a master's degree in education and certification in school district administration, as well as experience as a high school teacher, elementary school principal, and assistant superintendent of schools, reached the glass ceiling by 1959. She described being the only woman in a room filled with men educators at the New York state capital, Albany. Having got that far, she could go no further. According to the American Association of School Administrators (Glass, 2010), in the 1980s, only about 1.2% of U.S. superintendents were women. The picture appears to be changing today. According to the ILO Group, women now hold one-third of the superintendent positions in the nation's 500 largest school districts, the highest levels since the launch of the ILO Group's *Superintendent Research Project*, and superintendent turnover continues at historic levels, reaching a three-year high in 2025 (ILO Group, 2025, p. 12). As a postscript, my aunt continued her interest in education and served as a school board member in her community after retirement.

As late as 1971, my wife, Patricia, although a school social worker, not a teacher, was required to begin maternity leave when she was 4 months pregnant with our first son. The idea was that women should not "show" that they were pregnant at school. By the time our daughter was born in 1979, things had changed, and that restriction had been removed.

Education of African Americans

The history of African Americans' education is complex and shaped by systemic racism, segregation, and ongoing civil rights battles. During the period of slavery, Africans were portrayed as incapable of higher intellectual functioning, as an obvious way of justifying their treatment. For many reasons, they were not allowed to learn to read. In fact, South Carolina passed a law in 1740 making it illegal to teach a slave to read, and several other southern colonies (and later states) passed similar laws. But even where formal laws were not enacted, teaching slaves to read was against the norms of Southern society.

After slavery ended, the path to education was filled with challenges, as many Black people faced significant barriers to learning. The creation of historically Black colleges and universities (HBCUs) in the late 1800s was a key step, offering vital educational opportunities for Black students during a time of exclusion. Booker T. Washington, a famous, educated, former slave, was called to create a black normal and agricultural school at Tuskegee, Alabama, in 1881- a time when hundreds of African-Americans were being lynched annually. Here, he practiced the philosophy of education that he hoped would reduce white opposition to black schooling (Warikoo & Jacoby-Senghor, 2016).

The Jim Crow era in American history began in the 1870s and lasted until the Civil Rights era of the 1960s. The Supreme Court's decision of Plessey v. Ferguson in 1896 established what was called the separate but equal doctrine. It allowed states to segregate based on race as long as facilities were available for white and black citizens. States, primarily in the Southern United States, passed various laws ranging from separate drinking fountains to separate schools. They became collectively known as Jim Crow laws. The name "Jim Crow" originated from a song made popular by Thomas Dartmouth Rice, a white character in a minstrel show of the early 1800s who painted his face black while performing. The song Jim Crow made a mockery of blacks (Cockrell, 1996).

During the Jim Crow era, segregation laws enforced separate and unequal educational systems, which severely disadvantaged African American students and created significant disparities in resources and quality. While the focus has been on local control of education, the federal government has played a substantial role in establishing and ensuring educational equality. The landmark Supreme Court case Brown v. Board of Education in 1954 was pivotal, declaring racial segregation in public schools unconstitutional and paving the way for gradual desegregation across the country. Carlson states, "African Americans, especially the generation that came of age during the 1950s and 1960s, implemented and expanded the limited scope of the Brown decision through individual and collective challenges to the entire Jim Crow system" (Carson, 2004/2005, p.10). The Civil Rights Act of 1964 was the landmark legislation that outlawed discrimination and enforced integration in public places, employment, and schools. The 14th Amendment created the legal principle of equal protection. Still, discriminatory laws persisted until the Civil Rights Act provided specific, federal enforcement to dismantle segregation and guarantee civil rights, including the right to desegregation (Williams, 2004).

Despite notable progress since then, disparities in educational attainment and access to resources persist. Factors such as socioeconomic status, the conditions of neighborhoods, and the enduring impact of discrimination continue to influence the quality of education available to African Americans. Ongoing efforts to rectify these inequities focus on advocating for equitable funding, ensuring access to high-quality teachers, and promoting culturally relevant curricula that resonate with the histories and experiences of Black students.

Paul Green in *The Paradox of the Promised Unfulfilled: Brown V. Board of Education and the Continued Pursuit of Excellence in Education*, sums it up best, "Despite notable progress since then, disparities in educational attainment and access to resources persist. Factors such as socioeconomic status, the conditions of neighborhoods, and the enduring impact of discrimination continue to influence the quality of education available to Black Americans. Ongoing efforts to rectify these inequities focus on advocating for equitable funding, ensuring access to high-quality teachers, and promoting culturally relevant curricula that resonate with the histories and experiences of Black students" (Green, 2004, p.280)

Special education and federal legislation

Following quickly, and some would say developing out of, the Civil Rights legislation of the 1960s was two pieces of legislation that would change education across all fifty states. By banning recipients of federal funds from discriminating against people with disabilities, the Rehabilitation Act of 1973, for the first time in federal law, established a definition of disability. That definition broadly includes any person who has a physical or mental impairment that substantially limits one or more major life activities. It was followed two years later by the Individuals with Disabilities Education Act (IDEA). "The IDEA established the right of children with disabilities to attend public schools, to receive services designed to meet their needs free of charge, and, to the greatest extent possible, to receive instruction in regular education classrooms alongside nondisabled children" (Aron & Loprest, 2012, p.99). The number of students aged 3–21 served under IDEA in the United States was 7.5 million in the 2022–23 school year. As a percentage of total public school enrollment, this amounts to 15 percent of students (NCES, 2025b).

It is fair to say that no single piece of federal legislation has changed the daily life of schools in America as much as the IDEA. Through establishing the requirement of the least restrictive environment, students are now only removed from the general education classroom when their needs cannot be met there, even with supplemental aids and services. The law also requires the writing of an individualized education program (IEP) for each student with a disability. This document outlines their specific educational goals, services, and accommodations. The law also requires schools to involve parents in all IEP planning. Ultimately, the IDEA ensures that states are accountable for delivering services to students with disabilities. The U.S. Department of Education can withhold federal funding if a state does not comply with the law.

As Aron and Loprest point out, "the many legal conflicts that arise between parents and schools can be counterproductive for children and their educational success and costly for school systems. To some extent, these conflicts arise because parents play an integral role- one that is required by law - in the team that develops their child's individualized service plan. The incentives for parents to obtain the most help for their child may differ from those for school systems that are trying to balance educational needs and budgets" (p.118). The enactment of the IDEA has posed challenges, both legal and educational. It has impacted instruction and has played a role in teacher education, supervision, and evaluation. Meier reports that responsibility for smoothly integrated inclusion secondary programs often rests on the principals' ability not only to schedule students appropriately but also, through knowledge of the law, to provide teachers and the community with the tools to adapt to changes in how services are provided as they occur (Meier, 2023). Since the enactment involves specific planning and instruction, the federal government, for the first time in American history, has had a particular role in what happens in every classroom throughout the country.

Native American education

The history of the treatment of Native Americans in the United States has been interwoven with notions of American exceptionalism, political expediency, and economic gain. As Lomawaima and McCarty (2025) describe it in *To remain an Indian: Lessons in democracy from a century of Native American education,* "mission and federal schools were established as laboratories for a grand experiment in cultural cleansing, Christian conversion, and what has been termed the 'proletarianization' of menial laborers and domestic workers into the workforce" (Lomawaima & McCarty, 2025, p.1957). They dispute the commonly used term, "assimilation," in that it is too benign a term for the treatment of Native Americans and instead propose "domestication." They point out that the term better describes the transformation of Native Americans for the use and benefit of settlers. Further highlighting that definition by further stating, "the list of synonyms for *domesticate* on Thesursus.com makes explicit its implications: subdue, break, yoke – and, also, teach and train" (Lomawaima & McCarty, 2025, p. 1958). Those authors highlight Native American communities' efforts to reclaim control over their educational systems and to promote their languages and traditions.

President Richard Nixon signed the Indian Education Act of 1972 into law, and it is recognized today as being the first legislation to address the disparities in outcomes between Native American and Non-Native American students. This legislation enabled greater tribal control over education and is a shift toward recognizing tribal sovereignty. Additionally, the inclusion of Native American history, culture, and languages into the curriculum not only improved educational relevance for Native American students but also contributed to the preservation of Native American cultures. This Act was far-reaching, including provisions for hiring Native American teachers and staff, creating role models within the educational system who understood students' cultural backgrounds (U.S. Department of Health, Education, and Welfare, 1974).

Where we are today

Data compiled by the National Indian Educational Association (2026) presents a challenging picture of the current situation. Demographics indicate that youth represent the highest percentage of the Native population compared to the general US population. Policymakers should take this into account by ensuring that educational resources and programs are adequately funded and supported. The National Indian Educational Association (NIEA, 2026) reports that 93% of Native American students attend public schools, which indicates that these communities rely heavily on public education systems, and that underscores the need for public schools to have culturally relevant education. Furthermore, 49% of Native youth attend schools where they are a minority, and only 24% attend schools where they represent the majority of students enrolled. One implication of this is that students may not see their heritage reflected in their school environment, as the creators of the 1972 legislation anticipated.

Disparities exist in the success rates of Native American students. According to NIEA data, the high school graduation rate increased from 67% in 2012 to 74% in 2019 (NIEA, 2026), but this increase still falls short of the current national average of 87% for all public schools (National Center for Educational Statistics, 2025b). Efforts must be made to continue and increase this positive trend.

Native youth face higher rates of poverty, with 37% of those students attending high-poverty public schools as compared with 8% of white public-school students. The majority of Native American students qualify for free or reduced-price lunch, further emphasizing the socio-economic challenges their communities face in educating them (NIEA, 2026).

While school safety is a national concern, NIEA data indicate that 14% of students aged 12-18 are afraid of being attacked or harmed at school. That is twice that of any other racial or ethnic group and over three times the national average. School safety is an area that needs attention in general but is particularly critical for Native youth (NIEA, 2026).

Despite the stated aim of the 1972 Act, Native students are less likely than their white peers to have a teacher who shares their racial and ethnic background. The majority of teachers in schools that are predominantly Native American in composition are white (61%). In schools where Native youth are the majority, only 29% of the faculty are Native Americans - clearly, more needs to happen to attract Native Americans to the teaching profession.

Education of non-English speaking students

America has always thought of itself as a nation of immigrants. With that comes the challenge of educating a large, linguistically diverse population. Aside from its immigrant population, there is also a substantial bilingual Mexican-American population. Growing out of the Civil Rights legislation of the 1960s was the movement by Mexican-Americans to develop bicultural and bilingual programs. Responding to this concern, Texas Senator Ralph Yarborough, a former educator himself, led the passage of the Bilingual Education Act of 1968, known as Title VII of the Elementary and Secondary Education Act (ESEA) (Gamson et al., 2015). As in the case of special education, federal laws served as an overarching umbrella for state laws, and local school districts were mandated to implement these mandates regarding the education of non-English and bilingual students.

These programs required targeted instruction to develop English language proficiency among multilingual learners. Holding non-English and bilingual students to the same expectations and outcomes as their peers also required equitable access to the whole curriculum and educational standards. To accomplish those ends, schools were required to offer additional support services to facilitate academic success for these students. This might include bilingual education programs, English as a Second Language (ESL) programs, and various resources to support students as they acquire English language skills (U.S. Department of Education, 2015).

Opinions on the necessity and success of such programs are currently in dispute. Some point to the costs and the burdens it places on schools; others highlight its impact on overall school performance rates (Gunderson, 2021). Regardless, local school districts will always have the option to supply services for non-English-speaking students. We have the obligation of providing educational programs that are productive and equitable for all our students if we are to progress as a nation. Like so much in schools, it all comes down to teachers. Almendarez-De Bello put it this way, "There is no question that teachers have the greatest impact on student achievement. This is especially the case for Latino students who are entering our school systems as English Language Learners (ELL) with minimal access to bilingual and relatable educators" (Almendarez-De Bello, 2019, p.3).

Reaction to 2022 PISA scores

The Program for International Student Assessment (PISA) measures 15-year-olds' skills in math, science, and reading. It is administered every three years through the 38 member nations of the OECD (Organization for Economic Cooperation and Development. In summary, the USA students scored lower in math in 2022 than in 2018 and showed somewhat improved scores in reading and science (Long, 2024).

While the United States could be said to have maintained or slightly increased scores in reading and science, math scores fell below. Of course, the pandemic has a lot to answer for, but the US scores were well below those of other nations with similar economic levels. "The United States has more students in the bottom group and fewer students in the top group than most other industrialized countries that are part of the OECD" (Barshay, 2023).

Andreas Schleicher, director for education and skills at the OECD, emphasized that the inequities in the U.S. are often misunderstood to be primarily a problem of weak schools in poor neighborhoods. He focuses on identifying gaps and providing the resources to fill them. Additionally, Schleicher states, " There is actually good research, good evidence, out there, and they're good practices, but how this actually happens, I guess the harder part is, when it comes to the quality of teaching and teachers and again, the U.S. spends a lot, but teachers are not paid really well, and teaching is not an attractive career choice. And the quality of education can never be better than the quality of your teachers" (Robinson & Green, 2023).

Some Americans tend to see the issue through the lens of a fragmented, locally controlled educational structure that highlights economic disparities. Others point to the need for a greater emphasis on critical thinking. And still others feel that the tests and their results are irrelevant to Americans. According to Harry Federer, executive director of the National Center for Fair & Open Testing, "The information tested on international tests is not the information children will need to compete in the innovation economy, and the results do not tell us important information about student proficiency with the vocational competencies necessary to create, innovate, and pursue entrepreneurial opportunities" (Long, 2024).

Teachers' salaries

It is interesting to note that, according to the Pew Research Center, both the general public in America and teachers themselves believe that teaching is a difficult job. To be more precise, "And about three-quarters of Americans (74%) say teachers should be paid more than they are now, including 39% who say teachers should be paid *a lot* more" (Braga et al., 2024). But does this match up to reality?

When it comes to teachers' salaries, it is back to that very local control. Thirty-eight states have school districts that mirror county boundaries; the others either have combinations of county boundaries and other units, such as cities or townships, or, as in the case of New York, a mixture of five different ways that school districts are organized to account for historical factors, local needs, and patterns of growth (Proximity One, 2025). Each district decides the pay scale for its teachers. New York State has 730 school districts; New York City alone has 32, with two special city-wide districts (New York State Education Department 2025). During the 2023-2024 school year, there were 13,303 public school districts. (Institute of Education Sciences. (2024)

For the 2023-2024 school year, the National Education Association (NEA) reported that the average schoolteacher annual salary in the nation was $72,030, with California and New York paying the highest salaries, $ 101,084 and $95,615, respectively. At the other end of the scale were Mississippi ($53,704) and Florida ($54,875) (National Education Association, 2025). Those averages represent such diverse considerations as cost of living, level of subject taught, and wealth of the school district as defined by local school tax revenue. Many school districts have a sliding scale that increases salary based on years of service and teachers' educational levels. That has been my personal experience as a teacher in New York State. In some states, school districts have decided that elementary teachers, the majority of whom are women, should earn less than high school teachers. Implicit in whatever system is employed is a judgement regarding the value of teachers. Sometimes the overriding factors are education and experience; other times, the level at which the teacher works. The NEA released data clearly showing that teachers earn 24% more on average in states with collective bargaining (National Education Association, 2025).

As for post-secondary education, the situations vary just as widely, with salaries for US university and college teachers determined by rank, institution, and field, ranging from $70s to over $100,000, with median wages around $84,000 (Bureau of Labor Statistics, October, 2025) for all postsecondary teachers. The NEA reported, "Faculty salaries rose by an average of 4.3 percent between 2022-23 and 2023-24, exceeding the 3.3 percent inflation rate. As a result, faculty purchasing power increased by 1 percent. Despite this improvement, purchasing power in 2023-24 was 6.8 percent below pre-pandemic levels" (National Education Association, 2025). Post-secondary educators face the same situation as their public school counterparts regarding location being a critical factor, but, as reported in the same NEA publication, there is a persistent disparity in salaries between men and women.

Allegretto (2024) and Neuber and Beckstein (2022) highlight the painful truth that there is a wide pay gap between teachers at any level and those with the same degree working in other professions. And that gap widens in those states where teachers receive the lowest average incomes! No wonder teachers resort to having second and third jobs to pay their rent. Given the cost of higher education, we have to ask ourselves, what motivates people to go into teaching? Clearly, the notion of paying teachers much more, as mentioned above, is aspirational given the realities of financing education and the value associated with being a teacher.

Concluding remarks

How is it possible that fifty unique states with separate educational systems, linked through relatively recent federal legislation, manage to function as an academic system? The answer lies within each teacher. America's efforts to provide education for its vast and diverse student population have posed unique systemic and, at times, personal challenges for teachers. It is a tribute to the spirit of American teachers that the system operates as well as it does. Teachers continue to face challenges, which they have learned to overcome individually and collectively in different ways.

Despite those pressures, legions of teachers have made a difference in their students' lives and have contributed to the fabric of American education. Teachers like Karen Van Dover, over the course of her career, reached out to students who, because of family problems, were bounced from school to school. Bertha Marsh, a state normal school graduate who not only insisted that her students learn to write effectively but also spent hours with them after school, working towards that end. June Lanham, whose individualized approach to her students involved visiting their homes to encourage greater parental involvement. William Hurd, a beloved high school English teacher, like many other academics, took advantage of the ten-month cycle to work as a postman during the summer holidays to supplement his salary. Joseph Baldino and Sarah Miller, unknown to each other, in different places and at various times, taught students how to understand and express what they were learning through the lens of theater. Angelo Ditta teaches adult learners in the General Education Development (GED) program, helping them earn a high school equivalency diploma and open doors to improved employment opportunities or even college education. His students are often immigrants, for whom English is a second or third language, or students who, for a variety of reasons, could not finish high school. Each is drawn into a classroom that soon becomes a new world family for them as they learn academic subjects in an open and trusting environment. Seth Meier, a high school art teacher following in his mother's footsteps, engages his students in all aspects of art, including set design and the production of the annual school musical. Georgette Bowling, with her colleagues, has integrated learning experiences across three grade levels in a unique program that allowed students to advance in specific areas at their own pace. And many continue beyond retirement to contribute to the profession that they love and have devoted their lives to. Chuck Triolo, an elementary school teacher, continued as a school board member in retirement. Louise Miller continues her love of teaching by training teachers in the Socratic method. And Diane Wrobleski, although retired as an English teacher, continues to impact young people's lives through mentoring, making the dream of a college education a reality for those who might never have thought it possible. American education is facing many challenges, some a product of its historical roots, others caused by its present circumstances. The one constant over time is the nation's capable and caring teachers. These individuals I've mentioned represent a few of the 3.3 million American teachers whose resiliency and commitment extend well beyond their employment statistics. Like all teachers throughout the world, they live forever in the memories of those lives they have touched.

TEACHING WASN'T WHAT I WAS PLANNING TO DO

Thomas C. De Bello

As a person involved in teacher education, I have always been interested in what motivates people to become teachers. My path toward my lifelong profession was not direct or straightforward.

As a student, things did not always come easily for me. However, I had supportive parents, especially a father who patiently helped me understand my math assignments. I was motivated to succeed, and that helped me overcome some difficulties I might have had. Also, early on, I discovered that I really liked to read.

I was raised in a traditional Italian-American family, including the ritual Sunday luncheon at my grandparents' home, where all the family gathered routinely. Among my relatives was an uncle who had been a high school science teacher, coach, and athletic director for a school district. Also, I had an aunt who was a high school English teacher, principal, and the district director of curriculum in the same district as my uncle. My aunt and uncle often had intense conversations about things happening in the school district. Sometimes, these discussions included students, programs, discipline policies, etc. They frequently disagreed about how things should be handled. As a kid, I didn't want to be a teacher. There was so much controversy and disagreement.

As I entered college, I wasn't sure of what I wanted to be, but I was sure teaching would not be for me! My high school was great; it reflected many U.S. suburban high schools in the 1950s, and it didn't have much of a social studies curriculum beyond history. I was hooked when I got to college and took my first anthropology course! My college offered a dual major in anthropology and sociology, and I signed up. I was particularly drawn to all aspects of anthropology and worked on an archeology dig as part of a course I took. After graduation, I was accepted into a graduate program in anthropology, and I was on my way to a career in anthropology, or so I thought.

My program was intense, and I loved it. However, I soon realized that to be an anthropologist, I needed to be able to live in another culture, learn its language, and function effectively in a different physical and societal environment. The thing was that I had never traveled outside of the U.S.; in fact, I had barely ventured outside of my home state, New York! Most of the other students in the program had experienced some overseas travel; my roommate had just returned to the U. S. from two years abroad teaching in Norway. Before that, he had been a Peace Corps Volunteer in Nepal. He hoped to continue his studies in anthropology, specializing in Nepalese society. It was his experience that encouraged me to join the Peace Corps. I realized that if I committed myself to years of study in anthropology, I'd better know if I was suited for that kind of life!

I was accepted into the Peace Corps and assigned to a training group at Stanford University, preparing volunteers to teach English as a Second Language in the Philippines. Dwight W. Allen, the director of our program, developed a teacher training system known as micro-teaching at Stanford. In ten short weeks, we were taught a method of English as a Second Language teaching, given opportunities to practice teaching Filipino American children, and immersed in the Tagalog language and Filipino culture. After a one-week orientation in Manila, I was sent to a rural community in southern Mindanao, a large island in the south part of the Philippines. The townspeople spoke Cebuano, Tagalog being a second language to most of them, the same way English was. So, I had to learn Cebuano!

Two years later, I discovered I could live in another culture, learn a new language, and feel part of the community. In short, I acquired the initial skills necessary for successful fieldwork in anthropology. But, along the way, I also discovered that I loved teaching. With my background in social sciences and a new curriculum in New York State social studies, I was hired to teach ninth-grade social studies! I was fortunate that my principal was a former social studies teacher, and my chairperson was really grounded in instructional design, I was given the support I needed to make the transition to teaching back in the USA.

I have always found teaching exciting and challenging. Once you think you've got something down, the tectonic plates shift beneath you, and there are new things to consider and adjust to. My commitment to the content I teach has always been important, but the students I teach are equally important, and while it may seem trite, I have always learned from them. One experience in my second year of teaching influenced me greatly and shaped my approach to students.

Ray wasn't the best student academically, but he was enthusiastic. He liked to argue about the topics I taught, and he was relentless when he found a topic that excited him. He would go to the library and research things on his own. Sometimes, he got so caught up in the topic that his regular class assignments suffered.

Towards the end of the year, we studied Ancient Egypt, and Ray brought me a copy of National Geographic about the Aswan Dam. He was really into it and wanted me to read it. He put his name on the front cover and handed it to me, saying I could take it home over the weekend. That's just how Ray was. He gave me a homework assignment!

For some reason, I packed up and put Ray's National Geographic in a plastic bag, not in my briefcase. I tossed the bag and my briefcase into the dark pit, which was the trunk of my car. Then, I headed home for a quick meal and a change before returning to school to chaperone the 9th-grade dance.

The dance was its usual crazy mix of kids. Some students tried to act older than their age, while others struggled to mature even to their chronological years. They were just typical ninth graders. There was the usual parking lot check, and it ended almost as quickly as the dance began. The cleanup crew stayed until about midnight, and it was then that I noticed Ray hadn't come to the dance.

Ray was usually at every student council activity and always volunteered to do the jobs others didn't want, so I expected him to be at clean-up. I asked one of the kids, who told me that Ray was worried about an English test on Monday and decided to stay home and catch up with his readings.

I never could have expected the call from the principal on Sunday evening. He called to tell me that Ray died sometime Saturday night. It seems that Ray's mom left him in the living room reading a novel Saturday night, and when she awoke, he was still in the chair with a book in his hands. All efforts to wake him failed. It was later determined that Ray had an undetected heart problem.

Early on in my teaching, I learned that the lives of our students can't be taken for granted and can be very fragile. I also learned that enthusiasm for a subject could count more than actual grades. By traditional assessments, Ray was only a moderately successful student, but through his interest, he excelled. I realized that part of my job would be to nurture the interest and support the enthusiasm of my students. This more holistic approach to teaching is the core of who I am as a teacher and administrator.

In the back of my mind, my 10th-grade English teacher, Miss Marsh, serves as a model of commitment. As a 9th grader in 1957 I had heard stories of the infamous Miss Marsh, how strict, stern, and exacting she was. Not at all like the young, laid back and popular Miss Hackett. I thought these were all exaggerations. After all, I had eight years of nuns teaching me at Catholic school. How bad could she be?

I soon discovered what the rigors of Miss Marsh's class could be like. I could handle the reading assignments, and I enjoyed them, but it was the writing that got to me. Every week, we would be given a writing assignment. "Write an essay about…" was how it typically began. However, before the essay could be completed, each student had to have an outline approved. In those days, an outline meant a full-sentence alphanumeric outline, not something with Venn diagrams or arrows. Each week, we had to submit an outline based on the topic. Before we could start our essay, our outline needed to be approved. We could not begin a new essay until we had completed the previous week's essay. It wasn't long before I was two weeks behind in my essays.

Miss Marsh had a cure for that: an after-school review. Each afternoon, students from any of her sections could come to this review session to make up work. So, at three-thirty on a blistery fall afternoon, I found myself, with about twenty others, sitting in a classroom working on an outline. The week's topic I was behind was

"Teaching someone to…" The choice that I regretted making was "Teaching Someone to Dance the Cha-Cha." Three times, I went up to Miss Marsh's desk, and three times, I was sent back with additional notes written across the page in red! I was getting frustrated. Why didn't I understand what she meant? On the fourth go-round, no doubt equally frustrated Miss Marsh decided to take another tack.

Let me describe Miss Marsh to you. She began teaching in the 1930s in the town's original schoolhouse. She was a slight woman, well into her sixties at the time, about five feet, one inch tall, with a commanding presence. She looked up at me from her desk, her eyes above her rimless glasses, and said, "All I'm asking is that you describe the movement step by step." Then she looked at me, got up, and said. "Pretend I'm your partner, and you're showing me the steps. Show me what to do first." So there I was, face to face with Miss Marsh; she put out her hands for me to hold. Just then, the entire Varsity football team passed the classroom door, and I heard, "Miss Marsh's boyfriend. Look, everyone!" She said, "We haven't got all afternoon; show me as though you are my dance teacher." Those familiar with the cha-cha may know that the steps are compact and based partly on the rumba and mambo, with plenty of hip and pelvic movements. There is a basic forward movement. I began my illustration, and Miss Marsh began to follow me, then suddenly, she stopped short.

Recall that I mentioned Miss Marsh first began teaching in the 1930s and that she taught at the town's original school. The story was that one winter, when the snow and ice were awful, Miss Marsh was leaving school after a late review session and unfortunately fell on the ice, breaking her hip and damaging her lower spine. As a result of that fall and the inadequate treatment available locally at the time, she walked with a pronounced limp. Back to my lesson. Miss Marsh quickly realized that her body lacked the dexterity to complete the move. She looked up at me and said, "You've got the idea now. Go back to your seat and write it down as you would teach it step by step."

What has always stayed with me over the years, aside from anything I might have learned about the writing process, was what it meant to be a teacher. Sure, she had standards for her students; believe me, she was exacting, but she also offered all her students a means to achieve those standards. She extended herself to me at the risk of personal embarrassment, and I have never forgotten that lesson. I have tried to bring that same attitude to all my classes. Later in graduate school, I had the good fortune to work with Rita and Ken Dunn, and to quote Ken, "If students can't learn the way we are teaching them, then we need to teach them in the way that they learn."

For 18 years, I taught social studies in grades 7 – 9, and I loved the challenge of seeing young people grow in skills and sometimes even maturity! I believed that if I could provide challenging and meaningful lessons that involved my students, classroom management would not be a significant issue.

Armed with a newly minted doctorate in education, I expanded my professional activities by teaching evenings at a community college and speaking at conferences. At a conference in upstate New York, I was scheduled to give two workshops on the writing process. After the first, some participants asked me to join them in the banquet room for lunch. We were randomly seated at large round tables. To my left was the popular children's author, Tomie dePaolo, and to my right was my oldest son's reading teacher. Tomie and I compared our grandmother's tomato sauce recipes, but the conversation with my son's teacher took a more serious turn. She attended my workshop, and during the discussion, she mentioned an opening for an elementary school principal in another district and encouraged me to apply. I had not thought about that direction at all. I had been a social studies department head and secondary school summer school principal, but going to the elementary school would be a return to my elementary school roots long ago in the Philippines. That chance encounter led to my being an elementary school principal at three entirely different schools over the next sixteen years.

Throughout this journey, I was fortunate to have the support of my wife, who was a school social worker. Although we never worked in the same school district, her experiences and knowledge provided a seasoned perspective that usually helped me see things differently. Not to say we always agreed, but we could appreciate where each other came from and be supportive.

My goal was always to support teachers, understand their concerns, and work with them to find solutions. As I understood, every student has a learning style, so too, teachers had a preferred way of teaching, which made them effective. What worked well for one person might not suit another. To me, teachers come to the profession wanting to make their students the best and most successful they can be. Working with teachers to minimize the gap between their beliefs about teaching and learning and their daily practice was more important than trying to make them fit a mold of what a teacher should be. Using different approaches, supporting teacher initiatives, and helping pick up the pieces when things didn't go as planned were all part of the principal's job.

Initially, being an elementary school principal was a one-person show, especially in my first two schools. Sometimes, I felt like the guy in the circus who would get a long stick and spin a plate on top and then another, and then another until ten plates were spinning- he would keep plates spinning as he added another. If one fell, there was a good chance it would knock others down. Watching him was exhausting but being him was even more draining. Our superintendent, a very student-centered leader, introduced us to site-based leadership. A team approach with principals, teachers, support staff, parents, and community members coming together, analyzing issues, and, in collaboration, developing a plan to address those issues! Wow! Finally, there would be helping to keep those plates spinning!

Like every classroom, every school has its issues and concerns, and I became familiar with each one and loved my experiences in each school where I worked. At the core are always the students and how they can best be served. At my previous school, we developed a site-based team that included parents, custodians, and community members. Additionally, we had many student teachers and talented, experienced teachers willing to help train them. Rather than seeing these young people as just passing through, we collaboratively developed our school into a professional development school, working with a local university. Our experienced teachers not only took in student teachers but also became adjuncts to the college, teaching the student teaching seminar in-house and supervising and even developing the skills to evaluate those fledgling teachers effectively. This was a great way to recognize the talents and achievements of teachers and encourage young people in their careers.

I sometimes found myself in a position of counseling teachers who were faced with making the life-altering decision to retire. Retirement incentives were not routinely offered. You never knew if there would be one much in advance, and most times there weren't. There were teachers I hated to lose because of their well-deserved popularity. The reality was that for some, they would have to work an additional four years to make up the difference if they did not take the incentive package.

Early on, as a principal, I saw what happened to a solid teacher who did not take the incentive because he felt he had "more productive years" ahead. In two years, all his professional friends were gone. Instead of seeing him as the sage mentor, new teachers saw him as a dinosaur, and his classroom performance began to suffer. He left without making up the financial difference, somewhat embittered.

That colored my view of the decision process. When teachers came to me saying that they felt they were at the top of their game, I'd say, "What a great time to go, when all around you will remember you as one of the best! If you miss it that much, you can always tutor or come back as a substitute teacher." Some did that briefly, but most either enjoyed retirement or found another part-time job to pass the time. The complex nature of teachers' attachment to their profession should not be overlooked.Working with colleagues, support staff, and parents in these ways takes time and good listening skills. People's experiences must be validated, but what works well in one situation may not work well in another. There needs to be a vehicle for productive exchange between all the people important to a student's education. With that, there must be give-and-take and an understanding that respectful disagreements can develop. That way, an inclusive community of learners can be created, and our profession can be respected and grown.

That brings me back to those Sunday luncheons at my grandparents' home. Over the years, I understood that my aunt and uncle's intense conversations about school issues came from a love for what they were doing and a genuine care for students' learning and welfare. We need to replicate my grandmother's lunches, where discussions, even disagreements, can be aired in an environment that recognizes each person's worth and commitment.

Additionally, we need to provide vehicles for teachers to not only have a voice but also to grow in their profession and for the school community to address concerns together productively. No school and no classroom will ever be perfect. As one educator years ago put it, "You're either getting better or getting worse. There's no standing still." Those plates won't stay spinning on their own, and the moment we become complacent, you know what happens.

A STORY OF OPPORTUNITY AND PASSION FOR TEACHING

Reginald O. York

My journey into teaching as my profession did not take the usual path. I grew up in the late 1940s, before rock-n-roll had entered the music scene, and throughout the 1950s, when rock-n-roll became king. I vaguely remember thinking that Dwight Eisenhower would be the better president because he had been a *General* in the Army and his opponent had only been a Governor.

My life started in a working-class environment where people got jobs as mechanics or plumbers or truck drivers. No one was a teacher, and no one went to college. I gave little thought to what I would do as an adult when I was growing up in this environment. My mother insisted that all her children graduate from high school, something that was not always true for my neighborhood friends, nor had it been true for either my mother or father.

My family was very religious, my father being a Baptist minister. He was not an educated minister. In fact, he never got beyond the ninth grade in school. But in my neighborhood, going to college was not required of this position.

Both of my parents had slightly greater aspirations than the typical person who lived on our street. My father decided to become a preacher, a job that had a higher prestige than that of a truck driver, which was another option for him, given his education. My mother finished only the ninth grade but was determined that all her children would graduate from high school.

My mother taught us to respect everyone, because we are all God's children. Thus, we would not use the n word when referring to black people, something that was very common in our neighborhood. Using the n word to refer to a black person was disrespectful.

As a child, I have a vivid memory of an incident in a small restaurant where blacks were not allowed to sit but could order take-out. A teenage black boy had ordered a take-out meal and was waiting for it to be delivered when he leaned against a stool at the counter, close enough to look like he was almost sitting on it. The manager came out of the back and yelled that he could not sit on that stool. I got really mad. It seemed cruel and extremely disrespectful. I had not yet learned to use the word racism, but I had learned about respect and about not being cruel to others.

That Reggie will never amount to anything!

These words were spoken by the vice-principal of West Mecklenburg High School (Charlotte, N. C.) to my mother when I was in the tenth grade. I had gotten into some light trouble, like bringing a switch-blade knife to school, which had followed a few times when I was in trouble because of guilt by association. At that time, I had plenty of friends who got into serious trouble, and I was sometimes spotted as being in the crowd or identified as being one of their friends.

Those words from the vice-principal were preceded by the statement "Now Ron and Claude were fine students at this school, but……" That's because I had two elder brothers who had gone to West Mecklenburg High School and had not gotten into any trouble. In fact, one of those brothers had won the award as being the best actor in the drama program offered by the school and another had been given the senior superlative of "best looking" as well as "biggest heart breaker." Now the school had to deal with me, the member of the family who seemed to be heading in a different direction.

That statement made my mother so mad I thought her head was going to explode. But it did not. It did not because my mother had embraced the social norms of the community and one of those rules was to respect authority and another was to be nice. My mother was one of the nicest people you could meet. But she never forgot this incident and much later really wanted to see this vice principal somewhere to tell her I had gotten a PhD degree. She really wanted that!

When I was in the tenth grade, I had a long way to go before getting into any kind of a respected profession like teaching or anything else that would require a college degree. The first step on that journey was my decision to follow my brother in taking a high school course in dramatics which led to my getting the Thespian Award in my senior year, as the best actor.

A key part of that experience was that it changed my social network of friends. Before this action, my best friends were not heading for college. In fact, at least one headed for prison. These new friends were more compatible with my tendency to be such a thinker about stuff and to be very curious about the world in which I lived.

I laughed when my brother announced that he was going to college

My elder brother, Ron, had a role to play in another part of my story. We lived in a neighborhood where no one went to college, and some did not graduate from high school. One day he announced that he was going to college. My response was to laugh. We were not the kind of people who went to college! Was he going to get *too big for his britches*?

This announcement influenced me, but that influence was not immediate. It took me a while to go from laughing at such a journey to going there myself. My experience with acting in school plays had changed my primary social network where I now had friends who were going to college. When I entered my senior year in high school I had decided to give college a try, but I had not taken college preparation courses, so I was not ready for a normal college.

As you can see, the first phase of my journey to becoming a teacher reflected the enormous advantage I had, not because of wealth, of which we had little, but because of the message from my parents to live a good life and aspire to be your best. The second major advantage I had was the opportunity to become educated, which you will see in the next section.

Community college was my first opportunity

Fortunately, my city had a community college where employed people took night classes. And it had a good English teacher who knew just how to teach a guy like me. She emphasized the fundamentals I had not gotten in high school. And I liked her. She was warm and experienced and expected that her students would get the fundamentals no matter how long it took. There were no excuses, and it was quite clear what you had to do to pass her courses. She was just what I needed at the time.

Next came a transfer to a four-year college. By then, I had matured a lot, especially regarding how to study. More importantly, I began to take courses in my major, the courses I enjoyed. My progression in grades in college got better with each step on the ladder, from community college to the courses in my undergraduate major, to the courses in graduate school. The more I liked the course, the more motivated I was to perform well. Increasingly, I was doing what I wanted, not just what the professor wanted me to do.

A few years later, Charlotte College became the University of North Carolina Charlotte and had acquired an impressive array of newly-minted PhD professors in my major, political science. I got to know several of them, including the chair of the department who had the skills I admired in a college professor - he cared about the growth of his students which was expressed by warmth and genuineness. He respected his students as demonstrated by his regard for their well-being, and by a tendency not to live by a social hierarchy where people were treated differently because of where they were on the hierarchy. The embrace of equality is a major indicator of respect in my opinion. He was my model for the good teacher.

I discovered social work as my career by accident

I did not know what to do with a political science degree. I took the necessary courses to become a teacher in the school system of North Carolina, but I was not the normal education major, my love was political science. In the summer after graduating from college, a friend indicated there was a job opening in the child welfare program of the Mecklenburg County Department of Social Services. It was a social work job. I did not know what social work was. I had never known a social worker. My college did not have a social work major nor any courses in this profession.

I went for a job interview and was impressed with the social worker who interviewed me. She seemed intelligent and competent and had good social skills, just like a good social worker should have. The person in this vacant social work position would have a caseload of older boys who had gotten in trouble with the law and had been placed in foster care. This job looked interesting to me. And most importantly, I got it!

My experiences as a social worker were profound in my development. I worked with boys who had grown up in an environment worse than mine, where crime was commonplace. I went into many black neighborhoods, places with which I was unfamiliar. In my school experience, I had no black classmates. My high school, when I graduated, had never had a black student. There were no black people living in my neighborhoods. So, I had never had a black friend.

I quickly learned basic principles about social work, both from my experiences and the excellent social work supervision I had received. I learned that progress with clients would not come without empathy and genuineness and positive regard. I learned how boys can get into trouble when this was common for their friends. I also learned how some parents had done much to be good parents and had faced a lot of obstacles to doing the right thing. These learnings were good for my skills as a social worker, but skills in teaching had to come later.

Graduate School is where I soared

I got a scholarship from the state of North Carolina to attend the Master of Social Work program at Tulane University, with the provision that I would work in the welfare system in this state for one year for every year I was in graduate school. Tulane University is in New Orleans, a city with an environment that I was not familiar with. It was a great experience. I learned to drink strong coffee, eat gumbo and shrimp remoulade, and walk in the French Quarter which was replete with history. I also learned a lot about social work, its history, methods, and how to evaluate practice.

I achieved good grades and engaged in fun projects such as taking a faculty member's dissertation a step further in a research study. I was really motivated, and this was a major key to my success. And this was a lesson I learned about teaching and learning - maybe we teachers should back up a bit on making sure students learn a specific piece of content and give students the freedom to do what is exciting to them. This observation, of course, has its limits, given the educational environment in which we work.

I was encouraged by the Assistant Dean of the School of Social Work at Tulane to enter the doctoral program. I was flattered. I had not considered myself to be PhD material. After all, I had grown up where many people did not even graduate from high school. So, this encounter became very important to my eventual development as a college professor.

My transition to my teaching career

After I received the MSW degree, I returned to my previous employer, a county social services agency, where I served as supervisor for child protective services, another leg in my professional development. Then I became a County Department of Social Services Director, a job I held only 2 years before I returned to school in the PhD Program at Tulane where my thirst for knowledge and the intellectual challenge were well satisfied.

My earliest experience with college teaching came in the PhD Program at Tulane University. One part of that experience was a teaching internship. It was brief, much too brief, but it gave me an appetite for the teaching role, a role that combines educational planning with the classroom teaching experience.

After receiving my PhD degree from Tulane University I took a job as director of a human service agency, but this job failed to provide the intellectual challenge that I craved. So, I took a job at UNC-Chapel Hill. Next, I was a professor at East Carolina University, followed by the University of North Carolina Wilmington, where I retired, but kept teaching because I really love it.

Why did I become a teacher?

I became a teacher because I had great opportunities in my life. I had subtle guidance from my parents that I could be something different from others in my neighborhood. I had the opportunity to go to college, which opened my world. I had the opportunity to get scholarships for graduate school to do something I did not have the ability to finance on my own. I had the opportunity to engage in some early teaching experiences that illustrated how much I loved this role. And I got a full-time teaching job at a university. I now teach part-time even though I have retired from my last job as a college teacher.

I have had many roles in my social work career, first as a caseworker, then a supervisor, then an agency administrator, then as a college teacher, then as an academic administrator, then, again, as a teacher, because I loved it the most. In fact, when I was an academic administrator, I only taught one course each week. After about 5 years in that role, I realized that the happiest day of the week was the one when I was teaching. So, I resigned my role as administrator and returned to teaching and have not stopped yet, even though I retired from full-time teaching five years ago. While each of the various roles mentioned above helped form who I am, they did not equal the joy I get from teaching.

I enjoy all aspects of teaching, from preparation of content, to developing exercises, to engaging students in class discussions, to giving feedback to students on written assignments…Wait! I made a mistake. I do not like every aspect of teaching - I do not like giving grades. I realize that grades are a matter of justice, not mercy, but it is not easy getting students to see this is the reason their grades were not as high as they wanted.

I have often told people that I love teaching because I love learning. I love the intellectual challenge of preparing for the course in a way that motivates every student. I love the classroom challenge of revising my explanation on the spot when my previous explanation seems not to be communicated to all students.

I believe in learning by doing. I get students involved in a learning activity early in the class experience and move from experience to discussion. For example, I might give them a tool for measuring their preference for the male sex-role stereotype in describing the good human service agency manager before they engage in the descriptive and explanatory study of this theme. I might pose discussion questions about the nature of the spirit of scientific inquiry before they are assigned to read a chapter in the course text on this theme. These preliminary activities tend to open their minds to better understanding of the content they are learning.

In my opinion, the best teachers are those who clarify expectations, demonstrate empathy, engage students in meaningful learning activities that include teacher feedback, and evaluate student achievement in a transparent manner that truly measures learning outcomes.

When my days in this life are done, I hope that students will remember my love of teaching, my desire for them to embrace learning as I have done. And I hope they continue to embrace the learning experience every day in their lives.

Are teachers going to become extinct?

We are now in a new technological revolution, one that is akin to the emergence of computers into everyday life several decades ago. But this one might be even bigger… a lot of people seem to think so. What should we expect and what should we do?

Information and the analysis of information will be at our fingertips like we have never seen before. A major difference is that this information will also be available to students in our classes. They can just ask AI what the answer to the question on the exam is and get an excellent response. They can get AI to write their course papers in a way that is not only adequate, but also goes beyond what we teachers might expect of our students. A few years ago, my first encounter with this phenomenon was the example of a student who seemed really weak on knowledge needed in the course based on class discussions. But this student presented excellent answers to the graded written assignments in this class. The clue to her cheating was that many parts of her answers, while excellent, used terminology that was not in the textbook that students were using, which helped me guess that the answers might have come from AI.

Cheating is a theme for many teachers I know. But a bigger challenge for me is how we can use AI to the advantage of students learning. My general recommendation is *Lean In*, a phrase I got from Sheryl Sandberg's book by this title. Her definition of this term is actively pursuing opportunities rather than waiting for them to be offered. Often when a revolutionary new technology comes on the scene, too many of us wait until someone tells us what to do about it. And some of us even just wish for it to go away. There was a time when you could make a living making buggy whips, but then that stinky, noisy, horseless carriage came on the scent and buggy whip makers had to find a new craft.

What do I mean by *lean in*? I mean energetically looking for the good in AI. Be ready to drop those lesson plans or charts or statistical analysis software in favor of letting AI do it. But we must make sure that it is what students really need. We must be the decision-makers; AI is not appropriate for that.

I am teaching a course on research methods for social work students at a university in the United States. There is a good deal of emphasis on the use of statistics to analyze data in that course. Previously, I created a set of Excel spreadsheet files for students to simplify the endeavor of analyzing their data from their studies evaluating their social work practice. But I learned that AI could do this job even more efficiently. You just state your hypothesis, enter the data and ask AI if the data supports the hypothesis. You will get a great answer. And this is just the beginning. I am constantly finding ways that AI can improve the learning process for students. So, I am teaching students to use AI appropriately. That is my solution!

THE TRIALS AND TRIBULATIONS OF A CAREER PEANUT BUTTER SANDWICH MAKER

Richard J. Guez

When I began my 31st year teaching, uprooted from my forever elementary existence into a massive middle school with bells, deans, and sports teams, I presumed the change was either going to be a professional recharge or truly the beginning of the end - I could simply retire and start living off my pension. My school district, as prominent and pretentious as they come from Long Island's Gold Coast, had decided two years prior to move the entire 6th grade, my boxed fiefdom for most of my teaching career, into the Junior Highs - making them stereotypical American middle schools. This move was seen by many as natural, others saw it as a change for change's sake, and still others saw it as a doorway into sheer chaos. Most significantly, for me at least, I saw it placing me in a new box entirely - a box with dimensions and weight for which I was unfamiliar and perhaps unprepared. Was it a move from "Handle with Care," "Fragile" and "This end is up" to "Lift with legs," "Heavy Load" and "Caution: Fire Hazard"? I was understandably anxious, somewhat ignorant about the move and a bit indignant.

At 17 - some time ago, I decided to become a therapist. That was a fine profession. I was confident that I had what it takes - strong, righteous opinions based on my life, superior analytical skills tested in a High School setting, and I had logged numerous hours watching Phil Donahue and Oprah Winfrey (American daytime talk show hosts from the 80s/90s). Much like my peers at the time, I thought I saw the world as it really was, and I could, should, and would enlighten it - high confidence with low competence.

Middling grades, immaturity, and a serious lack of focus were descriptors most used to describe me - but I didn't claim those titles or dispel them. I just didn't really care. I wasn't wholly apathetic - just a friendly, polite, and generally aloof American teen. Typical.

When I entered my first commuter college after graduating high school, I began working toward becoming a therapist. I liked the remedial math class I had to take and the psychology course. And as the semester holiday approached, I felt confident that I was going to perform quite well as a freshman (as a side note, I received the Highest GPA in my major, Psychology, that semester). I was still that overconfident kid, but I felt I was really making it happen. And then, as with all of life's stories, the bottom dropped out. My mother and first mentor, who had successfully battled with malignant melanoma since I was four, fell ill at Christmas and died two weeks later. I thought nothing would ever be the same. And it wasn't.

I changed colleges and made education my major, keeping psychology as my minor. I was working, as well as volunteering, at Arrowhead Elementary in their child care center. In my second job at a retail company, I received recognition for foiling crimes and for using my charm to get people to sign up for credit cards. In hindsight, I feel guilty about that - the cards had a high interest rate. Soon after, I started my student teaching at Setauket Elementary (K-6). I had even made a name for myself at my college - my professors liked my participation and saw me as an asset to their classes, and I was an excellent student.

Sitting at her desk, basked from behind from an open window by a bright sun, was Mrs. Carlin. She was the unapproachable, theatrically stoic, and yet endearing elder principal of Arrowhead Elementary School. I knocked at her giant, solid oak door, a door which in my four years working there, I had never even dared to approach. She was reading her oversized New York Times and, upon hearing the knock, peered over the paper with the tops of her hallmark spectacles. She called me forward with just one finger. With the newspaper now folded but still in hand, she asked me one question. As always, she was direct. This turned out to be the most she ever said to me in my tenure there. She asked me, "If they ask you what school you would like to teach at, what would you tell the hiring committee?" Perhaps because it was true, perhaps because my mother's spirit was on my shoulder whispering to me, or maybe it was just a miracle, I didn't fumble or run out of the room. I said with one calm, clear, and purposeful sentence, "I think of Arrowhead as my home, and I'd like to come home." A few weeks later, I was hired to teach 5th grade at Setauket Elementary School - same district.

The first lesson I taught as a teacher, and every first day of school thereafter, has been about peanut-butter and jelly - sort of. Students and their teachers tend to be a bit anxious that first day and an out-of-the-box lesson can make all the difference. I begin by asking a student to get a book from the class library. When they get to the class library they aren't sure which book. I clarify by giving some direction - but not enough. And so on till they eventually pick the 'correct book.' This leads to a natural conversation about concise and general directions. I then ask students to be as concise as they can - asking them to write directions for making a peanut butter and jelly sandwich for a space alien. I present to the class the main ingredients and supplies I have on hand and then remind them to be very deliberate in their instructions. As they write their directions I scan their work. I stop after a few minutes and then pull their entries… and try to follow their directions as written. Students always write "put the jelly on the bread," and "spread the jelly on the peanut-butter." And so I carry out their directions as written - word for word. As the jar of jelly destroys the bread still in its bag and the jelly jar bounces off the peanut-butter jar the students' laughter gets louder and louder - but remains sincere, constant and endearing. The messy part begins when they instruct me, the directions follower, to take the jelly out - this is why I wear plastic gloves and cover the table with a disposable table cover. Then we begin round two - they eagerly go back to their desks and revise - again and again. Reluctant writers, poets and lovers of peanut butter want to have their sandwich made (or want me to make a mess). Either way this lesson is affectionately remembered years, even decades later, by former students and has allowed me to garner a legendary status as an instructor and amateur comedian. Over the years I've added smashing near successful creations on the window. And paper towels - lots of paper towels.

My first principal and mentor as a teacher was Dr. Thomas De Bello. His insatiable interest in research-based education, learning, and bad jokes is ingrained in my professional life even today. He introduced me to progressive practitioners, researchers, and one - entirely by accident - cult. We did some of our own research, wrote a research paper that was later published, created learning style presentations, tools, and even fostered a teacher-driven parent presentation on Learning Styles. My experience with Tom at the time taught me that teaching requires continuous learning. Over time, I revised it to mean teaching is addressing each and every learner, and you must know your craft to do that well. My true take, long after Tom's retirement and me entering my own retirement conversations, is that if learning isn't pleasurable for the student and the teacher, it isn't really learning. It's just stored memories, mostly short-term. Learning is where seamless associations of the concrete and abstract mingle and where new and beautiful ideas, dreams, and wisdom merge.

Like all veteran teachers I have noticed the subtle, and sometimes not so subtle, changes in our young learners over time. Most notably, educators have identified significant student challenges with mental health, the formation of authentic social relationships and issues related to an unhealthy diet of video screens and social media. As one "starfish" in the sea I decided to create a workshop for teachers to generate tools and methods to address our uniquely modern challenges in this realm. The workshop filled immediately and was a dynamic professional experience for all attendees. When it was over, the cohort wanted to utilize the work completed. We decided to share the materials, information, and wisdom generated in a well-crafted teacher-led presentation for the fifth and sixth grade parents. The very well attended presentation included teacher presenters, videos, a question and answer session, a live digital survey, a student-read passage on self-esteem, and a helping of current research. Parents found the experience comfortable and even enjoyable as well as accessible and actionable. We had generated an educational nexus addressing parents' need for direct and applicable information and tools with teachers' professional obligation to convey concerns for their students and support the home-front. It also placed our teachers in a setting beyond the four walls of a classroom. The following year we presented to a larger audience and even more teachers and staff eagerly enhanced our educational community.

Thirty-one years into my profession, still learning and enjoying my experiences, I began my new path at a middle school. In preparation for that detour, I looked over my professional journey, from its origin to the present day, and noted that events, people, and happenstance have shaped and reshaped me as an educator - time and again. Some professional alterations over the years were intrinsically generated - advancing age, maturing perspectives, continuous and cumulative learning and realigning priorities. Other amendments, extrinsic in form, exposed an ever changing educational vista. Each year a new class, once unwrapped and revealed, presents its own vibrant personality, emotional needs, academic demands and social dynamics. These factors, each year, mingled with fluid curriculum, administrative turnovers, societal pressures and parental concerns/whims/perceptions. And, currently, the inception of AI as a savior, destroyer and guardian of everything and anything. My proficiency with AI, albeit as a neophyte, has led to faster revisions of labs, assignments, activities, selections, research, assessment generation and analysis. AI, as compared to all other extrinsic forces I have encountered, has most enhanced my limited time and energy allowing me to spend more of the school day teaching and fostering engaging, powerful and meaningful experiences, learning and relationships. It is an invigorating new part of my path and a noteworthy element of my evolution as an educator.

Although my transition to middle school is still a work in progress, I am, truth be told, loving it so far. In my educational journey, I've surmised that middle school is certainly a new box, but that boxes come in all shapes and sizes. They can carry a lot of weight - but we can determine what goes in the box and what comes out. And sometimes it's OK to shelve a box or two, look at new boxes, and even design and craft your own box. Lastly, and perhaps most significantly, stepping out of your box is usually a risk worth taking. I just need to remember to leave room in the box for the peanut butter.

REFERENCES

Allegretto, S. (2024, September 12). *Teacher pay rises in 2023 - but not enough to shrink pay gap with other college graduates.* Economic Policy Institute. Retrieved from https://www.epi.org/publication/teacher-pay-in-2023/

Almendarez-De Bello, B. (2019). *A place for me: An analysis of Latinas' journeys into educational administrative positions on Long Island* (Publication No. 13812522) Doctoral dissertation. St. John's University. ProQuest Dissertations and Theses Global.

Aloe, A., Barends, E., Besharov, D., Bhutta, Z., Cai, X., Gaarder, M., Garside, R., Haddaway, N., Kristjansson, E., Maynard, B., Mazerolle, L., Mildon, R., Miller, S., Minx, J., Neyroud, P., O'Connor, A., Rousseau, D., Saran, A., Starks, J., & White, H. (2020). Editorial: Fifty Campbell systematic reviews relevant to the policy response to COVID-19. *Campbell Systematic Reviews, 16*(3), e1107. DOI: 10.1002/cl2.1107 PMID: 34234882

Aron, L., & Loprest, P. (2012). Disability and the education system. *The Future of Children, 22*(1), 97–122. DOI: 10.1353/foc.2012.0007 PMID: 22550687

Barney, H. H. (1851). *Report on the American system of graded free schools.*

Barshay, J. (2023, December 18). *What the new PISA results really say about U.S. schools.* Future Ed. Retrieved from https://www.future-ed.org/what-the-new-pisa-results-really-say-about-u-s-schools/

Brackett, M. A., Rivers, S. E., & Salovey, P. (2011). Emotionally intelligent classroom management. *Educational Psychologist, 46*(4), 245–257.

Braga, D., Hurst, K., Greenwood, S., Zanetti, N., & Mandapat, J. C. (2024, April 4). *What public K-12 teachers want Americans to know about teaching?* Pew Research Center. Retrieved from https://www.pewresearch.org/social-trends/2024/04/04/what-public-k-12-teachers-want-americans-to-know-about-teaching/

Carson, C. (2004/2005). The fateful turn toward Brown v. Board of Education. *Washington History, 16*(2), 6–10.

Cockrell, D. (1996). Jim Crow, demon of disorder. *American Music, 14*(2), 161–184. DOI: 10.2307/3052351

Cohen, D. K. (1998). Dewey's problem. *The Elementary School Journal, 98*(5), 427–446. DOI: 10.1086/461907

Cole, J. R. (2011). The Great American University. *Bulletin - American Academy of Arts and Sciences. American Academy of Arts and Sciences, 64*(3), 27–35. https://www.jstor.org/stable/41149417

Dedham Museum & Archive. (2025). *Mann right to free public school.* Retrieved from https://www.dedhammuseum.org/lesson-plan/mann-right-to-free-public-school/

Dewey, J. (2015). *The collected works of John Dewey.* Pergamon Media (Kindle Edition.)

Gamson, D. A., McDermott, K. A., & Reed, D. S. (2015). The elementary and secondary education act at fifty: Aspirations, effects, and limitations. *RSF: The Russell Sage Foundation Journal of the Social Sciences, 1*(3), 32–50.

Glass, T. E. (2010, June 17). *Where are all the women superintendents?* American Association of School Administrators. Retrieved from https://www.aasa.org/resources/resource/where-are-all-the-women-superintendents/

Goldstein, D. (2014). *The teacher wars: A history of America's most embattled profession* [Kindle edition]. Knopf Doubleday Publishing Group.

Green, P. (2004). The paradox of the promised unfulfilled: Brown v. Board of Education and the continued pursuit of excellence in education. *The Journal of Negro Education, 73*(3), 268–284. DOI: 10.2307/4129611

Group, I. L. O. (2025, September). *The Superintendent Research Project: Update 2025* [PDF]. Retrieved from https://www.ilogroup.com/wp-content/uploads/2025/09/Superintendent-Research-Project-Update-2025.pdf

Gunderson, L. (2021). The consequences of English learner as a category in teaching, learning, and research. *Journal of Adolescent & Adult Literacy*, *64*(4), 431–439. DOI: 10.1002/jaal.1116

History of normal schools. (1860, August). *The Massachusetts Teacher*, 13(8), 284–295. https://www.jstor.org/stable/45025109

Hopkins, E. A. (2017). John Dewey and Progressive Education. *The Journal of Educational Thought (JET). Revue de La Pensée Éducative*, *50*(1), 59–68.

Huffman, G. E. (2013). Teacher perceptions regarding the relationship of modified year-round school calendars with student achievement, student behavior, and teacher efficacy. Doctoral dissertation. University of Southern Mississippi. Retrieved from https://aquila.usm.edu/dissertations/185

Labaree, D. F. (Ed.). (2008). *Handbook of research on teacher education* (3rd ed.). Routledge.

Lomawaima, K. T., & McCarty, T. L. (2025). *To remain an Indian: Lessons in democracy from a century of Native American education*. Teachers College Press.

Long, C. (2024, January 19). What can we really learn from the 2022 PISA test results? *NEA Today*. Retrieved from https://www.nea.org/nea-today/all-news-articles/pisa-2022

Meier, G. M. (2023). *An investigation of the secondary principals' role in developing and implementing successful inclusion programs*. Doctoral dissertation, St. John's University.

National Center for Education Statistics. (2018). *Table S1-N: Percentage of public schools operating on any type of 12-month cycle and percentage of schools with all students attending on the same year-round cycle, by selected school characteristics: 2007–08, 2011–12, 2017–18*. In the *National Teacher and Principal Survey, 2017–18*. U.S. Department of Education. https://nces.ed.gov/surveys/ntps/tables/ntps1718_20050401_s1n.asp

National Center for Education Statistics. (2025a). *Documentation for the NCES Common Core of Data School-Level Finance Survey (SLFS), School Year 2021–22 (Fiscal Year 2022)* (Provisional File Version 1a) (NCES 2025-047d). U.S. Department of Education. https://nces.ed.gov/use-work/resource-library/data/data-file/documentation-nces-common-core-data-school-level-finance-survey-slfs-school-year-2021-22-fiscal-year-0

National Center for Education Statistics. (2025b). *Fast facts. U.S. Department of Education*. Retrieved from https://nces.ed.gov/fastfacts/display.asp?id=64

National Education Association. (2025). *Educator pay data*. Retrieved from https://www.nea.org/resource-library/educator-pay-and-student-spending-how-does-your-state-rank

National Indian Education Association. (2026, January). *Data on Native students*. Retrieved from https://www.niea.org/native-student-data

Neem, J. N. (2017). *Democracy's schools: The rise of public education in America* (How things worked). Johns Hopkins University Press.

Ogren, C. A. (2005). *The American State Normal School: An instrument of great good*. Palgrave Macmillan. DOI: 10.1057/9781403979100

Ohio School Commissioner. (1856). *Second annual report of the School Commissioner, for the year 1855*. State Printer.

Paterson, W. A. (2021, December 8). *From 1871 to 2021: A short history of education in the United States*. SUNY Buffalo State. Retrieved from https://suny.buffalostate.edu/news/1871-2021-short-history-education-united-states

Proximity One. (2025, December 19). *Proximity One*. Retrieved from https://proximityone.com/sdstate.htm#:~:text=In%20the%20District%20of%20Columbia,%2C%20municipal%2C%20or%20state%20government

Robinson, G. (Host) & Green, J. (2023, February 22). *K-12 global education Interview with Andreas* Schleicher [Podcast episode]. Pioneer Institute Podcast. Retrieved from https://pioneerinstitute.org/podcast-episode/oecds-andreas-schleicher-on-pisa-k-12-global-education/

Rudolph, F. (2021). *The American college and university: A history*. University of Georgia Press.

Secaur, M. (2022, March 16). *District position paper: Social and emotional learning*. Smithtown Central School District. Retrieved from https://www.smithtown.k12.ny.us/Files/Community/Important-Issues-in-Education/SCSD_Position_Paper__SEL_3-16_-_Google_Docs.pdf

Soldner, M. (2025). *Learn about the new condition of education 2025*. Part 1. National Center for Education Statistics.

Thomas, S. (2010). *Marriage vows and economic discrimination: The married teacher problem* (master's thesis). Marshall University. Retrieved from https://mds.marshall.edu/cgi/viewcontent.cgi?referer=&httpsredir=1&article=1286&context=etd

US Bureau of Labor Statistics. (October, 2025). *Kindergarten and elementary school teachers*. Occupational Outlook Handbook. Retrieved from https://www.bls.gov/ooh/education-training-and-library/kindergarten-and-elementary-school-teachers.htm

US Census Bureau. (2020). *2020 census - School district reference map*. Retrieved from ttps://www.census.gov/geographies/reference-maps/2020/geo/2020pl-maps/2020-schdist-map.html#:~:text=These%20county%20(or%20county%20equivalent,are%20labeled%20as%20scale%20permits. US Department of Education. (2015). *Fact sheet: English learner students*. Retrieved from https://www.ed.gov/sites/ed/files/about/offices/list/ocr/docs/dcl-factsheet-el-students-201501.pdf

U.S. Department of Health, Education, and Welfare. (1974). *The Indian Education Act of 1972 (DHEW Publication No. OE 74-02400)*. U.S. Government Printing Office. Retrieved from https://files.eric.ed.gov/fulltext/ED103175.pdf

Warikoo, N., Sinclair, S., Fei, J., & Jacoby-Senghor, D. (2016). Examining racial bias in education: A new approach. *Educational Researcher*, *45*(9), 508–514. DOI: 10.3102/0013189X16683408

Whitney, W. F. (Ed.). (1860). History of normal schools. *The Massachusetts Teacher, 13*(8), 284–295.

Williams, J. (2004). The 1964 Civil Rights Act: Then and now. *Human Rights (Chicago, Ill.)*, *31*(3), 6–8, 15.

Chapter 3
Teachers' Voices From Canada

Arooj Farooqi
http://orcid.org/0009-0001-5989-2766
Dalhousie University, Canada

Jonathan Shaw
The Studio for Teaching and Learning, Saint Mary's University, Canada

Eric Bird
http://orcid.org/0009-0004-1239-3742
Greater Victoria School District # 61, Canada

ABSTRACT

This chapter provides an overview of the Canadian education system, including both K–12 and post-secondary education. It outlines the structure and functioning of educational systems across Canada's provinces and territories, as well as the federal government's responsibilities. The chapter examines licensing requirements within Canadian education and the stringency of professional certification processes. In addition, it explores the future of teaching, particularly in relation to the growing influence of artificial intelligence. The chapter further highlights Canada's standing as one of the world's most educated nations, with an internationally respected education system. The discussion concludes with reflective accounts from Canadian teachers.

THE CANADIAN EDUCATION SYSTEM: A SHORT OVERVIEW FROM INSIDE

Arooj Farooqi

Introduction

To see the deeper lens on the Canadian education system, it is impossible not to consider its massive landmass, or to avoid examining its origins. It is likely that this beautiful country's name, 'Canada', comes from the Huron-Iroquois word 'kanata,' meaning 'village' or 'settlement.' Furthermore, the first official use of the name Canada dates back *to 1791* (Government of Canada, 2020).

As the name suggests, this is a land of settlement, a concept that is reflected in Canada's vast geography and its division into provinces and territories, which makes Canada unique. Being the world's second-largest country by territory, it has a massive land. Canada consists of ten provinces and three territories, totalling 13 self-governing regions, with provinces having more autonomy and territories being federally administered, each with unique capitals and characteristics.

Thus, "many teachers' education programs in Canada have incorporated curriculum content related to various aspects of cultural awareness and equity, such as multicultural, culturally responsive, intercultural, anti-racist, and global citizenship education" (Levent & Sağlam, 2024, p. 275).

DOI: 10.4018/979-8-3373-8983-7.ch003

The Council of Ministers of Education, Canada (CMEC, n.d.) represents the education interests of Canada's provinces and territories through intergovernmental cooperation. While all provinces and territories conduct education-related internal activities independently, CMEC provides them with the means to speak, act, and intervene collectively on the world stage. As the federal government controls the country's primary functions, it allocates federal funds; each province and territory then allocates funds according to its needs, immigration, and plans through its own internal Education Ministry. There is no federal education ministry in Canada; however, the Canadian education system allocates significant funds to immigration-linked programs and research beyond the mainstream education.

Despite each province and territory having an individual education system, Canadian education ranks among the highest in the world. However, the other side of the coin is that it is this vast geographical location, various provinces and territories' huge immigration influx and various communities that Canada's education system is not as simple as it may seem. The various studies and analyses of several authors will help to understand the systemic challenges in Canadian education, especially regarding equity and education outcomes.

Racialised Students (Cultural Barriers)

According to a study published by the University of Ottawa (2023), it underscores that higher education institutions must recognise and address the specific needs of their racialised student communities and create inclusive learning environments that better meet these needs. It was further added that failing to do so could affect the overall psychological well-being and academic performance of racialised students. These students are a bigger portion of immigrant communities, and hence it is a great challenge for the educators and policy makers to bring everyone to the same platform when it comes to performance due to the cultural and religious differences, personal challenges, apart from simply language disabilities

Lack of Planning (Policymakers)

It is equally important to discuss a study published by Alyass and Buist (2025). The paper examined McCrimmon's work, which was published in 2015, and the issues raised by him are influenced by government policy. Worth noting is that it unpacks several issues and challenges that teachers face. These challenges stem from the lack of planning for diverse learners in the education system, as well as the mention of reduced funding, larger class sizes, and demands by administration and/or parents to meet or exceed curricular demands, which communicate two vital points. Firstly, it is a reality that these challenges are a result of policy and its role in allocating funding and influencing class sizes. Secondly, it also highlights that "teachers must adapt their educational practices to meet the needs of an increasingly diverse student population, particularly students with exceptional learning needs" (McCrimmon, 2015, p. 234). The adaptations that teachers are being asked to make are policy-guided, and any constraints that the government creates, such as 'reduction of funding' and ' long working hours', are as well.

Disabled Students (Case from Ontario)

Another major issue regarding policy and its role is in addressing the persistent lack of planning for students with disabilities. Let us have a look at an example from Ontario's K-12 education system. In this policy, statements are in place to guide inclusive education practices. However, Campbell (2020) writes that educators are not provided with guidance on implementing these policy guidelines and enacting them in their teaching practices within Ontario's K-12 Education System. As a result of this lack of knowledge as it pertains to enacting policy in teaching practices, which concludes that there is a lack of planning for students with disabilities and racialised students to be included in Ontario K-12 classrooms.

The Canadian public school system, commonly referred to as K–12 education, is structured as follows:

Canadian Public School System (K-12)

Since Canada has a decentralised education system, each province's ministry has established school boards that oversee education from kindergarten to grade 12. Each province's and territory's schools from grades 1 to 8 are called elementary, and grades 9-12 are called high schools. However, some school boards consider grade 9 to be part of elementary. All government-funded schools in Canada are called public schools, and no fees are charged (FutureLearn, 2021).

This education is mandatory and free for all school-age children. This means 13 public school systems across the country provide free education to Canadians from kindergarten to grade 12.

The Council of Ministers of Education (CMEC) established standards, national frameworks and assessments to create common goals and measures for students across Canada, alongside provincial curricula. In this reading, math and science are closely monitored through the Pan-Canadian Assessment Program (PCAP) across all provinces and territories. This helps compare outcomes and improve curricula at provincial or territorial levels to maintain learning standards for every Canadian student, regardless of the different programs in public schools.

PCAP promotes shared educational objectives, such as scientific literacy and global competencies, while allowing provinces flexibility in implementation (CMEC, 2026).

Each province has language support programs for newcomers, known as English as a Second Language (ESL) programs, that help newcomers understand the challenges they face in Canada and help them adjust to the school system. Similarly, to pass high school, all students must take a literacy exam, which varies by province and territory. For instance, Ontario's Grade 10 literacy test (OSSLT) is unique in its structure (EQAO, n.d.), British Columbia also has a mandatory Grade 10 literacy assessment (GLA) as a graduation requirement (Curriculum BC), making them similar in purpose (British Columbia Ministry of Education, 2025), though specific tests differ; other provinces like Alberta and New Brunswick have provincial assessments, but not always at the Grade 10 level or with the same focus as Ontario's OSSLT (New Brunswick Education).

Also, Canada is a bilingual country with English and French as official languages; a few provinces have school systems that primarily use French, such as Quebec. At the same time, New Brunswick is an officially bilingual province. Quebec, the province-wide standardised tests overseen by the Ministry of Education are called the "épreuves uniques". These are exit exams in a variety of courses administered in grade 10 (Secondary IV) and grade 11 (Secondary V), the last two years of high school. Additionally, all grade 6 students are required to write exams in English or French Language Arts and Mathematics. Quebec's province-wide assessment is long-standing and stable. In the list of "unique exams," the Ministry occasionally changes the cohort of courses to be examined (Cowley & MacPherson, 2022).

Additionally, all the provinces have French Immersion boards, too, and regardless of the school board, all students are required to study French from grades 4 to 8 and must earn at least one French credit to graduate from secondary school.

The blend of this student-oriented curriculum is providing top performances of Canadian K-12 students around the world. Canada, being the largest country in terms of geographic area, and a country that welcomes immigrants and refugees, still ranks among the top performers globally in Mathematics, according to the OECD report (Council of Ministers of Education, Canada, 2023).

Consequently, Canada has taken significant steps to modernise teacher education and curriculum to meet evolving societal needs. Educational reforms emphasise 21st-century skills, multiculturalism, equity, and inclusion. It is important to note that technology in Canada is not a new or sudden development, and this is evident from research by Knapper and Wills in 1980, published by UNESCO, which shows Canada's advancement in digital literacy, The Canadian academic environment is in many ways uniquely affected, as it is by the size of the country, its population, federal system, etc. This situation, to a certain extent, had stimulated interest in educational technology and the directions of its application.

Among Canadian educational authorities and teachers, as Bennett (2016) states, there is a growing realisation that 'digital literacies' are becoming essential in preparing students for full participation in the emerging post-industrial 'knowledge society' of the 21st century.

Thus, seeing provinces have introduced policies that promote technology integration, global citizenship, competency-based learning, and flexible classrooms is not an abrupt change. Such frameworks prioritise personalised learning, creative thinking, and collaboration, reduce rigid learning outcomes, and empower teachers while leaving students to make meaningful educational choices.

Now, this digital learning is on the rise in Canada and is exerting an impact upon education policy in most of the nation's ten provinces and three territories. Without a national education department, the promotion of 21st-century skills, technology and learning falls to provincial and territorial education authorities with varying degrees of commitment to K-12 technology education reform and classroom integration. National advocacy groups such as 21C Canada do hold sway over provincial ministers of education, but, so far, the implementation of 21st-century learning and the explicit teaching of 'digital literacies' is very uneven, particularly outside of the recognised eLearning leaders among the provinces Ontario, British Columbia and Alberta (Bennett, 2016).

For some, computer technology can be used as a powerful and flexible tool for learning. Indeed, there is sufficient optimism in the potential of technology to have a positive impact on learning that governments have established task forces and dedicated substantial research funds to identifying and promoting ways to deliver or enhance instruction with the use of technology. At the same time, there is sufficient scepticism about the use of technology to improve learning and beliefs that it may even represent serious threats to education, as noted in research by Sclater et al. (2006).

The truth is, the digital divide is exacerbated by rapid technological adoption. According to the University of Waterloo, Cybersecurity and Privacy Institute (n.d.), the technology streams are very specialised studies in education that require explicit training for teachers to become subject experts for their students and in their own professional practice. Staple core subjects such as math and the arts were practised long before the digital age. With the rising and rapidly changing digital age and economy, and the lack of knowledge in understanding these principles in great depth, the need for cybersecurity education is unparalleled. Teachers lack knowledge and expertise regarding cyberspace. Schools and government ministries may lack resources and facilities to implement cybersecurity education. The speed of technological change results in new risks, requiring new solutions. Teachers may face problems in developing their knowledge of the latest technology and thus ensuring students are safe. A solution to the gaps in cybersecurity education lies in reshaping and rethinking education practices and methodology to normalise digital literacy within the existing K-12 curriculum through cross-curricular learning and providing adequate training to educators.

This requires maintaining consistent and high-quality information on education from all provinces and territories to support informed decision-making, policy development, and program creation of the education system and keep it abreast with the International Standard Classification of Education (ISCED), the Pan-Canadian Education Indicators Program (or PCEIP, which presents a statistical portrait of the Canadian education system (UNESCO, n.d.). ISCED provides a globally agreed framework for categorising education programmes and qualifications, enabling cross-national comparison of education systems. Though PCEIP does not directly apply ISCED, it presents data in various formats, including tables, fact sheets, and reports. This keeps improving Canadian K-12 education as the world's top class. Education policymakers and governments rigorously monitor the education system to ensure that the standards of curriculum delivery and teaching quality are not compromised (Statistics Canada, 2025).

To what extent is it meaningful to compare Canada with other countries as if they are necessarily performing better? It is important not to frame Canada in comparison with other countries in simplistic terms. A common global narrative often highlights the so-called 'top-performing' education systems that have emerged on the world stage. Although international comparisons frequently place countries such as Canada, Finland, and Singapore side by side, research suggests that such comparisons can be misleading.

The OECD cautions that differences in students' educational experiences may make comparisons across countries 'unfair' (OECD, 2019). Furthermore, studies highlight that socio-economic, cultural, and structural factors significantly influence educational outcomes, meaning that results must be interpreted within context. As a result, directly comparing Canada's K–12 system with those of Finland or Singapore oversimplifies complex educational realities.

Teaching Profession

While the federal government plays a role in education investments and policies, the responsibility for teacher education programs in Canada lies with the individual provinces and territories (Levent & Sağlam, 2024). So, gaining a general understanding of Canada's teacher preparation system is essential for comprehending how the Canadian education system operates.

To become a teacher, it is mandatory to have a teaching license, three years of post-secondary education (a Bachelor of Education 3-4-year program), and four or more semesters of a teaching education program. A criminal record check/background check and other suitability requirements, such as an English language test, are required to teach in public schools in Canada. However, the K-12 education system is decentralised, and each province has its own regulatory body to monitor teaching licensing requirements.

For example, "to teach in Ontario's publicly funded schools, you must be certified by the Ontario College of Teachers and pay an annual membership fee to keep your membership in good standing" (Ontario College of Teachers).

The perks for these school teachers' salaries in Canada vary by experience, location, and role, but teachers can expect to earn roughly $55,000 to $100,000 annually over their careers (Remitly, 2025).

Internationally Educated Teachers, commonly referred to as IETs, are also accepted in Canada, but they must comply with the standards of Canadian education and the certification system.

However, Internationally Educated Teachers (IETs) often face challenges in Canada related to educational standardisation and the licensing process. This issue is further examined in a recent study by Marom and Xu (2025):

- IETs encounter systemic obstacles in hiring and employment.
- IET's international experience is seen as a deficiency in schools.
- IETs must work harder to establish professional legitimacy.
- Assumptions about IETs' professionalism intersect with race and accent.
- IETs enhance culturally responsive teaching and bring international perspectives.

This research further states that in a study, CMEC identified several key barriers to IETs' school integration. These include language competence, unfamiliarity with classroom technology, lack of confidence, lack of local classroom management experience, and difficulty working with parents. This study on 13 IETs and five school leaders supports some of the CMEC findings, but, also underscores the importance of professional networks and resilience in facilitating integration.

Post-secondary Education

Similar to the K-12 education system, the post-secondary education system is also not centralised. The provinces and territories, rather than the federal government, control their own institutions, and unlike in other countries, the education system in each province has no strict "national hierarchy"; instead, there are clear categories (CMEC, n.d.).

As the Canadian provincial and territorial governments are primarily responsible for higher education, they hold exclusive legislative power over education policy, funding, and quality assurance. In contrast, the federal government plays a supporting role, mainly through funding programs and specific areas such as military colleges and indigenous education, as outlined in the Canadian Constitution Act, 1867 (Government of Canada, 2026).

Indigenous Education in Canada: Federal, Provincial, and Community Roles

In Canada, education in Indigenous communities follows a slightly different structure compared to mainstream public education. While education is generally a provincial or territorial responsibility, the federal government plays an important role in supporting First Nations education on reserves *(First Nations communities living on designated lands)* through funding and policy oversight. On the other hand, provinces and territories are responsible for Indigenous students living off-reserve *(outside these designated communities)*, as well as Métis *(people of mixed Indigenous and European ancestry)* and Inuit *(Indigenous peoples primarily from northern regions of Canada)* learners. In recent years, there has been a stronger focus on self-governance and culturally relevant education. Many Indigenous communities are gradually taking control of their own education systems, ensuring that teaching practices reflect their languages, traditions, and Ways of Knowing *(Indigenous knowledge systems and perspectives)*. Indigenous-led research and national reports also emphasise the need to address historical inequalities caused by past policies, particularly the long-term impact of 'the residential school system' *(a former government-supported schooling system for Indigenous children)*. Across different regions of Canada, especially in northern and remote areas *(geographically distant communities with limited access to services)*, efforts are being made to improve access to education, provide better teacher training, and develop community-based schooling models.

Overall, these initiatives show that Canada is moving towards a more inclusive and responsive education system, where Indigenous voices and leadership play a central role, particularly through ongoing commitments to culturally relevant education and community-based approaches (Truth and Reconciliation Commission of Canada, 2015; Assembly of First Nations, 2010; Council of Ministers of Education, Canada, 2019)

A Brief Look at the Hierarchy and Structure of Tertiary and University Education in Canada for Teaching Purposes

In Canada, the federal government supports post-secondary education primarily through funding transfers, student financial assistance, and research funding (Government of Canada, 2025b). National research councils such as SSHRC, NSERC, and CIHR provide substantial support for research and training at universities and colleges across the country (Government of Canada, 2025). SSHRC, in particular, funds research, scholarships, and institutional initiatives that strengthen post-secondary education (Social Sciences and Humanities Research Council of Canada, 2025). These agencies, together, function as part of the federal Tri-Agency system, supporting researchers and students nationwide (Government of Canada, 2025b). However, despite this federal involvement, post-secondary education remains under provincial and territorial jurisdiction, ensuring provincial independence in governance and administration (Library of Parliament).

Individual Provincial/Territorial Policies

Post-secondary teaching requirements in Canada are not federally regulated, but are set by each institution and province/territory. For instance, in the Humber College Faculty Credential Policy (Ontario, Canada). This official policy from a Canadian post-secondary institution shows how teaching qualifications are defined for faculty:

- Teaching staff must hold recognised academic or professional credentials.

For breadth (general) courses, instructors usually need an advanced degree (e.g., master's or terminal degree). At least 50% of faculty in degree programs must hold a terminal academic credential in the relevant field. (Humber College)

Important to note is that "In Canada, as a regulated profession, teacher professionalism is codified through certification policies and professional standards. However, standards and competencies may vary or have different interpretations across jurisdictions. Certification policies are susceptible to job market needs, changes in priorities, and migration waves. International players, such as the Organization for Economic Co-operation and Development (OECD), also play a growing role in shaping global benchmarks for teacher professionalism" (Marom & Xu, 2025).

So, those looking to come to Canada as teachers must meet the federal requirement under the National Occupational Classification (NOC) for the Faculty/University Professors & Post-Secondary Instructors (Statistics Canada, 2024).

- A doctoral degree is generally required for university professors.
- A master's degree may be required for college instructors or specific academic fields, depending on the institution and position.

In addition to this official Canadian government classification, typical educational requirements for faculty and post-secondary instructors may include provincial requirements as well.

Seeing this broader spectrum of education, it is inevitable to assume that the teaching profession could be extinct. With the advent of AI, the Canadian government is expanding and investing more in research, paving the way and improving teaching requirements for the 21st century. The research and advocacy support efforts to mitigate the effects of AI, thereby strengthening and advancing teaching in Canada.

LINC and Adult Settlement Education

Settlement services are a distinctive feature of Canada's immigration model, and the Government of Canada heavily funds the Language Instruction for Newcomers to Canada (LINC) programme, a bridge system and an essential part of immigration and adult education. It is a support programme for newcomers with language disabilities to help them assimilate well into Canadian culture and lifestyle. The Government of Canada (2025a) states that permanent residents and protected persons can take no-cost language classes to improve their English or French skills.

Apart from the multiple benefits of taking these language classes, the foremost important is instruction from qualified, experienced teachers, to teach in a Canadian LINC program, teachers need a university degree(ideally in Teaching English as a Second Language – TESL - or Lingusitics), a TESL Canada accredited TESL certification, experience with adult ESL learners, cultural awareness, knowledge of settlement program, strong technology skills, and proficiency in the Canadian Language Benchmarks (CLBs) and Portfolio-Based Language Assessment (PBLA), and a teaching license and the teacher must maintain good standing. However, it varies from province to province and territory to territory.

In this, the teacher qualifications, accountability, and curriculum are the responsibility of the federal government, which partially oversees the provinces that provide these services.

Conclusion

In short, the Canadian education system reflects a complex balance of decentralisation, diversity, and high global performance. While it faces ongoing challenges related to equity, policy implementation, and inclusion, it continues to evolve through reforms focused on digital literacy, multiculturalism, and student-centred learning.

Despite rapid technological advancements, teaching in Canada is not becoming obsolete but is instead adapting to new demands. Teachers remain essential in shaping critical thinking, supporting diverse learners, and creating meaningful educational experiences that extend beyond what technology alone can provide.

TEACHING: MY FOREVER LOVE!

Arooj Farooqi

"Choose a job you love, and you will never have to work a day in your life" (Confucius)

A calling or a carefully chosen path?

Standing here today as a seasoned educator and English specialist, it feels like the blink of an eye. It all started when I was in high school - highly motivated, ambitious, and ready to conquer the world.

Like many other teenagers, I was overwhelmed by the numerous possibilities before me. I was drawn to fashion design, with a particular fondness for Victorian styles, which I found enchanting. At the same time, I cherished reading literature and engaging in thoughtful discussions about ideas, a habit influenced by my grandmother, a professor who greatly impacted me. Despite these interests, I was uncertain about my future career path. During this time, my mother gently suggested, "How about you become a teacher... an English teacher? Since you already enjoy English literature and love history, why do you want to limit it to fashion?" This suggestion struck me as the direction that felt most right and resonated with me. I began to view teaching not just as a job but as a calling that perfectly intertwined my passion for literature, history, and meaningful interactions with others. This decision brought clarity and peace, setting me on a path that, after 24 years - through life's ups and downs - I am grateful to have chosen. Facing challenges and exploring various positions in my career, the idea of leaving it has never crossed my mind.

The Weight and the Worth of the Work

All these years, I have had the immense pleasure of teaching around the world, making substantial impacts in various communities. Having my schooling at one of the most prestigious schools in Pakistan and a combined MA in Applied Linguistics & English Literature was the beginning of this endless journey.

Originally from Pakistan, but having lived most of my life abroad, I had the privilege of teaching in different educational systems and seeing multiple classroom realities. From Pakistan to Dubai, other parts of the Middle East, the UK, and

Canada - everywhere I have been teaching, I have never had problems - surprised?! Yes, this is what I have learned after extensive experience - as my dad always says, problems are experiences, learn from them and keep enjoying your journey.

Each country has its own culture, work ethic, and educational rules. Student behaviour, policies, staff, curriculum, and teaching methods all differ. My ability to adapt and stay up to date with educational trends has been essential to my success. I further pursued my professional growth in the UK, completing additional teaching specialisations at the University of Cambridge and the London Teacher's College, in addition to my MA in English *(major with Linguistics & Literature).* These experiences have helped me develop strategies for thriving in diverse settings. Not only this but also flexibility and open-mindedness enabled me to embrace new methods and understand cultural differences, resulting in a more results-oriented approach to teaching and an inclusive classroom environment where students from diverse backgrounds felt engaged. Active listening fostered collaboration with students and colleagues, leading to more effective problem-solving and a harmonious teaching environment. Patience and flexibility allowed me to adapt practices to each environment, improving student outcomes and satisfaction. Recognising that one approach may not suit every community helped me manage the challenges of change, ensuring that I maintained high teaching standards across various educational settings. Teaching is never easy; it is a continual challenge.

My journey of learning and growth continued when I completed another specialisation in adult education with teaching English as a Foreign Language (EFL) in Pakistan. Because of my good results, I was offered a teaching job at the same university. However, I had other commitments, so I stayed for only a year to finish my studies. Then I returned to Dubai and joined the Ministry of Education as a lead teacher and English teacher trainer. This also meant saying goodbye to my long career teaching International General Certificate of Secondary Education (IGCSE) and *A* levels, a British curriculum I have always loved.

I am often surprised when people claim teaching is the easiest profession. Teaching is, in fact, the foundation for all other professions. I am motivated both internally and externally, and my strong professional commitment keeps me focused on my goals, undeterred by minor setbacks.

Moments that Shaped my Work

With this, how can I miss the struggling learners, language disabilities, challenges, and behavioural issues? As a high school teacher, I have always encountered such problems. Not because high schools inherently have issues, but because it is the age; the behaviour, impulsivity, and emotional responses are natural parts of this stage of life. As a teacher, it is vital to understand that these growing adults require different strategies. Family socioeconomic status also plays a crucial role, but we must recognise each student's potential without bias.

One effective method I always use in my class is clear instructions and student engagement. I design flexible lesson plans that allow bursts of creativity while maintaining the teaching environment and learners' autonomy. These plans often start with a clear lesson outline that specifies activities and goals. However, I leave room within the structure for students to explore their creativity, fostering engagement and self-discovery, while maintaining students' autonomy.

I also create Individualised Educational Plans (IEPs) that cater to students' unique needs, ensuring they can build confidence without feeling left out. By maintaining students' profiles, I can better understand their challenges and adapt my teaching methods accordingly. The strategy for controlling impulsivity and offering tailored support significantly contributes to effective classroom management.

Once in Dubai, I remember tackling a fierce situation with calmness, when a group of young high schoolers got into a fight - they were hitting and kicking and picked up water bottles, to throw water on each other - I jumped in to stop them as others were afraid to. Clearly, it was not my place to be scared. As soon as I jumped, they threw water on each other, chilled icy - and instead of each other and in a few seconds I was all drenched in wet. From my high pony and bangs, to my stiletto pencil heel sandals. All in water - and then there was this big silence in the class. At the same time, one of the boys called the administrator who looks after these boys and disciplines them.

I am always very keen on handling matters myself rather than running to ask for help over minor issues. Class administration and organisation are my keen areas. I immediately realised that this was an accident. I covered for the boys and told the administration that nothing like that had happened; it was just a spill.

And it changes all - the boys who were boisterous, non-serious, and not completing their work are now my best students - working hard and being punctual. So a lesson learnt, what kindness can do, harsh punishments definitely cannot.

We all must step out of our traditional roles as teachers, feel the presence of these individuals, own them, and think that this is what we are giving the world. Time is changing, and we, as teachers, must keep learning and understanding these changes each day. We are forming students; we are creating the future of this world. Students need to be informed, loved, trusted, and cared for. Teachers are role models. I always heard this as I was growing up, but why? In these complex situations, I realised and felt proud of myself. This personal commitment goes hand in hand with a broader mission: to advocate for systemic changes that support and empower educators to prepare our students for the future. As I discuss, our educational policies should evolve to require continuous learning and licensure renewal. This will ensure teachers stay equipped for the rapidly changing academic landscape, especially with technological advancements. Through these efforts, we can collectively work towards a future in which education adapts to serve our students and society better.

Trust me, this was not easy. However, I love challenges, and I have always wanted to learn and teach.

Similarly, on another occasion, when one of my students in an adult teaching classroom in my LINC (Language Instruction for Newcomers to Canada) class came from a war-torn country, she was an early childhood educator in her home country and worked with the Ministry of Education. But sadly, when she went to a new country to save herself and her family, she ended up working as a cleaner and refused to accept government funds. I cannot forget the day she stood, with a small bag of gifts, tears filled her eyes, and she hugged me so tight, saying - I thought I was dead in the war, I was only living, but you gave me life again. I helped her learn English, complete her designated level, and reach her goal of starting her career again as an early childhood educator.

These examples are from my teaching class and are essential for me to keep practising empathy in my teaching. Teaching is a holistic job; it is not merely teaching and checking students' work, but also building broken confidence and supporting its building, building together!!

Reflections Earned Over Time

> "Those people who develop the ability to continuously acquire new and better forms of knowledge that they can apply to their work and to their lives will be the movers and shakers in our society for the indefinite future." - Brian Tracy (n.d.), Motivational Speaker.

My personal experience has further channelled my ideology, and I completed another specialised Master of Education in Educational Leadership and Policy from Canada. This supports my idea of bringing in changes and renovations to train teachers. I am a big supporter of the idea that teachers are the 'guardians of our future', says UN deputy chief Amina J. Mohammed (UN News, 2025). Soon after, I completed another specialisation in adult education in Teaching English as a Foreign Language (TEEFL) and attained the most prestigious Adult English teaching license in Canada. This is to support and adapt myself in the education industry, like a river flows, no stopping!

Having had such encounters and professional commitments, I train teachers through multiple webinars and conference presentations, sharing insights and supporting them in addressing classroom matters, and also teach about AI and its importance. I am a big fan of technology, but not at the cost of the environment I share with teachers. For instance, I integrated a learning management system that personalises learning experiences for my students. This system provides a great online community and a blended learning experience, supporting them in using technology for English learning. This approach not only enhances student engagement but also helps me to streamline my teaching methods. Specifically, it reduces printing hassle and allows me to focus more on direct student interaction and tailored educational development. Achieving a high-level certification in an elite instructional design course and acquiring certification from Ontario is another feather in my cap. And now, I am eagerly awaiting the start of my doctoral studies!

Reimagining Teaching in a Changing World

"AI won't replace humans - but humans with AI will replace humans without AI-" Karim Lakhani (2023) is a professor at Harvard Business School.

Honestly, with so much happening so fast, I am deeply interested in seeing teachers' evolution and professional training that intrinsically motivates them. Having acquired a bachelor's degree in teaching and then entered the profession will not suffice; we, the teachers, must keep the ball rolling.

The technological invasion, especially AI, has transformed traditional teaching styles into more advanced models, yet teachers still prefer traditional models. Modern teaching is not simply about using computers, but about preparing students to become digital citizens; this requires greater investment and more rigorous preparation for teachers.

There should be strict regulations requiring teachers to renew their teaching licenses every 2 years, similar to a driver's license, to keep up with changes, especially in learning technology, its use, and its implications. Along with cultural integration, bridging courses are a component of teacher licensing that policymakers must not overlook to mitigate the growing risk of AI. Teachers must actively invest in their learning!

From Charlatan to Midwife: A Reflection on Teacher Identity

Jonathan Shaw

Seeking respite from the meat-eating sun of Southern Taiwan (and knowing that I might be sick at any moment), I stand on the third-floor outdoor hallway of the high school. My stomach churns, and my hands tremble so violently I can hardly sip my water. I check my watch.

Nine minutes. I have nine minutes to become an English language teacher. How did I get here? I already regret letting myself be talked into this. I've been in the country for three days, still swirling from seven connecting flights booked by my friend, who bought the cheapest possible ticket. He knew my promises to "think about" coming here were empty, so he simply booked the flight and called to say I'd be flying out in two weeks.

Eight minutes to become a teacher. What do I know about teaching the English language? What do I know about teaching? Someone in the office downstairs handed me a textbook this morning. I crack it open. It's in Chinese. I stare at the characters, inducing a fresh wave of panic. My instructions are simple and terrifying: deliver six consecutive 50-minute lessons using pages 88 to 94. I'm not a teacher. I'm a fraud. My only qualification is that I'm a "native" speaker of English, which isn't a qualification at all. It's an accident of birth.

Seven minutes. If I take the fire escape, nobody will notice. But I'd have to walk past the principal's office. He picked me up from the train station at 7:15 this morning and spent the last hour elegantly serving me green tea picked from the hills above us. He played Side A of a Miles Davis LP on an ancient record player. He knew I was just substituting for the day, and I'm sure he could sense my mounting panic. He was cultured and elegant, patient and kind, wise and learned. Everything I'm not. I'm a charlatan in a cheap nylon tie clutching an empty satchel, trying to pass for an educator. What a joke. Maybe I could scale the school's perimeter wall.

Six minutes before the charade starts. They're going to notice my hands shaking. My voice will quiver, and then I'll start hyperventilating until the room goes gray. It happens every time I speak in front of others. This feels like a nightmare from which I can't wake. The sweat is dripping down my forehead, and I'm not even in the classroom yet. The humidity is stifling; my shirt is already soaked. I loosen my tie, but the air provides no relief. What am I going to do?

The school buzzer jolts me to my senses. Five minutes. Why am I so full of doubt? You know who wasn't full of doubt? Miss Graham. Mr. Morrison. Mrs. Ferguson. Mrs. Hambrick. Mrs. Warlow. They were just like the principal here: warm, patient, calm, and wise. Why am I so different? Am I so different?

Mrs. Hambrick was my Grade 11 history teacher back in Canada. She knew a lot about the Greeks and Persians and Akkadians, but that's not why I loved her. Her classes were full of long pauses, giving us time to actually think. She smiled. She laughed. She tilted her head back in thought. I didn't get nervous speaking in her class because she made me feel like a person. She said things like, "Johnny, now that's an interesting thought. Let's follow it. Where does it take us, class?" No teacher had ever said things like that to us before. Sometimes she'd admit, "I don't know the answer to that. I'm going to think about it and get back to you." And she always did. In her class, learning wasn't a competition, or listening and repeating, or filling out worksheets. It was sitting in groups, thinking, exchanging, talking, and looking for answers to a stream of difficult questions. "Put away your books," she said on the first day. "We read at home, but in class we think and talk."

Can I learn to apply something from this in the next four minutes? I ask myself, as a boy in a blue and white uniform walks toward me and into the classroom. "Hello, Teacher!" he says cheerfully as he walks past. I look behind me to see who he's addressing. There's nobody else on the balcony. He thinks I am a teacher.

I walk into the classroom as he's finding his seat. "Good morning, I'm Joh… I'm Mr. Shaw, your teacher for today's class." He nods. I've fooled him. Is this my strategy? Just keep up the charade. Fake it 'til I make it to 4:00 pm. It's better than fainting, I suppose.

For the next three minutes, I'll act like a teacher. I wipe the blackboard with a dusty cloth. I sit down and flip through the pages of the textbook and tilt my head back in thought. More kids shuffle into class and address me as "Teacher." This could work, but it only gets me to the start of class. Then what? "Open your books on page 88, which I can't read"? I still haven't solved anything other than this performance. The panic returns.

Two minutes before the class starts, everything starts to happen in slow motion. My awareness of noise abates. I begin to have a moment of clarity. The next seven hours might be a nightmare, but they don't have to be. I can determine this outcome, but it depends on me solving the central problem of my life. I am a deeply insecure person, and all my personality flaws are defensive mechanisms to hide this. I can be aloof, guarded, arrogant, impatient, cynical, and sarcastic. My friends see past this, but most people don't. I'm the opposite of the principal and all the teachers who made me love learning and encouraged me to go to university. In one minute, I'm going to have to reinvent myself.

Fifty-five seconds. I came to Taiwan to get away from myself. This is what I wanted: a new start. But I thought the changes would be gradual, not the result of a panic attack a few days after landing. I can't stop it now. The buzzer rings. I feel my pulse in my neck. Time speeds up again and my sense of hearing sharpens. I exhale slowly. My heart rate drops. I close my eyes, and as I open them, I scan the room. "My name is Mr. Sh… My name is Johnny, and I'm your substitute teacher today," I say. "Now, put away your books. We read at home, but in class we think and talk."

The next 50 minutes were Side B of the Miles Davis album in the principal's office. Improvisational, but not chaotic; based on a framework and a few ideas. Our time is filled with pauses, careful listening, laughter, nodding, refrains, and riffs. I had pretended to reinvent myself, but it became real. I pretended to be a teacher, but that becomes real, too. Seven hours later, I'm still vibrating. I am in a trance as I'm dropped off at the train station. I don't remember going home.

The euphoria I felt on the train ride home eventually faded into the routine of a career, but the lessons of that morning remained etched in my psyche. I knew something transformational had happened, but I wasn't quite ready to confront myself to understand it. That took another 12 years, including a decade-long hiatus from the classroom, when I found myself in a graduate education degree back in Canada. The program was built around exploring teacher identity, reflection, and cultivating a professional practice, and we were challenged to explore the reasons we became educators. This culminated in drafting a teaching philosophy statement for our teaching portfolios. As the deadline approached, I started to feel like I was back outside that classroom in Chiayi County at 8:50 am. "And this time, I can't fake it," I thought. And so, I went through it all again, only this time it took weeks and months, not minutes. In the end, I completed my first draft of my teaching philosophy two years after I graduated. In what has become an annual ritual, I am now working on Draft 11.

Tracing the arc from that panicked substitute English teacher to the university lecturer I am today, I've come to realize that my career has been an extended meditation on two specific ideas I stumbled upon that morning. In Chiayi, I saw emulating these factors as survival tactics, but I now see cultivating them as the core of our craft.

Intellectual Character

I earlier described the teachers who I admired as being "warm, patient, calm, and wise". I now see these qualities as being a byproduct of something far more important: intellectual virtue. Perhaps nobody has articulated this more lucidly and concisely than Richard Paul and Linda Elder (2010) who describe the intellectual dispositions of critical thinkers: humility, autonomy, integrity, courage, perseverance, confidence in reason, empathy, and fairmindedness. The transformational moments I experienced in Mrs. Hambrick's classroom were not a result of her being nice. Rather, they were because she exemplified these dispositions and sought to cultivate them in us.

Intellectual Midwifery

In Plato's *Theaetetus*, Socrates describes his maieutic method as a form of "midwifery," emphasizing his role in helping others develop and deliver their own insights. When Mrs. Hambrick said, "Johnny, now that's an interesting thought. Let's follow it," she was stepping away from the role of a giver of knowledge and instead adopting the role of a midwife. For me, this was a first, tentative step into a liminal intellectual state, what Shelagh Crooks (2017) identifies as the "strategic adaptation" prompted by the disorientation of leaving a "closed epistemology" behind (pp. 11-12).

The next step came when she admitted, "I don't know the answer to that." In that moment, she was signaling that knowledge is not a commodity to be transferred, but something constructed through a process of evidential inquiry and reflection. She was drawing me out of an *absolutist* conception of knowledge towards an *evaluative* stance (Kuhn & Park, 2005). By "piercing the veil" of her educational practice, she showed us that the goal was not to receive the truth from an expert, but to enter the "lifeblood of the classroom" through active reflection and argumentation (Crooks, 2017, p.7).

When I look back to morning in Chiayi (as I still often do), I am reminded that my research and teaching practice is an attempt to map the terrain I stumbled onto by accident at 08:50 one morning. I am no longer that trembling (and skinny) young man on the balcony, but I carry him with me. He reminds me that every class is an improvisation, every student is a thinker, and every day is an opportunity to practice the intellectual virtues that make true learning possible. I am still working on my teaching philosophy, and perhaps I will be for the rest of my life. But I no longer feel like a charlatan. I feel like a midwife.

How I came to be a teacher

Eric Bird

As I contemplate my journey of becoming a teacher and making education a place to land, I marvel at the experiences, opportunities, and adventures that I have had. I have always dreamed about foreign lands, learning about people who live differently than me, and dreamt of seeing and experiencing all the wonders of the world. Growing up, my heart yearned for new cultural experiences, adventures and people! It's been a long-term dream to learn about people and everything that makes them tick.... I love connecting and building relationships with people and cultures from around the globe. One experience that shaped me through childhood was living at Michener Park in Edmonton, Alberta. My dad attended the University of Alberta, where he completed a PhD in educational administration. This was during the late 70s and early 80s, and as a family, we lived in a global community. Students had come to study at the University of Alberta and needed a place to live with their families; Mitchner Park was that place. On one side was a family from Italy, on the other, a family from Iran. Kitty-corner to us was another family who came from Nairobi, Kenya. Together as kids, we laughed and played, and studied at school, while our parents worked hard to better themselves. To complete their education was their dream ...to then return home or begin a new adventure somewhere new.

My experience living in Michener Park shaped me and had a profound impact on the rest of my life. I wanted to go to Italy; I wanted to visit Iran and learn more about Muslim culture. I wanted to experience parts of Canada that were different from British Columbia, to go to places I'd never seen before. Speaking a foreign language was something that tickled my fancy. Both of my parents are highly educated. My father has a PhD, and my mother has a Master's degree, both of which are in educational administration. Both of them were teachers and retired as elementary school administrators. I never considered education or thought teaching would be the profession for me. In fact, I tried to avoid it because I thought a household full of teachers was weird! I valued the learning, the conversations and insights that I gleaned from my childhood, but I was not so sure about the "being a teacher" part.

As I grew up, I've always been connected with education. When my dad finished his doctorate and we returned to Victoria from Edmonton, the world took an economic turn, and both my parents lost their jobs at the University of Victoria. With both parents, now unemployed, and a family to provide for, my parents went out on a limb and purchased a small retail business that sold goods and supplies and games and products for teachers. *Teachers' Corner* quickly became the go to place in Victoria for educational resources, supplies, and classroom accoutrement. I would work in the store on weekends and support families who had a heart for supporting their children's learning. I also worked alongside teachers, providing them with resources to enhance their classroom and their teaching practice. We often took our products on the road and would have a table or two and some of the out of the reach schools and school districts that needed resources for their classrooms and schools. Manned by my father and me, we drove many kilometres to sell our wares and connect with families and schools throughout British Columbia.

During high school I never would've considered becoming a teacher. I was restless and unsure of next steps. I was quite unclear about what I was going to do with my life, but I knew I wanted to do something far away in a foreign land. To that end, I took a gap year and did some volunteer work in Hong Kong and throughout Asia, which was such a rewarding and life shaping experience. I was able to work with the poor and needy, teach English to Vietnamese refugees, work with malnourished children on the garbage dump of Manila, Philippines and bring light and life to those without hope, by way of drama and dance and the visual arts. These experiences solidified my love for new places and great food and for interesting people worldwide. It also began to develop the sense of compassion and empathy that has been at the core of my being since I was a child.

After an extended "gap" year that lasted around four years, I reached some clarity about what I wanted to be when I grew up. It was at this point in my journey then that I decided, yes, I truly wanted to be a teacher. My experiences created the opportunities to learn more about culture and the things that people truly value: family, being loved unconditionally and having ownership and agency over one's own learning journey. There were numerous times where I witnessed people discovering and learning new things…having "ah ha" moments. These times made me realize I wanted to be someone who taught and guided others to grow, discover and be their best.

I knew then, beyond a shadow of a doubt, that teaching was something I wanted to pursue. I had fallen in love with the people of Asia, specifically Hong Kong and the Philippines. I knew that the next step was to get some training to become a teacher and head out into the world once more. Following some upgrading of my high school courses I came to the realization that I could study and do well in school. My academic results in high school were less than exemplary, which meant I needed to redo several courses so that I could study at university and build a solid foundation for my newfound dream of becoming a teacher.

I have had good teachers throughout my own educational experiences, and they reminded me of my strengths and abilities. It was their support of my academic endeavours that reminded me of who I wanted to be as a teacher. I wanted to be someone who valued their students, gave them a voice and provided a space for them to learn, no matter what their learning styles or learning needs were. I wanted to be that teacher who helped my students access concepts they may never have understood before. I wanted to be fun!

After some upgrading at Camosun College, I moved to university and began my Bachelor of Education studies. I have always loved school and studying, but at times, the demands of rigorous study have been challenging. It's often obstacles at work that reshape and reframe who we are and bring newness to the areas in our lives that need challenging. I loved many of my courses. I particularly loved theater in education. The drama courses that I was taking inspired me and encouraged me. I realized what a valuable tool the arts can be to connect people with each other and themselves. Playing different roles within a play or exploring the nuances of a text through creating drama, help to deepen meaning and bring about greater understanding for those creating the work. Whether participants enjoy taking part in the creative process or use drama as a tool for learning, drama creates a safe space for people to explore themselves more fully. Drama and theater work well cross-culturally because they transcend the barriers of language, and class.

During my BEd, there was a period where I struggled to stay focused, and then I was inflicted with glandular fever/mononucleosis, which wiped me out. I decided to take a break from my studies and quickly took a position teaching English in Japan. It's not ideal to stop studies partway through, so I quickly found my feet again when I moved to the small Japanese town called Furukawa. It was a trying and difficult experience that restored my belief in myself and developed a strength in me that I never knew I had. I was one of four English-speaking foreigners in the town, and I quickly made friends with locals, learned Japanese, and participated in a multitude of festivals and cultural events that were important to the community where I was living. This filling of my bucket encouraged me to participate more and become a part of the community. It filled my soul and helped me to refocus my goals of becoming a teacher.

After a year and a half of working in Japan, I returned to Canada to complete my degree before the end of 2000. I had a short time to complete all of my degree requirements, or the program requirements would have changed drastically. I worked through the summer session; the fall and spring sessions were earmarked for practicum. By the middle of July, I finished my last course of a Bachelor of Education. My last University of Victoria course was on a Tuesday, by Friday I was on a plane to Taichung, Taiwan, ready to teach on Monday. I had multiple levels of English classes during my first summer school at the Royal English language school, where I spent two years teaching English as a Second Language (ESL), cramming school or __ (b xíbān).

My time in Taiwan was wonderful, but I quickly realized that I wanted to land a position as a teacher in the classroom, or I could end up solely teaching English. I wanted the diversity that comes from working in the classroom and teaching all subjects. I pursued new international jobs, but that was quickly shut down because I did not have the Primary Years Program (PYP) training that so many schools were looking for. They wanted to employ teachers who could foster inquiry and use concept-based curriculum instruction to propel their students towards growth and depth and resilience.

Jakarta Indonesia was the place where I continued to grow as an educator. I landed at a school called Sekolah Pelita Harapan that provided me with the PYP training that is so desperately needed. I spent five years in this close community learning about Indonesia, its history and its amazing people. I loved my time in Jakarta and seeing students flourish when they participated in the arts was an amazing memory of my time there. Working with the production team as stage manager, it was a huge group effort to pull off such shows as the King and I and the Sound of Music. After five years, I knew it was time for another adventure, and the Philippines called my name. My parents ended up moving to Jakarta and taught at Universitas Pelita Harapan, which kept me connected to both the place and my people, and my parents.

International School Manila was the place where many dreams came true for me as an educator. Our classes were home to students from at least 14 different countries or more and there were boundless opportunities for learning, service, and community building. The arts were beyond plentiful as well, from music to theatre, drama and dance! Teachers were spoiled for opportunity and choice when it came to professional development. I said yes to every professional development opportunity that I could because I wanted to grow and become the best teacher I could be. I completed a counselling certificate and a Master of Science in Interdisciplinary Studies from the State University of new York (SUNY), Buffalo State. It wasn't just what the place offered; Manila and ISM were home; they built community, friendships, and connections that have stood the test of time. In turn, I gave back to my school community, devoting my time to my grade 5 team and both middle and high school drama productions.

I left Manila after 12 years feeling blessed, fulfilled… equipped, ready for whatever lay ahead back home in Canada, the place I left 19 years prior, thinking I would be living overseas for life… and then plans changed. I felt an urgent desire to reconnect with my family and my country of origin, so this time, it was Canada that called me home. I decided to place roots in Vancouver, a large city full of promise and adventure, close to Victoria home and family. And then, COVID hit, with the world getting turned on its end. My school in Vancouver provided safety and employment during the pandemic. Its community rallied during those challenging days that were felt throughout the world. COVID days as a teacher were exhausting and relentless. Filled with uncertainty and fear, making school a place for kids to connect with others and feel safe. It was a place where teachers so often were the only stable force, for those in their care. With great responsibility came much sacrifice, and COVID times took their toll on many, and on me. I was left feeling exhausted and burned out.

With that, my journey took me full circle back to Victoria and even more ironically, Sidney, BC. Having lived in some of the largest cities in the world and now living in a community of around 12,000 is somewhat surreal, but I would never change it ever. I have come to realize moving at a slower pace has proved space to grow, change and be more reflective. I've been home for just over three years now and my work as a Teacher Teaching on Call (TTOC) has been rewarding in so many ways. Moving between schools ranging from elementary to high school, from kindergarten to counseling to French immersion grade one have shaped my vision and dreams once more. These experiences have given me insight into what the future and education might look like and what kids still need. They need to be valued and cared for, loved for who they are, and encouraged to take risks, to try everything, do it all… at least once. Moving from school to school can be challenging at times; being able to experience a diversity of school cultures definitely outweighs the challenges.

My role in education has morphed once again. I've recently finished a Master of Arts Counselling Psychology (MACP) and I'm newly qualified to work as a counselor with the Victoria School District, while building my own clinical counselling practice. The lesson I have learned, and the stories I have collected along the way continue to shape what the twilight of my career will look like as it unfolds. We are once again living in uncertain times and students and teachers alike need a sense of purpose and a strong sense of identity to help them weather the challenges. I am thrilled to be working in this new role as a counselor within the schools because so many children and youth struggle with anxiety and fear that needs nurturing and care. They need to begin reclaiming who they are and be challenged to do and be their best because they are the future of our world. This is why I became a teacher, to encourage, lead and inspire!

REFERENCES

Alyass, G., & Buist, A. (2025). Inclusive education in Ontario, Canada: An overview. *Educational Planning, 32*(3), 107–116.

Assembly of First Nations. (2010). *First Nations control of First Nations education: It's our vision, it's our time*. Retrieved from https://education.afn.ca/afntoolkit/wp-content/uploads/2021/04/2010-AFN-First-Nations-Contol-of-First-Nations-Education_sm.pdf

Bennett, P. W. (2016). Digital learning in Canadian K–12 schools: A review of critical issues, policy, and practice. In Marcus-Quinn, A., & Hourigan, T. (Eds.), *Handbook on digital learning for K–12 schools* (pp. 293–315). Springer., DOI: 10.1007/978-3-319-33808-8_17

British Columbia Ministry of Education. (2025). *Curriculum, British Columbia. Grade 10 literacy assessment.* Retrieved from https://curriculum.gov.bc.ca/provincial/grade-10-literacy-assessment

Campbell, C. (2020). Educational equity in Canada: The case of Ontario's strategies and actions to advance excellence and equity for students. *School Leadership & Management, 41*(4–5), 409–428. DOI: 10.1080/13632434.2019.1709165

Council of Ministers of Education. Canada. (2019). *CMEC Indigenous education plan, 2019–2022.* Retrieved from https://www.cmec.ca/719/CMEC_Indigenous_Education_Plan%2C_2019%E2%80%9322_.html

Council of Ministers of Education. Canada. (2023, December 5). *OECD report ranks Canadian students among top performers globally in mathematics.* Retrieved from https://cmec.ca/278/OECD_REPORT_RANKS_CANADIAN_STUDENTS_AMONG_TOP_PERFORMERS_GLOBALLY_IN_MATHEMATICS

Council of Ministers of Education. Canada. (2026). *Pan-Canadian Assessment Program (PCAP).* Retrieved from https://www.cmec.ca/240/Pan-Canadian_Assessment_Program (PCAP).html

Council of Ministers of Education. Canada. (n.d.). *International.* Retrieved from https://cmec.ca/148/International.html

Council of Ministers of Education. Canada. (n.d., a). *Postsecondary education in Canada: Jurisdiction and authority.* Retrieved from https://cmec.ca/158/Postsecondary_Education.html

Cowley, P., & MacPherson, P. (2022). *Testing Canadian K-12 students: Regional variability, room for improvement: A cross-Canada comparison of K-12 provincial assessment programs.* Fraser Institute. Retrieved from www.fraserinstitute.org/sites/default/files/testing-canadian-k12-students-regional-variability.pdf. (fraserinstitute.org)

Crooks, S. M. (2017). Finding a place in higher education: An epistemological analysis. *The Canadian Journal for the Scholarship of Teaching and Learning, 8*(1). Advance online publication. DOI: 10.5206/cjsotl-rcacea.2017.1.2

Education Quality and Accountability Office (EQAO). (n.d.) *Ontario Secondary School Literacy Test (OSSLT).* Retrieved from https://www.eqao.com/the-assessments/osslt/

FutureLearn. (2021, 3 Sept.). Explore: *The Canadian education system by province and territory.* Retrieved from https://www.futurelearn.com/info/futurelearn-international/canada-public-education-by-province

Government of Canada. (2020). *Origin of the name "Canada". Canadian Heritage.* Retrieved from https://www.canada.ca/en/canadian-heritage/services/origin-name-canada.html

Government of Canada. (2025). *Understand the Canadian education system.* Retrieved from https://www.educanada.ca/study-plan-etudes/system-education-systeme.aspx?lang=eng

Government of Canada. (2025a). *Language classes funded by the Government of Canada. Retrieved from* https://www.canada.ca/en/immigration-refugees-citizenship/services/settle-canada/language-skills/classes.html

Government of Canada. (2025b). *Canada's research funding ecosystem. Innovation, Science and Economic Development Canada.* Retrieved from https://www.canada.ca/en/research-coordinating-committee/corporate/canadas-research-funding-ecosystem.html

Government of Canada. (2026). *Constitution Act 1867.* Retrieved from https://laws-lois.justice.gc.ca/eng/const/page-1.html

Humber College Institute of Technology and Advanced Learning. (2021). *Faculty academic/professional credential requirements Policy.* Legal, Risk and Privacy Office. Retrieved from https://humber.ca/legal-and-risk-management/policies/academic/faculty-academic-professional-credential-requirements-policy.html

Knapper, C. K., & Willis, B. (1980). Educational technology in Canada: Recent developments and future trends. *Higher Education in Europe*, *5*(3), 10–15. https://unesdoc.unesco.org/ark:/48223/pf0000042428. DOI: 10.1080/0379772800050304

Kuhn, D., & Park, S.-H. (2005). Epistemological understanding and the development of intellectual values. *International Journal of Educational Research*, *43*(3), 111–124. DOI: 10.1016/j.ijer.2006.05.003

Levent, A. F., & Sağlam, M. H. (2024). More internationalisation, more innovation: The case of Canadian teacher training programs. In Akgün, B., & Alpaydın, Y. (Eds.), *Global agendas and education reforms* (pp. 271–287). Palgrave Macmillan., DOI: 10.1007/978-981-97-3068-1_14

Marom, L., & Xu, H. (2025). "I had to prove myself a hundred times more than the other teachers": The experiences of internationally educated teachers in the Canadian school system. *Teaching and Teacher Education*, *145*, 105196. DOI: 10.1016/j.tate.2025.105196

McCrimmon, A. W. (2015). Inclusive education in Canada: Issues in teacher paration. *Intervention in School and Clinic*, *50*(4), 234–237. DOI: 10.1177/1053451214546402

Ontario College of Teachers. (2026). *Requirements — Becoming a Teacher.* Retrieved from https://www.oct.ca/en-ca/becoming-a-teacher/requirements

Organisation for Economic Co-operation and Development (OECD). (2019). *PISA 2018 results (Volume II): Where all students can succeed.* OECD Publishing. DOI: 10.1787/b5fd1b8f-en

Organisation for Economic Co-operation and Development (OECD). (2022). *PISA 2022 results (Volume I): The state of learning and equity in education.* OECD Publishing. DOI: 10.1787/53f23881-en

Paul, R., & Elder, L. (2010). *The miniature guide to critical thinking concepts and tools.* Dillon Beach: Foundation for Critical Thinking Press.

Remitly. (2025). *Teacher salary in Canada: What educators can expect in 2025.* Retrieved from emitly.com/blog/en-ca/jobs-and-careers/teacher-salary/

Sclater, J., Sicoly, F., Abrami, P. C., & Wade, C. A. (2006). Ubiquitous technology integration in Canadian public schools: Year one study. *Canadian Journal of Learning and Technology*, *32*(1). Advance online publication. DOI: 10.21432/T2W897

Social Sciences and Humanities Research Council of Canada. (2025). *Our Mandate.* Government of Canada. Retrieved from https://sshrc-crsh.canada.ca/en/about-sshrc/mandate.aspx

Statistics Canada. (2024). *National Occupational Classification (NOC) for the faculty/university professors & post-secondary instructors.* Retrieved from https://www23.statcan.gc.ca/

Statistics Canada. (2025). *Education Indicators in Canada: Handbook for the Pan-Canadian Education Indicators Program.* https://www150.statcan.gc.ca

Truth and Reconciliation Commission of Canada. (2015). *Calls to action.* National Centre for Truth and Reconciliation. Retrieved from https://nctr.ca/records/reports/

UNESCO. Institute for Statistics. (n.d.). *International Standard Classification of Education (ISCED).* Retrieved from https://www.uis.unesco.org/en/methods-and-tools/isced

University of Ottawa. (2023, September 18). *New research highlights the importance of equity in education.* Retrieved from https://www.uottawa.ca/en/media/news/new-research-highlights-importance-equity-education

University of Waterloo, Cybersecurity and Privacy Institute. (n.d.). *Technology and the need for integration in public education.* Retrieved from https://uwaterloo.ca/cybersecurity-privacy-institute/technology-and-need-integration-public-education

Chapter 4
Teachers' Voices From Brazil

Schayana Suelin Schreiber
http://orcid.org/0009-0004-6627-1089
Serviço Nacional de Aprendizagem Comercial-SENAC RS, Brazil

Fabiana Diniz Kurtz
Universidade Regional do Noroeste do Estado do Rio Grande do Sul, Brazil

Maria Alice da Silva Brandão
Universidade Regional do Noroeste do Estado do Rio Grande do Sul, Brazil

ABSTRACT

This chapter examines education and the teaching profession in Brazil, situating them within historical, social, and political contexts. It outlines the structure of the Brazilian education system and key reforms in teacher education, highlighting persistent inequalities, professional challenges, and policy tensions. Drawing on legislation, international assessments, and the authors' professional experiences, the chapter discusses teaching in Brazil as a field marked by both recognition and resistance.

EDUCATION AND THE TEACHING PROFESSION IN BRAZIL: BETWEEN RECOGNITION AND RESISTANCE

Fabiana Diniz Kurtz
Schayana Suelin Schreiber

Education System and Structural Context

Brazil has one of the largest and most complex education systems in the world. As a federal and deeply unequal country, it offers a paradigmatic case for understanding how teacher education reflects broader social, economic, and political tensions. According to the National Institute for Educational Studies and Research Anísio Teixeira (Brazil, 2023) there are more than 47 million students and around 2.2 million teachers across basic and higher education. Education is a constitutional right, and over the past three decades several national reforms have sought to strengthen it - from the Law of Guidelines and Bases of National Education (LDB No. 9,394/1996) to the National Education Plan (PNE 2014–2024), the National Common Curricular Base (Brazil, 2018), and its Complement on Computing (Brazil, 2022), which integrates digital culture and computational thinking across all stages of schooling, and, more recently, the National Digital Education Policy (PNED) (Brazil, 2023b).

These transformations reflect broader debates on pedagogical innovation and the role of digital technologies in reshaping educational cultures, as discussed by Kurtz et al. (2021), who argue that innovation in education must be understood cross-culturally and through the lens of reflective and transformative teaching practice. These documents

DOI: 10.4018/979-8-3373-8983-7.ch004

show an ongoing effort to expand access, ensure equity, and rethink the role of teachers in contemporary Brazil. Yet, teaching in Brazil continues to be a profession of paradoxes. On the one hand, there is an enormous social demand for qualified educators. On the other hand, teachers still face low salaries, fragile working conditions, and limited professional recognition in some contexts. As the Organization for Economic Co-operation and Development (OECD, 2024) highlights, the mismatch between ambitious national goals and the daily conditions of teachers has deepened, exposing structural inequalities and weak professional valorization.

In structural terms, the Brazilian education system is organized into Basic Education and Higher Education. Basic Education comprises Early Childhood Education, a nine-year compulsory Elementary Education (ages 6 - 14), and a three-year Upper Secondary Education (ages 15 - 17) as established by national legislation (Brazil, 1996; Brazil, 2009; Brazil, 2023). Thus, students are expected to complete 12 years of compulsory schooling, though the quality and continuity of this trajectory vary widely across regions. Despite near-universal enrollment in the 6 - 14 age group, inequalities persist: rural areas, indigenous and quilombola (Afro-Brazilian resident of quilombo settlements first established by left behind and escaped slaves in Brazil) communities, and low-income urban peripheries continue to face barriers related to infrastructure, transportation, digital access, and school permanence. Such disparities illustrate that while Brazil's education system nominally reaches almost all children, equitable and meaningful access remains uneven and strongly shaped by social class, race, and geography.

Historical roots and persistent inequality

This landscape is also rooted in the country's educational history. Schooling in Brazil began with Jesuit missions in the sixteenth century, primarily oriented toward catechesis and colonial administration. After the Jesuits' expulsion in the mid-eighteenth century, state-led education developed slowly, and only in the nineteenth century did the country establish its first higher-education institutions. The first officially recognized university was created in 1920 in Rio de Janeiro (today the Federal University of Rio de Janeiro – UFRJ). Importantly, enslaved Africans and their descendants were systematically excluded from schooling throughout the colonial and imperial periods. The "Lei do Ventre Livre" (Law of the Free Womb), enacted in 1871, declared that children born to enslaved women would be legally free, yet it did not guarantee access to education or social inclusion. Likewise, the abolition of slavery in 1888 did not include provisions to ensure educational access, leaving a legacy of racialized exclusion that continues to shape inequalities in teacher preparation, professional opportunities, and student outcomes today.

Current international assessments further illuminate these disparities. In the 2022 cycle of the Programme for International Student Assessment (PISA), Brazilian students scored 379 in Mathematics, 410 in Reading, and 403 in Science, remaining below OECD averages and revealing persistent challenges in foundational learning (OECD, 2023; Brazil, 2023). Less than half of Brazilian students reach basic proficiency levels according to OECD benchmarks for minimum competency. Moreover, results vary significantly across regions and between public and private schools, reflecting deep structural inequalities in the education system (Brazil, 2023; OECD, 2023; Todos Pela Educação, 2023). These indicators underscore how the historical inequities embedded in Brazil's educational structure continue to constrain learning opportunities and the professional conditions of teachers.

In quantitative terms, Brazil has more than 1,300 higher education institutions offering teacher-education programs (licenciaturas), but less than 60% of in-service teachers hold a degree exactly in the field in which they teach (Brazil, 2023a). That mismatch between initial training and classroom reality is one of the main challenges we face, especially in regions where public investment is historically uneven.

This structural gap is not recent but rather the outcome of a long historical process. Historically, teacher education has been shaped by policy reforms and ideological disputes. Diniz-Pereira (2013) traces the emergence of teacher-education research in Brazil as a "field of struggles," influenced by Bourdieu's notion of symbolic capital, in which universities, ministries, and international agencies compete for legitimacy. This insight helps explain why Brazilian policies oscillate between valuing critical pedagogy and imposing technocratic models.

Reform cycles and policy disputes in teacher education

Since the mid-1990s, international agencies such as the World Bank, United Nations Educational, Scientific and Cultural Organization (UNESCO), and the Organization for Economic Co-operation and Development (OECD) have strongly influenced national reforms. During 1995–2002, Brazil adopted a neoliberal policy agenda emphasizing managerial efficiency, standardized assessment, and accountability in education.

With the turn of the century, however, a new political cycle began. In the following decade, the political orientation shifted. The government expanded public investment in education and sought to democratize access to higher education through programs such as *University for All Program* (ProUni, 2004) and the *Program for the Restructuring and Expansion of Federal Universities* (Reuni, 2007). Nevertheless, even though these initiatives emphasized social inclusion and equity, they coexisted with the persistence of managerial models introduced in the 1990s. As Oliveira and Leiro (2019) observe, the federal executives maintained centralized control over teacher education policy through legislative mechanisms, revealing contradictions between participatory discourse and technocratic implementation.

Subsequently, in 2015, the new National Curriculum Guidelines for Teacher Education (CNE/CP Resolution 2/2015) (Brazil, 2015) represented a significant attempt to realign teacher education with school realities, emphasizing the integration of theory and practice, social commitment, and pedagogical reflection. However, the implementation of these guidelines soon collided with Brazil's 2016 political crisis. The country entered a period of institutional instability and policy realignment.

At the same time, regional and socioeconomic inequalities remain among the most decisive factors shaping Brazil's educational landscape. Educational resources and opportunities are unevenly distributed across the country: the South and Southeast concentrate higher levels of infrastructure, connectivity, and teacher-training provision, while the North and Northeast experience persistent deficits in school facilities, technological access, and investment.

At the same time, recent studies from Southern Brazil (Kurtz et al., 2024) highlight that teacher knowledge is socially and territorially situated, emphasizing continuing education as a space for professional reflection and epistemic resistance within unequal contexts.

Moreover, as Santos and Diniz-Pereira (2016) demonstrate, these regional asymmetries intersect with growing attempts to standardize curriculum and teacher education. The authors caution that the drive for national standardization - through instruments such as the BNCC - often erodes teacher autonomy, reduces curricular diversity, and subjects teachers to managerial control derived from business logic.

Culturally, the image of the teacher in Brazil remains deeply ambivalent. Teaching is admired as a moral calling - associated with dedication, affection, and service - yet rarely acknowledged as an intellectual profession. Consequently, this contradiction still echoes in the way society evaluates education: teachers are essential, yet their voices are often silenced in decision-making spaces.

From a personal standpoint and based on our own experiences as teacher educators and researchers, this duality defines much of what it means to work in education in Brazil: to live constantly between recognition and resistance. Nevertheless, we persist because we believe that the classroom, even with its limitations, remains a space of transformation - a place where social inequalities can be challenged and new meanings of citizenship and learning can emerge.

In the years that followed, educational policy became increasingly fragmented. Two previous administrations consolidated a more centralized and technocratic agenda, culminating in the approval of the National Common Curricular Base (BNCC, 2017) and the National Common Base for Teacher Education (BNC-Formação, 2020). These initiatives deepened the standardization of curricula and reinforced performance-oriented models. Only recently, from 2023 onward, has the government sought to restore a more dialogic and humanistic vision of teacher education.

So, the approval of the National Common Curricular Base (BNCC) in 2017 and the National Common Base for Teacher Education (2020) further intensified this debate. According to Costa et al. (2019), these policies are part of a wider process of curricular standardization that promotes what they call the "dis-intellectualization of teaching." In their view, teachers are being reduced to technicians who execute pre-defined competencies, while their critical and creative roles are systematically undermined.

Following this trajectory, in 2019 the National Board of Education (CNE) approved Resolution CNE/CP No. 1/2019, which amended Article 22 of the 2015 guidelines to adapt teacher-education programs to the new National Common

Curricular Base (BNCC). Subsequently, Resolution CNE/CP No. 2/2019 established the National Common Base for Teacher Education, setting a uniform competency framework across licensure programs. However, the implementation of these norms faced resistance from universities and educators who viewed them as excessively prescriptive and misaligned with the diverse realities of Brazilian schools (Santos & Diniz-Pereira, 2016; Costa et al., 2019).

In an attempt to mitigate these tensions, Resolution CNE/CP No. 1/2024 (Brazil, 2024a) extended the implementation deadline by 90 days, giving higher-education institutions more time to adapt their curricula. More importantly, the most recent Resolution CNE/CP No. 4/2024, enacted on 29 May 2024 (Brazil, 2024b), entirely redefined the National Curriculum Guidelines for Initial Teacher Education. This new resolution revokes all previous ones and emphasizes a more integrated, humanistic, and critical approach to teacher education. Specifically, it restores the articulation between theory and practice, reaffirms the social and ethical mission of teaching, and explicitly incorporates digital competencies and technological innovation as essential to contemporary professional formation. In addition, it requires that all teacher education curricula include supervised practicum, community-based extension, and the development of digital-pedagogical skills, establishing a new baseline for the professional profile of teachers in Brazil. In this sense, teacher education policies are now entering a new phase - one that seeks to overcome the technocratic model of the 2020 National Common Base for Teacher Education and re-centers teacher training on critical, inclusive, and context-responsive pedagogical practices.

Digital transformation and the future of teaching

The COVID-19 pandemic then made these tensions even clearer. In 2020, when schools closed, teachers all over the country reinvented themselves overnight. Without infrastructure or training, teachers turned their homes into classrooms, learned to record and edit lessons, and reached students by every possible means. It was exhausting, but also revealing. Ultimately, it showed how creative, generous, and resilient Brazilian teachers are - and how fragile our policies remain in supporting them.

By November 2020, more than five million children between six and seventeen were out of school (UNICEF, 2021), exposing the depth of digital exclusion. Teachers, however, emerged as central figures in sustaining learning and emotional connection. This crisis, as Leite et al. (2018) argue, demonstrated that curricular reforms alone are insufficient without structural investments in working conditions, connectivity, and continuing education.

In recent years, new discussions have emerged around artificial intelligence and the digital culture of education. The question, therefore, is no longer whether to use technology, but how to integrate it responsibly and meaningfully. Following the legacy of Paulo Freire, the world-known Brazilian educator, many educators now defend a critical and human-centered approach: technology should be seen as a cultural artifact, not a replacement for human mediation. This approach resonates with Vygotskyan perspectives on mediation and metacognition, which view digital tools as extensions of human thinking rather than substitutes for it (Silva et al., 2024).

In this regard, Brazil's new teacher-education legislation has also redefined the role of distance education. After a decade of rapid growth in online teacher education programs, often marked by low levels of supervision and interaction, the 2024 National Curriculum Guidelines for Initial Teacher Education (CNE/CP Resolution No. 4/2024) now establish that teacher-preparation courses can no longer be offered fully online (EaD). Instead, higher-education institutions must ensure significant face-to-face engagement, supervised practicum, and community-based extension activities.

This policy shift reflects a broader pedagogical understanding that teaching is not a purely cognitive or technical activity but a social, dialogic, and relational practice. Technology remains essential, yet its integration must strengthen - not replace - human interaction and critical reflection in the learning process.

This ongoing debate intersects with the newly implemented PNED (Brazil, 2023b). As Kurtz (2023) argues, digital policies can only become emancipatory if teacher education promotes critical digital literacy - that is, the capacity to analyze technological mediation ethically, politically, and pedagogically, rather than as merely operating tools.

Today, therefore, teacher education in Brazil faces the challenge of forming professionals capable of acting ethically and critically in digital contexts. We must prepare future educators to understand not only how to use technologies but also why and for what purposes - because, as we often tell our students, education will always need technology, and technology will always need educators.

Looking forward, the renewal of teacher education depends on restoring its intellectual prestige and ensuring fair professional conditions. Ultimately, as Costa et al. (2019) emphasize, the future of teaching in Brazil will rely on reconciling innovation with criticality and reaffirming Freirean principles of autonomy, dialogue, and hope. As Kurtz et al. (2021) remind us, rethinking innovation in education requires both intercultural awareness and a commitment to human-centered digital pedagogy - a balance that continues to define the struggles and possibilities of teacher education in Brazil.

Teacher voices: narratives of becoming

Despite the social centrality of teaching, the profession has struggled to consolidate itself as a consistently attractive first career choice in many contexts in Brazil. Discussions on teacher recruitment and retention frequently point to low salaries, demanding working conditions, and limited social prestige as factors shaping entry into licensure programs and early-career permanence (Brazil, 2023a; b; OECD, 2024; Todos Pela Educação, 2023). This tension helps explain why teaching is sometimes narrated as a "second option" or a path shaped by contingency rather than an early vocational project - an issue that the narratives below make visible through lived experience.

The narratives that follow are presented as situated accounts that illuminate how structural reforms, professional conditions, and cultural expectations are experienced in everyday trajectories. Read alongside the contextual discussion above, these voices serve as analytical evidence of the paradox between recognition and precarization, highlighting how teachers negotiate career choice, identity, and agency within unequal and increasingly technologized educational contexts.

EVERY DETOUR LED ME HERE - TO TEACHING

Schayana Suelin Schreiber

Since the very beginning, the only thing I was sure about my adult life was that I did not want to become a teacher. Before talking directly about myself, let me share a little about my family.

I was born in a small town in the northwest part of southern Brazil. I was the only child of a young couple who were both surprised and delighted when they heard they were expecting me. At that time, my parents worked in a grain cooperative in a small countryside village: my mother as a supermarket cashier and my father in the grain receiving area. Later, my father was transferred to a different cooperative in the city, and my mother started working as a cleaning lady in a private school, which later became the school where I studied and which I graduated with a scholarship.

Seeking new paths, my father started a Business Administration degree at UNIJUÍ (Regional University of Northwestern Rio Grande do Sul State, a private university). He graduated after eight years, studying whenever our family could afford it. He now holds an MBA in Marketing and Human Resources. Inspired by him and by my Mom's experience of working in a school education, my mother pursued a degree in Pedagogy and later a postgraduate certificate in Inclusive Education.

Almost everyone in my family is a teacher: my three godmothers are teachers of math, robotics, and biology, and in kindergarten), my aunt teaches history, and my uncle teaches IT. Growing up surrounded by constant conversations about classrooms, lesson plans, students' behavior, and assessments, I eventually got tired of hearing about teaching all the time. Maybe that is why I never pictured myself teaching as I grew up surrounded by educators talking about classrooms, students, and endless assessments.

Yet, as a child, I used to play with my dolls, and I was always teaching them. In the third grade, I joined a study club and started helping classmates with Portuguese lessons. One student used to come to my house every Tuesday morning so we could review together. When he passed the school year without taking make-up exams, his grandparents brought me a Christmas gift which became my first "teacher reward". I will never forget that feeling.

In my last year of high school, my goal was clear: I wanted to study medicine. I even spent a semester in Canada studying English as a Second Language. But when I came back, things changed. I decided to give up on that dream and started looking for something new. That is when I went to a language school to take an English exam and, unexpectedly, they invited me to teach kids. I accepted, thinking it would be temporary. I also began a health-related course, planning to go back to med school soon. But after two years teaching and in the middle of a pandemic, I realized that education had already found me. So, I decided to study Portuguese and English (Letras - Português e Inglês).

During my undergraduate studies, I moved to another city, lived on my own for the first time, and faced new professional challenges. I received a scholarship that allowed me to work closely with professors teaching Portuguese as a Foreign Language, and I even had the opportunity to study abroad at UMCS (Maria Curie-Skłodowska University), in Poland. I finally graduated in December 2024 and I recently completed my post-graduation in School Management and Neuropsychopedagogy and as I look back, I can see how every detour led me here - to teaching.

Becoming a teacher in Brazil is both a privilege and a challenge. It is a privilege because we work directly with people's goals and help them express ideas, learn a new language, and believe in their potential. But it is also a challenge because our educational system still struggles with inequalities, lack of resources, and limited recognition of teachers' work.

Throughout my journey, I have realized that being a teacher means constantly balancing expectations and realities. Sometimes, it means facing a class that does not seem interested at all, or adapting lessons for students who learn in completely different ways. Other times, it means staying up late correcting assignments or preparing engaging lessons. And, perhaps most challenging of all, it means continuing to give your best even when society often undervalues the role of teachers despite the fact that we are the very people who help shape every other profession.

Still, the classroom is where I find meaning. Every time a student who once said *"I can't do it"* suddenly starts speaking with confidence, or when someone proudly shows me they understood a grammar point that used to be impossible, those are the moments that remind me why teaching matters. I have learned that progress in education does not always happen loudly. It often happens in silence: in the way a shy student raises their hand for the first time, or in how a group starts collaborating instead of competing.

The greatest joy of teaching is witnessing transformation, not only in students but also in ourselves. I am not the same person I was when I entered the classroom for the first time. Teaching has taught me patience, resilience, and empathy. It has shown me that knowledge is not something we deliver; it is something we build together.

In recent years, technology has changed the way we teach and learn. Interactive platforms, apps, and artificial intelligence tools have become part of our daily routines. Many people wonder if, in the future, technology will replace teachers. Personally, I believe that the opposite is true: technology makes teachers even more essential. AI can generate content, translate texts, and provide instant answers, but it cannot truly *teach*. It does not feel compassion when a student struggles or pride when someone finally succeeds. Teaching is not only about providing information; it is about connection, care, and guidance. These are deeply human abilities that no machine can replicate. I have seen how technology can enhance learning when used with intention. For instance, digital tools can make lessons more dynamic and interactive, but it is our empathy, creativity, and flexibility as teachers that truly keep education alive. We become facilitators, designers, and emotional supporters, proving that teaching goes far beyond screens and slides.

In my view, the teacher's role in this technological era is to act as a mediator, someone who helps students interpret, question, and humanise the digital world. Our mission is not to compete with technology, but to give it meaning. We teach our students how to think critically, how to use digital tools ethically, and how to recognize what is true, useful, or harmful in an ocean of information. Technology can teach you *what* to think, but only education can teach you *how* to think and *why* it matters.

When I look back at my story, I smile at the irony of life: I once said I would never become a teacher, and now I cannot imagine being anything else. Teaching did not just become my career; it became part of who I am. I have learned that being a teacher means choosing again and again every day. Choosing to stay hopeful even when circumstances are difficult. Choosing to believe in people's capacity to change. Choosing to see potential where others see limitation.

If I could go back to the moment when I was invited to teach for the first time, I would say "yes" all over again without hesitation. Because teaching has given me much more than I could ever give back. It has given me stories, voices, and countless lessons that go beyond textbooks. Teaching is not about perfection; it is about presence. It is about being truly there for someone who is trying to learn, to find their voice, or to rebuild their confidence. And that, I believe, is the most beautiful and necessary human act of all.

No matter how advanced technology becomes, learning will always require human connection. Education will always need teachers not only to transmit knowledge, but to nurture empathy, creativity, and hope.

So yes, I once said I did not want to be a teacher. But today, I would not trade it for anything.

TEACHING AS SHOWING PEOPLE THE WORLD

Maria Alice da Silva Brandão

I have been an English teacher for 18 years. It is bizarre to think about all that time teaching, and not really to have an idea of how it all began. Maybe because I thought I was lost, when in reality, teaching had found me all along.

When I was a kid I never had a specific career I wanted to pursue. I was always changing my mind and exploring all the possibilities. But I did think that, in the end, I would be a doctor, just like my father, and that was encouraged in my home. My sister was already certain of becoming a doctor in the future, and her and I would spend time with our father in the hospital and be in awe of his profession, of taking care of people.

But with time, I realized I didn't really fit in in that world, and that was sad. I remember feeling so hopeless and alone, especially because my sister was very certain of it. But my wise and loving mother said: "There are many ways to help people and take care of them, you don't have to be a doctor, you know?". That made me feel better, and I went back to exploring.

I loved stories since I was a child. Both reading and listening to them. Books were everything to me, and I didn't have a preference: I would read anything I could put my hands on. My father still had his books from the time he was a medical student, so I read all of those (and they possibly influenced me into thinking I would be a doctor). Since my father's favorite sport was tennis, he had books about that, and I read them all. My mom liked cooking, knitting and nature, she had books about that, and I read them all too. My grandfather loved historical facts, had a bunch of books about it, and once again, I read them all, besides everything else, I was reading at school.

Pretty soon it became quite clear to me that I loved learning. All those books gave me so much information, different perspectives, new angles to look at life in general. And I loved sharing all of that. And because I was such a big reader, friends were always asking for my help with homework and with writing. That may have been a clue that I was going to be a teacher.

When the time came to choose a college course, I knew I wanted something related to language. Maybe journalism, because I loved writing too. I did consider a degree in English language, because that would open up so many doors to me, as a translator, for example, but my university didn't offer that course, so they instructed me to start pedagogy and later on transfer to English in the other campus.

When the time came to do the transfer, I was in love with all the possibilities and incredible things I was learning in pedagogy, another course that made me see lots of doors opening up to me. Thinking back, it was a very conscious choice, and the one I am really happy to have made. But I do remember not seeing myself as a teacher, but more so as someone who would enjoy school administration.

And then, I started working as an English teacher in a Social Project, with teenagers that would not be able to pay for a formal language course. That was an incredible experience, where I learned much more than I have taught. Being able to help students that never considered learning another language because of their life circumstances, and seeing firsthand how much that was enabling them to see more opportunities in their future, was incredibly rewarding. I was so young then and I had never thought I could help someone see a better future for themselves. That was finally when I thought "Hey, I can be a teacher".

While studying in college and also teaching in different schools, the biggest challenge has always been the limitations. Of course, as teachers we are already doing so much more than we think we are, but for me I have always felt like I could do more. Not just in teaching students (grammar, vocabulary, and pronunciation), but giving them more support in their learning journey. Unfortunately, we usually do not have the time to do that for the whole class.

In Horizontina, Brazil, where I live, we have a factory owned by the multinational company John Deere, which brought foreigners to live and work here. Sometimes, the whole family comes with them, and that gave me the opportunity of working with North American kids, who needed help adapting to a new language, school system, and culture. The experience of going to school with them and seeing the process of learning a language by immersion so up-close was interesting. The connections made, how much their personalities played a part, and the differences in the process for the outgoing and the shy ones. That sparked my curiosity and got me even more interested in teaching English.

Another very rewarding experience - probably one of the best ones - was when I had a chance to accompany students in an exchange program in Canada. We spent a month in Vancouver. Again, being able to see students exploring and speaking English, their excitement understanding native speakers after so much studying, was amazing. Every day they had different stories of challenges they overcame by speaking English, of interacting with the world, of dealing with being away from their parents, their home country and mother tongue for the first time.

As a person and as a teacher it has always being important to me to show people the world. We are in a vast world that is growing smaller as we share so much. We have much more commonalities than differences. And the more we evolve, the more I believe it is important to respect each other, respect our differences, and celebrate how much we can learn from one another.

TEACHING FOUND ME: A BRAZILIAN STORY OF LEARNING AND BECOMING

Fabiana Diniz Kurtz

I grew up in a small town in southern Brazil, the daughter of a divorced mother who worked as a federal civil servant and raised two children on her own. Our life was modest; money was often scarce, but there was always discipline, perseverance, and love. From an early age, I learned that independence and education were the only reliable paths toward a different future. My mother always made sure of that. She never studied beyond the fourth grade, yet her handwriting remains the most beautiful I have ever seen.

To be honest, in my teenage years, choosing a profession felt like choosing a destiny. In my city, entering a federal university was the only viable way to build a stable career. Yet, the competition for admission was fierce, and my family could not afford private education. Like many Brazilian middle-class families, ours believed that careers such as Medicine or Law guaranteed both prestige and financial security, especially during the 1990s. Teaching, on the other hand, was seen as a noble but poorly rewarded calling. I never imagined myself as a teacher - at least not until my early twenties, when life itself redirected my path.

Coming from public schools whose instruction was strong yet not enough to secure admission in competitive exams, I faced several disappointments. After two unsuccessful attempts at the entrance exams for Law and Medicine, I had to confront reality and myself. That was a turning point. What could I study that would still open doors, connect to my interests, and perhaps allow me to work soon? I had always admired the English language - its rhythm, its possibilities - and was fascinated by how people could connect through it. I often watched movies and listened to music with my mother; looking back now, I realize how profoundly those evenings shaped my choices. Then, almost by chance, I applied for a degree in Portuguese and English Studies (Letras – Português e Inglês). To my surprise, I was accepted among the top candidates. In retrospect, that moment changed everything.

Discovering meaning in the unexpected

During my undergraduate years, I received a research scholarship that allowed me to work closely with my professors - and to help with household expenses as well. My supervisor was a nationally recognized scholar in Applied Linguistics, and under her mentorship I discovered that research could be as creative and transformative as teaching itself. During that time, I attended conferences, read voraciously, and learned that behind every lesson there is theory, design, and intention.

However, university life was not always peaceful. I also witnessed competition, vanity, and favoritism among colleagues. I believe that such a meaningful experience taught me early that knowledge and generosity do not always walk together. Still, I stayed. I learned to navigate these contradictions and to hold on to what truly mattered: curiosity, ethics, and empathy.

After completing my Master's in Linguistics - ranking first in my field and second overall, a result not necessarily celebrated by all - I began teaching as a substitute lecturer at my own university, while also working part-time at a private institution and several language courses. Ironically, I often found myself teaching in the very franchises whose pedagogical models I questioned - experiences that later motivated me to leave that commercial world and devote myself to education as a social practice. Eventually, I passed every public-service exam I applied for, and soon I was teaching at the very institution that once seemed out of reach. Two decades later, many colleagues have become lifelong friends. I love what I do, and I love the university where I belong.

Teaching and technology: learning to mediate

Over the years, my career evolved alongside profound transformations in Brazilian education. I earned my Doctorate in Education and later a Post-Doctorate in Scientific and Technological Education. I also spent time abroad - in Lisbon, through a national doctoral sandwich fellowship, and in Latvia, through the Erasmus+ teaching mobility program. Most recently, I was awarded a Fulbright Visiting Researcher grant - a rare and deeply meaningful milestone in my academic journey. These international experiences widened my view of education as a global, dialogical, and profoundly human endeavor.

My research has always revolved around one central question: How can technology serve learning without dehumanizing it? I have drawn upon Vygotsky's historical-cultural theory, particularly his concepts of mediation, scaffolding, and the Zone of Proximal Development. These ideas have helped me understand that technology is not the center of the learning process - people are. Tools, even artificial intelligence, are extensions of human intention and creativity. In my view, the teacher remains the heart of education – building relationship with and among students, where meaning is negotiated and knowledge is built collaboratively.

This belief has guided every project I coordinate, from teacher-training initiatives to digital-literacy observatories. I see the classroom - physical or virtual - as a living organism, constantly reshaped by its participants. A class is never merely a transmission of content; it is an encounter of histories, emotions, and worldviews.

Lessons from the classroom

If there is one lesson my students have taught me, it is that teaching is not about control - it is about presence. Students rarely remember perfect slides or grammatical explanations; they remember how you made them feel capable of thinking and expressing themselves. In Brazil, where inequalities remain vast and access to quality education is still uneven, every classroom is a microcosm of society. We face outdated curricula, low salaries, and the persistent misconception that teaching is a natural gift rather than a profession - an idea that sustains low remuneration and weak social recognition. Even so, we keep going, because we know that without teachers there is no democracy, no cultural continuity, and no future.

I often remind my students, future language teachers, that the classroom is not a stage where teachers perform but a laboratory of life where everyone experiments with meaning. This belief was reinforced during a class in an undergraduate English teacher-education course, when a heated discussion emerged between students with different levels of oral proficiency. Some of the more fluent speakers began to dominate the interaction, turning the activity into an implicit competition. I paused the class, redesigned the task, and invited students to reflect on how language can function as power. What began as tension became a collective learning moment. From that episode, I learned that teaching is not about displaying expertise, but about creating conditions in which all voices can legitimately emerge. Over the years, I have seen brilliant students struggle with insecurity, and others once labeled "weak" blossom when given the chance to speak. These transformations reaffirm my conviction that education is, above all, a process of shared becoming.

In contrast, another recurring experience reminds me why I remain deeply committed to teaching. Over the years, I have witnessed students from economically disadvantaged backgrounds, often with limited prior exposure to English, excel through creativity rather than formal accuracy. I remember a student who struggled with grammar but produced a multimodal project combining images, music, and personal narrative with remarkable sensitivity and originality. That work moved the entire class. It taught me that learning does not follow a single path and that creativity, when valued, can become a powerful form of resistance against educational inequality. From this experience, I learned that the role of the teacher is to recognise potential where traditional metrics fail to look.

Remaining human in a technological world

Today, as digital tools and artificial intelligence reshape the way we teach and learn, I sense both fascination and fear among my colleagues. Some believe technology will replace us; others resist it altogether. Personally, I believe the truth lies somewhere in-between. AI can process data, simulate dialogues, and even generate content, but it cannot feel compassion, build trust, or read the unspoken emotions of a student. Those capacities - empathy, ethical judgment, intuition - remain uniquely human.

This is why teacher education must evolve. We need to prepare educators who understand not only how to use technology but also why and when to use it. In my courses and research groups, I encourage pre-service and in-service teachers to reflect critically on their digital practices - to see technology not as a threat but as a cultural artifact to be interpreted, reimagined, and humanised.

Choosing again

Looking back, I realise that I did not choose teaching - it chose me. It entered my life through detours, disappointments, and serendipity. Yet if I could go back in time, I would make the same decisions all over again. Teaching gave me not only a career but also a lens through which to see the world - a world where knowledge is not a possession but a relationship.

Yes, the challenges remain: low salaries in basic education, precarious working conditions, and the persistent under-valuing of the profession. But teaching continues to be essential because learning is, above all, a human act. Knowledge does not exist without mediation, and mediation requires presence - someone who listens, questions, and believes in the learner's potential.

Education will always need technology, but technology will always need educators. Ultimately, it is through teachers that humanity translates its knowledge, emotions, and hopes into forms the next generation can understand and renew.

I became a teacher almost by accident, but remaining one has been a deliberate and passionate choice. Teaching, to me, is not simply a profession - it is a way of existing in the world, of building bridges between what is and what could be.

Looking toward the future of the teaching profession, I believe that our greatest challenge will be to remain human in increasingly complex, technologized, and unequal educational contexts. Teachers will continue to navigate tensions between innovation and tradition, efficiency and care, performance and meaning. In this landscape, our professional identity is constituted by multiple forms of knowledge - pedagogical, disciplinary, and technological - which shape how we design, mediate, and interpret learning experiences. Yet, despite the growing centrality of digital tools, I am convinced that teaching will endure as a relational, ethical, and profoundly transformative profession. What sustains education is not the tool, the platform, or the curriculum alone, but the teacher's capacity to listen, to mediate conflicts, to recognize invisible talents, and to believe in learners even when they doubt themselves. The future of teaching, in my view, depends less on mastering every new technology and more on cultivating wisdom, empathy, and critical hope.

REFERENCES

Brazil. Presidency of the Republic, Civil House, Sub-Chief of Legal Affairs (1988). *Constitution of the Federative Republic of Brazil.* Retrieved from https://www.planalto.gov.br/ccivil_03/constituicao/constituicao.htm

Brazil. Presidency of the Republic, Civil House, Sub-Chief of Legal Affairs. (1996). *Law No. 9,394, of December 20, 1996 (Law of Guidelines and Bases of National Education – LDB).* Retrieved from https://www.planalto.gov.br/ccivil_03/leis/l9394.htm

Brazil. Presidency of the Republic, Civil House, Sub-Chief of Legal Affairs. (2004). *Provisional Measure No. 213, of September 10, 2004 (PROUNI Program).* Retrieved from https://www.planalto.gov.br/ccivil_03/_ato2004-2006/2004/Mpv/213.htm

Brazil. Presidency of the Republic, Civil House, Sub-Chief of Legal Affairs. (2007). *Decree No. 6,096, of April 24, 2007 (REUNI Program).* Retrieved from https://www.planalto.gov.br/ccivil_03/_ato2007-2010/2007/decreto/d6096.htm

Brazil. Presidency of the Republic, Civil House, Sub-Chief of Legal Affairs. (2009). *Constitutional Amendment No. 59/2009 – Establishes compulsory schooling from ages 4 to 17.* Retrieved from https://www.planalto.gov.br/ccivil_03/constituicao/emendas/emc/emc59.htm

Brazil. Presidency of the Republic. Civil House. Sub-Chief of Legal Affairs. (2014). *Law No. 13,005 of June 25, 2014: Approves the National Education Plan (PNE 2014–2024).* Retrieved from https://www.planalto.gov.br/ccivil_03/_ato2011-2014/2014/lei/l13005.htm

Brazil. Presidency of the Republic, Civil House, Sub-Chief of Legal Affairs (2015). *CNE/CP Resolution No. 2/2015: National Curriculum Guidelines for Initial and Continuing Teacher Education.* Retrieved from https://www.gov.br/mec/pt-br/cne/resolucoes/resolucoes-cp-2015

Brazil. Presidency of the Republic, Civil House, Sub-Chief of Legal Affairs. (2018). *National Common Curricular Base (BNCC).* Retrieved from https://basenacionalcomum.mec.gov.br/

Brazil. Presidency of the Republic, Civil House, Sub-Chief of Legal Affairs. (2022). *Complement to the National Common Curricular Base: Computing.* Retrieved from https://www.gov.br/mec/pt-br/escolas-conectadas/BNCCComputaoCompletodiagramado.pdf

Brazil. Presidency of the Republic, Civil House, Sub-Chief of Legal Affairs. (2023a). Instituto Nacional de Estudos e Pesquisas Educacionais Anísio Teixeira (INEP). *Resumo técnico do censo escolar 2020-2023 [In Portuguese: Basic Education Census 2020-2023. Technical summary.* Retrieved from DOI: 10.56238/sevened2024.031-083

Brazil. Presidency of the Republic, Civil House, Sub-Chief of Legal Affairs. (2023b). *LAW No. 14,533, OF JANUARY 11, 2023. National Digital Education Policy (PNED).* Retrieved from https://www.planalto.gov.br/ccivil_03/_ato2023-2026/2023/lei/l14533.htm

Brazil. Presidency of the Republic, Civil House, Sub-Chief of Legal Affairs. (2024a). *CNE/CP Resolution No. 1, of January 2, 2024.* Retrieved from https://www.in.gov.br/en/web/dou/-/resolucao-cne/cp-n-1-de-2-de-janeiro-de-2024-541121652

Brazil. Presidency of the Republic, Civil House, Sub-Chief of Legal Affairs. (2024b). *CNE/CP Resolution No. 4, of May 29, 2024.* Retrieved from https://www.in.gov.br/en/web/dou/-/resolucao-cne/cp-n-4-de-29-de-maio-de-2024-555507198

Costa, M. C. S., Farias, M. C. G., & Souza, M. B. (2019). *A Base Nacional Comum Curricular (BNCC) e a formação de professores no Brasil: retrocessos, precarização do trabalho e desintelectualização docente* [In Portuguese: *The National Common Curricular Base (BNCC) and teacher education in Brazil: Setbacks, work precarization, and the disintellectualization of teaching].* Retrieved from https://periodicos.uff.br/revistamovimento/article/view/32665

da Silva, D. R., Kurtz, F. D., & Pansera-de-Araújo, M. C. (2024). *A metacognição e o pensamento computacional na perspectiva histórico-cultural de Vygotsky* [In Portuguese: *Metacognition and computational thinking in Vygotsky's historical-cultural perspective].* Retrieved from https://ojs.upf.br/index.php/rep/article/view/15264

Kurtz, F. D., & da Silva, D. R. (2023). *Amplitude conceitual acerca do ensino híbrido na educação brasileira: inovação, modalidade ou "nome fantasia"?* [Conceptual amplitude of hybrid teaching in Brazilian education: Innovation, modality, or a fantasy label?]. Revista Insignare Scientia., Retrieved from https://periodicos.uffs.edu.br/index.php/RIS/article/view/13160

Kurtz, F. D., Silva, D. R., & Krajka, J. (2021). Rethinking innovation in education from a cross-cultural perspective: The role performed by digital information and communication technologies (DICT) in pedagogy change. *Humanidades & Inovação, 8*(1), 114–131. Retrieved from https://revista.unitins.br/index.php/humanidadeseinovacao/article/view/4869

Kurtz, F. D., Silva, D. R., & Pansera de Araújo, M. C. (2024). *Teacher knowledge: Insights for continuing education in Southern Brazil.* Retrieved from https://doaj.org/article/f3c8fed9277340b79278e8cdf1a7f49e

OECD. (2023). *PISA 2022 Results (Volume I): The State of Learning Worldwide.* Retrieved from https://www.oecd.org/pisa/publications/pisa-2022-results.htm

OECD. (2024). *Education at a Glance 2024: OECD Indicators.* Retrieved from https://www.oecd.org/education/education-at-a-glance/

Oliveira, D. A., & Leiro, A. C. R. (2019). *Políticas de formação docente no Brasil: referências legais em foco [In Portuguese: Teacher training policies in Brazil: legal references in focus].* Retrieved from https://www.scielo.br/j/pp/a/R3qWFzj9Kjcztng7YgJtwxc/?format=pdf&lang=pt

Santos, L. L. C. P., & Diniz-Pereira, J. E. (2016). *Tentativas de padronização do currículo e da formação de professores no Brasil [In Portuguese: Attempts at standardizing curriculum and teacher education in Brazil].* Retrieved from https://www.scielo.br/j/ccedes/a/SqHHMdWVCV9Fwpgq4GRnb7B/?lang=pt

Todos Pela Educação. (2023). *Brazilian Education Yearbook 2023.* Retrieved from https://todospelaeducacao.org.br/

UNICEF. (2021). *Out-of-school children in Brazil: A warning about the impacts of the COVID-19 pandemic on education.* Retrieved from https://www.unicef.org/brazil/media/14881/file/out-of-school-children-in-brazil.pdf

Chapter 5
Teachers' Voices From Colombia

Ruth Monica Allen
http://orcid.org/0009-0001-0567-5002
The Columbus School, Colombia

Alejandra Villa Galvis
The Columbus School, Colombia

Andres Julian Zuñiga Tirado
http://orcid.org/0009-0008-0704-1864
The Columbus School, Colombia

ABSTRACT

This chapter presents an overview of education in Colombia by situating current systems, policies, and practices within their historical, legal, and socio-economic context. It traces the development of education from pre-colonial community-based learning and Catholic-influenced formal schooling to the contemporary framework established by the 1991 Constitution and the General Education Law of 1994. The chapter describes the structure of the school system, teacher education pathways, assessment and accountability mechanisms, and recent reform initiatives, while identifying ongoing challenges related to inequality and uneven implementation. It concludes with personal narratives from three educators, illustrating diverse professional pathways and providing practical insight into how national policies related to areas such as bilingual education, assessment, school climate, and technology integration are enacted in school contexts.

AN OVERVIEW OF EDUCATION IN COLOMBIA

Education in Colombia is defined by the Ministry of Education as a "permanent process of personal, cultural, and social formation, grounded in a comprehensive understanding of the human person, including dignity, rights, and duties" (Republica de Colombia, 1994, art. 1). The aims of education, as set out in this foundational law, include the holistic development of the individual and the formation of citizens who value human rights and democratic participation. In addition, the law establishes that education should foster critical and creative capacities, promote scientific, technical, and cultural knowledge, and prepare individuals for meaningful participation in economic and social life through work.

This definition offers a helpful way to understand education in Colombia today, as it shows that national priorities have long gone beyond academic achievement to include moral development and responsible citizenship. However, the extent to which these aspirations have been translated and continue to be translated into practice is shaped by a long-standing context of social and economic inequality. According to the OECD (2024: 1), Colombia continues to exhibit high levels of income inequality, significantly higher than the OECD average. This pattern of inequality is reflected in educational outcomes, with OECD analyses of education in Colombia (2023; 2024: 1) showing that socio-economic background remains a strong predictor of student performance.

DOI: 10.4018/979-8-3373-8983-7.ch005

Historical background

Before the colonial period, the societies that inhabited what is now Colombia organized education as an integral part of everyday life rather than through formal systems of schooling. Knowledge was transmitted through social practice and valued not on an individual basis, but as the expression of cultural knowledge that sustained community and a sense of shared identity (Reichel-Dolmatoff & Reichel-Dolmatoff, 1961). As Flores (2018) note, many of the indigenous communities in Colombia today continue to transmit cultural knowledge orally through participation in social life, rituals, and community practices.

Formal education, understood as the establishment of schools as distinct institutions, did not begin in Colombia as a state project but as a religious one. During the colonial period (1500-1810), schooling was largely controlled by catholic religious orders and oriented toward the formation of obedient subjects and moral Christians (Helg, 2001). The dominant role of the church established cultural expectations about schooling that persists to the present day, including an emphasis on strong moral expectations and the idea that education is as much about character formation as it is about academic learning.

New educational ideals were introduced after independence in the 19th century. Leaders of the new republic recognized that it was necessary to prepare students to be effective citizens, skilled workers, and good Catholics. Subjects such as "reading, writing, arithmetic, and grammar", were emphasized together with "religion, moral education, and civic instruction" (Helg, 2001: 37). However, the emerging republic lacked both the funds and the institutional strength to fully separate the state from the church. Despite various reforms, the constitution of 1886 reinforced Catholicism as at the heart of national life and stated that public education should be organized and directed in accordance with the Catholic religion (Helg, 2001). As a result, while the responsibility for education was increasingly shared between the church and the state, moral authority remained anchored in catholic values.

Increased urbanization and social change in the early 20th century created pressure for a more technical approach to education with a view to better preparing the workforce for economic development. While the church remained highly influential in public schooling and continued to focus on social order and moral education, the need to form the individual as a contributor to economic productivity became increasingly important (Cifuentes Medina & Camargo, 2016). The authority and influence of church gradually diminished as the state expanded public schooling, modernized teacher training, and promoted scientific and technical knowledge. Helg (2001) argues that this tension between the church and the state was a significant factor in the evolution of a dual public and private education system, which persists to the present day. State schools serve the majority of the population and are tasked with guaranteeing universal access and coherence across diverse regions. Private schools, many of them religious in nature, operate with greater autonomy, and are often associated with tradition, prestige and the formation of moral character.

The constitutional reform of 1991 marked a decisive turning point by redefining education as both a fundamental right and a public service (Cifuentes Medina & Camargo, 2016). This constitutional shift placed education within a democratic framework, explicitly recognizing the rights of children and ethnic minorities and establishing educational provision as a shared responsibility of the state, society, and the family. The subsequent General Education Law (República de Colombia, 1994, Law 115) reinforced the parallel public and private system, with private institutions being granted broad autonomy in pedagogical orientation and curriculum, provided they complied with national standards. Significantly, ethnoeducation was recognized as a distinct educational approach. Education for ethnic groups was no longer to be considered an adaptation of mainstream schooling, but a model that "respects and develops their cultural identity, language, traditions, and forms of social organization" (República de Colombia, Law 115, art. 55).

CURRENT SITUATION

The structure of schooling

The structure of formal schooling in Colombia is defined by the General Education Law (República de Colombia, 1994, Law 115) and is organized into pre-primary, basic education, and upper secondary education. Pre-primary education typically serves children aged 3 to 5, while compulsory education spans ages 5 to 16 and includes basic primary education (grades 1–5) and lower secondary education (grades 6–9). Upper secondary education (grades 10–11) culminates in the bachillerato, the national school-leaving qualification that enables entry into higher education as well as technical and vocational pathways.

Alongside this national structure, there are a number of international schools that operate parallel systems aligned with European or North American educational models. While these institutions operate within Colombian regulatory frameworks, they typically extend upper secondary education to age 18, leading to internationally recognized qualifications such as the US High School or the International Baccalaureate Diploma.

Similarly, the education system in Colombia operates under two academic calendars: Calendar A, which runs from January to December, and Calendar B, which runs from August to July. While public schools follow Calendar A, many private schools follow Calendar B, reflecting their alignment with European and North American academic cycles.

In terms of instructional time, students in Colombia receive approximately 1,000 hours of compulsory instruction per year in primary education and 1,200 hours in lower secondary education, exceeding the OECD averages of 804 hours and 909 hours, respectively (OECD, 2025: 1).

Teacher training

Teacher training in Colombia has developed through two main pathways. Teachers may enter the profession either through university-based education programs or through the Escuelas Normales Superiores (OECD, 2016). The Escuela Normal Superior usually begins training students during the last year of secondary school and continues with post-secondary teacher preparation focused mainly on early childhood and primary education. In contrast, university programs train teachers only at the higher-education level and place more emphasis on academic disciplines and educational theory alongside pedagogy. This dual system has helped expand the teaching workforce and ensure coverage across the country, including rural and disadvantaged areas. However, it has also led to differences in the content and quality of initial teacher training, as well as uneven levels of professional recognition and career opportunities (OECD, 2016).

Alongside the national training pathways, the Colombian education system also incorporates international teachers, particularly in private bilingual and international schools. According to Bettney (2022), international teachers are most commonly recruited to teach through English and to support international or foreign curricular frameworks, and their inclusion is often linked to schools' bilingual or global profiles. In practice, this results in differentiated professional roles, with international teachers typically associated with English-medium instruction and Colombian teachers more closely linked to Spanish-language subjects and the national curriculum.

Teacher salaries

School teacher salaries in Colombia vary notably by sector and institutional context. Public-sector teachers are paid according to nationally regulated salary scales linked to qualifications, years of service, and merit-based progression (monthly average: US$500-1,350) (Glassdoor, 2026). The OECD (2016) observed that policies such as merit-based recruitment, as implemented in 2005, were aimed at strengthening the teaching profession in Colombia. However, the studies of these hiring reforms show that although new recruitment mechanisms succeeded in attracting candidates with stronger academic profiles, they also resulted in a significant loss of experienced teachers, with unintended negative consequences for student learning outcomes (Busso et al., 2024).

In contrast, private-sector schools set salaries independently, leading to greater variation across institutions. Within the private sector, particularly in bilingual and international schools, there is frequently an additional distinction between national and international teachers. According to Bettney (2022), international teachers are often employed under separate contractual arrangements, and these contracts may include higher salaries or different benefit structures than those offered to Colombian teachers working in similar roles.

The average lecturer university gross annual salary in Colombia is $ 59,000 or an equivalent hourly rate of $ 28 (SalaryExpert, 2026).

Assessment and accountability

From the early 2000s onward, reforms strengthened Colombia's capacity to define and assess learning outcomes through national standards and large-scale testing systems. Curriculum guidelines were closely aligned with external assessments, most notably the Pruebas SABER, creating a coherent framework for measuring student learning. At the primary and lower secondary levels (Saber 3°, 5°, and 9°), the tests were designed to assess foundational competencies and to identify gaps within and across schools. At the upper secondary level, the Saber 11 test serves as a high-stakes assessment required for high school graduation and may be used for university admissions, scholarships, and institutional comparisons. SABER 11 results are also used to assign official performance categories to schools, which are widely reported in national media through rankings and league tables. These classifications shape public perceptions of quality and, particularly for private schools, may have financial implications, as tuition increases are often linked to performance categories established by education authorities.

In parallel, Colombia participates in international assessments such as PISA to benchmark national performance. While the 2022 results show some long-term progress in mathematics and reading, overall achievement remains below OECD averages, and performance is closely related to socio-economic background (OECD, 2023).

Overall, these national and international assessments reflect a results-focused approach to education, with evaluations being used to promote accountability, enable comparisons, and identify differences across schools and student populations.

Convivencia

Historically, an orderly school climate in Colombia was closely associated with discipline, obedience, and respect for authority. Historical research shows how disobedience was "managed, curtailed, and even suppressed through threats, intimidation, and punishment" (Loaiza Zuluaga, 2013, p. 24), reflecting a disciplinary model grounded in authority and coercion. This approach was closely linked to the traditional maxim *"la letra con sangre entra,"* which translates literally as "learning enters through blood", a widely cited expression used to justify harsh disciplinary practices (ibid, 2013:23). Subsequent research on school climate in Colombia acknowledged that punitive, rule-based disciplinary approaches fell short, generating resistance and negativity rather than meaningful socialization (Valencia Murcia & Mazuera, 2006). This led to calls for a more formative, values-based model of discipline, and resulted in a national framework of *"convivencia"* that protects children's rights and is designed to ensure that responses to conflict, bullying, and school violence are preventative, pedagogical, and restorative rather than sanction-driven.

"*Convivencia*" is often translated as "coexistence" or "living together," but in the Colombian educational context, it refers more broadly to the quality of relationships and everyday social life within a school community. Schools are expected to develop a Manual de Convivencia (Guidebook of behaviour) that offers clear guidance on promoting positive relationships, managing conflict, and creating a respectful and participatory school climate. Within this approach, conflict is not seen as a breakdown of school order, but as a formative and pedagogical opportunity that can be addressed through dialogue, negotiation, and recognition of difference (Miranda Medina et al., 2022).

More recently, increasing concern about students' mental health has shaped how *"convivencia"* is understood and put into practice in schools. Current research highlights the importance of developing students' social and emotional skills as a key part of a positive school environment, placing socio-emotional learning at the core of school life (Martínez et al., 2024). At the same time, recent Colombian legislation recognizes socio-emotional education as an essential part of students' overall development and makes its implementation a legal requirement for schools.

Inclusion

Post-1991 policies for inclusion (Republica de Colombia, 1996 and 2017) expanded access for students with disabilities and special educational needs within mainstream schooling. While these reforms redefined diversity as a structural feature of the education system, they also exposed gaps in teacher preparation, as educators were increasingly required to address complex learning needs without consistent training in inclusive pedagogical practices. Inclusion became not only a question of access and rights, but also a pedagogical challenge (UNESCO, 2020). In the recent OECD TALIS

2024 report, 65% of teachers (similar to the OECD average of 62%) felt that they are capable of designing learning tasks to accommodate the special educational needs of students (OECD 2024:2).

Bilingual education

Bilingual education in Colombia can be traced to the early 20th century, when a small number of private schools, often founded by foreign communities or inspired by international educational models, introduced instruction in another language (most commonly English) as well as Spanish. These early bilingual initiatives were largely concentrated in the private sector and became closely associated with elite education, access to international universities and global cultural capital (De Mejia, 2002). Over time, English–Spanish bilingualism came to dominate the bilingual landscape, reinforcing distinctions between private bilingual schools and the largely monolingual public education system. De Mejía (2002) argues that this historical pattern positioned bilingualism not as a universal educational right, but as a differentiated resource, unevenly distributed across socio-economic contexts.

In the early 2000s, the Colombian state began to pursue a more equitable system-wide approach to bilingual education. The Ministry of Education launched the National Bilingual Program (Republica de Colombia, 2004) with the aim of extending English language learning into public education and framing bilingualism as a driver of educational quality and national competitiveness. This program sought to establish national standards, teacher development initiatives, and proficiency targets aligned with international frameworks. However, limited oversight and uneven funding structures resulted in inconsistent implementation and inequalities in learning across the country (Bettney, 2022; Cardona-Escobar et al., 2023).

Alongside its global focus on English, Colombia's education system also has a distinct linguistic responsibility related to the education of indigenous populations. According to Cely Betancourt et al. (2023), there are 68 indigenous languages spoken across different regions of the country. The 1991 Constitution introduced ethnoeducation as an approach intended to preserve these languages, along with community knowledge and culturally grounded curricula. However, Cely Betancourt et al. (2023) indicate that as a result of the more consistent policy, attention and support given to Spanish–English bilingualism, Spanish–English bilingualism has become more visible and socially valued, whereas other forms of bilingualism, particularly those involving indigenous languages, have remained largely invisible and undervalued (Cely Betancourt et al., 2023; Bettney, 2022; de Mejía, 2020).

Technology

From the late 2000s onward, digital technology became an explicit focus of educational reform in Colombia, with policies prioritizing access, digital content development, and teacher professional development (Departamento Nacional de Planeación [DNP], 2020). These priorities were shaped in part by persistent inequalities in digital infrastructure, which required policy attention on connectivity and basic use. Unfortunately, despite overall improvements, inequalities in access have remained. In 2023, 90% of students in private schools had internet access at home, compared with only 68% of students in public schools (Vanegas-Giraldo, 2025).

Studies of technological education in Colombia, including those by Cárdenas Salgado (2012) and Velasco Sánchez (2024), indicate limitations in that policies have tended to emphasise the development of skills for the use of existing tools, rather than on fostering the creative and critical capacities needed to generate innovative technological solutions. This approach differs from wider national and local efforts to promote innovation outside the school system. In Medellín, for example, initiatives such as Ruta N have focused on supporting entrepreneurship, research, and technological innovation through collaboration between universities, industry, and government. Schools, however, have often been only marginally involved in these efforts, creating a gap between broader innovation strategies and the role of schools in building the foundational skills and mindsets that support those strategies.

In 2025, in response to advances in artificial intelligence (AI), the government introduced a National Policy for Artificial Intelligence (Departamento Nacional de Planeación [DNP], 2025). This policy acknowledges ongoing inequalities in access to technology and reliable connectivity, while also emphasizing AI's potential to support national development. Importantly, it represents a positive shift beyond a purely technical focus by incorporating ethical considerations into its framework. However, research indicates that teacher preparation remains a key constraint on the meaningful and equitable use of AI in education, demonstrating that even in schools with adequate connectivity, many teachers lack the training and institutional support needed to integrate AI in transformative ways (Vanegas-Giraldo, 2025). This is reflected in the fact that while 53% of teachers in Colombia report having used AI in their work, 80% of this use is limited to lesson planning and activity design rather than its use for pedagogical innovation (OECD, 2025: 2).

CONCLUSION

Helg (2001) observes that educational reforms in Colombia have often been additive rather than transformative, with new policies and programs layered onto existing structures without fully addressing underlying inequalities or institutional capacity. Indeed, despite successive reform efforts, persistent gaps in learning and equity remain evident (OECD, 2023). In a similar way, de Zubiría Samper (2013) argues that meaningful educational change is unlikely to emerge from the accumulation of reforms alone, and that true transformation will depend on sustained pedagogical development and attention to the conditions that support learning.

These perspectives point to the importance of examining the underlying structures that shape educational practice, rather than relying primarily on the accumulation of new reforms. Current discussions of educational change, including those related to technology, increasingly emphasize that sustainable improvement depends on strengthening the human and relational foundations of teaching and learning. As UNESCO (2023) notes, educational innovation should support but not "supplant the human connection on which teaching and learning are based" (p. v). This position is fully aligned with the Colombian Ministry of Education's definition of education as grounded in a comprehensive understanding of the human person (República de Colombia 1994) and suggests that Colombia already has the educational vision and principles needed to support meaningful educational change. The central task lies in ensuring that this vision and these principles are translated into practice in ways that are consistent, equitable, and effective throughout the country.

AI tools were used to support Spanish - English translation and to enhance the readability of this manuscript. The author retains full responsibility for the content, interpretation, and final wording of all sections.

Teaching is About Learning how to Reach Others

I am not descended from teachers. In fact, my father, one of four boys who went straight from an all-boys naval school into the Royal Navy often said that his two greatest fears growing up were teachers and women. Somewhat ironic, then, that he went on to have four daughters, all of whom, at one point or another, have become educators.

It wasn't until much later in life that I understood how my father´s experience of school had shaped his outlook and, as a result, my own. He spent his formative years on *The Mercury*, a naval training establishment moored on the River Hamble in the UK. Life on board was strict and often unforgiving. It was a hard education, designed to instill discipline, but it also bred a sense of responsibility, resilience, and self-control. Thankfully, my own upbringing was gentler, though it was not without echoes of that world. My sisters and I were taught the value of self-discipline and respect for authority, the importance of being outdoors, and the significance of a well-kept routine. Books were encouraged, television was rationed (it would rot our brains, we were told) and learning itself was treated as a privilege.

My earliest memories of my own schooling belong to the 1970s, a time when education in the UK was experimenting with "child-centered" and progressive approaches. In the hands of the right teachers, this meant freedom. At primary school, we mixed oil and water in glass jars, puzzling over why they refused to blend, and spent afternoons testing, wondering and discovering. Learning felt like play, and curiosity was not only encouraged, but expected.

Secondary school, however, was a different story and the experimentation gave way to routines, rules and an expectation of compliance. Ours was a largely vocational school and most of my classmates were destined for the local shipyard. The focus was on passing exams and getting the right qualifications. In some subjects, such as English and the humanities, curiosity still had a small place, but in others such as math and science, the focus was mainly on memory and tests. I was told it didn´t matter if I didn´t understand something so long as I could remember it for the test. On the whole, I did what I was told, followed the rules and tried not to stand out.

As a teenager, my need to belong began to overshadow my desire to learn. I was shy, eager to please, and terrified of drawing the wrong kind of attention. When being good at something made me different, I pretended not to care, downplayed effort, and faked indifference. It worked, at least on the surface. I belonged but, in the process, I stopped pushing myself. My curiosity was replaced by compliance. The cost of that choice came at the end of secondary school. My school leavers' certificate described me as someone who would "*float unhurriedly through life*." It was meant to be gentle, but it felt judgmental. On top of that, my final exam results were a disappointment, and my father's silence when he read them was harder to bear than any reprimand. He didn't need to say a word, his expression said enough. That moment, quiet, painful, and private, was the turning point.

For the first time, I felt the sting of failure not as shame but as something else, a challenge. I realized that the comfort of fitting in had cost me the satisfaction of achievement and I began to study again, to reclaim the curiosity I had once taken for granted. Looking back, I see now that this was my first real lesson in learning: that growth rarely happens without discomfort, and that failure, faced honestly, can become a catalyst for progress.

At university, where I studied English Language and Literature, the world opened up. Here, once again, learning wasn't about memorizing or repeating, it was about thinking. I began to see that meaning wasn't something handed down from authority but was something constructed through close attention and analysis. I learned to listen for my own response, to trust my instincts, and to defend an interpretation not because it was right, but because it was mine. That shift, from imitation and repetition to analysis and authenticity, was pivotal. It was here, without realizing it, that the foundation of my philosophy as an educator began to take root. I came to understand that the learning is not about transferring knowledge, but about giving others the confidence to form their own ideas and gain an understanding of the world around them.

After completing my undergraduate studies, I went into teaching, for the most part, I must admit, because I loved words. I loved the rhythm of language, the richness of literature and the way stories could open new ways of seeing. I wanted to share this, and I imagined classrooms filled with discussion and discovery but my experience as a student teacher swiftly brought me back to reality. I spent hours preparing each lesson and would arrive early, armed with carefully designed handouts and high hopes. Within minutes, though, many of my lessons would fall apart. What I had imagined as a lively discussion would dissolve into silence, blank faces, or sniggers that spread from one corner of the room to the other. Sometimes, an activity that I thought would fill the entire period was completed in minutes, leaving me wracking my brain for what to do next. Those early months were exhausting, but they reinforced that teaching was not about showcasing what I knew, but about learning how to reach others.

After qualifying as a teacher, one of my first roles was in a large secondary school. Nothing in my teacher training had prepared me for the sheer intensity of it all, the constant demands on time, the need to shift gears from teaching energetic eleven-year-olds to skeptical sixteen-year-olds, to earnest 18-year-olds. The range of teachers I worked with was also as varied as the students. At one end were those who seemed to have given up entirely, reading the newspaper at their desks while chaos unfolded around them. At the other were the strict disciplinarians, with sharp voices and rigid rules. Both extremes seemed to leave little room for learning, one through neglect, the other through fear.

Somewhere between the two, I noticed a different kind of teacher, the ones whose classrooms were filled with quiet purpose and whose students respected them without being afraid. There was structure, but also a sense that relationships drove the learning. They didn't raise their voices, but they were listened to and respected. I soon realized that what looked effortless was anything but. Behind that calm confidence lay careful planning, consistent routines, and, most of all, genuine respect for the students in their care. Watching them, it became apparent that control achieved through fear is temporary while respect built through relationship endures.

Following this, I took on a series of short-term substitute teaching roles. This was a different kind of experience, one that demanded flexibility, humility and a sense of humor. Each morning brought a new classroom, a new set of names to learn and a new group of personalities to get to know. I would walk into rooms where no one knew me and where respect wasn't assumed but had to be earned, every single day. There were moments of quiet triumph, a lesson that caught fire in all the right ways, and the occasional one that caught fire rather more literally (thankfully I wasn't asked to pay for the damage). In those transient classrooms, no two groups ever responded the same way. It was clear that being a good teacher wasn't a constant you carried with you, it was something you had to rebuild, again and again in different contexts and circumstances. Those months of walking into unfamiliar classrooms, of negotiating new dynamics each day, became the best possible preparation for what was to come.

When I moved to Colombia, I thought I was bringing experience and, in many ways, I was. My experience in unpredictable classrooms had taught me to slow down, pay attention, and build trust gradually. Still, nothing could have prepared me for just how different it would feel. The language was new, everyday life was unfamiliar, and the culture of schooling, though wrapped in the same familiar words, was very different.

On paper, the curriculum was recognizable with the same types of learning objectives and assessments but beneath the surface, the dynamics in the classroom diverged. Where in England I had struggled to draw students out into discussion, in Colombia the challenge was the opposite. Silence was rare, not because students were driven by academic passion (although sometimes they were), but because they were endlessly social. They would ask personal questions, tell stories, and try to make me part of their world. It was charming, disarming, and at times exhausting to keep them on task and I learned that maintaining focus in Colombian classrooms required a different kind of approach. More so than in the UK, teaching and learning were profoundly relational. Students needed to feel seen and understood, to sense that their teacher cared about them before they would fully engage as learners.

What I found most difficult to adjust to, however, was not the students themselves, but the way the education system operated. In the UK, progression from one grade to the next is automatic, and teacher assessments are used mainly to indicate progress toward external examinations rather than as formal records that affect university entry. In contrast, in Colombia, like the US, student promotion depends directly on teacher grades and internal evaluations play a significant role in determining whether students advanced or repeated a year. This made me much more aware of the responsibility I carried as a teacher and led me to reflect on some common assumptions about schooling, particularly in terms of whether a grade can fully represent a student's skills and abilities or how far we can expect students to learn within the same time scale. Gradually, I became more aware of how strongly educational structures shape students' experiences, and how frequently compliance is equated with learning or progress.

Teaching in Colombia also showed me that education is as much a reflection of culture as it is of curriculum. I had arrived as a teacher, but I became a learner again, grappling with new paradigms and perspectives. The distance between teacher and student in this school was diminished. It was normal for students to call teachers by their first name, and to speak using an informal, conversational tone rather than a hierarchical one. It wasn´t enough just to be the adult in the room to have authority, instead authority had to be earned through respect and the development of positive relationships. In this, language was both my bridge and my barrier. I taught in English, but each lesson required translation, not just of words, but of meaning, tone, and intent. A single mistranslation could derail a poem or shift the nuance of a discussion entirely. I spent as much time learning from my students as they did from me.

When I became Head of Year at the school, a role responsible for the social and emotional wellbeing of a group of students (akin to a dean of students), Colombia was living through turbulent times. Violence was not a daily reality for us, but it was always present in the background and that year, seven students in my cohort lost their parents, some through natural causes, others under more violent circumstances. I attended every one of the funerals. Each one left a mark but also revealed something I hadn't expected. The school was clearly a refuge, a place where the routines of lessons and daily rituals offered a fragile but vital sense of normality. In a country where things could change overnight, the predictability of school was a kind of anchor. We began each day not pretending that everything was fine but choosing to carry on together. What struck me most was the sense of community. In England, grief had often been private and contained but here, it was collective and visible. When tragedy struck, people didn't retreat behind closed doors, they gathered and shared their feelings. Emotion was not seen as weakness but as proof of care, an act of solidarity. During that year, I learned that teaching is as much about presence as it is about pedagogy. The continuity of showing up each day, the lessons, the greetings at the door, the structure of the day, became its own form of resilience. The school's strength lay not in shielding students from the world, but in helping them face it together.

After several years in Bogota, I moved to Cartagena. Though it was the same country, it was an entirely different world, moving from the cool mountains to the heat of the Caribbean. The Colombian coast carries its own rhythm. Music and dance are never far away and the culture is even more open and expressive. While time seems slower, the energy can be higher, and the heat reflected in the warmth and generosity of the people.

The school where I worked lay just outside the city, surrounded by open fields and low trees. It was never quiet. We taught with windows open to the heat, our voices competing with the sounds of nature, the hum of ceiling fans, and the distant whir of old air conditioners. It was exhausting, and sustaining focus was never easy. The students brought with them the same coastal energy, expressive, and endlessly social, however, by mid-morning, concentration would drift and at times, lessons felt like an act of endurance. I learned to adapt, to shift lessons into shorter bursts, and to use stories and conversation to pull their attention back to the task at hand. Teaching required patience, persistence, and imagination, a constant balancing act between the climate and the classroom.

It was in this school that I first stepped into administration, becoming the Academic Coordinator for the implementation of the IB Middle Years Program (MYP), a program designed to promote interdisciplinary learning and to connect subjects through broader, conceptual understanding. Doing so demanded balance between structure, flexibility, control and creativity. Coordinating the MYP meant helping teachers see links between disciplines, encouraging collaboration, and translating ideals into daily practice. It was, at times, hard to encourage teachers to move away from the silo of their own subject area towards more collaborative learning structure but once they were there, the benefits were clear and there was no going back.

After this experience, I became a head of school, at another school in La Guajira, no longer directly leading the learning in the classroom but orchestrating the learning environment and looking to impact student growth from a more strategic perspective. Being a head of school, gave me increased access to and understanding of what is often referred to as the "educational eco-system" in Colombia. Although ours was a private school, we were still subject to the same laws and regulations as other public schools in the country. This could sometimes be frustrating, particularly in terms of internal assessment systems designed to support student learning and external testing systems designed as indicators of school quality. As a graduation requirement, all students must take what is known as the Test of knowledge (Prueba Saber). To give some context, this is a test of endurance, an eight-hour exam with multiple-choice questions on a range of subjects. While designed as a system for quality control of schools and used by some universities as a filter for entrance, its real significance was given by the media who would take the results of these exams and produce league tables of the "best" schools in the country. The temptation was, of course, to focus on exam preparation and it took a leap of faith to maintain the focus on learning skills rather than going through drills.

La Guajira was probably the place where the inequalities within Colombia were most apparent. The school and its community were inside what can only be described as a "bubble", air-conditioned, comfortable and organized in a way that most of the schools in the area could never achieve. As a private school we were rich in resources, while public schools in the area struggled to maintain staff, to stock libraries or to introduce technology. Theirs was a completely different world.

I saw the power and potential of bringing these different worlds together during a chance encounter on a local beach. My parents were visiting from the UK, and we were sitting by the sea when a young boy approached us barefoot, selling mango from a small tray. My father, always curious, began practicing his Spanish with him. Before long, they were kneeling in the sand, my father drawing coastlines with a stick and turning the beach into a simple map of the world to show where we had come from. The boy listened closely, asking questions as he followed along. I watched them from a short distance, two people from very different backgrounds sharing a brief but meaningful moment. It reminded me how much potential exists when people are given the chance to learn, connect, and imagine beyond their immediate context, and of the responsibility we carry to recognize and nurture that potential when and where we can.

So, while I did not come from a family of teachers, perhaps that is why I became one. Whether in the England or Colombia, teaching, for me, has never been about authority or expertise; it has been about curiosity, about discovery, about learning how to listen and how to see the world through others' eyes.

Back to the Classroom: my Journey Toward the Essence of Teaching

I never imagined that the place where I learned cognitive and emotional skills, so crucial for life, would also be the stage where I would discover my true vocation and passion. The school where I attended and that saw me grow up since I was four years old, that space full of laughter, fears, learning, friends, and memories, opened its doors to me again, this time not as a student, but as a teacher and lifelong learner. Sometimes I think life was preparing me, without me knowing it, to return to this place, with a different perspective, and with more love and interest in learning than ever.

I am the only child of a second marriage, I have eight half-siblings, where my nephews seemed more like my siblings and my siblings seemed more like my uncles. Since an early age, I have been surrounded by different personalities, ages, and perspectives, which in a way helped me understand the importance of communication and empathy.

My father, due to his work and profession, had to offer speeches or transmit information in the manner of a discourse to different audiences. I was fortunate enough that he took me with him to some of these, I always admired his way of captivating, involving, and inspiring people, with what he said and how he said it. Being very young, I understood that I had a sensitivity to easily read body language and read the emotions of others. For this reason, what my father did as part of his job caused a great positive impact on me. Thanks to this, years later I understood the importance of assertive communication and how there are other ways to communicate differently than speaking or writing, but by feeling and observing.

My mother is a deeply sympathetic person and has always shown herself to be full of joy. She enjoys music and dancing with a sincere passion, just as my father did. I definitely inherited that sensitivity to rhythm and art from both of them. When I was younger, it was very easy for me to learn a song and immediately capture its beat to dance to it. Dancing has been part of my life since I can remember. I also played the piano for a few years. Perhaps because of that, or perhaps because that is how I was raised at home, today I feel that my senses are especially active and connected to my inner self. My hearing, my voice, my sight, and my touch have become channels through which I perceive, remember, and feel the world with an intensity that, I am sure, is also a legacy from my parents.

When I was in the second grade at school, in the year 1986, I remember, and not with much happiness, the teacher I had back then. Unfortunately for me and for her, most of my memories are not very positive, because we were children seven to eight years old and we were in a crucial stage of development. This teacher did not have the slightest intention of knowing us as people, as human beings, she was only interested in us always following her great and selfish ego. If we didn't do it the way she thought it should be... TTAAAZZZZ the ruler sounded against the desk. You might think that those times were in the past where teachers punished their students with "humiliations," but no, this teacher still applied these "educational" methods toward her students. I was afraid to participate, she blocked my thoughts, I did not develop my potential that school year because of a disconnection with my teacher. Thanks to her, I learned what a teacher should definitely not be or do and what they should not fail to do.

I remember a teacher I had in the sixth grade with great affection and appreciation. My memories of her, more than my academic learning that school year, are the way she took the time to get to know her students as individuals. She knew what examples and connections to make between academics and our experiences, and everything definitely made more sense. In this particular class, I did not feel afraid to participate, nor to present my ideas, nor to make mistakes, because I knew there would be no repression for my errors, but rather more opportunities for growth. From her, I learned to see my students not only as learners but as integral humans.

I am fortunate to have studied at a school that offers us infinite opportunities to develop and enhance our skills. As you may have read, since an early age my senses have been very connected. We had a theater and choir group focused on musicals. For me, this moment was the most wonderful part of the day, because I could be on stage, dancing, singing, communicating, and transmitting emotions. Being an only child, as can happen to many of us who grew up in this position, I grew up being a little introverted, but not shy, and I realized I wasn't shy thanks to my theater and choir teachers, and I value this with great affection.

With all this, it might seem that I am a teacher of some artistic discipline, but that is not the case. When I entered university to study Law, my educational and personal process took an unexpected turn. This career demands abundant reading, memory, critical thinking, argumentative capacity, and, above all, the ability to defend ideas with foundation. That complemented the aspects I already recognized in myself, such as sensitivity, deep interpretation, and the ability to see beyond the superficial. During this time, I learned to be more disciplined and to cultivate a true love for reading. As the years passed, I understood that this was not the profession I wished to pursue, although I continue to thank my teachers for converting such literal and theoretical legal content into meaningful, and sometimes even fun, learning experiences. Although there were times when theory was inevitable, when applying and transferring knowledge, teamwork became fundamental. From this process, I take an invaluable lesson: no matter how serious or complex a topic is, it is always possible to teach it in a creative, humane, and empathetic way.

My path to teaching was not planned. I have a degree in marketing and advertising. For several years, I worked in the world of marketing and advertising, a vibrant environment, full of creativity and competition. It was a stimulating world, where I learned about communication, strategy, and human relations. I liked the energy of creating, of connecting with people through ideas and messages. However, although I enjoyed what I was doing, I felt that something inside me was not complete. There was professional satisfaction, but not fulfillment. Over time, I understood that, although my career offered me many opportunities, my heart longed for something deeper, something that would connect me with the purpose of serving, contributing, and transforming.

It was one of those coincidences that seem to be written into life that changed my destiny. One day, unexpectedly, I was called by the school where I graduated and where my eldest daughter graduated and my son still studies, to substitute for a kindergarten teacher. I accepted without imagining that, that day would mark a before and after in my professional history. I clearly remember that first day, the nerves of entering the classroom, making sure I remembered everything in the teacher's plans, and putting my second language, English, back into practice. Looking back, I think it was the perfect opportunity for me to realize that this was my passion. I entered the room and the curious eyes of four-year-old boys and girls marked me; they looked eager to know, understand, and comprehend what I was doing there and why their teacher wasn't. When I started explaining to them, I felt the appropriate words flowed for interacting with these students. Then, since it was their English class, I had to read a book and sing a song that went with it to them in English. I took advantage of the moment to put my creative communication into practice and did an artistic presentation (at least, I see it that way) for this lesson, I spoke, danced, and sang, with the result that I made the students part of the "show". I knew that the kinesthetic element was fundamental for learning. Thus, the objective was achieved, which was for the students to name body parts in their second language, English. While I spoke with them and felt their curiosity and energy, I had a certainty that this is what I want to do for the rest of my life. That day I knew I had found my place.

That is how I began my studies to certify myself as a teacher, and subsequently, I pursued a Master's degree in Educational Sciences. I believe that teaching is a gift that some of us possess, but also a responsibility that requires permanent training and recognizing ourselves as lifelong learners. In the educational institution where I currently work, there are multiple opportunities to participate in committees that work to make the school's mission a reality. I have been part of several of them, experiences that have enriched my professional development and allowed me to contribute to our community from my own perspectives.

We know that, as teachers, we are permanent learners. Theory is fundamental, so that we can later adapt it to our reality and our educational environment. For this reason, certifying myself as a *Teacher Leader* has also been a crucial step in my professional growth. The world is constantly changing and, for this reason, we must stay updated in this marvelous science that is education.

Educating is an ART - it requires all our creativity to motivate and connect with students and make processes dynamic and even personal. When we are teaching, we put on our best performance to keep our audience captivated. As artists, we are sensitive; we must be able to read glances that go beyond the surface, glances that communicate when they fail to understand a topic or an idea, or when they have an unexpressed feeling. We must be ears that listen to silences that say more than any word, and narratives that propose, transmit, and affirm learning.

Although my two worlds, marketing and education, seem distant, today I know they are more connected than I imagined. In marketing, I learned the power of communication, listening, and empathy. I learned to recognize that every message needs to understand the other person to make sense. I transfer that same idea to my daily life as a teacher. Communicating is not just speaking, it is also understanding, listening, observing, and building bridges from the intangible to the tangible. These bridges are not limited only to the classroom, they also extend to families. Over time, I have learned that a fundamental part of the educational work is strengthening the bond with parents. They are not a third party or external observers, they are our most indispensable allies. When the family and school walk hand in hand and work as a team, the educational process becomes more powerful and more coherent. All my previous training has helped me build that relationship of trust. Assertive communication, learned in my advertising years, has become an essential tool for working with my students' families. Listening, guiding, recognizing, and validating their emotions creates the foundation of a solid relationship. In elementary education, where children are still forming their identity, this alliance is invaluable. The child who feels coherence between what is taught at home and what is experienced at school. What better teaching than coherence?

Throughout these years, I have been constructing a teaching philosophy. I firmly believe that educating is not just teaching how to read, write, or add. Those are merely the visible and tangible means. True education occurs when we help students think, understand, connect, and, above all, be good human beings. Educating is forming integral, empathetic, and reflective people, beings capable of solving problems, however simple they may seem. Teaching, then, is not just educating, but accompanying in the task of being.

I have witnessed that when a teacher manages to connect emotionally with their students, the transformation is profound. That connection is what converts teaching into a meaningful experience. It is not about being perfect or having all the answers, but about showing ourselves to be authentic, allowing ourselves to feel, and building trust. Teaching is an act of love toward humanity. Having the disposition to look at the other, to accompany them, to believe in all their potential. When a student feels that their teachers believe in them and get to know them, everything changes, fears disappear and the desire to learn emerges. Believe me, this is also reflected in academic result, in my case, for most of the years I have been teaching, the data shows that my students have had significant growth. In that process of accompanying, we, teachers, also transform. Every student who passes through my classes teaches me something new: patience, humility, creativity, and respect. They remind me that education is a constant exchange and that, in reality, we are all learners.

Education is also creating community. The most powerful learning occurs when respect, teamwork, and a sense of belonging are built. From the first day of class, I work with my students to create and generate an environment where everyone feels included, where they understand that we are a team or like a family, and that respect is the basis of everything we do. We create our rules together, we talk about the importance of asking for forgiveness, of being thankful and educated, and of listening to each other. I do not seek for my students to only be academically good, but that they be good companions, that they learn to coexist, to be empathetic. I have verified that when the classroom becomes a community, fear disappears. Children dare to make mistakes, to ask questions, to think differently. In that climate of trust and belonging, the most genuine learning arises.

The physical space also teaches. I like the place where we learn to be cozy, organized, and full of meaning. An organized classroom inspires tranquility and respect, transmitting the silent message that what we do here matters. When students participate in the care of the space, they learn responsibility and a sense of belonging. Although they may not consciously perceive it, a structured and aesthetically pleasing environment strengthens their executive functions, helping them to organize, plan, and take care of what belongs to everyone.

In a time characterized by rapid technological advancement, which significantly influences learning and interpersonal dynamics, the fundamental importance of human connection endures. After fourteen years as a teacher, I believe teaching remains a profoundly human act, centered on accompanying, inspiring, and growing alongside students. The essence of education, the physical encounter cannot be replaced by digital tools, critical elements like the comforting word, shared laughter, and the glance that conveys confidence are irreplaceable. Consequently, regardless of technological innovation and artificial intelligence, the purpose of educators is to safeguard the vitality of human relationships.

Artificial intelligence (AI) is now integrated into daily life and is rapidly gaining presence within the educational system. I do not see or feel AI as a competitor, I consider it a vital partner and ally, a tool necessary for advancement. Specifically, AI offers transformative potential for inclusion in an increasingly diverse world by facilitating the personalization of learning experiences for all students. In a world characterized by the immediate and abundant availability of information, the educator's role must be redefined. Our primary duty shifts to guiding students to become critical thinkers who are both ethical and responsible in their use of information and acquired knowledge. Ultimately, core human attributes like intuition, emotions, moral judgment, and the essential bond between student and teacher are beyond the scope of AI. Therefore, the path forward requires learning to coexist with AI, ensuring it remains a service tool for humanity.

I know that everything I have written about education and being an educator sounds very romantic, but I always try to look at the glass as half-full. Of course, we must be sincere, there is also the half-empty part of the glass. There are moments where you question if you are doing things right. The "I wish I had" plays a large part in your thoughts, where the behavior and educational processes of some students make you think that you definitely don't want to continue doing this and exhausting yourself emotionally and physically, because yes, teaching requires all your physical and emotional energy. There are times when administrative work requires an investment of time that you don't have when you should be attentive to the education and lives of a number of students, and also when there are families that make you question your abilities and knowledge. When you start on this path of education, it takes a while to find that balance between your personal and professional life, since most of the time we have to take work home, carry students who are in difficult processes in your thoughts, and your personal life is almost secondary. But those of us who love this profession manage to find that balance, that is for sure!

Fourteen years after that first day as an educator, I continue to feel just as fortunate. Every morning, waking up, I feel happy knowing that I am going to dedicate the day to something I am passionate about, something that fulfills me not only professionally but also spiritually. Being a teacher has allowed me to look at life with more calm and more gratitude. Furthermore, my school has a special meaning, it was my home as a student, it is today as a professional, and also as a parent. Sometimes, when my children ask me why I enjoy teaching so much, I tell them that in the same place where they received their first academic education, I also did, and that just like them who are full of dreams, I also dreamed of being many things. I tell them that life, with its wisdom, brought me back here to show me my purpose. I tell them that the greatest learning is that vocations are not always sought out or what you thought they were; sometimes they just find us, and when that happens, everything makes sense. Today I know that teaching is my way of contributing to the world.

Walking through the school, among the laughter of my students, fills me with happiness. I feel that everything fits, the student, the mother, and the teacher that I am, intertwined in the same purpose. Teaching has brought me back to my essence, it has taught me to look with compassion, to listen with patience, and to believe in the power of small things. Every time a class ends and a student smiles at me, I confirm that I chose well.

The Human Spark: An Autobiography of Connection and Transformation

My name is Andrés Julián Zúñiga, and I am 43 years old. My education journey, however, did not begin as a planned endeavor. It unfolded naturally, almost accidentally, driven by circumstance and, ultimately, sustained by an unexpected calling. Today, after 22 years in the classroom, I recognize that teaching is the profession that truly fulfills me, offering a boundless adventure in every class. This path has taught me that education is the most powerful tool for humanizing individuals, transforming lives, and ultimately re-dignifying the role of the teacher in society.

I come from a family rooted in teaching. My mother dedicated her life to the craft and is now a retired teacher from the Colombian public education system, known as the 'magisterio'. For her, teaching was not merely a job; it was her vocation and her passion. My father, too, was a teacher for many years. Yet his story holds a bitter element of disappointment. He became discouraged with the financial realities of being an educator, specifically the meager pay, and eventually ceased teaching altogether, changing his occupation. This contrast, the enduring passion of my mother against the profound disappointment that drove my father away, was the backdrop against which I eventually made my own choice.

My initial direction was entirely different. I pursued and completed a degree in Electronic Engineering and began working in a car manufacturing company. When I finally decided to become a professor, my mother, perhaps recalling the difficulties my father had faced, was skeptical. She did not believe I could find complete fulfillment or successfully carry out my life's work as a teacher. How wrong she was, and how grateful I am that she underestimated the capacity of this profession to satisfy the deepest needs of the soul. Twenty-two years later, I stand firmly convinced that teaching was my best decision.

The actual start of my teaching career was born out of a transitional period. After living in the United States for about ten years, my family and I returned to Colombia. My father, in conversation with a lady he drove to the airport, learned of an opening: they needed an assistant in a classroom. The ideal candidate needed to be polite, responsible, caring, and, crucially, fluent in English. I was given the opportunity to serve as a teacher assistant in an English as a Second Language classroom.

This seemingly minor role provided enormous advantages. By observing the mechanics of the classroom and the strategies that proved successful, I began to acquire the tools necessary to develop into a teacher rich in alternatives for delivering lessons. The combination of my practical classroom experience and my engineering background began to shape a teaching philosophy centered on innovation and real-world application.

The blend of Electronic Engineering and technological innovation, with the fundamental need to empathize and connect with students quickly, became my hallmark. My objective every day is to show students that truly wonderful things are possible when they seize ownership of their learning. When learning becomes engaging, pleasant, and clearly serves a future purpose, it becomes empowering.

My career trajectory has been varied, providing a panoramic view of the educational landscape. I began by teaching mathematics to second-grade students, then moved to fourth grade. Later, I taught calculus in upper high school. I spent time as a professor of basic sciences at the university level. Finally, I returned to school as a high school pre-engineering teacher.

This diverse experience solidified my vision: What is education for? Why do we teach? The answer, without a doubt, is to humanize every one of our students. To humanize them means ensuring that everything we do in the classroom is geared toward improving the quality of human life, regardless of the specific occupation or path they choose.

Students approach learning with varied motivations. Some view education through the lens of entrepreneurship. Others are simply curious about knowledge itself. Still others are motivated by the desire to 'do'; to create, to apply skills. And then there are students who, at any given moment, are not connected to the information we are trying to convey. This disparity in connection cannot, however, lead to frustration or defeat for us, the educators. It must never create barriers to continuing our mission. Recognizing this reality is part of what makes teaching challenging but infinitely rewarding.

One of the greatest joys of my professional life lies in witnessing the profound transformation education offers, particularly when opportunities are extended to those who might otherwise be overlooked. My experience leading extracurricular projects - specifically in robotics and technological innovation allowed me to meet students driven by powerful internal motivation. These students registered for these projects because they were genuinely interested in topics like robotics, programming, or mechanical design. They were captivated by these subjects.

It was within this context that I had the privilege of meeting a young man named Jairo. Jairo became a crucial member of the robotics team. His participation was made possible by a scholarship from the 'Argos Group', a major Colombian cement company. This scholarship enabled him to fully participate in the robotics project. At the time, Jairo was just 12 years old, and his fascination with technology was contagious, in a word, incredible. Jairo's family background provided an unusual, yet potent, starting point for his technological curiosity: both of his parents were recyclers. They often received discarded appliances, some electronic and other mechanicals. Jairo had the extraordinary advantage of being able to take these devices apart, attempting to figure out what had gone wrong with each one. This practical, hands-on disassembly was his introduction to the world of technology and electronics, and it generated immense satisfaction for him.

I had the opportunity to spend a significant amount of time with Jairo. He possessed an insatiable hunger for depth; whenever I mentioned a new topic, he wanted to explore it further, understand the 'why', and immediately find ways to apply it. Jairo's mind worked by connecting the dots, trying to integrate them into a complete picture. My role was simple yet vital: I was the professor who helped him keep motivated so that he could construct his own knowledge. Unfortunately, his parents passed away, and he was stranded with a distant sibling. This did not by any means deter him from pursuing his personal pursuit of success. He completed his high school years and, due to his excellent reputation, was granted a full scholarship at a very well-known university in Medellín. Not long after, he worked his way to become the university's international ambassador. He traveled to countries and recruited students for this university. He now owns an important technological startup for hospitals and clinics.

Jairo's story embodies the transformative power of humanized education. He possessed the raw internal motivation and curiosity, but education provided the framework, mentorship, and opportunities (such as the scholarship) that channeled his interest into skill and achievement. A teacher is fundamentally a guide, a scaffold, intended to empower students to take command of their own learning.

The modern educational landscape has shifted dramatically. Years ago, a teacher might have hoped to impart much of the available knowledge; today, that is impossible. Our function has evolved. Students have moved past the role of passive receptors of information; they are now eager to collaborate and create innovative solutions for real-world problems.

This evolution brings profound joy. The greatest rewards I have found in life flourished from education: the satisfaction of providing exemplary and excellent instruction, the ability to meet diverse people, and the chance to share with individuals from different cultures, countries, and languages. Education fosters meaningful and intelligent debates in which individuals form well-argued opinions.

These deep, intellectual conversations are not dictated by our job titles or our societal positions; they are accessible to everyone through the shared pursuit of knowledge. I live it every day at the teacher's lounge. The question sometimes arises: Why do we do what we do? Why choose this path, especially when the payment structure might echo the disappointment my own father felt? We choose it not merely for the abstract concept of vocation, but for connection. We are human beings whose role is to connect not just people to each other, but knowledge to a specific purpose.

For some people, the thrill, the adrenaline, might be found in extreme sports or high-speed racing. For me, the adrenaline surge, the true sense of professional reward, comes at the end of a class when a student says, 'Wow, today was really a spectacular class, and this is going to stay with me'. That feedback - that visible spark of comprehension and empowerment in the student's eyes - is the real satisfaction of a teacher. It is the feeling of being motivated every day to step into the classroom.

This internal reward is what re-dignifies the profession, elevating it far beyond the constraints of salary or public perception. It's a job where we are paid in epiphanies, in moments where potential is unlocked, and where connections are shielded.

In my journey, there have inevitably been many mistakes and continuous opportunities for learning. But having the opportunity to create significant learning experiences for my students over the years has solidified my path. I believe, with absolute conviction, that I will never stop being a teacher. Even if circumstances prevent me from standing in a physical classroom, I hope that life grants me the continued chance to keep motivating others and to keep lighting that essential spark in my students' eyes.

Whenever we sit down with students and engage in discussions about knowledge and life, we are fostering that crucial connection. Though I perhaps didn't fully anticipate the deep reflection and difficulty of this task when I began this autobiography, I know that the rewards of seeing a life transformed by learning like Jairo's, or countless others who have discovered their entrepreneurial spirit or their intellectual curiosity, make every challenge worthwhile.

Teaching is not merely delivering content; it is about building a bridge between the students' current reality and their future potential, using empathy, innovation, and connection as the primary construction materials. It is the purest form of human endeavor, creating better human beings and, consequently, improving the quality of life for all.

Note: AI tools were used to support Spanish - English translation and to enhance the readability of this manuscript. The authors retain full responsibility for the content, interpretation, and final wording of all sections.

REFERENCES

Bettney, E. (2022). Examining hegemonic and monoglossic language ideologies, policies, and practices within bilingual education in Colombia. Íkala. *Revista de Lenguaje y Cultura*, *27*(1), 249–270. DOI: 10.17533/udea.ikala.v27n1a12

Busso, M., Brutti, Z., & Sánchez Torres, F. (2024). Teacher hiring reforms and student outcomes: Evidence from Colombia. *Journal of Public Economics*, *233*, 104727. DOI: 10.1016/j.jpubeco.2024.104727

Cárdenas Salgado, E. D. (2012). El camino histórico de la educación tecnológica en los sistemas educativos de algunos países del mundo y su influencia en la educación tecnológica en Colombia [In Spanish: The historical path of technological education in the educational systems of some countries of the world and its influence on technological education in Colombia]. *Informador Técnico*, *76*, 108–123. DOI: 10.23850/22565035.35

Cardona-Escobar, E., Barnes, M., & Pruyn, M. (2023). The enactment of the Colombian National Bilingual Program: Equal access to language capital? Profile: Issues in Teachers'. *Professional Development (Philadelphia, Pa.)*, *25*(2), 95–110.

Cely Betancourt, B. L., Zea Jaimes, K. D., Bohórquez Quesada, L. M., & Gil Rodríguez, E. D. (2023). Reflections on the role of indigenous languages in the context of bilingualism policies in Colombia. *Ciencia Latina: Revista Científica Multidisciplinar*, *7*(6), 2497–2516. DOI: 10.37811/cl_rcm.v7i6.8872

Cifuentes Medina, F., & Camargo Silva, A. (2016). La historia de las reformas educativas en Colombia [In Spanish: The history of educational reforms in Colombia]. Cultura. *Educación y Sociedad*, *7*(2), 9–28.

De Mejía, A.-M. (2002). *Power, prestige and bilingualism: International perspectives on elite bilingual education*. Multilingual Matters. DOI: 10.21832/9781853595929

De Zubiría Samper, J. (2013). *Cómo aprender mejor: Educación para el desarrollo de la inteligencia* [In Spanish: How to learn better: Education for the development of intelligence]. Cooperativa Editorial Magisterio.

DNP Departamento Nacional de Planeación. (2020). *Política de integración de tecnologías digitales en el sector educativo (CONPES Documento No. 3988)* [In Spanish: Policy for integrating digital technologies in the education sector]. Gobierno de Colombia.

DNP Departamento Nacional de Planeación. (2025). *Política Nacional de Inteligencia Artificial (CONPES Documento No.4144)* [In Spanish: National Artificial Intelligence Policy]. Gobierno de Colombia.

Flores, H. (2018). Cultural and intercultural education: Experiences of ethnoeducational teachers in Colombia. *The Australian Journal of Teacher Education*, *43*(7), 62–81. DOI: 10.14221/ajte.2018v43n7.4

Glassdoor (2026). Teacher: Average salary & pay trends 2026 - Colombia Retrieved from https://www.glassdoor.com/Salaries/colombia-teacher-salary-SRCH_IL.0,8_IN54_KO9,16.htm

Helg, A. (2001). *La educación en Colombia, 1918–1957: Una historia social, económica y política* [Education in Colombia, 1918-1957: A social, economic, and political story]. Universidad Pedagógica Nacional.

Instituto Colombiano para la Evaluación de la Educación ICFES. (2024). Advances and challenges of the PISA 2022 assessments: Colombian students improve in mathematics and reading.

Loaiza Zuluaga, Y. E. (2013). Disciplina en las escuelas normales de Caldas durante las décadas de 1960 y 1970: Poder y autoridad para vigilar y castigar. [Discipline in normal schools from Caldas during the 1960s and 1970s: power and authority to control and punish]. *Revista Educación y Pedagogía*, *25*(65), 137–152.

Miranda Medina, C. F., Rodríguez Burgos, K. E., & Morcote González, O. S. (2022). Política pública de convivencia escolar colombiana desde la perspectiva de los docentes [In Spanish: Colombian public policy on school coexistence from the perspective of teachers]. *Justicia*, *27*(41), 13–30. DOI: 10.17081/just.27.41.5677

OECD. (2016). Education in Colombia: Reviews of national policies for education. OECD Publishing. Retrieved from https://www.oecd.org/content/dam/oecd/en/publications/reports/2016/04/education-in-colombia_g1g63511/9789264250604-en.pdf

OECD. (2023). PISA 2022 results (Volume I and II): Country notes – Colombia. OECD Publishing. Retrieved from https://www.oecd.org/en/publications/pisa-2022-results-volume-i-and-ii-country-notes_ed6fbcc5-en/colombia_dd5f34d9-en.html

OECD. (2024:1). Colombia Education at a glance 2024 country note. In Education at a glance 2024: OECD indicators. OECD Publishing. Retrieved from https://www.oecd.org/en/publications/education-at-a-glance-2024-country-notes_fab77ef0-en/colombia_0eba06c5-en.html

OECD. (2024:2). TALIS 2024 results: Colombia (Country note). OECD Publishing. Retrieved from https://www.oecd.org/en/publications/results-from-talis-2024-country-notes_e127f9e2-en/colombia_8f1df220-en.html

OECD. (2024:3). OECD Economic Surveys: Colombia 2024. OECD Publishing. https://www.oecd.org/en/publications/2024/09/oecd-economic-surveys-colombia-2024_7b382d76.html

OECD. (2025:1). Education at a glance 2025: Country note – Colombia. OECD Publishing. Retrieved from https://www.oecd.org/en/publications/education-at-a-glance-2025_1a3543e2-en/colombia_32e069b7-en.html

OECD. (2025:2). Results from TALIS 2024: The State of Teaching, TALIS. OECD Publishing. Retrieved from https://www.oecd.org/en/publications/results-from-talis-2024_90df6235-en.html

Reichel-Dolmatoff, G., & Reichel-Dolmatoff, A. (1961). *The people of Aritama: The cultural personality of a Colombian Mestizo village*. University of Chicago Press.

República de Colombia. (1994) Ley 115 de 1994: Ley General de Educación. [In Spanish: Law 115 of 1994: General Law of Education]. Diario Oficial No. 41.214. Retrieved from https://www.funcionpublica.gov.co/eva/gestornormativo/norma.php?i=292

República de Colombia. (1996, agosto 5). Decreto 2082 de 1996: Por el cual se reglamenta la atención educativa para personas con limitaciones o con capacidades o talentos excepcionales [In Spanish: Decree 2082 of 1996: Regulating educational services for people with disabilities or exceptional abilities or talents]. Retrieved from https://www.funcionpublica.gov.co/eva/gestornormativo/norma.php?i=1519

República de Colombia. (2004). Ministerio de Educación Nacional. Programa Nacional de Bilingüismo [In Spanish: National program of bilingualism]. Retrieved from https://www.mineducacion.gov.co/1621/articles-132560_recurso_pdf_programa_nacional_bilinguismo.pdf

República de Colombia. (2017, agosto 29). Decreto 1421 de 2017: Por el cual se reglamenta en el marco de la educación inclusiva la atención educativa a la población con discapacidad (Diario Oficial No. 50340) [Decree 1421 of 2017: By which the educational attention to the population with disabilities is regulated within the framework of inclusive education]. Retrieved from. https://www.funcionpublica.gov.co/eva/gestornormativo/norma.php?i=87040

SalaryExpert. (n.d.). Lecturer salary in Colombia. Retrieved from https://www.salaryexpert.com/salary/job/lecturer/colombia#:~:text=The%20average%20lecturer%20gross%20salary,an%20average%20bonus%20of%20%24%201.394

UNESCO. (2020). *Global Education Monitoring Report: Inclusion and education – All means all*. UNESCO.

UNESCO. (2023). *Global Education Monitoring Report 2023: Technology in education*. UNESCO.

Valencia Murcia, F., & Mazuera, V. (2006). La figura del manual de convivencia en la vida escolar [In Spanish: The role of the code of conduct in school life. *Revista Científica Guillermo de Ockham*, *4*(1), 119–131.

Vanegas-Giraldo, J. J. (2025). Impacto de la inteligencia artificial en la brecha educativa en Colombia [In Spanish: Impact of artificial intelligence on the educational gap in Colombia'. [RIIEP]. *Revista Interamericana de Investigación Educación y Pedagogía, 18*(2), 11–30.

Velasco Sánchez, M. (2024). Transformando la educación en Colombia: Políticas de innovación con TIC en la era digital [In Spanish: Transforming education in Colombia: ICT innovation policies in the digital age]. Discimus. *Revista Digital de Educación, 3*(1), 121–150. DOI: 10.61447/20240601/art05

Chapter 6
Teachers' Voices From Nigeria

Eseoghene Elsie Adeniji
http://orcid.org/0009-0003-8028-2617
Doyens School, Nigeria

Muazu Omeji
Nigerian Tulip International College, Nigeria

Abdulsalam Adeyemi Ahmed
Nigerian Tulip International College, Nigeria

ABSTRACT

The chapter includes the pre-colonial, colonial, and independent history and the contemporary state of Nigerian education. The structure of the educational system is revealed (pre-school primary-secondary - tertiary). Also, teacher education and development in Nigeria are presented. Literacy rates and level of education according to international assessments are discussed. Personal stories of three teachers will conclude the sub-chapter. Their views on the perspective of the teaching profession will be presented.

THE NIGERIAN EDUCATION SYSTEM AND TEACHER EDUCATION: A COUNTRY OVERVIEW

Eseoghene Adeniji

Introduction

With Nigeria being the most populous nation in Africa, it is concurrently faced with high challenges and great opportunities for its educational sector. Education plays a core role in the nation's struggle for social integration, economic development, technological advancement, and national cohesion. Given its rapidly growing and youthful population, Nigeria depends on its education system to actualize human capital, reduce inequality, and prepare its citizens for productive involvement in society.

The Nigerian education system has changed over the years in response to social change, political developments, and economic pressures. Successive governments have issued reforms to expand access, improve quality, and align education more directly with national priorities. To this end, teacher education is a major supportive subsystem within the system. Teachers translate educational policy, curricula, and reform into classroom practice; hence, their preparation and professional competencies are crucial to effectiveness in education. National policy documents consistently recognize this reality, emphasizing that educational outcomes are closely linked to the quality of teachers at all levels (Federal Republic of Nigeria [FRN], 2013).

DOI: 10.4018/979-8-3373-8983-7.ch006

This paper offers a descriptive overview of the country's system of education and teacher education in Nigeria. It thus outlines the general trend of the historical development, structure, governance, and key institutional features of the education system, with special attention being paid to the main teacher education pathways and the regulatory frameworks. Major challenges and recent reform efforts are also discussed. It, therefore, presents a general contextual reference to comparative studies, policy discussions, and academic research that may focus on education in Nigeria.

Structure and organization of the Nigerian education system

Historical context and policy evolution

The Nigerian education system has evolved through three major historical phases: indigenous, colonial, and post-independence education. Before colonial contact, the indigenous systems of education existed in various Nigerian societies. These were informal, community-based, and closely connected with cultural values, moral development, vocational skills, and social responsibilities. This was the practice wherein people learned through observation, imitation, storytelling, and apprenticeship with the end purpose of being prepared for a functional role within the community.

It was Christian missionaries, in the mid-nineteenth century, with the later support of the British colonial administration, who introduced colonial education. The mission schools concentrated on literacy, numeracy, and religious instruction, with teacher training colleges established to supply the necessary personnel for the rapidly expanding school system. But there was certain unevenness in the way this colonial policy produced educational development, with much greater expansion across southern Nigeria than in the north.

Following the 1960 independence, Nigeria took sole responsibility for education and embarked on reforms that aimed at integrating the nation and ensuring development. In 1976, the Universal Primary Education scheme was launched, being a major effort to expand access. It was followed by the adoption of the National Policy on Education in 1977, which stipulated national educational objectives and regulated the structure of the system. The NPE has undergone several revisions, reflecting changing national priorities and global trends (FRN, 2013).

The 6-3-3-4 system of education

The Nigerian education system is based on a 6-3-3-4 pattern, meaning six years in primary school, three years in junior secondary, another three years in senior secondary, and four years in higher education institutions. This structure is supposed to provide a clear guidance from basic education to the advanced levels of academic and professional training.

The Early Childhood Development and Education (ECCDE) caters for children between 0–5 years, through institutions such as crèches, nursery schools, and pre-primary classes. ECCDE is meant to prepare children to cope with formal schooling through the development of simple cognitive, social, and emotional capabilities. While ECCDE is recognized in national policy, provision is highly dominated by private operators, leading to variability in accessibility, affordability, and quality.

Primary education is to last for six years and is compulsory and free under the Universal Basic Education (UBE) programme introduced in 1999 by the government. The curriculum stresses literacy, numeracy, basic science, social studies, and moral instruction. Junior secondary education continues with the provision of pre-vocational subjects and broad academic exposure. The completion of this level leads to the Basic Education Certificate.

The three years of senior secondary education provide for further specialization in the sciences, arts, and commerce, as well as technical courses. The culmination of this program leads to the Senior Secondary Certificate Examination, conducted by such bodies as the West African Examinations Council and the National Examinations Council (NECO).

It targets universities, polytechnics, and colleges of education. This prescribes that universities will be emphatic on academic and professional degree programs, the polytechnics on technical and vocational, while colleges of education focus on teacher education. Despite this structured framework, implementation challenges persist due to funding constraints, regional disparities, and infrastructural limitations, particularly in rural and peri-urban areas (Janghorban et al., 2024; UNESCO Institute for Statistics, 2022).

Governance and quality assurance

Education governance in Nigeria is based on a federal system, with shared responsibilities between the federal, state, and local governments. It includes policy formulation, coordination, and national planning from the Federal Ministry of Education, while the state governments are responsible for managing the secondary level of education and the local governments for primary education.

Regulatory agencies coordinate quality assurance and standard-setting. The National University Commission (NUC) supervises universities; colleges of education are regulated by the National Commission for Colleges of Education (NCCE), while the National Board for Technical Education (NBTE) supervises polytechnics and technical institutions. These agencies establish minimum academic standards, accredit programmes, and monitor compliance (National Commission for Colleges of Education, 2012; National Universities Commission, 2018).

Despite these arrangements, differences in implementation and allocation of resources are still clear across the states. While decentralization fostered local participation, at the same time, this widened disparity in curriculum delivery, staffing, and infrastructure.

Education financing in Nigeria

Various governments in Nigeria, namely the federal, state, and local levels, provide finance to education, supplemented by households, communities, and the private sector. In principle, public financing of education comes mainly from government budgetary allocations, which are then apportioned to the different levels of education and among administration responsibilities. The federal government largely funds tertiary institutions and national education agencies, while state and local governments bear primary responsibility for financing basic and secondary education (Federal Republic of Nigeria, 2020).

Despite these long-standing policy commitments to education, the levels of funding have remained constrained relative to the size and needs of the system. This is because larger conditions of the macro-economy, competing development priorities, and fluctuations in government revenues underpin education budgets. Consequently, many public schools face shortfalls in financial allocations, which impact their infrastructural maintenance, availability of instructional materials, and welfare of teachers. These constraints are particularly evident in rural and underserved areas, where schools often lack basic facilities and learning resources (UNESCO, 2015).

Households play an important role in financing education through school fees, levies, and private contributions, especially at the secondary and tertiary levels. The growth in private education has also transferred some of the costs to households. Private schools and institutions of higher learning have expanded access and the diversity of provision but have raised equity concerns, with access to higher-quality institutions often linked to household income and location.

Teacher education institutions are also similarly challenged in financing. Public colleges of education and faculties of education within universities often suffer from low capital investment, less research funding, and low input in the supervision of teaching practice. In turn, such financial constraints impact staff recruitment, professional development, and overall teacher preparation quality. Those conditions notwithstanding, some institutions have tried to supplement public funding by generating revenues internally and other donor-supported projects, though these are uneven and often inadequate.

Generally, the financing of education in Nigeria mirrors the close linkage between resource availability and the quality of education. Predictable funding flows, efficient mechanisms for the allocation of resources, and enhanced financial management at all tiers of government are essential preconditions to ensure the sustainability of improvements in general and teacher education.

Teacher education in Nigeria

Historical development

Teacher education in Nigeria grew concurrently with the expansion of formal schooling. Initially, teacher preparation was left to informal apprenticeship and Grade II Teacher Certificate programmes. As the need for certified teachers grew, formal training colleges were established. The Ashby Commission of 1959 recommendations on professional teacher training led to an increase in the number of colleges of education and university faculties of education.

The National Policy on Education underscores the importance of teacher education, stating that no education system can rise above the quality of its teachers (FRN, 2013). This policy framework mandates comprehensive preparation that integrates academic knowledge, pedagogical skills, and professional ethics.

Teacher education institutions and qualifications

The institutions that are basically responsible for teacher training in Nigeria are the colleges of education. Colleges of education award the Nigeria Certificate in Education, NCE, which is the minimum qualification a person needs to teach at the junior secondary and primary school levels. Programs leading to the award of the NCE generally last for three years and combine subject specialization with professional studies and teaching practice.

The universities, therefore, offer BEd, BA or BSc in Education, and Postgraduate Diploma in Education - PGDE. These qualifications prepare teachers for senior secondary education, educational administration, and research roles. The National Teachers' Institute, NTI, provides other routes through distance learning and in-service programs, especially for unqualified or underqualified teachers.

Curriculum and teaching practice

Teacher education curricula are formulated based on a delicate balance between subject matter knowledge, pedagogical competence, and studies in general education. Representative courses include educational psychology, sociology of education, curriculum studies, assessment, classroom management, and teaching methods in the subject area.

Teaching practice is an integral part and compulsory component of all teacher education programmes. It gives student teachers hands-on classroom experience in real school settings, thus providing a practical application of the theories considered. At the same time, teaching practice is widely recognized as highly valuable, though the quality of supervision and length of placement also vary between institutions.

Professional regulation and development

The teaching profession in Nigeria is regulated by the Teachers Registration Council of Nigeria, which ensures that only qualified teachers are registered and professional standards are upheld. Continuous Professional Development is promoted through workshops, seminars, and in-service training, though these opportunities are very unequal.

Challenges facing the education and teacher education systems

Literacy rate of adult (aged 15 and above) literacy in Nigeria, according to the World Bank, was at 70.41% level (World Bank, 2024). According to UNICEF (2023), only 74% of children aged between six and eleven attend primary school, while 61 percent regularly attend it. Overall, 27% of children aged 7 to 14 have foundational reading skills, 25% have foundational numeracy skills, and only 7% of 15- to 24-year-olds have Information and Communication Technology (ICT) skills. Average teacher salaries in public schools are $650 per month (Etateach, 2024), while lecturer's average monthly salary is from $1,000 for entry-level positions to over $4,000 for top professors (Academic Jobs, 2024). The statistics differ according to public/private schools, living area and gender for schools, and higher education institution/ position at universities.

Nigeria's education system faces persistent challenges, including inadequate funding, poor infrastructure, overcrowded classrooms, and shortages of qualified teachers. These challenges are more pronounced in rural and underserved areas, where limited access to electricity, ICT, and basic facilities constrain effective teaching and learning (Janghorban et al., 2024; UNESCO Institute for Statistics, 2022).

The provision and retention of teachers continue to be a problem at all levels, especially in science and technical fields. Low salaries, limited prospects for advancement, and poor working conditions are all factors contributing to inequitable teacher distribution and attrition. Teacher education institutions have their related challenges in outdated facilities, limited research capacity, and insufficient opportunities for faculty development.

Technology and recent reform efforts

Most recent reforms have placed emphasis on review of the curriculum, integration of ICT, and enhancement of teacher professional development. The digital tool adoption and online platforms have increased access to more learning and training opportunities; however, infrastructural deficits remain a limitation to full implementation.

Technological change has increased expectations for teachers to develop digital skills and adapt to new modes of instruction. Teacher education programmes are gradually incorporating ICT training to prepare teachers for contemporary classroom environments (Ajao et al., 2023).

Conclusion

The Nigerian system of education and teacher education is a reflection of the size, diversity, and historical evolution of the country. From its colonial foundations to contemporary reforms, the system has expanded significantly in terms of access and institutional coverage, yet it continues to face persistent challenges related to quality, equity, and capacity. While the formal structure of education - from early childhood through tertiary levels - provides a clear framework for learning progression, disparities in implementation across regions, and socio-economic contexts remain evident.

Within this system, teacher education occupies a central place. The creation of colleges of education, university faculties of education, and specialist institutions like the National Teachers' Institute represents sustained national recognition of the role of teachers in educational development. Minimum qualification standards, professional registration through the Teachers Registration Council of Nigeria, and accreditation by national agencies all point toward a steadily more regulated profession. However, in areas like supply, instructional quality, and continuous professional development, there are noticeable disparities between policy intent and reality.

These continue to be shaped by resource constraints, infrastructural deficits, and uneven deployment of qualified teachers. Rapid population growth, technological change, and rising societal expectations regarding the role of education in supporting economic competitiveness and social cohesion add further complexity to these challenges. Recent initiatives do focus on digital learning, quality assurance, and professional standards, but their impact is uneven and often constrained by funding and administrative capacity.

In sum, the Nigerian education system and its teacher education sub-sector remain works in progress. Sustained attention to quality, relevance, and strengthening institutions has to go hand in hand with expanded access. A more detailed awareness of the country's educational structures, multiple approaches for preparing teachers, and binding constraints provides an essential foundation for subsequent reform efforts, comparative studies, and policy dialogue. As Nigeria furthers development through education, the effectiveness of the teacher education system is destined to be a key determinant of improved learning outcomes and long-term societal progress.

BECOMING A TEACHER – MAKING A DIFFERENCE

Eseoghene Adeniji

Although the journey started quietly and early in my childhood, I didn't actually plan to become a teacher. Growing up with a father who was a lecturer and a mother who was a teacher, learning was always around me. Our home was full of books, lesson notes, and conversations about students-some who excelled, some who struggled, and some who surprised my parents in ways no one expected. Without realizing it, I absorbed not just knowledge but also the values and habits that would later shape me as a teacher. This is where I learned how to break down ideas, explain them clearly, and see potential in people even when they didn't see these things in themselves.

A long-cherished dream of mine was to be a doctor. I loved the idea of helping people directly, of making a tangible difference in someone's life. But then, I noticed something about myself: I found joy in sharing what I knew, guiding others to understanding, and breaking complex questions into simple solutions. Watching someone's face light up when they finally understood something gave me a satisfaction that no medical career could match. Slowly, I realized my calling wasn't to heal bodies -it was to nurture minds. Teaching was where I could truly make a lasting impact.

This classroom has become my platform for building confidence, curiosity, and character. I wanted to open doors for children, help them see their potential, and give them the courage to step through. Teaching comes with immense rewards; it is pure joy to watch a child finally grasp a concept or discover a strength. However, teaching has its challenges too. Progress may be slow, some days may feel overwhelming, and not every child will respond as you might have hoped. Yet these challenges have taught me patience, resilience, and humility. They have shown me that the heart of teaching is not perfection but persistence and care.

Some experiences have deeply marked me. I remember this one girl who was labeled a 'slow learner.' She rarely believed in herself, and it showed from her work. So, I just made it my mission to show her love, celebrate her every small stride, and keep telling her that she could do it. Her confidence grew bit by bit, and so did her progress. Watching her grow into a successful learner taught me that belief and encouragement can unlock potential in ways talent alone cannot.

Another instance is about a boy who could not read at all. Many had assumed that he would always struggle, but I approached him differently. I made learning fun and approachable using the playway method: games, songs, and hands-on activities. In one week, he could read short sentences. Before long, he became one of the strongest readers in the class. His transformation reminded me that children blossom when learning is personalized, engaging, and full of encouragement.

For me, teaching is not about conducting lessons but about understanding each child, building their confidence, and enabling them to see what they are capable of. The successes have taught me to celebrate small victories, the failures to be patient and adapt. Each child I have ever taught has left an imprint on me, shaping in some way my growth and my perspective.

Through the years, I have grown not only as a teacher but also as a person. I have learned to listen deeply, approach challenges creatively, and to value progress over perfection. Teaching has taught me empathy, patience, and resilience in ways no other profession could. I find continued inspiration from the children I teach, just as I hope they are inspired by me.

I became a teacher to make a difference, and every day in the classroom reaffirms that choice. Each lesson, each challenge, and each success is a reminder that teaching is not just a profession; it's a chance to change lives, one child at a time.

I view teaching as a profession that must evolve while remaining grounded in its mission of influencing and changing lives. Teaching is an art that involves more than just imparting information; it requires talent, understanding, and a tremendous sense of accountability. A teacher today needs to be more than a teacher; one needs to be a mentor and a guide who leads children through a rapidly changing and challenging world. They help students build confidence, resilience, and the ability to think independently.

I believe the future of teaching relies on continuous growth and purposeful adaptation. Considering that learners and societies change, the teachers should be lifelong learners themselves, always refining their practice to address the challenges but preserve all those human values at the heart of education. It is through effective teaching that every child is acknowledged as an individual; above all, steady progress is valued; learning environments support curiosity, effort, and personal development.

In order for the profession to flourish, teachers must be valued, respected, encouraged, and empowered to lead and innovate. This enables teaching to make a profound difference and be a positive force for life. This view inspires me and enhances my sense of purpose. Indeed, I strongly believe that teaching is one of the most powerful professions that go beyond influencing the classroom and affect the future lives they touch.

MY 20 YEARS JOURNEY INTO THE PROPHETS' WORK: TEACHING PROFESSION

Abdulsalam Adeyemi Ahmed

As someone who has experienced the teaching profession from multiple perspectives - as a subject teacher at secondary level, as a hostel supervisor at secondary level, as a classroom teacher at primary level, and now as an administrator who has served through the ranks; Discipline master, Vice principal academics, principal for 8years. I have come to appreciate both the timeless value and the evolving challenges that define the prestige of our noble calling.

I had always wanted to be a medical doctor from my early childhood, however, the love and passion for teaching grew during my year 1 at the university while studying clinical biochemistry. I found myself teaching my mates, juniors and seniors in some courses during tutorial classes at the university.

The passion drove me to secure a teaching appointment with Hill-crest International School while still an undergraduate. After completing my university education and compulsory national youth service which was also on teaching, I secured a permanent teaching job with a French-based private secondary school in Jos, Plateau state, Nigeria.

After teaching Biology, Integrated science and Agricultural science for 4 years in Jos, I secured a teaching job with Nigerian Tulip International Colleges in Abuja, Nigeria where I have been working for 16 years now. Presently, servicing as Head of Primary Academics after raising through the ranks from hostel supervisor, biology, agricultural and integrated science teacher, Vice principal academics, first Nigerian principal for 8 years and now, in my third year as national head of primary academics at the NTIC headquarters servicing as Educational quality assurance officer.

My teaching's enduring roles from Jos to Abuja

For me, teaching remains one of the most vital professions in shaping the human mind and society's moral compass. I have been privileged to produce students who went ahead to become doctors, engineers, lawyers, or leaders in various fields of human discipline. The profession's true prestige, therefore, lies not in material reward, but in its immeasurable influence on human potential and national development.

Shifting perceptions of the teaching profession

Despite its sacred importance, the popularity of the teaching profession has fluctuated in recent years. In many societies, particularly in developing nations like Nigeria, teaching has lost some of its societal glamour due to limited financial incentives, heavy workloads, and inadequate recognition. Yet, within educational circles, the respect for committed teachers remains unshaken. This is undoubtedly true. My parents and students still hold deep admiration for me as teacher who teaches with passion, integrity, and excellence.

My view as a supervisor

From a supervisory standpoint, I managed students' hostel, prep and accommodation system for years. I observe that teachers who continuously upgrade their skills, embrace innovation, and maintain ethical standards are those who elevate the profession's image. Professional development, mentorship, and peer collaboration are key factors that helped me throughout my supervision years sustaining my dignity of teaching. As a supervisor, I celebrated excellence and promoted a culture that recognizes teaching as both an art and a science.

My personal reflection as a primary and secondary school teacher

As a primary and secondary teacher, I have always believed that prestige is earned through my dedication, empathy, and professionalism. My teacher's influence extends far beyond the classrooms - into the character, values, and future of all learners who ever stepped into my classrooms. When I teach with sincerity and purpose, I command respect and admiration, not just from students but also from my institution and my society at large.

Perspective as an administrator, discipline master, academic and principal

My academic leadership journey is one of grace not effort, privilege not entitlement, and humility not pride. As an administrator, I strongly believe that institutional support is essential in rebuilding the prestige of the teaching profession. Competitive remuneration, conducive work environments, and opportunities for career progression must be prioritized. Administrators and policymakers must communicate that teaching is not a fallback job but a front-line profession - the foundation upon which every other discipline stands.

The way forward

To enhance the popularity and prestige of teaching, there must be a collective effort to:

1. Rebrand the image of teaching as a prestigious and impactful career;
2. Encourage teacher's professionalism through certification and continuous learning;
3. Recognize and reward excellence publicly;
4. Integrate modern teaching technologies that enhance both status and effectiveness;
5. Celebrate teachers of long service in teaching with better standard of living: house, car, health/life insurance, and his children's future education.

In my view, the teaching profession will always remain the mother of all professions. While its popularity may ebb and flow with time, its prestige is eternal - grounded in the sacred responsibility of shaping lives and futures. When teachers teach with dignity, and societies value them accordingly, education becomes the strongest pillar of progress. When I think about the teaching profession, I think about purpose - not just a job, but a calling. I've had the privilege of walking this path as a teacher, a supervisor, and now as an administrator. And from each of these lenses, one truth stands out clearly: teaching remains the heartbeat of every developed society.

THE ROAD FILLED WITH CHALLENGES

Muazu Omeji

I am Muazu Omeji from Nigeria, and I have been a teacher for nearly twenty-four years, serving in schools across the northern and central regions of the country. I hold a Bachelor's, Master's, and Doctoral degree in Mathematics Education.

It is a great honor to share my journey, reflections, and insights on the teaching profession.

Growing up, teaching was the very last profession I envisioned for myself. I regarded it with a sense of disdain, seeing it as a fallback option for those who had failed to realize their true ambitions. This perception was further reinforced by the appearance and demeanor of some of my high school Mathematics teachers, which left much to be admired.

I mistakenly assumed that their attitude reflected both the subject and the teaching profession itself. Consequently, I made a firm decision never to study mathematics or consider teaching as a career. My aspiration was to study pharmacy. When I was denied admission into the program, I enrolled in a remedial course at the University of Jos, hoping it would eventually serve as a pathway to my desired field. However, upon completing the program, events did not unfold as I had anticipated - I was instead offered admission to study mathematics, the very course I had once vowed never to pursue.

However, this time, my perspective had changed. My university lecturers presented both mathematics and the teaching profession in a new and inspiring light. For the first time, I came to regard teaching as a deeply noble and highly respectable vocation.

After completing my undergraduate degree, I enrolled in a postgraduate program and took up part-time teaching jobs to support myself. At that point, teaching was more of a necessity than a passion. I moved from one school to another in search of better pay rather than purpose.

My journey took a significant turn in 2005 when I joined Nigerian Turkish International Colleges (NTIC). There, I encountered educators who viewed teaching not merely as a profession, but as a noble calling - an act of service to humanity and a force for societal transformation. Their passion was deeply inspiring. For the first time, I no longer perceived teaching as a mere accident of circumstance. Rather, I came to see it as a sacred responsibility entrusted to me.

Since then, guiding and shaping young minds has become my true vocation. I have devoted my time, energy, and personal comfort to nurturing a responsible and enlightened generation. My fulfillment now stems not from material rewards, but from the hope that one day, at least one of my students will ascend to a position of influence and serve as a catalyst for meaningful change, both in Nigeria and beyond.

Nothing brings me greater joy than witnessing the growth of my students, especially those who once struggled, as they gain confidence, excel in their chosen fields, and later return to express their gratitude. The emotional reward that comes from such moments is beyond measure - it is the very essence of the teaching profession.

Nevertheless, my journey has not been without challenges. At times, the attitudes of students, parents, and even society have deeply eroded my sense of worth. Many students see teachers as little more than servants; some parents equate our value with the fees they pay; and society often relegates us to the status of second-class citizens – people to be pitied rather than respected.

In Nigeria today, teachers are undervalued and looked down upon. In short, perpetual struggle and poverty now define the teaching profession. It is not uncommon for people to respond with pity rather than admiration when they learn that one is a teacher.

I recall a painful personal experience during the COVID-19 pandemic, when public transportation was scarce. A junior police officer, who used his motorcycle for commercial purposes, offered me a ride from AYA to Tipper Garage in Abuja. Upon the arrival, I offered to pay the fare, but he had no change. As I searched for some, he called out to me and asked,

"Oga, where do you work?"
"I teach at a nearby school," I replied.
"Teacher?" he repeated.
"Yes," I confirmed.

Immediately, he started his motorcycle and rode off, refusing to collect the fare. In that moment, I felt a deep sense of worthlessness - as though, in his eyes, a teacher was too poor to be charged a fare.

Another painful memory dates back to 2007 and 2008, when one of my students, Henri Aniobi, won gold medals at the Pan African Mathematics Olympiad in Côte d'Ivoire and Tunisia. He later represented Nigeria with distinction, earning two bronze medals at the International Mathematics Olympiad in Argentina and the Netherlands. Despite these remarkable achievements, neither Henri nor I received any form of recognition from government officials - not even a handshake or a letter of commendation.

This, unfortunately, is the harsh reality faced by many Nigerian teachers. I often hesitate to discuss our salaries, as doing so only deepens the sense of despair. In truth, even unskilled laborers live far more comfortably than qualified, dedicated teachers. It almost feels as though the system is designed to keep educators in perpetual struggle and obscurity.

Broadly speaking, there is a widespread misconception about teachers and the teaching profession - that teachers merely transmit information, a task that machines can now perform. This notion, however, is deeply flawed. Teachers do far more than convey knowledge; they shape lives. We nurture young minds intellectually, morally, and socially. While technology can deliver information, it cannot cultivate empathy, instill values, or build character. It cannot discern a child's silent struggles or tailor instruction to individual needs. Only a teacher can!

Technology may enhance education, but it can never replace the transformative power of human connection—the very soul of teaching.

No matter how advanced technology becomes, teachers will always remain the heartbeat of education. We are not merely producing knowledgeable students; we are cultivating responsible, empathetic, and visionary leaders - the true foundation of every thriving society.

In conclusion, teaching found me when I least expected it. What began as a reluctant journey has become my life's purpose. Though the road has been filled with challenges, I remain proud and steadfast in this calling.

When all is said and done, teachers are not just workers, we are builders of nations.

REFERENCES

Academic Jobs. (2024). *University salaries in Nigeria: Detailed guide & insights for all higher ed jobs.* Retrieved from https://www.academicjobs.com/ng/salaries

Ajao, Q. M., Oludamilare, O., & Sadeeq, L. (2023). Drivers of mobile payment acceptance: The impact of network externalities in Nigeria. *OAlib, 10*(6), e10240. DOI: 10.4236/oalib.1110240

Etateach (2024). *Teacher salaries around the world 2024.* Retrieved from https://etateach.com/teacher-salaries-around-the-world-2024.html

Federal Republic of Nigeria. (2013). *National policy on education* (6th ed.). NERDC Press.

Federal Republic of Nigeria. (2020). *Education sector analysis.* Federal Ministry of Education.

Janghorban, P., Sesan, T., Salihu, M.-K., Ohunakin, O., & Chinichian, N. (2024). Willingness to pay for an electricity connection: A choice experiment among rural households and enterprises in Nigeria. *arXiv Preprint,* arXiv:2407.15757v1.

National Commission for Colleges of Education. (2012). *Minimum standards for Nigeria certificate in education.* NCCE.

National Universities Commission. (2018). *Benchmark minimum academic standards for education.* NUC.

Nigerian Informer. (2025). *Teachers' salaries in Nigeria.* Retrieved from https://nigerianinformer.com/teachers-salaries-in-nigeria/

Teachers Registration Council of Nigeria. (2019). *Professional standards for Nigerian teachers.* TRCN.

UNESCO Institute for Statistics. (2022). *Nigeria education profile.* UIS.

UNICEF. (2023). *Nigeria education fact sheets.* Retrieved from https://www.unicef.org/nigeria/reports/nigeria-education-fact-sheets

World Bank. (2024). *Literacy rate, adult total (% of people ages 15 and above) – Nigeria.* Retrieved from https://data.worldbank.org/indicator/SE.ADT.LITR.ZS?locations=NG

Chapter 7
Teachers' Voices From Kenya

Gladys Jebet Cheserem
http://orcid.org/0009-0000-4833-4200
Salawa Junior Secondary School, Kenya

Yahuma Martin Yahuma
Kabarnet High School, Kenya

Mary Josephine Amimo
Ulanda Comprehensive School, Kenya

ABSTRACT

The chapter includes history and the contemporary state of Kenyan education, structure of the educational system is revealed, teacher education and development in Kenya will be presented. Personal stories of three teachers will conclude the sub-chapter. Their views on the perspective of teaching profession will be presented. Overviewing the book's purpose and themes. It discusses the situation in education, increasing demands in and towards educators, lack of support offered to educators by society, views on humans versus technologies roles in education, etc. It explains why teacher stories are part of the book. Teacher roles throughout history are discussed, from just a servant, to a highly respected, even sacred profession, back to a less respected job,how teachers shape the world, that no other professions can be gained without qualified and inspiring teachers. The paradox everybody understands teachers are needed, but nobody wants their children to become teachers, The goal of the book is to open society's eyes and change their paradoxical attitude towards teaching and teachers.

The system of education in Kenya

Gladys Cheserem

The goal of education is not only to provide literary and scientific knowledge but also to help students acquire knowledge, skills, and values, and to prepare them for life. Therefore, the informal education of indigenous peoples in precolonial African countries, Kenya among them, cannot be undermined. Knowledge was passed from generation to generation through social practice and valued as the expression of cultural knowledge that sustained community and a sense of shared identity.

During the colonial period, formal education in Kenya was introduced. In 1985, the British Empire declared its protectorate over Kenya. Initially, Christian missionaries carried out elementary education. Starting from 1911, the colonial government started to subsidise the existing missionary schools and opened some public schools (Mwria, 1991). During the colonial era, education, like society, was stratified along racial lines; there existed an 'African education', a 'European Education', and an 'Asian Education'; three separate systems divided by rigid boundaries (Ominde, 1964).

DOI: 10.4018/979-8-3373-8983-7.ch007

Independence brought sweeping reforms to the educational system. Between 1964 and 1985, the 7-4-2-3-system was applied. This does not include the 'pre-primary' schooling provided to children under the age of six. The first education system after Kenya's independence was 7-4-2-3 (seven years of primary, four years of lower secondary, two years of upper secondary school, and three years of university, implemented only in some territiries), while the second one, introduced in 1985, the 8-4-4 system (primary–secondary–university), was implemented everywhere in independent Kenya (Wanjohi, 2011). According to Amutabi (2019), the Competency Based Curriculum (CBC) under the 2-6-3-3 system of education in Kenya was introduced in 2017 to replace the 8-4-4 system of education which served Kenya for 32 years.

Besides general and higher education, a great role in Kenyan education has been played by technical and vocational education, which has been extremely important for the employment of Kenyan youth. Anzaya (2024) mentions that over the last 100 years, the Technical and Vocational Education and Training (TVET) in Kenya equipped the youth with the much-needed industrial skills and knowledge to thrive in the job market. This has fostered innovation, entrepreneurship, and self-reliance. TVET in Kenya developed during three stages: pre-colonial (traditional TVET), colonial, and post-colonial. It has always played a fundamental role in the socio-economic development of Kenya. During the pre-colonial era, traditional TVET was practiced by blacksmiths, potters, herbalists, carpenters, and other skilled practitioners. In 1914, the colonial Government opened the first Government African School (GAS) in Machakos for vocational trades. Later, in 1924, the Native Industrial Training Depot (NITD), now known as Kabete National Polytechnic, was established. In the post-colonial era, the TVET sector in Kenya has achieved key milestones, opening four SAGAs, a Kenya School of TVET (KSTVET), Kenya National Qualification Authority (KNQA), TVET Curriculum Development, Assessment and Certification Council (TVET CDACC), and Technical and Vocational Education Training Authority (TVETA), all contributing to the skilling of the Kenyan youth. The importance of TVET in Kenyan society cannot be overstated. It trains industry-ready graduates with the skills demanded by the job market. This has been achieved through the implementation of Competency-Based Education and Training (CBET) and Dual Training, a component of CBET.

Higher education also took into consideration country requirements. Egerton, the oldest Western-type institution of higher learning in Kenya, was founded as a Farm School in 1939. In 1950, the School was upgraded to an Agricultural College offering diploma programmes. The University of Nairobi, independent Kenya's first university, was inaugurated on 25 March 1970 (Higher Education in Kenya: Strides and Trends, n.d.). One of the major problems of Kenyan higher education is the lack of funding. Although the percentage of GDP spent on education (on all levels) grew from 4.82% in 1971 to 6.67% in 2010, this is obviously not enough. Due to it, teaching quality and higher education teacher motivation is insufficient (Higher Education in Kenya: Strides and Trends, n.d.). McCowan (2018) claims that lecturers in Kenyan universities are poorly and unstably paid. Financial difficulties characterize not only public but also private universities (Sa'diyah, 2025). While the need in higher education for the improvement of life quality is growing, and so are the admissions to universities, the quality of teaching is decreasing, due to the insufficient number of PhD holders among university academic staff and their low motivation. Higher education should shift from the "graduate-mill" approach, to the country's development goals (Chege, 2015).

Becoming a teacher in Kenya

For one to become an early childhood teacher, he or she must have a Kenya Certificate of Secondary Education (KCSE) minimum grade D+ (Plus),or its approved equivalent, plus a Certificate in Early Childhood Development and Education offered by Kenya National Examinations Council or the Ministry of Education or its approved equivalent. A diploma in Early Childhood Development and Education offered by KNEC or its approved equivalent (Digger Jobs (n.d.).

In Kenya, for one to become a school teacher, the person has to be a Kenyan citizen, have either a minimum P1 certificate for primary school (the basic qualification for one to be employed to teach in primary school only, obtained as result of two-year study) or a two-year diploma in Education which enables to teach at any level of school, and be registered with the Teacher Service Commission. They must hold a Bachelor of Education Degree with two teaching subjects. Alternatively, they must hold a Bachelor of Science or Arts Degree plus a Post Graduate Diploma in Education (PGDE) with two teaching subjects. If they are Bachelor of Science with Education or Bachelor of Arts with Education holders, they must have two teaching subjects (Teachers' Service Commission, n.d.).

To teach at a vocation education institution, one must possess a bachelor of Education or a technical sphere or else a Craft Certificate (awarded by an approved qualification awarding institution or an accredited university (local or foreign) (TVETA, n.d.). To become a lecturer in Kenya, it is necessary to have a master's degree in the corresponding discipline.

Teacher and lecturer salaries in Kenya

According to *The Kenya Times* (2026), primary teacher II (Grade B5) will earn Ksh 28,600-37,100 (US$222-288), while senior teachers will earn Ksh 49,781-66,233 (US$386-513). According to Glassdoor (n.d.), *the average salary for a lecturer is $116920 per year in Kenya.*

Private schools and universities pay better, while governmentally-financed educational institutions do not pay such good salaries, but offer job security, which is an important factor to make working for them attractive. Public universities often offer benefit packages, including comprehensive retirement plans and generous health coverage. Public universities often provide greater job security, particularly in tenured positions, which can be appealing to academics seeking long-term stability. Academic staff may receive research grants, professional development funding, and benefit from the prestige of working at a top-tier institution.

In 2025, the divide between public and private schools and university salaries remains evident, though both sectors face unique challenges and opportunities. Public institutions continue to navigate funding constraints, while private universities balance high tuition costs with competitive salaries. Lecturers' salaries in Kenya are based on title and rank in a training institution. Those employed by the government are graded differently from those in private sector.

Teachers' trade unions

School teachers as well as university lecturers in Kenya have unions. They are needed to protect teachers' rights. The Kenya National Union of Teachers (KNUT) is the largest teachers' trade union in Kenya. It was formed on December 4, 1957. The union held its first strike in 1963, before Kenyan independence. Other major strikes have been held in 1966, 1969, 1997, 1998, 2002, and 2009. The Kenya Union of Post-Primary Education Teachers (KUPPET) plays a vital role in championing teachers' welfare and contributing to reforms in secondary and tertiary education. Formed in 1993, KUPPET was established to specifically address the needs of teachers in secondary schools, technical institutions, and tertiary colleges - distinct from the broader representation offered by the Kenya National Union of Teachers (KNUT).

In 1966 University College Academic Staff Association was registered. Initially established as a social body to support expatriate and local academic staff, it gradually evolved in response to the need for stronger representation and advocacy. In the early 1970s, lecturers' dissatisfaction grew over the limitations of staff associations in negotiating key matters affecting welfare and academic freedom. This led to the transformation of the association into a full-fledged trade union. In 1993, the Universities' Academic Staff Union (UASU) was formally established, and its constitution was officially registered on May 2, 2003.

Throughout its history, UASU has stood as a pillar of strength for university lecturers, challenging unfair labour practices, participating in policy dialogue, and fighting for the dignity, recognition, and empowerment of academic staff in Kenya. Today, we continue to build on this legacy—firmly committed to justice, equity, and educational progress. Technical and Vocational tutors have a union too, but formerly they were in KUPPET.

Some important statistics on enrolment, literacy, and expenditure on education

According to UNICEF (n.d.), "before the COVID-19 pandemic, nationwide enrolment in primary education stood at 93 per cent, but at secondary level was only 71 per cent". According to the Global Economy.com (2022), the literacy rate among Kenyan citizens aged 15 and above is 82.9%. One of conditions to provide a higher enrolment to schools and, consequently, a higher level of literacy, is a better funding. According to the Economic Survey (2024), national expenditure on the education sector has been steadily growing between 2019 and 2023 (in 2023, it amounted to 690 billion Kenyan shillings (about US$5,351 billion).

Kenya in international assessments of education quality

Kenya took part in the Programme for International Student Assessment (PISA) for the first time ever, the Kenya National Examinations Council (KNEC) has announced. The evaluation brings together over 90 countries in an effort to assess the quality and effectiveness of their education systems. According to KNEC, the assessment which is run by the Organisation for Economic Cooperation and Development (OECD) was conducted in September 2025, however, the results are not available so far.

Teacher development and governmental support to teachers

The Kenyan government supports teachers through training and capacity building; however, science and language teachers are more privileged in those capacity building sessions compared to the humanities. With the introduction of Competency-Based Education (CBE) in 2017, the government is trying its best to support teachers. The junior school teachers' career progression is still in the shadows, but they are looking forward to the light at the end of the tunnel when CBE is more stabilized.

The transition from the 8-4-4 system to the CBE is one of the most ambitious educational reforms in the country's history. The priorities of CBE underscore the development of core competencies/transferal skills, including critical thinking, creativity, problem-solving, communication, collaboration, digital literacy, and ethical reasoning, thus making school leavers better prepared for future life. According to Mauti et al. (2024), the teacher role has dramatically changed in the CBE from a deliverer of content to facilitator of learning. Such teacher need both pedagogical knowledge and practical skills. However, teacher training programs often lag behind these requirements.

The Government has reaffirmed its commitment to transforming teacher education to ensure the successful delivery of Competency-Based Education (CBE) in Kenya. Speaking during the opening of the Teachers' Education Conference 2025 in Mombasa, Education Cabinet Secretary Julius Ogamba emphasized the urgent need to harmonize teacher preparation across all levels of education. "This is not just a routine engagement. It is a timely and critical platform that brings together key education stakeholders as the country undertakes major reforms to align teacher education with national development goals and the evolving needs of the education sector," said Ogamba. The conference, convened under the theme *Status of Pre-service Teacher Training and Teacher Employment in Kenya*, sought to review current pre-service teacher education programmes, evaluate placement systems, assess teacher demand and employment, and chart policy reforms to sustain the implementation of CBE. Ogamba said the government is working to ensure that teacher education programmes across universities, TVET institutions, and teacher training colleges are effectively aligned with the new curriculum framework and labour market expectations. The government has already implemented key reforms in entry requirements and training standards. All P1 and Early Childhood Development Education (ECDE) certificate holders are now required to upgrade to diploma level. "In addition, a minimum Kenya Certificate of Secondary Education (KCSE) grade of C (Plain), with subject-specific requirements - especially in Science, Technology, Engineering, and Mathematics (STEM) - is mandatory for admission to teacher training programmes," he said. Additionally, the Ministry is implementing recommendations from the Presidential Working Party on Education Reform (PWPER), including the establishment of the Kenya Teacher Training College and the Kenya School of Teacher and Education Management, which will help coordinate both pre-service and in-service teacher education. Amb. Prof. Julius Bitok, the Principal Secretary in the State Department for Basic Education, echoed the CS's sentiments, describing the conference as the culmination of months of consultations involving Vice Chancellors, Teachers Service Commission (TSC) officials, and education stakeholders (Kepsha, 2025).

In conclusion, the Kenyan education system has undergone various changes to suit the current needs of a post-modern student and pupil in a dynamic society, whereby technology is taking over. Teachers' and lecturers' salaries are improving thanks to the unions, which have always been at the forefront of advocating for the rights of teachers, tutors, and lecturers. The government is trying to adjust to the current education system, too, and is hopeful to achieve its dreams and goals of education.

The way of acting with empathy and understanding

Gladys Cheserem

In the late 90s, I would be glued to our small black-and-white TV. I admired the international journalists from DW and CNN reading the news. I didn't know English very well at that time, given that we mostly spoke Swahili, and our native language Kalenjin. I would read storybooks and newspapers. Over time, my English improved, and I would now know what was happening around my little world. I would read stories about Africa and overseas, about colonial Africa and post-colonial Africa, and about Iraq, Iran, and Afghanistan refugees (from the UNHCR booklets my father got from his human rights organization). I would read the Bible and tell my grandfather about Jesus. He would laugh and tell me those were just stories. He was a staunch African Traditionalist. He would then tell me stories about the World Wars, the liberation of our land from foreigners, and we would laugh at times, even feel like crying. He joked and told me I was a child of Europe (because I spoke English to him). We would sing songs about going to war and gospel hymns. I was now torn between being a news anchor, a diplomat, a lawyer, a teacher, an author, or should I be all of them? After school, I would come home and mimic the news anchors, reading the news with a newspaper in my hand. I would also mimic my teachers, teaching stones and trees. I would perform poems at school and outside school.

I finished primary school and joined my secondary school. I was privileged to attend one of the best high schools in Kenya. I started well with good grades in form one, but with time, I started dropping due to various factors surrounding me, especially the sickness of my mother. My dreams vanished, but I remembered the motivational books I read, Gifted Hands by Ben Carson, among others. I told myself I won't give up on my dreams, and I kept moving on towards my goals and ambitions. I finished high school, eagerly waiting for my results. When they were finally out, I felt like the whole world was on my shoulders. I didn't get grades that would give me direct entry into the government university program for a bachelor's degree.

I started figuring out that maybe I would venture into business, but I didn't have any capital. I worked for my relative as a waitress at a small hotel. Some of my clients would question me, "Why are you working here?" I asked myself why? They would tell me you are too bright to be here. That's when I knew that's not my destiny, but now money was a problem, my family could not afford a self-sponsored program at the university. I stayed for about 1.5 years as a waitress, then came back home and worked as a shopkeeper at a nearby shop. I applied for a diploma course on Health Records, and I got a letter of invitation (from a top referral hospital in Kenya) after some time, but my heart wasn't at medical field at all. I applied for a self-sponsored program at a public university for a Bachelor of Education degree, and I received the invitation letter as well. My mother was now recovering a bit, and she told me my dream would come true, which gave me a ray of hope in my hopelessness, but where would we get money for my studies? We had to raise funds, and I applied for a HELB (Higher Education Loans Board) loan, which helped me cover my studies.

I was enrolled at the university, and I started my education journey as a teacher in the School of Education faculty of Arts and Social Sciences. I chose the History/Religion option for my studies. My literature lecturer in my first year asked why I did not choose English/Literature (I was doing well in Literature), but I told him I was more comfortable with the History/Religion option. I successfully finished my four years at the university and graduated with Second Class Honors Upper Division and started my job hunt. I was employed at a private school. I was expectant at a young age, just at the beginning of my career. I was to continue working, but the working conditions were too demanding and tiresome, given the situation I was in. I had to quit.

I returned to job seeking again, but finding a job in a public school was like a fairy tale; they were mostly employing science teachers, and for humanities, if you didn't have a connection, you would not be employed. Luckily, I secured a teaching job after 2 years of graduation, but it was on contract with the school board, not the government (meaning the salary would be peanuts). It was a local secondary school in the remote villages of Kenya along the Kerio Valley of the Great Rift Valley. I dedicated myself to teaching History and Christian Religious Education (CRE). Teaching in a remote school had its own challenges and successes. In 2020, in February, unfortunately, the coronavirus struck not only Kenya but the entire globe. Schools closed, and people stayed home with minimal movement. We returned to teaching the same year, but with restrictions like social distancing, sanitization, and wearing a mask. It was hard to do so in my location because the Kerio Valley is so hot and temperatures are so high, but we soldiered on.

Corona virus disrupted the education calendar and, when studies resumed fully for all forms (Form 1-4), the holidays were squeezed so as to recover the time lost during the quarantine period, meaning we would spend a lot of time with students at school, but on my side it was a blessing as a non-government teacher, because I would be paid (most schools in Kenya don't pay non-government employed teachers during holidays). During this period, it was hard for parents to cater to school fees for students, because in the normal calendar, holidays would be an opportune time to go and fend for their children for the next term of their studies. Absenteeism was high because I was teaching in a day school where students arrived in the morning and left in the evening.

Socio-cultural factors were a major challenge to me during my teaching in the remote secondary school, the community around me were pastoralists and farmers, they kept livestock like cows, goats, and sheep. Some students would miss school to look after cattle, while others would go home early to attend to their livestock. The economic status of their community was also low for some students, as some would go to the market days during school days to sell commodities so that they might get money for their upkeep. In a remote village set-up, culture is deeply rooted, every end of year around December in the Kalenjin community, boys undergo circumcision as a rite of passage, marking an end of childhood to adulthood. I remember an instance where I was still new in the school, and boys who underwent the circumcision rituals almost became unruly and undisciplined just because of the rite of passage they underwent. At the passage, women are regarded lesser and men who have undergone the ritual are seen as the only ones who can discipline them. I would try to maintain control of discipline during my duty as a teacher and as a subject teacher, but they were uncontrollable until they were summoned to the deputy principal's office for a disciplinary case and given some suspension, which is when they accepted to heed whatever I instructed them. Teenage pregnancies were also a challenge, maybe due to the low socio-economic status and being in a day school rather than a boarding school.

Despite the challenges in the remote secondary school, I worked there up to 2023. I had a hope that through education, they would still conquer the opportunities around them, away from the village or even in the village setup. Because education empowers one with knowledge and skills. I became their Christian Union (CU) Patron, and we would meet every Wednesday to share God's word, and I would motivate them during those moments, and through spiritual guidance, it impacted good morals in most of them. Even those who seemed not to change made me happy that, after finishing school, some communicated with me in a composed and friendly manner, meaning the morals we shared during school days positively impacted them in their later life. 2023 February, a critical phase in the history of the Kenyan education system, a new model of education came into reality, the 2-6-3-3-3, the CBC, currently called CBE Competency Based Education (Competency-Based Curriculum; Pre-Primary, Primary, Junior Secondary, Senior Secondary, and Tertiary-College and University) that replaced the 8-4-4 system that had earlier been implemented in the year 1985. I secured a chance to be employed as a Junior Secondary teacher on a permanent and pensionable basis by the Kenyan Government, under the Teachers Service Commission (TSC), and I harmoniously exited my working station to my new working station, not so far away, meaning climatic and environmental changes were the same, only the new model and working environment changed. It is common knowledge that change is gradual, and it needs patience and optimism. We became the pioneers of the new model of education, surrounded by a myriad of hurdles. We taught without textbooks at grade 7(Junior Secondary starts from grade 7-9), that year we just used curriculum designs and depended on online notes and research. We taught what we didn't specialize in at our universities; that is, the two teaching subjects for a high school teacher, we were expected to deliver our best. We taught 12 subjects and 2 optional subjects, making a total of 14 subjects or so. I finished teaching grade 7 in 2023 Social Studies, Life Skills, CRE, Health Education, Computer Studies, and Agriculture. In 2024, new books were introduced and some subjects were merged to reduce their number to 9. We were only two teachers in Junior Secondary (understaffed) school, primary school teachers had to chip in and help where possible. At the verge of term three, 2023, new intern teachers were employed (two of them) to help ease our workload.

In 2024, there was a nationwide strike for the Junior School intern teachers. It was a hard time, I remained in school alone since I was on a permanent basis, and controlling the whole grade 7 and 8 was not easy. It lasted a few weeks, and the government promised to confirm the intern teachers. Teaching in Junior School is not a walk in the park. First of all, a Junior School teacher teaches in a primary school compound, yet they are post-primary teachers; it is only the physical structures that make them separate from the primary. Most of them are mainly not represented in the Board of Management this the board members are discussing issues or matters concerning Junior School in their absence this not promoting equity and equal representation. The age gap challenge to junior secondary teachers is a problem.

When we were posted in primary schools (where most of the teachers are old), we were seen as young teachers. In a nutshell, this tries to express the challenges of being junior secondary school teacher in a primary environment, headed by one administrator with no clear leadership structure that separates junior school as a phase of its own rather than being merged with primary school (these challenges has seen KNUT; Kenya National Union of Teachers and KUPPET; Kenya Union of Post-Primary Teachers both claiming junior school as belonging to them, meaning we are hanging in between and is still there up to date). Junior School teachers recently marched peacefully, demanding autonomy of the Junior Secondary School.

"Teacher, teacher," some small students called me at the top of their voices one morning, "Come and see, we've killed a snake!" I gazed at them with wonder. I briskly walked to see, indeed, they've killed a snake on their own! They are grade 1 pupils, being a Junior Secondary School(JSS) teacher means you must control all grades, not only grades 7-9 but also 1-6 (Primary), I don't take this as a challenge but as an opportunity to learn from little children, because as JSS teachers we were taught how to handle adolescents. The young children from my jurisdiction of teaching taught me that the environment shapes us. The snake they killed is a symbol of bravery and self-efficacy. These are children who have grown up in a harsh environment, and it has shaped their confidence.

Just like my previous local secondary school, their socio-economic activities are not different at all, they are pastoralists and farmers. The challenges they face are similar to those of the previous level (secondary school). But I have to act with empathy and understanding, because working along the savannah in a rural set-up is not like an urban set up where children can access urban life, if a child comes late to school I have to understand why, some come late because there was no firewood for cooking, some maybe because they were fetching water for use during the dry season, during rainy seasons the roads might be muddy making the students to come late to school and for those whose parents drink liquor, they come late because they were cooking on their own in the morning or afternoon. Some do not finish homework due to limited access to Information and Communication Technologies' (ICT) services. In the new CBE (Competency-Based Education) model, which was previously CBC, in 2023, learning is more ICT-integrated, and most of these children's parents don't have smartphones, and even if they do, electricity is an issue.

One of the successes in the new model of education for me as a teacher in JSS is that the textbooks have now been distributed, and learning is becoming stabilized. JSS is now complete from grades 7-9; grade 9 did their national assessment in 2025. The teaching methods are learner-centered rather than teacher-centered, like in the 8-4-4 system. Learning is ICT-integrated, on my end, I usually incorporate ICT during my lessons to mold a technologically empowered child. Despite being in a rural set-up, I use projectors and tablets where needed, and the school's WIFI. I am optimistic that the children will have a bright future and explore the world using education as a key to success in their lives, whether in white-collar jobs or in entrepreneurship. Down the savannah along the Kerio Valley, not only do animal ecosystems but also plants thrive (although climate change due to human activities endangers them). In every season, pupils and students always share the wild fruits with their teachers. This is the virtue of generosity in them; it creates a social bond.

Regarding the future of education as a teacher in Kenya, unless Junior School has autonomy with clear administrative structures, the new model will not fully come into being. Did I want to become a teacher? I was uncertain, but I had a teaching passion in me. Who is a teacher? A teacher is a guide, mentor, instructor, disciplinarian, a second parent away from home, a friend, and a role model. In short, a teacher is well-rounded.

My story isn't just about not becoming what I wanted from my dilemma in career pathway, I am all that I wanted to be, I am a teacher by profession. As for law, I do apply paralegal aspects in the movement I am in, that is the Kenyan Peasants League, they use Kenyan Constitution for legal pathways alongside international laws and treaties, in becoming a news anchor. I use my social media accounts to share messages with the world, covering politics, socio-economic issues, and emerging issues in our society. The diplomatic career dream is realized when I meet foreigners, build strong diplomatic ties with them, and talk about my authorship through my social media. Incorporating my story of being a mother at an early age at the beginning of my career is a reflection of women and their professional journey. It is the women who always leave job hunts to take care of their children if they are unemployed. This shows that women struggle in job markets to achieve their dreams. Do I love teaching? Yes, I do love my work, and I don't regret becoming a teacher. I teach the younger generation to realize their dreams and become what they want to. That's my journey.

The teaching profession deals with the desire to change students' lives positively

Mary Josephine Amimo

Like most children, I grew up changing career choices every now and then. This would happen any time I admired someone in their different fields of work. From medicine, mechanics, to art. I wanted to do it all. Among all the things I wanted to be when I grew up none came even remotely close to teaching. During my last year in high school, I was fortunate to attend a retreat that would later prompt me to pursue teaching as a profession. For me, teaching has not only become a profession but also a platform that can be used to shape young minds and help mold them in preparation for tomorrow.

Being a teacher does not only consist of going to class and delivering lessons. Teaching involves many things, one of them being trying to know and understand your learners. In order to achieve this, at times a teacher is required to 'think like the learner'.

This profession has its advantages and disadvantages. Some of the advantages include the following:

- The teaching profession offers a profound sense of purpose that makes us want to create a lasting impact on the learners. The reward lies in witnessing those moments when learners achieve their goals, potential careers, or when they contribute to society as informed citizens.
- Due to the dynamic nature of the classroom, teachers must constantly update their knowledge and adapt to new information creatively so as to be able to engage with diverse perspectives. This also helps make their lessons more enjoyable and less monotonous.
- For many schools in Kenya, be it the public-school systems or private educational institutions, this profession comes with a strong union that protects teachers, such as KNUT and KUPPET, comprehensive health care insurance, and pension plans. This acts as a powerful motivator that offers long-term financial security, especially during uncertain economic climates.
- Schools in Kenya have a predictable daily routine. They operate on fixed schedules, such as term dates, class periods, time–in, time–out, and sports and games timelines. This helps both personal and professional management and planning.

The disadvantages include:

- At times, teachers may experience emotional labour or emotional burnout due to the demanding nature of their work. Their duties include administrative work, which may extend to late evenings or even during the weekends, managing the classroom dynamics, planning lessons, parent communication, and supporting the learners' socio-emotional needs.
- Despite the importance of teaching, it is often undervalued, especially in terms of the acquired salaries. In this sector, teachers of early education often find themselves with the short end of the stick. Despite their workload, their salaries tend to be lower than those of the average teacher. This, paired with stagnant income amid rising inflation, can lead to financial stress, prompting them to seek alternatives in other fields of work to meet their needs. Apart from that, it may also erode the profession's morale.
- Besides limited resources, underfunded systems also act as a hindrance in the quest to deliver and acquire education. In some areas, teachers experience shortages of teaching and learning materials (textbooks, chalk), toilets, laboratories, and even classrooms. Especially during this transition period from 8 - 4 - 4 to CBE this creates an environment that makes teaching and learning difficult.

Experiences and lessons learnt in teaching

Inasmuch as planning is essential, in order to survive in this field, one must be flexible. A teacher can meticulously plan a lesson only to be interrupted by unplanned moments. They can be sudden events that capture learners' attention or unexpected questions from learners (which may or may not be relevant to the lesson). In such cases, a teacher is expected to be able to pivot and adapt the situation into the lesson. These events may also contribute to the class liveliness, therefore reducing boredom and classroom monotony. In situations where these events do not correspond to class-related activities, they can be incorporated into the day-to-day life activities.

Learners find it difficult learning from a person that they do not like, feel seen by, or even trust. For learning to take place, a teacher first creates a good rapport between themselves and the learners. This can be done by first knowing the names of the learners, their interests (whether personal, academic, or co-curricular), the challenges they face, be it in school or at home, celebrating their victories, and encouraging them when they need encouragement. Doing this helps create a trusting environment where the learners feel heard and seen.

The most painful part of being a teacher is not about the salary or the little respect shown by society. It's about not being able to get through to all your learners. Even though it's impossible to reach all the learners, as a teacher, you would want to positively impact all their lives. Some of them have challenges that are beyond the capabilities of a teacher to solve, and yet we are expected to act as if we can make a difference for each one of them. But even knowing this, we try our very best for each and every one of them.

A few years ago, while I was still new to this field, I happened to come across a very heartbreaking case. There was a young learner who had successfully completed her primary level education and was called to join one of Kenya's most popular high schools for her secondary education. To the student, this was a dream come true. An opportunity many strive to get, but only a few are selected. On the first day of admission, she arrived late after the day's work was done and most of the teachers had already left the compound. Due to this, she was urged to go back home and come the next morning, which she adamantly refused, stating she would rather sleep at the gate than go back. This prompted the security guard to inform the school principal. When the principal arrived at the gate and saw the state of the girl, she could send her back.

The girl was an orphan, and her only caring guardian was her maternal grandmother. She wore her primary uniform, which had so many patches that it was impossible to identify its original state. She had walked over 40km with nothing but an empty box on her head and mismatched, worn-out slippers. School was the only refuge the young girl had: if she dared to return home, her uncles would marry her off. After hearing her story, the principal talked with the teachers and board members. The girl was provided with everything that she needed in order to make her learning comfortable. For four years, she never went back, but during the holidays, her grandmother would come visit her in school, where she stayed with one of her teachers. She completed her Kenya Certificate of Secondary Education and is in her first year of medical school.

Teaching is not always easy; it has its challenges, and so does acquiring education. But if teachers, government, and community come together, the process of teaching and getting education will become a little bit easier.

The switch from journalism to teaching

Martin Yahuma

"No printed word nor spoken plea can teach young minds what men or women should be, not all the printed books, but what the teachers themselves are." William Butler Yeates

Journalism was the mirage I chased after high school. Like any young man in my time, inspired by the American rappers Jaheim and Tupac Shakur, I wanted popularity, a great name, and money. I wanted to hit and be legendary. Journalism was my key – the key that education was to hand me to unlock my future.

Before the future, there is always history: I was born and raised in a family of seven, and several relatives. My father, a retired doctor, and my mother, a nurse, wanted all their children and relatives under their care to join the medical field. As a middle child, I was lucky to look up to two older sisters who naturally gravitated toward what our parents didn't want. Teaching was, therefore, a concept I only experienced at school.

School was a cocktail of things – I still try to find the needles of good times in the hay of trouble, pain, and suffering that I encountered, from the time I joined a boarding school at the age of 9. What did I ever do to my parents! Ironically, in this very cocktail of things - bullying, undeserved punishments, the rods for the child and hunger, sneaking contraband items, selling slippers and dictionaries, sleeping on a foolscap for a mattress – I stumbled upon my inspiration, and made my first step towards my future - being a teacher.

So, two years after high school, I was yet to find a career path. I was still set on being a journalist after several rejections from the colleges I applied to. I would not pursue a career in nursing or medicine. It wasn't just for me. I applied for everything else - human resource management, hospitality management, tourism and travel, food production, you name it. Nothing came through.

I even had a business running, a hand in entrepreneurship.

Then one day, I went to visit my younger brother at my alma mater. Naturally, I met many of my former teachers, and one question kept coming up -

"What do you do nowadays?"

It was a difficult question, as all teachers would like to hear success and accomplishment stories from their former students. I did not have an answer!

I pictured myself back in class, a flashback of this question, to which many of us back then had responded with doctors, lawyers, engineers – none of us had wanted to be teachers. I still did not want to be one.

Afterwards, I found my parents talking to the then Deputy Headteacher. She gallantly smiled at me as I approached.

"Martin! See how big you have grown!"

I smiled back.

"I am guessing you followed in your father's footsteps: A Doctor, right?"

I felt my heart race. Smiling was suddenly a struggle. I knew it was time to once again respond to the awkward question to which I had no answer. And yes, she asked the question. And yes, I fumbled again.

This was my teacher of English. Her smile was as new as it was six years ago when I had left Primary School. Her voice: still reassuring. I loved English Lessons.

"Have you ever considered teaching, Martin?"

I said yes and that I had dismissed it as inconceivable.

"Why so? You were an excellent presenter during English Lessons."

I thought then of a thousand reasons not to be a teacher, but I said none out of the respect, maybe, that I had for her and my parents there.

"Come on, I can assure you that teaching will not only be good for you but will present you with an avenue of being any other thing you would like to be. Firms out here hire people with a background in Education. Consider it as a stepping stone to what you want to pursue. What was it again…?

"Journalism, madam."

"A degree in English and Literature can be a start."

I did not want to hear more. My parents were paying keen attention, and from their faces, I could tell their decision.

I still had my heart in journalism, but a seed had been planted in my mind. The rest is history.

Teaching would be described as a journey for some, but for me, it is a collection of unique stories. The very first time I stepped into a classroom full of teenage boys, stays with me to date, fresh in my mind.

It was an interview: I had 10 minutes to prepare for a topic and teach a Form Two class in the presence of my Head of Department. I had travelled so far to be here, miles away from home, trained and eager to start. Those twenty minutes washed every doubt I had about being a teacher. The boys, neat in their white shirts, green sweaters, and grey trousers, sat in silence and waited. In that silence, at their expectation, I felt my doubt disappear. I was in charge. I had the Key. I enjoyed the uninterrupted attention of about fifty young minds, and the Head of Department, all engrossed in what I was saying, responding to my questions, and laughing at my jokes.

There and then, I knew this was all I was meant to be. They say a good teacher merely explains, but a great teacher inspires. I was determined to be a great teacher.

I have had a share of great experiences, twists and turns, and there are days I have felt like I made a horrible decision. I have been overworked, overwhelmed, both underutilized and overutilized, I have questioned the system and even the curriculum itself once in a while – but I have always lived by one principle: Living the Lesson I want to Teach.

I would easily say that the first lesson was my best; however, there have been many other lessons where impact was made, lives were changed, dreams were hatched, and narratives re-written.

As a teacher, you are naturally entangled in the personal lives of the students. You have many mini hearts dished out to each boy and girl. The story of one boy I taught, his heart set on being an oncologist, stands out in this moment. His mother, the only parent, had cancer, and all the boy ever wanted was to save her. Sadly, the mother died. The hopelessness was so solid, the poverty and bleakness in his future were not just his, but mine as well. He is still in school, and the burden of fanning his flame of being who he wants to be for the sake of other cancer patients, even though his mother did not live long enough to be treated by him, sits on my shoulders. This is just one case of many other personal stories of orphans, terminal illnesses, and divorce that surround the lives of my students. It is not possible to make them go away, but empathy and presence are roles a teacher needs to play well. No university prepares a teacher for this.

I have enjoyed walking the journey with many individual boys and girls over the years, each story a unique journey for the students I have handled. I have learned patience, mentoring, setting pace, and most importantly, being an example. I have learnt to be different things in one person to fit in the shoes of every aspiring doctor, engineer, pilot, nurse, and future teacher in the classrooms that I have taught. I have seen the live fruits of teaching from the students I have taught over the years. It is a clear demonstration of the nobility of the teaching profession, after all, a preacher's mistakes only come to light on judgment day, a doctor's mistake lies cold in the grave, a lawyer's mistake is serving prison time, but a teacher's mistake is always roaming the world.

Globally, the teaching profession is considered crucial in societal development and shaping future generations. The widespread challenges, including burdensome workload and inadequate professional recognition leads to its unpopularity. Most teachers chose it as the last resort when everything else they wanted failed to come true. In Kenya, teachers are almost the least paid public servants, yet a lot is expected from them. However, due to a lack of alternatives and the high cost of training in other fields, teaching remains a popular choice, as it is accessible and affordable for the masses. Many trained teachers in Kenya chose to work in other fields for a while before eventually returning to teaching for retirement benefits.

Africa is still grappling with technological advancement and is highly reliant on what Western countries have to offer. The ICT integration in the Education System relies heavily on teachers to implement it. It is highly unlikely for teachers to be replaced by Machines. Education is alive. No machine or robot can replace a teacher.

REFERENCES

Amutabi, M. N. (2019). Competency Based Curriculum (CBC) and the end of an era in Kenya's education sector and implications for development: Some empirical reflections. *Journal of Popular Education in Africa*, *3*(10), 45–66.

Anzaya, J. (2024). Celebrating 100 years of TVET success in Kenya. *TVET Magazine,* special edition 1(1), 1-69.

Chege, M. (2015). Re-inventing Kenya's university: From a "Graduate-mill" to a development-oriented paradigm. *International Journal of Educational Development*, *44*, 21–27. DOI: 10.1016/j.ijedudev.2015.07.002

Economy, G. com. (2022). *Literacy rate.* Retrieved from https://www.theglobaleconomy.com/Kenya/Literacy_rate/

Higher Education in Kenya: Strides and Trends. (n.d.). Retrieved from https://publication.codesria.org/index.php/pub/catalog/download/28/53/144?inline=1

Jobs, D. (n.d.). Retrieved from https://jobs.digger.co.ke/37451/ecde-teacher-iii#:~:text=Kenya%20Certificate%20of%20Secondary%20Education%20(KCSE)%20minimum%20grade%20D+%20(,P.O.%20Box%2049%20%2D%2090300.
Glassdoor. (n.d.). *How much does a lecturer make in Kenya?* Retrieved from https://www.glassdoor.com/Salaries/kenya-lecturer-salary-SRCH_IL.0,5_IN130_KO6,14.htm

KEPSHA. (2025). The 2025 KEPSHA-KCB National Annual General Meeting and Conference. Retrieved from https://kepsha.or.ke/kepsha-kcb-national-agm-2025/

Mauti, J. M., Moindi, R., & Masagara, G. A. (2024). Teacher education in the advent of transition of education systems in Kenya. *Journal of the Kenya National Commission for UNESCO*, *5*(2), 1–15.

Mwria, K. (1991). Education for subordination: African education in colonial Kenya. *History of Education*, *20*(3), 261–273. DOI: 10.1080/0046760910200306

Ominde, S. H. (1964). *Kenya education commission report.* Republic of Kenya. Nairobi: Government Printers.

Sa'diyah, R. R., Aprilya, E., & Wahjono, S. I. (2025). Organizational structure of private higher education institutions and their development patterns. *Golden Ratio of Data in Summary*, *5*(3), 566–572. DOI: 10.52970/grdis.v5i3.1254

Teachers' Service Commission. (n.d.). *Recruitment of teachers on permanent and pensionable terms of service.* Retrieved from https://gaa.go.ke/sites/default/files/2024-10/TSC%20Recruitment%20of%20Teachers%20on%20Permanent%20and%20Pensionable%20Terms%20of%20Servicepdf.pdf#:~:text=i)%20Be%20a%20Kenyan%20citizen;%20ii)%20Must,a%20registered%20teacher%20with%20Teachers%20Service%20Commission

The Kenya Times. (2026, January 16). *New salaries and allowances for Kenyan teachers by job groups.* Retrieved from https://thekenyatimes.com/latest-kenya-times-news/new-salaries-and-allowances-for-kenyan-teachers/

TVETA. (n.d.). *Application for registration and licensing of trainers.* https://www.tveta.go.ke/trainer-application-process/#:~:text=The%20application%20is%20done%20online,a%203%2Dyear%20expiry%20period

UNICEF. (n.d.). *UNICEF for every child. Kenya. Education. Providing inclusive and equitable quality education for every child.* Retrieved from https://www.unicef.org/kenya/education

Wanjohi, A. M. (2011). *Development of education system in Kenya since independence.* Kenpro. Retrieved from https://kenpro.org/papers/education-system-kenya-independence.htm

Chapter 8
Teachers' Voices From South Africa:
Teaching in Crisis, Not in Extinction – Structural Pressures and Uncertainty in South Africa

Sibhekinkosi Anna Nkomo
http://orcid.org/0000-0002-7428-9017
University of the Witwatersrand, South Africa

Bhekuyise Zungu
http://orcid.org/0000-0001-9196-8196
University of the Witwatersrand, South Africa

ABSTRACT

This chapter argues that teaching in South Africa faces a crisis of sustainability rather than extinction. Drawing on insights from teacher educators in higher education, it examines how structural constraints, policy decisions, and deteriorating working conditions reshape professional trajectories, particularly for early-career teachers. Despite continued teacher production, provincial budget cuts and frozen posts create employment insecurity, undermining morale and workforce planning. Student teachers report excessive workloads, large classes, administrative burdens, and emotional strain, leading to burnout and self-doubt even before formal entry into the profession. Many are increasingly viewing postgraduate study as an exit strategy rather than as professional advancement, signalling early attrition. The chapter concludes that sustaining teaching requires coherent employment policies, manageable workloads, and stronger alignment between teacher education and labour market realities to prevent further erosion of professionalism.

INTRODUCTION

Across global debates about the future of teaching, scholars question whether the profession is declining, transforming, or becoming obsolete (Hargreaves & Fullan, 2015; UNESCO & International Task Force on Teachers for Education 2030, 2024). The teaching profession is increasingly framed through the language of crisis, with concerns about declining morale, shortages in key subject areas, growing workloads, and retention problems, particularly among early-career educators (Ingersoll et al., 2018). In South Africa, however, these debates take on a different urgency; the issue is not teacher extinction but professional sustainability. Teaching jobs are not disappearing because they are no longer needed;

DOI: 10.4018/979-8-3373-8983-7.ch008

rather, the profession is being undermined by policy contradictions, employment insecurity, and deteriorating working conditions (Pitsoe, 2013; Van der Berg et al., 2022).

South Africa presents a striking paradox. The education system continues to face large class sizes, uneven learner outcomes, and deep inequalities across provinces and schools, all of which sustain demand for qualified teachers. Yet newly qualified teachers struggle to secure permanent posts, while those already in classrooms report intensified administrative and professional workloads (Van Broekhuizen, 2015; 2016; Tonder & Fourie, 2015). Studies of attrition consistently identify increased workload, low salaries, weak incentives, contractual employment, and limited resources as central reasons why teachers leave or contemplate leaving the profession (Lumadi, 2011; Mampane, 2012; Mafukata & Mudau, 2016). Burnout research in South African schools reinforces this pattern: excessive demands and limited support are associated with emotional exhaustion, anxiety, and work-related stress (Bernstein & Batchelor, 2022; Emsley et al., 2009).

From the perspective of teacher educators, these dynamics are visible in supervision, informal classroom discussion, and reflective work, where student teachers express anxiety about employment prospects, exhaustion linked to workload expectations, and uncertainty about long-term professional commitment. While existing research has extensively documented teacher attrition, burnout, and working conditions in South Africa, much of this literature focuses either on in-service teachers or on quantitative patterns of turnover, with limited attention to how these structural pressures are experienced and interpreted during the transition from teacher preparation into the profession. This points to a critical gap in the literature: insufficient attention to how student teachers and early-career educators experience and make sense of these structural pressures before fully entering the profession, and how this shapes their professional intentions. In particular, less is known about how early-career teachers and student teachers make sense of the contradiction between the strong national demand for teachers and weak employment absorption within the system.

Addressing this gap, this chapter argues that structural pressures, employment insecurity, workload intensification, emotional strain, and policy-practice misalignment are reshaping teachers' professional trajectories, particularly among early-career and newly qualified educators. Its key contribution lies in foregrounding the pre-employment and early-career phase as a critical yet underexplored site where the sustainability of the teaching profession is already being negotiated. By linking teacher education experiences with broader systemic constraints, the chapter extends current debates beyond attrition statistics to show how burnout and early exit are not only outcomes of workplace conditions but are also shaped earlier through training-to-work transitions. Taken together, the South African literature suggests that teaching is being weakened by cumulative structural strain, with burnout and early exit emerging as central mechanisms of attrition.

Background: Teaching and Teacher Education in South Africa

Teacher education in South Africa has undergone a significant transformation, shifting from apprenticeship-style and college-based preparation to university-based professional training. Historically, prospective teachers were trained primarily through vocational models focused on practical classroom readiness, often within colleges of education that emphasised immediate preparation for teaching practice (Rusznyak et al., 2016). During the early 2000s, major higher education reforms resulted in teacher training colleges being incorporated into universities, aligning teacher education more closely with academic and research-based knowledge (Hofmeyr, 2016). While this transition strengthened the professional and academic status of teaching, it also introduced tensions between theoretical preparation and the realities of under-resourced and unequal schooling contexts.

Today, initial teacher education (ITE) is firmly located within higher education institutions and is offered through both public and private universities in face-to-face and distance learning formats. Contemporary programmes typically combine disciplinary knowledge, pedagogical training, and supervised teaching practice. Two primary pathways into teaching exist in South Africa: the concurrent model, in which students complete a four-year Bachelor of Education (BEd) degree integrating pedagogy and school-based experience, and the consecutive model, where students first complete a disciplinary bachelor's degree followed by a one-year Postgraduate Certificate in Education (PGCE) (Hofmeyr, 2016). These pathways reflect broader international trends toward university-based professional preparation.

Teacher education has also expanded through distance learning institutions such as the University of South Africa (UNISA) and North-West University (NWU), improving access for students unable to attend residential universities. In addition, universities and research centres have introduced curriculum innovations aimed at strengthening literacy, mathematics, multilingual education, and African language pedagogy (Taylor & Mawoyo, 2022; Davids, 2023). These initiatives reflect ongoing efforts to improve teacher preparation and respond more effectively to the linguistic and educational realities of South African classrooms.

Despite these developments, significant structural challenges continue to shape the profession. Although universities graduate new teachers annually, employment opportunities do not increase proportionately, contributing to uncertainty and disillusionment among graduates (BOSA, 2024b). Public discourse continues to position teachers as central to national development, social cohesion, and post-apartheid transformation. However, this symbolic recognition often contrasts with the lived realities of teaching, which are increasingly characterised by large class sizes, resource shortages, administrative overload, and limited professional support (Independent Online [IOL], 2025).

These pressures have intensified amid fiscal constraints and growing accountability demands within the education system. Teacher unions have repeatedly raised concerns regarding workload intensification, mental health pressures, and inadequate institutional support. Consequently, a widening gap has emerged between policy rhetoric surrounding teacher importance and the everyday realities experienced within schools (Van der Berg et al., 2016).

It is within this broader context that student teachers begin forming professional identities and expectations about the profession. Teaching practice or work-integrated learning (WIL) placements frequently provide early exposure to the pressures associated with classroom teaching, including professional precarity, emotional strain, and concerns regarding long-term sustainability. These experiences play an important role in shaping how future teachers understand the profession and their place within it (Ingersoll et al., 2018).

Overall, teacher education in South Africa reflects ongoing efforts to professionalise teaching while responding to persistent structural inequalities and changing educational demands. Although reforms, technology and curriculum innovations continue to strengthen professional preparation, the sustainability of teaching as a profession remains deeply affected by broader social, institutional, and policy pressures.

Conceptual Framing: Burnout, Professional Sustainability and Professional Identity

This chapter is conceptually grounded in three interrelated bodies of scholarship: teacher burnout, professional sustainability, and professional identity. Together, these frameworks provide a lens for understanding how structural conditions within education systems shape teachers' experiences, commitments, and decisions to remain in or exit the profession. Rather than treating teacher attrition as an individual failing or a natural outcome of technological change, these perspectives foreground the systemic, relational, and ethical dimensions of professional life. Importantly, the chapter also situates these debates within growing discussions surrounding artificial intelligence (AI), digitalisation, and the future of teaching. While technological developments are often presented as solutions to educational inefficiency and teacher workload, this chapter argues that the core crisis facing teaching is not professional extinction through automation, but increasing professional unsustainability under intensifying institutional, technological, and policy pressures.

Teacher Burnout, Emotional Labour, and Digital Intensification

Teacher burnout is a well-established concept in educational research, commonly defined as a psychological response to chronic workplace stress characterised by emotional exhaustion, depersonalisation, and a reduced sense of professional efficacy (Maslach & Leiter, 2016; Maslach, 2018). Teaching is widely recognised as a profession highly vulnerable to burnout due to its intensive emotional labour, relational demands, and moral responsibility. Teachers are required not only to deliver curriculum content but also to care for learners, manage behaviour, respond to trauma, and navigate complex social dynamics, often simultaneously.

In contexts such as South Africa, where teachers work within conditions of inequality, poverty, and under-resourced schooling, these pressures are intensified. The expectation that teachers will compensate for systemic shortcomings places sustained emotional and cognitive demands on individuals, increasing the risk of burnout (Van der Berg et al., 2016). Importantly, burnout is not simply a matter of individual resilience or coping skills, but is strongly shaped by organisational and structural conditions, including workload, support, recognition, and job security (Maslach & Leiter, 2016).

Contemporary discussions surrounding AI and digital technologies further complicate these dynamics. AI-driven systems are increasingly promoted as mechanisms for improving efficiency through automated marking, data analytics, lesson planning, and administrative management (Biesta, 2017; Holmes et al., 2019). In some respects, these technologies may reduce aspects of teachers' administrative workload and provide useful pedagogical support tools. Teachers may use AI to generate lesson ideas, draft feedback, develop moderation rubrics, or organise learning materials more efficiently (Biesta, 2017; Holmes et al., 2019).

However, the assumption that AI can substantially replace the intellectual, relational, and ethical dimensions of teaching remains deeply problematic. Assessment, for example, is not merely a technical process of grading learner performance. Effective assessment requires teachers to interpret student thinking, identify misconceptions, monitor developmental progress, and adapt pedagogy in response to learners' needs. These processes rely heavily on professional judgement, contextual understanding, and relational engagement. While AI may assist with administrative aspects of assessment, the meaningful interpretation of learner growth remains deeply connected to human pedagogical expertise (Selwyn, 2019; 2021).

Furthermore, the expansion of digital systems may intensify forms of administrative surveillance and algorithmic accountability within schools. Teachers increasingly operate within data-driven environments where performance metrics, reporting systems, and digital monitoring tools shape professional practice. Rather than reducing pressure, these technologies can contribute to workload intensification, reduced professional autonomy, and heightened anxiety surrounding performativity and accountability. In this sense, technological integration may simultaneously support and strain the profession.

This conceptualisation is particularly relevant to this chapter, as it helps explain why exhaustion and disengagement are evident not only among in-service teachers but also among pre-service teachers during teaching practice. When student teachers encounter school environments characterised by overload, digital administrative demands, and limited support, they begin to internalise burnout as an expected feature of professional life. Burnout thus becomes anticipatory, shaping intentions and aspirations even before formal entry into the workforce.

PROFESSIONAL SUSTAINABILITY AND EARLY-CAREER ATTRITION

While burnout focuses on individual experience, the concept of professional sustainability shifts attention to the conditions under which a profession can retain its workforce over time. Professional sustainability is concerned with whether teachers can maintain meaningful, healthy, and stable careers within existing systems, rather than merely entering the profession (Ingersoll et al., 2018). Research consistently shows that early-career teachers are particularly vulnerable to attrition, with a significant proportion leaving within the first five years of employment (Ingersoll et al., 2018). Factors contributing to this trend include heavy workloads, inadequate mentoring, employment insecurity, and a lack of professional autonomy. From a sustainability perspective, attrition is not interpreted as a problem of recruitment alone, but as evidence of systemic failure to support teachers across their professional lifecycle.

In the South African context, professional sustainability is further undermined by labour market instability and provincial disparities in employment practices. Post freezes, short-term contracts, and delayed appointments disrupt the transition from teacher education to employment, weakening professional commitment and confidence. At the same time, increasing digitalisation within education has generated additional expectations that teachers continuously adapt to new technologies, online systems, and platform-based forms of accountability, often without sufficient training or institutional support.

The sustainability lens is therefore critical for understanding why teaching persists as a socially necessary profession while simultaneously losing its capacity to retain those trained to practise it. Crucially, this framework also accommodates the idea of "hidden" or "anticipatory" attrition. When student teachers plan exit strategies, such as pursuing postgraduate study outside of school teaching, before formally entering the profession, the system loses potential long-term educators without this loss being reflected in official attrition statistics. Professional sustainability thus requires attention to teacher education spaces as key sites where retention is either strengthened or eroded.

Importantly, technological advancement does not eliminate the need for teachers. Rather, it reshapes expectations surrounding the profession. Teaching involves ethical judgement, emotional responsiveness, cultural interpretation, and relationship-building, dimensions that cannot be fully automated through AI systems. The growing reliance on digital technologies, therefore, raises important questions about how education systems can integrate technological support without reducing teaching to a purely technical or data-driven function (Williamson, 2017; Zawacki-Richter et al., 2019).

Professional Identity, Relational Pedagogy, and the Meaning of Teaching

Professional identity refers to how individuals understand themselves as professionals, including their sense of purpose, belonging, and recognition within a field. For many teachers, professional identity is strongly linked to moral purpose, social contribution, and relational engagement with learners. Teaching is often framed as a calling rather than simply an occupation, particularly in contexts where education is associated with social justice and transformation. However, professional identity is not fixed; it is shaped and reshaped through experience, institutional culture, policy environments, and increasingly, digital educational contexts.

In South Africa, student teachers frequently enter the profession with strong ideals about making a difference, contributing to community upliftment, and supporting learners beyond academic instruction. These ideals are reinforced during teacher education but are often challenged during teaching practice or WIL, where structural constraints limit teachers' capacity to enact their values. Employment insecurity, workload intensification, digital administrative pressures, and limited recognition undermine teachers' sense of professional worth, destabilising identity and weakening long-term commitment.

At the same time, contemporary educational discourse increasingly frames teaching as a function that can be supplemented or replaced through AI technologies, online learning platforms, and automated instructional systems. This chapter challenges such reductionist perspectives by arguing that teaching is fundamentally relational and human-centred. Teachers do not simply transmit information; they mediate values, build trust, recognise emotional needs, respond to social complexities, and cultivate belonging within classrooms. These relational dimensions remain central to effective pedagogy and cannot be meaningfully replicated through algorithmic systems alone (Biester, 2017; 2019).

The ethical implications of AI integration in education are therefore significant. While AI may support aspects of teaching practice, excessive reliance on automated systems risks narrowing conceptions of teaching to measurable outputs and technical efficiency. Such approaches may marginalise the emotional, ethical, and relational labour that defines much of teachers' professional work. Human-centred pedagogy consequently remains critical within increasingly digitised educational environments.

Professional identity tensions emerge when teachers experience a persistent mismatch between their values and the institutional conditions under which they work. Research suggests that these tensions contribute to disengagement, disillusionment, and eventual exit from the profession (Ingersoll et al., 2018). In this sense, the crisis facing teaching is not that teachers are becoming obsolete, but that the conditions necessary to sustain meaningful professional practice are becoming increasingly difficult to maintain.

Methodological Positioning and Reflective Approach

As teacher educators, we occupy a distinctive position at the intersection of policy, preparation, and practice. Our engagement with student teachers occurs across multiple sites, including coursework, teaching practice supervision, assessment of reflective assignments, and informal conversations regarding professional aspirations and concerns. These interactions provide insight into how student teachers interpret the profession they are preparing to enter and how structural conditions shape their expectations and decisions.

This chapter adopts a qualitative, interpretive approach informed by practitioner inquiry (Cochran-Smith & Lytle, 2009). More specifically, the chapter is situated within reflective practitioner scholarship, which recognises professional experience and sustained pedagogical engagement as valuable sources of analytical insight. It does not report on a formally designed empirical study, nor does it draw on systematically collected research data requiring prior ethical clearance. Instead, the analysis is informed by sustained engagement with pre-service teachers across multiple academic cohorts within a South African teacher education programme. The reflections presented emerged inductively through ongoing teaching, supervision, mentoring, and critical engagement with recurring student concerns over time.

Ethical considerations have guided the use of these insights. Because the reflections arise from everyday teaching practice rather than a formal research project, the chapter operates within the boundaries of professional reflective scholarship. This positioning aligns with scholarship recognising the value of practitioner knowledge and reflective inquiry in understanding professional practice (Ingersoll et al., 2018). No individual student voices are quoted directly; instead, composite representations are used to protect anonymity. The aim is not to present personal narratives but to illustrate how broader structural conditions are experienced during professional formation. This approach avoids the risks associated with extracting detailed accounts from potentially vulnerable participants while still allowing student perspectives to inform the analysis.

Although the absence of formal interview or survey data limits the ability to make population-level claims, this methodological stance offers important analytical value. Teacher education spaces are often overlooked as sites where professional disengagement begins. Yet research indicates that early experiences strongly influence long-term retention and career trajectories, making insights from initial teacher education particularly important for understanding patterns of attrition and sustainability in the profession (Ingersoll et al., 2018).

To contextualise these reflections within broader scholarly debates, a focused literature review was conducted using Google Scholar and related academic databases. A series of carefully selected keywords was used, including "teaching profession," "teacher burnout," "teacher retention," "teacher education," "teacher identity," "AI in education," "algorithmic pedagogy," and "early-career teachers." The review revealed a comparatively limited body of recent peer-reviewed scholarship focused specifically on teacher education and professional sustainability within the South African context. As a result, the review was expanded to include credible online sources, including newspaper articles and official reports, to provide a more comprehensive and current understanding of the topic. While the review primarily focused on literature published within the last twelve years to ensure the relevance and currency of evidence, preference was given to sources addressing teacher education, workforce sustainability, and changing classroom conditions in South Africa.

The chapter, therefore, presents contextualised professional reflections rather than empirical findings derived from human subject research. This distinction ensures ethical responsibility while contributing critically to professional discourse. By situating the analysis within teacher education contexts, the chapter offers a reflective yet analytically grounded perspective on how systemic pressures begin to shape perceptions of the teaching profession during its earliest stages.

Institutional Context

The reflections informing this chapter emerged within a school of education at a large, urban, research-intensive university in Johannesburg. The institution is widely recognised for its role in preparing teachers for diverse and often challenging schooling contexts across South Africa.

Historically, the institution reflects broader inequalities embedded within South Africa's apartheid education system, where access, resources, and educational quality were racially differentiated. Post-apartheid transformation initiatives significantly widened access and diversified the student population, although structural inequalities within schooling and higher education continue to shape educational experiences and opportunities.

Its initial teacher education programmes, offered at both undergraduate and postgraduate levels, combine theoretical coursework with practicum placements in a range of school environments, including under-resourced and high-density urban schools. This context is particularly significant given the broader structural pressures shaping the South African education system, including resource inequalities, workforce instability, policy reform, and increasing administrative demands on teachers. As a site of teacher formation, the school provides insight into how pre-service teachers encounter and interpret the realities of teaching as a profession under strain. It is within this context that student teachers begin to engage with issues such as employment uncertainty, workload intensification, professional precarity, digital and administrative pressures, and long-term career sustainability, making it a critical setting for examining how perceptions of a "crisis" in teaching emerge even before entry into the workforce.

Reflective insights

The insights presented here are derived from recurring patterns observed across multiple cohorts rather than isolated anecdotes. Student teachers consistently raise concerns related to employment insecurity, workload intensification, teacher burnout, and postgraduate study as an alternative career pathway or potential exit strategy from classroom teaching. The recurrence of these concerns suggests broader structural pressures shaping professional expectations rather than isolated individual dissatisfaction.

Importantly, these concerns increasingly intersect with anxieties about technological change, evolving accountability demands, and uncertainty regarding the future role of teachers within increasingly digitised educational environments. These patterns also point to a gap in existing research, which has not sufficiently examined how professional uncertainty and disengagement begin to emerge during teacher preparation rather than only after entry into the profession. Such an interpretive approach is consistent with qualitative traditions that prioritise contextual depth, professional insight, and analytical richness over statistical generalisability (Van der Berg et al., 2016).

EMPLOYMENT INSECURITY AND THE TEACHER LABOUR MARKET

Teaching is a profession that has a long and interesting history, from being a preferred career with high social status (Wolhuter et al., 2012) to being regarded as a career selected by young people, based on the extent that teaching is judged to be useful (Watt et al, 2012). This issue is particularly important because in the past 15 years, there has been a revived interest in studying teaching with an increase in students enrolling in initial teacher education programmes at both undergraduate and postgraduate levels (OECD, 2019; Van Broekhoven, 2015). However, in South Africa, the challenge facing teaching is best understood as one of retention and professional sustainability rather than outright extinction. Studies consistently link teacher exit to structural pressures: increased workload, low salaries, insecure employment, weak incentives, and limited resources (Mafukata & Mudau, 2016; Lumadi, 2011).

Work on attrition and early retirement likewise shows that these conditions demoralise teachers and contribute to resignation, while research on burnout finds that excessive demands and poor support are associated with emotional exhaustion and work-related stress (Bernstein & Batchelor, 2022; Mafukata & Mudau, 2016; Emsley et al., 2009). National supply-and-demand analysis further suggests that the problem is not only whether teachers are being produced, but whether graduates are being matched to demand and moved into stable posts in time to meet need (Van der Berg et al., 2022; Van Broekhuizen, 2015; 2016). Employment insecurity has emerged as one of the most significant threats to the sustainability of the teaching profession in South Africa. Despite ongoing discourse around teacher shortages, newly qualified teachers frequently encounter limited employment opportunities due to provincial budget constraints and post-provisioning freezes. This contradiction has produced a labour market characterised by both unmet classroom needs and unemployed or underemployed qualified teachers (BOSA, 2024a).

In recent years, several provinces, most notably the Western Cape, have implemented austerity measures that resulted in the freezing or reduction of teaching posts. For example, the Western Cape Education Department (WCED) reported a R3.8 billion budget shortfall, leading to a plan to cut 2,407 educator posts effective January 2025 (Damons, 2024). The KwaZulu-Natal province is facing a crisis with over 12,000 vacant teaching and administration posts, and at least 2,000 filled posts that it cannot afford (Magubane, 2025). The Gauteng province is experiencing a hiring freeze on middle-management posts and is struggling to manage a massive vacancy list. In addition, reports of non-renewal of contract teachers and delays in permanent appointments have heightened anxiety among graduating teachers, many of whom anticipate unemployment upon qualification (Bakharia, 2024). These conditions erode confidence in teaching as a stable career and undermine the perceived value of teacher education qualifications. Short-term contracts have become an increasingly common feature of the teacher labour market. While such arrangements may offer temporary relief for staffing shortages, they contribute to professional precarity by limiting job security, career progression, and access to benefits. Research suggests that employment instability is a key factor influencing early-career teachers' decisions to leave the profession or seek alternative career pathways (Ingersoll et al., 2018).

The persistence of unemployed qualified teachers alongside overcrowded classrooms raises serious questions about workforce planning and policy coherence. From a systemic perspective, the issue is not an oversupply of teachers, but a misalignment between training, budgeting, and deployment. This misalignment signals structural inefficiency rather than professional redundancy. For student teachers, awareness of these labour market realities shapes their professional orientation. Conversations during final-year courses frequently reflect concern about whether teaching offers a viable future. Such uncertainty weakens professional commitment and contributes to anticipatory attrition, where individuals plan exit strategies even before formally entering the profession.

Workload Intensification, Teacher Burnout, and Digital Pressures

Workload intensification is consistently identified as a central challenge facing the teaching profession in South Africa. Teachers are expected to fulfil multiple roles beyond instructional delivery, including administrative reporting, learner support, parental engagement, curriculum compliance, and pastoral care. These demands are particularly acute in under-resourced schools, where limited support structures amplify the burden placed on individual teachers (Van der Berg et al., 2016). Student teachers' experiences during teaching practice offer early insight into the cumulative effects of these pressures. Many report being overwhelmed by large class sizes, extensive administrative tasks, and the emotional demands of managing diverse learner needs. These experiences align with international research identifying workload and emotional labour as key contributors to teacher burnout (Maslach & Leiter, 2016).

In recent years, technological and AI-driven systems have increasingly been introduced into education with the promise of improving efficiency, streamlining administration, and reducing teacher workload. Digital platforms can assist teachers with lesson preparation, automated marking, attendance tracking, moderation support, data management, and drafting feedback. In some instances, these tools may alleviate repetitive administrative tasks and provide valuable professional support. However, the growing integration of AI into schooling has also introduced new forms of pressure and accountability. Teachers are increasingly required to engage with digital reporting systems, performance tracking tools, online learning platforms, and data-driven accountability measures, often without sufficient training or institutional support (Selwyn, 2019).

Importantly, while AI may support aspects of administrative work, it cannot replace the deeply relational and pedagogical dimensions of teaching. Assessment, for example, involves far more than assigning marks or generating feedback. Teachers must interpret learner thinking, identify recurring misconceptions, monitor developmental progress, and adapt instruction in response to learners' individual needs. These processes require contextual understanding, professional judgement, and sustained relational engagement. As Biesta (2021) argues, education cannot be reduced to processes of efficiency and measurable outcomes alone, because teaching fundamentally involves ethical judgement, human interaction, and the formation of persons. Excessive reliance on AI systems therefore, risks narrowing teaching to technical performance indicators while overlooking the intellectual and emotional labour central to effective pedagogy.

Burnout is characterised by emotional exhaustion, depersonalisation, and a diminished sense of professional efficacy. Teaching is especially vulnerable to burnout due to its relational nature and moral responsibility. In contexts where teachers are expected to address social problems such as poverty, trauma, and behavioural challenges without adequate support, the risk of burnout increases significantly (Maslach & Leiter, 2016). Of particular concern is the emergence of burnout symptoms among pre-service teachers. Student teachers often interpret their practicum experiences not as temporary challenges, but as indicators of what awaits them in full-time employment. This anticipation of chronic stress contributes to early disengagement and shapes intentions to leave the profession (Ingersoll et al., 2018).

The integration of digital technologies may also intensify professional anxiety by contributing to forms of administrative surveillance and algorithmic accountability. Data-driven schooling environments increasingly position teachers within cultures of measurement, monitoring, and performativity, where professional value becomes tied to quantifiable outputs and compliance with digital systems (Williamson, 2017). Rather than reducing pressure, these developments may deepen feelings of exhaustion, reduce professional autonomy, and reinforce perceptions of teaching as an increasingly unsustainable profession.

Teacher unions and education stakeholders have increasingly raised concerns about mental health and well-being, calling for greater institutional support and realistic workload expectations (IOL, 2024). However, systemic responses remain limited, and responsibility for coping with stress is frequently individualised. Such approaches obscure the structural origins of burnout and reinforce narratives of personal resilience rather than collective responsibility. The persistence of workload intensification and burnout undermines not only individual well-being but also the long-term sustainability of the profession. Without meaningful intervention, these conditions threaten to perpetuate cycles of attrition, further exacerbating staffing challenges and destabilising the education system.

Rather than signalling the extinction of teaching, these conditions suggest a profession under increasing strain from intersecting institutional, technological, and social pressures. While AI and digital technologies may provide important support tools, they cannot replace the relational, ethical, and human-centred dimensions that remain fundamental to teaching and learning.

Postgraduate Study as an Exit Strategy

One of the most striking patterns observed among pre-service teachers is the framing of postgraduate study as a pathway out of classroom teaching rather than as professional advancement within the profession. While further study has traditionally been associated with career progression, leadership development, or specialised expertise, many student teachers articulate postgraduate education as a means of escape from what they perceive as an unsustainable professional environment.

Conversations with final-year students frequently reveal aspirations to pursue Honours, Masters, or doctoral studies in fields adjacent to education, such as policy analysis, educational technology, psychology, or higher education teaching. Others express intentions to transition entirely out of education into sectors perceived as offering greater stability and work-life balance. These aspirations are often articulated alongside explicit concerns about workload, burnout, and employment insecurity within school teaching. Research on early career teachers indicates that intentions to leave the profession often emerge well before actual exit and are shaped by perceptions of future working conditions (Ingersoll et al., 2018). In the South African context, awareness of post freezes, short-term contracts, and limited career progression reinforces the perception that classroom teaching offers limited long-term prospects. As a result, postgraduate study becomes a strategic response to structural uncertainty rather than a purely academic pursuit.

This trend reflects what may be described as "anticipatory attrition," in which individuals begin planning their exit before formally entering the profession, often after early encounters with workload pressures, limited prospects, and professional disillusionment during teacher preparation (Struyven & Vanthournout, 2014; Ingersoll et al., 2018). Such patterns are rarely captured in official attrition statistics, which typically focus on teachers who have already entered and left the workforce. This highlights a conceptual gap in attrition research, which tends to focus on exit after employment while overlooking pre-entry withdrawal and intention formation. However, the loss of potential long-term teachers at the point of entry represents a significant, if largely invisible, challenge to professional sustainability. The emotional dimension of this phenomenon is also notable. Student teachers often describe feelings of guilt or ambivalence about leaving a profession they once viewed as a calling (Struyven & Vanthournout, 2014). This tension highlights the disjuncture between the moral purpose associated with teaching and the material conditions under which it is practised. When commitment is met with precarity, further study becomes both a protective strategy and a means of preserving professional identity.

From a systemic perspective, the use of postgraduate study as an exit strategy raises important questions for teacher education and policy. If initial teacher education programmes increasingly serve as transitional spaces rather than pipelines into sustained classroom practice, then current models of workforce planning are insufficient. Addressing this issue requires not discouraging further study but improving the conditions that make continued classroom teaching a viable and attractive option. This pattern also has implications for how success is measured within teacher education. High graduation or postgraduate enrolment rates may mask underlying dissatisfaction with classroom teaching. Without attention to the structural drivers of exit, efforts to strengthen the profession risk addressing symptoms rather than causes.

DISCUSSION: TEACHING IN CRISIS, NOT EXTINCTION

The evidence presented in this chapter does not suggest that teaching is disappearing. Rather, it points to a profession experiencing structural weakening and increasing unsustainability. The South African case challenges dominant extinction narratives surrounding the future of teaching, particularly those suggesting that technological advancement and artificial intelligence (AI) will render teachers obsolete. Teaching persists because it remains socially necessary and institutionally central to schooling systems. Teachers continue to play critical roles in social cohesion, ethical formation, emotional support, and contextualised learning, dimensions of education that cannot be fully automated or replicated through algorithmic systems (Biesta, 2017).

At the same time, the findings reveal a profession under significant strain. Research consistently demonstrates that employment precarity, declining morale, workload intensification, and inadequate institutional support contribute to professional disengagement and attrition (Ingersoll et al., 2018; Maslach & Leiter, 2016). In South Africa, these pressures are further intensified by overcrowded classrooms, uneven resource distribution, administrative overload, and unstable employment pathways for newly qualified teachers. The issue, therefore, is not that teaching is becoming irrelevant, but that the conditions necessary to sustain teachers are steadily deteriorating.

Importantly, contemporary debates surrounding AI and digital technologies risk oversimplifying the nature of teaching by framing it primarily as the transmission of information or the management of measurable outcomes. While AI-driven technologies may assist with lesson preparation, administrative tasks, assessment moderation, and data management, the evidence presented in this chapter suggests that teaching involves forms of relational, ethical, and emotional labour that remain fundamentally human. Teachers do not simply deliver curriculum content; they interpret learner needs, respond to emotional and social complexities, exercise professional judgement, and cultivate meaningful relationships within classrooms. These dimensions of teaching cannot be reduced to automated processes without fundamentally altering the nature and purpose of education itself.

Furthermore, technological integration may simultaneously alleviate and intensify professional pressures. Although AI has the potential to reduce some administrative workload, it may also contribute to increased forms of digital surveillance, performativity, and algorithmic accountability within schools. Teachers are increasingly expected to comply with data-driven reporting systems, online platforms, and performance monitoring mechanisms that expand administrative demands rather than reduce them. In this sense, technological change does not necessarily resolve the sustainability crisis facing teaching, but may in some contexts deepen existing tensions surrounding workload, autonomy, and professional identity (Selwyn, 2019; Williamson, 2017).

Framing teaching as a profession facing extinction therefore risks misdiagnosing the problem. Such narratives shift attention away from the structural conditions undermining the profession and toward technologically deterministic assumptions about replacement. By contrast, understanding teaching as a profession in crisis foregrounds the possibility of institutional intervention, professional renewal, and systemic reform. The evidence discussed in this chapter suggests that professional disengagement begins early, often during teacher preparation itself. Student teachers encounter the realities of schooling during practicum placements and interpret these experiences as indicators of their future professional lives. Overcrowded classrooms, limited mentoring, emotional exhaustion, digital administrative pressures, and insecure employment prospects shape their professional identities and influence long-term career intentions. Research indicates that such early experiences strongly affect teacher retention and professional sustainability (Ingersoll et al., 2018).

The South African case therefore, reveals a profession weakened not by irrelevance, but by persistent misalignment between expectations, institutional support, and working conditions. Public discourse continues to position teachers as central agents of national development, social justice, and educational transformation, yet these symbolic expectations are rarely matched by material support or sustainable professional conditions. This contradiction contributes to burnout, anticipatory attrition, and declining professional confidence among both pre-service and practising teachers.

Ultimately, this chapter argues that the future of teaching should not be understood through binary debates about human replacement versus technological advancement. Rather, the central issue concerns how education systems can integrate technological innovation while preserving the relational, ethical, and human-centred dimensions of teaching. AI may support aspects of professional practice, but it cannot replace the interpersonal, moral, and contextual work that defines meaningful education. The challenge facing education systems is therefore not whether teachers will disappear, but whether the profession can remain sustainable under increasingly complex institutional, technological, and social pressures. This distinction is critical for reframing global debates about the future of teaching and for designing interventions that address the structural causes of teacher disengagement and attrition.

FUTURE RESEARCH DIRECTIONS

Future research should move beyond describing teacher dissatisfaction and trace how exit intentions are formed across the full pathway from teacher education into the early career years. The South African literature already points to the main pressures "unsatisfactory remuneration, lack of resources, uninvolved parents, learner diversity, and an overwhelming workload" (Botha et al, 2023) while other work suggests that "the greatest threat to the retention of teachers in the teaching profession appears to be ways in which provincial and regional education offices appropriate teacher appointment policies and procedures" (Diko & Letseka, 2009, p. 228). At the same time, studies of teacher well-being and early attrition show that burnout and leaving are not sudden events, but processes shaped by work stress, emotional exhaustion, and discontent over time (Harmsen et al, 2018; Botha et al, 2023). Future studies should therefore be longitudinal, following student teachers into their first appointments to examine how mentoring, induction, school placement, workload, and contract security shape retention intentions and professional identity. They should also move from description to evaluation by testing interventions that are likely to matter in practice, such as reduced administrative burden, stronger early-career support, mentoring, and more coherent appointment processes, because the current evidence base mostly identifies the problem rather than showing which responses improve retention and well-being. A further priority is the policy-to-practice gap in South African staffing, since the literature suggests that retention depends not only on teacher motivation but on how posts are filled, supported, and sustained in provincial systems.

CONCLUSION

This chapter has argued that the teaching profession in South Africa is not becoming extinct but is confronting a growing crisis of sustainability driven by structural neglect, institutional pressures, and changing educational conditions. Employment insecurity, workload intensification, emotional exhaustion, and policy incoherence signal systemic strain rather than professional obsolescence. While debates about artificial intelligence (AI) and digital technologies increasingly shape discussions about the future of education, the evidence presented here suggests that the central challenge is not technological replacement, but the erosion of the conditions necessary to sustain meaningful professional practice over time.

Although AI may assist with administrative tasks, lesson preparation, and assessment support, teaching remains fundamentally relational work requiring emotional labour, ethical judgement, contextual responsiveness, and sustained human engagement (Maslach & Leiter, 2016). Teachers continue to play indispensable roles in supporting learners, mediating values, and responding to the social and emotional complexities of classrooms. At the same time, technological integration may intensify professional pressures through increased surveillance, performativity, and data-driven accountability demands.

The chapter further demonstrates that these pressures begin shaping professional identities and career intentions during teacher education itself. Student teachers frequently interpret practicum experiences as indicators of future working conditions, confirming research that attrition is often seeded early in professional formation (Ingersoll et al., 2018). Reimagining the future of teaching therefore, requires more than technological innovation or recruitment-focused policies. It requires coherent employment policies, manageable workloads, meaningful institutional support, and greater alignment between teacher education and labour market realities.

Ultimately, the South African case demonstrates that teaching is not threatened by irrelevance, but by the normalisation of unsustainable working conditions. For policymakers and global audiences alike, the key challenge is not whether teachers will disappear, but whether education systems can sustain the relational, ethical, and human-centred dimensions of teaching in increasingly complex institutional and technological environments.

PERSONAL NARRATIVES

Narrative 1- Researcher 1

How I became interested in education, obstacles, and problems:

Well, my grandmother was a teacher- I am told. My elder sister was a teacher as well. So, teaching runs in the family- I guess. I became interested in education, obstacles, and problems from an early age, growing up in Soweto, South Africa. This was during the height of apartheid, when the education of a black child was treated as inferior. I became interested in education when looking up to our teachers as role models was just heartbreaking because the teaching profession at the time was viewed as starving for dignity. I became interested in education even when graduating from high school was a challenge on its own, let alone going to university. Yes, it was difficult. At that point, it was difficult to even go to the teachers for support, for they themselves were afraid of their own lives. We did, however, have teachers who never gave up on us. One for me was my Biology teacher. For some reason, she saw a future for me. One day, she made me teach Biology lessons in class because she said that I had potential. She was aware of my stuttering but said that I should not let that bother me because she saw a teacher in me. Later, when I was in matric, my mother said to me that I would not be rich in monetary value, but through me and my teachings, children would be educated. 21 years later, I am still in the classroom teaching and loving it. I guess I was meant to be in the classroom.

Narrative 2- 4th Year Bachelor in Education (Foundation Phase) Undergraduate Student

My interest in education developed gradually through experiences of helping younger children in my family and community with schoolwork and everyday learning. I realized that I enjoyed explaining ideas, encouraging children, and seeing their confidence grow when they understood something new. Those moments made me recognise that teaching was more than a job; it was a meaningful way to make a difference in people's lives. Choosing Foundation Phase teaching (Grade R- 3- Elementary/ Kindergarten) as a male was not easy because many people see it as a female-dominated field, and they questioned me every time as to why a man would want to teach young children (5-9-year-olds). At times, I had to overcome doubt, stereotypes, and the pressure to choose a career that others considered more suitable for men. However, these challenges helped me become more determined and confident in following a path that matched my passion and values.

My early teaching experiences taught me that working with young learners requires patience, creativity, and genuine care. I quickly learned that successful teaching is not only about presenting content, but also about creating a safe and supportive environment where children feel valued and ready to learn. Some lessons went well, while others required me to adapt and think differently, which helped me grow professionally. Being a male Foundation Phase teacher has also shown me the importance of representation, as learners benefit from seeing positive male role models in nurturing educational spaces. I hope my presence helps challenge stereotypes and shows children that kindness, guidance, and care are qualities that belong to everyone. These experiences have shaped my growth as a teacher and strengthened my commitment to helping young learners build a strong foundation for their future learning.

Narrative 3- 1st Year Masters in Education (Foundation Phase)- Inservice Teacher

When having to choose a career path, one is drawn to the impact of their role, the incentives that will be gained, and the possibility of more opportunities that may come. The list of career choices was endless, and I was caught between passion and job security. I choose the latter. The decision was based on hoping I would not struggle to secure a job as soon as I graduated. Education became the path I chose. It was a selfless choice as I've always been told that one does not become a teacher to be rich, but rather to impact lives. In hindsight, I still agree that job security is important. I found that I grew to find passion in ways that I did not expect. Teaching changed from being a job title to being a transformative role I actively poured myself into each day as I stood in front of my class. I realised the importance of my passion and how it impacted the little children I was entrusted with.

Like any role, being a teacher has its challenges. Personally, the one I still find challenging to date is being expected to be a *"jack of all trades"*. I am expected to fulfil certain duties I feel I am not qualified for; I may have been exposed to the skills, but not enough to confidently deliver. An example within the classroom setting would be the expectation to be able to teach the home language and the additional language the school offers. I have the basic communication skills of the additional language; however, it is not enough to adequately teach it. This is a major challenge, and as a result, I had to intentionally avoid teaching at a state school, as I would be regarded as not being able to fulfil the requirements of the post. Therefore, I had to look for a job within the private sector, as they often have a designated individual who is natively exposed and fluent in the additional language.

This has served as a challenge because, as a lifelong scholar, exposure to different settings is important. I have found that my views about educational settings are not as vast because I have only had teaching experience in the private sector. The private sector has its challenges, yes; they, however, are nothing compared to state schools. At times, I desire to be in a state school not only to gain experience but to bring about the change I would like to see and potentially address some of the learning issues that are there. Another challenge I have encountered with the *"jack of all trades"* is the role that is outside the classroom, which are extra murals. These are what I call contractual obligations that require filling hours that are non-related to my teaching qualification. They are a slow passion killer, especially for individuals such as myself who managed to finish 12 years of academic schooling, not playing sports but being invested in other forms of school activities. Now, due to filling hours, I "teach" sport even though I am inadequately trained, as my teaching degree did not have an extramural or sport module; this is the part of my role I had to teach myself.

Apart from the challenges, I have sought to overcome them in ways that I find fulfilling, and this is through furthering my studies, hence I have proceeded to pursue a postgraduate degree. I have found that teaching has become a skill that I have perfected, but with each new academic year, I find that children are not the same. They seem to be evolving in ways that could not solely be sustained by the skills I have perfected and those I have acquired during my undergraduate qualification. Their interests, needs, and challenges vary. As a result, I needed to pursue and engage in what is current in education and what could inform my teaching practice beyond skill. I have found that I may not be able to teach in a state school, but through furthering my studies, I may potentially suggest teaching practices that may impact the change I wish to see. Being able to work with and be guided by experienced supervisors in the higher institution I am at has been meaningful to my growth as a teacher. The lectures have exposed me to so much content that I can apply to my practice.

As a result, I envision myself being a lecturer one day and instilling the same passion for growth and change. In conclusion, although my teaching journey began as a pursuit of job security, it has turned out to be far more meaningful. Through positive impact on each learner, I grew in passion. Apart from the challenges and opportunities, I continue to teach because I am committed to making a difference.

Narrative 4- 2nd Year Masters in Education (Pre-service Teacher)

Becoming the Teacher I Once Needed

From an early age, I started to understand that different students experience education in different ways. My experience growing up in a socioeconomically disadvantaged area gave me insight into the different ways learners receive support and encouragement to succeed. Although I could not describe it, I always wanted learning to become an exciting and valuable experience that everyone could enjoy. The desire, which I had developed through my teaching experiences, eventually transformed my teaching identity and professional goals. The classroom design I wanted to create would deliver a completely different educational experience. My path to becoming a teacher began many years ago.

My education journey was not straightforward, as I initially worked in marketing and wealth management. The two fields helped me develop my communication skills and my ability to interact with others, but I wanted to perform work that had greater significance. Education attracted me because it enabled me to work directly with students while establishing connections through my innovative approaches to teaching. I have always valued empathy and human connection, and teaching gave me a space to express these qualities. Choosing education as my career path meant two things for me: I wanted to develop myself personally, and I wanted to help others. My entry into the profession created a crisis of confidence for me because it demonstrated that passion alone would not enable success in the field.

Adjusting to existing school structures and expectations was one of my biggest challenges. As a new teacher entering the field, I found myself surrounded by veteran educators who were often reluctant to embrace new ideas. My efforts to put into practice what I had learned from my education met with resistance and created a degree of conflict between the desire to implement change and the desire to contribute positively to the school environment. Additionally, I found myself overcompensating by attempting to give students the same experience I had when I was attending school. Consequently, I used a great deal of energy to ensure that the learning experience would be enjoyable for students, sometimes overlooking the practical aspects of delivering instruction, such as time and the constraints of the curriculum. As a result of these experiences, I began to reflect on the challenge of blending my passion with the realities of being a teacher.

My educational path reached its critical moment when I started teaching at an international Muslim school. The school environment made me feel like an outsider because I was the only Black person who practiced Islam at that time. The space developed into my primary development location after an extended period of time. I developed skills for connecting with people who possess diverse cultural and religious identities, which led to my increased understanding of different cultures. My experiences with students from low-income backgrounds solidified my dedication to providing equal educational opportunities for all learners. I discovered that true inclusion requires two elements, which include providing access to resources and establishing authentic spaces where people can feel at home.

My tutoring experience taught me more about inclusion, which I learned through language studies. I worked with students who struggled to express themselves in English and allowed them to use their home languages. The students developed better self-assurance and classroom involvement, which helped them grasp academic material. I discovered that language usage determines whether it helps or prevents learning. The anti-bullying drama activity in the Life Skills class became one of my strongest teaching experiences. The entire classroom stopped talking when a quiet student used a puppet to say, *"I don't like coming to school because they laugh at me."*

Through these experiences, I have come to see teaching as a continuous journey of learning and reflection. I see empathy, patience, and collaboration as essential skills, which I practice every day. I now approach teaching with a greater sense of balance, which combines my passion with my deliberate teaching methods. I consider myself an educator who continues to develop my teaching skills through perpetual learning. My goal is to create a space where every learner feels seen, heard, and valued. I am developing into the teacher that I needed during my school years, and this process leads my professional development.

REFERENCES

Bakharia, U. (2024, September 3). Western Cape education says no teacher retrenchments despite loss of 2,400 jobs due to budget cuts. Mail & Guardian. Retrieved from https://mg.co.za/education/2024-09-03-western-cape-education-says-no-teacher-retrenchments-despite-loss-of-2400-jobs-due-to-budget-cuts/#:~:text=3%20September%202024-,Western%20Cape%20education%20says%20no%20teacher%20retrenchments%20despite%20loss,jobs%20due%20to%20budget%20cuts&text=The%20Western%20Cape%20education%20department,teachers%20won't%20be%20reappointed

Bernstein, C., & Batchelor, T. (2022). Qualitative exploration of workplace demands, resources, and bullying among teachers in South African schools: Implications for individual and organisational well-being. *South African Journal of Education*, *42*(2), 2081. DOI: 10.15700/saje.v42n2a2081

Biesta, G. (2017). *The rediscovery of teaching*. Routledge. DOI: 10.4324/9781315617497

Biesta, G. (2021). *World-centred education: A view for the present.* Routledge. [100.1] DOI: 10.4324/9781003098331

BOSA. (2024a). Over 32,000 teachers lost in five years as teaching shortage crisis spirals. Retrieved from https://bosa.co.za/over-32-000-teachers-lost-in-five-years-as-teaching-shortage-crisis-spirals/

BOSA. (2024b). Teaching shortage crisis: 1,200 Western Cape teachers quit as 12,700 remain jobless. Retrieved from https://bosa.co.za/teaching-shortage-crisis-1-200-western-cape-teachers-quit-as-12-700-remain-jobless/

Botha, M., De Jager, S., & Evans, R. (2023). 21st-century South African teachers in turbulent educational waters. Journal of Education (University of KwaZulu-Natal), 92, 6-22. DOI: 10.17159/2520-9868/i92a01

Cochran-Smith, M., & Lytle, S. L. (2009). Teacher research as stance. In Noffke, S. E., & Somekh, B. (Eds.), *The SAGE handbook of educational action research* (pp. 39–49). SAGE. DOI: 10.4135/9780857021021.n5

Damons, M. (2024, August 27). Thousands of teaching posts to be cut in the Western Cape: Schools are expected to receive their 2025 staff allocations on Friday. Ground UP. Retrieved from https://groundup.org.za/article/2400-teaching-posts-will-be-cut-in-western-cape-in-2025/#:~:text=In%20the%20circular%2C%20the%20WCED's,are%20now%20proposed%20for%202025

Davids, L. (2023). *Faculty of Education-CALT Launch 25 October 2023.* University of the Western Cape.

Diko, N. N., & Letseka, M. (2009). Policy appropriation in teacher retention and attrition: The case of North-West Province. *Perspectives in Education*, *27*(3), 228–236.

Emsley, R., Emsley, L., & Seedat, S. (2009). Occupational disability on psychiatric grounds in South African school-teachers. *The African Journal of Psychiatry*, *12*(3), 223–226. DOI: 10.4314/ajpsy.v12i3.48498 PMID: 19750252

Hargreaves, A., & Fullan, M. (2015). *Professional capital: Transforming teaching in every school.* Teachers College Press.

Harmsen, R., Helms-Lorenz, M., Maulana, R., & Van Veen, K. (2018). The relationship between beginning teachers' stress causes, stress responses, teaching behaviour and attrition. *Teachers and Teaching*, *24*(6), 626–643. DOI: 10.1080/13540602.2018.1465404

Hofmeyr, J. (2016). International literature review on alternative initial teacher education pathways. [102.1]Prepared for the Zenex Foundation, Johannesburg. JET Education Services. Retrieved from https://www.zenexfoundation.org.za/international-literature-review-on-alternative-initial-teacher-education-pathways/initial-teacher-education-learning-briefs/

Holmes, W., Bialik, M., & Fadel, C. (2019). *Artificial intelligence in education: Promises and implications for teaching and learning*. Center for Curriculum Redesign. [103.1]

Independent Online (IOL). (2025, 06.10). Teachers face burnout as austerity measures spark crisis in education. Retrieved from https://iol.co.za/capetimes/news/2025-06-10-teachers-face-burnout-as-austerity-measures-spark-crisis-in-education/

Ingersoll, R. M., Merrill, L., & Stuckey, D. (2018). Seven trends: The transformation of the teaching force. CPRE Research Reports. University of Pennsylvania. Retrieved from https://repository.upenn.edu/cpre_researchreports/108

Lumadi, M. (2011). Teachers' exodus in South African schools: A smoke with burning fire. *Contemporary Issues in Education Research, 1*(3), 31–40. DOI: 10.19030/cier.v1i3.1192

Mafukata, M. A., & Mudau, A. V. (2016). [104.1]Exploring teacher mass resignation and early retirement from public schools. *Human and Social Sciences, 3*(2), 2243–2255.

Magubane, T. (2025, November 12). 12,000 vacant teaching, admin posts in KZN Department of Education impacting on operations. IOL News (The Mercury). Retrieved from https://iol.co.za/mercury/2025-11-12-12000-vacant-teaching-admin-posts-in-kzn-department-of-education-impacting-on-operations/

Mampane, P. M. (2012). The teacher turnover crisis: Evidence from South Africa. *Business Education & Accreditation, 4*(2), 73–83.

Maslach, C. (2018). Burnout: A multidimensional perspective. In Professional burnout (pp. 19-32). CRC Press.

Maslach, C., & Leiter, M. P. (2016). Understanding the burnout experience: Recent research and its implications for psychiatry. [105.1]. *World Psychiatry; Official Journal of the World Psychiatric Association (WPA), 15*(2), 103–111. DOI: 10.1002/wps.20311 PMID: 27265691

Organisation for Economic Co-operation and Development (OECD). (2019). [106.1]TALIS 2018 Results (Volume I): Teachers and school leaders as lifelong learners. Department of Basic Education, Pretoria, South Africa. Retrieved from www.education.gov.za/Portals/0/Documents/Reports/Talis%20Teachers%20and%20Principals%20as%20Lifelong%20Learners%20Final.pdf?ver=2019-07-02-090156-000[107.1]

Pitsoe, V. (2013). Teacher attrition in South Africa: Trends, challenges and prospects. *Journal of Social Sciences, 36*(3), 309–318. DOI: 10.1080/09718923.2013.11893197

Rusznyak, L., Balfour, R., Van Vollenhoven, W., & Sosibo, L. (2016). Why academic depth and rigour in university-based coursework matter for prospective teachers. [108.1]. *Perspectives in Education, 34*(1), 1–9. DOI: 10.38140/pie.v34i1.1939

Selwyn, N. (2019). *Should robots replace teachers?: AI and the future of education.* John Wiley & Sons. [110.1]

Selwyn, N. (2021). *Education and technology: Key issues and debates.* Bloomsbury Publishing. [109.1]

Struyven, K., & Vanthournout, G. (2014). Teachers' exit decisions: An investigation into the reasons why newly qualified teachers fail to enter the teaching profession or why those who do enter do not continue teaching. *Teaching and Teacher Education, 43*, 37–45. DOI: 10.1016/j.tate.2014.06.002

Taylor, N., & Mawoyo, M. (2022). Professionalising teaching: The case of language and literacy. In Spaull, N., & Pretorius, E. (Eds.), *Early Grade Reading in South Africa Reading* (pp. 164–178). Oxford University Press.

Tonder, D. V., & Fourie, E. (2015). Alleviating the intensification of educator workload through internships: The Relieve Educators' Administrative Demands (READ) model. *International Journal of Educational Sciences, 9*(2), 219–232. DOI: 10.1080/09751122.2015.11890312

UNESCO, & International Task Force on Teachers for Education 2030. (2024). Global report on teachers: Addressing teacher shortages and transforming the profession. UNESCO. DOI: 10.54675/FIGU8035

Van Broekhuizen, H. (2015). Teacher supply in South Africa: A focus on initial teacher education graduate production. Stellenbosch: Stellenbosch University Department of Economics Working Paper 07, 2015. Retrieved from https://ideas.repec.org/p/sza/wpaper/wpapers239.html

Van Broekhuizen, H. (2016). [111.1]Graduate unemployment, higher education access and success, and teacher production in South Africa. Doctoral dissertation. Stellenbosch University. Retrieved from https://resep.sun.ac.za/wp-content/uploads/2017/10/VAN-BROEKHUIZEN-H.-2015.-Graduate-unemployment-Higher-Education-access-and-success-and-teacher-production-in-South-Africa.pdf

Van der Berg, S., Gustafsson, M., & Burger, C. (2022). School teacher supply and demand in South Africa in 2019 and beyond[112.1]. Social Science Research Network. DOI: 10.2139/ssrn.4213003

Van der Berg, S., Spaull, N., Wills, G., Gustafsson, M., & Kotzé, J. (2016). Identifying binding constraints in education. [113.1]. *The South African Journal of Economics*, *84*(4), 1–20. DOI: 10.1111/saje.12108

Watt, H. M., Richardson, P. W., Klusmann, U., Kunter, M., Beyer, B., Trautwein, U., & Baumert, J. (2012). Motivations for choosing teaching as a career: An international comparison using the FIT-Choice scale. *Teaching and Teacher Education*, *28*(6), 791–805. DOI: 10.1016/j.tate.2012.03.003

Williamson, B. (2017). Big data in education: The digital future of learning, policy and practice. *Sage (Atlanta, Ga.)*. Advance online publication. DOI: 10.4135/9781529714920

Wolhuter, C., Van der Walt, H., Potgieter, F., Meyer, L., & Mamiala, T. (2012). What inspires South African student teachers for their future profession? *South African Journal of Education*, *32*(2), 178–190. DOI: 10.15700/saje.v32n2a570

Zawacki-Richter, O., Marín, V. I., Bond, M., & Gouverneur, F. (2019). Systematic review of[114.1] research on artificial intelligence applications in higher education: Where are the educators? *International Journal of Educational Technology in Higher Education*, *16*(39), 1–27. DOI: 10.1186/s41239-019-0171-0

ADDITIONAL READING

Barkhuizen, N., Lesenyeho, D. L., & Schutte, N. (2020). Talent retention of academic staff in South African higher education institutions. *International Journal of Business and Management*, *12*(1), 191–207.

Books, S., & Ndlalane, T. (2011). What the US could learn from South Africa about education and social justice. *Educational Foundations*, *25*, 83–102.

Bush, T., & Glover, D. (2016). School leadership and management in South Africa: Findings from a systematic literature review. *International Journal of Educational Management*, *30*(2), 211–231. DOI: 10.1108/IJEM-07-2014-0101

Fourie, A., & de Klerk, W. (2024). The psychological well-being of schoolteachers in South Africa: A critical review. *Journal of Psychology in Africa*, *34*(1), 95–105. DOI: 10.1080/14330237.2024.2311989

Governder, L., Hoffmann, N., & Sayed, Y. (2016). *Teacher professionalism and accountability in South Africa: A review of the literature*. Cape Peninsula, University of Technology. Retrieved from https://hdl.handle.net/10779/uos.23471291

Hoadley, U. (2012). What do we know about teaching and learning in South African primary schools? *Education as Change*, *16*(2), 187–202. DOI: 10.1080/16823206.2012.745725

Lotz-Sisitka, H. (2011). Teacher professional development with an education for sustainable development focus in South Africa: Development of a network, curriculum framework, and resources for teacher education. *Southern African Journal of Environmental Education*, *28*, 30–71.

Mkhwanazi, S. (2014). Crossing the past political boundary: Teacher professional learning in a South African reform context. *Mediterranean Journal of Social Sciences*, *5*(10), 425–432. DOI: 10.5901/mjss.2014.v5n10p425

Moloi, K. (2007). An overview of education management in South Africa. *South African Journal of Education*, *27*(3), 463–476.

Msibi, T., & Mchunu, S. (2013). The knot of curriculum and teacher professionalism in post-apartheid South Africa. *Education as Change*, *17*(1), 19–35. DOI: 10.1080/16823206.2013.773924

Sayed, Y., Singh, M., Bulgrin, E., Henry, M., Williams, D., Metcalfe, M., . . . Mindano, G. (2021). Teacher support, preparedness and resilience during times of crises and uncertainty: COVID-19 and education in the Global South. *Journal of Education (University of KwaZulu-Natal)*, (84), 125-154.

KEY TERMS AND DEFINITIONS

Foundation Phase: First few years of the child's formative formal education (Grade R- Grade 3)

Intermediate Phase: In the South African context, this is the introductory phase to theory, where reading for learning is introduced (Grade 4 - Grade 7)

Senior Phase: In the South African education context, this is the continuation of reading for learning in terms of progression; the concepts are getting harder compared to the others (Grade 8 - Grade 12).

Work Integrated Learning (WIL): It is learning by doing, while studying. Instead of only applying theory in a classroom, students also apply what they have learned in a real workplace setting.

Chapter 9
Teachers' Voices From Greece

Konstantinos Haskis
http://orcid.org/0009-0003-0065-9155
University of Ioannina, Greece

Tatiani Gkatsa
http://orcid.org/0000-0002-2060-7171
University of Ioannina, Greece

Panagiota Papanikolaou
http://orcid.org/0009-0007-4252-5111
University of Ioannina, Greece

ABSTRACT

The Greek education system has evolved through a long historical trajectory closely linked to the political, cultural, and social development of the Greek state. From its origins in ancient philosophical thought to its contemporary alignment with European educational policies, education has functioned as a central pillar of national identity, social cohesion, and civic formation. This chapter examines the historical foundations, modern structure, reform initiatives, teacher education, professional development mechanisms, and current challenges of Greek education within a European context. It explores governance, curriculum reform, digital transformation, inclusive education, and higher education modernization, while highlighting persistent challenges related to student performance, teacher status, and institutional effectiveness. The chapter concludes with personal narratives of three university lecturers, offering critical perspectives on the teaching profession and its future in Greece.

EDUCATION IN GREECE: HISTORICAL EVOLUTION AND LIVED EXPERIENCES ACROSS EDUCATIONAL LEVELS

Konstantinos Haskis
Tatiani Gkatsa

Introduction

Education constitutes a dynamic and multifaceted institution, reflecting the social, cultural, and political transformations of each era. In the Greek context, the evolution of the educational system is closely intertwined with the country's historical trajectory, reform efforts, and the contemporary challenges emerging from globalization and technological advancement.

However, understanding education cannot be confined to institutional or historical analyses alone. Its deeper meaning unfolds through the voices of educators themselves - those who experience, interpret, and shape educational reality in their

DOI: 10.4018/979-8-3373-8983-7.ch009

everyday practice. Their personal trajectories act as a bridge between theory and practice, shedding light on dimensions of education that often remain overlooked in macro-level approaches.

This chapter is part of a broader collective effort to highlight the experiences of educators from diverse educational systems and cultural contexts. Within this framework, three complementary perspectives are presented, offering a multidimensional view of education in Greece. The first part focuses on the historical development of the Greek educational system, outlining key milestones and reforms. The second part shifts attention to the lived experience of a primary school teacher, emphasizing her relationship with the school environment and everyday educational practice. The third part broadens the perspective by presenting the longitudinal journey of a university educator, tracing her path from early schooling to the academic environment, including significant transitions across different educational settings and stages.

Through this synthesis, the chapter seeks to highlight both the continuity and the transitions that characterize education as a system and as a lived experience. At the same time, it aims to underscore the central role of the educator as an agent of change, adaptation, and meaning-making within an ever-evolving educational landscape.

Laying the foundations of European education and modern reforms of Greek education system

The Greek education system has undergone profound transformations throughout its long history, reflecting the nation's complex political, cultural, and social evolution. From its ancient philosophical traditions to contemporary European integration efforts, education in Greece has consistently functioned as a cornerstone of national identity and social development. This report explores the historical trajectory of the Greek education system, its modern structure and reforms, the processes of teacher education and training, and the mechanisms of professional development and certification within the teaching profession.

Historical overview of education in Greece

Education in Greece has deep historical roots and has played a foundational role in the cultural and political formation of Greek city-states. In ancient Athens, education had a humanistic and philosophical orientation. Its purpose was not limited to the transmission of knowledge but aimed at shaping the "good citizen," who would combine intellectual cultivation, moral integrity, and physical fitness. Teaching music, grammar, and rhetoric sought to develop logical and aesthetic judgment. The contribution of philosophers to the evolution of educational thought was significant. Socrates, through what later became known as Socratic teaching, Plato, through the Academy, and Aristotle, through the Lyceum, systematically established pedagogical and epistemological models that profoundly influenced Western tradition.

During the Hellenistic and Roman periods, education spread throughout the broader Greek-speaking world. The founding of the Library of Alexandria and other intellectual centers elevated the Greek language as an international medium of science and knowledge (Fraser, 1972). Greek education also deeply influenced Roman culture, as Roman aristocrats adopted the Greek educational model and employed Greek teachers.

After the Roman period, Byzantine education acquired a strongly religious character. The Church assumed responsibility for disseminating knowledge and preserving the Greek language. Education was divided into three levels: elementary, secondary, and higher. Elementary education focused on writing, reading, and chanting; secondary education studied classical authors; and higher education covered rhetoric, philosophy, and theology (Bouzakis, 2002).

During the Ottoman period, after the fall of Constantinople in 1453, Greek education faced significant restrictions, though it was not eradicated. The Church maintained a central role in preserving the Greek language and faith through schools operating near monasteries and bishoprics (Dimaras, 1973). At the same time, significant schools were established in major commercial and intellectual centers such as Ioannina, Smyrna, and Mount Athos, where philosophy, theology, and sciences were taught. The term "secret school," though largely symbolic, reflects the struggle to preserve education under foreign domination (Nirvanas, 2010).

After the Greek War of Independence in 1821 and the establishment of the independent Greek state, education was reorganized on a national basis. Ioannis Kapodistrias is considered the founder of organized education in Greece (1828–1831). He established the Central School of Aegina (1829), the first teacher-training school of the new state, and strengthened the operation of mutual-teaching schools in the provinces. He also created orphanages with an educational character, combining intellectual and vocational training (Dimaras, 1978; Bouzakis, 2002). His initiatives laid the foundation for the development of a national education system.

After the establishment of the Greek state (1830), the educational system was organized according to the Bavarian model. The 1834 law established primary, Greek-language, and secondary education, while the University of Athens (1837) became the first higher education institution in the Balkans (Fragoudaki, 1985). Despite modernization efforts, poverty and the lack of schools limited access to education (Bouzakis, 2002).

During the 20th century, new pedagogical approaches and the linguistic conflict between Katharevousa and Demotic Greek profoundly influenced schools (Tsoukalas, 1981). In 1917, Eleftherios Venizelos introduced the use of Demotic Greek in teaching and renewed the school curriculum (Dimaras, 1978). However, political turmoil during the interwar period and the Occupation led to the degradation of schools (Bouzakis, 2002).

Postwar education was characterized by centralization and ideological control. The 1964 reform established free education, the use of the Demotic language, and nine-year compulsory schooling (Papanoutsos, 1976). These reforms were suspended during the Military Dictatorship (1967–1974).

After 1974, education in Greece became democratized. In 1976, Demotic Greek was definitively established as the language of instruction (Law 309/1976). During the 1980s and 1990s, the Unified Lyceum and the Panhellenic examination system were introduced for admission to higher education, while higher education itself was expanded (Matsagouras, 2007).

From 2010 onwards, educational reforms in Greece have focused on digital modernization, the evaluation of teaching performance, the enhancement of early childhood education, and the reform of teaching practices based on the principles of STEM, differentiated learning, and experiential learning (Ministry of Education, 2019). At the same time, inclusive policies have been promoted to create a school without exclusion, where all students - regardless of socio-economic, cultural, or learning background - have equal opportunities to participate and learn (UNESCO, 2020; Soulis, 2015).

Contemporary Greek education has undergone continuous reforms, reflecting the social and ideological developments of the country. Despite the challenges, it remains a cornerstone of Greek society and a key factor in the nation's progress and cohesion.

The modern education system and its reforms

Today, the Greek education system is governed by the Ministry of Education, Religious Affairs, and Sports. It is divided into four main levels: preschool education, primary education, secondary education, and tertiary education. Education is compulsory from the ages of 4 to 15, encompassing preschool (Νηπιαγωγείο), primary (Δημοτικό), and lower secondary (Γυμνάσιο) levels (OECD, 2020). Upper secondary education (Λύκειο) is optional but essential for university entry.

The system remains highly centralized, with the Ministry defining curricula, textbooks, and teacher appointments. However, in recent years, there has been a gradual shift toward decentralization and school autonomy (OECD, 2018). The introduction of all-day schools, digital learning platforms, and competency-based curricula mark significant modern developments (Alexiadou, 2020).

The performance of Greek students in the international PISA assessments consistently shows lower results compared to the OECD average. According to 2022 data, Greece ranks 44th among approximately 80 participating countries (OECD, 2023), with students scoring around 430 points in mathematics, 438 points in reading comprehension, and 441 points in science, compared to OECD averages of approximately 472, 476, and 485 points, respectively (OECD, 2023). A significant proportion of students (~26%) falls below the minimum proficiency level, while only a small proportion (~4%) reaches the highest skill levels (OECD, 2023). These results indicate a need to improve education in Greece, with an emphasis on developing fundamental skills in mathematics, reading comprehension, and scientific thinking (OECD, 2023).

Higher education is exclusively public and tuition-free for undergraduate studies. It is organized into Universities (πανεπιστήμια) and technical universities (πολυτεχνεία), while the Hellenic Authority for Higher Education (HAHE) ensures quality assurance and accreditation. Since Greece joined the Bologna Process in 1999, its higher education structure follows the three-cycle system - Bachelor's, Master's, and Doctorate - with ECTS credits applied (Verdis, 2017).

Key recent reforms include the digital transformation of schools through the "*Digital School*" initiative, inclusive education policies for students with disabilities, and efforts to internationalize Greek universities by offering English-taught programs. In 2023, reforms emphasized the modernization of vocational education, promoting apprenticeships and aligning qualifications with labor market needs (European Commission, 2024).

Teacher education and training in Greece

Teacher education in Greece has evolved from traditional teacher seminaries to university-based programs aligned with European standards. Primary school teachers are trained in four-year university departments of education, while secondary school teachers typically graduate from discipline-specific faculties (e.g., Mathematics, Philology, Physics) and subsequently complete pedagogical and teaching training programs (Kazamias & Mattheou, 2008).

Since 2013, pedagogical competence has been formally required for teaching positions in secondary education. This competence can be acquired either through postgraduate studies in education or through completion of certified pedagogical courses (Alexiadou, 2019).

Practical training, though often criticized for its limited scope, constitutes a key component of teacher preparation. Many universities have developed partnerships with schools for supervised teaching practice, combining theoretical coursework with classroom experience (Kassotakis & Verdis, 2013).

Recent years have seen a growing emphasis on developing teachers' digital literacy, critical thinking, and inclusive education skills. The National Center for Public Administration and Local Government (EKDDA) and the Institute of Educational Policy (IEP) offer seminars and training programs aimed at equipping teachers with competencies relevant to the digital era and intercultural education.

Teachers' professional development and certification

Professional development and certification are crucial elements in maintaining educational quality in Greece. Teachers are appointed through national examinations conducted by the Supreme Council for Civil Personnel Selection (ASEP). This competitive process assesses both subject knowledge and pedagogical skills.

Once employed, teachers are expected to engage in lifelong learning through continuous professional development (CPD) programs. The Ministry and regional educational centers (PEKES) provide workshops, online courses, and mentoring programs to enhance teachers' professional capacity (Verdis, 2020).

A certification system introduced in recent years aims to ensure continuous evaluation and progression. Teachers undergo assessment based on their teaching effectiveness, contribution to school life, and engagement in professional development activities (Alexiadou & Zmas, 2021). Although this system has faced criticism for bureaucratic rigidity and insufficient support, it represents a step toward aligning Greek education with European quality assurance frameworks.

Furthermore, European-funded programs such as Erasmus+ have expanded opportunities for teacher mobility, international cooperation, and exposure to innovative pedagogical practices. Digital learning environments and professional networks have also gained prominence, especially after the COVID-19 pandemic, which accelerated the digitalization of Greek education.

Teacher compensation system

The salary progression of teachers in Greece is determined by the unified public sector pay scale. It includes specific salary grades linked to years of service and academic qualifications. Permanent teachers are promoted to higher grades over time, while holding postgraduate or doctoral degrees can lead to additional salary increases. Furthermore, assuming positions of responsibility, such as school principal or education advisor, comes with extra allowances and additional points in performance evaluations.

According to the OECD report "Education at a Glance 2024", teachers in Greece are among the lowest paid in OECD countries. Starting salaries for newly appointed teachers' amount to approximately €13,104 per year, placing Greece near the bottom of the ranking, with only Slovakia and Latvia reporting lower salaries. Additionally, between 2015 and 2023, real teacher salaries in Greece decreased by 9%, while the average in other countries increased by 4%.

At the same time, a significant number of teachers work as substitutes, who are assigned each year to different schools and regions based on the system's needs. Substitutes perform the same educational work as permanent teachers, but job insecurity and frequent relocations affect their professional stability and quality of life. Low pay combined with the high cost of living, especially in tourist areas (islands) and Athens, creates considerable difficulties for teachers in finding suitable housing. Many teachers are forced to travel long distances or share accommodations, which burdens their daily lives and affects their well-being.

This situation highlights the need to revise salaries and improve working conditions to ensure the professional dignity of teachers and the quality of education.

Salaries of Higher Education instructors and faculty

In Greece, the salaries of teaching and research staff (faculty) at universities remain limited, with the basic salary for full professors around €3,420 gross, and lower salaries for lecturers and assistant professors, depending on experience and position. The salary scale is narrow and allowances are limited, which restricts differentiation and the competitiveness of Greek higher education institutions.

At the international level, according to the OECD report "Education at a Glance 2025," average salaries for higher education staff are significantly higher, with $61,958 for junior staff, $73,682 for intermediate staff, and $108,255 for senior staff, corresponding to approximately 59% higher earnings than those of workers with tertiary education overall. Similarly, in many European countries, university salaries far exceed Greek salaries, especially at higher ranks.

This comparison highlights that Greece ranks low in faculty salaries, which may affect the attraction and retention of high-quality academic personnel. Adjusting salaries to international levels is considered an important step for enhancing the quality and competitiveness of Greek higher education.

Conclusion

The evolution of Greece's education system reflects the nation's ongoing effort to balance its rich historical legacy with the demands of modernization and globalization. The reforms of recent decades demonstrate a commitment to inclusivity, quality assurance, and lifelong learning. However, persistent challenges - such as excessive centralization, limited practical training, and unequal access to resources - continue to affect the efficiency of educational outcomes.

Looking forward, the continuous professional development of teachers, the modernization of curricula, and the cultivation of digital and intercultural competencies will be key to ensuring that Greek education meets the needs of the 21st century. The alignment with European educational standards and the embrace of innovation will determine the country's success in transforming education into a truly dynamic and equitable system.

THE POWER OF TEACHING: FROM ANCIENT GREEK LITERATURE TO STUDENTS' LIFE STORIES

Konstantinos Haskis

The historical overview presented above highlighted the key transformations and milestones that have shaped the evolution of education in Greece, emphasizing the broader institutional and socio-political context. However, understanding education cannot be limited to macro-level analysis alone; it gains depth and meaning when viewed through the lived experiences of those who actively participate in it.

In this light, the following section shifts the focus from a collective historical narrative to the personal account of a primary school teacher, offering insight into her relationship with the school environment, her students, and her professional role.

My professional and academic journey is deeply connected to my passion for education and my firm belief that teaching constitutes the most important factor in shaping the future of our society. From my very first steps in the field of classical philology, my aim has been not only to transmit knowledge, but also to cultivate an environment that fosters growth, self-confidence, and creativity in students.

My journey into education was far from predetermined. As a teenager, I aspired to become a lawyer, following in the footsteps of my elder brother. Yet life often leads us along unexpected paths. It was a secondary school teacher of Ancient Greek, during my preparatory courses for university admission, who first awakened in me a profound love for language, intellectual inquiry, and pedagogy. That encounter marked the beginning of my lifelong engagement with philology.

I pursued my undergraduate studies in Philology at the University of Ioannina, where my academic identity began to take shape. Immersing myself in the texts of ancient Greek literature, with their intricate layers of meaning, inspired me to continue my studies abroad. At Royal Holloway, University of London, I undertook a postgraduate program specializing in ancient comedy, focusing particularly on the works of Aristophanes. This period was intellectually transformative: the academic environment, the dialogue with scholars and students from diverse cultural backgrounds, and the use of modern interpretive frameworks offered me fresh perspectives on classical texts.

Subsequently, I completed my doctoral dissertation at the University of Ioannina, Department of Philology, focusing on ancient Greek tragedy. My thesis, entitled "*Myth and Fragmentation: Mythological Adaptations in Minor Tragic Poets of the 5th and 4th Century BC*", examined how lesser-known tragic poets of the classical period reworked mythological narratives to serve their dramatic compositions. This demanding yet rewarding research journey allowed me to engage deeply with a rich and multifaceted literary tradition.

Although my initial ambition was to pursue an academic career in higher education, the scarcity of positions led me to secondary education - a decision I have never regretted. In schools, I discovered a dynamic environment where knowledge meets everyday life, and where teaching acquires its fullest meaning through the eyes and aspirations of young people. A classroom is not merely a space for instruction; it is a shared arena of encounter, intellectual growth, emotion, and dreams.

One of the most poignant experiences of my career occurred during my work at a Greek school in Germany. There, I met Eliza, a student of Russian origin. She was exceptionally bright, fluent in Greek, English, and German. Her personal circumstances were difficult: her father had passed away, her mother had remarried, and her financial resources were limited. To support herself, she worked every Saturday at a fish shop. Despite these obstacles, her dedication to learning was remarkable. She dreamed of becoming an engineer and asked me to tutor her in Greek. I declined any payment - her passion and determination were rewarding enough.

Years later, Eliza was admitted to Aristotle University of Thessaloniki. I vividly recall the moment when she offered me a small gift and invited me to dinner as a gesture of gratitude. That encounter captures, for me, the very essence of teaching: the profound human bond that can emerge within a school community.

Another dimension of the teaching vocation that I deeply cherish is meeting former students' years after their graduation. It is a source of genuine joy to encounter them as adults - university graduates, professionals, and parents - who approach me with warmth and respect, eager to share their life journeys. These encounters affirm, in the most tangible way, the lasting resonance of a teacher's words and presence during their formative years.

I vividly remember one such instance: a young man visited the school to meet his brother, who was completing his teaching practicum. This young man was my student at the University of Ioannina during the two semesters in which I delivered a philosophy course on the work of the Stoic philosopher Marcus Aurelius, "*Meditations,*" to students of the Department of Philology. He remembered me clearly and expressed how much he had enjoyed that course. Such moments of unprompted recognition remain among the most meaningful rewards in a teacher's career.

Today, I serve as the principal of a secondary school. Although administrative responsibilities have reduced my classroom hours, daily interaction with students remains a cornerstone of my professional life. I take time to talk with them, to listen to their concerns, and to understand their challenges. The role of the contemporary educator extends far beyond the dissemination of knowledge: it encompasses mentorship, empathy, and the cultivation of students' confidence and agency.

Assuming the role of school principal was, for me, the natural evolution of my professional path. I perceive school leadership not merely as an administrative task but primarily as an educational responsibility. The functions of a principal include a vital link between students, teachers, parents, and the wider community. The principal's role is to inspire, to encourage, to form a vision, and to foster a culture of cooperation and respect.

From the very first day I undertook the duties of principal, I set as my main objectives:

- the creation of a safe and inclusive school environment for every student,
- the enhancement of creativity and innovation in teaching practice,
- the support of teachers through continuous dialogue, training, and collaboration,
- and the strengthening of the relationship between school and society, so that the school functions as a living organism within its broader social context.

My experience to date has taught me that educational leadership is, above all, an act of service. It means listening, understanding, supporting, and creating the conditions under which every member of the school community can thrive. It means addressing challenges with responsibility, cultivating a climate of trust, and reinforcing the spirit of collectivity.

Looking back on my journey so far, I feel that the common thread connecting each stage - from my studies and research to my teaching and leadership - is my love for children and my unwavering belief in the transformative power of education. As a principal, I continue to learn every day, not just from theory and experience but mainly from my interactions with students and fellow educators.

Education, after all, is a continuous journey of learning and growth. For me, the greatest achievement is not only professional advancement but also the ability to contribute, with all my strength, to the creation of a school community that supports, inspires, and cultivates the future.

Meanwhile, I continue to engage in research and publish in academic journals. My scholarly identity has not diminished; rather, it enriches my pedagogical practice. Classical education, which has shaped my intellectual journey, remains a foundation for critical thought, analytical rigor, and meaningful dialogue.

I profoundly love the teaching profession. It is a vocation that keeps one intellectually alive and renewed through continuous contact with young people who dare to dream of the future. Together with them, one dreams as well. This shared journey - within and beyond the classroom - remains the most precious gift of my life.

Looking ahead, the teaching profession faces both significant challenges and promising opportunities. In an era marked by rapid social change, technological advancement, and increasing complexity in students' needs, educators are called upon to assume multifaceted roles that extend well beyond traditional instruction. The future of teaching lies in the epistemic integration of deep disciplinary knowledge, pedagogical innovation, and reflective practice, grounded in ethical responsibility and professional judgment. Within this framework, teaching emerges as an experiential, dialogical, and critically reflective process, in which educators continuously reinterpret knowledge in relation to learners' lived realities. At the same time, sustained professional development and institutional support are essential in enabling teachers to navigate evolving educational paradigms and to exercise professional autonomy. Despite systemic constraints, the profession retains its profound social mission: to cultivate critical thinking, resilience, and intellectual agency in learners. Ultimately, for those who approach teaching as a vocation rooted in lifelong learning, reflective inquiry, and genuine human connection, its prospects remain not only viable but deeply meaningful and socially indispensable.

ALWAYS AT SCHOOL – NEVER JUST AT WORK

Panagiota Papanikolaou

My name is Panagiota Papanikolaou and I am a primary education teacher. I have been serving in primary schools in Greece for 22 years, having worked in a variety of educational and social environments. For the last three years I have had the honor and responsibility of acting as a principal in a primary education school.

For me, school is not just a place of professional activity. It is a community, a living organism that constantly challenges, motivates and educates me.

Every time I'm asked:

"What do you do for a living?" I answer with a small, but meaningful variation:

"I don't go to work....I go to school!"

First of all, I would like to emphasize that public and free education was decisive for my path. It gave me the opportunity to be who I am today. Looking back in time as a student of a small primary school, in a mountainous village in Tzoumerka in Epirus, I realize that I could not have imagined that I would be able to overcome the obstacles and difficulties and achieve my goals. Perhaps the fact that my father was a teacher played a decisive role and so, in a natural and effortless way, the idea of following the same path took root in me. Years later, in the national exams that I took, studying at the pedagogical department was one of my first choices. Becoming a teacher was then simply a choice of profession for me, but along the way I realized that it was something that I deeply desired and that perfectly expressed me.

When I started studying at the Department of Primary Education of the University of Ioannina, I was full of dreams, enthusiasm and impatience. I believed that university studies were enough, however, I realized that it was only the beginning of my studies. Real development comes through practice, constant critical thinking and continuous training.

I am grateful that I had the opportunity to continue my studies at the same University, free of charge, obtaining a Master's Degree in "Social Sciences and Education", Postgraduate Education, a second degree in the Department of Philosophy, Pedagogy and Philosophy and a PhD in Philosophy of Education and at the same time teaching in primary schools. The University of Ioannina and in particular the Department of Pedagogy remains for me a place of knowledge, collaboration and lively dialogue. I maintain close contact with the Department, participate in programs and actions and continue to be inspired - just like back then, at the beginning of my journey. It is a dynamic process that makes me redefine my role as a teacher and enrich my epistemological and teaching background.

As part of my master's degree in "Social Sciences and Education", I chose to focus on the study of the phenomenon of bullying, which, in 2005, was a relatively unknown field in the Greek educational discourse. My research engagement with this phenomenon provided the theoretical background for the design and implementation, over a number of years, of prevention, awareness-raising and intervention programs on issues of school violence and bullying in the schools where I worked. These interventions were implemented with basic pedagogical principles of active student participation, teamwork and role-playing. An important part of this process was the creation by Filanagnosia of the program "With Books We Defeat Violence", whose thematic axis were school violence and bullying. The students borrowed relevant literary works, presented the stories, dramatized them and discussed them, approaching the phenomenon in an experiential way. Through this action, text comprehension emerged as a valuable tool for emotional education, the development of empathy and the cultivation of critical thinking, acting as a bridge between theory and educational practice. The implementation and long-term operation of the text comprehension program in my classes was presented at scientific conferences as a good practice.

In 2010, I completed my studies at the Department of Philosophy, Pedagogy and Psychology, specializing in Psychology, obtaining my second university degree. This specialisation significantly enhanced my pedagogical work, as it provided me with a deeper understanding of the psycho-emotional needs of students, contributed to more effective classroom management and strengthened my communication and interpersonal skills at school.

Furthermore, after successfully completing the written exams, I participated in the two-year training program (Teachers' Institute- didaskaleio), during which I studied for two academic years at the Department of Pedagogy. During the training, I delved into issues of pedagogical theory, teaching methodology and modern educational approaches, further strengthening my scientific and teaching background.

A pivotal point in my educational and research journey was the completion of my PhD in Philosophy of Education. This experience provided me with a solid epistemological foundation, which helps me interpret and understand in depth the educational reality, theoretical approaches and educational policies. Through philosophical analysis, my ability to reflect, ask critical questions and seek transformative practices in education was cultivated.

If I had to choose certain stages that empowered and shaped me as an educator and as a personality - beyond my continuous training and studies - I would focus on the following. An important milestone in my professional career was the school where I taught for eleven years. It was a real "school" for me in the broadest sense: a creative environment, full of opportunities for learning, development and innovation. There I learned to "stand on my own two feet", to experiment, to plan, to collaborate and to deal with crisis situations. My students, colleagues and I working together implemented many educational programs, participated in Erasmus+ programs, developed extroverted actions and cultivated a culture of trust, support and joint creation. Erasmus+ programs are European educational initiatives funded by the EU that promote mobility, intercultural cooperation, and the professional development of educators, providing opportunities for training and the exchange of best practices among teachers from different countries. There I felt - and learned - that when there is mutual respect and a shared vision, anything is possible. Our participation in Erasmus+ programs has been especially crucial for managing professional stress and enhancing the mental resilience of both educators and students. Particularly significant was the mobility experience in Braga, Portugal, within the framework of the "Mindfulness in Nature" program, which focused on improving mental well-being through the practice of mindfulness in natural settings. Through experiential workshops and outdoor activities, we developed skills that promote concentration, relaxation, and self-awareness, while simultaneously strengthening social cohesion and inclusion within the educational community. We exchanged experiences, practices, and initiatives with colleagues from other countries and recognized the value of mindfulness as a tool for managing both personal and professional stress.

Furthermore, mindfulness techniques help students develop self-regulation skills, improving their individual performance as well as the collaborative atmosphere in the classroom.

Of course, I would single out the school principal who was a source of inspiration for me. Always supportive in the collaboration we had during those years and I would dare to say my mentor in my later career as a principal. She was the one who encouraged me to apply for the position of principal, believing that I possessed all the qualifications and the strength to lead a new school unit. I will never forget the day I had to submit my application and found a note from her on my classroom desk: "Take the next step… you deserve it!"

A special place in my professional and personal career is occupied by my participation in the innovative program "Role Models", of the Greek Social Security Institution, which highlighted the power of education as a lever for overcoming social and economic obstacles. Through this action, individuals who inspired students were presented, acting as role models. They encouraged their students to dream, to dare and to claim their future, overcoming the limits that are often set by the social and not only starting point and that they can overcome through education. In the innovative program, I collaborated with an excellent professor, who was also the reason for me to reflect on my role as a teacher. Our paths once again crossed and the proposal to take part in this action was deeply honorable. Education is, in my opinion, the most valuable social good. For vulnerable socio-economic groups, it is often the only realistic opportunity for progress, equal participation and a life with dignity. A good teacher is not just a carrier of knowledge; he/she is a companion of students on the path to thought, values and self-determination. He/ She is the one who will inspire, listen, activate the dynamics of critical thinking and action, cultivate empathy through everyday pedagogical practice.

I deeply believe that the role of the teacher must primarily be human-centered with respect for diversity, commitment to the values of democratic education and a willingness to continuously learn and reflect.

Teaching, for me, is much more than the transmission of knowledge; it is the creation of a relationship, a relationship of empowerment, trust and inspiration. It is a continuous and open dialogue with students, with colleagues, with society, but also with myself. I do not experience it as a static process, but as a living and dynamic interaction, which evolves over time and is influenced by the needs and conditions of the time.

The teacher, in my personal opinion, must be an intellectual in practice: connecting theory with educational reality, reading the social context and intervening in a reflective but also practical way.

In an era where public education is being tested by successive crises and the role of the teacher is often questioned, I consider it crucial to preserve and strengthen the right of everyone to quality public education. At the same time, it is necessary to recognize in practice the value of educational work and to strengthen the role of the teacher as a carrier of knowledge, morality and social change. Empowering teachers is not a luxury, but a prerequisite for an education that responds to the challenges of the era. There is a need for substantial recognition of their mission and support, so that they can carry out their role with freedom, reflection and prestige.

It is not self-evident – nor easy – to reflect on my journey as a teacher. And yet, looking back, I can say with certainty that I would not change a thing. Every experience, every difficulty, every success and failure has brought me here, has developed me both as a person and as a professional as well.

If you had asked me in my early steps how I imagined my professional life, I certainly could not have predicted its evolution. I remember my first year as a teacher being the most difficult. In fact, I had thought that this profession might not be the one for me. Now I cannot imagine myself not being a teacher, not being in a public school - despite the difficulties, frustrations and challenges that inevitably accompany the teaching role.

The most hopeful thing for me is that I continue to strive in ominous times for the autonomy and freedom of educational discourse. I insist on fighting for a better school, more open, more just, more collaborative and more democratic. I hope there are many of us in this fight.

But what is the future of the teaching profession?

Global narratives surrounding the teaching profession often raise the question of whether teaching jobs are likely to disappear, mainly as a result of technological advancement and the expansion of digital learning. In the international context, artificial intelligence, digital platforms, and distance education are frequently presented as factors that may reduce the need for human teaching. However, the case of Greece demonstrates that the role of the teacher is not being abolished but rather transformed.

Despite the severe demographic challenge and the decline in the student population, Greek society continues to attribute a significant social role to teachers. Teaching is not confined to the transmission of knowledge; rather, teachers contribute substantially to students' socialization, to the management of social inequalities, and to the cultivation of democratic awareness. The digital era reinforces the need for teachers with pedagogical competence and the ability to use technology critically, rather than for their replacement.

In Greece, the prospects of the teaching profession depend to a large extent on political choices and public investment in education. Although the profession is being questioned in terms of its modes of practice, it remains necessary and socially decisive. The future of the teacher does not lie in disappearance, but in adaptation to new social, technological, and pedagogical conditions.

I have to go now… I have to go to SCHOOL!!!

STEPS OF THE MIND, STEPS OF THE HEART: MY EDUCATIONAL JOURNEY

Identity of a Greek educator – psychologist

Tatiani Gkatsa

The personal narrative of the primary school teacher underscored the significance of everyday educational practice and interpersonal relationships within the school context. It also illustrated how professional identity is shaped through experience, challenges, and continuous interaction with the educational environment.

Expanding this perspective, the third section moves into a different yet interconnected domain: higher education. Through the lived experience of a university educator, it presents a longitudinal journey of learning and professional development, tracing a path that begins in early schooling and extends into the academic world, including formative transitions across diverse educational settings and stages.Today, I work as a permanent teaching and laboratory support staff member at a University of Education and Primary School Pedagogy in Greece. Looking back, I feel that my path was not simply a series of events or professional choices; it was a journey of identity, through which the traits that define me today were gradually built: as a teacher, as a psychologist, as a human being.

Childhood: family, play, and early learning

As a child, I grew up in a two-story house with a yard and garden, in a provincial town with a flourishing economy, where the majority of residents were involved in fur manufacturing and trade. My parents ran a fur workshop on the ground floor; my father was simultaneously a merchant, while my mother worked in the workshop with dedication. Together with my two siblings, I had the opportunity to enjoy both parental supervision and the freedom to explore, play, and discover the world around me.

I was very diligent and consistent in my studies from an early age, but I also had a strong need for play. I enjoyed team games that held my interest, quickly losing interest in those that did not inspire me. Very early, I realized that reading fascinated me far more than most games; my mother's magazines and the newspapers she brought home offered new images, stories, and knowledge that captivated me more than any game. I remember spending Sundays with my pocket money to buy an adventure magazine, reading it in two hours, and then returning it so that I could access a second one, demonstrating both discipline and my early love for reading.

My love for knowledge expanded when I discovered the public lending library in my small town, which, fortunately, was the fourth largest in the wider area. During my elementary school years, I would read up to three books per week, a habit that continued into middle school, although later my focus shifted to preparing for university admission.

At home, my study routine in elementary school usually lasted 30–45 minutes at midday, and before bedtime, I reviewed the lessons for the next day. Studying was an obligation I carried out independently, without supervision, but always with discipline. Play remained my top priority. I was a good student, with consistent performance across all subjects.

School years: early responsibilities and teaching

In middle school, my focus shifted even more toward academic subjects. By the end of the second year, I began helping classmates and local children, primarily in French and written composition. My first teaching experience arose when family friends asked me to support their son, who had failed French in the first year and was preparing for a retake exam. Despite my own difficulties with physics, I excelled in languages, history, mathematics, and chemistry.

Through these early teaching experiences, I began to understand the joy of transmitting knowledge and the responsibility an educator has toward their students. I realized that teaching is not merely conveying information, but a process of empathy and support, where each student is treated as an individual with their own life, priorities, and dreams.

My choice to pursue studies in the Faculty of Philosophy with a focus on Psychology was deliberate. It reflects my love for knowledge, my need to understand people, and my desire to support others in their personal development. At the same time, I maintained curiosity and dedication in my studies, seeking answers through books, encyclopedias, and discussions with older peers. My parents fully supported this path, providing me with the resources and stimuli needed for further growth.

Good teachers for me were those with knowledge, respect, and vision, who inspired us and gave us space to get to know them personally. Conversely, there were examples of poor teachers, mainly at university, where some experiences left me in uncomfortable situations, something that had never occurred during my childhood or adolescence. These experiences strengthened my determination to become an educator who respects and inspires her students.

Childhood: the first seeds of respect and admiration

In my childhood, my first teachers did not serve as conscious role models. They did not directly influence my thinking about the future. Yet, they were steady figures who evoked respect and admiration in me. My first teacher had something that fascinated me - the calmness she carried, her presence, the way she stood in the classroom. Sometimes, I would imitate her, not in matters of teaching, but in simple gestures, in the way she spoke.

Later, during higher grades, I met teachers who influenced me more deeply. They were not only knowledgeable; they were people with vision and humanistic ideals. From them, the hidden charm of education was born within me, almost unconsciously. A feeling that followed me quietly, pushing me toward a path that had already begun to take shape within my identity.

Adolescence - high school: the first conscious choices

In high school, when the time came to think about the profession I would pursue, my eyes were already turned toward education. It was not a sudden decision, but the result of everything I had felt until then: the respect I had for my teachers, the fascination for knowledge, the sense that the classroom is a living space of learning and relationships.

University years: dreams and limitations

As a university student, I encountered professors whom I admired deeply, even though they often seemed distant and unapproachable. My greatest desire was to continue toward a PhD. However, circumstances did not allow it: the professor I was most interested in as a supervisor was in another city, and I, already married, could not bear the expenses of maintaining a second life elsewhere.

That deprivation taught me my first great lesson: that life brings obstacles, but those very obstacles can become starting points for new paths. So, I was led to begin working in private tutoring schools.

Tutoring years: passion and awareness

I started working as a tutor with a deep desire to help my students achieve their goals. My dedication was so strong that sometimes I did not realize how fully I involved myself in their efforts. I remember a particularly talented and committed student who ultimately chose a different path than expected. Years later, when we met again, she spoke to me with love and admiration, acknowledging my effort and faith in her. It was then that I realized that what truly remains is not grades or exam success, but the relationship, the belief, and the support the student felt. For me, that moment was a profound reminder that our role as educators is not only to guide students toward academic achievement but also to respect their personal choices and the unique paths they follow.

Postgraduate studies and family: resilience

Later, I decided to pursue an MSc in Child and Adolescent Mental Health. This experience was marked by national recognition and a scholarship, even though I was already married and expecting my first daughter. My thirst for learning became immense. I felt that I was living simultaneously for my family and for my work. During this period, I developed resilience - the ability to balance multiple roles, to continue learning despite challenges, and to persevere in demanding circumstances.

Special education: embracing diversity

Being appointed as a special education teacher in secondary education was a turning point. I was among the first educators in the country with specific qualifications, working with students with diverse and atypical learning difficulties in inclusive classrooms. This experience fostered a deep understanding that each student is unique. I learned that there is no single 'normal'; there are many forms of learning and life paths.

Parallel roles: Social contribution

My career expanded to include parallel roles: I worked as a mental health counselor, as coordinator at the Observatory for the Prevention of School Violence and Bullying, and I led educational programs in mainstream middle and high schools. These experiences developed my sense of social contribution. Education is not confined to the classroom; it is a social responsibility and an intervention that can impact entire communities.

University teaching: The Joy of collaboration

After many years of work, research, and writing, I joined the university in a permanent teaching position. Teaching university students was a new challenge. I did not want to merely transmit knowledge; I wanted to walk alongside them. We researched together, wrote together, and published collaboratively. This experience strengthened my belief that knowledge is a collective process. As a university educator, I am not only a transmitter of knowledge but also a fellow traveler in learning.

Books: cultivating the love of knowledge

My deep love for knowledge was cultivated through extensive reading: literary works, world classics, philosophy, essays, and poetry - especially by Greek poets. This extensive reading was not a luxury; it was a necessity.

Through books, I developed critical thinking, structured reasoning, and the ability to question and reshape ideas. Reading became my mental nourishment and the defining trait that drives me to this day: an unending thirst for knowledge.

Today: the identity that has emerged

Looking back at my narrative, I can see that each stage added a defining trait. Childhood instilled respect and admiration, while adolescence brought vision and the power of early choices. During university years, perseverance became essential in overcoming obstacles, and later, through tutoring, passion and empathy were cultivated. Postgraduate studies and family life nurtured resilience, while working in special education fostered the acceptance of uniqueness. Parallel roles emphasized the value of social contribution, and university teaching highlighted the importance of collaboration. Finally, extensive reading has continuously fueled a deep thirst for knowledge.

Together, these traits form my current identity: a teacher, psychologist, and researcher. I am not focused on earning a lot of money; I am fulfilled by continuing to teach, research, write, and share knowledge.

Teaching and research, for me, are forms of therapy: they create meaning, shape identity, and open new pathways. Through my personal journey, I understand that what defines me is not only what I have done but also how these traits were cultivated within me, shaping my desire to continue contributing, learning, and supporting others.

Tomorrow: the transformation

Concerns about how teaching and research may evolve in the future, amid rapid developments and the growing dominance of artificial intelligence, remain strong and highly relevant. In my view, the profession of the educational/school psychologist is not expected to disappear, but rather to be strengthened and to evolve substantially. The increasing psychosocial needs of students, the rise of anxiety, school bullying, and emotional difficulties, as well as the growing emphasis on prevention and early intervention within the school context, make this role essential. Although technology can provide supportive tools for assessment and intervention, it cannot replace human connection, empathy, and collaboration with students, teachers, and families, which lie at the core of the school psychologist's role.

Similarly, in my opinion, the teaching profession will not disappear but will be transformed to meet the demands of contemporary society. Technology and digital tools can support and enrich the teaching and learning process; however, they cannot replace the pedagogical role of the teacher, the interpersonal relationship with students, or the ability to inspire, guide, and support learners in a holistic way. The teacher of the future will assume a more complex and multifaceted role, acting as a facilitator of learning and a promoter of students' social and emotional skills.

Conclusion (Epilogue)

Bringing together the historical evolution of education in Greece and the lived experiences of educators across different educational levels, this chapter highlights the dynamic and multifaceted nature of teaching as both a profession and a social mission. The historical trajectory reveals a system in constant transition, striving to reconcile tradition with innovation, while the personal narratives illuminate how these broader transformations are experienced, interpreted, and enacted in everyday educational practice.

Across all three accounts, a common thread emerges: the enduring significance of the teacher. Despite structural challenges, policy constraints, and the rapid advancement of technology, the teacher remains at the core of the educational process. The profession is not diminishing; rather, it is evolving -requiring adaptability, continuous learning, and the ability to navigate increasingly complex educational environments.

At the same time, the narratives demonstrate that education is not merely a system of policies and reforms, but a deeply human experience shaped by relationships, emotions, and personal journeys. From the classroom of primary education to the halls of academia, the path of the educator is marked by transitions, challenges, and ongoing professional and personal growth.

Looking ahead, the future of education in Greece - and globally - will depend on the capacity to support teachers in this evolving role. Investment in professional development, openness to innovation, and a sustained emphasis on social and emotional learning will be essential. Yet, beyond all structural changes, what remains constant is the uniquely human dimension of teaching: the ability to inspire, connect, and transform lives.

In this sense, the voices presented in this chapter do not merely describe education; they embody it. They remind us that education is, ultimately, a lived experience - one that continues to unfold, adapt, and endure.

REFERENCES

Alexiadou, N. (2019). *Policy learning and Europeanization in education: The governance of teacher education in Greece*. Springer.

Alexiadou, N., & Zmas, A. (2021). *Europeanization and education policy: Governing by soft law in the EU*. Palgrave Macmillan.

Bouzakis, S. (2002). *Education in Greece: Historical overview*. Gutenberg.

Dimaras, A. (1973). [32.1]The reform that never happened. Ermis European Commission. (2024). Education and training monitor: Greece 2023. Publications Office of the European Union.

Fraser, P. M. (1972). *Ptolemaic Alexandria*. Clarendon Press. [33.1]

Kassotakis, M., & Verdis, A. (2013). *Teacher education in Greece: Challenges and perspectives*. Pedio Publications.

Kazamias, A. M., & Mattheou, D. (2008). *Education and the European identity: Historical and contemporary perspectives*. Metaixmio.

Ministry of Education and Religious Affairs. (2021). *Guide to special education and training*. Ministry of Education and Religious Affairs.

Nirvanas, K. (2010). *History of Greek education*. Papazisis.

OECD. (2018). *Education policy outlook*. OECD Publishing.

OECD. (2020). *Education at a glance 2020: OECD indicators*. OECD Publishing.

OECD. (2023). PISA 2022 Results: Country Note Greece. OECD Publishing. Retrieved from https://www.oecd.org/publication/pisa-2022-results/country-notes/greece-a24e696b

OECD. (2024). *Education at a glance 2024: OECD indicators*. OECD Publishing., DOI: 10.1787/c00cad36-

OECD. (2025). *Education at a glance 2025: OECD indicators*. OECD Publishing., DOI: 10.1787/1c0d9c79-

Papanoutsos, E. P. (1976). *The educational reform of 1964*. OEDB.

Soulis, S. (2015). *Applied social policy: Design of health and social protection services*. Papazisis.

Tsoukalas, K. (1981). *Dependence and reproduction: The social role of educational mechanisms in Greece*. Themelio.

UNESCO. (2020). *Global education monitoring report 2020: Inclusion and education: All means all*. UNESCO., DOI: 10.1787/1c0d9c79-

Verdis, A. (2017). Higher education in Greece: Structure, governance and reform. In Curaj, A. (Eds.), *European higher education area: The impact of past and future policies* (pp. 345–361). Springer.

Verdis, A. (2020). Quality assurance and professional development in Greek education. Athens: National and Kapodistrian University of Athens.

Chapter 10
Teachers' Voices From Poland

Izabela Olszak
http://orcid.org/0000-0002-8504-7814
The John Paul II Catholic University of Lublin, Poland

Sylwia Niewczas
http://orcid.org/0009-0002-2058-0535
The John Paul II Catholic University of Lublin, Poland

Małgorzata Anna Tetiurka
Lubelskie Samorządowe Centrum Doskonalenia Nauczycieli, Poland

ABSTRACT

Education in Poland has played a pivotal role in shaping the nation's social, cultural, and economic development. From the establishment of the Jagiellonian University in 1364 through periods of political upheaval, education has been a key instrument for national preservation, social cohesion, and modernization. Following the democratic transition of 1989, extensive reforms focused on decentralization, modernization, and alignment with European standards, particularly after Poland's accession to the European Union in 2004. This study also highlights the experiences of teachers on their path to becoming foreign language educators, providing firsthand insights into the challenges and opportunities within the evolving Polish education system.

A SHORT OVERVIEW OF EDUCATION IN POLAND

Izabela Olszak,

Education in Poland plays a crucial role in shaping the nation's social, cultural and economic development. Rooted in a long intellectual tradition dating back to the founding of the Jagiellonian University in 1364, one of the oldest in Europe, the Polish education system has evolved over centuries of political change and social transformation. During the partitions of the eighteenth and nineteenth centuries, education served as a key instrument of national preservation. At the same time, the post-war socialist period introduced a centralized system emphasizing universal access and ideological conformity. Following the democratic transition of 1989, Poland undertook extensive reforms aimed at decentralization, modernization, and alignment with European standards, especially in the context of its accession to the European Union in 2004 (European Commission, 2024; GUS, 2023; OECD, 2023). From a policy-analysis perspective, these reforms can be understood as a shift from input-oriented governance toward outcome- and quality-oriented regulation, increasingly embedded in European accountability and benchmarking frameworks.

Today, the structure of Polish education reflects both historical continuity and adaptation to modern demands. The system begins with early childhood education (*przedszkole*) for children aged three to six, followed by compulsory eight-year primary education (*szkoła podstawowa*), which provides a general foundation in key academic and social competen-

DOI: 10.4018/979-8-3373-8983-7.ch010

cies. After primary school, students can choose among general secondary schools (*liceum ogólnokształcące*), technical secondary schools (*technikum*), or vocational schools (*branżowa szkoła I stopnia*), depending on their career aspirations. Students who complete the national *matura* examination (*matriculation examination*, which can be compared to A-Level *exams*, the Abitur or the Baccalauréat) gain access to higher education, which follows the Bologna Process framework, offering bachelor's, master's, and doctoral degrees (European Commission, 2024). This multilevel governance model reflects broader European trends toward decentralization combined with centralized quality assurance and external evaluation mechanisms. Governance of education in Poland combines national oversight with local autonomy. The Ministry of Education and Science defines curricula, quality standards and teacher qualifications, while municipalities and counties administer and finance schools. This decentralized model aims to enhance flexibility and efficiency. Moreover, Poland's participation in the European Union has expanded international cooperation, notably through the Erasmus+ program, which promotes student and staff mobility. Over the last two decades, Polish students have demonstrated remarkable improvement in the OECD's Programme for International Student Assessment (PISA) rankings, performing above the OECD average in reading, mathematics and science, which reflects the success of reforms introduced in the late 1990s (European Commission, 2024; Jakubowski et al., 2010; OECD, 2023). When compared with selected OECD and EU systems of similar socioeconomic profile, Poland's performance gains are notable for their consistency across cohorts, indicating not only short-term reform effects but also sustained system-level impact.

Despite these achievements, several challenges persist. Educational inequalities between rural and urban areas continue to affect access and outcomes, while teacher shortages, low salaries, and limited professional development opportunities remain pressing concerns. Issues of equity and social justice, particularly related to gender, students with migrant backgrounds and learners with special educational needs, remain unevenly addressed across regions. Furthermore, critics argue that the curriculum is still overly theoretical and needs a greater emphasis on digital literacy, creativity and civic education. The inclusion of students with disabilities and migrant backgrounds, though improving, requires stronger institutional support and resources. Meanwhile, universities face the task of balancing academic quality, financial stability and international competitiveness, as global rankings are becoming increasingly important indicators of performance (European Commission, 2024; OECD, 2023).

Looking ahead, Polish education policy prioritizes digital transformation, lifelong learning and the development of STEM competencies to meet labour market needs. More recently, policy discourse has also begun to address the implications of artificial intelligence, data literacy and advanced educational technologies for teaching, assessment and teacher professionalism. There is also a growing emphasis on environmental education, entrepreneurship and global citizenship, aligning national strategies with the United Nations Sustainable Development Goals. In this broader context, education in Poland is understood not only as a means of individual empowerment but also as a foundation for sustainable and inclusive national progress. Finally, the Polish education system stands as a dynamic and evolving structure that successfully blends historical legacy with modern innovation. While equity, teacher development and curricular modernization remain ongoing priorities, Poland's steady progress since the 1990s illustrates how education can serve as a driving force for democratic values, economic resilience and social cohesion in an increasingly interconnected world (OECD, 2023).

Teacher education and professional development in Poland: evolution, structure and policy context

Teacher education in Poland has undergone a profound transformation over the past several decades, reflecting broader social, economic and political shifts that have shaped the country since the late twentieth century. During the communist period, teacher preparation was centralized and ideologically driven, emphasizing uniformity and conformity over pedagogical innovation (Komorowska, 1994). The systemic reforms following the democratic transition of 1989 marked a decisive move toward decentralization, professionalization and alignment with European educational standards. These reforms can be analytically framed within a policy-learning and Europeanization perspective, whereby national teacher education models increasingly respond to transnational norms, benchmarks and accountability mechanisms. These changes redefined the teacher's role, emphasizing autonomy, pedagogical creativity and responsiveness to diverse learners' needs.

Contemporary teacher education in Poland integrates academic, pedagogical and practical components within a coherent system designed to equip future educators with both disciplinary expertise and instructional competence. Initial teacher preparation is primarily delivered through higher education institutions, particularly university faculties of education and philology, which offer programmes combining subject-specific study with theoretical and methodological instruction. Curricula typically blend disciplinary courses (e.g., mathematics, languages, sciences, or humanities) with modules on developmental psychology, didactics, classroom management and inclusive pedagogy (Białek, 2021; Grzyb & Pituła, 2019; Konieczka-Śliwińska, 2016; Michalak-Dawidziuk, 2021; Wiłkomirska & Zielińska, 2015). Increasingly, these curricula also incorporate components related to digital pedagogy, ethical use of technology and data-informed teaching practices, reflecting broader European competency frameworks.

Primary education programmes provide broad-based preparation across multiple subjects, whereas secondary-level pathways emphasize disciplinary specialization. Practical experience, introduced through supervised teaching placements, remains a central element of teacher training, fostering reflective practice and professional self-efficacy. The reflective elements discussed later in this chapter are methodologically grounded in narrative and practice-based inquiry, allowing practitioners' experiences to be interpreted as situated professional knowledge rather than purely autobiographical accounts. Although many independent teacher-training colleges were incorporated into universities following the 1999 reform, their legacy persists in the sustained focus on practice-oriented education and early classroom engagement (Giebułtowska, 2018; Karbowniczek & Zdybel, 2022; Madalińska-Michalak, 2020).

Certification and licensing procedures further formalize professional status. Graduates must obtain a teaching licence confirming both theoretical and practical readiness to teach, while subsequent career advancement depends on documented experience, evaluations, and continuing education, as specified by the Teacher's Charter (*Karta Nauczyciela*), the principal legal framework regulating teachers' rights, obligations and promotion pathways. This framework also functions as a national accountability mechanism, linking professional development, appraisal and career progression. This system underscores lifelong learning as a professional standard (Wiłkomirska & Zielińska, 2015; Giebułtowska, 2018).

Recent statistics illustrate the demographic and structural characteristics of the profession. According to the OECD's *Education at a Glance 2025*, Polish lower-secondary teachers are on average 48 years old, with nearly half aged 50 or above, considerably higher than the OECD average, while only 4% are under 30. These trends raise concerns regarding early-career attrition, long-term workforce sustainability and teacher well-being, which are increasingly recognized as critical policy challenges across OECD systems. Nevertheless, teacher qualifications remain exceptionally high: only 0.4% of teachers are not fully qualified, and the share of unfilled positions is 1%. In 2023/24, approximately 525,200 full-time-equivalent teachers were employed nationwide

The development of teacher education and professional growth in Poland has been driven by a succession of national reforms and international initiatives. Since 1989, policy efforts have sought to enhance educational quality, professionalize teaching and align national frameworks with European Union expectations. The decentralization of school governance granted institutions greater autonomy while extending teachers' responsibility for curriculum design, innovation, and inclusion (Michalak-Dawidziuk, 2021; OECD, 2025).

A pivotal milestone was the Education Reform Act of 1999, which restructured the school system and created a tiered framework for teacher training and career progression. It extended compulsory schooling, established the three-level structure (primary, lower-secondary, upper-secondary) and reinforced the requirement for continuous professional development. The Teacher's Charter, first enacted in 1982 and later amended, continues to define teachers' professional rights, responsibilities, salary scales and promotion procedures, serving as a cornerstone of the profession's legal identity (Madalińska-Michalak, 2019; Wiłkomirska & Zielińska, 2015).

Recent government strategies emphasize digital literacy, inclusion and lifelong learning. The National Education Development Programme 2017-2022 set explicit objectives for expanding teacher-training opportunities and fostering innovation. According to the Ministry of Education and Science (*Ministerstwo Edukacji i Nauki, 2023*). *Nauka w Polsce 2023 Report* approximately 65% of Polish teachers participated in ICT-oriented workshops in 2022, reflecting the system's adaptation to digital transformation. European Union engagement has been equally influential. Participation in Erasmus+ and other EU-funded projects has enhanced teacher mobility, collaborative research and intercultural exchange. In 2023, about 1,450 teachers took part in EU-supported mobility programmes, integrating innovative pedagogical strategies upon return. Moreover, EU structural funds have financed regional teacher-training centres, especially in rural areas, helping to reduce disparities in professional development access.

Evidence from TALIS 2024 shows that 85% of Polish teachers engaged in at least one professional-development activity during the preceding year, surpassing the OECD average of 78%. This attests to the effectiveness of national and EU-supported initiatives in cultivating a culture of lifelong learning. Nonetheless, several challenges persist: unequal access to high-quality training between urban and rural contexts, limited funding for sustained professional learning, and uneven relevance of available courses. Policy responses increasingly target these issues through improved quality assurance, greater equity, and responsiveness to teachers' evolving professional needs (Białek, 2021; Kamińska, 2023; Mercer & Pawlak, 2024).

The evolution of teacher education and development in Poland demonstrates a continuous effort to balance content mastery, pedagogical competence and professional growth. By combining rigorous academic study with structured practical experience, clearly defined career frameworks and robust lifelong-learning policies, Poland has built a teacher-education model consistent with European standards and responsive to twenty-first-century challenges Ongoing reforms, supported by national strategies and EU programmes, continue to strengthen the profession's resilience and adaptive capacity, ensuring that educators are equipped to foster meaningful learning, engage critically with innovation, and sustain the continuous improvement of the national education system (Giebułtowska, 2018; Boczkowska, 2023; Madalińska-Michalak, 2020).

Professional development of teachers

Professional development is widely recognized as a cornerstone of teacher quality in Poland, ensuring that educators maintain up-to-date knowledge, refine instructional strategies and respond effectively to evolving student needs. Unlike initial teacher preparation, which provides the foundational knowledge and competencies required for teaching, professional development in Poland is conceived as a continuous and career-long process encompassing formal in-service training, mentoring, collaborative learning, and engagement with research-informed practice (Giebułtowska, 2018; Karbowniczek & Zdybel, 2022). According to the OECD's TALIS 2024 survey, approximately 85% of lower-secondary teachers in Poland participated in at least one professional development activity in the preceding 12 months, significantly above the OECD average of 78%. This high level of engagement reflects a strong institutional culture of continuous learning supported by both national and EU policies (Mercer & Pawlak, 2024). In-service teacher education in Poland is diverse and strategically aligned with national and regional priorities. Teachers may participate in workshops, seminars, and accredited courses organized by universities, pedagogical centres, and educational NGOs. These initiatives commonly focus on curriculum updates, innovative teaching methodologies, digital literacy, inclusive education, and classroom management. For instance, the National Centre for Supporting Vocational and Continuing Education (KOWEZiU) offers over 1,200 accredited courses annually, covering both general and vocational education. Such initiatives are essential for addressing gaps in pedagogical and technological knowledge, particularly in fast-changing fields such as STEM and ICT integration (Karbowniczek & Zdybel, 2022; Wiłkomirska & Zielińska, 2015).

Mentoring and induction programmes represent a key element of teacher development in Poland. Newly appointed teachers typically undergo a probationary period of 18-24 months, during which they are supported by experienced mentors. This process helps them navigate classroom practices, assessment procedures, and institutional expectations. As observed by Giebułtowska (2018), structured mentoring substantially improves teacher retention and professional confidence, with approximately 72% of novice teachers reporting greater preparedness following their induction. Moreover, mentoring promotes reflective practice, encouraging teachers to analyse and refine their instructional strategies based on classroom outcomes. Teacher appraisal and evaluation systems in Poland also play a critical role in promoting professional growth. Evaluations are conducted at both school and national levels and include classroom observation, self-assessment, and analysis of student performance. Beyond measuring teacher effectiveness, these evaluations identify professional learning needs and link appraisal outcomes to tailored development opportunities. Kamińska (2023) reports that 64% of Polish teachers found formal evaluations helpful in identifying their professional development goals - a figure notably higher than the OECD average of 51%. This indicates that appraisal systems function not merely as accountability mechanisms but also as integral components of the professional learning cycle (Wiłkomirska & Zielińska, 2015; Madalińska-Michalak, 2020).

Participation in professional networks, conferences and communities of practice further strengthens teacher learning in Poland. Subject-specific teacher associations, online forums, and local learning communities allow educators to share best practices, develop collaborative projects, and stay informed about emerging pedagogical trends. European Union–funded programmes, particularly *Erasmus+*, have played a crucial role in supporting teacher mobility, innovation, and intercultural competence. In 2023, around 1,450 Polish teachers took part in EU mobility projects, gaining experience in different European educational contexts. Such international exposure enriches domestic practice and strengthens teachers' global awareness (Mercer & Pawlak, 2024; Madalińska-Michalak, 2019).

Recent empirical and thematic research further deepens our understanding of professional development within both Polish and global contexts. For example, Pawlak and Mercer (2024) highlight the role of teacher professional curiosity as a driver of sustained engagement with ongoing learning, linking it to higher adaptability in navigating digital and inclusive pedagogies. Mróz et al. (2025) provide evidence on pre-service teacher competencies, emphasizing sustainable development and ecological literacy as emerging dimensions of teacher preparation aligned with international frameworks. The latest OECD TALIS 2024 analyses underscore the complex interplay between teacher well-being, job satisfaction, and career intentions, noting that positive professional thriving correlates with participation in reflective professional learning communities and mentorship structures. Moreover, conceptual reviews by Kurrle and Warwas (2025) synthesize evidence on teacher well-being and retention challenges globally, advocating for integrative policy approaches that combine workload management, targeted support for early-career teachers, and digital competence development, including AI-enhanced instructional practice. Together, these studies broaden the empirical foundation for professional development policy, particularly around well-being, retention, digital skills and sustainable teacher education.

EU structural funds have also supported the establishment of regional teacher training centres, particularly in rural or underserved regions, which have contributed to reducing territorial disparities in access to high-quality training. These initiatives demonstrate Poland's commitment to equitable professional learning opportunities for all teachers, regardless of geographic location. Despite strong engagement and institutional support, persistent challenges remain. Regional inequities, limited funding, and variability in training quality continue to constrain the full potential of professional development in Poland. Teachers in rural areas, in particular, face barriers related to time, travel and access to in-person workshops, often relying instead on online learning options that may not fully replicate the benefits of interactive, face-to-face experiences. Addressing these challenges requires sustained policy commitment, systemic coordination, and sufficient financial support to ensure that all educators have equitable access to meaningful, high-quality professional development (Mercer & Pawlak, 2024; Boczkowska, 2023; Konieczka-Śliwińska, 2016). Professional development in Poland represents a comprehensive and evolving system combining formal training, mentoring, appraisal and collaborative learning. The consistently high level of teacher participation, combined with strong institutional and policy frameworks, underscores the country's commitment to lifelong learning within the teaching profession (Madalińska-Michalak, 2020; Mercer & Pawlak, 2024). However, continued attention to equity, relevance, and sustainability remains essential. By investing in inclusive, evidence-based professional learning, Poland reinforces the professional capacity of its educators, supports improved student outcomes, and contributes to the ongoing modernization of its education system (Giebułtowska, 2018; Boczkowska, 2023; Kamińska, 2023).

Challenges and opportunities in teacher development

Despite significant progress in teacher education and professional development, the Polish education system continues to face several structural and practical challenges. Understanding these challenges is crucial for informing policy, enhancing teacher effectiveness, and ensuring equitable educational outcomes across the country. At the same time, emerging opportunities provide avenues for improvement and innovation, allowing Poland to strengthen its teaching workforce and modernize its educational practices. One of the most pressing challenges is the issue of teacher shortages, particularly in subjects such as mathematics, science, and foreign languages. According to the Central Statistical Office of Poland, in the 2023/24 school year, approximately 12% of schools reported difficulties in filling teaching positions, with rural areas disproportionately affected. This shortage has implications for workload, teacher stress, and student learning outcomes. TALIS 2024 data indicate that 48% of Polish teachers report moderate to high levels of workload-related stress, higher than the OECD average of 42 % (OECD, 2023).

Regional disparities further compound these challenges. Teachers in smaller towns and rural areas often have fewer opportunities for professional development, limited access to modern teaching technologies, and reduced networking possibilities compared to their urban counterparts. As a result, students in these regions may experience lower-quality instruction, creating equity gaps that persist despite national reforms aimed at inclusive education. According to the Ministry of Education and Science (2023), only 58% of teachers in rural areas participated in digital-skills training programs in 2022, compared with 72% in urban centers. The integration of digital technologies presents both a challenge and an opportunity. The COVID-19 pandemic accelerated the need for digital competence among teachers, highlighting gaps in training and access to resources. While initiatives such as national e-learning platforms, ICT workshops, and EU-funded projects have expanded teachers' technological capacities, effective integration into daily classroom practice remains uneven. Approximately 65% of teachers reported feeling confident in using digital tools for teaching, suggesting progress but also the need for ongoing support.

Inclusion of students with diverse needs is another area of both challenge and opportunity. Poland has expanded policies for inclusive education, providing specialized training for teachers, adapted curricula, and additional support services. Nevertheless, teachers often report feeling insufficiently prepared to manage classrooms with students exhibiting a wide range of learning difficulties or disabilities. Data from Mercer and Pawlak (2024) indicate that 39% of teachers feel inadequately trained to address the needs of students with autism spectrum disorder or other neurodiverse profiles, emphasizing the ongoing necessity of targeted professional development. Career progression and professional motivation also represent areas for improvement. While the Teacher's Charter provides structured pathways for advancement, including the categories of contract, appointed, chartered, and expert teacher, recent surveys indicate that younger teachers may feel demotivated due to limited salary increases and high workloads. Opportunities for strengthening the system include leveraging EU mobility programs, expanding digital literacy training, and promoting collaborative professional networks. By addressing workload, regional disparities, and subject-specific shortages, Poland has the potential to create a more equitable and effective system for teacher development. Initiatives focusing on mentorship, inclusive pedagogy, and innovative classroom practices are already demonstrating positive outcomes, as evidenced by increased teacher retention in pilot programs and improvements in student achievement in participating schools (Giebułtowska, 2018). Teacher development in Poland is shaped by a complex interplay of challenges and opportunities. While shortages, workload pressures, regional inequities, and the integration of inclusive and digital practices present ongoing difficulties, targeted policies, professional networks, and EU-supported initiatives provide pathways to strengthen the teaching profession. Addressing these issues will be critical for ensuring that Poland continues to enhance educational quality and provide all students with equitable access to high-quality learning experiences.

Case studies and examples of innovative teacher training programs

Poland has implemented a range of innovative teacher training programs in recent years, designed to enhance professional competencies, promote inclusive and digital pedagogy, and foster continuous professional growth. These programs provide valuable insights into effective practices in teacher development and demonstrate how targeted interventions can address both systemic challenges and individual professional needs. Examining case studies from various regions reveals the interplay between policy, institutional support, and teacher engagement in fostering high-quality education.

One notable example is the nationwide initiative *"School for the Future" (Szkoła Przyszłości*), implemented in collaboration with the Ministry of Education and Science and several pedagogical universities. Launched in 2020, the program aimed to improve digital literacy, STEM teaching competencies, and innovative pedagogical strategies among teachers of primary and secondary schools. By 2023, approximately 7,500 teachers across 450 schools had participated in the program. Evaluations indicated that 82 % of the participants reported increased confidence in integrating digital tools into their teaching, while 74 % reported improvements in student engagement and learning outcomes following implementation of new instructional strategies (Ministerstwo Edukacji i Nauki, 2023).

Another illustrative case is the *"Mentoring and Peer Collaboration Program"* initiated by the Warsaw Centre for Teacher Development. This program pairs novice teachers with experienced mentors and encourages collaborative learning communities within schools. Between 2021 and 2023, 1,200 early-career teachers participated in structured mentoring sessions, classroom observations, and joint lesson planning workshops. Surveys conducted post-program revealed that 68 % of novice teachers felt significantly better prepared for classroom challenges, and teacher retention rates in participating schools increased by 12 % over two years, indicating the program's effectiveness in supporting professional growth and mitigating early-career attrition (Giebułtowska, 2018).

In the field of inclusive education, the program *"Supporting Diverse Learners" (Wspieranie Uczniów o Różnorodnych Potrzebach)* has been particularly impactful. Focused on training teachers to meet the needs of students with disabilities, neurodiverse profiles, and language learning difficulties, this initiative provides both in-person workshops and online modules. As of 2023, over 3,200 teachers had completed the program, with 77 % reporting increased competence in designing individualized educational plans, adapting teaching materials, and employing inclusive classroom strategies. Case studies from participating schools indicate that the program has contributed to a measurable increase in student participation, reduced classroom disruptions, and higher achievement among students with special educational needs (Mercer & Pawlak, 2024).

International collaboration has also enriched teacher training in Poland. *Erasmus+* programs and other EU-funded projects have enabled Polish teachers to observe educational practices in other European countries and apply them in domestic contexts. For instance, the 2022–2023 Erasmus+ mobility project *"Innovative Pedagogy in European Schools"* involved 1,450 teachers from 120 schools, allowing them to participate in workshops on inquiry-based learning, collaborative assessment, and digital classroom management. Follow-up surveys indicated that 65% of participants implemented at least one new teaching strategy upon returning to Poland, with reported improvements in student motivation and learning outcomes (Ministerstwo Edukacji i Nauki, 2023).

These case studies illustrate how targeted, well-structured professional development programs can address specific challenges in teacher education, foster innovation, and enhance student outcomes. The programs share common characteristics: alignment with national and EU educational priorities, integration of practical classroom experiences, structured mentorship or peer collaboration, and ongoing evaluation to measure effectiveness. They provide a model for scaling up professional development initiatives across Poland and offer insights for other countries seeking to strengthen teacher competencies in dynamic and diverse educational contexts.

Looking ahead, the trajectory of education in Poland is shaped not only by national reform imperatives but also by rapidly evolving international educational policies and global trends. Increasingly, strategic frameworks such as UNESCO's Education 2030 Agenda, the OECD Future of Education and Skills 2030 initiative and the European Commission's Strategic Framework for European Cooperation in Education and Training (ET 2030) emphasize the development of future-ready competencies, holistic well-being, equity of access, and sustainable, inclusive learning ecosystems. In response, Poland is likely to further align policy priorities with these transnational agendas by strengthening digital and data-informed pedagogies, enhancing competency-based curricula and embedding sustainable development goals more deeply into both pre-service and in-service teacher education. Emerging policy discourse also underscores the potential of artificial intelligence and adaptive learning systems to support tailored instruction, while highlighting the need for ethical, equity-centered governance of educational technologies. Future reforms may thus intensify focus on teacher professional thriving, retention systems and workload sustainability, areas increasingly recognized as essential for long-term system resilience in OECD analyses. Moreover, Poland's participation in international assessment and networking platforms provides opportunities for cross-national learning and comparative benchmarking that can continuously refine teacher development pathways and student learning outcomes. Altogether, these trends point toward an integrated policy vision in which educational quality, equity, technological fluency and sustainable development are interwoven to support lifelong learning for all learners in an interconnected global context.

BETWEEN WORDS AND MINDS: MY JOURNEY THROUGH LANGUAGE LEARNING AND TEACHING

Izabela Olszak

My journey into the world of foreign languages began in a seemingly ordinary classroom, yet it marked the beginning of a lifelong fascination. As a child, I encountered both English and German at school. At first, the unfamiliar sounds and structures seemed puzzling, but their rhythm and melody drew me in. What began as an academic requirement soon became a genuine passion - an invitation to see the world through a different linguistic lens.

During my high school years, I realized that learning a language is far more than memorizing vocabulary and mastering grammar; it is a deeply cognitive and emotional process. The first moment I understood a song without translation or held a spontaneous conversation with a native speaker brought an almost tangible sense of discovery. I began to perceive language as a bridge, connecting not only words, but also cultures and ways of thinking. This realization naturally led me to pursue philological studies, where English and German became the foundation of my academic path.

University life opened the door to applied linguistics and language pedagogy. Courses in teaching methodology fascinated me the most: for the first time, I saw the complexity of the learning process and the delicate balance between cognition, motivation, and emotion. During my first teaching practicum, I discovered that effective teaching is not simply about transferring knowledge — it is about guiding, inspiring, and helping learners believe in their own potential.

I vividly recall one of my earliest lessons: a group of twelve-year-olds staring at me expectantly while I struggled to explain the difference between *some* and *any*. My explanations failed, and the class quickly descended into confusion and laughter. It was a humbling moment — but also a turning point. That day taught me that successful teaching requires flexibility, empathy, and the courage to learn alongside one's students.

It was then that the key question shaping my research emerged: *How can we adapt language teaching to the individual perceptual and cognitive capacities of each learner?* This question also reflects broader concerns in international educational policy regarding personalized learning, digital adaptation, and equity, linking personal experience to global trends

After graduation, I began teaching in a secondary school, where I encountered the true diversity of learners. Some students absorbed new structures with ease; others struggled, despite equal effort. This experience made me aware of the enormous variability in learning styles and processing speed. My curiosity led me toward psycholinguistics and neurodidactics, fields that offered a scientific lens through which to understand these differences.

During my doctoral studies, I investigated individual differences in foreign language acquisition, focusing on working memory, attention, and automatization. A pivotal moment in my academic career came with the development of a model supporting learners with varying perceptual efficiency, grounded in principles of individualized instruction. Presenting these findings at international conferences confirmed that adaptive strategies, respecting cognitive diversity, can significantly enhance language learning outcomes.

"What a child can do in cooperation today, he can do alone tomorrow."

Lev Vygotsky

Parallel to research, I pursued my work as a university lecturer, preparing future teachers of foreign languages. This experience was transformative: watching my students evolve from hesitant beginners into reflective practitioners reaffirmed my belief that language teaching transcends transmission of content. A teacher is a mediator - between cultures, ideas, and human experiences.

In recent years, my academic interests have turned toward the emotional and motivational dimensions of language learning. My studies highlight the crucial role of positive classroom climate and teacher–student relationships in fostering language acquisition. I have also become increasingly involved in exploring digital tools and artificial intelligence as allies in creating personalized, learner-centered environments.

"Teaching is not about transferring knowledge but creating possibilities for the production or construction of knowledge." Paulo Freire

Looking back, I see my career as an evolving dialogue between theory and practice, research and empathy. Each stage, from my first fascination with English and German, through classroom experiences, to advanced research, has deepened my understanding of what it means to learn and to teach. Today, I strive to integrate the perspectives of teacher, researcher, and mentor, which convinced that effective language education begins with understanding the learner — their emotions, cognition, and individual rhythm of discovery.

Future perspectives

In conclusion, I view the teaching profession as one that stands at a decisive crossroads, shaped by rapid social, technological, and cultural change. Teachers today are no longer mere transmitters of knowledge, but designers of learning experiences, guides in an information-saturated world and guardians of human connection in increasingly digital environments. The future of teaching lies in adaptability, lifelong learning, and ethical responsibility, particularly, in how educators integrate technology while preserving empathy, critical thinking, and inclusivity. Despite its challenges, the profession retains a unique power: the ability to shape minds, identities and possibilities. It is precisely this responsibility and potential for meaningful impact that make teaching, now and in the years to come, not only relevant but also indispensable. Future perspectives should also consider the integration of AI and advanced digital tools to complement individualized learning while supporting teacher well-being.

BECOMING THE TEACHER I NEEDED

Małgorzata Tetiurka

Early influences

My journey into teaching has never felt like a single decision. Instead, it has been a long, quiet unfolding - shaped by childhood experiences, mentors, disappointments, and, most importantly, the children and teachers I have met along the way. Reflecting on this journey through the lens of teacher education research, early experiences, mentorship, and exposure to reflective practice significantly contribute to professional identity formation (Pawlak & Mercer, 2024). Reading the stories of others who found their way into the profession, I realise that my own narrative echoes theirs in many ways: teaching often begins not in a university lecture hall but in the early, intimate spaces of family, community, and identity.

As a child, I never wanted to be a teacher. My best friend did, and I wondered quietly why she aspired to what I saw as such an unaspiring position: even then I was fully aware of the hardships and challenges that teaching carried. I loved reading from a very early age and, as I would spend hours reading bound annuals of children's magazines at my great aunt's house - the only teacher in my family - they all declared that I would become either a journalist or a lawyer, which I accepted as a kind of revealed truth.

First encounters with English

I started learning English at the age of ten - my family's decision, after I consistently showed no interest in the ballet classes I had been attending. In those days, in the early 1970s in Poland, Russian was the only modern foreign language taught at school, and sending a child to private English lessons was considered an oddity, art for art's sake. Travelling abroad, especially to an English-speaking country, was more difficult than the biblical camel passing through the eye of a needle. Yet my family, my grandmother in particular, must have had a kind of intuition, because that small, unusual decision became the quiet beginning of my life's path.

My first English teacher was an ex-RAF pilot who had stayed for some time in the UK after the war and picked up some English along the way. He had no idea how to teach ten-year-olds. I still remember the first page of my first English notebook: in my neat handwriting, Lesson one written at the top, and underneath, in a column, those mysterious sentences: I have a book, You have a book, She has a book, He has a book, It has a book…

Strangely enough, these methods (or the lack of them) did not discourage me from learning English. The teacher was doing his best; he soon taught us the song *Pussy cat, Pussy cat, where have you been*, giving us a little cultural background by explaining who the Queen was—and since then I have never had problems with the infamous Present Perfect. When in doubt, I would hum the song and everything fell into place. This informal learning experience aligns with research highlighting learner autonomy and the role of situated practice in early language acquisition (Mróz et al., 2025).

Interestingly, my first English coursebook, *My English Book*, was written by Jan Mickunas, who - just like my ex-RAF pilot teacher - had also been a soldier before becoming a teacher. He too learned his English outside any formal pedagogical framework, building his proficiency as a self-motivated learner navigating the limited possibilities of the post-war Poland. The coincidence of being taught by one former soldier while learning from another through his book only deepens my sense that my path into English was shaped by people whose journeys into teaching were anything but conventional.

School years and early motivations

Then English was introduced into my primary school curriculum, and I remember a succession of teachers who whizzed through our classrooms, treating the job more as a temporary stopover than a career. The contrast between these experiences and later structured mentorship highlights how early exposure to reflective and supportive teachers can shape professional identity, a point consistently observed in longitudinal teacher development studies (Pawlak & Mercer, 2024; Kurrle & Warwas, 2025). The teacher who stayed with us a little longer was not very popular and struggled with discipline. His way of motivating us was to paint dazzling pictures of what the profession could offer if only we studied hard. You will be able to sit in your own flat, warm slippers on your feet, translating books for a living, he would say - a vision not particularly appealing to young teenagers. We could not help wondering why he himself preferred wrestling with children every day rather than embracing this supposedly lucrative translator's life, especially since he so visibly disliked being in the classroom.

In my secondary school I continued learning English, this time taught by a qualified teacher, but I wasn't particularly inspired. We wanted to translate the Beatles' songs, but she could only offer us *Que Sera Sera* sung by Doris Day. So, following in the footsteps of thousands of teenagers worldwide, I translated and learned *Yesterday* all by myself. I had some grammar issues, especially with the phrase „She wouldn't say", and no one to ask for help, but the satisfaction - and the lyrics - have stayed with me to this day.

I also continued attending private one-to-one lessons taught by a university student. I loved those. Looking back, I think she tried out on me quite a lot of the material they were covering at university, in due proportion. She once asked me to interpret Robert Frost's *Stopping by Woods on a Snowy Evening*, giving me my first informal lesson on poetry in English.

Choosing English by chance

Until two months before my matura exam (matura is a matriculation examination and can be compared to A-level exams, the abitur or the baccalauréat), I was convinced I would take the entrance exam to a medical academy. This pivotal decision illustrates how chance, coupled with systemic access policies and mentorship, can shape professional pathways—a theme reflected in international teacher education research (OECD TALIS 2024). Then, as one of the top students in my secondary school, an unexpected opportunity appeared: I could be offered direct admission to university, provided I chose a pedagogical faculty. English philology fell into that category, so I gave up my plans to study medicine without any regrets and happily embraced the chance to become a student of English - without the daunting experience of competing with fifteen other candidates for every single place in what was then an extremely prestigious and popular faculty.

University: challenge and survival

My studies were extremely difficult and demanding, far beyond our actual abilities at the time, as the department's policy was to eliminate the weaker students after the first year. I was too focused on surviving to truly enjoy the learning. Asking first-year students to read and discuss *Beowulf* and follow lectures in phonology while they were still struggling with basic grammar and vocabulary was probably not pedagogically justified, but it certainly made us appreciate the fact that we were still students.

I got married at the beginning of my studies, and sometime during my second year I began giving private lessons to support our family budget. I relied on intuition, and my priority was to avoid all the mistakes my former teachers had made - especially not to demotivate my learners by making them believe that English was so difficult that they would never manage to learn it. Since I felt responsible for not harming my pupils through misguided methods, the course in methodology was the one I looked forward to most eagerly. Now they'll show me how to explain the Present Perfect and other grammar points, I thought, and I will finally know how to teach. I couldn't have been more wrong. The course turned out to be a history of EFL rather than a practical introduction to teaching methods. I was extremely disappointed, but I concluded that I simply needed to study on my own.

First job: a trial by fire

Soon I graduated with honours and got my first job, which was quite an achievement at the time, albeit in the secondary school with the worst reputation in town. Some of the final-year students, who had had the misfortune of repeating a year once or twice, were almost my age. I was also appointed a class tutor. Because I was so young, I identified more with my pupils than with the teachers in the staff room. I was particularly disgusted by the way some teachers gossiped about students, called them names, and constantly complained about them.

I had two main worries in this first job: whether I would be able to explain all the English issues clearly and accurately, and whether I would manage to fulfil my pastoral responsibilities without overlooking any student who needed help. I could deal with the first worry by preparing very carefully for every lesson, checking all the grammar and lexis I was going to teach, and making sure I knew the answers to any questions that might arise. The second worry was much harder to prepare for, but I did my best to trust my students, to be honest with them, and to listen whenever they wanted to talk.

I must have been at least partially successful, because I stayed in touch with many of my students even after I left that school - and this was long before social media. They would simply drop by for a chat and to complain about various injustices they experienced at school. Quite recently, one of those former students found me on Facebook and confessed that she had learned more with me than with anyone else later on. Even if she was just being kind, such moments are what make us teachers tick and give us the strength to try even harder.

Becoming a practitioner

After that, I worked for several private language schools, and this was where I truly developed my teaching craft. Without the constraints of a strict syllabus or curriculum, with students' satisfaction and good results as priorities, and with learners who were willing and motivated, I could try out different approaches, experiment with various methods, and develop techniques that matched my students' needs. Free from the limitations of school hierarchy, I could also build friendlier, more genuine relationships with my learners. Not infrequently they would invite me for a pint after a Friday class or to a café at the end of term. This was when I realised how profoundly beneficial deeper positive relationships can be for the learning process. As Rita Pierson said in her TED talk: "Children don't learn from people they don't like." I believe this is true for learners of every age.

Fighting impostor syndrome

At that time, in my pursuit of excellence in teaching, I was attending every possible workshop, conference or training session, usually offered by publishers. These events were also a rare opportunity to listen to native speakers, talk to them, and, apart from drawing on their experience, put to the test my own ability to communicate with someone for whom English was a first language. Because I still suffered from a stubborn impostor syndrome (a problem related to constant self-doubt and/or fear of being preceived as pretending to be more knowledgeable than one really is, according to Bravata et al., 2020). How can I be a good teacher if I have spent only two months in the UK? Is my English good enough for me to call myself a teacher? Am I teaching them the right things? Those questions pushed me to try even harder and to be constantly on the lookout for new ideas.

Becoming a mentor

My next career step was working in the Foreign Languages Department at Maria Curie-Skłodowska University in Lublin, Poland. We provided English for Specific Purposes classes to students from different faculties, and I happily embraced the challenge of mastering Business English, English for Lawyers, and English for maths or geography students. I was also chosen as the head of the English section and gradually moved into a teacher training and mentoring role. My duties involved observing colleagues' lessons and giving them feedback. I needed to learn how to offer constructive, supportive feedback, and I benefited enormously from those observations -both the excellent lessons and the ones that could, or should, be improved.

Before any of that could happen, however, I had to earn my colleagues' trust and convince them that each observation was a meeting of two professionals, not a supervisor visiting a subordinate to find fault with their teaching. I am immensely indebted to all my friends and colleagues for sharing their expertise and their doubts with me so generously.

Working with future teachers

I was then offered a job at a neighbouring university, in the English Philology Department. I specialised in Teaching English to Young Learners but also taught conversation classes and other language skills courses. Working with future teachers opened a new chapter in my career - probably the one I enjoyed the most. My classes were practice-based, following Kolb's cycle of learning, as I firmly believe in learning by doing. My ambition was to show these future teachers that, contrary to what some literature may suggest, there is no single correct way of doing things. Everything depends on whom you teach, in what circumstances, and what your aims are. I like to believe I was successful in this role, judging by the number of former students who occasionally get in touch to tell me how interesting they found my classes and how useful their notes were in helping them survive at least the first months of their own teaching.

Supporting practising teachers

Rather naturally, somewhere along the way I began working on a major British Council teacher development project, and when this ended, I took a part-time position in a regional in-service teacher development centre. Here I run workshops, organise conferences, and offer guidance whenever teachers need it. Working with practising teachers has offered yet another perspective on education, as it constantly confronts theoretical underpinnings with the realities of everyday school life.

Although this job is extremely rewarding and brings me a great deal of satisfaction, it is also a source of many dilemmas and frustrations. As in many other contexts worldwide, the teaching profession is undergoing numerous unfavourable changes. Teachers' authority is diminishing, eroded by a lack of respect from political and educational authorities, from parents, and consequently from children. Despite repeated promises from consecutive governments, bureaucracy is increasing, and teachers' autonomy is shrinking. They are required to implement one new pedagogical idea after another, often without any financial support or meaningful training. All this, combined with unsatisfactory pay and the negative public perception of the profession, discourages new people from entering teaching.

Nevertheless, despite these obstacles and difficulties, there are hundreds of teachers who excel at their work and devote their time and effort to ensuring that every child benefits as much as possible from the education they receive. I feel extremely privileged to be working for such people. I try to make their lives a little easier by researching and exploring various areas of ELT and then offering training based on what I discover. I hope this saves them precious time and helps them stay up-to-date. In a way, I am doing what I wish someone had done for me when I was a novice teacher.

Looking back

Looking back at this long path, I can see how each stage of my professional life shaped me into the teacher I needed when I was young: the confused learner looking for clarity, the shy student seeking encouragement, the novice teacher craving guidance, the practitioner searching for fresh ideas, the mentor striving to support others, and finally the teacher educator navigating the shifting landscape of our profession. Each role added a new layer to my understanding of what it means to teach: from the ex-RAF pilot who unknowingly sparked my curiosity, to the university student who opened the door to poetry, to my early pupils who taught me humility, to the colleagues who trusted me in their classrooms, and the teachers I now work with who remind me daily why this work matters. Becoming a teacher has been less about mastering methods and more about learning to listen, reflect, adapt, care, and persist - often against the odds. If there is one conclusion I draw from all these experiences, it is that teaching is never a finished identity but a continuous becoming, shaped by the people we meet and the responsibilities we choose to carry. And perhaps, in supporting others on their journeys, I am still, in some way, becoming the teacher I once needed myself.

Future perspective

Looking ahead, I see the future of the teaching profession as both demanding and profoundly human. Teachers will be asked to do more than ever before: to design learning rather than deliver it, to respond to diversity with sensitivity and skill, and to navigate technologies that can support learning but never replace relationships. Yet none of this will be sustainable unless teaching is recognised as a profession that requires trust, autonomy and time to think. The greatest challenge may not lie in adapting to change, but in retaining committed teachers in systems that too often exhaust rather than empower them. If teaching is to remain a viable and meaningful career, it must offer not only responsibility but also respect, realistic working conditions and opportunities for continued growth. I remain cautiously hopeful that, despite shortages, reforms and uncertainties, there will always be people who choose this work because it allows them to make sense of complexity, to care, and to accompany others in their learning. And if we succeed in supporting such teachers, the profession will not merely survive the future - it will shape it.

Closing reflection

In the end, my journey has taught me that teachers are always in the process of becoming - shaped by the people they meet, the challenges they face, and the responsibilities they choose to carry. If today's education system sends out an SOS, it is a reminder not of failure but of how vital teachers are. And if I can strengthen even a few teachers along the way, then I am fulfilling the very purpose that once shaped me.

AM I STILL MEANT TO BE A TEACHER? PRACTITIONER NARRATIVE AS REFLECTIVE INQUIRY

Sylwia Niewczas

The following narrative is offered as a reflective and autoethnographic account of professional identity development across different stages of a teaching career. Drawing on the tradition of narrative inquiry and reflective practitioner research, this account does not aim to provide a comprehensive autobiography, but rather to illuminate how systemic conditions, institutional expectations, and learner interactions are experienced at the micro level of everyday educational practice. The narrative serves as an illustrative lens through which broader themes discussed in this chapter—such as teacher motivation, professional identity, emotional labor, and lifelong learning—can be more deeply understood.

Early professional identity formation

Ever since I can remember, I wanted to be a teacher of English. I was fascinated by words - by their rhythm, sound, and power to connect people across borders. While my peers dreamt of careers in medicine, business, or law, I dreamt of a classroom - of chalk on the board, the murmur of students, and the quiet joy of learning together. That dream became more tangible in high school, where I met a remarkable English teacher - a woman whose classes felt like stories brought to life. She had a gift for awakening curiosity, for making even grammar feel meaningful. Watching her, I thought: *This is what I want to do. This is who I want to be.*

But as with all dreams, reality soon introduced its complexity. University studies in English philology turned out to be far more demanding than I had expected. The workload was intense; the expectations were high. Yet, those years taught me discipline and humility - two qualities every teacher needs. After graduation, I started working with teenagers. I was full of passion and idealism, eager to change the world one lesson at a time.

Disillusionment and systemic constraints

And then came the first disillusionments. The classroom was not always a space of inspiration; sometimes, it was a battlefield of attention, motivation, and fatigue. I learned that teaching is not about perfect lessons or flawless methodology - it's about people, emotions, and the unpredictable rhythm of human interaction. Still, I stayed committed. But in Poland, teachers often face ambivalent or even dismissive public attitudes. The social image of the profession, burdened by stereotypes and systemic neglect, began to weigh heavily on me. At some point, I started to wonder: *Is this really the path I was meant to follow?*

Temporary exit and return to teaching

Eventually, I stepped away. I joined the corporate world - a place where results could be measured, efforts rewarded, and silence rarely broken by teenage energy. Yet, despite the order and stability, I felt an emptiness I couldn't ignore. I missed my students. I missed their laughter, their questions, and their small daily victories. I missed the sense of shared purpose — that subtle but powerful feeling that something meaningful was happening in the classroom. This period of professional doubt reflects patterns widely reported in the literature on early-career teacher attrition, where emotional overload, lack of institutional support, and negative public discourse contribute to temporary or permanent exits from the profession.

Teaching across the lifespan: adults and older learners

So I returned. And this time, I returned differently - more aware, more grounded, and more curious. I began working not only with young learners but also with adults and seniors. Teaching older adults opened my eyes to something profoundly human: the courage to learn despite fear, the joy of progress no matter the age, the beauty of late-blooming curiosity. My students' stories — of rediscovering themselves through language, of chasing dreams long postponed - deeply moved me. I will never forget one of my senior students, a retired engineer in his seventies, who once stood up after a class presentation and said with tears in his eyes, 'I never thought I'd speak English in public.' That moment reminded me that teaching is not about how much we teach, but how much we empower. This encounter exemplifies findings from adult education and geragogy research, which highlight the role of affective factors, self-efficacy, and identity reconstruction in later-life language learning.

Not long after returning, I worked with a teenage student who had almost given up on English. Each class seemed like an uphill battle — until one day, I asked him to bring a song he liked in English. We translated and discussed the lyrics together, line by line. For the first time, his eyes lit up. He began to see language not as a subject, but as a bridge to something personal. That moment reminded me how powerful it can be to meet students where their interests truly lie.

From practice to research: reflexivity and academic inquiry

These encounters inspired me to look beyond practice and toward research. I entered a doctoral program in linguistics, driven by one central question: *How does the aging mind learn, and what can language teachers do to support it?* My PhD explored English language learning in later adulthood - a topic that became not only my academic pursuit but also a mirror of my own growth. In studying my learners, I found myself studying the essence of teaching: patience, empathy, and the art of listening. This transition from practice to research illustrates the reciprocal relationship between experiential knowledge and academic inquiry, positioning practitioner reflection as a legitimate source of research questions and theoretical insight.

When I defended my dissertation this year, it felt like closing a long, winding circle - from a high school dream to an academic reality, from doubt to rediscovery. Fourteen years in education have taught me that being a teacher is less about standing at the front of a class and more about walking beside others. It is about noticing small changes, celebrating invisible progress, and finding meaning in the everyday.

Professional identity as an ongoing process

There were moments when I questioned everything - my choices, my strength, even my worth. But each time, the answer returned to me through the faces of my students, through their stories, through the quiet gratitude that comes when learning changes a life, even in small ways.

Today, as a university lecturer and researcher, I try to bridge science and practice - to show that theory and empathy can coexist, that reflection can make teaching more human. I draw inspiration from neuroscience, psychology, and the ever-changing landscape of education. Every class, every project, and every article I write reminds me that teaching is a lifelong dialogue - between mind and heart, between past and future.

My guiding motto has become: "*Education is not about filling a vessel, but about lighting a flame.*" And that flame - fragile, bright, and alive - continues to guide me through each new stage of my journey.

Being a teacher, I have learned, is not a title one earns once and for all. It is a calling that must be renewed every day - through reflection, compassion, and courage. And so, after all these years, I no longer ask whether I am still meant to be a teacher. I know that I am, because teaching is not what I *do*. It is who I *am*.

From an analytical perspective, this narrative illustrates how teacher identity is continuously negotiated across institutional contexts, learner groups, and career stages. It underscores the importance of reflective practice not only as a personal coping strategy but as a source of insight into systemic strengths and tensions within teacher education and professional development frameworks.

From today's perspective, my professional path has taught me that teaching is not a fixed role but a dynamic process of becoming. Its future, at least as I see it, depends less on external reforms and more on the inner readiness of teachers to reflect, adapt, and remain attentive to their learners' changing needs. Despite moments of uncertainty and fatigue, I continue to experience teaching as a meaningful space of encounter — with others and with myself. This reflective stance allows me to look ahead with calm rather than certainty, trusting that as long as learning remains relational and purposeful, the teaching profession will continue to evolve alongside those who practice it.

REFERENCES

Białek, K. (2021). Teachers' development standards in the school of education, Warsaw. A Case Study (pp. 122-124). [Article in Polish / English]. In E. Kowalska & M. Nowak (Eds.). *Teacher education and professional development in Poland.* Foundation for the Development of the Education System (FRSE). DOI: 10.47050/66515314.124-144

Boczkowska, M. A. (2023). Teachers' resilience in Poland – the role of sociodemographic and professional factors. *Lubelski Rocznik Pedagogiczny*, *42*(3), 53–69. DOI: 10.17951/lrp.2023.42.3.53-69

Bravata, D. M., Watts, S. A., Keefer, A. L., Madhusudhan, D. K., Taylor, K. T., Clark, D. M., Nelson, R. S., Cokley, K. O., & Hagg, H. K. (2020). Prevalence, predictors, and treatment of impostor syndrome: A systematic review. *Journal of General Internal Medicine*, *35*(4), 1252–1275. DOI: 10.1007/s11606-019-05364-1 PMID: 31848865

Central Statistical Office of Poland (GUS). (2023). *Education in the school year 2022/2023.* Warsaw: Statistics Poland. Retrieved from https://stat.gov.pl/en/topics/education/education/education-in-the-school-year-20222023-preliminary-data,13,1.html

European Commission. (2024). *Education and training monitor 2024: Poland.* Directorate-General for Education, Youth, Sport and Culture. Retrieved from https://op.europa.eu/webpub/eac/education-and-training-monitor/en/monitor-toolbox/country-page/poland.html

Giebułtowska, J. (2018). Teachers' professional development in the professional learning community model. *Labor et Educatio*, *5*, 57–72. DOI: 10.4467/25439561LE.17.003.7978

Grzyb, B., & Pituła, B. (2019). Prospects of professional development of teachers in light of current changes in the education system. *Przegląd Pedagogiczny, 2,* 121-133. DOI: 10.34767/PP.2019.02.09

Jakubowski, M., Patrinos, H. A., Porta, E., & Wiśniewski, J. (2010). *The impact of the 1999 education reform in Poland.* OECD Education Working Papers, No. 49. Paris: OECD Publishing. https://doi.org/DOI: 10.1787/5kmclwphxg90-en

Kamińska, M. (2023). Teachers' working conditions in times of professional crisis: Evidence of Poland. *The Modern Higher Education Review*, *8*(8). Advance online publication. DOI: 10.28925/2617-5266.2023.83

Karbowniczek, J., & Zdybel, D. (2022). Connective learning as teachers' approach to one's own professional development: The case of Poland. *Multidisciplinary Journal of School Education*, *11*(21), 189–210. DOI: 10.35765/mjse.2022.1121.10

Komorowska, H. (1994). Curriculum development for in-service teacher education in Poland. *Studia Anglica Posnaniensia*, *28*, 113–121.

Konieczka-Śliwińska, D. (2016). Higher education reform in Poland. An example of training for candidates of teacher profession. *Czech-Polish Historical and Pedagogical Journal*, *8*(1), 43–54. DOI: 10.5817/cphpj-2016-005

Kurrle, S., & Warwas, J. (2025). Teacher well-being, professional resilience, and retention: Conceptual frameworks and international evidence. *Teaching and Teacher Education*, *136*, 104421. DOI: 10.1016/j.tate.2024.104421

Kurrle, A., & Warwas, J. (2025). *Teacher well-being, retention, and professional thriving: A contemporary conceptual review. Educational Research Review*, *40*, 100–120.Mercer, S., & Pawlak, M. (2024). *Teacher professional curiosity and development in Poland: Insights from reflective practice. Teaching and Teacher Education*, *123*, 104872.

Madalińska-Michalak, J. (2019). Shaping the future of teaching profession. *Labor et Educatio, 7,* 29-42. https://doi/org/DOI: 10.4467/25439561LE.19.002.11519

Madalińska-Michalak, J. (2020). Teacher education policy issues in Poland: Recommendations for building a high-quality teaching profession. *Kultura-Społeczeństwo-Edukacja*, *18*(2), 7–25. DOI: 10.14746/kse.2020.18.1

Mercer, S., & Pawlak, M. (2024). Language teacher professional curiosity: Understanding the drive for professional development. *Studies in Second Language Learning and Teaching*, *14*(3). Advance online publication. DOI: 10.14746/ssllt.39293

Mercer, S., & Pawlak, M. (2024). Teacher professional curiosity as a driver of lifelong learning, adaptability, and well-being. *System*, *120*, 103210. DOI: 10.1016/j.system.2023.103210

Michalak-Dawidziuk, J. (2021). Selected aspects of the teaching profession in Poland. *Studia Edukacyjne*, *60*(60), 135–160. DOI: 10.14746/se.2021.60.8

Ministerstwo Edukacji i Nauki. (2023). *Nauka w Polsce 2023* [Report] [In Polish: Ministry of Education and Science. Science in Poland]. Ośrodek Przetwarzania Informacji (OPI) przygotowany na zlecenie Ministerstwa Edukacji i Nauki. https://radon.nauka.gov.pl/analizy/nauka-w-Polsce-2023?utm

Mróz, A., Nowak, E., & Kwiatkowska, M. (2025). Pre-service teacher competencies for sustainable development: Empirical evidence from Polish higher education. *Sustainability*, *17*(3), 1452. DOI: 10.3390/su17031452

OECD. (2023). *Education at a glance 2023: OECD indicators – Poland*. OECD Publishing., DOI: 10.1787/69096873-

Wiłkomirska, A., & Zielińska, A. (2015). The system of teachers' professional development in Poland. *Kultura Pedagogiczna*, *1*, 65–78.

Chapter 11
Teachers' Voices From Georgia

Natela Doghonadze
http://orcid.org/0000-0001-7333-8692
International Black Sea University, Georgia

Eka Tkavashvili
Ilia State University, Georgia

Rusudan Chachanidze
http://orcid.org/0009-0009-6793-5568
Zvare Public School, Georgia

ABSTRACT

Georgia has centuries-old traditions in education. Georgian alphabet is believed to have been developed in the 3rd-4th centuries, however, there are material proofs only from the 5th century In ancient times, children of nobility received their education at home and/or at schools existing in palaces and churches. Schools and academies were opened in churches and monasteries for representatives of all social layers. Nowadays, after joining the Bologna Process and carrying out intensive education reforms to modernize the Georgian education system and bring it into correspondence with international standards the education sector has become a star performer in the Georgian economy, worth around $3.3 billion and accounting for seven per cent of the Georgian economy. According to the World Bank, the literacy rate of the population aged 15 or more is 100%. However, the PISA results of Georgian school graduates on international assessments are not so good. Georgian secondary education is free and inclusive. The sub-chapter also contains three personal teacher stories.

A SHORT OVERVIEW ON EDUCATION AND TEACHER ROLE IN GEORGIA: FROM GLORIOUS HISTORY TO VULNERABLE PRESENT AND FUTURE

Natela Doghonadze

History of Education in Georgia

Georgia has centuries-old traditions in education. In ancient times, children of nobility received their education at home and/or at schools existing in palaces and churches. Following the sample of the ancient Greeks, they studied philosophy (including the scientific knowledge of those times), history, rhetoric, and various arts. They knew the Greek and Aramaic languages as early as in the 3rd-4th centuries of our era. With the adoption of the Christian religion, Georgian monasteries and churches were not only religious but also educational centers. Georgian alphabet is believed to have been developed in the 3rd-4th centuries, however, there are material proofs only from the 5th century (Vasadze, 2015). It was twice modified and the version used today comes from the 10th century. "Georgian scripts were granted the national status

DOI: 10.4018/979-8-3373-8983-7.ch011

of intangible cultural heritage in Georgia in 2015 and inscribed on the UNESCO Representative List of the Intangible Cultural Heritage of Humanity in 2016" (Chelidze, 2019). Schools and later academies (as higher education institutions) were opened in churches and monasteries for representatives of all social layers. Education has traditionally been viewed as one of the central values among Georgians, together with personal dignity, kinship, love of life, hospitality, tolerance, faith, language, family, and respect for women (mothers) (Britannica, n.d.; Lindner & Tsertsvadze, 2018).

To have an idea of Georgian education within the Russian Empire and, further, in the USSR, there are few Western publications on the topic. According to one such author, Tanguiane (1979), three-quarters of the population [in the Russian Empire] were illiterate; certain peoples were 98% illiterate; most children did not attend school (4 out of 5); and there were only 127, 000 students in the higher-education system. In 1919 compulsory, free education, both general and polytechnical (providing theoretical and practical initiation in the main production sectors), for all children and adolescents of both sexes up to the age of 17 was established; for the development of a network of pre-school establishments (day nurseries, kindergartens, play centres), with a view to improving public education and liberating women; the complete implementation of the principles of the common school was introduced, incorporating work experience within its curriculum and providing teaching in the pupils' native tongue, co-educational and non-clerical. By the end of the 1930s, only 12% of the population remained illiterate. By 1959, despite the consequences of WWII, illiteracy had been completely eradicated. Universal 10-year secondary education was achieved by the mid-1970s. The great majority of tertiary education students received scholarships.

The education system in Soviet Georgia was very similar to that of all Soviet republics. There was only one higher education institution that bore the name of a university – Tbilisi State University, established in 1918. By 1988, there were 19 higher education institutions (HEIs) enrolling some 86,400 students with more than 100 specialisations and 4to 16 faculties at each university. With a gross tertiary enrolment ratio of 30 per cent, Georgia had one of the highest participation rates in the Soviet countries by the time it gained independence" (Chakhaia & Bregvadze, 2018).

On the other hand, according to Chankseliani (2013), there were problems of Russification of the population (Russian was *the lingua franca in the USSR* and the second official language of the Georgian SSR, similarly to other republics), education was mostly teacher-centered, and Marxist ideology was visible in textbooks, especially on history.

The Bologna process

After regaining independence in 1991, in 2005, Georgia joined the Bologna process, and the government have taken many steps to bring Georgian higher education in line with international standards. Student and teacher exchange became easier in Georgia through Erazmus+ programs (Kitiashvili, 2024). Georgian diplomas have become recognized in EU member states. Quality mechanisms have been introduced for both public and private higher education institutions; the authorization of HEIs and the accreditation of programs have contributed to improving quality. However, it is impossible to deny that they are too bureaucratized and do not always, due to it, reflect the real picture. Again, much has been done to stress research, innovation, and technology application in HEIs, however, the measures are not always effective enough, varying from HEI to HEI (World Bank, 2014). Inclusive education for children with physical and/or mental impairments (students with special needs) became compulsory for schools. It facilitated greater socialization for children with special needs, however, done in a haste, for Georgia to be recognized as part of international educational community, without relevant psychological, pedagogical, and financial support, it brought about much teacher and sometimes parents' dissatisfaction, as well as decrease in teaching quality.

Nowadays, after joining in the Bologna process (an intergovernmental higher education reform process launched in 1999 that includes 48 European countries and a number of European organisations; it aims at better recognition of each other's degrees and stimulating student, academic staff and specialists' international mobility), and carrying out intensive education reforms to modernize the Georgian education system and bring it into correspondence with international standards, according to White (2024), "the education sector has become a star performer in the Georgian economy, worth around $3.3 billion and accounting for seven per cent of the Georgian economy and rising." According to the World Bank (as cited by Trading Economics, 2022), based on official sources, the literacy rate of the population aged 15 or more is 100%. According to some other sources (Macrotrends, 2025), it is 99.58%. With 53 per cent of 19-20-year-olds enrolled in higher education, Georgia is among the leading nations in this regard (World Bank, 2018).

However, the performance of Georgian school graduates on international assessments (PISA, 2022; OECD, 2022) is not strong, indicating that education must be substantially improved. The overall knowledge level of Georgian school graduates does not currently meet international standards (380 points compared to the world average of 470 points). PIRLS results reveal that compared to their peers in other post-socialist countries, school students in Georgia receive lower grades and have lower achievement rates in all three areas (World Bank, 2014).

The Salamanca Statement (1994) and the UN Convention on the Rights of Persons with Disabilities (CRPD) (UN, 2006) introduced a new vision for the education of persons with special needs. In 2006, inclusive education was introduced in Georgia. However, there are many obstacles to the effective application of the inclusive education model in Georgia (MES, 2015). "The most commonly discussed obstacles are the lack of specialists and funds, and sometimes negative attitudes toward diversity" (Tchintcharauli & Javakhishvili, 2017). The existing legislation does not ensure the right to inclusive education at the higher education level. According to the National Curriculum, parents are responsible for the decision-making process concerning the placement of their child in a mainstream or special education school; however, not all parents make a thoughtful decision, and, placing the child in a mainstream school, are not involved in helping the child to learn. Not all classrooms are adapted for children with special needs. While direct costs are covered by the government (free-of-charge education), indirect costs (transportation) are covered by parents, and they are high, to say nothing about the fact that at least one care-taker should have free time to accompany the child to and from the school. One special teacher and one psychologist per school (who sometimes do not have a relevant training) are not sufficient to provide the necessary support.

Tabatadze (2017) research has revealed that the quality of education of ethnic minorities in the territories of their compact habitation is generally lower than in other regions of Georgia. The author sees the outcome in better education of teachers for minorities' schools as well as in the improvement of National Curriculum in this direction.

In 2022, the Ministry of Education and Science of Georgia presented its Unified National Strategy of Education and Science of Georgia for 2022-2030. Within the framework of the 'Better Education for a Better Future' project, an element of the 2022-2030 strategy, focus will be placed on the preparation of professional resources based on modern teaching methodology, support of professional development and teacher training programs of higher educational institutions, professional development of school principals and teachers, and sharing of international expertise. The strategy dwells on three main pillars of Quality, Equity, and Good governance in Education.

According to MES (2022), "during the development and subsequent implementation of the 2022-2030 education and science strategy, significant attention will be paid to improving the quality and availability of data related to the education and science system. The strategy will promote the implementation of an evidence-based approach and the compatibility of data analysis with the standards established by the UNESCO Institute for Statistics" (p.5). By the beginning of 2026, little progress in this direction had been observed.

Mitaishvili-Rayyis (2023) states that "key educational metrics have significantly improved as a result of these efforts, including the achievement of nearly universal primary enrollment and a modest improvement in student performance on international assessments. Nevertheless, despite these advancements, a sizable portion of Georgian students continue to leave school without having mastered basic competencies for life and work" (p. 11).

Since 2014, the European Training Foundation (2025) has been supporting Georgia to develop education and training to boost employability, increase access to opportunities, and promote social cohesion. In 2024, according to them, key reforms in general education included a major secondary-level curriculum overhaul, increased infrastructure investment—with construction set to begin on 75 new public schools—and a shift toward greater school autonomy, decentralising decision-making to individual schools. In 2024, significant efforts were made to enhance the professional development framework for teachers. Furthermore, around 70% of educators received a salary increase, reinforcing efforts to make teaching a more attractive profession (ETF, 2025).

According to Narmania et al. (2023), however, among the unemployed population in Georgia (18.5% of the working-age population) 32.3% are graduates from higher education institutions and over 40% of vocational schools. This inevitably leads to the conclusion that orientation to graduates' employability is insufficient in the tertiary education process.

"Despite notable progress in democratizing education, improving teaching quality, and introducing digital technologies, the system continues to struggle with issues such as regional disparities, corruption, inadequate infrastructure, and insufficient funding" (Gelashvili et al., 2025). Economic difficulties, an authoritarian mindset, and a lack of empirical studies aimed at improving educational quality may be among the main reasons for the limited effectiveness of education reforms undertaken to date.

Further reform plans

The Ministry of Education, Science, and Youth (2025a, b) publicised conceptions of higher education reform and then of general education system reform according to which general education is going to be transformed from a 12-year education to an 11-year one, four year Bachelor studies (except some specialties, such as medicine) into 3-year ones, and two-year Master studies into one-year ones. Later, after receiving criticisms, some modifications were offered: private schools permitted to provide a 12-year education and adding a special, 12th class in a school or district for preparation for learning abroad, and two types of Master's courses (one-year, just to get a certificate, and 2-year including a thesis, for those who want to continue their studies on Doctoral level. Although the quality of education, besides its duration, depends on many factors, such as the quality of curricula, syllabi, and educational materials, contemporary and effective teaching methods, teacher qualifications, equipment and other resources, and, especially important, the effort applied by students to learning, shortening of the study period can significantly (negatively) impact the quality of the obtained knowledge and skills. Such cardinal changes should have been carried out based on research. Besides, this may have an impact on the recognition of Georgian certificates and diplomas within the Bologna Process (e.g., there may be confusion between certificate types). And many teachers may lose their jobs. Another plan, dealing with minimising the number of international students at public universities under the motto 'public universities should mostly teach Georgian citizens' seems weird, as this will bar the internationalisation process (most international students want a public university diploma to avoid problems of its recognition in their home countries). The recent MES initiative concerning the merger of the two oldest and largest universities in Georgia has caused contradictory reactions in Georgian Society and abroad (Georgia Today, 2026; Georgian Business Consulting, 2025; GTU, 2026).

Structure of education

Schooling in Georgia lasts 12 years, 9 of which are compulsory (from autumn 2026, it will be 11 years of schooling, 9 of which are compulsory). It is free and inclusive. The first six years cover primary school, the seventh through ninth grades are termed 'basic school', and 10th through 12th grade are secondary school. Education in public schools is free and available to everybody. There are many private schools in the country that are authorised by the government and issue certificates accepted in Georgia, and some international private schools that offer certificates of International Baccalaureate (IB). Vocational education is of two levels: equivalent to secondary school and post-secondary education provided either in colleges or at higher education institutions HEIs). Tertiary education includes vocational and higher education. Higher education is provided by colleges of higher education (only Bachelor programs), Study Universities (Bachelor and Master programs) and Universities (Bachelor, Master, and Doctorate levels) (National Center for Education Quality Enhancement, n.d.).

How to become a teacher in Georgia

There are two main ways to become a teacher in Georgia: to get a Bachelor's degree in some area and then to complete a one-year 60-credit teacher training educational program or to get a Bachelor's degree with an integrated 60-credit program. Teachers, when hired, are required to submit a document of criminal background check. There are four qualification categories of teachers: practicing, senior, leading, and mentor. Not all practicing teachers meet the contemporary educational requirements, so step by step these positions are being cut. As teacher population is getting too old, to enable young teachers start their career, in 2019, retirement-age practitioner teachers who could not or did not want to take the qualification exam in a specialty that would promote them to senior teacher status were offered a retirement incentive (two-year salaries). About half of them benefitted from this suggestion (Ministry of Education and Science of Georgia, 2019). For those who had worked only due to money (and their students) it was a good chance, as they got money, while their students got an opportunity to have more intrinsically motivated and qualified teachers.

Senior teachers possess an exam-based certificate which attests to their teaching subject and methodological competence. Candidates for the status of lead teacher and mentor have to create various clubs at school, attend conferences and trainings, organize professional development events for colleagues, and much more. Additionally, they have to conduct model lessons evaluated by a special group and compile a portfolio that is also reviewed. A mentor teacher serves as a consultant for other teachers and supervises the pedagogical practice of undergraduate and teacher certification program students as well as early career teachers.

Teacher qualifications, professional development, and student achievement are closely interrelated (Darling-Hammond, 2000). Before 2015, teacher professional development activities were conducted in specific parts of schools and therefore had a local character. In 2015, significant changes were implemented at the national level to the system of professional development and teacher performance assessment in Georgia's general education schools. The National Center for Teachers' Professional Development was founded. The system became centralized. This has simultaneously positive and negative consequences: on the one hand, free professional development is offered to all public school teachers throughout the country, on the other hand, taking into consideration that the offered training sessions are not always of adequate quality, it causes dissatisfaction of many teachers who view these sessions as a waste of time. There are training sessions offered by different universities and training centers, which are often of higher quality, but their certificates are not 'valued' by school administration for promotion reasons. Kirvalidze and Lobzhanidze (2023) studied the efficiency of teacher professional development in Georgia through teacher collaboration. They found that the centralized system of professional development and assessment focused on developmental assessment helps to strengthen the teachers' professional relations, however, mistrust among colleagues, changes being constantly introduced to the education system, and shortage of time were revealed as hindering factors for teacher development.

Teacher and lecturer income and well-being

Till July 2024, teachers at public schools received the salaries calculated as follows:

Final Salary = Base Salary + Seniority Bonus + Qualification Bonus + Status Bonus

The base salary (teacher practitioner) was quite low - up to GEL 30 (about $11) per hour, totaling approximately GEL 500-600 (about $184-221) per month. This is low, compared to average Georgian monthly salary (GEL 2,500≈ $900) (Remote people, 2026). This was supplemented by a modest monthly amount based on seniority (for five/10/more than 10 years + GEL 15/about $6 on each stage) and qualifications (Master's degree GEL40/$15 and Doctorate degree GEL 100/$37) (Narimanishvili, 2024). Lead (GEL 150) and mentor teacher (GEL160) received status bonuses (Ministry of Education, Science, and Youth of Georgia, 2011). Supplementary payment was previewed for teaching students with special needs (annual GEL370-570, depending on the number of such students from 1 to 5). Lead and mentor teacher salaries, especially if they received some supplements, were tolerable (official subsistence minimum in Georgia in 2024 was GEL 250, which is an unrealistic sum with which one can hardly make both ends meet, and the official average monthly salary was GEL1,943, according to Geostat, 2025a, b). The average teacher salary in Europe is 25,000 Euro per year, making it more than three times less in Georgia than across Europe, but Georgian teachers' salaries are a little higher than in Albania (Business Media, 2026). Even given the country's relatively low level of economic development, teachers are clearly underpaid.

According to the July 2024 reform, which had to increase all teachers' salaries, as it was preliminarily announced, by a minimum of GEL 500 (1TV, 2024), in reality, the only category of teachers who significantly benefited were practicing teachers. The new salary calculation formula is as follows: Final Salary = Base Salary + Seniority Bonus + Qualification Bonus + Functional Bonus (only for Lead Teachers and Mentors). The base salary (hourly rate) for teachers working up to 15 hours per week, the hourly rate is 96 lari (about $35). But there is no longer be an allowance for status. Instead, senior teachers, according to the new formula, do not receive any supplementary payments, while leading teachers and mentors receive a small functional bonus: Leading teacher — 150 lari [about $55]; Mentor — 300 lari [about $110.5]. Therefore, the emphasis is now on the teaching load rather than on qualification or status, which has left lead and mentor teachers disappointed.

According to World Salaries (2025), a lecturer at a HEI earns, on average, GEL 125,100 annually (GEL 10,425 monthly), with salaries ranging from GEL 4,801 to 57,200 (GEL 58 hourly). According to Economic Research Institute (n.d.), average annual Professor's salary is GEL 159,697 (GEL 77 hourly). Taking into consideration the fact that the majority of HEIs do not offer any bonuses for publications, participation in international conferences, etc. (or, at best, offer them once a year), which is a requirement during once-in-four or five-year competitions for academic positions, Professor's positions do not offer really good incomes, which trigger many lecturers with doctorate degrees combine jobs at 2-3 HEIS as invited lecturers rather than occupy an academic position. This cannot have a positive impact on the quality of teaching, as excessive teaching hours leave them with little time for professional development. The ongoing educational reform plans to increase professors' salaries, but it will occur at the expense of a reduction in the number of professors.

Teacher burnout, especially after the COVID-19 pandemic, is quite an issue in Georgia. Tavdgiridze et al. (2024) report that teachers face diverse challenges daily. Factors such as student behavior, special-needs instruction, parent engagement, and regulatory compliance contribute to burnout. So do frequent meetings, complex requests, and continuous reforms that consume teachers' time. Fatigue can strain teacher-student relationships and diminish teaching motivation. External pressures from school, parents, and society may become overwhelming, contributing to emotional stress and professional burnout.

Teacher education

The document called *2022-2030 Unified National Strategy of Education and Science of Georgia* states that "as part of the education system reform, significant changes were introduced to increase the accessibility of education and improve the quality, inclusiveness, and development of the labor market-oriented system. In the reform framework, the government started implementing the third-generation national curriculum… New, improved, and modern learning resources are created. The program 'New School Model' was launched" (MES, 2022).

According to the World Bank (2014), the quality of teacher education varies from HEI to HEI and may not be the best. Although teacher development opportunities exist, teachers are not obliged to undergo training. Teacher development programs offered by the state are free for public school teachers, but private school teachers have to pay for their professional development (some private schools cover some of these expenses). Educational Resource Centers opened in all regions are the bridges between the Ministry and the schools that have to support the implementation of the National Curriculum. However, only 37% of teachers surveyed in the PISA frame reported participation in professional development activities, which is lower than the OECD average of 53%. Salaries, especially compared to responsibilities, may not attract the best teachers to work at schools (World Bank, 2014).

As noted above, teaching is unpopular in Georgia. "Since 2011 only 1 to 3% of university students study in the field of education, compared to social sciences and business which attract 37-40% of university students each year" (Burduli, 2021). To try to improve the image of the teaching profession, the Education for All Coalition, Georgia (EFA), an NGO, together with the Teacher Development National Center, started the National Teacher Award. It awards 10,000 Georgian Laris to one teacher annually and the person is given an opportunity to win the Global Teacher Awards ($1 mln). The first recipient of the award was selected as a finalist, which is a significant recognition for Georgian educators. In 2023, the National Teacher Award was established by the Government of Georgia, with the aim of recognizing the best teachers (according to the subjects taught) annually for their outstanding contributions to society and the education system. Winners receive a specially designed badge and a monetary award of 10,000 GEL (Ministry of Education, Science, and Youth, 2024).

Technologies in education

The emergence of new technologies has always had an impact on education. Much has been done to introduce computers in Georgian educational institutions during the past two decades (Tavdgiridze et al., 2023). The COVID-19 pandemic prompted widespread adoption of technologies, even among teachers who had previously been reluctant to do so (Doghonadze et al., 2020). Considering the limited availability of the internet and computers, as well as mobile devices, "Georgia was among the global firsts to introduce curriculum-based TV programmes by joint efforts of Ministry of Education and Science and Georgian Public Broadcasting, which still enjoys growing popularity and serves to the best interest of the society as a whole" (UNESCO, n.d.). The document recognises the problem of digital divide and equity, especially for schools located in remote areas. "Georgia is resolved to support the introduction and development of innovative models of distance and hybrid learning at all levels of education in order to ensure equal access to quality education for schools located far from cities, for families with low socio-economic opportunities without access to the Internet or digital technologies as well as create equal learning opportunities for persons with special educational needs" (UNESCO, n.d.). It was planned to build and renovate up to 800 schools in need by 2026 in accordance with modern standards and universal design requirements – a promise more or less fulfilled. "Georgia underscores its commitment to support the cultivation of 21st century skills and competences in learners at all levels of education, such as literacy, multilingualism, quantitative literacy, financial literacy, scientific, engineering and green skills, digital and technology-based competences, interpersonal skills and active citizenship, entrepreneurship, creativity, initiative, intercultural sensitivity and expression" (UNESCO, n.d.).

However, nowadays, it is insufficient just to integrate technologies in the educational process. Using artificial intelligence (AI) is a new stage of technologies' application. Undeniable is the role of AI in personalized learning, as with its help students can "communicate" in a foreign language, practice to compensate for their weak points, even be guides in research (Moralishvili, 2023). In Georgia, the ethics and legislation related to AI applications are still in the development stage. This, on the one hand, hinders the efficient application of AI in education, and, on the other hand, enables lazy and dishonest students and even teachers to "benefit" from doing the job instead of them (essay-writing, etc.). Therefore, much remains to be done to integrate AI into education in such a way that it rather stimulates creativity and critical thinking than created barriers to their development.

Personal viewpoint

This is an overview of official data. As for my personal opinion based on observation and communication with numerous colleagues both at schools and HEIs, I can mention that there is a high competition for teaching jobs both at schools and HEIs, as these are among the few numerous job opportunities in Georgia (others include banks, police, army, and governmental structures; a lot of people in Georgia are self-employed in small businesses). This high competition does not imply that teaching jobs are 'popular', for many people with higher education, these are simply one of the few they can get at all. Besides having an intrinsic motivation of sharing one's knowledge with younger generation (which is characteristic of maybe 30% of teachers and lecturers), teachers, especially female teachers, who are in majority at school, have extrinsic motives of guaranteed summer vacations, a flexible timetable, and relatively short working day (if we forget about correcting students' homework and getting ready for classes at home, and many, non-intrinsically motivated 'teachers' do forget it). While their children study at the school where they work, this provides an additional extrinsic motive: the opportunity to better care for their own children.

Unmotivated, even sometimes hating their students, teachers, even if qualified, cannot – will not – teach well. Instead of professionally developing (attending training sessions and conferences, at least online, reading up, etc.), teachers serve as private tutors for children whose parents are either too busy or not educated enough to help their children learn and/or to prepare for national entrance exams. Only intrinsically most motivated teachers manage to combine this with professional growth. Concerning school teachers' qualifications. The US Embassy and British Council do a lot to increase English teachers' qualifications. English Teachers' Association of Georgia (ETAG), supported by them, is also doing a great job across Georgia. *The Goethe-Institute* supports teachers of German, and *the* DAAD created good conditions for university academic staff to do research in Germany. The situation is much worse for mathematics and physics teachers; their qualifications, on average, are below all standards (I do not want to hurt some wonderful, enthusiastic, and knowledgeable teachers). I can bring an example of my niece's math teacher, who explained only algebra to her and her classmates, as she said she did not like geometry; they were only given homework, with no explanations or practice in class. Many math teachers several times failed qualification exams needed to become senior teachers. National Center for Teachers' Professional Development holds free-of-charge training sessions for public school teachers. However, many teachers complain about the qualifications of trainers. Some universities used to offer better training, however, only the certificates issued by NCRPD have value for job promotion at school, due to which teachers are no longer motivated to attend other training. And one more grave problem – the majority of school teachers are aged 40 or older, which means that in about 30 years, Georgia, like many other countries, will face a shortage of school teachers.

There is the Educators' and Scientists' Free Trade Union of Georgia (ESFTUG), a professional, voluntary public association of educators. The ESFTUG is a member of global federation of education trade unions - Education International (EI) and EI European Region- European Trade Union Committee for Education (ETUCE) and the Georgian Trade Union Confederation (GTUC) (Educators' and Scientists' Free Trade Union of Georgia, n.d.). However, so far, it (or any other professional organization) has not done much to support teachers, either in their professional development or in defending their rights.

At HEIs, especially private ones, administration often creates conditions that students fail courses, as this means they will have to pay for retaking them. In this situation, some lecturers either give undeserved high grades to students in order to be assessed by them positively, and increase their chances to maintain the jobs, or try to please the administration by failing a lot of students. Many professors write articles, attend conferences, and get acquainted with innovations in the field only the year before the academic competition, not because professional development is their intrinsic desire, but because it is a formal requirement. Many lecturers are good specialists in their field but have minimal pedagogical knowledge and cannot teach well. Although giving higher education to their children is still very popular in Georgia (about 80% of school graduates are entering national entrance exams), nowadays, money is a greater value than education, so fewer people care about getting a university diploma and especially getting knowledge together with the diploma (why learn – the internet and AI will answer all your questions!), which I personally view as a very dangerous trend.

Don't get so frightened after reading these lines – things are not so bad. There are still many good teachers and lecturers in Georgia, and those who are really motivated to learn, have more possibilities to do so today, due to the possibilities offered by the internet. But educating, training, and supporting good teachers must be a priority of a nation which wants to be successful.

I HAVEN'T CHOSEN TEACHING – TEACHING CHOSE ME

Natela Doghonadze

As a child, I lived in a yard of three two-storied wooden houses. Mostly railway station and textile factory workers lived there. My mother's uncle used to be a boss at the railway, so he had a three-bedroom flat where he lived with his two sisters. When my parents married, they lived in one room of a communal flat. After my granduncle's death, my grandma and her sister swapped the flat with my parents so that the younger family could live in better conditions. By then, my Dad had defended his PhD in theoretical physics and my Mum worked as a lawyer. We were the most educated family in the yard, so many kids below and of my age and even one year older came to me to help them with homework. I eagerly did – it was easy and pleasant for me. I studied well at school, knew equally well all subjects, and read a lot, as I was interested in everything: plants, animals, minerals, geography, history, travels, adventures, people's relations, poetry, fiction, etc. My father greatly contributed to my multilateral education. Every workday he studied with me for a couple of hours something – chess, math, history and so on. On Sundays, we dedicated more time to studies. Therefore, I knew more than children of my age according to the school program and could help children older than me.

In the ninth grade, I started thinking about choosing my profession. Although my relationships with math (especially, geometry) and chemistry were fine, I had problems with physics. I liked mathematical logic, but in physics, it irritated me to hear "Let's ignore this and that" and also those formulae which jumped out of nowhere (as we didn't know enough math to understand them). I was good at languages (Russian, Georgian, and English) and loved literature. I was thinking of becoming a writer, but for that one needs life experience. Eventually, I decided to study English.

When I was graduating, I was sure that was not enough for me and I wanted to continue. In fact, I saw two directions: linguistics and language teaching. I liked both. By that time I could, additionally to Russian, Georgian and English, tolerably communicate in French and Spanish. I was not only able to learn languages from books (I learned French in three years as my second specialty at university and Spanish by myself, covering six grades' textbooks in half a year, as I was charmed with songs from a Spanish musical) but also could pick them up seeing similarities among languages (I understood a lot of Italian and Portuguese from the series on television). I had read some books on linguistics and they were extremely fascinating for me. I read plenty of books by English and American authors and O. Henry, Maugham and Fitzgerald were among my favorites. I could do good literary analysis and enjoyed it. However, I thought "Who am I to find something out in the English language or literature? If I study some phenomenon in the English language or literature, would anybody care? So many native speakers are doing it. Should I do it only for my pleasure?" I have always wanted to do something useful. That is why I decided to work on a dissertation on teaching English to Georgian schoolchildren, hoping that somebody would benefit from my findings. That decided my choice. Later I understood that I wanted to dedicate myself to a wider area – teaching in general.

When I graduated, I was ready to teach at school, but, paradoxically, it was easier to be employed part-time at a university than to get a position at school. My first experience was taking to school practice a group of students who had been a year below me when I was studying. I couldn't sleep the night before. I thought about how to dress to look solid, how to address them (in Georgian, there are different pronouns for friendly "thou" – shen - and formal "thee" – tqven- like tu/usted in Spanish and tu/vous in French)), and how to prove to them that, besides the position of a teacher, I had the right to assess the lessons they held. I was very lucky. The group was very friendly. They accepted the rule of calling one other "tqven" to show respect (we moved to "shen" as soon as they were no longer my students). I abandoned my efforts to pretend that I was older than them – they were very happy to have a young friendly teacher, and I dressed exactly like them, so, when they made the practice album, under the group photo they wrote "Find the teacher". During the lessons that were not assessed they got from me such useful feedback which permitted them to score maximum in the graded lessons. Therefore, nobody was strained or unhappy – we did our best.

During my school years, I gained some memorable experiences which taught me how to teach and how not to teach ever. I had a Russian teacher who did her best to teach well, however, she came from not very educated family and sometimes made language mistakes. It's normal when a human, even a teacher, (seldom) makes mistakes. It's a problem when s/he refuses to self-correct and admit the mistake. I did the written homework correctly, and she corrected one word for the wrong variant. We had to self-correct in the next homework, to memorize the correct writing, which I believe to be good practice (too often students care about the grade and ignore teacher feedback, so they may make the same mistake dozens of times). However, I could not write wrong, so I wrote that word the same way again. I got an "F" for that homework (normally, homework was not graded, only feedback was provided). Today, when a good student corrects something that I say/write, I always check myself, even if I am 100% sure that I am right. I tell him/her "I know this like that, but let me check and then tell you". I check and if (one case out of a hundred) the student is right, I always admit it. I did not want to quarrel with her, to humiliate her in front of the class, I just wanted the truth. The next day, during the break, when nobody else was in the classroom, I came up to her with an orthographic dictionary and showed her the right variant. Her face color changed from green to purple, but she had to admit her mistake. She collected the exercise books that day and never returned them to the whole class saying they were completed and we had to start new ones. Probably she expected me or my parents to go to the principal with the proof of her incompetence. After that, she kept asking me difficult questions at every lesson. I always answered. If before that case, I rather intuitively (based on abundant reading) knew how to spell and punctuate, from then on I became a mixture of synthetic and analytical language learner. I am finally grateful to her – she taught me three important lessons: 1) be very knowledgeable (a head 'taller' than your students) on the subject; 2) don't be too self-confident, and always check yourself, especially when a good student says you re wrong; 3) never fight/revenge on your students, that only proves your meanness; admitting your mistakes is not a shame, fighting your students (against whom your social position, experience, and knowledge protect you) is unfair, fight your equals or those above you, if fighting is so important for you.

However, the majority of my school teachers were knowledgeable specialists and good people. On the example of my chemistry teacher, I realized what it means for a teacher to be a good psychologist and to know your students well. I was learning easily and never struggled with subjects. I had a good memory and didn't need to spend hours trying to memorize materials. Neither my parents nor I cared too much about grades. I mostly got 'A's, sometimes a 'B'. I perceived 'B's calmly, they were dignified grades. This was how I started learning chemistry till the moment when it turned out that I needed to understand, not simply memorize it. We had a test consisting of a theoretical issue and two problems. I did OK with theory, but got stuck with the problems which I couldn't solve to the end. The test was poorly done, but it deserved some low, but positive grade. Had she given me a positive grade, I would have ignored it – just one ‘C’ among so many ‘A’s and a few ‘B’s! The teacher had understood my resilient character and realized that only a shock would change my study style, so she failed me on that test. That sobered me. I had never before got an ‘F’. I asked the teacher what I could do to improve my semester grade and she said “Two lessons are left to the end of the semester. Sit down and relearn the material with deep understanding. If you can’t do it independently, I’m ready to help.” So I did and I realized that not only math is about deep understanding. After that, all my grades in chemistry to the end of schooling were ‘A’s, and till today I remember a lot from the course. The lesson I later concluded from that experience was that students should be graded flexibly and individually – struggling students need support for their effort, while easily learning superficial students need to be put down to earth.

We had a wonderful history teacher. She believed that all students could get at least ‘B’s in her subject. That was why she never gave a lower grade but was re-asking the student who didn’t study well again and again until s/he was able to receive a ‘B’. She split us into groups, with at least one very successful student in each group. We had to study together for the semester summing up, and if somebody in the group received a low grade, the whole group did. That was at the end of the 1960s, don’t forget. I don’t know whether she developed this approach herself or read/heard somewhere about it, but it was so different from what other teachers did. We all loved history lessons and history in general.

The English teacher who taught us in the 8th grade knew English well – spoke English with us, she had rich vocabulary and accurate grammar, and her pronunciation was good, but I didn’t have a feeling she cared. She honestly presented all the material under study, but regularly engaged in activities only average students. She believed low achievers were hopeless and she hated listening to them, she was sure high achievers (including myself) could do without much practice, so she concentrated on students with average results. In a language, if one does not speak, his/her speaking skills decay. This is what happened to me. Luckily, the next year we got a teacher whose English (especially, pronunciation) was not that perfect, but who understood that she had to let us enjoy the learning. She permitted us to translate poetry instead of newspaper (it was our idea), just on condition we really did it. She let us choose discussion topics and even make up our own grammar and vocabulary drills. We enjoyed a lot of learner autonomy (I remind you once more, it was 1969/70 in the Soviet Union).

At the Institute of Foreign Languages, the majority of lecturers were friendly, communicable, helpful, and knowledgeable. There were some exceptions, of course. For example, the Vice-Rector and a lecturer on political economy whom we called Pinochet for his rudeness, even cruelty, under a mask of intelligence. He wrote a denunciation of our beloved lecturer of philosophy who permitted us to express our own ideas in connection with Marxism on condition that we could prove them logically or by evidence.

My first experience of an open-book exam which now is often viewed as an innovation was in my history of the English language class – our demanding but fair and understanding lecturer believed most of us would not become history of language specialists, however, we needed the general understanding where irregular verbs, for example, came from, etc. That is why her exam included practical questions to answer which we could apply our course notes as guidebooks. She did not demand us to memorize Old English conjugations, etc., just to be able to understand old language (especially in literature) with the help of our notes. We were so grateful to her. She contributed so much to our linguistic thinking. She could look strictly at us when we did not follow, but she never raised her voice. She always spoke calmly and we listened attentively. She was my role model and was one of the arguments I decided to work in methods of teaching English. She recommended the institute administration to invite me as a part-time lecturer. Later, as a teacher, I have, like her, done my best to promote my outstanding students. I have never been afraid of the possibility of them occupying my place. I have been self-confident enough, as I have kept learning during my teaching career. But if they could do better, it would mean for me I have not taught them in vain. Now, getting older and more tired, I passed over my positions to them – no pressure on me, I understand that younger people need to be promoted, as they have more energy. But I’m at their side as long as they need my support.

My PhD course was not more difficult (like many people state) than he previous levels. The main difference was that it definitely taught me to be more autonomous. I have always been ready to take up responsibilities and to help others. It so happened that in Georgia at the time I graduated, there were only three people with a Doctor Nauk degree (it’s something like post-doctoral degree in other countries, which permitted to supervise PhD dissertations) in methods of teaching foreign languages, and I was the only one in teaching English. I just had to help other people who wanted to do their PhDs in the field, so next year after my defense I started supervising PhD dissertations. Now I am the ex-supervisor of 42 defended PhD dissertations, some in English language teaching and some in education.

I love teaching – I want to share what I know and not sit on it like a dog in the manger, I like young people, and communicating with them helps me feel young, too. I am quite artistic, and I hope I manage to present materials well enough. Teaching is two-sided – I learn many things from my students, too. I do my best to treat them with respect – to let them express their opinions, to treat them as people first and then as students. I am inspired by interested and motivated students, then my classes are at my maximum. Their initial preparation is often of a lower level than I would like, but I try to compensate for it as much as time permits. My goal is to help them grow professionally and as people (the teacher's profession is first of all about being humans). I prefer to overestimate than to underestimate them – life will put things right, anyway. I disrespect teachers whose goal is to catch (mistakes or misbehavior), punish, fail, and prove that they are the power and the most knowledgeable ones. The more knowledgeable people in the world, the kinder it becomes.

I am generally optimistic, but there are moments when I feel desperate. There are always one or two students in the group who cannot be motivated by any means, unfortunately, this is the reality. But I had two cases which made me doubt my career choice. The first I had while I was teaching Business English to Business freshman students. The group was too big for a language class, the majority in the group were male students, noisy, and undisciplined (unfortunately, in our high schools discipline is a huge problem – democracy is understood by students and often their parents as the right to do anything they want), but they were just crazy kids. They wouldn't listen, were not engaged in activities, and did not react to my requests to tell me what kind of classes they wanted – total chaos. I warned them they could fail midterm – no reaction. Their general English was tolerable and they believed they could do with it without study. All I managed to do was to provide good slides and handouts so that those who wanted to study for the midterm would be able to get a good grade. Half of the group got very poor results. When they came to the next class, they asked me "Why?" They were sincerely surprised. They were even silent hoping to hear my answer. I explained that Business English is the language used for specific purposes, it is not so difficult, but it has to be studied, and I know how to teach it if they want to learn. They came to senses, they learned and they passed the final. Happy ending. But it required all my experience, knowledge, and patience. Next year, Rector heard from many subject teachers complaints about students' level of English. I was the Vice-rector for Education then. He asked me to accompany him to classes. He entered rooms and asked questions to students. In some groups, students couldn't answer well. He asked who their English teacher was. Then we entered my former group. I had a cold sweat on my forehead and my knees were shaking. He spoke to my former students and they responded well enough. He was satisfied and asked who their English teacher was and they looked at me. "You see, good teaching matters," Rector said. I could exhale calmly. I passed the exam together with my former students.

The other case was worse. They were Juniors or Seniors, I'm not sure now. They were noisy, and undisciplined, and not only hated learning themselves but also despised those who wanted to learn. Twenty-four of them – seven who wanted to learn American Literature and seventeen who didn't (by the way, the course was elective, nobody made them choose the course, but they didn't want to study at all. They made a hell of the lives of those students who wanted to learn and mine, of course. They stood up, talked aloud from one corner of the room to another, threw objects, and called names those students who tried to listen and answer to me. Dumb guys, idiots, bookworms, and many worse nicknames. I did what I have never done – I begged them not to come to my class and promised not to register their absence. They came! Coming to class was their sadistic entertainment! I begged them to entertain silently so that others could learn – nay! I, of course, could address the disciplinary board, but I do not believe in such things. Fourteen of them failed my course – and they didn't care. It looks like others were more or less well-read before they became university students or they managed to cheat during the exam, I don't know. Next year some of them took a different elective course, hoping to pass there more easily, some even transferred to another university, and some of them retook my course, but this time they were in the minority now and couldn't ruin my classes. Several never graduated. The funny thing is the majority of them are my Facebook friends and regularly congratulate me on holidays. Nothing personal, it looks like. They simply didn't want to study. It was my only professional fiasco in life. I thought might be I was too old to teach young people, and I could no longer establish rapport with them. But the next batch of students revealed I was not a bad teacher.

Teaching is not an easy job, it is connected with a lot of challenges – large classes, various levels of knowledge and aptitudes among students, discipline, a lack of motivation, misunderstandings with administration and the Ministry who are still too authoritarian, too much load, especially paperwork... Some of these depend on me and I do my best to tackle them: I develop various materials and activities according to sub-groups inside the group, use tasks with keys, simplify the language while explaining things, find out interesting facts, and create optimal conditions for all students who really want to study (and not simply somehow get the grade and forget the subject the next day after the exam) to pass the exam. We discuss, debate, analyze, and try to find the root of phenomena. Primary school teachers are in a better position – their kids have not had the negative impact of bad teachers yet. At university, we get some students who only want diplomas to please their parents or to be employed or even those who are at university just to have a good time with peers, not to join the army and not to start to be responsible for somebody or something. They are disappointed in education – they think it's useless (Google knows all the answers, why to work hard instead of leading an idle life), boring (a lot of textbooks, I have to admit, are horribly boring), and little related to life. I let them learn the way they like and can (if they truly learn and not loaf), give them hints on how to improve their memory and use mnemonics, how to compare and come to conclusions based on evidence, not emotions…

Teaching and learning have become an inseparable part of my life over the years. It's my horizon, my outlook on life – I read fiction books, watch movies, travel, and listen to people talk, and it becomes a rich soil for my examples when I teach Education/Pedagogy. Teachers need to know so much – not only their subjects and how to teach them – they need to know life and relate their teaching to life – then it is interesting and motivating. I absorb such information like a sponge intuitively in case one day I need it to exemplify or explain something.

Some teachers say they do not work at their best and are not engaged in professional growth, as their pay is low and they have to make money for their families. Don't go to professions like teachers and doctors if you don't like your job not only in the beginning but also after a few years! This is not yours. Please do not ruin children's lives. I will not give technical (professional) recommendations here – they are too numerous, and volumes and volumes are dedicated to them. My only recommendation is: quit, if you hate (or are indifferent to) the process, both you and your students will be much happier.

By character I am neither a leader nor a lead person. I, however, realize that, if you are not a leader for your students, they will hardly learn well. As for administrative leadership positions, I have never cared for them. Somehow, I was assessed for my ability to do work responsibly, knowledgeably, and thoughtfully, and to ignite hearts, so I was promoted to a Vice-Rector's position and occupied it for ten years (after ten years, I quit myself, as I was too tired of the job), and author of four programs (English Philology, BA, Higher Education Management, MA, Teacher Certification 60-credit program, and Education Sciences, PhD), and then, for 12 years, the coordinator of these successful programs. I did my best to be education-centered, student-centered, and colleague-centered. I left the positions when I got tired and realized a younger person should continue. However, I perceive myself much more as a teacher and researcher than as an administrator.

I am not very happy with the changes that are taking place in contemporary education, however, having met many wonderful enthusiastic teachers during my career helps me remain optimistic concerning the perspectives of teachers and teaching. There will always be teachers with their original, creative approaches, despite all vehement efforts of 'standardisation' and seeing teachers as technicians fulfilling the given program. And technologies, including AI, will be tamed and applied for the benefit of teachers and learners, I believe. However, society has to support them emotionally and financially, instead of discrediting.

A JOURNEY OF TRANSFORMATION

Eka Tkavashvili

Many teachers say they have always dreamed of becoming one, but for me, teaching was not a childhood plan - it was something that found me unexpectedly. I was born into a family of primary school teachers. My parents studied in the same group at the Pushkin Tbilisi State Pedagogical Institute (Now Ilia State University), however, they never taught at school. Yet, even without their direct example, something within me was drawn to the act of teaching. When my father brought home a green board while I was still in kindergarten, I began to write numbers on it with great enthusiasm. I preferred that to playing with dolls, which puzzled everyone. While other children in my yard were busy with their toys, I gathered them as "pupils," wrote their names in a notebook I called my "register," and played the role of their teacher.

Looking back, I now realize that this early fascination was not mere play - it was the first sign of my vocation. I loved organizing, explaining, and seeing others understand. At that time, I had no concept of what it meant to be a "teacher by birth" or "by vocation," but the impulse was already there.

I began school at the age of five, a year earlier than my peers did. My first day has remained vivid in my memory. My mother accompanied me; she and my future teacher had been institute group mates. As the new pupils entered the classroom one by one, I was inexplicably left outside. No one explained anything. After standing alone for a few minutes, I quietly walked back home - fortunately, it was nearby. My mother was astonished to see me return so soon. Even now, as someone who understands the importance of children's rights, I often ask myself how it could have been acceptable to leave a five-year-old child unattended. That small episode made me sensitive to children's emotions and aware of the importance of protection, inclusion, and empathy – the values that later shaped my understanding of what a teacher should be.

Throughout my school years, I encountered many types of teachers. Some inspired me deeply; others merely went through the motions. Among those who left a lasting impression was my first English teacher - a kind, soft-spoken woman with impeccable manners. I was astonished that she always thanked us for our answers, something no other teacher had done before. Her courtesy and appreciation for each student's effort created an atmosphere of respect that fostered genuine motivation.

Another model teacher was our Georgian literature teacher, an elderly man of calm temperament and quiet authority. Even when faced with noisy or disruptive students, he never raised his voice. His patience taught me that dignity, not humiliation, is the key to discipline. Those two teachers - one gentle, the other steady - shaped my earliest sense of what good teaching means: respect, composure, and humanity.

As a teenager, I did not dream of teaching. My ambition was to become a lawyer; I wanted to establish justice and stand for what was right. I was naturally law-abiding, yet critical of vague or illogical rules. This sense of fairness has followed me throughout my professional life. When time came to choose a career, my family gathered to discuss options. My father objected to my becoming a doctor - though my mother was proud of the idea, as medicine was then considered a prestigious profession for women. It was my brother who suggested a middle path: "Why not study foreign languages?"

We had always loved English, perhaps because we travelled together as Georgian dancers and often interacted with foreigners. My father supported the idea, and I took the exams and was admitted to the Institute of Foreign Languages. I was fascinated by English and American literature, and I admired our professors' erudition. However, it was only in the third year that a pedagogy lecturer casually mentioned, "You know, you are training to become teachers." The entire class was stunned. None of us had paid attention to the sign above the entrance that said 'Pedagogical Institute'. We just thought we were going to be language specialists.

Our first school practice came soon after. The lesson we observed was conducted by a highly educated teacher who had just returned from the United States. I was impressed by her confidence and the rapport she had with her students. When the supervisor asked, "Who would like to conduct the first lesson?" I raised my hand without hesitation.

I prepared meticulously - studied every phrase, every question, rehearsed every possible answer. I entered the classroom certain of success. Yet, the lesson did not go as I had imagined. The students were confused by my questions, and the flow I had planned so carefully collapsed. Afterward, my lecturer told me bluntly that the lesson was a failure. I did not feel devastated; rather, I sensed that something important had happened. I realized that I had strong knowledge but lacked the practical strategies to engage learners. Unfortunately, my mentor at the time admitted that he had grown tired of teaching and no longer found joy in it. His indifference became a silent warning to me: never to lose interest, never to allow routine to extinguish passion.

That early failure became my turning point. It was the moment when I began to search for the how of teaching - not only what to teach, but how to reach minds and hearts.

Shortly afterward, I was invited to work as a laboratory assistant at the Chair of Didactics of Foreign Languages. The lecturer who offered me the position was a truly inspirational woman. Although advanced in years, she was remarkably open-minded and forward-looking. Her progressive ideas and human warmth made a deep impression on me. She often told me, “You must share if you want to have followers and like-minded people around you. Don’t keep your thoughts to yourself - share them with others. Only then will you find those who live by the same vision.”

Those words have stayed with me ever since. They became a guiding principle in my life: knowledge grows when shared, and teaching is one of the most generous acts a person can perform.

This opportunity came at a turbulent moment - the early 1990s, the period of the Tbilisi war and severe social hardship. There was no electricity, no gas, and the universities were often closed. Winters were dark and cold, and yet my desire to learn burned even stronger.

In those difficult years, teaching became my form of resistance. When there was no light, I read by candle; when there was no stability, I built it in my classroom. I realized that education could serve as both survival and hope. My perseverance was soon rewarded with a discovery that changed my professional path: a colleague told me that a new teachers’ association was being established by the British Council - the English Teachers Association of Georgia (ETAG).

ETAG became a bridge between Georgian teachers and the international community. Through it, I attended workshops led by American and British experts, gaining access to modern methodologies that were otherwise unavailable in Georgia at the time. Every Saturday session brought not only knowledge but also inspiration. I began to understand what my mission as a teaching methodology lecturer truly was - to help future teachers see methodology not as theory, but as a practical art of communication and learning.

The experience with ETAG opened new horizons for me. I tested new ideas in my university classes and shared them with my students, encouraging them to view teaching as creative problem-solving. A few years later, another milestone followed: I received a scholarship to Cambridge for a Trainer-to-Trainer summer workshop. Standing in front of fifty teachers from twenty-three countries, I delivered a short presentation - my first international public speech. Among the participants was Keith Morrow, a leading figure in communicative language teaching. That moment was life-changing. I realized that my passion for teaching connected me to something universal - a global community of educators committed to human growth and understanding.

It was in Cambridge that I experienced a deep retrospection. I remembered the childhood moments when I explained lessons to my classmates and felt the same quiet joy I now felt as an adult professional. The circle was complete. Teaching, I understood, was not just a job but a lifelong dialogue between giving and learning.

Later, my academic life took another profound turn when my first scientific adviser, Professor Natela Doghonadze, encouraged me to explore reflective teaching in my dissertation. Her intuition proved transformative. Reflection became not just a research topic but a personal way of living for me. Through reflective practice, I began to examine my own thoughts and actions critically. It was never easy - constructive criticism can be painful - but it opened pathways to self-awareness that no theoretical course could have offered.

I learned that real professional growth requires courage: the courage to face one’s weaknesses, to listen to students’ feedback, and to question one’s assumptions. Gradually, I came to see that the process of developing as a professional was inseparable from developing as a person. Teaching, more than any other profession, requires constant moral vigilance and emotional balance. A teacher’s words can heal or wound; their attitude can empower or silence. For that reason, a teacher must cultivate patience, empathy, and self-control every day.

Over the years, I have realized that my students have taught me as much as I have taught them. Each new generation has helped me see the world through different eyes. Teaching is not a one-way process - it is a dialogue, a continuous exchange of perspectives. I often tell my students that teaching and learning are two sides of the same coin, both rooted in curiosity and generosity.

I have always sensed within myself the spirit of social constructivism. I believe deeply in mutual learning - to give and to take, as I often describe it. This principle keeps me attached to teaching to this day. It is what keeps me learning, reflecting, and staying intellectually young.

Throughout my career, I have met many educators - some brilliant, others indifferent. Both have influenced me. The inspiring ones showed me what to emulate: calmness, empathy, and professionalism. The uninspired ones taught me what to avoid: monotony, arrogance, and emotional detachment. Every encounter, positive or negative, has contributed to shaping my own professional ethics.

I have come to believe that no teacher should ever stop learning. The day we think we “know enough” is the day our teaching begins to decline. True educators remain humble, open-minded, and reflective throughout their lives.

Among many memorable experiences, one remains especially dear to me. Years ago, while travelling on the metro, a young woman approached me with her mother. Smiling shyly, she said, "Mother, this is my lecturer, Eka Tkavashvili, who taught me and made me love teaching." In that brief moment, I felt that my years of dedication, effort, and self-doubt were all worth it. No award or certificate could compare to the quiet fulfillment of seeing one's influence reflected in another human being. That is when I fully grasped what it means to make a difference - not on a grand stage, but in the hearts of students.

As I look back now, I no longer think badly of the schoolteacher who once left me standing outside the classroom on my first day. My experience as a teacher has taught me to be more tolerant and understanding of other people's drawbacks. We all make mistakes, and it is impossible to be one hundred percent perfect. What matters is the willingness to learn, to reflect, and to grow from every imperfection - our own and others'.

Looking back on decades of teaching, I see not a career, but a journey of transformation. Teaching has been both my challenge and my reward, my discipline and my joy. It has required intellectual rigor and emotional resilience, but it has also given me a sense of purpose that no other profession could provide.

In one of my favorite books, Training Foreign Language Teachers by Michael J. Wallace, the author reminds us that the word "profession" originally meant "a profession of faith." It implied a calling, a dedication to the welfare of others. That definition resonates deeply with me. Teaching, at its core, is an act of faith - faith in human potential, in learning, and in the belief that knowledge can make the world a better place.

Today, after many years of teaching, I still feel the same excitement I did as a child writing numbers on my green board. Each lesson is a new beginning; each student is a new story. I believe that as long as we give and take, teach and learn, we remain alive, curious, and forever young.

My journey as a teacher is far from over. New collaborations and experiences continue to shape my understanding of education. Each new encounter, whether with students, colleagues, or fellow educators across borders, reminds me that teaching, like life itself, is a continuous unfolding story.

A teacher may not change the world with a single lesson, but they can change the life of a single student - and that student may one day change the world.

As a concluding reflection, I would like to briefly share my views on the future perspectives of the teaching profession.

Predicting the future of the teaching profession is not an easy task in the modern era, when educational, technological, and social changes occur at unprecedented speed. What seems clear, however, is that teaching and learning will no longer remain the same. In the age of artificial intelligence, when learners have immediate access to vast amounts of information, policymakers may be tempted to believe that reducing direct contact hours with teachers in physical classrooms is economically reasonable.

Despite this temptation and the growing role of digital and virtual learning environments, I firmly believe that real teaching cannot - and should not - be replaced. This is not because virtual learning lacks value, but because human interaction is fundamentally irreplaceable. Learning is not solely a cognitive process. As Benjamin Bloom's taxonomy reminds us, learning involves cognitive, affective, and psychomotor domains. Learning without emotional engagement is comparable to perceiving the world without a heart.

Teachers create learning contexts rooted in the "here and now," where students engage intellectually, emotionally, and socially. The absence of genuine human interaction may result in

For this reason, I believe that the teaching profession will remain in high demand in the future. However, its focus will inevitably evolve. Teachers will increasingly emphasize the development of learners' socio-emotional skills, critical thinking, and adaptability. We are likely to see more integrative approaches to teaching, incorporating topics such as sustainable development, financial literacy, entrepreneurship, digital competence, and life skills, rather than an overemphasis on memorization and factual recall. In this changing landscape, the role of the teacher will not diminish; instead, it will become more complex, more human-centered, and intellectually demanding.

I PLAYED AN IMPORTANT ROLE IN MY STUDENTS' DECISION-MAKING, ASSESSING THEIR ABILITIES AND DOING THEIR BEST

Rusudan Chachanidze

As a child, I grew up in Georgia, in the Imereti region, in a village situated in the mountains at about 2000 meters above the sea level. The area is fascinating, with its nature, beauty, history, tradition, culture, relationships among people, and resort Nunisi.

Georgia is a traditional country. In villages, there are extended traditional families, and children grow up with grandparents who are actively involved in the process of raising them. They have a very close relationship, love, connection, and attitudes towards each other. Children are involved in family work, gardening, and farming, and learn these activities from a very early age. We had cattle, pigs, chickens, grew grapes, corn, potatoes, some vegetables, and fruit. When I was 7, I knew everything about these matters, and I think it is gratifying and beneficial for development if doing too much farming does not negatively impact children's learning. In fact, knowledge of everyday life can be the building blocks of future learning.

My mother grew up in the Ukraine. She didn't receive a university education, but her school education was good. She loved world literature and often read books even after a long day of work at home. Mom loved learning and was a good mother who taught us to love school, teachers, and learning. My father was a very talented man with a university education. He was a war participant and a public figure. At an early age, he did a lot of social projects as an active citizen. He established and built a railway station in my village, a football pitch, a church, built automobile roads, and seven bridges in my village. He was a very active and respected figure and was involved in every social issue that mattered in regional development and progress. He was an authoritative figure whom people respected greatly.

Dad was an affectionate parent towards us, his three daughters, and had high expectations from us. He believed in our abilities and was sure that we would study well and achieve a lot in our lives. He encouraged us, and so we grew up courageous and independent. He was honest towards everyone and treated us with respect, and therefore, he was an authoritative figure for us, his daughters. For my father, education was the highest value, and he often told us stories about successful people and heroes, bought valuable books for us, and sometimes read heroic and patriotic poems with emotion and explanation. I think Dad had a great parental style and managed to raise us so that later we were able to continue our studies despite the fact that it was almost impossible financially.

When my elder sister and I were about to finish school and start our university education, my father's business failed because he had some disagreement with the government. My father had a legal conflict with a project of a German company, which intended to restrict Georgian people's traditional right of cattle herding and mowing the lawns in their own land. My father lost his business because he did not stop his litigation despite the fact that Georgian officials demanded that he stop. People got back their traditional rights, but my father lost his income, and it was impossible for our family to pay education expenses or hire private tutors for university exam preparation. In Georgia at that time, it was almost impossible (especially in villages) to pass university admission exams without studying with private tutors. When my elder sister finished school and had to cope with the situation of not being able to dream about university, I was really sorry. Almost every classmate of my sister was admitted to the university. My sister had good grades at school. I started acting and planned my day to prepare myself and gain a study grant. My father reminded me later that I had told my family I would definitely get a grant, and indeed I did! My sister got encouraged and started preparing for admission as well. Due to my hard work and dedication, I passed exams with distinctions and gained a grant. My sister got a 20% discount on university fees. I graduated from the faculty of law with distinction. I think my father's high expectations, values, and attitudes made us able to try and achieve. The parental style, bringing up and teachers' role are incredibly high. I think my father would have been a good example of how teachers should be to encourage and motivate students and increase their self-esteem.

Soon after my graduation, there was a staff competition in the judicial system in Georgia, and I passed the exams with distinction, but I was not chosen for the position because, as the letter informed me, of my age. I was not 21 years old yet. Only 2 days remained before my 21st birthday! I thought it was a very weak pretext for not choosing me. Instead, a woman with a degree in history, not law, was chosen.

For me, independence has always been very important, so I decided not to waste time in the unfair field like that and started studying English from my elder sister. My sisters had quite contemporary English books, and I studied the English course for the bachelor's program by myself. I often listened to my sister's classes with her private students and was fascinated by this profession and how she loved and motivated her students. During 7 years, I studied hard and at the same time I had to give lessons to my sister's pupils as she had moved to Tbilisi to continue her studies. I continued learning English at the Caucasus University course and earned a C1 certificate (the 5th of 6 levels of language knowledge, according to the acknowledged Common European Framework of Reference for languages). I got married and divorced after my unsuccessful eight-month relationship with my husband, who started gambling, and I realized it would be impossible to raise my child with him. I was 5 months pregnant when I left him, and then my daughter was born. I continued private tutoring and passed the national teachers' exam in English and pedagogy. After certification, I got a teacher's job in my village. By this time, my daughter was 1 year old. I did not stop thinking about further development and started preparing for the MA entrance exams. Again, I gained the state grant and completed my MA degree with distinction. During this period, I taught at a state school in my village and prepared pupils for university exams and other purposes. I got the status of a leader teacher in English and in civic education, I passed TKT exams (Cambridge certificate for teachers) and enriched my experience as a teacher and educator. I attended many training sessions and worked as an assessor for mentor teachers. I started my PhD in Education at the International Black Sea University and finished the first year, but I had to stop due to financial reasons. However, I continue learning on my own. I always use different contemporary books to enrich my teaching methods at school and in my private teaching.

During my teaching career (18 years as a private tutor and 12 years as a public school teacher), I have met and worked with many different pupils, changed my teaching methods, and my relationship style with them. My father's character influenced my teaching style. The characteristics that make me successful and cause students to choose me as their private teacher are my positive expectations, care, and affection towards them. I always believe that every child is unique and has some specific talent and ability. Not only teaching the subject is important, but it is also essential to get to know their characters, attitudes, interests, and listen to their opinions with respect. When a teacher is a good friend, has a good relationship with students, and is involved in their everyday growth, students try to do their best. We, schoolteachers, sometimes play games with them after school, go on excursions with them, listen to stories about their experiences, and tell ours. Pupils respect this kind of relationship; it influences their discipline, behavior, and motivation to learn.

I remember when I taught 4th-grade pupils: a hyperactive student moved into our class, which made the whole class chaotic and disrupted their behavior and learning. I did my best and worked both with the entire class and to each student individually to maintain their motivation and discipline. There was a boy, G., in that class who was adopted by his uncle's family because his parents could not take care of him. One day, after an exhausting lesson with this class, the bell rang, and all the pupils left the class noisily. But I noticed the boy looked a bit sad as he left the classroom. I called him, took his hand, and told him warmly: "My dear G., I know that you are a very good boy and you can learn really well. Your uncle is a very successful and clever man, and your grandparents were a good family and hardworking, good people. I will always be by your side and pay close attention to your learning, and if you let me help with it, you will be very successful in life." He looked at me with hope, and after this day, he never again wasted his time during my lessons. He always listened carefully to my words, wrote, read and fulfilled grammar exercises. He got more serious and respectful to all teachers, though he had critical opinions of some of them. His English level improved a lot. After every school year, he asked me to recommend a self-study book, and I always did. He studied during the summer holiday. After every summer, he used to return to school with better language skills, and he did his best during every school year. I learned that students need support not from time to time but continuously in order to be successful.

When this class moved to grade 5, their class tutor allowed them to blame teachers for their poor academic achievement and bad behavior. They got even noisier during their 10th, 11th, and 12th grade, they got absolutely lazy and spent the whole year fighting each other during lessons, being entertained with mobile phones, and arguing with their teachers. All teachers got frustrated and hopeless with them. All those pupils hoped that their parents would hire the best private tutors for them, and help them to become university students, so they didn't care about learning at school. I did not agree to teach any of them privately. In their last school year, they had to go to the nearest city to be prepared for admission in 4 subjects, so they often missed classes. Only G. could not afford to have private tutors for university exams, and so he was alone in most lessons. When I first entered the class with only one pupil, it was the first time I had done my best and conducted a proper lesson. I checked G's level in English and was sure that he had perfect readiness to pass university exams with distinction. I was really sorry for him, and he did not stop trying even though no one could help him use this knowledge.

One day, I arrived at school with my colleague M. When we met G. in the hall, M. smiled at G. and told him that he was a very good boy. "What a sweet-hearted woman she must be" I thought. I knew her as a very strict teacher. This experience made me express my true encouragement with G. after I finished a great lesson with only one child in the classroom. I was really pleased with his knowledge, attention, motivation, and attitude towards my subject. The lesson ended. When I was leaving the class, I looked back and asked him what his brother, who finished school the year before, was doing. He answered that he had started a job. I looked at G. and said, "You are a very hard-working, clever, and good boy. Everything will be well in your life. There is everything in the universe for the people of your kind. There is a job, there is education, money, and people who appreciate your personal qualities and your dedication." He looked at me with hopeful eyes, and I left the class. The next evening, his adoptive mother called me and told me that G. had asked her to prepare for university exams, and he promised that he would do everything, work, and have his own money to pay the expenses during his university studies. I was really pleased, thanked her for her kindness, and told her that I would teach G. without money so that they could afford to pay for other subjects. G. passed the exams and gained a state grant. Two of his classmates were not admitted to university at all, and many of them were admitted, but didn't get state grants. G. is a successful and very active student now, and I hope he will be successful all his life and will help many people with his professional knowledge and skills.

I have had many examples of this kind, and I learned from my experience that students need authoritative parents and teachers who believe in their abilities and success, believe in their unique qualities, and support them.

Also, I have learned that critical thinking is important; however, students should not mistakenly perceive critical thinking as criticizing everything and everybody. They should be critical of themselves first, not only of their teachers. They need to respect teachers to learn the best from them. Also, parents and teachers should show respect for other teachers. Blaming others for one's problems is not an effective way; in this way, it is difficult, if possible at all, to learn anything. Critical thinking is about (fair, objective) analysis, abut requiring empirical proofs/arguments for ideas and not just being nihilistic about everything and everybody (except oneself).

In conclusion, the role of teachers, educators, and parenting style (viewing parents as our first teachers) is immeasurable. Teachers play a great role in students' self-assessment formation that is essential for setting goals and making destination, also in keeping trying and making effort to achieve. Students' attitude and motivation formation is also a meter of human interference that cannot be done by any technology. Without my father's attitude I would have never been able to have such a strong desire and determination to achieve educational aims, I would have never believed in my abilities. On the other hand, I played an important role in my students' decision-making, assessing their abilities and doing their best. Students need close relationship, parents' and/or teachers' care and encouragement that only humans can do. Technologies should help teachers, they should not be advertised teachers' competitors. So, it is very important for the governments to care about teachers' prestige and make their role more effective.

To improve, the chapter should delve more deeply into these broader determinants, incorporating data and case studies that illustrate how socio-economic, cultural, and infrastructural factors impact educational outcomes. It should also highlight successful interventions or pilot programs aimed at improving teacher training, student engagement, and resource allocation, providing a more holistic and balanced view. Including perspectives from teachers, students, and policymakers on these issues would enrich the narrative, making it more comprehensive and strategically oriented toward actionable solutions.

REFERENCES

1TV. (2024). Education Minister announces plans for salary raise for teachers from July 2024. Retrieved from https://1tv.ge/lang/en/news/education-minister-announces-plans-for-salary-raise-for-teachers-from-july-2024/

Britannica, The. Editors of Encyclopaedia. (n.d.). Georgia: Cultural life. Encyclopaedia Britannica. Retrieved June 4, 2025 from https://www.britannica.com/place/Georgia/Cultural-life

Burduli, T. (2021, 31 May). The 'Oscars of Education': How a competition is helping boost prestige for Georgia's undervalued teachers. Retrieved from https://civil.ge/archives/423804

Business Media. (2026). Teachers' salaries: Which countries pay the most and the least in Europe? Retrieved from https://bm.ge/en/news/teachers-salaries-which-countries-pay-the-most-and-the-least-in-europe/122519

Chakhaia, L., & Bregvadze, T. (2018). Georgia: Higher education system dynamics and institutional diversity. In J. Huisman et al. (eds.). 25 years of transformations of higher education systems in post-Soviet countries. Palgrave.

Chankseliani, M. (2013). Higher education access in Post-Soviet Georgia: Overcoming a legacy of corruption. In Meyer, H.-D., St.John, E. P., Chankseliani, M., & Uribe, L. (Eds.), *Fairness in access to higher education in a global perspective: Reconciling excellence, efficiency, and justice* (pp. 171–187). SensePublishers. DOI: 10.1007/978-94-6209-230-3_10

Chelidze, A. (2019). The three lives of the Georgian alphabet. Retrieved from https://blogs.bl.uk/european/2019/08/the-three-lives-of-the-georgian-alphabet.html

Darling-Hammond, L. (2000). Teacher quality and student achievement. *Education Policy Analysis Archives*, *8*, 1–1. DOI: 10.14507/epaa.v8n1.2000

Doghonadze, N., Aliyev, A., Halawachy, H., Knodel, L., & Adedoying, A. S. (2020). The degree of readiness to total distance learning in the face of COVID-19 - Teachers' view (Case of Azerbaijan, Georgia, Iraq, Nigeria, UK and Ukraine). *Journal of Education in Black Sea Region*, *5*(2), 2–41. DOI: 10.31578/jebs.v5i2.197

Economic Research Institute. (n.d.). Professor salary. Retrieved July 29, 2025 from https://www.erieri.com/salary/job/professor/georgia/tbilisi#:~:text=The%20average%20pay%20for%20a,of%20education%20for%20a%20Professor

Educators' and Scientists' Free Trade Union of Georgia. (n.d.). About organisation. Retrieved from https://www.educator.ge/en/about-en/about-esftug

European Training Foundation (2025). Georgia. Developing education and training to improve youth employment. Retrieved from

Gelashvili, N., Bakradze, M., & Chikvaidze, E. (2025). Educational reforms in post-Soviet Georgia: Achievements and challenges. American Journal of multifunctional publishing, 2(6), 6-10.

Georgia Today. (2026, January 29). Government announces merger of Tbilisi State University and Georgian Technical University. https://georgiatoday.ge/government-announces-merger-of-tbilisi-state-university-and-georgian-technical-university/

Georgian Business Consulting. (2025, December 18). Professors from 65 leading universities around the world call on Kobakhidze to reconsider the concept of education.

Geostat. (2025a). Subsistence minimum. Retrieved from https://www.geostat.ge/en/modules/categories/791/subsistence-minimum

Geostat. (2025b). Wages. Retrieved from https://www.geostat.ge/en/modules/categories/39/wages

GTU. (2026, January 29). An expanded meeting of academic staff and students held at GTU. Retrieved from https://gtu.ge/en/News/29715/

Kirvalidze, M. & Lobzhanidze, S. (2023). Professional development and performance assessment system focused on strengthening teachers' collaboration: The case of Georgia. Problems of Education in the 21st century, 81(1), 66-89. DOI: 10.33225/pec/23.81.66

Kitiashvili, A. (2024). Bridging the gap: Institutional readiness and barriers to Erazmus + participation in Georgia. *Education Sciences and Psychology*, *73*(4), 10–33.

Lindner, H. G., & Tsertsvadze, Z. (2018). *Verte Georgiens / Values of Georgia*. Mitteldeutscher Verlag.

Macrotrends. (2025). Georgia literacy rate 2002-2025. Retrieved from https://www.macrotrends.net/global-metrics/countries/geo/georgia/literacy-rate

Ministry of Education and Science of Georgia. (2019). About 6,000 registered retired teachers will receive cash awards in the beginning of October. Retrieved from https://mes.gov.ge/oldmes/print.php?id=9344&lang=eng

Ministry of Education and Science of Georgia. (2022). 2022-2030 Unified national strategy of education and science of Georgia.

Ministry of Education, Science, and Youth of Georgia. (2011). Contest of mentor teachers was announced. Retrieved from https://mes.gov.ge/content.php?id=2789&lang=eng&csrt=5264965610508141570

Ministry of Education, Science, and Youth of Georgia. (2024). Winning teachers of the 2024 teacher prize honored. Retrieved from https://mes.gov.ge/content.php?id=13861&lang=eng

Ministry of Education, Science, and Youth of Georgia. (2025 b). Zogadi ganatlebis sistemis reformis erovnuli konceftsia [at the moment the information is available only in Georgian: General education system reform conception]. Retrieved from https://www.mes.gov.ge/content.php?id=14304&lang=eng&csrt=5413917047265440953https://mes.gov.ge/uploads/files/zogadi_ganaTlebis_sistemis_reformis_erovnuli_koncefcia.pdf?csrt=4552110965314880402

Ministry of Education, Science, and Youth of Georgia. (2025a). Umaghlesi ganatlebis reformis konceftsiis prezentacia [at the moment the information is available only in Georgian: Presentation of higher education reform conception]. Retrieved from https://www.mes.gov.ge/content.php?id=14304&lang=eng&csrt=5413917047265440953

Mitaishvili-Rayyis, Y. (2023). Educational reforms in Georgia: Past progress and future directions. Retrieved from https://www.researchgate.net/publication/371911209_Educational_Reforms_in_Georgia_Past_Progress_and_Future_Directions#fullTextFileContent

Moralishvili, S. (2023). AI and personalized learning in higher education instructions in Georgia. *International Scientific Journal Diplomacy and Law*, *2*(10), 111–114.

Narimanishvili, N. (2024). Georgian teachers complain about injustice: Why the "unprecedented pay raise" isn't enough? Retrieved from https://jam-news.net/teachers-salary-in-georgia/

Narmania, D., Kharkheli, M., Vardiashvili, N., & Makasarashvili, M. (2023). The role of education in the growth of the Georgian economy. *The Business and Management Review*, *14*(1), 88–95. DOI: 10.24052/BMR/V14NU01/ART-10

National Center for Education Quality Enhancement. (n.d.). Education system. Retrieved from https://eqe.ge/en/page/parent/7/ganatlebis-sistema

OECD. (2022). PISA 2022 Results (Volume I). Retrieved from https://www.oecd.org/en/publications/pisa-2022-results-volume-i_53f23881-en/full-report.html

Remote people. (2026). Average salary in Georgia. Retrieved from https://remotepeople.com/countries/georgia/average-salary/

Tabatadze, S. (2017). Minority education in Georgia: Is it delivering what is expected? *Diaspora, Indigenous, and Minority Education, 11*(1), 17–30. DOI: 10.1080/15595692.2016.1245658

Tanguiane, S. (1979). Some lessons from Soviet experience in educational development. International Institute for educational planning. UNESCO. Retrieved from https://unesdoc.unesco.org/ark:/48223/pf0000070277#:~:text=The%20USSR%20was%20moving%20towards,exceptional%20social%20and%20cultural%20significance

Tavdgiridze, L., Katamadze, G., & Bolkvadze, M. (2023). School education, technologies, challenges – practice, analysis and perspectives based on the Georgian example. In *Inted2023 Proceedings* (pp. 1658–1662). IATED., DOI: 10.21125/inted.2023.0467

Tavdgiridze, L., Sherozia, N., Beridze, K., Meskhidze, S., & Khasaia, I. (2024) Enhancing the pedagogical climate in schools: A crucial factor in mitigating teacher burnout (Illustrated by Georgian schools), INTED2024 Proceedings, pp. 2132-2137. https://doi.org.DOI: 10.21125/inted.2024.0587

Tchintcharauli, T., & Javakhishvili, N. (2017). Inclusive education in Georgia: Current trends and challenges. *British Journal of Special Education, 44*(4, 12b), 465–483. DOI: 10.1111/1467-8578.12188

Trading Economics. (2022). Georgia - literacy rate, adult total (% of people ages 15 and above). Retrieved from https://tradingeconomics.com/georgia/literacy-rate-adult-total-percent-of-people-ages-15-and-above-wb-data.html#:~:text=15%20And%20Above)-,Literacy%20rate%2C%20adult%20total%20(%25%20of%20people%20ages%2015%20and,compiled%20from%20officially%20recognized%20sources.

UN. (2006). Convention on the rights of persons with disabilities, Annex 1. Retrieved from http://www.un.org/esa/socdev/enable/rights/ ahcfinalrepe.htm]

UNESCO. (1994). The Salamanca statement and framework for action on special needs education. Retrieved from https://www.right-to-education.org/sites/right-to-education.org/files/resource-attachments/Salamanca_Statement_1994.pdf

UNESCO. (n.d.). Georgia's national statement of commitment. Retrieved from https://media.unesco.org/sites/default/files/webform/ed3002/Georgia_National_Statement_of_Commitment_0.pdf

Vasadze, N. (2015). *Georgian chronicles of education.*

White, S. (2024, 12 May). Georgia's education sector positioned for growth based on increased domestic, foreign demand. Retrieved from https://www.investor.ge/2024/12/05/georgias-education-sector-positioned-for-growth-based-on-increased-domestic-foreign-demand/#:~:text=The%20education%20sector%20has%20become,the%20Georgian%20economy%20and%20rising

World Bank. (2014). Georgia. Teachers. SABER country report. Retrieved from https://documents1.worldbank.org/curated/en/788461468198234275/pdf/105634-WP-ADD-SERIES-PUBLIC-SABER-Teachers-Georgia-CR-Final-2014.pdf

World Bank. (2018). Technical assistance to support reforms to the higher education financing system in Georgia (P164779). Final report. Retrieved from https://documents1.worldbank.org/curated/en/895021551184190719/pdf/Report-on-Georgia-Higher-Education-Funding-Reform.pdf

World Salaries. (2025). Average lecturer salary in Tbilisi, Georgia for 2025. Retrieved from https://worldsalaries.com/average-lecturer-salary-in-tbilisi/georgia/

Zedginidze-Jishkariani, N., & Gachechiladze, S. (2024). EDUCATION POLICY AND KNOWLEDGE BASED ECONOMY: CASE OF GOERGIA. STUDIJOS–VERSLAS–VISUOMENĖ. *DABARTIS IR ATEITIES ĮŽVALGOS, 1*(IX), 207–216.

Chapter 12
Teachers' Voices From Azerbaijan

Aydin Aliyev
http://orcid.org/0000-0002-4914-3788
Odlar Yurdu University, Azerbaijan

Gulhayat Abdullayeva
Azerbaijan State Pedagogical University, Azerbaijan

Aysel Aghamaliyeva
http://orcid.org/0009-0003-0778-5576
Khirdalan School N1, Azerbaijan

ABSTRACT

This paper analyzes the historical development and modern structure of Azerbaijan's education system, focusing on the transition from traditional foundations to contemporary policy reforms. It outlines the structural stages of the national system and its alignment with international standards, while placing a heavy emphasis on the professional lifecycle of educators including their recruitment and certification processes. By addressing systemic challenges such as regional inequality and the gap between theory and practice, the paper uses qualitative narratives from practicing teachers to offer a grounded perspective on the future of the profession.

AZERBAIJAN'S EDUCATION SYSTEM: HISTORY, REFORMS, AND TEACHER PROFESSIONALISATION

Aydin Aliyev

The history of education in Azerbaijan is diverse and complex. From the 10th to 16th centuries, education was primarily based on religious institutions, but secular subjects (science, mathematics, astronomy, and medicine) were also delivered. Initially, the languages of instruction were Persian and Arabic, and later, the Azerbaijani, referred to as Turkish at that time (Suleymanova, 2025), became the medium of instruction. Madrasas (traditional Islamic religious schools) and palace schools provided training for state officials, doctors, and scientists, while the waqf system (an Islamic charitable endowment used to fund education and public welfare) provided funding for teachers and learners. During this period, the mobility of teachers and learners built a vast intellectual network, transforming Azerbaijan into a prominent cultural center in the Islamic world (Najaf & Najafov, 2025). During the period from the 16th to 18th centuries, in spite of feudal division and external invasions, primary schools and madrasas retained the foundation of education, with curricula covering both religious and secular sciences (Abdullayeva & Gasimova, 2021). In the period between 1828 and 1918, northern Azerbaijan was absorbed into the Russian Empire, leading to the formation of national, religious, and bilingual schools; learners were sent to Russia and Europe to pursue their higher education (Isakhanli, 2005). During the short period (1918-1920) of the Azerbaijan Democratic Republic, a national education system was created, the Azerbaijani

DOI: 10.4018/979-8-3373-8983-7.ch012

language was declared the state and language of instruction, teacher training courses were opened, and Baku State University was established. Significantly, within this short time, the government funded 100 Azerbaijani students to continue higher education abroad, expecting that they would return to aid the advancement of their homeland (Isakhanli, 2018).

From 1920 to 1945, under Soviet rule, the education system changed completely. Teacher insufficiencies were met by short-term pedagogical courses. Literacy improved through educational initiatives (Aliyeva, 2024). New higher education and specialized institutes were created, primary education became mandatory, and after World War II, infrastructure was updated. During 1969-1982, reforms were implemented in educational infrastructure, national and moral values were promoted, the Azerbaijani language was recognized as the state language, and the establishment of schools increased educational opportunity (Hasanov, 2024; Ahmadov et al., 2018). From 1982 to 1991, in the last years of the Soviet Union, the introduction of global teaching methods clashed with economic challenges and ideological restrictions, harming the quality of education.

After gaining independence, Azerbaijan's education system went through significant reforms. Starting in 1991, the country began to establish a national education policy, shifting from existing Soviet structures and seeking to create a modern system compatible with international standards. School curricula were renewed, Azerbaijani was enforced as the main language of instruction, and teacher training and professional development programs were reinforced (Suleymanov, 2020).

The modern Azerbaijani education system includes several stages and is run by the Ministry of Science and Education. Preschool education typically starts at ages 5 or 6 and serves as a foundation for primary school, which is not mandatory. General education has three levels: primary education lasts 4 years (grades I–IV), general secondary education lasts 5 years (grades V–IX) and is mandatory, and complete secondary education lasts 2 years (grades X–XI). Students who finish general and complete secondary education receive a state-issued certificate. After completing general secondary education, students can attend vocational or technical colleges for 2 to 4 years to gain the knowledge and skills needed for the job market. According to the Constitution, every citizen has the right to education, and the state provides free and mandatory general secondary education (Azerbaijan Republic, 2019).

In 2005, the country joined the Bologna Process, which connected its higher education system to the European Higher Education Area. The higher education framework includes Bachelor's degree (4–5 years), Master's degree (1.5–2 years), and Doctoral degree (3–5 years). The European Transfer Credit System (ECTS) is in use. University management and quality assurance methods have also been updated. Joining the Bologna Process expanded international exchange opportunities for Azerbaijani students, raised the quality of higher education, and secured international recognition for diplomas (European Higher Education Area, n.d.).

Key legislative acts on education include the “Law on Education” (Azerbaijan Republic, 2009) and the “Law on General Education” (Azerbaijan Republic, 2019). The language of instruction is primarily Azerbaijani (in approximately 92% of schools), but instruction in Russian, English, or mixed languages is also possible in some schools. Additionally, according to Baku International Multiculturalism Centre (2024) in some regions, the languages of minority peoples (e.g., Lezgian, Talysh, and Avar) are taught as native languages.

In Azerbaijan, teacher training is principally carried out in the pedagogical fields of higher education institutions. Prospective teachers must first fulfill secondary education (grade XI) and then take part in admission exams conducted by the State Examination Center to be accepted into the pedagogical faculties of universities. Key institutions are Baku State University, Azerbaijan State Pedagogical University, Nakhchivan State University, Ganja State University, and some other universities. Teacher preparation programs are commonly organized as 4-year Bachelor's degrees (equivalent to a B.Ed.). At this level, students acquire theoretical and practical knowledge in subjects such as pedagogy, psychology, teaching methodology, subject teaching, educational technologies, and school practice. Pedagogical practice is usually performed in the final year (mainly final semester), where teacher candidates engage in the teaching process in real schools to practice and develop their teaching abilities.

Students who complete their undergraduate degree must take part in the Teacher Recruitment Exam (MİQ) held by the Ministry of Science and Education after obtaining a state-approved diploma. This exam evaluates candidates' subject knowledge, pedagogical abilities, and methodological preparation. Successful candidates are appointed as teachers in general education schools based on their scores and preferences across the country (Azerbaijan Republic, 2019).

Also, since 2021 teacher's certification process has been introduced. It includes both a written test and an interview, and the results can influence salary increases and career advancement. The process is managed through the Institute of Education (ARTİ) and aims to ensure that teachers meet modern educational standards and demonstrate continuous professional growth. Teachers are required to participate in this certification process every five years to maintain their professional status (Azerbaijan Republic, 2019).

The teacher development projects in Azerbaijan, implemented by the Ministry of Science and Education, Azerbaijan Teacher Development Centre (ATDC), the Institute of Education (ARTİ), and other local partners, aim to enhance the overall quality of education by strengthening teachers' professional competencies. These initiatives focus on improving lesson-planning skills, digital literacy, and modern pedagogical practices, while promoting competency-based learning and STEM education. They also seek to develop inclusive teaching approaches, support continuous professional growth through certification and assessment, and foster leadership and management skills among school administrators. Programs like "Teach for Azerbaijan" additionally aim to attract talented young specialists to the teaching profession and provide students with enriched learning opportunities, particularly in underserved regions (Ministry of Science and Education, 2016). Overall, these projects are designed to create conditions for effective teaching, innovation, and equitable access to quality education across the country.

Furthermore, regular professional development and skill-renewal courses are held in collaboration with international partners for active teachers. In recent years, for example, through British Council programs, special attention has been paid to contemporary teaching methods, communicative learning, and the improvement of digital skills (British Council, 2024).

Even though important reforms have been made in teacher training and certification systems, criticism remains (Huseynova, 2019; Allahverdiyeva, 2024; European Training Foundation, 2025). Research shows that in pedagogical programs, theoretical knowledge and practice often do not align with real school experience. Moreover, collaboration between universities and schools is not strong enough, and teacher candidates do not gain sufficient practical experience. In many cases, it can be said that the content of teacher preparation programs is quite outdated and does not address contemporary skills such as digital literacy technologies, diversity, and critical thinking. Apart from this, teacher candidates and teachers living in regions of Azerbaijan do not have the same opportunity in terms of reaching educational resources. While teacher certification exams are seen as a significant step for quality assessment, there are still questions about the fairness, objectivity, and reliability of this process. Some teachers state that this exam is not conducted within a sufficient time frame, and sometimes they believe that this assessment is subjective (Huseynova, 2019; Allahverdiyeva, 2024).

Researchers (Talafian et al., 2025; Darling-Hammond et al., 2017), on the other hand, maintain that to make teacher profession successful, teacher training must be aligned with broader reforms, such as the quality of training, resource provision, teachers' motivation, and the prestige of the teaching profession. I believe that enhancing teacher quality cannot be achieved solely through formal exams and certifications. We need ongoing, long-term professional development, practice, and mentoring.

THE TRUTH BEHIND MY BECOMING A TEACHER

Aydin Aliyev

"The teacher is a sacred master and unmatched by any other being on earth". I came across this statement in one of the scholars' articles about teaching, and I adopted it as a motto for my profession from the very beginning of my career. Although teaching was not my childhood dream, when I studied in high school, I decided to become a teacher thanks to the teachers I had.

My name is Aydin Aliyev, and I am from Ganja, Azerbaijan. I hold a Doctor of Philosophy in Education Sciences, specializing in teaching English. I come from an educated family. My father was an engineer and my mother was an accountant. Since childhood, I have always had great respect for teachers, as my grandmother was a math teacher. I witnessed respect for her and other teachers from my parents. Teachers were acknowledged as role models in my surroundings. I remember that teachers were believed to hold a unique and respected status, setting them apart from other members of society. However, this is not the reason why I wanted to become a teacher.

I started school in 1993, when there was a war in Azerbaijan. I remember seeing soldiers, tanks, displaced people, and hearing news of casualties everywhere. This situation made me want to join the Azerbaijani army. However, the teachers at the Private Turkish high school where my parents sent me to study in another city (Mingachevir) aroused my interest in the teaching profession.

The subject I enjoyed the most at school was mathematics. My grandmother was a math teacher, and she probably played a role in shaping my interest in the subject. She seemed to encourage me to enjoy math, and I grew up liking it. However, English was quite different for me. Back in high school, I found English difficult, and I'm not entirely sure why - it just seemed harder to learn compared to other subjects. Despite this, I eventually became an English teacher, specializing in English and pedagogy.

Outside of school, I often read children's encyclopedias and various works of literature. At home, we had a bookshelf filled with many different books, and I frequently spent time exploring them, including selections from world literature. I believe these books strongly influenced my worldview and education, helping me develop curiosity, imagination, and a broader understanding of the world. My father and his highly educated family were very cultured, with extensive knowledge of different subjects, foreign cultures, music, and people. Their influence had a great impact on me, shaping my interests and perspective.

There were several teachers who inspired me in a positive way, especially during my time at the Turkish high school I attended. Most of the teachers there had a great influence on me and motivated me to become a teacher myself. They treated us with respect and created a warm, supportive environment. One of them, Mr. Bülent Görel, our physics teacher, left a particularly strong impression on me. He was patient, calm, and never got angry with students. I deeply admired his personality and often thought that if I would ever become a teacher, I would want to be like him.

The teachers at my school didn't just teach us academic subjects - they spent extra time with us outside the classroom as well. They talked with us about our personal issues, played football with us, and even organized reading sessions. I really loved those moments and those teachers. I always wanted them to notice me, to ask me questions, to show that they cared. They truly inspired me to become a teacher, and now I believe that I'm doing my best to follow their example - or at least to carry the same spirit they showed us.

I started thinking about my future profession, particularly about becoming a teacher, when I was in high school, around the 9th or 10th grade. That was during my time at the Turkish high school, where I was surrounded by inspiring teachers who greatly influenced my decision to pursue teaching as a career.

When it came to deciding whether to study education or English, to be honest, the decision wasn't entirely mine. I had a feeling that I would become a teacher one day, but I didn't know exactly which subject I would teach. After receiving my exam results, I decided to apply to study in another country — Turkey. During that time, one of the teachers responsible for advising students about university choices told me something that truly stayed with me. He said, "I can see that you're meant to be a teacher. You have the talent to become an excellent English teacher." His words influenced me deeply, and that's how I decided to study English and education.

At first, I felt uncertain about my choice, especially because my English wasn't very good at that time, and studying in a foreign country was challenging. However, during my university years, I worked hard to improve both my English and my understanding of teaching methodology. By the time I graduated, I realized that I had truly chosen the right path — teaching became not only my profession but also my passion.

After graduating, some of my friends invited me to work as an English teacher at the foundation school of Kafka University in Azerbaijan. I started working there in 2010. At first, I felt a mix of excitement and nervousness, wondering if I would be successful in my new role. However, it didn't take long for me to realize that I was exactly where I needed to be, and that teaching was truly the right path for me.

One of my first challenges as a new teacher, and something I still occasionally face, has been dealing with documentation. At the university, there are many forms, papers, and formalities that need to be completed, which can take a lot of time. When I first started teaching, this was a significant challenge because it often prevented me from focusing on what I truly wanted to do — improving students' learning and working on my professional development. Even now, I sometimes feel the same way, as these administrative tasks can be time-consuming and distract from the core work of teaching.

There have been many challenges I faced as a teacher, but I will mention one or two significant ones, mainly related to administrative issues. As an English teacher in Azerbaijan, I have noticed that many administrators are still "old school" and resistant to change. For example, sometimes I ask for basic classroom technologies, such as speakers, to enhance my lessons, but it can be difficult to convince administrators that they are really necessary. In such cases, I often have to provide the equipment myself, spending my own money to make the lessons effective and engaging. Another example occurred when I was teaching a pedagogy class for Master's students. I assigned essays and suggested that we compile them into a book. However, the head of the department did not allow us to proceed, and afterward, I was not assigned any classes the following semester. Situations like this illustrate how administrative decisions can sometimes hinder teachers' initiatives and professional development. I have found that many administrators tend to be authoritarian, resist change, and may even feel threatened by new ideas rather than seeing them as constructive. These experiences have shown me that navigating administrative challenges is an ongoing part of being a teacher.

From these challenges, I learned two important lessons. Regarding administrative issues, I realized that sometimes it is necessary to wait for the right moment or the right person. Convincing administrators to accept new ideas can take a long time, and patience is essential. More importantly, I learned that I am ultimately responsible for my own professional development as well as my students' growth. I cannot rely on others to solve problems for me. Even if it requires spending my own resources or extra effort, it is my responsibility to ensure that I continue to improve as a teacher and provide the best possible education for my students.

Although many teachers left a strong and positive impression on me, there were also some whose approaches made me promise myself that I would never repeat their mistakes. One common issue I observed was teachers insisting that students simply memorize material and reproduce it during the exams. I believe teaching should go beyond rote learning; students' understanding, interpretation, critical thinking, and analysis are much more important, even if their responses are not fully academic. Another mistake I noticed was when teachers neglected students' personal issues. While teachers do not need to know every detail of a student's life outside the classroom, they should at least be aware of and sensitive to challenges that may affect their learning. Unfortunately, some teachers treated students as if they were insignificant, ignoring their needs as human beings.

I also observed teachers who doubted students' potential from the very beginning. They complained constantly, saying students would not succeed or become well-educated. I believe this is extremely harmful. Teachers must first believe in their students' abilities. That belief shapes how they prepare for lessons, motivate students, and approach teaching in general. I have made it a principle to always encourage and motivate my students while maintaining my self-motivation, because a teacher's attitude profoundly influences the students' learning experience and their confidence.

There are many positive qualities I learned from my teachers that I now try to apply in my teaching. One key lesson is patience. I remember several of my teachers being incredibly patient, and I learned from them that no matter what happens in the classroom, it's important not to react immediately but to remain calm and composed. Another is motivation. My teachers always encouraged us, and I try to do the same with my students. I motivate myself by believing in their potential, and then I work to convince my students that they are capable and that the work we are doing together truly matters. Equally important is respect. I saw many teachers treating me with respect, acknowledging my importance as a person. I strive to do the same with all my students, regardless of their abilities or English proficiency. Respecting students helps them feel valued and strong, and it is essential for fostering their growth and confidence.

Although I am generally a very motivated person when it comes to teaching, there have been times when I seriously considered quitting. One of the main reasons was feeling that I didn't receive what I deserved. At times, I encountered administrators who seemed to try to stop me simply because I was ambitious and trying to do more. It often felt like they were afraid I might challenge their position, and this lack of support felt unjust and discouraging. Another challenge was seeing situations where people with lower qualifications or less experience were given authority over me. For example, someone with a master's degree trying to direct a PhD holder can be frustrating and demotivating. These injustices sometimes made me question whether I should continue teaching. Despite these challenges, I chose to continue because teaching is my passion and my life's work. Over time, I realized that perseverance pays off, and eventually, I achieved the goals I had set for myself. These experiences taught me resilience and the importance of staying committed to my professional values, even in difficult circumstances.

As a teacher, I strive to create a friendly and respectful environment in the classroom. I show my students that I respect them, and in return, they understand the importance of mutual respect. When they feel that I genuinely care for and value them, it helps break the traditional, rigid image of teaching that many may have. My goal is to make the classroom a place where students feel supported, valued, and comfortable to engage.

When I see my students struggle or fail, I try to empathize with them and help them understand that setbacks are a normal part of learning. I encourage them to keep going and not see failure as the end. On the other hand, when my students succeed, I feel a deep sense of pride and accomplishment, as if their success were my own. I celebrate these moments publicly, sharing them on social media or among colleagues, because their achievements reflect our joint efforts and inspire others as well.

I try to make my classes engaging and meaningful by creating a friendly and supportive environment for my students. I take into account their interests and the demands of the modern world, integrating technology, movies, videos, and social media into my lessons. I also avoid being an authoritarian teacher, instead focusing on a student-centered approach. Today's students want to actively participate and speak in the classroom, so I give them space to do so. This approach not only encourages their involvement but also makes learning more interactive and meaningful for them.

In my view, some of the biggest problems in today's education system are related to technology and inequality. Technology is advancing rapidly, but unfortunately, not all parts of the world are prepared to keep up. This creates significant disparities between countries and within societies. Another major issue is the high cost of education, which leads to injustice. Wealthy students often have access to high-quality education, while many talented students cannot afford the same opportunities. Today, gaining admission to prestigious institutions often depends more on financial resources than on intelligence or effort. This creates a system where only a small percentage of capable students can access the best education, leaving many others behind despite their potential.

Another problem, particularly in Azerbaijani society, is the gender imbalance among teachers. In high, middle, and elementary schools, the majority of teachers are female. Teaching is often not seen as a prestigious profession for men unless they achieve higher positions, such as becoming university lecturers or administrators. Because of this perception, many young men are discouraged from pursuing a teaching career, which affects the diversity of the educational workforce.

Teaching is not just about instructing students; it is also about continuous self-improvement. Over my 15 years as a professional teacher, I have participated in various trainings and professional development opportunities each year. I believe that this process of growth should continue throughout my life. Regardless of age, I intend to keep teaching and learning, constantly enhancing my skills and knowledge to ensure that I provide the best possible education for my students.

For me, teachers are those who shape both individuals and society. In many cases, teachers have a greater influence on learners than parents. I believe that whatever teachers pass on - whether verbally or through practice - is absorbed by learners and later applied, consciously or subconsciously. In this sense, the influence of teachers on society cannot be denied.

I believe that good teachers recognize the importance of their work and take their responsibilities seriously. They always prepare lessons in advance and strive to make material clear and understandable for students. Good teachers motivate their students, communicate in an engaging way, and are approachable so that students feel comfortable speaking with them. Most importantly, good teachers genuinely care about and love their students, showing respect and support in all aspects of their learning and personal development. In addition, good teachers continually work on themselves. They pursue professional development, participate in trainings, and strive to meet the requirements of the modern world, ensuring that their teaching remains relevant and effective.

My advice to young people who want to become teachers is that teaching is a serious and important profession. You must be knowledgeable and skilled in your subject, no matter what you teach. Today's students are different — they want teachers who are competent and credible, and they often verify what they learn through the internet or other resources. A teacher's knowledge is essential to gain students' trust and respect. In addition to being knowledgeable, teachers should focus on building strong connections and networks, both locally and internationally. In today's globalized world, being able to communicate in English and engage with international networks is increasingly important. Preparing for these demands will help young teachers become effective, modern educators who can inspire and guide their students successfully.

A RELATIONSHIP OF MUTUAL COMMITMENT

Aysel Aghamaliyeva

Sometimes in life, we wonder whether we make a choice or life makes it for us. Teaching is one of those professions that often feels like it chooses the person rather than the other way around.

My name is Aysel Aghamaliyeva. I am an English teacher and currently I am in my eighteenth year of teaching career in a public school in Khirdalan, the town situated near Baku, the capital of Azerbaijan. I studied English Philology as a Bachelor degree and Linguistics as MA at the University of Languages in Baku. Now I am a PhD student of the same university conducting research on language theory.

As I remember, being a teacher wasn't my choice. When I went to primary school, my mother told me I was going to be an English teacher. I didn't understand what that meant at that time. Because I was just in the first grade. But it was 'engraved' in my mind. To be an English teacher in my case was very challenging, as we didn't have an English teacher at our school. But eventually my mother's dream came true. She even made her decision that it would be Azerbaijan University of Languages. I just followed my mother's dream. The reason why she wanted to see me as an English teacher was her own love for this language and her English teacher, though she always wanted to be a doctor.

Though being a teacher wasn't my dream, my English grammar teacher at university became my idol and at first sight I understood that I would be a teacher like her if I chose teaching. I remember my first lesson at university when my grammar teacher entered the room. I should admit that I found English very difficult to speak and understand at that time. Even after my first day at university I cried, because it seemed to me very hard to understand and express myself in English. However, my teacher's way of teaching grammar using real situations to explain helped us, students, to master a foreign language better. She asked us to make up a lot of sentences using different kinds of grammar and patiently explained our mistakes. Language learning for teaching it became interesting. While getting ready for her lessons, I always imagined how *I* would teach English like her. Now after having seventeen years of teaching practice I feel that I always use her methodology, her treatment of students in the teaching process. So wanting to be like her automatically prepared me for being a teacher.

When I graduated, I started teaching English at one of public schools located in Khirdalan and I am still teaching there. I teach mainly high school students. My teaching career is not limited with school only; I taught English at Azerbaijan State Academy of Physical Education and Sport for one year and at different language courses for several years. At present, alongside with school, I teach General English lessons online.

Although teaching English is my only aim, it differs according to where and whom I teach. In my opinion, teaching at school is more complicated because the needs, abilities, and behaviors of students are very different. At school, students are younger and still developing both academically and personally. Teachers must not only explain lessons but also guide students in social behavior, emotional development, and moral values. Teachers need to adjust their teaching methods to suit every student, which requires patience and creativity. Younger students may get distracted, misbehave, or need constant supervision. Emotional support is a bigger part of school teaching. Teachers act as mentors and role models, helping students cope with personal problems or build confidence.

So teaching is a challenging profession, as it deals with human beings. We don't only teach students new things, we prepare them for real life. Sometimes a teacher can be a person who they imitate. Students should feel confident with their teacher, should believe and trust him/her. Teaching and being a teacher is a complicated profession. It means you need not only to know your specialization but also you need to know the psychology of your students, to adjust to them in different situations.

Being a teacher means you can be everybody, not only a teacher at school. Depending on the age of students, a teacher takes responsibility for everything during the teaching period. Sometimes you act like a mother, showing care and patience when a student feels discouraged or struggles to keep up. Sometimes you try to act like a friend to understand their problems, sometimes you are a leader, and sometimes they show you the reality when you listen to them. For example, I once had a student who was shy and afraid of speaking English in class, so I encouraged her step by step until she gained confidence.

At other times, you become a friend to understand their personal problems - like when a student shared that he was having trouble at home, and I simply listened and helped him stay motivated.

A teacher is also a leader, guiding students through challenges. I remember organizing a school debate where I led my class to prepare arguments and work as a team, which made them feel proud and united. And sometimes, when I listen to my students, they show me reality, their honesty and curiosity often remind me why I chose this profession.

Teaching at school is a great responsibility. A teacher shapes the students' worldview, instills a love for learning, and encourages patriotism. When a teacher explains lessons in an interesting and understandable way, students become more eager to learn. Moreover, a teacher should not rely only on textbooks but also provide real-life examples and stimulate students' critical thinking. Teaching at school also means preparing the future builders of society. The students sitting at desks today will become engineers, doctors, teachers, and scientists tomorrow. Their growth into knowledgeable, responsible, and useful members of society depends largely on the efforts of their teachers.

Alongside all the above, teaching at school means tackling many challenges, teaching at school means tackling with many challenges. As for me, one of the main challenges is managing students with different learning abilities in one class. In one of my English classes, I faced a situation where students' language proficiency varied greatly. To address this, I organized a collaborative storytelling activity. I paired advanced learners with those who needed more support. Each group created a short story using the target grammar point — the past tense. Through peer learning and group discussion, students not only improved their grammar but also developed teamwork and communication skills. This experience showed me the importance of differentiation and collaboration in language teaching. Every student is unique; some understand lessons quickly while others need more time and attention. Balancing these differences can be difficult.

Another challenge is keeping students motivated. It is one of the most important and challenging aspects of teaching. For instance, when I realized that several of my students were losing interest in English, I incorporated project-based learning. Each student chose a topic they were passionate about - music, sports, or technology - and prepared a short presentation in English. This method not only improved their language skills but also increased their engagement, as they were working on subjects they truly cared about. Many students get easily distracted or lose interest in the subject, especially when they don't understand a foreign language. A teacher must find creative ways to make lessons engaging and ensure that every student participates actively.

Classroom discipline is also a common challenge in teaching. Sometimes students may misbehave, interrupt lessons, or not follow rules. Handling such situations without hurting anyone's feelings requires patience and strong communication skills. In most cases, instead of raising my voice, I calmly pause and look toward the noisy students. This quiet, firm attention often refocuses the class without confrontation. Sometimes I make eye contact and make a subtle gesture to remind them to be quiet. Often, this alone helps students correct their behavior. Once as I remember, during my lesson a few students in the back were talking while I was explaining a new grammatical concept. I calmly used eye contact and a gentle verbal reminder to redirect their attention, then spoke with them privately after the class to understand their perspective. By focusing on the behavior rather than labeling the students, I maintained a positive learning environment, and they became more attentive and engaged in subsequent lessons.

So for me, the journey into teaching has been a mix of both conscious decision and destiny. On the one hand, teaching chose me, on the other hand, I chose teaching. Certain experiences, people, or moments in my life naturally guided me toward the classroom. Perhaps it was a mentor teacher, a rewarding tutoring session, or the joy of explaining a concept to someone struggling to understand it. These moments made me realize that teaching is not just a career for me - it is a calling. I may have chosen teaching because I love helping others, sharing knowledge, and making a positive impact on young minds. The idea of shaping the future generation and seeing students succeed inspired me to step into this profession. Teaching gives me a sense of purpose and fulfillment that few other jobs can provide. I believe that while I may have chosen teaching, teaching also chose me. It is a relationship of mutual commitment: I spare my knowledge, care, and time, and in return, teaching fills my life with meaning and purpose.

From my personal perspective, whoever says whatever, the teaching profession has strong and promising prospects. Based on my long-term teaching experience, I believe that teachers will play an even more important role in the future. Modern society needs individuals who can think critically, adapt to change, and communicate effectively. Teachers are responsible for developing these skills. Although technology is becoming an essential part of education, it cannot replace human interaction, emotional support, and moral guidance that a teacher provides. I believe that teachers who continue professional development and remain open to innovation will always be needed. Therefore, teaching will remain a meaningful and respected profession with strong future perspectives.

TEACHING IS A JOURNEY OF SERVICE, REFLECTION, AND ONGOING LEARNING

Gulhayat Abdullayeva

Why I decided to be a teacher is a question I've often thought over. At first, I believed I chose this profession drawn by a desire to make a difference, to ignite curiosity, and to help students find their mind. But over time, I've come to realize that teaching has a way of choosing those who are meant for it. It tests your patience, pushes your limits, and shapes your identity in unexpected ways. Teaching found me not only in the classroom but also in the quiet, unseen moments - the early mornings spent planning, the late nights reflecting, and the countless in-betweens where learning and growth happen for both a student and a teacher.

I grew up in a family that valued education, even if they couldn't always help directly with schoolwork. Their encouragement motivated me to take learning seriously. I was a naturally curious child, especially drawn to language and literature, and I enjoyed exploring new ideas.

From an early age, I liked helping classmates understand their schoolwork. Looking back, that's when my interest in teaching and mentoring began. I had a few inspiring teachers who encouraged creative skill and critical thinking, and they made learning exciting. I also had some supportive teachers, who taught me the importance of empathy and connection in education.

Overall, my early experiences shaped my love for learning and helped me realize the kind of teacher and learner I wanted to be.

While I briefly considered other careers, I always found myself drawn back to teaching. I realized that I wanted a career where I could make a meaningful impact and help others grow - and teaching offered exactly that. I was trained to become a teacher, where I earned my degree.

During training, one key experience that shaped my teaching philosophy was working with diverse groups of students. It taught me the importance of patience, flexibility, and understanding each student's unique needs. I also learned how critical it is to build a supportive and comprehensive classroom environment.

Some of the most valuable skills I gained during this time include lesson planning, classroom management, and strategies for differentiated instruction. These continue to guide my teaching practice today.

I still remember the nervousness on my first day in the classroom - excited but anxious, unsure if I was truly ready. Standing in front of my first group of students was both overwhelming and energizing.

There were definitely challenges. I struggled at first with classroom management and adapting materials to meet different learning styles. Navigating school policies and administrative expectations also took some adjustment. But each challenge taught me something valuable.

One early success that stands out was helping a struggling student improve significantly in reading. Seeing their confidence grow reminded me why I chose this path. I also had setbacks - lessons that didn't go as planned or moments when I questioned my approach - but they pushed me to reflect and improve.

These early experiences taught me the importance of flexibility, patience, and constant learning. They helped shape a more student-centered and merciful teaching style that I still carry with me today.

One memorable case was a student who entered my class reading well below grade level. He was quiet and withdrawn, often avoiding class participation. I started working with him one-on-one, using materials that matched his interests. Over time, his reading improved, but more importantly, so did his confidence. By the end of the year, he volunteered to read aloud - a small moment, but a powerful reminder of how personal connection can drive progress.

I also remember a particularly difficult day when disagreements and disorderly conduct emerged around a group assignment. Rather than responding right away, I stopped the lecture and called the class together to talk about what went wrong. I learned from that experience how important it is to have an open dialogue about the classroom atmosphere and support students in taking charge of their education.

There were times early on when I questioned if I had chosen the right path - especially after tough days where nothing seemed to go right. But those doubts were always outweighed by the moments of growth, both mine and my students'.

These experiences taught me that teaching is not just about delivering content - it's about relationships, adaptability, and resilience. Every challenge is a chance to grow, and every success, no matter how small, has a lasting impact.

Seeing children develop not only intellectually but also in confidence and curiosity is what I love most about teaching. It is very satisfying to witness the moment when a topic "clicks" or a pupil feels pleased of their effort.

Meeting each student's unique demands is one of the most difficult tasks. It can be challenging to handle differences in aptitude, drive, and conduct, but I've discovered that it's important to treat every kid with tolerance, compassion, and adaptability.

I try to make classes relevant and involving participation in order to inspire and involve pupils. To arouse attention and encourage critical thinking, I employ practical exercises, real-world examples, and open-ended questions. In order to assist children feel more accountable and in control of their education, I also give them some choices.

I employ a variety of teaching strategies when working with students of varying abilities, which involve changing activities, providing different forms of support, and promoting peer cooperation.

Along with establishing a classroom culture that values work and respect, I also established clear standards for conduct.

My teaching is primarily based on creativity. I make an effort to make learning engaging and applicable to students' lives, whether it be through conversations, project-based learning, or cross-curricular connections. My objective is to provide an environment in the classroom where students feel free to express themselves, engage in critical thinking, and take chances with their education.

Since my training, my development as a teacher has continued. I frequently attend seminars, take professional development classes, study and do educational research to keep current. I can improve my techniques and keep up to date with best practices thanks to these encounters.

My perspective on student potential and the teacher's role in fostering it has been greatly impacted by some books. Colleagues who exhibit empathy, inventiveness, and fortitude in the classroom also serve as role models for me.

Whether it's via resource sharing, encouragement, or just listening, I think it's important to help novice educators. In addition to being gratifying, mentoring also enables me to evaluate my own work.

Above all, I am still learning from my students. Their questions, viewpoints, and difficulties force me to change the way I think and adjust. I view every day as an opportunity to develop with my students, since teaching is a continuous process.

Like many educators, I've had to deal with issues like big class numbers, hefty workloads, and variable student enthusiasm. It may occasionally be quite difficult to strike a balance between administrative responsibilities and the actual teaching activity.

I've learned to prioritize, maintain organization, and rely on teamwork to overcome these obstacles. Colleagues have greatly benefited by exchanging resources and tactics. Additionally, I've seen that developing close bonds with children promotes motivation and classroom management.

I would advise inexperienced or struggling educators not to attempt to accomplish everything by themselves. Seek assistance, maintain your flexibility, and keep in mind that progress takes time. Celebrate your own and your children's success and concentrate on the little victories.

Smaller class sizes, more mental health services, and less focus on standardised testing are all examples of structural changes that education has to make to better support teachers. Instead of simply meeting the targets, teachers need time to prepare, think, and develop. Assisting teachers entails assisting students, and when both are given priority, real change may start.

Teaching is a way of life for me, not just a profession. It has changed my perspective on the world and improved my patience, empathy, and comprehension of other people. I have learned something from each of my students, which has aided in my development as a person and as a teacher.

It is my desire that my students would remember me as someone who made them feel observed, pushed them, and believed in them. More than everything I taught them, I want them to continue to believe in their own abilities.

I want to keep developing as a teacher in the future by assuming leadership positions, coaching others, and being receptive to new information. My goal is to establish classrooms where learning is meaningful rather than merely required and each student feels appreciated.

I believe that being a "true" teacher is being dedicated to both your own and your students' personal development. It entails putting forth effort, empathy, and moral character each and every day, despite difficulties. I'm pleased to be a teacher because it's a journey of service, reflection, and ongoing learning.

REFERENCES

Abdullayeva, S., & Gasimova, S. (2021). XVII century Azerbaijani culture through the eyes of European travelers. *Grani, 24*(2), 41–45. DOI: 10.15421/172113

Ahmadov, H., Zeynalova, N., & Suleymanov, F. (2018). Heydar Aliyev's heritage in education. Norwegian Journal of Development of the International Science, (17), 5–17. Retrieved from https://cyberleninka.ru/article/n/heydar-aliyevs-heritage-in-education

Aliyeva, A. (2024). The formation of a new Soviet education system in Azerbaijan SSR. *Metafizika Journal, 7*(3), 59–75. DOI: 10.33864/2617-751X.2024.v7.i3.59-75

Allahverdiyeva, A. F. (2024). Effects of teacher certification in Azerbaijan on increasing their motivation. *Khazar University Journal of Education, 8*(1), 45–60.

Azerbaijan Republic. (2009). On education (Law No. 18343). Retrieved October 23, 2025, from https://e-qanun.az/framework/18343

Azerbaijan Republic. (2019). On general education (Law No. 1532-VQ). Retrieved October 23, 2025, from https://e-qanun.az/framework/42543

Baku International Multiculturalism Centre. (2024, November 26). Report on the fight against racism and discrimination in the Republic of Azerbaijan 2024. Retrieved from https://multikulturalizm.gov.az/en/post/2850/report-on-the-fight-against-racism-and-discrimination-in-the-republic-of-azerbaijan-2024.html?utm_source

British Council. (2024). Azerbaijan teacher development programme - 2022-23. Retrieved October 22, 2025, from https://www.britishcouncil.az/en/english/project/future-english/azerbaijan-teacher-development-programme-2022-2023

Darling-Hammond, L., Hyler, M. E., & Gardner, M. (2017). Effective teacher professional development. Learning policy institute.

European Higher Education Area. (n.d.). Azerbaijan. Retrieved October 23, 2025, from https://ehea.info/page-azerbaijan

European Training Foundation (ETF). (2025). The teacher management system in Azerbaijan. Retrieved from https://www.etf.europa.eu/sites/default/files/2025-08/Azerbaijan_Teacher%20Management%20System.pdf

Hasanov, U. (2024). Heydar Aliyev and youth policy. Retrieved from https://www.researchgate.net/publication/382351890_Heydar_Aliyev_and_Youth_Policy

Huseynova, F. (2019). Challenges and new perspectives of teacher training in Azerbaijan: Assessment of pedagogical activities of English language teachers. *Azerbaijan Journal of Educational Studies, 688*(III), 23–37. DOI: 10.29228/edu.28

Isakhanli, H. (2018). Higher education transformation, institutional diversity, and the role of the Azerbaijan Democratic Republic. In Higher Education in the Caucasus: Challenges and Opportunities (pp. 45–58). Springer. https://link.springer.com/chapter/10.1007/978-3-319-52980-6_4

Ministry of Science and Education of the Republic of Azerbaijan. (2016). "Teach for Azerbaijan" project. Retrieved October 23, 2025, from https://edu.gov.az/en/programmes/azerbaycan-ucun-oyret-layihesi

Najaf, A. N., & Najafov, R. (2025). Historical perspectives on education in medieval Azerbaijan (10th–16th centuries): Curriculum, methodology, and student mobility. Science. *Education and Innovations in the Context of Modern Problems, 8*(11), 16–33.

Suleymanov, T. (2020, December 28). Transformation of higher education in Azerbaijan: Reforms, policies and current trends. *The Journal of Economic Sciences: Theory and Practice, 77*(2), 40–60.

Suleymanova, G. (2025). A systematic review about the historical development of the Azerbaijani language. Proceedings of the 4th Conference on Central Asian Languages and Linguistics (ConCALL-4), 249–258.

Talafian, H., Lundsgaard, M., Mahmood, M., Shafer, D., Stelzer, T., & Kuo, E. (2025). Responsive professional development: A facilitation approach for teachers' development in a physics teaching community of practice. Teaching and Teacher Education, 153, 104812. DOI: 10.1016/j.tate.2025.104812

Chapter 13
Teachers' Voices From Iraq

Huda F. Halawachy
http://orcid.org/0009-0003-9223-0275
University of Mosul, Iraq

Huda Abdullah Al-Hassani
http://orcid.org/0000-0002-8562-479X
University of Mosul, Iraq

Shamal Sh. Taher
http://orcid.org/0009-0004-2615-5219
University of Mosul, Iraq

ABSTRACT

The current chapter is dedicated to showcasing the gaps in the education system of Iraq, some of which were highlighted by three Iraqi teachers' stories with decades of experience. Asst. Prof. Dr. Huda Halawachy from the University of Mosul, Iraq, her story began with her typical primary school in Mosul and the qualified administration and teaching staff in the 1970s. From her perspective, the war crisis truly crippled the education system. Lecturer Huda Al- Hassani, a staff member at the University of Mosul, Iraq, she spent her school and university years in Basra. Al- Hassani addresses some gaps in the education system of Iraq. Shamal Taher (MA holder in Linguistics, University of Mosul) is actively engaged in teaching at Trbaspi Primary Coed School, Kurdistan Region of Iraq (KRI), where he currently teaches grades 1-6. He ultimately finds the lack of economic and social motivation to be the key reason behind the decline of the teaching system in his region.

A BRIEF SUMMARY FOR IRAQI EDUCATIONAL SYSTEM

Historical Background: From the "Golden Age" to War

Iraq is an ancient country whose history dates back 8,000 years. Iraq was known as Mesopotamia and was the cradle of the first human civilizations known to man. "Baghdad remained throughout the ages the lighthouse of culture, civilization, and ingenuity, attracting seekers of education from all places, attracting men of thought and literature from all around the world" (Mikhailov & Mohammed, 2012). However, the history and system of education were not officially recorded until the creation of the official state in 1919. In 1923, its educational system was established, including the public and private sectors. The modern universities in Iraq were established beginning with the University of Baghdad in 1957, after the opening of large oil companies in the country. Their goal was first of all to meet the demand for qualified engineering employees. During this economic boom in the country, education also flourished.

Iraq's educational system, once a premier model in the Middle East, earned the UNESCO Prize for Literacy in the 1970s and early 1980s following the success of the "National campaign for the eradication of illiteracy" (Akrawi, 1935).

DOI: 10.4018/979-8-3373-8983-7.ch013

During this "Golden Age," academic achievement was the primary driver of social mobility and national pride; however, decades of conflict systematically dismantled this foundation. The system first weakened as funds were diverted to the Iran-Iraq War (1980–1988), followed by the devastating 1990s embargo, which categorized basic school supplies as "prohibited materials" (UNESCO, 2019).

Two periods are marked in Iraqi education:

- Before 2003, with a highly centralized system and emphasizing reaching education goals;
- After 2003, with control transferred to the Iraqi governorates (the provincial education council), which caused a decrease in the level of education in some regions (Abdullah et al., 2023).

There have been recent attempts to centralize the education system which has led to certain improvements (Abdullah et al., 2023).

Most recently, the UNICEF (2020) reports indicate that the occupation of Mosul and other cities by ISIS caused a total infrastructure collapse and mass displacement, leaving the nation's educational framework profoundly traumatized and damaged (UNICEF, 2020).

Historical Temporal/Context of Teaching in Iraq

The education system in Iraq was somewhat consistent prior the invasion of Iraq in 2003 although it witnessed a dramatic decrease in wages during the sanctions in 1990s (EPIC, 2016). Post-invasion reforms increased salaries to make the career more desirable and worthwhile (Education International, 2025). During the post-ISIS reconstruction era, unpredictable pay and worsening working conditions eroded motivation and led to the departure of qualified instructors (Shafaq News, 2020). The teaching experience of Dr. Huda Halawachy, one of the teachers' voices mentioned in this chapter, is contextualized around these changes, particularly, those related to wars and invasion. Later, modest economic improvements and reforms rarely addressed the fundamental problems, making teaching less desirable than other professions. Overall, these temporal shifts have a direct effect on Iraqi's educational system's recruitment, retention, and general well-being.

The Popularity of Teaching in Iraq

Teaching is popular in Iraq mainly because of steady state employment; high teacher enrollment and numbers show the ongoing need, with job stability outweighing personal preferences. In Iraq, teaching is still a major source of employment, according to Almasra (2024) and MOHESR (2024). As of 2022-2023, there were more than 750,000 school teachers and staff, and an additional 219,000 were hired through contracts, making the total number of instructional professionals more than one million. More than 126 institutions and colleges of higher education employ thousands of academic staff, including over 4, 180 at the University of Mosul. This indicates that teaching in schools and universities plays a major role in recent employment. Yet, the popularity of teaching for Huda Al-Hassani, one of teacher's voices in this chapter, has another inspiring approach that begins since she was a pupil at school. In view of that, Al-Hassani displays the profession of teaching as a childhood's unrecognized dream as she affectionately used to imitate the role of a teacher while playing with other kids at home with no future plans to be a teacher; yet, she by chance becomes a teacher!

The Structure of the Education System in Iraq

The Ministry of Education regulates K–12 education, while the Ministry of Higher Education and Scientific Research regulates higher education.

Table 1. The Structure of the Education System in Iraq

Education Level	Timeframe	Age	Notes
Primary	6 Years	6–11	Mandatory; culminates in a national baccalaureate exam.
Intermediate	3 Years	12–14	General curriculum leading to secondary education.
Preparatory	3 Years	15–17	Split into Scientific or Literary tracks.
Higher Education	4+ Years	18+	Entry is determined by the final Baccalaureate score (World Bank, 2021)

Teacher Education: The Three Pillars

In Iraq, the three primary educational pillars represented by College of Education, College of Basic Education, and College of Education for Girls, graduate future teachers (see Table 2). Each has a unique curriculum, specialization, and prestige. Admission standards vary, and only few graduates become teachers. This important information helps readers to comprehend both the teaching channels and the recruiting and placement systematic issues.

Table 2. Overview of Teacher Education Institutions in Iraq

Institution	Duration	Focus	Entry	Employment
Colleges of Education	4 yrs	Theory + pedagogy	High scores (~74–83 %)	~20 %, mostly urban
College of Basic Education	4 yrs	Practical skills	Moderate scores (~67–73 %)	<25 %, underserved areas
College of Education for Girls	4 yrs	Subject-specific pedagogy	Moderate (~61–66 %)	<25 %, subject-driven

This table shows primary teacher education colleges, including program focus, entry requirements, and employment rates. Besides, it reveals the large gap between the number of accepted graduates and those who is actually able to attain positions in teaching professions. Therefore, graduates usually criticize Iraq's schools, especially primary and girls' schools, but most of them stays either unemployed or under employed. What is worth mentioning is the fact that the employed graduates are taking a great part in both teaching provision and literacy, maintaining their status in the workplace, invaluable impact, and worth in the prosperity of the country in addition to showing the significant gap between training and employment.

Teacher Salaries and Professional Status

Iraqi teachers' motivation and professional status are negatively impacted by their sometimes low and delayed salary. For Paradise (2024), the insufficient salaries and inadequate compensation along with severe hardship circumstances can be regarded as the main reason behind the decreasing of teachers' motivation and does reduce motivation and destabilizing the professional performance. Despite these challenges, "a majority of teachers [...] did not want to stop teaching" (Paradies, 2024), indicating a high level of commitment that is closely linked to retention and motivation. According to Glassdoor (n.d.), the average salary for a teacher in Iraq is Iraqi Dinar 754181 (US$576) per month in Iraq. Of course, the salary received by a teacher depends on the school level (primary, intermediate, or preparatory), teacher qualification, and experience, as well as on the type of school (private or government-funded). The average salary range for a lecturer in Iraq is between IQD 19,708,556 (US$ 15,000) and IQD 33,710,538 (US$25,760) annually, depending on their academic degree (ERI, n.d.). As a matter of fact, low and delayed salaries hinder the motivation and career retention of Iraqi teachers, forcing many to seek alternative sources of income and affecting student performance. Yet, Shamal Sh. Taher, one of the teachers' voices included in this chapter and his story has a changing career phase as an officer of health, safety and environment at an Oil Company into a teacher at school in spite of the low income compared with his previous workplace. He committed to continue his career as a teacher despite of all the difficulties and challenges and even pursued his MA degree. Ultimately, teachers' stories in this chapter illustrate the need for institutional support by demonstrating that commitment alone is insufficient to alleviate financial strains.

The Recruitment in Fragile and Post–Conflict Context

Teaching in Iraq sometimes takes place in challenging conditions, such as packed classrooms, subpar facilities, and inconsistent remuneration, especially in post-conflict areas. According to a research, "teachers' living conditions have been negatively impacted by conflict and displacement [...] with implications for teacher retention and performance" (Paradies, 2024). In addition, current employment regulations have created a troubling trend, thereby teaching is seen less as a vocation and more as a solid employment. Teachers also confront "severe teacher shortages" and inefficient hiring procedures, "inadequate compensation [...] diminishes motivation and professional status" (INEE, 2021). In such an environment, many students flock to these colleges not because they feel a calling to teach, but as a desperate pursuit of financial security. For many, a teaching degree is merely a ticket to a government paycheck in a landscape where most non-medical graduates struggle to find employment (MOHESR, 2023).

Iraqi Students in International Assessments

Iraq's participation in the Trends in International Mathematics and Science Study (TIMSS) 2023, conducted in the fourth and eighth grades in 64 countries, is an advanced step toward raising the level of education in Iraq, although Iraqi students did not match the intermediate results (TIMSS, 2023).

Educational Governance and Quality Assurance

Public school education is free of charge, and the government bears the expenses of materials and supplies. The Ministry of Education is responsible for formulating educational policies and developing the curriculum, in addition to approving it. Student assessment includes daily classroom tests, monthly written tests, quarterly and annual exams, and attendance is strictly monitored to avoid students' dropout. National ministerial exams are held in grades 6 and 9, and the Baccalaureate exam is held in grade 12 (Abdullah et al., 2023).

The Renaissance of Iraqi Science: A Modern Success Story

As a staff member at the College of Arts, University of Mosul, Halawachy has witnessed many crises that my country faced. Still, scientific research progress in Iraqi universities proves to be there in the global scientific ranking. MOHESR (2024) states that by 2025, the total balance of Iraqi scientific research in global repositories will have surpassed 111,600 research papers.

As an illustration, the University of Baghdad, the nation's premier institution, currently records a research publishing rate of approximately 9 papers per day in the Scopus database, totaling over 18,000 indexed works (University of Baghdad, 2024). Despite the severe challenges Mosul faced during the 2014–2017 conflict, the University of Mosul has undergone a "scientific resurrection," consistently competing for the top national rank in research quality and innovation. In a landmark achievement, the University of Mosul was ranked first in Iraq by the Scimago Institutions Rankings (SIR, 2024) in terms of the quality and impact of its Scopus-indexed research.

Vision for the Future

Based on our experiences in the classroom and the research halls, we believe we must bridge the existing gaps with a focused, seven-point strategy:

- **Regulate Private Education:** It is necessary to establish strict quality controls for the growing number of private institutions to ensure they serve the mind, not just the wallet.

- **Continuous Professional Development:** Teachers are in dire need of consistent, high-level training sessions to modernize their skills.
- **A Global Syllabus:** Textbooks and syllabi should be redesigned from the ground up, starting with the youngest learners and moving through the university level.
- **Clear Pedagogical Guidelines:** Teachers need standardized, clear manuals to guide them through every item in the syllabus.
- **Holistic Learning:** Education must move beyond the desk. Outdoor activities and practical applications should be integrated into every curriculum.
- **Empowering Research Centers:** The research centers should be the primary problem-solvers for academic hurdles, particularly in the vital field of English Language Teaching and Learning.
- **Methodological Mastery:** It should be mandatory that teachers at all levels attend recurring sessions on modern teaching methodologies.

Teachers' Voices from Iraq

This section combines three Iraqi educators' perspectives to provide multifaceted view of education in a precarious and post-conflict setting. Two of these educators, Huda Halawachy and Huda Al-Hassani, are instructors at the Department of English, College of Arts, University of Mosul, Iraq, while the former is Assistant Professor in Linguistics, the latter is a Lecturer in English Literature. The other educator, Shamal Taher, who holds an MA in Linguistics, is an English Language teacher at a school in Kurdistan Region of Iraq. When taken as a whole, these perspectives emphasize common difficulties as well as challenging circumstances of teaching setting, reflecting the variety of educational experiences seen in different institutions.

The first voice is the Linguistics university professor, Dr. Halawachy, and her insightful essay entitled "Syllabus of Survival: The Hook, the Prophecy, and the Beautiful Minds of Mosul." In her essay Dr. Halawachy focuses on her journey across the extraordinary circumstances of Iraq during war times. Her experience illustrates the challenges of academic life, teaching, and research in a post-conflict institutional setting. The professor manages issues with resources, workload, and academic expectations while attempting to uphold scholarly norms and promote student growth in the face of structural limitations and ongoing recovery efforts.

The second voice is that of an English Literature university lecturer, Huda Al-Hassani, and her inspiring essay entitled "From A Child's Chalkboard to University Classrooms: My Journey of Teaching English and Literature in Iraq." The teaching journey of Al-Hassani begins as an adorable acting role of a teacher in childhood with other kids at home and a real school teacher also at home to eventually end up as a lecturer at university classrooms. Her experience, yet, provides stimulating perspectives on teaching literary studies in an environment shaped by institutional, linguistic, and cultural limitations. She concentrates on the shifts of the educational system before, during, and after the COVID-19 pandemic reaching to the age of AI in teaching. Also, she highlights on the part of creativity and performance that she incorporates with teaching both English literature and English as a foreign language at college and different institutions. Besides, her point of view extends to emphasize both practical challenges of maintaining student engagement and research effort in a constrained supportive environment and the intellectual importance of literary education.

The third voice, Shamal Taher, is an English language school teacher with an MA degree in Linguistics. His interesting essay is entitled "From Oil Fields to Blackboards: An Unexpected Career Change." In his essay, Shamal Taher's experience is constructed on a career shift from an officer in an Oil company into a teacher at school. His journey shows how he chose teaching career though it provides low salaries compared to his previous company. He maintained teaching as a desired profession which has a great contribution to the advancement of the country all the times. In addition, Shamal Taher reveals the reality of teaching the English Language in schools, and the challenges he faced with large classes, uneven student proficiency, and limited resources by bridging advanced academic training with everyday classroom practice. It also shows how despite of difficult situations, academic knowledge may help design successful teaching practices.

Taken together, these teacher voices and perspectives paint a complicated picture of education in Iraq, where great personal devotion coexists with structural limitations. The three educators demonstrate dedication and resilience to their career in spite of the differences in their institutional positions and places. Their experiences, then, not only clarifies the teaching's challenges in a fragile context, but also underlines the ongoing significance of teachers and educators in maintain and constructing the educational system in Iraq.

SYLLABUS OF SURVIVAL: THE HOOK, THE PROPHECY, AND THE BEAUTIFUL MINDS OF MOSUL

Huda Halawachy

From Crayons to Preparatory School

...And who cannot recall the nursery rhymes, songs, and fables one learns in kindergartens, preschools, and schools? Although I did not join kindergartens, the hook of being acquainted with the teaching atmosphere was school; the smell of chalk and dust, the sound of a bell, the authoritative voice of the teacher, rote memorisation, morning assembly on the school ground, strict rules, the uniform on which the logo of the school is fixed, and the strict administration will remain but a part of my academic biography as long as I live. According to the Ministry of Education in Iraq, the legal age to join the primary school is six years. Yet, there is a chance for smart youngsters to join at five or five and a half years old. Due to this reason and also because of the proof exhibited by my two elder sisters that they were ideal pupils, it was when I was five and a half years old that I entered the first ever educational institution of my life in the year 1976. I had entered Alfalaah Alnamoothajiya Primary Public School situated at Altayaaran Quarter of the Southeastern region of Mosul, which incidentally was and remains my native town, located in Nineveh, Iraq. I resided in the same Quarter. My residence was just so close to the school. It was one of three typical public schools found in Mosul with a special teaching system: we got four classes starting from (8:00 a.m. -12:00 p.m.). Then, we had a break to start the other two classes (1:00 p.m.-3:00 p.m.), as my memory recalls. It is in early childhood that youngsters are introduced to strict systems through their early teaching programmes and the joy and fun of outdoor learning (in the school garden), music classes, artwork activities, camping, and operettas as well. Going over the preceding details, I reminisced about the big hall of artwork in my typical primary school and the drawing class with the fruity smell of crayons. At that time, colours were a source of excitement for me as a child, as the present story intends to clarify the golden age of education at that time. In the seventies, youngsters were taught English in Grade 3; unfortunately, I did not get such a chance at my time compared to my two elder sisters, who spent their primary school years in the same school. The hook for my journey may have been starting to learn in a typical school. Who knows!

Having lived three grades of my typical public school, 1976-1979, my family decided to move to another house, situated in a quarter far from my school. My parents found I had to move to another school, situated near our new house. This obliged me to move to the new school. Al-Thawra Quarter, the new place, is another nice quarter situated to the west of Mosul, on the west bank of the city. Honestly, I did not like to move to another school, whatever. I told my mom, "I do not like to be in another school!" My parents were against the idea, being worried about me moving from the house to my old school, as it would take time for transportation. A new journey embarked from 1979-1982 in a Public Primary school, Al-Kawaakib for Girls, to spend the grades 4, 5, and 6. The system at this school was different: the classes started at 8:00 a.m. and ended at 11:30 a.m. because two more schools shared the same building. I did not like that atmosphere. This held for one year, as I remember, till one of the schools moved to a new building. What matters is the strict administration and the teachers' intellect in most of the classes. I came to know English in grade 5. The teacher was an amazing person. The name that I still remember while writing this story is that of Miss Muntaha Kashmoola. Believe it or not, I did not encounter any problems in learning the English language like any other subject. I proved I got the highest grades in class. My Miss continued teaching me English in Grade 6. Her classes strengthened the hook subconsciously.

A new academic stage was in Umu Salama Al-A'nsaariya, a Public Intermediate School, to spend three years (1982-1985); according to the General Exemption System in the Ministry of Education in Iraq, I did not take the final exams in Stages 1 and 2 as I scored high marks. Stage 3 involves exams following the Baccalaureate System. The school was somehow new, and it was not that distinguished compared to other old schools in Mosul, which were rich in their education history with reputed teachers and distinguished students. Still, I will be unfair if I skip mentioning the teachers' capacity, surely not all of them, in teaching math, social sciences, Arabic, English, biology, and sports classes. Mrs A'ayda was from Egypt; she was lovely and used to speak a mixture of Egyptian and Mosuli dialect. The Administration, with strict rules and different characters of ladies practising teaching as a job, added to my interest in a teaching career. I was unaware of this!

Now, it is the Preparatory School that is the pivot for any student to determine their future job. Al-Maysaloon Public School was not that good, but I was obliged again to join it as it was in the surrounding area of my house. No matter, some teachers proved to be good. At stage 4, I did not take the final exams due to my high scores, following the General Exemption System mentioned earlier. The student has two choices: either to choose a scientific speciality or a literary speciality to move to stages 5 and 6. It was the first choice for me and for all my sisters, too. It was a shock for me not to get the required high scores at stage 5 because of biology classes, and the teacher, who was so odd, addressed us as if we were college students; the questions in the monthly exams were odd too! I took some final exams, and it was the first time for me to do so. I felt it was not me; that summer was gloomy. My three sisters and I had never before taken final exams because of our high scores.

And the drama had to start at stage 6, the Baccalaureate. I achieved only 84%, which was a shudder for me, my family, and my teachers at school. I was expected to get higher marks than this. Here is the departure point for my arena, which I have never thought of! In a family of high-achievers, I had always been expected to soar; instead, I felt I had fallen. That summer, I truly became the 'black sheep of the white flock'.

Outside my window, the world was changing too. The drums of war, which had provided the soundtrack to my childhood since 1980, finally fell silent. On August 2, 1988, as I held my 'tragic' Baccalaureate certificate, the eight-year horrible war between Iraq and Iran ended. It was a surreal junction in the psyche: one nation's relief that the slaughter was over, mixed with my own private melancholy over a score that somehow came across like defeat.

This disappointment, however, worked to become a starting point for an area I had not previously considered. With my two elder sisters already established in Dentistry and Chemistry, the pressure of choosing a path was immense.

Unfair Scores and the University of Mosul Campus

And now it was time to launch a new academic life at the University of Mosul, a very reputable university locally and internationally. But the big question was which college to choose? My two elder sisters were discussing the matter of choosing the college with me; different choices were at the table, but the 'English' in me had the upper hand. So, it was the College of Arts; still, what to join? Is it the Department of English? Or the Department of Translation? I made up my mind and chose the Department of English, took the entrance exam, and I was accepted. Here is the pivot of my arena.

As a new college student, I found the linguistic and literary classes captivating. Exams began, and my teachers soon recognized me as a top student, but it was the 'Composition Class' that became my foundation stone. Prof. Dr. Dinha T. Gorgis, my teacher, helped me discover the inner teaching and linguistic skills in me. After classes on practising how to write sentences of different structures, Dr. Gorgis taught us how to choose topics to write the 'topic sentence'. One morning, Dr. Gorgis announced our first exam. The topic was 'My Teacher.' I knew immediately I would write about him. Dr. Gorgis was a man of immense charisma. I can still see his glasses, the specific way he carried his bag, and hear the refined tone of his British English - a legacy of his PhD studies in England. He was the first university teacher I ever saw sitting directly on the desks among us, checking our drafts; the same notebook was just like the *fair copy* and the *draft copy* (two terms were added to my dictionary for the first time). He was strict - misspelling a word might earn you the task of writing it correctly 100 times - but his sense of humour was as indescribable as his grading was unpredictable.

A week later, Dr. Gorgis joined the class with a pile of notebooks. I easily spotted mine due to its bright pink colour, covered in floral designs in white. My notebook was right on top. As he went through calling names, it was like a horror movie.

On the inside, on the first page itself, I had written—carefully, though—with my name and department name: "Huda Fadhil, First-Year, English Department, Mosul University." And reading this today, I see all the signs of the passing years and the writing that marked the beginnings.

'Who is Huda?' he asked, holding my notebook.

'Yes!' I answered, my heart racing.

'Go to the board,' he commanded, 'and write your composition, mistakes and all.'

I was confused, desperately trying to flip the pages to see my score before I reached the front of the room. When I finally saw it, I gasped. 7.5 out of 10. From a pioneer professor like Dr. Gorgis, this was a remarkable triumph. In that moment, the hook was not just set - it was strengthened for a lifetime.

That 7.5 score, and the stimulating comments that followed, became a benchmark for my time in his class. From then on, Dr. Gorgis began suggesting one topic after another for us to write. He would have my peers write their topic sentences and titles on the board, turning our classroom into a workshop of ideas.

Looking back, I still treasure the cover page of that notebook and the handwritten notes within it. To some, it is just an old college book; "to me, it is a golden medal that marks the moment I found my voice."

The "Golden Medal" and "teacher's prophecy" are both registered in my composition "My Own Opinion about Composition Class ", where I wrote a letter to my friend Jane in Florida, in which I confessed that my opinion about Dr. Gorgis was "a lovely teacher even though he always gets angry with us", but at the same time I knew that his real intention was "to make us good writers". At the last page, I saw his handwriting as a golden medal, which included the notes: "Keep this work in your copy-book" and "We shall have it as a sample work on the board", but the most important part of the golden medal was his prophecy that I carried with me for years: "I reckon that you will become one of the top students in your 3rd & 4th years". Consequently, at that moment, the 'hook' was not just a hobby or an interest, but a destiny that was confirmed.

The Prophecy: Dr. Gorgis and the Score that Confirmed My Path at Mosul University

The end of the first year was not the last time I met Dr. Gorgis, because he was my instructor again when he taught me Phonetics and Phonology in my second year and Linguistics in my fourth year. I was as eager as I could be to get the highest score, and it was like magic to get the highest scores in three groups in the toughest subjects, such as Linguistics, Drama, Novel, Poetry, and Literary Criticism. It was my fourth year, and my year of graduation, which I thought would be the turning point of my life; however, I was wrong. The graduation year was special for so many things.

I was going on with my monthly exams in the second course, and my concentration on my studies was high; then, I was in a car accident, which resulted in a broken thumb, and although it was not that bad, I had to undergo general surgery. Very soon, the pain in my body was forgotten. I can't jump to more details, skipping the 1990-1991 academic year, where I was in the third year. It was the year in which the drums of war started to be heard, because my country was facing all kinds of threats in the world. The war, which the American army named the Second Gulf War, was coming closer. I was asking myself, where does my future and my career place me in this world at conflict and at war?

"Jane Eyre" by Lantern Light

After the war officially began at dawn on January 17/18, 1991, my world had diminished to the size of my basement, where I was holed away with my parents and two sisters, while my eldest sister, a dentist, stayed at her post at Sinjar finishing her compulsory service. I did my best to maintain my wits and my sanity by immersing myself in Jane Eyre, the first course book we started in Novel Class, by the flickering light of a lantern. I spent hours diligently working away at the questions at the end of the textbook, scoring away with a red ink pen. The scratching sound was a rhythmic accompaniment to the uncertainty all around us. After the ceasefire, the prevailing rumors said: "The academic year was 'deleted,' and all our progress was for naught". However, in July 1991, the Ministry of Higher Education and Scientific Research in Iraq reopened the universities. My path was uncertain, built under the gun of missiles and the embargo, but I attained success. I graduated the following year for the 1991-1992 session, scoring a total of 76.28%. On the above pages, I set the stage for what I will achieve in the future.

The Return to My Roots-The Interview Moment

I submitted my file to the College of Arts, University of Mosul to join the Postgraduate Programme; I took the entrance examination in early 1993, which was in March or April, if I can remember, and I applied for a regular job at the University of Mosul during the summer. My classmate, who graduated third in our class, was appointed to the College of Education, while I was asked to return to our own college. The answer was quite simple but very important because, during the interview, the committee asked me a question: "Huda, tell us, how did you come from your house to the university? Answer in English." The command of the language, which I enriched even during the war, brought me back to the University, and therefore, on 18 August 1993, I became an employee.

The Spare List and the Struggle

But success was a double-edged sword. When the results of the Postgraduate Program were announced, I was the second on the spare list, and I was saddened, of course, but quietly grateful that I could stay on campus. In 1995, I was finally granted study leave to pursue my Master's degree, by which time life in Iraq had become an existential nightmare, because the embargo had made the "unbearable" the "normal". Simple tools of learning like notebooks and clean sheets of paper were luxuries, so we had to improvise, writing our notes on the blank side of printed documents, and use every available space. Pens and pencils were also on the list of prohibited objects, therefore, after finishing my coursework, I went back to work with my dear teacher Dr. Gorgis on my thesis: "Markedness Theory and Antonymy in Arabic with Reference to English", which was not only a matter of academic guidance but an exercise into deeper levels of analysis and critical thinking.

He pushed me relentlessly. "Huda, this is great," he would say, "but I need you to write better!"

The feedback he gave was an emotional rollercoaster, and sometimes I felt like I was flying through the air, carried on the wind of his warm and generous praise, while other times I felt uneasy, pressed to justify the high expectations he held for me. To this day I still feel that productive tension whenever I write, and my proudest moment was when he looked at a figure I had drawn of antonyms and exclaimed, "This is a major contribution to lexical semantics!"

Research in Isolation

No Internet in the 1990s to connect us to the world, and no Google, no online journals, therefore research was hours at the Central Library, or hours in the dusty corners of the college halls, searching for old books. My colleagues and I shared one friend's post office box so that we could write to scholars whose names we found in the Current Contents journals, and the replies we got were tragicomically representative of our times. I would open the long-awaited letter from a scholar to read: "I am sorry, I cannot help you, my country has an embargo on yours," which is a kind of heartbreak only an academic would know, being refused access to knowledge because of politics. While the world closed its doors, my mind opened wider, and it was "Huda's cognition" - no AI, no international databases, no digital libraries - that managed to win the trust of my supervisor's brilliant mind, and consequently, on 23 November 1998, I received my MA, which was the day I truly started my life as a teacher.

A New Chapter Begins: Entering the Department of Translation

In 1999, two months after my viva, I chose the more formal one, and the head of the Department of Translation, who had been a member of my examination committee and watched me defending my thesis, was so impressed by my performance that he went to the Dean and told him that I had to be in the Department of Translation. It was not long before I received an official letter sending me to my new academic "home", which I did not really want, and therefore my first teaching assignment was a translation course for the first-year morning students. I did not teach the course alone, but shared it with one of my most brilliant former teachers, the late Lecturer Maan M. Ahmed, who had taught me essay writing and translation and now stood by my side as a colleague in the same classroom.

The Challenge of the "Ghost" Textbooks

Before my first lecture of the second semester, a maelstrom of questions swirled in my head, where I wondered where to start, what teaching method to use, and how to control a class of 40 students. The materials I received were a stark reminder of the embargo, and the textbooks were old, not just in terms of content, but also in their physical condition, being ghost books that were already filled with handwritten notes and translated answers from generations of students, which meant that using them would be no challenge or benefit to my class. Then I turned to Mr Ahmed, and he gave me a pile of old magazines and journals, from which I extracted all the fragments and sentences that were syntactically complicated and had modern vocabulary. When I showed Mr Ahmed the material I had prepared so painstakingly, he looked at me with his stunning green eyes and smiled.

"Huda, where did you get all of this?" he asked. "It was all right there in the journals you gave me!" I replied.

My "hook" was growing stronger. I was no longer just a student of linguistics; I was a curator of knowledge, updating a stagnant syllabus through sheer willpower.

The Peer or the Professor?

I was a young teacher, and one time I was reading the schedule on the wall in the corridor when a Yemeni student approached me. He gave me a greeting of the common casual salutation of the students and talked to me as if I were a student, because I was small and looked young. He had no idea that I was the one who would be standing in front of the class the next day and teach him; however, I just smiled to myself and knew that it would not take long before he would see me standing in front of the class.

The Trial of the Blackboard

The final hurdle was the "Eligibility for Teaching" exam, a mandatory rite of passage for all new postgraduates at the University of Mosul. I stood before a formidable committee of nine members, including deans and English language specialists. My task: present a fifteen-minute lecture on my thesis using nothing but a piece of chalk and a blackboard.

After I finished, the room was silent as they prepared their critiques.

"Your eye contact was not good," one member remarked. "You focused on one side of the room and left the others behind."

My heart sank for a moment, but then he continued:

"However... I was watching your hands as you wrote on the board. They never shook. Not once."

Despite my internal tremors, my hands had betrayed a confidence I didn't yet know I possessed. I passed with a score of **89%**—a score that became the anchor of my career. I was no longer a "spare list" candidate (I recalled my first attempt as a postgraduate candidate); I was a teacher.

Defending the Word Amidst the War: The Doctor of Resilience

Returning to My Roots

I continued teaching at the Department of Translation for one and a half years; the classes I taught were composition, general English for non-departmental students (*Department of Sociology* and *Department of French*).I returned to the Department of English for the 1999-2000 academic year. My days were full, teaching everything from Comprehension and Composition to Research Methodology and Essay Writing. I began to take on the mantle of a mentor myself, supervising fourth-year undergraduate theses and providing linguistic assessments for candidates across various fields. I was no longer the young girl writing by lantern light; I was a cornerstone of the department.

The PhD and the Invasion

In 2003, the head of my department, Prof. Dr. Hussain A. Ahmed—who would eventually become my supervisor—recommended me for the Postgraduate Program to pursue my PhD. Once again, my academic milestones were destined to be marked by the sounds of conflict. This time, it was the 2003 American invasion. It was a hard road. While I was investigating avoidance in the use of American native speakers in their daily talk, the streets of Mosul were filled with death and destruction. It was a painful irony: I was researching avoidance of certain topics or structures in language, and in reality, I was trying to avoid the death and destruction, because my study dealt with American native speakers, I needed to access a world that was physically closed off to me. Collecting what I can only describe as "data under digital siege" was a high-risk endeavour, however, with the help of resourceful friends in Mosul, I learned how to navigate the fragile and unreliable internet connections at the time and managed to distribute my questionnaires electronically, which was a small victory, but a powerful one: technology and friendship defying the isolation that war had brought upon me.

My final defence took place on February 13, 2008, when I stood before the committee and presented my dissertation, A Synthetic Approach to the Study of Avoidance in Language Production, and when I was done, I looked at my supervisor and saw in his eyes the same pride that I felt in myself. The examining committee spoke positively about the size and depth of the work and about my choice of topic, as it was being tackled for the first time in the field of linguistics, meanwhile, outside the walls of the university, Mosul was still a center of conflict, however, inside, there was the air of academic debate, of careful analysis and of the discipline of linguistics. When I was awarded my PhD, the title was far more than a number of years of study, because it was evidence that I had refused to allow the circumstances of my country to silence my voice.

In my mind, this was the pinnacle of my teaching career.

The Changing Icon of the Teacher

But my teaching continued, though the long shadow of war and 13 years of embargo still loomed, and then, of course, came the ISIS occupation of Mosul and other cities, which led to three years that did not only change the borders but also the social fabric, consequently, thousands of families were displaced, students were forced to flee their homes, and the trauma people carried with them left the education system in tatters.

The most painful change has been in the "icon" of the teacher, once a figure of great respect and intellectual authority, because the profession has been debased by our halls of learning being filled with unqualified staff and ill-prepared students, and private kindergartens, schools and universities mushrooming like mushrooms after the rain. Some of these institutions are sincerely dedicated to the cultivation of the mind and character, but far too many are interested in profit rather than pedagogy, thereby turning education into a business rather than a sacred trust.

A Final Word

The story of teaching goes on, and the journey is long, strewn with the remnants of the past, but our hope is the greatest of our weapons. In 2014, even after the ravages of war in Mosul, I was ranked first in the Social Sciences / Linguistics and Literature in the total H-index rankings, with the University of Mosul, which is not just a personal achievement, but a quiet testament to our capacity to survive such devastation. The "beautiful minds" of Iraq are still here, waiting to be helped, and if we believe in them, if we invest in them, then a brighter future for education is not just a dream, but a reality. We can believe in them, and therefore, our classrooms can be again a place where minds are formed, dignity is restored, and futures are rebuilt.

FROM A CHILD'S CHALKBOARD TO UNIVERSITY CLASSROOMS: MY JOURNEY OF TEACHING ENGLISH AND LITERATURE IN IRAQ

Huda Al-Hassani

Since childhood, I have been imitating the role of a teacher with other girls and kids at home. I had a blackboard, chalkboard, eraser, and so on. I was taking it seriously as I was teaching, making exams, and giving marks to other kids stirred by my teachers at school. Yet, my journey as a teacher began coincidentally after earning a Bachelor of Arts in English Language from the University of Basra in 2004. At that time, the educational process in Iraq was dominated by traditional learning, where in-person lectures, notebooks, and chalkboards prevailed in classrooms. The classroom soon became clear as a platform and a laboratory, a place where learning, expression, and ideas were all interwoven. As a private teacher, I was invited to teach secondary school girls the English language subject. I was able to combine my passion for language, literature, and interpersonal relationships by becoming a teacher. Over the years, I've found that knowledge becomes more than just memorized content; it becomes lived experience when students engage with materials in a creative and personal way. I instructed first-year university students in my Introduction to Literature course in creating short stories that were motivated by themes, styles, or characters. In addition to fostering their analytical skills, this kind of activity was able to sharpen their narrative craft, creativity, and self-confidence.

As a matter of fact, teaching has always been a kind of an interesting adventure for me, a reciprocal journey between learners and educators. As for my earlier teaching years, I privately taught the English Language subject for secondary school pupils, enhancing their vocabulary, reading comprehension, grammar, and speaking fluency. My great experience and achievement was with Zahraa, who used to fail regularly in the English Language exams at secondary school. Yet, I was able, with constant direction and specialized assistance, to raise her level to the extent that she excelled in her studies. She eventually obtained a BA in the English Language after passing her university-level exams, too. Knowing that I was a role model for her and seeing her positive change was so touching; it confirmed for me that teaching is not just a job, but an appealing call.

Throughout my experience with Zahraa, I also noticed that many students are struggling in their studies, mainly due to a lack of motivation or engagement, rather than a lack of intelligence. Therefore, I was keen to create activities that can promote conversation, involvement, and individual expression. For example, exercises that include sentence construction can be developed into mini dialogues and conversational activities in authentic situations, giving the experience of language learning purpose and usefulness. Besides, I discovered that teaching should necessarily involve emotional support, as it is as important as instruction. For that reason, a safe learning environment, encouragement, and praise frequently released more potential than just lessons. These early teaching experiences became the base for my later methodology that combines creativity, confidence, and competence.

By 2018, I was teaching the *Speak Now* curriculum at the Cambridge International School, which placed a strong emphasis on interactive learning and communicative competence. The lessons focused on role-plays, group discussions, and pair work, providing students with real-world opportunities to practice their English in relevant settings. During the summer of 2019, I worked with children aged six to eleven at the Universal Education Centre in Mosul, Iraq. This time, I employed dramatization, songs, and storytelling. One shy pupil, Ali, played the Prince during the lessons and rehearsals of Cinderella; by the end of the performance, he delivered his lines easily and with confidence. These encounters, however, fostered transformative creativity, in which literature became a medium for self-confidence, social skills, and cultural compassion. I found out that an interactive, immersive, and playful atmosphere is ideal for language acquisition.

After completing my MA in Contemporary Literature and Culture at Brunel University in 2011, I joined the University of Mosul in 2013. During tht time, Iraq's Higher Education Reform Strategy (2013–2023) was in effect, with a focus on student-centred learning, faculty development, and curriculum renewal (MOHESR, 2013). I taught English literature, including poetry, novels, and drama, along with literary criticism, in addition to EFL for non-departmental students. All the time, I was aspiring to make learning experience engaging and appealing for my students. My classes focused on different storytelling activities, literary discussions, and critical debates. More interestingly, my pedagogy was significantly influenced by my talent as a literary writer and director. In this respect, I was able to incorporate various literary activities like poetry and fiction into the class because I authored several literary books like *Ten Short Stories*,

Love & Life: Forty English Songs, *Thoughts and Feelings*, and *A Poetical Voyage in the Arabic Singing*. As part of the Introduction to Literature subject, I lead a workshop for writing fiction, encouraging students to write their own short stories influenced by personal experiences, literary themes, or moral issues. Thereby their individual voice, narrative awareness and styles were marvellously developed.

My teaching experience, nevertheless, was further enhanced by directing and performing plays. In addition to adapting Shakespeare's *Macbeth* and *Malvolio's Trap*, adapted from *Twelfth Night*, I wrote and directed one-act plays like *Masquerade* and *Unfinished Crime*. Through these performances, literature was elevated from text to living art. For instance, soliloquy was used by the students while performing *Macbeth* in order to examine the protagonist's psychological conflict: "Is this a dagger which I see before me, / The handle toward my hand? Come, let me clutch thee." (Act2, Scene 1), seeing the dagger as an expression of Macbeth's internal conflict. On the other hand, students used the statement of Malvolio, "Some are born great, some achieve greatness, and some have greatness thrust upon'em," (Act 2, Scene 5), to analyse irony and social satire.

Actually, I frequently employed performance as a teaching strategy and pedagogical tool in the classroom. In this respect, I encouraged students to perform several scenes from plays like Goldsmith's *She Stoops to Conquer* to investigate the text deeper, make sense of its tone, and trace the characterisation of the protagonists. In Act 3, Kate Hardcastle decides to be a "barmaid" at the "inn" to uncover the humour of mistaken identity and irony in real time. She says, "O! sir, I must not tell my age. They say women and music should never be dated." Here, Kate, disguised as a barmaid, modestly resists the filtration of Charles Marlow. This scene is performed by the students while discussing gender roles, disguises, and social hypocrisy in the comedy of the 18th century.

Beyond Shakespeare and Goldsmith, I also presented contemporary European examples of realist and psychological drama through August Strindberg's *Facing Death* and Anton Chekhov's *The Boor*. Through Smirnov's unwavering statement, "As I've got to pay the interest on a mortgage tomorrow, I've come to ask you, madam, to pay me the money today," we can explore the conflict between mourning and evoking emotion in *The Boor*. By acting out this scene, students investigated how emotional repression, along with confrontation, feeds the Chekhovian discourse. In Strindberg's *Facing Death*, the students were engaged with Monsieur Durand's statement, "I am not dead yet, but I will be soon." They explored his intentions while confronting existential matters, the human condition, and moral sacrifice. By performing this play on stage, their appreciation of the tragic realism was enhanced. All of *the Boor*, *Hope*, and *Facing Death* were one-act plays edited, directed, and performed, transforming literature from a written text into a living art experience. Through stage discipline, teamwork, expressive delivery, and interpretive analysis, students were able to gain knowledge and wonderful learning outcomes. "The experience of acting of *Facing Death* made me finally understand the difference between reading and feeling literature," said Samir, a student.

Moreover, from 2018 to 2023, I founded and worked as editor-in-chief of *English Flowers Magazine*, which featured student translations, writings, and essays. This activity enhanced the creativity and scholarship of the students while encouraging them to be up-and-coming writers, authors, and critical thinkers. Students learned to develop their professional and academic skills needed for promoting their education by learning how to write, edit, peer-review, and publish their work through the magazine.

At the university level, creative education and pedagogical skills can be achieved by a balanced wisdom and novel ideas. I motivated students to explore with interpretation, performance, and multimedia while ensuring that they can understand the theoretical foundations and literary canon in order to promote both creative thinking and intellectual rigor.

Since 2013, I have supervised undergraduate research in theatre, cinema, and literature, first in person and then via hybrid digital platforms. *Great Expectations'* social critique, *Lord of the Flies'* symbolism, Shakespeare's comedy, *The Shining's* Gothic doubles, *Othello's* racism and identity, *As You Like It's* eco-criticism, and Atwood's *The Handmaid's Tale's* biblical references were among the subjects covered. While incorporating digital tools to develop technological literacy and lifelong learning habits, these projects fostered critical thinking, scholarly rigor, and independence (Al-Husseini, 2021).

Before the pandemic, I also instructed postgraduate students in English for Academic Purposes, with a focus on academic communication, reading, writing, speaking, and listening. Group discussions, peer presentations, and debates strengthened critical thinking, cooperation, and argumentation. I completely embraced digital teaching with the start of COVID-19, using Google Classroom and Google Meet to create hybrid models and recording lectures for YouTube.

Although they necessitated innovative solutions for limited internet access, varying digital literacy, and technical disruptions, digital tools allowed for continuous assessment, asynchronous access, and personalized learning. These difficulties served as a reminder of the importance of flexibility, fortitude, and creativity.

As I think back on my experience, I see the enormous influence of educators, both excellent and bad. I learned the value of profound comprehension from a chemistry teacher, while the inflexibility of an English teacher brought to light the necessity of openness, justice, and humility. These teachings influenced my philosophy, which is to respect students, encourage independent thought, uphold academic integrity, and promote inclusivity (Al-Husseini, 2021). Large classes, unequal motivation, and administrative demands are just a few of the difficulties that come with teaching in Iraq. To overcome these obstacles, I use interactive, student-centred methods, activities that are adapted to a range of skill levels, and techniques that foster intrinsic motivation. In addition to imparting knowledge, my goal is to promote creativity, critical thinking, and lifelong learning. I work to make learning immersive, meaningful, and interesting, whether that means incorporating multimedia, guiding original writing, or adapting Shakespeare for the stage.

From the 2004 chalkboards to the hybrid classrooms of today, my experience reflects the development of education in Iraq. My ongoing objective is to promote inclusive, engaging, and creative learning environments by advancing digital pedagogy, curriculum design, and academic communication. I hope to empower students to confidently and creatively handle academic, professional, and cultural problems by fusing literature, theatre, creative writing, and technology. For me, teaching is still a constant process of introspection, adjustment, and development—a place where human connection, creativity, and knowledge come together.

Nowadays, the profession of teaching is increasingly impacted by technological change, especially the integration of Artificial Intelligence (AI) in education. In my opinion, it becomes a must to put AI applications into consideration in teaching, particularly with the excessive use of AI by students in their homework, essay writing, seminars, and different kinds of studies. Recently, I've presented a worksheet in a symposium about the use of AI in teaching Drama. I found out that AI does have advantages and disadvantages in learning, as it sometimes makes mistakes and yields wrong information. For that, I believe it is the responsibility of a teacher to show the right way for students to use AI in an ethical, accurate, and effective way. And thus, I think AI should be recognized as a supportive tool that can enhance the experience of teaching through personalized learning, improved instructional planning, and efficient assessment, rather than as a substitute for teachers. Yet, the role of educators remains essential in promoting ethical awareness, critical thinking, and human interaction. For this reason, the future of teaching relies on integrating AI literacy with a very strong pedagogy and human values.

FROM OIL FIELDS TO BLACKBOARDS: AN UNEXPECTED CAREER CHANGE

Shamal Sh.Taher

I was born on one of the hottest days of July 4, 1990, in a hospital located in Mosul, Nineveh. My early childhood was spent primarily in the countryside, where the houses were built of mud, and the rooms were designed in traditional Middle-Eastern styles, contrasting sharply with today's architectural designs. My family consisted of seven brothers and five sisters, all cohabiting under one roof with our parents. We had access to electricity for merely one hour each day, necessitating reliance on lanterns, candles, and oil lamps for illumination. All family members slept in a row, with my mother meticulously arranging our beds on the ground side by side. During the evenings, we would recount frightening tales to amuse and, at times, scare our younger sisters. The boys engaged in target games, known locally, to pass the time during the dreary nights. My parents earned their livelihood through agriculture, cultivating a diverse array of crops including tomatoes, cucumbers, okra, eggplants, courgettes, melons, and watermelons. As children, we rose early each morning to accompany them to the farm, referred to as "bistan." Each year, the farm was located in a different area; on occasions, my dad was unable to secure nearby farmland, resulting in treks of approximately eight kilometres to reach our agricultural site.

I started school at the age of six in 1996. During my childhood, kindergartens were not available in my area. I had to walk for half an hour to reach my rural school. We used to wear sacks on our shoes so that the headmaster wouldn't get upset because we walked in the mud, which made our shoes dirty. Consequently, the classrooms would also get dirty. It was a really harsh time for families with more than a couple of pupils because, in my area, having children mainly meant helping with family chores, not attending school; thus, not many people could get out of school successfully. Luckily, my dad was a very open-minded man; he usually encouraged all family members to pursue their studies, even in tough times. He was our only source of light at home, working hard, worrying, and supporting us. I started primary school as a very shy boy and was not interested in math at all. I was really frustrated with math and didn't even like those who talked about it, including the math teachers. During my time, English was included in the fifth-grade syllabus, i.e., it was studied from the age of eleven, which made the learning process even more difficult. At first, I struggled to differentiate the English alphabet; I always wrote English dialogues in the Kurdish alphabet to help with reading skills. Speaking was not given much importance. Reading and writing were the main focus, and most teachers adopted the audiolingual method, as well as the traditional methods. Finally, after a lot of effort, I reached sixth grade, where we had the national exam. In Iraq, we take the bachelorette exam at the end of sixth primary and twelfth secondary school, which are final exams for all subjects, written and scored by the Ministry of Education. I failed my first attempt in math, but my dad didn't let me quit, so I tried my best and could pass on my second attempt in July 2002 with a grade fair which was only 50 points.

Amazingly, my school journey took a remarkable turn when I entered the 7th grade. I made a significant leap in my understanding of various subjects, and I found it easier to grasp different situations and behaviours. I started the year as a top student, as if some divine power had awakened me from my previous laziness. My teachers' attention was focused on me in all subjects, and I became the recipient of abundant praise. I was often presented as a typical example of a good student in my school, demonstrating commitment, cleanliness, hard work, and dedication to my studies. During most Thursday flag salutation ceremonies, I was frequently called up and praised in front of my peers for my behaviour and intelligence, which made me a role model for others.

Eventually, I scored 100 points in all subjects, and I was fortunate enough to be exempted from my final examinations. Bypassing final examinations was a technique used to motivate students to strive for excellence. I was even sent home with perfect grades one month before the end of the school year, which made me immensely proud in front of my classmates and family. This way, I passed the 8th grade as well with a perfect result. In the 9th grade, again as in the 6th grade, we had a national exam; I passed it successfully with a good mark. In the 10th grade, in the Kurdistan Region of Iraq, we had to decide whether to go into the scientific or literary branch of knowledge. Unfortunately, I struggled to find schools with specialized teachers, nor could I select schools that offered both literary and scientific branches. We had one literary school in the area where I lived. No other options were available; worse than that, transportation was a significant problem during my school years, as not many people had their own cars, and our village was somewhat isolated from big cities. We had to accept the literary branch. I passed the tenth and eleventh grades successfully with excellent results, again being exempted from final examinations as had happened in my 7th and 8th grades. I entered the 12th grade enthusiastically and studied very hard, well prepared for the national exam. I scored 100 in the first three examinations. Sadly, my oldest brother passed away in a terrible incident, and at the same time, my grandmother, who raised and cared for all of us, also passed away. The deaths of my two dearest people greatly affected my scores; in the last three subjects, I could only score in the eighties, so I ended up with an overall score of 85 in the 12th grade, which was a good grade. All literary branches accepted my result, meaning I could enter whatever literary branch I wanted with this grade.

I wanted to study law, but my dad told me that it is not a very nice and modest job; being a lawyer for villagers meant to be a hypocrite and do injustice to humanity, as they thought lawyers don't care about the kind of crime, they just have to defend whatever or whoever becomes their client. In 2008, the Department of English was the best choice after law. I really had an interest in learning new languages, and I loved English. I could be admitted to the Department of English, College of Arts, at the University of Duhok. I began studying and faced many struggles, particularly financial ones. This situation prevented me from going home except during lengthy holidays like summer holidays, Ramadan, the Qurban feast, and Newroz. As a result, I stayed in the dormitory for more than two months at a time. To help cover my college expenses, I worked during the summer. One reason my family was unable to support me financially was that my dad had been seriously ill for over seven years due to a severe backache, which prevented him from working. Consequently, one of my elder brothers had to quit school, sacrificing his future to help care for our family. We had a large family, and my dad couldn't provide for every single member. Additionally, I wanted to become independent and build my own character, striving for economic freedom. I aimed to be the kind of man who could manage all aspects of his life by himself. I pursued what I wanted to achieve.

After gaining my BA degree in 2012, I was recruited by an oil company as a Health, Safety, and Environment officer, and I was happy with the job as it provided enough to stand on my feet. In 2014, I received a call from the Directorate of Education telling me that I had been employed as a primary teacher. It was a devastating news because in Iraq once you are employed by the government you can't reject it or postpone it, you immediately need to serve for at least two years; in case of rejecting an employment your chance is going to be below zero to be reemployed in other ministries. I had to accept school and quit the oil company.

I started my new career as a teacher on May 7, 2014, teaching basic school, which includes grades one to nine in the Kurdistan Region of Iraq education system. I was not really content with the job, but it was something I had to do. Teaching and educating might be the hardest profession in the world. I taught in a basic school for two years. At first glance, I realized that most teachers have taken the job as something routine just to pass the days. Using traditional methods of teaching for years has led to nothing but laziness. Students were not motivated enough to study hard. Teachers were not enthusiastic about teaching their students; working with them negatively affected me, making me like them, but it distressed me.

As a result, I transferred to a secondary school, which includes grades 10 to 12. The new school was modern in terms of the building only. I remember my first day with students in grade 12; I entered my new class and said, "Hello, Good morning, how are you doing?" The students were like, "Oh, he speaks English with us." One student raised his hand and said, "Teacher, we don't want to learn English, just teach us how to get good scores in English". I replied, "I teach English, I don't cheat English." I worked for one more year in that school. A very critical point about the teachers was that they were not receiving their salaries on time, nor do they now. Sometimes it was delayed by up to 90 days, and at other times, it was cut significantly due to the unstable economic situation the government was facing, which greatly impacted teachers' outlook and perspective.

Motivation for both teachers to teach and learners to learn is pivotal and the main ingredient of an effective and healthy education. What I notice in our system is insufficiency in various categories of motivation. For instance, a child studies for 12 years, but they are not sure if they can be admitted to a good university; even if they are admitted, it will still be unclear if they can get a job or be employed by the government. This paralyses the student's mind as he can see their brothers and sisters who have made it with a very good grade, but they are jobless. From my perspective, teaching and education are a triangular process that requires the presence of a child, teacher, and parent. A vivid obstacle to successful teaching in the KRG education system is the lack of constant relationship and interaction between the child, teacher and parents. Nevertheless, the pedagogical system in the KRG is amazingly dedicated, providing every possible opportunity for learning and supporting teaching with the best modern methods. The problem lies in the application of these ingredients. The idea of motivation, which I previously mentioned, can best be illustrated through my current students I am teaching in my new school. I teach in an isolated village with around forty primary students, ranging from grades 1 to 6. The students' level of academic performance is below average. I often ask them why they do not try harder in school and give them advice that extends beyond just what is in the textbook. I dedicate the first five minutes of each class to motivating them, yet they still respond negatively. Many of them claim that after completing grade 6, they will quit school and work with their families and friends. The situation in the village where I am teaching now doesn't reflect a broader trend across schools in KRG, where many excellent private schools have emerged since 2010. However, what I wish to emphasize is that when there is insufficient motivation for any job, task, or activity, the results are unlikely to be satisfactory. Let us cross our fingers for the near future for development in the Iraqi education system.

Throughout my eleven years of teaching, I have noticed that people have different ideas about the teaching profession. Some believe that a good teacher can influence students positively. At the same time, they do not fully realize how difficult it is. Teachers must handle students with diverse learning styles, support students with emotional issues, and keep up with new technology and societal changes. They can influence positively if students (and their families) cooperate with them: are engaged and motivated.

I believe that most teachers themselves genuinely care about their work. They feel it is their calling. They enjoy their work because they want to help students learn and develop. There are small number of teachers who also feel tired and underappreciated. It is worth mentioning that the teaching profession requires a great deal of skill and patience. Thus, the process of teaching can also be very stressful, exhausting, and overwhelming at times. Therefore, it is a complex issue with many different perspectives and challenges. From my perspective, successful teaching integrates investment and strategic development. We need to fundamentally change the narrative from one of sacrifice to one of professional respect and capacity-building. Viewing teaching as a high-stakes intellectual pursuit, deserving of society's best efforts and full financial support, is the only sustainable way to ensure quality education for future generations.

REFERENCES

Abdullah, R. K., Kareem, H. S., Mahawas, A. A., & Haibes, E. K. (2023). *TIMSS encyclopedia. Iraq.* Retrieved from https://timss2023.org/wp-content/uploads/2024/11/Iraq.pdf

Akrawi, M. (1935). The new educational system in Iraq. *The Open Court, 1935*(3), 162–176.

Al-Husseini, S. (2021). E-learning in Iraqi universities: Challenges and opportunities. *Journal of Educational Technology and Innovation, 12*(3), 45–58.

Almasra, (2024). *The Ministry of Education announces statistics on the number of students and teaching staff across the country.* Retrieved from https://almasra.iq/16405/

Education for peace in Iraq Center (EPIC). (2016, December 16). Empty classrooms and black market textbooks. Retrieved from https://enablingpeace.org/empty-classrooms/

Education International. (2025). *Iraq: Educators' historic strike leads to salary increases and progress for education.* Retrieved from https://www.ei-ie.org/en/item/29965:iraq-educators-historic-strike-leads-to-salary-increases-and-progress-for-education

ERI (Economic Research Institute). (n.d.). *Lecturer salary in Iraq.* Retrieved from https://www.erieri.com/salary/job/lecturer/iraq#:~:text=The%20average%20pay%20for%20a,of%20education%20for%20a%20Lecturer

Glassdoor. (n.d.). *How much does a Teacher make in Iraq?* Retrieved from https://www.glassdoor.com/Salaries/iraq-teacher-salary-SRCH_IL.0,4_IN122_KO5,12.htm

Inter-agency Network for Education in Emergencies (INEE). (2021). *Teacher management in conflict and protracted crisis: Addressing resource gaps and enhancing support.* Retrieved from https://inee.org/resources/teacher-management-conflict-protracted-crisis

Mikhailov, L., & Mohammed, K. A. (2012, October 24–25). History of education in Iraq. Paper presented at the *International Scientific and Practical Conference: Modern Problems of Mathematics and its Application in Natural Sciences and Information Technology.* Kharkiv, Ukraine. Retrieved from http://www.confcontact.com/2012_10_24/4_Mikhaylov_Karam.htm

Ministry of Higher Education and Scientific Research (MOHESR). (2023). *The national strategy for higher education in Iraq 2023–2031: Enhancing the quality of outputs and alignment with the labor market.* Republic of Iraq.

Ministry of Higher Education and Scientific Research (MOHESR). (2024). *Higher education: One hundred & twenty-six Iraqi universities & colleges in Webometrics ranking.* Republic of Iraq. Retrieved from https://mohesr.gov.iq/en/post/higher-education-one-hundred-amp-twentysix-iraqi-universities-amp-colleges-in-webometrics-ranking-2024-07-19-21

MOHESR (Iraqi Ministry of Higher Education and Scientific Research). (2013). *Higher Education Reform Strategy in Iraq (2013–2023).* MOHESR.

Paradies, M. (2024). "I do not want to stop teaching": The impact of conflict and displacement on teachers in southern Mosul. *Prospects, 54*(3-4), 769–787. DOI: 10.1007/s11125-023-09666-5

SCImago Institutions Rankings (SIR). (2024). *University rankings - Iraq 2024.* SCImago Research Group. Retrieved from https://www.scimagoir.com/rankings.php?country=IRQ

Shafaq News. (2025, April 6). *Iraq's education meltdown: Pennies for professionals.* Shafaq News. Retrieved from https://shafaq.com/en/Report/Iraq-s-education-meltdown-Pennies-for-professionals

TIMSS. (2023). *International results in mathematics and science*. Retrieved from https://www.iea.nl/publications/timss-2023-international-report

UNESCO. (2019). *Iraq Spotlight Report 2019: Global Campaign for Education*. UNESCO Digital Library.

UNICEF. (2021, January 20). *UNICEF Iraq humanitarian situation report (IDP crisis): End-year 2020*. Retrieved from https://reliefweb.int/report/iraq/unicef-iraq-humanitarian-situation-report-idp-crisis-end-year-2020

University of Baghdad. (2024). *Research performance and Scopus indexing annual report 2023-2024*. Quality Assurance and Academic Performance Department. [Internal Report/Official Statistical Release]

World Bank. (2021). *Republic of Iraq: Human capital index 2020 brief*. World Bank Group. Retrieved from https://openknowledge.worldbank.org/handle/10986/34415

Chapter 14
Teachers' Voices From Iraqi Kurdistan

Venera Ulker
http://orcid.org/0000-0002-9094-7729
Tishk International University, Iraq

Lanja Abdul razzaq Dabbagh
http://orcid.org/0000-0001-6757-5691
Salahaddin University, Iraq

Harman Qarani
RISE International School, Iraq

ABSTRACT

Abstract This chapter examines the development and current structure of the education system in the Kurdistan Region of Iraq, situating it within its historical, political, and socio-economic context. It traces the evolution of education from informal religious instruction to a modern system shaped by de facto autonomy, post-conflict reconstruction, and rapid institutional expansion after 2003. The chapter outlines the organization of pre-primary, compulsory, secondary, and higher education, with particular attention to the national high-school examination system and its role in shaping university access. It also explores the growth of private and international schools and their implications for educational equity. Central to the analysis is teacher education and the teaching profession, highlighting enrollment trends, employability, and labor-market dynamics. Using a sociological and human capital perspective, the chapter offers insights into how education in Kurdistan reflects broader processes of state-building, social stratification, and workforce development.

THE EDUCATION SYSTEM IN THE KURDISTAN REGION OF IRAQ

Venera Ulker

Historical background of education in Kurdistan

The education system in the Kurdistan Region of Iraq (KRI) has evolved through a complex and politically charged history marked by periods of suppression, conflict, and later reconstruction and expansion. Prior to the 20th century, education in the Kurdish regions was largely informal and centered on religious institutions. Learning took place mainly in mosques and *madrasas*, where instruction focused on Qur'anic studies, Arabic grammar, ethics, classical Persian

DOI: 10.4018/979-8-3373-8983-7.ch014

literature, and basic numeracy (Kurdistan Regional Government, 2025) . Educational opportunities were limited mainly to males in urban areas, while rural communities had minimal access, resulting in low literacy levels across the region.

Following the establishment of the modern Iraqi state in the early 20th century, formal schooling gradually expanded to the Kurdish provinces. However, throughout this period, education was highly centralized under Baghdad, and the system reflected a nation-building project grounded in Arab nationalism. Kurdish-language instruction was restricted or banned, Kurdish history and culture were omitted from school curricula, and teachers were expected to promote a unified Arab identity (Stansfield, 2003). This period of 'Arabization' reached its peak in the 1970s and 80s, leading to the systematic marginalization of Kurdish intellectual life. Despite these limitations, Kurdish intellectuals advocated mother-tongue education and produced early Kurdish textbooks, though their use was often prohibited (Bengio, 2020).

A short period of political opening in 1959 allowed for the establishment of the Directorate General of Kurdish Studies within the Ministry of Education, enabling limited Kurdish-language instruction in some areas (Khdhir, 2015). Higher education also began to develop in Kurdish-majority regions, culminating in the founding of the University of Sulaimani in 1968 - an important milestone that provided Kurdish students access to disciplines such as literature, education, and sciences within their region (Ali, et al., 2021).

However, subsequent decades were characterized by instability and violence. The 1970s and 1980s saw renewed conflict between Kurdish forces and the Ba'athist regime, culminating in the Anfal campaign (1987–1988), during which thousands of villages were destroyed. This resulted in the closure of hundreds of schools, widespread displacement of teachers and students, and deep setbacks in educational development, especially in rural areas (Vernez et al., 2014).

A transformative shift occurred after the 1991 Gulf War, when the Kurdistan Region came under international protection and gained de facto autonomy. The establishment of the Kurdistan Regional Government marked a new era in Kurdish education. The newly formed Ministry of Education (MOE) adopted Kurdish as the official language of instruction and initiated the development of curricula that incorporated Kurdish history, geography, and culture (Vernez et al., 2016). After 2003, following the fall of Saddam Hussein's regime, the KRG accelerated its education reforms. Between 2003 and 2015, the number of K–12 schools increased by more than 30%, and the number of higher education institutions expanded from three public universities to more than twenty-five public and private universities (Ministry of Planning, 2015).

By 2024, illiteracy rates in the Kurdistan Region had dropped from 24% in 2018 to 16% (Kurdistan 24, 2024a). These advancements reflect not only improved access to education but also the use of schooling as a vehicle for strengthening Kurdish cultural identity and regional development.

Despite these gains in literacy and institutional expansion, the education system in the Kurdistan Region continues to face persistent structural challenges. Rapid population growth, large-scale internal displacement, and prolonged political and fiscal disputes between the Kurdistan Regional Government (KRG) and the federal government in Baghdad have placed considerable strain on educational infrastructure. Many public schools operate on double or even triple-shift systems, particularly in urban centers, reducing instructional time and negatively affecting learning outcomes (Vernez et al., 2016). In addition, shortages of qualified teachers - especially in science, mathematics, and English - remain a concern, compounded by delayed salary payments during periods of budgetary crisis. These challenges underscore that post-1991 reconstruction has been uneven, with access expanding more rapidly than quality and sustainability.

Private, national, and international schools

The private education sector in the Kurdistan Region has grown significantly since the early 2000s, driven by economic expansion, increased demand for English-medium schooling, and the presence of international workers. National private schools follow the Kurdish curriculum while offering enhanced English-language programs, modern instructional materials, and smaller student-teacher ratios.

The growth of the private education sector has also proven highly sensitive to political and economic stability. During the 2014–2017 financial crisis and again during the COVID-19 pandemic, many private schools experienced sharp enrollment declines as household incomes contracted and families struggled to meet tuition costs. Some institutions were forced to reduce staff, freeze salaries, or temporarily close. This volatility highlights the dependence of private schooling on broader fiscal conditions, distinguishing it sharply from the more stable - though resource-constrained - public sector.

International schools serve both expatriate and local families seeking global curricula. Many follow the Cambridge IGCSE, Pearson Edexcel, or International Baccalaureate (IB) programmes. Examples include the Classical School of the Medes (CSM), the British International Schools, and the International School of Choueifat, all of which use English as the primary medium of instruction.

Staffing patterns in private and international schools differ notably from those in public institutions. International schools often employ a mix of expatriate teachers - particularly for core subjects delivered in English - and locally trained graduates, many of whom receive higher salaries and more regular payments than their counterparts in public schools. This wage differential has contributed to a growing internal labor market within the teaching profession, where experienced teachers increasingly migrate from public to private institutions, intensifying staffing shortages in the public sector (Chali & Karimi, 2023).

While international schools have contributed to improved educational quality and diversified opportunities, their high tuition fees have created disparities in access between socioeconomic groups. Tuition fees in elite international schools commonly range from approximately USD 3,000 to over USD 10,000 per year, effectively restricting access to affluent families and expatriate communities. This has contributed to the emergence of a tiered educational landscape, in which socioeconomic status increasingly determines access to English-medium instruction, international curricula, and global higher education pathways. In response, a growing number of locally owned private schools have adopted hybrid Kurdish–English curricula, positioning themselves as a middle-ground option for urban middle-class families. The Ministry of Education plays a regulatory role in licensing, curriculum approval, and teacher credentialing for these institutions, although enforcement capacity varies (Kurdistan Regional Government, 2025).

Structure of the education system

The education system in the Kurdistan Region consists of four main levels:

1. Kindergarten (pre-primary)
2. Basic education (grades 1–9)
3. Secondary education (grades 10–12)
4. Higher education (universities and technical institutes)

The Ministry of Education (MOE) oversees pre-university education, while the Ministry of Higher Education and Scientific Research (MOHESR) manages tertiary institutions.

Kindergarten (KG) level

Early childhood education in the Kurdistan Region typically begins with kindergarten (KG), which includes two levels: KG1 (age 4) and KG2 (age 5). Attendance at the kindergarten level is not compulsory but is increasingly recognized as vital for children's cognitive and social development (Ali et al., 2021; UNICEF, 2023). Many private and international schools provide English-based kindergarten programs that follow international curricula such as the British Early Years Foundation Stage (EYFS), Montessori model, or the International Baccalaureate (IB) Primary Years Programme (Ali, et al., 2021). However, the lack of qualified preschool educators and uneven rural access remain challenges (World Bank, 2024).

Basic education (Grades 1–9)

Basic education is compulsory and free in all public schools. It consists of two stages - primary (grades 1–6) and intermediate (grades 7–9). The curriculum includes Kurdish, Arabic, English, mathematics, science, social studies, and Islamic education. Schools in minority communities, such as Turkmen or Assyrian areas, may offer instruction in their own languages (Kurdistan Regional Government, 2025).

The KRG has made significant investments in expanding access to schooling, particularly for girls. According to UNESCO (2024), gender parity at the primary level has improved substantially, though rural disparities persist.

Secondary education (Grades 10–12)

Secondary education lasts three years and leads to the national *Baccalaureate Examination*, a standardized assessment that determines university eligibility. Students choose either the scientific or the literary track. In 2024, more than 115,000 students participated in the final exams, with 73% in the science stream, 25% in the literature stream, and 2% in vocational education (The National Context, 2025).

High-School Graduation and University Entrance

The Baccalaureate Examination

The high-school final exam, known as the *Baccalaureate*, determines students' eligibility for higher education. In 2023, approximately 122,015 students sat for the Grade 12 final exams across the main provinces of Erbil (39,547), Sulaimani (27,376), and Duhok (28,285) (Rudaw, 2024). For the 2024–2025 academic year, more than 115,787 students registered for the exams: 72.8% in the science stream, 24.9% in the literature stream, and 2.3% in vocational programs (The National Context, 2025). These examinations are decisive, as the results directly affect students' university placement.

University admission and placement

According to the Kurdistan Regional Government's Ministry of Higher Education and Scientific Research, more than 44,000 students were accepted into universities in the first round of admissions in the 2024–2025 academic year—representing 96% of all applicants (Kurdistan 24, 2024c). During that same period, there were approximately 56,130 high-school graduates (Science: 41,277; Literary: 13,541; International: 410; Vocational: 902), while the government had prepared 64,761 university seats (Kurdistan 24, 2024c).

Private and public universities, and teacher training institutions

Higher education in the Kurdistan Region has expanded rapidly over the past two decades, with more than 66 officially recognized public and private universities and institutes operating under the supervision of the Ministry of Higher Education and Scientific Research (MoHESR) (Chali & Karimi, 2023). Public universities generally have larger student bodies and provide subsidized tuition fees. Private universities often offer modern facilities and English-medium programs, though their tuition fees are comparatively higher.

However, the quality of private higher education institutions is uneven. While some universities maintain strong academic standards and international partnerships, others have been criticized for limited research output, reliance on part-time or underqualified staff, and exceptionally low failure rates, raising concerns about grade inflation and academic rigor (Zangana, 2025). The primary attraction of many private universities remains English-medium instruction rather than curricular depth. In parallel, public universities have expanded fee-based "parallel" programs, allowing students to access competitive departments through paid tracks, thereby creating a hybrid system that blurs the boundary between public and private provision.

Teacher-training universities and colleges

Teacher preparation primarily occurs at the following institutions:

- Colleges of Education at Salahaddin University–Erbil, University of Sulaimani, University of Duhok, Soran University, Raparin University, and Tishk International University.
- Teaching Institutes (two-year programs) supervised by the MOE
- Pedagogical Training Centers, offering postgraduate pedagogical diplomas

These institutions prepare teachers for pre-primary, primary, and secondary schools. Colleges of Education train subject-specific teachers (e.g., English, mathematics, physics), while Teaching Institutes focus on primary-school educators.

However, faculties of education are often less preferred by top-scoring students. Fields such as medicine, engineering, and business continue to attract the highest achievers, leading to concerns about the long-term quality and motivation of incoming teachers (Zangana, 2025; Invest Kurdistan, 2023; Basa et al., 2019).

Enrollment trends by faculty

Although specific recent statistics comparing the number of students in faculties of education to other faculties are limited, reports indicate that around 40,000 students graduate from universities in the Kurdistan Region annually (Kurdistan 24, 2024b). Anecdotal evidence and ministry statements suggest that faculties of medicine, engineering, and business attract higher-achieving students, while faculties of education often receive lower preference among applicants - a reflection of the declining popularity of the teaching profession (Chali & Karimi, 2023).

Implications for the teaching profession: enrollment, employability, and labor market dynamics

Enrollment patterns in the Kurdistan Region's higher education system reveal important insights into how students perceive the teaching profession and how labor-market incentives shape their choices. Although the teaching profession is often considered less prestigious than careers in medicine, engineering, or law, it offers several structural advantages that continue to attract significant numbers of students - especially in public universities and scholarship-supported private institutions.

One notable factor is employability. Compared to other professional fields, the competition for teaching positions is significantly lower; public schools continue to experience periodic teacher shortages, particularly in rural districts and many new private schools open every year. As a result, graduates of Colleges of Education often secure employment more quickly than their peers from other faculties. In many cases, teaching remains one of the few professional pathways in the region with a relatively predictable route to employment, especially for graduates willing to accept positions outside major cities.

Anecdotal evidence from university career centers and staff interviews indicates that fresh graduates entering the teaching profession sometimes receive higher initial remuneration than new graduates in medicine, pharmacy, or engineering. This is because medical graduates must complete several unpaid or low-paid internship years before qualifying for professional licensure and full placement in hospitals or clinics. In contrast, graduates of education programs - once appointed - immediately begin receiving a salary, which, although modest in the long term, provides early financial stability.

This creates an incentive for some students to view teaching as a "faster-return" profession compared to fields with prolonged specialization pathways.

The economic dimension becomes even clearer when examined through the lens of human capital investment. A four-year bachelor's degree in education completed at a private university represents a moderate but meaningful financial investment for many families. According to interviews with administrators and financial estimates derived from tuition structures, the expected financial return on this investment often materializes only after approximately 20 years of employment. Because the return-on-investment (ROI) period is long, students and families frequently prefer educational programs in public universities, where tuition is fully subsidized, or in those private universities that offer significant scholarships, reducing overall educational costs. Consequently, public universities consistently enroll larger cohorts in their Colleges of Education than in several private universities.

Another structural factor influencing enrollment is the university admission system. The acceptance grade for admission to educational departments is often similar to - or only marginally lower than - the grade required for admission to fields such as engineering, law, and business administration. As a result, many students who achieve the required threshold for multiple programs opt for non-education fields that are perceived as more prestigious or more financially rewarding in the long term. This phenomenon reinforces the perception of education as a "fallback" option for those who either prefer stable employment or do not prioritize entering more competitive faculties.

Together, these dynamics illustrate a complex picture: the teaching profession offers early employment opportunities and relatively high initial financial security, yet long-term financial returns and societal prestige lag behind other professional fields. The combination of employment stability, scholarship availability, and moderate academic entry barriers continues to influence enrollment patterns across the region's public and private universities.

WHEN TEACHING BECOMES A CALLING

Venera Ulker

Early life and first teachers

I was born in a small city near the Caspian Sea, in a multinational neighborhood where most families worked at the airport. My father was a pilot, often away flying passenger and cargo planes across the Soviet Union and beyond, while my mother was a baker who stayed home to raise me and my two brothers.

My mother became my first teacher. She introduced me to the alphabet and basic knowledge even before I started school. Later, she guided me not by giving answers but by teaching me *how to learn*. She had once dreamed of becoming a Russian language and literature teacher but could not pursue that path due to some life circumstances she never told us about. Perhaps because of this, she encouraged me to explore different interests - dancing, drama, music school, and science olympiads - allowing me to discover my own strengths and passions.

Choosing my path

When I reached grades nine and ten, I faced the big dilemma of choosing a career path. I was a successful student and knew my strengths and weaknesses well. The English language was very popular then, and I had already participated in English competitions and attended English-speaking camps. Like many of my peers, I dreamed romantically of traveling the world and initially wanted to become a translator or interpreter. So, I applied to the English Department, Faculty of Romanic and Germanic Languages, Institute of World Languages, Ashgabat, Turkmenistan.

Later, during my practicum at a language center, I had a chance to teach. I was surrounded by passionate teachers in a positive environment, and when I saw my own students start speaking and writing in English, I felt an incredible joy. That moment, I knew teaching was more than a profession. It was a calling. On top of that, fate intervened when I met my future husband - also a teacher. Slowly, my path toward education became clear, and I embraced it wholeheartedly.

Becoming a teacher

My BA program was more philological than pedagogical. Of course, we had courses in pedagogy, but the real school where I learned to teach was my practicum. Since my second year, I had already been working as a teacher: first as a private tutor, then as a teacher assistant at a language course. But teaching had been a part of me long before. As the eldest child, I had always helped my younger brothers - guiding them with homework, keeping the house in order, and taking care of them whenever our parents were away. Without realizing it, I was already practicing being a teacher.

My mother also instilled in me the belief that all subjects mattered. She taught me not to ignore any discipline, to give my best effort in everything. This approach bore fruit: I graduated with honors, earning the highest grades in all my courses. Still, my deeper interest always leaned toward language - its history, word formation, and structure fascinated me endlessly.

Further studies: Master's and PhD

After graduating in 2002, I longed to continue my education. Life, however, brought marriage, children, and work responsibilities, and I had to postpone my academic dreams. Finally, in 2013, I resumed my studies at the International Black Sea University in Tbilisi, Georgia, where I completed both my Master's and PhD in Language Teaching.

Returning to studies after a long break was difficult. Balancing academic work with a full-time job and two children in primary school was a daily challenge. In many ways, the Master's program was even harder than the PhD course. What sustained me was the support of the university staff and professors. Among them, Professor Dr. Natela Doghonadze left an ever-lasting impact on me. She was both strict and immensely caring - her feedback on my thesis often made my heart race before I opened her emails, yet behind her firmness was the encouragement of a true mentor. She became a role model for me as a researcher and academic.

For both my theses, I focused on assessment, a subject I had long felt passionate about. I had observed a troubling gap between what and how students were taught and the way their knowledge was assessed. I believe teachers must be properly trained in assessment, as it is central to fairness and quality in education.

Memorable stories

There are many moments in my teaching journey that remain close to my heart, but a few stand out.

Once, I became sick and could only whisper. I didn't cancel my classes and entered the classroom, greeting my students silently. I still remember the surprised looks on their faces; at first, they thought I was tricking them, since I often enjoyed playful interactions. When I explained that I was unwell, something remarkable happened: the whole class fell into an extraordinary silence. Normally, my classes were lively and noisy, and I would often have to ask students to quiet down. But that day, every single student did their best to remain absolutely silent, straining to hear my whispered words. Their support and understanding moved me deeply. What could have been a difficult day turned into one of the most heartwarming experiences of my career.

Another memory comes from teaching a group of international students — from Tajikistan, Dagestan (Russia), and Turkey. On the very first day, I decided to speak only English, pretending not to know their native languages. In reality, Russian is my first language, Turkish is my second, and I am also fluent in Turkmen and Azerbaijani. My students tried their best to speak English, and it was a delight to see their efforts. The hardest part for me was keeping a straight face when they spoke Russian and Turkish about me, thinking I could not understand. For nearly half a semester, they had no idea I understood every word. When they finally realized, their shock turned into laughter, and that shared moment brought us closer together as a group.

These episodes remind me that teaching is not just about knowledge transfer but about building trust, empathy, and joy in the classroom.

Role models

At different stages of my life, I have drawn inspiration from different people. My mother was my first role model, embodying patience, curiosity, and perseverance. My primary school teacher, Ms. Yelena Rudolphovna Pchelnikova, the daughter of a German prisoner of war, combined professional discipline with maternal warmth. At university, I learned from many professors - not only what to do but also what *not* to do as a teacher. Later, during my postgraduate studies, Dr. Natela Doghonadze became a powerful example of academic rigor paired with care and encouragement.

University lecturer experience

My career as a university lecturer has allowed me to teach a wide range of courses - English language skills, linguistics, research methodology, and teacher education. Supervising student theses and preparing future teachers has been one of the most rewarding parts of my journey.

University students bring both independence and high expectations. This dynamic challenges me to continually learn and grow. Watching my students develop into confident professionals is one of my proudest achievements.

Joys and challenges of teaching

For me, the greatest joy of teaching lies in my students' accomplishments. My teaching happiness is measured by their victories. Yet, teaching is also demanding — a profession without weekends or holidays, requiring constant dedication 24/7.

In today's world, teachers are no longer mere transmitters of knowledge. With information so easily accessible, the real task is to help students evaluate, interpret, and apply it critically. My guiding principle is to treat students as I would want to be treated - with empathy, fairness, and respect. I aim to train teachers I would trust with my own children's education.

The future of the profession

Sadly, the popularity of teaching is declining. Fewer students choose teacher-training departments, even though the demand for qualified teachers is increasing. This is alarming, especially when the demand for teachers is only increasing. For example, in Iraqi Kurdistan alone, dozens of new schools have opened in recent years, and schools call us almost daily searching for teachers.

I hope that society will restore respect and prestige to the teaching profession, as the future of education depends on it. For me, the greatest reward remains the same: to see the spark of curiosity, confidence, and achievement in my students' eyes.

Conclusion

Looking back, I can see how my path to teaching was shaped by many influences - my mother's dedication, my teachers' examples, my own early experiences with siblings and students, and the joy I found in seeing others grow. Teaching has never been an easy job, but it has always been a meaningful one.

For me, being a teacher is not just about transferring knowledge; it is about shaping lives, inspiring confidence, and passing on the values of empathy, discipline, and curiosity. It is about building bridges across cultures and generations. And it is about ensuring that when students leave our classrooms, they are not only more knowledgeable but also better human beings.

Teaching, despite all its challenges, remains one of the most rewarding professions I can imagine. My journey into education may not have followed the straight path I once dreamed of, but I cannot imagine my life any other way.

I HAD ONLY ONE THING IN MY MIND AND THAT WAS BECOMING A TEACHER

Lanja Abdul Razzaq Dabbagh

My name is Lanja Abdul Razzaq Dabbagh, and I am a university teacher. I was born in Erbil (also known as Hawler, the Kurdish name for the city) in the Kurdistan Region of northwestern Iraq, to a very well-known family. My ancestors lived in the Citadel, a famous historical site in the centre of Erbil. My grandparents were landlords and worked in trading business. They spoke Kurdish, Arabic, and Turkish. Since, likely, the rest of the world is aware of our situation, we have lived in and continue to live in various challenging environments. Surrounded by unexpected circumstances that force us to change our plans consistently. Nonetheless, I was brought up with three plans in advance for everything I wanted to do: plans A, B, and C. I have learned to have one more plan: an open plan. In my career, I did not follow this procedure because I had only one thing on my mind: becoming a university English language teacher. Education, studying, and getting degrees played a vital role in our lives. My siblings and I grew up knowing that these three aspects should be the primary considerations when we plan our future. My parents played a greater role in ensuring that we never neglected this fact. So, the atmosphere in our house was like that: during school months, we all did our tasks to the best of our ability without anyone asking us. During the holidays, we spent most of our time reading. My late father was a keen reader; he encouraged us to read in English and Arabic, because, at that time, no Kurdish schools were available. We were educated in Arabic schools, which made it difficult for us to read Kurdish books, even though they were generally unavailable. Ultimately, that was one of the reasons my Arabic skills improved so significantly. No complaints, knowing as many languages as possible is a privilege. Having the opportunity to go deep into other languages is a blessing. I tried my best to keep up to my father's standard. He knew it, which is why he stood by my side later when I decided to study the English language and literature, rather than medicine. My late mother, on the other hand, did not have the opportunity to complete her education, as was the case for the majority of females at that time. Nonetheless, she was extremely clever and self-educated. Being in her presence, no one could believe that she had not finished school or obtained a degree. She used to say that your degree and certificate are your ID in life.

We all loved classical music because my father listened to it frequently. So, we grew up hearing all the beautiful masterpieces of famous, talented composers. I remember my father once asking me if there was a story behind the music I was listening to. Of course, I answered yes. I imagined every tone as being a tale and transformed it into words. That is how I became certain that I would have a job related to writing.

My family is very medical; my father was a very famous surgeon and a Fellow of the Royal College of Surgeons of Edinburgh. I have two elder brothers, both of whom are doctors: one is an anesthesiologist, and the other is a surgeon. My younger sister is also a doctor; she specializes in otolaryngology. My elder sister is an engineer; two of her sons are doctors: a plastic surgeon and a surgeon. Both my sisters-in-law are doctors too, a pathologist and an ophthalmologist. My aunt was a doctor, now retired. I have several cousins who are also doctors of different specialties. Yet, medicine was never my desired field.

When I finished high school, I broke the news to my parents. I told them I wanted to study a field that would make me happy and doesn't require much studying. I told them that I like to listen to the lectures, enjoy them, and absorb the information. Lectures, topics, lessons, etc. that do not require me to study too hard and for a long time. I said to them, "I want an easy job, a job that does not require me to be brave or have guts." Well, I was young and naive. As soon as I finished my talk, my mother said everyone expected me to become a medical doctor. My father supported my decision, but my mother was against it. I told them that I wanted to study the English language and literature to become a teacher. People around me, for example, the driver and the gardener, used to call me 'doctor'. My mother was so disappointed, she used to say, "Listen, everyone is calling you a doctor." Hence, I promised her that I would get an MA, then a PhD, so that people could call me 'doctor' just for her sake. I fulfilled my promise; both my parents were very proud of me and constantly mentioned it to others. I enjoyed every second of my college lectures. I thought to myself, "Yes, I made a perfect choice." This is exactly what I want. After graduation, I spent a few years as a translator at the College of Medicine library because I did not yet have a master's degree and did not want to become a high school teacher. Due to several personal, social, and political circumstances, my dream of becoming a university teacher was delayed for a few years. But I did not give up. Finally, I became a teacher, and from there, my academic journey began. As a teacher, you learn from others' mistakes as well as your own. Yet, you learn from others' success, too. When I first started lecturing, I constantly sought advice from my late teacher, who was my MA and PhD supervisor and mentor. I used to tell him that I wanted to have half of his proficiency. He would often reply, "You can if you want to." I learned a lot from him; he was a perfect teacher, an expert, and an excellent, talented supervisor. So, I tried my best to adopt his teaching and supervising methods. It was also he who advised me to combine language and literature for my PhD. Knowing my passion for literature, he was right as usual.

At the beginning of primary school, our teachers were nuns; they maintained a friendly class atmosphere while also preserving discipline. They were gracious and strict. As a pupil, I was happy. I learned how to be sociable and how to follow rules. The classes were constructive and pleasant. Other teachers, on the other hand, were very harsh on us and sometimes used language that was uncomfortable. Yes, you can learn from primary school teachers, from both their successes and failures, as you follow your path to becoming a university teacher. I realized that as a teacher, you should never underestimate your students, never compare them to others (students or siblings), never belittle them, and never force them to do a task that they are unable to accomplish. In intermediate and high school, I was not very happy, maybe because I thought I was forced to study topics I did not like, not realizing that all these topics are useful in one way or another for educating any human being. Teachers were so good, yet they lacked understanding of what teenagers go through. Teenagers require more attention. As a teacher, you need to know their 'language'. Unfortunately, that was not the case at that time. Here, I learned that junior college students still have a teenage mentality. As university teachers, we should not ignore this phase. Rewarding and punishing (by giving more tasks) is also a method I learned from my high school teachers. Out-of-class activities helped me engage shy students in classes, which is also something I learned from my high school teachers.

In intermediate and high school, I was not very happy, maybe because I thought I was forced to study topics I did not like, not realizing that all these topics are useful in one way or another for educating any human being. Teachers were so good, yet they lacked understanding of what teenagers go through. Teenagers require more attention. As a teacher, you need to know their 'language'. Unfortunately, that was not the case at that time. Here, I learned that junior college students still have a teenage mentality. As university teachers, we should not ignore this phase. Rewarding and punishing (by giving more tasks) is also a method I learned from my high school teachers. Out-of-class activities helped me engage shy students in classes, which is also something I learned from my high school teachers. Ultimately, I attended university and studied the subject I had long desired: the English language and literature. My goal was to complete college, earn my MA and PhD, and become a university professor. I greatly admired my university professors, and I learned a great deal from them. They were so talented at teaching that it made me more eager to become one. I used to listen, observe, comprehend, and absorb whatever they mentioned in the class. They made me cherish every moment. This is what I promised to do for my students when I became a teacher.

The same thing happened while I was studying for my MA and PhD. I valued every class, especially those delivered by my mentor. Again, I assured myself that I would become just like one of them. Balancing life's struggles and job tasks was one of the significant things I have learned from them. My parents used to tell me: Do not perform anything, even if you like it, under stress. So, I tried my best not to do so. I took maternity leave plus one year of unpaid leave for each of my children. That is how I managed to be in control of the job I like most. One important fact we should not forget is that I went through all the above while living in a country filled with struggles, wars, and life-threatening situations. Well, that did not stop me from becoming a teacher.

Teaching is a very difficult job. Some may not be aware of or acknowledge this. As a teacher, you face numerous struggles, obstacles, and challenges on a continuous basis. Besides the material you teach, you need to cope with every dilemma that comes with it. Each student needs your full attention. Psychological, sociological, and economic, among other aspects, entail a complete indulgence as you work with new generations each year. Still, I am tremendously blissful. Underpaid or not paid at all (in our case), I am proud to say that I am a teacher. During the COVID19 pandemic, when the world was locked down, teachers and medical doctors continued to work on the ground and online. The most important thing to note is that I would not have accomplished anything without my husband's support. He always encouraged me to fulfil my dream. Even when plans did not go well and obstacles were scattered in my path, he was there to fortify my path to success. He helped me in every step, taught me how to cope, and boosted my ego in all the breakdowns.

My advice is to follow one's dreams and become a teacher. No words can describe the feelings when you see one of your former students praising you and telling you how much they have learned from you. Seeing them successful with great jobs is a reward that makes you forget all the struggles you face as a teacher.

The future perspectives of the teaching profession depend on how much we believe in ourselves. Each teacher has their own views about the way of teaching that involve techniques or strategies to achieve the target whether it is the curriculum, the syllabus, the materials, classroom management, among others. Techniques that are used by some teachers could be appropriate with the contexts and contents of syllabus. This may not be the case for other teachers. Reflection, investigation, assessment should vary from one class to another to enhance the teaching learning process. If these points and the fact that teachers are the core of the teaching learning process are taken into consideration, our jobs will be safe and easier.

SOME TEACHERS ARE LUCKIER THAN OTHERS

Harman Qarani

In horse racing, the horses from parents that have won races are said to have a pedigree. They are sometimes 100 times more expensive than horses without the said pedigree. Analogously, in human societies, from antiquity, there has been a certain prestige given to artisans and craftsmen who come from generations of the same craftwork. Modern professions are not given the same consideration, but it is something to be said about a person choosing the same profession as their parents. If you have not guessed yet, both my parents were teachers.

Since I was very small, I have been surrounded by education. It was the main topic spoken about in our household. When I was a student, any issue that occurred in school, I had to see from a teacher's perspective. That is how things were explained to me. Also, I have some very good memories of my mother grading papers. At the same time, we sat together watching television, or she hunched over the kitchen table trying to figure out the weekly class schedule as the vice-principal. At dinner, my father was usually talking about his job in the Ministry of Education.

When it was my time to become a teacher, I was already marinated in education, learning and teaching theories and methods. Besides the reformative atmosphere at home, there were some teachers and circumstances that had a great impact on who I became and what kind of teacher I am. Honestly, I don't remember ever having an impactful moment or situation in primary school. The only overarching feeling about primary school, unfortunately, is very negative. I come from the last generation to whom corporal punishment, beating children, was allowed. My vivid memories of that time are being very afraid of certain teachers who used wooden sticks to beat the students. Sometimes, you didn't even have to do anything wrong to be punished; if the class was quite noisy, we could get collectively punished, and every student would be beaten. I remember the dark cloud that covered the class for the rest of the day after a beating, and I can say with great certainty that no learning happened after any punishment. My takeaway from primary school was that I would never let any student experience that feeling. The friendly relationship that I have with my students, probably, consciously or subconsciously, is due to me not wanting that feeling from any of my students.

In secondary and high school, I had a teacher who had a lasting impact on me. It might be a coincidence, but I like to think there is a correlation between all my favorite teachers being English teachers and my own decision to become an English teacher. After a public primary school I went to a private school in which the language of instruction was English. This opened a whole new world for me. The first teacher who had a great impact on me was my 7th-grade English teacher (Mr. Ahmet Ceylan). In his class, we used movies and real songs in learning. This was the first time I realized that lessons and learning can be fun. I thought if this were my career, then I could live with it. Sadly, I am no longer in touch with him. The other teacher was Mr. Ozgur Kucuk, who was my 11th-grade English teacher. He was a university teacher who also taught us part-time. I learned quite a lot from him, his expertise and work opened my eyes to the number of opportunities available to teachers in their careers, as he worked with many different organizations. This made the job of the teacher even more attractive to me. It was during my spring vacation in grade 11 that I visited the USA with Mr. Kucuk. During the trip, we visited some American high schools, and this up-close experience, and talking with their teachers deepened the conviction that a teaching career was my future. I am still in contact with Mr. Kucuk. When it was time to choose a major at university, the decision was an easy one. While most of my friends were waiting for the results of college acceptance exams to decide their fate, I had already picked the ELT (English Language Teaching) department at Tishk University.

My memories of my time at Tishk University are overwhelmingly positive. I learned a lot from my professors. All the theories that I had heard from my father in Kurdish, I would now learn them in correct and precise terminology in English. I learned how to do lesson planning and exam preparation, I saw my mother do all the time with scientific accuracy. Most of my professors were great, and I learned a great deal from them. One of them, Dr. Basil Qahtani, stands out from the rest in my memory, since he was the one who introduced me to English literature. The in-depth learning and studying during his class made me feel like I was learning something that even a native English speaker might not know. I realised that with enough practice a person whose native language is not English can teach it successfully. That awareness made me very proud of my major and the subsequent degree. However, the most beneficial thing l was taught that served me in my future job was how to teach anything. The theories and practical methods of learning and teaching were the best thing about my degree.

After graduation, I applied for a teacher's position to the same organisation that owned my private high school. I was hired, and I have been a teacher there for the past eight years. My experience in this regard is quite unique, since I am part of the same organisation where I studied in high school and some of my old teachers are my colleagues now, and a lot of their children are my students now. One more peculiarity about my teaching experience is that I started teaching with grade 12. So, while I have only been a teacher for 8 years, I already have students who have graduated from college and have jobs, and, as it is an international school, I have former students worldwide, from Japan to the USA. The sense of pride and satisfaction that comes with that is indescribable.

I alluded that learning how to teach any topic was the most beneficial aspect of my degree from Tishk University. That is why, besides the English language, I have taught sociology, political science, psychology, world history, human rights, and economics. Each of these subjects came with their special set of challenges. In my first year of teaching, I only had four students, I taught sociology and political science in grade 12 as elective subjects. It was an excellent experience because it eased me into my teaching career. So, I was pretty lucky in my first year, however not so lucky in the second year, because COVID-19 started and all my classes went online. Online classes were not a good experience for me, since I was teaching grades eleven, twelve, four, five, and six. The high-schoolers were difficult but still manageable. Teaching social sciences (history and geography) to primary school students, however, proved to be one of the hardest things I have done. It was very difficult to keep their attention on the lesson. I suffered in the first two weeks, but the clutch came when I asked them to teach one another and they became responsible for each other's grades. I conducted quizzes and exams as open-book quizzes and exams. Initially, they complained about these tactics, they said it was too easy. Later, they understood that I wanted them to think critically, rather than simply demonstrate memorization.

Those same students are now in grade 11, and I teach them sociology. They say they have learned a lot from my online lessons since they had to hold each other accountable. In my fourth year, the classes returned to classrooms, so by that time I had taught more online than in class (with only four students). Predictably, classroom management became an issue.

Among many things I have tried, the two which have given me consistent success and results are: the first, joining in with their jokes and banter, and allocating time for that, and then coming back to the subject matter. The second is conducting student-centered classes. When students have to teach each other, the class feels more exciting, time passes more quickly, and the students take on a greater sense of responsibility for their own learning. I have been very lucky to have had very few issues with my classes and students. The only minor issue I face every year occurs at the beginning of each school year trying to convince my students that subjects like sociology and psychology are beneficial for them. Once this conviction is established during the first two weeks (which I do by relating the topics to their daily lives and problems), the rest of the year becomes easy.

Now I must confess my experience as a teacher may not be that representative of the usual teacher experience in Erbil, since I have only taught in one very specialised and expensive international school. But my experience has been overwhelmingly positive, so much so that I have struggled to remember and come up with negative experiences in my teaching career. So either I am very lucky or maybe, since I have been brewing in the field of education since I can remember, teaching might be easier for me. The issues that other teachers might have may not be problems for me. Of course, I am not saying I have a better pedigree than other teachers, but that my sculptors (mom and dad) were excellent educators.

REFERENCES

Ali, B. J., Gardi, B., Othman, B. J., Ismael, N. B., Sorguli, S., Sabir, B. Y., Ahmed, S. A., Hamza, P. A., Aziz, H. M., & Anwar, G. (2021). Educational system: The policy of educational system in Kurdistan Region in public kindergarten. *International Journal of English Language & Translation Studies*, *6*(3), 62–71. DOI: 10.22161/ijels.63.10

Basa, F., Qadir, S. A., Alsilefanee, H. H., Alhanabadi, L. H., Salih, S. O., Akhshirsh, G. S., Azeed, B., & Moramarco, S. (2019). Updates in human and health sectors in Iraqi Kurdistan: A war-torn region. *Biomedicine and Prevention Issues*, *1*(212). Advance online publication. DOI: 10.19252/0000000D4

Bengio, O. (2020). Reclaiming national identity in Kurdish school textbooks. *The Middle East Journal*, *74*(3), 359–378. DOI: 10.3751/74.3.11

Chali, A., & Karimi, E. (2023). Kurdistan's boost for science and higher education. *Nature*, *616*(433), 433. Advance online publication. DOI: 10.1038/d41586-023-01274-9 PMID: 37072515

Invest Kurdistan. (2023, July 25). The ninth cabinet's impact on Kurdistan's economic growth. Retrieved from https://invest.gov.krd/news-and-events/the-ninth-cabinets-impact-on-kurdistans-economic-growth/

Khdhir, D. H. (2015). Dynamics of Kurdish identity formation in the Kurdistan Region-Iraq between 1991 and 2014. Doctoral dissertation. University of Nottingham. https://eprints.nottingham.ac.uk/47221/

Kurdistan24. (2024c, August 30). Kurdistan Region universities accept 96% of high school graduates in first round. Retrieved from https://www.kurdistan24.net/en/story/809032

Kurdistan 24. (2024a). Education. Retrieved from K24: https://www.kurdistan24.net/en/story/396575

Kurdistan 24. (2024b, February 2). Retrieved from Kurdistan24: https://www.kurdistan24.net/en/story/393925/40%2C000-annual-university-graduates-in-Kurdistan-Region%2C-says-KRG-official

Kurdistan Regional Government. (2025, October 5). Ministry of Education. Retrieved from https://gov.krd/MOE-en/system-and-education/basic-and-secondary-systems/

Ministry of Planning. (2015). Reforming the economy for shared prosperity. Erbil: Kurdistan Regional Government. Erbil, Kurdistan Regional Government. Retrieved from https://cdn.gov.krd/Ministries/Ministry%20of%20Planning/English/Publications/Reports/Ministry%20Reports/10.%20Reforming%20the%20KRG%20Reforming%20the%20Economy%20for%20Shared%20Prosperit.pdf

Rudaw. (2024, June 20). Education ministry releases grade 12 exam results. Retrieved from Rudaw: https://www.rudaw.net/english/kurdistan/200720242

Stansfield, G. R. (2003). *Iraqi Kurdistan: Political development and emergent democracy.* Routledge., DOI: 10.4324/9780203398302

The National Context. (2025, June 1). Grade 12 preparatory students - Kurdistan Region. Retrieved from The National Context: https://thenationalcontext.com/portal/115787-students-begin-exams-in-kurdistan-73-science-25-literature-2-vocational/

UNESCO. (2024). Planipolis: International Institute for Educational Planning. Retrieved from UNESCO: https://planipolis.iiep.unesco.org/en/2024/national-education-strategy-iraq-2022-2031-ines

UNICEF. (2023, November). Iraq. Retrieved from UNICEF: https://www.unicef.org/iraq/media/3276/file/Report%20ECE%20Investment%20Case%20in%20Iraq.pdf

Vernez, G., Culbertson, S., & Constant, L. (2014, April 4). Strategic priorities for improving access to quality education in the Kurdistan Region — Iraq. Retrieved from https://www.rand.org/pubs/monographs/MG1140-1.html

Vernez, G., Culbertson, S., Constant, L., & Karam, R. (2016, February 26). Initiatives to improve quality of education in the Kurdistan Region — Iraq. Retrieved from https://www.rand.org/pubs/research_reports/RR960.html

World Bank. (2024, September 18). National education strategy for Iraq 2022-2031 (English). Report. Washington, Iraq. Retrieved from https://documents.worldbank.org/en/publication/documents-reports/documentdetail/099091824091030738

Zangana, G. (2025, June 5). Unemployment of doctors in Kurdistan: A ticking time bomb for healthcare. Retrieved from https://www.internationalhealthpolicies.org/featured-article/unemployment-of-doctors-in-kurdistan-a-ticking-time-bomb-for-healthcare/

Chapter 15

Teachers' Voices From Kuwait

Laila A. Addasi
http://orcid.org/0009-0003-2393-1799
Al Hayat Universal Bilingual School, Kuwait

Omar Wardere
American International School of Kuwait, Kuwait

Sara Talal Alessa
Alruya Bilingual School, Kuwait

ABSTRACT

This chapter centers on the lived experiences of three educators—Laila Addasi, Omar Wardere, and Sara Al-Essa—whose professional journeys offer a rich, practice-based perspective on teaching in Kuwait. Through their narratives, the chapter explores themes of career progression, cross-cultural engagement, instructional practice, and leadership within diverse school settings. Their stories highlight the personal and professional dimensions of teaching, including challenges, growth opportunities, and the evolving expectations placed on educators. While grounded in the broader context of Kuwait's education system and its ongoing reforms, the primary focus remains on how these developments are experienced in practice. Together, these accounts provide valuable insight into the realities of education in Kuwait, emphasizing the human element behind policy and reform.

OVERVIEW OF EDUCATION IN KUWAIT

Introduction

Kuwait is a small yet affluent nation whose economy has historically depended on oil as its primary natural resource and export. Despite this reliance, the country has increasingly prioritized educational development as a strategic tool for economic diversification and long-term national sustainability. Recognizing education as central to national progress, policymakers aim to equip students with the knowledge, skills, and competencies necessary to compete in a global knowledge-based economy rather than to rely solely on oil revenues (Al-Senafi & Alsabbagh, 2024). Consequently, Kuwait's education system seeks to balance the preservation of cultural heritage with modernization efforts that promote critical thinking, innovation, and technological literacy. This overview examines the historical evolution and current educational initiatives in Kuwait, highlighting the nation's commitment to building an effective and forward-looking education system capable of preparing future generations for global challenges.

Teaching in Kuwait is undergoing significant transformation as certification requirements increase and educational institutions become more competitive. The country's education system is divided into public schools, which primarily serve Kuwaiti nationals, and private schools, which cater largely to expatriate residents. In the public sector, hiring processes and educational pathways are regulated by the Kuwait Ministry of Education, which has aligned reforms with

DOI: 10.4018/979-8-3373-8983-7.ch015

Kuwait Vision 2035 (Government of Kuwait, 2017) to enhance teaching quality and infrastructure. A key contributor to teacher preparation is the Kuwait University College of Education, established in 1966 and later developed into an independent institution, offering specialized tracks in primary, intermediate, and secondary education (Kuwait University College of Education, n.d.). In the private sector, a Bachelor's degree is typically required, with teaching certifications and experience considered highly desirable as institutions seek globally competitive educators. Professional development opportunities have expanded in recent years, including postgraduate certification programs in collaboration with United Kingdom institutions and training provided by the Public Authority for Applied Education and Training, particularly in areas such as artificial intelligence and educational technology (Public Authority for Applied Education and Training, 2024). Additionally, the Kuwait Ministry of Education has introduced initiatives such as the program *Using Professional Standards to Improve Teacher Performance in Light of Future Competencies*, aimed at enhancing teacher effectiveness (Kuwait Times, 2023). With competitive salaries ranging from approximately $1,600 to $4,500 USD per month, Kuwait continues to attract educators, reflecting a growing and promising market for teaching professionals.

Historical Overview of Education in Kuwait

The evolution of Kuwait's education system can be broadly categorized into three phases: traditional and cultural education, the establishment of formal schooling institutions, and the expansion of postsecondary education. During Kuwait's early development, education was primarily delivered through *kuttab* schools, which emphasized Islamic studies and Arabic literacy. This model reflected the nation's religious and cultural foundations. Over time, educational practices evolved into formal institutional structures aligned with modern schooling systems.

In 1911, Kuwait established its first formal school, followed by the rapid expansion of more than 300 schools within the subsequent decade (Al-Senafi & Alsabbagh, 2024). Early curricula focused on foundational subjects such as mathematics, commerce, reading, and writing taught in Arabic. However, in 1921, the introduction of English-language instruction marked a significant milestone in educational modernization. The establishment of the Ministry of Education in 1935 further strengthened centralized educational governance and policy development (Al-Senafi & Alsabbagh, 2024). Education has since been regarded as a "fundamental requisite for the progress of society, assured and promoted by the state" (Hafsyan, 2023, p. 4).

With the expansion of primary and secondary schooling, Kuwait enacted legislation guaranteeing free and compulsory education through the ninth grade. Additionally, the diversification and privatization of the education sector contributed to institutional development. British, American, bilingual, and nonsegregated schools were introduced under the Ministry of Education's regulatory framework. Specialized administrative divisions were also created to promote national identity, preserve religious instruction, and maintain academic quality across public and private institutions.

Higher education became a central component of Kuwait's national development strategy. The government implemented scholarship programs that enabled academically talented students to pursue higher education abroad, contributing to national capacity building (Hafsyan, 2023). In 1966, Kuwait University was established, providing citizens with free access to postsecondary education. This development was followed by the emergence of private universities and colleges, which expanded academic offerings, diversified professional pathways, and enhanced Kuwait's competitiveness in the international academic and labor markets.

Kuwait has developed a comprehensive educational system that spans from early childhood education to postsecondary and doctoral-level programs. Contemporary institutions provide diverse learning opportunities for both citizens and residents. These advancements demonstrate the country's ongoing commitment to educational reform, workforce development, and sustainable socioeconomic progress.

Structure of the Education System

Kuwait's education system is characterized by the presence of both public and private education sectors, which together contribute to the overall educational landscape. Public schools follow the national curriculum and provide free education for Kuwaiti citizens, ensuring broad access and continuity across the system. In parallel, private schools offer a range of international curricula and languages of instruction, serving both expatriate and Kuwaiti families. This diversity reflects Kuwait's openness to global educational models while maintaining national oversight and standards (The Borgen Project, n.d.).

Kuwait's education system is organized into clearly defined stages that guide students from early childhood through higher education. The system is centrally regulated by the Ministry of Education of Kuwait, which oversees public schooling and ensures alignment with national standards.

Kindergarten in Kuwait consists of two years and focuses on early childhood development for children typically between the ages of 4 and 6. At this stage, emphasis is placed on social, emotional, cognitive, and physical development. Learning experiences are designed to build foundational literacy and numeracy skills while encouraging creativity, cooperation, and independence. Although not compulsory, kindergarten is widely attended and serves as an important preparatory phase for formal schooling (UNESCO, 2007).

Primary education spans five years and provides students with essential foundational skills in Arabic, Islamic studies, mathematics, science, and social studies, along with English as a second language. This stage aims to establish core academic competencies, critical thinking skills, and responsible citizenship. Successful completion of primary education allows students to progress to the intermediate level (TIMSS, 2023a).

Following primary school, students enter intermediate education, which lasts four years. During this stage, the curriculum becomes more specialized and academically rigorous. Students deepen their understanding of core subjects and begin preparing for the academic and career pathways available in secondary education (TIMSS, 2023a).

Secondary education in Kuwait is three years in duration and plays a pivotal role in preparing students for higher education or entry into the workforce. Students may pursue general academic tracks or specialized pathways, including scientific or literary streams. In addition, vocational and technical pathways are offered through institutions such as the Public Authority for Applied Education and Training, which provides applied and career-oriented programs aligned with labor market needs (Public Authority for Applied Education and Training, 2024; TIMSS, 2023a).

Higher education in Kuwait includes both public and private institutions that foster professional growth and advanced academic study. The primary public university, Kuwait University (n.d.), offers undergraduate and graduate programs in medicine, engineering, law, business, arts, and sciences. The Public Authority for Applied Education and Training (PAAET) operates colleges and training institutes that grant applied degrees, diplomas, and technical certifications.

The private sector includes institutions such as American University of Kuwait (n.d.) and Gulf University for Science and Technology (n.d.), which offer programs in business, engineering, information technology, media, and other professional disciplines, often following international models.

Level of Education in Kuwait

According to The Borgen Project (n.d.), adult literacy rate (ages 15+) is 97%, while practically all young people aged 15-24 are literate. The Integrated Education Reform Program constitutes part of Kuwait's national vision 2035. In 1995, 2007, 2011, 2015, 2019, and 2023 Kuwaiti students participated in TIMMS (Trends in International Mathematics and Science Study) assessment. According to TIMSS 2023 (TIMSS, 2023b) assessment, in Science, in the 5th percentile Kuwaiti 8th graders received 248 points (benchmarking result: Dubai: 359) and in Math they received 253 points (Dubai: 370). These results have prompted further efforts to improve the quality of education and implement additional reforms.

Current Initiatives and Reforms

In recent years, Kuwait has intensified its efforts to modernize the education system in alignment with national development priorities. Education occupies a central position within Kuwait Vision 2035 (New Kuwait), which identifies human capital development as a key pillar for sustainable growth and economic diversification. Within this vision, education is viewed as a strategic investment aimed at preparing learners with the knowledge, skills, and values required for a knowledge-based economy (Government of Kuwait, 2017).

A major focus of recent reforms has been the continuous development of national curricula and textbooks. The Ministry of Education regularly reviews curricular frameworks to ensure alignment with international educational standards and benchmarks. In 2015, for instance, a renewed curricula in Math and Science were introduced (TIMSS, 2023a).

At the same time, national identity is preserved through Arabic language and Islamic studies (Kuwait Times, 2026). Updated textbooks increasingly emphasize critical thinking, problem-solving, and real-world application, supported by interdisciplinary approaches and digital learning resources.

Teacher development remains an important element of educational reform. National initiatives place emphasis on continuous professional development, instructional improvement, and reflective teaching practices. Teachers are encouraged to adopt learner-centered approaches and to integrate technology into classroom instruction in ways that support curricular goals and student engagement (TIMSS, 2023a).

Technology integration has also become an important component of recent initiatives. Efforts to expand digital platforms, e-learning tools, and educational technologies aim to enhance digital literacy and support more flexible learning environments that prepare students for higher education and future employment (AlQenaei, 2021; Karkouti, 2023).

Challenges Facing Education in Kuwait

As Kuwait continues to implement educational reforms, certain areas remain central to ongoing development. One key area relates to teacher professional development. While training opportunities are available, the evolving demands of contemporary education require sustained investment in professional learning that supports instructional practice, curriculum implementation, and classroom effectiveness. Opportunities for mentoring, collaboration, and skills development remain important in supporting teachers' professional growth.

Another consideration is the length of the academic year. Compared to some international education systems, the relatively shorter school year can place pressure on curriculum pacing and instructional planning. Teachers are often required to balance curricular objectives within limited instructional time, which may affect opportunities for reinforcement, enrichment, and extended learning activities.

Cultural influences also shape educational expectations and practices. In some contexts, parents place strong emphasis on students' academic grades as the primary indicator of success, sometimes giving less attention to learning processes and skill development. This focus on grades can create pressure on both students and teachers, influencing classroom dynamics and assessment practices.

Future Perspectives

One initiative that reflects this future-oriented direction is the "From Here We Shall Set Sail" (Min Hena Nabhur) national campaign, launched in the period following the COVID-19 pandemic (Aleisa et al., 2021 as cited in Cochrane, 2026). The initiative was developed by a group of Kuwaiti academics, educators, and education stakeholders to support the education sector in addressing pandemic-related challenges and reinforcing long-term educational planning. It seeks to inspire educators to embrace ambition and leadership and presents developmental proposals that emphasize updating curricula and assessment systems, as well as strengthening educational governance. As noted in the campaign's publication, it promotes a forward-looking vision for education that prepares learners and institutions for future challenges through strategic planning and sustainable reform.

Kuwait Vision 2035 outlines the future directions of the education sector in Kuwait. Kuwait Vision 2035 emphasize efficiency and inclusivity, with a focus on meeting the diverse needs of learners. Within this framework, inclusive education is a key priority, aimed at ensuring equitable access to learning opportunities and appropriate support for students across school settings.

At the practical level, future efforts are expected to continue shifting curricula toward skill development, including analytical thinking, problem-solving, communication, and collaboration, alongside stronger connections between learning and real-life contexts. Assessment practices are also anticipated to evolve through greater use of varied tools that capture student understanding, application, and ongoing progress, rather than relying solely on traditional examinations.

The vision further supports integrating students with diverse educational needs into mainstream education where appropriate, while strengthening special education services and in-school academic and psychological support. Attention is also directed toward enhancing teacher professional development to better align training with classroom realities and to support teachers in managing learner diversity. Collectively, these directions point toward a gradual and structured approach to strengthening educational practice in line with national development priorities.

Teachers in Kuwait

The profession of teaching in Kuwait is rapidly evolving as the certification demands continue to increase while the quality of students and rate of educational institutes raises in competitiveness. As noted there are two streams of education in Kuwait - Public (Government Schools) for Kuwaiti Nationals and Private Schools for Residents. In public schooling, the educational path and hiring procedure is sanctioned by the Ministry of Education. In alignment with the country's Vision 2035 there has been significant advancement in teaching pedagogies endorsed by the government which include the infrastructural enhancement of the Kuwait University College of Education which was established in 1966 as part of the College of Arts. The Kuwait College of Education gained its independence in the 1980s where it finally had its own building in 2019 where educators follow three paths - primary, intermediate and secondary education (Kuwait University College of Education, n.d.). In the private sector, a bachelor's degree requirement is mandated with experience and teaching certification being optimal. With advancement in certification and the development of more rigorous standards, the private education sector is also looking to hire well qualified educators all around. Many opportunities for certification, furthering degrees and training courses have emerged in the last decade to support teachers in Kuwait. Namely there are the Post-Graduate Certification Courses with the United Kingdom, Institutes such as Public Authority for Applied Education & Training (PAAET) offer courses to support the development of AI and teaching technologies. Furthermore, the Kuwait Ministry of Education also launched a program to support educator's professional development, *Using Professional Standards to Improve Teacher Performance in Light of Future Competencies'* (Kuwait Times, 2023). With a country driving the future of education so strongly, Kuwait also offers competitive teaching salaries and good international contract packages to teachers. A typical teaching salary in Kuwait can range from $1631.66USD to $4568.66USD based on experience, level of teaching and package negotiated. Over the years, the need for teachers in Kuwait continues to grow allowing for a competitive and promising marking for future educators.

CONCLUSION

In conclusion, Kuwait's education system reflects a sustained commitment to development and modernization. Through curriculum reform, national initiatives, and investment in human capital, education continues to play a vital role in shaping future generations. The country overview provides a contextual foundation for understanding the broader educational landscape in which educators and learners operate.

Laila's Story: A Journey Through Teaching

My story starts at the age of twelve, middle school. That's the year I decided I was going to be a teacher.

I spent most of my childhood stacking up teddy bears and dolls, arranging them in neat rows, playing "classroom." I'd line them up on my bedroom floor, hand each a pencil, and announce in my most serious voice, "Good morning, class!" I created makeshift homework, worksheets, and even marked their "tests" with bright red pens. My mother used to walk into my room, laugh, and say, "Who are you talking to, Laila?" But I couldn't help it - it felt real to me.

Being the youngest in my family, I was determined to become a teacher. You can imagine my envy when, while I was still in high school, both my older siblings "fell into teaching" before I did - already collecting stories from classrooms while I was still sitting in one. I remember thinking, no fair - this was supposed to be my dream!

When university applications opened, I approached them with determination. I had the grades, the drive, the extracurriculars to pursue anything - medicine, law, you name it. But teaching called me. I believe it was a predetermined purpose of who I was meant to become. My teachers' college entrance essay asked for the top five skills a teacher should have, so I proudly wrote: "Empathy, Compassion, Communication, Leadership, and Adaptability." I was so sure… I had planned it all.

Upon completing my studies, I was eager to embark on my teaching journey. But life had other plans. The path I had envisioned so clearly since I was twelve - shaped during high school and carefully mapped out through every career test and undergraduate course - didn't unfold as expected.

Yes, I became a teacher. But not in Canada, as I had imagined. Instead, I found myself in Kuwait - teaching not biology, but Grade 1. You prepare and plan for certain goals you are so sure of in life, only to have destiny sidetrack you. I can still remember my first day in the classroom - the smell of freshly sharpened pencils, the faint echo of Arabic phrases I did not yet understand, and a sea of tiny faces staring up at me: some curious, some shy, some already crying [secretly, I was too!]. It wasn't what I'd prepared for or imagined it would be. Students, staff, and parents - even I questioned my abilities because I was a young graduate. I still remember my director saying, "Don't divulge your age — just dive in!" And so, I dove straight in, turbulent waves and all.

Though I am of Middle Eastern descent, I was raised in the West - born in the U.S. and raised in Canada, speaking both fluent English and French. I did speak some Arabic, but not the Kuwaiti dialect, and couldn't read or write Arabic to save myself. You can imagine the surprise on parents' faces when they'd speak to me fluently in Kuwaiti and I'd smile, completely lost - or when I'd receive a handwritten note and couldn't tell if it was upside down or right-side up! In those moments, I regretted my childhood Saturday Arabic class that I'd skipped for sports tournaments and weekend outings. But there was no time for regret - I had a classroom waiting, and a promise to keep to my twelve-year-old self: I was going to make it. I was going to be the best teacher possible. I remember standing there thinking, I studied mitochondria, ecosystems, anatomy, physiology, biomechanics, and genetics - not circle time and phonics'. Plus, the last time I did phonics was in French Immersion! How on earth would I reach these little ones???

Luckily, my childhood "teddy bear classroom" instincts and little league coaching kicked in and took over my university training. With limited technology and no access to online resources, I would scan the book, roll out my giant projector, whose ancient, rambunctious wheels could be heard from miles away when it was being rolled along, and I would fire up my beat-up university laptop. I'd loudly announce, "Turn to page 35," only to realize that some of these kids didn't even know how to recognize numbers past 20 yet!

So, I learned to be creative - scanning books to be projected on the board to help the students flip pages, I would find, sometimes invent or create songs, videos, jingles and dances… Anything to get my students to learn. I was improving day by day. And just as I began finding my rhythm amidst the chaos of phonics, finger counting, developing a daily math fluency booklet and teaching the five senses, our next challenge arrived - International Day. My class was assigned the country of Turkey… Another language and another culture to learn and teach! To my amazement, all 24 of my students learned to count in Turkish, and I took pride in having completed my first feat of the year successfully.

Then came the class production: A Jungle Story. Amidst the animal costumes and chaos, songs and lines, I found myself building confidence in my students as they not only spoke but also acted and danced on stage — in front of a crowd of parents with Samsung and Sony digital cameras.

They say the first five years of teaching are the hardest (Lindqvist et al., 2014; Ávalos & Valenzuela, 2016). They couldn't have been more right. Two years into teaching Grade 1, I was burned out and didn't think I could face another group of six-year-olds or their parents again. Instead of celebrating my students' firsts — their first reading success, first concert, first sentences - I kept lists of what they should be doing. I was exhausted emotionally, mentally, and creatively. I was done. It wasn't the teaching I had trained for, nor the environment I had envisioned. I felt displaced, as if I had arrived at the proposed intended final stop, but I had gotten on the wrong flight that took me to a parallel dimension of my original target destination.

I used to tell myself in the past, "I don't do little kids!" and I truly believed that. But here I was, teaching grade one and adding to that, in a new country, with a new dialect, and a completely new culture. I dove in and tried to sail the waves; nothing was going to stop me from being that teacher I dreamt of. I refused to give up. Deep down, I knew I just needed to keep my foot in the door. There had to be light at the end of the tunnel, if only I could be patient enough. So rather than crumble and become another statistic of the "first-five-year syndrome," I seized every opportunity to show that I could teach science.

Being young did have its perks - I was naïve enough to believe that with hard work and willpower, I could make the transition from Grade 1 to middle school Science. I ensured that all my classroom observations took place during science lessons. I stayed late preparing creative demonstrations on the rock cycle and minerals, plant life cycles, and all about the five senses - showcasing creativity in lesson planning and delivery, hoping someone would notice.

And slowly, they did. Along the way, I discovered that I was not much of a risk-taker. I had what I call a "baby boomer workhorse mindset" - steady, loyal, and committed. Rather than looking for the next opportunity elsewhere, I kept investing in the one in front of me - staying late, taking on new responsibilities, and waiting patiently for doors to open.

So, I stayed. I got married, started my family, put my kids in the same school I was teaching at, and I kept going. At times, I compared their childhoods with mine, and I worried they were not getting the same carefree experiences. But over time, those comparisons faded. I found myself paying less attention to what was missing and more attention to the life we were building.

Eventually, I got my breakthrough - Grade 5 and 6 Science. My third year of teaching was about to begin, and I was finally stepping into the world I had dreamt of since I was twelve. From there, my "Go big or go home" attitude carried me through the years - to teaching Grade 12 Biology, becoming a team lead, and eventually a Head of Department building curricula.

Looking back, it might seem like I climbed the ladder quickly - but those years were filled with exhaustion, long nights, and fear. Yes, fear…Fear of quitting. Fear of underperforming. Fear of standing in front of my students and not reaching them. Fear became my fuel. It kept me preparing, revising lessons, and showing up the next day determined to do better. It drove me to become better but to also continue questioning myself - my decisions, my career, my impact.

The good teachers inspired me to be like them. The bad ones pushed me to fix the wrongs I had experienced as a student. Beneath it all was a deep desire to make a difference - to "be the change I wish to see in the world" (the phrase attributed to Mahatma Gandhi: as cited in Phillips, 2021). Now, decades later, I still wonder: Have I been that change? I may not have made the sweeping change I once imagined, but over the years I began to appreciate the impact that unfolds one student at a time.

A few years into being a Head of Department, I decided to pursue my Master's - and that is when I met Dr. De Bello, a jolly man who had been in education longer than I had been alive! Seeing his continued passion reminded me that there is more to teaching than what I was perceiving. Dr. De Bello was a breath of fresh air on my teaching journey. His courses came at a time when I was questioning everything: What else is there? Am I on the right path? Have I reached my goal? Is teaching just burnout and self-doubt?

Dr. De Bello's classes were rooted in reflection and connecting educators from around the world. One week we were discussing classroom challenges in Kuwait; the next, we were hearing from educators working in entirely different systems. Despite the distance, many of the same questions kept surfacing. Each discussion left me with new ideas to test in my own classroom. As my career progressed and I stepped into new roles, I found myself drawing on those conversations. Each position brought challenges and lessons I hadn't anticipated, and I approached them with a renewed sense of curiosity and purpose.

My teaching practices broadened, and I experimented with countless approaches - from traditional instruction and jigsaw learning to skits, differentiation, and even clown performances. What worked for one group didn't always work for another. I developed a habit of reflecting on lessons after they ended—asking what worked, what didn't, and what I would do differently next time. That habit stayed with me, shaping how I approached every new class, curriculum, and leadership role.

Teaching biology became more than a career; it became part of who I am. On the first day of class, I would tell my students, "Everything is biology." They laughed at first, but eventually they understood. The rewards came years later, when one student sent me a picture of his IV from the hospital and asked, "Hey Miss, isotonic, hypotonic, or hypertonic?" Former students - now doctors and parents - still stop me to sing "enzyme, enzyme, gotta catalyze reactions!" and call me "the enzyme that catalyzed their career path." It is in moments like these that I am reminded that teachers rarely see the full impact of their work, but only in ripples through time and chance meetings does it become apparent.

Then came COVID. Moving from the physical classroom to online Zoom was both intimidating and exciting. I still remember that first online class, filled with silent screens, uncertain faces, and the question, "Can you hear me?"

I was determined to keep my students connected. Those challenging months pushed me to become more than a teacher - I became a coach, troubleshooter, and motivator. Most importantly, they changed the way I viewed education. It became a conversation rather than a monologue.

Even now, I often ask myself, was my tunnel vision at twelve the right strategy? And every time, I come full circle and realize - this is exactly where I was meant to be. After teaching every science course under the sun - from Grade 4 to 12 - serving as Head of Department, I grew to be a Vice Principal. I can say the journey has been turbulent, but I wouldn't trade it for anything.

Leaving the classroom to become a Vice Principal did not end my teaching journey - it revolutionized it. I learned that teaching is not only what happens between a teacher and students; it is the shared effort of an entire community. As the African Proverb says, "It takes a village to raise a child," and to that I'd say, it also takes a community standing behind teachers and students to make learning possible.

Do I miss the classroom? Sometimes. The laughter, the "aha" moments, and the excitement when an experiment worked still tug at my heart. However, I now see teaching through a broader lens. Education does not stop at the classroom door; it is the work of a community. An educator, in the truest sense, is not someone who teaches but someone who guides, illuminates, and ignites curiosity. Maybe that 12-year-old girl with her teddy bears was onto something - she knew that teaching wasn't just about lessons. It was about the connection, the passion, the patience, and never giving up on learning - no matter how grown up we get.

When I think about the future of teaching - about AI, technology, and all the innovations still to come - I'm not worried about the profession disappearing. No matter where you are in the world, what era you live in, or what generation you belong to, teaching has always been defined by its humanity. Technology can give instant feedback, track progress, and monitor performance with incredible precision. AI can support learning in powerful ways. But it cannot replace the human connection at the heart of education, the community and humanity we all so carefully harness.

An educator sees more than data. We notice the quiet student who's struggling, the spark of confidence when understanding clicks, the emotions behind behavior, and the encouragement a learner needs at just the right moment. That empathy, that presence, that belief in another human being, those are things no algorithm can truly replicate. As the world advances, I believe the role of the teacher becomes even more important in the classroom. Technology can never replace the emotional connection between a teacher and the students being taught. Teaching will always be about people first, and that is what makes this profession timeless and irreplaceable.

So, if you ever find yourself doubting your path, remember - you're not alone on this journey. The education community is vast and deeply connected. Someone out there shares your story, your struggle, and your hope.

Look for the light. And when you find it, let your flame illuminate someone else's path. Because the journey may start with you, but it never ends there.

Omar's Story: A Journey of Constant Growth

When people imagine teachers, they often picture individuals who dreamed of the classroom from a young age - people who spent their childhood lining up imaginary students, writing pretend grades, or explaining concepts to siblings whether they wanted to listen or not. My own path could not have been more different. I did not walk into education because I planned it, prepared for it, or even considered it. In fact, teaching first came into my life as an accident. Or, perhaps more accurately, teaching arrived at a time when I was lost, unsure of my direction, and desperately searching for the next step. What I thought was a detour turned out to be the road I was meant to take.

Part of what shaped my path was the unique mix of places that formed my identity. I was born in Italy, grew up in Canada, and come from a Somali family. Those three worlds - East African, European, and North American - blended into how I see people, community, and learning. Moving between cultures taught me to be adaptable, empathetic, and aware that people's experiences shape their needs in ways you don't always see at first glance. That background has influenced my teaching more than I ever realized. I have been a middle school science teacher in Kuwait since 2014, but the roots of that journey trace back to my undergraduate years studying microbiology. At that time, I was determined - almost single-mindedly focused - on pursuing a career in laboratory science. I imagined myself working in a sterile lab environment doing quality control or quality assurance, contributing to public safety, product development, or clinical research. My bachelor's degree in microbiology was my ticket into that world, or so I believed. But reality did what it often does: it challenged my expectations.

The job market was tight, and I quickly found that getting into the field was much more difficult than I anticipated. Week after week, I searched for opportunities. I updated résumés, filled out applications, sent emails, and waited. Nothing moved. With each rejection, I felt a deeper sense of frustration and uncertainty. There is a unique type of discouragement that comes from feeling prepared but unwanted, qualified yet invisible. I was caught in that space, unsure of what to do next. One day, in the middle of this confusion, I decided to visit my former college professor to ask him for a reference. I thought that having his recommendation might give my job search the push it needed. I walked into his office expecting nothing more than a conversation and perhaps a signed letter. Instead, his response changed the trajectory of my life. "We're hiring," he said. I immediately assumed he meant the laboratory preparation room - some technical or support position connected to the department. It made sense. I had the background. I had the familiarity. It would be a way to stay connected to science while continuing my job search. But that wasn't what he meant. He meant teaching.

The idea stunned me. I remember sitting there, confused and almost uncomfortable at the thought. Teaching? Me? I was a science graduate who preferred microscopes to microphones, petri dishes to presentations. I had never imagined myself at the front of a classroom explaining scientific concepts to a group of students. My professor saw the hesitation on my face and reassured me. "You would be teaching material you already know," he said. "You would be helping students excel at things you already excel in." His confidence in my ability was both comforting and intimidating. I walked out of that office with a mixture of curiosity, fear, and a strange sense of possibility. I did not know what to do, but then a question came to mind: What do I have to lose? In the absence of other opportunities, perhaps I should try. Perhaps this accident was not as random as it seemed. So I decided to go for it. The first month was a period of intense observation. I shadowed my professor - now my mentor - and closely watched his teaching style. What surprised me most was how effortless he made it appear. His lessons were filled with humor; his classroom echoed with laughter and smiles. Students were relaxed yet engaged, focused yet joyful. I realized that he wasn't simply teaching science - he was teaching people. He was forming connections, inspiring curiosity, and nurturing confidence. His approach was human, warm, and alive. I studied how he paced lessons, how he handled misunderstandings, and how he created an environment where students felt safe to make mistakes. Even now, years later, I continually reflect on that experience. Much of my own teaching style is shaped by those early observations. Humor has become part of my classroom language. I've learned that students learn best when they feel comfortable, welcomed, and valued. That lesson remains with me. I ended up working at that college for three years, and I loved every minute of it. Those years were filled with personal growth, professional discovery, and a deepening sense of purpose. Somewhere along the way, amid the labs, lectures, and laughter, I realized something important: teaching was not a temporary solution or a placeholder job. It was my calling. With this newfound clarity, I began searching for international teaching opportunities. I wanted to broaden my experiences, challenge myself, and truly commit to this profession. Unfortunately, the college I was working at was not hiring permanent positions, so I knew I had to seek opportunities elsewhere. After a year and a half of searching, interviewing, and waiting, I finally received an offer to teach in Kuwait. I accepted the job with excitement and optimism - but I had no idea what awaited me. My first year in Kuwait was… eye-opening, to say the least. I quickly realized that teaching children is far different from teaching adults. The shift was so dramatic that it felt like entering an entirely new profession. My previous experience had not prepared me for the complexities of middle school students - their energy, their unpredictability, their emotions, their restlessness, and their need for structure and boundaries. Every day, for the first month, I thought about quitting. I struggled with classroom management. I struggled with redirecting behavior. I struggled with maintaining control without losing my patience. I had come from a world where students sat quietly, took notes, and listened. Suddenly, I was in a world where classroom management was not just a skill - it was a necessity for survival. I felt overwhelmed, unprepared, and sometimes even defeated. On top of that, I did not speak Arabic, which made everything more complicated. Simple misunderstandings became major challenges. Students would express themselves in ways I didn't fully grasp, and I would struggle to interpret their emotions and needs. The language barrier magnified my fear of failing them and made me feel like an outsider in my own classroom. But what kept me going were the people around me. Staff members who shared their experience and advice. Colleagues who arrived in Kuwait with me and understood what I was going through. Friends who helped me navigate the challenges of adjusting to a new country and a new teaching environment. They supported me back to my feet every time I stumbled. Most importantly, I realized how little I truly understood about teaching. Knowledge of content is not the same as knowledge of pedagogy. I knew science, but I did not yet know how to teach science to young learners in a way that was structured, engaging, and developmentally appropriate. I knew how to communicate facts, but not how to inspire curiosity in a room full of twelve-year-olds who wanted to talk, move, joke, and test limits. So I decided to learn. Truly learn. That first year became a year of listening, absorbing, and humbling myself. I spent hours with experienced teachers, asking questions, seeking feedback, and watching their lessons. I learned strategies for engagement, methods for structuring lessons, and approaches to classroom management. I learned how to connect with students without sacrificing authority. I learned how to balance warmth with structure, and flexibility with consistency. By the time my second year came around, everything felt different. I was more confident, more prepared, and more aware of what my students needed from me. And in that transformation, I discovered something profound: teaching is not a profession where you ever truly "arrive." It is a journey of constant growth. Every year, every class, every student teaches you something new. The moment you stop learning is the moment your teaching begins to weaken. My dedication to learning carried me forward into new opportunities for professional development. After several years of growing in the classroom, I pursued my master's degree in educational leadership. It was during this program that I had the privilege of meeting Dr. Tom De Bello. One of the most influential concepts I learned from him was the philosophy of holistic teaching - also known as educating the "whole child." This approach emphasizes that students are not simply academic beings; they are emotional, social, physical, and moral beings as well. The whole-child framework recognizes that intellectual growth cannot be separated from well-being, identity, relationships, and a sense of belonging. A student may excel academically but struggle emotionally, or succeed socially yet feel unseen in the classroom. Holistic teaching reminds educators that learning becomes meaningful only when all parts of a child are nurtured. It reframed how I saw my role - not just as a science teacher, but as someone responsible for supporting the full development of the young people in my classroom.

That idea deeply resonated with me and continues to influence the way I teach. It pushed me to think beyond test scores and content mastery. It encouraged me to look at students as individuals with stories, strengths, vulnerabilities, and potential. It taught me to ask not only "What are they learning?" but also "Who are they becoming?" A few years later, I pursued my teaching license, which required me to record and submit lessons for evaluation. This process challenged me to reflect even more deeply on my teaching practices. Watching myself teach - seeing the things I did well and the things I needed to improve. But the feedback I received was invaluable. It reaffirmed my strengths, highlighted my blind spots, and pushed me to become more intentional, reflective, and effective in the classroom. Looking back, the journey from microbiology graduate to middle school science teacher seems almost unbelievable. I entered the field by accident, unsure and unprepared. But with every step, every challenge, every student, and every mentor, I discovered more of what it means to be an educator. Teaching became not only my career, but my identity. Today, more than a decade after stepping into my first classroom, I still feel that sense of purpose. Teaching continues to surprise me, challenge me, and fulfill me in ways no laboratory job ever could have. Every year brings new students with new personalities, new questions, new stories, and new opportunities for growth. And with each group, I learn something new - not just about them, but also about myself. Looking back on my journey, I've come to understand something deeper about the teaching profession itself. I've come to understand that teaching is no longer just about delivering content - it's about connection, adaptability, and continuous growth. I entered the profession believing that strong subject knowledge was enough, but experience quickly taught me otherwise. What truly matters is understanding students as people and creating an environment where they feel safe, supported, and willing to take risks. I believe the future of teaching will demand even more empathy, flexibility, and cultural awareness, as classrooms are becoming increasingly diverse. It will be more difficult, but at the same time more exciting. My experiences have shown me that students learn best when they trust their teacher, and that trust is built through consistency, care, and genuine human connection. When it comes to AI, I don't see it as a threat to our profession, but as a tool. AI can support planning, organization, and access to information, but it can never replace the human side of teaching—the relationships, the emotional awareness, and the ability to truly understand students. If anything, AI will push teachers to focus more on what matters most: mentoring, guiding, and supporting students as whole individuals. If there is one thing my journey has taught me, it is that education is a living, breathing profession. You never truly master it, because the world keeps changing, students keep changing, and you must keep changing with them. Teaching requires humility, curiosity, resilience, and above all, heart. It demands that you keep learning - not for yourself alone, but for the students who look to you for guidance, understanding, and inspiration.

What started as an accidental career has become one of the greatest blessings of my life. It has taken me across borders, introduced me to incredible mentors and colleagues, and connected me with students who have shaped my worldview. It has shown me moments of frustration and moments of joy, moments of doubt and moments of absolute clarity. But through it all, teaching has remained a constant source of meaning and purpose. And the journey is far from over. I look forward to the years ahead - the new classrooms, the new ideas, the new challenges, and the new stories that will unfold. If the past decade has taught me anything, it's that the most unexpected paths often lead to the most fulfilling destinations. I cannot wait to see where this path takes me next.

Sara's Story: Shaping Minds Before Constructing Buildings

I began my professional journey in civil engineering. I chose this field because my father owned a construction company, and the initial plan was for me to work in the company. However, life took an unexpected turn. Shortly after graduating, personal circumstances beyond my control made it difficult for me to continue in field-based work. I found myself searching for a meaningful way to remain productive and contributive despite these limitations. During that period, I noticed that there was a teaching position available at Al-Ruya Bilingual School as a Life Skills teacher. The role seemed both purposeful and suitable for my circumstances. Once I entered the classroom, I discovered an unexpected sense of fulfillment. I quickly realized the depth of influence a teacher's words, presence, and instructional choices can have on students. Teaching revealed itself not merely as a profession, but as a powerful means of shaping lives. Fortunately, the Life Skills curriculum at the school was strong and well-designed, and it supported my growth by allowing space for creativity and meaningful engagement in my teaching.

What affected me most was the emotional dimension of teaching. Some of the most meaningful moments in my career emerged through students' reflections and responses. A student would say, "This lesson changed something in me," or "This topic really affected the way I behave," or "You changed the way I think about this."

Even at the end of the year, students would express sentiments such as, "This was the subject that had the greatest impact on me," or "You're the best teacher we've ever had." These statements were deeply impactful, reinforcing my belief that education extends far beyond curriculum delivery; it is about emotional engagement, personal growth, and lasting influence.

One particular experience remains especially vivid in my memory. A student in my class was withdrawn, emotionally distressed, and unwilling to communicate verbally with anyone. Rather than forcing dialogue, I introduced a simple reflective practice at the beginning of each lesson: personal diary writing. She was encouraged to write freely about her thoughts, concerns, and emotions, and I responded thoughtfully in writing. There was no spoken interaction - only silent communication through reflection and written response. Over time, this simple strategy helped her regain emotional balance. She later shared with me that she had been frustrated, and that this silent form of connection had helped resolve significant personal struggles. This experience reaffirmed my belief that small, compassionate human interventions can have a profound emotional and educational impact.

Motivated by these experiences, I committed myself to continuous professional development. I pursued a Diploma in Effective Teaching and participated in numerous workshops focused on instructional strategies, pedagogical practices, and school management. This was followed by the completion of a Master's degree in Multidisciplinary Science from Buffalo State University. Throughout this process, I remained guided by my own childhood experiences - particularly my struggle with concentration and my desire for learning environments that were engaging, inclusive, and responsive.

These experiences shaped my educational philosophy as both a teacher and an administrator. I consistently sought to reach every student, especially those who struggled to maintain focus or engagement. When a student appeared distracted, I did not interpret it as a lack of ability or motivation, but rather as a signal to adjust my instructional approach. As an administrator, I emphasized to teachers that true instructional success lies not in engaging only the visibly responsive students at the front of the classroom, but in reaching all students - especially those at the back, the quiet, the distracted, or the seemingly disengaged - and enabling them to connect meaningfully with the lesson.

Conversations with former engineering colleagues often highlighted the contrast between my professional paths. They would ask, sometimes with surprise:

"You were an engineer- how did you become a teacher? That's such a significant career shift."

My response was always clear: "Engineers build structures, but teachers build human beings. There is a fundamental difference between constructing buildings and shaping people. When individuals are developed thoughtfully and effectively, they become capable of building anything in the world."

Ultimately, I believe that effective teaching is grounded in human connection - care, empathy, and emotional presence. Authentic learning cannot occur in the absence of these elements. When students feel genuinely valued and supported, they engage more deeply, reflect meaningfully, and internalize what they learn. Reflection transforms information into understanding, and understanding into personal growth. This reflective process lies at the heart of true education.

For this reason, I find it difficult to envision artificial intelligence fully replacing the role of the teacher. While technology can enhance and support learning, it cannot replicate human care, emotional awareness, or relational trust. Education is not simply the transmission of knowledge; it is the transformation of the learner. That transformation remains, at its core, a deeply human connection.

REFERENCES

Al-Senafi, B., & Alsabbagh, S. (2024). An educational history of Kuwait: A focus on schools. *Study in English Language Teaching*, *12*(3), 44–54. DOI: 10.22158/selt.v12n3p44

Aleisa, E., Al-Asfour, A., Alkandari, A., Alhashem, F., Alfailakawi, A., & Alhouti, L. (2021). *From Here We Shall Set Sail: A national initiative to reform and advance education in Kuwait* [In Arabic: Min Hena Nabhur]. 1st ed.). Kuwait City.

AlQenaei, Z. M., Khalil, O., & Aldekheel, A. Y. (2021). Integrating information technology in precollege education in Kuwait: Teachers' perspectives on a botched initiative. *Journal of Information Technology Education*, *20*, 529–558. DOI: 10.28945/4890

American University of Kuwait. (n.d.). Who we are. https://www.auk.edu.kw/

Ávalos, B., & Valenzuela, J. P. (2016). Education for all and attrition/retention of new teachers: A trajectory study in Chile. *International Journal of Educational Development*, *49*, 279–290. DOI: 10.1016/j.ijedudev.2016.03.012

Cochrane, L., Al-Mohannadi, D., Aleisa, E., & Al Nasiri, N. (2026). The Arabian peninsula at the forefront of climate change - setting the research agenda. *Frontiers in Sustainability*, *7*, 1833682. DOI: 10.3389/frsus.2026.1833682

Government of Kuwait. (2017). Kuwait Vision 2035: New Kuwait. General Secretariat of the Supreme Council for Planning and Development. Retrieved from https://www.mofa.gov.kw/en/pages/kuwait-vision-2035

Gulf University for Science and Technology. (n.d.). Your journey begins at GUST: Preparing you for success. https://www.gust.edu.kw/home

Hafsyan, A. S. M. (2023). Gifted education in the State of Kuwait: Review from a learning-resource perspective. *Cogent Education*, *10*(1), 2224518. Advance online publication. DOI: 10.1080/2331186X.2023.2224518

Karkouti, I. M. (2023). Integrating technology in Qatar's higher education settings: What helps faculty accomplish the job. Technology. *Knowledge and Learning*, *28*(1), 279–305. DOI: 10.1007/s10758-021-09553-y

Kuwait Times. (2023, September 30). Ministry organizes program to enhance teachers' performance. Retrieved from https://kuwaittimes.com/article/19546/kuwait/other-news/ministry-organizes-program-to-enhance-teachers-performance/

Kuwait Times. (2026, February 12). Ministry of Education reaffirms commitment to Arabic language. Retrieved from https://kuwaittimes.com/article/39787/kuwait/other-news/ministry-of-education-reaffirms-commitment-to-arabic-language/

Kuwait University. (n.d.). About Kuwait University. Retrieved from https://www.ku.edu.kw/about-us/about-kuwait-university

Kuwait University College of Education. (n.d.). About the College of Education. Retrieved from https://edu.ku.edu.kw/about

Lindqvist, P., Nordänger, U. K., & Carlsson, R. (2014). Teacher attrition the first five years – A multifaceted image. *Teaching and Teacher Education*, *40*, 94–103. DOI: 10.1016/j.tate.2014.02.005

Public Authority for Applied Education and Training (PAAET). (2024). About PAAET and academic programs. from https://www.paaet.edu.kw/en/main/overview-the-public-authority/

Phillips, J. L. (2021, February 24). Origin story: Be the change. https://jenniferlphillips.com/blog/2021/2/24/origin-story-be-the-change

The Borgen Project. (n.d.). Education in Kuwait. Retrieved from https://borgenproject.org/education-in-kuwait/

TIMSS. (2023a). Kuwait. Retrieved from https://timss2023.org/wp-content/uploads/2024/10/Kuwait.pdf

TIMSS. (2023b). Exhibit D.3: Percentiles of Mathematics Achievement (Grade 8). Exhibit D.4: Percentiles of Science Achievement (Grade 8). https://timss2023.org/results/appendices/

UNESCO. (2006). Kuwait: Early childhood care and education (ECCE) programs. https://unesdoc.unesco.org/ark:/48223/pf0000147218

Chapter 16
Teachers' Voices From Qatar

Riyam Chaar
http://orcid.org/0009-0009-5780-3174
Arkansas State University, Qatar

Manal Mostapha
Heritage International Academy, Qatar

Caroline Tomossian
Global Academy International, Qatar

ABSTRACT

Social stability, economic expansion, and national progress are all fundamentally influenced by education. The State of Qatar has made education a key pillar in line with Qatar National Vision 2030. Over the past 20 years, the system has evolved from mostly conventional models to one that is benchmarked globally. The following aspects are examined in this essay: the historical transition from informal learning to formal government schooling paths into the teaching profession, including academic credentials and regulatory obligations; the structure and stages of the current education system; the income and employment benefits of educators and professors; significant national accomplishments; and a professional perspective based on lived experience. Overall, the analysis portrays Qatar's educational system as a quickly evolving model that seeks to strike a compromise between cultural and linguistic preservation and global competitiveness.

EDUCATION IN QATAR

Riyam Chaar

Introduction

Education is the source of social stability, economic growth and the basic pillar for any nation's rise. The State of Qatar has placed education as a strategic national priority and a central pillar of development, as articulated in Qatar National Vision 2030 (Ehsan, 2025) Over the past 20 years Qatar has shifted the education system from the traditional approach to an internationally benchmarked system that balances global standards with the preservation of national identity.

This essay will demonstrate in detail education in Qatar, as it will cover six interconnected areas: the historical development of education, pathways to becoming a teacher, the structure of the education system, teacher and lecturer income, major achievements of the Qatari education sector, and a personal professional viewpoint grounded in lived experience.

DOI: 10.4018/979-8-3373-8983-7.ch016

Historical development of education in Qatar

Traditional and Informal Education

Education in Qatar before the mid-twentieth century was informal, not uniform and focused mainly on learning religion. Quranic schools named Kuttab were the primary source of education, accompanied by family instruction, apprenticeships, and everyday social practices that reflected the cultural, economic, and religious life of Qatari society. The Kuttab was the most popular type of regular schooling. These were modest learning places, sometimes housed in mosques or private homes, where children - usually boys - were instructed by a religious instructor known as a mutawa'a or mu'allim. Mutawa'a's teaching was mainly based on Qur'an memorization, basic reading and writing in Arabic, simple arithmetic, and moral education rooted in Islamic values. Instructional strategies depended on rote learning, repetition, and recitation, with a strong emphasis on discipline and respect for elders (Nasser, 2017).

As mentioned earlier, education was not structured or uniform; it differed greatly based on gender, family background, and geographic location. Girls, unlike boys, were not allowed access to Kuttab; instead, they received home instruction and acquired religious concepts as well as household practices from their mothers or other female relatives. However, some girls who were of capable families that believed in the importance of education received literacy education (Al-Qadi, 2021).

While girls were supposed to practice domestic tasks at home with their families, boys were meant to learn the profession of their fathers; they acquired pearling, fishing, trade, and craftsmanship from their fathers and other male figures around them. This kind of practical learning or learning by doing was in place to prepare children to be responsible adults in their communities (Fromherz, 2012).

These early educational practices played a pivotal role in maintaining Arabic language proficiency, religious identity, and cultural values. Education was seen as a moral and social responsibility rather than a state system.

Emergence of Formal Schooling

The mid-twentieth century marked a turning point in Qatar's education. The discovery of oil led to a speedy economic progress, eventually affecting the education system. As a matter of fact, the first government school for boys was established in 1952. The Qatari government, under the leadership of Sheikh Ali bin Abdullah Al Thani, has founded the Al-Athariyya School in Doha for boys. This initiative was also followed by another where a school for girls was set up. This marked a transformation of the old, previously traditional, unstructured approach toward an institutionalized education. With this shift, the government also made schooling free of charge and accessible to the population (Nasser, 2017).

Between the 1960s and the 1970s, the education sector expanded rapidly; many teacher training institutes were formed, curricula were standardized, and administrative offices were developed under the Ministry of Education. Education became obligatory at the elementary level, reflecting the state's devotion to literacy, social movement, human capital growth, and national progress (Qatar National Library, 2020; MOEHE, 2018).

Qatar Education System Nowadays

Qatar has a well-established and robust education system that offers a wide range of schooling options, including public, private, and embassy schools. These schools follow diverse curricula such as the National Curriculum, International Baccalaureate (IB), American, and British programs, providing expatriate families with multiple educational choices. The Ministry of Education and Higher Education (MOEHE) has mandated a national values program and unified the curriculum for three compulsory subjects - Arabic, Islamic Studies, and Qatar History - across all schools to preserve the mother tongue and national heritage.

Qatari schools are monitored by frequent inspections, national accreditation systems such as QNQA/QNSA, and, in many instances, foreign accreditation agencies such as Western Association of Schools and Colleges (WASC), Cognia, and the foreign Baccalaureate. These inspections are carried out to ensure that academic standards are being met.

Accountability, continual progress, and conformity with international standards are all promoted by these processes (UNESCO, 2021).

In addition, the Ministry requires schools to upload student assessment data to the national learning management system, ensuring continuity, data security, and quality assurance.

All of these procedures taken by the State of Qatar convey Qatar's dedication to quality education and coincide with its national vision 2030 (General Secretariat for Development Planning, 2008) of building a solid, knowledgeable, skilled, and globally competitive society.

Educational Stages

The stages of Qatar educational system are as follows:

- Early childhood education: kindergarten (KG1–KG2)
- Primary education: grades 1–6
- Preparatory education: grades 7–9
- Secondary education: grades 10–12
- Higher education: universities and colleges

This structure ensures a comprehensible progression of learning and skill development in students across years (MoEHE, n.d.). Universities and colleges in Qatar serve not only the citizens of the country but also international students, especially from the Gulf region. Besides the major higher education institution – Qatar University - there are 27 public and private universities and colleges.

Pathways to Becoming a Teacher in Qatar

Academic and Professional Qualifications

There are several routes that would qualify a candidate to be a teacher in Qatar. The traditional approach requires having a Bachelor of Education (B.Ed.) degree, which assures that teachers are equipped with the essential pedagogical knowledge as well as subject specialization. This path complies with the international models used (Romanowski & Nasser, 2012).

Another route to become a teacher would require candidates who hold a Bachelor's degrees in disciplines other than education to attain teaching diplomas or qualifications such as Postgraduate Certificate in Education (PGCE) or the Postgraduate Diploma in Education (PGDE). Such diplomas ensure preparing candidates with the skills needed to transition into the teaching profession (Ellili-Cherif & Romanowski, 2013).

Additionally, the Ministry of Education and Higher Education (MoEHE) in Qatar has also set a Professional Licensing System (PLS). This system determines professional standards where teachers are said to show specific competencies, qualifications, and performance levels to obtain and maintain their licenses (MoEHE, 2023).

Applicants who are to be hired in the government schools should be proficient in the use of computers as they should complete the required assessments and interviews. They should be having an experience ranging between 3 to 5 years depending whether they were graduates from Qatar or foreign countries. Candidates must submit verified academic credentials, identification documents, and experience certificates and are appointed according to the Ministry's employment regulations (Ministry of Education and Higher Education, 2022).

Individuals who aim at having a position as a lecturer at higher education are required to have a Master's degree, whereas assistant professors and senior academics must hold a doctoral degree, research experience, and a record of scholarly publication (Qatar University, n.d.).

Regulatory and Legal Requirements

As per the regulatory requirements, teachers are supposed to submit these documents: attested academic certificates and transcripts, a CV, a passport copy, an experience letter, police clearance, medical fitness certification, and an approval from the Ministry of Education and Higher Education (MoEHE). These documents guarantee professionalism, safeguarding, and compliance with national education policies (MoEHE, 2023).

Teacher and Lecturer Income in Qatar

Qatar's focus on appointing qualified teachers has led it to allocate competitive salaries compared to the region. Monthly salaries for school teachers typically range between QAR 8,000 (around US$ 2,000 and QAR 15,000 (around US$4,000), depending on experience, qualifications, and school type. Adding to the monthly salaries, educators receive multiple benefits such as accommodation, transportation, health insurance, annual airfare, and end-of-service gratuity. University lecturers receive higher salaries ranging between QAR 15,000 (around US 4,000) and QAR 25,000 (around US $7,000) per month, while senior professors can earn up to QAR 30,000 (around US $ 8,000) or more, depending on rank and organization (Teach Across Asia, 2025).

Achievements of Education in Qatar

Education City and Global Engagement

An outstanding educational achievement in the State of Qatar is that of the establishment of Education City, which hosts branch campuses of leading international universities. This initiative has positioned Qatar as a regional hub for higher education and research, attracting students and scholars from around the world (Qatar Foundation, 2022). Universities in the educational city offer a range of internationally accredited programs with diverse disciplines (Qatar Foundation, n.d.).

The universities affiliated with Qatar Foundation in Education City are:

1. Hamad Bin Khalifa University (HBKU)
2. Weill Cornell Medicine – Qatar
3. Texas A&M University at Qatar
4. Carnegie Mellon University in Qatar
5. Georgetown University in Qatar
6. Northwestern University in Qatar
7. Virginia Commonwealth University School of the Arts in Qatar (VCUarts Qatar)
8. HEC Paris in Qatar

This establishment is a flagship initiative that positioned Qatar as a local and global center for higher education, research, and innovation.

Quality Assurance and Values Education

In 2018, the Department of Evaluation and School Accreditation at the Ministry of Education and Higher Education (MoEHE) officially started the Qatar National School Accreditation (QNSA) framework. This initiative has mandated accreditation for all private schools in the same way as it constituted a system of accountability for public schools. This system introduced structured accreditation cycles, regular inspections, and compliance monitoring to ensure consistency and educational quality nationwide.

Adding to that, another milestone in Qatar's achievement was the launching of the Values Education program, which was imposed by MoEHE's Curriculum Standards and Teaching Resources Department in 2019 and targeted implementing citizenship, ethics, Islamic values, national identity, and social responsibility across all schools. All of these frameworks of quality assurance and civic education have set Qatar as a landmark in education, seeking continuous development and enhancement toward quality education, emphasizing both academic excellence and societal values (Qatar News Agency, 2021).

Qatar's Most Recent Achievements in Education

Another recent achievement for Qatar was the record that Qatar has registered in the Global Knowledge Index, where in 2023 the country ranked 39th out of 133 countries demonstrating an enhanced global standing and transition toward a knowledge-based economy.

Significant public investment in education - roughly USD 4.91 billion, or over 9% of all government spending - has backed this success, demonstrating a persistent national commitment to high-quality education across all levels (Qatar Government Communications Office, 2024; United Nations Development Programme, 2023).

Honoring 79 outstanding students, educators, and researchers in the 18th Education Excellence Awards in 2025 was another indicator on the country's approach to recognizing academic achievement, innovation, leadership, and professional excellence within the education sector (The Peninsula Qatar, 2025).

Additionally, the state has performed exceptionally well in educational competitions held at the regional level. The fact that Qatari educators and public schools were able to acquire six honors at the 2025 Hamdan bin Rashid Al Maktoum Award for Distinguished Academic Performance is a clear indication of Qatar's increasing competitiveness and educational excellence on the regional level (Qatar News Agency [QNA], 2025).

At the policy level, the Ministry of Education and Higher Education (MOEHE) unveiled its 2024–2030 Strategic Plan, Igniting the Spark of Learning, in late 2024. The plan emphasizes curriculum development, quality assurance, capacity building, and better student outcomes in all areas of education. A methodical, long-term strategy to improving educational quality across the country is reflected in this strategic framework (MOEHE, 2024).

Qatar has reaffirmed its commitment to actively supporting international education initiatives outside of its own borders. Qatar's dedication to accomplishing Sustainable Development Goal 4 (Quality Education) was reiterated in 2024 through national consultations carried out in cooperation with UNESCO and regional partners. According to reports, Qatar has achieved most of the Sustainable Development Goal 4 (SDG 4) goals and metrics through consistent investment in education, cross-sector cooperation, and well-coordinated policy implementation (UNESCO, 2024).

Qatar's Performance in International Standardized Assessments

Qatar's participation in international standardized assessments, such as the Program for International Student Assessment (PISA), the Trends in International Mathematics and Science Study (TIMSS), and the Progress in International Reading Literacy Study (PIRLS) mirror a comprehensive national strategy for assessing educational outcomes against global standards and to drive continuous system-wide improvement. These evaluations are utilized as diagnostic and evaluative instruments for the purpose of directing policy change, design of curriculum, and teacher professional development in accordance with Qatar National Vision 2030 (Ehsan, 2025).

PISA tests 15-year-olds on their reading, math, and science skills. The results show that Qatar's overall score is still less than the OECD average. But trend data show that results continue to improve over time, especially in math and reading, with each testing cycle. These improvements are important because the student body is so diverse linguistically, and compulsory education has just recently been expanded. Qatar has made progress toward enabling more students to attain foundational competency levels, which is an indication that learning outcomes are steadily enhancing. However, the number of high-performing students is still low compared to the best-performing systems (OECD, 2023).

On the other hand, Qatar's results in TIMSS, which assesses students' proficiency in science and math in Grades 4 and 8, show better results, especially in primary school. Qatar's performance in mathematics and science has improved significantly over previous assessment cycles, placing it among the top Arab nations (International Association for the Evaluation of Educational Achievement, 2024). These findings indicate that concentrated curriculum alignment, specific instructional practices, and ongoing investment in enhancing the skills of teachers are producing favorable outcomes. The considerably better TIMSS scores show that timely intervention and organized instructional frameworks yield positive outcomes in lower-grade levels.

Qatar's involvement in PIRLS, which evaluates reading proficiency at the fourth grade level, underscores the country's initiatives to enhance early literacy development. Reading achievement is still an area that needs work, but PIRLS statistics have given us important information on the problems students have acquiring languages and the best ways to teach them, especially in classrooms where students speak more than one language (International Association for the Evaluation of Educational Achievement, 2023). These results have influenced early literacy programs and emphasized the significance of basic reading abilities as a requirement for future academic achievement.

Qatar's performance in worldwide standardized examinations indicates an education system undergoing purposeful reform rather than being static. Global standards like PISA highlight persistent difficulties in higher-order thinking and applied problem-solving, although enhancements in TIMSS and consistent development over time suggest that reform measures are starting to yield quantifiable learning improvements. Qatar views international evaluations not solely as grading tools but also as evidence-based systems that facilitate data-driven decision-making, enhance equity, and improve educational quality across all school sectors (MOEHE, 2023).

Personal Professional Viewpoint

The education system in Qatar reflects a purposeful, future-oriented vision that places equal importance on excellence and identity, as seen from a professional point of view. The Qatari context has provided evidence of how policy frameworks are put into reality through the implementation of accountability mechanisms, regular audits, and professional development programs.

The commitment of Qatar to maintaining local traditions while adhering to international norms is one of the country's most distinguishing characteristics. It is important to recognize that education not only helps students acquire academic skills but also helps them create their identities. This is why the mandated inclusion of Arabic language, Islamic values, and national history is viewed as so important.

As an additional benefit, Qatar provides educators with important professional possibilities, competitive salary, and access to the best practices from around the world. With its emphasis on continuous improvement, Qatar's educational system is positioned to serve as a model for educational reform in the region, despite the fact that challenges still exist, particularly in terms of maintaining innovation and managing rapid growth.

Conclusion

Education in Qatar has developed from informal and traditional learning contexts into an elaborate system that is recognized internationally and is connected with the goals of national development that Qatar has set for itself. Qatar has built an educational paradigm that fosters the development of human resources while simultaneously conserving cultural identity. This model was established via persistent investment, legislative clarity, and strategic change. There is an abundant description showing that the educational system is organized and diversified, educators are recognized and encouraged, and quality assurance procedures promote accountability and growth. The education system will continue to play a pivotal role in the formation of citizens who are educated, skilled, and active in global affairs as Qatar continues to work toward the objectives of Qatar National Vision 2030 (General Secretariat for Development Planning, 2008).

THE TEACHER'S MISSION IS TO TEACH EVERY STUDENT

Riyam Chaar

An American entrepreneur, author, and motivational speaker, Jim Rohn, says, "You are the average of the five people you spend the most time with." This statement truly reflects how I became the teacher I am today. As a matter of fact, in my childhood, I was encircled by grown-ups who believed in the power of knowledge, words, and service to others. These early exposures planted the seeds of my passion for learning and teaching, gradually shaping my character as a teacher.

Becoming a teacher was never a coincidence in my case. The environment in which I was brought up molded my decision and led me to choose teaching as my career path. A flashback to my first memories takes me back to grandma who was among the few educated adults in the neighborhood at that time. In fact, my grandma, "Najah" was a school supervisor and was fond of reading and educating others. She used to call on all the kids in the neighborhood who were from poor families and started teaching them how to read and write. Grandma Najah would make me sit with those kids and learn with them whatever she was covering. My Grandma's love of books was contagious; books became my passion and my way to escape into fairy tales, adventures, biographies, and other genres.

Moving to my aunt from my mom's side, Aunt "Hayat" was also a passionate reader who used to give lessons in religion to ladies in the area. Attending her gatherings used to empower me as I also felt how impactful she was with her words and how her approach motivated women to challenge their battles and cling to faith and patience to overcome the impediments they were facing in their daily struggles. Her approach has inspired me as I recognized the power of words and knowledge and how they can influence others and change their lives for the better.

During my school years, and particularly in grade 8, my parents decided to appoint a tutor to help in my studies, Miss Fadia, who was genuine by all means. I would never forget how Miss Fadia used to pick me up to go study at her home with treats, candies, and chocolate, Chocolate Fingers in specific, in the back seat to reward me at the end of the session. Her small gestures took the relationship with her beyond the experience of teaching. Her belief in my potential and the way she pushed me to achieve is beyond description. The way she blended discussions and play while studying was so amusing that I acquired the sense that teaching and learning are fun experiences and not daunting ones.

Again in grade 11, I had the opportunity to attend classes with an amazing English teacher, Miss Nisreen, who made me fall in love with literature. I used to wait for her classes eagerly, as she explained Shakespeare's plays and William Wordsworth's poems. Surprisingly, this teacher's style of dressing and lifestyle made me driven to want to be like her in the future. She was the perfect example of this quote by an American television, newspaper, and radio journalist and author Charles Kuralt, "Good teachers know how to bring out the best in students", since she drew out my strength, as she always mentioned to my parents that she sees a talent in me.

I don't want to forget my parents' proud remarks when they used to brag about my capabilities, mentioning to our relatives that I was an achiever. These statements that they uttered put me under a responsibility of not putting them down. Besides, my dad, Badih, was a constant reader who would read books of different genres and bring endless conversations to our evenings. All of these members built my eagerness to pursue a degree that qualifies me to teach.

Early in my university years, I got the opportunity to teach vocational baccalaureate students. This experience has put me in a situation where some of my students in the class were even older than me. This encounter has challenged me to sharpen my skills and trained me into varying my styles of instruction to attract different age categories and keep them engaged in class.

Once I was done with my bachelor's degree, I got a teaching position in Doha, Qatar. I left my homeland to start as a grade 4 teacher, which was a totally different experience from the one I had previously. One incident that I will never forget during my first year of teaching was when I asked my students to write a compare-and-contrast paragraph about living in the village and in the city. This task made my students puzzled since in Qatar, there are no villages, making them all fail in the test. This has made me understand that as a teacher, I have to consider the backgrounds of my students and what fits in one country might not be applicable to the other. This has also made me realize that at times when students fail a test, this might not be due to their capacities but to the inappropriate questions or expectations set by the teacher.

Years later, after attaining my master's and doctoral degrees, I held a position as an adjunct professor, where I taught master's candidates pursuing educational leadership. This experience led me to recognize that my role extended beyond teaching, as I continuously learned from the diverse perspectives, professional insights, and real-life leadership experiences that my master's candidates brought into the classroom. Engaging in rich discussions with practicing and aspiring leaders deepened my understanding of educational leadership and reinforced my belief that effective teaching and leadership are mutual processes grounded in shared learning.

When speaking of the challenges of being a teacher, I would like to bring to attention the fact that teaching students from various nationalities is definitely a challenge, since a norm that is acceptable by one nationality might not be acceptable for another. Furthermore, teachers might have students with learning difficulties or even gifts in classes and their mission is to cater to all students' needs. When classes are crowded, tailoring for all these differences becomes a frustrating experience.

When I started teaching in Qatar, for instance, I noticed a wide diversity in my classes with a blend of high achievers and low achievers. I also witnessed that a lot of emphasis was directed toward struggling students, and gifted learners were often neglected. This has caused me, as an English teacher, to find ways to quench the thirst of bright students. I took an individual initiative, and I created a writing enrichment program to nourish the talents of the young writers present in my classes. This program spanned approximately eight months and targeted middle school students who demonstrated a strong aptitude for writing. The selected students participated in hands-on writing sessions that blended experiential learning with literacy development through purposeful excursions and field visits. Throughout the program, students explored a variety of writing genres while visiting key local institutions, including Al Jazeera TV Channel, *The Peninsula Newspaper*, a commercial bank, a sewage treatment plant, Msheireb Museums, and local soap factories.

During these visits, students engaged with industry professionals, keynote speakers, and storytellers, gaining authentic insights that enriched their understanding of audience, purpose, and real-world contexts. Following each experience, students returned to the school setting to write, reflect, and refine their work. This initiative was presented as a key evidence-based practice during the school's accreditation process and was fully implemented as part of the institution's quality assurance framework. This was the PhD project that I did at the International Black Sea University, Georgia. The program received commendation and positive recognition in the accreditation report, highlighting its impact on student engagement, experiential learning, and the development of advanced writing skills. In addition to strengthening students' literacy competencies, the program provided meaningful, lasting learning experiences, with children and their parents expressing high levels of satisfaction.

I would also like to highlight one of the barriers that I personally faced in my career as an English teacher. The fact that I am an Arab and a non-native has prevented me from applying to various jobs in schools because of the misconceptions about the qualifications and competence of English teachers of Arab origin when compared to native speakers.

On the other hand, this profession brings daily rewards. Nothing would make a teacher happier than seeing a low achiever building progress and developing. Seeing once struggling students graduating and heading to universities to start building for their future leaves teachers with a sense of achievement. Parents' praise and words of gratitude are also rewarding and motivate teachers to move on and give their best, despite difficulties and hardships.

The role of teachers extends beyond the delivery of academic content. On the students' level, teachers play a major role in character building, in developing students' skills socially and emotionally, and also in preparing them to face the challenges of tomorrow. Regarding teachers' responsibilities toward parents, it is crucial that teachers maintain transparency and open respectful discussions with them. Teachers ought to help parents and guardians understand their children's progress, strengths, and needs, as teachers should show parents' willingness to support students. At the level of the wider community and society, teachers have the responsibility of exposing students to various community service opportunities. They should equip students to be prepared for the everlasting changes in the future, to accept differences, seek continuous growth, drive change, and play a positive role in societies.

When reflecting on my experiences as a teacher, I would like to mention that all experiences, whether positive or difficult, have contributed to refining my teaching philosophy and strengthening my approach to education. As a teacher, I learned that taking into account students' age, backgrounds, culture, talents, and needs is essential to building profiles of my pupils. These profiles will aid me later on in catering for the various needs and implementing differentiation that best fits each individual difference available in my class. Moreover, I learned that one approach of teaching is not enough, as much as that student-centered learning is emphasized nowadays to promote students' critical thinking, while direct instruction is needed for students with limited abilities. Adding to all that, another key lesson was the significance of relationships and emotional intelligence in education. Strong teacher–student relationships enhance motivation, engagement, and trust. This realization shifted my focus from control and discipline toward guidance, understanding, and restorative practices. My journey over the last 23 years has developed my teaching philosophy grounded on the belief that every student is teachable and that students learn at their own pace. Teachers should utilize empathy, adaptability, and continuous improvement to continue to positively impact students' lives.

As the world advances into the digital era, Qatar is likewise progressing in alignment with Qatar National Vision 2030, which emphasizes innovation, bilingual education, critical thinking, and global citizenship. Within this evolving context, the teaching profession remains the first and most enduring profession and is often regarded as the profession of the prophets, as it is the foundation upon which all other professions are built. While artificial intelligence is reshaping educational practices, it cannot replace teachers, since it does not address character building and value formation - core responsibilities that extend beyond academic instruction. Instead, AI serves as a supportive tool that empowers teachers to meet the demands of a fast-paced world.

Looking back on my journey, I realize that I envision teaching as more than a profession. It is a sacred mission that consists of a mixture of passion blended with empathy, and is focused on creating meaningful impact on the students in particular and society in general. It is a process of continuous learning and evolving and having that growth mindset and adaptability for change, since what would work today might not be fit tomorrow. I also believe that students have various capabilities, and everyone learns at their own pace and teachers shouldn't give up on that, but rather have high expectations and be armed with consistency and optimism to lift students up.

MY TEACHING JOURNEY

Manal Mostapha

Albert Einstein said, "I never teach my pupils, I only attempt to provide the conditions in which they can learn." To become a teacher was my dream. It started when I used to play the role of a teacher with my siblings. I used to ask them to sit down, write in notebooks, correct for them, and use chalk with a small blackboard. Not to forget that I was inspired by lots of great teachers like Mrs. Reem, Mrs. Soad, Mrs. Hadia, and Mrs. Ihsan (Math and English teachers). Since that time, I knew that I would be a teacher and nothing else. So, I finished my high school and headed to join the English Language and Literature Faculty at Beirut Arab University, Lebanon. Those four years were of the best in my life. In the last year, I had to do my observations at schools, so I chose the school where I studied from kindergarten to grade nine and for sure I met some of my teachers. Now I am visiting them as a teacher where they showed great feeling seeing their student as a teacher. I graduated, then moved to live in Qatar which was a totally new experience in both my life and career. I still remember my first day at school, I was happy but nervous and worried at the same time. It was challenging for me to immerse into the Qatari society and work with people of numerous nationalities.

Becoming a teacher may be an easy decision to make, but not an easy job. Though teaching is a profession, it is also a journey of learning and self-discovery. To start, I can say that teaching helped me shape my personality, my understanding of education, and the responsibilities of a teacher. Teaching is not about explaining and making corrections. It is completely different of what many people think. Back to my first year of teaching, I taught students of various nationalities and cultural backgrounds. Some students were confident and smart, while others were struggling to keep up. So, I quickly realized that teaching requires patience and creativity. In addition to that, teaching is not only about learning the subject but a teacher also must know how to explain and make sure that every student understands; she has to have differentiated instructions that suit the learning style of each student. Moreover, we are not only teaching but we are also educating minds and preparing generations to be of great impact in community. For example, one of my students, Fahad, was so shy and didn't like to participate or talk to his classmates. With time, and by encouraging and engaging him, I helped him to overcome his shyness. He really showed a great change, and I will never forget when his mum came and hugged me thanking me for helping him. Such incidents play a very important role in shaping our personality because it's a great achievement for the teacher.

Becoming a teacher is a meaningful and rewarding career choice. We as teachers play a vital role in shaping the future by guiding students not only in academics but also in values, manners, confidence, and life skills. I would like to mention another example that I will never forget. My grade four Qatari student, Jamal Al Naimi, had a special case due to very weak eyesight. He couldn't read 14 font size, so what I did was to print his worksheets and assessments in A3 paper size. He was so happy and showed great academic progress. One day, while I was driving to school, I was listening to the morning broadcast as usual (a program where kids can call and choose someone to thank or give the morning flower to), I suddenly heard Jamal, he called and thanked me, he said, " I want to thank Mrs. Manal for helping and supporting me!" I was really so contented and grateful to have a student who appreciates what his teacher did for him. So, we can inspire and affect young minds and help them discover their potential. We can affect the new generations and build their personalities. Not to forget that teaching is a continuous learning career. Every class brings different challenges, ideas, and perspectives, which help teachers to grow both professionally and personally. Teachers keep on developing their careers by learning from other teachers, attending different professional development programs, and visiting other schools.

Teaching is a respected career, but, like other careers, it has advantages and disadvantages. To talk about its advantages, teaching is a profession that makes a positive difference in students' lives. It is a job that offers stability and a healthy life balance. Teachers build good friendships throughout their careers. Teachers talk not only about teaching, we also share parts of our lives. We are both learning and growing in this profession. Moreover, we are heroes to some students; they know they can rely on us and feel safe with us. Sometimes, we are their source of strength and inspiration. Another advantage is that teachers have strong communication, leadership, and problem-solving skills. One more important advantage is the summer vacation and the monthly vacations, which no other profession will have.

Another example of the challenges that I faced was Mariam, a French-educated student who came with her family to live in Qatar last year. Her parents were so worried about her academic development, especially in using English, because she had never been to an English class. Her parents contacted me, and we had a plan to help her use English. Actually, I started with her from scratch: teaching her colors, objects' names, and numbers. Day by day, week by week, Mariam started to speak English, write simple sentences, and do her assignments by herself, without any assistance. It took about six months to notice the difference. At the end of the year, she was able to do her exams successfully. It was really a great achievement for me. Watching your students succeed and grasp new concepts is the best feeling. So, we must never give up. We must keep on trying to achieve our goals.

Despite its advantages, teaching can be a demanding and stressful profession. A teacher's day does not end at school. She must continue preparing at home, working on plans, correcting tests, and finding new techniques to use. Sometimes, I see students, lesson plans and other stuff at school in my dreams. A teacher must handle diverse learning needs and maintain discipline. Moreover, we may face heavy overloads, such as writing lesson plans, preparing exams, grading, correcting exam papers, etc. Another disadvantage is the salary; we are not paid for working hours after school. Teachers deserve higher salaries according to their efforts and time dedicated to work. Problems can extend to dealing with parents who usually have high expectations, and sometimes they are uncooperative. One of the struggles that a teacher can face is students' misbehavior, which is about how to find solutions to such behaviors and how to affect such students positively. We really suffer to have an ideal classroom. Besides, though professional development plays a very important role in developing the teaching process, it is sometimes a burden because it takes up our time that we have to dedicate to other tasks.

To conclude, I realized after 20 years of teaching that being a teacher needs passion, patience, and empathy. It is more than a profession; it is a deep calling, a mission to ignite curiosity, foster growth, and light the way for generations to come. It is a mission that builds the future of students. There are moments when you wonder why you chose this career, but also, there is nothing else in the world you would rather do. For me, I can't be anywhere else except at school, in the classroom, with students, and among books. Good teachers are the ones who can challenge young minds without losing their own.

As a teacher, I have my own views on the teaching perspective, which is making a difference in students' performance and behavior, and developing engaging ways of teaching that affect students' development. For me, teaching is a continuous process that never ends, and every student deserves a quality education since we are raising good citizens and critical thinkers. Moreover, teachers have to provide different techniques that meet students' needs and improve their performance.

Personally, I do not think technologies will substitute teachers; technologies are facilities to help teachers in being up-to-date, preparing their lessons, and using different techniques. This is also because teaching is a relationship between the teacher and her students; it is a way of communicating with the teacher who is a safe person for students to talk with and express their feelings, fears, and personal issues. Teaching will never be replaced by technologies or disappear. It is the mission of prophets that will never disappear. Therefore, teaching is a profession that will always be needed.

To end, I would like to thank Dr. Riyam Chaar, the Vice Principal at Heritage International Academy, for giving me the opportunity to write about my teaching journey.

GIVING THE SPARK OF HOPE FOR ALL GENERATIONS WHO WILL PASS BY MY PATH THROUGHOUT THE YEARS

Caroline Tomossian

"When there's a will, there's a way!" This simple phrase that was written by my instructor on the board every day of my grade 12 school year has made Mrs. Caroline Tomossian the person who I am today. This motivational quote became a mindset and reminded me every day that determination and persistence are and will always be the key to success. That perception has driven and empowered me to be the fun and knowledgeable role model that my students are expecting to meet annually. Before I recognized that my school years had come to an end, I was no longer sitting at students' desks anymore, but I was the one who should be ready to be the leader and mentor of yesterday, the educator and guide of today, and the exemplar of tomorrow who will give the spark of hope for all generations who will pass by my path throughout the years. Yes, my instructor fueled my drive to enter this profession and encouraged me to pursue my new dream that will always be the vital career, as it paves the way for all others despite its many challenges. As a French-educated pupil for 17 years, becoming an English-certified teacher presented a significant challenge for me. Transitioning from French to English can be so hard for a student especially when it happens at university level. It was hard to master grammatical rules, academic vocabulary, and pronunciation. It took me time also to be fluent and build confidence while speaking. The homework that took two hours from my friends' time to finish, took from me days and sleepless nights. However, I kept on daunting myself and never lost hope. I dedicated myself to hard work, reading books, writing diaries, and watching movies to enhance my language skills. I realized that it is never about the certificate that you gain, but success in this career is about the deep enthusiasm that will drive a positive, nurturing, and inspiring professional journey. This formidable experience had also carved and grown the passion that was innate in being a great lecturer. My university professor always used to tell me I was born to be a teacher, as I have always shown my love for teaching.

The vision that a teacher envisions today will shape the great leaders of tomorrow. We teach students to be strong, independent learners by helping them acquire knowledge in every aspect. Using diverse teaching methods, encouraging creativity and curiosity, linking the lessons to daily life examples, integrating technology, having discussions, and many more examples will foster critical thinking and will help shape the students' ways of thinking. From my 11 years of educational expertise, I have learned that we should not only give abstract definitions, explain the books' rules, or abide by a specific teaching method, but we should always be clever to engage all students' learning styles in the same period. Visual, auditory, and kinesthetic learners, gifted ones, students with special needs, and others who struggle - all have the right to be pioneers. Our job is to facilitate learning by guiding pupils to understand new skills and concepts through different methods. We also encourage them to capture the idea through a fun game or activity. As a team in the class, we build a positive and safe classroom environment that will help our students develop values and demonstrate responsibility and love for learning. Monitoring their work and assessing them will always provide us, them, and their guardians feedback to help in overcoming their daily challenges on all academic levels. As education is always evolving, professional growth also ensures teachers stay up-to-date with the speedy world to become more effective educators who positively impact students' success. You should always put yourself in the shoes of the students and always keep in mind to never be theoretical, but always practical. Even though a lesson plan is important in organizing and managing your time, you should never limit your creativity during times that arise spontaneously during the lesson explanation. Deeper discussions, flexibility, and real-life examples allow teachers to adapt lessons to students' needs, which will always lead to having a positive, engaged, student-centered class and ensure that learning goals are met effectively. Beyond the classroom walls and academic duties, mentors undertake a crucial role in shaping students' social behavioral part that extends into a broader surrounding. My influence as a teacher plays a vital role in developing their communication skills and promotes positive values. My mission leads to an impactful mission in teaching respect and tolerance for others' opinions and differences by understanding and giving standpoints without judging and hurting their feelings. We as teachers play a key role as well in training them to hold responsibilities, be trustworthy, and be accountable for their actions, whether they are positive or negative. Teaching moral values like being kind and compassionate to others will also teach pupils to manage their discipline and behavior effectively. Finally, showing perseverance, determination, and hard work will help them in crossing challenges and never giving up easily. As Albert Bandura said, most human behavior is learned through observation and imitation of others, not just direct experience, involving the cognitive processes like attention, retention, reproduction, and motivation, where people form ideas and later use coded information as guides for action (Bandura, 1986). As a result, as teachers we should strive to be positive influencers, as modelling embodies a significant purpose in shaping the young minds that we guide through our actions and behaviors.

With the dynamic world that we are living in nowadays, generations' mentality is changing. It is becoming very hard for us to keep them interested in the curricula that are taught. The rise of social media and technology is decreasing the enthusiasm shown and delaying the process of learning itself, as many students are also demotivated from the overload and the stress of exams that are pressuring them, leading to a great disconnection between school curricula and future aspirations. In addition, many obstacles appear when it comes to education apart from the progressive era. The parents' stress on scoring is always a great factor in lessening the student's motivation and teachers. An A+ student is a rubric for them, and obliging them to offer such grades will help in boxing students' creativity and only thinking about how to achieve this mark, forgetting the main purpose of learning. I always say to both parties that the grade is a factor of success, but it is not everything. What defines us are our actions and not our evaluations' marks; however, we should fulfill our responsibilities and do our best in exams to prove to ourselves that hard work pays off. Mistakes teach us and should never put us down. Certain students' behaviors can also negatively affect the class environment in general, so some teachers might find managing different personalities and misbehavior hard. Many barriers come up when entering the class; being thoughtful and wise will always make a difference. The workload in planning, grading, assessing, and preparing tests can be overwhelming; therefore, teachers must be passionate about their profession to thrive. In spite of the fact that we as educators are tackling many problems, this occupation holds many moral and advantageous sides. Observing students' academic progress will always give teachers the motivation to reach the job satisfaction. This emotional reward on social, cognitive, and academic parts throughout the years will always bring a unique sense of fulfillment and sense of pride. Seeing the light in one's students' eyes by understanding abstract concepts and achieving goals will also be gratifying. Every encouragement, word, and support will help in making a difference, leaving a lasting uplifting impact on both of us. We are remembered for years as the ones who gave high self-esteem to students to believe in themselves. In the long run, our job will help us in growing constantly and help us stay relevant in a changing world. Our dedication, hard work, and persistence will always keep us committed to our duties and give us a great sense of accomplishment.

Furthermore, I have encountered numerous rewarding experiences that have greatly contributed to my growth. One of my students had always feared talking in class, as she had a mispronunciation of the letters p and b. I used a tissue to help her visualize and distinguish between both sounds. I explained and showed that while puffing air to pronounce the letter "p," the tissue will move as it is an unvoiced sound. However, the "b" sound will barely move the tissue, as it is a voiced sound. Later we practiced using different words like "pen" vs. "ben," "pat" vs. "bat," and "park" vs. "bark." It took her three months to learn to differentiate sounds, but this practical approach in a hands-on way helped the student overcome her anxiety and boosted her confidence.

I also underwent pressure during corona virus times because we hadn't had any experience of online teaching. Keeping students engaged during the sessions was a real challenge without the usual face-to-face interaction. Despite these obstacles, I worked hard to adapt and support my students' needs, learning remotely through different new games and strategies. To maintain students' engagement, PowerPoint presentations, videos, songs, and games like Jeopardy made the students more engaged. With time and consistency, they learned to speak in turns, participate more, and freely express their opinions about different topics. These tools not only broke the monotony of online learning but also made the lessons more enjoyable and interactive. Regardless of the effort that I was making, teaching writing remained a struggle, as I could not monitor their work live. That's why the Google Classroom platform and homework helped a lot to track their progress, provide feedback, and maintain a record of their development. Despite the challenges, these tools helped me a lot in strengthening my digital skills.

Over time, I also dealt with students who struggled with speaking skills during tests. This anxiety caused them to feel stressed and not express their ideas clearly. I have worked hard on these students by going up the ladder step by step. I incorporated weekly speaking activities and encouraged them to speak in a less pressured environment so they could feel safe. Such steps showed great progress. One of my students in the class was hesitant to stand and talk in class. She often froze or struggled to express herself clearly when asked to speak. Every time she came prepared, and suddenly she forgot what she had written at home. I gave her the opportunity to stand and talk every day in front of her peers and improvise three sentences about a topic of her choice. With time this barrier was broken and she was able to express her ideas and feelings and talk about what she loves and what she is passionate about. She felt more confident and comfortable. I helped her in improvising simple sentences instead of memorizing complex ones, which gave her the freedom to express herself naturally without the pressure of being perfect. Gradually, she began speaking fluently. This experience has shown me that with encouragement, simple ways, and continuous support, a student can build self-confidence.

From my perspective, teaching is not merely a job or the act of delivering lessons, it is a deep commitment to raising wise, collaborative, kind, and respectful generations, while making a lasting impact on both education and society. A professional educator views teaching as a meaningful mission to inspire, guide, and empower students while meeting their diverse learning needs. Our role is far from easy. We evaluate the work of kids, collaborate with peers, follow up with parents, and work on sustaining all the needs of the kids. We foster critical thinking, promote lifelong learning, and shape responsible and independent learners. To succeed, a teacher must be patient enough to attain all the goals needed throughout the year, work on emotional intelligence, and grow on both levels, personally and professionally. We should always remember that our greatest skills are not teaching what we know, but bringing happiness, excitement, and encouragement when we teach. However sophisticated, artificial intelligence will not be able to do it all, therefore, it is not our competitor – it is out assistant which we need to apply wisely. Our profession has all the time been modified, but it has always been and will always remain needed.

REFERENCES

Al-Qadi, A. M. (2021). *Qatari women educated yet unemployed.* Qatar National Library. Retrieved from https://manara.qnl.qa/ndownloader/files/52430411/1

Bandura, A. (1986). *Social foundations of thought and action.* Prentice Hall.

Ehsan, M. M. (2025). International standardised tests and Qatar's educational development. In E. Zaidan, E., Tok, A. Al-Fadala, & L.Cochrane (Eds.). *The future of education policy in the state of Qatar* (pp. 45–67). Springer. DOI: 10.1007/978-981-97-9667-0_3

Einstein, A. (n.d.). Quotes. Retrieved from https://www.goodreads.com/quotes/253933-i-never-teach-my-pupils-i-only-attempt-to-provide

Ellili-Cherif, M., & Romanowski, M. H. (2013). Education for a new era: Teacher preparation in Qatar. *Journal of Education and Learning*, *2*(3), 158–171. DOI: 10.5539/jel.v2n3p158

Fromherz, A. J. (2012). *Qatar: A modern history.* Georgetown University Press.

General Secretariat for Development Planning. (2008). *Qatar National Vision 2030.* Government of Qatar. Retrieved from https://www.npc.qa/en/QNV/Documents/QNV2030_English_v2.pdf

International Association for the Evaluation of Educational Achievement. (2023). PIRLS 2021 international results in reading. Retrieved from https://pirls2021.org/results/

International Association for the Evaluation of Educational Achievement. (2024). TIMSS 2023 international results in mathematics and science. Retrieved fromhttps://timss2023.org/results/

Kuralt, C. (n.d.). Brainy Quote. Retrieved from https://www.brainyquote.com/quotes/charles_kuralt_364247

Ministry of Education and Higher Education. (2022). *Announcement for the recruitment of teachers in government schools for the academic year 2022–2023.* Ministry of Education and Higher Education, Qatar. Retrieved from https://www.edu.gov.qa/en/News/Details/4987800

Ministry of Education and Higher Education. (2023). *Professional licensing system for teachers and educational leaders in Qatar.* Retrieved from https://www.edu.gov.qa/en/News/Details/15330600

Ministry of Education and Higher Education. (2024). *Education sector strategy 2024–2030: Igniting the spark of learning.* Retrieved from https://moewebprod.edu.gov.qa/en/News/Details/10424400

Ministry of Education and Higher Education. (n.d.) *Education in Qatar.* Retrieved from https://www.edu.gov.qa/en/Content/EducationinQatar

Nasser, R. (2017). Qatar's educational reform: Past and future. *Open Review of Educational Research*, *4*(1), 1–15. DOI: 10.1080/23265507.2016.1266693

Organization for Economic Co-operation and Development. (2023). *PISA 2022 results (Volume I): Student performance and equity in education.* OECD Publishing. DOI: 10.1787/53f23881-en

Qatar Foundation. (2022). *Education City: Advancing education, research, and innovation.* Retrieved from https://www.qf.org.qa/education/education-city

Qatar Foundation. (n.d.). *Universities and programs in Education City.* Retrieved from https://www.qf.org.qa/education/education-city/universities

Qatar Government Communications Office. (2024). *Qatar's education sector: A journey of growth and excellence*. Retrieved from https://www.gco.gov.qa/en/focus/education/

Qatar National Library. (2020). *The history of education in Qatar*. Retrieved from https://www.qnl.qa/en/articles/history-education-qatar

Qatar News Agency. (2021). Ministry of Education and Higher Education Launches "My values draw my identity" project. Retrieved from https://qna.org.qa/en/news/news-details?id=0025-ministry-of-education-and-higher-education-launches-%27my-values-draw-my-identity%27-project&date=24/10/2021

Qatar News Agency. (2025, December 2). *Qatar wins six awards at the Hamdan bin Rashid Al Maktoum Award for Distinguished Academic Performance*. Retrieved from https://qna.org.qa/en/news-bulletins-details?id=0093-qatar-wins-6-awards-in-2025-hamdan-bin-rashid-award-for-distinguished-academic-performance&date=3/12/2025#:~:text=Doha%2C%20December%2002%20(QNA),the%20institutional%20and%20individual%20levels

Qatar University. (n.d.). *Faculty handbook* (Part 1). Qatar University. https://www.qu.edu.qa/siteimages/static_file/qu/offices%20and%20departments/vpaa/documents/vpaa_faculty_handbook_-_part_1.pdf

Rohn, J. (n.d.). You are the average of the five people you spend the most time with. Retrieved from https://personalexcellence.co/blog/average-of-5-people/

Romanowski, M. H., & Nasser, R. (2012). Teacher preparation and educational reform in Qatar. *International Journal of Educational Management*, *26*(2), 144–157. DOI: 10.1108/09513541211201938

Teach Across Asia. (2025). *Teaching jobs in Qatar: Salary and benefits*. Retrieved from https://teachacrossasia.com/teaching-locations/teaching-jobs-in-qatar/

The Peninsula Qatar. (2025). Education Excellence Award winners announced. Retrieved from https://thepeninsulaqatar.com/article/10/01/2025/education-excellence-award-winners-announced

UNESCO. (2021). *State of Qatar. Education policy review.* Retrieved from https://unesdoc.unesco.org/ark:/48223/pf0000211627

UNESCO. (2024). *National SDG 4 consultations and progress report: Qatar*. https://www.unesco.org/en/articles/qatar-national-consultations-follow-commitments-transforming-education-summit-and-achieving-sdg-4

United Nations Development Programme. (2023). *Global Knowledge Index 2023*. Retrieved from https://www.undp.org/publications/global-knowledge-index-2023

Chapter 17
Teacher Voices From South Korea:
Educational Achievement, Digital Transformation, and the Fragility of Professional Authority

Hanul Jang
http://orcid.org/0009-0004-2526-670X
Seoseon Elementary School, South Korea

Yeonjung Kim
http://orcid.org/0009-0002-4968-7256
Sinchang Elementary School, South Korea

Namyoung Kim
http://orcid.org/0009-0002-0106-1692
Seoul Ansan Elementary School, South Korea

ABSTRACT

South Korea is widely recognized as a high-performing education system, noted for strong student achievement, near-universal access to schooling, and high results in international assessments. At the same time, teachers face tensions related to declining professional authority, expanding workloads, and emotional strain. This chapter examines South Korean education through teacher voices, focusing on how structural reforms, social expectations, and digital transformation are experienced in everyday practice. It outlines the historical development and institutional structure of Korean education, with attention to the homeroom teacher system. The chapter then reviews major educational achievements alongside recent policy initiatives, including the 2022 Revised National Curriculum. Drawing on teacher narratives, it illustrates how policy changes shape classroom practice, relationships with students, and professional identity. The chapter concludes that sustaining educational success requires restoring conditions that allow teachers to teach without fear, supported by institutional trust.

A SHORT OVERVIEW ON EDUCATION AND TEACHER ROLE IN SOUTH KOREA

Hanul Jang

The history of education in Korea

The history of education in Korea stretches back to the earliest state formations, with records noting the conferment of scholarly titles in the Gojoseon period, which, according to tradition, is dated from 2333 BCE to 108 BCE. Over many centuries, Confucian ideals shaped the aims and institutions of Korean learning. During the Joseon dynasty, for

DOI: 10.4018/979-8-3373-8983-7.ch017

example, state-run Seonggyungwan, the highest national Confucian academy located in the capital, and local Hyanggyo, government-established schools in each province, functioned alongside private village schools (Seodang) and Confucian academies (Seowon) that emphasized classical Chinese texts and moral instruction. The primary purpose of education in that era was moral cultivation and preparation for the civil service examinations (Gwageo).

Modern, Western-style education began to be institutionalized in the late nineteenth century. The establishment of the first modern private schools (e.g., Wonsanhaksa in 1883), the Gabo Reform of 1894, and missionary-founded schools such as Ewha Hakdang and Paichai Hakdang introduced new curricula and pedagogies. After the liberation in 1945 and the enactment of the Education Act in 1949, Korea adopted a single-track structure (see details in the section 'Structure of the education system). State-led expansion of schooling during industrialization (1960s–1980s), coordinated with Five-Year Economic Development Plans, produced dramatic increases in secondary and tertiary enrollment. Since the 1990s, education policy has emphasized democratization, university autonomy, ICT integration, and diversification of higher education. More recently, policy attention has shifted toward preparing learners for the Fourth Industrial Revolution and addressing demographic change through measures such as the 2022 Revised National Curriculum and digital education strategies (Ministry of Education, 2022).

Achievements of Korean education

Compulsory elementary and lower-secondary education guarantees near-universal basic schooling, strengthening the public character of Korea's education system. High societal emphasis on schooling has translated into rapid expansion of educational attainment and high tertiary progression rates. Internationally, South Korea's students consistently perform near the top on major comparative assessments. For instance, Programme for International Student Assessment (PISA) 2022 results show Korean students outperforming the OECD average in mathematics, reading, and science (OECD, 2023). In mathematics, a substantially larger share of Korean 15-year-olds reached the highest proficiency levels compared with the OECD mean. Trends in International Mathematics & Science Study (TIMSS) 2023 likewise placed Korean fourth- and eighth-grade students among the world leaders in mathematics and science (IEA, 2024). These results reflect both high average performance and relatively narrow tails at the low end of the achievement distribution.

Structure of the education system

South Korea's formal pre-tertiary system follows a single-track arrangement: six years of elementary school, three years of middle school, and three years of high school, followed by tertiary programs (typically four-year universities). Elementary and secondary schooling is delivered through both public and private schools, alongside alternative and special-purpose institutions and a growing number of international schools. Higher education includes four-year universities, two-year colleges, graduate schools, and distance/cyber universities. In 2024, official statistics reported over 100,000 graduate degrees awarded (Ministry of Education & Korean Educational Development Institute, 2024), with the number of doctoral degrees increasing substantially over the last two decades.

Compulsory education, guaranteed constitutionally and under the Framework Act on Education, covers nine years (elementary + middle school). Since 2019, the government has phased in free high school tuition (beginning with 12th graders in fall 2019 and expanding to full implementation in 2021), significantly reducing direct costs for families (Ministry of Education, 2019). The 2022 Revised National Curriculum introduced student-centered instruction and competency frameworks aligned with the high-school credit system (Ministry of Education, 2022).

Teacher preparation and certification

Teacher education in Korea is structured by license type. Prospective elementary teachers are typically trained at national universities of education (or at university elementary-education departments), while secondary teachers are prepared through colleges of education, subject departments at comprehensive universities, or graduate education programs. The legal criteria for teacher certification (coursework, practicum, subject-specific requirements) are set out in the Regulations on the Qualification Examination for Teachers (Republic of Korea, Presidential Decree, n.d.-a). After obtaining initial certification, candidates must pass provincial or metropolitan teacher employment examinations - procedures that often include written tests, teaching demonstrations, and interviews - before being appointed to public school posts.

Competition for appointment has increased in recent years: for example, provincial employment competition rates for elementary posts rose from roughly from 1.62:1 in 2018 to about 2.44:1 in 2024, while overall competition for secondary posts remains substantially higher (with marked variation by subject and region) at around 8:1 on average (Ministry of Education & Korean Educational Development Institute, 2024). Structural differences in training pathways contribute to this gap: graduates of national universities of education are trained specifically for elementary positions and the admission quotas of those institutions interact closely with government elementary teacher supply policies. In contrast, secondary teacher applicants come from a broader set of pathways - undergraduate education faculties, graduate schools of education, and lateral entrants - intensifying competition for subject-specialist secondary posts.

Roles by certification and promotion pathways

Teachers' roles in Korea evolve with experience and formal appointment. Beginning teachers typically serve as classroom teachers, responsible for both subject instruction and homeroom duties, which include managing students' daily life at school, maintaining communication with parents, overseeing moral and emotional guidance, and coordinating class-level events or administrative matters. In Korean schools, the homeroom teacher provides overall guidance for a specific class of students, supervising both their academic progress and personal development while communicating closely with parents and managing classroom affairs. In elementary schools, one homeroom teacher usually teaches most subjects to the same class of students, ensuring holistic instruction and care. In contrast, middle and high schools operate on a subject-specialist system, where different teachers handle different subjects, and the homeroom teacher's role focuses more on student counseling, guidance, and career advising. With experience and demonstrated competence, teachers may be assigned by school leadership to roles such as department head or subject coordinator. Formal promotion paths—governed by the *Regulations on the Promotion of Educational Public Officials*—allow qualified teachers to progress into specialist or administrative positions (e.g., educational supervisors, vice-principals, principals), contingent upon years of service, completion of required training, performance evaluations, and other criteria (Republic of Korea, Presidential Decree, n.d.-b). This tiered career structure is designed both to reward professional development and to ensure that those in leadership positions meet institutional standards for school management and educational oversight.

Teacher remuneration system

Teachers' pay in Korea consists of a statutory base salary determined by a seniority-based scale (hobong), plus a range of allowances. These allowances are additional payments provided to compensate for specific responsibilities or working conditions, such as homeroom management duties, research activities, or long-term service in the profession. The statutory pay framework and associated allowances are administered under the Regulations on the Remuneration of Educational Public Officials and reflected annually in the pay tables published by the Ministry of Personnel Management (Republic of Korea, Ministry of Personnel Management, 2025).

Comparative data highlight a distinctive pattern: statutory starting salaries for teachers in Korea (2023 figures) were lower than the OECD average, while salaries for mid-career teachers (e.g., 15 years of service) were among the higher end within the OECD (OECD, 2024). For example, OECD figures place Korea's statutory beginning teacher salary for 2023 at approximately 33.99 million (roughly USD 24,200 or EUR 20,600), whereas salary levels for teachers with 15 years of service were markedly higher (OECD, 2024). These figures refer to statutory (gross) salaries; take-home pay is reduced by taxes and statutory deductions. A disclosure published by the Korean Federation of Teachers' Associations (KFTA) indicated a net monthly take-home pay for a beginning elementary teacher of approximately 2,309,160(roughly USD 1,645 or EUR 1,403)—only modestly above Korea's 2025 legal monthly minimum wage of 2,096,270(roughly USD 1,495 or EUR 1,274) (The JoongAng/aggregated press reporting, 2024). Surveys of younger teachers reveal that salary is a major retention concern: a KFTA survey of teachers under age 39 found that a large majority had considered leaving the profession because of pay (Korean Federation of Teachers' Associations, 2024). Beyond salary, teachers also face demanding working conditions. In many schools, teachers spend substantial time on administrative tasks, student counseling, and communication with parents in addition to regular teaching duties. These responsibilities often extend beyond official working hours and reduce the time available for lesson preparation and professional development.

Salaries of higher-education instructors and faculty

Faculty compensation in higher education varies according to institution type. Salaries for faculty at national universities are determined under seniority-based pay tables and administrative regulations issued by the Ministry of Personnel Management, with differences according to rank and appointment. Private universities set faculty wages according to internal regulations and collective bargaining, producing substantial cross-institutional variation. Adjunct/part-time lecturers have seen improvements in statutory protections since the Higher Education Act (revised 2019), but hourly lecture fees and employment stability remain concerns; for example, national averages for part-time lecturer pay in recent years were reported to be modest relative to living costs and academic workloads.

National education reform strategies

To respond to rapid social and technological change, the South Korean government has pursued multiple education reform initiatives focused on preparing learners for a complex, digitalized future. The 2022 Revised National Curriculum sets out aims to cultivate future-oriented core competencies—creativity, autonomy, collaboration, and digital literacy—and to operationalize student-centered, competency-based learning aligned with the full rollout of the high-school credit system (Ministry of Education, 2022; Han, 2022). Notably, the 2022 revision involved an unusually participatory development process, framed as "A future-oriented curriculum made with the people"—which emphasized stakeholder engagement, decentralization, and curricular autonomy (Han, 2022).

In February 2023 the Ministry unveiled a Digital-Based Education Innovation Strategy that established a roadmap for nationwide digital textbooks, the phased introduction of AI-enhanced learning assistants (AI tutors), and the construction of a national education platform (Ministry of Education, 2023). The strategy foregrounds personalized learning through learning-analytics and aims to provide teachers with new tools for instruction and assessment; pilot projects (e.g., 2023 digital lead schools and AI courseware trials) have informed implementation planning and professional development models (Ministry of Education, 2023).

By 2025, implementation activities have included expansion of digital infrastructure, piloting of AI digital textbooks in selected grades and subjects, and targeted teacher professional development to support blended and AI-assisted pedagogies. These reforms carry a potential to improve differentiated instruction and formative feedback, but they also raise challenges related to data governance, teacher workload, equity of access, and safeguarding of student privacy that require ongoing policy attention (Ministry of Education, 2023; An, 2024).

Understanding these developments also requires attention to the concept of teacher agency and professional identity. Teacher agency refers to teachers' capacity to make professional judgments and act purposefully within structural constraints (Priestley et al., 2015). In contexts where policy reforms, social expectations, and institutional structures rapidly change, teachers' professional identity becomes a key factor shaping how they interpret and respond to these pressures.

Contemporary challenges facing teachers

Teachers in Korea face multifaceted pressures. First, demographic decline and falling school-age populations have accelerated school mergers and closures (e.g., 49 schools slated to close in 2025), with disproportionate impact in non-metropolitan areas (The Straits Times, 2025; Korea Herald, 2025). Teachers in these regions often experience additional professional isolation due to shrinking school communities and reduced access to professional networks. Second, teachers report high administrative loads and frequent burdens associated with parental complaints and non-instructional tasks, which reduce time for lesson planning and professional development. Teaching and Learning International Survey

(TALIS) and national surveys indicate that Korean teachers experience elevated levels of work-related stress relative to OECD averages (Ainley & Carstens, 2018; Shim et al., 2024).

Recent national surveys of teachers have highlighted student misconduct and parental complaints as a leading source of stress and an obstacle to effective instruction (Korean Federation of Teachers' Associations, 2024). In 2023–24, public concern and debate intensified after high-profile incidents involving alleged parental pressure and teacher well-being; these episodes fueled policy discussions about strengthening legal protections for teachers and restoring professional authority.

Particularly, following the 2023 incident in which a teacher in Seoul died after alleged parental pressure and complaints, public debate on violations of teachers' rights intensified. Teachers organized mass rallies, demanding stronger protection of teacher authority and calling for its restoration. This eventually led to revisions in legal frameworks such as the Teacher Status Act; however, many educators still report that the impact of these reforms at the ground level remains minimal (Ministry of Education, 2023). These issues have serious implications for teacher job satisfaction and the long-term sustainability of education.

In response to increasing concerns about teacher well-being, the Korean government has introduced several institutional support mechanisms. For example, local education offices operate Teacher Healing Support Centers that provide psychological screening, counseling services, and referrals to mental health professionals for teachers experiencing severe stress. In addition, the Ministry of Education introduced a dedicated hotline (1395) that allows teachers to report violations of teacher rights and receive legal consultation as well as psychological recovery support. Furthermore, the government has launched nationwide programs offering free mental health counseling for teachers, reflecting growing recognition of the need to support educators facing emotional distress and the fear of complaints or false accusations (Asia Economic News, 2023; The Straits Times, 2024).

Although there has been movement toward legislative adjustment, such as consideration of teacher status and protection measures, many teachers report that improvements have been limited in practice (Ministry of Education, 2023).

Changing social valuation of teachers and the status of education

Historically, teachers in Korea were accorded considerable social respect as custodians of knowledge and moral exemplars. Over time, however, structural changes - marketization of education, expansion of private supplementary schooling, shifting notions of rights and accountability, and a more litigious parental culture - have altered perceptions of the profession's prestige. Public opinion still recognizes education as a crucial vehicle for social mobility (Korean Educational Development Institute, 2023), but many teachers report a perceived decline in societal respect and reduced participation in policy deliberation (Shim et al., 2024). The combination of perceived de-professionalisation, workload pressures, and demographic effects undermines the attractiveness and perceived stability of teaching as a long-term career.

Physical punishment in schools was officially banned with the revision of the Enforcement Decree of the Elementary and Secondary Education Act on March 18, 2011, but it was allowed until 2010. In particular, from the 20th century to the early 2000s, not only teachers but also parents, elders, and students widely believed that corporal punishment was necessary for education. The generation that experienced such punishment as students is now parents, and some appeal to current teachers with a sense of compensation based on their own past experiences, often making excessive demands or complaints. When news reports emerge of students assaulting teachers or teachers physically disciplining students, online comments sometimes reflect ironic reactions, such as, "Back then, we were hit with by teachers, and now teachers are being hit by students. Serves them right." Interestingly, many teachers today were once students who experienced corporal punishment, while most teachers who administered the punishment have retired. As a result, current teachers face the reality of having been punished as students while now experiencing abuse or unfair treatment from students.

False reports related to emotional child abuse, excessive parental complaints, and low salaries are major factors that undermine teachers' ability to conduct educational activities. Some parents secretly place recording devices in their child's bags or cabinet in the classroom and behavior management processes, reporting even minor incidents as emotional child abuse (G-Standard, 2024). Although the Teacher Status Protection Act has been enacted (Ministry of Education, 2024), teachers in the field do not feel its effectiveness, leading many to become disillusioned with teaching or leave the profession. Teachers' starting salaries have also been effectively frozen for long periods relative to inflation. In 2024, approximately 7,900 teachers nationwide resigned mid-career, a 19% increase compared to 2020, and among teachers with less than five years of experience, mid-career resignations increased by 30% over the past five years. Within teacher communities, the saying "Those who leave the teaching profession tend to be the more intelligent ones" circulates, reflecting a bitter yet understandable reality for teachers preparing to leave the profession.

Conclusion

Over recent decades, South Korea has achieved exceptional educational outcomes and a broadly accessible schooling system. Yet teachers contend with converging problems - intensive workloads, concerns about pay and professional respect, mounting administrative duties, and demographic shifts - that threaten the sustainability of those achievements. Three policy priorities are critical for going forward: (1) implementing digital transformation in ways that support classroom realities and teacher practice; (2) redesigning workload and administrative arrangements to allow teachers to prioritize instruction and professional growth; and (3) developing systemic responses to demographic change that protect educational equity and maintain high standards across regions. Strengthening teacher professionalism and social recognition must remain central to any strategy for sustaining Korea's educational performance in the decades ahead (OECD, 2024; Shim et al., 2024).

While the policy discussions and statistical trends described above illustrate structural challenges facing the teaching profession in Korea, they cannot fully capture how these changes are experienced by teachers in their everyday practice. The personal narratives presented in this chapter illustrate how these structural challenges are experienced at the classroom level. Addressing policy reform without considering teachers' lived experiences risks overlooking the human dimension of educational change.

AM I TRULY WORTHY OF BEING CALLED A "TEACHER"?

Hanul Jang

I am currently in my fifth year as an elementary school teacher in South Korea. I earned my master's degree in Practical Arts Education from Korea National University of Education, and I am now in the Second semester of a doctoral program in the same field. I would like to express my gratitude to Prof. Dr. Natela Doghonadze for giving me the opportunity to reflect on my journey as an educator through this essay.

In fact, my childhood dream was not to become a teacher - I wanted to be a TV producer. When I was in my third year of middle school, I organized a comedy sketch for the school festival - writing the script, casting my friends, and directing the performance. That experience brought me so much joy that it sparked my interest in media and led me to enroll in a foreign language high school.

However, everything changed when I met a Korean literature teacher in high school. Her classes were like theatrical performances. At times, she would become a child; at others, a tragic heroine. She brought literature to life, making stories feel vibrant and real. I was captivated by her teaching. I began to imitate her tone and questioning techniques, and gradually, I developed a deep admiration for the role of a teacher.

It was then that I had a realisation: "A teacher is like a producer." Planning and delivering a lesson that immerses students is a creative process - one that deeply appealed to me. After much discussion with my family, I decided to pursue teaching. Since elementary school teachers cover multiple subjects, I felt this career aligned well with my diverse interests, and I began preparing to become one.

After two years of preparation, I was admitted to the Department of Elementary Education at Korea National University of Education. My time in college was a critical period for developing the skills I would need as a teacher. In addition to various arts and physical education courses, I studied horticulture, animal husbandry, software, and video production through my major in Practical Arts Education. One course in particular—"Software Education and Video Production"—opened new possibilities for me.

After graduating and passing the teacher certification exam, I entered the teaching profession just as the COVID-19 pandemic began. I couldn't meet my students in person. With all lessons moved online, I used the video production skills

I had learned in college to create lesson videos for my students. These videos soon spread by word of mouth among fellow teachers, prompting me to launch a YouTube channel, which now has around 800 subscribers.

Even though I had limited teaching experience, I was invited to lead training sessions on video production and online instruction. This motivated me to pursue a Master's degree to gain more professional expertise, focusing on software education. I also joined a local ICT teacher research group to further develop my skills. Currently, in my doctoral program, I continue researching digital literacy and educational technology.

Looking back, I can say that I have worked with passion and commitment to professional growth throughout my teaching journey. However, as I was writing this reflection, I realized there's one element that has been missing in my story: my students.

Of course, I enjoy teaching and treasure my time with children. But upon reflection, I wonder - have I been viewing education primarily as a "job" or "career path"? That question gave me pause.

In Korean, the word "seonsaengnim" (teacher) is not merely a job title - it carries deep connotations of respect and trust. But do I truly deserve to be called by that name? Am I a teacher worthy of such reverence? These questions began to surface within me.

When I first entered the profession, my ideal was to "guide children and learn with them." But reality has been far from ideal. Teacher authority has eroded rapidly in Korea, while parents' complaints have grown more aggressive and irrational. Late-night and weekend calls left me with little personal time and significant stress.

Currently, I am the homeroom teacher of first graders. The children are lovely and endearing. Yet I find myself hesitating to give my heart fully to teaching. The reason is fear - fear of false accusations of child abuse and of parents' complaints. Under current law, even a mere suspicion of abuse can be reported, and if a parent uses this as a weapon, teachers must undergo investigation regardless of their innocence. I, too, have faced similar threats.

One parent once stormed into the principal's office, shouting that I should be fired - simply because I did not greet them in the hallway. Another parent, upset by a message I sent suggesting we work together to address their child's behavioral issues, accused me of "insulting their child" and filed a complaint. Later, I learned this parent had even called others to find more grounds to legally challenge me. Since then, I have lived with constant anxiety: *"What if a parent complains because I raised my voice during guidance? What if they report me for emotional abuse because a child says they were scared of me?"* Even when children run to me saying, "Teacher, I love you," I find myself unable to respond with a hug, a pat on the shoulder, or even a high five simple gestures of encouragement that could now be misinterpreted. This is the painful reality for many teachers in Korea.

In such circumstances, I have turned to graduate study and research as a way to overcome feelings of helplessness and low self-efficacy. The inability to guide students as I wish, or to withstand harsh parental complaints, has often made me feel small. Yet, through research - passing on knowledge to undergraduates, and striving to learn and grow - I have been able to rediscover my sense of purpose as a teacher.

In 2023, a tragedy struck close to home: a teacher just one year younger than me committed suicide after relentless complaints from a parent. This heartbreaking event sparked nationwide teacher protests. I too joined, holding a sign that read, *"Teachers just want to teach."*

That experience forced me to confront a difficult question: *"In a reality where teacher authority is so diminished, why do I continue to be a teacher? What does it truly mean to be one?"*

Eventually, I arrived at a profound realisation. A teacher is not simply someone who delivers lessons well. A true teacher is someone who builds trust with students, empathizes with their emotions, and walks alongside them through confusion and hardship. Sometimes a teacher is a listener, sometimes a counselor, but always, a trustworthy adult present in a child's life.

This role extends far beyond the classroom and is embodied in the very way a teacher lives. And to fulfill this role, teachers themselves must continue to grow.

I now understand that the identity of a "teacher" is not something given once and for all - it must be cultivated continuously. A teacher is someone who learns every day, grows with their students, and reflects on their own teaching and presence. Amidst a changing society, a teacher is one who listens to students' voices, questions the essence of education, and reassesses their own practices.

So, I no longer define myself solely as someone who teaches. I want to be someone who learns alongside my students. Education is not about reaching a destination; it is about walking a journey together. And on that journey, I believe I am gradually becoming someone truly worthy of being called a "teacher."

And I also believe this: teachers across Korea share the same wish. None of us wants to remain just "instructors of knowledge." We long to be true *seonsaengnim* - teachers in the deepest sense of the word. Yet, like me, many feel powerless in the current reality. They love their students dearly, but the weight of unjust complaints and fear of false accusations makes their voices grow faint. I sincerely hope for the day when teachers in Korea can live with joy in their profession, when they can embrace their students without fear, and when they can proudly call themselves "teachers" once again. May the teaching environment in Korea improve, so that every teacher can walk this journey with happiness, alongside the children they cherish.

Through this journey, I have come to realize that the crisis facing the teaching profession should not be understood as a matter of individual teachers' shortcomings. Rather, the difficulties teachers experience today stem largely from the erosion of social trust surrounding the profession and the lack of adequate institutional protection. Education is not a responsibility that teachers should bear alone; it is a shared task that must be carried collectively by schools, families, and society. Yet in reality, teachers are becoming increasingly isolated and are often left to carry this burden on their own. The current situation, in which teachers hesitate to build genuine relationships with children out of fear of misunderstandings or complaints, leaves lasting wounds on both teachers and students. For teachers to meet children without fear and to grow through trial and error, social respect for the teaching profession and substantial institutional safeguards must be firmly in place.

In today's Korean educational landscape, teachers ranging in age from 23 to 65 stand side by side, each bringing different life paths and professional experiences into the classroom. Regardless of age or years of experience, a society in which every teacher can uphold their educational ideals and aspirations is ultimately one in which both children and teachers can learn and grow together in safety and mutual trust.

A RESOLUTION BORN FROM DISILLUSIONMENT WITH MY TEACHERS

Namyoung Kim

Sadly, throughout my years in elementary, middle, and high school, I rarely encountered teachers I could truly respect. I felt this way as a student, and even now, as a teacher myself, that impression has not changed. I still remember a few exceptions: my sixth-grade homeroom teacher, my first-year high school homeroom teacher, and the Chinese language teacher I had in my second year of high school. They were good people - teachers who sincerely considered their students' perspectives, guided us with care, and consistently set an example of integrity and kindness.

Apart from those few, however, what comes to mind are teachers who lacked both instructional skill and professional integrity - some even resorting to emotional punishment under the guise of discipline. They were not only unhelpful to their students, either academically or in character formation, but, in fact, harmful. Not long ago, I was shocked to learn that one of those very teachers had been appointed as an assistant professor at a teacher training university. Perhaps the passage of time has transformed that person into an educator who treats students with dignity, but knowing how rarely people truly change, I cannot help but doubt whether such a person can provide quality guidance to future teachers. All I can do, from a distance, is hope that they no longer act as they once did and that they do not further burden public education.

The decision to become a teacher myself was shaped largely by my experience of having been taught by such unqualified educators. I often asked myself whether I had judged them unfairly in my immaturity, but even as an adult and now as a teacher, my conclusion has remained the same. From a young age I believed that teachers hold enormous power to influence lives at decisive moments, and I still believe that today. Seeing how some teachers squandered that responsibility, I felt a strong conviction that schools should treat students with dignity and nurture their growth - and that someone had to contribute to making that happen.

As long as those who misuse authority and suppress students are allowed to call themselves teachers, true education cannot exist. That is why I chose this path with a promise to myself: at the very least, my students will never suffer from the kind of misguided teaching I once endured.

To me, teaching is not merely about delivering content. It is about possessing strong subject expertise while also walking alongside students as they search for direction in their lives, helping them discover their potential. Had I not become a teacher, someone else would surely have stepped into the role. But what drove me forward was the belief that the students I meet should not be harmed by teachers who lack both skill and integrity. That conviction has held me steady and given me a deep sense of purpose. Even now, I remind myself of this every time I step into the classroom: *If I cannot help my students experience a better form of education, then who will?*

In the end, my decision to become a teacher was never simply about choosing a profession. It was about taking responsibility to do what I could to set right what had been broken by poor teachers. I know one person cannot reform an entire education system, but I can ensure that my classroom is a place of fairness, care, and growth. That is my mission, and that is the deepest reason why I became a teacher.

Finding meaning in practical arts: lessons from the garden and beyond

When I first began teaching Practical Arts in elementary school, I knew it was a subject with enormous potential to shape young lives in concrete and lasting ways. Unlike abstract theories that often remain confined to the classroom, Practical Arts touches directly on the routines of daily living - planting seeds, cooking food, fixing household items, or learning how to manage simple tools. Over the years, I have come to see this subject not only as a set of useful skills but as a powerful way to nurture confidence, cooperation, and joy in children.

One of the most vivid experiences comes each spring, when my students and I begin planting a small vegetable garden on the school grounds. At first, many of them are hesitant to dig into the soil. Some wrinkle their noses at the dirt under their fingernails, while others plant seeds impatiently, not quite believing that anything will come of it. But slowly, day by day, their skepticism turns into curiosity, and their curiosity into genuine care. They water the seedlings, weed the small beds, and protect the fragile sprouts from pests. And then, almost suddenly, one morning a student will shout with delight: "Look, teacher, it's growing!" That single moment of discovery never fails to remind me of why I love teaching this subject.

The harvest season is even more rewarding. When the time comes to harvest the crops they have planted, the students rush to pick what they have nurtured for months. I often see in their eyes a kind of wonder that textbooks alone could never inspire. They do not just learn where food comes from; they experience it with their own hands. The joy of carrying home a small basket of vegetables, sharing it with their families, or tasting it during class brings them a sense of accomplishment that no exam score can replicate. These moments of harvesting embody what I believe education should be - practical, joyful, and deeply connected to life itself.

Beyond gardening, Practical Arts opens countless opportunities for students to master useful skills. I recall teaching a unit on simple sewing, where the task was to repair a small tear in a piece of fabric. At first, the needles slipped, and the threads tangled. A few children wanted to give up, frustrated by their lack of dexterity. But with encouragement, they tried again and again. When they finally managed to stitch the fabric securely, the pride on their faces was unmistakable. In that instant, they discovered that patience and persistence could transform failure into success. I have seen similar breakthroughs when students learn how to cook a basic meal, handle a screwdriver safely, or plan a simple household budget. These activities might appear ordinary, but in the hands of children, they become stepping-stones toward independence and maturity.

As a teacher, what moves me most is not merely the acquisition of skills, but the transformation in attitude that accompanies them. Children who once hesitated to try something new begin to approach challenges with confidence. Students who were indifferent to group work learn to cooperate, because in the garden, no plant thrives without shared responsibility. The subject may be called "Practical Arts," but I have found that it is also an art of cultivating responsibility, respect, and resilience.

Looking back, I realize that my own enthusiasm for this subject has grown alongside my students' experiences. I have learned that education does not always require grand innovations or complex theories. Sometimes, the simple act of guiding a child's hands in the soil, or showing them how to fix a broken clasp, is enough to spark curiosity and joy that will stay with them for years.

In the end, what I find most important and interesting in my teaching is the way Practical Arts bridges the gap between school and everyday life. It reminds students that learning is not confined to textbooks but is embedded in every meal they cook, every seed they plant, and every small problem they solve. Watching them discover this connection has been one of the greatest privileges of my career. If education's purpose is to prepare children not just for exams but for life itself, then I believe Practical Arts holds a uniquely vital place in the curriculum.

The value of feedback: lessons from role models and cautionary examples

Looking back on my own years as a student, I can clearly distinguish between two types of teachers: those who gave meaningful feedback and those who did not. The difference, I have come to realize, was not merely a matter of style but of substance. A teacher's willingness - or refusal - to engage with a student's work beyond a simple grade left lasting impressions on me. It shaped not only how I understood learning, but also how I now approach teaching as a profession.

Some of the most disappointing experiences came from teachers who believed their job ended with a test. They handed out exams, marked them quickly, and returned the papers with nothing but a score written in red ink. For them, evaluation was final, like a stamp of approval or disapproval, and once the score was given, the learning process was over. As a student, I felt invisible in their classrooms. My efforts, my struggles, my progress - all of these were flattened into a single number that told me nothing about what I had done well or where I needed to grow. Over time, I realized how discouraging this was. Without feedback, learning became a one-sided performance rather than a dialogue. These teachers, whether they knew it or not, taught me a painful lesson: that education without reflection or guidance is incomplete.

In contrast, I was fortunate to meet teachers who believed in the power of feedback. They took the time to look closely at my work, to underline strengths, and to point out areas for improvement. Sometimes their comments were detailed, filling the margins of my essays or projects; other times they were brief but thoughtful, a few sentences that acknowledged my effort and nudged me toward a new perspective. What mattered most was not the length of their remarks but the fact that they cared enough to respond. Their feedback told me that my learning process mattered, that my mistakes were not failures but opportunities to grow.

I remember one teacher in particular who transformed how I thought about learning. After grading an essay, she sat down with me and explained why my argument was unclear in certain sections. Instead of dismissing it as poor work, she helped me see how I could reorganize my ideas to make them stronger. That conversation stayed with me, because it revealed two things at once: that I was capable of more than I thought, and that a teacher's role was not to judge from a distance but to walk alongside me as I improved. She became a role model for me, not simply because she was kind, but because she showed me what it meant to treat feedback as part of education itself.

These contrasting experiences taught me that feedback is not an optional extra but the very essence of meaningful teaching. Without it, assessment reduces students to static labels. With it, learning becomes dynamic, a process of ongoing reflection and growth. Feedback bridges the gap between where a student is and where they could be, and it gives them the confidence to keep moving forward.

Now, as a teacher myself, I hold firmly to this conviction. I cannot imagine reducing my students' progress to a number on a test without explaining what it means. Instead, I see feedback as a form of respect. It is a way of telling students, "I see your effort. I value your progress. Here is how you can grow further." Providing feedback takes time and energy, but I believe it is one of the most important investments I can make.

In the end, the lesson I carry with me is simple: bad teachers taught me how damaging silence can be, while role-model teachers showed me how powerful thoughtful words can become. If education is about guiding young people toward their potential, then feedback is the compass that points the way. That is why I aspire to be the kind of a teacher who never withholds it.

MY JOURNEY TO BECOMING A UNIVERSITY LECTURER

Yeon Jung Kim

Childhood and the seeds of learning

My parents have always carried a deep passion for education. From the beginning of my school life, they paid attention not only to my academic progress but also to the values reflected in my words and behavior. In the first and second grade, I attended a local public elementary school. Around that time, my parents spent a long time thinking about what kind of environment would help me learn and grow with greater ease. They eventually decided that an educational setting offering a wider range of experiences might suit my temperament well, and after careful consideration, I transferred to a private elementary school.

That transition changed my life in profound ways. The private school offered subjects and activities that public schools did not usually provide. There, I was able to receive an education that combined the arts, sports, and academics in a balanced way. I learned to play the flute, the piano, and the violin - each representing a different category of instruments: wind, percussion, and string. The school even had a swimming pool, and in summer we practiced swimming, while in winter we had skating and skiing lessons. This wide range of activities ignited a hunger in me to learn more, to push myself, and to excel in everything I tried.

Yet one of the most formative moments came during my very first swimming class. I had just transferred, and unlike most of my classmates, I had never swum before. While everyone else glided through the water with ease, I found myself clumsy, struggling to keep up, and painfully aware that I was the only one who couldn't do it. When I went home that day, I cried bitterly. My pride was wounded, and I hated the feeling of being left behind. My mother, sensing both my pain and my determination, immediately arranged for me to have private lessons. With her support and my persistence, I soon caught up. Before long, I not only swam comfortably but began to enjoy it. The more I practiced, the more confident I became, and eventually I was able to compete in school swimming competitions. That experience planted an important lesson in me: setbacks can be overcome with hard work and support, and sometimes failure can become the very foundation of growth.

Middle and high school: a culture of study

When I moved on to middle school, I entered a community where academic enthusiasm was deeply ingrained. The atmosphere was highly competitive, but in a constructive way. Many of my classmates were preparing for foreign language high schools, and in nearly every class there were two or three students aiming for science high schools. The environment itself seemed to breathe passion. At home, at school, and among peers, the culture was one of relentless study.

During this time, group study became a common practice in my neighborhood. We would organize ourselves into small study circles: one group for essay writing, another for mathematics, yet another for history. These were not passive sessions but spaces full of dialogue and debate. We challenged one another, exchanged ideas, and grew together. After school, it was natural for friends to gather at study rooms or libraries. We would study late into the night, eat together, and then return home around midnight.

I can still recall the smell of the night air as I walked home at that hour. It was cool and clear, carrying something quietly earned at the end of the day. To me, that night air was the scent of pride. Even now, when I leave the laboratory late at night after research, I sometimes catch a similar fragrance. In an instant, I am transported back to those middle school years, walking home with books in hand and dreams of the future.

High school continued much in the same spirit. Since most of my middle school peers advanced together, the academic culture persisted. It was simply expected that we would all attend four-year universities, and indeed most of us achieved that goal. The combination of personal determination, peer influence, and cultural expectation made studying not just a duty but a way of life.

Choosing my path in university

When the time came to choose my career, I was influenced both by societal expectations and family guidance. In those years, it was widely believed that teaching in elementary schools was a particularly suitable career for women. The reasons were practical: stable pay, guaranteed retirement, reasonable work-life balance, and long vacations. My grandfather, who himself had worked as a university lecturer, also encouraged me to pursue a teaching profession. He hoped I would follow a path where I could pass knowledge on to others. With these influences, I chose to attend a teacher's college with the aim of becoming an elementary school teacher.

Even within that choice, I faced another decision: which major to pursue. Personally, I had always enjoyed arts and physical education, and part of me considered choosing a field simply for the joy it could bring. On the other hand, I wanted a subject where I could engage not only my mind but also my hands - a field where I could create, experiment, and apply ideas in practice. For that reason, I chose to major in Practical Arts. It was a decision that aligned with both my interests and my personality, allowing me to experience education not as abstract theory but as something lived and applied.

One class during my undergraduate years remains vivid in my memory even today. The professor was giving a lecture on family studies. Sunlight streamed through the window behind her, and the atmosphere of the classroom seemed almost poetic. She spoke about why family is important, how families are structured, and the meaning of family education. I remember not only her words but also the feeling of that moment - the way the light filled the room, the way the textbook felt in my hands. That day's lesson stayed with me, and I often look back at it as a turning point. It was one of the reasons I grew to love my major and developed a passion for teaching.

Doctoral studies: learning through struggle

When the time came to consider further study, I decided to pursue a doctoral program. It was not an easy choice, because I knew that doctoral work would be very different from anything I had experienced before. During my early attempts, I realized how unprepared I was for academic writing at that level. I vividly remember the first paper I submitted. I had poured my effort into it, believing that hard work alone would carry me through. Yet when my professor read it, I was met not with praise but with stern criticism. I had not truly understood how to write in a scholarly way.

At the time, the criticism felt devastating. I thought I had tried my best, but in hindsight, my efforts were misguided. The experience was painful, but it was also transformative. That harsh lesson forced me to recognize the depth of care and precision required in academic writing. Since then, whenever I write, I do so with greater caution and seriousness. I read and reread, checking every line, knowing that my words must be clear, accurate, and meaningful. That moment of failure, though difficult, shaped me into a more disciplined scholar.

Doctoral life also demanded resilience beyond writing. There were countless nights spent rereading articles until their meaning became clear, countless revisions of ideas that never seemed to reach perfection. Yet those struggles taught me endurance and humility. They reminded me that learning never stops, even for a teacher. In fact, the very struggles I faced as a student made me more empathetic toward my future students.

Becoming a lecturer: fear and growth

It was during this doctoral journey that my professor first offered me the chance to teach as a lecturer. The opportunity was exciting, but it also filled me with fear. I worried that my shortcomings would be exposed in front of a classroom full of students. What if they noticed my lack of confidence? What if I failed to answer their questions? The thought of standing on the other side of the desk, no longer as a student but as a teacher, felt almost overwhelming.

To mask my insecurities, I prepared endlessly. I revised my lecture notes again and again, rehearsed my explanations, and tried to anticipate every possible question. Even so, my first class did not go as I hoped. The evaluations from the students were harsh, and reading them was a painful experience. I felt ashamed and discouraged. Questions crowded my mind: Was I truly cut out for this profession? Had I made a mistake?

Yet amidst the disappointment, I found sources of strength. Colleagues offered me words of encouragement. Even more importantly, a few undergraduate students reached out to me personally, offering kindness and support. Their simple words - telling me not to give up, that they appreciated my efforts - gave me the determination to try again.

I told myself: *Everyone struggles at the beginning. No one is perfect from the start. This is not the end; it is the first step toward becoming better.* With that mindset, I pressed forward. Year after year, I refined my lectures. Slowly, my confidence grew, and the quality of my teaching improved. Each semester brought new challenges, but also new rewards.

One of the most memorable rewards came in the form of letters from students. Some wrote to thank me for my dedication; others shared how much my classes had inspired them. Among these, one note stood out: *"I want to become a teacher like you."* Reading those words moved me deeply. It reminded me that teaching is not about perfection but about sincerity, effort, and the willingness to grow alongside one's students.

Building bonds with students today

Now, as a lecturer, I feel fortunate to work closely with my students, many of whom are preparing for the teacher certification exams. I teach fourth-year undergraduates who are on the threshold of becoming teachers themselves. These students are among the kindest, most genuine, and most responsible young people I have ever met. Each one of them is precious to me.

What makes our relationship special is that it goes beyond the traditional boundary between lecturer and student. I see them not only as learners but also as future colleagues. One day, they will stand in classrooms of their own, shaping the next generation. When that time comes, I hope to cheer them on not only as their former teacher but also as their fellow educator. In turn, they support me as well, encouraging me in ways that give me strength on difficult days. This mutual respect and encouragement from the heart of my teaching experience today.

My teaching philosophy

Through all these stages - childhood, schooling, university, doctoral struggles, and teaching experience - I have come to hold one conviction above all others: a teacher must be honest. Words, actions, and attitudes must align. If I tell my students that they must study diligently, read books, and practice self-discipline, then I must do the same myself. To instruct others while neglecting those principles personally would be hypocrisy.

For me, education is not merely the transfer of knowledge. It is the responsibility to embody the values one teaches. It is about modeling integrity, demonstrating care, and guiding others not only through words but also through example. I believe that students can sense authenticity, and when they see it, they are inspired to cultivate it within themselves.

Conclusion

Looking back, I realize that I did not simply choose to become a lecturer. Rather, each stage of my life - my parents' dedication to education, the challenges I faced as a child, the long nights of study in the middle and high school, the inspiration of professors during my university years, the humbling lessons of doctoral study, and the fears and triumphs of my first lectures - quietly but steadily pushed me toward this path.

Teaching is not always easy. It requires patience, preparation, and perseverance. But it is also one of the most rewarding journeys a person can take. Every day I spend with my students reaffirms my belief that education is both a privilege and a calling. As I continue this journey, I carry with me the lessons of my past and the hopes of my students' future, striving always to teach with honesty, humility, and heart. And if there is one promise I want to keep, it is this: to remain a lifelong learner - so that my students, too, can believe that growth is always possible.

Moreover, education today is entering a future in which the simple transmission of knowledge is no longer sufficient. As artificial intelligence and digital technologies reshape how people learn, schools can increasingly become places where students develop not only what to know but also how to ask meaningful questions, think critically, and act with integrity and purpose. Rather than accelerating competition and measuring learning only by speed or scores, education should move toward a deeper understanding, reflection, and a shared sense of responsibility - honoring the different backgrounds and learning paces of each learner.

In this changing landscape, the relationship between teachers and students also needs to evolve. Teachers should not remain merely providers of answers, but become thoughtful guides who design learning experiences and walk alongside students as they grow. Students, in turn, should not be passive receivers, but active agents who connect learning to their lives, shape their own questions, and expand their understanding through curiosity and effort. Ultimately, what will matter most is not technology or policy alone but also the strength of respectful relationships - seeing one another as whole persons. I hope to keep learning with my students, and to contribute to classrooms where curiosity is protected, dignity is honored, and growth is nurtured over time.

REFERENCES

Ainley, J., & Carstens, R. (2018). Teaching and Learning International Survey (TALIS) 2018 Conceptual Framework (*OECD Education Working Papers*, No. 187). OECD Publishing. Paris. DOI: 10.1787/19939019

An, S. H. (2024, September 2). Three concerns about AI digital textbooks. *Korean Educational Newspaper*. https://www.hangyo.com/news/article.html?no=102462

Asia Economic News. (2023, September 15). South Korea expands psychological support programs for teachers after classroom crisis. Retrieved from https://cm.asiae.co.kr/en/article/2023091511433066026

G-Standard. (2024, July 24). *Compilation of 2,077 Cases of Parental Complaints Infringing on Teacher Rights*. Retrieved from http://www.gstandard.net/news/articleView.html?idxno=528

Han, Y. O. (2022). Analysis of the meaning of the 2022 revised curriculum. *The Journal of the Convergence on Culture Technology*, *8*(5), 59–69. DOI: 10.17703/JCCT.2022.8.5.59

International Association for the Evaluation of Educational Achievement. (2024). *TIMSS 2023 international results*. IEA. https://timss2023.org/results/

Korea Herald. (2024, September 10). *Korean teachers handling larger classes, but starting pay lags behind OECD average*. https://www.koreaherald.com/article/3472092

Korean Educational Development Institute. (2023). *Brief research report, No. 24*. KEDI. https://www.kedi.re.kr/khome/mobile2/research/selectKediBriefForm.do?selectTp=0&board_sq_no=41&article_sq_no=35407

Korean Federation of Teachers' Association. (2024, November 20). *When asked about the advantages of teaching, 'professionalism' in 2004 vs. 'job security' in 2024… Why?* [Press Release]. https://www.kfta.or.kr/usr/wap/detail.do?app=16527&seq=270000381212

Ministry of Education. (2019, April 9). *Ruling party and government approve plan for free high school education – Starting with 3rd-year students in the second semester of 2019, full implementation in 2021* [Press Release]. Retrieved from https://share.google/IiSOf85gjOtgDv7qX

Ministry of Education. (2022). *2022 revised national curriculum* [Policy overview]. Ministry of Education.

Ministry of Education. (2023). *Digital-based education innovation strategy*. Ministry of Education.

Ministry of Education. (2023). Measures to strengthen protection of teachers' educational activities. Ministry of Education, Republic of Korea. Retrieved from https://english.moe.go.kr/boardCnts/viewRenewal.do?boardID=265&boardSeq=96720

Ministry of Education. & Korean Educational Development Institute. (2024). *Brief statistics on Korean education* (Contract Statistics Material CSM 2024-08, ISSN 2093-6990). MOE & KEDI.

OECD. (2023, December 5). *PISA 2022 results (Volume I and II): Country note – Korea*. OECD Publishing. https://www.oecd.org/en/publications/pisa-2022-results-volume-i-and-ii-country-notes_ed6fbcc5-en/korea_4e0cc43a-en.html

OECD. (2024). *Education at a Glance 2024: OECD Indicators*. OECD Publishing., DOI: 10.1787/c00cad36-

Priestley, M., Biesta, G., & Robinson, S. (2015). *Teacher agency: An ecological approach*. Bloomsbury.

Republic of Korea. (2019). *Higher Education Act* [Act No. 11212, partial amendment effective August 1, 2019]. National Law Information Center. https://www.law.go.kr

Republic of Korea. (2023). *Special Act on the Improvement of Teachers' Status and Protection of Educational Activities*. National Law Information Center. https://www.law.go.kr

Republic of Korea. Presidential Decree. (n.d.-a). *Regulation on teacher certification ( ).* National Law Information Center.

Republic of Korea. Presidential Decree. (n.d.-b). *Regulation on promotion of education public officials ( ).* National Law Information Center.

Republic of Korea, Ministry of Personnel Management. (2025). *Allowance Scheme*. Government of Korea. https://www.mpm.go.kr/mpm/info/resultPay/bizSalary/2025/

Shim, T., Jun, M., & Lee, S. Y. (2024). How do Korean secondary school teachers perceive psychological burnout in their teaching careers? *Behavioral Sciences (Basel, Switzerland), 14*(12), 1210. DOI: 10.3390/bs14121210 PMID: 39767351

The JoongAng. (2024, September 10*). Korean teachers' starting salary at 2.83 million, below OECD average — " 2.31 million after tax"*. https://www.joongang.co.kr/article/25277014

The Straits Times. (2024, September 20). South Korea offers free mental health treatment for teachers amid rising stress concerns. https://www.straitstimes.com/asia/east-asia/free-mental-health-treatment-for-south-korean-teachers-amid-suicide-cases

The Straits Times. (2025, February 23). *49 schools in South Korea to shut down amid declining population.* https://www.straitstimes.com/asia/east-asia/49-schools-in-south-korea-to-shut-down-amid-declining-population-data

Chapter 18
Teachers' Voices From Australia

Lori Kate Nichols
http://orcid.org/0009-0007-7257-1709
DET, Australia

Kerry Huke
DET, Australia

Linda Parish
Australian Catholic University, Australia

Heather Huke
DET, Australia

ABSTRACT

Australian education began thousands of years ago, and continues today, albeit vastly different but equally important. Beginning with Australia's First Nations people educating each generation in how to care for culture and "Country", Australian schools began in communities, but there was little formal education, and was nonexistent in many areas. Religion and missionaries brought education to many communities, but it was not until the late 1800s that the Education Act was established, bringing compulsory education for children. Public and private schools were educating Australian children with secondary schooling becoming more widespread as the need for skilled workers increased. Universities were established, providing opportunities for degrees in teaching. Now, there are 4 areas of education in Australia: Early Childhood, Primary and Secondary, Vocational Tertiary education and Higher Education at Universities. Behind every teacher is a journey, a background, a lightbulb moment, and a decision to make a difference. This section includes 4 teacher narratives.

A BRIEF OVERVIEW OF SOME SIGNIFICANT DEVELOPMENTS IN THE HISTORY OF AUSTRALIAN EDUCATION

Heather Huke

Linda Parish

The history of Australian education began many many years prior to colonisation in the 1700s, but significant changes since Federation in the early 1900s have seen both increased educational outcomes for students and increased challenges for teachers and educators. A brief history provides a contextual background for the teacher stories that follow.

DOI: 10.4018/979-8-3373-8983-7.ch018

Pre-Colonial Education

The history of education in Australia began tens of thousands of years ago, as First Nations communities recognised their role in teaching future generations in caring for 'Country' and culture.

This education system lasted for thousands of years prior to colonisation and continues today as First Nations knowledge of kinship, culture, and Country are shared. What colonists would consider a 'societal structure' has been shared for at least 70,000 years from one generation to the next. First Nations ways of knowing, being and doing continue to be cyclical and living epistemologies (Moreton-Robinson, 2011). The perception from the colonial settler lens that groups of First Nations peoples had no connection with each other, due to the vast geographical land mass is one with many truths, these groups had their own social structures, languages and cultures, passing on cultural knowledge from one generation to the next. But, despite the large land mass, vast language and family, the groups did interact like any other society for resource sharing, knowledge and kinship.

Colonial Expansion

Education changed when Europeans invaded these lands now called Australia. Settlers brought ideas of land ownership, which resulted in the oppression and dispossession of First Nations peoples from their lands. British colonists brought their structured and Eurocentric view of education to these lands with promises of free education for all, which would provide opportunities for social advancement. Ex-convicts, settlers, soldiers and landowners exerted pressure on the fragile environment which brought them into conflict with the First Nations peoples already living on these lands. For the settlers living off the land was a difficult experience, mainly due to the extreme climate and isolation. Ex-convicts with some skills were used as teachers in some settings, community-led schools were difficult to maintain or non-existent in remote areas.

Some wealthy families employed tutors from overseas to live with and teach their families, others set up small schools which were governed by churches and their missionaries in the tradition of other British colonies. This ad-hoc arrangement continued during the 1800s as towns and settlements grew more established and the general population grew.

Tension existed between different religious groups looking for favour from various colonial governments as they offered a variety of education models, sometimes staffed by missionaries or clergy. Meanwhile, according to Heffernan (2021), "the Nation's wealthiest required religious and grammar schools that prepared children for secondary education and for universities overseas".

In 1872 free public education was established and the Education Act turned Victoria into the first British colony (and one of the first regions in the world) to offer free, secular, and compulsory education to children.

This is all with a widening gap in educational disadvantage and health for Aboriginal and Torres Strait Islander peoples since colonisation (Heffernan & Maxwell, 2019), and links between poorer education outcomes and health broadly (Biddle, 2006). It is essential to understand and make the connection between pedagogy, educational practice, and their effects on perpetuating disadvantage within a colonised education system. This understanding is crucial for recognising why the oldest living cultures in the worlds' knowledge and education systems should be given a rightful and legitimate agency from a pedagogical standpoint. The benefits these hold for Australian society are broadly significant. It is also important to consider that the power-knowledge relation in settler-colonial knowledge systems is also interconnected and woven into cultural relations in Australia at multiple layers within educational practice, including the curriculum and pedagogy (Weuffen et al. 2023).

Federation Impact

The Federal Government of Australia was established in 1901 under Federation. Meanwhile, the 6 state legislatures provided funding for education as it continued to prepare children for the predominantly labour-focused workforce. In 1900, there was a total of 6900 schools for all colonies which serviced an estimated 3.8 million people. There were approximately 628,000 pupils enrolled in government schools and reportedly 154,000 enrolled in private education. In 1900 secondary education was only available to a small minority of children (Lake et al., 2022).

It is important to recognise that the idea of free and secular education for all children was not for First Nations children. For First Nations children it was for their civility, enlightenment and conformity to colonial values rather than education, with many First Nation children leaving these schools early as they were a "doomed race", sent out to work for the colonies. Alongside the development of schools in the colonies, legislation was passed to allow the forcible removal of thousands of Indigenous children from their families on the order of such colonists as Lachlan Macquarie. This process of churches and welfare bodies taking the 'care' of children who had been removed became known as the Stolen Generations. This practice continued into the 1960s through all states and left very few Indigenous families intact and unaffected. In some families, children from three or more generations were taken. The removal of children broke important cultural, spiritual and family ties and has left a lasting and intergenerational impact on the lives and wellbeing of Aboriginal and Torres Strait Islander peoples (Australian Institute of Aboriginal and Torres Strait Islander Studies, 2025)

The forcible removal of children and disruption to First Nations families caused by these policies has resulted in profound and long-lasting harms, affecting thousands of children and adults. These actions not only created significant education disadvantages but also inflicted deep intergenerational trauma, the impacts of which remain evident in Australian society today (*Timeline*, 2012)

Since Federation, the Australian education system continued to adapt, as policies developed in a system influenced by both private and public sectors. Private and religious schools were able to maintain a significant influence and attract government funding as institutions that provided instruction and education during decades to come.

During the early 20th century, significant advancements were made in education through the introduction of free state primary schooling. Schools became increasingly structured, teachers were formally qualified, and government education departments implemented monitoring systems to ensure standards. However, teacher shortages emerged during both World Wars as large numbers of men enlisted for overseas service. Additionally, students from economically disadvantaged backgrounds often left school after completing primary education to undertake paid manual work, helping to support their families.

Participation in secondary education expanded significantly, particularly after World War II. Technical colleges were established to develop an industrial and trade-oriented workforce, reflecting the growing demand for skilled labour. Education increasingly became a pathway to social mobility, enabling individuals to attain higher qualification and access better-paid professions. However, gender disparities persisted during this period, as many opportunities remained restricted for female students and other groups including First Nations peoples, limiting their access to certain fields and career prospects.

Teachers' colleges were established in the 1890s to provide consistent standards for teacher training, alongside the establishment of universities - one in Sydney in 1850 and one in Melbourne in 1853.

Women who trained as teachers were often required to resign once married, creating inequity and lack of continuity in the teaching profession. Significant changes occurred much later in the 1980s when married women having children were able to take periods of leave, allowing them to continue their chosen profession. Education Unions in various states during the 1980s were active in pressuring various levels of government to allow flexibility and significant numbers of women to remain in the teaching workforce.

By 1895, four universities enrolled 0.16% of the population. By 1914, 3,300 students (almost 1.0% of the population) were enrolled at six universities. By 1939, however, universities enrolled only 14,000 students, or 0.20% of the population (Lake et al., 2022).

Contemporary Education Systems

In the 1980s and 1990s governments realised the inequalities that made education less accessible to a significant group of students and trialled various types of disadvantaged school funding. Attempts at national consistency began, with individual states initially introducing their own frameworks (e.g., CFS in Victoria, NSW Syllabus) prior to the introduction of a partially successful national curriculum in the early 2000s. This provided a higher rate of secondary school completion and gave opportunities for a larger cohort to attend university with assistance. Universities became more supportive of accepting students from a wider range of social, ethnic and economic backgrounds.

This focus on addressing educational inequality and the provision of alternative pathways to university has changed the landscape for many aspiring young people and reduced barriers to educational completion and success. Curriculum reform during this time also acknowledged systematic issues related to racism and recognising Australia as a multicultural nation.

The four distinct areas of structured education in Australia today are as follows:

1. Early childhood education
2. Primary and Secondary schooling
3. Vocational education and training (VET)
4. Higher education
    1. The role of early childhood education is to provide care and supervision of children, to prepare children for school, and to ensure that children can participate effectively in subsequent learning opportunities. Early childhood education programs are conducted in community programs, pre-schools, and other child-care settings.
    2. Primary and secondary schools in Australia are either government- or privately-funded. The Australian Government is responsible for: allocating funding to States and Territories to support service delivery and reform to meet nationally agreed outcomes; ensuring that the funding arrangements for the non-government school sector and schools are consistent with, and support, the responsibilities of the States and Territories in regulation, educational quality, performance and reporting on educational outcomes

It is compulsory for children to have commenced school by the time they have turned six years of age. Children generally attend primary school until they are 11 or 12 years of age. Primary schools offer programs from Foundation (also referred to as kindergarten or reception) to Year 6 or 7 depending on the State or Territory. Australian primary and secondary schools follow a national curriculum whether they are state, federal or privately-funded.

3. Australia has an innovative model of Vocational Education and Training which is continually changing to meet the demands of industry and workplace requirements. TAFE (Technical and Further Education) colleges providing pathways to employment and training.
4. Higher education requires intensive study over a number of years to achieve a recognised high-level qualification. Higher education takes place within accredited universities or similar tertiary-level institutions. Australia has 43 registered universities. A significant feature of the tertiary education landscape in Australia is the large proportion of international students (approximately 32% of the student body at Australian universities). Even with reduced numbers in the past two years, Australia continues to have the highest ratio of international students per capita in the world. International education is within Australia's top-five exports, contributing $53.6 billion in export income during the 2024-25 financial year. The majority of international student enrolments are from the Asia/India sub-continent region (ICEF, 2025).

More detailed information about Australian school structures can be seen in the ACARA National Report on Schooling in Australia found at https://www.acara.edu.au/home.

It's appropriate at this point to briefly acknowledge that post-formal education environments including higher education, continue to work toward authentically and respectfully breakdown barriers and incorporating Indigenous perspective and knowledges into their course curricula, albeit slow and driven by First peoples (Bennett & Menzel, 2025; Fricker, 2025)

In conclusion, teachers in all areas continue to work to a high standard expected by both state and Federal Government authorities. There is a high level of accountability and constant expectation to apply and improve professional teaching skills. Teaching in the 21st century aims to provide a more inclusive education experience for the community, however remoteness, disadvantage and poverty is a reality and significant gaps exist in both the funding required and funding received to address these areas of disadvantage. The future continues to be shaped by the actions and decisions of political forces, with teachers regularly feeling that their professional ability to provide best practice as identified by educational research is being ignored.

Federal Government reports from 2025 highlight the success of the current education system, however, the recurring themes of class distinction, privatised education and discrimination still create divisions and inequality for parts of Australian society. This, together with increased monitoring of schools through mandated government assessments (National Assessment Program – Literacy and Numeracy (NAPLAN)) and mandated structured pedagogies (e.g., Victorian Teaching and Learning Model (VTLM 2.0)), are among the reasons many teachers are leaving the profession early. There is currently a teacher shortage in most Australian public schools, prompting the Australian Government to develop a National Teacher Workforce Action Plan for addressing the national issue of teacher workforce shortages (Australian Government, Department of Education, 2025). Ever increasing monitoring systems leading to teacher burnout and mental health issues, conflicts with difficult students and lack of support for their behaviours will likely continue to contribute to this shortage if not addressed appropriately. This is evident in the teacher accounts that follow.

A LIFELONG LEARNER'S AND COMMITTED EDUCATOR'S EDUCATIONAL JOURNEY

Heather Huke

My own family's involvement with education began as my parents arrived in Australia as part of the sponsored immigration program during the 1950s. My father, having completed Social Work subjects at an English university and my mother as a trained Mothercraft Nurse, were keen to find opportunities for a new life in Australia. Their initial sponsorship involved support from a church organisation, helping with social support and help with accommodation. My father visited the Department of Education with his university transcripts and was employed immediately as a teacher in a nearby secondary school. This was quite ironic, as he was required to teach Australian Geography as a new arrival from England – a very steep learning curve. In subsequent years this saw him qualify with a Diploma of Teaching while he worked full time for the Department of Education.

My father applied through the Department of Education for teaching positions in primary schools which also provided a house. This experience as a single teacher in a small school sent my parents to some remote locations where they became part of the local communities they were working in. Most of these were farming communities supportive enough to provide a sense of belonging, while my parents continued to find connection in local organisations and through friendships.

Over the next few years, they moved from school to school developing strong ties with some families who lived in the area. My father's development as a teacher was guided by his study and experience, however, it was many years before he worked alongside others in the profession.

In some ways this would have been an unusual teaching experience, as they developed family life and professional lives in small towns. My memories from these times were also somewhat unusual. My father was my teacher throughout all my primary school years in a one-room school in East Gippsland. My mother was his teaching assistant and helped in the mornings with younger children.

The school population was about 20 children, and I was grateful for the years that we stayed in that community. I remember one general store, one petrol station, a school, a memorial hall and tennis courts. Our house was across the road alongside the ten other houses that were part of the town - this was also a farming community. I have memories of travelling to visit other schools for sports days and combined school visits. However, most of our school days were spent in one large room with a wonderful area for play and exploration outside. I commend my father on his gentleness, creativity and tolerance over the years. It was somewhat ideal to experience education from this perspective. I think I was privileged to be protected from the harsh experiences some students of the 1960s and 1970s had to endure. Some great memories included our singing lessons, our yearly productions, where my father taught us all the songs from contemporary musicals, and we were expected to perform and act an abridged version of the musical for the local community. Gardening was also a regular part of the curriculum. We also went walking down to the river for our swimming lessons, where the community had built a wooden pool structure in the deep river and with careful supervision, we all survived - unheard of today.

I also commend my father for our regular physical education sessions. Although he had no enthusiasm for sport, the whole school formed 2 teams to participate in softball and cricket matches. I remember folk dancing, tree climbing and great games of hide and seek around the school property. I can't imagine working as a teacher in those days. I wonder where his peer support came from and how he managed his workload alone. His curriculum documents and course of study were probably a guide, but his enthusiasm to innovate was a real gift. I guess I would label him as a life-long learner who tried to create a supportive learning environment, rather than a heavily structured formal education setting.

Later, our family moved to the suburbs of Melbourne, where I encountered my first experience of a larger primary school with multiple classrooms, teams of teachers, and a sense of transition into the wider world. My high school years were also spent at a state school, where specialist subjects were taught by different teachers. However, this was during a period when qualified mathematics teachers were allocated only to senior classes, leaving many of us disadvantaged by the lack of proper instruction. As a result, we were often forced to teach ourselves, enduring years of frustration and inadequate guidance.

Fortunately, my parents moved from Melbourne suburbs to a Northern Victoria country town where the social and work pressures for our family were reduced. I completed Year 12 in a public high school and planned to move to Melbourne for University. However, at the time the Department of Education was providing free tertiary education and a living allowance for country students to live away from home while they studied. I decided to enrol in a Teacher's College for a 3-year Diploma of Teaching (Primary) and experienced life as an independent student from the age of 17 to 20. I would say that by the end of the 1970s there was a 70% majority of female students in our teaching course, with a higher number of males in areas like Outdoor and Physical Education.

As a 21-year-old with little life experience, I was totally unprepared for the transition to teaching. I was allocated to an outer Melbourne primary school which was built of portable classrooms, either single or double rooms which housed about 500 students. Teachers were unprepared, isolated, and unsupported for the most part. I remember 2 or 3 dedicated teachers within the whole school, but none of them were in leadership positions. There was no mentoring or professional support. It was sink or swim for all the graduates. Those first 3 years were very difficult and as a result I looked for a way out…choosing to travel overseas for 9 months in 1983. Subsequently I took a family leave and worked on and off as I had 3 children. During this time, I studied subjects towards a Graduate Diploma in Early Childhood, and as a parent and interested student I really benefitted from the knowledge gained during this time.

Around the age of 30, I felt ready to return to teaching, this time in another disadvantaged school, focusing on the early years. Fortunately, I had supportive colleagues who offered valuable feedback and guidance. During the 1990s, the Department of Education began investing more heavily in teacher development and professional learning, which proved transformative for my practice. I was finally able to engage with current research, work alongside knowledgeable coaches, and evolve into an informed practitioner - rather than remaining a participant in an under-resourced and seemingly disinterested education system. Through this process, I observed that some teachers were content to contribute little, learn minimally, and repeat the same practice year after year. In contrast, I recognised within myself a strong need to deepen my understanding of child development and best practice, and I embraced every opportunity for professional learning offered to teaching staff.

In subsequent schools I worked with teams of teachers who met regularly and shared ideas. This was helpful in sharing skills, knowledge and expertise. Sub school leaders were chosen, not for seniority, but for their leadership skills and ability to function well with a team. Team planning became a priority, with professional learning a weekly event. So different from those earlier days in my career. Within a school that had a 70% non- English-speaking background we were able to tailor play programs that encouraged conversation and language skills as well as reading and numeracy.

In 1995, I moved to another outer Melbourne location where people were generally better paid and worked there full-time for many years in various roles. I was rewarded by the experience of training to be a Reading Intervention teacher, where I was able to spend daily sessions with individuals or small groups of students who experienced reading difficulties. This experience significantly strengthened my understanding of effective teaching practices, enabling me to apply strategies and continuously refine my approach to support student learning. I also became interested in using literature and children's books to teach global concepts as many of our students had a limited world view. During a time of swift global change, I started to study a Graduate Diploma of Information Studies, hoping to train as a librarian in the later years of my career. While working full time I was able to engage in the challenge of study and appreciate opportunities Library Studies provided. Fortunately, I was able to gain a part-time role in a community library and work alongside some talented librarians, who assisted me in a transition from full-time teaching to part time teaching and part-time library work. This provided variety, challenges and opportunities to work with dedicated staff in the library and information sphere.

Rather than become disheartened and discouraged by our continuously under-resourced education system, I was able to balance my work with the rewards of a new career in a well-funded Council environment where my skills and experiences as a teacher were valued. During the next five years I was able to contribute to this world of libraries, offering free services and programs to people of all ages.

During the COVID-19 lockdowns, which were severe in our state of Victoria, I worked from home developing videos on teaching reading, book collections and staff training via Zoom meetings. I also worked part-time in a Specialist School for 3 years as a literacy coach where I worked with young classroom teachers and taught alongside them in a mentor role. I was also able to establish a new library within the school. I say thank goodness for the variety and the richness of a varied career. Forty years is a long time to work in education and the frustrations of poorly resourced state education, lack of funding, poor leadership and mentoring, high stress levels and many unpaid hours of work.

My experience has led me to look beyond the failures of the current system, knowing I have done my best and value the part I have been able to play in supporting other teaching colleagues, pre-service teachers, parents and students over time. I hope that as a lifelong learner and committed educator I can continue to share my experience outside of paid work and look forward to a future where I can continue to be a support to others.

DO YOU WANT TO BE A TEACHER OR AN EDUCATOR?

Kerry Huke

Writing my story, it's difficult to know where to begin and goodness knows where it will end. But so far, I've enjoyed the process. It has been such a long time since I've taken the chance to write and reflect. There was a time when I would pause at least twice a day, simply to think about what had happened or what my next idea or project might be. Those moments feel like only yesterday. Yet here I am, 38 years old more than ten years since those reflective days, more than twenty since starting high school, and over six years of living in my own home. Still, the memories remain alive in my thoughts and, often, in my heart.

Last night, I dreamed again not a Dr. King kind of dream, but the kind that makes you wake up and take a moment to remember where, and when you are. I woke thinking of friends who have come and gone. I often wake with emotions still fresh, as though I've just stepped out of an old memory. Sometimes I catch my breath, my heart full from revisiting moments that mattered. Those feelings stay with me through the day, soft and warm reminders of where I've been.

Moonee Vale was an interesting place for its time. The school, connected to a large church - now a healthcare centre sat just up from Moonee Ponds train station, across the car park from Woolworths. The schoolyard was all bitumen: hard, hot, and unforgiving. The only patch of grass sat beside a block of flats, and we weren't allowed near it. We were told off constantly for even trying.

Mum and Dad had sent us there with a group of families from our church in Dallas, so every day we'd carpool but that's a story for another time.

The playground sat near the church and was home to endless games of Octopus and British Bulldog. I lost plenty of skin from my hands and knees on that rough black surface. On the far side stood another yard with a large brick wall that became our goalposts and our imagination's canvas. Along the fence line grew small clusters of trees with benches beneath them, and on the ground, a white-painted square where we played down ball for hours.

Oh, how I loved that playground. The cold, slippery bitumen in winter, dangerous and unforgiving, and in summer, so scorching that if you weren't careful, the backs of your legs would burn. It was brutal, but it was ours.

The highlight, though, was the giant truck tyres. Maybe they were just normal truck tyres, but to us preppies, they were enormous. The best fun was climbing into them and having a friend roll you so fast you'd stick to the inside walls. If you were brave, you'd ride and roll over the top as your feet dangled in the air. We played with tin cans and rope, walked on wooden stilts, and best of all chased spinning bicycle wheel hubs, hitting them with sticks to make them roll faster.

I laugh about it now, but this was the early 90s. In fact, in Grade 5 at my new school in Sunbury, a visitor once came to teach us about schools in the 18th and 19th centuries - their games, toys, and equipment. Everything he showed us looked exactly like what we'd had at Moonee Vale. Everything except, of course, the truck tyres.

So many early memories linger. I remember music classes in the hall with the bright purple carpet, playing the glockenspiel and singing a song about Aiken Drum. I can still picture Timothey, Kim, Florence, Stephen, and Karl but what I remember most is rubbing the side of my hand on that purple carpet, really fast, until my skin turned bright green. I never knew why, but I did it again and again, fascinated by the magic of it.

I'm not sure about the scientific or psychological reasons, but I'm convinced I remember more from my early primary school years than from high school. I can recall more German from those early classes than I ever could learn Italian later on.

But one memory stands out more sharply than any other and given the time and the year, it probably shouldn't have been allowed. If you were caught swearing, you had to take a bite out of a bar of soap. We were made to brush our teeth after every meal, and the girls always had to wear skirts or dresses.

And then there was Ms F.

For the purpose of this story, no full names will be used.

Her punishments were something else. She used a rounders bat (small wooden cricket bat) used to strike the backs of our legs when we misbehaved. This is where I start to wonder how much of this is memory, and how much is dream? Still, I see it clearly: Timothy with his long legs and blond afro, running as though he had no control of his limbs. We were told to stand at the end of the playground, hands and legs spread against the wall, before she hit the backs of our thighs with that bat.

It feels impossible now like something that couldn't have happened, yet the sting, the fear, and the shame feel real enough that I can still recall them.

I know I wasn't a good kid at school, and I was definitely a handful as a teenager. But my educational journey seems marked by negative encounters. I still remember standing in choir in Grade 6, trying to sing my part, when my English teacher laughed at me in front of everyone and said, "What, can't you read?"

Moments like that - unkind, unnecessary interventions - shaped me in unexpected ways. In spite of them, I learned to make different choices, to change my path. Even now, some memories feel almost too unreal to have happened.

Despite my negative experiences in Australian education, I've built a kind of synergy in my own teaching practice taking the good and the bad from every teacher I've ever encountered. These stories help me remember the true impact we can have on a young person's life.

I've been incredibly privileged as a teacher to be mentored by remarkable people. But none have been more important than my grandfather, who patiently taught me to read after I was diagnosed with dyslexia and Irlen Syndrome (Scotopic Sensitivity Syndrome) in Year 8.

It was around that time I began finding a sense of calm and a deeper connection to my art. Reflection, journaling, and getting the chaos out of my head and onto a page became a lifeline a way to externalise the mess and finally breathe.

I can still see myself at the kitchen table with my grandparents, talking about creativity, my grandfather looking at me with quiet certainty and saying, "Imagine what you could do with this."

His kindness and belief in me laid the foundation for the educator I would become.

My mother, also a teacher, helped pave my path into education by recognising and nurturing my strengths. She saw how my art could open doors, and how it could lead me into teaching through an alternative pathway, especially when a traditional education degree felt out of reach due to my learning difficulties. Her support helped me achieve what I could never have managed alone.

That's why, as a careers practitioner, I often tell students to "use your parents for good instead of evil" to lean on the people who want the best for them.

As I entered the profession, I worked alongside four outstanding educators - people I watched, studied, and learned from daily. During my postgraduate studies, I was guided by a phenomenal lecturer who implemented Tribes training and developed learning communities built on collaboration.

I know now, as an adult, how vital the creative process is in helping someone discover a love of learning. My role as an educator is to facilitate that learning to ignite passion, enthusiasm, and the natural curiosity at the heart of being human.

My grandfather used to ask, "Do you want to be a teacher or an educator?" He meant: do you want to impart knowledge, or do you want to inspire a love of learning? That distinction has guided me ever since.

Over the years, I've seen countless educational theories come and go. But my philosophy has remained constant: every young person should be empowered through education, empowered to find their voice, take ownership of their learning, and shape their own educational journey.

Early Teaching Career

At 21, as I obtained my postgraduate degree, an unexpected opportunity came: to support my younger sister on a month-long trip to an orphanage on the Thai–Burma border. Immersed in the lives of Korean refugees, I encountered stories of resilience and hardship largely hidden from Western media. This sparked a new curiosity, a desire to understand history not just as dates and events, but as lived human experience. It reminded me that the way we do things in the West is not always the only, or the best, way.

This lesson followed me into my first substantive teaching position. I stepped into the shoes of a highly experienced history teacher, someone with vast, precise, intimidating knowledge. My task: Year 12 Russian Revolutions, War and Society, and 20th Century Australian History. At 21, with many students already 18, I often found myself panicking at night, learning the content before teaching it the next day.

One of the first textbooks I was given, *The Triumph of the Nomads* by Geoffrey Blainey (1975), struck me as ironic, given my lifelong interest in First Nations history and culture. It felt like a test of endurance, a trial by fire, yet I couldn't shake the fascination that kept me returning each day.

After seven weeks, it became clear just how deeply my predecessor had influenced these young people. His impact was quiet, profound, and enduring. When he returned, I knew I had found someone I needed to learn from not just about history, but about being a kind, devoted, realistic educator. He was cynical, yes, but in a way that forced me to confront the realities of education with clarity and resilience.

Looking back, I see how these early experiences shaped my approach. I must have been sixteen when someone told me that experiences can make us victims, or we can choose to treat each day as a lesson. That idea has guided me ever since.

Now, Mr. Savv, the only identifiable name I'll use here, was not the only profound influence in my early career. My first school was a rural high school in central Victoria. I still remember sitting in the staffroom with a remarkable man who spun gently in a roller chair and greeted me in a thick American accent: "Welcome to teaching, it's the best job in the world." Around him sat eight colleagues all different, all engaging, charismatic, and deeply supportive.

People often say education moves in cycles: what was new becomes old, and what was old becomes new again. I've only been in education for fifteen years, and I've already seen those cycles. The challenge comes when education becomes politicised, but I was fortunate to begin in a school where leadership and colleagues were influential, supportive, and pragmatic.

However, within Australia, the education system can often feel like a political football. With both State and Federal governments shaping direction, educators can find themselves at the mercy of shifting policies and changing priorities. Each new government can bring a new agenda, leaving schools to continually adapt, often within short timeframes and without sustained consistency.

A clear recent example of this politicisation can be seen in Victoria through ongoing debates around curriculum content and system reform. In 2025, discussions intensified following the Yoorrook Justice Commission, where calls were made to strengthen the teaching of First Nations history in schools. These recommendations sparked broader public and political debate about what should be prioritised in the curriculum and how history should be taught.

At the same time, education became entangled in wider political tensions, with arguments about curriculum "balance," values, and priorities emerging across media and political spheres. This was further compounded by funding negotiations between State and Federal governments, where agreements were tied to specific reforms in teaching and learning approaches, reinforcing how policy direction can shift depending on political priorities.

Timing matters

Timing matters. You might enter a school at the right moment, surrounded by people who lift and challenge you or in the wrong place at the wrong time, where survival feels impossible. You cannot navigate this profession alone. You grow through collaboration in ways you can't with a partner or friend. It is, in many ways, a shared experience not unlike surviving conflict a kind of shared trauma.

I was lucky to witness exceptional educators working together, creating a culture in which leadership, wellbeing, classroom management, careers, and community all aligned. It wasn't a harmonious time in the community; we experienced losses and hardships common in rural areas, including youth suicide and drug and alcohol issues. But we sought training, we banded together, and I remain grateful for the professional learning that still shapes my practice.

A few years in, I was asked to take on the Year 10 careers programme, supporting students with work experience and work exposure. This sparked a new passion. I was mentored by a Careers Practitioner with more than fifteen years in the field, and together, with our team, we won awards for our work engaging students in vocational pathways.

I completed a postgraduate qualification in careers education, which opened opportunities to work on a national scale at a time when Australia was investing in a national curriculum. Becoming a Careers Practitioner probably surprised no one, given my father's influence in vocational education and his dedication to supporting the local community.

For some time he worked for the local health organisation and three of the local high schools in the region as a youth worker. He was even the Vet placement officer for my friends when I went through high school. Eventually, we worked side by side supporting young people to explore employment and training pathways. It is still a time I think of with positivity. One clear example of our partnership was the development of Project Ready. I remember sitting in a room with my father and members of the Local Learning and Employment Network (LLEN), discussing gaps in education and opportunities young people needed. I still feel a deep sense of pride knowing my nephew is now participating in the programme more than seven years later.

I've never seen Project Ready as a magic bullet, but I'll never forget those early conversations advocating for young people, pushing for change, and knowing our voices contributed to a programme that still supports them today. It reinforced for me the power of collaboration, advocacy, and persistence.

As I began to reflect, I realised how quickly the years had passed. Looking in the rear-view mirror, it became clear it was now my turn to support those coming after me. Some of the people I've mentored have gone into leadership roles I never aspired to, and watching them grow has been one of the quiet joys of my career.

Now, there's something important to talk about: burnout. It is real. It is silent. And it is critical to recognise. A colleague once sat with me and gently suggested I needed to change my approach to reconsider the effort I was putting in and perhaps make different choices. She saw what I couldn't: I was overdoing it. I was undervaluing myself. I was arriving at school at 6:00 AM and leaving after 7:00 PM, still working at home, still marking.

For a long time, I blamed leadership. But eventually, I recognised my own part in it. I had created the situation as much as they had facilitated it. I wanted everything to be better. I wanted the best for every kid. But in doing so, I forgot to take care of myself.

This experience is not unique. Current data from the Australian Institute for Teaching and School Leadership highlights the growing challenge of teacher retention across Australia. Recent workforce reports show that more than one third of teachers are unsure whether they will remain in the profession until retirement, with many working an average of around 50 hours per week during term time. More broadly, research suggests that up to 50 per cent of graduate teachers leave within their first five years, with workload and burnout cited as key factors. These figures point to a profession under sustained pressure—one where passion and commitment are too often outweighed by unsustainable demands. They reinforce a difficult truth: if we do not address the conditions in which teachers work, we risk losing not only educators, but the relationships and continuity that sit at the heart of meaningful learning.

A Lucky Move

In 2019, I made a leap. My sister was working as a social worker at the local special school, and I knew I needed change. I was disillusioned with the integration support our students received in mainstream schools, particularly in careers and pathways, so I decided to learn on the job.

It turned out to be one of the most virtuous decisions I've made. I went from managing careers and pathways for over 1,200 students and teaching Year 12 Legal Studies, to working in a classroom with eight beautiful young men. Learning from them, laughing with them, working alongside them it became a healing experience. They helped me reprioritise myself at exactly the right time, as COVID hit in 2020. I quickly recognised how privileged I was to be working with them during such a dynamic and challenging time.

After a few years in the special school, I was offered an opportunity to work for the Education Department in careers and pathways. Though my time in the education department was short-lived, it sharpened my understanding of where I truly belong. The value I bring the part of the work that feels meaningful and authentic is in the classroom.

When I return to my grandfather's question now - do you want to be a teacher or an educator? - the answer feels both clearer and more complex than it once did. A teacher can deliver content, follow curriculum, and keep the system moving. An educator, however, carries memory, experience, and responsibility. An educator understands that learning is never neutral; every interaction, every word, every moment of care or cruelty leaves a mark that can last a lifetime. In the end, teaching comes down to one essential thing: relationships.

As conversations emerge about the future of education and the fear that artificial intelligence will replace us, we risk forgetting the deeply human core of what education means. Technology may support learning, but it cannot replace connection, trust, or the quiet power of being truly seen by another person.

My own story is proof of this truth. I carry the warmth of encouragement and the weight of harm in equal measure, and both have shaped the educator I am today. They remind me that young people may not remember every lesson we teach, but they will remember how we made them feel - whether they felt safe to be curious, to fail, and to grow, and whether someone genuinely believed in their potential.

Across classrooms, career offices, rural schools, special education settings, and policy spaces, I have learned that education is not about having all the answers. It is about walking alongside learners, advocating when systems fail them, and knowing when to step back and care for yourself so you can continue to care for others. It requires collaboration, humility, creativity, and the courage to change course when something no longer serves students - or yourself.

One of the ongoing challenges our profession faces is that education remains highly politicised. With each change of government come new priorities, reforms, and initiatives. School leaders are often forced to decide how closely to follow political directives versus responding to the lived realities of their school communities. In navigating this tension, leadership must recognise that the greatest asset in any school is its people. Staff are not interchangeable, just as students are not uniform. Effective leaders know their staff, value their differences, and understand that supporting educators as individuals is fundamental to supporting students.

I now know where I belong. I belong in spaces where relationships matter, where learning remains human, and where education empowers rather than diminishes. I choose, again and again, to be an educator - not because it is easier, but because it is meaningful. And if my story leaves anything behind, I hope it is this: a quiet reminder that what we do in education matters deeply, and that choosing to educate with compassion can change lives, including our own.

MY TEACHING STORY: TEACHING PEOPLE, NOT JUST TEACHING A CURRICULUM

Linda Parish

My teaching journey has spanned 40 years, bridging two centuries! I commenced the profession in the mid-1980s, teaching in Primary schools; after a family-growing hiatus I returned to teaching "at risk" youth and adults for a number of years before returning to Primary school teaching. I rounded up my career in a university setting as a lecturer/researcher focused specifically on Primary mathematics education and pre-service teacher mathematics knowledge. This is my story.

Early Aspirations

Teaching was something that was never on my radar growing up (apart from playing schools in my bedroom with my next-door neighbour when I was around six or seven). Towards my late teens, however, I became fascinated with children – how they develop language, how they communicate with each other, how they grow and change. I was also fascinated with all things medical and saw myself working with children within a medical field. My preference would have been as a doctor, but my final year of schooling was not a good one, and my grades fell far short of what I needed to get into a medical degree. I was well and truly over the whole school experience after a disastrous year during which I did almost no studying outside the classroom, so I decided to pursue nursing instead. In those days nurse training was hospital-based, with only a 6-week classroom block before being let loose on the wards with real-life patients. Technically we were not meant to do anything without supervision, but with a combination of understaffing and 20-year-old Sisters who liked to boss us, 17-year-old newbies, around, I found myself more often than not doing things on my own, and some of those things I still cringe about nearly 50 years later!

I lasted in my illustrious nursing career for all of eight months.

I also discovered that 80% of general hospital nursing is with geriatric patients, and that my goal of specialising in paediatrics and working with children would be years away. The obvious second career choice that would have me working primarily with children – was teaching!

Teacher Education in the 1980s in Tasmania

I commenced my teaching degree, a Bachelor of Education (Primary), the following year as neither a school-leaver nor a mature-age student (the concept of a gap year was not something people were familiar with in those days). The benefits of having that year off from studying, however, were immediate. I loved the university experience and the tertiary style of teaching and learning and decided I could easily have become a professional student, if I could have afforded it.

My university cohort was the first to go through as a 4-year bachelor's degree course. Prior to this teaching was a 3-year Diploma of Teaching, with an optional 4th year to upgrade to a Bachelor of Education. I loved the study; I loved the theory. I was not so in love with the actual teaching on placements, though, even though I absolutely loved working with the children. I think in those days I was too much of a perfectionist and was far too discontented with my imperfect approach to teaching, not recognising or understanding that I was still just learning myself.

I still vividly remember some of the experiences from those very early days of "teaching rounds", especially in some little rural schools in northern Tasmania, the state I grew up in.

There was a Grade 2 boy who came to school really excited one day because, "They came and put the poles up yesterday, and next week we're going to get 'lectricity'!" This was in the early 1980s, which may seem like a long time ago to some, but most people had had electricity for at least 50 years by then, thanks to Tasmania's infamous hydro-electric scheme. There were, however, still some small and isolated farming areas that were connecting to the grid for the first time. Probably the biggest significance of this was that these children had not grown up with television.

Then there was Keithy, a Grade 1 boy who wore a patch over his good (right) eye to encourage his lazy eye to strengthen. Keithy invariably managed to sit to the far left of the class group, so was constantly oblivious to what the other students were doing. When asked to line up at the door the class managed to line up with one line of girls and one line of boys, and Keithy standing to the left in his very own individual line. The teacher pulled him up and said, "Have a look around, Keithy, what do you think?" His reply was, "What do I think?... I think I'm happy!" How can you not love children!

Beginning my Teaching Career: A Baptism by Fire

My teaching degree came to a very anti-climactic end when there were very few teaching jobs available in Tasmania. As a non-school leaver student, I did not have a studentship, which was common for school-leavers in those days, which included a guaranteed one-year teaching contract on completion of the degree.

As an early 20s "Taswegian" this didn't bother me too much as I was very keen to leave Tasmania spread my wings. I ended up in Adelaide, the capital city of South Australia, where I had an aunt and uncle I could stay with. I hand-wrote

42 letters and posted them to schools all across Adelaide and finally secured a job teaching Reception (first-year of formal schooling), starting one week into the new year.

This was certainly a baptism by fire for me. As a naïve 22-year-old I assumed that having a teaching degree meant that I had a teaching degree, full stop. I had no comprehension that a teaching degree from one state could look very different to a teaching degree from another state. There were no common state curricula in those days, let alone a common Australian Curriculum. There were no Career Start programs, no induction support materials, no graduate mentoring, just a class of 21 fresh-faced and bright-eyed five-year-olds. To put things bluntly, I floundered! But I loved those kids! I can still name most of the children from my very first class, and even Facebook-stalk some at times (they are now well into their 40s).

Another thing that was different with the Adelaide students I taught was their lack of experience with the kinds of winter weather I took for granted growing up in Tasmania. I once casually mentioned fog, which I then had to explain to them. There was laughter and complete disbelief when I described fog as, "like a cloud sitting on the ground". I'm sure these students imagined clouds being white, fluffy and tangible like cotton-wool. In Tasmania a thick fog could linger until midday and I had experienced yard duty during these times where I knew there were children around me playing, but only because I could hear them, the denseness of the fog hiding anyone more than a few feet away completely from view.

Teaching Hiatus: Family came first

Several years later my teaching career was put on hold when I got married and started having my own children. I chose to be a stay-at-home mum with just the occasional stint at relief teaching. During that time, due to my husband's employment, we moved interstate twice – first to Alice Springs (in the very heart of Australia) in the Northern Territory, where my two oldest children started school and my youngest was born, then to Victoria where my teaching re-commenced. I had come almost full circle – back close to Tasmania, but still on mainland Australia.

Back to Teaching and a Change in Direction

By the mid-90s it still wasn't easy to procure a teaching position in a Primary School, so as well as applying for regular classroom teaching jobs I also applied for a Certificate of General Education for Adults teaching position at TAFE (the Australian government-run system that provides vocational education beyond compulsory Secondary School). The clientele in this course were primarily "at-risk youth", students who had been unsuccessful in completing a School Certificate, even after 10 or 11 years of mainstream education. These young adults still required some sort of education certificate in order to get job-seeker payments. Some of these students were still functionally illiterate; many were convinced they were just "dumb". In my entire career this is by far the best teaching experience I have had – those students taught ME so much about the importance of teaching *people*, not just teaching a curriculum. Ninety percent of my role was to re-build confidence in these young adults, and to see dimmed lights starting to shine, and shattered confidences beginning to repair, was hugely rewarding. This insight into focusing on teaching the learner, not just content, had a powerful impact on all my subsequent teaching experiences – both with children and adults, an in general classroom and intervention practice (including learners who struggle and gifted learners).

Back to Primary Teaching and Further Education

Another move (intrastate this time) saw this chapter in my teaching come to an end, but a fire had been lit! I was back teaching in a regular Primary School classroom, where I had the privilege of teaching Tyler, a 7-year-old who taught me a thing or two. Tyler came from a disadvantaged family background. Not only was he left-handed, but he had possibly never held a pencil before starting school. He also has a severe lisp, which wasn't helped by his missing two front teeth. To watch Tyler trying to write (then try to decipher what he'd written) and to hear him speak (and try to interpret what he'd said) gave many the impression that he was a student who would struggle academically. The reality couldn't have been further from that truth. Tyler was one of the most insightful students I taught and with an exceptional grasp of number. After an experience with snails as part of a unit on minibeasts, while other students wrote about snails being "slimy" or "I like snails", Tyler's barely legible sentence stated, "I thought it was heavy but it was the suction". He also taught me how to multiply by 5 mentally with ease when he recognised that, "I don't know what 24 fives are, but I know ten 24s are 240, so I think five 24s will be half of that." I lost touch with Tyler after he left the school. I really hope other teachers were able to recognise his potential and support his learning appropriately.

At this same time I also enrolled to do a Master of Education, specialising in early-years mathematics. On completion of this degree, I was invited to take on a one-year teaching contract at the university teaching pre-service teachers' mathematics pedagogy. This work was extended year by year until I completed my PhD and was offered a permanent, ongoing position of Teaching and Research. My career finally reached what had been my core passion – basically being a full-time "student" (researcher) while also teaching what I loved the most: mathematics and mathematics pedagogy.

A Mathematics Education Research Focus

My research focus for the past 15+ years has been on supporting the mathematics learning of students who are vulnerable in a regular classroom setting – both those who do not learn at the expected rate required by the curriculum, and those who learn much faster than the curriculum suggests.

My PhD topic was on young mathematically gifted students, those who I call the "forgotten vulnerable". These students learn at a faster rate, both requiring fewer learning experiences to construct new concepts, and readily generalising these concepts to other, more sophisticated concepts. This can give the impression that they just "know" things without ever being taught. The solution to this is not to simply bump them up a grade or give them the next grade-level work to complete – they will still learn quickly and generalise readily leaving them under-challenged and probably underachieving. It's important to recognise that gifted students consistently receiving A+ grades with no effort are still underachieving.

Contrary to popular belief, the danger of being under-challenged is not simply boredom, potentially resulting in behaviour issues. The bigger danger is that these students come to believe that learning is easy, and that "successful learning" is measured by not having to struggle when presented with something new. "I know they are good at maths because they can answer the questions quickly and they're always right", is a quote from one of the students I worked with for my PhD research. This 9-year-old student's learning was severely impaired by this belief. Confrontation with something new that she couldn't do straight away resulted in overwhelming and debilitating feelings of failure and distress. She felt that she was "not good at maths" because she was a thinker, not a fast worker, and she sometimes got answers wrong (even when her "wrong" answers were not mathematically incorrect, but because she had gone above and beyond the task at hand so had a different answer to others). This was a result of the core-belief (mindset) that she had developed from her own life and school experiences.

After working with this student for three months on challenging this self-limiting mindset and providing sufficient support with suitably challenging work, her mindset shifted noticeably: "I know I'm good at maths because I didn't think I could do that (pointing to a task that took 30-minutes of sustained effort to complete), but I did it!" Note that her comment had changed from "I know *they* are good at maths" to "I know *I* am good at maths".

Teaching Pre-Service Teachers

Throughout my career I have taught 5-year-olds right through to mature adults. Pedagogy and andragogy may differ, but learner needs are the same – all students need teaching approaches that take their individual differences into consideration (and I'm not talking about the different "learning styles", a theory that was first debunked nearly 20 years ago in an extensive review of decades of research).

I very clearly remember one Bachelor of Education (Primary) student coming to see me at the end of the first week in the first year of her course in tears. She confided in me that she thought she had made a mistake, and that tertiary education was not accessible for her as she had been diagnosed with severe dyslexia as a child. She had spent time during a gap year, after completing Year 12, working as a teacher aide in a Year 6 classroom where she had spent much of her time working with some boys with dyslexia. She felt as though she was able to really connect with these boys because of her own experience, and thought, as a teacher, she could really have a positive impact on other students like them.

Once the reality of the study-load required for tertiary learning hit her, however, she began to second guess her decision. The first step was to remind her that the strategies she had developed to overcome the challenges of dyslexia had had enabled her to not only successfully completed Year 12 but to completed it with a high enough score (better than 70% of that year's student population) to get into a teaching degree. Through sheer determination and support from the university's disability services and staff, the student completed her degree within the standard four years. She procured a teaching position at a school in a very disadvantaged area, and within a year was appointed as the school's literacy leader. She is an amazing teacher, making a huge difference in the lives of students who have historically been misunderstood and often left behind.

It is the stories of the students I have taught that have made my teaching career so fulfilling. It is not about the grades students get, it is about their successful learning, and that can look very different from one student to the next.

The Last Chapter (for now...)

I am now heading into retirement and looking back; one regret is that I did not know, in my early years of teaching, what I know now! The only reason for this is that I feel I could have helped more students more effectively over the years.

My biggest sorrow, however, is that education in parts of Australia currently seems to be following a trend of distrusting, disregarding and discrediting research, especially obvious in mathematics education, with the introduction of mandated direct instruction approaches to reportedly "reduce cognitive load". Having fought so hard over the years to encourage teachers to have high expectations of their students, to challenge them with tasks that require both sustained effort and creativity, and to understand mathematics as concept-based, not skill-based, this is devastating. Teaching mathematics can be a very effective vehicle for teaching students how to solve any problem in life (1. identify what the problem is, 2. come up with a plan that may work to solve the problem, 3. implement the plan, 4. assess the outcome of the plan, then repeat from step 2 if necessary). Mathematics should be a way of learning how to think critically and reason logically; it is not a list of rules and procedures to memorise. However, schools are now being encouraged to use a direct-instruction, rote-based approach – "I do, we do, you do" This approach sees mathematics as the skills, not that the skills enable mathematics to be done. The skills required to be able to do the mathematics are best learnt by doing the mathematics (we don't teach music theory for years before getting students to actually make music).

A recent lesson with a class of Foundation students, late in the school year, required them to explore how many popsicle sticks would be required to make a number chart (for the new Foundation students due to start school soon), representing the numbers from 1-10. The solution to this task requires adding 1+2+3...+10. Working either individually or in pairs the class came up with several different ways to approach the task, with most drawing up a chart and adding physical popsicle sticks before counting/adding them all. Most came to the conclusion that 55 popsicle sticks were needed. One student recognised he could add the numbers 1-10 without having to use the materials. He was encouraged to explore the 1-10 pattern until he realised he could add the numbers more efficiently by pairing them into partitions of 10 – 1+9, 2+8, 3+7, etc. Another student spent time simply counting out 10 popsicle sticks and recording the number sequence, which was still an appropriate learning experience for him. This one task was then built upon by the classroom teacher over a series of lessons to help students notice the place values structure of 2-digit numbers – the two 5s in the number 55 are represented by 5 (bundles of) tens and 5 ones.

Students cannot learn how to problem-solve if they are first shown how to solve the problem and then asked to replicate that. I have learnt that students can be capable of much more than we often give them credit for if they are given the opportunity to show us what they know first, and not just expected to remember something they have just been shown.

In some ways it is sad that I am finishing my career within this current state, but I am choosing to celebrate that the later decades of my career, especially, spanned a time where mathematics education research was so vibrant and exciting. I observed students as young as five doing some incredible mathematics. Teaching students number sense and learning to think and reason mathematically rather than just dispensing my own knowledge has meant that I have been able to learn from my students just as they have been able to learn from me. And continuous learning is what makes life so fruitful.

Final Thoughts

Throughout my many years of experience I have discovered effective teaching is about nurturing confidence, curiosity, resilience and the development of individual people; it is not about delivering perfect lessons. From the rural schools of Tasmania to the "city kids" in Adelaide, to TAFE classrooms filled with at-risk youth, back to teaching six- and seven-year-olds in Victoria, and finally to teaching tertiary, pre-service teachers, where I explored mathematics education in depth, I have learnt that teaching is as much about listening and learning about students' lives as it is about guiding and educating them. My greatest reward has been witnessing those moments of transformation when a learner discovers their own strengths and their own unique abilities, and are excited about learning more. Teaching has been my career, but more profoundly, it has been a wild, exciting and fulfilling ride.

MY TEACHING STORY: I WOULDN'T HAVE IT ANY OTHER WAY

Lori Nichols

What did I want to be when I grew up? Lots of things. A dancer, a dance teacher, an actor, a flight attendant, an architect (yep! Loved drawing house plans) and at one time, a drama teacher. I was discouraged from this, so after school I entered the work force in hospitality, became a dental nurse very briefly, worked in an airport checking people on and off flights to places all over the world, learned Auslan (Australian Sign Language), and worked as an interpreter… What am I today? I am a Visual and Performing arts teacher in a special education school. How did I manage to end up exactly where I thought I might like to be? I'll take you back and explain.

I had a fairly normal Australian life growing up. We lived in the suburbs of Melbourne Victoria, not too far from both of my grandparents, my aunt, uncle and cousins and I could see my primary school at the end of my street. My dad worked very hard in the air freight business, sending perishable foods overseas. He started super early and worked most weekends, travelled for work, but was an excellent dad. My mum worked in childcare and as an integration aide (as they were known then) in a school with students with special needs. I have possibly the most boring of heritages… nearly everyone I have traced arrived in Australia in the late 1800s or early 1900s from Britain. I don't even think I can claim a convict as an ancestor. The most interesting story involves a cattle farmer who got chased up a tree by an angry bull, getting stuck there long enough for a small town to be named Nichols Point in his honour. It's a nice place to visit if you are ever near Mildura in the north of Victoria with the story written on the side of the local shop to read.

If I had to use one word to sum up my childhood, it would be "dance". I started dancing lessons when I was 3. I remember begging to accompany my mum to aerobics classes and doing the moves at the back of the room (Mum actually won aerobics competitions back in the day!) I started dance classes around about that time and barely looked back. I remember idolising my dance teachers and doing well from early on, often moving up a class to dance with slightly older girls. While I was good at dancing, I was probably average at school. I was mostly well behaved, really only told off for talking too much. I had good teachers most of the time with the exception of a rather cranky and strict grade 5 teacher that will go unnamed. Mostly I liked to laugh with my friends and dance. I also really loved art classes. I can still picture the art room from primary school and even some of the artwork I created. There were two teachers who taught grade 5 and 6 every year called Mr Oliver and Mr Uren. They worked so well together and created some fun end-of-year concert items, and I remember doing Grease when I was in grade 6. In Australia, primary school is from Prep (first year of school) to grade 6 and then secondary schooling begins at Year 7 and finishes with year 12. In Victoria, students complete Victorian Certificate of Education (VCE) (there are other options now) and then those results allow entry to university courses.

Secondary school was much the same. I did ok and once I was allowed to start choosing my subjects, I was able to do all the things I liked. Art and Drama. Well, I did have to continue with the core subjects of maths, science, history and English. Also, because of a deal with my dad, ICT (Information Communication Technology – Computer classes in the mid 1990's). You see, my school did not offer Dance as a VCE (year 11 and 12) subject, so I had to attend and pay for it through my dance school. My dad agreed but I had to continue with maths and ICT as he knew it would be good for my future. But I have gotten ahead of myself.

My favourite subjects in secondary school were Art and Drama. My drama teacher Ms Brown was a tiny but mighty woman who I thought was awesome. I also really loved graphics classes. I liked using T squares and rulers and learning about one- and two-point perspectives and drawing things like houses, etc. In fact, I really enjoyed drawing interesting house plans. When I dislocated my knee in year 8, and had to stay home for a while, my dad brought home an architect's drawing table with a ruler on an arm. It was so cool, and I was thinking that maybe I could be an architect when I grew up. That was fairly quickly put to bed when I realised that I would need to learn much more maths than I cared for.

If Dance was my first love, then Drama was my second. I loved being on stage and participated in all the school rock eisteddfods and productions, becoming the choreographer and assistant director of the final school production when I was in year 12. I even received an award for contribution to the school at the year 12 awards night that I did not see coming. I loved drama so much that I had the idea to do a Drama degree in university and then complete a Diploma of Education and become a Drama teacher. When I told my mum, she discouraged it… not that she did not think I could do it, but she worked with teachers and saw how hard it was and that the pay was terrible and I think she thought I would be happier doing something else. So, I did not apply for uni and planned to work. My final subjects for my VCE were English, Maths, ICT, Drama, Art, and Dance. VCE (Victorian Certificate of Education) is what we graduate with at the end of secondary school. Did I do well? Not overly, but by that stage I was determined to be a Flight Attendant. I loved flying and had been on planes a few times and thought that job looked great.

I started working in Hospitality and was a pretty good waitress. It turns out that while too much talking in school gets you told off, being able to talk to anyone about anything is an asset when you work in hospitality and retail. I applied once and came close to becoming a Flight Attendant when Virgin Atlantic came to Australia in the late 1990s but it turns out I am on the short side, and I decided I didn't want that anymore anyway. After a detour into dental nursing (not for me) I continued working in hospitality and then someone I knew started a two-year course learning AUSLAN (Australian Sign Language) and I thought that sounded pretty awesome and signed up to start the next semester. Life changing is a strong phrase but doing this changed the direction I went in and is ultimately the reason I am where I am today so I'm going to say it. This course was life changing. I was good at Auslan, and I did not even have to try to be good at it. I decided to continue to become qualified to be an Auslan Interpreter and make this my career.

By the time I qualified as an interpreter, I was working at the Melbourne Airport as a check-in agent for a company that supplied staff to multiple airlines. It was here that I met a colleague who introduced me to my partner, and we are together 20 years later. It was her who encouraged me to take the leap of faith to try free-lance interpreting full time and leave the airport job. It was also around this time that I began experiencing panic attacks and I was diagnosed with an anxiety disorder. I worked very hard to manage this and working for myself helped a lot. Interpreting is an interesting job where you are almost a fly on the wall to things that would not normally involve you. I interpreted doctors' appointments, university lectures, meetings, graduations, presentations… The list goes on. I even interpreted a funeral in the middle of the bush. One of my regular gigs was at Furlong Park School for Deaf Children. I would interpret their weekly meeting as they had both Deaf and Hearing staff. After a while I was asked to interpret other things that involved the young students and it occurred to me that maybe I could work directly with the deaf students, rather than interpreting for another person to work with them. With encouragement from my partner, I applied for university at the age of 30 and attended a regional campus for 4 years to attain my teacher's degree for primary school teaching. I had plans to continue studying after and become a Teacher of the Deaf but by the time I finished the 4 years, I had had enough.

Auslan helped me get my first teaching job. (See? Life changing). The principal from a school called Sunshine Harvester Primary School had heard from Furlong Park School for Deaf Children that I was graduating and that I had an Arts and Auslan background and they happened to be looking for a teacher to teach Auslan as well as Art. I jumped at it as getting a job as a graduate teacher can be difficult. It turns out that I was not super comfortable teaching Auslan as I did not feel it was my language to teach, but I loved the school and the students. It was a VERY multicultural school with over 70 different first languages spoken by the students. I ended up teaching Prep or Foundation year and then grade 1 in the classroom. I learned so much from the teachers and students. Nearly all of the students had come to Australia as a refugee and most had some kind of trauma in their background. Many students were also from families that had been affected by drug abuse as the area the school was in was known for low-income families. I remember one day some staff going through a box of books that had been gathered through a book drive. One of the books was found to have hollowed out pages and a bag of white powder was found inside. It seems a student had traded a book that they had no idea contained drugs that belonged to someone in their family.

I also fondly remember teaching a boy called Harvey (name changed) whose mum had been in prison and had been given a second chance to have custody of her children and seemed to be trying hard to support him at school. I firmly believe he was undiagnosed Attention Deficit Hyperactivity Disorder (ADHD) and possibly had Alcohol Foetal Syndrome (AFS), or something along those lines, but he was a challenge to teach, and I thoroughly enjoyed trialling new reward systems with him or finding ways to engage him in his learning. It was the beginning of a career filled with the enjoyment of finding ways to engage challenging students. After leaving Sunshine Harvester PS, I found out a few years later that Harvey's mum had relapsed and that he had ended up in foster care. I sometimes still wonder how he has grown up.

My next school was Goonawarra Primary school. It was much closer to home, and it felt great not having a long commute and being able to arrive at work early to get work done or get home before dark during winter. It was quite different from Sunshine Harvester, which was an open plan, team teaching, collaborative school. Goonawarra was individual classrooms with each teacher planning for themselves. This changed over time, but it was an adjustment for me. My first role was as the Art teacher while their usual Art teacher took a year off. I loved it and I really enjoyed teaching across the school and getting to know all the students. The following years were spent in grade 1 and foundation, and eventually I was asked to become a team leader of a team of three teaching grade 1. This was also the year 2020. COVID-19 struck, and my team and I ended up navigating the weird and frustrating world of teaching six-year-old students through a computer screen.

I have NEVER relied so heavily on my students' parents, nor have I ever felt so out of my comfort zone. We had to think through every step of what we were asking our students to do, making sure their parent or guardian would be able to facilitate the lessons. We needed to think about what would be in each of the houses. Do they have blocks to count? Do they have paper to write on? Can they print anything? We managed to sort it all out and started to think a little differently. Students could count and categorise socks by colour, type and size. They could use things like toys or cars to help with their adding, and we found some great online games and websites to support phonics, reading and numeracy. I even managed to rope my Dad into delivering writing books to each of the grade 1 students so that they had something to write on! My Dad was bored out of his brain and very happy for a job to do. We had very strict rules in Melbourne during the first lockdown and we had to get my school to sign a form stating that he was doing essential work for the school in case he was found more than 10km from his home.

It was at this school that I had started teaching Max (name changed). He was a super special kid. I taught him his first year of school and it was clear early on that his ability to focus and manage his emotions was impaired. It took some time to convince his mum to seek some support and eventually he was diagnosed with ADHD. Some medication began to help but it also altered his personality and his appetite. His mum didn't like this and so began a few years of interrupted treatments and some fairly severe behaviours.

During 2020 Max was taught by a colleague who did not understand how to manage his behaviours, and he spent most of that year in and out of the classroom and having consequences forced on him for just being himself. In 2021 he returned to me as a grade 2 student. I had a lot of work to do regaining the trust that he had lost in teachers. This particular group of students was a challenge for me. There were 4 students who had received funding, or was applying for funding, for severe behaviour, but very little of that funding was used by the school to allocate support staff in the classroom. I was managing 22 students, with Max and another student using a tier 3 behaviour management strategy of working 10 minutes on and 10 minute off, others with tier 2 interventions such as personal reward strategies and programs. Nearly half of the class were in and out at different times to reading intervention programs after the year of covid lockdowns had put them behind, while also trying to ensure the rest of the class was engaging in lessons that were differentiated, had multiple exposures and delivered the curriculum.

I did everything I could that year for Max and the other students who had developed behavioural concerns, but with more lockdowns, an increasing workload, more leadership roles and my own existing anxiety disorder, I was very close to burnout. I was experiencing panic attacks again and at school. During one of the lockdowns in 2021, I found a job advertised for Sunbury and Macedon Ranges Specialist School (SMRSS) as the art teacher. I began thinking increasingly about it. Maybe this would be better for my anxiety? Leadership was stressful and as much as I loved working with students like Max and doing everything I could to help them, the lack of support coming from my own leadership was defeating. I applied and got the job, so beginning the next chapter.

Sunbury and Macedon Ranges Specialist School is a school for students who have a disability. They are required to have an IQ score below 70 to qualify but may also have any other disabilities such as autistic spectrum disorders (ASD), ADHD, physical disabilities and many others. Because I wanted to be sure of what I was walking into the next year, I arranged to be absent from my school for a day and spent it at SMRSS, going into each class to get an idea of what I needed to plan for. I distinctly remember walking into the front office and my new principal Jo walking out of her office to ask me if I would be involved in the school production at the senior campus, and that someone had asked if they could make a documentary of it and would that be OK with me. I of course said yes and thought it might be a guy and his cameral sometimes. Boy, was I wrong.

I started the following year and settled into the new role. I loved working one-on-one with the student's making art and soon discovered that abstract art was my best friend – anything goes then! I was spending Thursdays at the senior campus starting the production and we met the director making the documentary. His name was Thomas Charles Hyland and he was so lovely and really keen to make a great documentary as we developed the production from start to finish. There was a meeting with a production company called Truce Films and they discussed financing and how they would be looking for funding from the ABC or from Screen Vic. We still had no idea of what was to come. We just focused on coming up with our production story and were asking our students for some ideas.

The one hitch was that Thomas told us we needed to be careful what our story was about if we wanted to do the documentary, due to the film needing to pay for the rights to songs and concepts. After a few ideas were vetoed by Thomas, we landed on Australian songs and then narrowed to John Farnham and created a story about four school kids who travel back in time to meet John Farnham in different decades and experience his music. I wrote it with input from my partner in crime at school Darcy Nolan and we got on with it. So did the documentary crew. It started with one camera, then two, and before we knew it, there were sound guys, producers and multiple cameras.

Our students were amazing. Even though they had not yet stood in front of an audience, our students really took being filmed at school in their stride. Thomas was careful to ensure that the camera crew and sound guy were consistent, so the students got to know them and while there were 4 students who were chosen to be featured, all students knew that they were going to be on TV at some stage and embraced it. The actual production was also really wonderful for our students. They had lines and dances to learn, costumes and makeup for the dress rehearsals and confidences soared. They became a little team and their support for each other was incredible. It was something that the documentary captured beautifully, showing the small moments of support that we didn't see as their teachers. Even now, two productions later, it is a big deal to be in the production, with so many students wishing to a part of it, that I need to write in extra lines and parts so that no one misses out.

The documentary "This is Going to Be Big" premiered at the Melbourne International Film Festival and after that was released all over the world. I was lucky enough to be asked to go to London for the premier along with one of the students that had been featured. Later it was released on the ABC as a 2-part Limited series and the movie is on Netflix in Australia and New Zealand. I have been recognised in shops, and it is all a bit surreal… I am just an art teacher after all! I have continued teaching Visual arts at both campuses and a production every second year and couldn't be happier!

I really don't think I would be the teacher I am today if I had done that drama degree and started teaching way back when I was in my twenties. I think that all the life experience I bring to the job today is what makes me the teacher I am. It is almost like every part of my journey was meant to happen or was all leading me in a very roundabout way to where I am and where I was meant to be. I love being a teacher. I laugh every day, I am tired at the end of every day, and I see wonderful things every day. Teaching is hard, harder than many people realise, but all that hard fades away when a student holds a paint brush independently by themselves, or says your name for the first time, or is just so proud of the artwork they have created that they hold it all day waiting to show their mum. Seeing students say a line they have been practicing for months and get it right all by themselves is amazing and it is just so rewarding.

I can't really imagine a world without teachers and schools. I do wonder if the sudden rise of AI and all that it can do will impact how we teach, but I just can't imagine a world where students do not go to school to learn all the literacy and numeracy skills they need to be able to succeed in life. People still need to be literate and numerate to engage in technology and we still need to foster creativity and physical activity to produce well-rounded people. I do think that the people who are in decision-making positions for schools and education probably need to rethink the role of a teacher and how much of the work load they really can take. Thinking back to my final year at Goonawarra and how challenging it was to manage the different needs in that classroom, I can understand why so many teachers are leaving the profession. I didn't leave, but so easily could have. A workplace that causes panic attacks is not healthy. I am still teaching because I had a different skill set I could use and took the leap to something different. Students like Max are the ones who suffer when their teachers are burnt out. The constant introduction of new curriculum or updated teaching models, mandating things like Individual Learning Plans and asking for more evidence when providing funding for students who need it is exhausting and distracting from the act of actually teaching. I agree that we need to be looking at evidence-based practices and using them in schools, but it does not always mean more work for teachers or higher expectations when little is given in return. More funding is needed to be able to provide the appropriate supports for teachers because we really cannot do it all and still produce literate and numerate humans who will contribute positively to society.

You know so many people say to me that I must be so special to do what I do every day, but really, I could not think of anything worse than sitting behind a desk and looking at a computer all day long. My job is fun, and I wouldn't have it any other way.

REFERENCES

Australian Government, Department of Education. (2025). *National Teacher Workforce Action Plan, Retrieved from* https://www.education.gov.au/national-teacher-workforce-action-plan

Australian Institute of Aboriginal and Torres Strait Islander Studies. (2025). *AIATSIS 20. Summit 2025.* Retrieved from https://aiatsis.gov.au/whats-new/events/aiatsis-summit-2025

Bennett, B., & Menzel, K. (2025). *Indigenous research knowledges and their place in the academy* (Vol. 7). Springer. DOI: 10.1007/978-3-031-92703-4_1

Biddle, N. (2006). The association between health and education in Australia: Indigenous/non-indigenous comparisons. *The Economic and Labour Relations Review*, 2023/01/01, 17(1), 107-141. DOI: 10.1177/103530460601700105

Fricker, A. (2025). Yarning as decolonial praxis in initial teacher training: An Australian context. *Frontiers in Sociology, 10*, 1561532. Advance online publication. DOI: 10.3389/fsoc.2025.1561532 PMID: 40672972

Heffernan, T. (2021, May 26). *The History of Education in Australia*. Oxford Research Encyclopedia of Education. Retrieved from https://oxfordre.com/education/view/10.1093/acrefore/9780190264093.001.0001/acrefore-9780190264093-e-1459

Heffernan, T. A., & Maxwell, J. (2019). The media's coverage of "Closing the Gap" in Australian education. *Discourse (Abingdon), 41*(6), 1–14. DOI: 10.1080/01596306.2019.1592365

ICEF. (2025). *ICEF Monitor: Global trends in international enrolments and policies as we head into 2026*Retrieved from https://monitor.icef.com/2025/12/global-trends-in-international-enrolments-and-policies-as-we-head-into-2026/

Lake, S., Joannes-Boyau, R., Lucas, A. M. C., Callum, A., O'Connor, J., Pelizzon, A., Tregear, P., & Vodeb, O. (2022). A brief history of Australian universities. *Social Alternatives, 41*(1), 8–16.

Moreton-Robinson, A. (2011). The white man's burden. *Australian Feminist Studies, 26*(70), 413–431. DOI: 10.1080/08164649.2011.621175

Timeline. (2012). The national inquiry into the separation of aboriginal and Torres Strait Islander children from their families, bringing them home. Retrieved from https://humanrights.gov.au/?a=51075

Weuffen, S., Maxwell, J., & Lowe, K. (2023). Inclusive, colourblind, and deficit: Understanding teachers' contradictory views of Aboriginal students' participation in education. *Australian Educational Researcher, 50*(1), 89–110. DOI: 10.1007/s13384-022-00517-4

Chapter 19
Summing Up and Content Analysis of Teachers' Voices

Natela Doghonadze
http://orcid.org/0000-0001-7333-8692
International Black Sea University, Georgia

ABSTRACT

While Chapter 3 involves 49 teachers' stories from all continents (15 countries), this sub-chapter presents content analysis of these personal stories. Although the number of teachers involved in the project cannot be viewed as representative of teachers in the world, however, due to the variety of the participants' backgrounds, the stories (and their content analysis) enable the author of this sub-chapter to have some grounded insights into the problem discussed in the book. The objective of the sub-chapter was to sum up and analyse the ideas expressed in the chapter Teacher Voices. Based on the content analysis, the following themes were identified: family, teachers' and environment impact on choosing their profession, features of effective and poor teaching, insights of what teaching and education is, the advantages and challenges of the teaching jobs, the reasons to become a teacher, the components and the role of professional development, what sort of support teachers need, and, most importantly, what teacher mission is.

INTRODUCTION

Initially, the personal stories of becoming a teacher were not planned as part of a research, but further, while editing them, I perceived them as wonderful material for qualitative research on teacher views on their jobs (I do not use the word 'profession', as many of them are/view themselves as mathematicians, IT specialists, chemistry, literature specialists and so on who teach at schools or universities). I realized that the content analysis of these stories (teacher reflections) will substantially enrich this book.

The objective of the sub-chapter was to sum up and analyse the ideas expressed in Chapter 3 *Teacher Voices* concerning the essence of teaching, its advantages and challenges, as well as future perspectives. The given subchapter is an effort to conduct content analysis of teacher stories included in Chapter 3. The introduction to the whole book is at the same time an Introduction to this sub-chapter. Chapter 2 is in fact its literature review. This is why (being only a chapter part) it does not have a traditional chapter structure (literature review is absent) - it includes the research (content analysis) per se.

METHOD

It is very conditionally possible to speak about sample selection in this case, as teachers just told their stories, they were not involved in research. However, having involved 49 teachers from all continents (15 countries, and one of them with a separately represented autonomy), the book enables to get an overall idea of teachers' carriers, their problems and

DOI: 10.4018/979-8-3373-8983-7.ch019

joys, their perceptions of their jobs and the future perspectives of teaching. Of course, teachers from various countries, depending on the countries' socioeconomic and cultural development, have various problems, but they also have very much in common.

Although the teachers were given an approximate list of what issues they were expected to discuss, all of them emphasised different aspects, most important for them personally or in the context of their country. Separating topics in their writings was easy enough, while with sub-topics, keywords and sentences illustrating them, was more complicated, as there seemed to be much overlap (such as, for instance, advantages of being a teacher overlapped in their texts with the mission of the teaching profession), so, although I did my best, I could not avoid some overlaps.

RESULTS AND ANALYSIS

The tables below represent the demographic data of the teachers in the chapter, the themes and the sub-themes that arose in the process of content analysis, and keywords. The analysis also involves some quantification. Some exemplary sentences are presented and discussed.

Table 1. Demographic data of teacher stories' authors

The number of countries	15 (and one autonomy)
The number of teacher stories analysed	49
School teachers (only):	16
Higher education teachers (only) Involved in teaching both at school and at University	18 12
Other	3
Degrees held	Bachelor (9), Master's (20), Doctoral (20)
Subjects taught	Math (2), arts (2), English (22), History (2), Primary/elementary School (4), Inclusive Education (1), ICT (2), Pedagogy/ Education (1), Drama (1), Pedagogy (1), Teaching Methods (1), Literature (1), Sociology (1), Political Science (1), Social Sciences (2), Biology (1), Science (1), Agriculture (1)
Teaching experience	5-10 years (5); more than 10 years (44)
Gender	Males (13), females (36)
Possessing teaching around the globe experience	5
Doing some other job/receiving a different education before becoming a teacher	11

Although the number of teachers involved in the project cannot be viewed as representative of teachers in the world, however, due to the variety of the participants' backgrounds, the stories (and their content analysis) enable the author of this article to have some grounded insights into the problem discussed in the book. To provide a higher reliability of the content analysis, which is generally quite subjective, as themes, sub-themes, and keywords may be selected differently by different people, I read the stories very carefully three times.

The following themes were distinguished, based both on teacher personal stories and the theoretical analysis in the book: family, teachers' and environment impact on choosing their profession, features of effective and poor teaching, insights of what teaching and education is, the advantages and challenges of the teaching jobs, the reasons to become a teacher, the components and the role of professional development, what sort of support teachers need, and, most importantly, what teacher mission is.

Table 2 includes the results of the most popular theme findings – **teacher mission** (42 participants discussed the topic). Three teachers called teacher mission their sacred responsibility. Ten teachers spoke about humanising education and recommended teaching people, not teaching curriculum (teachers mentioned curriculum much less than they mentioned human relations, however, 'subject' was more often mentioned). Two teachers mentioned that teachers have to ensure student safety (within their possibilities, first of all, in the classroom) as an absolute precondition for learning. Love for students and/or their respect are another precondition. The sub-topics of teacher mission deal with learning/cognition (inspiring love of learning and curiosity and discovery, providing subject and general knowledge and interest towards the subject taught, creating a productive learning environment, mediation between curriculum, syllabus, textbook and the student), contribution to student development (learner autonomy, success, growth, character building, resilience, self-confidence, creativity, socialization, empowerment) and to society (because students are/will become society members).

When counting the keywords, the context was taken into consideration, for instance, 'love' was used in collocation 'of profession/teaching' and 'of children/students'. Correspondingly, only the second type of collocations were taken into consideration. Love and respect for students were often mentioned by teachers. Some people believe that learning depends on the intellectual ability – well, it does, but if there is no curiosity, just the genetic ability to learn does not help much. This is why teachers dedicated much attention to developing curiosity and the sense of discovery as a component of teacher's mission. And making learning interesting is, of course, important. Although teachers wrote much about the greater importance of relations compared to knowledge provision, still the word 'knowledge' referring to their subject and general education was mentioned by them quite often. And this is natural, let alone the importance, teachers have to teach (=provide knowledge). And, whatever is said today about technology able to provide knowledge, learning environment can be provided only by teachers, and it occupies a huge place in teacher mission.

Providing students' growth is also often mentioned by the teachers as an important teacher mission. By growth, of course, they mean intellectual and moral growth/development. Special attention was paid to developing students' cooperative/collaborative skills. And, finally, via student development teachers' mission is to contribute to society development.

The findings are in line with Larsson et al. (2025), Leatemia et al. (2025);. Situations that prompt teachers in problem-based curricula to reflect on their beliefs, identity and mission. *Medical Teacher*, *47*(1), 64-72.

Table 2. Analysis of sub-themes within the "Teacher mission" theme

Sub-themes	# of teachers who discussed the sub-theme	Keywords	# of teachers who used the keyword	# of times the keyword was used
Humanising education (teaching people, not teaching curriculum)	10	Human/humanize/humanity/humanistic curriculum subject	24 12 18	75 23 75
Love for students and their respect	17	Love (for children/students) Respect (for children/students)	13 12	22 25
Ensuring safety	4	Safety/safe	12	15
Inspiring the love of learning	8	Inspire Ignite Love of learning	9 4 1	15 6 2
Developing curiosity and discovery	11	Spark Curiosity Discover/(self-)discovery	5 13 6	7 36 45
Encouraging the interest in his/her subject	10	Interest/interesting	13	18
Providing subject knowledge	10	(subject/content) knowledge transfer	12 5	29 7
Shaping the students' worldview/knowledge (in general)	7	Worldview (general knowledge)	15	56
Mediation (between curriculum, syllabus, textbook and the student; between cultures)	3	Mediation/mediator	3	7
Creating a productive/positive/supportive learning environment	10	Learning environment	19	36
Helping students grow	11	Grow/growth	19	39

continued on following page

Table 2. Continued

Sub-themes	# of teachers who discussed the sub-theme	Keywords	# of teachers who used the keyword	# of times the keyword was used
Empowering young people	8	Empower Give a voice	8 5	11 7
Leading students to success/achievement	10	Success/succeed Achieve/achievement	18 12	29 15
Character building/formation	6	Character	6	7
Developing resilience/persistence in students	4	Resilience/resilient Persistence/persistent	4 2	5 2
Developing collaboration/cooperation	20	Social behavior Collaboration/cooperation	8 22	20 36
Building students' self-confidence	10	(self-)Confidence	15	37
Nurturing hope	6	Nurture Hope	11 6	15 7
Developing creativity	10	Creative/creativity	16	34
Emotional development	8	Empathy	8	9
Developing moral values	7	Values	9	12
Developing patriotism	1	Patriotism	1	1
Positive influence on society	8	Influence Impact Society	5 5 19	8 5 29
Stimulating national development	2	National development	1	1

For those who have not read the personal stories or read them superficially, here come the especially interesting statements by the teachers:

- My role as an educator is to facilitate that learning to ignite passion, enthusiasm, and the natural curiosity at the heart of being human.
- A teacher can deliver content, follow curriculum, and keep the system moving. An educator, however, carries memory, experience, and responsibility. An educator understands that learning is never neutral; every interaction, every word, every moment of care or cruelty leaves a mark that can last a lifetime. In the end, teaching comes down to one essential thing: relationships.
- Young people may not remember every lesson we teach, but they will remember how we made them feel - whether they felt safe to be curious, to fail, and to grow, and whether someone genuinely believed in their potential.
- Education is not about having all the answers. It is about walking alongside learners, advocating when systems fail them, and knowing when to step back and care for yourself so you can continue to care for others. It requires collaboration, humility, creativity, and the courage to change course when something no longer serves students - or yourself.
- Teachers not only must explain lessons but also guide students in social behavior, emotional development, and moral values.
- A teacher is also a leader, guiding students through challenges.
- Some of these students were still functionally illiterate; many were convinced they were just "dumb". In my entire career this is by far the best teaching experience I have had – those students taught ME so much about the importance of teaching *people*, not just teaching a curriculum.
- It is my desire that my students would remember me as someone who made them feel observed, pushed them, and believed in them.
- In my view, the teacher remains the heart of education – building relationship with and among students, where meaning is negotiated and knowledge is built collaboratively.

- In my view, the teacher's role in this technological era is to act as a mediator, someone who helps students interpret, question, and humanise the digital world. Our mission is not to compete with technology, but to give it meaning.
- We are creating the future of this world.
- The foundation of my philosophy as an educator began to take root: that the purpose of education is not to transfer knowledge, but to give others the confidence to form their own ideas and understanding of the world around them.
- A teacher may not change the world with a single lesson, but they can change the life of a single student - and that student may one day change the world.
- I hope to keep learning with my students, and to contribute to classrooms where curiosity is protected, dignity is honored, and growth is nurtured over time.

Table 3 deals with the second by popularity themes of features of **good and poor teaching** (41 teachers spoke about it). Their sub-themes include personal features, professional qualification, and attitude towards teaching. Some features were viewed by me as both personal and professional (e.g., care). Numerous personal features of good teachers were named, but the especially popular keywords were 'caring, 'supportive', 'empathetic', and 'patient'. Concerning strictness, it was used four times in a positive manner (strict but fair, strict but calm and never raised her voice, strict, but with a sense of humour, strict and caring) and twice in a negative way. When used in a positive way, it rather stood for "demanding" than for "stern". Not too much was spoken about poor teaching. What is interesting, several teachers mentioned that dealing with poor teaching also played a kind of a positive role in their lives: they learned how not to teach.

Among professional characteristics of good teaching knowledge of the subject, teaching methodologies and theories, respect and trust of every student, as well as learning from experience were stressed. Besides, student-centrered approach, with its different features, was underscored.

Table 3. Features of good and poor teaching

Sub-theme	# of teachers who named this feature	keywords	# of teachers who used the keyword	# of times the keyword was used
Personal features of good teachers	38	Gentle Kind Caring	2 9 31	2 9 38
		Creative/possessing imagination	17	30
		Tolerant (toward mistakes/opinions…)	2	2
		Motivated	16	26
		Committed/loyal/devoted	17	23
		Supportive	25	43
		Friendly	7	8
		Emotional	11	21
		Empathetic	26	51
		Emotionally balanced/calm	13	17
		Realistic/pragmatic	1	2
		Knowledgeable (having a broad understanding of the world)/ loving reading	11	23
		Curious	14	18
		Patient	22	39
		Fair/objective	8	8

continued on following page

Table 3. Continued

Sub-theme	# of teachers who named this feature	keywords	# of teachers who used the keyword	# of times the keyword was used
		Flexible	9	12
		Possessing a sense of humour/laughing/joking	15	19
		Adaptable/Open-minded	16	29
		Wise	6	9
		Humble (humility)	11	15
		Honest	5	6
		Communicative (establishing good rapport)	16	22
		Feeling a need to learn/ Continuous learning	6	6
		Confident	11	15
		Generous	4	5
Personal features of bad teachers	3	Unkind	1	1
		Inflexible	1	1
		Cranky	1	1
		Sharp voice	1	1
		(too) Strict	2	2
		Low qualification/competence	3	3
Professional features of good teachers	45	Knowledge of the subject	44	55
		Innovation	9	10
		Pedagogical and psychological knowledge: Informed practitioner (teaching/pedagogical) Strategies Approaches Teaching methodology, theories, Social Constructivism Kolb's cycles of learning	14 1 4 19 38 1 1	23 1 4 38 71 1 1
		Involvement in research	24	55
		Reflection	15	24
		Commitment/loyalty to the profession	8	13
		Teamwork skills (1)/ collaboration (3)	21	43
		Readiness to share knowledge and skills with other teachers	17	24
		Enthusiasm/positive thinking/optimism (3)	17	19
		Student-centeredness: Individualized instruction Dedicating extra time to students Respect/trust of every student considering students' learning styles, age culture and needs Inclusion Care/nurture	6 3 1 31 9 4 26 3 11	7 5 1 52 10 10 38 3 12
		Learning from experience, positive or negative(13)/Life experience	46	269
		Critical thinking	10	21
		Responsibility for one's own professional development	1	1
		Responsibility for students' growth	13	25

continued on following page

Table 3. Continued

Sub-theme	# of teachers who named this feature	keywords	# of teachers who used the keyword	# of times the keyword was used
		Ethical judgment/integrity	14	20
		Effective leadership	7	11
		Effective classroom management	8	12
		Planning	10	15
		Variety of teaching methods/styles/approaches/activities: Pair work Discussion/debate Project-based learning Problem solving Games Teamwork Open-book exams/quizzes Movies/videos Songs Outdoor activities Performing plays	4 1 10 13 3 6 10 1 5 11 2 4	11 1 16 16 3 7 14 2 5 18 2 13
Professional features of bad teachers	7	Explaining poor teaching by low pay	1	1
		Lacking teaching methods	1	1
		Stressing rote memorization/learning	3	3
		Punishment (including corporal punishment) Discipline/respect based on fear/afraid; disciplinarian (too) Strict rules Misusing authority Suppressing students Humiliation Unnecessary interventions	5 4 5 1 1 2 1	6 4 5 1 1 2 1
		Unprepared Chaotic	3 4	5 4
		Resisting change and innovations	2	3
		Demotivated	2	2
		Teacher-centered	1	1
		Ignoring students' problems	1	1
		Underestimating students' potential	1	1
		Isolated	1	1
		Gossiping about students	1	1

Here are some important statements about efficient teachers:

- I was finally able to engage with current research, work alongside knowledgeable coaches, and evolve into an informed practitioner - rather than remaining a participant in an under-resourced and seemingly disinterested education system.
- I hope that as a lifelong learner and committed educator I can continue to share my experience outside of paid work and look forward to a future where I can continue to be a support to others.
- Sometimes I catch my breath, my heart full from revisiting moments that mattered. Those feelings stay with me through the day, soft and warm reminders of where I've been.
- I've built a kind of synergy in my own teaching practice taking the good and the bad from every teacher.
- I still remember sitting in the staffroom with a remarkable man who spun gently in a roller chair and greeted me in a thick American accent: Welcome to teaching, it's the best job in the world."

- Today's students are different — they want teachers who are competent and credible, and they often verify what they learn through the internet or other resources.
- Some of the most valuable skills I gained during this time include lesson planning, classroom management, and strategies for differentiated instruction.
- Time is changing, and we, as teachers, must keep learning and understanding these changes each day.
- Behind that calm confidence lay careful planning, consistent routines, and, most of all, genuine respect for the students in their care.
- I was lucky to witness exceptional educators working together, creating a culture in which leadership, wellbeing, classroom management, careers, and community all aligned.
- Their students respected them without being afraid. There was structure, but also warmth and authenticity. They didn't raise their voices, yet they were listened to.
- I knew there would be no repression for my errors, but rather more opportunities for growth. From her, I learned to see my students not only as learners but as integral humans.
- I realized that as a teacher, you should never underestimate your students, never compare them to others (students or siblings), never belittle them, and never force them to do a task that they are unable to accomplish.
- A good teacher is not just a carrier of knowledge; he/she is a companion of students on the path to thought, values and self-determination.
- Communicating is not just speaking, it is also understanding, listening, observing, and building bridges from the intangible to the tangible. These bridges are not limited only to the classroom, they also extend to families.
- The day we think we "know enough" is the day our teaching begins to decline.
- A teacher is required to 'think like the learner'.
- I can see how each stage of my professional life shaped me into the teacher I needed when I was young: the confused learner looking for clarity, the shy student seeking encouragement, the novice teacher craving guidance, the practitioner searching for fresh ideas, the mentor striving to support others, and finally the teacher educator navigating the shifting landscape of our profession.
- Good teachers are the ones who can challenge young minds without losing their own.
- A teacher must be honest. Words, actions, and attitudes must align.

And these are some statements about poor teaching:

- I observed that some teachers were content to contribute little, learn minimally, and repeat the same practice year after year.
- It feels impossible now like something that couldn't have happened, yet the sting, the fear, and the shame feel real enough that I can still recall them.
- Control achieved through fear is temporary while respect built through relationship endures.
- Those who seemed to have given up entirely, reading the newspaper at their desks while chaos unfolded around them.
- I disrespect teachers whose goal is to catch (mistakes or misbehavior), punish, fail, and prove that they are the power and the most knowledgeable ones.
- Some teachers say they do not work at their best and are not engaged in professional growth, as their pay is low and they have to make money for their families. Don't go to professions like teachers and doctors if you don't like your job not only in the beginning but also after a few years! This is not yours.
- The lesson was a failure. I did not feel devastated; rather, I sensed that something important had happened. I realized that I had strong knowledge but lacked the practical strategies to engage learners.
- I remember the dark cloud that covered the class for the rest of the day after a beating, and I can say with great certainty that no learning happened after any punishment.
- Treating the job more as a temporary stopover than a career.

The next by popularity theme was how the teachers (34) see the future of their profession – see Table 4. Although the popularity of the teaching profession is decreasing and those who produce educational technologies contribute to this decrease, the teachers are quite optimistic and believe that the profession is changing, but it will be maintained, probably, even become more valued. It is common opinion that technologies are just supportive tools, they cannot substitute human teachers who can interact, trust and be trusted, and demonstrate and support creativity.

Table 4. Future of teaching (teachers vs. technologies)

Sub-themes	# of teachers who discussed the theme	keywords	# of teachers who used the keyword	# of times the keyword was used
Integration of technologies into the educational process	34	Integration	9	11
		Technologies	34	80
Role of AI in education		AI	13	45
Supportive tool/ally		Support/supportive Ally	3 1	3 1
Technology cannot substitute teachers		Substitute	2	2
Teacher advantages compared to technologies		Connection/interaction	3	5
		Trust	3	3
		Creativity	1	1

Here are some importance citations on the theme:

- As conversations emerge about the future of education and the fear that artificial intelligence will replace us, we risk forgetting the deeply human core of what education means. Technology may support learning, but it cannot replace connection, trust, or the quiet power of being truly seen by another person.
- [during the COVID-19] I ended up navigating the weird and frustrating world of teaching six-year-old students through a computer screen.
- I just can't imagine a world where students do not go to school to learn all of the literacy and numeracy skills they need to be able to succeed in life. Regardless of how technology may or may not take over the world, people still need to be literate and numerate to engage in technology and we still need to foster creativity and physical activity to produce well-rounded people.
- Vygotsky's historical-cultural theory and the Zone of Proximal Development have helped me understand that technology is not the center of the learning process - people are. Tools, even artificial intelligence, are extensions of human intention and creativity.
- AI can process data, simulate dialogues, and even generate content, but it cannot feel compassion, build trust, or read the unspoken emotions of a student.
- Education will always need technology, but technology will always need educators.
- It is through teachers that humanity translates its knowledge, emotions, and hopes into forms the next generation can understand and renew.
- I am convinced that teaching will endure as a relational, ethical, and profoundly transformative profession… The future of teaching, in my view, depends less on mastering every new technology and more on cultivating wisdom, empathy, and critical hope.
- Technology makes teachers even more essential. AI can generate content, translate texts, and provide instant answers, but it cannot truly *teach*. It doesn't feel compassion when a student struggles or pride when someone finally succeeds.
- Technology can teach you *what* to think, but only education can teach you *how* to think and *why* it matters.
- I am a big fan of technology, but not at the cost of the environment I share with teachers.

- . In a world characterized by the immediate and abundant availability of information, the educator's role must be redefined. Our primary duty shifts to guiding students to become critical thinkers who are both ethical and responsible in their use of information and acquired knowledge.
- Every morning, waking up, I feel happy knowing that I am going to dedicate the day to something I am passionate about, something that fulfills me not only professionally but also spiritually. Being a teacher has allowed me to look at life with more calm and more gratitude.
- In the age of artificial intelligence, when learners have immediate access to vast amounts of information, policymakers may be tempted to believe that reducing direct contact hours with teachers in physical classrooms is economically reasonable.
- Despite this temptation and the growing role of digital and virtual learning environments, I firmly believe that real teaching cannot - and should not - be replaced. This is not because virtual learning lacks value, but because human interaction is fundamentally irreplaceable.
- AI may lead to a more mechanistic, robotic form of learning, which could have a detrimental effect on learners' development as social beings. Education, after all, is not merely about acquiring information, but about shaping personalities, values, and identities.
- Technology and digital tools can support and enrich the teaching and learning process; however, they cannot replace the pedagogical role of the teacher, the interpersonal relationship with students, or the ability to inspire, guide, and support learners in a holistic way.
- Viewing teaching as a high-stakes intellectual pursuit, deserving of society's best efforts and full financial support, is the only sustainable way to ensure quality education for future generations.
- The future of teaching lies in adaptability, lifelong learning, and ethical responsibility, particularly, in how educators integrate technology while preserving empathy, critical thinking, and inclusivity.
- Technologies that can support learning but never replace relationships.
- Teaching is not a fixed role but a dynamic process of becoming. Its future, at least as I see it, depends less on external reforms and more on the inner readiness of teachers to reflect, adapt, and remain attentive to their learners' changing needs.
- Teaching is not about perfection but about sincerity, effort, and the willingness to grow alongside one's students.
- Rather than accelerating competition and measuring learning only by speed or scores, education should move toward a deeper understanding, reflection, and a shared sense of responsibility - honoring the different backgrounds and learning paces of each learner.

Table 5 includes the data concerning the second by popularity (28 teachers discuss it) theme: **what is teaching?** It includes the following sub-themes: teaching as art, service, educating, way of living, meaningful job, platform that can be used to shape young minds, learning, calling/vocation, science, dialogue between theory and practice, self-discovery, continuous process. It was underlined by one teacher that teaching is not about perfection, it is about presence. Teaching is a continuous process which is not over when the lessons end, it is an endless process of growth and improvement, of overcoming barriers and mistakes, self-discovery and innovation. It is strange enough that only one teacher compared teaching to art, as it is often compared to it. However, besides being a kind of art (the opinion I share), teaching is many other things as well, and, probably, this is the reason why only one teacher expressed this opinion. On the other hand, teaching as science (pedagogy/education, psychology, classroom management) was mentioned quite often. At the same time, the teachers emphasized that effective teaching unites science (knowledge) and experience. Very many teachers underline the importance of relationships/dialogue between teacher and students in the process of teaching – twice as much as spoke about the importance of providing knowledge (educating). They also often mentioned care for their students. Not only care, but also guidance was stressed by many teachers.

Table 5. Teaching is ...

Sub-themes	# of teachers who discussed the sub-theme	Keywords	# of teachers who used the keyword	# of times the keyword was used
Service	6	Service	6	6
Way of living/identity	3	Way of living	3	3
A meaningful job (2)	13	Meaningful Noble	13 7	14 8
Calling/vocation	13	Calling Vocation	13 6	16 11
A platform that can be used to shape young minds	1	Platform	1	1
Educating	10	Educating/education	10	31
A continuous process	22	Continuous	22	35
Learning	8	Learning	10	25
Self-discovery	1	Self-discovery	1	1
Art	1	Art	1	1
Science	13	Science/scientific Pedagogy/Pedagogical/Education Psychology/psychologist (classroom/education) Management	4 9 6 12	4 22 10 18
Dialogue between theory and practice/experience	3	Theory and practice/experience	3	4
Dialogue with students	24	Connection / bridge Dialogue/relationships	5 24	10 43
Care	24	Care	24	35
Guidance		Guide/guidance	23	45

Describing teaching as service, a way of living, a meaningful/noble job, a calling/vocation, and a platform to shape young minds reveals that educators realize the great role of teaching – and that is why they choose/stay in the profession.

Throughout the stories, teaching and education/teachers and educators are often used synonymously. However, the difference between teaching and education was interestingly explained by one teacher: while teaching may be limited by the subject content, education is developing a person. In a sense, all great teachers are educators. Several teachers expressed similar ideas.

Here are some very important ideas on the sub-theme:

- Teaching is not just about instructing students; it is also about continuous self-improvement
- Teaching is one of those professions that often feels like it chooses the person rather than the other way around.
- I have learnt that teaching is as much about listening and learning about students' lives as it is about guiding and educating them.
- My job is fun, and I wouldn't have it any other way.
- Teaching tests your patience, pushes your limits, and shapes your identity in unexpected ways.
- Teaching is a way of life for me, not just a profession. It has changed my perspective on the world and improved my patience, empathy, and comprehension of other people.
- Teaching is not about control - it is about presence.
- Teaching, to me, is not simply a profession - it is a way of existing in the world, of building bridges between what is and what could be.
- Throughout my journey, I have realized that being a teacher means constantly balancing expectations and realities.
- Teaching became not only my career, but my identity.
- Teaching is as much about presence as it is about pedagogy.

- Educating is an ART - it requires all our creativity to motivate and connect with students and make processes dynamic and even personal. When we are teaching, we put on our best performance to keep our audience captivated.
- After fourteen years as a teacher, I believe teaching remains a profoundly human act, centered on accompanying, inspiring, and growing alongside students.
- Teaching, I understood, was not just a job but a lifelong dialogue between giving and learning.
- Teaching, at its core, is an act of faith - faith in human potential, in learning, and in the belief that knowledge can make the world a better place.
- Teaching involves many things, one of them being trying to know and understand your learners. In order to achieve this at times a teacher is required to 'think like the learner'.
- Teaching is not a fallback job but a front-line profession - the foundation upon which every other discipline stands.
- Successful teaching requires flexibility, empathy, and the courage to learn alongside one's students.
- I view the teaching profession as one that stands at a decisive crossroads, shaped by rapid social, technological, and cultural change.
- Education is not a responsibility that teachers should bear alone; it is a shared task that must be carried collectively by schools, families, and society.
- Education is, in my opinion, the most valuable social good.
- Education will always need teachers not only to transmit knowledge, but to nurture empathy, creativity, and hope.

The next two most popular themes were the **challenges of teaching** (25 teachers pondered on it) and **the advantages of being a teacher** (24 teachers discussed it). Table 6 presents them. Trying to classify the challenges and advantages was difficult due to the overlapping nature of some of them, for example, the challenges caused by COVID-19 pandemic were organisational/management (the institutions had problems organising the online educational process), but they also were psychological (stress) and pedagogical (changing the methods of teaching), therefore, I had to choose the dominating (to my mind) feature to classify some sub-themes. Among challenges, pedagogical ones were leading, especially dealing with classroom discipline and teaching in multicultural classes. Among psychological challenges, most important were low student motivation/interest, the need to adapt to fast changes, and coping with stress. Political challenges, especially, war and instability on the country were also often mentioned. Among economic/financial challenges the teachers emphasized low salaries and lack of funding in education. Social challenges were mostly stressed by the teachers from countries where these challenges characterize society in general. The teachers paid much more attention to intrinsic advantages of their work (such as pride for your students' success/achievement/accomplishment) than to extrinsic ones (such as having a guaranteed summer vacation).

Table 6. Challenges and advantages of being a teacher

Sub-theme	# of teachers who named this challenge/advantage	keywords	# of teachers who used the keyword	# of times the keyword was used
Pedagogical challenges	15	(managing students with) Different learning abilities/ knowledge level (in one class)	5	5
		Classroom discipline	14	20
		Adapting materials to learners' needs	5	6
		Class size/large classes	3	3
		Teaching in multicultural classes/environments	7	9
		Increasing complexity of students' needs	4	4
		Grading system perceived as indicator of quality	6	13

continued on following page

Table 6. Continued

Sub-theme	# of teachers who named this challenge/advantage	keywords	# of teachers who used the keyword	# of times the keyword was used
Psychological challenges	12	Tensions between innovation and tradition (1),	2	2
		Lack of student interest/motivation	11	14
		Burnout	4	4
		Isolation (lack of support)	6	7
		Adapting to change	12	15
		Fear of false accusations	1	2
		Stress	11	12
		Various learning styles of students	6	6
Social challenges	6	Gender imbalance among teachers	1	1
		Lack of support and understanding from administration	1	7
		Inequality (as a problem for application of technologies)	5	6
		Society undervaluing teachers' role	4	4
		Bullying	3	6
		Attitude of parents and students	5	6
		Teenage pregnancy	1	1
		Lack of respect	4	4
Political challenges	10	Education being politicized	3	5
		War and instability	10	22
		Systemic neglect	1	1
		Lack of educational research support/funding	1	1
		Lack of research-based (reform) decisions	1	1
Economic/financial challenges	10	High cost (fees) of education	4	5
		Low salaries	7	10
		Lack of resources and funding	10	14
		Limited technologies and educational materials	5	6
		Physical conditions (heat)	4	4
Organizational (management) challenges	9	Administrators with low qualification	1	1
		Overload	1	1
		Work-life balance	1	1
		Having to teach what one hasn't specialized in	1	1
		COVID-19/pandemic	9	11
Advantages				

continued on following page

Table 6. Continued

Sub-theme	# of teachers who named this challenge/advantage	keywords	# of teachers who used the keyword	# of times the keyword was used
Intrinsic advantages: Social	23	Pride for your students' success/achievement/ accomplishment	10	11
		Meeting diverse people	1	1
		Meeting former students years after their graduation	1	1
		Joy of collaboration	1	1
Cognitive		Enjoyment of finding ways to engage challenging students	1	1
		Learning from one's students	1	1
		The joy of transmitting knowledge	1	1
		Shaping minds, identities and possibilities	1	1
Psychological		Feeling young and enjoying communication with the young	1	1
Extrinsic advantages: Financial Social/organisational		Financial security	1	1
		Summer vacation	1	1
		Letters of appreciation from (former) students	1	1

Some important statements on the topic of the challenges of being a teacher were as follows:

- I believe that our greatest challenge will be to remain human in increasingly complex, technologised, and unequal educational contexts.
- Becoming a teacher in Brazil is both a privilege and a challenge. It is a privilege because we work directly with people's goals and help them express ideas, learn a new language, and believe in their potential. But it is also a challenge because our educational system still struggles with inequalities, lack of resources, and limited recognition of teachers' work.
- Perhaps most challenging of all, it means continuing to give your best even when society often undervalues the role of teachers despite the fact that we are the very people who help shape every other profession.
- The air vibrated with the steady chorus of cicadas, the hum of ceiling fans, and the distant whir of old air conditioners struggling against the humidity. We taught with windows open to the heavy air, our voices competing with the sounds of nature and the occasional storm rolling in from the sea. It was exhausting at times, and sustaining focus in the heat was never easy.
- I have verified that when the classroom becomes a community, fear disappears. Children dare to make mistakes, to ask questions, to think differently. In that climate of trust and belonging, the most genuine learning arises.

The sayings dealing with the advantages of being a teacher included:

- Learning from them [students], laughing with them, working alongside them it became a healing experience.
- Because teaching has given me much more than I could ever give back. It has given me stories, voices, and countless lessons that go beyond textbooks. Teaching is not about perfection; it's about presence… This internal reward is what re-dignifies the profession, elevating it far beyond the constraints of salary or public perception. It's a job where we are paid in epiphanies, in moments where potential is unlocked, and where connections are shielded.
- I like young people, and communicating with them helps me feel young, too.
- Teaching is two-sided – I learn many things from my students, too.
- The teaching profession offers a profound sense of purpose that makes us want to create a lasting impact on the learners.

- Nothing would make a teacher happier than seeing a low achiever building progress and developing.

The further by popularity themes were their definitions of a teacher (23) and a classroom (22) – see Table 7.

Table 7. Definitions of what a teacher and a classroom is

Theme	# of teachers who provided their definitions	keywords	# of teachers who used the keyword	# of times the keyword was used
A teacher is…	23	A carrier of knowledge, morality and social change	23	73
		A mentor/guide	23	33
		A sacred master/prophet	2	2
		A disciplinarian	1	1
		A role model/ example/exemplar /exemplary/sample/ best	13	17
		My childhood dream	1	1
		A continuous learner	6	6
		The 'guardians of our future'	1	1
A classroom is …	15	Laboratory	2	2
		Safe place	8	9
		A shared arena of encounter, intellectual growth, emotion, and dreams	1	1

Find below some especially important definitions of teacher roles:

- Teachers are the 'guardians of our future'
- The school was clearly a refuge, a place where the routines of lessons and daily rituals offered a fragile but vital sense of normality. In a country where life could change overnight, the predictability of school was a kind of an anchor.
- A teacher is a guide, mentor, instructor, disciplinarian, a second parent away from home, a friend and a role model.
- Teachers today are no longer mere transmitters of knowledge, but designers of learning experiences, guides in an information-saturated world and guardians of human connection in increasingly digital environments.
- Becoming a teacher has been less about mastering methods and more about learning to listen, reflect, adapt, care, and persist - often against the odds.
- A teacher is like a producer. Planning and delivering a lesson that immerses students is a creative process.

As for the classroom, they characterize is as follows:

- The classroom is not a stage where teachers perform but a laboratory of life where everyone experiments with meaning.
- My goal is to make the classroom a place where students feel supported, valued, and comfortable to engage.
- Teaching didn't just become my career; it became part of who I am. I've learned that being a teacher means choosing again and again every day.
- Classrooms hummed with quiet purpose.
- The classroom soon became clear as a platform and a laboratory, a place where learning, expression, and ideas were all interwoven.

The further theme was **the choice of profession**: who (22) and what reasons (23) impacted their path. Family members have a positive impact on some of the teachers' desire to become teachers. Teachers, good and even bad, also inspire their desire to become teachers. Realizing the social importance of the job, love for helping others, and the hope to be able to make a difference are named as the major reasons for choosing the teaching careers.

Table 8. The choice of teaching

Sub-themes	# of teachers who named this reason	keywords	# of teachers who used the keyword	# of times the keyword was used
Family impact on choosing the profession: One or both parents are/were teachers	9	Father Mother/Mom	7 9	22 15
Family member(s) (informally) teaching them (5)		Father Mother Grandfather Grandmother	1 2 1 3	1 6 3 3
Family members recommending the profession/ supporting the choice of the teaching profession		Father Mother Grandfather Godmother Aunt Great aunt Uncle	2 1 2 1 3 1 2	2 1 2 1 4 1 2
Impact of their teachers on choosing their profession and the way of teaching	13	Role model	4	5
		Idol	2	2
		Advice	2	3
		Inspiring	13	23
		Encouraging	6	7
Reasons to become teachers	23	Social importance of the job/a noble profession	23	32
		Love for helping students	13	43
		Love for working with children	5	8
		Having bad teachers (wishing to change this situation)	3	3
		Making a difference/introducing change	12	14
		Desire to develop curiosity	10	20
		retirement benefits (1)	1	1
		economic stability (if one works in a public school)	3	3

Find below some exciting quotations on the theme:

- She [my mother] saw how my art could open doors, and how it could lead me into teaching through an alternative pathway, especially when a traditional education degree felt out of reach due to my learning difficulties.
- As a careers practitioner, I often tell students to "use your parents for good instead of evil" to lean on the people who want the best for them.
- When it was my time to become a teacher, I was already marinated in education, learning and teaching theories and methods.
- I've been incredibly privileged as a teacher to be mentored by remarkable people.
- I know now, as an adult, how vital the creative process is in helping someone discover a love of learning.
- I have had good teachers throughout my own educational experiences and they reminded me of my strengths and abilities.
- I choose, again and again, to be an educator - not because it is easier, but because it is meaningful.

- Why I decided to be a teacher is a question I've often thought over. At first, I believed I chose this profession drawn by a desire to make a difference, to ignite curiosity, and to help students find their mind
- We keep going, because we know that without teachers there is no democracy, no cultural continuity, and no future.
- We choose it not merely for the abstract concept of vocation, but for connection. We are human beings whose role is to connect not just people to each other, but knowledge to a specific purpose.
- For some people, the thrill, the adrenaline, might be found in extreme sports or high-speed racing. For me, the adrenaline surge, the true sense of professional reward, comes at the end of a class when a student says, 'Wow, today was really a spectacular class".
- [Viewing] digital tools and artificial intelligence as allies in creating personalized, learner-centered environments.
- There were moments when I questioned everything - my choices, my strength, even my worth. But each time, the answer returned to me through the faces of my students, through their stories, through the quiet gratitude that comes when learning changes a life, even in small ways.

Sufficient attention was also paid to the theme of professional development (Table 9).

Table 9. The theme of professional development discussed by the teachers

Sub-themes	# of teachers who discussed the theme	keywords	# of teachers who used the keyword	# of times the keyword was used
Continuous learning	20	Continuous	18	26
Self-education		Self-education Studying (independently) online Committed/dedicated myself to ... understanding/study/ development Self-improvement	1 1 5 1	1 1 5 1
Training sessions & workshops		Training Workshop Seminar Webinar	16 6 2 1	28 9 2 1
Conferences		Conference	7	8
Upgrading/ professional certification/ increasing the level of formal education (Master's, Doctoral)		Certificate Diploma Degree	3 5 17	5 8 25
Developing alongside students		Developing/learning alongside students	8	12
Membership in professional unions, being a member of a professional group		Union Professional/research group	2 3	3 3
Maintaining contacts with the program one graduated from		Maintain contacts	1	1
Participation in exchange programs		Exchange program	2	2
Observing how your colleagues teach		Observation/observe	6	9
Reflection		Reflect/reflection	20	52
Doing research		Research	20	55

These two quotations are notable on the theme:

- I learned that real professional growth requires courage: the courage to face one's weaknesses, to listen to students' feedback, and to question one's assumptions.
- Shaped by the people they meet, the challenges they face, and the responsibilities they choose to carry.

The remaining themes were less popular, however, also important: the support that teachers need (16), teacher workload (12), experiences as a novice teacher (8), and Novice teacher's experiences () were described as simultaneously exhausting and exciting, eventually transforming.

Table 10. Support that teachers need

Sub-themes	# of teachers who discussed the theme	keywords	# of teachers who used the keyword	# of times the keyword was used
Empowering teachers/ recognition of their mission/valuing them	16	Empower Value Recognise Award Demonstrate respect	6 7 12 4 16	6 10 12 5 29
Organising training sessions and seminars		Training Seminar	4 1	4 1
Providing educational materials and technological equipment		Provide Educational materials Technologies Equip	4 1 2 3	5 1 2 3

Here come two quotations on the theme:

- Assisting teachers entails assisting students, and when both are given priority, real change may start.
- Empowering teachers is not a luxury, but a prerequisite for an education that responds to the challenges of the era. There is a need for substantial recognition of their mission and support, so that they can carry out their role with freedom, reflection and prestige.

Table 11. The theme of teacher workload

Sub-themes	# of teachers who discussed the theme	keywords	# of teachers who used the keyword	# of times the keyword was used
Dealing with documents/papers	**12**	Papers/paperwork	2	2
		Bureaucracy	1	1
		Documentation	1	1
Involvement in extracurricular activities		Extracurricular	1	1
Overload		Overload	1	1
Assessment / grading		Assessment Grading Correcting tests/assignments	1 4 3	1 4 4
Preparing/planning lessons and tests		Preparing Developing Design/designer Making up Adapting Materials Lesson plans Tests	12 3 5 2 6 2 3 2	16 3 6 2 7 2 8 3
Classroom management/organisation/discipline		Classroom management Organising Discipline	7 8 10	12 10 15

And this quotation seemed especially important to me:

- I think that the people who are in decision-making positions for schools and education probably need to rethink the role of a teacher and how much of the work load they really can take.

Table 12. The theme of experiences as a novice teacher

Sub-themes	# of teachers who discussed the theme	keywords	# of teachers who used the keyword	# of times the keyword was used
Emotions	8	Nervousness	3	3
		Worrying about clear explanation	4	4
		Anxiety	2	3
		Panic	1	6
		Overwhelming	3	3
		Energising	1	1
Self-perception		Low/lack of self-confidence	1	2
		Low self-efficacy	1	1
		Helplessness	1	1
		Doubt	3	5
		Hesitant	2	2
		Shortcomings	1	1
		Transformation/transformative	5	6
Physical state		Exhaustion	3	6
		Stomach ache	1	1
		Hands tremble/shake	1	1
Degree of preparedness		Trial/baptism by fire	2	2
		Endlessly preparing	1	1

Below find some quotes how teachers describe their experiences of being novice teachers:

- This was certainly a baptism by fire for me.
- I would advise inexperienced or struggling educators not to attempt to accomplish everything by themselves. Seek assistance, maintain your flexibility, and keep in mind that progress takes time.
- Why am I so full of doubt?... Seven hours later, I'm still vibrating. I am in a trance as I'm dropped off at the train station.... I knew something transformational had happened, but I wasn't quite ready to confront myself to understand it.
- Those early months were exhausting, but they were also transformative.
- In that silence, in their expectation, I felt my doubt disappear. I was in charge. I had the Key. I enjoyed the uninterrupted attention of about fifty young minds, and the Head of Department, all engrossed in what I was saying, responding to my questions, and laughing at my jokes.
- I worried that my shortcomings would be exposed in front of a classroom full of students. What if they noticed my lack of confidence? What if I failed to answer their questions? The thought of standing on the other side of the desk, no longer as a student but as a teacher, felt almost overwhelming.

CONCLUSION

The teachers discussed the following topics in their reflections: teacher mission, features of good and poor teaching, future of teaching, what teaching is, challenges and advantages of teaching, what are teachers and classroom, what and who had an impact on their choice to become teachers, professional development, support that teachers need, workload, and their experiences as novice teachers. These are eternal topics of research on teaching and discussion in teachers' rooms. What is a relatively new topic is the threat of teaching being completely entrusted to AI. And here, teachers demonstrate great optimism (otherwise people cannot stay in this profession/occupation, as you like) – the teachers cannot (should not!) be substituted by technologies and education should not be dehumanised. Education decision makers should listen to teachers' voices while distributing the roles of teachers and technologies in the educational process.

To sum up, teachers from all over the world have shared their thoughts about their profession – how they understand it, what the social perception of their profession is, and whether a bright or a gloomy perspective awaits the profession. They expressed some individual views and various attitudes related to the traditions of their societies, however, what is important, they very much hope that teachers will maintain an important position in society and will be enabled to fulfil their honorable mission. The editors, authors and contributors of this book express the desire for teachers to be heard and supported in their efforts. If the book can help this positive attitude to and care of the teaching jobs at least a little, their goal will be reached.

REFERENCES

Larsson, A., Ledman, K., & Lindmark, T. (2025). Controversial issues in Swedish citizenship education: Teachers' strategies. *Citizenship. Social and Economics Education*, *24*(2-3), 169–181. DOI: 10.1177/14788047241309555

Leatemia, L. D., Compen, B., Dolmans, D. H., van Merrienboer, J. J., & Susilo, A. P. (2025). Situations that prompt teachers in problem-based curricula to reflect on their beliefs, identity and mission. *Medical Teacher*, *47*(1), 64–72. DOI: 10.1080/0142159X.2024.2316853 PMID: 38395030

Section 3

Chapter 20
Future Perspectives of the Teaching Profession

Akhilesh Pandey
http://orcid.org/0000-0002-9172-9328
Galgotias University, India

Rahul Bharadwaj
http://orcid.org/0000-0001-9502-5048
SOHT, India

Himanshu Sharma
SOH, India

Sudhanshu Bhushan
http://orcid.org/0009-0008-8420-0734
SOH, India

Shankar Kumar
SOH, India

ABSTRACT

The teaching profession stands at a pivotal crossroads, profoundly shaped by rapid technological advancements, shifting societal expectations, and unprecedented global interconnectedness. As we stand in early 2026, the reverberations of AI proliferation, post-pandemic recovery, and climate imperatives continue to redefine educational landscapes worldwide. This comprehensive chapter embarks on an expansive exploration of teaching's evolution—from its ancient origins as communal knowledge-sharing rituals to its anticipated future trajectories as a hybrid, human-AI symbiotic endeavor. By meticulously tracing historical patterns and projecting forward with evidence-based foresight, the analysis identifies pivotal drivers of change, including artificial intelligence's role in hyper-personalized learning ecosystems, sustainability imperatives that embed ecological stewardship into curricula, and the inexorable rise of data-driven pedagogies that prioritize learner agency over rote memorization.

INTRODUCTION: REFRAMING THE TEACHING PROFESSION

Teaching as a Civilizational Institution

Teaching has historically functioned as a foundational institution of civilization, facilitating the intergenerational transmission of knowledge, cultural values, and social norms. Across diverse historical contexts - from oral knowledge systems and classical philosophical traditions to modern institutional schooling - educators have played a central role

DOI: 10.4018/979-8-3373-8983-7.ch020

in shaping human capital and societal continuity (Darling-Hammond, 2017; Dewey, 1938). Beyond cognitive development, teaching has consistently contributed to ethical formation, identity construction, and civic participation, thereby positioning the profession at the core of social reproduction and transformation.

However, the structural conditions under which teaching operates have never been static. Educational systems have historically evolved in response to broader socio-economic configurations, including agrarian economies, industrialization, and the rise of knowledge societies. In the contemporary era, this adaptive function is being tested at an unprecedented scale.

Contemporary Disruptions and Structural Transformation

The early twenty-first century is characterized by the convergence of multiple systemic disruptions that collectively challenge traditional conceptions of teaching. First, the rapid advancement of artificial intelligence and data-driven technologies is redefining knowledge production, access, and dissemination. Second, escalating climate instability and sustainability imperatives are reshaping curricular priorities and pedagogical goals. Third, economic restructuring - marked by automation, gig economies, and shifting labor market demands -necessitates new forms of skills development and lifelong learning (World Economic Forum, 2023).

These transformations do not merely require incremental pedagogical adjustments; rather, they signal a paradigmatic shift in the nature and purpose of teaching. The conventional model, which positions teachers primarily as transmitters of standardized knowledge, is increasingly inadequate in addressing the complexity, uncertainty, and interdisciplinarity of contemporary challenges. Instead, teaching is being reconstituted as a dynamic, context-responsive profession embedded within broader socio-technical systems.

Central Thesis

This chapter advances the argument that the future of the teaching profession lies in its evolution from a content-delivery function to an adaptive, system-level role. In this emerging paradigm, teachers are not confined to classroom instruction but operate as:

- Ecosystem designers, structuring learning environments that integrate technological, social, and experiential dimensions;
- Ethical mediators, guiding learners through normative dilemmas associated with technology, sustainability, and globalization;
- Human development facilitators, fostering cognitive, emotional, and social capabilities necessary for navigating complex futures.

This reconceptualization aligns with contemporary scholarship emphasizing teacher agency, professional autonomy, and the integration of human-centered competencies in education systems (Fullan, 2020; Biesta, 2015).

Conceptual Framework: Adaptive Ecosystem Teacher Model (AETM)

To systematically analyze this transformation, the chapter introduces the Adaptive Ecosystem Teacher Model (AETM). This framework conceptualizes teaching as a dynamic interaction between structural forces and professional capacities, organized around four interdependent dimensions:

Drivers

These refer to macro-level forces shaping educational change, including:

- Technological advancements (e.g., artificial intelligence, digital platforms)
- Demographic transitions (e.g., aging populations, migration)

- Ecological pressures (e.g., climate change, sustainability goals)
- Economic shifts (e.g., automation, knowledge economies)

Constraints

Constraints represent systemic limitations that mediate the impact of these drivers:

- Policy and governance structures
- Institutional rigidity and curriculum standardization
- Teacher labor conditions and workload intensification
- Persistent inequities in access and resources

Competencies

Competencies denote the evolving skillset required of teachers:

- Digital and data literacy
- Socio-emotional intelligence
- Adaptive leadership and innovation capacity
- Global and intercultural competence

Agency

Agency captures the capacity of teachers to act as transformative professionals:

- Autonomy in pedagogical decision-making
- Participation in institutional and policy processes
- Engagement in research and innovation
- Professional voice and collective action

Analytical Proposition

The AETM framework posits that meaningful transformation in teaching emerges when professional competencies and agency are strengthened in ways that effectively respond to systemic drivers while navigating structural constraints.

Chapter Structure and Analytical Approach

The chapter is organized to progressively build and substantiate this central argument through a structured analytical sequence:

- Section 2 synthesizes key historical developments to demonstrate the adaptive nature of teaching across socio-economic transitions.
- Section 3 examines the major structural drivers currently reshaping the profession, with emphasis on their interdependencies.
- Section 4 delineates the competencies required for future-ready educators within complex learning ecosystems.
- Section 5 critically analyzes systemic constraints, including governance limitations, labor conditions, and equity challenges.
- Section 6 explores strategic pathways for transformation, focusing on institutional innovation and policy alignment.

- Section 7 presents comparative global case insights to illustrate context-specific adaptations.
- Section 8 consolidates the discussion through a formal articulation of the Adaptive Ecosystem Teacher Model.

Concluding Perspective

By integrating historical analysis, structural examination, and conceptual modeling, this chapter seeks to reposition teaching as a strategic profession central to societal resilience and transformation. The emphasis is not on expanding the scope of teacher responsibilities in an unstructured manner, but on redefining the profession through coherence, adaptability, and systemic alignment.

HISTORICAL EVOLUTION OF TEACHING: PATTERNS OF ADAPTATION AND TRANSFORMATION

Selective Historical Framing

While the history of teaching spans millennia and encompasses diverse cultural traditions, this section adopts a selective analytical approach, focusing only on those transitions that illuminate the chapter's central argument: that teaching evolves in response to broader socio-economic and political transformations. Rather than offering a descriptive chronology, the discussion emphasizes structural shifts in the purpose, organization, and epistemology of teaching across key historical phases.

This approach aligns with contemporary historiographical perspectives that view education systems not as autonomous institutions but as embedded within wider societal configurations (Cuban, 1993; Labaree, 2008). Accordingly, four major epochs are examined: oral-traditional systems, scholastic and religious institutionalization, industrial mass schooling, and progressive educational reform.

Pre-Industrial Pedagogies: Relational and Contextual Learning

In pre-industrial societies, teaching was primarily informal, relational, and context-dependent. Knowledge transmission occurred through oral traditions, apprenticeship models, and community-based practices. Learning was embedded within everyday life, with elders, artisans, and community leaders functioning as educators.

These systems were characterized by:

- Integration of cognitive, moral, and practical knowledge
- Emphasis on imitation, participation, and experiential learning
- Strong alignment with local cultural and ecological contexts

From a structural perspective, teaching in this era reflected decentralized social organization, where knowledge authority was distributed rather than institutionalized. As a result, pedagogy was adaptive and responsive, though limited in scalability and standardization (Goody, 1987).

Scholastic and Religious Institutionalization: Authority and Canon

The emergence of formal institutions during the medieval period marked a significant shift toward centralized and hierarchical models of teaching. Religious institutions - such as monasteries, madrasas, and early universities - became primary sites of knowledge production and dissemination.

The key characteristics of this phase included:

- Codification of knowledge into canonical texts

- Teacher authority grounded in religious or philosophical legitimacy
- Emphasis on memorization, commentary, and dialectical reasoning

This period reflects a broader socio-political context of centralized authority and stratified social order, where education served to preserve ideological continuity and institutional stability. While intellectual traditions such as scholasticism advanced critical inquiry within defined boundaries, innovation was often constrained by doctrinal orthodoxy (Durkheim, 1977).

Industrial Schooling: Standardization and Mass Education

The industrial revolution introduced a transformative reconfiguration of education systems, giving rise to mass schooling models designed for efficiency, uniformity, and scalability. Influenced by the needs of industrial economies, education systems adopted bureaucratic structures resembling factory organization.

Defining features included:

- Age-graded classrooms and standardized curricula
- Emphasis on discipline, punctuality, and routine
- Centralized administration and assessment systems

Teachers in this model functioned primarily as implementers of prescribed curricula, with limited autonomy. The objective was to produce a workforce equipped with basic literacy, numeracy, and compliance skills necessary for industrial production.

Scholars have argued that this model reflects the logic of industrial capitalism, where education systems are aligned with labor market demands and state governance structures (Bowles & Gintis, 1976). While mass schooling significantly expanded access, it also entrenched rigid pedagogical practices that prioritized uniformity over individualization.

Progressive Education: Reclaiming the Learner

The late nineteenth and early twentieth centuries witnessed a critical response to industrial schooling through the emergence of progressive education movements. Influenced by thinkers such as John Dewey, these movements emphasized experiential learning, critical thinking, and democratic participation.

Core principles included:

- Learner-centered pedagogy
- Integration of theory and practice
- Education as a process of inquiry and reflection

Progressive education redefined the teacher's role from an authority figure to a facilitator of learning, thereby reintroducing elements of adaptability and responsiveness. However, despite its conceptual influence, the progressive model often remained constrained by institutional structures rooted in industrial-era standardization (Tyack & Cuban, 1995).

Analytical Synthesis: Patterns Across Historical Phases

A comparative analysis of these epochs reveals several recurring patterns that are central to understanding the evolution of teaching:

Alignment with Socio-Economic Structures

Teaching systems consistently reflect the dominant economic and political arrangements of their time. Decentralized societies foster flexible pedagogies, while centralized systems produce standardized and hierarchical models of teaching.

Cycles of Rigidity and Innovation

Periods of institutional stability often lead to pedagogical rigidity, characterized by standardized practices and reduced professional autonomy. Conversely, moments of social disruption - such as industrialization or democratization - create opportunities for innovation and reform.

Tension Between Standardization and Individualization

A persistent tension exists between the need for scalable education systems and the desire for personalized, meaningful learning experiences. This tension remains unresolved across historical periods and continues to shape contemporary debates.

Implications for Contemporary Transformation

The historical trajectory outlined above provides a critical insight into the current moment of transformation. The convergence of technological, ecological, and economic disruptions mirrors earlier periods of systemic change, but with greater complexity and global interconnectedness.

Key Implication

The present context does not call for incremental reform within existing institutional frameworks. Instead, it necessitates a structural reconfiguration of the teaching profession, analogous to previous paradigm shifts.

This reinforces the central thesis of the chapter:

Teaching must evolve beyond its industrial era foundations toward a model that is adaptive, integrative, and responsive to complex socio-technical environments.

STRUCTURAL DRIVERS OF TRANSFORMATION

Technological Acceleration

Reconfiguring the Educational Landscape

Technological acceleration constitutes one of the most significant structural drivers reshaping the teaching profession in the twenty-first century. The rapid advancement of artificial intelligence (AI), learning analytics, and immersive technologies such as virtual and augmented reality is fundamentally altering how knowledge is produced, accessed, and transmitted. Unlike earlier technological interventions that primarily supplemented teaching, contemporary innovations are restructuring the epistemological and pedagogical foundations of education itself (Selwyn, 2022).

Artificial intelligence systems, for instance, enable real-time personalization of learning pathways by analyzing student performance data, identifying gaps, and recommending targeted interventions. Learning analytics platforms extend this capability by generating predictive insights regarding student engagement, progression, and risk of attrition (Siemens & Baker, 2012). Simultaneously, immersive technologies facilitate experiential learning environments that transcend physical and geographical limitations, allowing learners to engage with complex scenarios in simulated contexts.

These developments collectively signal a shift from content-centric instruction to data-driven and experience-based learning ecosystems, thereby redefining the operational environment in which teachers function.

Automation and the Redistribution of Cognitive Labor

A central implication of technological advancement is the automation of routine cognitive and administrative tasks traditionally performed by teachers. Activities such as grading objective assessments, tracking attendance, and delivering standardized instructional content are increasingly managed by intelligent systems.

This redistribution of labor has two significant consequences. First, it enhances efficiency by reducing time spent on repetitive tasks. Second, and more importantly, it repositions teachers within the educational process. Rather than functioning as primary sources of information, teachers are increasingly required to engage in higher-order professional functions, including interpretation, contextualization, and pedagogical design (Luckin et al., 2016).

From a theoretical perspective, this shift aligns with the broader transformation of work in knowledge economies, where automation displaces routine tasks while amplifying the value of complex, non-routine human capabilities (Autor, 2015). In education, this translates into a redefinition of professional expertise, where the teacher's role becomes less about information delivery and more about facilitating meaning-making and critical engagement.

Emergence of Interpretive and Ethical Roles

As technological systems assume greater responsibility for content delivery and assessment, the teacher's role expands into domains that require human judgment, ethical reasoning, and contextual sensitivity. AI-driven educational tools, while powerful, are not neutral; they are shaped by underlying algorithms, data sets, and design assumptions that may embed biases or reinforce inequalities (Williamson, 2017).

Consequently, teachers must act as ethical mediators, critically evaluating the outputs of technological systems and ensuring that their use aligns with principles of equity, inclusion, and pedagogical integrity. This includes:

- Interpreting algorithmic recommendations within specific learner contexts
- Identifying and mitigating biases in data-driven systems
- Guiding students in understanding the ethical implications of technology use

In addition, teachers assume an increasingly important role in fostering digital criticality among learners. This involves not only teaching technical skills but also cultivating the capacity to question, evaluate, and responsibly engage with digital information and systems.

Relational and Human-Centered Pedagogy

Despite the growing influence of technology, the importance of relational dimensions in teaching remains undiminished. On the contrary, as digital systems mediate more aspects of learning, the human elements of education - empathy, trust, and interpersonal connection - gain greater significance.

Research in educational psychology consistently demonstrates that teacher-student relationships are central to motivation, engagement, and learning outcomes (Hattie, 2009). Technological tools, while efficient, cannot replicate the nuanced understanding and emotional responsiveness that characterize effective teaching.

As a result, pedagogy in technologically enriched environments becomes increasingly human-centered, with teachers focusing on:

- Building supportive learning communities
- Facilitating collaborative inquiry
- Addressing socio-emotional dimensions of learning

This reorientation underscores a critical insight: technology enhances but does not replace the relational core of teaching.

Data-Informed but Professionally Mediated Practice

The integration of data analytics into education has given rise to the concept of data-informed teaching, where instructional decisions are guided by evidence derived from student data. While this approach offers significant potential for improving learning outcomes, it also raises important questions regarding professional autonomy and decision-making.

Effective use of data requires teachers to engage in interpretive judgment, rather than relying on automated recommendations. Data must be contextualized within broader pedagogical, social, and cultural frameworks to ensure its meaningful application (Mandinach & Gummer, 2016).

Thus, the emerging model of teaching is not data-driven in a deterministic sense, but data-informed and professionally mediated, where teachers retain authority over instructional decisions while leveraging technological insights to enhance practice.

ANALYTICAL SYNTHESIS

The analysis of technological acceleration reveals a fundamental restructuring of the teaching profession. Three key insights emerge:

- Automation reduces routine cognitive labor, enabling greater efficiency but requiring role redefinition
- Teachers transition toward interpretive, ethical, and relational functions, emphasizing uniquely human capabilities
- Pedagogy evolves into a data-informed yet human-centered practice, balancing technological potential with professional judgment

These shifts collectively reinforce the argument that technology does not render teachers obsolete; rather, it reconfigures their professional identity and expands their strategic importance within educational systems.

Implications for Professional Transformation

The implications of technological acceleration extend beyond classroom practice to the broader structure of the profession. Teacher education programs must integrate digital literacy, ethical reasoning, and data competence as core components. Similarly, institutional policies must support continuous professional development and provide the necessary infrastructure for effective technology integration.

Ultimately, the challenge lies not in adopting technology, but in aligning technological innovation with pedagogical purpose and professional values. This alignment is essential for ensuring that technological advancement contributes to meaningful and equitable educational transformation.

FUTURE COMPETENCIES: THE PROFESSIONAL RECONFIGURATION

Reframing Teacher Professionalism in a Complex Era

The transformation of education systems in the twenty-first century necessitates a fundamental reconfiguration of teacher professionalism. Traditional models of teaching, which emphasized subject mastery and instructional delivery, are increasingly insufficient in addressing the complexities of contemporary learning environments. Instead, the emerging teacher profile reflects a shift toward integrative professionalism, characterized by the ability to synthesize multiple domains of knowledge, skills, and dispositions.

This shift is driven by the convergence of technological advancement, socio-cultural diversification, and evolving labor market demands. As a result, teachers are required to operate not only as disciplinary experts but also as data interpreters, emotional facilitators, institutional collaborators, and global citizens. The following subsections outline the core competency domains that define this reconfiguration.

Digital and Data Competence

AI Literacy and Algorithmic Awareness

Digital competence in contemporary education extends beyond basic technological proficiency to include critical engagement with artificial intelligence systems and algorithmic processes. Teachers must understand how AI-driven platforms function, including their underlying data structures, decision-making logics, and potential biases.

AI literacy enables educators to:

- Evaluate the reliability and limitations of automated recommendations
- Identify algorithmic bias and its implications for equity
- Integrate AI tools in ways that enhance rather than constrain learning

Scholarly work emphasizes that without such awareness, educators risk becoming passive users of technology rather than informed professionals capable of exercising pedagogical judgment (Holmes et al., 2019).

Data Interpretation for Personalized Learning

The increasing availability of student data through learning management systems and analytics platforms has introduced new possibilities for personalized and adaptive learning. However, the effective use of data requires interpretive competence rather than mere technical access.

Teachers must be able to:

- Analyze learning patterns and identify areas of need
- Translate data insights into targeted pedagogical interventions
- Balance quantitative indicators with qualitative understanding of learners

Data literacy thus becomes a critical professional skill, enabling teachers to move from intuition-based decision-making to evidence-informed practice (Mandinach & Gummer, 2016).

Ethical Technology Use

The integration of digital tools in education raises significant ethical considerations, including issues related to privacy, surveillance, and data ownership. Teachers must therefore develop the capacity to navigate these concerns responsibly.

Key aspects include:

- Ensuring informed consent and data protection
- Promoting responsible digital behavior among students
- Critically assessing the ethical implications of EdTech platforms

Ethical competence is essential for maintaining trust and safeguarding the integrity of educational processes in increasingly digitized environments (Selwyn, 2022).

Socio-Emotional Competence

Managing Affective Dynamics in Learning Environments

Learning is not solely a cognitive process; it is deeply influenced by emotional and social factors. Teachers must therefore possess the ability to manage classroom affective dynamics, including student motivation, engagement, and interpersonal relationships.

Effective socio-emotional competence involves:

- Recognizing emotional cues and responding appropriately
- Creating inclusive and supportive classroom climates
- Facilitating collaboration and conflict resolution

Research indicates that emotionally supportive teaching environments significantly enhance student outcomes, particularly in diverse and high-stress contexts (Jennings & Greenberg, 2009).

Addressing Mental Health Challenges

The growing prevalence of mental health concerns among students places additional responsibilities on teachers. While educators are not mental health professionals, they play a crucial role in early identification and support.

This requires:

- Awareness of common mental health issues such as anxiety and depression
- Ability to provide initial support and referral where necessary
- Integration of well-being practices into classroom routines

Such competencies are increasingly recognized as essential components of effective teaching in contemporary educational settings (OECD, 2019).

Building Psychological Safety

Psychological safety - the perception that one can express ideas and take risks without fear of negative consequences - is a critical condition for meaningful learning. Teachers must cultivate environments where students feel valued, respected, and empowered.

This involves:

- Encouraging open dialogue and questioning
- Validating diverse perspectives
- Reducing fear of failure

By fostering psychological safety, teachers enable deeper engagement, creativity, and critical thinking among learners.

ADAPTIVE LEADERSHIP

Curriculum Innovation

In rapidly changing knowledge environments, static curricula quickly become outdated. Teachers must therefore engage in continuous curriculum innovation, adapting content and pedagogy to emerging needs.

This includes:

- Integrating interdisciplinary approaches
- Incorporating real-world problem-solving
- Aligning learning objectives with future competencies

Curriculum innovation reflects a shift from implementation to design-oriented professionalism, where teachers actively shape educational experiences (Fullan, 2020).

Institutional Collaboration

Teaching is increasingly recognized as a collaborative rather than individual endeavor. Effective educators engage with colleagues, administrators, and external stakeholders to enhance learning outcomes.

Collaborative competence involves:

- Participating in professional learning communities
- Engaging in cross-disciplinary initiatives
- Contributing to institutional decision-making processes

Such collaboration strengthens organizational capacity and supports systemic improvement.

Continuous Professional Learning

Given the pace of change, teacher learning must be ongoing. Continuous professional development is no longer optional but a core professional responsibility.

Key dimensions include:

- Engagement with research and evidence-based practices
- Participation in formal and informal learning networks
- Reflective practice and self-evaluation

This orientation toward lifelong learning aligns teaching with other knowledge-intensive professions.

GLOBAL AND CULTURAL COMPETENCE

Intercultural Communication

Globalization has transformed classrooms into culturally diverse spaces. Teachers must develop the ability to communicate effectively across cultural boundaries.

This includes:

- Sensitivity to cultural differences in communication styles

- Awareness of implicit biases
- Ability to foster inclusive dialogue

Intercultural competence enhances both equity and educational effectiveness in diverse settings.

Contextual Pedagogy

Effective teaching requires adaptation to local contexts, including socio-economic conditions, cultural practices, and community needs. Contextual pedagogy ensures that learning is relevant and meaningful.

Teachers must:

- Align content with learners' lived experiences
- Incorporate local knowledge systems
- Adapt strategies to specific educational environments

This approach bridges the gap between global frameworks and local realities.

Global-Local Knowledge Integration

The contemporary teacher operates at the intersection of global knowledge flows and local contexts. This requires the ability to integrate international perspectives with indigenous and community-based knowledge.

Such integration:

- Enriches curriculum content
- Promotes critical global awareness
- Supports culturally responsive teaching

Synthesis: Toward Integrative Professionalism

The competency domains outlined above collectively signal a fundamental shift in the nature of teaching. Rather than functioning within narrowly defined areas of expertise, teachers are increasingly required to operate across multiple domains simultaneously.

This transition reflects the emergence of integrative professionalism, characterized by:

- The ability to synthesize diverse forms of knowledge
- Flexibility in responding to complex and dynamic contexts
- Balance between technological capability and human-centered practice

Analytical Conclusion

Effectiveness in contemporary teaching is no longer determined solely by subject expertise, but by the capacity to integrate digital, emotional, organizational, and cultural competencies into a coherent professional practice.

This reconfiguration reinforces the broader argument of the chapter: the future of teaching lies not in incremental skill enhancement, but in a systemic redefinition of professional identity aligned with the demands of complex, adaptive educational ecosystems.

STRUCTURAL CONSTRAINTS AND SYSTEMIC CHALLENGES

Governance and Political Economy of Education

Structural Limits to Educational Transformation

Educational transformation is not solely a pedagogical challenge, it is fundamentally shaped by the political economy of education systems. Governance structures determine how resources are allocated, how policies are implemented, and how accountability is enforced. In many contexts, these structures are characterized by centralized decision-making, where policy directives are formulated at national or state levels with limited responsiveness to local institutional realities.

Centralized policy systems often prioritize uniformity and scalability, which can constrain innovation at the school or classroom level. While standardization may enhance comparability and control, it frequently limits teachers' capacity to adapt pedagogy to diverse learner needs (Ball, 2012).

Funding Constraints and Resource Allocation

Financial limitations represent a critical barrier to meaningful reform. Education systems in many regions operate under resource constraints, affecting infrastructure, teacher recruitment, and professional development opportunities. Insufficient funding also restricts the integration of technological tools and the maintenance of equitable learning environments.

Moreover, funding models are often disconnected from actual institutional needs, leading to inefficiencies and inequities. Schools serving marginalized populations frequently experience systematic under-resourcing, thereby reinforcing existing disparities (OECD, 2020).

Bureaucratic Accountability Structures

Accountability mechanisms, while intended to ensure quality and transparency, can produce unintended consequences. High-stakes testing regimes and performance metrics often incentivize compliance over innovation, encouraging teachers to focus on measurable outcomes at the expense of deeper learning.

Bureaucratic systems may also generate excessive administrative demands, reducing the time and autonomy available for pedagogical work. As a result, teachers operate within constrained environments where professional judgment is subordinated to procedural requirements.

Analytical Insight

A critical insight emerging from this analysis is that educational reforms frequently fail not due to deficiencies in pedagogical design, but due to misalignment between policy frameworks and institutional capacity. Without coherence between governance structures, resource allocation, and professional conditions, reform initiatives remain fragmented and unsustainable.

TEACHER SUSTAINABILITY AND LABOR CONDITIONS

The Centrality of Teacher Well-Being

Teacher sustainability has emerged as a critical concern in contemporary education systems. While policy discourse often emphasizes innovation and reform, the well-being of teachers as primary agents of change remains insufficiently addressed. Sustainable transformation requires a stable and motivated workforce capable of engaging with complex professional demands.

Workload Intensification and Burnout

One of the most significant challenges facing teachers is workload intensification, characterized by increasing instructional, administrative, and extracurricular responsibilities. This intensification is associated with high levels of stress and burnout, which negatively impact both teacher performance and student outcomes (Skaalvik & Skaalvik, 2017).

Burnout manifests through emotional exhaustion, depersonalization, and reduced professional efficacy. These conditions not only affect individual teachers but also contribute to systemic issues such as attrition and teacher shortages.

Administrative Overload and Reduced Autonomy

Administrative tasks, including documentation, reporting, and compliance requirements, consume a substantial portion of teachers' time. This administrative overload reduces opportunities for lesson planning, student engagement, and professional development.

Simultaneously, low levels of professional autonomy limit teachers' ability to exercise judgment and creativity in their practice. Research indicates that autonomy is a key determinant of job satisfaction and professional commitment (Ingersoll, 2003).

Technological Intensification of Labor

While technological integration offers significant benefits, it also introduces new forms of labor. Teachers are required to manage digital platforms, interpret data analytics, and respond to increased expectations for availability and responsiveness. This results in cognitive and emotional intensification, extending the scope of professional responsibilities.

Analytical Expansion

The cumulative effect of these pressures leads to:

- Role strain, as teachers navigate competing demands
- Identity fragmentation, arising from conflicting expectations
- Reduced retention, particularly among early-career educators

These dynamics highlight the need to reconsider the structural conditions under which teaching is practiced.

Positioning Statement

Teacher sustainability must be understood as a precondition for educational innovation, rather than a secondary consideration. Without addressing labor conditions and well-being, reform efforts are unlikely to achieve long-term impact.

EQUITY AND ACCESS

Persistent Structural Inequalities

Despite global efforts to expand educational access, significant disparities persist in terms of infrastructure, resources, and learning opportunities. These inequalities are particularly evident along socio-economic, geographic, and demographic lines.

Students in under-resourced contexts often lack access to:

- Qualified teachers

- Adequate learning materials
- Digital technologies and connectivity

Such disparities limit the effectiveness of educational reforms and exacerbate achievement gaps (UNESCO, 2021).

The Digital Divide

The expansion of digital learning has introduced new dimensions of inequality. The digital divide encompasses not only access to devices and internet connectivity but also differences in digital literacy and support systems.

As education systems increasingly rely on technology, unequal access risks reinforcing existing inequalities rather than mitigating them.

Implications for Transformation

Addressing equity requires systemic interventions that extend beyond classroom practice. Policies must prioritize inclusive resource allocation, targeted support for marginalized communities, and equitable access to digital infrastructure.

ETHICAL CHALLENGES IN EDUCATIONAL TECHNOLOGY

Data Privacy and Surveillance

The use of digital platforms in education involves the collection and analysis of large volumes of student data. This raises concerns regarding privacy, consent, and data security. Inadequate safeguards can expose students to risks associated with data misuse and unauthorized access.

Algorithmic Bias and Fairness

AI-driven systems are susceptible to biases embedded in training data and design processes. Such biases can lead to unequal learning opportunities and discriminatory outcomes, particularly for marginalized groups (O'Neil, 2016).

Teachers must therefore play a critical role in identifying and mitigating these biases within educational technologies.

Commercialization of Education

The growing influence of private EdTech companies introduces market dynamics into education systems. While innovation may be accelerated, there is a risk that commercial interests may prioritize profitability over pedagogical value.

This raises important questions about the governance and regulation of educational technologies.

CURRICULUM INERTIA

Structural Rigidity in Curriculum Design

Curriculum structures in many education systems remain rooted in traditional disciplinary boundaries. These structures often prioritize content coverage over conceptual understanding and application.

Rigid curricula limit the capacity to address complex, interdisciplinary challenges such as climate change, public health, and technological ethics.

Assessment-Driven Constraints

Assessment systems further reinforce curriculum inertia by emphasizing standardized testing and measurable outcomes. This focus discourages innovation and constrains pedagogical flexibility.

Teachers may feel compelled to "teach to the test," thereby limiting opportunities for creative and inquiry-based learning (Au, 2007).

Implications for Pedagogical Innovation

Overcoming curriculum inertia requires:

- Integration of interdisciplinary approaches
- Adoption of flexible assessment models
- Empowerment of teachers in curriculum design

Such changes are essential for aligning education with the demands of contemporary society.

Synthesis: Interconnected Constraints

The challenges discussed in this section are not isolated; they are deeply interconnected. Governance structures influence funding and accountability, which in turn shape teacher working conditions, equity outcomes, and curriculum design.

Analytical Conclusion

Structural transformation in education requires a system-level approach that addresses these constraints in an integrated manner. Without such alignment, reform efforts risk remaining superficial and fragmented.

PATHWAYS FOR TRANSFORMATION

Reimagining Educational Change

Transforming the teaching profession requires more than the adoption of new tools or isolated reforms; it necessitates a systemic reorientation of educational practices, institutional structures, and policy frameworks. The pathways outlined in this section emphasize coordinated strategies that align pedagogy, professional development, and governance mechanisms. Rather than treating innovation as a technological imperative, these pathways foreground the centrality of human agency, professional collaboration, and policy support in enabling sustainable change.

Personalized and Hybrid Learning Systems

Integration of Digital and Physical Learning Environments

The emergence of hybrid learning systems represents a significant shift in the organization of educational experiences. By combining face-to-face instruction with digital platforms, hybrid models enable flexible, adaptive, and learner-centered approaches. These systems facilitate access to diverse resources, support asynchronous learning, and allow for differentiated pacing.

Digital technologies, such as adaptive learning platforms and learning management systems, provide opportunities for tailoring instruction to individual learner profiles. At the same time, in-person interactions remain essential for fostering social engagement, collaboration, and mentorship.

Differentiation and Inclusion

Personalized learning systems are particularly valuable in addressing learner diversity. By leveraging data and flexible instructional strategies, teachers can design learning experiences that accommodate varying abilities, interests, and backgrounds. This approach enhances both equity and effectiveness, moving beyond one-size-fits-all models of instruction (Pane et al., 2017).

However, the success of such systems depends on teachers' capacity to interpret data, design differentiated activities, and maintain a balance between technological efficiency and human interaction.

Collaborative Professional Ecosystems

Communities of Practice

Professional collaboration is a cornerstone of educational transformation. Communities of practice provide structured spaces where teachers can share knowledge, reflect on practice, and engage in collective problem-solving. These communities foster continuous learning and support the dissemination of innovative practices across institutions (Wenger, 1998).

Collaboration enhances professional capacity by:

- Encouraging peer learning and mentoring
- Promoting reflective practice
- Supporting the integration of new pedagogical approaches

Networked Professional Development

Advances in digital communication have enabled the development of networked professional learning ecosystems, where educators connect across institutional and geographical boundaries. Online platforms, webinars, and collaborative research initiatives facilitate access to diverse perspectives and resources.

Such networks contribute to the development of distributed expertise, reducing professional isolation and enabling teachers to engage with global best practices while adapting them to local contexts.

Policy and Funding Innovations

Increased Public Investment

Sustainable transformation requires adequate and equitable funding. Public investment in education must extend beyond infrastructure to include teacher development, technological integration, and support systems for innovation. Without sufficient resources, even well-designed reforms are unlikely to achieve meaningful impact (OECD, 2020).

Incentive Structures for Innovation

Policy frameworks can play a critical role in encouraging innovation by establishing incentive structures that reward experimentation, collaboration, and professional growth. These may include grants for innovative teaching practices, recognition systems, and career advancement opportunities linked to professional development.

Such incentives help shift institutional cultures from compliance-oriented models to innovation-oriented environments.

Public–Private Collaboration

Collaboration between public institutions and private organizations can enhance resource availability and accelerate innovation. Partnerships with technology providers, research institutions, and industry stakeholders can support the development of new learning tools and pedagogical models.

However, these collaborations must be governed by clear regulatory frameworks to ensure alignment with educational objectives and to prevent the undue influence of commercial interests.

Teacher Agency and Practitioner Research

Teachers as Designers

In transformed educational systems, teachers are not merely implementers of externally designed curricula; they are active designers of learning environments. This involves creating contextually relevant instructional strategies, integrating interdisciplinary content, and adapting pedagogy to evolving learner needs.

Teachers as Researchers

Practitioner research enables teachers to systematically investigate their own practice, generate evidence, and contribute to professional knowledge. Action research, in particular, provides a framework for iterative improvement and reflective inquiry (Cochran-Smith & Lytle, 2009).

By engaging in research, teachers enhance their capacity to:

- Evaluate the effectiveness of interventions
- Adapt strategies based on evidence
- Contribute to broader educational discourse

Teachers as Change Agents

Empowering teachers as change agents is essential for sustainable transformation. This requires not only professional competence but also institutional support for autonomy, leadership, and participation in decision-making processes.

Teacher agency enables:

- Innovation at the classroom and institutional levels
- Alignment between policy and practice
- Development of responsive and adaptive education systems

Synthesis: Agency-Driven Transformation

The pathways outlined above collectively underscore a critical insight: educational transformation is not fundamentally technology-driven, but agency-driven. While technological tools and policy frameworks provide important enabling conditions, the effectiveness of reform ultimately depends on the capacity of teachers to interpret, adapt, and implement change within their specific contexts.

Analytical Conclusion

Sustainable transformation emerges from the alignment of three key elements:

- Empowered teachers with the competencies and autonomy to innovate

- Collaborative professional ecosystems that support continuous learning
- Enabling policy environments that provide resources and incentives

This integrated approach ensures that transformation is not imposed from above but co-constructed through professional practice, thereby enhancing both its legitimacy and its long-term impact.

Global Case Insights: Contextual Adaptation

Framing Comparative Educational Analysis

Global education systems provide valuable insights into how teaching professions evolve in response to diverse socio-political, economic, and cultural contexts. However, comparative analysis must avoid simplistic policy transfer and instead focus on contextual adaptation, recognizing that educational effectiveness depends on alignment between institutional structures and local realities (Steiner-Khamsi, 2014).

This section examines selected national contexts—Finland, Singapore, Kenya, and Brazil—to illustrate how different systems operationalize teaching transformation. These cases are not presented as ideal models, but as contextually grounded examples that highlight varied pathways toward strengthening the teaching profession.

Finland: Trust, Autonomy, and Professionalization

High Teacher Autonomy

Finland's education system is widely recognized for its emphasis on teacher autonomy and professional trust. Teachers are granted significant discretion in curriculum implementation, assessment design, and pedagogical approaches. This autonomy is supported by a culture that views teaching as a high-status profession requiring advanced expertise.

Research-Based Teacher Education

A defining feature of the Finnish model is its research-oriented teacher education system, where all teachers are required to complete master's-level qualifications. This preparation emphasizes inquiry, critical reflection, and evidence-based practice, enabling teachers to function as informed professionals rather than technical implementers (Sahlberg, 2011).

Trust-Driven Governance

Governance in Finland is characterized by low-stakes accountability and high institutional trust. Standardized testing is minimal, and evaluation systems prioritize formative assessment and professional responsibility. This environment fosters innovation and reduces administrative burden, allowing teachers to focus on pedagogical quality.

Singapore: System Coherence and Professional Development

Skills-Focused Curriculum

Singapore's education system is notable for its strategic alignment with national economic priorities. The curriculum emphasizes future-oriented skills, including critical thinking, problem-solving, and adaptability. This focus reflects a deliberate effort to prepare learners for a rapidly changing global economy (Tan, 2017).

Structured Professional Development Systems

Singapore has developed a comprehensive framework for continuous professional development, including mentoring programs, career pathways, and leadership training. Teachers are supported throughout their careers through systematic opportunities for skill enhancement and specialization.

Centralized but Adaptive Governance

While governance in Singapore is relatively centralized, it is also characterized by strategic flexibility and responsiveness. Policies are implemented with a focus on coherence and long-term planning, ensuring alignment between curriculum, assessment, and teacher development.

Kenya: Innovation Under Resource Constraints

Low-Cost Technological Innovation

Kenya provides an example of how educational systems can leverage cost-effective technological solutions to expand access and improve learning outcomes. Mobile learning platforms and digital content delivery systems have been utilized to address infrastructural limitations and reach underserved populations (Piper et al., 2016).

Accessibility-Focused Approaches

Educational initiatives in Kenya often prioritize equity and accessibility, focusing on rural and marginalized communities. Programs are designed to overcome barriers related to geography, socio-economic status, and resource availability.

Contextual Adaptation

The Kenyan case highlights the importance of context-sensitive innovation, where solutions are tailored to local conditions rather than imported from high-resource settings. This approach underscores the role of adaptability in educational transformation.

Brazil: Socio-Emotional Learning and Inclusive Reform

Integration of Socio-Emotional Learning

Brazil has increasingly emphasized the integration of socio-emotional competencies within its curriculum. Recognizing the role of emotional and social factors in learning, educational reforms have incorporated skills such as resilience, empathy, and collaboration (OECD, 2015).

Context-Sensitive Policy Reforms

Brazil's education system operates within a context of significant socio-economic diversity. As a result, reforms are often designed to be flexible and context-responsive, allowing for adaptation at regional and local levels.

Challenges and Progress

While Brazil continues to face challenges related to inequality and resource distribution, its focus on inclusive and holistic education reflects a broader shift toward human-centered learning models.

Comparative Insight: Alignment over Imitation

A cross-case analysis of these systems reveals that there is no universal model for educational transformation. Instead, successful systems share a common characteristic: alignment across key dimensions.

Policy Alignment

Effective systems ensure coherence between national policies, institutional practices, and classroom implementation.

Cultural Alignment

Educational approaches are consistent with societal values, norms, and expectations, enhancing legitimacy and sustainability.

Professional Alignment

Teacher preparation, development, and working conditions are aligned with the demands placed on the profession.

Analytical Conclusion

The comparative analysis underscores that educational transformation is inherently context-dependent. While global trends such as technological integration and competency-based learning are widely observed, their implementation varies significantly based on local conditions.

Final Insight

Sustainable reform requires not the replication of external models, but the strategic alignment of policy, culture, and professional structures within specific contexts. This reinforces the broader argument of the chapter: the future of teaching depends on adaptive, system-level approaches that are responsive to both global pressures and local realities.

CONCEPTUAL FRAMEWORK: ADAPTIVE ECOSYSTEM TEACHER MODEL (AETM)

Framing the Need for a Conceptual Model

The preceding sections have examined the historical evolution, structural drivers, emerging competencies, systemic constraints, and global variations shaping the teaching profession. While these dimensions provide valuable analytical insights, their interrelationships require a unifying conceptual framework to enable systematic understanding and application.

The Adaptive Ecosystem Teacher Model (AETM) is proposed as an integrative framework that captures the dynamic interaction between external forces and internal professional capacities. Rather than viewing teaching as a static role, the model conceptualizes it as an adaptive function within a complex educational ecosystem, influenced by continuous feedback between structural conditions and professional agency.

This approach aligns with systems thinking in education, which emphasizes interdependence, non-linearity, and contextual responsiveness (Fullan, 2020; Bronfenbrenner, 1979). The AETM framework thus provides both an analytical lens and a practical guide for understanding how teaching can evolve in response to contemporary challenges.

Core Dimensions of the AETM Framework

The AETM is structured around four interdependent dimensions: Drivers, Constraints, Competencies, and Agency. These dimensions are not discrete categories but interact dynamically to shape the effectiveness and sustainability of teaching systems.

Drivers: Forces of Systemic Transformation

Drivers represent the macro-level forces that necessitate transformation within education systems. These include technological, demographic, ecological, and economic dynamics that redefine the context in which teaching occurs.

- Technological Drivers: The proliferation of artificial intelligence, data analytics, and digital platforms reshapes knowledge access and pedagogical possibilities.
- Demographic Drivers: Increasing diversity, migration, and changing learner profiles demand inclusive and flexible teaching approaches.
- Ecological Drivers: Climate change and sustainability imperatives require interdisciplinary and future-oriented education.
- Economic Drivers: Shifts toward knowledge economies and automation emphasize higher-order skills such as creativity and adaptability.

These drivers function as external pressures that disrupt traditional educational models and create the conditions for transformation. Importantly, they are interconnected, amplifying complexity and uncertainty within teaching environments.

Constraints: Structural and Institutional Limitations

Constraints refer to the systemic barriers that mediate the impact of drivers and influence the extent to which transformation can occur. These include governance structures, policy frameworks, resource distribution, and labor conditions.

- Governance and Policy Constraints: Centralized decision-making and rigid accountability systems may limit local innovation and responsiveness.
- Inequity and Resource Constraints: Disparities in infrastructure and funding restrict access to quality education and technological integration.
- Labor Conditions: Workload intensification, administrative demands, and limited autonomy affect teacher motivation and sustainability.

Constraints are not merely obstacles; they are structural realities that must be strategically navigated. Effective reform requires alignment between policy intentions and institutional capacity (Ball, 2012).

Competencies: Professional Capacities for Adaptation

Competencies represent the skills, knowledge, and dispositions required for teachers to operate effectively within evolving educational ecosystems. These extend beyond traditional subject expertise to encompass multidimensional professional capabilities.

- Digital Competence: Ability to engage with technology, interpret data, and integrate digital tools into pedagogy.
- Socio-Emotional Competence: Capacity to manage relationships, support well-being, and create inclusive learning environments.
- Adaptive Competence: Skills related to innovation, problem-solving, and responsiveness to change.
- Global Competence: Understanding of cultural diversity and the ability to integrate global and local perspectives.

These competencies enable teachers to respond proactively to external drivers while maintaining pedagogical integrity. They reflect the shift toward integrative professionalism, where effectiveness depends on cross-domain expertise (Darling-Hammond et al., 2020).

Agency: Professional Autonomy and Transformative Capacity

Agency refers to the capacity of teachers to act as intentional and influential professionals within educational systems. It encompasses autonomy, decision-making authority, and the ability to initiate and sustain change.

- Pedagogical Autonomy: Freedom to design and adapt instructional strategies based on learner needs.
- Innovative Capacity: Ability to experiment with new approaches and integrate emerging practices.
- Professional Voice: Participation in institutional and policy-level decision-making processes.

Agency is a critical mediating factor within the AETM framework. Even in the presence of strong competencies, transformation is limited if teachers lack the authority or support to enact change (Biesta et al., 2015).

Dynamic Interactions within the Framework

The AETM framework emphasizes the dynamic interplay between its four dimensions. Drivers create pressures for change, while constraints shape the conditions under which responses are possible. Competencies provide the capacity to respond, and agency determines the extent to which these capacities are enacted.

This interaction can be understood through three key relationships:

1. Drivers–Constraints Interaction: External forces are filtered through institutional structures, determining the scope and direction of reform.
2. Competencies–Agency Interaction: Professional skills must be complemented by autonomy and empowerment to produce meaningful outcomes.
3. Systemic Alignment: Effective transformation occurs when all dimensions are aligned toward shared goals.

The absence of alignment results in fragmentation (for example, high competencies without agency lead to underutilization of professional capacity, while strong policy initiatives without institutional support lead to implementation gaps).

Framework Proposition

The central proposition of the Adaptive Ecosystem Teacher Model is as follows:

Effective future teaching systems emerge when professional competencies and teacher agency are strengthened, while structural constraints are strategically managed in response to evolving systemic drivers.

This proposition highlights three critical principles:

- Capacity Building: Investment in teacher competencies is essential for adapting to complex environments.
- Empowerment: Agency enables teachers to translate competencies into practice.
- Strategic Governance: Constraints must be addressed through coherent policy and institutional alignment.

Implications for Policy and Practice

The AETM framework offers several implications for educational stakeholders:

- For Policymakers: Design flexible and responsive governance systems that support innovation and reduce unnecessary constraints.

- For Institutions: Foster collaborative cultures and provide resources for continuous professional development.
- For Teacher Education: Integrate interdisciplinary competencies and emphasize reflective and research-based practice.

By aligning these elements, education systems can create environments where teachers function as adaptive professionals capable of navigating complexity and driving transformation.

Concluding Integration

The Adaptive Ecosystem Teacher Model provides a comprehensive and integrative lens for understanding the future of the teaching profession. It moves beyond fragmented analyses by situating teaching within a broader ecosystem of interacting forces and capacities.

Final Analytical Insight

The future of teaching is not determined by any single factor - technological, institutional, or individual - but by the alignment and interaction of multiple dimensions within a dynamic system. The AETM framework thus offers a foundation for both scholarly inquiry and practical reform, contributing to the development of resilient and future-ready education systems.

CONCLUSION: FROM EXPANSION TO PRECISION

Reframing the Trajectory of the Teaching Profession

The analysis presented throughout this chapter underscores a critical shift in how the teaching profession must be understood in the contemporary era. While earlier reform efforts have often focused on expanding the roles and responsibilities of teachers, such an approach risks overextension without structural coherence. The future of teaching, therefore, is not defined by the accumulation of additional functions, but by a strategic restructuring of its core identity.

This restructuring reflects the transition from a relatively bounded, classroom-centered profession to one embedded within complex, adaptive educational ecosystems. Teachers are no longer positioned as isolated actors delivering predefined content; instead, they operate within interconnected systems shaped by technological innovation, socio-cultural diversity, and policy dynamics.

From Knowledge Transmission to System Navigation

Limitations of the Transmission Model

The traditional conception of teachers as knowledge transmitters is increasingly insufficient in a context where information is widely accessible through digital technologies. The authority of the teacher is no longer derived primarily from content ownership, but from the capacity to interpret, contextualize, and facilitate learning.

This shift challenges long-standing pedagogical assumptions and necessitates a redefinition of professional expertise. Teaching is no longer centered on delivering standardized knowledge, but on enabling learners to engage critically with complex and evolving information landscapes (Biesta, 2015).

Emergence of System Navigators

In the emerging paradigm, teachers function as system navigators, capable of operating across multiple domains and managing the interplay between technological tools, institutional structures, and learner needs. This role involves:

- Coordinating diverse learning resources and environments
- Interpreting data and adapting instructional strategies
- Mediating between policy expectations and classroom realities

System navigation requires a high degree of adaptive expertise, enabling teachers to respond effectively to uncertainty and change.

Teachers as Human Development Specialists

Expanding the Scope of Educational Outcomes

Contemporary education extends beyond cognitive achievement to encompass holistic human development, including emotional well-being, social competence, and ethical awareness. As a result, teachers are increasingly recognized as human development specialists who support multiple dimensions of learner growth.

This expanded role reflects growing recognition of the importance of socio-emotional learning, mental health, and identity formation in educational success (Darling-Hammond et al., 2020).

Integrating Cognitive and Affective Dimensions

Effective teaching in this context requires the integration of cognitive and affective domains. Teachers must create learning environments that are not only intellectually stimulating but also emotionally supportive and inclusive.

This integration involves:

- Fostering resilience and motivation
- Supporting diverse learner identities
- Encouraging collaboration and empathy

Such practices contribute to the development of learners who are not only knowledgeable but also capable of navigating complex social and ethical challenges.

Teachers as Ethical Anchors in Technological Environments

Navigating Ethical Complexity

The increasing integration of technology in education introduces new ethical challenges related to data privacy, algorithmic bias, and the commercialization of learning. In this context, teachers assume the role of ethical anchors, guiding both their own practice and student engagement with technology.

This role requires:

- Critical evaluation of digital tools and platforms
- Promotion of responsible and ethical technology use
- Advocacy for equity and fairness in digital learning environments

Preserving Human-Centered Education

As educational processes become increasingly mediated by technology, there is a risk of reducing learning to data-driven transactions. Teachers play a crucial role in preserving the human-centered nature of education, ensuring that technological innovation serves pedagogical and ethical purposes rather than undermining them (Selwyn, 2022).

Toward Systemic Alignment

The Necessity of Multi-Level Coherence

A central conclusion of this chapter is that sustainable transformation in education depends on alignment across multiple systemic dimensions. Isolated reforms, whether technological, curricular, or professional, are insufficient if they are not supported by coherent structures and policies.

Effective transformation requires alignment across:

- Policy Systems: Governance frameworks that enable flexibility, innovation, and responsiveness
- Institutional Structures: Organizational environments that support collaboration and professional growth
- Professional Conditions: Sustainable workloads, autonomy, and opportunities for development
- Teacher Agency: Empowerment of educators as active participants in shaping educational practice

Risks of Fragmented Reform

In the absence of such alignment, educational innovation is likely to remain fragmented and unsustainable. For example:

- Technological initiatives may fail without adequate training and support
- Curriculum reforms may be undermined by rigid assessment systems
- Professional development efforts may have limited impact without institutional backing

These challenges highlight the importance of adopting a systems perspective, where change is coordinated across multiple levels rather than implemented in isolation (Fullan, 2020).

Integrating the Adaptive Ecosystem Perspective

The Adaptive Ecosystem Teacher Model (AETM) introduced in this chapter provides a framework for understanding how alignment can be achieved. By integrating drivers, constraints, competencies, and agency, the model emphasizes the need for balanced and coordinated development.

From this perspective, the transformation of teaching is not a linear process but a dynamic interaction between external pressures and internal capacities. Success depends on the ability of education systems to:

- Anticipate and respond to emerging challenges
- Support teachers in developing relevant competencies
- Create conditions that enable professional agency

Final Analytical Position

The future of the teaching profession is defined not by expansion alone, but by precision in role definition, coherence in system design, and alignment across structural dimensions.

Teachers are no longer:

- Knowledge transmitters operating within fixed instructional frameworks

They are becoming:

- System navigators managing complex educational ecosystems
- Human development specialists supporting holistic learner growth

- Ethical anchors guiding responsible engagement with technology

Concluding Insight

Sustainable transformation in education requires a deliberate and coordinated effort to align policy systems, institutional structures, professional conditions, and teacher agency. Without such alignment, even well-intentioned innovations risk remaining superficial, fragmented, and ultimately ineffective.

By contrast, when alignment is achieved, the teaching profession can evolve into a resilient, adaptive, and strategically positioned force capable of addressing the challenges of an increasingly complex and uncertain world.

REFERENCES

Au, W. (2007). High-stakes testing and curricular control. *Educational Researcher, 36*(5), 258–267. DOI: 10.3102/0013189X07306523

Autor, D. H. (2015). Why are there still so many jobs? The history and future of workplace automation. *The Journal of Economic Perspectives*, *29*(3), 3–30. DOI: 10.1257/jep.29.3.3

Ball, S. J. (2012). *Global education Inc.: New policy networks and the neo-liberal imaginary*. Routledge. DOI: 10.4324/9780203803301

Biesta, G. (2015). *Good education in an age of measurement: Ethics, politics, democracy*. Routledge. DOI: 10.4324/9781315634319

Biesta, G., Priestley, M., & Robinson, S. (2015). The role of beliefs in teacher agency. *Teachers and Teaching*, *21*(6), 624–640. DOI: 10.1080/13540602.2015.1044325

Bowles, S., & Gintis, H. (1976). *Schooling in capitalist America: Educational reform and the contradictions of economic life*. Basic Books.

Bronfenbrenner, U. (1979). *The ecology of human development*. Harvard University Press. DOI: 10.4159/9780674028845

Cochran-Smith, M., & Lytle, S. L. (2009). *Inquiry as stance: Practitioner research for the next generation*. Teachers College Press.

Cuban, L. (1993). *How teachers taught: Constancy and change in American classrooms, 1890–1990* (2nd ed.). Teachers College Press.

Darling-Hammond, L. (2017). *Empowered educators: How high-performing systems shape teaching quality around the world*. Jossey-Bass.

Darling-Hammond, L., Flook, L., Cook-Harvey, C., Barron, B., & Osher, D. (2020). Implications for educational practice of the science of learning. *Applied Developmental Science*, *24*(2), 97–140. DOI: 10.1080/10888691.2018.1537791

Dewey, J. (1938). *Experience and education*. Kappa Delta Pi.

Durkheim, E. (1977). *The evolution of educational thought: Lectures on the formation and development of secondary education in France*. Routledge.

Fullan, M. (2020). *Leading in a culture of change* (2nd ed.). Jossey-Bass.

Goody, J. (1987). *The interface between the written and the oral*. Cambridge University Press.

Hattie, J. (2009). *Visible learning: A synthesis of over 800 meta-analyses relating to achievement*. Routledge.

Holmes, W., Bialik, M., & Fadel, C. (2019). *Artificial intelligence in education: Promises and implications for teaching and learning*. Center for Curriculum Redesign.

Ingersoll, R. M. (2003). *Who controls teachers' work? Power and accountability in America's schools*. Harvard University Press.

Jennings, P. A., & Greenberg, M. T. (2009). The prosocial classroom. *Review of Educational Research*, *79*(1), 491–525. DOI: 10.3102/0034654308325693

Labaree, D. F. (2008). The winning ways of a losing strategy: Educationalizing social problems in the United States. *Educational Theory*, *58*(4), 447–460. DOI: 10.1111/j.1741-5446.2008.00299.x

Luckin, R., Holmes, W., Griffiths, M., & Forcier, L. B. (2016). *Intelligence unleashed: An argument for AI in education*. Pearson.

Mandinach, E. B., & Gummer, E. S. (2016). What does it mean for teachers to be data literate? *Teachers College Record*, *118*(11), 1–25.

O'Neil, C. (2016). *Weapons of math destruction: How big data increases inequality and threatens democracy*. Crown.

OECD. (2015). *Skills for social progress: The power of social and emotional skills*. OECD Publishing.

OECD. (2019). *Educating 21st century children: Emotional well-being in the digital age*. OECD Publishing.

OECD. (2020). *Education at a glance 2020: OECD indicators*. OECD Publishing.

Pane, J. F., Steiner, E. D., Baird, M. D., & Hamilton, L. S. (2017). *Informing progress: Insights on personalized learning implementation and effects*. RAND Corporation.

Piper, B., Zuilkowski, S. S., & Ong'ele, S. (2016). Implementing mother tongue instruction in the real world. *Comparative Education Review*, *60*(4), 776–807. DOI: 10.1086/688493

Sahlberg, P. (2011). *Finnish lessons: What can the world learn from educational change in Finland?* Teachers College Press.

Selwyn, N. (2022). *Education and technology: Key issues and debates* (3rd ed.). Bloomsbury. DOI: 10.5040/9781350145573

Siemens, G., & Baker, R. S. (2012). Learning analytics and educational data mining. In *Proceedings of the 2nd International Conference on Learning Analytics and Knowledge* (pp. 252–254).

Skaalvik, E. M., & Skaalvik, S. (2017). Teacher stress and burnout. *Teaching and Teacher Education*, *67*, 152–160. DOI: 10.1016/j.tate.2017.06.006

Steiner-Khamsi, G. (2014). Cross-national policy borrowing: Understanding reception and translation. *Asia Pacific Journal of Education*, *34*(2), 153–167. DOI: 10.1080/02188791.2013.875649

Tan, C. (2017). *Education policy borrowing in China: Looking west or looking east?* Routledge.

Tyack, D., & Cuban, L. (1995). *Tinkering toward utopia: A century of public school reform*. Harvard University Press.

UNESCO. (2021). *Reimagining our futures together: A new social contract for education*. UNESCO.

Wenger, E. (1998). *Communities of practice: Learning, meaning, and identity*. Cambridge University Press. DOI: 10.1017/CBO9780511803932

Williamson, B. (2017). Big data in education: The digital future of learning, policy and practice. *Sage (Atlanta, Ga.)*. Advance online publication. DOI: 10.4135/9781529714920

World Economic Forum. (2023). *The future of jobs report 2023*. World Economic Forum. Retrieved from https://www.weforum.org/publications/the-future-of-jobs-report-2023/digest/?gad_source=1&gad_campaignid=22228224717&gbraid=0AAAAAoVy5F66uqFyHM-LPF6TKNqGhVWAW&gclid=Cj0KCQjw4a3OBhCHARIsAChaqJMxHTIGdl465EureErYKd8Y9fvg0cP92JL1YyRzv3CFMhCPZWA1EYgaAplEEALw_wcB

Chapter 21
Teaching on the Margins, Leading at the Center:
An Urban Community College Adjunct's Reflection on the Enduring Necessity of Teachers in an AI Age

Marvin Espinoza
http://orcid.org/0009-0009-5662-8239
East Los Angeles College, USA

ABSTRACT

This chapter examines the evolving role of teachers in an era shaped by artificial intelligence, declining professional prestige, and increasing labor precarity. Drawing on nearly two decades of adjunct faculty experience in an urban community college, it integrates reflective practitioner scholarship with recent research (2023–2025) on educational technology, labor conditions, and equity-driven pedagogy. The chapter argues that technological expansion intensifies rather than diminishes the need for teachers as relational, ethical, and interpretive professionals. Findings highlight teaching as a critical institutional infrastructure, particularly in access-oriented institutions serving historically marginalized students. The chapter concludes with implications for policy, faculty development, and the ethical integration of artificial intelligence in education.

1. INTRODUCTION AND BACKGROUND

This chapter contributes to ongoing debates by bridging practitioner experience with contemporary scholarship on artificial intelligence, labor precarity, and equity in higher education. Across global education systems, the teaching profession is experiencing a pronounced erosion of social prestige, material support, and institutional authority. This decline is occurring at a moment of intensifying demand, as student enrollments grow while the pipeline of qualified, motivated educators continues to shrink (Cochran-Smith et al., 2024; Schleicher, 2024; UNESCO, 2024).

Shortages are no longer limited to specific disciplines or geographic regions but reflect a systemic crisis shaped by deteriorating working conditions, stagnant compensation, and diminishing professional autonomy (Darling-Hammond, 2024; Ingersoll et al., 2023). In urban, under-resourced, and access-oriented institutions, these pressures are magnified, placing unprecedented strain on educators who serve students with the greatest structural barriers to success.

Concurrently, public discourse surrounding education has shifted in ways that further destabilize the professional standing of teachers. Political rhetoric and media narratives increasingly frame teaching as a task that can be automated, outsourced, or simplified through technological intervention, positioning educators as facilitators rather than experts (Selwyn, 2024; Knox, 2024).

DOI: 10.4018/979-8-3373-8983-7.ch021

Artificial intelligence has become a symbolic centerpiece in claims that learners can acquire knowledge independently through AI tutors, adaptive platforms, and algorithmic feedback systems (Kasneci et al., 2023; Zawacki-Richter et al., 2024). While such technologies offer potential instructional benefits, their popular framing often minimizes or ignores the relational, ethical, and interpretive labor that defines effective teaching (Holmes et al., 2023; Noddings, 2024).

Recent scholarship has traced these narratives to broader neoliberal governance frameworks that redefine education as a market commodity rather than a public good. Within this paradigm, teaching labor is evaluated primarily through cost efficiency, scalability, and performance metrics, leading to the reclassification of educators as expendable inputs rather than central institutional actors (Marginson, 2023, 2024; Ball, 2023).

This logic has accelerated the casualization of academic labor, particularly in higher education, where adjunct faculty now constitute the instructional majority while remaining structurally marginalized (Kezar & Holcombe, 2023; Kezar et al., 2024). The erosion of prestige is therefore not simply cultural but deeply embedded in policy, funding, and governance decisions.

Studies of AI-assisted learning environments demonstrate that students frequently over-trust algorithmic outputs, struggle to evaluate accuracy, and conflate fluency with understanding in the absence of guided instruction (Bearman et al., 2024; Mollick & Mollick, 2024).

Without teachers to contextualize, challenge, and ethically frame AI-generated information, learning risks becoming superficial, inequitable, and misaligned with democratic educational aims (Williamson & Eynon, 2023; Knox, 2024). Rather than diminishing the need for teachers, AI expands the scope of pedagogical responsibility by requiring educators to cultivate critical AI literacy, epistemic humility, and ethical reasoning (Dede et al., 2024; Holmes et al., 2023).

This chapter intervenes in these debates by foregrounding the lived experience of an adjunct faculty member who has taught in an urban community college for nearly twenty years (Clandinin, 2023; McAlpine & Amundsen, 2024).

Community colleges occupy a paradoxical and often overlooked position within higher education systems. They enroll a disproportionate share of students facing economic precarity, linguistic marginalization, immigration-related stress, and interrupted educational trajectories, yet they operate with constrained funding and heightened accountability pressures (Bailey et al., 2023; Jenkins & Fink, 2024; Levin & Hernandez, 2023).

Instruction in these institutions is overwhelmingly delivered by contingent faculty, whose labor sustains access while remaining institutionally undervalued (AAUP, 2024; Kezar & Maxey, 2024). The decline in teaching prestige is therefore most visible at the community college level, where the moral and civic dimensions of teaching are most pronounced yet least rewarded.

Research consistently demonstrates that faculty-student relationships are among the strongest predictors of persistence, belonging, and academic success for community college students (Felten & Lambert, 2024; Rendón, 2023; Museus & Chang, 2024). These outcomes are not produced through content delivery alone but through sustained human interaction, trust, and recognition, capacities that cannot be automated or scaled without loss (Zembylas, 2024; Palmer, 2024).

Higher education systems globally have mirrored these trends through the expansion of contingent academic labor. Studies from Europe, Australia, and Latin America document parallel processes of casualization in which instructional responsibilities are shifted to non-tenure-track faculty under short-term contracts, often justified through discourses of efficiency and flexibility (Courtois & O'Keefe, 2024; Rhoades et al., 2023). These dynamics suggest that the U.S. adjunct experience is not anomalous but indicative of a transnational restructuring of teaching labor.

Within this global context, community colleges and equivalent access-oriented institutions function as early indicators of how teaching roles are redefined under conditions of austerity and technological expansion. As governments increasingly promote digital solutions to educational access, the risk emerges that teacher labor is framed as scalable content delivery rather than situated professional practice (Williamson, 2024).

The U.S. community college case thus offers insight into global futures of teaching, particularly where equity-oriented institutions are asked to do more with fewer resources while absorbing the social consequences of inequality. I recall moments in my classroom when students arrived unsure not only of the content, but of whether they belonged in college at all. In those moments, the role of the teacher was not to deliver information, but to interpret uncertainty, build trust, and create conditions for learning to begin.

This chapter argues that understanding teaching as relational and infrastructural work is essential for designing equitable and sustainable education systems in an AI-driven era.

2. METHODOLOGICAL ORIENTATION: REFLECTIVE PRACTITIONER SCHOLARSHIP

Methodological legitimacy in reflective practitioner research also depends on transparency regarding analytic boundaries. Recent methodological scholarship emphasizes that practitioner reflection gains rigor when it is explicitly connected to theory building and institutional analysis (Knaflic & Martin, 2023). In this chapter, reflection operates as an analytic site where professional identity, labor conditions, and pedagogical change intersect.

Furthermore, reflective methodology allows for temporal depth that cross-sectional research often lacks. Longitudinal practitioner insight reveals patterns of institutional behavior that may not appear in short-term studies, particularly in relation to adjunct labor stability and evolving technology mandates (Boud & van der Meer, 2024). This temporal perspective strengthens claims about systemic rather than episodic challenges in teaching.

Finally, reflective practitioner scholarship supports epistemic justice by legitimizing knowledge produced by educators whose labor is structurally marginalized. By situating adjunct faculty experience within peer-reviewed research, this chapter contributes to a more inclusive knowledge base capable of informing policy and institutional reform (Fraser & Bartlett, 2023). Reflective practitioner scholarship also creates space to examine contradiction and tension rather than resolve them prematurely (Boud & van der Meer, 2024; Fraser & Bartlett, 2023).

2.1 Reflective Narrative as Scholarly Knowledge

This chapter is grounded in reflective practitioner scholarship, a methodological approach that recognizes professional experience as a legitimate source of knowledge when critically examined and situated within existing research (Clandinin, 2023; McAlpine & Amundsen, 2024). Reflective narrative does not replace empirical analysis; rather, it complements it by revealing how policy, labor structures, and pedagogical theories are enacted in lived practice.

Within education research, reflective and narrative methodologies have gained renewed legitimacy, particularly in studies of teaching identity, emotional labor, and professional ethics (Brookfield, 2023; Zembylas, 2024). Such approaches are especially valuable in examining adjunct faculty work, which is often underrepresented in institutional data yet central to student learning outcomes (Kezar & Holcombe, 2023).

This chapter makes three primary contributions to the literature. First, it integrates reflective practitioner scholarship with contemporary research on artificial intelligence in education, offering a grounded perspective on how technological change is experienced in real classrooms. Second, it reframes adjunct faculty not as peripheral actors but as central to institutional functioning, positioning teaching as critical infrastructure. Third, it advances a human-centered framework for understanding the future of teaching, emphasizing relational, ethical, and interpretive dimensions that resist automation.

2.2 Positionality and Teaching Context

In my own teaching practice, this has meant navigating conversations that extend beyond course content, including supporting students managing work schedules, family responsibilities, and, at times, crises that directly affect their ability to engage academically. This experience is informed by my positionality as a long-serving adjunct faculty member in an urban community college, where I teach primarily first-generation college students who often balance employment, caregiving responsibilities, and financial insecurity. These realities have underscored the limits of purely autonomous or technology-mediated learning models, revealing that, in these contexts, teaching necessarily extends beyond content delivery to include mentoring, advocacy, cultural translation, and emotional support (Rendón, 2023; Felten & Lambert, 2024).

Acknowledging positionality is essential not only for transparency but also for ethical scholarship. As Tronto (2023) argues, care-based professions require reflexivity about power, responsibility, and relational accountability. This chapter, therefore, situates personal narrative within broader labor and policy frameworks, avoiding individual exceptionalism while highlighting systemic patterns.

Methodological rigor in reflective practitioner scholarship is strengthened when narrative is explicitly linked to analytic interpretation. Rather than presenting experience as anecdotal evidence, reflective inquiry situates lived practice within theoretical and empirical frameworks that render individual experience intelligible as a social phenomenon (Brookfield,

2023; McAlpine & Amundsen, 2024). In this chapter, reflection functions as an analytic bridge between macro-level policy dynamics and micro-level instructional realities.

Recent scholarship emphasizes that practitioner narratives are particularly valuable in examining labor conditions and pedagogical change under technological transformation (Kreber, 2023; Zawacki-Richter et al., 2024). Quantitative indicators of teacher attrition or technology adoption cannot capture how educators interpret institutional mandates, negotiate ethical tensions, or adapt pedagogy in real time.

This methodological stance also resists false binaries between objectivity and subjectivity. Rather than positioning experience as bias, reflective inquiry treats experience as data that requires interpretation and contextualization (Brookfield, 2023; Clandinin, 2023). This approach is particularly relevant in studying adjunct labor, where institutional metrics often fail to capture the full scope of instructional, relational, and emotional work performed (Santoro, 2024).

Finally, reflective practitioner scholarship supports ethical accountability. By situating personal narrative within broader institutional patterns, the chapter avoids exceptionalism and instead emphasizes how individual experiences reflect systemic design choices (McAlpine & Amundsen, 2024; Tronto, 2023). This orientation strengthens the chapter's contribution to understanding teaching as structured labor rather than individualized vocation.

3. BECOMING A TEACHER: IDENTITY AND COMMITMENT

Entering the teaching profession was not the result of accident or convenience but of a deliberate commitment to education as a public good, grounded in the belief that education can alter life trajectories, particularly for students historically excluded from traditional pathways of academic success (Darling-Hammond, 2024). Like many educators working in access-oriented institutions, this commitment has required navigating ongoing uncertainty, including semesters when returning to the classroom demanded a conscious decision to remain despite unclear future course assignments, reinforcing that persistence in teaching is often an ethical choice rather than a structural guarantee.

Early teaching experiences revealed that community college classrooms are sites of profound complexity. Students arrive with diverse levels of academic preparation, uneven access to technology, and lived experiences shaped by structural inequality. Teaching in this environment requires adaptability, cultural responsiveness, and emotional intelligence, capacities that extend far beyond standardized curricula or automated instructional tools (Hargreaves & O'Connor, 2023; Zawacki-Richter et al., 2024).

Over time, professional identity became less tied to institutional status and more grounded in relational impact. Remaining in the profession despite adjunct precarity was not an act of resignation but of ethical resolve. As Palmer (2024) suggests, teaching is sustained not by external validation alone but by an internal alignment between values and practice. This alignment has been repeatedly tested by declining prestige, stagnant wages, and narratives suggesting that teachers are increasingly unnecessary.

Yet it is precisely these conditions that reveal the enduring necessity of teaching. When students struggle to interpret feedback generated by artificial intelligence tools, navigate institutional bureaucracy, or reconcile academic expectations with lived realities, it is the teacher, not the algorithm, who provides context, judgment, and care (Mollick & Mollick, 2024; Holmes et al., 2023). Becoming a teacher in this context also involved learning how to navigate ambiguity.

Expectations surrounding curriculum, assessment, and student support were often communicated implicitly rather than formally, a condition common in access-oriented institutions with high reliance on contingent faculty (Kezar & Maxey, 2024). This required developing professional judgment grounded in responsiveness rather than rigid adherence to policy, reinforcing the role of discretion as a core teaching competency (Biesta, 2023).

These experiences illustrate that becoming a teacher is not a discrete moment, but an ongoing process shaped by institutional context. Professional identity evolves through repeated negotiation between values, constraints, and student realities (Day & Gu, 2024; Palmer, 2024), underscoring why teaching cannot be reduced to technical skill acquisition alone.

Purpose-driven identity formation can mask institutional accountability. Scholars warn that systems benefiting from teachers' vocational commitment often externalize responsibility for sustainability onto individuals (Kelchtermans, 2023). This dynamic places educators in a double bind, where leaving the profession is experienced as moral failure rather than structural consequence.

3.1 Teaching as Invisible Institutional Infrastructure

Teaching in higher education is often conceptualized as a service delivered to students. This aligns with emerging scholarship that conceptualizes academic labor itself as institutional infrastructure rather than service delivery (Shin & Jung, 2024). Recent scholarship argues that instructional labor provides the connective tissue through which institutional missions are realized, especially in contexts where students rely on faculty to navigate bureaucratic, academic, and cultural systems simultaneously (McCowan, 2023; Benabou et al., 2024).

In community colleges, adjunct faculty often perform this infrastructural role without formal recognition, stabilizing student experiences across fragmented support systems. Their work ensures continuity in advising, curriculum interpretation, and institutional memory despite high turnover and limited structural investment. The invisibility of teaching as infrastructure contributes directly to its devaluation.

When instructional labor is taken for granted as endlessly elastic, institutions normalize precarious employment structures while relying on faculty goodwill to absorb systemic shortcomings (Berg & Seeber, 2024). This dynamic mirrors broader patterns in care work, where relational labor is essential yet undercompensated due to its association with moral commitment rather than professional expertise (Tronto, 2023).

Reframing teaching as infrastructure rather than service has significant implications for policy and institutional design. Infrastructure requires sustained investment, maintenance, and collective responsibility. Applying this logic to teaching challenges models that treat adjunct labor as disposable and instead positions educators as central to institutional resilience and equity outcomes.

Professional commitment to teaching is increasingly understood as a form of ethical identity rather than institutional allegiance. Research on teacher motivation suggests that educators who persist in access-oriented institutions often do so because teaching aligns with deeply held values related to justice, care, and community responsibility (Biesta, 2023; Palmer, 2024). This form of commitment persists even as external validation declines.

For adjunct faculty, this ethical orientation frequently compensates for the absence of formal professional recognition. However, scholars caution that ethical commitment should not be conflated with tolerance for inequitable conditions (Santoro, 2024). When institutions rely on teachers' moral resolve to sustain under-resourced systems, professional identity becomes both a source of resilience and a site of vulnerability.

Understanding why educators enter and remain in teaching, therefore, requires attention not only to personal motivation but to the institutional contexts that shape professional meaning. This chapter situates individual commitment within these broader structures, resisting narratives that individualize responsibility for systemic failure. Conceptualizing teaching as infrastructure also reframes how institutions measure effectiveness. Infrastructure is evaluated not by short-term outputs but by durability, reliability, and capacity to absorb strain.

Teaching labor in community colleges functions in this way by absorbing the consequences of policy volatility, student precarity, and technological disruption (McCowan, 2023; Berg & Seeber, 2024). Adjunct faculty frequently stabilize learning environments through informal mentoring, curricular adaptation, and emotional support that remain undocumented yet essential. This infrastructural role becomes most visible during periods of crisis when instructional continuity depended heavily on faculty improvisation and relational labor rather than institutional preparedness (Zembylas, 2024; Felten & Lambert, 2024).

Institutional reliance on invisible teaching infrastructure often becomes apparent only when it is disrupted (AAUP, 2024; Levin & Hernandez, 2023). While teaching infrastructure is essential to institutional functioning, it is treated as infinitely flexible. Such assumptions obscure the cumulative toll of sustained precarity, a pattern consistent with research on academic labor erosion and organizational fragility (Berg & Seeber, 2024; Rhoades et al., 2023). Over time, the erosion of teaching infrastructure manifests as diminished continuity, weakened student trust, and reduced instructional coherence.

Moreover, infrastructural labor is deeply tied to equity. When teaching infrastructure erodes, marginalized students experience disproportionate harm, as they rely more heavily on faculty mediation to navigate institutional complexity (Perna & Finney, 2023). This reinforces the argument that teaching infrastructure is not merely operational but justice-oriented. Recognizing teaching as infrastructure, therefore, requires rethinking funding models, evaluation metrics, and governance structures that currently obscure instructional labor behind efficiency rhetoric.

4. THE ADJUNCT CONDITION: STRUCTURAL PRECARITY

I have experienced this dissonance directly, being entrusted with student success outcomes while simultaneously navigating semester-to-semester employment uncertainty, a condition that also reshapes how adjunct faculty engage with professional growth. Opportunities for sustained professional development, curriculum leadership, and pedagogical innovation are often limited or informal, despite expectations that adjunct instructors maintain instructional quality equivalent to full-time faculty (AAUP, 2024; Kezar & Holcombe, 2023). This misalignment reinforces a system in which professional responsibility is decoupled from professional investment, positioning adjunct faculty as implementers of institutional priorities rather than contributors to their design and intensifying the professional dissonance between expertise and authority (Marginson, 2024).

The emotional consequences of this arrangement extend beyond workload and compensation. Research on emotional labor highlights that educators working under conditions of uncertainty experience heightened vigilance, self-monitoring, and role strain as they attempt to meet student needs while navigating institutional ambiguity (Hargreaves & O'Connor, 2023; Zembylas, 2024). For adjunct faculty, this emotional labor is compounded by limited access to support structures and exclusion from decision-making spaces. Over time, the cumulative effect of these conditions contributes to moral injury, particularly when instructors are unable to act in accordance with their ethical commitments due to structural constraints (Santoro, 2024; Tronto, 2023).

Despite these challenges, adjunct faculty often sustain high levels of instructional commitment and student engagement. This persistence is frequently rooted in relational accountability to students and alignment with the access-oriented missions of community colleges (Rendón, 2023; Cochran-Smith et al., 2024). However, scholars caution that institutional reliance on this commitment risks normalizing inequity when dedication is treated as a substitute for structural support (Kezar et al., 2024; Palmer, 2024). Addressing the adjunct condition, therefore, requires shifting from narratives of individual resilience to institutional responsibility, recognizing that professional dissonance is not a personal failure but a predictable outcome of organizational design.

4.1 Adjunctification as Structural Norm in U.S. Higher Education

Over the past several decades, adjunctification has shifted from a temporary staffing strategy to a structural norm within higher education, particularly in community colleges. Recent research indicates that contingent faculty now teach most undergraduate courses in the United States, with community colleges relying on adjunct instructors for as much as seventy percent of their instructional labor (Kezar & Holcombe, 2023; AAUP, 2024). This reliance reflects broader neoliberal governance models that prioritize flexibility, cost containment, and managerial efficiency over professional stability and faculty development (Marginson, 2024).

Despite their central instructional role, adjunct faculty often occupy a marginal institutional position. Contracts are typically semester-based, compensation is frequently calculated per course rather than per hour worked, and access to benefits, professional development funding, and shared governance remains limited or nonexistent (Kezar et al., 2023). These conditions contribute to what scholars have described as professional dissonance, a misalignment between the responsibility's adjuncts carry and the recognition or support they receive (Santoro, 2024).

From a practitioner perspective, this dissonance is experienced not as abstraction but as daily reality. Adjunct faculty are expected to uphold institutional learning outcomes, maintain academic rigor, integrate technology, support student retention initiatives, and respond to increasingly complex student needs, all while navigating uncertainty regarding continued employment. The contradiction between institutional dependence and disposability shapes how adjunct faculty experience their professional identity and sense of belonging.

4.2 Emotional and Cognitive Labor in Contingent Teaching

Teaching has long been recognized as emotionally intensive work, but recent scholarship emphasizes that contingent faculty experience disproportionate emotional and cognitive burdens due to their employment status (Hargreaves & O'Connor, 2023; Zembylas, 2024). Adjunct instructors often teach students facing housing insecurity, food insecurity, immigration related stress, and mental health challenges, particularly in urban community college settings. Responding effectively to these realities requires emotional presence, relational attentiveness, and ethical judgment.

At the same time, adjunct faculty frequently lack access to institutional resources that support this labor. Limited office space, unpaid advising time, and exclusion from student support networks create structural barriers that increase cognitive load. Research suggests that this combination of high emotional demand and low institutional support contributes to burnout, moral distress, and attrition among contingent faculty (Schutz et al., 2023; Santoro, 2024).

Moral injury is an increasingly used framework for understanding these experiences.

Moral injury occurs when professionals are constrained from acting in accordance with their ethical commitments due to systemic conditions (Santoro, 2024). For adjunct faculty, moral injury emerges when instructors recognize student needs but lack the authority, time, or institutional backing to address them fully. The result is not disengagement but sustained ethical tension.

4.3 Professional Identity Without Institutional Security

Professional identity for adjunct faculty is often constructed in the absence of traditional markers of academic status. Titles, tenure pathways, and promotion structures that historically signaled professional legitimacy are frequently unavailable. Yet research demonstrates that adjunct faculty often maintain a strong sense of professional purpose rooted in student relationships and instructional impact rather than institutional recognition (Kreber, 2023; Palmer, 2024).

In long-term adjunct teaching, professional identity becomes anchored in continuity of service rather than contractual permanence. Teaching multiple cohorts of students over many years allows adjunct instructors to witness longitudinal student outcomes, including transfer, degree completion, and career advancement. These experiences reinforce a sense of vocational commitment that persists despite material insecurity.

However, this form of identity construction carries risk. When professional worth is sustained primarily through personal resilience rather than structural support, institutions may inadvertently normalize exploitation. Recent literature cautions against romanticizing adjunct dedication, emphasizing the need to distinguish between individual commitment and systemic responsibility (Kezar & Maxey, 2024).

4.4 Why Adjunct Faculty Stay

Given the documented challenges of adjunct teaching, a central question emerges: why do faculty remain in these roles for extended periods? Research suggests that decisions to stay are rarely driven by optimism about institutional reform. Instead, they are shaped by relational accountability to students, identification with community-centered educational missions, and a belief in teaching as civic work (Rendón, 2023; Tronto, 2023).

In urban community colleges, adjunct faculty often serve students whose educational journeys are fragile and nonlinear. Instructors become anchors of stability in otherwise fragmented institutional experiences. Leaving the classroom can feel like withdrawing support from students who already experience systemic abandonment. This sense of responsibility is not mandated by contract but emerges from ethical commitment.

Yet remaining should not be interpreted as consent to precarity. Contemporary scholarship increasingly calls for reframing adjunct persistence as evidence of professional dedication rather than justification for continued marginalization (Cochran Smith et al., 2024). Supporting adjunct faculty is therefore not only a labor issue but a student success imperative. The adjunct condition also shapes how faculty relate to institutions over time, limiting long-term planning, professional development, and reinforcing marginalization. (Kezar et al., 2024; Courtois & O'Keefe, 2024).

Despite these conditions, adjunct faculty often develop deep institutional knowledge through sustained presence. This knowledge, however, is rarely leveraged in decision-making processes, reflecting a persistent disconnect between expertise and authority (Marginson, 2024; Rhoades et al., 2023). The result is a system that depends on instructional expertise while structurally excluding those who possess it.

The adjunct condition thus represents not only an employment category but an organizational design choice. Institutions that normalize contingency embed instability into instructional systems, with direct consequences for student learning and institutional coherence (Kezar & Maxey, 2024). Addressing adjunct precarity, therefore, requires reexamining how institutions define faculty roles, distribute authority, and conceptualize instructional responsibility.

5. ARTIFICIAL INTELLIGENCE AND TEACHING

This chapter contends that artificial intelligence does not diminish teaching but redefines the forms of expertise required. This shift reflects broader transformations in professional work under digital conditions, where expertise is reconfigured rather than eliminated (Susskind & Susskind, 2023). In practice, I have observed students confidently present AI-generated responses that were incomplete or inaccurate, requiring guided dialogue to unpack misconceptions and rebuild understanding.

This experience reflects a broader shift in how authority and expertise are perceived within educational environments, as algorithmic systems increasingly generate explanations, feedback, and recommendations that can lead students to conflate fluency with accuracy and assume technological outputs carry neutral or superior authority (Selwyn, 2024; Mollick & Mollick, 2024). In response, teachers play a critical role in interrupting this assumption by modeling critical engagement with AI-generated content, demonstrating how to question sources, identify limitations, and contextualize information, thereby reinforcing that AI amplifies the need for educators who can guide epistemic judgment rather than simply transmit information.

The integration of AI further complicates assessment practices. Automated tools promise efficiency in grading and feedback, yet research highlights the risk of narrowing evaluative criteria to what can be easily quantified or standardized (Bearman et al., 2024; Holmes et al., 2023). Teachers remain essential in interpreting student work holistically, recognizing learning that unfolds through struggle, iteration, and partial understanding. Without human mediation, assessment risks prioritizing surface-level performance over deeper cognitive and developmental outcomes, particularly for students navigating unfamiliar academic norms (Zawacki-Richter et al., 2024).

Finally, framing artificial intelligence as an amplifier rather than a replacement underscores the ethical responsibility of institutions to support teachers during technological transitions. When AI is introduced without a clear pedagogical purpose or faculty involvement, it can intensify workload, blur professional boundaries, and exacerbate existing labor inequities (Selwyn, 2024; Williamson, 2024). Conversely, when educators are positioned as co-designers and critical interpreters of AI tools, technology can enhance instructional capacity while preserving professional autonomy. This distinction reinforces the chapter's central claim that technology does not diminish the role of teachers but instead heightens the importance of their judgment, relational expertise, and ethical leadership.

5.1 The Myth of Autonomous Learning

A dominant narrative shaping contemporary discourse on education technology is the promise of autonomous learning. Proponents argue that artificial intelligence systems, adaptive platforms, and algorithmic feedback tools enable learners to acquire knowledge independently, rendering traditional teaching roles increasingly unnecessary. While such claims are rhetorically powerful, recent scholarship challenges their pedagogical validity, particularly in equity-oriented educational contexts (Selwyn, 2024; Williamson & Eynon, 2023).

Autonomous learning presumes that learners possess the metacognitive skills, disciplinary literacy, and contextual knowledge required to evaluate information, monitor understanding, and apply feedback effectively. Research demonstrates that these capacities are unevenly distributed and strongly correlated with prior educational opportunity, socioeconomic status, and cultural capital (Marginson, 2023; Jenkins & Fink, 2024). In community colleges, where many students are first-generation and navigating unfamiliar academic norms, the assumption of learner autonomy risks deepening rather than mitigating inequality.

Studies of AI-mediated instruction further indicate that without teacher mediation, students often misinterpret automated feedback, overtrust algorithmic outputs, or disengage when systems fail to account for their lived realities (Kasneci et al., 2023; Bearman et al., 2024). Autonomous learning, when detached from human guidance, becomes less a pathway to empowerment and more a mechanism of stratification.

5.2 Artificial Intelligence in the Community College Classroom

Within community college classrooms, artificial intelligence is already embedded in everyday instructional practice. Students use generative tools for drafting, summarizing, translating, and problem-solving. Faculty employ AI-assisted systems for plagiarism detection, learning analytics, and formative assessment. The presence of AI is therefore not speculative but immediate and consequential (Zawacki-Richter et al., 2024).

However, empirical studies emphasize that the effectiveness of AI tools is contingent upon teacher framing and pedagogical intent. When instructors explicitly teach students how to interrogate AI outputs, recognize bias, and use tools as supports rather than substitutes, learning outcomes improve (Mollick & Mollick, 2024; Holmes et al., 2023). Conversely, when AI use is unstructured or implicitly encouraged as a shortcut, students demonstrate reduced conceptual understanding and weakened epistemic judgment (Bearman et al., 2024). From a practitioner's perspective, AI has increased the interpretive labor of teaching.

5.3 Teachers as Ethical and Epistemic Guides

One of the most significant limitations of artificial intelligence in education lies in its inability to exercise ethical judgment. AI systems generate outputs based on probabilistic patterns rather than moral reasoning. They cannot assess the social consequences of knowledge use, recognize harm, or respond with care to student vulnerability (Noddings, 2024; Zembylas, 2024).

Teachers serve as ethical and epistemic guides who help students navigate not only what they know but also how and why knowledge is used. This role has become more critical as AI blurs boundaries between original thought, assisted production, and algorithmic reproduction. Research highlights that students require explicit instruction in epistemic humility, source evaluation, and responsible technology use, all of which depend on teacher modeling and dialogue (Holmes et al., 2023; Selwyn, 2024).

In this sense, artificial intelligence amplifies rather than replaces teaching. The more complex the technological environment becomes, the greater the need for educators who can contextualize information, mediate meaning, and uphold ethical standards.

5.4 Artificial Intelligence and the Risk of Pedagogical Deskilling

Beyond questions of student learning, artificial intelligence introduces significant risks related to the deskilling of teaching labor. Pedagogical deskilling occurs when professional judgment, curricular decision-making, and assessment expertise are progressively displaced by standardized tools and automated systems. Recent studies caution that AI-driven instructional technologies may shift authority away from educators by embedding pedagogical assumptions within opaque algorithms (Perrotta & Selwyn, 2024; Knox & Williamson, 2024).

In higher education, the automation of feedback, grading, and content generation risks redefining teaching as system supervision rather than intellectual practice. When instructional decisions are increasingly mediated by AI platforms, faculty may experience reduced agency over curriculum pacing, assessment design, and pedagogical responsiveness (Castañeda & Williamson, 2023). Over time, such shifts can erode professional expertise, particularly for contingent faculty whose instructional autonomy is already constrained.

Importantly, deskilling does not occur through technology alone but through institutional choices about implementation. Research demonstrates that when AI adoption is driven by efficiency rather than pedagogical enhancement, teachers are positioned as end users rather than co-designers of educational systems (Williamson, 2024; Dede et al., 2024). This dynamic reinforces existing hierarchies and exacerbates labor precarity.

Addressing the risk of deskilling requires deliberate investment in faculty agency, professional development, and participatory governance. Teachers must be supported not only in using AI tools but in shaping their pedagogical purpose, ethical boundaries, and evaluative criteria. Technology integration also reshapes temporal expectations of teaching. Technology integration extends instructional labor beyond scheduled teaching time, often occurring without compensation for adjunct faculty (Selwyn, 2024; Williamson, 2024).

Artificial intelligence further accelerates instructional cycles. Drafting, feedback, and revision occur more quickly, increasing pressure on instructors to respond at a comparable speed. While efficiency is often framed as a benefit, research cautions that acceleration can erode opportunities for reflection and pedagogical deliberation essential to high-quality teaching (Bearman et al., 2024; Mollick & Mollick, 2024).

Moreover, technology mediates power relations within institutions. Decisions about platform adoption, analytics, and data use are frequently centralized, limiting faculty agency (Selwyn & Jandrić, 2024). When teachers are excluded from these decisions, technology functions as a governance mechanism rather than a pedagogical tool, reinforcing the chapter's argument that technology redistributes rather than eliminates labor (Zawacki-Richter et al., 2024).

6. RELATIONAL PEDAGOGY AND THE IRREPLACEABLE HUMAN DIMENSION OF TEACHING

Studies demonstrate that students are more willing to engage in complex reasoning when they perceive instructors as credible, caring, and responsive (Yeager et al., 2024). This trust is particularly critical in AI-mediated environments where students must evaluate competing sources of information. Furthermore, relational teaching mitigates stereotype threat and academic disengagement among historically marginalized students (Murphy & Destin, 2023). These effects cannot be replicated through automated systems, as they rely on nuanced human recognition and affirmation. Relational pedagogy should therefore be understood as a core instructional competency rather than an interpersonal disposition.

Relational pedagogy supports cognitive development by fostering trust, confidence, and active sense-making, particularly in AI-mediated environments. When instructors engage students with care, consistency, and intellectual respect, they model how knowledge is constructed, questioned, and revised. This modeling encourages students to move beyond passive consumption of information toward active sense-making, a capacity that is especially important in environments saturated with automated feedback and algorithmic recommendations.

By cultivating epistemic trust and reducing stereotype threat, relational teaching enables students to engage more deeply with uncertainty and complexity rather than retreat from challenge. In this way, relational pedagogy strengthens both cognitive resilience and academic agency, reinforcing its role as an essential dimension of effective teaching that cannot be separated from learning itself (Yeager et al., 2024; Murphy & Destin, 2023).

6.1 Teaching as Relationship Work

A consistent finding across contemporary education research is that learning is fundamentally relational. Students' sense of belonging, trust, and recognition strongly predict engagement, persistence, and academic success, particularly in access-oriented institutions (Felten & Lambert, 2024; Rendón, 2023). In community colleges, where students often experience fragmented institutional support, faculty relationships frequently serve as the primary site of connection.

Relational pedagogy involves more than approachability or friendliness. It requires intentional practices that affirm student identity, acknowledge external pressures, and create psychologically safe learning environments. These practices are not ancillary to instruction but integral to cognitive engagement and persistence (Hargreaves & O'Connor, 2023).

Artificial intelligence systems can simulate responsiveness but cannot establish mutual recognition or shared meaning. Students readily distinguish between automated interaction and human presence, particularly when navigating academic uncertainty or personal challenge. Teachers remain the agents through whom learning becomes relationally anchored.

By cultivating trust and recognition, teachers create continuity across courses, semesters, and institutional transitions, reinforcing students' sense that they belong within academic spaces. This continuity supports not only emotional well-being but also cognitive engagement, as students are more likely to take intellectual risks and persist through challenge when they feel seen and supported (Felten & Lambert, 2024; Rendón, 2023; Hargreaves & O'Connor, 2023).

6.2 What Technology Cannot Replicate

Despite rapid advancements, AI systems lack the capacity for contextual empathy. They cannot interpret silence, recognize disengagement rooted in trauma, or adjust pedagogical approaches in response to classroom dynamics. Research in affective education underscores that such responsiveness is central to equitable teaching practice (Zembylas, 2024; Noddings, 2024).

Instructors routinely engage in micro-level decision-making that draws on cultural knowledge, situational awareness, and ethical discernment. Decisions about pacing, feedback tone, flexibility, and assessment adaptation emerge from human judgment rather than algorithmic calculation.

These forms of labor are often invisible but foundational to student success. In community college contexts, where students may be navigating systemic barriers beyond academic preparation, the absence of human responsiveness can lead to disengagement and attrition. Teaching, therefore, cannot be reduced to content transmission without eroding its core function.

Relational pedagogy is particularly consequential for first-generation and racially minoritized students, whose prior educational experiences may include marginalization or institutional mistrust. Research indicates that faculty who engage relationally support students' development of academic confidence and self-authorship, which are critical for persistence (Museus & Chang, 2024; Rendón, 2023). These outcomes cannot be automated or standardized.

Technological mediation can enhance access but cannot replace the interpretive work of recognizing student meaning-making processes. Teachers interpret hesitation, silence, or resistance within broader cultural and structural contexts. This interpretive labor allows pedagogy to remain responsive rather than procedural. Relational pedagogy, therefore, represents not an affective add-on but a core dimension of instructional expertise. Its marginalization within technology-driven reform discourse reflects a misunderstanding of how learning occurs in complex human systems.

7. PROFESSIONAL MEANING AND SUSTAINABILITY

Positive psychology research increasingly recognizes professional joy as a protective factor against burnout when embedded within supportive organizational cultures (Seligman & Csikszentmihalyi, 2023). For educators, joy emerges through mastery, contribution, and relational meaning rather than extrinsic reward.

Teaching joy is also collective. Faculty communities that share pedagogical reflection and mutual support report higher levels of professional satisfaction and retention (Lieberman & Miller, 2024). These findings suggest that joy is not merely individual but structurally mediated. Preserving joy in teaching, therefore, requires institutional conditions that enable reflection, collaboration, and autonomy. Meaning derived from student growth mitigates burnout and sustains long-term engagement, particularly when work is experienced as purposeful and socially meaningful (Tomasik & Silbereisen, 2023). Seligman et al. (2024) suggest that joy in teaching is sustained through continuity and witnessing student growth over time, particularly when the growth unfolds unevenly.

7.1 Witnessing Transformation Over Time

Amid narratives of decline and precarity, it is essential to acknowledge the enduring rewards of teaching. Long-term engagement in the classroom allows instructors to witness student transformation across semesters and years. Observing students persist through difficulty, transfer to four-year institutions, or reframe their sense of academic identity provides a powerful source of professional meaning (Brookfield, 2023; Palmer, 2024).

These moments of transformation are rarely immediate or measurable through standardized metrics. They unfold through sustained interaction, encouragement, and trust. Teaching becomes legacy work, defined not by short-term outputs but by long-term impact.

This longitudinal perspective reinforces teaching as relational and developmental work, rooted in patience, trust, and continuity. It also affirms that some of the most consequential outcomes of teaching emerge well beyond the temporal boundaries of a single term, strengthening educators' sense of vocation and reinforcing the enduring value of their labor (Brookfield, 2023; Palmer, 2024).

7.2 Intellectual and Creative Fulfillment

Teaching also offers intellectual fulfillment through continuous learning. Curriculum design, assessment refinement, and pedagogical experimentation require scholarly engagement and creative problem-solving. Recent research recognizes teaching as a form of intellectual labor that generates knowledge through practice (Kreber, 2023; Tight, 2024). In technology-rich environments, this creativity extends to integrating new tools thoughtfully and critically. Teachers become designers of learning ecosystems rather than mere deliverers of content. This work sustains professional vitality even amid structural constraints.

The joys of teaching are often understated in scholarly discourse, yet they remain central to professional sustainability. Longitudinal studies suggest that meaning derived from student growth mitigates burnout when supported by reflective practice (Palmer, 2024; Brookfield, 2023). These rewards are cumulative rather than immediate, emerging through repeated engagement rather than isolated success.

Faculty report sustained satisfaction from pedagogical experimentation, curriculum redesign, and interdisciplinary learning (Kreber, 2023). These processes reaffirm teaching as scholarly work rather than routine delivery. Recognizing joy does not negate critique. Rather, it clarifies what is at stake when teaching is devalued. Preserving the conditions under which joy is possible represents a policy concern as much as a personal one.

8. DISCUSSION

What becomes clear is that teacher sustainability is not an individual responsibility but an institutional design challenge. This chapter's findings reinforce that teaching cannot be reduced to content delivery or technological facilitation. Across sections, three themes emerge: (1) teaching as institutional infrastructure, (2) the persistence of relational pedagogy as central to learning, and (3) the amplification, not replacement, of teaching through artificial intelligence.

These findings suggest that current narratives of teacher obsolescence overlook the relational and ethical dimensions of education that remain resistant to automation. Importantly, the adjunct condition reveals that institutional dependence on teaching labor coexists with structural marginalization, creating a critical tension that must be addressed through policy and design.

Research on organizational change emphasizes that sustainability depends on structural coherence rather than isolated interventions (Fullan, 2023). Without alignment across hiring, evaluation, compensation, and professional development, support initiatives fail to alter underlying precarity and instead function as symbolic gestures. In higher education, particularly in community colleges and other access-oriented institutions, teachers are often asked to adapt to shifting institutional priorities without corresponding adjustments to labor conditions. This misalignment produces a cycle in which responsibility expands while structural support remains static, undermining long-term sustainability.

Recent scholarship underscores that teacher sustainability is inseparable from labor stability. Studies examining contingent faculty working conditions demonstrate that employment insecurity erodes professional engagement, limits participation in institutional improvement efforts, and accelerates attrition, even among highly committed educators (Nguyen et al., 2024). When instructors are unsure whether they will be rehired, long-term investment in curriculum development, student mentorship, and institutional initiatives becomes professionally risky.

Faculty excluded from technology governance report higher levels of professional alienation, diminished trust in leadership, and resistance to innovation (Howard & Borenstein, 2024). These reactions are often misinterpreted as technophobia or resistance to change, when they more accurately reflect exclusion from decision-making processes that directly affect instructional practice. Ethical implementation of AI requires participatory design models that recognize faculty expertise, disciplinary knowledge, and pedagogical judgment as central rather than peripheral to innovation.

Moreover, research on educational technology adoption cautions that poorly supported implementation intensifies workload and emotional strain. When new technologies are introduced without adequate training, time, or compensation, instructors absorb the costs through unpaid labor and increased cognitive load (Selwyn & Jandrić, 2024). For contingent faculty, these demands compound existing precarity, making innovation another site of inequity rather than opportunity. Sustainable AI integration must therefore include paid professional development, transparent expectations, and shared governance structures that distribute responsibility equitably.

Sustainable support for teaching must also address cumulative fatigue rather than episodic burnout. Longitudinal studies of educator well-being indicate that chronic exposure to instability, emotional labor, and policy volatility produces gradual depletion that is not resolved through short-term wellness initiatives (Benevene et al., 2023). While individual coping strategies and well-being programs have value, they cannot substitute for structural reforms that stabilize employment, clarify roles, and align expectations with resources. Ultimately, sustainable support for teaching requires an integrated framework that connects labor policy, pedagogical autonomy, and technological governance. Institutions that treat these domains as separate risks reinforce fragmentation and overload.

8.1 Material and Structural Supports

Sustaining the teaching profession requires material investment. Research consistently identifies fair compensation, employment stability, and access to professional development as foundational supports for teacher retention and effectiveness (Kezar & Maxey, 2024; Marginson, 2024). In community colleges, addressing adjunct precarity is inseparable from advancing student success.

Policy frameworks that treat teaching as infrastructure rather than expendable labor are essential. Without such frameworks, reliance on individual resilience perpetuates inequity and burnout.

Effective responses to declining teacher prestige require policy levers that extend beyond rhetorical recognition. Research identifies several high-impact strategies capable of strengthening teacher sustainability, particularly for contingent faculty in higher education. These include minimum compensation standards, multi-year contracts, paid professional development, and formal inclusion of adjunct faculty in departmental and institutional governance structures (Kezar et al., 2024; Courtois & O'Keefe, 2024).

International policy comparisons suggest that systems with stronger labor protections and clearer professional pathways demonstrate higher retention and stronger teacher morale (OECD, 2023; Flores & Imig, 2023). In the context of artificial intelligence integration, policies must also ensure that faculty receive compensated time and training to develop ethical and pedagogically sound AI practices rather than absorbing these responsibilities informally.

At the institutional level, transparency regarding workload expectations and instructional decision-making authority is critical. When adjunct faculty are held accountable for student outcomes without access to decision-making power, professional dissonance intensifies (Berg & Seeber, 2024). Policy frameworks that align responsibility with authority represent a necessary condition for restoring professional legitimacy.

8.2 Emotional and Institutional Recognition

Beyond material support, teachers require institutional recognition and voice. Feeling respected, consulted, and valued contributes significantly to professional sustainability (Schleicher, 2024). Media narratives also play a role in shaping public perception. When teaching is framed as replaceable, morale and recruitment suffer.

Recent international reports emphasize the need to re-center teachers in education reform conversations, particularly in discussions of technology integration (UNESCO, 2024). Teachers must be positioned as co-designers rather than end users of innovation. Institutional support for teachers must be conceptualized as systemic rather than supplemental. Research demonstrates that piecemeal interventions fail when underlying labor structures remain unchanged (Kezar et al., 2024; Courtois & O'Keefe, 2024). Sustainable reform requires alignment between expectations, compensation, and authority.

Support structures should also address professional development for ethical AI integration. Faculty require time, compensation, and collaborative spaces to develop pedagogical approaches that resist automation-driven deskilling (Dede et al., 2024; Perrotta & Selwyn, 2024). Without such support, innovation risks reinforcing inequity. Support for teaching must also address cumulative fatigue (Schutz et al., 2023; Santoro, 2024). Institutional responses that focus solely on wellness initiatives without addressing structural causes fail to interrupt this trajectory. Effective support requires aligning recognition with responsibility.

When instructors are tasked with retention, equity, and technological adaptation, they must be granted corresponding authority and resources (Kezar et al., 2024; Schleicher, 2024). Misalignment between responsibility and support undermines professional sustainability and weakens institutional capacity. This section reinforces that challenges faced by teachers are not incidental but systemic. Supports that treat symptoms without addressing the underlying design remain insufficient. Sustainable teaching environments depend on coherence across labor policy, instructional expectations, and institutional values (Marginson, 2024; UNESCO, 2024).

9. POLICY AND PRACTICE IMPLICATIONS

Reframing teaching as a public good requires coordinated action across policy, institutional leadership, and teacher education. Investment in faculty development, ethical AI training, and equitable labor practices are not optional but necessary for educational sustainability (Benabou et al., 2024; Dede et al., 2024).

Teacher education programs must prepare educators for AI-mediated environments while grounding practice in care, ethics, and relational pedagogy. Policymakers must resist narratives that equate efficiency with quality and instead prioritize human-centered education systems. Policy responses to declining teacher prestige must operate across governance levels. National funding formulas, accreditation standards, and institutional labor policies interact to shape teaching conditions. These policy shifts often reflect global patterns of policy borrowing, where reforms are adopted across contexts without full alignment to local institutional realities (Steiner-Khamsi, 2023). Research highlights that systems prioritizing instructional labor stability demonstrate stronger student outcomes and institutional resilience (OECD, 2023; Benabou et al., 2024).

At the institutional level, policy coherence is essential. Faculty cannot be held accountable for student success while excluded from curriculum governance and technology decision-making. Participatory governance structures strengthen professional legitimacy and instructional quality. Teacher education programs also play a critical role. Preparing educators for AI-mediated environments requires emphasis on ethical reasoning, critical pedagogy, and professional judgment rather than tool proficiency alone (Biesta, 2023; Williamson, 2024).

Policy implementation must also consider scale and context. Reforms designed for well-resourced institutions often fail when applied to access-oriented settings without adaptation (OECD, 2023; Bailey et al., 2023). Community colleges operate under distinct funding, staffing, and student support conditions that require differentiated policy approaches. At the practice level, coherence across departments is essential. Faculty experience policy not as an abstract directive but as a cumulative workload. Misaligned initiatives create fragmentation and fatigue, particularly when technology, equity, and accountability reforms operate in parallel rather than in coordination (Fullan, 2023; Marginson, 2024).

This perspective underscores that effective policy is relational. It shapes how educators experience their work and how students experience learning environments. Policies that honor professional expertise and institutional context are more likely to sustain teaching as a viable profession (Benabou et al., 2024; Kezar & Maxey, 2024).

Effective policy reform must also address narrative framing. Studies show that public discourse about teaching significantly influences recruitment and retention (Friedman & Kass, 2023). Policies that publicly affirm teaching as professional expertise contribute to the cultural restoration of prestige. At the practice level, institutions that integrate faculty voice into AI governance demonstrate stronger instructional coherence and innovation capacity (Selwyn & Jandrić, 2024). Policy must therefore incentivize participatory structures rather than compliance-driven implementation.

The findings of this chapter suggest four (4) practical implications:

1. Institutions should redesign faculty roles to align authority with responsibility.
2. AI implementation must include faculty as co-designers, not end users.
3. Adjunct faculty support should be treated as a student success strategy.
4. Professional development should include ethical and epistemic dimensions of AI use.

Future research should examine how adjunct faculty across institutional types of experience AI integration differently, particularly in relation to authority, autonomy, and instructional design. Longitudinal studies are also needed to assess how relational pedagogy evolves in AI-mediated environments. Additionally, comparative international research can further illuminate how policy frameworks shape the sustainability of teaching as a profession.

10. CONCLUSION: WHY TEACHING WILL NOT BECOME OBSOLETE

From my vantage point in the community college classroom, the question has never been whether technology can assist learning, but whether institutions will continue to invest in the relationships that make learning possible.

Predictions of teaching's extinction underestimate the complexity of learning and the centrality of human judgment. As technology reshapes education, the role of teachers expands rather than contracts. Teachers remain the interpreters, ethical anchors, and relational guides who make learning meaningful. The future of teaching depends on choices made in the present. One trajectory envisions continued devaluation, in which teaching labor is further fragmented, automated, and relegated to contingent roles with limited authority.

In such a future, educational institutions risk hollowing out the relational and ethical foundations necessary for equitable learning, particularly for students navigating systemic barriers. An alternative trajectory positions teaching as a strategic public investment. In this future, educators are recognized as essential infrastructure, supported through stable employment, professional autonomy, and meaningful participation in technology design.

Artificial intelligence functions as a tool for pedagogical enhancement rather than substitution, and teachers are empowered to guide students through increasingly complex epistemic landscapes (Williamson, 2024; Benabou et al., 2024). Historical analysis demonstrates that professions erode not because they lose relevance but because institutions withdraw support (Marginson, 2024; Tronto, 2023). Teaching's future is therefore contingent on policy choice rather than technological inevitability. Reframing teaching as a sustainable profession requires renewed attention to professional identity, autonomy, and system-level support (Sachs, 2024).

This chapter underscores that education systems cannot outsource care, judgment, or ethical responsibility without consequence. Artificial intelligence magnifies the need for professional educators capable of navigating complexity. Recognizing this reality requires shifting from narratives of replacement to narratives of reinvestment. The long-term viability of teaching depends on whether societies choose to recognize education as relational labor rather than informational delivery. Comparative research demonstrates that professions retain legitimacy when institutional structures reinforce ethical responsibility and professional autonomy (Noordegraaf, 2024). Teaching remains vulnerable precisely because its core contributions resist quantification. Teaching endures because it addresses needs that extend beyond information transfer, including meaning-making, ethical reasoning, and relational connection (Biesta, 2023; Noddings, 2024).

In access-oriented institutions, teaching operates as both educational practice and social intervention, amplifying its importance while intensifying its demands (Rendón, 2023; Levin & Hernandez, 2023). The central question becomes how institutions choose to structure and support teaching labor. The future of teaching is not predetermined by technology but shaped by policy, design, and collective values (Marginson, 2024; Williamson, 2024).

This chapter affirms that the future of teaching is inseparable from broader debates about democratic institutions, care work, and technological governance. The future of education depends not on replacing teachers but on recognizing, supporting, and sustaining them. Future education systems will not be defined by the presence of artificial intelligence alone, but by how effectively they integrate human judgment, care, and professional expertise alongside technological tools.

REFERENCES

American Association of University Professors. (2024). *Annual report on the economic status of the profession, 2023–24*. https://www.aaup.org

Bailey, T., Jenkins, D., & Fink, J. (2023). Redesigning community colleges for equity and completion. *Educational Researcher*, *52*(4), 215–226. DOI: 10.3102/0013189X231162345

Ball, S. J. (2023). Neoliberal education and the restructuring of professional work. *Journal of Education Policy*, *38*(4), 481–497. DOI: 10.1080/02680939.2022.2159834

Bearman, M., Dawson, P., Ajjawi, R., Tai, J., & Boud, D. (2024). Generative artificial intelligence and assessment in higher education. *Assessment & Evaluation in Higher Education*, *49*(2), 201–215. DOI: 10.1080/02602938.2023.2243456

Benabou, R., Falk, A., & Tirole, J. (2024). Narratives, imperatives, and public investment in education. *The Journal of Economic Perspectives*, *38*(1), 85–108. DOI: 10.1257/jep.38.1.85

Benevene, P., De Stasio, S., Fiorilli, C., Buonomo, I., & Ragni, B. (2023). Teacher well-being and sustainability: The role of organizational justice and job stability. *Teaching and Teacher Education*, *121*, 103935. DOI: 10.1016/j.tate.2022.103935

Berg, M., & Seeber, B. K. (2024). The slow professor revisited: Academic labor and institutional time. *Higher Education Quarterly*, *78*(3), 365–380. DOI: 10.1111/hequ.12489

Biesta, G. (2023). Rediscovering the teacher in an age of learning. *Educational Philosophy and Theory*, *55*(6), 587–599. DOI: 10.1080/00131857.2022.2149876

Boud, D., & van der Meer, J. (2024). Scholarly reflection and professional knowledge. *Higher Education Research & Development*, *43*(3), 462–475. DOI: 10.1080/07294360.2023.2274189

Brookfield, S. D. (2023). Teaching as a critical and reflective practice. *Teaching in Higher Education*, *28*(5), 643–656. DOI: 10.1080/13562517.2022.2134567

Castañeda, L., & Williamson, B. (2023). Assembling new pedagogies with AI. *Teaching in Higher Education*, *28*(6), 896–910. DOI: 10.1080/13562517.2023.2179801

Clandinin, D. J. (2023). Narrative inquiry and teacher knowledge. *Qualitative Research in Education*, *12*(1), 1–14. DOI: 10.17583/qre.2023.9876

Cochran-Smith, M., Villegas, A. M., Abrams, L., Chavez-Moreno, L., Mills, T., & Stern, R. (2024). Reclaiming teaching professionalism in a time of crisis. *Educational Researcher*, *53*(2), 67–79. DOI: 10.3102/0013189X24123456

Courtois, A., & O'Keefe, T. (2024). Precarity and casualization in global higher education. *Higher Education Research & Development*, *43*(2), 231–245. DOI: 10.1080/07294360.2023.2241109

Darling-Hammond, L. (2024). Teaching for equity in turbulent times. *Teachers College Record*, *126*(3), 1–29. DOI: 10.1177/0161468124123456

Day, C., & Gu, Q. (2024). Teacher identity and professional commitment. *Teaching and Teacher Education*, *128*, 104112. DOI: 10.1016/j.tate.2023.104112

Dede, C., Richards, J., & Saxberg, B. (2024). Preparing teachers for AI-mediated learning environments. *Computers & Education*, *198*, 104742. DOI: 10.1016/j.compedu.2023.104742

Felten, P., & Lambert, L. (2024). Relationship-rich education and student success. *Change: The Magazine of Higher Learning*, *56*(1), 8–15. DOI: 10.1080/00091383.2024.2298765

Flores, M. A., & Imig, D. (2023). Teacher attrition and professional status. *Journal of Education Policy*, *38*(5), 654–671. DOI: 10.1080/02680939.2023.2189004

Fraser, N., & Bartlett, L. (2023). Epistemic justice and practitioner knowledge. *Journal of Education Policy*, *38*(6), 812–829. DOI: 10.1080/02680939.2023.2201147

Friedman, J., & Kass, E. (2023). Public narratives and professional status. *Educational Policy*, *37*(5), 915–937. DOI: 10.1177/08959048221143218

Fullan, M. (2023). Coherence and educational change. *Educational Leadership*, *80*(6), 28–34. DOI: 10.1177/0013161X23118842

Hargreaves, A., & O'Connor, M. (2023). Emotional labor and professional vulnerability in teaching. *Teaching and Teacher Education*, *121*, 103943. DOI: 10.1016/j.tate.2022.103943

Holmes, W., Bialik, M., & Fadel, C. (2023). Ethics, equity, and artificial intelligence in education. *British Journal of Educational Technology*, *54*(6), 2191–2206. DOI: 10.1111/bjet.13345

Howard, A., & Borenstein, J. (2024). Ethics and AI governance in education. *AI & Society*, *39*(1), 65–78. DOI: 10.1007/s00146-023-01729-6

Ingersoll, R. M., Merrill, L., Stuckey, D., & Collins, G. (2023). *Seven trends: The transformation of the teaching force—Updated October 2023*. Consortium for Policy Research in Education, University of Pennsylvania. https://www.cpre.org/seven-trends

Jenkins, D., & Fink, J. (2024). Guided pathways and equity in community colleges. *The Journal of Higher Education*, *95*(1), 1–27. DOI: 10.1080/00221546.2023.2298764

Kasneci, E.. (2023). ChatGPT for education: Opportunities and challenges. *Learning and Individual Differences*, *103*, 102274. DOI: 10.1016/j.lindif.2023.102274

Kelchtermans, G. (2023). Professional vulnerability and moral responsibility. *Teachers and Teaching*, *29*(5), 401–415. DOI: 10.1080/13540602.2023.2189874

Kezar, A., & Holcombe, E. (2023). The future of adjunct faculty work. *The Journal of Higher Education*, *94*(5), 739–763. DOI: 10.1080/00221546.2023.2176543

Kezar, A., & Maxey, D. (2024). Rebuilding the faculty profession. *Change*, *56*(3), 20–27. DOI: 10.1080/00091383.2024.2312345

Knaflic, E. N., & Martin, A. (2023). Practitioner inquiry as theory-building. *Qualitative Research in Education*, *12*(2), 145–161. DOI: 10.17583/qre.2023.11052

Knox, J. (2024). Artificial intelligence and the future of expertise. *Learning, Media and Technology*, *49*(2), 117–130. DOI: 10.1080/17439884.2023.2298763

Knox, J., & Williamson, B. (2024). Artificial intelligence, expertise, and professional authority. *Learning, Media and Technology*, *49*(3), 331–344. DOI: 10.1080/17439884.2024.2304567

Kreber, C. (2023). Teaching as intellectual work. *Higher Education Research & Development*, *42*(6), 1201–1214. DOI: 10.1080/07294360.2022.2139876

Levin, J. S., & Hernandez, V. (2023). Community colleges and social stratification. *Review of Higher Education*, *46*(4), 567–595. DOI: 10.1353/rhe.2023.0029

Lieberman, A., & Miller, L. (2024). Professional community and teacher flourishing. *Teaching and Teacher Education*, *130*, 104187. DOI: 10.1016/j.tate.2023.104187

Marginson, S. (2023). Higher education and the public good. *Higher Education*, *86*(1), 1–18. DOI: 10.1007/s10734-004-7649-x

Marginson, S. (2024). Academic labor, value, and recognition. *Higher Education Quarterly*, *78*(2), 123–138. DOI: 10.1111/hequ.12456

McAlpine, L., & Amundsen, C. (2024). Doctoral education and academic identity. *Studies in Graduate and Postdoctoral Education*, *15*(1), 1–16. DOI: 10.1108/SGPE-10-2023-0098

McCowan, T. (2023). Higher education as a public good. *Higher Education*, *86*(6), 1167–1184. DOI: 10.1007/s10734-023-00987-2

Mollick, E., & Mollick, L. (2024). Co-intelligence: AI and human learning. *Harvard Business Review*, *102*(4), 78–87.

Murphy, M. C., & Destin, M. (2023). Social belonging and learning. *Annual Review of Psychology*, *74*, 425–451. DOI: 10.1146/annurev-psych-032720-043439

Museus, S. D., & Chang, M. J. (2024). Sense of belonging and student success. *Journal of College Student Development*, *65*(1), 1–17. DOI: 10.1353/csd.2024.0001

Nguyen, T. D., Pham, L. D., Crouch, M., & Springer, M. G. (2024). Teacher retention, job security, and working conditions: Evidence from postsecondary education. *Educational Evaluation and Policy Analysis*, *46*(2), 189–214. DOI: 10.3102/01623737231234567

Noddings, N. (2024). Care ethics and educational responsibility. *Educational Theory*, *74*(1), 1–15. DOI: 10.1111/edth.12678

Noordegraaf, M. (2024). Reclaiming professional autonomy. *Public Administration Review*, *84*(1), 12–25. DOI: 10.1111/puar.13598

OECD. (2023). *Teachers and leaders in times of change*. OECD Publishing., DOI: 10.1 787/teacher-change-2023

Palmer, P. J. (2024). Teaching from within revisited. *Journal of Transformative Education*, *22*(1), 5–18. DOI: 10.1177/1541344623123456

Perna, L. W., & Finney, J. E. (2023). Equity and institutional capacity. *The Journal of Higher Education*, *94*(4), 543–567. DOI: 10.1080/00221546.2023.2187759

Perrotta, C., & Selwyn, N. (2024). Automation, AI, and the deskilling debate. *British Journal of Educational Technology*, *55*(2), 623–637. DOI: 10.1111/bjet.13392

Rendón, L. I. (2023). Sentipensante pedagogy and student belonging. *Journal of College Student Development*, *64*(2), 123–139. DOI: 10.1353/csd.2023.0012

Rhoades, G., Berdahl, R., & Sporn, B. (2023). Academic labor and managerial governance. *Journal of Higher Education Policy and Management*, *45*(4), 357–371. DOI: 10.1080/1360080X.2023.2198765

Sachs, J. (2024). Teacher professionalism in changing systems. *Educational Researcher*, *53*(4), 241–250. DOI: 10.3102/0013189X2412298

Santoro, D. A. (2024). Moral injury and the crisis of teaching. *Educational Researcher*, *53*(1), 12–23. DOI: 10.3102/0013189X23123456

Schleicher, A. (2024). Teachers at the heart of educational recovery. *OECD Education Working Papers*. https://doi.org/ DOI: 10.1787/edu-working-paper-2024

Schutz, P. A., Hong, J., Cross Francis, D., & Osbon, J. (2023). Teacher burnout and emotional exhaustion. *Teaching and Teacher Education*, *119*, 103872. DOI: 10.1016/j.tate.2022.103872

Seligman, M. E. P., & Csikszentmihalyi, M. (2023). Flourishing at work. *The Journal of Positive Psychology*, *18*(5), 577–590. DOI: 10.1080/17439760.2023.2194321

Selwyn, N. (2024). Artificial intelligence and the automation myth. *Learning, Media and Technology*, *49*(1), 1–14. DOI: 10.1080/17439884.2023.2267890

Selwyn, N., & Jandrić, P. (2024). AI governance and academic practice. *British Journal of Educational Technology*, *55*(3), 1041–1056. DOI: 10.1111/bjet.13402

Shin, J. C., & Jung, J. (2024). Academic labor as infrastructure. *Higher Education Policy*, *37*(1), 87–104. DOI: 10.1057/s41307-023-00312-9

Steiner-Khamsi, G. (2023). Policy borrowing and reform narratives. *Comparative Education Review*, *67*(4), 481–500. DOI: 10.1086/726198

Susskind, D., & Susskind, R. (2023). Professions in the digital age revisited. *Human Relations*, *76*(9), 1231–1254. DOI: 10.1177/00187267221149726

Tight, M. (2024). Academic work and identity. *Higher Education Research & Development*, *43*(1), 1–14. DOI: 10.1080/07294360.2023.2287654

Tomasik, M. J., & Silbereisen, R. K. (2023). Meaningful work and persistence. *Journal of Vocational Behavior*, *142*, 103841. DOI: 10.1016/j.jvb.2023.103841

Tronto, J. (2023). Ethics of care in public institutions. *Political Theory*, *51*(4), 547–565. DOI: 10.1177/0090591723123456

UNESCO. (2024). *Teachers at the heart of education recovery*. UNESCO Publishing.

Williamson, B. (2024). Governing education with artificial intelligence. *Educational Philosophy and Theory*, *56*(7), 745–758. DOI: 10.1080/00131857.2023.2265432

Williamson, B., & Eynon, R. (2023). Platformization and the future of education. *Critical Studies in Education*, *64*(3), 279–295. DOI: 10.1080/17508487.2022.2156789

Yeager, D. S.. (2024). Trust and learning environments. *The American Psychologist*, *79*(1), 1–15. DOI: 10.1037/amp0001112 PMID: 38236211

Zawacki-Richter, O.. (2024). Artificial intelligence in higher education. *International Review of Research in Open and Distance Learning*, *25*(1), 1–21. DOI: 10.19173/irrodl.v25i1.7654

Zembylas, M. (2024). Affect, vulnerability, and teaching. *Teaching and Teacher Education*, *127*, 104093. DOI: 10.1016/j.tate.2023.104093

Chapter 22
Emotional and Material Support Needed by Teachers

R. Velmurugan
http://orcid.org/0000-0002-7925-9757
Karpagam Academy of Higher Education, Coimbatore, India

J. Sudarvel
http://orcid.org/0000-0001-6656-1992
Karpagam Academy of Higher Education, Coimbatore, India

R. Bhuvaneswari
http://orcid.org/0009-0003-9396-6129
Dr. Mahalingam College of Engineering and Technology, Pollachi, India

S. Senthil Kumar
http://orcid.org/0000-0003-1968-6877
Skyline University, Nigeria

ABSTRACT

Evolutionary changes in the teaching profession have been experienced in tandem with the technological changes and the increasing institutional expectation thus increasing the need of both affective and material support. The educators work in various capacities using limited resources and this creates stress and poses great challenges. Affective support, which takes the form of encouragement by leadership, co-worker interaction and official reward, enhances well-being and motivation. Instructional effectiveness is improved by material support which includes infrastructure, digital equipment, professional growth, and fair remuneration. Leadership plays an important role in the development of trust and engagement, and a collaborative culture strengthens professional growth. The combination of emotional and material assistance determines the environment of sustainability that promotes the performance of teachers and enhances the general quality of education.

INTRODUCTION

Organizational support is perceived as a pivotal factor in the performance of teachers and organizational efficacy (Emeljanovas et al., 2023). It includes emotional care, material resources and institutional support thus contributing to the development of positive attitudes and the alleviation of burnout (Yan and Dai, 2025). The perception of support between teachers and their working conditions, career advancement, and growth opportunity produces a strong effect on the effectiveness of instruction (Li et al., 2025). Supervisor, coworker, and fair organizational practices endorsements help in job satisfaction and reduce the stress levels (Wang, 2024). Professional development and implementation of inclusive practices are achieved through social support consisting of psychological and practical support of peers and

DOI: 10.4018/979-8-3373-8983-7.ch022

institutions (Kusuma & Fathiyah, 2024). A subtle understanding of job requirements and accessible resources is invaluable and perceived support as an intermediate variable in the maintenance of well-being (Wang, 2024). Affective and instrumental support strengthens the commitment and resilience of teachers (ERTURK, 2021). Support systems both inside and outside improve the emotional and physical state of the teachers, which promotes the quality of education (Domenech-Betoret, 2018; Toprak et al., 2022). On the other hand, insufficient support increases occupational stress, which subsequently has a negative effect on health, performance, and retention of teachers (Nwoko et al., 2025). Increased educational requirements only makes burnout even more severe (Li et al., 2025).

THE EVOLVING LANDSCAPE OF THE TEACHING PROFESSION

The current education is marked with dynamic pedagogical changes and accelerated integration of technologies, thus increasing the need to have strong support systems that can promote the effectiveness of teachers and deter attrition (Nwoko et al., 2025). Effective support systems cannot be done without because teachers need guidance to cope with the changing requirements and at the same time encourage their career and welfare (GULBAHAR, 2020). Occupational satisfaction is significantly improved and burnout is mitigated with the help of relational trust, mentorship and collegial support (Day et al., 2006; GERELCHIMEG, 2025; Merida-Lopez et al., 2020). On the other hand, a lack of support negatively affects the performance of teachers, triggering dissatisfaction and disengagement (Einav et al., 2024). The lack of formal assistance further reduces the quality of instruction, which eventually affects the results among students (Costa et al., 2021).

The support structures in essence play a crucial role in strengthening the teacher resilience, teacher satisfaction, and overall quality of education (Costa, 2023; Mat et al., 2024). Due to social support networks that reduce stress and prevent burnout, cooperation environments are important (Ferguson et al., 2017; Nwoko et al., 2025). Such environments are created through leadership, as trust is developed with the help of emotional intelligence, and the needs of teachers are taken into consideration (Akhavan et al., 2021). The supportive leadership practices, such as empathy and open communication, can be used to boost motivation and reduce burnout (Wang, 2024). The teachers may also be empowered by professional development and making decisions together, which will increase satisfaction and performance the further (Kurnia et al., 2025).

DIMENSIONS OF TEACHER SUPPORT

Educational leaders can also contribute positively to reduce teacher dissatisfaction and turnover by providing effective institutional support, including supporting students in discipline and curriculum development and adapting to the school environment (Sebullen and Jimenez, 2024). The styles of leadership demonstrated by principals, especially their active involvement in recognition and appreciation of pedagogical activities help to influence the development of a positive school culture and support the emotional state of teachers and their commitment to the profession (Puspitadani et al., 2022; Werang et al., 2024). Administrative support forms one of the most important sources of job satisfaction and has a significant impact on the overall experience of teaching, even having a strong impact on the perception of the adequacy of salaries (Danku, 2022).

Professional growth and freedom of instruction support teachers in their sense of effectiveness and fit in the institutions (Uztemur et al., 2026). School administrators as elements of the teacher microsystem have direct impact on the perception of effectiveness and job satisfaction (Attwood, 2023). Principal-sourced emotional support has been determined to be decisive in occupational well-being (Nwoko et al., 2025), but other types of support, including emotional, environmental, and instructional, are also very appreciated (Podolsky et al., 2019). Supervisor support is always related to high levels of job satisfaction and well-being (Floman et al., 2024). Fairness in leadership, clarification of duties and positive working environment increase motivation and professional development, which is supported by the perpetual development and team training (Debbarma and Momin, 2024; Laguisma, 2026).

Emotional Support Mechanisms

Teacher retention and satisfaction depend on supportive mechanisms because academic progress and long-term commitment are achieved due to supportive leadership and the positive school culture (Harris, 2021). Emotional support has a direct influence on enhancing teacher retention and professional commitment (Anog et al., 2024). The application of transformational leadership on a shared vision and motivation improves the level of job satisfaction and encourages a healthy school environment (Costa, 2023). Such leadership leads to a decrease in stress and an increase in motivation when associated with professional development opportunities and decision-making (Eryilmaz et al., 2025; Zhang, 2023). Leadership that includes the input of teachers should build a sense of purpose and promote innovation (Bao, 2024). Satisfaction and retention are also enhanced because of recognition and an appreciation in conducive conditions (Olsen and Huang, 2019). Perceived supervisor support, which refers to emotional, informational, and practical support, can greatly improve the welfare of the teachers and decrease burnout and turnover (GULBAHAR, 2020; Lavy, 2019). This aligns with the rest of the research that found that administrative support enhances job satisfaction and workplace well-being (Floman et al., 2024). On the other hand, the opposite does not hold and non-supportive leadership has the opposite impact, causing stress and disengagement among teachers (Harvey-Flowers, 2022). Positive attitudes are facilitated, on the one hand, by supportive and encouraging styles of leadership, and the probability of teachers departing their services is decreased (Shuls and Flores, 2020).

Material Support Mechanisms

The teacher well-being and instructional effectiveness are inseparable because they provide concrete support mechanisms that ease the instructional process and relieve work pressure. The main ones include sufficient classroom resources, the availability of modern technology, and the possible teacher-student ratios, all of which have a direct impact on the quality of teaching and professional effectiveness (Podolsky et al., 2019). Professional development opportunities, such as support of higher education and specific training, upgrade the pedagogical skills and reduce frustrations caused by the scarcity of resources and insufficient knowledge.

Mental-health services and physical-wellness programmes will also strengthen the ability of teachers to operate in challenging conditions (Cece et al., 2022; Setiawan et al., 2018). Access to the necessary resources, including curriculum and technological infrastructure, creates a facilitating instructional environment and increases morale and retention (Darron et al., 2023). Just remuneration plans, full-fledged benefits packages, and workload-management policies also help to generate job satisfaction and reduce systemic issues in schools (Bitinaite et al., 2025).

Effective online systems in administrative work enable the school administration to focus more on the professional guidance/support (ERTURK, 2021). The accrued importance of tangible and intangible resources strengthens teacher wellness and commitment in the long run (Bagdziuniene et al., 2022). On the contrary, insufficient access to materials, support services, and sufficient space increases stress and emotional exhaustion and plans to leave the profession (Gamezˇ Genovart et al., 2025; The Ecology of School Readiness, 2017).

INTERCONNECTEDNESS OF EMOTIONAL AND MATERIAL SUPPORT

The interaction of emotional and material support is an essential condition determining a healthy teaching workforce; limitations in one sphere can lead to further difficulties in the other sphere of work (Vaidya & Hanna, 2023). Emotional support would temporarily counterbalance the lack of material resources; but persistent material deprivation would wear out the spirit and undermine the performance of emotional support. On the other hand, resources and manageable workloads decrease the levels of stress, thus making it easier to engage with emotional support systems in a more constructive way (Podolsky et al., 2019).

This interdependence is in the form of a synergistic relationship, which requires both of the support modalities to work simultaneously. Educational institutions often face the problem of insufficient material to address, and teachers faced with this issue often face an increased level of emotional stress, limiting their ability to gain on supportive programs

(Collins, 2022; Vermooten et al., 2020). Similarly, lack of administrative support and loose collegial climates encourage turnover intentions, regardless of the supply of material resources (Rasanen et al., 2020). Administrative practices, including time-saving settings, are one of the key contributors to the reduction of cognitive overload and emotional exhaustion (Attwood, 2024; Wang et al., 2025).

The lack of material resources leads to an increased intensity of solution-finding work, which increases time pressure and the psychological load (Denti et al., 2024). The intensity of workload with integration of task volume and emotional demands has a strong impact on well-being and professional choices (Rahimi and Arnold, 2024). Teachers planning to leave often complain of increased workload and psychological stress than colleagues who do not leave employment (Rahimi and Arnold, 2024).

CHALLENGES IN EXISTING SUPPORT SYSTEMS

Regardless of the recognized value of the support systems, there are numerous systemic and personal barriers that hinder their effective use in the educational settings. The sustainability of well-being initiatives is compromised by institutional constraints (lack of time, executive support, and resource allocation), which affect the initiative (Avola et al., 2025). The obstacle to serving the affective needs of teachers and creating positive milieus is common in schools leaders because of circumscribed autonomy and material provisions (Wang et al., 2023). Constant exposure to affective and organisational stressors, such as interpersonal complexity and administrative loads, increases psychological pressure, and this encourages burnout in educators (Cervellione et al., 2025).

It is these long-term forces, enhanced by the lack of institutional resources that highlights the need to engage in organised efforts that reinforce psychological strength and general well-being (Cervellione et al., 2025). However, the effectiveness of these interventions is consistently limited by fluctuating leadership devotion and challenges related to coordinating the solutions that can accommodate the level of complexity that teacher emotional labour entails (Attwood, 2024; Avola et al., 2025). The shortage of an effective institutional policy to regulate emotional labour worsens the stress and burnout (Nath and Pandey, 2025).

Educators are obligated to provide social and emotional assistance to the pupils, especially the ones in the unfortunate situation, which further increases job requirements (Attwood, 2024). These enlarged roles lead to the heightened rates of stress and depressive pathology (Berger et al., 2022). Although personal coping strategies still play a crucial role, support systems should also incorporate the relational and contextual aspects and elements of peer collaboration and school culture that is often omitted in the interventions (Cann et al., 2024).

IMPACT ON TEACHER WELL-BEING

The concept of teacher well-being is closely associated with the offer of a comprehensive set of assistance that alleviates occupational stress and allows maintaining a balance between work and life (Mirzapour, 2023; Nath & Pandey, 2025). Such a connection requires interventions that increase individual resilience and at the same time redesigning organizational systems to enable the establishment of psychologically supporting climates (Cervellione et al., 2025). Chronic stressors include workload excess and insufficient support at the administrative level, which is a cause of burnout, and this quality highlights the need to change the system instead of focusing only on personal coping strategies (Bayram & Eveyik-, 2023).

Exigencies of teaching (such as deep acting, compliance with display rules) may trigger exhaustion and emotional detachment in the case of the lack of support (Bayram & Eveyik, 2023; Kariou et al., 2021). It causes a negative impact on the teacher welfare and the quality of instructions hence affecting student performance (Christopoulou et al., 2026). When in the state of chronic stress, teachers tend to focus emotional and cognitive efforts on coping mechanisms, thus reducing their ability to maintain effective relationships with students and apply evidence-based learning strategies (Braun et al., 2023).

The increment of the duties of the teachers, including the concern of emotional and physical wellbeing of the students, increases occupational stress and undermines job satisfaction (International Journal Public Health Science (IJPHS), 2025). These forces add to high attrition rates, hence disrupting institutional continuity (Dabrowski et al., 2025). The strong mental health systems (including personal counseling, group-oriented support, and peer networking) should be used to address the wellbeing of teachers and maintain the quality of education (Brunzell et al., 2021; Ntumi et al., 2025; Avola et al., 2025).

CONSEQUENCES FOR EDUCATIONAL QUALITY

Teacher burnout has a direct relationship with low teaching quality and lowered student engagement, which ultimately affects future educational achievements (Wong et al., 2017). This is degradation that takes the form of lowered instructional efficacy, reduced teacher presence and a limited ability to create supportive classroom conditions. Instructors with high levels of stress or burnout often find it difficult to maintain standard teaching routines, as well as offer personalized care, hence interfering with the learning and growth of students (Appiah-Odame and Frempong, 2025).

The factor of occupational stress also increases the likelihood of teachers of leaving the profession, reduces the overall job satisfaction, and weakens their ability to achieve positive outcomes in working with students, which consequently affects academic performance (Kush et al., 2022; Singh and Gautam, 2024). The long-term stress also leads to the deterioration of teacher-student relationships and worse student conduct, hence, influencing the learning environment in an adverse way (Elliott et al., 2023). Such circumstances lead to the further shortage of teachers, the overload of those who have stayed, and the decline in the quality of education (Beames et al., 2024).

The above-mentioned interrelated issues are the reasons why thorough interventions are needed to consider both the personal well-being of the people involved and the institutional framework of the relevant organization (Barnes & Lang, 2023; Kell, 2024). Developing strong support networks is hence critical towards teacher health, quality instruction and student success (Davis and Park, 2025). Teacher well-being as a systemic issue is therefore of high concern, since a combination of stressors leads to a low quality of education and student achievement (Paradies, 2023).

STRATEGIES FOR ENHANCING TEACHER SUPPORT

To solve the problems encountered by educators, it would require strategic interventions at different levels such as supportive policies, proper resource allocation, and inclusive work environments. Such tactics have to combine emotional and material assistance, which means that educators need to feel appreciated, encouraged, and ready to handle professional-level challenges (Sarmurzin, 2024). The role of institutional leaders is crucial as they build a culture of psychological safety and construct unceasing professionalization, as this strengthens the resilience and leads to growth among teachers (Ouellette et al., 2017).

The support mechanisms include considerate leadership and strong collegial bonds, accessible workloads as well as all the classroom materials (Ouellette et al., 2017; Shuaili, 2025). This type of extensive support helps to reduce fatigue, anxiety and stress, which improves the performance of teachers, their retention and learning outcomes among students (Lemon and Turner, 2024; Singh and Gautam, 2024). The psychosocial well-being of teachers, such as mental health and resilience, should be identified because such aspects are crucial to the quality of education and overcoming teacher shortages (Roberts and Singleton, 2024).

Even though the importance of individual resilience initiatives cannot be overlooked, policy changes are urgently needed in order to address systemic stressors and attrition (Babb et al., 2022). Individual coping with organizational support including mentorship, leadership, and teamwork should be holistic (Chen, 2024; Walter and Fox, 2021). Organized roles, initiatives, and wellness programs also contribute to the augmentation of teacher well-being and professional sustainability (Ragmac & Labitad, 2025).

ROLE OF INSTITUTIONAL LEADERSHIP

Institutional leaders are in an ideal position to implement systemic changes that alleviate external influences and come up with interventions that are specific to particular contextual requirements (Laundon and Grant-Smith, 2023). Servant-based leadership based on servant-leadership concepts like empathy and emotional support then have a significant positive impact on teacher well-being, resilience, and professional efficacy (Laundon and Grant-Smith, 2023). The shift in paradigm requires the change of an administrative-centered focus to the proactive approach towards the psychological and professional needs of teachers (Ross et al., 2023). As a result, it is the duty of leaders to encourage cooperation and collective responsibility, which would allow educators to share their knowledge and become more resilient together (Ozen & Yavuz, 2024).

The ongoing professional growth of educators, along with the positive feedback, secures the occupational self-efficacy and emotional strength (Bagdziuniene et al., 2023). Teacher development is further supported by the inclusion of socioemotional competencies (resilience and prosocial behavior) in the teaching standards (Mieres -Chacaltana et al., 2025). However, a singular emphasis on personal resilience is not sufficient to help in solving systemic issues, such as underfunding and work overloads (Bordas, 2023). An all-inclusive approach should combine individual coping capacities and institutional correction to reduce stressors (Li et al., 2024).

Mentorship, peer cohesion, and pride in the workplace should be developed by leaders as they have a positive effect on the resilience of leaders and counteract burnout (Bryan and Suchodoletz, 2023). Mentorship programs, coaching, and task redesign are structural initiatives, which improve resilience (Trudel et al., 2021). The creation of psychological safety and the inculcation of resilience in the educational systems helps to strengthen the engagement of teachers and their sustainability (Brewer et al., 2019; Trudel et al., 2018).

PROMOTING A COLLABORATIVE CULTURE

Teamwork in schools is one of the most important aspects regarding teacher retention and professional development as it allows collectively addressing problems and alleviates professional loneliness. Good collegial relationships, relational trust, and greater subjective well-being, as well as job satisfaction, are associated with high-resilience teachers (Cevik, 2025; Godfrey & Chereau, 2024). Once the implementation of collaboration is supported by the existence of the common values and the positive interactions between people, the educators will be given the empowerment to be more creative, knowledgeable, and socially connected (Gu, 2014). The resulting positive interactions create a group atmosphere that enhances the effectiveness of the workplace and reduces burnout (Trudel et al., 2018).

Professional agency and reduced role ambiguity are reinforced by openness of communication as well as the involvement of teachers in decision-making processes (Pretorius & Padmanabhanunni, 2025). This culture can be developed by education leaders through redistributing non-instructional tasks, which will provide a specific area to collaborate and engage with each other on a professional level (Chua et al., 2025; Pollock et al., 2023). This business management tool increases independence and confidence, which are unsustainable in psychological health and workplace (Cann et al., 2023; Uztemur et al., 2026).

Peer-collaboration networks can be formal as well as informal, which are effective coping skills, positively affecting the well-being, self-efficacy, and satisfaction, particularly in dynamic learning environments (Paradies, 2023). Principals may support these networks with the help of distributed leadership and open communication, which will help to develop supportive relations between teachers and administrators (Acton & Glasgow, 2015).

POLICY IMPLICATIONS

Policy implications provide reasons why teacher well-being has to be a primary focus and specific resources are to be assigned that would address cognitive, subjective, physical, mental, and social aspects of occupational health (Duong et al., 2023). Strong support systems that clump instrumental, informational, and emotional resources are essential to enhancing resilience and reducing professional stress (Soncini et al., 2022). This means that the policies should support cooperative and relationally-oriented school conditions, thus increasing the level of teacher innovativeness and job satisfaction due to collaborative activities, exchange of knowledge, and mutual support (Hu et al., 2024).

Sound structures must have proactive measures to deal with stressors and provide ready support systems to reduce the stigma about mental health. Distributed leadership must be promoted, which will enable educators and enhance autonomy, which is closely linked with job satisfaction and collaboration with colleagues (Lin, 2022). The promotion of self-efficacy by providing autonomy in the design of the curriculum and the instructional practices contributes to maintaining motivation and developing innovation further (Mat et al., 2024).

The continuous professional growth and participation in learning communities is essential in the development of a shared purpose and collective efficacy. The policymakers must work towards ensuring that the work environments are conducive to increase well-being and satisfaction (Nwoko et al., 2025). The well-being of educators directly affects the level of instructional performance and student achievement, which makes the psychological support an important driver of educational progress (Emeljanovas et al., 2023). A holistic paradigm should also have to deal with workload, stress management, and work life balance through systemic interventions and it is supported by coordinated efforts by the policymakers and administrators (Nwoko et al., 2025; Labial, 2025; Ntouka et al., 2026).

IMPACT ON STUDENT OUTCOMES

The mental well-being of teachers, which is often mentioned as unimportant, plays a central role in determining the learning experience and academic performance of students, which makes it an important policy priority (Ntumi et al., 2025). High anaesthetics of burnout, emotional exhaustion and stress reduce the effectiveness of the teacher, retention and student achievement (Ntumi et al., 2025). This highlights the urgent need to have policies that address the mental health through its strong correlation with the quality of education and the school environment (Singh & Gautam, 2024).

Psychosocial well-being of teachers promoted by developing positive work conditions, reasonable workload distribution, and full access to mental-health services increases job satisfaction and professional effectiveness (Lima et al., 2024; Mat et al., 2024). The improved teacher well-being, in its turn, can also be attributed to increased student engagement and better academic outcomes (Wang, 2024). The inspired teachers create favorable classroom environments and create strong relational relationships that form the foundation of successful academic and social growth of students (Chamani et al., 2023).

Psychological well-being of teachers also affects the confidence of teachers to meet the needs of students with mental-health and maintain positive relationships with them, thereby enhancing learning outcomes (Savage & Woloshyn, 2022). Systemic support, including counseling and stress-management interventions, contributes to the improvement of the quality of education and student achievement (Beames et al., 2024; Schneider et al., 2024). Based on that, the organizations have to implement extensive policies to reduce the number of workplace risks and promote constructive organizations as they understand that well-being of teachers and students is deeply interdependent (Rahimi Arnold, 2024; Brailovskaia et al., 2024; Chen et al., 2024).

FUTURE DIRECTIONS AND RECOMMENDATIONS

The future studies will focus on the effectiveness of intervention programmes to improve the mental health and well-being of teachers, and, at the same time, measure the effect on the student outcomes (GERELCHIMEG, 2025; Harding et al., 2019). The latter can only be achieved through longitudinal studies that would prove causal relationships among the teacher-well-being programs and academic outcomes as well as psychological well-being among students (Harding et al., 2018; Rahmi, 2024; Wang, 2024). Subjective well-being of teachers should also be better understood because when high levels are achieved they do not always lead to better results (Renteria and Silva, 2025).

The supportive teachers often develop caring and intellectually stimulating environments that promote learning and success among students (Cavioni et al., 2023). Well-being of teachers is linked to higher levels of self-efficacy and job satisfaction which ultimately lead to better teacher-student relationships and psychological growth of students (Li et al., 2025; Wang, 2023). The given relationship highlights the significance of putting the well-being of teachers first in the quality of education (Goktas and Kaya, 2023; Zhou et al., 2024).

The only way to maintain positive results is to employ an interdisciplinary method that involves psychological training, institutional support, and digital well-being strategies (Adade et al., 2024; Tran et al., 2024). Another aspect is the well-being of teachers in terms of the productivity, innovation, and relational processes in educational settings (Hidayati et al., 2025). In future studies, heterogeneous methodological models should be applied over self-reports to include the student views and objective measures to attain an all-embracing comprehension (Dreer, 2023).

CONTINUOUS EVALUATION AND ADAPTATION

Continuous monitoring is essential to the optimisation of learning environments as well as to the sustenance of applicability of support systems in response to the changing needs of instructors and students (Zhang, 2024). Close understanding of teacher well-being, including positive, negative, and professional aspects, will help recognize factors that can be subject to specific interventions (Ozturk et al., 2024). This undertaking requires the conceptualisation of teacher well-being as a multi-dimensional concept that represents not only individual and professional aspects but also interdependence between them and the teaching profession (Ozturk et al., 2024).

Enhancing teacher agency in the management of professional experiences in combination with the integration of positive-psychology concepts like gratitude can improve occupational satisfaction and well-being in general (Xue et al., 2024). Strong well-being structures that are supported by an adequate level of resources and perpetuated feedback systems create prosperous conditions in the teaching and learning processes (Qi et al., 2025). Integration of well-being training into the sphere of professional development, including the training of first-year teachers, provides them with skills that allow achieving pedagogical effectiveness as well as ensuring personal balance (White & McCallum, 2022).

Since the stress experienced by teachers is cyclical during the academic year, the empirical research should investigate the timing of well-being interventions to ensure the greatest effectiveness (Berger et al., 2022). The future studies should thus use the heterogeneous sources of data, such as semi-structured interviews, reflective journals, and structured classroom observations, to achieve an overall outlook (Ao et al., 2023). Furthermore, it is necessary to distinguish between the interventions that should be developed to promote well-being and those aimed at reducing ill-being because every area requires a different methodological approach (Avola et al., 2025).

INNOVATIVE MODELS OF SUPPORT

The heterogeneous nature of the challenges faced by educators requires models that integrate a vast range of interventions, such as, but not limited to, mindfulness-based stress-management courses and school-level programs that lead to the development of supportive cultures (Zhou et al., 2024). Coping capacities of teachers are consolidated through individual-professional-development programmes based on well-being, which are accompanied by mentoring, coaching and learning communities (Lemon and Turner, 2024). This enhances perseverance and positively affects occupational well-being as the promotion of a growth mindset using these programmes enriches it (He et al., 2023). In turn, these initiatives provide the teachers with the resilience strategies and encourage proactive approach to the professional requirements (Liu, 2023).

Systemic changes are also the key to building the supportive education atmosphere that includes resources, resources, proper leadership communication, and the professional development that is situation-specific (Nwoko et al., 2024). The policy alterations should reduce burnout through the regulation of workloads and the establishment of incentives that strengthen psychological capital (Liu and Du, 2024). Specialized programmes that focus on stress management, mindfulness and resilience are invaluable to the reduction of emotional fatigue and distress (Angelini et al., 2024; Chaudhry and Chhajer, 2023; Onan and Aydin, 2024).

Such system and policy-level approaches are of critical significance to maintaining teacher well-being and improving student outcomes (Nwoko et al., 2024). The attitudes of teachers to different types of social support in diverse educational settings can provide information on effective mechanisms to develop supportive climate (Costa, 2023).

CONCLUSION

This synthesis highlights the need for multifaceted interventions addressing both individual and systemic factors influencing teacher well-being, given its central role in educational effectiveness. Interventions should combine psychological support with institutional practices that promote growth mindset and reduce burnout (Cervellione et al., 2025; He et al., 2023). Programs focusing on emotional regulation, mindfulness, and reflective capacity enhance emotional competence and resilience among teachers (Cervellione et al., 2025). These efforts strengthen psychological resources and improve self-regulation, helping educators manage occupational stress (Cervellione et al., 2025; Qiu et al., 2025).

Social support through peer learning and mentoring reduces burnout and professional isolation (Einav et al., 2024). School leadership plays a vital role in creating supportive environments where teachers feel valued, heard, and psychologically safe (Katz & Moè, 2024; O'Toole & Dobutowitsch, 2022; Rahimi & Arnold, 2024). Embedding empathy into administrative practices and recognizing teacher challenges without punitive responses further strengthens engagement (Ntumi et al., 2025).

A holistic strategy that integrates individual interventions, institutional support, and policy reforms is essential for building a resilient and effective teaching workforce. Such an approach enhances teacher well-being and improves educational outcomes (Kusuma & Fathiyah, 2024). Incorporating emotional intelligence training into teacher education equips educators with skills to manage emotions and build positive relationships, supporting both teacher and student development (Wang, 2023).

REFERENCES

Acton, R., & Glasgow, P. (2015). Teacher Wellbeing in Neoliberal Contexts: A Review of the Literature [Review of *Teacher Wellbeing in Neoliberal Contexts: A Review of the Literature*]. *˜The œAustralian Journal of Teacher Education, 40*(40). Edith Cowan University. DOI: 10.14221/ajte.2015v40n8.6

Adade, J. R. D., Antwi-Danso, S., Amos, P. M., Bedu-Addo, P. K. A., & Antwi, T. (2024). Relationships among counselor trainees emotional intelligence, stress and empathy. *Journal of Pedagogical Sociology and Psychology*. DOI: 10.33902/JPSP.202426287

Akhavan, N., Walsh, N., & Goree, J. (2021). Benefits of Mindfulness Professional Development for Elementary Teachers. *Journal of School Administration Research and Development*, *6*(1), 24–42. DOI: 10.32674/jsard.v6i1.2462

Angelini, G., Mamprin, C., Borrelli, I., Santoro, P. E., Gualano, M. R., Moscato, U., & Fiorilli, C. (2024). Engaged teachers and well-being: The mediating role of burnout dimensions. *Health Psychology and Behavioral Medicine*, *12*(1), 2404507. DOI: 10.1080/21642850.2024.2404507

Anog, M. D. I., Vera, J. V. D., & Peteros, E. D. L. (2024). Examining Teacher Retention through the Lens of Job Satisfaction and Commitment in a Philippine Private School. *International Journal of Learning Teaching and Educational Research*, *23*(9), 242–264. DOI: 10.26803/ijlter.23.9.13

Ao, N., Zhang, S., Tian, G., Zhu, X., & Xiao-wei, K. (2023). Exploring teacher wellbeing in educational reforms: A Chinese perspective. *Frontiers in Psychology*, *14*, 1265536. Advance online publication. DOI: 10.3389/fpsyg.2023.1265536

Appiah-Odame, D. E. K., & Frempong, D. G.Appiah-Odame. (2025). The Silent Crisis of Teacher Burnout: Systemic Challenges and Coping Mechanisms. *Educational Point*, *2*(2). Advance online publication. DOI: 10.71176/edup/17638

Attwood, A. I. (2023). Semantic Uses of Emotional Intelligence in K-12 Teacher Roles: Discussing Concepts Across Social Cognitive Context. In *IntechOpen eBooks*. IntechOpen. DOI: 10.5772/intechopen.1002761

Attwood, A. I. (2024). A perspective on psychological factors affecting the emotional labor of teachers. *Frontiers in Education*, *9*, 1291698. Advance online publication. DOI: 10.3389/feduc.2024.1291698

Avola, P., Soini, T., Jyrkiäinen, A., & Pentikäinen, V. (2025). Interventions to Teacher Well-Being and Burnout A Scoping Review [Review of *Interventions to Teacher Well-Being and Burnout A Scoping Review*]. *Educational Psychology Review*, *37*(1). Springer Science+Business Media. DOI: 10.1007/s10648-025-09986-2

Babb, J., Sokal, L., & Trudel, L. E. (2022). THIS IS US: Latent Profile Analysis of Canadian Teachers' Burnout during the COVID-19 Pandemic. *Canadian Journal of Education / Revue Canadienne de l Éducation*, *45*(2), 555. DOI: 10.53967/cje-rce.v45i2.5057

Bao, Y. (2024). A dual mediation model of the association between principal inclusive leadership and teacher innovative behavior. *Scientific Reports*, *14*(1), 12320. Advance online publication. DOI: 10.1038/s41598-024-63332-0

Barnes, S. P., & Lang, J. E. (2023). Supporting School Staff: Insights From Employee Health and Well-Being Programs [Review of *Supporting School Staff: Insights From Employee Health and Well-Being Programs*]. *Journal of School Health*, *93*(9), 842. Wiley. DOI: 10.1111/josh.13377

Bayram, P. E., & Eveyik-Aydın, E. (2023). THE RELATIONSHIP BETWEEN THE EMOTIONAL LABOR AND BURNOUT LEVELS OF EFL TEACHERS AT UNIVERSITY PREPARATORY SCHOOLS. *TEFLIN Journal - A Publication on the Teaching and Learning of English*, *34*(2), 226. DOI: 10.15639/teflinjournal.v34i2/226-244

Beames, J. R., Roberts, A., Deady, M., O'Dea, B., & Werner-Seidler, A. (2024). 'Very little is done other than the odd reminder'...'look after yourself': A mixed-methods evaluation of what Australian teachers need and want from a wellbeing program. *Australian Educational Researcher*, *51*(5), 2117–2139. Advance online publication. DOI: 10.1007/s13384-023-00684-y

Berger, E., Reupert, A., Campbell, T. C. H., Morris, Z., Hammer, M., Diamond, Z. M., Hine, R., Patrick, P., & Fathers, C. (2022). A Systematic Review of Evidence-Based Wellbeing Initiatives for Schoolteachers and Early Childhood Educators [Review of *A Systematic Review of Evidence-Based Wellbeing Initiatives for Schoolteachers and Early Childhood Educators*]. *Educational Psychology Review, 34*(4), 2919. Springer Science+Business Media. DOI: 10.1007/s10648-022-09690-5

Bordás, A. (2023). Investigation of Resilience among Teachers and in Teacher Education. *Central European Journal of Educational Research*, *5*(1), 24–36. DOI: 10.37441/cejer/2023/5/1/11119

Brailovskaia, J., Duscha, A.-L., Kreyelkamp, G. M., & Margraf, J. (2024). Teachers' competence: How to protect teachers' mental health from the burden caused by students' private in-class use of technical devices? *PLoS One*, *19*(6), e0305114. Advance online publication. DOI: 10.1371/journal.pone.0305114

Braun, S. S., Bradshaw, C. P., Beahm, L. A., Curhan, A., Downer, J. T., Ialongo, N. S., & Tolan, P. H. (2023). Predicting implementation of the PAX Good Behavior Game + MyTeachingPartner interventions. *Frontiers in Psychology*, *14*, 1059138. Advance online publication. DOI: 10.3389/fpsyg.2023.1059138

Brewer, M. L., Lane, M., Carter, A., Barnard, S., & Ibrahim, O. (2019). Evaluation of a leadership development program to enhance university staff and student resilience. *Journal of Teaching and Learning for Graduate Employability*, *10*(2), 136–151. DOI: 10.21153/jtlge2019vol10no2art882

Brunzell, T., Waters, L., & Stokes, H. (2021). Trauma-informed Teacher Wellbeing: Teacher Reflections within Trauma-informed Positive Education. *The Australian Journal of Teacher Education*, *46*(5), 91–107. DOI: 10.14221/ajte.2021v46n5.6

Bryan, C., & von Suchodoletz, A. (2023). *Teachers' Resilience and Burnout in the United Arab Emirates: Teaching Through the COVID- 19 Pandemic. Gulf Education and Social Policy Review*. GESPR., DOI: 10.18502/gespr.v4i1.13805

Cann, R., Sinnema, C., Daly, A. J., & Rodway, J. (2024). Swimming against the Tide: A Mixed-Methods Study of how the MARKERS Educator Wellbeing Program Changed Educators' Relational Space. *International Journal of Applied Positive Psychology*, *9*(2), 799–826. DOI: 10.1007/s41042-024-00153-6

Cann, R., Sinnema, C., Rodway, J., & Daly, A. J. (2023). What do we know about interventions to improve educator wellbeing? A systematic literature review. *Journal of Educational Change*, *25*(2), 231–270. DOI: 10.1007/s10833-023-09490-w

Cavioni, V., Toto, G. A., & Ornaghi, V. (2023). Portraits of pre-service special education teachers: Perspectives on well-being and its association with self-efficacy and work engagement. *The International Journal of Emotional Education*, *15*(2), 21–36. DOI: 10.56300/VHRV8364

Cece, V., Martinent, G., Guillet-Descas, E., & Lentillon-Kaestner, V. (2022). The Predictive Role of Perceived Support from Principals and Professional Identity on Teachers' Motivation and Well-Being: A Longitudinal Study. *International Journal of Environmental Research and Public Health*, *19*(11), 6674. DOI: 10.3390/ijerph19116674

Cervellione, B., Lombardo, E. M. C., & Iacolino, C. (2025). Psychological resources and interventions for teachers' emotional competence and well-being: A systematic review. *Frontiers in Psychology*, *16*, 1640968. DOI: 10.3389/fpsyg.2025.1640968

Çevik, M. N. (2025). The relationship of distributed leadership with teachers' subjective well-being and professional satisfaction in Türkiye: Does psychological resilience make a difference? *BMC Psychology*, *13*(1), 1227. DOI: 10.1186/s40359-025-03555-6

Chamani, S., Safaeizadeh, F., & Xodabande, I. (2023). Investigating the relationship between language teachers' occupational self-efficacy, satisfaction and meaning at work, and their subjective wellbeing. *Frontiers in Psychology*, *14*, 1219130. Advance online publication. DOI: 10.3389/fpsyg.2023.1219130

Chaudhry, S., & Chhajer, R. (2023). Enhancing psychological well-being of school teachers in India: Role of energy management, thriving, and stress. *Frontiers in Psychology*, *14*, 1239587. Advance online publication. DOI: 10.3389/fpsyg.2023.1239587

Chen, J. (2024). Reimaging Teacher Resilience for Flourishing. *The Asia-Pacific Education Researcher*, *33*(6), 1363–1372. DOI: 10.1007/s40299-023-00810-5

Chen, X. hui, Bailey, R., Xie, H., & Samsudin, N. (2024). The Relationship between Teacher-Students Relationships and Academic Grades Among High School Student: The Role of Perceived Teaching Quality and Student's Mental Health Symptoms. Research Square (Research Square). DOI: 10.21203/rs.3.rs-4871554/v1

Christopoulou, S., Antonopoulou, H., Zapantis, R., Gkintoni, E., & Halkiopoulos, C. (2026). Teacher Well-Being and Burnout Resilience: Dimensional Independence, Pandemic Burden, and Profile Analysis in Primary Education. *International Journal of Environmental Research and Public Health*, *23*(2), 190. DOI: 10.3390/ijerph23020190

Chua, C. S. K., Soo, L. M. J., & Chng, H. S. E. (2025). Quality Education in Singapore: Bridging Teacher Leadership with Teacher Wellbeing. *International Journal of Education Policy and Leadership*, *21*(3). Advance online publication. DOI: 10.22230/ijepl.2025v21n3a1543

Collins, C. (2022). "There is Something to be Said for Actually Being There:" Experiences of Elementary General Music Teachers in High-Poverty Schools. *Deep Blue (University of Michigan)*. DOI: 10.7302/6846

Costa, C. (2023). Teacher Well-Being: Investigating Barriers and Facilitators Using the Job Demands-Resources Framework. *Deep Blue (University of Michigan)*. DOI: 10.7302/7344

Costa, C., Park, N., & Kira, M. (2021). #ArmMeWith: Resources for Teacher Wellbeing. *International Journal of Wellbeing*, *11*(2), 20–37. DOI: 10.5502/ijw.v11i2.1365

Dabrowski, A., Hsien, M., Zant, T. V. D., & Ahmed, S. K. (2025). "We are left to fend for ourselves": Understanding why teachers struggle to support students' mental health. *Frontiers in Education*, *9*, 1505077. Advance online publication. DOI: 10.3389/feduc.2024.1505077

Danku, B. E. M. (2022). EVALUATING ORGANISATIONAL FACTORS AND TUTOR BURNOUT IN AKATSI COLLEGE OF EDUCATION, GHANA. *International Journal of Applied Research in Social Sciences*, *4*(5), 190–202. DOI: 10.51594/ijarss.v4i5.357

Darron, L. S., Hurt, C. S., & Hiraetta, W. (2023). Principal characteristics effect on teacher retention: A systematic review [Review of *Principal characteristics effect on teacher retention: A systematic review*]. *Educational Research and Reviews, 18*(6), 104. Academic Journals. DOI: 10.5897/ERR2023.4318

Davis, T., & Park, E. (2025). A Systematic Review of Early-Career Teacher Wellbeing, Stress, Burnout and Support Mechanisms During and Post COVID-19 Pandemic. *Education Sciences*, *15*(8), 996. DOI: 10.3390/educsci15080996

Day, C., Stobart, G., Sammons, P., Kington, A., Gu, Q., Smees, R., & Mujtaba, T. (2006). Variations in Teachers' Work, Lives and Effectiveness [Data set]. In *PsycEXTRA Dataset*. DOI: 10.1037/e615332007-001 de Lima, D. F., Sampaio, A. A., & de Souza, D. C. (2024). Taxas de mortalidade por suicídio entre professores brasileiros: Ano base 2020. *Olhar de Professor*, *27*, 1–22. DOI: 10.5212/OlharProfr.v.27.23249.053

Debbarma, D., & Momin, P. N. S. (2024). Factors Influencing the Performance of Elementary School Teachers: a Systematic Review [Review of *Factors Influencing the Performance of Elementary School Teachers: a Systematic Review*]. Research Square (Research Square). Research Square (United States). DOI: 10.21203/rs.3.rs-4450710/v1

Denti, L., Sturén, E., & Johansson, L. (2024). Scarcity mindset among schoolteachers: How resource scarcity negatively impacts teachers' cognition and behaviors. *Frontiers in Psychology*, *14*, 1333735. Advance online publication. DOI: 10.3389/fpsyg.2023.1333735

Doménech-Betoret, F. (2018). The Educational Situation Quality Model: Recent Advances [Review of *The Educational Situation Quality Model: Recent Advances*]. *Frontiers in Psychology, 9*. Frontiers Media. DOI: 10.3389/fpsyg.2018.00328

Dreer, B. (2023). On the outcomes of teacher wellbeing: a systematic review of research [Review of *On the outcomes of teacher wellbeing: a systematic review of research*]. *Frontiers in Psychology, 14*. Frontiers Media. DOI: 10.3389/fpsyg.2023.1205179

Duong, A. C., Nguyen, H. N., Tran, A. T. N., & Trinh, T. M. (2023). An investigation into teachers' occupational well-being and education leadership during the COVID-19 pandemic. *Frontiers in Education*, *8*, 1112577. Advance online publication. DOI: 10.3389/feduc.2023.1112577

Einav, M., Confino, D., Geva, N., & Margalit, M. (2024). Teachers' Burnout – The Role of Social Support, Gratitude, Hope, Entitlement and Loneliness. *International Journal of Applied Positive Psychology*, *9*(2), 827–849. DOI: 10.1007/s41042-024-00154-5

Elliott, A. C., Reddy, L. A., Lekwa, A., & Fingerhut, J. (2023). Teacher stress and supports, classroom practices and student outcomes in high poverty urban elementary schools. *Psychology in the Schools*, *61*(1), 29–42. DOI: 10.1002/pits.23023

Emeljanovas, A., Sabaliauskas, S., Mežienė, B., & Istomina, N. (2023). The relationships between teachers' emotional health and stress coping. *Frontiers in Psychology*, *14*, 1276431. Advance online publication. DOI: 10.3389/fpsyg.2023.1276431

Ertürk, R.ERTÜRK. (2021). Analysis of the Relationship between School Administrators' Supportive Behaviors and Teachers' Job Satisfaction and Subjective Well-Being. *International Journal of Contemporary Educational Research*, *8*(4), 184–195. DOI: 10.33200/ijcer.956667

Eryılmaz, N., Kennedy, A., Strietholt, R., & Johansson, S. (2025). Teacher job satisfaction: International evidence on the role of school working conditions and teacher characteristics. *Studies in Educational Evaluation*, *86*, 101474. DOI: 10.1016/j.stueduc.2025.101474

Ferguson, K., Mang, C. F., & Frost, L. (2017). Teacher Stress and Social Support Usage. *Brock Education Journal*, *26*(2). Advance online publication. DOI: 10.26522/brocked.v26i2.606

Floman, J. L., Ponnock, A. R., Jain, J. P., & Brackett, M. A. (2024). Emotionally intelligent school leadership predicts educator well-being before and during a crisis. *Frontiers in Psychology*, *14*, 1159382. DOI: 10.3389/fpsyg.2023.1159382

Gámez-Genovart, M., Trobat, M. F. O., & Ramón, M. R. R. (2025). Research on teacher well-being: A systematic review. *Teaching and Teacher Education*, *168*, 105264. DOI: 10.1016/j.tate.2025.105264

GERELCHIMEG. B. (2025). The Impact of Teacher Well-Being, Joy, and Effectiveness On Student Outcomes and Sustainable Education. *ResearchWorks at the University of Washington (University of Washington).* https://hdl.handle.net/1773/54581

Godfrey, D., & Chereau, B. M. (2024). School improvement and peer learning partnerships: Building organizational resilience in primary schools in England. *Frontiers in Education*, *8*, 1339173. Advance online publication. DOI: 10.3389/feduc.2023.1339173

Göktaş, E., & Kaya, M. (2023). The Effects of Teacher Relationships on Student Academic Achievement: A Second Order Meta-Analysis. *Participatory Educational Research*, *10*(1), 275–289. DOI: 10.17275/per.23.15.10.1

Gu, Q. (2014). The role of relational resilience in teachers' career-long commitment and effectiveness. *Teachers and Teaching*, *20*(5), 502–529. DOI: 10.1080/13540602.2014.937961

Gülbahar, B.GÜLBAHAR. (2020). Investigation of The Relationship Between Perception of Supervisor Support, Perceived School Effectiveness, Work Engagement, Job Satisfaction and Organizational Cynic Attitude of Teachers. *Participatory Educational Research*, *7*(3), 1–20. DOI: 10.17275/per.20.32.7.3

Harding, S., Morris, R., Gunnell, D., Ford, T., Hollingworth, W., Tilling, K., Evans, R., Bell, S., Powell, J., Brockman, R., Campbell, R., Araya, R., Murphy, S., & Kidger, J. (2018). Is teachers' mental health and wellbeing associated with students' mental health and wellbeing? *Journal of Affective Disorders*, *242*, 180–187. DOI: 10.1016/j.jad.2018.08.080

Harding, S., Morris, R., Gunnell, D., Ford, T., Hollingworth, W., Tilling, K., Evans, R., Bell, S., Powell, J., Brockman, R., Campbell, R., Araya, R., Murphy, S., & Kidger, J. (2019). Is teachers' mental health and wellbeing associated with students' mental health and wellbeing? *Journal of Affective Disorders*, *253*, 460–466. DOI: 10.1016/j.jad.2019.03.046

Harris, W. Jennifer. (2021). Administrative Support: What Teachers Say They Need. *Scholar Commons (University of South Carolina)*. https://scholarcommons.sc.edu/etd/6854

Harvey-Flowers, M. E. (2022). Secondary Educators' Socioemotional Well-Being Throughout the COVID-19 Pandemic: A Narrative Inquiry. *Deep Blue (University of Michigan)*. DOI: 10.7302/6738

He, J., Iskhar, S., Yan, Y., & Aisuluu, M. (2023). Exploring the relationship between teacher growth mindset, grit, mindfulness, and EFL teachers' well-being. *Frontiers in Psychology*, *14*, 1241335. Advance online publication. DOI: 10.3389/fpsyg.2023.1241335

Hidayati, D., Imama, M. L., Hilhamsyah, H., Maysaroh, A., & Kartiwi, A. P. (2025). Digital Life Among Teachers: From Burnout to Well-Being. *Educational Process International Journal*, *15*(1). Advance online publication. DOI: 10.22521/edupij.2025.15.93

Hu, B., Park, K., & Xu, Z. (2024). The Mediating Effect of Teachers' Collective Innovativeness Between School Climate and Job Satisfaction. *European Journal of Educational Research*, *1573*(volume-13-issue-4-october-2024), 1573–1585. Advance online publication. DOI: 10.12973/eu-jer.13.4.1573

International Journal of Public Health Science (IJPHS). (2025). *International Journal of Public Health Science*. IJPHS., DOI: 10.11591/ijphs

Kariou, A., Koutsimani, P., Montgomery, A., & Lainidi, O. (2021). Emotional Labor and Burnout among Teachers: A Systematic Review. *International Journal of Environmental Research and Public Health*, *18*(23), 12760. DOI: 10.3390/ijerph182312760

Katz, I., & Moè, A. (2024). Exploring teachers' psychological needs, motivating styles, emotion regulation and self-compassion: A comparative study before and during the COVID-19 lockdown. *Teaching and Teacher Education*, *148*, 104706. DOI: 10.1016/j.tate.2024.104706

Kell, S. (2024). University Students' Perceptions of a 30-Minute Break During Class: A Realistic Practice for Wellness? *Teaching & Learning Inquiry*, *12*, 1–30. DOI: 10.20343/teachlearninqu.12.17

Kurnia, N., Permana, J., Kurniady, D. A., & Novebri, N. (2025). The Power of Leadership: A Systematic Review on Enhancing Teacher Self-Efficacy to Overcome Burnout. In *Advances in Social Science, Education and Humanities Research/Advances in social science, education and humanities research* (p. 1019). DOI: 10.2991/978-2-38476-489-1_82

Kush, J. M., Badillo-Goicoechea, E., Musci, R. J., & Stuart, E. A. (2022). Teacher Mental Health During the COVID-19 Pandemic: Informing Policies to Support Teacher Well-being and Effective Teaching Practices. *arXiv (Cornell University)*. https://doi.org//arxiv.2109.01547DOI: 10.48550

Kusuma, R. Y., & Fathiyah, K. N. (2024). Self-Efficacy and Social Support: Two Predictors of Teachers Resilience in Inclusive Elementary School. *Journal An-Nafs Kajian Penelitian Psikologi*, *9*(1), 150. DOI: 10.33367/psi.v9i1.5448

Labial, R. J. D. (2025). Breaking the Silence: A Phenomenological Study on the Mental Health Concerns on Teachers in the Modern Educational Landscape. *International Journal of Research Publication and Reviews*, *6*(7), 2261–2291. DOI: 10.55248/gengpi.6.0725.2588

Laguisma, G. (2026). *Administrative support as a predictor of job satisfaction and performance among senior high school teachers*. DOI: 10.21203/rs.3.rs-8497299/v1

Laundon, M., & Grant-Smith, D. (2023). Defining and Advancing a Systems Approach to Achieving Educator Wellbeing: An Integrative Review of Wellbeing in Higher Education. *Student Success*, *14*(3), 104–119. DOI: 10.5204/ssj.3191

Lavy, S. (2019). Daily Dynamics of Teachers' Organizational Citizenship Behavior: Social and Emotional Antecedents and Outcomes. *Frontiers in Psychology*, *10*, 2863. Advance online publication. DOI: 10.3389/fpsyg.2019.02863

Lemon, N., & Turner, K. (2024). Unravelling the wellbeing needs of Australian teachers: A qualitative inquiry. *Australian Educational Researcher*, *51*(5), 2161–2181. Advance online publication. DOI: 10.1007/s13384-023-00687-9

Li, K., Xu, X., Zhang, Y., & Xin-yu, X. (2024). The influence of environmental factors on the job burnout of physical education teachers in tertiary education. *Scientific Reports*, *14*(1), 9126. Advance online publication. DOI: 10.1038/s41598-024-59748-3

Li, L., Kanchanapoom, K., Deeprasert, J., Duan, N., & Zhou, Q. (2025). Unveiling the factors shaping teacher job performance: Exploring the interplay of personality traits, perceived organizational support, self-efficacy, and job satisfaction. *BMC Psychology*, *13*(1), 14. DOI: 10.1186/s40359-024-02324-1

Li, Y., Chen, J., Lu, J., & Xiang, W. (2025). A meta-analysis of teacher well-being: A job demands and resources perspective. *Educational Research Review*, *49*, 100719. DOI: 10.1016/j.edurev.2025.100719

Li, Y., Nie, Y., Ma, Z., Liu, C., Cao, Y., Qu, G., Hou, L., Du, K., Guo, M., Wang, T., & Zhu, X. (2025). A network analysis of the relationship between perceived social support, emotion regulation, and job burnout among elementary and middle school teachers. *Frontiers in Psychology*, *16*, 1704862. Advance online publication. DOI: 10.3389/fpsyg.2025.1704862

Lin, Q. (2022). The relationship between distributed leadership and teacher innovativeness: Mediating roles of teacher autonomy and professional collaboration. *Frontiers in Psychology*, *13*, 948152. DOI: 10.3389/fpsyg.2022.948152

Liu, D., & Du, R. (2024). Psychological capital, mindfulness, and teacher burnout: Insights from Chinese EFL educators through structural equation modeling. *Frontiers in Psychology*, *15*, 1351912. Advance online publication. DOI: 10.3389/fpsyg.2024.1351912

Liu, Z. (2023). Transforming teaching: Wellbeing and professional practice. *Frontiers in Psychology*, *14*, 1192148. Advance online publication. DOI: 10.3389/fpsyg.2023.1192148

Mat, C. M. P. C., Johari, K. S. K., & Mahmud, M. I. (2024). Testing the Healthy School Organisation Instrument (i-OS) and the Holistic Psychological Well-Being Model of School Organisations. *International Journal of Learning Teaching and Educational Research*, *23*(2), 113–144. DOI: 10.26803/ijlter.23.2.6

Mieres-Chacaltana, M., Salvo-Garrido, S., & Domínguez-Lara, S. (2025). Resilience and prosociality: Pathways to strengthen teachers' self-efficacy in the classroom. *Frontiers in Psychology*, *16*, 1660879. Advance online publication. DOI: 10.3389/fpsyg.2025.1660879

Mirzapour, F. (2023). Tapping into Teachers' Voices and Technology with the Lens of Wellbeing. *Research Square (Research Square)*. DOI: 10.21203/rs.3.rs-3500049/v1

Nath, R., & Pandey, C. (2025). The Hidden Burden: Emotional Labor and Well-being of School Teachers. *Asian Journal of Education and Social Studies*, *51*(2), 500–510. DOI: 10.9734/ajess/2025/v51i21802

Ntouka, E., Antonopoulou, H., Rekka, E. A., Gkintoni, E., & Halkiopoulos, C. (2026). Employment Precarity as an Organizational Determinant of Teacher Burnout and Mental Health: Validation of the Maslach Burnout Inventory-Educators Survey Among Greek Primary Education Teachers. *Societies (Basel, Switzerland)*, *16*(2), 52. DOI: 10.3390/soc16020052

Ntumi, S., Amos, P. M., Antwi, T., Nimo, D. G., Ofori, D. M., & Sarfo, P. O. (2025). Linking Burnout Emotional Exhaustion and Assessment Related Stress to Mental Health Outcomes Among Early Career Teachers: Counselling Support as a Dual Mediating and Moderating Factor. *Research Square (Research Square)*. DOI: 10.21203/rs.3.rs-7003152/v1

Nwoko, J. C., Adegboye, O. A., Malau-Aduli, A. E. O., Anderson, E., & Malau-Aduli, B. S. (2025). The influence of school environment and demographics on teacher wellbeing. *Scientific Reports*, *15*(1), 34970. DOI: 10.1038/s41598-025-18970-3

Nwoko, J. C., Anderson, E., Adegboye, O. A., Malau-Aduli, A. E. O., & Malau-Aduli, B. S. (2024). Navigating Teachers' Occupational Well-Being in the Tides of Classroom Processes and School Structures. *Education Sciences*, *14*(11), 1225. DOI: 10.3390/educsci14111225

Nwoko, J. C., Anderson, E., Adegboye, O. A., Malau-Aduli, A. E. O., & Malau-Aduli, B. S. (2025). From passion to pressure: Exploring the realities of the teaching profession. *Frontiers in Public Health*, *13*, 1505330. DOI: 10.3389/fpubh.2025.1505330

O'Toole, C., & Dobutowitsch, M. (2022). The Courage to Care: Teacher Compassion Predicts More Positive Attitudes Toward Trauma-Informed Practice. *Journal of Child & Adolescent Trauma*, *16*(1), 123–133. DOI: 10.1007/s40653-022-00486-x

Olsen, A. A., & Huang, F. L. (2019). Teacher job satisfaction by principal support and teacher cooperation: Results from the Schools and Staffing Survey. *Education Policy Analysis Archives*, *27*, 11. DOI: 10.14507/epaa.27.4174

Onan, A. M., & Aydın, S. (2024). Well-Being, Burnout, and Teaching Anxiety among EFL Teachers. *Journal of Language Research*, *8*(1), 17–35. DOI: 10.51726/jlr.1376451

Ouellette, R. R., Frazier, S. L., Shernoff, E. S., Cappella, E., Mehta, T., Maríñez-Lora, A. M., Cua, G., & Atkins, M. S. (2017). Teacher Job Stress and Satisfaction in Urban Schools: Disentangling Individual-, Classroom-, and Organizational-Level Influences. *Behavior Therapy*, *49*(4), 494–508. DOI: 10.1016/j.beth.2017.11.011

Özen, H., & Yavuz, P. (2024). A Theoretical Analysis for Resilience: Developing a Complex Adaptive Leadership Model in Schools. *DergiPark (Istanbul University)*. https://dergipark.org.tr/tr/pub/ajeli/issue/85313/1494652

Ozturk, M., Wigelsworth, M., & Squires, G. (2024). A systematic review of primary school teachers' wellbeing: room for a holistic approach [Review of *A systematic review of primary school teachers' wellbeing: room for a holistic approach*]. *Frontiers in Psychology, 15*. Frontiers Media. DOI: 10.3389/fpsyg.2024.1358424

Paradies, M. (2023). "I do not want to stop teaching": The impact of conflict and displacement on teachers in southern Mosul. *Prospects*. Advance online publication. DOI: 10.1007/s11125-023-09666-5

Podolsky, A., Kini, T., Darling-Hammond, L., & Bishop, J. (2019). Strategies for attracting and retaining educators: What does the evidence say? *Education Policy Analysis Archives*, *27*, 38. DOI: 10.14507/epaa.27.3722

Pollock, K., Nielsen, R., & Singh, S. (2023). School Principals' Work Intensification and Resilience: A Call for Structural Change. *Canadian Journal of Educational Administration and Policy*, *203*(203), 2–12. DOI: 10.7202/1108429ar

Pretorius, T. B., & Padmanabhanunni, A. (2025). Teaching identification as a protective and risk factor for teacher burnout in the context of role stress. *Discover Psychology*, *5*(1), 133. Advance online publication. DOI: 10.1007/s44202-025-00467-9

Puspitadani, E., Yudea, F., & Loo, F. (2022). Educational Leadership and Learning Quality: The Influence of the Princi-pal's Leadership Style on Teacher Performance. *Jurnal Ilmu Pendidikan Dan Humaniora*, *11*(3), 206–220. DOI: 10.35335/jiph.v11i3.24

Qi, W., Zhang, Y., & Arshad, M. Z. (2025). Sustainable education in action: Principal leadership, teacher wellbeing, and altruism in the sports context. *Acta Psychologica*, *254*, 104846. DOI: 10.1016/j.actpsy.2025.104846

Qiu, S., Qiu, J., Xu, J., & Wang, L. (2025). Effective emotion regulation and positive psychological capital as coping strategies to alleviate teacher burnout: a narrative review [Review of *Effective emotion regulation and positive psychological capital as coping strategies to alleviate teacher burnout: a narrative review*]. *Frontiers in Psychology, 16*. Frontiers Media. DOI: 10.3389/fpsyg.2025.1639037

Ragmac, C., & Labitad, G. (2025). Work-life Imbalance and Well-being among Public Secondary School Teachers. *International Journal on Science and Technology*, *16*(3), 8076. Advance online publication. DOI: 10.71097/IJSAT.v16.i3.8076

Rahimi, M., & Arnold, B. (2024). Understanding Australia's teacher shortage: The importance of psychosocial working conditions to turnover intentions. *Australian Educational Researcher*. Advance online publication. DOI: 10.1007/s13384-024-00720-5

Rahmi, K. H. (2024). Teachers' mental health and well-being in education: What can be improved for the education system in Indonesia? *Multidisciplinary Reviews*, *7*(12), 2024301. DOI: 10.31893/multirev.2024301

Räsänen, K., Pietarinen, J., Pyhältö, K., Soini, T., & Väisänen, P. (2020). Why leave the teaching profession? A longitudinal approach to the prevalence and persistence of teacher turnover intentions. *Social Psychology of Education*, *23*(4), 837–859. DOI: 10.1007/s11218-020-09567-x

Rentería, J. M., & Silva, D. S. (2025). The parabolic path of teacher well-being and student learning achievement in Peru. *Humanities & Social Sciences Communications*, *12*(1), 1391. Advance online publication. DOI: 10.1057/s41599-025-05736-5

Roberts, T., & Singleton, E. (2024). The Impact of Educational Leadership Standards on the Teacher Shortage Crisis: A Call for Change. *Open Journal of Leadership*, *13*(1), 1–5. DOI: 10.4236/ojl.2024.131001

Ross, P. M., Scanes, E., & Locke, W. (2023). Stress adaptation and resilience of academics in higher education. *Asia Pacific Education Review*. Advance online publication. DOI: 10.1007/s12564-023-09829-1

Sarmurzin, Y. (2024). Enhancing Teacher Status in Kazakhstan: The Role of School Leaders and Legislative Measures. *Research Square (Research Square)*. DOI: 10.21203/rs.3.rs-4195846/v1

Savage, M. P., & Woloshyn, V. (2022). Coping is crucial : Exploring relations between K-12 educators and staff coping strategies, perceived stress and psychological wellbeing. *The International Journal of Emotional Education*, *14*(2), 3–18. DOI: 10.56300/QBVZ8040

Schneider, A., Stegall, M. S., Sirotiak, Z., Herrmann, F., & Thomas, E. B. K. (2024). Just as Essential: The Mental Health of Educators During the COVID-19 Pandemic. *Disaster Medicine and Public Health Preparedness*, *18*, e6. Advance online publication. DOI: 10.1017/dmp.2023.231

Sebullen, M. T., & Jimenez, O. B. (2024). Examining the Impact of Administrative Support on Transformational Leadership and Teacher Job Satisfaction. *International Journal of Innovation and Scientific Research*, *840*(X), 840–863. Advance online publication. DOI: 10.51244/IJRSI.2024.1110066

Setiawan, D., Sitorus, J., & Natsir, M. (2018). Inhibiting Factor of Primary School Teacher Competence in Indonesia: Pedagogic and Professionalism. *Asian Social Science*, *14*(6), 30. DOI: 10.5539/ass.v14n6p30

Shuaili, A. S. T. A. (2025). Occupational Stress and Job Satisfaction: Unveiling Challenges in Teachers' and Doctors' Work Environments. *World Journal of Education*, *15*(1), 37. DOI: 10.5430/wje.v15n1p37

Shuls, J. V., & Flores, J. (2020). *Improving Teacher Retention through Support and Development. 4*(1). https://files.eric.ed.gov/fulltext/EJ1282763.pdf

Singh, Y. K., & Gautam, D. N. S. (2024). The Impact of Job Satisfaction on Teacher Mental Health: A Call to Action for Educational Policymakers. *Open Education Studies*, *6*(1), 20240008. Advance online publication. DOI: 10.1515/edu-2024-0008

Soncini, A., Floris, F., & Matteucci, M. C. (2022). Feeling supported and engaged during COVID-19: The role of family and colleagues in promoting teachers' well-being. *Teachers and Teaching*, *29*(1), 37–51. DOI: 10.1080/13540602.2022.2144820

The Ecology of School Readiness. (2017). *Routledge eBooks*. Informa., DOI: 10.4324/9781315562544-3

Toprak, E., Durmuşçelebi, M., & ORMAN, P. (2022). Öğretmenlerin Mesleki Tükenmişlik Düzeylerini Azaltmada Öncelenmesi Gereken Mesleki Sosyal Destek Faktörleri. *Pamukkale University Journal of Education*. DOI: 10.9779/pauefd.1142792

Tr n, T. T., Luong, D., & Nguyen, T. T. D. (2024). A Bibliometrics Analysis of Scopus-Indexed Research on Teachers' Well-Being from 1995-2022: Emerging Research Trends. *European Journal of Educational Research*, *457*(volume-13-issue-2-april-2024), 457–478. Advance online publication. DOI: 10.12973/eu-jer.13.2.457

Trudel, L. E., Sokal, L., & Babb, J. (2018). *Interdisciplinary Education and Psychology*. Interdisciplinary Education and Psychology., DOI: 10.31532/interdiscipeducpsychol

Trudel, L. G. E., Sokal, L., & Babb, J. (2021). Planning for Teacher Recovery from the COVID-19 Pandemic: Adaptive Regulation to Promote Resilience. *Interdisciplinary Education and Psychology*, *3*(1). Advance online publication. DOI: 10.31532/InterdiscipEducPsychol.3.1.001

Üztemur, S., Gökalp, A., İlğan, A., & Dinç, E. (2026). Leadership, autonomy, and organizational trust as predictors of teacher wellbeing and job satisfaction: A cross-cultural study based on PISA 2022 data. *Frontiers in Psychology*, *16*, 1703458. DOI: 10.3389/fpsyg.2025.1703458

Vaidya, S. R., & Hanna, C. (2023). The Four-Capital Theory as Framework for Teacher Retention and Attrition. *International Education Studies*, *16*(6), 21. DOI: 10.5539/ies.v16n6p21

Vermooten, N., Malan, J., & Boonzaier, B. (2020). Variance in employee engagement: A qualitative analysis amongst public school teachers in the Cape Winelands education district. *SA Journal of Industrial Psychology*, *46*. Advance online publication. DOI: 10.4102/sajip.v46i0.1568

Walter, H. L., & Fox, H. B. (2021). Understanding Teacher Well-Being During the Covid-19 Pandemic Over Time: A Qualitative Longitudinal Study. *Journal of Organizational Psychology*, *21*(5). Advance online publication. DOI: 10.33423/jop.v21i5.4716

Wang, H., Burić, I., Chang, M., & Gross, J. J. (2023). Teachers' emotion regulation and related environmental, personal, instructional, and well-being factors: A meta-analysis. *Social Psychology of Education*, *26*(6), 1651–1696. DOI: 10.1007/s11218-023-09810-1

Wang, K., Huang, T., Lin, X., & Tan, R. (2025). Time poverty and teacher subjective well-being in an accelerated society: A three-wave longitudinal analysis of emotional exhaustion, psychological resilience, and gender. *Frontiers in Psychology*, *16*, 1728219. Advance online publication. DOI: 10.3389/fpsyg.2025.1728219

Wang, T. (2023). Teachers as the agent of change for student mental health: The role of teacher care and teacher support in Chinese students' well-being. *Frontiers in Psychology*, *14*, 1283515. Advance online publication. DOI: 10.3389/fpsyg.2023.1283515

Wang, X. (2023). Exploring positive teacher-student relationships: The synergy of teacher mindfulness and emotional intelligence. *Frontiers in Psychology*, *14*, 1301786. Advance online publication. DOI: 10.3389/fpsyg.2023.1301786

Wang, Y. (2024). Exploring the impact of workload, organizational support, and work engagement on teachers' psychological wellbeing: A structural equation modeling approach. *Frontiers in Psychology*, *14*, 1345740. Advance online publication. DOI: 10.3389/fpsyg.2023.1345740

Werang, B. R., Rati, N. W., Leba, S. M. R., Asaloei, S. I., & Imbang, D. (2024). On Emotional Exhaustion, Job Satisfaction, and Job Performance of Indonesian Elementary School Teachers. *International Journal of Religion*, *5*(5), 248–261. DOI: 10.61707/2syk5m87

White, M. A., & McCallum, F. (2022). *Transforming Teaching: Wellbeing and Professional Practice*. DOI: 10.1007/978-981-19-4945-6

Wong, V., Ruble, L. A., Yu, Y., & McGrew, J. H. (2017). Too Stressed to Teach? Teaching Quality, Student Engagement, and IEP Outcomes. *Exceptional Children*, *83*(4), 412–427. DOI: 10.1177/0014402917690729

Xue, Z., Huang, H., & Yu, Q. (2024). The associations among gratitude, job crafting, teacher-student relationships, and teacher psychological well-being. *Frontiers in Psychology*, *15*, 1329782. Advance online publication. DOI: 10.3389/fpsyg.2024.1329782

Yan, J., & Dai, X. (2025). Double marginalization: An ethnographic-ecological analysis of rural PE teachers' professional development between urban and underdeveloped areas. *Frontiers in Public Health*, *13*, 1645977. Advance online publication. DOI: 10.3389/fpubh.2025.1645977

Zhang, H. (2024). Psychological wellbeing in Chinese university students: Insights into the influences of academic self-concept, teacher support, and student engagement. *Frontiers in Psychology*, *14*, 1336682. Advance online publication. DOI: 10.3389/fpsyg.2023.1336682

Zhang, J. (2023). Exploring the Impact of Transformational School Leadership on Teacher Job Satisfaction. *International Journal of Education and Humanities*, *8*(1), 39–42. DOI: 10.54097/ijeh.v8i1.6875

Zhou, S., Slemp, G. R., & Vella-Brodrick, D. (2024). Factors Associated with Teacher Wellbeing: A Meta-Analysis. *Educational Psychology Review*, *36*(2), 63. Advance online publication. DOI: 10.1007/s10648-024-09886-x

Chapter 23

Teaching Values in the Age of Artificial Intelligence:
A Narrative-Discursive Study of Teachers as Irreplaceable Moral Agents

Ruhan Güçlü
http://orcid.org/0000-0002-2748-8363
Gaziantep University, Turkey

Vildan İnci Kavak
http://orcid.org/0000-0001-7249-9048
Gaziantep Islam Science and Technology University, Turkey & Khoja Akhmet Yassawi International Kazakh-Turkish University, Kazakhstan

ABSTRACT

This chapter aims to foreground the value-based and moral dimensions of the teaching profession at a time when teaching is increasingly framed as a function that can be replaced by digital platforms and artificial intelligence (AI). This chapter challenges that reductionist view by arguing that teachers play a fundamentally irreplaceable role as carriers and mediators of values. The study involves 22 practising teachers working in public secondary schools in Türkiye. It adopts a qualitative, narrative-based research design with a qualitative narrative inquiry based on written narrative elicitation. The primary aim is to explore how teachers construct their professional identities and articulate values education within contemporary debates on technology and artificial intelligence (AI). Drawing on teachers' own narratives, the chapter seeks to demonstrate that teaching is not merely a cognitive activity but a deeply human, relational, and ethical practice through which core values such as responsibility, justice, respect, patience, and empathy are enacted and transmitted.

INTRODUCTION

The use of artificial intelligence (AI) in education has increased rapidly in recent years, raising important questions about the future of teaching. Most discussions focus on how AI can support teaching through faster feedback (Hattie & Timperley, 2007; Shute, 2008), automated assessment (Redecker & Johannessen, 2013; Williamson, 2017), and personalized learning (Holmes et al., 2019; Luckin & Holmes, 2016), as well as more recent developments in AI-supported educational systems (Chen et al., 2020; Garzón, 2025). In these approaches, teaching is often characterized as a cognitive or technical activity that can be enhanced by digital tools. While such systems can support instructional tasks, this view tends to oversimplify what teaching entails. However, teaching is not limited to delivering information or managing learning tasks. It is a social and ethical practice that develops through interaction between teachers and students (Biesta, 2016; Noddings, 2003). Teachers make decisions not only about what to teach, but also about how to guide, support, and respond to learners. These decisions are shaped by values such as fairness, care, responsibility, and respect (Sockett,

DOI: 10.4018/979-8-3373-8983-7.ch023

2012; Campbell, 2014). Linguistic research shows that such values are communicated through language in everyday classroom interaction. Through explanations, feedback, and comments, teachers express evaluations and stances that influence how students understand both knowledge and behaviour (Halliday, 1978; Hyland, 2005).

From a linguistic and discourse-based perspective, teacher identity is formed through language use (Gee, 2001; Varghese et al., 2005). These scholars argue that identity is not a fixed personal trait but is constructed and negotiated through discourse, interaction, and self-representation. Teachers construct their professional identities through talk and writing about their experiences, challenges, and beliefs, particularly in reflective and narrative forms. Research on teacher narratives has examined these accounts from several perspectives, including professional development, moral agency, emotional labour, and ideology (Barkhuizen, 2016; Connelly & Clandinin, 2012; Barkhuizen, 2021). Narrative studies demonstrate that teachers' stories serve as a key resource for understanding how they interpret their work, justify their decisions, and position themselves ethically within educational contexts. Narrative accounts produced by teachers often foreground moral concerns and value-based judgments about students, learning, and professional responsibility. These narratives show that values are not separate from teaching practice; rather, they are closely tied to how teachers understand their role and how they act in educational settings (Kelchtermans, 2009).

This article challenges views of teaching that focus mainly on technical efficiency by emphasising teachers' roles as carriers and mediators of values. It argues that teaching is not only a cognitive activity but also a human practice grounded in relationships and ethical judgment (Biesta, 2020). Through an analysis of teachers' narratives, the study shows that values education is inseparable from teachers' identities and professional practices. For this reason, it represents an aspect of teaching that cannot be transferred to AI-driven systems, which lack the capacity to engage with human experience, moral reasoning, and relational meaning. In addition, from a narrative discourse perspective, teachers' accounts are not treated as transparent reflections of experience, but as discursive acts through which professional identity, moral authority, and technological boundaries are constructed. Narratives function not merely as descriptive reports, but as sites of positioning in which speakers claim legitimacy, responsibility, and interpretative authority. Central to this chapter's argument is a distinction between instruction and education: while the former can be supported or replicated by AI systems, the latter, as a moral, relational, and identity-forming practice cannot. This distinction runs through all four research questions and is foregrounded consistently across the findings.

LITERATURE REVIEW

This section reviews the theoretical and empirical foundations underpinning the study across four interrelated areas: the relationship between values, moral agency, and teaching in an era shaped by artificial intelligence; theoretical perspectives on values and values education, including moral development theory, pedagogical approaches, and values education frameworks; and the specific institutional context of values education in Türkiye. Together, these strands establish the conceptual basis from which the study's research questions and analytical framework are derived.

Values, Moral Agency, and Teaching in the Age of AI

The growing presence of artificial intelligence in educational contexts has recently led to debates about what teaching is and what it should become. In much of the current literature, AI is discussed in relation to teaching, its efficiency, and data-driven decision-making. Scholars highlight its potential to assist teachers through learning analytics, automated feedback, and adaptive learning systems (Selwyn, 2019; Zawacki-Richter et al., 2019). As a result, teaching is frequently conceptualised as a process that can be optimised through technological intervention. However, this focus often leaves aside the ethical and relational dimensions of teaching.

Teaching is inherently value-laden because it involves constant judgments about students, learning, and appropriate behaviour. Teachers must decide how to treat learners fairly, respond to failure, and balance institutional demands with individual needs. As Hansen (2001a) argues, teaching is a moral activity in which values are reflected through everyday pedagogical choices. For example, Fenstermacher and Richardson (2005) emphasise that good teaching cannot be understood solely in terms of effectiveness, since ethical responsibility and practical wisdom play a central role in professional practice.

Moreover, these ethical dimensions of teaching are realised primarily through interaction and communication. Classroom talk, feedback, and explanations are not neutral forms of information exchange; they are sites where authority, care, and responsibility are negotiated. Research in educational discourse shows that teachers routinely express evaluations, expectations, and attitudes through language, shaping how students understand both academic content and social norms (Mercer, 2004; Walsh, 2011). For this reason, values are not external to teaching practice but embedded in the communicative routines of classrooms. From a discourse-based perspective, teacher identity is closely linked to these communicative practices. Identity is understood not as a stable personal attribute but as something that is constructed through repeated patterns of language use and social interaction. Studies on professional identity highlight that teachers come to understand who they are as educators by narrating their experiences, reflecting on dilemmas, and positioning themselves in relation to students and institutions (Beijaard et al., 2004; Varelas, 2012). Narrative inquiry, in particular, has shown that teachers' stories frequently foreground moral concerns, emotional investment, and value judgments, revealing how ethical considerations shape professional self-understanding (Connelly & Clandinin, 2012).

Against this background, claims that artificial intelligence can replace key aspects of teaching appear conceptually limited. While AI systems may support instructional decision-making, they do not engage in moral deliberation or relational understanding. They cannot interpret situations in light of lived experience, nor can they assume responsibility for the consequences of pedagogical action. As Selwyn (2021) cautions, the expansion of AI in education risks promoting a technocratic view of teaching if ethical and human dimensions are ignored. Similar concerns are raised in studies examining the broader implications of artificial intelligence for educational practice and governance (Knox, 2020; Williamson & Eynon, 2020). Ethical concerns surrounding AI integration in education increasingly focus on issues such as data privacy, algorithmic bias, and accountability (Lim et al., 2025; Wiese et al., 2025). Therefore, values, moral agency, and identity remain central to teaching and represent aspects of educational practice that cannot be delegated to AI-driven systems. Recent developments in generative AI, including large language models capable of producing contextually coherent text, further complicate this picture by blurring the boundary between automated and human-like interaction (Holmes & Tuomi, 2022). Posthumanist perspectives additionally challenge essentialist distinctions between human and machine agency, arguing that the professional boundaries teachers draw around AI are themselves discursively produced rather than technologically given (Knox, 2020). This study engages with these perspectives by examining how teachers actively construct and maintain such boundaries through evaluative language and narrative positioning.

From a discourse-analytic perspective, values are not treated as abstract entities in this study but as socially constructed through language. Teachers' narratives are therefore examined not only for thematic content but also for how moral positioning is linguistically realised through evaluative language, modality, metaphor, and boundary construction. This allows the study to explore how teachers discursively construct professional identity and delimit the scope of artificial intelligence in education. Despite the growing body of research on AI in education, relatively few empirical studies have examined how practising teachers discursively construct the limits of AI through their professional narratives. This study addresses that gap by foregrounding teachers' first-person accounts as the primary site of both values enactment and boundary construction.

Theoretical Perspectives on Values and Values Education

Values are fundamental principles that guide behaviour and reflect what is deemed important in community life, shaping individuals' lifestyles and serving as the moral foundation of collective well-being (Cevizci, 2006; Güngör, 1998; Jimenez, 2008; Özlem, 2010). Across the philosophical literature, a shared understanding emerges: values are not merely private preferences but socially-embedded commitments that moderate behaviour and enhance collective well-being (Ulusoy & Dilmaç, 2012; Yel & Aladağ, 2009).

Kohlberg's (1958) cognitive-developmental model traces moral reasoning across pre-conventional, conventional, and post-conventional levels, demonstrating that moral judgement evolves through experience, reflection, and social engagement. This developmental perspective underpins the present study's understanding of values education as an ongoing, context-sensitive process. Freire (1998) similarly argues that teaching is inherently social and moral, and that the affective dispositions teachers embody, including humility, courage, and care, constitute the relational authority through which values are transmitted. Crucially, Freire insists that personal character and professional commitment must be integrated rather than conflated, a distinction central to this study's understanding of moral agency.

Values are cultivated from birth, beginning in the family and transitioning to formal schooling (Ceka & Murati, 2016; Long, 1999). In schools, values education operates through both explicit curricular instruction and the implicit messages of everyday pedagogical practice (Elkatmış, 2009; Thornberg, 2016). Beyond school, religious organisations and mass media also shape children's values, making the teacher's mediating role particularly critical (Ülavere & Tammik, 2017). Pedagogically, values education encompasses several orientations: direct virtue instruction (the trait approach), student-centred values clarification, Kohlberg's (1975) cognitive-developmental reasoning, and experiential methods such as role-playing (Shaftel, 1967). Rather than treating these as competing frameworks, this study is primarily concerned with how such orientations manifest implicitly within teachers' everyday practice and narrative self-positioning.

At a broader level, values education is organised around conventional (transmission-based) and progressive (constructivist) orientations, though Sanger and Osguthorpe (2005) caution that this binary oversimplifies a continuum of approaches (Berkowitz, 2011). Critical perspectives further attend to the hidden curriculum through which values are implicitly reproduced in school routines and disciplinary practices (Bernstein, 2000; Giroux & Penna, 1983). These orientations inform this study's attention to both explicit and implicit forms of values mediation in teachers' practice.

Values education aims to enhance learners' academic engagement, promote ethical social behaviour, and support character development (Berkowitz, 2011). It is discussed globally across the West, Asia, and Latin America, under terms including character education, moral education, citizenship education, and the pedagogical mission of education (Veugelers & Vedder, 2003). Cultural context shapes its content: each culture establishes core values to guide members' behaviour (Barragan, 2008), and educators and policymakers construct value frameworks typically including justice, solidarity, self-discipline, autonomy, empathy, and critical thinking, which are integrated into curricula (Veugelers & Vedder, 2003). Values education may be explicit, through a formal program, or implicit within the hidden curriculum of everyday practice (Akbaş, 2004; Halstead, 1996; Tarman & Kuran, 2014). Howard et al. (2004) argue that educating students in values and ethical principles is the most effective means of cultivating strong character and reinforcing social cohesion. It is therefore crucial for educators to internalise the goals and significance of values education throughout their professional practice.

Values Education in Türkiye

In Türkiye, values education was an implicit component of the formal education system until 2005, when it became explicitly integrated into the official curricula. The Ministry of National Education (MoNE) issued the First Class Circular numbered 53 in 2010, which defines the objectives of the Turkish education system. This circular emphasizes the development of individuals who acknowledge national, spiritual, and universal cultural values, integrate these values into their behavior, and feel a sense of responsibility for transmitting these values to future generations. Additionally, it aims to enhance students' academic success (MoNE, 2010). Distributing this circular to all primary and secondary schools marked a significant milestone for values education in Türkiye. Its multidisciplinary and historical content helps explain various cultures and histories, reflecting accumulated cultural knowledge. The objectives of the 2018 curriculum emphasize the importance of students valuing democratic, secular, national, and modern principles while adopting national, spiritual, and universal values. It aims to cultivate virtuous individuals by instilling 18 core values: justice, caring for family, unity, independence, peace, scientific thinking, diligence, solidarity, sensitivity, honesty, aesthetics, equality, freedom, respect, love, responsibility, thriftiness, patriotism, and helpfulness, as outlined by MoNE (2018a, 2018b).

Türkiye's most recent curricular initiative is the Maarif Model (MM), implemented from 2024 onward. Rooted in the term 'maarif' (knowledge and culture), the MM aims to cultivate 'competent and virtuous individuals' by integrating national consciousness with 21st-century skills (MoNE, 2024). The model defines ten interrelated character traits, moral, wise, courageous, aesthetic, willful, compassionate, healthy, questioning, productive, and patriotic, that together constitute its vision of human development (MoNE, 2024). Crucially for this study, these traits overlap substantially with the values that participating teachers articulate in their professional narratives, reinforcing the argument that values education is both a systemic and deeply relational project.

A key focus of the new model is the integration of 21st-century skills, such as digital literacy, STEM education, and technology, into the MM. This theme demonstrates MM's strategic goal of preparing students for contemporary societal and workforce needs through curriculum updates and skill development. Multiple studies highlight the increasing inclusion of digital literacy concepts in MM curricula, particularly in Turkish language instruction and secondary education. Banaz (2024) examined the 2024 Secondary School Turkish Curriculum and observed frequent use of "digital" terminology and content reflecting technological progress, indicating the curriculum's adaptation to the digital age. Similarly, Kuzu et al. (2024) identified digital literacy as vital within the Virtue-Value-Action model, but noted deficiencies in media literacy and information technology skills.

All of these principles complement one another and are compatible with UNESCO's (2000) universal values, which operate in 84 countries (including Türkiye) across five continents (LVEP, 2005). These national principles and their substances share a common aim: cultivating competent and virtuous people.

To summarise, teachers play a key role in achieving these national and universal educational goals. Their attitudes toward teaching, learning, and curricula, along with their preferred teaching methods and the knowledge gained during the learning process, significantly influence students' academic success and the implementation of curriculum objectives (Brown, 2008). Teachers with positive attitudes towards this area are believed to deliver values education more effectively. The aim of this study is to examine how teachers conceptualise values education and moral responsibility in their professional practice amid increasing technologisation and the growing use of artificial intelligence (AI) in education. Drawing on teachers' narratives, the study seeks to highlight the value-based and ethical dimensions of teaching and to explore why teachers continue to view values education as a domain that cannot be replaced by technological or AI-driven systems. To achieve these aims, the study is guided by the following research questions:

1. How do teachers describe their roles and responsibilities in mediating values within educational settings?
2. Which values emerge most prominently in teachers' professional narratives, and how are these values enacted in everyday teaching practices?
3. How do teachers position themselves in relation to digital technologies and artificial intelligence in education?
4. What limits do teachers attribute to AI in values education, and what makes teachers irreplaceable as moral agents?

METHODOLOGY

Research Design

This study adopts a qualitative, narrative-based research design with supportive descriptive survey elements. The primary aim is to explore how teachers construct their professional identities and articulate values education in the context of increasing technologisation and the growing presence of artificial intelligence (AI) in education. A qualitative approach is particularly appropriate for this purpose, as values, moral reasoning, and emotional positioning are complex, context-sensitive phenomena that cannot be adequately captured through predefined categories or purely quantitative measures.

A narrative approach was adopted to explore teachers' lived experiences and professional meaning-making. This approach enables an in-depth examination of how teachers organise lived experience, professional meaning, and ethical judgement through personal accounts. By foregrounding teachers' own voices, narrative inquiry allows values to emerge not as abstract principles but as enacted practices embedded in everyday teaching situations. This design aligns with the study's theoretical position that teaching is a moral, relational, and identity-forming practice rather than a purely technical activity.

Participants and Sampling

The study involves 22 practising teachers working in public secondary schools in Türkiye. Participants were selected through purposive sampling to ensure diversity in teaching experience, educational level, and institutional context. Such variation was considered essential for capturing a broad range of value-related experiences and professional perspectives.

To be eligible for participation, teachers were required to (a) have a minimum of three years of professional experience and (b) be actively engaged in classroom teaching at the time of data collection. Participation was voluntary, and respondents self-selected into the study. A sample size of 22 participants was deemed sufficient to achieve thematic saturation while remaining consistent with established standards in qualitative narrative research.

Data Collection Instruments

Data were collected through a written narrative elicitation instrument specifically designed for this study. The instrument consisted of two complementary sections intended to contextualise participants' professional backgrounds while eliciting reflective narrative responses.

The first section, titled *Participant Profile*, included closed-ended items gathering non-identifiable professional information such as years of teaching experience, educational level, subject area, institutional type, frequency of digital technology use, and experience with AI-based educational tools. These items were included solely to situate the narratives within relevant professional contexts and to enhance interpretative depth. They were not treated as a statistical dataset, nor were they subjected to quantitative analysis. The second and primary section comprised a *Narrative-Based Reflective Survey* organised thematically around teaching identity, values education, emotional and moral responsibility, and perceptions of artificial intelligence in education. The survey included open-ended questions prompting participants to describe concrete classroom experiences, articulate the values they prioritise, reflect on morally challenging situations, and evaluate the pedagogical capacities and limitations of AI.

Questions were deliberately designed to encourage detailed reflection rather than brief descriptive responses. No length restrictions were imposed, allowing teachers to construct meaning in their own terms and to express values as lived and enacted practices rather than abstract declarations.

DATA COLLECTION PROCEDURE

Data were collected through an online questionnaire designed and distributed via Google Docs. The online format was preferred both for practical accessibility and for its suitability to reflective inquiry. By allowing teachers to complete the survey in their own time and setting, the digital environment supported thoughtful engagement with questions that required ethical consideration and personal introspection.

Before beginning the questionnaire, participants were provided with a brief informed consent statement outlining the purpose of the study, the voluntary nature of participation, and the principles of anonymity and confidentiality guiding the research. Participation proceeded only after consent had been explicitly indicated. Importantly, the survey was completed without any imposed time restrictions. This was particularly relevant given that many of the prompts invited participants to recount emotionally challenging experiences and articulate nuanced value positions. The asynchronous format thus reduced potential performance pressure and offered a more reflective space for narrative expression.

Responses were recorded digitally and stored securely throughout the research process. The survey did not request identifying information, and participants were reminded to avoid including personal or institutional details in their written accounts.

DATA ANALYSIS PROCEDURE

The analysis was guided by Güçlü's (2026) integrated value framework, which brings together UNESCO's universal value categories (2000) and the core values articulated in the Turkish Ministry of National Education (MoNE, 2018a, 2018b) curriculum. Rather than treating these two systems as separate taxonomies, the framework consolidates them into a unified analytical structure comprising 17 values. This consolidated set includes five overlapping values common to both frameworks (honesty, love, respect, responsibility, and tolerance), seven values specific to UNESCO (cooperation, freedom, happiness, humility, peace, simplicity, and unity), and five values unique to the national curriculum (justice, friendship, self-control, patience, and helpfulness). This merging logic allowed for both global normative alignment and national curricular specificity, thereby providing a systematic yet context-sensitive analytical lens for examining how values are articulated and enacted in teachers' narratives.

The analytical process began with repeated holistic readings of the narratives to develop an overall understanding of recurring value patterns, emotional orientations, and modes of professional self-positioning. Following this familiarisation stage, explicit and implicit references to values were identified at the lexical and discourse levels. Explicit references included direct mentions of named values (e.g., responsibility, justice), whereas implicit references involved evaluative language, moral positioning, or descriptions of action reflecting underlying value orientations.

Value-related segments were then categorized according to the 17-value taxonomy. Coding decisions were made contextually, prioritizing narrative coherence and meaning-in-use rather than relying solely on surface-level keyword identification. In the final stage, coded segments were interpreted thematically by situating emerging patterns within broader discussions of teacher identity, moral agency, and perceptions of the pedagogical and ethical limits of AI and digital technologies. Particular attention was given to how teachers positioned themselves in relation to technology when reflecting on responsibility and the transmission of values. In addition to value categorisation, attention was paid to discursive features such as modality ("can", "cannot"), evaluative lexis, pronoun positioning, and metaphorical framing. These linguistic choices were examined as indicators of stance-taking and professional self-positioning in relation to artificial intelligence. This discursive layer of analysis was applied systematically across all four findings sections. In the first section metaphorical constructions (e.g., 'laying foundations,' 'leaving a trace') are examined as evidence of ontological boundary-drawing between human pedagogy and AI-supported instruction. In the second section, evaluative lexis and first-person pronoun positioning reveal how values such as justice and patience are enacted through relational accountability rather than abstract declaration. In the third and fourth sections, the systematic use of restrictive modality ('cannot') in AI-related utterances is read as a discursive act of professional authority and boundary maintenance, while enabling modality ('can support,' 'can help') signals the functional utility teachers concede to digital tools. This dual-modal pattern constitutes a central discursive finding: teachers construct AI as instrumentally capable but morally absent.

The Researchers' Positionality

The values we hold are shaped by our everyday interactions and cultural experiences, making them social constructs. Morality is understood as part of social identity, with individuals functioning as moral agents responsible for their actions and for others' judgments. These meanings and interpretations develop through social engagement, emphasizing that our behavior is often influenced more by perceptions than by an objective reality. The authors encourage the exploration of normative ethics and moral development in a broad manner, thereby promoting dialogue among diverse perspectives. They recognize that we can never have absolute certainty-known as fallibilism- and see knowledge as a process that is always evolving through reinterpretation and adjustment. This open and inclusive approach guides how they gather and analyze data. In practical terms, this positionality shaped the study in several ways. The researchers consciously bracketed prescriptive value judgements to ensure teachers' own framings remained analytically central. Interpretive decisions were grounded in textual evidence and cross-checked against the 17-value framework rather than imposed deductively. The researchers acknowledge that their professional contexts within Turkish higher education may have sensitised them to relational and linguistic dimensions of the data; these influences were managed through continuous reflexive discussion between co-researchers and by anchoring all claims in direct participant quotations.

Trustworthiness and Ethical Considerations

Throughout the analysis, careful attention was paid to ensuring interpretative consistency by grounding all readings in concrete textual evidence drawn directly from the teachers' narratives. Analytical decisions were informed by repeated engagement with the data and by ongoing reflexive consideration of the researcher's role in interpreting value-focused narratives. The study was conducted in line with institutional ethical guidelines. Participation was entirely voluntary, and all teachers were provided informed consent prior to data collection. To protect participants' privacy, pseudonyms were used in the dataset or the analysis.

FINDINGS AND DISCUSSION

This section reports and interprets the patterns emerging from the written narrative survey responses (n = 22). Across accounts, teachers described values education as a lived, relational practice embedded in everyday school life. While most participants acknowledged the instructional benefits of digital tools and AI, they consistently positioned moral agency, emotional attunement, and responsibility as teacher-bound dimensions of education.

TEACHERS' ROLES IN VALUES MEDIATION

The questionnaire findings reveal that participants overwhelmingly construct teaching as a morally grounded and relational profession. Rather than defining their role in narrowly instructional terms, teachers consistently articulate their professional identity in relation to character formation, social influence, and long-term human development. In this respect, mediating values is not described as an auxiliary responsibility attached to curriculum delivery; rather, it is positioned as constitutive of what it means to be a teacher.

Importantly, the values teachers refer to in their role constructions correspond closely to the consolidated 17-value framework guiding this study. In particular, responsibility, respect, justice, patience, and love, drawn from both UNESCO's universal value taxonomy and the Turkish MoNE curriculum, emerge implicitly and explicitly in teachers' accounts of professional purpose. This orientation is not confined to a particular level of experience or institutional context. Across middle school, high school, and higher education settings, teachers converge around a shared assumption: teaching inevitably involves shaping dispositions, attitudes, and ethical orientations, consistent with Hansen's (2001b) argument that teaching is inherently a moral practice.

A recurrent pattern in the data concerns the metaphors through which teachers describe their role:

1. *"For me, teaching is like placing a brick while laying the foundations of our future. Being able to touch children's lives is very special."* (Teacher 16)
2. *"To touch lives. To leave a trace."* (Teacher 5)

Such expressions indicate that teachers perceive their influence as extending beyond cognitive instruction into the moral and existential dimensions of students' lives. Metaphor analysis also reveals how teachers conceptualise their role in temporally extended and developmental terms ("laying foundations," "leaving a trace"). These metaphors construct teaching as an enduring moral influence rather than a momentary instructional performance. Such figurative language strengthens the ontological distinction teachers draw between human pedagogy and AI-supported instruction, and resonates with Biesta's (2010, 2021) conceptualisation of education as subjectification rather than mere qualification.

Moreover, several accounts frame the teacher as an ethical decision-maker responsible for ensuring fairness and accountability within complex classroom dynamics. Narratives of fair grading, resisting institutional bias, and protecting students from external criticism illustrate how justice (MoNE-unique) and responsibility (overlapping across frameworks) are enacted as professional obligations. Participants repeatedly stress that values are internalised through observation of lived example:

3. *"There is a saying: You cannot teach your child to be honest; you must be honest yourself, and they will learn by looking at you. What matters is not so much what you do, but who you are when you do it. A wrong person cannot instill the right values. Only the right person can impart the right way of living."* (Teacher 11)
4. *"Values begin in the family, and school reinforces and develops them; when they are firmly grounded, children learn more permanently through practice and lived experience."* (Teacher 17)

The emphasis on "who you are" underscores that moral authority emerges less from formal instruction and more from relational authenticity, consistent with findings that teachers' personal value systems shape the classroom's moral climate (Beauchamp & Thomas, 2009). The data further make clear that teachers experience moral responsibility as context-sensitive and situational. Values mediation is frequently narrated through specific classroom incidents requiring ethical judgement:

5. *"One day, two students were arguing. During their verbal confrontation, I intervened and first listened to them carefully and in detail. By listening to them and showing respect, I noticed that they calmed down. They realized from their own perspectives that the issue was actually something simple and not worth hurting each other's feelings over. As a result, the situation was resolved more quickly. Seeing that they viewed me as the teacher who solved the conflict also made me genuinely happy. I learned that it is not always necessary to provide a ready-made solution; sometimes listening with respect and patience is enough."* (Teacher 7)
6. *"A student who had come from the earthquake-affected region and had lost family members was a very difficult experience for me. I tried to help the student overcome this situation by approaching them with compassion."* (Teacher 2)

These examples suggest that teachers do not approach values education as rule enforcement but as interpretative engagement. Patience and respect frequently function as mediating dispositions in conflict situations, and decisions emerge from attentiveness to circumstance and relational meaning, consistent with Noddings' (1984, 2012) ethics of care framework. Participants additionally position trust and relational depth as enabling conditions for moral transmission:

7. *"A strong teacher–student relationship makes it easier for the values the teacher wishes to convey to be genuinely received. When a teacher builds an authentic relationship with students, free from artificiality, self-interest, or a distant and superior attitude, and engages with them on a human level, their lived experiences and expressions of values become credible and meaningful. Otherwise, students may observe the teacher as if watching a performance. They may even take part in the "play," fulfilling all required behaviors at school and in the classroom; however, outside of that setting, once they step out of their roles, they tend to act according to what they truly believe or aspire to be."* (Teacher 9)

This emphasis on relational strength supports the argument that values education operates within what Biesta (2020) terms a pedagogical encounter, an ethical space shaped by presence, recognition, and responsibility.

While participants predominantly describe values mediation as situational and relational, their accounts rarely reflect a structured approach aligned with formal character education models. Research suggests that proactive strategies, including shared norm-setting, a positive school-wide climate, and explicit reinforcement of expected social behaviours, strengthen moral climates more sustainably than incident-driven responses alone (Berkowitz, 2011; Freiberg & Lapointe, 2006; Solomon et al., 2001). The predominance of reactive engagement observed here is consistent with implementation studies showing that scarce training and assessment tools often keep values education at an *ad hoc* level (Muthanna et al., 2021). Thus, the findings indicate that participants construct their role as moral mediators who navigate complex interpersonal environments through example, discernment, and accountability. Values education emerges not as a discrete curricular objective but as a continuous moral process woven into the fabric of everyday pedagogical interaction.

Educators frequently describe values education as an ongoing, informal process embedded in daily interactions rather than as a formally scheduled curricular component. As Narvaez (2006) argues, values education is embedded in the fabric of instructional practice whether explicitly stated in the curriculum, and much of this moral mediation operates within what Halstead (1996) characterises as the hidden curriculum. Teachers also acknowledge that elements of their moral mediation may remain partly unreflective: routine actions, how they speak, listen, and resolve conflict, are often performed automatically, and unexamined moral influence can inadvertently produce inconsistencies (Colnerud, 2006). Beyond relational presence and moral example, participants implicitly construct their responsibility as protective, corrective, and accountable, assuming responsibility not only for transmitting academic knowledge but for safeguarding students' dignity, ensuring fairness, and modelling moral consistency.

Values in Practice

The second research question aimed not simply to identify which values teachers mention, but to understand how these values take form within the texture of daily pedagogical life. When examined closely, the questionnaire responses do not read like a catalogue of virtues. Instead, they reveal a lived moral vocabulary-one that is inseparable from classroom interaction, emotional labour, and practical decision-making.

When interpreted through the integrated 17-value framework underpinning this study, a clear concentration pattern becomes evident: the most prominently enacted values in teachers' narratives include empathy, compassion, justice, patience, respect, responsibility, and honesty, while UNESCO-specific values such as freedom, unity, humility, peace, simplicity, and happiness remain comparatively less visible in spontaneous professional discourse.

Across the narratives, certain values consistently surface; however, they rarely appear in isolation. Empathy, patience, justice, respect, compassion, and responsibility tend to emerge as interconnected commitments that shape how teachers interpret and respond to classroom realities. Empathy and compassion are articulated not as moral slogans, but as prerequisites for understanding student behaviour:

8. *"A sense of compassion and justice, an empathetic approach, and the ease of serving as a role model."* (Teacher 6)

What is striking here is the sequencing itself, compassion leads to empathy, which is operationalised through listening. In a similar vein, another teacher emphasises the centrality of emotional bonds:

9. *"Compassion, empathy, and the strong bonds that are formed."* (Teacher 16)

These expressions suggest that moral influence begins with affective attunement, resonating with Noddings' (1984, 2012) ethics of care, in which moral action is grounded in attentiveness rather than detached rule application. Justice appears repeatedly as a structuring principle of classroom life, not as an abstract civic concept but localised within daily pedagogical decisions:

10. *Justice and equality: A just and equal society is open to development and transformation; therefore, justice and equality are values that every student should internalize. Human-centeredness: An understanding that places human beings at the center rather than measuring them by money or material wealth brings happiness and well-being to society and supports growth and transformation; for this reason, every student deserves and expects to be treated in a human-centered way, first at school and then in all areas of society, and should be able to practice this approach when necessary. National values: Truly national values rooted in our deep historical heritage, in which justice, equality, and a human-centered understanding prevail. Republican values: I attach great importance to the values of this system of governance, which best reflects the free and egalitarian spirit of Turkish society and enables us to receive the respect we deserve, to have human rights, to raise objections, and to determine governance, recognizing the right to live with dignity as human beings."* (Teacher 9)

The emphasis shifts from ideological commitment to interpersonal fairness. Similarly, another teacher underscores the necessity of equal treatment:

11. *"Students should be educated with a strong sense of responsibility, and we should show them what they are capable of achieving based on what they learn and observe. Of course, while doing so, we must approach each student equally and fairly."* (Teacher 6)

The enactment of justice becomes visible in fair evaluation, calibrated discipline, and the preservation of student dignity, sustained through everyday modelling rather than formal declaration (Lickona, 1991). Patience, meanwhile, emerges as the quiet condition that makes other values operational:

12. *"Respect must definitely be mutual. Patience is indispensable in both learning and teaching. At times, whether among students themselves or between student and teacher, empathy must unquestionably be practiced."* (Teacher 16)

Patience operates as a stabilising mechanism, enabling teachers to balance competing values in real time through emotional self-regulation rather than rule enforcement alone. Teachers also consistently distance themselves from didactic approaches to values transmission, describing moral education as embodied practice:

13. *"Most people learn through lived experience, and I believe this is the right way; when someone experiences something directly, they understand its impact and act accordingly."* (Teacher 19)
14. *"If students grow up taking you as a role model and idealizing your actions, we must be careful about how we act."* (Teacher 22)

Modelling emerges as a primary mechanism of enactment, echoing Halstead and Taylor's (2000) observation that moral education operates implicitly through relational culture. Concrete narratives also reveal that teachers actively weigh competing considerations:

15. *"During a written exam, a student whom I had not expected performed very well. When I asked, "Did you cheat?" the student replied, "Yes, teacher." Because the student was honest, I did not lower the grade. I explained that honesty is more important than anything else, and this became an example for the other students as well."* (Teacher 5)

At this moment, institutional rules do not disappear; they are reframed through a developmental lens. The teacher interprets the incident not simply as a breach of policy but as an opportunity for moral growth. Such enactments illustrate what Arthur (2003) refers to as moral professionalism, the capacity to integrate ethical reasoning into immediate pedagogical judgement. This example demonstrates that values are not only expressed but prioritised contextually; teachers actively negotiate which value should take precedence in a given situation, thereby enacting values as situational hierarchies rather than fixed doctrines.

Equally significant is the way teachers describe experiencing tension between values. Several participants mention being "caught" between discipline and compassion, between maintaining distance and expressing closeness. These tensions suggest that values are not experienced as fixed and harmonious; rather, they coexist in dynamic and sometimes conflicting relationships. Schwartz's (1992, 2012) theory of value structures provides a useful interpretive frame here, as it emphasises that values operate in relational constellations rather than hierarchical isolation.

Overall, then, the data demonstrate that the most prominent values, empathy, compassion, justice, patience, respect, responsibility, and honesty, are enacted through specific pedagogical mechanisms: attentive listening, fair and proportionate decision-making, emotional restraint, consistent modelling, contextualised judgement, and relational accountability. Values education, in this sense, emerges not as a static curriculum component but as a living moral practice sustained within the everyday grammar of teaching. This finding is consistent with ethnographic evidence that moral learning is largely constructed through day-to-day routines and interaction rather than formal moral instruction alone (Thornberg, 2009).

At the same time, teachers' accounts suggest that this enactment is rarely organised around a predefined moral framework. Their approach to values education is primarily reactive and unplanned, integrated into daily school life as an informal, ongoing curriculum, much of it performed without conscious reflection. Teachers tend to focus heavily on classroom management and discipline, and such a narrow focus risks limiting attention to short-term student behaviour, potentially overlooking the broader moral influence they exert beyond the classroom (Boostrom, 1991). These negotiations are often framed in experiential rather than theoretical terms: teachers do not refer to research from education, psychology, or philosophy but draw instead on personal experience, common sense, and worldview (Muthanna et al., 2021). As Sockett and LePage (2002) argue, without a shared moral language, teachers may find it difficult to handle complex moral judgements confidently, develop coherent ethical foundations, or guide students in structured moral reflection. This is reflected in international survey findings where many teachers struggled to articulate a critically reflective stance toward values education (Stephenson et al., 1998). As Powney et al. (1995, p. 17) observe, the lack of precise language makes it difficult to professionalise values education, reducing it to something "everybody does but not something everybody has the tools to think about."

The relatively small and context-bound sample limits the generalisability of these findings, and broader cross-contextual research is needed. Nonetheless, the findings clearly indicate that the most prominent values cluster around overlapping and MoNE-specific categories, compassion, respect, responsibility, honesty, justice, and patience, while UNESCO-specific values remain relatively peripheral. The prominence of these values suggests that teachers' moral reasoning is anchored primarily in relational and regulatory classroom demands rather than in macro-level civic-humanistic ideals.

Teachers' Positioning toward AI

The third research question focused on how teachers position themselves in relation to digital technologies and artificial intelligence in educational contexts. Unlike the previous sections, which discussed values primarily through relational narratives, the responses here adopt a more reflexive tone. Teachers do not react to technology with categorical acceptance or rejection. Instead, what emerges is a calibrated and nuanced positioning, one that acknowledges instrumental utility while simultaneously preserving a clear boundary around the core of pedagogical authority.

At first glance, many participants openly recognise the practical benefits of digital tools and AI-supported systems. References to efficiency, access to information, visual enrichment, and time-saving functions recur across responses. For instance:

16. *"It has significant facilitating effects in terms of content production; its strongest contribution is that it encourages students, at least to some extent, to engage in producing their own work."* (Teacher 13)
17. *"It is beneficial in terms of easy access to information and obtaining concise summaries quickly."* (Teacher 21)
18. *"It enables multi-sensory learning."* (Teacher 3)

Such statements indicate that teachers do not perceive technology as inherently disruptive. On the contrary, they recognise its capacity to enrich instructional environments and diversify pedagogical techniques. In this respect, their responses resonate with broader scholarship suggesting that teachers increasingly integrate AI as a cognitive scaffold rather than as a replacement mechanism (e.g., Selwyn, 2019). However, as the responses unfold, a subtle distinction begins to take shape. While technology is described as supportive in instructional terms, it is rarely granted epistemic or moral centrality. Several teachers articulate this boundary explicitly:

19. *"AI can be used as a mere source of information, but the teaching–learning environment remains incomplete without emotions and thoughts."* (Teacher 2)
20. *Artificial intelligence cannot form an emotional bond."* (Teacher 3)
21. *"AI can provide lesson materials, but it cannot empathise with the student."* (Teacher 16)

These declarative constructions function as positioning acts (Davies & Harré, 1990), through which teachers allocate epistemic and moral authority to themselves while simultaneously defining the limits of technological agency. The narrative form allows participants to claim experiential legitimacy by grounding such assertions in lived examples. What becomes visible here is not technological anxiety but ontological differentiation. Teachers distinguish between tools that enhance cognitive processes and human presence that sustains relational and affective dimensions of learning. In other words, technology is framed as operationally useful yet existentially limited.

A central discursive finding emerges from this pattern. Across the narratives, teachers systematically employ restrictive modality, particularly "cannot", when describing AI in moral and relational contexts. This repeated negative modal construction functions as a discursive act of boundary maintenance and professional authority. In contrast, when referring to instructional utility, teachers employ enabling modality ("can help," "can support"), signalling a clear functional distinction between technological assistance and moral presence. This dual-modal pattern, AI as instrumentally capable but morally absent, constitutes one of the most consistent discursive findings of the study and directly reflects the instruction/education distinction foregrounded in its theoretical framework.

Even teachers who report regular AI use maintain this distinction. Their acceptance of technological integration does not translate into conceptual equivalence. Instead, they construct a dual-layered understanding of education: one layer associated with content, efficiency, and delivery; the other with relational presence, moral influence, and contextual judgement. This differentiation closely mirrors Biesta's (2020) distinction between qualification and subjectification: while AI may assist qualification, knowledge transmission and skill acquisition, teachers implicitly reserve subjectification for the human encounter, a limitation also highlighted in recent discussions on the boundaries of artificial intelligence in education (Holmes & Tuomi, 2022). At the same time, participants' voices measured concerns about overreliance:

22. *"It supports multi-perspective thinking, but it may lead to laziness."* (Teacher 5)
23. *"It can help teachers develop and reflect that development onto students, but it may also lead to passivity."* (Teacher 7)

These remarks signal a perceived risk, that overreliance may weaken students' engagement or independent thinking, and reflect teachers' tendency to advocate moderated and guided integration rather than unrestricted dependence. A further significant pattern concerns authority and boundaries. Several participants emphasise that AI operates within parameters set by human agency:

24. *"There are technologies that need to be included in education today, but they must be used very carefully and in a limited way."* (Teacher 18)

Rather than positioning themselves as subordinated to technological systems, teachers assert that AI remains contingent upon human control. Pronoun choices further reinforce this: teachers frequently employ the first-person singular when discussing moral responsibility, foregrounding human agency, while AI is treated as a non-agentive entity lacking intentional subjectivity.This asymmetry in agency attribution reflects a clear discursive construction of hierarchical authority, one in which the teacher remains the moral centre of the educational encounter.

The Limits of AI in Values Education

The fourth research question shifts the discussion from positioning to boundary setting. While the previous section showed that teachers integrate digital technologies in pragmatic ways, the present findings reveal a clear threshold: values education is widely perceived as a domain that cannot be delegated to artificial systems. This perception does not stem from technological resistance; rather, it is grounded in how teachers conceptualise moral responsibility, relational presence, and human accountability.

A central pattern that emerges from the responses concerns emotional absence. Teachers consistently describe AI as lacking affective depth, and this perceived absence becomes decisive when values are at stake. The following statements illustrate this shared concern:

25. *"It may support topic explanation and practice questions, but I do not think it can provide the emotional support a teacher offers."* (Teacher 21)

26. *"Artificial intelligence cannot give advice aligned with our culture and moral structure; it may misguide students."* (Teacher 7)

Within these narratives, emotional connection is not presented as an optional supplement to education but as its grounding condition. Teachers repeatedly imply that values are transmitted through lived relational encounters, through presence, consistency, and shared experience. In the absence of this relational dimension, moral instruction risks becoming procedural rather than transformative, consistent with Noddings' (2012) argument that care is a structural foundation of ethical pedagogy rather than a mere emotional add-on.

Equally significant is the emphasis on moral judgement under conditions of uncertainty. Several participants describe situations in which competing obligations had to be weighed: discipline versus compassion, fairness versus flexibility, institutional rules versus personal circumstances. In these accounts, moral action is portrayed as interpretative rather than algorithmic. For example, earlier narratives showed teachers choosing to moderate punishment when honesty was demonstrated or to adjust responses in light of trauma or hardship. These decisions were not framed as deviations from standards but as ethically responsible recalibrations. It is precisely this contextual discernment that participants perceive as uniquely human. It is important to note that the constraints attributed to AI throughout this section reflect teachers' perceptions rather than empirically tested technical capabilities. These perceptions are analytically significant as evidence of discursive boundary construction, but they should be read as subjective framings rather than definitive claims about what current or future AI systems can or cannot accomplish.

The findings resonate with Biesta's (2020) insistence that moral decisions in classrooms require situated judgement, an attentiveness to context, vulnerability, and long-term developmental consequence that cannot be reduced to technical problem-solving. Moreover, because moral meanings can be culturally and religiously embedded, values education in plural contexts demands cultural sensitivity and cannot be fully reduced to decontextualised, one-size-fits-all guidance (Halstead, 2007). This concern becomes more explicit in statements addressing replacement directly:

27. *"It may replace instruction. However, it cannot surpass education in terms of compassion, closeness, role modelling, and values education. Think of YouTube teachers: students do not love the teachers themselves, but their explanations. Yet, because there is no shared experience, no sense of attachment develops."* (Teacher 11)
28. *"It cannot support human emotions; after all, they are children and we try to understand them, though it can still be very helpful for activities and so on."* (Teacher 10)

These formulations articulate a conceptual distinction between instruction, associated with cognitive transfer, and education, associated with moral formation and relational influence. AI is seen as potentially effective within the former domain but structurally limited in the latter. The boundary, therefore, is not technological sophistication but human ontology. Teachers also repeatedly refer to accountability. Unlike AI systems, teachers experience themselves as answerable for their decisions, a sense captured implicitly in one participant's reflection that "a wrong decision can affect a child's life." Moral authority carries weight precisely because it entails answerability, while AI is perceived as operating without moral ownership. This aligns with Campbell's (2003) notion of teachers as moral agents whose authority derives not merely from knowledge but from ethical commitment. Another layer of meaning becomes visible when teachers discuss the possibility of technological overreach:

29. *"In values education, technology can support the source of instruction, making learning gains more effective and engaging. However, it is the practitioner's attitude and personality that ultimately establish the value."* (Teacher 11)

Rather than positioning themselves as subordinated to technological systems, teachers assert that AI remains contingent upon human control, authority is not ceded to the machine but remains anchored in professional judgement. This insistence on teacher-bound moral authority becomes even more meaningful when considered alongside participants' descriptions of their everyday practice. As earlier sections indicated, values education is often reactive, unplanned, and grounded in personal experience and intuitive judgement rather than systematic theoretical frameworks (Colnerud

& Granström, 2002; Klaassen, 2002). What is being protected from technological replacement is therefore not a fully theorised professional domain but a deeply personal, experience-based moral engagement. In this sense, the boundaries teachers draw against AI are ethically intuitive rather than conceptually systematised, grounded in relational conviction rather than in an explicitly theorised account of pedagogical ethics. Artificial intelligence systems are fundamentally rule-based and algorithmic; they excel at patterned responses and structured outputs. What teachers appear to defend is precisely the capacity to navigate moral ambiguity, emotional complexity, and contextual nuance, dimensions that resist procedural logic.

Overall, the data reveal a carefully balanced stance. Teachers neither romanticise nor demonise AI. Instead, they incorporate it into a pragmatic framework: useful for expanding the pedagogical repertoire, but insufficient for replacing the relational and ethical dimensions of education. The findings allow the limits of AI in values education to be articulated in structured terms. Teachers attribute to AI an affective limitation (absence of emotional reciprocity), a contextual limitation (inability to navigate moral ambiguity and competing obligations), an accountability limitation (lack of answerability for consequences), and an ontological limitation (absence of human relational presence).

In summary, teachers situate themselves not in opposition to artificial intelligence but above and around it, as professionals who integrate technological tools while maintaining moral, relational, and deliberative authority. Correspondingly, teachers' irreplaceability is constructed not in terms of content expertise but in terms of moral agency: the capacity to interpret context, assume responsibility for consequences, embody ethical commitments, and sustain relational continuity over time. AI may assist instruction, but values education is framed as irreducibly human, and the fourth research question is answered both in terms of attributed technological limits and in terms of the moral foundations of professional irreplaceability.

DISCUSSION

This section synthesises the findings reported in relation to the four research questions and the broader theoretical framework. The discussion situates emerging patterns within the existing literature on teacher identity, moral agency, and the pedagogical limits of artificial intelligence, and reflects on the implications of the findings for professional practice and future research.

With respect to the first research question how teachers describe their roles in mediating values, the findings confirm that participants construct teaching as an inherently moral and relational practice. Rather than defining their role in narrowly instructional terms, teachers consistently invoke character formation, long-term human development, and the shaping of ethical dispositions. This resonates with Hansen's (2001b) conception of teaching as an ethical calling, and with Biesta's (2020) distinction between qualification and subjectification. Crucially, moral authority is positioned as emerging from relational authenticity rather than formal instruction, a pattern well documented in the ethics-of-care literature (Noddings, 1984; 2012). The prominence of metaphors of durability ("laying foundations," "leaving a trace") reveals that teachers do not merely frame their role as moral but as ontologically distinct from what AI-supported systems can offer.

Turning to the second research question, which values are most prominently enacted and how the findings show a clear clustering around overlapping values (compassion, respect, responsibility, honesty) and MoNE-specific values (justice, patience), while UNESCO-specific macro-civic values (freedom, unity, peace, simplicity) remain comparatively peripheral. This distribution is consistent with Güçlü's (2026) integrated value taxonomy, which anticipated that relational and community-oriented values would dominate in school-based contexts due to their alignment with children's sociomoral development and the day-to-day regulatory demands of classroom life. The enactment patterns also align with Schwartz's (1992, 2012) model: values do not function as isolated ideals but as relational constellations in which empathy enables justice, patience sustains respect, and modelling operationalises honesty.

The third research question addressed how teachers position themselves in relation to AI and digital technologies. The findings reveal a calibrated stance: teachers acknowledge the instructional utility of AI (content generation, information access, multi-sensory engagement) while drawing a firm boundary at the level of moral and relational authority. This positioning is not technophobic; it is ontological. Teachers discursively construct AI as an operationally capable but morally inert tool, incapable of emotional reciprocity, contextual judgement, or accountability for developmental consequences. This mirrors Selwyn's (2021) caution against technocratic reductionism, and aligns with Holmes and Tuomi's (2022) analysis of the structural limits of AI in education.

Finally, the fourth research question, what limits teachers attribute to AI in values education is answered through four perceived constraints. Teachers attribute to AI an affective limitation (absence of emotional reciprocity and relational depth), a contextual limitation (inability to navigate moral ambiguity and competing obligations in real time), an accountability limitation (absence of answerability for developmental consequences), and an ontological limitation (the impossibility of inhabiting the relational space in which values become meaningful). All in all, these constraints define values education as irreducibly human: not because AI lacks content knowledge, but because it lacks the moral presence, ethical commitment, and relational continuity that make value transmission credible and lasting. This finding extends Campbell's (2003) notion of the ethical teacher and supports Biesta's (2020) argument for a world-centred, rather than technology-centred, vision of education.

CONCLUSION

This study has examined how teachers conceptualise their roles in mediating values, which values they foreground in their professional narratives, and how they position artificial intelligence in relation to the moral core of education. Rather than approaching these as isolated concerns, the findings reveal a deeply interconnected understanding: teaching, in participants' eyes, is inseparable from ethical responsibility.

Across the dataset, teachers do not describe values education as an additional curricular component that can be separated from instructional practice. Instead, they situate it at the heart of their professional identity. To teach is to influence; to influence is to assume responsibility. This orientation becomes particularly visible in how teachers speak of "touching lives," "leaving a trace," and shaping students' future. Such expressions indicate that education is understood not merely as qualification, acquisition of knowledge and skills, but as a formative process involving character, judgement, and relational depth.When read through the integrated 17-value framework guiding this study, it becomes evident that teachers' professional discourse clusters predominantly around overlapping values (such as compassion, respect, responsibility, and honesty) and MoNE-specific values (such as justice and patience), while UNESCO-specific macro-civic values remain comparatively peripheral. This distribution reflects the relational and context-bound demands of everyday classroom life rather than abstract civic idealism.

Equally significant is the manner in which values are enacted. Empathy, justice, patience, respect, compassion, and responsibility do not appear as abstract moral labels. They emerge through listening before judging, moderating punishment in light of honesty, balancing discipline with mercy, and maintaining fairness under pressure. Values education, therefore, is embedded in decision-making under conditions of uncertainty. It is in these moments-often invisible, routine, yet ethically charged- that teachers see their role most clearly. Within this framework, artificial intelligence is neither an enemy nor a saviour of education. Participants widely acknowledge its utility in enhancing instructional efficiency, generating content, and expanding access to information. However, they also draw a conceptual boundary: while AI may assist with cognitive processes, it does not assume the relational and moral dimensions that define education as a human encounter. Importantly, teachers' claims of irreplaceability are not grounded in professional protectionism. Rather, they arise from an understanding of education as accountable moral action. AI can simulate explanation, generate examples, and analyse data. Yet it does not bear responsibility for the consequences of classroom decisions; it does not navigate competing values in lived, embodied contexts; and it does not inhabit the relational space within which values become meaningful. For the teachers in this study, this distinction is decisive.

Overall, the findings suggest that contemporary debates on AI in education risk oversimplification when they frame the issue solely in terms of efficiency or automation. Empirically, this study contributes by grounding abstract debates on artificial intelligence in teachers' lived moral reasoning rather than in speculative technological scenarios. Conceptually, it clarifies that teachers' resistance to replacement is not driven by technophobia but by a differentiated understanding of instruction versus education, where the latter is inseparable from relational presence, contextual judgement, and moral accountability. The present study demonstrates that teachers themselves conceptualise their work in ontological terms, as a form of moral presence. Education, as described in these narratives, is not reducible to information transfer; it is sustained through relational authority, contextual judgement, and ethical accountability. Linguistically, teachers' narratives construct this boundary through evaluative language, restrictive modality, metaphorical framing, and agentive pronoun use, all of which position the human teacher as the locus of moral authority.

Finally, the findings raise important implications for professional preparation. This study highlights the absence of a shared ethical language and systematic engagement with relevant theory as a significant constraint on professional growth. Knowledge of conflict resolution, moral development, bullying prevention, aggression, social influence, ethics, and citizenship education should be considered core components of teacher competence, alongside subject teaching and learning skills, and therefore integrated into teacher training programmes. Yet several studies indicate that teachers often feel insufficiently prepared. National data suggest that many teacher candidates receive limited training in conflict management or ethics (Riksförbund, 2004). Internationally, research from the Netherlands (Willemse et al., 2005) and across Europe (Taylor, 1994) indicates that preparation for moral education frequently remains implicit and under-theorised.

In this respect, the enactment of empathy, justice, patience, and responsibility observed in this study reflects both strength and vulnerability: strength in the depth of relational commitment, and vulnerability in the relative absence of a shared professional meta-language to support systematic reflection and sustained moral pedagogy. To summarise, the study contributes to ongoing discussions on technology and schooling by grounding theoretical concerns in practitioner insight. It shows that the question is not whether AI can support teaching; it clearly can, but whether it can assume the ethical weight of educating. According to the voices represented here, the answer remains decisively human. In sum, this study makes three principal contributions. First, it provides empirical evidence that teacher moral agency is anchored in relational, contextual, and accountable practice, dimensions that remain structurally beyond the reach of current AI systems. Second, it validates Güçlü's (2026) eclectic value taxonomy as a viable analytical framework for cross-contextual values research, bridging UNESCO's universal standards with national curricular specificities. Third, it argues that professional preparation programs must treat moral reasoning, conflict resolution, and values pedagogy as core competencies rather than supplementary additions. The central question is not whether AI can support teaching; it clearly can, but whether it can assume the ethical weight of educating. According to the voices represented here, the answer remains decisively human. Nevertheless, the findings should be interpreted in light of certain limitations. The study is based on a qualitative and context-bound sample within a specific national education system. Broader cross-cultural and quantitative research may reveal alternative constructions of teacher identity and AI integration. Future studies may also explore how structured preparation in moral philosophy and values pedagogy shapes teachers' perceptions of technological boundaries.

REFERENCES

Akbaş, O. (2004). *Evaluation of the degree of reaching of affective goals at the elementery level in Turkish national education system* (Unpublished doctoral thesis). Gazi University, İstanbul.

Arthur, J. (2003). *Education with character: The moral economy of schooling*. Routledge Falmer. DOI: 10.4324/9780203220139

Banaz, E. (2024). 2024 Türkiye yüzyılı maarif modeli ortaokul Türkçe dersi öğretim programının dijital okuryazarlık açısından incelenmesi [In Turkish: An examination of the Turkish language curriculum for middle school students, a model of education in the 21st century, from the perspective of digital literacy]. *Kuram ve Uygulamada Sosyal Bilimler Dergisi, 8*(1), 279–290. DOI: 10.48066/kusob.1483671

Barkhuizen, G. (2016). *Reflections on language teacher identity research*. Routledge. DOI: 10.4324/9781315643465

Barkhuizen, G. (2021). *Language teacher educator identity*. Cambridge University Press. DOI: 10.1017/9781108874083

Barragan, P. C. (2008). *Happiness and education a research on values based education*. Retrieved from https://wor lddatabaseofhappines s.eur.nl/hap_bib/freetexts/cubas_barragan_p_2008.pdf

Beauchamp, C., & Thomas, L. (2009). Understanding teacher identity: An overview of issues in the literature and implications for teacher education. *Cambridge Journal of Education, 39*(2), 175–189. DOI: 10.1080/03057640902902252

Beijaard, D., Meijer, P. C., & Verloop, N. (2004). Reconsidering research on teachers' professional identity. *Teaching and Teacher Education, 20*(2), 107–128. DOI: 10.1016/j.tate.2003.07.001

Berkowitz, M. (2011). What works in values education? *International Journal of Educational Research, 50*(3), 153–158. DOI: 10.1016/j.ijer.2011.07.003

Bernstein, B. (2000). *Pedagogy, symbolic control and identity: Theory, research, critique*. Rowman & Littlefield Publishers.

Biesta, G. (2010). *Good education in an age of measurement: Ethics, politics, democracy*. Paradigm Publishers.

Biesta, G. (2016). *The beautiful risk of education*. Routledge.

Biesta, G. (2020). Risking ourselves in education: Qualification, socialization, and subjectification revisited. *Educational Theory, 70*(1), 89–104. DOI: 10.1111/edth.12411

Biesta, G. J. J. (2021). *World-centred education: A view for the present*. Routledge. DOI: 10.4324/9781003098331

Boostrom, R. (1991). The nature and functions of classroom rules. *Curriculum Inquiry, 21*(2), 193–216. DOI: 10.1080/03626784.1991.11075363

Brown, G. (2008). *Integrating teachers' conceptions: Assessment, teaching, learning, curriculum and efficacy*. Nova Science Publishers.

Campbell, E. (2003). *The ethical teacher*. Open University Press.

Campbell, E. (2014). Teaching ethically as a moral condition of professionalism. In Nucci, L., & Krettenauer, T. (Eds.), *Handbook of moral and character education* (pp. 117–134). Routledge.

Ceka, A., & Murati, R. (2016). The role of parents in the education of children. *Journal of Education and Practice, 7*(5), 61–64.

Cevizci, A. (2006). *Felsefe ansiklopedisi [In Turkish: Encyclopedia of philosophy]* (Cilt 4). Babil Yayıncılık.

Chen, L., Chen, P., & Lin, Z. (2020). Artificial intelligence in education: A review. *IEEE Access : Practical Innovations, Open Solutions*, *8*, 75264–75278. DOI: 10.1109/ACCESS.2020.2988510

Colnerud, G. (2006). Teacher ethics as a research problem: Syntheses achieved and new issues. *Teachers and Teaching*, *12*(3), 365–385. DOI: 10.1080/13450600500467704

Colnerud, G., & Granström, K. (2002). *Respekt för läraryrket: Om lärares yrkesspråk och yrkesetik* [In Swedish: Respect for the teaching profession: On teachers' professional language and professional ethics]. Studentlitteratur.

Connelly, F. M., & Clandinin, D. J. (2012). Narrative inquiry. In Green, J. L., Camilli, G., & Elmore, P. B. (Eds.), *Handbook of complementary methods in education research* (pp. 477–487). Routledge. DOI: 10.4324/9780203874769-30

Davies, B., & Harré, R. (1990). Positioning: The discursive production of selves. *Journal for the Theory of Social Behaviour*, *20*(1), 43–63. DOI: 10.1111/j.1468-5914.1990.tb00174.x

Elkatmış, M. (2009). Hayat bilgisi öğretiminde değer eğitimi. [In Turkish: Value education in life skills teaching]. B. Tay (Ed.). *Hayat bilgisi öğretimi.* (p. 335-365). Maya Akademi.

Fenstermacher, G. D., & Richardson, V. (2005). On making determinations of quality in teaching. *Teachers College Record*, *107*(1), 186–213. DOI: 10.1111/j.1467-9620.2005.00462.x

Freiberg, H. J., & Lapointe, J. M. (2006). Research-based programs for preventing and solving discipline problems. In Evertson, C. M., & Weinstein, C. S. (Eds.), *Handbook of classroom management: Research, practice, and contemporary issues* (pp. 735–786). Lawrence Erlbaum.

Freire, P. (1998). *Teachers as cultural workers: Letters to those who dare teach.* Westview Press.

Garzón, J., Patiño, E., & Marulanda, C. (2025). Systematic review of artificial intelligence in education: Trends, benefits, and challenges. *Multimodal Technologies and Interaction*, *9*(8), 84. DOI: 10.3390/mti9080084

Gee, J. P. (2001). Identity as an analytic lens for research in education. *Review of Research in Education*, *25*, 99–125.

Giroux, H., & Penna, A. (1983). Social education in the classroom: The dynamics of the hidden curriculum. In H. Giroux, H. & D. Purpel (Eds). *The hidden curriculum and moral education* (pp. 100–121). Mc-Cutchan Publishing Corporation.

Güçlü, R. (2026). Kosova'da Türkçe yayımlanan *Bahar* çocuk dergisinde değerlerin tutum odaklı değerleme çözümlemesi [In Turkish: An attitudinal appraisal analysis of values in Bahar children's magazine published in Turkish in Kosovo]. *ODU Journal of Social Sciences Research*, *16*(1), 1-17. DOI: 10.48146/odusobiad.1737029

Güngör, E. (1998). *Değerler psikolojisi üzerinde araştırmalar* [Research on the psychology of values]. Ötüken.

Halliday, M. A. K. (1978). *Language as social semiotic: The social interpretation of language and meaning*. Edward Arnold.

Halstead, J. M. (1996). Values and values education in schools. In Halstead, J. M., & Taylor, M. J. (Eds.), *Values in Education and Education in Values* (pp. 3–13). Routledge.

Halstead, J. M.J. Mark Halstead. (2007). Islamic values: A distinctive framework for moral education? *Journal of Moral Education*, *36*(3), 283–296. DOI: 10.1080/03057240701643056

Halstead, J. M., & Taylor, M. J. (2000). Learning and teaching about values: A review of recent research. *Cambridge Journal of Education*, *30*(2), 169–202. DOI: 10.1080/713657146

Hansen, D. T. (2001a). *Exploring the moral heart of teaching: Toward a teacher's creed.* Teachers College Press.

Hansen, D. T. (2001b). *The call to teach.* Teachers College Press.

Hattie, J., & Timperley, H. (2007). The power of feedback. *Review of Educational Research, 77*(1), 81–112. DOI: 10.3102/003465430298487

Holmes, W., Bialik, M., & Fadel, C. (2019). *Artificial intelligence in education: Promises and implications for teaching and learning*. Center for Curriculum Redesign.

Holmes, W., & Tuomi, I. (2022). State of the art and practice in AI in education. *European Journal of Education, 57*(4), 542–570. DOI: 10.1111/ejed.12533

Howard, R., Berkowitz, M., & Schaeffer, E. (2004). Politics of character education. *Educational Policy, 18*(1), 188–215. DOI: 10.1177/0895904803260031

Hyland, K. (2005). Metadiscourse: Exploring interaction in writing. *Continuum.*

Jimenez, J. C. (2008). *The significance of values in an organization.* Cograf Communications.

Kelchtermans, G. (2009). Who I am in how I teach is the message: Self-understanding, vulnerability and reflection. *Teachers and Teaching, 15*(2), 257–272. DOI: 10.1080/13540600902875332

Klaassen, C. A. (2002). Teacher pedagogical competence and values education. *Teaching and Teacher Education, 18*(2), 151–163. DOI: 10.1016/S0742-051X(01)00060-9

Knox, J. (2020). Artificial intelligence and education in China. *Learning, Media and Technology, 45*(3), 298–311. DOI: 10.1080/17439884.2020.1754236

Kohlberg, L. (1958). *The development of modes of moral thinking and choice in the years 10 to 16* (Doctoral dissertation, The University of Chicago).

Kohlberg, L. (1975). The cognitive developmental approach to moral education. *Phi Delta Kappan, 56*(10), 670–677.

Kuzu, O., Göçer, V., & Akçay, A. O. (2024). Türkiye yüzyılı maarif modeli kapsamında ilkokul matematik dersi öğretim programı'nın incelenmesi [In Turkish: Examination of the primary school mathematics curriculum within the framework of the 21st century Turkish education model]. *RumeliDE Journal of Language and Literature Studies*, (41), 640–667. DOI: 10.5281/zenodo.13337757

Lickona, T. (1991). *Educating for character: How our schools can teach respect and responsibility.* Bantam Books.

Lim, T., Gottipati, S., & Cheong, M. (2025). What students really think: unpacking AI ethics in educational assessments through a triadic framework. *International Journal of Educational Technology in Higher Education, 22*(1), 56. Long, B. K. (1999). *The value-able child: Teaching values at home and school.* Good Year Books.

Luckin, R., & Holmes, W. (2016). *Intelligence unleashed: An argument for AI in education.* Pearson.

LVEP. (2005). *Living values education.* Retrieved December 7, 2025, from http://www. livingvalues.net/

Mercer, N. (2004). Sociocultural discourse analysis. *Journal of Applied Linguistics, 1*(2), 137–168. DOI: 10.1558/japl.2004.1.2.137

Ministry of National Education (MoNE). (2010). *First lesson circular (No. 53).* Ministry of National Education.

Ministry of National Education (MoNE). (2024). *Türkiye Century Education Model (Maarif Modeli) curriculum framework.* Ministry of National Education. Retrieved from https://www.meb.gov.tr/the-century-of-turkiye-education-model-new-curriculum-draft-opened-for-public-opinion/haber/33489/enMoNE (2018a). İngilizcedersiöğretimprogramı: 2-8. Sınıflar [In Turkish: English Language Curriculum: Grades 2-8]. Ministry of National Education.

MoNE. (2018b). İngilizcedersiöğretimprogramı: 2-8. Sınıflar [In Turkish: English Language Curriculum: Grades 9-12]. Ministry of National Education. Retrieved from https://mufredat.meb.gov.tr/Dosyalar/201812020472656-OGM%20 INGILIZCE%20PRG%2020.012018.pdf

Muthanna, A., Alduais, A., & Ghundol, B. (2021). Challenges facing teacher education in Yemen: Toward better quality. In *Handbook of Research on Teacher Education Pedagogical Innovations and Practices in the Middle East* (pp. 411–425). Springer.

Narvaez, D. (2006). Integrative ethical education. In Killen, M., & Smetana, J. G. (Eds.), *Handbook of moral development* (pp. 703–732). Lawrence Erlbaum Associates.

Noddings, N. (1984). *Caring: A feminine approach to ethics and moral education*. University of California Press.

Noddings, N. (2003). *Caring: A feminine approach to ethics and moral education* (2nd ed.). University of California Press.

Noddings, N. (2012). The caring relation in teaching. *Oxford Review of Education, 38*(6), 771–781. DOI: 10.1080/03054985.2012.745047

Özlem, D. (2010). *Etik: Ahlak felsefesi* [In Turkish: Ethics: Moral philosophy]. Say Press.

Powney, J., Cullen, M.-A., Schlapp, U., Glissov, P., Johnstone, M., & Munn, P. (1995). *Understanding values education in the primary school*. Scottish Council for Research in Education.

Redecker, C., & Johannessen, Ø. (2013). Changing assessment: Towards a new assessment paradigm using ICT. *European Journal of Education, 48*(1), 79–96. DOI: 10.1111/ejed.12018

Riksförbund, L. (2004). En undersökning om den nya lärarutbildningens kvalitet [A survey of the quality of the new teacher education]. *Journal of Moral Education, 19*, 48–57.

Sanger, M., & Osguthorpe, R. (2005). Making sense of approaches to moral education. *Journal of Moral Education, 34*(1), 57–71. DOI: 10.1080/03057240500049323

Schwartz, S. H. (1992). Universals in the content and structure of values: Theoretical advances and empirical tests in 20 countries. In Zanna, M. P. (Ed.), Vol. 25, pp. 1–65). Advances in experimental social psychology. Academic Press., DOI: 10.1016/S0065-2601(08)60281-6

Schwartz, S. H. (2012). An overview of the Schwartz theory of basic values. *Online Readings in Psychology and Culture, 2*(1), 1–20. DOI: 10.9707/2307-0919.1116

Selwyn, N. (2019). *Should robots replace teachers? AI and the future of education*. Polity Press.

Selwyn, N. (2021). *Education and technology: Key issues and debates* (3rd ed.). Bloomsbury.

Shaftel, F. R. (1967). *Role playing for social values*. Prentice Hall.

Shute, V. J. (2008). Focus on formative feedback. *Review of Educational Research, 78*(1), 153–189. DOI: 10.3102/0034654307313795

Sockett, H. (2012). *Knowledge and virtue in teaching and learning: The primacy of dispositions*. Routledge. DOI: 10.4324/9780203155509

Sockett, H., & LePage, P. (2002). The missing language of the classroom: Teaching as a moral activity. *Teaching and Teacher Education, 18*(2), 159–171. DOI: 10.1016/S0742-051X(01)00061-0

Solomon, D., Watson, M. S., & Battistich, V. A. (2001). Teaching and schooling effects on moral/pro-social development. In V. Richardson (Ed.). *Handbook of research on teaching* (4th ed., pp. 566–603).

Stephenson, J., Ling, L., Burman, E., & Cooper, M. (1998). Values in education: A study of teachers' attitudes, beliefs and practices. *Educational Studies, 24*(1), 27–43. DOI: 10.1080/0305569980240102

Tarman, B., & Kuran, B. (2014). Teachers' perceptions about the relationship between learning levels of values in citizenship and human rights course and the environment. *Gazi University Journal Gazi Educational Faculty GUJGEF, 34*(2), 293–319.

Taylor, M., & Consortium of Institutions for Development and Research in Education in Europe. (1994). *Values education in Europe: A comparative overview of a survey of 26 countries in 1993*. Consortium of Institutions for Development and Research in Education in Europe.

Thornberg, R. (2009). The moral construction of the good pupil embedded in school rules. *Education, Citizenship and Social Justice, 4*(3), 245–261. DOI: 10.1177/1746197909340874

Thornberg, R. (2016). Values education in Nordic preschools: A commentary. *International Journal of Early Childhood, 48*(2), 241–257. DOI: 10.1007/s13158-016-0167-z

Ülavere, P., & Tammik, A. (2017). Value education in Estonian preschool child care institutions. *Journal of Teacher Education for Sustainability, 19*(1), 129–146. DOI: 10.1515/jtes-2017-0009

Ulusoy, K., & Dilmaç, B. (2012). *Değerler eğitimi* [In Turkish: Values education]. Pegem Press.

UNESCO. (2000). *Living values activities for children ages 3–7: Living Values Education Program*. UNESCO Publishing.

Varelas, M. (Ed.). (2012). *Identity construction and science education research: Learning, teaching, and being in multiple contexts* (Vol. 35). Springer Science & Business Media. DOI: 10.1007/978-94-6209-043-9

Varghese, M., Morgan, B., Johnston, B., & Johnson, K. A. (2005). Theorizing language teacher identity: Three perspectives and beyond. *Journal of Language, Identity, and Education, 4*(1), 21–44. DOI: 10.1207/s15327701jlie0401_2 PMID: 26913180

Veugelers, W., & Vedder, P. (2003). Values in teaching. *Teachers and Teaching, 9*(4), 377–389. DOI: 10.1080/1354060032000097262

Walsh, S. (2011). *Exploring classroom discourse: Language in action*. Routledge. DOI: 10.4324/9780203827826

Wiese, L. J., Patil, I., Schiff, D. S., & Magana, A. J. (2025). AI ethics education: A systematic literature review. *Computers and Education: Artificial Intelligence, 8*, 100405. DOI: 10.1016/j.caeai.2025.100405

Willemse, M., Lunenberg, M., & Korthagen, F. (2005). Values in education: A study on the preparation of student teachers for moral education. *Teaching and Teacher Education, 21*(6), 645–656.

Williamson, B. (2017). Big data in education: The digital future of learning, policy and practice. *Sage (Atlanta, Ga.)*. Advance online publication. DOI: 10.4135/9781529714920

Williamson, B., & Eynon, R. (2020). Historical threads, missing links, and future directions in AI in education. *Learning, Media and Technology, 45*(3), 223–235. DOI: 10.1080/17439884.2020.1798995

Yel, S., & Aladağ, S. (2009). Sosyal bilgilerde değerlerin öğretimi [In Turkish: Teaching values in social studies]. M. Safran (Ed.). Sosyal bilgiler öğretimi (s.118-145). Pegem Press.

Zawacki-Richter, O., Marín, V. I., Bond, M., & Gouverneur, F. (2019). Systematic review of research on artificial intelligence applications in higher education. *International Journal of Educational Technology in Higher Education, 16*(1), 39. DOI: 10.1186/s41239-019-0171-0

Chapter 24
Rethinking the Future of the Teaching Profession in the Age of Automation and Artificial Intelligence

Md. Ashrafuzzaman
http://orcid.org/0000-0003-2100-9998
University of Frontier Technology, Bangladesh

ABSTRACT

The rapid growth of automation and artificial intelligence (AI) is transforming educational systems, pedagogical practices, and teacher professional identity worldwide. Increasing public and political discourse regarding the potential replacement of human teachers by intelligent machines has intensified concerns about the declining attractiveness, status, and sustainability of the teaching profession. This chapter critically examines the assumption that AI can replace human teaching by advancing a human-centered perspective that positions teachers as essential to learning, socialization, and moral development. Drawing on a systematic narrative review of interdisciplinary research, the chapter analyzes how AI is reshaping instructional design, assessment, feedback, and classroom interaction while highlighting its limitations in addressing the cognitive, emotional, ethical, and sociocultural dimensions of teaching. It also discusses implications for professional development and policy reform, advocating collaborative human–AI models to support equitable and transformative education.

INTRODUCTION

The unprecedented expansion of automation and artificial intelligence (AI) is rapidly transforming social, economic, and educational systems worldwide (Tarafdar et al., 2025; Gidiotis & Hrastinski, 2024). Intelligent technologies have evolved over the last ten years to develop state-of-the-art generating models that can create human-imitating text, images, and instructional resources through sophisticated rule-based patterns and generative predictive coding. AI-based tools are now being used to offer personalized tutoring, automated grading, predictive analytics, and adaptive learning paths in the field of education, challenging conventional pedagogical approaches and practices (Ahmed et al., 2026; Kawoosa & Prashar, 2026; Ashrafuzzaman et al., 2025; Terantino et al., 2025; Holmes et al., 2019; Zawacki-Richter et al., 2019).

The accelerated technological growth has created a lot of debate on the relevance of teachers in the future. Major accounts have contained speculations that AI will soon substitute teachers and that teaching is a task that can be reduced to the transfer of information and acquisition of skills. The market-driven technology companies and the policy agenda focusing on efficiency, scalability, and data-driven governance tend to support such discourse (Williamson, 2017; Selwyn,

DOI: 10.4018/979-8-3373-8983-7.ch024

2022). These assertions, however, run the risk of simplifying the complexity of teaching into a multi-dimensional state and the loss of relationships, ethical and sociocultural underpinnings of teaching.

Meanwhile, world-education systems experience acute shortages in the number of teachers, worsening recruitment factors, and growing attrition. According to UNESCO (2023), more than 44 million additional teachers are needed by 2030 to achieve the targets in universal primary and secondary education. However, the teaching profession is increasingly less appealing because of workloads, emotional labor, low pay, lack of professionalism, and declining social status (Ingersoll et al., 2018; OECD, 2021). The implied notion that teachers will lose their jobs to machines can contribute to further undercutting of the professional identity and social status of teaching staff, which will increase the workforce instability.

Teaching is essentially a social career that is founded on human interaction, empathy, morality, and mediation of culture. The teachers assist not only the cognitive progress but also emotional well-being, socialization, identity formation, and moral reasoning (Biesta, 2015). These aspects of instruction are not susceptible to algorithmic replication, since they stand on the contextual knowledge, emotional sensitivity and moral judgment abilities that are distinctively human.

The chapter critically questions the arguments on teacher replacement by AI, developing a humanistic approach to intelligent technologies as pedagogical and not professional replacements. It discusses the way AI is transforming the method of instruction, the system of assessment, and the nature of the teacher, as well as the natural constraints of the automation process in relation to the social and ethical needs of education that cannot be fulfilled. The chapter seeks to offer a holistic perspective of how the relationship between teachers and intelligent systems has changed using the insights of learning sciences, sociology, educational technology, and policy research. Accordingly, this study addresses the following research objectives:

i. To critically analyze the impact of automation and artificial intelligence on the roles, identity, and professional autonomy of teachers.
ii. To examine the pedagogical, emotional, ethical, and sociocultural dimensions of teaching that resist full technological automation.
iii. To explore how AI-driven educational technologies are transforming instructional practices, assessment systems, and teacher-student interactions.
iv. To assess global policy responses and institutional strategies aimed at sustaining the teaching profession in the context of digital transformation.
v. To propose a human-centered conceptual framework for integrating artificial intelligence into education in ways that enhance, rather than diminish, the professional relevance of teachers.

The chapter also has implications on teacher education, continuing professional development, and educational policy, and cries out that educators must immediately develop AI literacy, ethical reasoning, and pedagogical design skills. Finally, it promotes the paradigm shift of technological determinism towards collaborative human-AI models, which can improve the quality of the teaching process without sacrificing professional autonomy and human agency.

CONCEPTUAL AND THEORETICAL FRAMEWORK: TEACHING IN THE AGE OF AI

To interpret the consequences of automation and artificial intelligence in teaching, a strong interdisciplinary approach to the analysis of educational theory, sociological viewpoints, and human-computer interactions research is needed. This chapter is based on four overlapping theoretical perspectives: sociocultural learning theory, teacher professional identity theory, critical digital pedagogy, and human-centered artificial intelligence.

Automation and Artificial Intelligence in Education

In educational contexts, the term 'automation' is used to mean delegating instructional, administrative, and evaluative functions to computational systems. AI-based educational technology currently includes automated grading, intelligent tutoring, adaptive learning, predictive analytics, and content generation (Holmes et al., 2019). Such systems are based on machine learning algorithms that are trained with the help of huge datasets, as they allow adapting to the behavior and performance of learners in real-time.

Large language models, machine learning and other generative AI models continue to expand automation through the generation of instructional content, academic performance, assessments, and feedback with significantly little human effort (Johora et al., 2025; Kasneci et al., 2023). Although these features provide better effectiveness and scalability, they also pose deeper concerns regarding the quality of pedagogy, ethical responsibility, and professional freedom (Selwyn, 2022; Williamson & Eynon, 2020).

From a critical perspective, technological innovation is not value-neutral. Educational technologies represent ideological suppositions of efficiency, standardization, and control, where measurement of results is commonly favored over comprehensive growth (Williamson, 2017). Therefore, the sociopolitical embeddedness of AI in education demands its analysis of the aspects of implications on professional relations of power.

Sociocultural Perspectives on Teaching and Learning

The sociocultural learning theory underlines that cultural tools, historical contexts and social interaction are the mediating factors in cognition (Vygotsky, 1978). Learning is a dialogic, collaborative, and guided process in communities of practice. The teachers are considered to be in the core mediational role, whereby they support the understanding of the learners and guide them through the zones of proximal development.

In this view, teaching is more or less relational and situational. It involves an awareness of the emotional conditions, cultural affiliations, social identities and lived experiences of learners (Rogoff, 2003). These subtle interactions cannot be completely modeled by algorithmic models, which work on probabilistic associations and not on social meaning.

Artificial intelligence-based systems can be similar to adaptive instruction, but in fact, they do not know human emotions, cultural sensitivity, and ethical decision-making. Therefore, AI may improve teaching and learning efficiency (Strzelecki, 2024), but it will not be able to reproduce the socially situated, affective, and ethical aspects of teaching (Darby, 2019).

Teacher Professional Identity and Agency

Teacher professional identity describes the way teachers view themselves and their place in larger institutional, cultural and political contexts. It is determined by individual beliefs, professional values, policy framework, and workplace circumstances (Beauchamp & Thomas, 2009).

The growth of AI in education carries with it important consequences of teacher identity. The automation of teaching activities also creates a danger of making teachers less professional and creative in their pedagogical choices by turning them into the facilitators of pre-programmed information (Selwyn, 2022). According to empirical research, overdependence on algorithmic systems may result in deskilling of teachers, surveillance, and loss of professional autonomy (Williamson & Eynon, 2020; Perrotta et al., 2021).

On the other hand, AI can assist teachers by enabling them in instructional design (Abualgasim & Ahmed, 2025) and formative assessment and differentiated learning when applied in human-centered frameworks (Terantino et al., 2025; Holmes et al., 2019). To maintain pedagogical quality, ethical accountability and professional motivation, the maintenance of teacher agency is therefore a priority.

Human-Centered Artificial Intelligence

Human-centered AI (HCAI) focuses on the design of intelligent systems that grow human capabilities without violating ethical values, transparency, accountability, and inclusivity (Shneiderman, 2020). Instead of substituting human expertise, HCAI aims to aid the process of decision-making, creativity, and social well-being.

Human-centered AI is actively used in the field of education, where teacher agency, pedagogical freedom, and learner-centered design are of primary importance (Holmes et al., 2022). This paradigm acknowledges teachers as co-designers of learning environments that are AI-enhanced, in that the use of technological systems does not impose learning requirements on teachers but supports them.

The ethical aspects of human-centered approaches are also anticipated, such as information privacy, algorithmic bias, monitoring, and fairness. In the absence of these measures, AI is likely to contribute to the growth of social inequality and the deterioration of trust in educational establishments (Williamson & Eynon, 2020; Selwyn, 2022).

Conceptual Model: Teaching in the Age of AI

Building on these theoretical foundations, this chapter proposes a multidimensional conceptual model of teaching in the age of automation and artificial intelligence, structured around four interrelated domains (see Figure 1):

Figure 1. Conceptual Framework: Teaching in the Age of AI

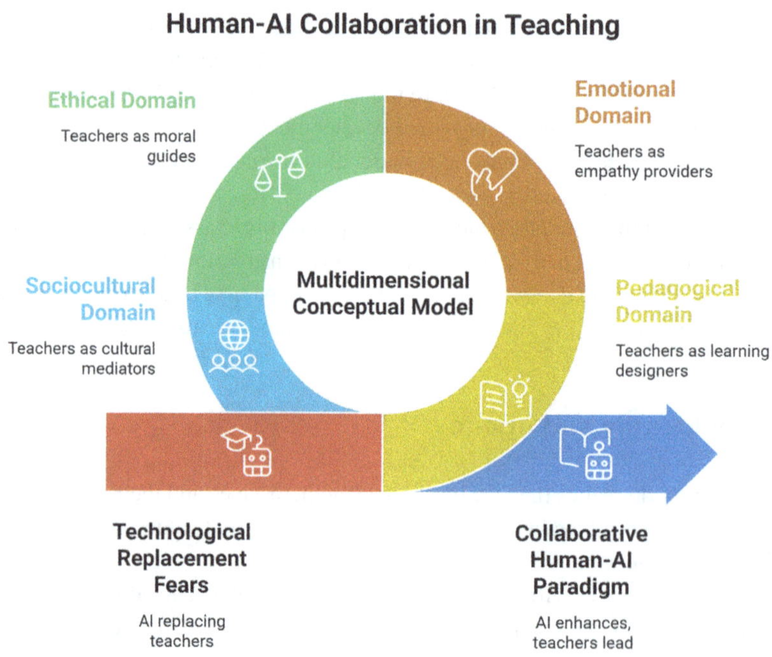

a) Pedagogical Domain: Teachers as learning designers, facilitators of inquiry, and cultivators of higher-order thinking.
b) Emotional Domain: Teachers as providers of empathy, motivation, care, and socio-emotional scaffolding.
c) Ethical Domain: Teachers as moral agents guiding value formation, ethical reasoning, and civic responsibility.
d) Sociocultural Domain: Teachers as mediators of cultural knowledge, identity development, and social belonging.

Although the conceptual model is effective in outlining four domains of teaching in the age of AI, it is analyzable in the sense that it seeks to examine the dynamic tensions and interdependencies among the four domains of teaching instead of treating the domains as distinct entities. Practically, pedagogical decisions cannot be made without emotional and ethical considerations; to elaborate, designing inquiry-based learning (pedagogical) will require sensitivity to student motivation and well-being (emotional), and fairness and inclusivity (ethical). Likewise, the sociocultural domain cuts across all the other domains by influencing the construction, interpretation, and valuation of knowledge in particular contexts. However, structural asymmetries of the human-AI relationship can also be observed by the model: although AI can be scaled to accommodate personalization and efficiency, it is still limited in addressing ambiguity, moral judgment, and cultural nuance. This leads to a dependency effect, where excessive dependence on algorithmic output may unintentionally constrain pedagogical flexibility or reinforce other biases unless critically mediated by teachers. Thus, the model can be construed as both a descriptive framework and a normative guide, which pre-empts teacher agency as a regulatory instrument. Its practical usefulness lies in its ability to negotiate these areas effectively in context by educators, to ensure that the integration of AI does not displace these relationship, ethical, and culturally embedded dimensions of teaching.

Within this model, AI functions as an enabling infrastructure that enhances efficiency, personalization, and access, while teachers retain primary responsibility for relational, ethical, and contextual dimensions of learning. This framework rejects deterministic narratives of technological replacement and instead advances a collaborative human–AI paradigm that preserves professional dignity and pedagogical integrity.

METHODOLOGY

This chapter uses a systematic narrative review approach (see Figure 2), which incorporates the critical synthesis of interdisciplinary literature to study how automation and artificial intelligence (AI) can influence the teaching profession. The review-based method serves specifically well in investigating new areas of research with diversity in concepts, pluralism of methods, and fast technological transformation (Snyder, 2019). This chapter draws a comprehensive view of the pedagogical, professional, ethical and policy implications of AI integration by synthesizing the outcomes of the field of educational technology, teacher education, learning sciences, sociology and policy studies. The analysis is directed by a critical interpretive synthesis approach that enables the development of concepts on a conceptual level rather than simply aggregating the empirical results (Dixon-Woods et al., 2005). This method allows more intense theoretical involvement, reevaluation of the existing evidence according to sociocultural, human-oriented, and ethical models.

Figure 2. Research Methodology for AI in Teaching

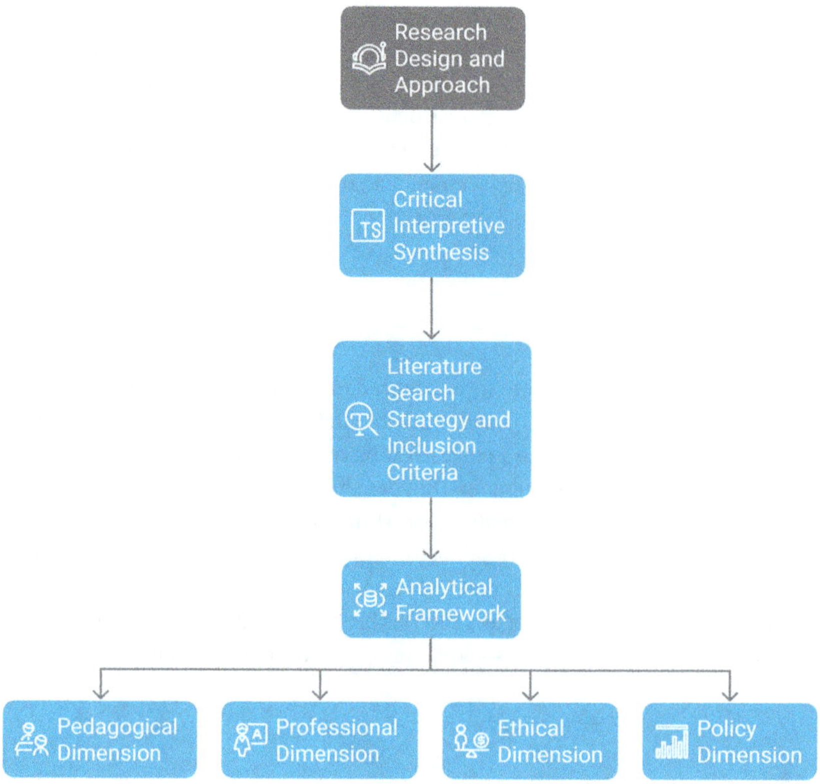

Search Strategy

This research uses the PRISMA framework (Figure 3), which ensures rigour, transparency and replicability in the synthesis of literature about artificial intelligence (AI) and teaching. The review process involved four stages: identification, screening, eligibility, and inclusion. During the identification phase, terms such as "artificial intelligence in education," "automation and teaching", "teacher professional identity", "human-AI collaboration", "AI pedagogy", "educational -automation", and "teacher education and AI" were used with Boolean operators to search Scopus-indexed databases Elsevier -ScienceDirect, SpringerLink, Routledge, Taylor & Francis, SAGE Journals, Emerald Insight, IEEE Xplore and ERIC for research published between 2019 and 2026. Boolean operators were employed with keywords including "artificial intelligence in education," "automation and teaching," and "teacher professional identity", resulting in 191 records. In the screening phase, 28 duplicates were removed, resulting in 163 records; 98 were excluded after reviewing titles and abstracts. During the eligibility stage, 65 full-text sources were appraised using inclusion and exclusion criteria, leading to the exclusion of 31 studies. A total of 34 studies were included for qualitative synthesis, including peer-reviewed journal articles and a range of scholarly books. They were reviewed using a multifaceted framework that incorporated pedagogical, professional, ethical, and policy perspectives, thereby increasing the validity and rigor of the review.

Figure 3. PRISMA Declaration for the Process of Searching and Filtering

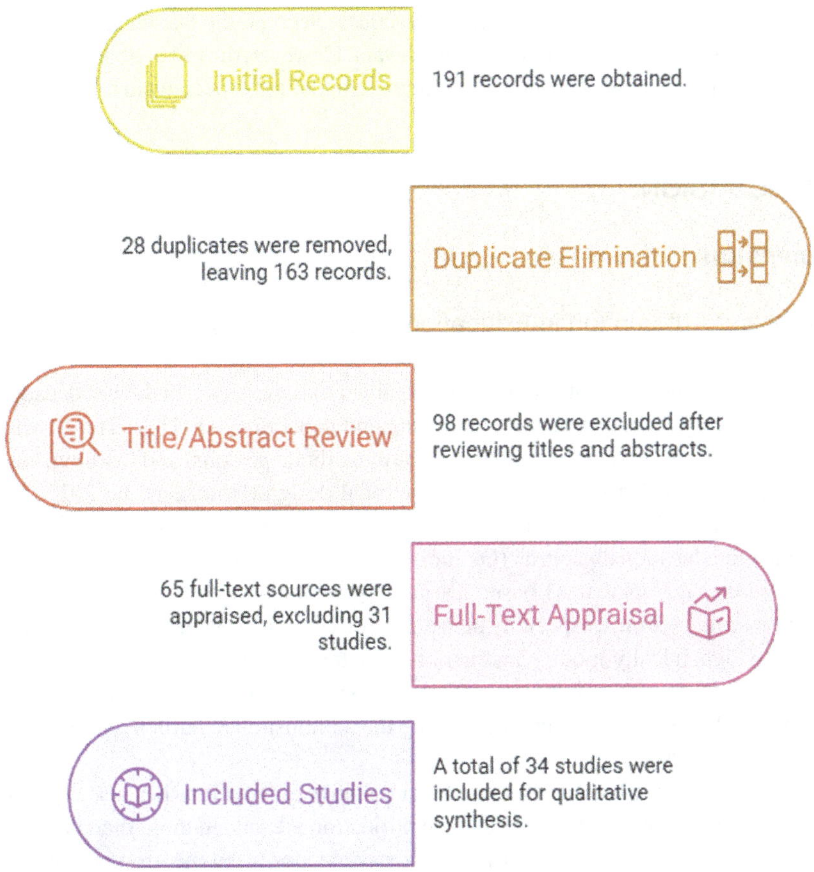

ANALYTICAL FRAMEWORK

The analytical framework formed in this chapter is a set of four dimensions that are interrelated and they are the following: pedagogical, professional, ethical, and policy. The pedagogical aspect focuses on the classroom dynamics, pedagogical design, learning and assessment in AI- mediated settings. The professional dimension underlines teacher identity, agency, autonomy, workload, and job satisfaction in the context of the impact of automation on the nature and meaning of professional practice. The ethical aspect covers the concerns of equity, algorithmic bias, data privacy, moral development, and social justice and brings up the normative duties involved in the integration of AI. The policy dimension is the set of policies of the government, labor market planning schemes, digital reform policies, and international education policies influencing the systemic implementation of intelligent technologies. Taken together, this multidimensional framework allows the balance of micro-level analysis of pedagogical processes, meso-level analysis of institutional practices, and macro-level analysis of policy impacts in the changing relationship between artificial intelligence and teaching profession.

Limitations of the Methodology

Although systematic narrative reviews allow deep conceptual integration, there are some limitations. First, use of secondary data limits first-hand observation of classroom practices. Second, the fast-changing aspect of AI technology implies that empirical evidence can soon be outdated and irrelevant. However, the review-based approach can greatly contribute to theory construction, policy examination, and conceptual modeling, especially in new interdisciplinary research.

RESULTS AND DISCUSSION

Pedagogical Dimension

Artificial Intelligence and Automation in Education: Global Trends

Introducing artificial intelligence (AI) into education has gained massive steam in the last decade, especially after the progress of machine learning and natural language processing and generative AI. There is a growing utilization of AI-powered technologies in educational systems around the globe to facilitate personalized learning, automated assessment, predictive analytics, intelligent tutoring systems, and instructional design (Holmes et al., 2022; Kasneci et al., 2023). These technologies suggest scalability, effectiveness, and general improvement of teaching and learning processes based on data, transforming the old educational patterns (Okulicz-Kozaryn et al., 2026).

Recent empirical research suggests that AI-based learning systems could greatly improve learning outcomes to be implemented in adaptive learning settings, especially in mathematics, science, and language learning (Wang et al., 2024). Adaptive learning systems dynamically modify instructional content in response to learner performance, facilitating differentiated instruction on a large scale (Chen et al., 2022). Likewise, automated feedback systems have the potential to employ immediate formative learning assessment, decreasing the administrative burden among teachers, and increasing learner participation (Zhai et al., 2023).

Nevertheless, critics believe that the fast spread of AI technologies is dangerous because it promotes instrumentalist attitudes to teaching and learning, where efficiency and quantification are valued more than holistic learning and moral growth (Selwyn, 2022; Williamson & Eynon, 2020). They are compounded by the growing involvement of individual technology companies in policy-making on educational matters and the frequent promotion of such policies to fulfill commercial goals instead of being founded on educational principles (Williamson, 2017; Perrotta et al., 2021).

Large language models and other generative AI systems have only exacerbated the discussions of teacher replacement. The models have the potential to create lesson plans, assessments, feedback, and explanatory material, which has resulted in claims that the functions of teaching can be automated completely (Kasneci et al., 2023). However, studies continually underscore the fact that these systems do not have the contextual awareness, moral reasoning, and emotional intelligence that are the key elements of effective pedagogy (Holmes et al., 2022; Darby, 2019).

Redefining the Role of Teachers in the AI-Driven Educational Ecosystem

The swift spread of artificial intelligence (AI) technologies in education has caused a profound reassessment of the roles, duties, and professional identities of teachers. Instead of replacing teachers, AI-based systems bring educators closer to the role of learning designers, facilitators, mentors, and ethical mediators (Oh & Ahn, 2024; Saravanan & Kamrozzaman, 2025). This shift is part of the general paradigm shift towards content transmission models to learner-centred, adaptive, and data-informed pedagogies (UNESCO, 2024).

According to recent empirical research, teachers view AI as an additive force that automates administrative functions and increases the elements of personalization and formative assessment, releasing the instructional time to higher-order pedagogic activities (Saravanan & Kamrozzaman, 2025). Oh and Ahn (2024) worked with 100 elementary teachers in South Korea, conducting a mixed-method research that showed that teachers were highly open to AI in terms of workload reduction but showed great fears regarding the inability of AI to mirror emotional intelligence, ethical judgment, and moral reasoning skills that teachers regarded as part of being a good teacher.

Such results support the concept of human-AI complementary relationships, according to which AI in education must complement professional pedagogical skills instead of replacing them (Holmes et al., 2024; Luckin, 2025). In this conceptualisation, educators will continue to be essential as emotional attachments, socio-cultural intermediaries, and epistemic mentors so that learning can be local, inclusive, and ethical.

Pedagogical Transformation in the Age of Intelligent Technologies

The use of AI in the classroom has led to a major change in pedagogy. Learner-centered, data-driven and personalized learning environments are slowly replacing traditional teacher-centered approaches to learning (Chen et al., 2022; Ifenthaler & Schumacher, 2023). The role of teachers has shifted towards being facilitators, mentors and designers of learning experiences, leading students through inquiry-based, collaborative and technology-mediated learning experiences. Instead of viewing AI as inherently oppressive, Chatzichristofis (2025) claims that, when placed in educator-led, dialogic, and culturally responsive settings, AI can facilitate inclusive and inquiry-based learning.

A number of studies pinpoint the pedagogical advantages of AI-enhanced learning especially to assist individualized learning paths, formative assessment, and learning analytics (Holmes et al., 2019; Wang et al., 2024a). The AI-enabled dashboards enable the teacher to track the progress of students in real time, which in turn allows targeted interventions as well as adaptive instruction. Besides, intelligent tutoring systems proved to be effective in scaffolding problem-solving knowledge and conceptual knowledge (VanLehn, 2011).

Although these benefits exist, pedagogical reductionism is discouraged, as it is the redefinition of teaching based on algorithmic optimization more than person-centered interaction (Selwyn, 2022). The practice of teaching, to a larger degree, requires emotional labour, moral judgment and socio-cultural mediation which cannot be formalized and automated. Over-dependence on algorithmic systems is associated with the risk of curricular narrowness, as well as prioritizing measurable skills over critical thinking, creativity, and ethical judgment (Darby, 2019; OECD, 2021).

Moreover, there is also an issue of datafication and surveillance in AI-powered classrooms. Learning analytics systems gather huge amounts of information about students, posing ethical challenges on the realm of privacy, consent, bias, and algorithmic governance (Williamson & Eynon, 2020; Zawacki-Richter et al., 2019). These practices can undermine trust, limit pedagogical autonomy, and strengthen inequities, especially when taking place in low-resource settings (Selwyn, 2022).

AI-Supported Pedagogical Innovation: Opportunities and Constraints Analysis

The intelligent tutoring systems, learning analytics applications, and generative AI tools have proven to be highly promising as AI-driven instructional technologies to improve instructional design, differentiated instruction, and engagement with learners (Ahmed et al., 2026; Zawacki-Richter et al., 2024). Individualized learning journeys, immediate feedback, and predictive analytics enable the teacher to detect learning deficiencies and modify teaching plans to meet them (Khosravi et al., 2025).

Nevertheless, there are also critical pedagogical limitations as noted in the empirical evidence. Educators have been noted to complain of the issues of algorithmic opacity, data confidentiality, pedagogical dissonance, as well as technological addiction (Saravanan & Kamrozzaman, 2025; UNESCO, 2024). Furthermore, the generative AI applications tend to perform poorly in context-sensitive thinking, academic fact-finding, and moral judgment-making features that serve to support the argument in support of the need to teach by humans (Oh & Ahn, 2024).

These problems are further complicated in the context of developing countries by infrastructural inequalities, digital disparities, and teacher training inadequacies (Nyaaba, 2025). The Ghana design case study found that localized AI tools can contribute greatly to the preparation of pre-service teachers in a culturally contextualized setting, a limitation to scalability exists due to the access barrier, insufficient linguistic datasets, and financial constraints (Nyaaba, 2025). This highlights the value of global artificial intelligence systems or glocalised AI models that combine world-sized technological norms and local pedagogical conditions.

PROFESSIONAL DIMENSION

Teacher Professional Identity in Digitally Mediated Environments

Digital transformation is changing teachers' professional identity. Research suggests that the spread of AI-driven technologies restructures the functions of teachers, professional agency, and professional relationships at work (Day & Gu, 2014; Beauchamp & Thomas, 2009). Whereas certain teachers feel empowered by AI, others feel anxious, deskilled, and deprived of professional control (Perrotta et al., 2021; Ifenthaler & Schumacher, 2023).

Empirical studies in various settings show that educators tend to have a peripheral role in the process of making decisions that may affect technology implementation, which is commonly spurred by a policy agenda or business interest (Williamson, 2017; Selwyn, 2022). This top-down practice undermines teacher autonomy and is one of the causes of professional alienation.

Recent longitudinal research also indicates that long-term experiences of algorithmic instructional systems can transform the pedagogical beliefs of teachers so as to promote adherence to standardized procedures instead of reflective practice (Zhai et al., 2023). Increasingly, teachers become the actors in the intermediary relationship between the learners and the algorithmic spaces, not interacting in the pedagogical engagement but acting as administrators of technical systems (Holmes et al., 2022).

Nevertheless, in situations where educators play an active role in the co-design and assessment of AI solutions, favorable professional impacts are created. The models of participatory design improve teacher agency, pedagogical creativity, or professional satisfaction (Ifenthaler & Schumacher, 2023; Holmes et al., 2022). These results highlight the significance of teacher-based AI integration models.

Can Teaching Be Automated? Cognitive, Emotional, and Ethical Dimensions

One of the most debated issues in the modern discourse is whether it is possible to entirely automate teaching. Although AI systems have proved to be exceptional in terms of processing data, recognizing patterns, and generating content, they are inherently restricted in terms of their relational and ethical aspects of education (Darby, 2019; Biesta, 2015).

The studies of cognitive science underline that learning is social, emotional, and embodied (Immordino-Yang et al., 2019). Emotional involvement has a great impact on memory, motivation and conceptual understanding. The educators have a strong role in developing positive emotional climate, building resilience and developing the identity of the learners- something that the AI systems cannot imitate.

The restrictions of automation are further shown by ethical reasoning and moral development. The teachers are modeling values, leading ethical reflection, and developing civic responsibility during dialog engagement and lived example (Biesta, 2015). Algorithms have no moral agency and cannot hold ethical consequences hence they do not make them the right moral educator (Holmes et al., 2022).

Moreover, the sociocultural orientations focus on the significance of culture, identity construction, and social connectedness in education (Rogoff, 2003). The teachers enable the learners to become part of the communities of practice, language growth, cultural understanding and social involvement. The processes are so entrenched in human relations and they are not computational rules.

Teacher Education and Professional Development in the AI Era

Teacher education and professional development would require significant change in order to integrate AI into education. According to the current frameworks, it is necessary to develop AI literacy, ethical reasoning, data-informed pedagogy, and instructional design among teachers (Ifenthaler & Schumacher, 2023; Holmes et al., 2022).

Educational technology, learning analytics, and digital pedagogy are courses that are increasingly being included in pre-service teacher education programs and undergraduate educational technology programs. Nevertheless, a study has shown that there has been an ongoing lack in the willingness of teachers to critically assess AI systems and their meaningful implementation in pedagogy (Zawacki-Richter et al., 2019; Chen et al., 2022).

Models of continuous professional development that place a high value on reflective practice, collaborative learning, and experiences in the use of AI tools show encouraging results (OECD, 2021). Micro-credentialing, blended learning, and professional learning communities provide scale, flexible skill development and the development of a professional identity through peer support and formation of professional identity.

However, the global inequality in teacher professional development exists as a result of disparities in digital infrastructure, institutional capacity, and policy supporting this development. Access to high-quality training is an acute issue in the low-resource context, which concerns equity and inclusion issues on a global level (UNESCO, 2023; Selwyn, 2022).

Teacher Professional Identity in the Era of Generative AI

The advent of AI technologies focused on generating content has added to the concerns of professional displacement, deskilling, and identity loss among educators (Zawacki-Richter et al., 2024). Nevertheless, recent studies indicate that this is a more complex truth, the use of AI is transforming, and it is not reducing the professionalism of teachers (Luckin, 2025).

Professional identity reconstruction consists of reconstructing teachers as facilitators of hybrid intelligence by incorporating human pedagogical skills into computational ability (Holmes et al., 2024). Such a hybrid model demands new skills, such as the ability to use AI, interpret data ethically, design instructional methods that are adaptive, and online leadership (UNESCO, 2024).

Programmes of professional development focused on AI pedagogical integration have reported encouraging results in terms of enhancing teacher confidence, instructional innovation and student engagement (Khosravi et al., 2025). Nevertheless, there is systemic disparity in teacher upskilling, especially when the context is low-resource (Nyaaba, 2025).

ETHICAL DIMENSION

Emotional Intelligence, Ethics, and the Irreplaceable Human Dimension of Teaching

No matter how far affective computing has progressed, AI still seriously lacks the capacity to simulate emotional, moral, and relational aspects of teaching (Holmes et al., 2024; UNESCO, 2024). The teaching competencies that are not computational are emotional intelligence, empathy, ethical sensitivity, and cultural responsiveness.

The results of a study by Oh and Ahn (2024) revealed that the socio-emotional support was the most replaceable skill that teachers considered to be the most important part of their professional job. Interpersonal relationships are highly dependent on emotional health, motivation, identity formation, and moral reasoning in students, which cannot be authentic in AI. On the same note, Saravanan and Kamrozzaman (2025) noted that teachers were worried that AI-mediated learning environments reduce student curiosity, intrinsic motivation, and critical thinking.

There are also ethical aspects that make integration of AI more difficult. There is a great threat of algorithmic bias, data surveillance, intellectual property questions, and automated decision-making to the educational equity and learner autonomy (Williamson & Eynon, 2025). Therefore, teachers can be considered as moral watchdogs, as they make sure that the use of AI can be in accord with democratic principles, human dignity, and inclusive pedagogy.

POLICY DIMENSION

Policy Perspectives and Global Workforce Implications for Teacher Sustainability

The educational policies progressively present AI as an innovation, efficiency, and competitiveness driver. International organizations promote the use of AI in the learning process to improve resource distribution and access and provide better learning outcomes (OECD, 2021; UNESCO, 2023). But critics warn that the policy agendas tend to focus on technological modernity at the expense of teacher health and professional sustainability.

One of the main challenges of the education systems all over the world is the shortage of teachers, their burnout, and the loss of professional prestige (Ingersoll et al., 2018; OECD, 2021). It is often argued that AI is the answer to the labor shortage, but empirical studies indicate that, with the advent of technology, a solution to the relational and emotional needs of teaching cannot be found (Holmes et al., 2022; Selwyn, 2022).

Policies that focus on the human-AI partnership, teacher empowerment, and ethical governance show more promise of sustainable teaching restructuring. The areas that require strategic investment in terms of teacher professional development, inclusive technology development, and building institutional capacity are necessary to connect AI integration with educational values and social equity.

To keep the teaching profession alive in the era of AI, a system of holistic reform, including teacher training, professional development, working conditions, and socio-cultural appreciation is needed (Williamson & Eynon, 2025). The absence of proper precaution measures makes the introduction of AI a threat of amplifying teacher workload, surveillance pressures and professional deskilling.

UNESCO (2024) notes that the frameworks of AI governance should be human-centered and suggests that teachers should be involved in the process of designing, evaluating, and implementing AI. The ethical-by-design AI models, agentic teacher, and participative decision-making systems should be a priority of the national education systems.

Recent global developments make it clear that AI will never substitute teachers but can change the teaching process (Saravanan & Kamrozzaman, 2025). The integration of AI is therefore not sustainable based on technological acceleration but under strong policies in teacher empowerment that do not destroy the professional autonomy, dignity, and socio-emotional labour.

Human-Centered AI Integration Framework for Education

The proposed Human-Centered AI Integration Framework (see Figure 4) in Education will help incorporate artificial intelligence in education in the form that assists, supplements, and maintains the professional activities of teachers, enhances learning results, equity, and moral responsibility.

Figure 4. Human-Centered AI Integration Framework for Education

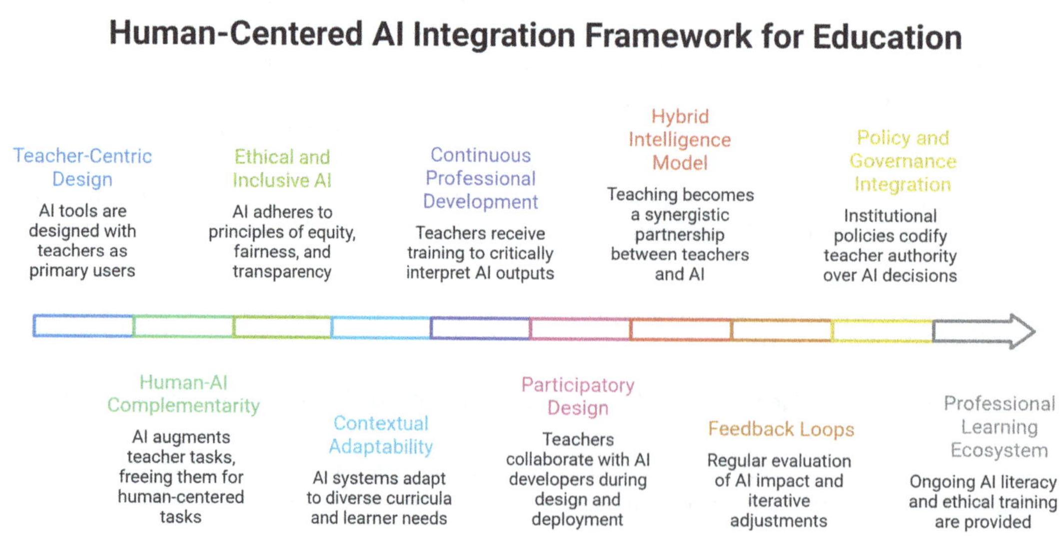

Core Principles

The process of implementing artificial intelligence in education must be informed with a number of principles that centralize and make teachers relevant to technology-enhanced learning environments. First, the teacher-centric design focuses on the idea that AI tools should be designed to have teachers as the main users and decision-makers in case pedagogical power does not fall into computers but rather stays in the hands of a teacher who can decide on instructional interventions. Second, human-AI complementarity emphasizes that AI is to complement, not supplant, human ability and support cognitive, analytical, and administrative capabilities, focusing on letting teachers concentrate more on the emotional, social, and ethical aspects of learning (Holmes et al., 2024). Third, ethical and inclusive AI states that educational technologies should be guided by the principles of equity, fairness, privacy, and transparency, and teachers should be able to monitor them to detect and eliminate possible biases in the algorithms (Williamson & Eynon, 2025). Fourth, contextual adaptability is the ability of the AI systems to be more flexible to suit various curricula, learner needs, and cultural contexts with the help of the teacher experience rather than strict algorithm prescriptions. Lastly, the ongoing professional growth is required to allow teachers to become AI-literate, critically evaluate the output of algorithms, create the activities based on AI support, and remain a pedagogical agent in the context of more and more digital learning.

Framework Components

The curriculum and learning design aspect is devoted to the creation of flexible and individualized learning streams that address the needs of different students. In this component, the teachers are very important in the process of mixing the curriculum objectives and the learning goals and contextualization of any given content with respect to the specific classroom setting and the backgrounds of the learners. This process can be assisted by artificial intelligence, which offers data-based knowledge and offers learning materials, as well as recommends an ideal content sequence. Instead of substituting teachers, AI serves as a decision-support system that will lead to improved instruction planning and allow teachers to compute more personalized and differentiated learning opportunities.

Formative assessment and feedback component underlines the idea of constant tracking of the learning process, along with the feedback. Teachers decode analytical observations that the AI systems produce, and apply them to modify the instructional techniques, detect the learning gaps, and offer insightful socio-emotional advice to learners. The value of AI technologies is that they help grade common things automatically, produce learning analytics, and provide predictive notifications in case students need extra help. Under this type of collaboration, AI is used to increase the efficiency in data processing, and teachers still have the responsibility of determining pedagogical judgement and personalized feedback.

Classroom interaction and collaboration component deals with student engagement, peer learning and collaborative construction of knowledge. Instructors lead discussions, encourage social-emotional learning and scaffold collaborative discussions that stimulate critical thinking and engagement. The AI tools are used to help suggest discussion points, track the participation trends, and discover the engagement trends in the classroom. In such a complementary interaction, teachers continue to be in control of creating valuable learning relationships and AI offers analytical support to enhance the participation and learning dynamics.

The professional development and decision Support element is based on enhancing the professional competencies and reflective practice of teachers. Teachers are engaged in AI literacy training, they take part in developing educational technologies co-designing them, and they assess the efficiency of AI-powered teaching tools. The AI systems facilitate these activities by monitoring the level of performance, suggesting corresponding continuous professional development (CPD) training, and assisting in assessing how the pedagogical process can be improved. This aspect shows that we need to empower teachers through technological knowledge to ensure that AI integration enhances professional autonomy and not erode it.

The ethics and equity governance element will make sure that the application of AI in education is ethical and leads to fair results. Teachers can be ethical guardians, protecting the privacy of the students, identifying possible biases in the algorithms, and providing equity in the educational processes that are facilitated by artificial intelligence. AI systems can help with this since they offer transparent mechanisms of decision-making and indicate irregularities or anomalies that need to be reviewed by people. Such joint supervision may serve as a way of keeping accountable and may also make sure that technological innovations are conducted in accordance with the rules of social justice and responsible educational practice.

Implementation Strategy

To introduce AI in education successfully, the implementation strategy must be well-structured based on collaboration and human-centered design. Participatory design is of paramount importance as it engages teachers directly in both the design and implementation of AI technologies so that those systems could constitute realistic classroom requirements and pedagogical priorities. Using hybrid intelligence models, AI and teachers exist in a mutually supportive relationship in which technology handles routine and data-intensive jobs, and teachers take on the more advanced duties of mentoring, ethical advice, and teaching decision-making. The feedback loops must also be continuous to track the impact of AI on teaching practice and learning outcomes to enable the institutions to make several changes and keep the pedagogy aligned. Moreover, it is required to integrate policy and governance to make it clear what institutional guidelines can substantiate teacher authority in decisions related to AI, what accountability structures can be identified, and what professional contributions are appreciated. Lastly, the creation of a professional learning ecosystem will guarantee that educators are continuously trained in AI literacy, ethical reasoning, and pedagogical innovation to be able to remain agile and flexible in a technology-enhanced learning setting.

Expected Outcomes

The adoption of a humanistic AI model in education can produce some valuable results. Firstly, it improves the relevance of teachers as it allows them to focus more on human-centered elements of teaching, including mentorship, creativity, and emotional support, which increases their professional identity and job satisfaction. Second, it helps to enhance student learning by integrating individualized AI-based learning analytics with the contextual knowledge and pedagogical experience of the teacher. Third, it encourages ethical and fair educational actions through the process of ensuring that educators maintain control over the AI engine and, therefore, provide a protective layer of fairness, transparency, and the privacy of students. Lastly, the framework sustains educational innovation by aligning technological development with teacher empowerment, institutional resilience and long-term educational development objectives. Such a balanced integration will make AI a valuable collaborator in education and not a replacement of the critical human position of teachers.

POLICY IMPLICATIONS

Reframing National AI-in-Education Strategies

Education policies must shift from technology-centric reform agendas toward teacher-centered AI integration models. National AI strategies should explicitly articulate the role of teachers as central pedagogical agents, ensuring that technological adoption strengthens rather than marginalizes professional autonomy (UNESCO, 2024).

The process of re-framing national AI-in-education strategies means to integrate pedagogical goals into technological planning. AI should not be viewed as a cost-cutting initiative but as an aid to enhance learning quality, equity, and access. Governments and educational institutions should have policies that define AI as a tool to support the improvement of learning quality, equity, and access, and not simply a way of saving money. Teachers should be involved in policy development, curriculum reform and procurement of AI to ensure alignment with the reality of the classroom. In addition, national policies need to incorporate ethical guidelines, mechanisms for accountability, and explicit data usage, privacy safeguarding and algorithmic transparency policies. Incorporating teachers at the heart of AI governance empowers education systems to foster sustainable innovation without compromising professional dignity and teaching integrity.

Reforming Teacher Education and Professional Development

The rise of artificial intelligence (AI) for educational purposes necessitates a profound transformation in the professional training of teachers and learning support staff. The advent of artificial intelligence (AI) in the educational field calls for a radical transformation of teacher education and professional development. Traditional teacher training programs tend to focus primarily on pedagogical and content knowledge, with little attention given to competencies in AI. However, in the digital context, teachers require skills which are both pedagogical, technological and ethical. Therefore, teacher education programs should include AI literacy, learning analytics, ethical technology use, human-AI pedagogical design, and data-informed instructional decision-making to equip teachers for AI-mediated learning environments.

Besides pre-service preparation, continual professional development (CPD) systems need to be transformed into lifelong learning systems to foster teachers' continuous adaptation to technological change. Educators can continually update their skills through micro-credentialing, online professional learning communities, collaborative networks of teachers, and digital workshops (Ifenthaler & Schumacher, 2023). Importantly, professional development should also reinforce teacher confidence and agency, and encourage reflective practice to ensure that the use of AI builds innovation and empowerment, not anxiety and professional dependency.

Strengthening Teacher Workforce Sustainability

One of the greatest challenges of education today is the shortage of teachers in almost every country in the world. In many countries, the rising workloads, the low status of the teaching profession, low salaries, and emotional exhaustion have been contributing factors to the profession's loss of interest. While AI technologies are often promoted as solutions to these shortages, overreliance on automation may unintentionally intensify professional dissatisfaction if teachers perceive technology as a threat to their roles and identities.

Policies aimed at strengthening teacher workforce sustainability must therefore prioritize teacher well-being alongside technological advancement. Without healthy working conditions, teachers won't be motivated and won't stay in the school. AI can have a positive impact by automating repetitive tasks like grading, attendance, and data management, freeing up time for teachers to focus on meaningful, instructional, and relational tasks. But these efficiencies must not be used instead of professional judgment and class discussion.

Competitive compensation and improved professional status are also essential. While there is a higher expectation of teachers across many educational systems to be better paid and to have opportunities for career progression, the reality is that this is not the case. Governments and institutions need to reinforce the profession of teacher as a highly skilled and socially valuable one once again. To reduce teacher burnout, mitigate teacher attrition, and support teacher professional development, public resources must be dedicated to teacher support services, mental health programs, workload management, and professional development. Without systemic investment in teacher well-being, technological innovation risks accelerating professional attrition (OECD, 2021; UNESCO, 2023). In addition to technological infrastructure, it is equally important to maintain a stable, respected and motivated teaching team to ensure the sustainable integration of AI.

Ethical and Social Considerations

The growth of AI also brings serious ethical concerns, such as bias in the algorithms, surveillance of data, invasion of privacy, transparency and online inequality (Wang et al., 2024b). Educational technologies are guided by ethical gatekeepers, who make sure that they include, promote equity, and democratic participation (Williamson & Eynon, 2025). To address these challenges, AI governance frameworks must ensure transparency, accountability, fairness, and cultural sensitivity. Failure to address these dimensions risks reinforcing global educational inequities and undermining public trust.

CONCLUSION

The chapter has critically looked at the future of teaching in the era of automation and artificial intelligence, and dismissed simplistic replacement accounts in favor of a human-centered collaboration paradigm. The discussion shows that the teaching profession is essentially a human discipline based on the idea of empathy, moral judgment, cultural intermediation, and trustful relationships. Although the possibilities of AI in pedagogy are unprecedented, it adds value to teacher experience but does not replace it. The only way to make education systems in the digital era sustainable is, therefore, to regain the teaching profession as one that is noble, intellectually engaging, and socially imperative. Finally, it is not about the substitution of teachers with AI, but rather about the empowerment of teachers to create the ethical, inclusive, and human-centered future of education by the society. The findings synthesized in this chapter are very critical of deterministic arguments that artificial intelligence will replace teachers. Instead, all arguments point to one direction, the human-AI cooperation paradigm, in which, pedagogical practice is not being substituted by the intelligent technologies, but rather aided by them. Education is also brought out as a multidimensional professional practice, which consists of cognitive facilitation, emotional mentoring, moral guidance and sociocultural mediation. The modern AI systems do not have the capability of calculating these aspects. Even though automation can effectively manage instructional logistics, adaptive learning, and formative feedback, empathy, moral judgment, identity creation, and relational trust, which form the focal point of the educational practice, cannot be replaced. This remodeling causes teachers not to be the traditional experts, but the architects of the worlds of hybrid intelligences, the coordinators of the relations between students and intelligent technologies. The future of teaching is not, however, in the struggle with technological change but in the roadmap of professionally redesigning the roles, competencies, and identities.

Note from Publisher

Correction Notice: A correction to this manuscript has been published.
Reason: Poor Image Quality
The author supplied better quality images after publication. All images in the chapter have been replaced.
Correction Date: 14th August 2026

REFERENCES

Abualgasim, S. D. A., & Ahmed, Z. E. (2025). Artificial intelligence in education: Partner or replacement for teachers? In Khan, S., & Pringuet, P. (Eds.), *Potential of AI to replace teachers' expertise: Ethics and challenges* (pp. 265–272). IGI Global Scientific Publishing., DOI: 10.4018/979-8-3373-0396-3.ch010

Ahmed, S., Shanta, M. I., Ashrafuzzaman, M., & Hossen, R. (2026). Integrating transformers to outperform classical and deep learning in ChatGPT-in-education sentiment analysis with an explainable web app. *Discover Artificial Intelligence*, *6*(1), 504. Advance online publication. DOI: 10.1007/s44163-026-01277-1

Ashrafuzzaman, M., Mimmo, S. S., Noyon, M. M. I., & Khan, M. R. (2025). AI as a learning partner: Exploring ethical awareness of engineering students. *INTI Journal*, *5*(18). Advance online publication. DOI: 10.61453/INTIj.202569

Beauchamp, C., & Thomas, L. (2009). Understanding teacher identity: An overview of issues in the literature and implications for teacher education. *Cambridge Journal of Education*, *39*(2), 175–189. DOI: 10.1080/03057640902902252

Biesta, G. (2015). *Good education in an age of measurement: Ethics, politics, democracy*. Routledge. DOI: 10.4324/9781315634319

Chatzichristofis, S. A. (2025). Reframing AI in education: A pedagogical opportunity, not a technocratic threat. *Journal of Research in Science Teaching*, *63*(1), 97–103. DOI: 10.1002/tea.70024

Chen, L., Chen, P., & Lin, Z. (2022). Artificial intelligence in education: A review. *IEEE Access : Practical Innovations, Open Solutions*, *10*, 75264–75278. DOI: 10.1109/ACCESS.2022.3188795

Darby, F. (2019). *Small teaching online: Applying learning science in online classes*. Jossey-Bass.

Day, C., & Gu, Q. (2014). *Resilient teachers, resilient schools*. Routledge.

Dixon-Woods, M., Agarwal, S., Young, B., Jones, D., & Sutton, A. (2005). Integrative approaches to qualitative research. *Journal of Health Services Research & Policy*, *11*(1), 45–52. DOI: 10.1177/1355819605010001110 PMID: 15667704

Gidiotis, I., & Hrastinski, S. (2024). Imagining the future of artificial intelligence in education: A review of social science fiction. *Learning, Media and Technology*, *51*(1), 35–47. DOI: 10.1080/17439884.2024.2365829

Holmes, W., Bialik, M., & Fadel, C. (2019). *Artificial intelligence in education: Promises and implications for teaching and learning*. Center for Curriculum Redesign.

Holmes, W., Bialik, M., & Fadel, C. (2024). *Artificial intelligence in education: Promises and implications for teaching and learning* (2nd ed.). Center for Curriculum Redesign.

Holmes, W., Tuomi, I., & Fadel, C. (2022). Ethics of AI in education: Towards a community-wide framework. *Educational Technology Research and Development*, *70*(1), 455–473. DOI: 10.1007/s11423-021-10044-2

Ifenthaler, D., & Schumacher, C. (2023). Teacher education in the age of AI. *Teaching and Teacher Education*, *125*, 104044. DOI: 10.1016/j.tate.2023.104044

Immordino-Yang, M. H., Darling-Hammond, L., & Krone, C. (2019). The brain basis for integrated social, emotional, and academic development. *Annual Review of Psychology*, *70*, 41–65.

Ingersoll, R., Merrill, L., & Stuckey, D. (2018). *Seven trends: The transformation of the teaching force*. CPRE.

Johora, F. T., Hasan, M. N., Rajbongshi, A., Ashrafuzzaman, M., & Akter, F. (2025). An explainable AI-based approach for predicting undergraduate students' academic performance. *Array (New York, N.Y.)*, *26*, 100384. DOI: 10.1016/j.array.2025.100384

Kasneci, E., Sessler, K., Küchemann, S., Bannert, M., Dementieva, D., Fischer, F., Gasser, U., Groh, G., Günnemann, S., Hüllermeier, E., Krusche, S., Kutyniok, G., Michaeli, T., Nerdel, C., Pfeffer, J., Poquet, O., Sailer, M., Schmidt, A., Seidel, T., & Kasneci, G. (2023). ChatGPT for good? On opportunities and challenges of large language models for education. *Learning and Individual Differences*, *103*, 102274. DOI: 10.1016/j.lindif.2023.102274

Kawoosa, A. I., & Prashar, D. (2026). The transformation of education: Artificial intelligence replacing traditional classroom teaching. In Kadry, S., & Balasubramaniam, S. (Eds.), *Artificial intelligence in education.*, DOI: 10.5772/intechopen.1012993

Khosravi, H., Kitto, K., & Gašević, D. (2025). Data-informed teaching: The role of learning analytics in adaptive pedagogy. *Computers & Education: Artificial Intelligence*, *6*, 100141. DOI: 10.1016/j.caeai.2024.100141

Luckin, R. (2025). *AI for school teachers: Transforming pedagogy and professional identity*. Routledge.

Nyaaba, M. (2025). Glocalizing generative AI in education for the Global South: The design case of 21st century teacher educator AI for Ghana. *Computers & Education: Artificial Intelligence*, *7*, 100167. DOI: 10.1016/j.caeai.2025.100167

OECD. (2021). *Teachers and school leaders as valued professionals*. OECD Publishing.

Oh, S.-Y., & Ahn, Y. (2024). Exploring teachers' perceptions of artificial intelligence: Socio-emotional deficiency as opportunity and challenge in human–AI complementarity. *Computers & Education: Artificial Intelligence*, *5*, 100129. DOI: 10.1016/j.caeai.2024.100129

Okulicz-Kozaryn, W., Artyukhov, A., & Artyukhova, N. (2026). Will AI replace us? Changing the university teacher role. *Societies (Basel, Switzerland)*, *16*(1), 32. DOI: 10.3390/soc16010032

Perrotta, C., Gulson, K., Williamson, B., & Witzenberger, K. (2021). Automation, big data and the politics of education. *British Journal of Educational Technology*, *52*(2), 467–482.

Rogoff, B. (2003). *The cultural nature of human development*. Oxford University Press.

Saravanan, T., & Kamrozzaman, N. A. (2025). Artificial intelligence in primary education: Teacher perceptions, instructional decisions, and integration challenges. *International Journal of Research and Innovation in Social Science*, *9*(10), 9393–9406. DOI: 10.47772/IJRISS.2025.909000772

Selwyn, N. (2022). *Should robots replace teachers? AI and the future of education*. Polity Press.

Shneiderman, B. (2020). Human-centered AI. *International Journal of Human-Computer Interaction*, *36*(6), 495–504. DOI: 10.1080/10447318.2020.1741118

Snyder, H. (2019). Literature review methodology. *Journal of Business Research*, *104*, 333–339. DOI: 10.1016/j.jbusres.2019.07.039

Tarafdar, S., Afroz, S., & Ashrafuzzaman, M. (2025). Artificial intelligence and the future of education in Bangladesh. In *Advances in educational technologies and instructional design book series* (pp. 287–320). DOI: 10.4018/979-8-3693-7949-3.ch011

Terantino, J., Zaheer, S., & Zhu, Y. (2025). Redefining the role of educators, not replacing them. In Khan, S., & Pringuet, P. (Eds.), *Potential of AI to replace teachers' expertise: ethics and challenges* (pp. 221–264). IGI Global Scientific Publishing., DOI: 10.4018/979-8-3373-0396-3.ch009

UNESCO. (2023). *Global report on teachers: Addressing teacher shortages*. UNESCO Publishing.

UNESCO. (2024). *Guidance on generative AI in education and research*. UNESCO Publishing.

VanLehn, K. (2011). The relative effectiveness of human tutoring, intelligent tutoring systems, and other tutoring systems. *Educational Psychologist*, *46*(4), 197–221. DOI: 10.1080/00461520.2011.611369

Wang, S., Wang, F., Zhu, Z., Wang, J., Tran, T., & Du, Z. (2024b). Artificial intelligence in education: A systematic literature review. *Expert Systems with Applications*, *252*, 124167. DOI: 10.1016/j.eswa.2024.124167

Wang, Y., Yang, J., & Li, H. (2024a). AI-driven adaptive learning environments. *Computers & Education: Artificial Intelligence*, *5*, 100145.

Williamson, B. (2017). Big data in education: The digital future of learning, policy and practice. *Sage (Atlanta, Ga.)*. Advance online publication. DOI: 10.4135/9781529714920

Williamson, B., & Eynon, R. (2020). Historical threads, missing links, and future directions in AI in education. *Learning, Media and Technology*, *45*(3), 223–235. DOI: 10.1080/17439884.2020.1798995

Williamson, B., & Eynon, R. (2025). Historical threads, missing links, and future directions in AI education governance. *Learning, Media and Technology*, *50*(1), 1–16. DOI: 10.1080/17439884.2024.2331007

Zawacki-Richter, O., Bond, M., & Marín, V. I. (2024). Systematic review of AI applications in higher education: A pedagogical perspective. *Educational Technology Research and Development*, *72*(1), 1–29. DOI: 10.1007/s11423-024-10345-8

Zawacki-Richter, O., Marín, V. I., Bond, M., & Gouverneur, F. (2019). Systematic review of research on AI applications in higher education. *International Journal of Educational Technology in Higher Education*, *16*(1), 39. DOI: 10.1186/s41239-019-0171-0

Zhai, X.. (2023). AI-assisted formative assessment. *Journal of Educational Technology & Society*, *26*(1), 31–45.

Chapter 25
Moving Beyond the "Teaching Jobs Are Going to Get Extinct in the Age of Generative AI" Narrative:
Making Teachers "Non-Substitutable"

Ashraf Alam
http://orcid.org/0000-0001-6178-1187
Department of Education, National Institute of Technology Calicut, Kozhikode, India

ABSTRACT

This chapter reframes the teacher extinction thesis as a platform-amplified socio-technical imaginary that mislabels legitimacy and work-design crises as automation destiny. Teaching is judgment-intensive, responsibility-bearing, relational public work, not content delivery. Drawing on professional jurisdiction, recognition economies, labour-process intensification, care ethics, audit culture, and algorithmic management, it shows how platformisation and proxy accountability compress discretion, externalise authority, and trigger moral injury and attrition. It reconstructs non-substitutable roles, autonomy scaffolders, safeguarding stewards, civic discourse moderators, inclusion-capability designers, and assessment interpreters under provenance uncertainty. The chapter ends with system levers, validity-aware accountability, protected time sovereignty, classroom-centred careers, and contestable ethical edtech governance.

1. INTRODUCTION

1.1 Teacher Extinction Discourse Inside Platformed Attention Economies

The teacher extinction narrative operates as a high-velocity social claim engineered by platform logics that privilege salience, virality, and performative certainty over institutional complexity. In these attention markets, generative AI demonstrations, productivity metaphors, and frictionless personalization rhetoric compress schooling into a transactional model of content acquisition, thereby obscuring the high-discretion, high-liability character of pedagogic work (Kaledio et al., 2024; Bukar et al., 2024). Extinction talk functions as a distributive device that reallocates responsibility for learning outcomes from public systems to individuals, families, and self-service platforms, normalizing the withdrawal of inclusive supports that make learning safe, equitable, and developmentally coherent. The core analytic move is to distinguish occupational prediction from professional devaluation, since the dominant risk is not elimination of teaching, but reclassification of teachers into low-autonomy operators governed by scripts, metrics, and vendor-defined workflows.

DOI: 10.4018/979-8-3373-8983-7.ch025

1.2 Prestige and Legitimacy as Contested Professional Public Goods

Prestige is treated here as a multidimensional composite of dignity, authority, autonomy, remuneration justice, role clarity, and socially conferred trust, rather than as a sentimental reputation index. Legitimacy is conceptualized as the normative license for teachers to exercise discretionary judgment under uncertainty, particularly where safeguarding, inclusion, epistemic integrity, and proportional discipline are at stake (Zadorina et al., 2024; Iqbal et al., 2024; Sharma et al., 2024). These constructs function as professional public goods because they stabilize the civic and distributive purposes of schooling that cannot be secured through market coordination alone, including capability expansion, social cohesion, and rights-literate participation. When prestige and legitimacy erode, institutional systems often substitute surveillance for trust, measurement for meaning, and compliance for ethical discernment, thereby weakening the very conditions that make teaching effective in heterogeneous classrooms. The chapter therefore treats legitimacy not as deference, but as accountable authority anchored in transparent standards and context-sensitive judgment.

1.3 Analytical Questions Linking Autonomy, AI, and Deprofessionalization

The chapter's analytical agenda centers on mechanisms that allocate symbolic capital, decision rights, and accountability across teachers, institutions, and technology infrastructures. Autonomy is examined through a bifocal lens that integrates *Self-Determination Theory*, *Self-Regulated Learning*, and *Metacognitive Scaffolding* with sociological constructs of responsibilization, risk transfer, and governability. A parallel question concerns how AI adoption interacts with audit regimes, scripted pedagogy, and platform governance to compress discretion, intensify clerical load, and externalize jurisdiction to vendors through procurement, analytics, and standardized pacing architectures. Teacher motivation and retention are framed as ecological outcomes shaped by *Job Demands-Resources* equilibria, *Organizational Justice*, psychological contracts, and moral injury dynamics arising from value conflict between care-based ethics and metric-driven imperatives. The forward question is which role families remain structurally non-substitutable because they entail relational authority, ethical liability, and live interpretive judgment.

1.4 Scope, Limits, and Recurring Category Errors

Conceptual precision is required to avoid category collapse between labour-market stress and technological mythology. Teacher shortage is treated as a capacity and work-design problem shaped by recruitment pipelines, attrition dynamics, and institutional incentives, while teacher extinction is treated as a cultural narrative about obsolescence. Task automation is distinguished from substitution of professional judgment, since routine assistance can coexist with persistent accountability for harms, equity safeguards, and developmental coherence. Autonomy is defined as scaffolded capability, not educational abandonment, because agency is produced through feedback loops, relational safety, and epistemic training that enable learners to evaluate sources, calibrate confidence, and resist manipulation in synthetic-media environments. Technology integration is separated from platformisation and algorithmic management, where tools become governance infrastructures that standardize work, datafy performance, and redistribute authority. The recurrent category error is to reduce learning to information transfer, thereby treating pedagogy as a mere interface problem.

1.5 Chapter Roadmap, Argument Logic, and Knowledge Claims

The chapter advances a conceptual-theoretical narrative review that synthesizes professional valuation, learning science, organizational control, political economy, care ethics, and critical data governance into a single explanatory architecture. Section 2 specifies how prestige is produced and eroded through jurisdictional politics, recognition regimes, labour-process intensification, gendered care penalties, and audit-centric managerialism. Section 3 interrogates autonomy and AI through socio-technical imaginaries, highlighting how hype dynamics, diffusion pressures, and platformisation can misframe governance choices as technological inevitabilities. Section 4 reconstructs teacher roles for complex learning ecologies, positioning teachers as autonomy architects, inclusion designers, civic facilitators, and assessment interpreters in AI-rich contexts. Section 5 treats professional formation as the reproduction of practical wisdom through coached rehearsal, inquiry ecologies, collegial infrastructures, and moral resilience. Section 6 identifies system conditions that restore attractiveness and legitimacy through trust-based accountability, time politics, career architecture, and ethical edtech governance, culminating in a conclusion that rejects extinction frames in favor of teacher-centered technological futures.

2. PRESTIGE AND POLITICAL ECONOMY OF TEACHING WORK

2.1 Professions, Jurisdictions, and Boundary Work in Schooling

Teaching secures professional standing when its core jurisdiction is recognized as high-discretion decision making under uncertainty, where curriculum enactment, assessment interpretation, safeguarding triage, and classroom governance require context-sensitive judgment rather than procedural execution. Within *Professional Jurisdiction* logics, prestige emerges from authorized discretion, ethical accountability, and control over the signature practices that convert policy texts into lived learning (Mouta et al., 2024; Davis et al., 2024; Alam, 2023a). Deprofessionalization begins when boundary work is reversed, with scripted pedagogies, mandated pacing architectures, and compliance-centric rubrics reclassifying teachers as implementers of external expertise and relocating interpretive authority into managerial protocols. In *Street-Level Discretion* conditions, rule following cannot anticipate heterogeneous classrooms, resource constraints, and value conflicts, so the erosion of discretion predictably degrades quality while amplifying blame. The mechanism map in Table 1 consolidates these jurisdictional dynamics with complementary prestige lenses, clarifying why extinction talk mislabels governance failures as technological destiny.

2.2 Symbolic Capital, Recognition Regimes, and Reputational Infrastructures

Prestige is not a private sentiment but a public recognition economy, where *Symbolic Capital*, institutional signaling, and interactional credibility co-produce the legitimacy that allows teachers to act decisively in ethically fraught moments. Recognition regimes operate across micro-level encounters, such as parent trust, student compliance, and peer standing, and macro-level discourses, such as policy frames, media moral panics, and platform commentary that re-script teachers as either heroic martyrs or disposable service workers (Al-Shorman et al., 2025; Stolpe & Hallström, 2024; Zawacki-Richter et al., 2024). When reputational infrastructures privilege visibility, quantification, and performative "impact" proxies, relational labor, inclusion work, and deliberative facilitation become structurally under-credited, even though they are causally upstream of learning stability and classroom order. This reputational drift becomes more acute under platformed metrics that convert complex pedagogic value into simplified dashboards, thereby rewarding what is easily countable and penalizing what is ethically necessary. Table 1 offers a compact crosswalk linking recognition logics to observable institutional symptoms and repair levers that re-anchor legitimacy in accountable discretion.

2.3 Labour Process Dynamics, Precarity, and Work Intensification

Prestige also has a material substrate shaped by *Labour Process* design, employment security, workload architecture, and the distribution of discretionary time. When wage structures compress, contracts become precarious, and staffing ratios deteriorate, professional dignity is undermined through a political economy that signals low societal valuation and converts expertise into replaceable labor. Work intensification follows a predictable pattern of task accretion, administrative creep, documentation overload, and role saturation, in which teachers absorb clerical production, compliance reporting, and social service substitution without compensatory resources or authority (Kong et al., 2025; Vieriu & Petrea, 2025; Choi et al., 2024). Under *Job Demands-Resources* logic, this design produces chronic depletion, burnout trajectories, and retention collapse, not as individual fragility but as system-level miscalibration of demands, control, and support. Table 1 synthesizes this labour-market pathway with parallel mechanisms, enabling a precise diagnosis of where extinction rhetoric masks redesignable work architectures.

Table 1. Conceptual Lenses for Teaching Prestige, its Erosion and Repair

Analytical Lens for Professional Valuation	Prestige Production Mechanism in Schools	Erosion Pathway Often Misread as Extinction	Observable Institutional Symptoms and Signal Failures	Restorative Design Lever for Dignity and Legitimacy
Professional Jurisdiction and Boundary Governance	Authorized discretion, ethical liability, and control over curriculum enactment, assessment interpretation, and safeguarding decisions	Scripted pedagogy and mandated pacing displace judgment, reframing teachers as operators of external templates	Narrowed decision rights, routine compliance rituals, and escalating conflicts over classroom authority	Decision-rights charters, protected interpretive space, and standards that formalize accountable discretion
Recognition Regimes and Symbolic Capital Allocation	Socially conferred credibility through trust, role clarity, and culturally legible professional authority	Teacher-blame frames and reputational downgrades convert structural failures into individual deficit stories	Declining public trust, parental escalation, and status anxiety within school interaction orders	Legitimacy renewal through transparent norms, respectful communication infrastructures, and recognition-linked career pathways
Labour Process Architecture and Workload Political Economy	Material justice via stable contracts, fair compensation, manageable caseloads, and protected planning time	Wage compression and intensification signal disposability, accelerating attrition and quality volatility	Chronic vacancies, expanding class sizes, excessive documentation, and depleted instructional bandwidth	Work redesign, staffing ratio commitments, time protection, and compensation aligned to responsibility load
Care Ethics and Emotional Labour Valuation	Skilled relational work that stabilizes belonging, motivation, and safety, treated as core expertise	Care work is moralized yet under-rewarded, producing gendered devaluation and hidden workload	Emotional exhaustion, unresolved conflict climates, and inequitable burdens in inclusion and safeguarding	Credentialing of relational competence, safeguarding supports, and workload credits for care-intensive functions
Audit Culture and Metric Governance Dynamics	Accountability aligned to meaningful constructs, with validity-aware indicators and professional trust	Proxy targets displace educational purpose, producing metric gaming and clerical overload	Indicator fixation, superficial compliance, narrowed curricula, and reduced professional initiative	Validity-first accountability, low-burden evidence systems, and teacher voice in indicator design
Platformized Reputational Economies and Datafied Control	Tools that augment professional judgment while preserving transparency, contestability, and autonomy	Vendor metrics and opaque analytics centralize authority, enabling algorithmic management of pedagogy	Workflow standardization, surveillance creep, and dependency on proprietary dashboards	Procurement governance, audit rights, data minimization, and limits on automated decision making

Table 1 clarifies that prestige erosion is a multi-causal systems phenomenon rather than a single technology shock, and it identifies repair levers that are immediately actionable through governance, work design, and accountability architecture. The most persistent misclassification occurs when platform metrics and audit regimes are treated as neutral efficiency instruments, even though they often re-engineer professional roles into compliance micro-tasks that displace relational and interpretive work. A coherent repair strategy therefore requires simultaneous intervention in decision rights, recognition infrastructures, material job quality, care valuation, validity-aware accountability, and platform governance, because partial reforms tend to relocate pressure rather than relieve it. This synthesis also explains why extinction narratives remain rhetorically compelling, since they compress a complex causality chain into a single deterministic storyline, while Table 1 re-expands the chain into discrete mechanisms that can be redesigned without sacrificing technological innovation.

2.4 Care Ethics, Emotional Labour, and Gendered Devaluation

Teaching contains intensive *Care Ethics* obligations, where relational attunement, affect regulation, and climate maintenance operate as high-skill labor that stabilizes learning readiness, behavioral regulation, and identity-safe participation. Emotional labour is not decorative empathy but a controlled professional performance that governs escalation, sustains belonging, and enables productive struggle without humiliation, particularly in classrooms shaped by trauma exposure, social polarization, and epistemic instability (Adeleye et al., 2024; Kumar et al., 2024; Martin et al., 2024). Devaluation emerges when care work is coded as natural disposition rather than expertise, producing a prestige penalty that is frequently gendered and compounded by stratification dynamics that redistribute the hardest emotional loads to the least resourced settings. This ethical invisibilization also distorts governance, because systems invest in measurement and surveillance rather than in safeguarding capacity, counseling interfaces, and time for relational repair. Table 1 foregrounds care valuation as a structural prestige mechanism, implying that legitimacy restoration requires explicit workload credits, role protections, and professional authority to enact safeguarding decisions without bureaucratic delay.

2.5 Managerialism, Audit Culture, and Metric-Driven Control

Managerialism operationalizes a governance imaginary where teaching is treated as monitorable output production, and professional trust is replaced by surveillance, targets, and compliance documentation that convert pedagogy into administrable fragments. Under *Audit Culture*, indicators become proxy currencies that reorganize attention, narrow curricular breadth, and incentivize performativity, producing validity loss when what is measurable crowds out what is educationally consequential (Ng et al., 2024; Alwaqdani, 2025; Walter, 2024). Metric-driven control also intensifies epistemic risk, because dashboards can create an illusion of objectivity while hiding construct underrepresentation, differential measurement error, and strategic gaming, thereby undermining fairness and professional judgment simultaneously. The institutional result is a paradoxical decline in quality alongside increased reporting, as discretionary time for planning, feedback, and inclusion design is displaced by clerical labor and reputational self-defense. The repair logic highlighted in Table 1 implies that accountability must be redesigned as validity-aware, low-burden, and teacher-voiced, with clear decision rights and contestability, so that metrics support, rather than govern, the ethical core of teaching.

3. AUTONOMY, GENERATIVE AI, AND SOCIO-TECHNICAL LEARNING IMAGINARIES

3.1 Scaffolded Autonomy, Self-Regulation, and Relational Safety

Autonomy is not an ontological default triggered by content abundance, it is a developmentally engineered competence produced through *Self-Determination Theory*, *Self-Regulated Learning*, and *Metacognitive Scaffolding* that converts dependence into calibrated agency. In rigorous learning ecologies, autonomy emerges from feedback-rich loops, strategy coaching, goal orchestration, and error-tolerant climates that protect epistemic risk-taking, particularly for learners navigating linguistic diversity, precarious home supports, and unequal access to quiet study infrastructures (Lin & Chen, 2024; Tashtoush et al., 2024; Mustafa et al., 2024). *Epistemic Cognition* adds a non-negotiable layer, autonomous learning in generative AI environments requires source evaluation, confidence calibration, and plausibility auditing, otherwise autonomy degenerates into credulity and tool-dependence. The prestige logic from Table 1 remains operative, when teachers are stripped of discretionary authority to scaffold autonomy, institutions silently reclassify learning as self-service, amplifying inequity through responsibilization and shifting failure costs onto households. Table 2 will later specify how autonomy imaginaries become governance scripts.

3.2 Hype Cycles, Diffusion Dynamics, and Institutional Isomorphism

Generative AI narratives diffuse through attention economies via amplification heuristics that reward novelty, certainty, and managerial legibility, producing a policy theatre in which rhetoric substitutes for capacity, and demonstration substitutes for governance. Under *Diffusion of Innovations*, adoption is frequently driven by prestige signaling, competitive mimicry, and perceived modernity, while *Institutional Isomorphism* explains why organisations converge on similar AI discourse even when local constraints, infrastructure fragility, and workforce readiness diverge sharply (Galindo-Domínguez et al., 2024; Alam, 2023b; Sperling et al., 2024). *Sociotechnical Imaginaries* clarify that replacement myths are not neutral forecasts, they encode preferred power arrangements, including vendor jurisdiction over curriculum pacing, analytics-defined quality, and procurement-led standardisation that compresses teacher discretion. This dynamic can produce a legitimacy inversion, institutions adopt AI to appear future-ready, yet the adoption path often intensifies audit load, expands clerical friction, and destabilizes professional identity through metric pressure, as Table 1 already anticipates. Table 2 will crystallize these imaginaries into actionable counter-frames that preserve teacher-centered legitimacy.

3.3 Automation Limits, Professional Judgment, and Accountability Allocation

The decisive analytic distinction is between task automation and responsibility-bearing judgment, because teaching is a high-variance inference practice enacted under uncertainty, where micro-decisions carry ethical, developmental, and distributive consequences. *Decision Theory* and cognitive architectures of expertise position pedagogic work as real-time hypothesis testing, teachers interpret partial signals, update beliefs, and select interventions under constraints of time, emotion, and heterogeneous prior knowledge. This is compounded by accountability asymmetry, even when tools propose, humans remain liable for harm prevention, equity safeguards, and proportional discipline, a structure captured by *Accountability Theory* and the logic of non-delegable duty (Almasri, 2024; Perkins et al., 2024; Guo et al., 2024). Automation also introduces epistemic hazards such as *Automation Bias*, over-trust, and error camouflage, especially when model outputs present fluent rationales that obscure uncertainty. Table 2 operationalizes these tensions by contrasting dominant imaginaries with counter-constructs that protect professional discretion and legitimacy while still enabling augmentation.

Table 2. AI Learning Imaginaries and Teacher-Centred Counter-Frames

Imaginary Claim	Latent Learning Ontology	Counter-Constructive Frame	Deprofessionalisation Failure Mode	Teacher-Centred Governance Reframing
AI Tutors Can Replace Teachers at Scale	Learning is explanation delivery plus practice optimisation, relational authority is optional	*Sociomateriality* and *Care Ethics* treat learning as participation, belonging, and normed interaction	Deskilling of live orchestration, safeguarding dilution, and responsibility diffusion	AI is bounded to augmentation, teachers retain final interpretive authority and duty-of-care accountability
Autonomy Means Self-Paced Self-Service Learning	Agency is presumed, guidance is a consumable add-on	*Metacognitive Scaffolding* and feedback literacy treat autonomy as coached competence	Responsibilization, inequity amplification, and silent exclusion through unmet support needs	Autonomy is governed through scaffold mandates, protected feedback time, and inclusion-sensitive pacing discretion
Dashboards Make Quality Visible and Controllable	What is measurable is what matters, proxies are equivalent to constructs	Validity reasoning and *Audit Culture* critique distinguish indicators from educational value	Metric fixation, performativity, clerical overload, and narrowing of pedagogy	Accountability is validity-aware, low-burden, and teacher-voiced, with contestability and interpretive latitude
Automated Assessment Is Objective and Fair by Design	Scoring equals judgment, bias is solvable through optimisation alone	Fairness, *Epistemic Justice*, and interpretability treat judgment as contextual and moral	Credibility harms, misclassification, and inequitable consequences masked by technical opacity	Teachers steward fairness, require auditability, and set limits on automated decisions in high-stakes contexts
Platforms Standardise Best Practice Across Contexts	Uniformity is quality, local variation is noise	*Professional Jurisdiction* and adaptive expertise treat context as constitutive, not residual	Jurisdictional capture by vendors, loss of curricular agency, and template lock-in	Procurement norms preserve discretionary space, local adaptation rights, and transparent change-control governance
Generative Content Makes Curriculum Design Secondary	Knowledge is modular content, sequencing is algorithmic optimization	*Curriculum-as-Practice* treats curriculum as ethical design and cultural mediation	Curriculum thinning, coherence loss, and fragmentation of learning progressions	Teachers lead sequencing, coherence, and cultural fit, AI assists drafting under clear quality criteria

Table 2 implies that the core risk is not computational capability but governance drift, where seductive ontologies of efficiency authorize jurisdictional capture, invalidate relational labour, and externalize accountability into opaque infrastructures. The counter-frame is not anti-technology, it is epistemically disciplined augmentation in which teacher discretion, contestability, and duty-of-care remain structurally protected, preventing responsibility laundering and equity erosion. When these governance constraints are absent, AI tools can become managerial substitutes for professional trust, intensifying the audit dynamics already mapped in Table 1 and producing brittle compliance rather than robust learning. The actionable synthesis is that automation should be restricted to low-liability support functions, while judgment-intensive domains, safeguarding, inclusion, and assessment interpretation remain teacher-led, with explicit decision rights and transparency requirements. Subsequent subsections extend this architecture into postdigital classroom assemblages and platformised control regimes.

3.4 Postdigital Classrooms as Sociomaterial Learning Assemblages

Classrooms are not delivery channels, they are postdigital assemblages of bodies, artefacts, routines, language practices, and authority relations that co-produce attention, participation, and legitimacy in real time. *Activity Theory* and *Practice Theory* treat learning as mediated action embedded in norms, tools, and role structures, so any AI insertion necessarily reconfigures who can speak, who is believed, what counts as evidence, and how conflict is regulated (Memarian & Doleck, 2024; Filgueiras, 2024; Linderoth et al., 2024). *Distributed Cognition* clarifies that expertise is not located solely in individuals or tools, it is enacted through orchestration, timing, and socio-material coordination, functions that demand professional vision and relational authority. In this ecology, the teacher is an institutional stabilizer who calibrates emotional climate, regulates discourse norms, and maintains epistemic integrity when synthetic media, misinformation, and performative antagonism destabilize shared realities. The postdigital implication is that AI is never simply additive, it is a re-mediator of power, attention, and responsibility, and therefore must be governed through the counter-frames in Table 2 rather than through procurement-only logics.

3.5 Platformisation, Algorithmic Management, and Datafied Governance

Platformisation is a structural shift from discrete instructional tools to governance infrastructures that standardise workflows, datafy performance, and relocate pedagogic authority into vendor analytics and managerial dashboards. *Algorithmic Management* and *Critical Data Studies* explain how metric-centric control can convert professional work into micro-task compliance, expanding surveillance surface area, intensifying documentation load, and narrowing curricular agency under the guise of transparency (Sămărescu et al., 2024; Alam & Mohanty, 2024; Guettala et al., 2024). This produces a dual legitimacy crisis, teachers are held responsible for outcomes while their decision rights are constrained by opaque scoring systems, predictive flags, and standardized pacing architectures that are difficult to contest. Table 2 indicates why this is a deprofessionalisation engine, the platform ontology privileges uniformity, measurability, and scalability, while undervaluing relational labour, inclusion design, and contextual judgment. A defensible governance response requires procurement as professional boundary work, including audit rights, data minimization, interoperability mandates, and explicit limits on automated decision making in high-liability domains. Without these constraints, platform systems can operationalize extinction talk by quietly substituting professional discretion with datafied control.

4. REIMAGINING TEACHER ROLES WITHIN COMPLEX LEARNING ECOLOGIES

4.1 Mandate Drift, Role Overload, and Boundary Maintenance

Contemporary schooling exhibits mandate drift in which education systems become de facto social-service interfaces, absorbing safeguarding escalation, psychosocial triage, digital citizenship mediation, nutrition insecurity spillovers, and community conflict regulation without commensurate staffing, time budgets, or jurisdictional clarity. Under *Role Theory*, the predictable outputs are overload, ambiguity, and conflict, where teachers carry simultaneous demands for attainment acceleration, therapeutic responsiveness, administrative traceability, and reputational self-defense, producing chronic strain and fragmented professional attention (Edwards-Fapohunda & Adediji, 2024; Bulut et al., 2024; Murdan & Halkhoree, 2024). *Institutional Logics* further destabilize role integrity by importing marketized customer-service expectations, bureaucratic compliance imperatives, and platform-led datafication norms that privilege auditability over pedagogic discernment. Boundary maintenance becomes a legitimacy practice that protects high-liability work, curriculum enactment, assessment interpretation, safeguarding judgment, from unfunded task dumping while enabling structured interprofessional collaboration. The role families consolidated in Table 3 provide a coherent boundary grammar for AI-rich schools, specifying which responsibilities must remain teacher-led to preserve dignity, discretion, and accountable authority.

4.2 Professional Identity, Organisational Justice, and Moral Injury

Teacher identity functions as an ecological construct stabilized by recognition, autonomy, competence, and belonging, and destabilized by institutional incoherence that fractures the moral narrative of professional purpose. *Self-Determination Theory* explains how autonomy deprivation and competence devaluation attenuate intrinsic commitment, while *Organisational Justice* and procedural legitimacy clarify that unfair evaluation architectures, opaque workload allocation, and constrained voice mechanisms generate disengagement even when resources appear nominally sufficient (Alam, 2022; Farooqi et al., 2024; Tang, 2024). Moral injury emerges when teachers are compelled to enact practices that violate care-based ethics, such as exclusionary discipline normalization, deficit framing, or uncritical compliance with surveillance-heavy platforms that erode trust and dignity. Psychological contract dynamics amplify this injury through repeated breaches in promised support, protected planning time, and professional respect, producing a betrayal schema that accelerates attrition. Table 3 is therefore not merely a taxonomy, it is an identity-stabilization instrument that makes non-substitutable responsibilities legible, shielding teachers from role erosion disguised as technological modernization.

4.3 Relational Pedagogy, Safeguarding, and Civic Formation

In complex learning ecologies, teaching is irreducibly relational and civic, where the classroom operates as a normative micro-polity requiring skilled governance of belonging, deliberation, conflict, and epistemic trust. *Relational Pedagogy* and *Care Ethics* treat instruction as interpersonal choreography that regulates emotion, attention, and participation, enabling cognitive demand without humiliation or exclusion, while safeguarding is high-stakes judgment under uncertainty requiring confidentiality calibration, proportional response, and trauma-sensitive repair (Sanusi et al., 2024; Airaj, 2024; Ramirez & Esparrell, 2024). Civic formation is embedded in discourse norms, rights literacy, and epistemic humility that equip learners to navigate polarised information ecosystems and synthetic media manipulation. These responsibilities are liability-bearing and context-sensitive, and their legitimacy depends on authorized discretion rather than scripted compliance. Table 3 operationalizes these role families as future-proof professional jurisdictions, specifying theoretical anchors, signature responsibilities, and enabling conditions that keep teachers central in AI-saturated schooling.

Table 3. Future-Proof Teacher Role Families and Non-Substitutability Anchors

Role Family Archetype	Theoretical Anchor Construct	Signature Responsibilities in Practice	Non-Substitutable Value Proposition	Dignity and Prestige Enabling Condition
Autonomy and Metacognition Architect	*Self-Regulated Learning, Metacognitive Scaffolding*	Designs feedback loops, strategy coaching, goal calibration, and error-tolerant learning climates for diverse learners	Requires live diagnostic judgment, relational trust, and adaptive scaffolding that cannot be fully pre-specified	Protected time for coaching, discretionary sequencing rights, and low-burden accountability
Safeguarding and Harm-Prevention Steward	*Duty-of-Care Accountability*, trauma-sensitive governance	Conducts risk triage, confidentiality judgments, proportional interventions, and restorative climate stabilization	Non-delegable liability, contextual discernment, and ethical proportionality in real-time interactions	Clear authority, specialist referral pathways, and institutional backing for safety-first decisions
Civic Reasoning and Discourse Moderator	*Deliberative Competence*, epistemic norm formation	Orchestrates dialogue norms, rights literacy, conflict mediation, and misinformation resistance practices	Depends on legitimate authority, situational mediation, and credibility calibration across contested truths	Policy protection against politicised pressure, civic mandate clarity, and trust-based governance
Inclusion and Capability Expansion Designer	*Universal Design for Learning, Capability Approach*	Engineers accessibility pathways, differentiated supports, and opportunity structures that reduce conversion barriers	Requires granular knowledge of learner variability, local constraints, and equity-sensitive adaptation	Resourcing for inclusion, reduced caseload volatility, and recognition of equity labor in evaluation

continued on following page

Table 3. Continued

Role Family Archetype	Theoretical Anchor Construct	Signature Responsibilities in Practice	Non-Substitutable Value Proposition	Dignity and Prestige Enabling Condition
Assessment Interpreter and Evidence Steward	validity reasoning, *Assessment for Learning*	Interprets evidence, safeguards fairness, manages provenance ambiguity, and delivers dialogic feedback that shapes agency	Judgment-intensive interpretation, accountability for consequences, and context-aware fairness calibration	Teacher-led assessment standards, contestable analytics, and integrity protocols without punitive surveillance
Curriculum Coherence and Cultural Mediator	*Curriculum-as-Practice, Pedagogical Content Knowledge*	Maintains sequencing coherence, disciplinary integrity, cultural fit, and developmental appropriateness under AI content abundance	Ethical design decisions and contextual mediation that resist template lock-in and fragmentation	Curriculum decision rights, collaborative planning infrastructure, and procurement rules aligned to pedagogy

Table 3 implies that teacher-centred modernization is a governance choice that preserves non-substitutable jurisdictions while allowing bounded augmentation in low-liability domains, thereby preventing responsibility laundering into opaque systems. The table also clarifies why extinction narratives persist, they collapse heterogeneous role families into a single content-delivery caricature, ignoring safeguarding liability, discourse governance, inclusion design, and interpretive assessment. When institutions operationalize these archetypes through decision-rights charters, protected time, and legitimacy-aware accountability, professional identity stabilizes and recruitment becomes structurally feasible. Conversely, when these archetypes are denied, platform workflows can convert teachers into monitored operators, producing deprofessionalisation through jurisdictional drift rather than through true substitution. The most actionable inference is that role clarity must be engineered upstream in policy, procurement, and workload design, so that AI tools are subordinated to professional ethics and contestable judgment.

4.4 Inclusion Architectures, Capability Expansion, and Epistemic Justice

Teacher roles must be reframed as equity-making design work in which inclusion is produced through anticipatory architecture rather than after-the-fact remediation. *Universal Design for Learning* treats variability as normative, requiring flexible pathways, multimodal representation, and responsive evidence practices, while culturally sustaining approaches emphasize that legitimacy and motivation depend on identity-safe participation and language-respectful interaction. The *Capability Approach* shifts evaluation from credential accumulation to expansion of real freedoms, positioning teachers as opportunity-structure engineers who reduce conversion barriers for learners facing disability, poverty, displacement, or stigma (Tahir et al., 2024; Leong et al., 2024; Yim & Su, 2025). *Epistemic Justice* adds a credibility lens, testimonial discounting and interpretive marginalisation undermine learner agency, and teachers perform recognition labor that restores epistemic standing within classroom micro-politics. In AI-mediated settings, misclassification risk, biased risk flags, and opaque recommendations can amplify exclusion, so inclusion requires teacher override authority and fairness-aware interpretation aligned with the inclusion designer archetype in Table 3.

4.5 Curriculum Authority and Assessment Interpretation Under AI

Curriculum in AI-rich schooling is enacted design rather than static documentation, where sequencing, coherence, and cultural fit are ethical decisions shaping what futures become thinkable for learners. *Curriculum-as-Practice* and *Pedagogical Content Knowledge* position teachers as interpretive designers who translate disciplinary epistemologies into developmentally coherent progressions while preserving conceptual integrity (Yim, 2024; Cukurova, 2025; Lee et al., 2024). Assessment is not mere scoring, it is validity-grounded interpretive judgment, where evidence must be contextualized, triangulated, and translated into feedback that shapes learner identity, agency, and metacognitive control. Generative AI introduces provenance ambiguity and synthetic text saturation, requiring integrity protocols such as process evidence, dialogic defense, and reasoning transparency, while avoiding punitive surveillance that corrodes trust and belonging. The assessment interpreter and curriculum coherence archetypes in Table 3 clarify non-substitutability, teachers remain accountable stewards of evidence and meaning, ensuring fairness across unequal tool access and sustaining legitimacy under postdigital uncertainty.

5. PROFESSIONAL FORMATION PATHWAYS FOR SUSTAINABLE TEACHING EXPERTISE

5.1 Practical Wisdom, Professional Vision, and Ethical Judgment

Professional formation is best conceptualized as the cultivation of *Phronesis*, *Professional Vision*, and ethically accountable discretion in environments saturated by uncertainty, heterogeneity, and consequential trade-offs. *Epistemology of Practice* clarifies that teaching expertise is not reducible to procedural fluency, it is a situated capability for rapid diagnostic inference, proportional intervention, and harm-minimizing decision making under bounded time, affective volatility, and competing institutional imperatives (Selwyn, 2024; Farahani & Ghasmi, 2024; Mao et al., 2024). *Normative Ethics* and duty-of-care architectures foreground the non-delegable liabilities embedded in safeguarding, inclusion, and assessment interpretation, thereby making ethical judgment a core competence rather than an optional disposition. Formation must therefore develop interpretive acuity, value-sensitivity, and evidence-calibrated action selection, while resisting the compliance trap that converts professional responsibility into checklist obedience. The developmental architectures synthesized in Table 4 are introduced here as a governance-relevant blueprint that protects discretion, stabilizes legitimacy, and prevents deskilling under datafied accountability.

5.2 Practice-Based Preparation, Cognitive Apprenticeship, and Rehearsal

Practice-based preparation operationalizes expertise as performance under constraints, aligning *Cognitive Apprenticeship*, coached rehearsal, and deliberate feedback loops with the cognitive science of expertise acquisition. In this architecture, knowledge is not merely stored, it is enacted through repeated, scaffolded performance of high-leverage instructional moves, including explanation design, questioning precision, feedback calibration, and classroom norm governance, all adapted to learner variability and linguistic diversity (Uygun, 2024; AlAli & Wardat, 2024; Alam & Mohanty, 2023). *Situated Learning* and *Deliberate Practice* emphasize that competency growth requires structured difficulty gradients, rapid error correction, and reflective meta-monitoring, rather than episodic exposure or generic observation. Clinical reasoning metaphors further clarify the diagnostic nature of teaching, where hypotheses about learner thinking are iteratively tested through formative evidence, then updated through professional judgment. Table 4 will later consolidate these preparation logics with misapplication hazards, showing how rehearsal cultures can degrade into scripting unless protected by autonomy, reflective rigor, and validity-aware accountability.

5.3 Practitioner Inquiry, Improvement Science, and Evaluation Literacy

Teacher expertise is sustained when teachers function as disciplined knowledge producers within *Practitioner Inquiry*, *Improvement Science*, and evaluation-literate professional cultures that treat variation as signal rather than noise. Inquiry routines translate classroom problems into actionable theories of change, specify measurable yet meaningful indicators, and iterate through structured cycles that privilege learning over blame (Salloum et al., 2024; Díaz & Nussbaum, 2024; Ifenthaler et al., 2024). Evaluation literacy adds epistemic safeguards by strengthening construct clarity, validity reasoning, and interpretive caution toward dashboards, thereby reducing proxy fixation and analytic overreach. In AI-mediated environments, inquiry must expand into epistemic vigilance, including plausibility auditing, provenance sensitivity, and bias-aware interpretation of automated recommendations, without collapsing into surveillance or techno-panics. Table 4 functions as an integrative map of formation models that convert inquiry from performative paperwork into a high-trust professional learning engine, clarifying which governance conditions keep inquiry intellectually honest, psychologically safe, and aligned with dignity-preserving discretion.

Table 4. Teacher Development Architectures Preserving Expertise and Prestige

Development Architecture	Theoretical Substrate	Capability Formation Outcome	Misapplication Hazard	Governance Safeguard for Prestige
Practice-Based Apprenticeship	*Situated Learning, Cognitive Apprenticeship*	Builds adaptive enactment, tacit noticing, and context-sensitive judgment through coached performance	Degenerates into mimicry, reproducing local routines without principled reflection or equity calibration	Protected mentoring time, transparent standards, and discretionary space for principled adaptation
Deliberate Rehearsal Cycles	*Deliberate Practice*, feedback-loop cybernetics	Accelerates precision in core moves, error correction, and feedback literacy under time pressure	Converts teaching into scripted micro-technique, weakening ethical discernment and relational attunement	Reflective debrief norms, autonomy over instructional design, and validity-aware performance evidence
Practitioner Inquiry Studios	*Improvement Science*, disciplined problem solving	Strengthens causal reasoning, measurement literacy, and iterative intervention design grounded in classroom realities	Becomes compliance research for audits, incentivizing superficial documentation and risk-avoidant reporting	Teacher-led inquiry agendas, low-burden evidence systems, and non-punitive learning accountability
Collegial Learning Infrastructures	*Communities of Practice, Distributed Cognition*	Stabilizes identity, shared standards, and collective efficacy through peer coaching and joint sensemaking	Collapses into meeting fatigue, ritual talk, and conformity pressures that suppress dissent and innovation	Protected collaboration time, psychological safety protocols, and leadership that rewards candor and learning
Transformative Moral Formation	*Transformative Learning*, moral psychology frameworks	Develops value coherence, civic professionalism, and resilience against moral injury through critical reflection	Drifts into coercive norming or politicised capture, triggering backlash and legitimacy erosion	Procedural fairness, pluralistic dialogue norms, and safeguards against ideological instrumentalization
AI-Era Epistemic Stewardship Practicum	*Epistemic Cognition*, responsible automation principles	Builds tool-audit competence, provenance reasoning, and contestable interpretation of AI outputs	Produces techno-dependence, automation bias, and responsibility laundering into opaque systems	Audit rights, contestability rules, and explicit limits on automated decisions in high-liability domains

Table 4 indicates that formation is a governance problem as much as a pedagogic one, because competence trajectories depend on time allocation, decision rights, and legitimacy-aware accountability rather than on training content alone. The most robust architectures are those that couple rehearsal with reflection, inquiry with validity reasoning, and collegiality with psychological safety, thereby preventing the compliance drift that converts professional learning into performative documentation. The table also clarifies why AI-era formation must include epistemic stewardship, not as a technical add-on but as an ethical competence that sustains responsibility, fairness, and interpretive authority under synthetic information conditions (Nikitina & Ishchenko, 2024; Predrag, 2023; Alam & Mohanty, 2022). When these safeguards are absent, platforms can capture jurisdiction by redefining quality through vendor metrics, while teachers remain liable for harms without the authority to contest automated recommendations. The actionable inference is that teacher development must be designed as an integrated system of coached performance, disciplined inquiry, and protected discretion, aligned to prestige restoration rather than to monitoring convenience.

5.4 Collegial Infrastructures, Learning Organisations, and Psychological Safety

Expertise reproduction is structurally collective, requiring collegial infrastructures that operationalize *Communities of Practice*, *Distributed Cognition*, and learning-organization dynamics as durable routines rather than episodic events. In such systems, professional knowledge is circulated through co-planning, peer coaching, instructional rounds, and calibrated moderation of assessment judgments, producing shared standards while preserving local adaptation (Ismail et al., 2024; Louis & ElAzab, 2023; Fitria, 2023). *Psychological Safety* is a precondition for this knowledge metabolism, because teachers must be able to surface uncertainty, disclose error, and contest weak indicators without reputational penalty. Organizational design constructs, including time sovereignty, workload fairness, and transparent decision rights, determine whether collegiality becomes an enabling infrastructure or a bureaucratic burden. Table 4 already specifies how collegial learning collapses into meeting fatigue when governance treats collaboration as a symbolic ritual rather than as protected deep work. A dignity-preserving system therefore funds collegiality through time budgets, mentoring recognition, and evaluation designs that reward learning behaviors, not merely performance optics.

5.5 Transformative Learning, Critical Pedagogy, and Moral Resilience

Moral resilience in teaching is an institutional product shaped by value coherence, recognition stability, and the capacity to act ethically under constraint, rather than a psychological demand for endurance under harm. *Transformative Learning* frames professional growth as perspective recalibration through critical reflection and dialogue, while *Critical Pedagogy* supplies analytic tools for examining power, voice, and inclusion as everyday classroom governance tasks. These constructs become professionally generative when they are anchored in pluralistic norms, procedural fairness, and non-coercive deliberation, because legitimacy collapses when moral formation is mistaken for ideological enforcement (Fischer & Dobbins, 2024; Mitev et al., 2024; Trevisan et al., 2024). Moral injury dynamics clarify why teachers exit when they are compelled to enact policies that violate care-based ethics, especially under metric regimes that reward exclusion, compliance, and reputational management. Table 4 positions transformative moral formation as a stabilizer of civic professionalism, provided that institutions protect voice, ensure workload realism, and maintain contestable accountability. Under these conditions, teachers sustain ethical agency, epistemic integrity, and commitment in AI-saturated, socially fractured learning ecologies.

6. SYSTEM CONDITIONS RESTORING PRESTIGE AND RECRUITMENT RESILIENCE

6.1 Complexity Dynamics, Feedback Loops, and Workforce Stability

Teaching attractiveness behaves as a coupled-systems output, shaped by reinforcing loops among workload, morale, vacancy rates, class-size inflation, behavioural complexity, and public dissatisfaction, rather than by any single isolated variable. Within *Complexity Science* and *Systems Dynamics*, shortages are not merely headcount deficits, they are amplifiers that increase task density, compress discretionary time, and elevate emotional load, thereby accelerating exit and reducing onboarding capacity, a self-exciting spiral that mimics inevitability (Clarke, 2023; Melweth et al., 2024; Kwihangana, 2025). *Path Dependence* explains why short-term fixes that privilege compliance and surveillance can lock systems into brittle governance, because they generate defensive routines, reputational anxiety, and measurement gaming, which further erode legitimacy. The restoration logic requires breaking negative feedback through workload re-engineering, staffing ratio commitments, and protected discretionary space, aligned with the prestige mechanisms in Table 1 and the role families in Table 3. Table 5 later operationalizes these system levers as governance-ready design choices.

6.2 Trust-Based Governance, Legitimacy Renewal, and Accountability Design

Legitimacy renewal depends on governance architectures that treat teachers as accountable professionals rather than monitored operators, replacing control-heavy compliance with trust-calibrated oversight grounded in *Procedural Justice* and *Legitimacy Theory*. Trust-based systems specify decision rights, escalation pathways, and ethical boundaries, then align accountability to valid constructs rather than to proxy convenience, directly countering the audit distortions mapped in Table 1 and the imaginary traps in Table 2. *Validity Reasoning* becomes a governance instrument, indicators must be construct-representative, low-burden, and interpretable, with teacher voice in design, review, and revision, otherwise measurement becomes a prestige-draining workload generator (Gao, 2025; Ghiasvand & Seyri, 2025; Alam, 2023c). Accountability should be contestable, with documented override authority, appeal mechanisms, and transparent interpretation rules, particularly where AI-mediated analytics create opacity and responsibility diffusion. These design commitments prefigure Table 5 by specifying how legitimacy becomes an infrastructural property of systems, not a motivational slogan, and how governance can preserve discretion without sacrificing public assurance.

6.3 Time Politics, Work Design, and Attention Governance

Time is a normative currency that signals value, and it is also the enabling substrate for the work that most strongly predicts learning coherence, namely planning, feedback, inclusion design, family communication, and collegial calibration. Under *Job Design Theory* and labour-process diagnostics, administrative creep, documentation inflation, and platform notification saturation fragment cognitive bandwidth, converting pedagogic attention into clerical throughput and eroding professional identity through constant interruption (Shao & Sun, 2025; Lan, 2024; Zavatta, 2024). Attention governance therefore requires explicit time budgets, task pruning protocols, and workload caps that protect deep work, reduce decision fatigue, and preserve interpretive judgment, especially for the non-substitutable role families specified in Table 3 and the formation architectures in Table 4. The system levers in Table 5 translate time politics into enforceable design commitments, specifying where protected time, staffing ratios, and accountability simplification must cohere, otherwise reforms merely relocate pressure across tasks without restoring dignity.

Table 5. Ecosystem Levers Rebuilding Teacher Prestige Through System Design

Lever Domain	Mechanism of System Change	Common Implementation Failure	Enabling Condition for Uptake	Intended Prestige and Retention Effect
Workload and Staffing Architecture	Breaks shortage-amplifying loops by reducing task density, stabilising class sizes, and recalibrating caseload complexity	Temporary staffing patches increase churn, while workloads remain structurally unbounded	Ratio commitments, task audits, and enforceable workload ceilings tied to role clarity	Lowers burnout risk, restores discretionary time, and stabilises workforce pipelines
Validity-Aware Accountability Architecture	Aligns oversight to construct-valid evidence, reducing proxy fixation and performativity under *Audit Culture* pressures	Indicator proliferation, dashboard fetishism, and compliance rituals displace pedagogic work	Teacher voice in indicator design, contestability rules, and low-burden evidence protocols	Rebuilds legitimacy, increases trust, and improves retention through fair governance
Protected Professional Time and Attention Governance	Allocates time sovereignty for planning, feedback, inclusion design, and collegial calibration, reducing fragmentation	Protected time is nominal, then cannibalised by meetings, reporting, and platform notifications	Time budgets embedded in timetables, meeting caps, and notification minimisation norms	Enhances quality, reduces cognitive overload, and signals institutional respect
Career Ladders and Compensation Justice	Creates classroom-centred advancement pathways that reward mentoring, curriculum design, inclusion leadership, and AI stewardship	Promotion requires leaving classrooms, while pay scales ignore responsibility load and hardship contexts	Multi-track ladders, transparent criteria, and compensation aligned to ethical liability and workload	Strengthens professional identity, improves recruitment, and reduces mid-career exit
Ethical Platform and AI Governance	Prevents jurisdictional drift by limiting opaque automation, requiring auditability, and constraining surveillance creep	Vendor lock-in, proprietary metrics, and responsibility laundering into non-contestable systems	Procurement standards, audit rights, interoperability, and limits on automated decisions	Preserves discretion, protects fairness, and reduces deprofessionalisation incentives
Public Narrative and Trust Infrastructure	Reorients discourse through credibility signals, respectful communication norms, and anti-blame governance that protects teachers	Symbolic praise without material reform, plus moral panics that fuel punitive policy	Communication protocols, stakeholder compacts, and coherent reforms that match rhetoric	Increases social respect, stabilises legitimacy, and improves recruitment sentiment

Table 5 clarifies that prestige restoration is an engineered property of institutional design, not a charisma-dependent outcome, because each lever targets a distinct failure mode that otherwise cascades across recruitment, retention, and instructional quality. The levers also demonstrate complementarity, workload redesign without validity-aware accountability can be re-eroded by indicator creep, while ethical platform governance without protected time can still amplify clerical burden through datafied workflows. A coherent implementation strategy therefore requires coupling staffing ratios with time sovereignty, aligning accountability to valid constructs, and embedding contestability so teachers can override, audit, and correct automated recommendations without punitive retaliation. The table also converts the earlier theoretical architecture into a system blueprint that is legible to policy makers, workforce planners, and technologists, while preserving the dignity-centred professionalism demanded by Table 1 and the non-substitutability claims specified in Table 3.

6.4 Career Architectures, Recognition Pathways, and Pay Justice

Career design is both material justice and symbolic recognition, and it becomes a prestige engine when advancement pathways reward expertise accumulation while keeping accomplished teachers anchored in classrooms rather than pushing them into managerial exit routes. A credible architecture differentiates role families, such as mentor-teacher, inclusion designer, curriculum coherence lead, and ethical AI steward, then aligns progression criteria to observable professional contributions, reducing the status vacuum that makes marketised alternatives appear attractive. Pay justice must track responsibility load, emotional labour intensity, and context hardship, otherwise compensation signals disposability, undermining the legitimacy composite defined in Section 1 and the labour-process dynamics in Table 1. *Professional Capital* logics require that expertise be made visible through peer-reviewed artifacts of practice, calibrated assessment moderation, and leadership in collegial learning routines, thereby linking Table 4 formation infrastructures to tangible recognition. This alignment also reduces credential inflation traps, because progression is anchored in demonstrated capability and ethical accountability, not merely in accumulating formal tokens.

6.5 Media Ecology, Edtech Ethics, and Procurement Sovereignty

Public discourse is a governance variable, because media frames, platform outrage cycles, and techno-saviour narratives can convert complex system failures into teacher-blame scripts, thereby legitimising punitive accountability and accelerating exit. Within *Framing Theory* and media-ecology dynamics, prestige restoration requires communication infrastructures that protect teachers from reputational volatility while making system reforms legible, coherent, and trust-generating. Ethical edtech governance must be treated as sovereignty over pedagogic jurisdiction, procurement should be teacher-informed, standards-driven, and interoperability-oriented, with strict limits on surveillance, data extraction, and opaque automated decision making in high-liability domains. *Contestability* is essential, teachers must have audit rights, override authority, and clear responsibility allocation, otherwise platforms operationalize deprofessionalisation by centralising control while externalising liability. These media and procurement commitments complete Table 5's ecosystem blueprint by ensuring that cultural respect is coupled to material redesign, so legitimacy becomes durable rather than performative in internationally diverse contexts.

7. CONCLUSION

7.1 Teaching Persists while Professionalism is Politically Contested

The extinction narrative misdiagnoses a legitimacy and work-design crisis as a technological inevitability, because the enduring core of teaching resides in responsibility-bearing judgment, relational authority, and ethically constrained discretion enacted within complex sociomaterial ecologies. When governance architectures compress discretion through scripted pedagogy, audit-centric metrics, and platformised workflows, they do not remove teachers, they reclassify them into monitored operators while preserving liability for safeguarding, equity, and developmental coherence. This is why teacher scarcity can coexist with replacement rhetoric, the system simultaneously demands more care, inclusion, and conflict mediation while stripping the professional conditions that make such work sustainable. The conceptual machinery assembled across Tables 1 through 5 demonstrates that prestige erosion is multi-causal, produced by jurisdictional capture, recognition downgrades, labour-process intensification, and validity loss in accountability regimes. A credible future therefore rejects deterministic automation myths and instead reasserts teaching as a professional public good whose legitimacy must be engineered through institutional design and ethical governance.

7.2 Integrated Propositions across Prestige, Autonomy, Roles, and Formation

A coherent synthesis follows from the chapter's architecture, prestige is produced through a coupled composite of symbolic recognition, material justice, and protected discretion, and it erodes when accountability systems substitute proxies for value and surveillance for trust. Autonomy is not self-service independence, it is scaffolded capability constructed through *Self-Regulated Learning*, feedback literacy, and relational safety, and it becomes responsibilization when institutions withdraw supports under the banner of personalization. Role reconstruction clarifies that non-substitutability resides in teacher functions that combine interpretive judgment, ethical liability, and live orchestration, including safeguarding stewardship, civic discourse moderation, inclusion design, curriculum coherence mediation, and assessment interpretation under provenance ambiguity. Professional formation is the reproduction engine of these roles, operationalized through practice-based rehearsal, inquiry studios, collegial infrastructures, and *Psychological Safety*, while moral resilience is an organisational output shaped by procedural fairness and value coherence rather than an individual endurance requirement. Together these propositions specify a governance agenda in which AI is subordinated to teacher-led standards, contestability, and validity-aware accountability, preserving legitimacy while enabling augmentation.

7.3 Policy, Workforce, and Technology Agenda for Prestige Renewal

A submission-ready agenda for international systems begins with system design levers that break shortage-amplifying feedback loops by stabilising staffing ratios, enforcing workload ceilings, and protecting time sovereignty for planning, feedback, inclusion design, and collegial calibration. Governance reform must pivot from audit inflation to validity-aware accountability with teacher voice, contestability, and transparent decision rights, ensuring that metrics inform rather than govern and that responsibility remains aligned with authority. Workforce architectures should establish multi-track, classroom-centred career ladders with compensation justice calibrated to responsibility load, safeguarding intensity, and context hardship, thereby converting expertise into visible recognition rather than forcing exit into managerial roles. Technology governance should treat procurement as professional boundary work, requiring interoperability, audit rights, data minimization, and strict limits on automated decision making in high-liability domains, while embedding ethical AI stewardship as a teacher-led jurisdiction. The end state is a teacher-centred socio-technical future where legitimacy, dignity, and public trust are designed properties of systems, not fragile outcomes of individual heroism.

REFERENCES

Adeleye, O. O., Eden, C. A., & Adeniyi, I. S. (2024). Innovative teaching methodologies in the era of artificial intelligence: A review of inclusive educational practices. *World Journal of Advanced Engineering Technology and Sciences, 11*(2), 069-079.

Airaj, M. (2024). Ethical artificial intelligence for teaching-learning in higher education. *Education and Information Technologies, 29*(13), 17145–17167. DOI: 10.1007/s10639-024-12545-x

Al-Shorman, H. M., Saatchi, S. G., Alanaziand, T., Alzboon, M. S., Alka'awneh, S. M. N., Wahed, M. K. Y. A., & Al-Momani, A. A. M. (2025). Evaluating Artificial Intelligence Integration in Education Through Integrating TAM and S–O–R. In *Intelligence-driven circular economy: Regeneration towards sustainability and social responsibility–Volume 1* (pp. 353–367). Springer Nature Switzerland. DOI: 10.1007/978-3-031-73899-9_28

AlAli, R., & Wardat, Y. (2024). Opportunities and challenges of integrating generative artificial intelligence in education. *International Journal of Religion, 5*(7), 784–793. DOI: 10.61707/8y29gv34

Alam, A. (2022). Impact of university's human resources practices on professors' occupational performance: empirical evidence from India's higher education sector. In Rajagopal, R. B. (Ed.), *Inclusive businesses in developing economies: Converging people, profit, and corporate citizenship* (pp. 107–131). Springer International Publishing. DOI: 10.1007/978-3-031-12217-0_6

Alam, A. (2023a). Media multitasking with M-learning technology in real-time classroom learning: Analysing the dynamics in formal educational settings for the future of E-learning in India. In *2nd International conference on smart technologies and systems for next generation computing (ICSTSN)* (pp. 1-6). IEEE. DOI: 10.1109/ICSTSN57873.2023.10151509

Alam, A. (2023b). The secret sauce of student success: Cracking the code by navigating the path to personalized learning with educational data mining. In *2nd International conference on smart technologies and systems for next generation computing (ICSTSN)* (pp. 1-8). IEEE. DOI: 10.1109/ICSTSN57873.2023.10151558

Alam, A. (2023c). Intelligence unleashed: An argument for AI-enabled learning ecologies with real world examples of today and a peek into the future. In *International conference on innovations in computer science, electronics & electrical engineering-2022* (Vol. 2717, No. 1, p. 030001). AIP Publishing LLC. DOI: 10.1063/5.0129803

Alam, A., & Mohanty, A. (2022, December). Facial analytics or virtual avatars: competencies and design considerations for student-teacher interaction in AI-powered online education for effective classroom engagement. In *International conference on communication, networks and computing* (pp. 252-265). Cham: Springer Nature Switzerland.

Alam, A., & Mohanty, A. (2023, January). Learning on the move: a pedagogical framework for state-of-the-art mobile learning. In *International conference on data management, analytics & innovation* (pp. 735-748). Singapore: Springer Nature Singapore. DOI: 10.1007/978-981-99-1414-2_52

Alam, A., & Mohanty, A. (2024). Integrated constructive robotics in education (ICRE) model: A paradigmatic framework for transformative learning in educational ecosystem. *Cogent Education, 11*(1), 2324487. DOI: 10.1080/2331186X.2024.2324487

Almasri, F. (2024). Exploring the impact of artificial intelligence in teaching and learning of science: A systematic review of empirical research. *Research in Science Education, 54*(5), 977–997. DOI: 10.1007/s11165-024-10176-3

Alwaqdani, M. (2025). Investigating teachers' perceptions of artificial intelligence tools in education: Potential and difficulties. *Education and Information Technologies, 30*(3), 2737–2755. DOI: 10.1007/s10639-024-12903-9

Bukar, U. A., Sayeed, M. S., Razak, S. F. A., Yogarayan, S., & Sneesl, R. (2024). Decision-making framework for the utilization of generative artificial intelligence in education: A case study of ChatGPT. *IEEE Access : Practical Innovations, Open Solutions*, *12*, 95368–95389. DOI: 10.1109/ACCESS.2024.3425172

Bulut, O., Beiting-Parrish, M., Casabianca, J. M., Slater, S. C., Jiao, H., Song, D., . . . Morilova, P. (2024). The rise of artificial intelligence in educational measurement: Opportunities and ethical challenges. *arXiv preprint arXiv:2406.18900*.

Choi, J. I., Yang, E., & Goo, E. H. (2024). The effects of an ethics education program on artificial intelligence among middle school students: Analysis of perception and attitude changes. *Applied Sciences (Basel, Switzerland)*, *14*(4), 1588. DOI: 10.3390/app14041588

Clarke, M. (2023). The subordination of teacher identity: Ethical risks and potential lines of flight. *Teachers and Teaching*, *29*(3), 241–258. DOI: 10.1080/13540602.2022.2144823

Cukurova, M. (2025). The interplay of learning, analytics and artificial intelligence in education: A vision for hybrid intelligence. *British Journal of Educational Technology*, *56*(2), 469–488. DOI: 10.1111/bjet.13514

Davis, C., Bush, T., & Wood, S. (2024). Artificial intelligence in education: Enhancing learning experiences through personalized adaptation. *International Journal of Cyber and IT Service Management*, *4*(1), 26–32. DOI: 10.34306/ijcitsm.v4i1.146

Díaz, B., & Nussbaum, M. (2024). Artificial intelligence for teaching and learning in schools: The need for pedagogical intelligence. *Computers & Education*, *217*, 105071. DOI: 10.1016/j.compedu.2024.105071

Edwards-Fapohunda, M. O., & Adediji, M. A. (2024). Sustainable development of distance learning in continuing adult education: The impact of artificial intelligence. *Iconic Research and Engineering Journals*, *8*(1), 113–114.

Farahani, M. S., & Ghasmi, G. (2024, July). Artificial intelligence in education: A comprehensive study. In *Forum for Education Studies, 2*(3), 1379-1379. DOI: 10.59400/fes.v2i3.1379

Farooqi, M. T. K., Amanat, I., & Awan, S. M. (2024). Ethical considerations and challenges in the integration of artificial intelligence in education: A systematic review. *Journal of Excellence in Management Sciences*, *3*(4), 35–50. DOI: 10.69565/jems.v3i4.314

Filgueiras, F. (2024). Artificial intelligence and education governance. *Education, Citizenship and Social Justice*, *19*(3), 349–361. DOI: 10.1177/17461979231160674

Fischer, I., & Dobbins, K. (2024). Is it worth it? How paradoxical tensions of identity shape the readiness of management educators to embrace transformative technologies in their teaching. *Journal of Management Education*, *48*(4), 829–848. DOI: 10.1177/10525629231201843

Fitria, T. N. (2023). The use of artificial intelligence in education (AIED): Can AI replace the teacher's role? *Epigram*, *20*(2), 165–187. DOI: 10.32722/epi.v20i2.5711

Galindo-Domínguez, H., Delgado, N., Losada, D., & Etxabe, J. M. (2024). An analysis of the use of artificial intelligence in education in Spain: The in-service teacher's perspective. *Journal of Digital Learning in Teacher Education*, *40*(1), 41–56. DOI: 10.1080/21532974.2023.2284726

Gao, R. (2025). The erosion and reconstruction of teachers' authority in the context of artificial intelligence. *Journal of Theory and Practice in Education and Innovation*, *2*(2), 26–33.

Ghiasvand, F., & Seyri, H. (2025). A collaborative reflection on the synergy of Artificial Intelligence (AI) and language teacher identity reconstruction. *Teaching and Teacher Education*, *160*, 105022. DOI: 10.1016/j.tate.2025.105022

Guettala, M., Bourekkache, S., Kazar, O., & Harous, S. (2024). Generative artificial intelligence in education: Advancing adaptive and personalized learning. *Acta Informatica Pragensia*, *13*(3), 460–489. DOI: 10.18267/j.aip.235

Guo, S., Zheng, Y., & Zhai, X. (2024). Artificial intelligence in education research during 2013–2023: A review based on bibliometric analysis. *Education and Information Technologies*, *29*(13), 16387–16409. DOI: 10.1007/s10639-024-12491-8

Ifenthaler, D., Majumdar, R., Gorissen, P., Judge, M., Mishra, S., Raffaghelli, J., & Shimada, A. (2024). Artificial intelligence in education: Implications for policymakers, researchers, and practitioners. *Technology. Knowledge and Learning*, *29*(4), 1693–1710. DOI: 10.1007/s10758-024-09747-0

Iqbal, M., Khan, N. U., & Imran, M. (2024). The role of artificial intelligence (AI) in transforming educational practices: Opportunities, challenges, and implications. *Qlantic Journal of Social Sciences*, *5*(2), 348–359. DOI: 10.55737/qjss.349319430

Ismail, A., Aliu, A., Ibrahim, M., & Sulaiman, A. (2024). Preparing teachers of the future in the era of artificial intelligence. *Journal of Artificial Intelligence. Machine Learning and Neural Network*, *44*, 31–41.

Kaledio, P., Robert, A., & Frank, L. (2024). The impact of artificial intelligence on students' learning experience. *Wiley Interdisciplinary Reviews: Computational Statistics*, *2*(01), 75–84.

Kong, S. C., Korte, S. M., Burton, S., Keskitalo, P., Turunen, T., Smith, D., Wang, L., Lee, J. C.-K., & Beaton, M. C. (2025). Artificial Intelligence (AI) literacy–an argument for AI literacy in education. *Innovations in Education and Teaching International*, *62*(2), 477–483. DOI: 10.1080/14703297.2024.2332744

Kumar, S., Rao, P., Singhania, S., Verma, S., & Kheterpal, M. (2024). Will artificial intelligence drive the advancements in higher education? A tri-phased exploration. *Technological Forecasting and Social Change*, *201*, 123258. DOI: 10.1016/j.techfore.2024.123258

Kwihangana, F. (2025). Teacher positioning in educational ICT policies: Implications for digital teacher identity development in under-resourced contexts. *Journal of Education Policy*, *40*(2), 242–265. DOI: 10.1080/02680939.2024.2386309

Lan, Y. (2024). Through tensions to identity-based motivations: Exploring teacher professional identity in Artificial Intelligence-enhanced teacher training. *Teaching and Teacher Education*, *151*, 104736. DOI: 10.1016/j.tate.2024.104736

Lee, Y. J., Davis, R. O., & Ryu, J. (2024). Korean in-service teachers' perceptions of implementing artificial intelligence (AI) education for teaching in schools and their AI teacher training programs. *International Journal of Information and Education Technology (IJIET)*, *14*(2), 214–219. DOI: 10.18178/ijiet.2024.14.2.2042

Leong, W. Y., Leong, Y. Z., & San Leong, W. (2024, October). Artificial Intelligence in education. In *IET International Conference on Engineering Technologies and Applications (ICETA 2024)* (Vol. 2024, pp. 183-184). IET.

Lin, H., & Chen, Q. (2024). Artificial intelligence (AI)-integrated educational applications and college students' creativity and academic emotions: Students and teachers' perceptions and attitudes. *BMC Psychology*, *12*(1), 487. DOI: 10.1186/s40359-024-01979-0 PMID: 39285268

Linderoth, C., Hultén, M., & Stenliden, L. (2024). Competing visions of artificial intelligence in education—A heuristic analysis on sociotechnical imaginaries and problematizations in policy guidelines. *Policy Futures in Education*, *22*(8), 1662–1678. DOI: 10.1177/14782103241228900

Louis, M., & ElAzab, M. (2023). Will AI replace teacher? *International Journal of Internet Education*, *22*(2), 9–21. DOI: 10.21608/ijie.2023.312491

Mao, J., Chen, B., & Liu, J. C. (2024). Generative artificial intelligence in education and its implications for assessment. *TechTrends*, *68*(1), 58–66. DOI: 10.1007/s11528-023-00911-4

Martin, F., Zhuang, M., & Schaefer, D. (2024). Systematic review of research on artificial intelligence in K-12 education (2017–2022). *Computers and Education: Artificial Intelligence*, *6*, 100195. DOI: 10.1016/j.caeai.2023.100195

Melweth, H. M. A., Alkahtani, A. S., & Al Mdawi, A. M. M. (2024). The impact of artificial intelligence on improving the quality of education and reducing future anxiety among a sample of teachers in Saudi Arabia. *Kurdish Studies*, *12*(2), 5741–5758.

Memarian, B., & Doleck, T. (2024). Human-in-the-loop in artificial intelligence in education: A review and entity-relationship (ER) analysis. *Computers in Human Behavior: Artificial Humans*, *2*(1), 100053. DOI: 10.1016/j.chbah.2024.100053

Mitev, A. Z., Tóth, R., & Vaszkun, B. (2024). Role transition of higher education teachers due to disruptive technological change: Identity reconstruction for a better teacher-student relationship. *International Journal of Management Education*, *22*(2), 100978. DOI: 10.1016/j.ijme.2024.100978

Mouta, A., Pinto-Llorente, A. M., & Torrecilla-Sánchez, E. M. (2024). Uncovering blind spots in education ethics: Insights from a systematic literature review on artificial intelligence in education. *International Journal of Artificial Intelligence in Education*, *34*(3), 1166–1205. DOI: 10.1007/s40593-023-00384-9

Murdan, A. P., & Halkhoree, R. (2024, June). Integration of Artificial Intelligence for educational excellence and innovation in higher education institutions. In *2024 1st International Conference on Smart Energy Systems and Artificial Intelligence (SESAI)* (pp. 1-6). IEEE. DOI: 10.1109/SESAI61023.2024.10599402

Mustafa, M. Y., Tlili, A., Lampropoulos, G., Huang, R., Jandrić, P., Zhao, J., Salha, S., Xu, L., Pnada, S., & Saqr, M. (2024). A systematic review of literature reviews on artificial intelligence in education (AIED): A roadmap to a future research agenda. *Smart Learning Environments*, *11*(1), 59. DOI: 10.1186/s40561-024-00350-5

Ng, D. T. K., Su, J., Leung, J. K. L., & Chu, S. K. W. (2024). Artificial intelligence (AI) literacy education in secondary schools: A review. *Interactive Learning Environments*, *32*(10), 6204–6224. DOI: 10.1080/10494820.2023.2255228

Nikitina, I., & Ishchenko, T. (2024). The impact of ai on teachers: Support or replacement? *Scientific Journal of Polonia University*, *65*(4), 93–99. DOI: 10.23856/6511

Perkins, M., Furze, L., Roe, J., & MacVaugh, J. (2024). The Artificial Intelligence Assessment Scale (AIAS): A framework for ethical integration of generative AI in educational assessment. *Journal of University Teaching & Learning Practice*, *21*(6), 49–66. DOI: 10.53761/q3azde36

Predrag, P. A. L. E. (2023). Which teachers should be replaced by AI. *Problems of Education in the 21st Century, 81*(3), 296-302.

Ramirez, E. A. B., & Esparrell, J. A. F. (2024). Artificial intelligence (AI) in education: Unlocking the perfect synergy for learning. *Educational Process: International Journal*, *13*(1), 35–51.

Salloum, S. A., Salloum, A., & Alfaisal, R. (2024). Objectives and obstacles of artificial intelligence in education. In Al-marzouqi, A., Salloum, S. A., Al-Saidat, M., & Aburayya, A. (Eds.), *Artificial Intelligence in education: The power and dangers of ChatGPT in the classroom* (pp. 605–614). Springer.

Sămărescu, N., Bumbac, R., Zamfiroiu, A., & Iorgulescu, M. C. (2024). Artificial intelligence in education: Next-gen teacher perspectives. *Amfiteatru Economic*, *26*(65), 145–161. DOI: 10.24818/EA/2024/65/145

Sanusi, I. T., Agbo, F. J., Dada, O. A., Yunusa, A. A., Aruleba, K. D., Obaido, G., Olawumi, O., & Oyelere, S. S.Centre for Multidisciplinary Research and Innovation (CEMRI). (2024). Stakeholders' insights on artificial intelligence education: Perspectives of teachers, students, and policymakers. *Computers and Education Open*, *7*, 100212. DOI: 10.1016/j.caeo.2024.100212

Selwyn, N. (2024). On the limits of artificial intelligence (AI) in education. *Nordisk tidsskrift for pedagogikk og kritikk, 10*(1), 3-14.

Shao, J., & Sun, S. (2025). Teacher identity in the era of intelligence. *Journal of Educational Theory and Practice*, *2*(1). Advance online publication. DOI: 10.62177/jetp.v2i1.141

Sharma, S., Singh, G., Sharma, C. S., & Kapoor, S. (2024). Artificial intelligence in Indian higher education institutions: A quantitative study on adoption and perceptions. *International Journal of System Assurance Engineering and Management*, •••, 1–17. DOI: 10.1007/s13198-023-02193-8

Sperling, K., Stenberg, C. J., McGrath, C., Åkerfeldt, A., Heintz, F., & Stenliden, L. (2024). In search of artificial intelligence (AI) literacy in teacher education: A scoping review. *Computers and Education Open*, *6*, 100169. DOI: 10.1016/j.caeo.2024.100169

Stolpe, K., & Hallström, J. (2024). Artificial intelligence literacy for technology education. *Computers and Education Open*, *6*, 100159. DOI: 10.1016/j.caeo.2024.100159

Tahir, M., Hassan, F. D., & Shagoo, M. R. (2024). Role of artificial intelligence in education: A conceptual review. *World Journal of Advanced Research and Reviews*, *22*(1), 1469–1475. DOI: 10.30574/wjarr.2024.22.1.1217

Tang, K. H. D. (2024). Implications of artificial intelligence for teaching and learning. *Acta Pedagogia Asiana*, *3*(2), 65–79. DOI: 10.53623/apga.v3i2.404

Tashtoush, M. A., Wardat, Y., Ali, R. A., & Saleh, S. (2024). Artificial intelligence in education: Mathematics teachers' perspectives, practices and challenges. *Iraqi Journal for Computer Science and Mathematics*, *5*(1), 20. DOI: 10.52866/ijcsm.2024.05.01.004

Trevisan, O., Christensen, R., Drossel, K., Friesen, S., Forkosh-Baruch, A., & Phillips, M. (2024). Drivers of digital realities for ongoing teacher professional learning. *Technology. Knowledge and Learning*, *29*(4), 1851–1868. DOI: 10.1007/s10758-024-09771-0

Uygun, D. (2024). Teachers' perspectives on artificial intelligence in education. *Advances in Mobile Learning Educational Research*, *4*(1), 931–939. DOI: 10.25082/AMLER.2024.01.005

Vieriu, A. M., & Petrea, G. (2025). The impact of artificial intelligence (AI) on students' academic development. *Education Sciences*, *15*(3), 343. DOI: 10.3390/educsci15030343

Walter, Y. (2024). Embracing the future of Artificial Intelligence in the classroom: The relevance of AI literacy, prompt engineering, and critical thinking in modern education. *International Journal of Educational Technology in Higher Education*, *21*(1), 15. DOI: 10.1186/s41239-024-00448-3

Yim, I. H. Y. (2024). A critical review of teaching and learning artificial intelligence (AI) literacy: Developing an intelligence-based AI literacy framework for primary school education. *Computers and Education: Artificial Intelligence*, *7*, 100319. DOI: 10.1016/j.caeai.2024.100319

Yim, I. H. Y., & Su, J. (2025). Artificial intelligence (AI) learning tools in K-12 education: A scoping review. *Journal of Computers in Education*, *12*(1), 93–131.

Zadorina, O., Hurskaya, V., Sobolyeva, S., Grekova, L., & Vasylyuk-Zaitseva, S. (2024). The role of artificial intelligence in creation of future education: Possibilities and challenges. *Futurity Education*, *4*(2), 163–185.

Zavatta, G. (2024). Reconsidering the role of teacher professional learning in shaping the social and professional identity of teachers: Reflections from an ongoing study in building teacher agency through digital technologies. In *INTED2024 Proceedings* (pp. 6756-6764). IATED.

Zawacki-Richter, O., Bai, J. Y., Lee, K., Slagter van Tryon, P. J., & Prinsloo, P. (2024). New advances in artificial intelligence applications in higher education? *International Journal of Educational Technology in Higher Education*, *21*(1), 32. DOI: 10.1186/s41239-024-00464-3

Chapter 26
The Pedagogical Soul:
Why Machines Can't Replace Teachers

Sneh Lata
http://orcid.org/0009-0007-8195-6491
G.C. Rithoj, Gurugram University, India

ABSTRACT

This chapter examines the growing influence of artificial intelligence in education and argues that technology cannot replace the moral, relational, and interpretive dimensions that define teaching. Drawing on philosophical, empirical, and policy perspectives particularly within the Indian context it analyzes how automation reshapes teacher autonomy, ethical responsibility, and democratic learning. The chapter concludes by proposing a framework for human-centered innovation, positioning technology as a pedagogical ally that supports, rather than substitutes, the teacher's irreplaceable role in fostering moral and civic growth.

1. INTRODUCTION

The acceleration of artificial intelligence (AI) and digital technologies across educational systems has revived a long-standing question: Can machines truly replace teachers? The discourse around this issue has intensified since 2020, when educational disruptions caused by the COVID-19 pandemic led to unprecedented reliance on learning management systems, algorithmic tutoring, and adaptive learning tools. In 2023, the *OECD Education Policy Outlook* reported that 72% of member countries had adopted AI-assisted learning systems or analytics platforms in their national strategies (OECD, 2023).

Across policy documents and EdTech marketing, a recurring claim is that AI systems can outperform teachers in efficiency, personalization, and scalability. The *World Bank's Education Technology Review* (2022) described AI as a "frontier solution" capable of addressing shortages in teacher supply and uneven quality across low- and middle-income nations. Similar enthusiasm characterizes UNESCO *Report* (2021) which highlights the potential of intelligent tutoring systems to "free educators from repetitive tasks." While these developments reflect legitimate aspirations for innovation, they also rest on a narrow interpretation of teaching as content delivery and learning as data optimization.

Such a perspective reflects what Selwyn (2019) terms "technological solutionism," the belief that complex social and moral practices can be resolved through technical intervention. Within this paradigm, teachers are reframed as facilitators of machine-curated knowledge rather than as agents of moral and interpretive judgment. The consequence is not merely professional displacement but an erosion of education's ethical and civic purposes. As Biesta (2017) observes, education involves not only *qualification* the acquisition of knowledge and skills but also *socialization* and *subjectification*, the processes through which learners become responsible, autonomous persons. Only the first of these dimensions can be meaningfully supported by automation.

The notion of a *pedagogical soul* emerges from this context as both a critique and an alternative. It captures those elements of teaching that resist codification: moral responsibility, empathy, contextual understanding, and interpretive

DOI: 10.4018/979-8-3373-8983-7.ch026

sensitivity. Dewey (1938) described education as a "reconstruction of experience," emphasizing the relational and situational nature of learning. Freire (1970) later expanded this view through the idea of dialogic pedagogy, where teaching is a moral act grounded in solidarity and mutual recognition. To describe this moral-interpretive dimension as a "soul" is not to invoke metaphysics but to affirm that teaching involves meaning-making, ethical presence, and emotional attunement qualities that cannot be engineered. While recent AI systems, such as large language models and affective computing tools, simulate conversational and emotional behaviors, they do not possess *intentionality* or moral accountability. Searle's (1980) "Chinese Room" argument illustrates this distinction: machines manipulate symbols according to rules but do not understand meanings. This absence of intentional consciousness renders AI incapable of genuine moral or pedagogical judgment. Dreyfus (1992) similarly contends that human expertise depends on embodied experience and situational awareness, which no computational process can reproduce.

Beyond philosophical considerations, empirical research reinforces the irreplaceable role of teachers in shaping learning outcomes. Studies in affective neuroscience reveal how emotional attunement and trust between teachers and students foster motivation and deeper learning (Immordino-Yang & Damasio, 2007). Machine-based learning environments, despite their adaptability, cannot replicate the subtle cues and empathic responses that constitute classroom life.

Contemporary policy debates often obscure these findings by emphasizing cost-effectiveness and scalability. The *OECD Report* (2021) warns that algorithmic systems may "redefine teaching work around data interpretation rather than pedagogical engagement." Similarly, the *UNESCO Recommendation on the Ethics of Artificial Intelligence* (2021) underscores the dangers of delegating educational authority to systems that lack transparency or ethical reasoning. In low-resource contexts, these systems risk reinforcing existing inequities. Studies from India's National Education Policy review (NEP, 2020) and Kenya's Digital Learning Programme indicate that technology adoption without corresponding teacher training widens achievement gaps (World Bank, 2022).

The central argument of this chapter, therefore, is that the irreplaceability of teachers lies not in their mastery of information but in their moral and relational capacities. Teachers do not merely deliver knowledge; they model ethical reasoning, interpret social meaning, and nurture the conditions for democratic citizenship. Palmer (1998) referred to this as "teaching from within," where authenticity and vulnerability shape the learning encounter. The human presence of the teacher transforms education into a moral dialogue rather than a transaction of data.

As AI becomes further embedded in educational governance through predictive analytics, automated grading, and curriculum optimization, there is an urgent need to reassert this humanistic foundation. The pedagogical soul, as conceptualized here, signifies education's moral consciousness. It insists that while technology can support and enrich teaching, it cannot replace the moral, affective, and interpretive dimensions that define it. The following section develops the theoretical scaffolding for this claim by examining how classical and contemporary educational philosophies contrast with the logic of machine learning and algorithmic optimization.

Research questions and methodological approach

The present chapter adopts a qualitative and interpretive research approach to examine the evolving relationship between artificial intelligence and human pedagogy. Rather than treating technology purely as a technical development, the analysis situates AI within philosophical, ethical, and educational debates concerning the role of teachers in contemporary learning systems. The study relies on a combination of conceptual analysis, policy review, and secondary empirical evidence drawn from international and Indian educational research.

The research design integrates three complementary methods. First, a **philosophical–analytical method** is employed to interpret classical educational theories of Dewey, Freire, Noddings, and Biesta in relation to contemporary developments in artificial intelligence. Second, a **policy analysis method** is used to examine major educational frameworks such as the National Education Policy (2020), UNESCO's Recommendation on the Ethics of Artificial Intelligence (2021), and OECD educational technology reports. Third, the chapter incorporates **secondary empirical evidence and illustrative case examples** from Indian classrooms, EdTech initiatives, and digital learning programs in order to contextualize the theoretical claims.

The chapter is guided by the following research questions:

- To what extent can artificial intelligence replicate or substitute the pedagogical functions performed by human teachers?
- How do ethical, relational, and emotional dimensions of teaching challenge the assumption that education can be automated?
- What are the implications of AI-driven education systems for teacher autonomy, student agency, and democratic learning in the Indian context?
- How can technology be integrated into education in ways that support rather than undermine the pedagogical role of teachers?

2. THEORETICAL FOUNDATIONS OF PEDAGOGY AND MACHINE LEARNING

Teaching and learning have long been examined not merely as acts of knowledge transmission but as complex moral, social, and epistemological practices. The philosophical traditions that shaped modern pedagogy pragmatism, critical humanism, and phenomenology converge on a central insight: education is inherently relational and dialogical. By contrast, the computational logic of AI is grounded in prediction, optimization, and replication of patterns derived from data. This section juxtaposes these two worldviews to reveal why machine intelligence cannot fully emulate pedagogical understanding.

Figure 1. Theoretical foundations of pedagogy and machine learning

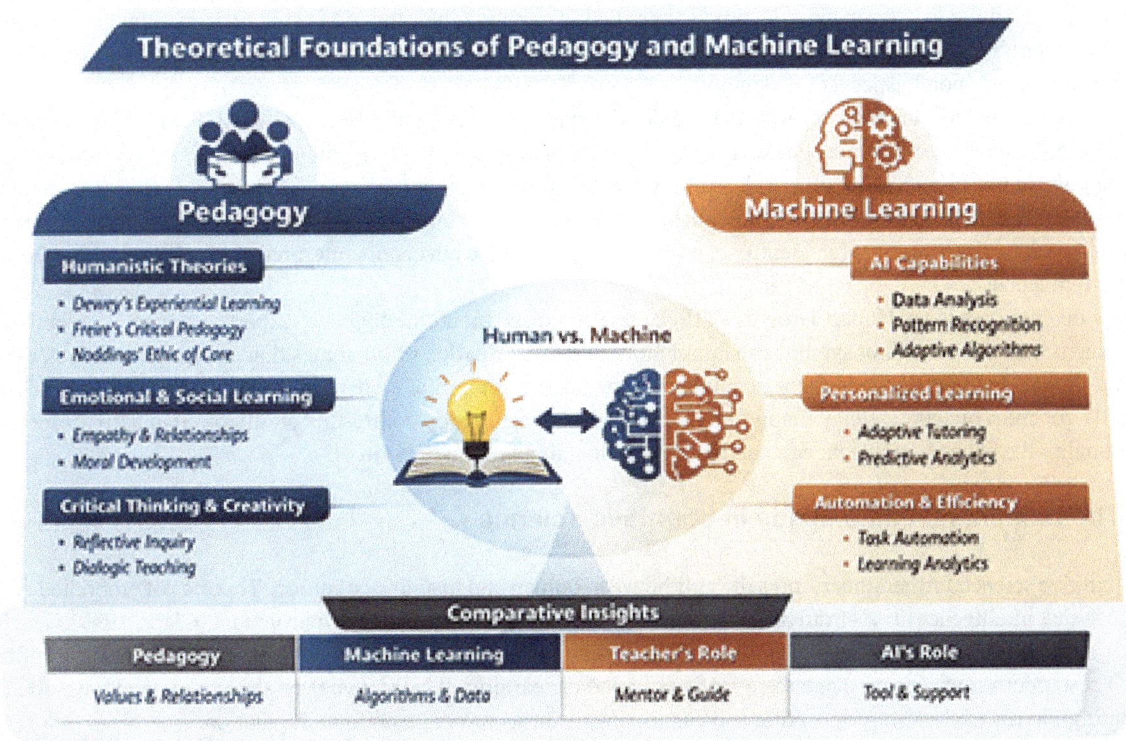

(Source: Author's estimate)

2.1. Education as moral and relational practice

John Dewey's *Experience and Education* (1938) positioned teaching as a process of experiential reconstruction, where knowledge emerges through inquiry embedded in social contexts. Dewey emphasized the teacher's role as a guide who mediates between the learner's experience and the collective aims of society. This mediating function requires ethical discernment and situational awareness, capacities that resist formalization. Paulo Freire (1970), writing from a critical perspective, reframed education as a dialogic process of humanization. For Freire, teaching is not a unidirectional act of information transfer but a mutual search for meaning grounded in empathy and ethical responsibility.

More recent work continues to highlight this moral dimension. Nel Noddings (2013) advanced an "ethic of care" as the foundation of educational practice, describing caring as both a relational and moral act. Caring teachers respond to students as unique beings, not as data points in an assessment matrix. Neuroscientific studies lend empirical support to these insights. Immordino-Yang and Damasio (2007) found that emotion is integral to reasoning and decision-making in learning contexts, implying that affective attunement is not ancillary but central to cognition. Machines, lacking emotion and embodied intersubjectivity, cannot replicate this dimension of human understanding.

Gert Biesta (2017) further conceptualized teaching as involving *subjectification* the formation of moral and autonomous persons. Technology can assist with *qualification* and *socialization*, but subjectification depends on encounters that disrupt, challenge, and affirm the learner's sense of agency. This relational event cannot be programmed, as it involves a teacher's moral presence and interpretive tact.

2.2. Machine learning and the logic of optimization

Artificial intelligence operates on an entirely different epistemic foundation. Machine learning systems are designed to detect statistical regularities in data and produce predictive outputs. Their function is not understanding but optimization. The underlying assumption is that learning can be modeled as pattern recognition - a notion sharply at odds with the interpretive and moral aspects of pedagogy.

AI's expansion into education began with behaviourist "teaching machines" developed by B. F. Skinner in the 1950s, which sought to automate reinforcement learning. Although contemporary systems employ sophisticated neural networks, the pedagogical premise remains similar: learning is treated as an input–output process. Holmes et al. (2022) note that adaptive learning platforms now use reinforcement algorithms to personalize instruction but still rely on quantifiable performance data. Such systems can identify gaps in factual knowledge but cannot interpret ambiguity, ethical dilemmas, or cultural nuance.

This distinction echoes Hubert Dreyfus's (1992) critique of artificial intelligence: expertise depends on embodied engagement with the world, not symbolic manipulation. Similarly, Searle (1980) argues that computational systems can simulate linguistic competence without genuine understanding a limitation evident in AI chatbots that produce grammatically coherent but contextually inappropriate responses. Teaching, by contrast, is an interpretive activity rooted in intentionality the capacity to mean, care, and judge within a lived moral horizon.

2.3. The human–machine divide in cognitive science

Cognitive science further underscores the gulf between human and machine cognition. Theories of embodied cognition posit that intelligence arises from the body's sensorimotor interaction with the environment (Clark, 1999). Teachers employ such embodied awareness in classroom dynamics modulating tone, gesture, and pacing in response to students' cues. These micro-interactions shape the affective climate of learning. AI systems, even those equipped with affective computing interfaces, lack proprioception and cannot engage in reciprocal emotional regulation.

Empirical findings support this distinction. Studies by Immordino-Yang (2015) and Jennings and Greenberg (2009) show that emotional resonance between teachers and students predicts engagement and academic resilience. In contrast, analyses of automated tutoring systems reveal limitations in sustaining motivation beyond short-term tasks (Luckin et al., 2016). The *OECD* report (2019) concludes that while AI can personalize pacing and content, it "cannot replicate the empathic, ethical, and cultural mediation central to teaching."

The cognitive limitations of AI are paralleled by epistemological ones. Human understanding is interpretive and context-sensitive; AI learning is inductive and data-bound. Machine learning, by contrast, functions through statistical correlations devoid of historical consciousness. Teaching, as a hermeneutic act, requires precisely this temporal and ethical situatedness.

2.4. Synthesis: Pedagogical understanding and machine intelligence

Across these theoretical strands pragmatism, critical pedagogy, ethics of care, phenomenology, and cognitive science a consistent pattern emerges. Teaching is characterized by moral intentionality, affective presence, and interpretive judgment. Machine intelligence, though increasingly capable of simulation, remains confined to procedural and predictive functions. The distinction is not one of degree but of kind.

The challenge for contemporary education, therefore, is not to resist technological advancement but to safeguard the pedagogical essence that defines human teaching. Theories of AI in education often emphasize scalability and personalization, yet they risk abstracting learners from the ethical and social contexts that give education meaning. Recognizing this tension invites a more integrated framework in which technology supports but does not supplant the moral and relational dimensions of teaching.

Table 1 consolidates the theoretical distinctions between pedagogy and machine learning, highlighting how humanistic education operates within ethical, contextual, and interpretive dimensions that data-driven systems can only approximate. The following section turns to empirical evidence from Indian classrooms to examine how these contrasts unfold in practice.

Table 1. Comparison of Pedagogical and Machine-Learning Foundations

Dimension	Pedagogical Foundations	Machine-Learning Foundations	Interpretation
Epistemology	Knowledge is constructed through experience, reflection, and dialogue.	Knowledge is extracted statistically from large datasets.	Pedagogy seeks *meaning*; ML seeks *correlation.*
Philosophical Orientation	Humanism and pragmatism—learning as growth and social transformation.	Positivism and computational rationality—learning as optimization.	Humanistic inquiry vs. algorithmic prediction.
Moral Dimension	Teaching entails moral responsibility, empathy, and care.	Systems lack intentionality or moral agency.	Ethical presence cannot be programmed.
Cognitive Model	Embodied and socially mediated cognition.	Abstract symbol manipulation and pattern recognition.	Human learning is contextual; ML is statistical.
Learning Process	Dialogic, iterative, and relational.	Feed-forward and feedback loops optimizing outputs.	Dialogue produces understanding; data loops produce prediction.
Role of the Teacher / Designer	Reflective practitioner and moral guide who interprets contexts.	System architect who defines parameters and metrics.	Judgment vs. configuration.
Role of the Learner / User	Co-creator of meaning and subject of transformation.	Data source generating behavioral traces for model training.	Learner as agent vs. learner as dataset.
Emotional Dimension	Integral to cognition and motivation; relationships drive learning.	Simulated through affective computing; lacks genuine empathy.	Emotional intelligence is lived, not coded.
Equity and Inclusion	Values diversity and cultural context.	Risks bias through non-representative data.	Equity requires ethical design and human oversight.
Goal of Education / System	Human formation—ethical, civic, and creative growth.	Performance optimization and predictive accuracy.	Human flourishing transcends efficiency.

(The table was designed by the Author, based on: Dewey (1938); Freire (1970); Biesta (2017); Dreyfus (1992); Noddings (2013); Immordino-Yang (2015); Searle (1980); Holmes et al. (2022); NITI Aayog (2021); UNESCO (2021); World Bank (2022); and Goleman (1995)).

1. **Meaning vs. Prediction** → Pedagogy interprets experience; machine learning models it.
2. **Ethics as Core, not Add-on** → Teachers embody care; algorithms lack accountability.
3. **Context Matters** → Indian multilingual, socio-economic diversity resists uniform algorithmic templates.
4. **Equity through Design** → AI inclusion requires participatory, local-language datasets (AI4Bharat 2022).

5. **Complement, Don't Replace** → Technology must augment reflective practice, not dictate it.

3. AI, SIMULATION, AND THE LIMITS OF AUTOMATION

The integration of artificial intelligence in education has gained increasing momentum globally and within India's rapidly expanding EdTech sector. From adaptive tutoring systems to automated grading tools, AI applications promise to make education more efficient, personalized, and accessible. But beneath these technological ambitions lie fundamental epistemic and ethical tensions. Education, as both an intellectual and moral enterprise, cannot be fully captured through computational simulation. While machines may imitate certain teaching behaviours, they cannot replicate the interpretive, ethical, and contextual intelligence that defines human pedagogy.

3.1. The rise of AI in Indian education

India's education system, serving over 265 million school students and 38 million higher education learners, faces acute challenges of scale and equity (Ministry of Education, 2023). The government's *National Education Policy (NEP) 2020* identifies digital learning and artificial intelligence as key drivers of transformation. Initiatives such as *SWAYAM*, *DIKSHA*, and *NPTEL* have expanded access to open educational resources, while AI-driven platforms like *Byju's*, *Toppr*, and *Vedantu* have redefined private digital learning markets (NITI Aayog, 2021).

According to a *KPMG India* (2022) analysis, the Indian EdTech industry was valued at USD 3.5 billion in 2022 and projected to grow at a compound annual rate of 39% through 2026. These platforms employ machine learning algorithms for personalized content recommendation, performance tracking, and predictive analytics. While this innovation aligns with India's *Digital India* vision, it also risks reinforcing socio-economic and linguistic inequalities. Research by the *Brookings Institution India Center* (Sharma & Sahni, 2021) found that 68% of rural students lacked stable internet access, limiting the reach of AI-enabled learning tools to urban, English-speaking populations.

The *AI for All* initiative launched by the *Ministry of Electronics and Information Technology (MeitY)* in collaboration with Intel (2021) seeks to enhance AI literacy among students and teachers. The reports from UNESCO (2023) and the *OECD* (2023) warn that the expansion of AI in education without robust ethical governance risks data exploitation, algorithmic bias, and de-professionalization of teachers. In India, these challenges are amplified by infrastructural disparities and weak regulatory oversight of private EdTech providers.

During the pandemic period, several schools in Delhi, Maharashtra, and Karnataka experimented with AI-enabled adaptive learning platforms to compensate for teacher shortages. While these platforms successfully provided structured practice exercises and automated feedback, field observations reported by state education departments indicated that students often disengaged in the absence of teacher interaction. Teachers noted that students required encouragement, contextual explanations, and moral guidance, particularly, when dealing with uncertainty or emotional stress. In many cases, the presence of a teacher during hybrid sessions significantly improved participation and comprehension.

A similar pattern was observed in government schools using DIKSHA-based digital learning modules. Although the platform improved access to learning materials, teachers remained central in interpreting content, translating concepts into local languages, and addressing the socio-cultural issues that digital platforms could not anticipate. These experiences demonstrate that technology can enhance access, but cannot substitute the relational and interpretive functions of teaching.

3.2. Simulation and the limits of understanding

The core limitation of AI in education lies in its reliance on simulation rather than genuine understanding. AI systems, whether rule-based or generative, operate through data-driven correlations rather than interpretive reasoning. Searle's (1980) argument remains instructive: computers manipulate symbols without comprehending their meaning. In the classroom context, this translates to systems that can deliver content, assess responses, and mimic conversational tone, but that cannot *understand* learners' emotions, intentions, or moral struggles.

Empirical evaluations corroborate this distinction. A meta-analysis by Holmes et al. (2022) found that while intelligent tutoring systems improved factual recall and test performance, their impact on critical thinking, creativity, and empathy remained negligible. Similarly, a 2022 *World Bank* report on *Learning in the Age of Digital Disruption* concluded that automated instruction enhances efficiency but not depth of understanding or civic learning.

These findings highlight the distinction between cognitive automation and moral formation. Machines excel at pattern recognition but fail to interpret ambiguity, irony, or ethical nuance qualities embedded in classroom discourse. As Dreyfus (1992) argued, human expertise involves embodied experience and situational sensitivity, which cannot be formalized as algorithms. Indian classrooms, often characterized by linguistic diversity and socio-economic heterogeneity, demand precisely this contextual responsiveness.

To summarise, we can say that teaching cannot be fully automated for three reasons. First, it requires **moral judgment**, which algorithms lack. Second, it depends on **contextual interpretation** of dynamic classroom situations. Third, it is inherently **relational**, built on trust and empathy. AI may optimize instruction, but it cannot replace the human presence that gives education meaning.

3.3. The mirage of emotional AI

Recent advances in affective computing claim to detect students' emotions using facial recognition, voice modulation, and physiological sensors. Indian EdTech companies such as *Embibe* and *iDream Education* have explored emotion-tracking features to personalize learning. But scholars caution that such applications raise serious ethical and epistemic concerns. Benjamin (2019) and Crawford (2021) warn that affect recognition often reflects Western psychological assumptions and may misread culturally diverse expressions. In India's multicultural classrooms, emotion detection algorithms risk misclassification and bias, particularly against marginalized groups.

The *UNESCO Recommendation on the Ethics of Artificial Intelligence* (2021) explicitly prohibits AI systems from making high-stakes decisions based on inferred emotions or behavioural surveillance. A 2023 report by the *Observer Research Foundation (ORF)* emphasized that India's nascent data protection framework lacks explicit safeguards for educational data collected through AI platforms (Sharma et al., 2023). Without transparency and accountability, emotional AI could transform classrooms into sites of surveillance rather than empathy.

3.4. Algorithmic pedagogy and dehumanization

The automation of teaching through data analytics also threatens the relational fabric of pedagogy. When algorithms mediate curriculum design, assessment, and classroom management, teachers risk becoming operators of pre-programmed systems. Selwyn (2019) describes this as "algorithmic pedagogy," where professional judgment is supplanted by predictive analytics. Indian teachers already face systemic constraints large class sizes, exam-oriented curricula, and administrative overload that reduce opportunities for reflective engagement. Introducing AI without redefining teacher agency may further narrow their role to data interpreters.

Another emerging concern in AI-driven education is the so-called **"black box" problem** of algorithmic decision-making. Many machine learning systems operate through complex models whose internal logic is not easily interpretable even by developers. When such opaque systems are used to recommend learning pathways, evaluate performance, or predict student outcomes, teachers may find it difficult to question or override these decisions. This opacity undermines the interpretive role of educators and raises ethical questions about accountability and fairness. Transparent and explainable AI systems are therefore essential if teachers are to maintain professional judgment and ensure that technological recommendations align with pedagogical values.

3.5. The human element beyond automation

Teaching involves more than transmitting knowledge; it entails cultivating curiosity, ethical reasoning, and community. These aspects are inherently dialogical and cannot be automated. Dewey (1938) viewed education as a moral process in which teachers model inquiry and democratic participation. In India, this vision resonates with Rabindranath Tagore's humanist philosophy, which emphasized experiential learning grounded in compassion and creativity (Tagore, 1917/2008). AI systems, designed for efficiency, are ill-equipped to nurture such dispositions.

The limits of automation thus reveal a deeper question about educational purpose. If the aim of schooling is not merely skill acquisition but human flourishing, then machines can only assist, not replace, teachers. As the *National Education Policy 2020* affirms, "technology must serve pedagogy, not the other way around." The next section elaborates this principle through the ethical, affective, and relational dimensions of teaching what may be called the moral architecture of the pedagogical soul.

4. ETHICS, CARE, AND RESPONSIBILITY IN EDUCATION

The ethical dimension of teaching defines the essence of education as a human practice. Beyond the transmission of knowledge, teaching involves moral responsibility, empathy, and care. In India's plural and stratified society, this ethical vocation carries additional weight, as teachers mediate between cultural diversity, social justice, and democratic inclusion. Understanding the pedagogical soul in this context requires examining how ethics and care inform the teacher–student relationship and why these cannot be replicated by machines.

4.1. Teaching as a moral responsibility

Teaching is an ethical act because it concerns the formation of persons. As Biesta (2017) argues, teachers are responsible not only for what students learn but also who they become. This responsibility entails moral discernment, the ability to interpret learners' needs within social and cultural contexts. In India, where classrooms often include wide variations in caste, language, and gender identity, pedagogical ethics also means recognizing and responding to systemic inequalities.

4.2. The ethic of care in Indian classrooms

Nel Noddings' (2013) ethic of care provides a powerful framework for reimagining pedagogy as relational practice. Caring involves attentiveness, responsibility, and reciprocity qualities that depend on emotional presence. Indian educators have long emphasized similar values. Gandhi's *Nai Talim* envisioned education as *sambandh* (relationship), rooted in compassion and community service (Gandhi, 1951). Tagore's *Santiniketan* model likewise celebrated affective connection between teacher and student as the basis of creativity.

Research confirms the relevance of care-based pedagogy in Indian contexts. *UNICEF India* (2021) study on girls' education highlighted the importance of caring teachers in supporting adolescent well-being during digital learning transitions. AI-driven systems, lacking emotional consciousness, cannot provide such moral anchorage.

4.3. Emotional intelligence and pedagogical presence

Teaching draws heavily on emotional intelligence the capacity to perceive, understand, and regulate emotions in oneself and others. Goleman (1995) described this as a crucial determinant of leadership and learning outcomes. Jennings and Greenberg (2009) demonstrated that teacher emotional competence predicts student engagement and classroom climate.

4.4. Ethical risks of delegating care to machines

Delegating caring functions to AI in education introduces ethical risks that extend beyond accuracy. First, it dilutes moral accountability. When algorithms decide interventions, it becomes unclear who bears responsibility for student well-being. Second, data-driven care invites surveillance. UNESCO's *Recommendation on the Ethics of Artificial Intelligence* (2021) insists that educational AI must protect human oversight and agency. Yet Indian EdTech firms operate in a regulatory grey zone. The *Digital Personal Data Protection Act* (Government of India, 2023) lacks sector-specific provisions for minors' data.

4.5. Care, equity, and social justice

The ethic of care is inseparable from social justice. In India's stratified society, caring pedagogy resists exclusion by recognizing students' lived realities. Freire's (1970) dialogic method finds resonance in Indian initiatives such as *Eklavya* and *Bharat Gyan Vigyan Samiti*, which foreground participatory learning among marginalized communities. Studies show that when teachers adopt relational approaches emphasizing empathy and dignity, students from disadvantaged groups exhibit stronger academic persistence (Govinda & Bandyopadhyay, 2019).

AI-driven education risks neutralizing these contextual sensitivities. Algorithms trained on homogeneous datasets often replicate existing biases. A 2024 *NASSCOM* report acknowledged that most Indian EdTech AI models use urban-centric datasets, underrepresenting rural and tribal learners. Without ethical oversight, such bias undermines inclusion the moral cornerstone of Indian education policy.

4.6. Teacher agency and ethical judgment

Ethical teaching depends on professional autonomy. Teachers interpret curricula and respond to ethical dilemmas using practical wisdom (*phronesis*). When automation dictates pacing or assessment, this agency erodes. This perspective echoes the NEP (2020) vision, which defines teachers as "designers of learning experiences and facilitators of inquiry." It emphasizes continuous professional development and reflective practice. Integrating AI ethically, therefore, demands participatory co-design where teachers remain decision-makers, not mere implementers.

4.7. Cultural ethics and the Indian pedagogical soul

The Indian philosophical tradition situates education within a moral cosmology of *seva* (service), *ahimsa* (non-harm), and *satyagraha* (truth-seeking). These principles frame teaching as a spiritual and ethical pursuit. Tagore, Gandhi, and Sri Aurobindo envisioned education as self-realization through empathy and community engagement. In this vision, the "pedagogical soul" reflects the unity of knowledge and compassion's synthesis, absent in machine logic.

The *AI4Bharat Initiative* at IIT Madras (2022) integrates ethical AI development rooted in linguistic diversity and social inclusion. Such efforts suggest that India's educational modernization need not sacrifice its moral foundations.

4.8. Synthesis: The moral architecture of teaching

Ethics and care are not peripheral virtues but the structural pillars of pedagogy. Teachers embody responsibility, empathy, and interpretive judgment capacities rooted in consciousness and moral freedom. Machines, by contrast, lack intention and accountability. Their operations are functional, not ethical. As the Indian context illustrates, delegating moral labor to AI risks undermining the very essence of education as human formation.

The challenge for Indian education is thus to harmonize innovation with ethical stewardship. AI can augment teaching but must remain subordinate to the teacher's moral and relational intelligence. The pedagogical soul endures not as a nostalgic metaphor but as a living ethical reality the conscience of education in a digital age.

5. TEACHER AUTONOMY AND PROFESSIONAL JUDGMENT

The vitality of any education system rests on the professional autonomy and moral judgment of its teachers. In India, where education serves as both a developmental and a democratizing project, teacher agency is not a luxury but a necessity. The emergence of artificial intelligence and data-driven education has complicated this terrain by reconfiguring the meaning of pedagogical decision-making. As algorithmic systems begin to shape assessment, content delivery, and classroom management, teachers face a subtle but pervasive erosion of professional discretion. This section explores the philosophical, institutional, and technological dimensions of teacher autonomy in the Indian context.

5.1. The meaning of professional judgment

Professional judgment in teaching refers to the capacity to interpret complex educational situations and act wisely amid uncertainty. Schön (1983) described this as "reflection-in-action," a process where practitioners draw upon tacit knowledge to respond to real-time challenges. In India, this reflective ability is essential because classrooms are deeply heterogeneous defined by linguistic diversity, varying socio-economic backgrounds, and differing levels of parental literacy. Teachers must therefore constantly adapt pedagogical strategies to fit the lived realities of their students.

The *National Council for Teacher Education (NCTE)* in its *National Curriculum Framework for Teacher Education (NCFTE)* (2009) emphasized that teachers are not mere "transmitters of information" but "transformative intellectuals" responsible for nurturing critical and democratic citizenship. However in practice, professional autonomy remains constrained by bureaucratic accountability, exam-oriented curricula, and now increasingly by the logic of automation. The integration of AI into school systems, while potentially easing clerical burdens, also introduces new forms of surveillance and control.

5.2. Algorithmic governance and pedagogical control

The shift toward AI-enabled education platforms has generated new power asymmetries. Teachers are increasingly managed by data dashboards that track attendance, performance, and "learning outcomes." The *Samagra Shiksha* program and *DIKSHA* platform central pillars of India's digital education strategy use analytics to monitor teacher performance across states. While these initiatives aim to ensure accountability, they also reconfigure autonomy by transforming qualitative pedagogical acts into quantifiable indicators. Selwyn (2019) cautions that algorithmic systems impose "data-driven performativity," where professional success is defined by metrics rather than moral or contextual judgment. Decisions previously based on student dialogue were now informed by algorithmic recommendations. In states such as Andhra Pradesh and Gujarat, where AI-based "performance monitoring" tools were piloted, educators expressed concern that human relationships were being replaced by digital feedback loops. The problem is not technology *per se* but its use as an apparatus of control rather than collaboration.

5.3. Teacher autonomy and educational equity

Professional judgment also serves a social function: it enables teachers to respond ethically to inequality. India's schooling system continues to mirror social hierarchies of caste, class, and gender (Govinda & Bandyopadhyay, 2019). A teacher's interpretive freedom allows for differentiated instruction that recognizes these inequities. When AI platforms standardize content and assessment, they risk deepening disparities by ignoring cultural and linguistic diversity. Research by Sharma and Sahni (2021) for *Brookings India* found that digital learning algorithms often favour English-speaking students and urban schools, perpetuating the marginalization of rural and tribal learners.

Autonomy thus becomes an ethical imperative: teachers must be free to adapt, translate, and contextualize technology for inclusive learning. The *National Education Policy (NEP) 2020* acknowledges this when it calls for empowering teachers as "designers of learning experiences" rather than implementers of fixed curricula. Yet realizing this vision requires institutional trust and investment in professional development, both of which remain uneven across states.

5.4. Reflective practice in Indian teacher education

The erosion of professional judgment is partly rooted in the structure of teacher education itself. For decades, training programs have emphasized compliance over inquiry. The Justice Verma Commission report (2012) noted that teacher preparation in India often prioritizes content delivery and procedural conformity, leaving little space for reflective engagement. Reforms initiated under the *NCTE Integrated Teacher Education Programme (ITEP)* (2021) seek to restore autonomy by embedding ethics, research, and reflection into teacher preparation.

AI tools could, in principle, support reflective practice by providing diagnostic insights or facilitating peer learning networks. When embedded within hierarchical systems of evaluation, these tools risk narrowing professional discourse. Teachers must therefore be trained not merely to use AI but to *critique* and *curate* it.

5.5. Reclaiming agency in a digital era

Empowering teachers in an age of AI requires rebalancing authority between human and machine intelligence. The *NITI Aayog Responsible AI for Social Empowerment (RAISE)* framework advocates a "human-in-command" principle, ensuring that educators retain decision-making power. Several Indian initiatives exemplify this balance. The *Central Board of Secondary Education (CBSE)*'s *AI Curriculum Integration Project* encourages teachers to use AI to design creative assessments rather than replace them.

5.6. Autonomy as moral responsibility

Teacher autonomy is not isolation; it is moral responsibility exercised in community. Biesta (2017) distinguishes between freedom *from* interference and freedom *for* responsible action. In India's educational ethos shaped by thinkers such as Tagore, Gandhi, and Aurobindo, autonomy is tied to *seva* (service) and ethical discernment. Teachers must remain accountable to learners and society, not to algorithms or bureaucratic targets. Restoring professional judgment, therefore, is essential to preserving education's ethical and democratic character.

As the Indian education system continues its digital transformation, the challenge is not to resist technology but to humanize it. The autonomy of teachers must be the axis around which innovation revolves. This autonomy, informed by reflection, empathy, and moral judgment, constitutes the living conscience of education the pedagogical soul that sustains democratic learning.

6. EDUCATION, DEMOCRACY, AND HUMAN FORMATION

Education and democracy share a moral covenant. Both rest on dialogue, critical inquiry, and respect for human dignity. In India, this connection is constitutionally enshrined: the *Right to Education Act (Government of India, 2009)* and the *National Education Policy* (Ministry of Education, Government of India, 2020) articulate education as a means of cultivating democratic citizenship and social justice. The rise of AI-driven education, however, poses new questions about how democratic and humanistic values can be preserved in an increasingly automated learning environment.

6.1. The democratic purpose of education

John Dewey's (1938) idea of education as the "foundation of democracy" resonates deeply with India's constitutional vision. Democracy, for Dewey, is not merely a political structure but a way of life, a mode of associated living that depends on communication and participation. In India, thinkers like Mahatma Gandhi and Rabindranath Tagore translated this philosophy into indigenous terms. Gandhi's *Nai Talim* emphasized self-reliance, moral character, and community service as the essence of education, while Tagore's *Santiniketan* promoted creativity and freedom as pathways to harmony. Both viewed education as the cultivation of ethical citizens capable of reasoning and compassion.

In the digital age, these democratic aspirations confront new challenges. AI-based systems often privilege efficiency and standardization, narrowing space for deliberation. When algorithms determine pacing and assessment, they shape what counts as knowledge and who counts as a successful learner. UNESCO's report (2021) cautions that AI-driven education, if left unchecked, may "redefine learners as data subjects rather than agents." In India, this risk is compounded by socio-economic stratification; digital learning may widen divides between privileged and marginalized communities, thereby weakening democracy's moral foundation.

6.2. Human formation and moral agency

Education's ultimate purpose is *human formation*: the nurturing of autonomy, empathy, and ethical reasoning. Biesta (2017) calls this process *subjectification,* i.e. the becoming of responsible persons. For Indian educators, this has historically been articulated as *man-making education*, a term popularized by Swami Vivekananda. It implies developing character and conscience alongside intellect. AI systems, while adept at optimizing performance, cannot cultivate such moral awareness. Their operations are rule-bound and devoid of intentionality.

While much of the debate on artificial intelligence in education focuses on teachers, it is equally important to consider its impact on students' agency. AI-based learning systems often structure educational experiences through predefined pathways, predictive recommendations, and standardized performance metrics. Although these tools may enhance efficiency, they can also limit opportunities for students to explore ideas independently or engage in critical dialogue.

Student agency involves the ability to question knowledge, interpret experiences, and participate actively in the learning process. In traditional classrooms, teachers facilitate this agency by encouraging discussion, disagreement, and reflection. When learning becomes heavily mediated by algorithms, there is a risk that students may internalize knowledge as something delivered by systems rather than constructed through inquiry. Strengthening student agency, therefore, requires teachers to remain active mediators who encourage critical engagement with technology rather than passive acceptance of algorithmic authority.

6.3. Democracy and digital inequality

The democratic promise of AI in education lies in access, but the reality often reproduces inequality. India's *Annual Status of Education Report (ASER)* (2022) revealed that while 77% of urban students had internet-enabled devices, only 31% of rural households did. Gender disparities remain stark: girls in rural areas are 20% less likely than boys to have access to digital learning tools. When AI-based education becomes the norm, these inequities translate into civic exclusion.

Policy responses acknowledge this risk. The *NEP 2020* and *NITI Aayog's Responsible AI for Social Empowerment (RAISE)* framework advocate inclusive AI design and local-language adaptation. However, implementation remains uneven. Studies by UNESCO (2023) and the *Observer Research Foundation* (Sharma et al., 2023) warn that unregulated private EdTech growth in India can commodify education and marginalize vulnerable learners. Democracy, understood as a collective endeavour, depends on ensuring that technological modernization does not erode equal participation.

6.4. Teachers as democratic agents

Teachers are central to the democratic mission of education. They model deliberation, respect, and critical questioning. Dewey (1938) described teachers as "agents of public intelligence," mediating between individual growth and societal good. In India, this role takes on added significance amid cultural and linguistic plurality. The teacher's interpretive presence enables democratic dialogue across difference.

Agorithmic instruction reduces dialogic interaction to a sequence of tasks, replacing conversation with computation. The relational essence of democracy -listening, disagreement and ethical persuasion, is lost, when learning becomes transactional.

So in contemporary digital learning environments, the democratic role of teachers becomes even more significant. Teachers not only guide academic learning but also help students critically understand the technologies shaping their lives. By facilitating discussions on data ethics, algorithmic bias, and digital citizenship, educators ensure that technological literacy is accompanied by democratic awareness. In this sense, the teacher's role evolves rather than diminishes in the age of AI, becoming a bridge between technological innovation and democratic responsibility.

6.5. Civic education in the age of AI

Civic education has traditionally been conveyed through discussion, storytelling, and moral exemplars. In India's social studies and political science curricula, teachers often mediate between abstract democratic ideals and lived realities of inequality. AI systems can deliver civic content but cannot model ethical commitment. UNESCO's *Report* (2021) emphasizes that "moral formation arises through encounter, not automation." Indian programs such as *Paryavaran Mitra* and *Youth Parliament* demonstrate the power of experiential learning in nurturing civic agency.

Integrating AI ethically into civic education would mean using it as a dialogic tool rather than a didactic authority. Virtual reality and simulation could, for instance, help students visualize democratic processes or environmental systems, but the interpretive guidance of the teacher remains indispensable.

6.6. Education as dialogue and human freedom

The relationship between education and democracy is ultimately a question of freedom to think, question, and act responsibly. Freire's (1970) dialogic pedagogy resonates powerfully in India's contemporary classrooms. Education, for Freire, is a practice of freedom where teachers and students co-create knowledge. This ethos aligns with the Indian philosophical concept of *anubhav* - knowledge born from lived experience. AI-based education, predicated on efficiency, risks displacing this dialogical mode with instrumental rationality.

Tagore warned a century ago that mechanized education produces conformity rather than creativity. His insight acquires new relevance in an era of algorithmic learning. To safeguard democracy, education must remain a space of unpredictability, where the human encounter between teacher and learner continues to generate meaning and moral growth.

6.7. Human formation as India's educational horizon

In the Indian context, human formation transcends academic achievement. It involves cultivating *karuna* (compassion), *satya* (truthfulness), and *sahishnuta* (tolerance) values embedded in the Constitution's Preamble. The *NEP 2020* reiterates these principles, envisioning education as "holistic, integrated, and value-based." AI systems, by contrast, optimize measurable outputs. When educational policy privileges efficiency over ethics, it risks divorcing learning from humanity.

Reclaiming education's humanistic mission requires policies that prioritize relationships over algorithms. Schools must empower teachers to engage students as moral agents and community members. Professional development programs should include ethics, dialogue, and reflective pedagogy alongside digital skills. Democratic education in India's future will depend not on how smart its machines become, but on how wise its teachers remain.

7. REFRAMING TECHNOLOGY AS PEDAGOGICAL SUPPORT

The question is not whether technology should have a place in education, but how it can support rather than supplant pedagogy. In India and globally, the proliferation of artificial intelligence (AI) and digital learning systems has generated both optimism and unease. The central argument advanced throughout this chapter that teaching possesses an irreducibly moral and relational dimension, it does not reject technology but calls for its principled integration. Reframing technology as pedagogical support means aligning innovation with the ethical, democratic, and humanistic purposes of education.

7.1. The principle of human oversight

UNESCO's *Recommendation on the Ethics of Artificial Intelligence* (2021) establishes a foundational principle: human oversight must remain central to all AI applications in education. Such policy statements reflect a growing consensus that teachers must retain authority over moral and interpretive decisions in classrooms. AI can analyze data, recommend resources, and streamline administrative tasks, but the final act of teaching the judgment of what is meaningful, just, or kind remains the domain of the human teacher.

Empirical examples affirm this approach. The *CBSE AI Curriculum integrations Project* launched in 2020 (Central Board of Secondary Education, 2020) trains teachers to use AI in designing creative assessments rather than delegating evaluation entirely to machines. The project emphasizes human-AI collaboration through problem-based learning, encouraging teachers to mentor students in understanding ethical dilemmas in AI applications. These initiatives illustrate how technology can expand pedagogical horizons without displacing the teacher's ethical agency.

7.2. Participatory design and co-agency

For technology to support pedagogy, teachers must participate in its design and governance. Studies in participatory technology design show that when educators are involved in shaping tools, they use them more creatively and responsibly (Williamson & Piattoeva, 2022). In India, the *DIKSHA* platform has begun implementing user-feedback loops that allow teachers to co-create and localize content in regional languages. Such co-agency transforms teachers from passive users into collaborators, ensuring that digital systems reflect diverse pedagogical cultures rather than enforcing uniformity.

7.3. Contextual adaptation and local knowledge

India's educational diversity demands context-sensitive technology design. Algorithms trained on global datasets often fail to accommodate local languages, pedagogies, or cultural nuances. The *AI4Bharat* initiative at IIT Madras (2022) exemplifies efforts to develop AI systems for Indian languages and inclusive education. By creating open-source datasets in Tamil, Hindi, Bengali, and other languages, it expands accessibility while preserving cultural integrity.

Local adaptation is equally critical for rural and marginalized communities. The Pratham Foundation's *(2022) Hybrid Learning Model* demonstrates how community facilitators can use low-cost digital tools to complement human instruction rather than replace it. Such initiatives affirm that pedagogical value arises when technology amplifies human connection within local realities.

7.4. Ethical digital pedagogy

Ethical digital pedagogy requires critical awareness of technology's moral implications. Teachers must be equipped to question algorithmic bias, data privacy violations, and inequities in access. A 2023 *Observer Research Foundation* study documented that several EdTech companies in India collected students' biometric and behavioral data without adequate consent (Sharma et al., 2023). Ethical training would enable teachers to identify and resist such practices. Moreover, integrating ethics of AI into curricula allows students to critically understand technology's societal impact turning classrooms into laboratories of democratic responsibility.

7.5. From automation to augmentation

The paradigm shift from automation to augmentation reframes technology as an ally of human creativity. Holmes et al., (2022) argue that AI should enhance human capacities for empathy, reasoning, and collaboration rather than replace them. In Indian classrooms, this might involve using adaptive platforms to differentiate instruction while freeing teachers to focus on mentoring and critical dialogue. AI can assist with administrative efficiency grading, attendance, and diagnostics allowing teachers to devote energy to emotional and ethical engagement.

The World Bank's *Report* (2022) underscores that the most effective educational technologies are those integrated with strong teacher support systems. In Government of the Indian state of Kerala's initiative *Hi-Tech School Programme* (KITE, 2026), digital tools are deployed alongside continuous professional development workshops. Teachers report that technology has improved their instructional flexibility and fostered peer collaboration. Such evidence supports the thesis that the pedagogical soul of education thrives when technology serves as scaffolding, not substitute.

7.6. Policy frameworks for human-centered innovation

Educational policy must translate these pedagogical insights into systemic safeguards. The *National Education Policy (NEP) 2020* (Ministry of Education, Government of India, 2020) emphasizes the "ethical and humanistic use of technology" and calls for the creation of a National Educational Technology Forum (NETF) to ensure participatory governance. This institutional mechanism can act as a bridge between research, classroom practice, and policymaking aligning technological development with democratic accountability.

International frameworks reinforce this direction. UNESCO (2021) envisions "technological humanism," while the *OECD Education Policy Outlook* (2023) recommends ethical auditing and open data standards for AI in education. India's adoption of similar norms could institutionalize transparency, teacher representation, and public trust in educational AI systems.

7.7. The future of human-AI collaboration in education

As India advances toward its vision of a digital knowledge society, the relationship between teachers and technology will increasingly define educational quality. The goal is not resistance but a partnership in which machines extend human capacity without diminishing moral agency. The next phase of educational innovation must therefore prioritize co-design, ethical reflection, and equity.

Universities and teacher education institutions should establish interdisciplinary programs on AI ethics and pedagogy, enabling future educators to navigate technological complexity with philosophical depth. Collaborative research between engineers, social scientists, and educators can generate culturally grounded AI models responsive to India's pluralism. Such collaboration embodies the spirit of *Vasudhaiva Kutumbakam,* the world as one family anchoring digital modernity in ethical universality.

Reframing technology as pedagogical support thus represents a reassertion of human purpose. It reminds policymakers, technologists, and educators alike that the ultimate goal of education is not to mechanize learning but to deepen understanding, empathy, and shared responsibility. When technology becomes a servant of these ends, it fulfils its true pedagogical promise.

In other words, a meaningful synthesis between artificial intelligence and pedagogy requires recognizing that both operate within different but complementary domains of intelligence. AI contributes to analytical efficiency, large-scale data processing, and personalized learning pathways, whereas teachers contribute to ethical judgment, contextual understanding, and emotional engagement. Educational innovation will be most effective when these strengths are integrated rather than treated as competing forces. Such synthesis reinforces the central thesis of this chapter: technology can enhance educational systems, but the pedagogical soul remains fundamentally human.

CONCLUSION

Education stands at a defining crossroads. The rise of artificial intelligence and automation has challenged humanity to reconsider what it means to teach and to learn. Across global systems and with particular urgency in India technological optimism has collided with ethical realism. This chapter has argued that while machines can process information, analyze data, and personalize instruction, they cannot embody the moral, relational, and interpretive essence that defines teaching. The "pedagogical soul" represents that irreducible human dimension empathy, judgment, and responsibility without which education loses its meaning.

Drawing upon philosophy, cognitive science, and empirical research, the analysis demonstrated that teaching is more than a technical function; it is a moral encounter rooted in care and dialogue. Dewey's vision of education as democratic growth, Freire's concept of dialogic liberation, and Noddings's ethic of care converge to affirm that learning is an ethical relationship, not an algorithmic process. In India's context, this relationship acquires special significance. The nation's educational traditions from Gandhi's *Nai Talim* to Tagore's humanism anchor pedagogy in compassion, creativity, and community. These values must guide India's digital transformation.

Empirical evidence from Indian schools, universities, and policy frameworks underscores both the promise and the peril of AI integration. Programs like *DIKSHA*, *SWAYAM*, and *AI for Youth* have expanded access and innovation, yet they also risk standardizing pedagogy and reducing teachers to data operators. The challenge lies not in rejecting technology but in redefining its purpose. When aligned with ethical oversight, participatory design, and contextual adaptation, AI can augment human capacities. When left unregulated, it threatens autonomy, privacy, and equity.

The future of education, therefore, depends on moral clarity. Teachers must remain the interpreters of meaning, not the servants of machines. Policy must protect their agency and embed ethics in technological governance. AI should amplify creativity, empathy, and inclusion - the very qualities that define the human vocation of teaching. As the *National Education Policy* (Ministry of Education, Government of India, 2020) asserts, technology must "serve pedagogy and not the other way around." In conclusion, this chapter reaffirms that the soul of pedagogy is not an abstraction but a living force, the conscience of education. Machines may simulate intelligence, but they cannot embody wisdom. Safeguarding that wisdom requires a human-centered vision of education in which technology is a means, not an end. India's democratic and spiritual heritage offers a profound template for this synthesis: progress guided by ethics, innovation grounded in humanity. Only by preserving this balance can education remain what it was always meant to be - a journey toward freedom, understanding, and human flourishing.

REFERENCES

Aayog, N. I. T. I. (2021). *Responsible AI for social empowerment (RAISE) framework*. Retrieved from https://www.niti.gov.in/responsible-ai

Annual Status of Education Report (ASER). (2022). *ASER 2022: Rural and urban education survey*. ASER Centre. Retrieved from https://asercentre.org/aser-2022/

Aurobindo, S. (1990). *The human cycle*. Sri Aurobindo Ashram.

Benjamin, R. (2019). *Race after technology: Abolitionist tools for the new Jim code*. Polity Press.

Biesta, G. (2017). *The rediscovery of teaching*. Routledge. DOI: 10.4324/9781315617497

Central Board of Secondary Education. (2020). *Artificial intelligence integration for school curriculum*. Retrieved from https://cbseacademic.nic.in/web_material/Curriculum20/AI_Integration_Manual_Introduction.pdf

Clark, A. (1999). An embodied cognitive science? *Trends in Cognitive Sciences*, *3*(9), 345–351. DOI: 10.1016/S1364-6613(99)01361-3 PMID: 10461197

Crawford, K. (2021). *Atlas of AI: Power, politics, and the planetary costs of artificial intelligence*. Yale University Press.

Dewey, J. (1938). *Experience and education*. Macmillan.

Dreyfus, H. L. (1992). *What computers still can't do: A critique of artificial reason*. MIT Press.

Freire, P. (1970). Pedagogy of the oppressed. *Continuum : an Interdisciplinary Journal on Continuity of Care*.

Gandhi, M. (1951). *Basic Education*. Navajivan Publishing House.

Goleman, D. (1995). *Emotional intelligence: Why it can matter more than IQ*. Bantam Books.

Government of India. (2009). *The Right of Children to Free and Compulsory Education Act, 2009*. Retrieved from https://www.indiacode.nic.in/bitstream/123456789/13682/1/rte_act_2009.pdf

Government of India. (2023). *Digital Personal Data Protection Act, 2023*. Retrieved from https://www.indiacode.nic.in/bitstream/123456789/22037/1/a2023-22.pdf

Govinda, R., & Bandyopadhyay, M. (2019). *Status of education in India report*. National University of Educational Planning and Administration (NUEPA). Retrieved from https://www.educationforallinindia.com/status_of_india_report_nuepa.pdf

Holmes, W., Bialik, M., & Fadel, C. (2022). *Artificial intelligence in education: Promises and implications for teaching and learning*. Center for Curriculum Redesign. Retrieved from https://curriculumredesign.org/wp-content/uploads/AI-in-Education.pdf

Immordino-Yang, M. H. (2015). *Emotions, learning, and the brain: Exploring the educational implications of affective neuroscience*. W. W. Norton.

Immordino-Yang, M. H., & Damasio, A. (2007). We feel, therefore we learn: The Relevance of Affective and Social Neuroscience to Education. *Mind, Brain and Education : the Official Journal of the International Mind, Brain, and Education Society*, *1*(1), 3–10. DOI: 10.1111/j.1751-228X.2007.00004.x

India, K. P. M. G. (2022). *Edtech trends -Based on conversations on Quora. KPMG*. Retrieved from https://assets.kpmg.com/content/dam/kpmg/in/pdf/2022/12/edtech-trends-based-on-conversations-on-quora.pdf

Jennings, P. A., & Greenberg, M. T. (2009). The prosocial classroom. *Review of Educational Research*, *79*(1), 491–525. DOI: 10.3102/0034654308325693

Justice Verma Commission. (2012). *Report of the High-Powered Commission on Teacher Education*. Ministry of Human Resource Development, Government of India.

Kerala Infrastructure and Technology for Education (KITE). (2026). *Hi-Tech school project for Secondary schools.* Retrieved from https://kite.kerala.gov.in/KITE/index.php/welcome/ict/1

Luckin, R., Holmes, W., Griffiths, M., & Forcier, L. B. (2016). *Intelligence unleashed: An argument for AI in education.* Pearson Education.

Madras, I. I. T. (2022). *AI4Bharat Initiative: Building inclusive AI for Indian languages.* Retrieved from https://ai4bharat.iitm.ac.in

Ministry of Education, Government of India. (2020). *National Education Policy*. Retrieved from https://www.education.gov.in/sites/upload_files/mhrd/files/NEP_Final_English.pdf

Ministry of Education, Government of India. (2023). *Education statistics at a glance 2023*. Retrieved from https://educationforallinindia.com/educational-statistics/

NASSCOM. (2024). *Strategic review 2024: India's tech sector performance.* New Delhi. Retrieved from https://nasscom.in/knowledge-center/publications/technology-sector-india-strategic-review-2024

National Council for Teacher Education. (2009). *National Curriculum Framework for Teacher Education (NCFTE): Towards preparing professional and humane teacher.* New Delhi: NCTE. Retrieved from https://ncte.gov.in/website/PDF/NCFTE_2009.pdf

National Council for Teacher Education. (2021). *Integrated Teacher Education Programme (ITEP): Policy framework.* NCTE.

Noddings, N. (2013). *Caring: A relational approach to ethics and moral education* (2nd ed.). University of California Press.

OECD. (2019). *Future of education and skills 2030: OECD learning compass 2030.* OECD Publishing. Retrieved from https://www.oecd.org/education/2030-project

OECD. (2021). *OECD Digital Education Outlook 2021: Pushing the Frontiers with Artificial Intelligence, Blockchain and Robots*. OECD Publishing., DOI: 10.1787/589b283f-

OECD. (2023). *Education policy outlook 2023: Transforming education in a changing world.* https://doi.org/DOI: 10.1787/7c7aaee3-en

Palmer, P. J. (1998). *The courage to teach: Exploring the inner landscape of a teacher's life*. Jossey-Bass.

Pratham Foundation. (2022). *Annual report 2021-22.* Pratham. Retrieved from https://www.pratham.org/about/annual-reports/

Schön, D. A. (1983). *The reflective practitioner: How professionals think in action.* Basic Books.

Searle, J. R. (1980). Minds, brains, and programs. *Behavioral and Brain Sciences*, *3*(3), 417–457. DOI: 10.1017/S0140525X00005756

Selwyn, N. (2019). *Should robots replace teachers? AI and the future of education.* Polity Press.

Sharma, P., Sarma, A., Basrur, A., & Tripathi, P. (2023, December 6). *AI Governance in India: Aspirations and Apprehensions*. Observer Research Foundation. Retrieved from https://www.orfonline.org/research/ai-governance-in-india-aspirations-and-apprehensions

Sharma, R., & Sahni, P. (2021). *Digital learning and inequality in India*. Brookings Institution India Center.

Tagore, R. (2008). *Personality (Reprint of 1917)*. Macmillan India.

UNESCO. (2021). *Recommendation on the ethics of artificial intelligence*. UNESCO. Retrieved from https://unesdoc.unesco.org/ark:/48223/pf0000381137

UNESCO. (2023). *Report on the implementation of Education for Sustainable Development (ESD) for 2030 and the Berlin Declaration*. UNESCO. Retrieved from https://unesdoc.unesco.org/ark:/48223/pf0000387344

Williamson, B., & Piattoeva, N. (2022). Education governance and datafication: Critical insights. *Critical Studies in Education*, *27*, 3515–3531. DOI: 10.1080/17508487.2022.2041678

World Bank. (2022). *The future of learning: Redefining education in a digital age*. https://doi.org/DOI: 10.1596/978-1-4648-1786-9

Chapter 27
Reframing the Teacher's Mission in a Changing World:
Evolving Roles, Responsibilities, and Professional Purpose

Andi Asrifan
http://orcid.org/0000-0002-9934-6129
Universitas Negeri Makassar, Indonesia

Dewi Furwana
UIN Palopo, Indonesia

ABSTRACT

The mission of education is experiencing considerable transformation due to global technological, social, and pedagogical shifts. This study investigates the evolution of teachers' professional duties and responsibilities in modern knowledge society. It examines historical viewpoints on pedagogy, the evolving functions of educators in digital and technology-oriented learning contexts, and the ethical obligations linked to inclusive and socially accountable education. Special emphasis is placed on educators as architects of learning experiences, digital navigators, and mentors for continuous education. The discourse underscores the significance of professional growth and adaptive skills in equipping educators for forthcoming problems. The research ultimately advocates for a revitalized professional role for educators as transformative agents who foster critical thinking, ethical consciousness, and global citizenship.

1. EDUCATION IN AN ERA OF TRANSFORMATION

1.1 Global Transformations Affecting Education

Global education systems are experiencing significant upheaval as civilisations confront rapid technological advancements, globalization, demographic shifts, and environmental issues. These global developments have redefined the expectations of educational institutions and, more specifically, of teachers as pivotal figures in influencing future generations. In the twenty-first century, education is no longer limited to the dissemination of established information (Rahimi & Oh, 2024). Rather, it must equip learners to manage ambiguity, complexity, and perpetual change.

Technological disruption is a fundamental force reshaping schooling. Progress in digital technology, artificial intelligence, big data analytics, and mobile connection has radically transformed the production, access, and dissemination of knowledge. Education is no longer confined to physical classrooms or conventional textbooks. Contemporary students engage with digital platforms, online knowledge libraries, and sophisticated learning systems that offer unparalleled

DOI: 10.4018/979-8-3373-8983-7.ch027

access to information (Khanduri & Teotia, 2023). Although these advancements enhance educational prospects, they also compel instructors to reconsider their roles in navigating students through extensive digital information landscapes.

Globalization intensifies these changes. Economic, cultural, and informational contacts increasingly surpass national borders, necessitating individuals to have intercultural competency, global awareness, and the capacity to work across varied contexts (Nopas & Kerdsomboon, 2024). Education systems must consequently equip learners for both local engagement and global citizenship. Educators are anticipated to develop competencies including communication, critical thinking, adaptability, and cross-cultural awareness that empower pupils to excel in interconnected communities.

Demographic changes also influence the changing dynamics of schooling. Numerous nations encounter increasing cultural and linguistic variety in educational settings as a result of migration and demographic shifts (Ivorgba, 2025). Educators must address these realities by implementing inclusive educational strategies that recognize varied identities, experiences, and learning requirements. This necessitates educators to transcend conventional teaching methods in favour of more adaptable and culturally attuned ways that foster equitable learning results.

Alongside technological and demographic transformations, environmental issues increasingly influence educational agendas. Challenges include climate change, environmental sustainability, and resource management necessitate novel kinds of knowledge and civic accountability. Education is essential for equipping learners to comprehend intricate environmental processes and engage in sustainable development initiatives. Consequently, educators are anticipated to cultivate environmental literacy, ethical consciousness, and responsible decision-making in pupils (Funa et al., 2022).

The cumulative global shifts have markedly heightened the complexity of the teaching profession. Educators have transitioned from being just transmitters of information to becoming facilitators of critical enquiry, architects of significant learning experiences, and mentors who navigate students through a swiftly changing environment. As educational demands increase, educators must consistently modify their teaching methodologies, professional identities, and sense of mission. Comprehending these worldwide changes is crucial for reevaluating the purpose of education in modern society.

1.2 The Changing Landscape of Teaching and Learning

Globalization has changed teaching and learning. Learner-centered methods that emphasise active engagement, collaboration, and critical analysis are replacing teacher-centric methods that focus on content transmission (Yoshida et al., 2023). These instructional changes reflect modern knowledge comprehension and learning processes. Many educational systems were industrial-model-based. In this method, teachers were authority who taught students standardized knowledge in ordered classrooms. Memorization and replication assessed learning (Gentile et al., 2023). While effective for mass instruction, this technique gave students few chances to develop higher-order thinking abilities or engage with real-world concerns.

In contrast, modern educational frameworks emphasize constructivist learning. This approach holds that students learn by actively engaging with concepts, experiences, and social relationships. Thus, educators must foster inquiry, experimentation, and collaborative problem-solving in learning environments.

Digital technology has accelerated this trend. Online learning platforms, interactive multimedia, and educational apps have expanded teaching tools. These technologies allow students to learn at their own pace and according to their needs (Vidal-Fernández et al., 2025). Digital platforms encourage global learning communities by enabling cross-border collaboration.

AI advances technology-enhanced education. Intelligent tutoring, automatic feedback, and adaptive learning platforms can assess and modify student support. These technologies can boost learning efficiency and reveal student progress (Zhang & Cao, 2025). AI raises questions about educators in technology-enhanced learning environments.

Digital technologies increasingly emphasize human guidance and pedagogical skill rather than replacing teachers. Teachers help students understand data, evaluate sources, and apply knowledge in meaningful circumstances. Teachers' knowledge mediation roles are becoming more important in a digital world with too much information (Kiryakova & Kozhuharova, 2024).

The rise of collaborative and project-based learning methods shows that many real-world situations require transdisciplinary thinking and collaboration (Soipimai & Sanrattana, 2023). Teachers are expected to create learning environments that encourage student engagement with complex problems, collaboration, and inventive solutions. Such methods better align education with current businesses and society.

The changing educational landscape requires instructors to be more flexible, creative, and reflective. Educators must balance technological advances with human qualities to keep learning meaningful, inclusive, and intellectually stimulating.

1.3 The Need to Reframe the Teacher's Mission

In light of the significant changes impacting education, there is a growing necessity to reevaluate the core purpose of teaching. Conventional notions of the teacher's job, focused mostly on imparting curriculum content, are inadequate for addressing the complexities of contemporary education (Bates et al., 2023). Teaching should be recognized as a dynamic and complex vocation that fosters intellectual growth, ethical consciousness, and social responsibility.

Reconceptualizing the educator's role entails acknowledging teachers as key architects of societal progress. Educators shape not only the knowledge students acquire but also their cognitive processes, interpersonal interactions, and responses to global issues (Melhim et al., 2023). The mission of education include not only academic instruction but also the development of critical thinking, empathy, and responsible citizenship.

A vital aspect of this redefined mission is promoting critical enquiry. In a time marked by swift information dissemination and extensive digital communication, learners must cultivate the capacity for critical analysis, evidence evaluation, and informed decision-making. Educators are essential in directing pupils through these processes, assisting them in differentiating between credible information and falsehoods (Moustaghfir & Brigui, 2024).

An further significant aspect is to ethical and social consciousness. Education is progressively anticipated to tackle intricate societal challenges, including inequality, environmental sustainability, and technological ethics. Teachers act as facilitators of debate and reflection, prompting students to contemplate multiple perspectives and engage carefully with moral and civic issues (Markauskaitė et al., 2023).

Lifelong learning has become a primary objective of modern education. As technological and economic transformations incessantly redefine the skills necessary for societal engagement, individuals must stay flexible and receptive to continuing education. Educators facilitate this objective by fostering curiosity, resilience, and a dedication to intellectual development in students (Sunde et al., 2022).

Altering the educator's mission necessitates modifications at both institutional and regulatory levels. Teacher education programs must provide educators with the information and skills necessary to traverse intricate educational settings (Petrychenko et al., 2023). Professional development opportunities must facilitate ongoing learning and innovation in teaching methodologies. Furthermore, educational systems must acknowledge and endorse the professional autonomy of teachers as reflective practitioners adept at addressing varied learning settings.

Ultimately, redefining the educator's mission signifies a wider acknowledgement that education is pivotal in tackling global concerns and fostering sustainable futures. Teachers are not only classroom teachers; they are architects of learning experiences that shape individuals' understanding of the world and their roles within it. By adopting this broadened role, educators may significantly aid in cultivating informed, ethical, and adaptable citizens equipped to manage an increasingly intricate landscape.

2. HISTORICAL PERSPECTIVES ON THE TEACHER'S ROLE

2.1 The Teacher as Knowledge Transmitter

Traditionally, educators have passed on knowledge from expert to student. Many early educational systems saw instructors as authoritative figures whose main job was to teach students organized knowledge in a disciplined environment. This approach reflected societal beliefs that knowledge was rigid, hierarchical, and managed by institutions (Bhardwaj et al., 2025). This framework made the classroom a one-way street for information.

This educational style evolved from mass education in the industrial age of the 19th and 20th centuries. Industrialization created education institutions to prepare students for new economic frameworks that required standardized skills, discipline, and efficiency. Educational institutions sometimes resembled factories, with identical curricula, scheduling, and centralized governance (Darling-Hammond et al., 2023). Teachers had to follow syllabi and ensure students learned industrial society skills.

Lectures, memorization, and recitation dominated training in this paradigm. Teachers controlled classroom discussions and assessed students' understanding. Assimilation, assessment, and institutional compliance were expected from students. Students are generally assessed on their capacity to memorize rather than critically or creatively apply knowledge (Masaiti et al., 2023). Discipline and order were important to traditional teaching. In large, overcrowded classes, classroom discipline is essential for effective learning. Thus, instructors were expected to govern student behavior by routines, hierarchies, and rules. Effective teaching required authority and discipline (Lucksnat et al., 2024). Despite its limitations, the knowledge transmission model improved educational accessibility in modern schooling systems. It standardized curricula, trained many instructors, and educated growing populations. This technique has increased reading rates and taught students foundational knowledge (Lillard, 2023).

This technique often limits pupils' creativity, critical thinking, and comprehension, critics say. The assumption that information could be passed from instructor to student ignored how humans perceive and create meaning. Educational theorists challenged this paradigm and proposed different pedagogy and cognition theories. Historical views of teachers as knowledge transmitters mark a turning point in educational practice. Modern classrooms still reflect this viewpoint, but educational theories and social changes have widened instructor expectations (Jurado & Jurado, 2024). Understanding this history helps explain the evolution of teaching roles.

2.2 The Teacher as Facilitator of Learning

The twentieth century experienced substantial transformations in educational philosophy that contested conventional teacher-centered instructional approaches. Inspired by advancements in psychology, sociology, and the philosophy of education, experts have increasingly highlighted the proactive role of learners in knowledge construction. The intellectual advancements facilitated the rise of constructivist viewpoints on learning, which regarded pupils as active participants instead of passive users of information (Ngo, 2024).

Constructivist theories propose that learning transpires through investigation, reflection, and engagement with the environment (Gono & Moraes, 2023). Knowledge is not merely conveyed from instructor to student but is constructed through cognitive engagement and social interaction. Consequently, the teacher's role transitioned from an authoritative knowledge provider to a facilitator who aids pupils in cultivating their own comprehension.

In this evolving framework, educators are tasked with creating learning settings that promote enquiry, dialogue, and problem-solving. Instead of presenting material just through lectures, educators facilitate activities that encourage exploration and critical reflection among students. Students are urged to pose enquiries, explore concepts, and engage with peers to cultivate a more profound comprehension (Sartika et al., 2023).

The supportive role of educators is most apparent in student-centered pedagogies, including project-based learning, inquiry-based learning, and collaborative learning methods. In these models, educators design learning experiences centered on real-world issues or genuine activities that necessitate students to utilize information in significant manners. Educators offer direction, materials, and evaluations while permitting students to actively influence their educational journey (Hughes et al., 2023).

The teacher as facilitator underscores the significance of discourse and engagement in the classroom. Learning is perceived as a social activity that transpires through communication and collective experience (Wang & AUTHOR_ID, 2024). Consequently, educators facilitate chances for dialogue, collaborative work, and peer learning, enabling students to express their thoughts and gain insights from each other.

This educational transition also signifies an increasing acknowledgement of the varied learning requirements and capabilities seen in modern classrooms. Educators must modify their teaching methodologies to cater to diverse learning styles, backgrounds, and levels of prior knowledge. Facilitating learning entails offering tailored help and establishing inclusive environments that enable all students to engage effectively (Goyibova et al., 2025).

Technology has further strengthened the supportive function of educators. Digital learning platforms, online resources, and collaborative technology enable students to autonomously access knowledge and interact with content in many manners. In these situations, educators act as facilitators, assisting students in traversing intricate information landscapes and cultivating critical evaluation abilities.

2.3 Professional Identity and the Evolution of Teaching

The changing roles of teachers are closely linked to their professional identities. Professional identity is teachers' understanding of their roles, duties, and values within the educational environment (Ambusaidi & Alhosni, 2023, p. 305). Educational studies, legislative reforms, societal expectations, and institutional structures have shaped this identity. Teaching was once considered a semi-professional career with limited autonomy and administrative oversight. Teachers had to teach standardized courses and follow institutional guidelines. Inflexible educational rules limited instructors' classroom decision-making and professional advancement (Deuchar, 2024, p. 4).

As learning and pedagogy research advanced in the 20th century, teaching became seen as a vocation requiring specific knowledge and competence. Smith & Vattøy (2022, p. 53) emphasize the importance of pedagogical knowledge, reflective practice, and continual professional growth for effective teaching. These advances recognized teaching as an intellectual occupation rather than a technical one.

Teachers' professional identity has also changed due to policy developments in many countries. Professional standards, accreditation systems, and teacher training programs that focused intellectual and pedagogical expertise were created to improve education. Reflective practice, peer collaboration, and professional learning groups were increasingly encouraged for educators (Meng, 2023, p. 24). Public expectations on educators also increased. Teachers are increasingly expected to assist student well-being, promote inclusive education, use technology, and engage with the community. The higher expectations show that education is crucial to addressing social, cultural, and economic challenges. Professional autonomy has become important to teachers. Many educational systems empower teachers to make educated pedagogical choices based on student and local factors. Teachers should be thoughtful practitioners who adapt their methods to diverse learners (Liang et al., 2024, p. 2).

However, teaching has presented new challenges. Education professionals sometimes face increased workloads, accountability standards, and statutory restraints that may limit their autonomy and well-being. Teachers across contexts struggle to balance institutional responsibilities with professional values (Lau et al., 2022, p. 4). Despite these issues, teachers' professional identity shows a growing recognition of their influence on society. Teachers are professionals whose competence, discernment, and ethical commitments improve educational systems and student welfare (Siminto et al., 2023, p. 150). Understanding the history of teaching roles and professional identity helps educators understand their contemporary difficulties and opportunities. The dynamic relationship between education and society will undoubtedly change teachers' professional goals.

3. EMERGING ROLES OF TEACHERS IN THE DIGITAL AND KNOWLEDGE ECONOMY

3.1 Teachers as Designers of Learning Experiences

The swift evolution of the digital and knowledge economy has profoundly altered expectations for education. In modern educational settings, educators are perceived not merely as information dispensers but increasingly as architects of significant learning experiences. This transition acknowledges that twenty-first-century learning necessitates more than just access to information; it demands meticulously designed educational settings that promote enquiry, creativity, collaboration, and critical thinking (Dangar, 2025).

Consequently, instructional design has emerged as a fundamental competency for contemporary educators. Educators must meticulously design and structure instructional activities that actively include students in the learning process. Educators are encouraged to establish dynamic learning settings that promote discovery and engagement, rather than depending exclusively on traditional lectures or textbook-based education. Effective instructional design entails the selection of suitable learning objectives, the creation of interactive activities, and the use of varied materials that enhance student comprehension (Mallillin et al., 2023, p. 41).

The incorporation of technology is essential in this design process. Digital tools enable educators to create multimodal learning environments that include text, video, interactive simulations, and collaborative platforms. These tools allow students to interact with knowledge in more adaptable and individualized manners (Dikilitaş & Noguera, 2023, p. 16). Online discussion forums, digital storytelling platforms, and interactive simulations enable learners to engage actively in knowledge construction.

Furthermore, the digital economy increasingly necessitates transdisciplinary cognition and practical problem-solving abilities. Consequently, educators are urged to create learning experiences that link classroom knowledge to real-world situations. Project-based, case-based, and problem-based learning methodologies offer students the chance to implement theoretical knowledge in practical contexts. These methodologies promote learners to explore intricate problems, engage in collaboration with peers, and cultivate unique solutions (Aithal & Maiya, 2023, p. 304).

In crafting such experiences, educators must take account for the varied needs and histories of their pupils. Effective learning environments are inclusive and attuned to diverse learning styles, cultural viewpoints, and existing knowledge. Consequently, educators must implement adaptable teaching methods that enable all students to engage meaningfully in the learning process (Nor et al., 2024, p. 52).

An additional crucial facet of the educator's work as a learning designer encompasses the use of formative assessment. Instead of depending exclusively on final tests, educators are progressively integrating continuous assessment techniques that offer feedback during the learning process. Digital platforms enable instructors to track student progress, recognize learning difficulties, and modify teaching approaches accordingly (Prastikawati et al., 2024, p. 244).

The creation of successful learning settings necessitates contemplation and modification. Educators must assess the efficacy of their teaching methods and adjust them according to student performance and feedback. This reflective technique facilitates ongoing enhancement of teaching practices (Nurhidayah & Wirza, 2024, p. 12). The position of instructors as architects of learning experiences underscores the increasing intricacy of modern education. Educators must integrate pedagogical expertise, technical proficiency, and creativity to develop learning environments that equip students for engagement in the knowledge economy.

3.2 Teachers as Digital Navigators and AI Collaborators

The proliferation of digital technologies and artificial intelligence has revolutionized the methods of accessing, analyzing, and applying knowledge. In this swiftly changing environment, educators increasingly function as digital navigators, guiding pupils across intricate information landscapes (Amin, 2023, p. 5). Given the abundance of information accessible online, learners must cultivate the capacity to critically assess sources, differentiate credible knowledge from falsehoods, and utilize digital tools judiciously.

Educators are crucial in facilitating the development of digital literacy abilities among pupils. Instead of merely guiding students to online resources, educators must instruct learners on how to evaluate the legitimacy, relevance, and correctness of digital information. This method include instructing students in discerning credible sources, recognizing biases in information systems, and employing critical thinking while interacting with digital content (Eden et al., 2024, p. 691).

The emergence of artificial intelligence has significantly broadened the technological framework of education. AI-driven solutions currently enhance multiple facets of education, encompassing automated feedback, adaptive learning systems, intelligent tutoring platforms, and data-informed learning analytics (Paiva et al., 2025, p. 3). These technologies provide potential to improve learning efficiency and tailor training to meet students' specific requirements.

The incorporation of AI in education necessitates meticulous pedagogical discernment. Educators must ascertain how to utilize these tools to augment learning while preserving critical thinking and student autonomy. AI solutions can facilitate mundane chores like grading and feedback provision, enabling educators to concentrate more on mentorship, discourse, and advanced learning activities.

Consequently, educators are progressively functioning as partners with AI technology. Instead of supplanting human educators, AI systems serve as supplementary instruments that enhance educational decision-making. Educators analyze the insights produced by learning analytics, modify instructional techniques according to student performance metrics, and guarantee the ethical and responsible utilization of AI tools (Saylam et al., 2023, p. 45).

Ethical considerations are paramount in the application of AI within the educational sector. Concerns include data privacy, algorithmic bias, and equal access to technology necessitate meticulous consideration (Devi, 2023, p. 1036). Educators must assist pupils in comprehending both the advantages and constraints of AI systems while promoting responsible digital citizenship.

Furthermore, educators act as intermediaries between technological systems and human learning processes. Although digital tools can disseminate knowledge effectively, substantive learning frequently necessitates human connection, discourse, and contemplation. Consequently, educators furnish the contextual direction and emotional support that technology alone is incapable of providing (Forsström et al., 2025).

As digital technologies advance, the role of educators as digital navigators and AI collaborators is expected to become increasingly important. Educators must consistently enhance their technical skills while upholding pedagogical principles that emphasize critical thinking, ethical consciousness, and learner-centered education.

3.3 Teachers as Mentors for Lifelong Learning

Learning is no longer limited to formal education or life stages in the knowledge economy. Rapid technological breakthroughs, changing job markets, and complex social challenges require constant learning. Therefore, education increasingly emphasizes lifelong learning abilities that enable people to adapt to changing environments ("International Journal of Research in Education Humanities and Commerce," 2023).

Teachers help pupils develop these skills. In addition to teaching, educators coach students to develop lifelong learning habits, attitudes, and skills. Mentoring involves helping students think independently, identify learning opportunities, set goals, and assess their progress (Nuis et al., 2023). Lifelong learning requires critical thinking. Learning to analyze complex issues, evaluate many perspectives, and make informed decisions is essential in a data-driven world. Educators foster these qualities through inquiry, discussion, and thoughtful analysis. Classroom discussions and problem-solving teach students to carefully consider ideas and evidence (Rap et al., 2023, p. 144).

Lifelong learning requires adaptability. Technology and society change quickly, thus people must always be ready to learn new skills and adapt (Gündüz, 2023, p. 795). By offering diverse learning experiences and encouraging problem-solving, educators can foster adaptation.

Mentoring promotes students' moral and personal development. Students must navigate complex social and technical landscapes with accountability, identity, and ethical decision-making. Teachers help students consider these issues and find purpose in their studies (Mouta et al., 2023, p. 28). Educators also help students value curiosity and intellectual inquiry. Lifelong learners seek knowledge beyond formal duties. Educators inspire pupils to learn independently by showing enthusiasm and intellectual curiosity (Jirout & Matthews, 2022).

Educators mentor outside the classroom. Educators often advise students on career paths, learning opportunities, and networking (Huot et al., 2024, p. 56). This advice helps students connect their education to life goals. In increasingly complex cultures, the ability to learn and adapt is crucial for individuals and communities. Teachers help students develop the intellectual, social, and ethical skills needed for lifelong learning (Sunde et al., 2022, p. 300). Educators as lifelong learning mentors indicate a shift in education goals. Education prepares students for lifelong learning in dynamic knowledge societies, not just academic accomplishment. Through mentorship, direction, and inspiration, teachers help students overcome the challenges of a changing world (Huot et al., 2024, p. 56).

4. ETHICAL RESPONSIBILITIES AND PROFESSIONAL PURPOSE IN CONTEMPORARY TEACHING

4.1 Teaching as a Moral and Ethical Profession

Teaching has historically been acknowledged as both an academic vocation and a profoundly moral and ethical endeavor. In contrast to numerous other professions, teaching necessitates direct and continuous involvement in the growth of individuals. Educators impact students' cognitive development, ethical principles, and social perspectives (İNCİ &

Çetin, 2022, p. 293). Consequently, the duties of educators encompass not just the transmission of academic knowledge but also the ethical mentorship and comprehensive development of students.

The ethical dimension of education fundamentally entails the obligation to provide equitable learning opportunities. Educational systems are frequently influenced by structural disparities associated with socioeconomic class, geographic location, language, gender, and cultural identity. Educators are often situated at the nexus of these disparities, engaging with students who introduce varied backgrounds and experiences into the classroom. Consequently, ethical pedagogy necessitates that educators identify and confront obstacles that may restrict students' access to significant learning experiences (Estefan et al., 2023).

Achieving equality in education necessitates the implementation of instructional strategies that accommodate various learners and mitigate gaps in educational results (Xiang-hui, 2024). Educators must be cognizant of variations in learning requirements, existing knowledge, and social situations. Ensuring equitable learning opportunities does not imply uniform treatment of all students; instead, it necessitates a tailored approach that addresses specific circumstances to successfully foster each student's development.

Another fundamental ethical obligation of educators pertains to the protection of student welfare. Classrooms serve not just as venues for intellectual engagement but also as habitats for social and emotional development among students. Educators must establish learning settings that are secure, respectful, and conducive to support. This encompasses safeguarding students against discrimination, bullying, or exclusion while cultivating positive interactions that promote trust and engagement (Wang et al., 2024, p. 4).

Ethical pedagogy encompasses the responsible distribution of knowledge. In an age marked by swift information dissemination and pervasive digital communication, educators are essential in directing pupils towards credible knowledge and critical comprehension. Educators must guarantee that the knowledge delivered in classrooms is precise, equitable, and based on reliable sources (Amin, 2023, p. 5). Simultaneously, educators must motivate students to interrogate assumptions, assess evidence, and engage critically with information.

Moreover, educators act as exemplars whose actions and dispositions shape students' views on ethical behavior. Educators exemplify principles such as fairness, respect, integrity, and responsibility via their relationships with students and coworkers. These ideals foster classroom climates conducive to ethical dialogue and reflection (BAYDAR & Levent, 2023, p. 933).

The ethical obligations of educators also encompass promoting civic consciousness and social responsibility in students. Education is essential for equipping individuals to engage actively in democratic society. Educators motivate students to confront social concerns, evaluate other viewpoints, and cultivate a feeling of accountability towards their communities (Melhim et al., 2023, p. 4). By fostering these attributes, educators facilitate the cultivation of knowledgeable and active citizens.

In modern education, when technology advancements and global interconnectivity generate new ethical challenges, the moral aspect of teaching gains heightened importance. Educators must address issues about digital ethics, information veracity, and ethical technology utilization. Resolving these difficulties necessitates careful contemplation and expert discernment (Örtegren, 2023). Ultimately, perceiving teaching as a moral and ethical vocation underscores the significant societal role of educators. Educators are responsible for imparting knowledge as well as cultivating the values and skills that inform individuals' engagement in society.

4.2 Inclusive and Culturally Responsive Teaching

Modern classrooms are increasingly defined by cultural, linguistic, and socio-economic variety. Migration, globalization, and demographic shifts have established educational contexts in which students contribute diverse experiences, identities, and viewpoints (Alshraah et al., 2024, p. 655). In these situations, inclusive and culturally sensitive teaching has emerged as a fundamental aspect of effective educational practice.

Culturally responsive pedagogy acknowledges that students' cultural backgrounds affect their interpretation of knowledge, engagement with learning resources, and interactions in the classroom. Conventional pedagogical methods frequently mirrored prevailing cultural viewpoints and neglected the experiences of marginalized populations. Inclusive teaching techniques aim to mitigate these limitations by recognising and appreciating the diversity that students provide to the learning environment (Stavrianos, 2023, p. 21).

Educators employing culturally responsive methodologies endeavor to link curriculum material with students' experiential realities. By integrating varied viewpoints, examples, and narratives into teaching, educators cultivate learning environments in which students recognize their identities within the educational process. This method increases student involvement and fosters a deeper comprehension by rendering information more pertinent and significant (Abdalla & Moussa, 2024, p. 92).

Inclusive teaching encompasses the examination of equity and representation in educational resources and classroom methodologies. Educators must rigorously analyze the presentation of knowledge and identify which perspectives are included or omitted in educational discussions. Promoting varied viewpoints enables pupils to cultivate a more thorough comprehension of intricate social and historical matters (Gajardo et al., 2022, p. 139).

The diversity of languages constitutes a significant aspect of inclusive education. Numerous classes have students who communicate in various languages or are acquiring knowledge in a second language. Teachers must consequently use measures that facilitate linguistic growth while ensuring that language differences do not impede participation. Strategies may encompass scaffolding, visual aids, collaborative learning, and multilingual resources (Alexandrowicz & Hansen, 2023, p. 74).

In addition to curriculum design, inclusive teaching entails cultivating classroom cultures in which all students feel esteemed and acknowledged. Educators must foster open communication, promote reciprocal respect, and confront discriminatory conduct as it occurs. Establishing inclusive classroom standards fosters a sense of belonging that enhances student engagement and well-being (Akintayo et al., 2024, p. 775).

Socio-economic disparities also affect students' educational experiences. Certain learners may encounter difficulties due to restricted access to educational resources, inadequate technical infrastructure, or unsupportive learning situations beyond the classroom setting. Educators are essential in identifying these issues and modifying teaching methods to assist students who may need extra support (Prasetyowibowo et al., 2023, p. 2).

Professional development and reflective practice are crucial for educators aiming to effectively adopt inclusive pedagogies (Barnard & Henn, 2023). Educators must consistently scrutinize their assumptions, prejudices, and teaching methodologies to establish equal learning environments. Engaging in research on culturally responsive education and engaging with colleagues can facilitate continuous professional development. Inclusive and culturally responsive pedagogy eventually fosters more egalitarian educational institutions. By appreciating diversity and confronting structural inequities, educators foster learning environments that enable all students to engage fully in educational activities.

4.3 Teachers as Agents of Social Transformation

Education has historically been seen as a potent catalyst for societal transformation. Education enables communities to convey knowledge, values, and cultural traditions, while also providing individuals with the necessary abilities for participation in communal decision-making (ERTUGRULOGLU et al., 2024, p. 137). In this overarching goal, educators serve as crucial agents of societal reform.

Educators shape pupils' perceptions of the world and their role within it. By imparting knowledge that fosters critical thinking, educators enable learners to interrogate assumptions, analyze societal institutions, and contemplate alternate viewpoints. This technique facilitates pupils in cultivating a more profound comprehension of societal concerns and their prospective involvement in resolving them (Taştı & Yıldırım, 2022, p. 566).

A crucial aspect of teachers' transformative function is promoting democratic engagement. Democratic civilizations depend on citizens who can engage in informed discourse, assess evidence, and partake in collective decision-making. Educators facilitate this process by promoting open dialogue, debate, and critical examination within the classroom (Dessingué & Wagner, 2024).

Through these techniques, children learn to express their thoughts, respect other perspectives, and engage constructively with intricate situations. These encounters foster the competencies essential for active citizenship and democratic participation.

Education is instrumental in promoting social fairness. Educators frequently engage with children facing diverse manifestations of social inequality associated with economic position, race, gender, or resource accessibility (Stubbs & Hullinger, 2022, p. 19). By tackling these challenges in educational settings, educators can assist students in comprehending the structural elements that influence social chances.

Advancing social justice in education does not necessitate that educators endorse particular political stances. It entails establishing educational settings in which students can critically analyze social issues, contemplate many viewpoints, and think on the ethical ramifications of social choices (Stubbs & Hullinger, 2022, p. 19). These methods foster empathy and a dedication to equity among learners.

Educators also participate in wider initiatives for sustainable development. Global issues including climate change, environmental degradation, and resource constraint necessitate informed and responsible response. Education for sustainability promotes students' comprehension of the interrelation among social, economic, and environmental systems. Educators are pivotal in directing students to investigate these matters and reflect on how personal and communal activities might foster sustainable futures (Melhim et al., 2023, p. 4).

Teachers, in addition to shaping student perspectives, engage in educational communities that impact policy and practice. Educators influence the development of educational systems that foster fairness and innovation through professional collaboration, research engagement, and community involvement (Eden et al., 2023, p. 142).

The function of educators as catalysts for social change thus underscores the greater societal importance of education. Teachers enhance societal development by equipping learners with information, critical awareness, and ethical understanding, fostering more democratic, inclusive, and sustainable communities (Melhim et al., 2023, p. 4). Acknowledging this transformative potential underscores the necessity of supporting educators as professionals endowed with educational skill and a profound sense of social responsibility. Educators influence both the future of individual students and the broader future of society through their job.

5. FUTURE DIRECTIONS FOR THE TEACHER'S MISSION

5.1 Preparing Teachers for Future Educational Challenges

As societies evolve in response to rapid technological, social, and environmental changes, the aim of education must likewise adjust to new realities. Equipping teachers for future educational problems necessitates a proactive strategy that endows educators with the skills to navigate complex and unexpected learning contexts (Mitina et al., 2024, p. 45). Modern teacher preparation programs must transcend conventional pedagogical training models and integrate broader competencies in digital literacy, multidisciplinary collaboration, and adaptive competence.

A vital competency for future instructors is digital literacy. The incorporation of technology in education has revolutionized the methods of accessing, generating, and disseminating knowledge. Educators must not only comprehend the utilization of digital tools but also cultivate the ability to meaningfully incorporate these technology into pedagogical activities. This encompasses the capacity to assess digital resources, create technology-enhanced learning activities, and instruct students in appropriate digital engagement (Diao et al., 2023, p. 67).

Digital literacy encompasses comprehension of developing technologies, including artificial intelligence, learning analytics, and immersive learning environments (Feng & Liu, 2024, p. 4). Educators must critically evaluate the impact of new technologies on instructional methodologies and student learning outcomes. Instead of perceiving technology as a substitute for human educators, teachers should acquire the skills to utilize digital resources strategically to augment pedagogical efficacy and accommodate varied learning requirements.

Interdisciplinary collaboration constitutes a crucial ability for prospective instructors. Numerous modern challenges—such as climate change, public health emergencies, and technology advancements—necessitate expertise that encompasses various academic fields (Āboltiņa et al., 2024, p. 2). Educators must be ready to cooperate across disciplines and create learning experiences that promote the integration of information from diverse fields.

Interdisciplinary teaching methodologies enable pupils to confront intricate issues that cannot be comprehended through a singular discipline lens (Wang, 2024, p. 2). Addressing environmental sustainability may require insights from science, economics, ethics, and social policy. Educators capable of facilitating interdisciplinary learning assist students in cultivating more holistic understandings of real-world situations.

Adaptive competence is crucial in equipping instructors for future educational environments. In contrast to regular expertise, which emphasizes the application of established approaches to common scenarios, adaptive competence include the capacity to respond innovatively to novel difficulties (Pelgrim et al., 2022, p. 1246). Educators must be adept at modifying teaching tactics in response to changing learning environments, student requirements, and technological advancements.

Teacher education programs must consequently prioritize adaptability, reflective practice, and problem-solving competencies. Future educators ought to be motivated to explore novel pedagogical methods, assess their efficacy, and enhance their practices informed by evidence and feedback (Donlon & Tiernan, 2023, p. 80).

Teacher training must encompass the development of technical and pedagogical competencies, as well as the ethical and social dimensions of education. Prospective educators must be prepared to address challenges pertaining to digital ethics, educational equity, and appropriate technology utilization. Equipping educators to confront these difficulties necessitates the incorporation of ethical thought and critical analysis into teacher preparation curricula. Ultimately, equipping teachers for forthcoming educational difficulties necessitates the development of educators who are both informed and flexible. By cultivating digital abilities, multidisciplinary viewpoints, and adaptive knowledge, educators will be more equipped to assist students in traversing the intricacies of the twenty-first century.

5.2 Professional Learning and Continuous Development

The dynamic evolution of education necessitates that teacher preparation extends beyond first certification or admission into the profession (Olivier, 2022, p. 151). Teaching should be regarded as a profession defined by perpetual learning and professional development. Continuous professional development is crucial for ensuring that educators remain attuned to evolving educational methodologies, technological advancements, and shifting societal demands.

Professional development allows instructors to enhance their teaching methodologies and augment their comprehension of topic matter. Teachers can investigate innovative pedagogical approaches, acquire knowledge of educational technologies, and remain updated on advancements in educational research through workshops, training programs, and advanced study (Adu et al., 2023, p. 545). Such chances enable educators to enhance their methodologies in ways that foster successful and engaging learning environments.

Reflective practice constitutes a fundamental element of ongoing professional growth. Educators gain from consistently assessing their pedagogical methods, analyzing student performance, and contemplating enhancements to instructional strategies. Reflection allows educators to transcend habitual routines and cultivate a profound comprehension of the impact of teaching decisions on learning processes (Juma, 2024).

Research-informed instruction enhances professional development by linking classroom practices with academic knowledge. Educators who utilize research findings are more adept at using evidence-based teaching methods that improve student learning outcomes. Engaging with academic literature, participating in research initiatives, and working with educational researchers might enhance informed pedagogical decision-making (Skedsmo & Huber, 2023, p. 167).

Professional learning communities significantly contribute to teacher development. These groups unite educators to exchange experiences, address instructional issues, and investigate innovative pedagogical methods. Collaborative discourse across professional networks enables educators to learn from each other and formulate collective solutions to shared educational challenges (Nor et al., 2024, p. 43).

The proliferation of digital communication technology has enabled the expansion of global professional learning networks. Educators can now engage in online forums, webinars, and virtual conferences that link teachers from various geographies and educational environments (Pedersen et al., 2023). These networks facilitate cross-cultural exchange and the dissemination of best practices within global educational communities.

Mentorship programs facilitate ongoing professional development, especially for novice educators. Seasoned educators can offer direction, feedback, and support to novice instructors as they confront the obstacles of classroom practice. Mentorship cultivates professional confidence and promotes introspective development (Diem et al., 2024, p. 560).

Institutional support is essential for the sustainability of professional learning initiatives. Educational systems must dedicate money, time, and infrastructure to facilitate teacher development. Policies that promote collaboration, research involvement, and professional independence can enhance the culture of ongoing learning inside educational institutions (Darling-Hammond et al., 2022). By fostering continuous professional development, educational institutions guarantee that educators stay adept at addressing changing educational requirements. Ongoing education not only improves instructional efficacy but also fosters educators' professional fulfilment and enduring dedication to their vocation.

5.3 Toward a Renewed Professional Purpose for Teachers

As educational environments alter, it is imperative to define a revitalised professional purpose for educators. The responsibilities of educators encompass much more than the transmission of curriculum material. Educators play a pivotal role in influencing the intellectual, ethical, and social growth of students, and their efforts substantially enhance societal advancement (Melhim et al., 2023, p. 4).

A revitalized perspective on education acknowledges teachers as transformative experts that assist students in navigating intricate global circumstances (Singh et al., 2025). In a rapidly evolving technological landscape, marked by environmental unpredictability and social variety, education must equip individuals to think critically, engage responsibly, and contribute significantly to their communities. Educators are crucial in fostering these abilities.

An essential component of this revitalized professional objective is cultivating ethical consciousness in learners. Students must cultivate the capacity to assess the ramifications of their acts, analyze ethical quandaries, and interact ethically with technical and social frameworks. Educators foster this understanding by establishing learning environments that facilitate conversation, reflection, and ethical reasoning (Krakowski et al., 2022).

Global citizenship education constitutes a significant aspect of modern pedagogy. As cultures grow more interconnected, learners must comprehend global concerns and value varied perspectives. Educators facilitate the development of intercultural competence, empathy, and collaborative skills across cultural barriers (Nopas & Kerdsomboon, 2024, p. 6).

A vital aspect of the teacher's revitalized role is to enable students to tackle intricate societal issues. Challenges such as climate change, economic disparity, and technological upheaval necessitate knowledgeable and active individuals adept at collaborative problem-solving. Teachers can promote active student participation in tackling these difficulties through inquiry-based learning, interdisciplinary investigation, and community engagement (McDiarmid & Zhao, 2022, p. 13).

The revitalized professional mission of educators underscores the need of fostering curiosity and promoting lifelong learning. In dynamic knowledge societies, individuals must always learn new skills and information. Educators foster this mentality by exemplifying intellectual curiosity, promoting autonomous exploration, and assisting students in cultivating self-directed learning practices (Karlen & Hertel, 2024).

Moreover, acknowledging teaching as a transformational vocation necessitates extensive social support for educators (Bates et al., 2023, p. 1407). Educational policies must recognize the intricacies of teaching and furnish educators with the autonomy, resources, and professional esteem essential for good performance. When educators receive professional assistance, they are more capable of innovating, collaborating, and enhancing educational outcomes.

The future of education ultimately relies on educators who perceive their profession as intellectually stimulating and socially significant (Ebby et al., 2024). By adopting a revitalized professional mission rooted in ethical accountability, global consciousness, and continuous education, educators can cultivate generations of students equipped to tackle the urgent issues of contemporary society. The changing mission of teaching signifies a wider revolution in the fundamental aim of education. Educators are not solely facilitators in classrooms; they are leaders in the continuous endeavor to develop knowledgeable, accountable, and empathetic citizens.

6. CONCLUSION

The function of educators has experienced considerable change due to shifting social, technical, and educational landscapes. Historically, educators were predominantly regarded as conveyors of knowledge within organized classroom settings intended for uniform education. Over time, advancements in educational theory, globalization, digital innovation, and evolving societal expectations have transformed the professional obligations and objectives linked to teaching. These advancements necessitate that educators embrace more dynamic, reflective, and varied responsibilities that transcend conventional classroom instruction.

Modern education increasingly entails the creation of significant learning experiences, navigating pupils through intricate digital information landscapes, and mentoring learners in acquiring skills essential for lifetime learning. Educators must traverse swiftly evolving knowledge domains while guaranteeing that pedagogical methods are inclusive, equitable, and attuned to varied student requirements. The ethical aspects of education are especially important in this situation. Educators are responsible for developing critical thinking, encouraging civic involvement, and nurturing ethical consciousness in students who will interact in progressively interconnected societies.

The analysis provided in this discussion underscores that teaching is not a static profession; rather, it continually adapts in reaction to wider societal changes. Equipping educators for these realities necessitates teacher education programmers that prioritize digital proficiency, multidisciplinary collaboration, reflective practice, and adaptive expertise. The building of supportive professional settings that foster continual learning, research involvement, and collaborative professional communities is equally crucial.

The role of teachers must be recognized as inherently transforming. Educators are essential in developing learners who can adeptly address intricate global issues, engage meaningfully with varied viewpoints, and contribute responsibly to societal advancement. By adopting a revitalised professional mission rooted in ethical accountability, intellectual inquisitiveness, and dedication to continuous education, educators play a pivotal role in cultivating knowledgeable, resilient, and globally responsible citizens.

REFERENCES

Abdalla, H. I., & Moussa, A. (2024). Culturally Responsive Teaching: Navigating Models and Implementing Effective Strategies. *Acta Pedagogia Asiana*, *3*(2), 91–100. DOI: 10.53623/apga.v3i2.432

Āboltiņa, L., Lāma, G., Sarva, E., Kaļķe, B., Āboliņa, A., Daniela, L., Rubene, Z., & Bernande, M. (2024). Challenges and opportunities for the development of future teachers' professional competence in Latvia. *Frontiers in Education*, *8*, 1307387. Advance online publication. DOI: 10.3389/feduc.2023.1307387

Adu, E. O., Duku, N., & Adu, E. O. (2023). Role of continuing professional teacher development (CPTD) on teachers' and learners' achievement in South Africa: A literature review [Review of *Role of continuing professional teacher development (CPTD) on teachers' and learners' achievement in South Africa: A literature review*]. *International Journal of Research in Business and Social Science (2147-4478)*, *12*(7), 542. Ümit Hacıoğlu. DOI: 10.20525/ijrbs.v12i7.2799

Aithal, P. S., & Maiya, A. K. (2023). Innovations in Higher Education Industry – Shaping the Future. *International Journal of Case Studies in Business IT and Education*, *294*, 294–322. Advance online publication. DOI: 10.47992/IJCSBE.2581.6942.0321

Akintayo, O. T., Eden, C. A., Ayeni, O. O., & Onyebuchi, N. C.Olateju Temitope AkintayoChima Abimbola EdenOyebola Olusola AyeniNneamaka Chisom Onyebuchi. (2024). Inclusive curriculum design: Meeting the diverse needs of students for social improvement. *International Journal of Applied Research in Social Sciences*, *6*(5), 770–784. DOI: 10.51594/ijarss.v6i5.1100

Alexandrowicz, V., & Hansen, B. (2023). Addressing Multilingual Learners' Language Needs Through Engaging Inquiry-Based Science. *English Language Teaching*, *16*(10), 73. DOI: 10.5539/elt.v16n10p73

Alshraah, S. M., Issa, S. H. M., Migdadi, H. F., & Nishat, A. S. (2024). Enhancing Pedagogical Strategies for Multilingual Classrooms in Foreign Language Education: Training Lecturers for Linguistic Diversity and Language Variation. *Journal of Language Teaching and Research*, *15*(2), 654–663. DOI: 10.17507/jltr.1502.34

Ambusaidi, A., & Alhosni, K. Z. (2023). MATHEMATICS AND SCIENCE TEACHERS' PERCEPTIONS OF THE FACTORS INFLUENCING TEACHING AND PROFESSIONAL IDENTITY. *Problems of Education in the 21st Century*, *81*(3), 303. DOI: 10.33225/pec/23.81.303

Amin, M. Y. M. (2023). AI and Chat GPT in Language Teaching: Enhancing EFL Classroom Support and Transforming Assessment Techniques. *International Journal of Higher Education Pedagogies*, *4*(4), 1–15. DOI: 10.33422/ijhep.v4i4.554

Barnard, R. W., & Henn, R. H. (2023). Overcoming Learning Obstacles: Strategies for Supporting Students with Diverse Needs. *OAlib*, *10*(8), 1–14. DOI: 10.4236/oalib.1110509

Bates, G., Fisher, R., Turner, K., Machirori, T. L., & Rixon, A. (2023). Raising the social status of teachers: Teachers as social entrepreneurs. *Australian Educational Researcher*, *51*(4), 1405–1424. DOI: 10.1007/s13384-023-00646-4

Baydar, F., & Levent, A. F.BAYDAR. (2023). Ethical Review on Teachers' Relations with the School Environment. *International Journal of Educational Research Review*, *8*(4), 932–946. DOI: 10.24331/ijere.1336456

Bhardwaj, V., Zhang, S., Tan, Y. Q., & Pandey, V. (2025). Redefining learning: Student-centered strategies for academic and personal growth. *Frontiers in Education*, *10*, 1518602. Advance online publication. DOI: 10.3389/feduc.2025.1518602

Dangar, H. N. (2025). Transforming Learning Spaces: Key Demands for 21st Century Classrooms. *Edumania-An International Multidisciplinary Journal*, *3*(1), 30–33. DOI: 10.59231/edumania/9095

Darling-Hammond, L., DiNapoli, M., & Kini, T. (2023). *The Federal Role in Ending Teacher Shortages*. DOI: 10.54300/649.892

Darling-Hammond, L., Flook, L., Schachner, A., Wojcikiewicz, S. K., Cantor, P., & Osher, D. (2022). *Educator Learning to Enact the Science of Learning and Development*. DOI: 10.54300/859.776

Dessingué, A., & Wagner, D. (2024). Promoting dialogical critical thinking in education: Examining teachers' practices and conceptualizations in the Norwegian school context. *Journal of Curriculum Studies*, *57*(2), 184–202. DOI: 10.1080/00220272.2024.2334937

Deuchar, A. (2024). Policy makers as experts and teachers in need of reform: A critique of 'evidence-based' reforms of initial teacher education in Australia. *Australian Educational Researcher*. Advance online publication. DOI: 10.1007/s13384-024-00757-6

Devi, A. (2023). Ethical Considerations in Using Artificial Intelligence to Improve Teaching and Learning. *Tuijin Jishu/Journal of Propulsion Technology, 44*(4), 1031. DOI: 10.52783/tjjpt.v44.i4.966

Diao, J., Tang, X., Ma, X., & Ding, X. (2023). An International Perspective on the Connotation, Framework, and Development Strategies of Teacher Digital Literacy. *Journal of Educational Technology Development and Exchange*, *16*(2), 66–78. DOI: 10.18785/jetde.1602.04

Diem, H. T. T., Thinh, M. P., & Lam, V. (2024). Exploring Practical Pedagogy in High School Biology Education: A Qualitative Study of Pre-Service Biology Teachers' Experiences in Vietnam. *European Journal of Educational Research*, *557*(volume-13-issue-2-april-2024), 557–571. Advance online publication. DOI: 10.12973/eu-jer.13.2.557

Dikilitaş, K., & Noguera, I. (2023). *Conceptual framework for flexible learning design: The Context of flipped classroom*. DOI: 10.31265/USPS.267

Donlon, E., & Tiernan, P. (2023). Chatbots and Citations: An Experiment in Academic Writing with Generative AI. *Irish Journal of Technology Enhanced Learning*, *7*(2), 75–87. DOI: 10.22554/ijtel.v7i2.125

Ebby, C. B., Hess, B., Pecora, L., & Valerio, J. (2024). Facilitating collaborative inquiry into practice around artifacts of mathematics teaching. *Journal of Mathematics Teacher Education*, *29*(1), 59–82. DOI: 10.1007/s10857-024-09649-z

Eden, C. A., Chisom, O. N., & Adeniyi, I. S.Chima Abimbola EdenOnyebuchi Nneamaka ChisomIdowu Sulaimon Adeniyi. (2023). Education policy and social change: Examining the impact of reform initiatives on equity and access. *International Journal of Science and Research Archive*, *11*(2), 139–146. DOI: 10.30574/ijsra.2024.11.2.0372

Eden, C. A., Chisom, O. N., & Adeniyi, I. S.Chima Abimbola EdenOnyebuchi Nneamaka ChisomIdowu Sulaimon Adeniyi. (2024). PROMOTING DIGITAL LITERACY AND SOCIAL EQUITY IN EDUCATION: LESSONS FROM SUCCESSFUL INITIATIVES. *International Journal of Management & Entrepreneurship Research*, *6*(3), 687–696. DOI: 10.51594/ijmer.v6i3.880

Ertugruloglu, O., Gülcan, N. Y., & Pi̇şki̇n Abi̇doğlu, Ü.ERTUGRULOGLU. (2024). The Impact of Culture on the Education System. *International E-Journal of Educational Studies*, *8*(16), 131–141. DOI: 10.31458/iejes.1436091

Estefan, M., Selbin, J. C., & MacDonald, S. (2023). From Inclusive to Equitable Pedagogy: How to Design Course Assignments and Learning Activities That Address Structural Inequalities. *Teaching Sociology*, *51*(3), 262–274. DOI: 10.1177/0092055X231174515

Feng, X., & Liu, H. (2024). I feel blue– teacher, can you help me? A study on the effect of digital literacies on language learners' technostress, on-line engagement, autonomy, and academic success. *BMC Psychology*, *12*(1), 143. Advance online publication. DOI: 10.1186/s40359-024-01637-5 PMID: 38481351

Forsström, S., Njå, M., Munthe, E., Álvarez-Galván, J.-L., & Houldsworth, L. (2025). The impact of digital technologies on students' learning. In *OECD education working papers*. DOI: 10.1787/19939019

Funa, A. A., Gabay, R. A. E., Ibardaloza, R. T., & Limjap, A. A. (2022). Knowledge, attitudes, and behaviors of teachers and students toward sustainable development of Pili (Canarium ovatum). *Jurnal Cakrawala Pendidikan, 41*(3), 569–585. DOI: 10.21831/cp.v41i3.42407

Gajardo, J. M., Garrido, F., Pinochet, S. P., & Castro-Palacios, G. (2022). Hate Speech and the Gender Perspective: A Problem from the Teaching of Social Sciences in School. *European Journal of Educational Research, 133.* Advance online publication. DOI: 10.12973/eu-jer.12.1.133

Gentile, M., Città, G., Perna, S., & Allegra, M. (2023). Do we still need teachers? Navigating the paradigm shift of the teacher's role in the AI era. *Frontiers in Education, 8*, 1161777. Advance online publication. DOI: 10.3389/feduc.2023.1161777

Gono, S., & Moraes, A. J. D. (2023). Student appraisals of collaborative team teaching: A quest for student engagement. *Journal of Applied Learning & Teaching, 6*(1). Advance online publication. DOI: 10.37074/jalt.2023.6.1.26

Goyibova, N., Muslimov, N., Sabirova, G., Kadirova, N., & Samatova, B. (2025). Differentiation approach in education: Tailoring instruction for diverse learner needs. *MethodsX, 14*, 103163. DOI: 10.1016/j.mex.2025.103163 PMID: 39897653

Gündüz, A. Y. (2023). The Importance of Investigating Students' Lifelong Learning Levels and Perceptions of 21st-Century Skills. *International E-Journal of Educational Studies, 7*(15), 788–796. DOI: 10.31458/iejes.1346220

Hughes, M. D., Riello, S., & Krause, A. (2023). Starting from Scratch: A Holistic Framework for Designing Digitally Delivered Graduate Programs for STEM Working Professionals. *International Journal of Higher Education, 12*(6), 63. DOI: 10.5430/ijhe.v12n6p63

Huot, S., Hok, C., Kumar, P., & Heng, L. (2024). Exploring the benefits of teacher involvement in guiding high school students' orientation toward personal and educational growth. *Cambodian Journal of Educational and Social Sciences., 1*(1), 49–66. DOI: 10.69496/cjess.v1i1.9

İnci, Ş., & Çetin, Ş.İNCİ. (2022). Professional Value-Oriented Life Tendency Scale Teacher Form Validity and Reliability Study. *International Journal of Educational Research Review, 7*(4), 292–306. DOI: 10.24331/ijere.1173727

International Journal of Research in Education Humanities and Commerce. (2023). *International Journal of Research in Education Humanities and Commerce.* DOI: 10.37602/ijrehc

Ivorgba, E. A. (2025). Multilingualism and Multiliteracies in 21st-Century Education. *International Journal of Research and Innovation in Social Science, 3243*(IIIS), 3243–3255. Advance online publication. DOI: 10.47772/IJRISS.2025.903SEDU0243

Jirout, J., & Matthews, S. E. (2022). Developing Intellectual Character: An Educational Perspective on How Uncertainty-Driven Curiosity Can Support Learning. In *Creativity theory and action in education* (p. 253). Springer International Publishing. DOI: 10.1007/978-3-030-98729-9_14

Juma, A. A.Ahmad Asad Juma. (2024). Self-reflection in teaching: A comprehensive guide to empowering educators and enhancing student learning. *International Journal of Science and Research Archive, 12*(1), 2835–2844. DOI: 10.30574/ijsra.2024.12.1.1113

Jurado, R. J. S., & Jurado, M. D. S. (2024). Educational Innovation in the 21st Century. *YUYAY Estrategias Metodologías & Didácticas Educativas, 3*(1), 35–52. DOI: 10.59343/yuyay.v3i1.60

Karlen, Y., & Hertel, S. (2024). Inspiring self-regulated learning in everyday classrooms: Teachers' professional competences and promotion of self-regulated learning. *Unterrichtswissenschaft, 52*(1), 1–13. DOI: 10.1007/s42010-024-00196-3

Khanduri, V., & Teotia, A. (2023). Revolutionizing Learning: An Exploratory Study on The Impact of Technology-Enhanced Learning Using Digital Learning Platforms and AI Tools on The Study Habits of University Students Through Focus Group Discussions. *International Journal of Research Publication and Reviews*, *4*(6), 663–672. DOI: 10.55248/gengpi.4.623.44407

Kiryakova, G., & Kozhuharova, D. (2024). The Digital Competences Necessary for the Successful Pedagogical Practice of Teachers in the Digital Age. *Education Sciences*, *14*(5), 507. DOI: 10.3390/educsci14050507

Krakowski, A., Greenwald, E., Hurt, T., Nonnecke, B., & Cannady, M. A. (2022). Authentic Integration of Ethics and AI through Sociotechnical, Problem-Based Learning. *Proceedings of the AAAI Conference on Artificial Intelligence*, *36*(11), 12774–12782. DOI: 10.1609/aaai.v36i11.21556

Lau, J., Vähäsantanen, K., & Collin, K. (2022). Teachers' Identity Tensions and Related Coping Strategies: Interaction With the Career Stages and Socio-Political Context. *Professions and Professionalism*, *12*(2). Advance online publication. DOI: 10.7577/pp.4562

Liang, W., To, J., & Lo, Y. Y. (2024). A journey towards teacher empowerment in differentiated instruction: Implications for a sustainable teacher professional development model. *Asia Pacific Education Review*. Advance online publication. DOI: 10.1007/s12564-024-09977-y

Lillard, A. S. (2023). Why the time is ripe for an education revolution. *Frontiers in Developmental Psychology*, *1*, 1177576. Advance online publication. DOI: 10.3389/fdpys.2023.1177576

Lucksnat, C., Richter, E., Henschel, S., Hoffmann, L., Schipolowski, S., & Richter, D. (2024). Comparing the teaching quality of alternatively certified teachers and traditionally certified teachers: Findings from a large-scale study. *Educational Assessment, Evaluation and Accountability*, *36*(1), 75–106. DOI: 10.1007/s11092-023-09426-1

Mallillin, L. L. D., Mallillin, J. B., Ampongan, Y. D., Lipayon, I. C., Mejica, M. M., & Burabo, J. Z. (2023). Instructional design for effective classroom Pedagogy of teaching. *Eureka Journal of Educational Research*, *1*(2), 41–52. DOI: 10.56773/ejer.v1i2.6

Markauskaitė, L., Carvalho, L., & Fawns, T. (2023). The role of teachers in a sustainable university: From digital competencies to postdigital capabilities. *Educational Technology Research and Development*, *71*(1), 181–198. DOI: 10.1007/s11423-023-10199-z PMID: 36779078

Masaiti, G., Kakupa, P., & Mupeta, S. (2023). Re-imagining assessment in higher education: Creating alternative pathways for inclusive and democratic assessments in Zambian higher education institutions. *Scholarship of Teaching and Learning in the South*, *7*(3), 46–77. DOI: 10.36615/sotls.v7i3.384

McDiarmid, G. W., & Zhao, Y. (2022). Time to Rethink: Educating for a Technology-Transformed World. *Carolina Digital Repository (University of North Carolina at Chapel Hill)*. DOI: 10.17615/aa8e-bd54

Melhim, M. A., Rababah, M. A., Rabab'a, Y. A., Zainelabdin, F. A., Dalaeen, I. A., Zaytoon, N. A. A., Alqiam, H. A. A., & Al-khatib, L. I. (2023). Teachers' Perspectives on Social Values and Their Influence on Sustainable Development in Ajloun Governorate. *Journal of Higher Education Theory and Practice*, *23*(14). Advance online publication. DOI: 10.33423/jhetp.v23i14.6389

Melhim, M. A., Rababah, M. A., Rabab'a, Y. A., Zainelabdin, F. A., Dalaeen, I. A., Zaytoon, N. A. A., Alqiam, H. A. A., & Al-khatib, L. I. (2023). Teachers' Perspectives on Social Values and Their Influence on Sustainable Development in Ajloun Governorate. *Journal of Higher Education Theory and Practice*, *23*(14). Advance online publication. DOI: 10.33423/jhetp.v23i14.6389

Meng, S. Y. (2023). Enhancing Teaching and Learning: Aligning Instructional Practices with Education Quality Standards. *Research and Advances in Education*, *2*(7), 17–31. DOI: 10.56397/RAE.2023.07.04

Mitina, L. M., Osadcheva, I., & Mitin, G. V. (2024). Teacher of the Future: New Scientific Approaches, Competency Matrices, Development Resources. *Vestnik Prakticheskoi Psikhologii Obrazovaniia, 20*(4), 43–56. DOI: 10.17759/bppe.2023200404

Moustaghfir, S., & Brigui, H. (2024). Navigating Critical Thinking in the Digital Era: An Informative Exploration. *International Journal of Linguistics Literature & Translation, 7*(1), 137–143. DOI: 10.32996/ijllt.2024.7.1.11x

Mouta, A., Llorente, A. M. P., & Sánchez, E. M. T. (2023). Uncovering Blind Spots in Education Ethics: Insights from a Systematic Literature Review on Artificial Intelligence in Education. *International Journal of Artificial Intelligence in Education*. Advance online publication. DOI: 10.1007/s40593-023-00384-9

Ngo, T. T. A. (2024). Perception of Engineering Students on Social Constructivist Learning Approach in Classroom. [iJEP]. *International Journal of Engineering Pedagogy, 14*(1), 20–38. DOI: 10.3991/ijep.v14i1.43101

Nopas, D., & Kerdsomboon, C. (2024). Fostering Global Competence in Teacher Education: Curriculum Integration and Professional Development. *Higher Education Studies, 14*(2), 1. DOI: 10.5539/hes.v14n2p1

Nor, A., Yusuf, M., & Arabi, I. (2024). Strategies for Improving the Professionalism of Islamic Education Teachers at University. *Tafkir Interdisciplinary Journal of Islamic Education, 5*(1), 40–61. DOI: 10.31538/tijie.v5i1.774

Nor, A., Yusuf, M., & Arabi, I. (2024). Strategies for Improving the Professionalism of Islamic Education Teachers at University. *Tafkir Interdisciplinary Journal of Islamic Education, 5*(1), 40–61. DOI: 10.31538/tijie.v5i1.774

Nuis, W., Segers, M., & Beausaert, S. (2023). Conceptualizing mentoring in higher education: A systematic literature review. *Educational Research Review, 41*, 100565. DOI: 10.1016/j.edurev.2023.100565

Nurhidayah, M. I., & Wirza, Y. (2024). Reflective practice in the teaching practicum program: Pre-service English teachers' reflections. *Journal of Applied Studies in Language, 8*(1), 11–19. DOI: 10.31940/jasl.v8i1.11-19

Olivier, J. (2022). Preparing education students for self-directed multimodal learning for the 4IR. In *Disruptions in higher education* (p. 35). DOI: 10.4102/aosis.2022.BK306.03

Örtegren, A. (2023). Philosophical underpinnings of digital citizenship through a postdigital lens: Implications for teacher educators' professional digital competence. *Education and Information Technologies, 29*(4), 4253–4285. DOI: 10.1007/s10639-023-11965-5

Paiva, R., Xisto, J., Sobrinho, Á., Silva, A., Sarmento, F., Recch, F., Tenório, S., Carvalho, A. M. X., Bittencourt, I. I., & Isotani, S. (2025). Expanding the resilience of the Brazilian education system by supporting the evaluation of digital textbooks. *Humanities & Social Sciences Communications, 12*(1), 1315. Advance online publication. DOI: 10.1057/s41599-025-05489-1

Pedersen, J., Long, C. E., Hollweck, T., & Kim, M. J. (2023). Professional learning in global networks: Lessons from ARC. *Journal of Educational Change, 25*(2), 271–303. DOI: 10.1007/s10833-023-09492-8

Pelgrim, E., Hissink, E., Bus, L., Schaaf, M. F. van der, Nieuwenhuis, L., Tartwijk, J. van, & Kuijer-Siebelink, W. (2022). Professionals' adaptive expertise and adaptive performance in educational and workplace settings: an overview of reviews [Review of *Professionals' adaptive expertise and adaptive performance in educational and workplace settings: an overview of reviews*]. *Advances in Health Sciences Education, 27*(5), 1245. Springer Science+Business Media. DOI: 10.1007/s10459-022-10190-y

Petrychenko, O., Петриченко, И. Е., Burmaka, I., & Vynohradova, A. (2023). Changes in modern university: Challenges of today and development trends. *Collection of Scientific Works of the State University of Infrastructure and Technologies Series Transport Systems and Technologies, 41*(41), 74–83. DOI: 10.32703/2617-9059-2023-41-6

Prasetyowibowo, A., Graha, A. S., Suherman, W. S., Rismayanthi, C., & Guntur, G. (2023). Developing an android-based learning media for physical education to enhance high School students' learning outcomes. *International Journal of Physical Education Sports and Health*, *10*(6), 152–157. Advance online publication. DOI: 10.22271/kheljournal.2023.v10.i6c.3148

Prastikawati, E. F., Adeoye, M. A., & Ryan, J. (2024). Fostering Effective Teaching Practices: Integrating Formative Assessment and Mentorship in Indonesian Preservice Teacher Education. [IJOLAE]. *Indonesian Journal on Learning and Advanced Education*, *6*(2), 230–253. DOI: 10.23917/ijolae.v6i2.23431

Rahimi, R. A., & Oh, G. S. (2024). Rethinking the role of educators in the 21st century: Navigating globalization, technology, and pandemics. *Journal of Marketing Analytics*, *12*(2), 182–197. DOI: 10.1057/s41270-024-00303-4

Rap, S., Geller, S., Katchevich, D., Gbarin, H., Blonder, R., Rap, S., Geller, S., Katchevich, D., Gbarin, H., & Blonder, R. (2023). "Chemistry, climate and the skills in between": Mapping cognitive skills in an innovative program designed to empower future citizens to address global challenges. *Chemistry Teacher International : Best Practices in Chemistry Education*, *5*(2), 143–154. DOI: 10.1515/cti-2023-0015

Sartika, W., Rahman, S. R., & Irfan, M. (2023). Empowering students' critical thinking skills using problem-based learning. *Inornatus Biology Education Journal*, *3*(2), 67–74. DOI: 10.30862/inornatus.v3i2.427

Saylam, S., Duman, N., Yildirim, Y., & Satsevich, K. (2023). Empowering education with AI: Addressing ethical concerns. *London Journal of Social Sciences*, *6*(6), 39–48. DOI: 10.31039/ljss.2023.6.103

Siminto, S., Lisnawati, S. D., & Muharam, S. (2023). Teacher Professionalism Development Strategy through ChatGPT Support in the Context of Education Management. [ADMAN]. *Journal of Contemporary Administration and Management*, *1*(3), 150–155. DOI: 10.61100/adman.v1i3.65

Singh, N. C., Gilead, T., Chakraborty, A., Herwegen, J. V., van Atteveldt, N., Borst, G., Bugden, S., Jasińska, K. K., Kay, J., Pugh, K. R., & Duraiappah, A. K. (2025). A new education agenda based on The International Science and Evidence Based Education Assessment. *NPJ Science of Learning*, *10*(1), 24. DOI: 10.1038/s41539-024-00288-w PMID: 40348805

Skedsmo, G., & Huber, S. G. (2023). Understanding academic resilience, equity, and research engagement to improve education. *Educational Assessment, Evaluation and Accountability*, *35*(2), 165–168. DOI: 10.1007/s11092-023-09408-3

Smith, K., & Vattøy, K.-D. (2022). 1. Developing a Platform for a Research- Based Teacher Education. In *Fagbokforlaget eBooks*. DOI: 10.55669/oa040301

Soipimai, W., & Sanrattana, W. (2023). Collaborative Practices to Empower Teachers' Capacities for the 21st Century. *World Journal of Education*, *13*(1), 30. DOI: 10.5430/wje.v13n1p30

Stavrianos, A., & Pratt-Adams, S. (2023). Experience as the Sought Outcome: From Foundational Skills to Inclusive and Holistic Learning. *Open Journal of Social Sciences*, *11*(10), 19–35. DOI: 10.4236/jss.2023.1110002

Stubbs, C., & Hullinger, H. (2022). Developing critical consciousness in students for cultural transformation. *Journal of the Scholarship of Teaching and Learning for Christians in Higher Education*, *12*(1), 9–31. DOI: 10.31380/sotlched.12.1.9

Sunde, J. I., Winter, P., Brunstad, P. O., Oliverio, S., Strand, G. M., Amdal, I. I., Ulvik, M., Tyrfingsdóttir, J., Jónsdóttir, A. H., Jenssen, M. M. F., Johannessen, W. H., Oltedal, E., Holst-Larsen, R., Veka, I., Wergedahl, H., Holthe, A., Hanssen, N. B., Klungeland, M., Waage, I. Ó., & Symeonidis, V. (2022). Validity and Value of Teacher Education Research. In *Fagbokforlaget eBooks*. DOI: 10.55669/oa0503

Sunde, J. I., Winter, P., Brunstad, P. O., Oliverio, S., Strand, G. M., Amdal, I. I., Ulvik, M., Tyrfingsdóttir, J., Jónsdóttir, A. H., Jenssen, M. M. F., Johannessen, W. H., Oltedal, E., Holst-Larsen, R., Veka, I., Wergedahl, H., Holthe, A., Hanssen, N. B., Klungeland, M., Waage, I. Ó., & Symeonidis, V. (2022). Validity and Value of Teacher Education Research. In *Fagbokforlaget eBooks*. DOI: 10.55669/oa0503

Taştı, Ö. Y., & Yıldırım, A. (2022). Critical Thinking Skills and Dispositions of Turkish Pre-service Teachers: A Systematic Review of Research [Review of *Critical Thinking Skills and Dispositions of Turkish Pre-service Teachers: A Systematic Review of Research*]. *Kuramsal Eğitimbilim, 15*(3), 561. Afyon Kocatepe University. DOI: 10.30831/akukeg.1062721

Vidal-Fernández, A., Martínez-Algora, C., & Román-González, M. (2025). Digital Tools to Support Personalized Education for Gifted Students: A Systematic Literature Review. *Education Sciences, 15*(9), 1257. DOI: 10.3390/educsci15091257

Wang, C.-C. (2024). Using design thinking for interdisciplinary curriculum design and teaching: A case study in higher education. *Humanities & Social Sciences Communications, 11*(1), 307. Advance online publication. DOI: 10.1057/s41599-024-02813-z

Wang, M. (2024). Rethinking how people learn: A holistic framework for effective learning design. *Knowledge Management & E-Learning An International Journal, 208*, 208–216. Advance online publication. DOI: 10.34105/j.kmel.2024.16.010

Wang, X., Li, Y., Chen, K., & Zheng, Y. (2024). Understanding teacher emotional exhaustion: Exploring the role of teaching motivation, perceived autonomy, and teacher–student relationships. *Frontiers in Psychology, 14*, 1342598. Advance online publication. DOI: 10.3389/fpsyg.2023.1342598 PMID: 38259554

Xiang-hui, M. (2024). Equity in Education: How Classroom Practices Can Promote Social Justice. *Journal of Education and Educational Policy Studies, 2*(1), 12–17. DOI: 10.54254/3049-7248/2/2024009

Yoshida, F., Conti, G. J., Yamauchi, T., & Kawanishi, M. (2023). Learner-Centeredness vs. Teacher-Centeredness: How Are They Different? *Journal of Education and Learning, 12*(5), 1. DOI: 10.5539/jel.v12n5p1

Zhang, H., & Cao, J. (2025). From digital disruption to mental health: The impact of AI-induced educational anxiety on teacher well-being in the era of smart education. *BMC Public Health, 25*(1), 4010. DOI: 10.1186/s12889-025-25372-7 PMID: 41250007

Chapter 28
Algorithmic Pedagogy:
When Data Decides What Teachers Teach

Kusum Lata
http://orcid.org/0009-0005-2938-4129
D.G.C. Gurugram, Gurugram University, India

ABSTRACT

This chapter examines the rise of algorithmic pedagogy and its implications for teaching, knowledge, and democratic education, with a specific focus on the Indian educational context. It analyses how data-driven systems increasingly shape curricular decisions, assessment practices, and instructional strategies, positioning algorithms as influential pedagogical actors. Drawing on sociotechnical theory, critical pedagogy, and empirical evidence from India and global contexts, the chapter evaluates both the benefits and risks of algorithmic interventions, including personalization, efficiency, bias, surveillance, and epistemic injustice. The discussion highlights how linguistic diversity, social inequality, and governance structures in India intensify these dynamics. The chapter concludes by advancing principles for human-centered educational AI that prioritize pedagogical primacy, teacher autonomy, equity, transparency, and democratic governance, arguing that reclaiming pedagogy is essential to ensuring ethical and inclusive educational transformation.

INTRODUCTION

Over the past two decades, education systems across the world have undergone a profound transformation driven by the growing reliance on data, digital platforms, and algorithmic decision-making. Teaching, once grounded primarily in professional judgment, disciplinary expertise, and contextual understanding of learners, is increasingly shaped by algorithmic systems that recommend content, sequence lessons, predict student performance, and evaluate instructional effectiveness. This shift marks the emergence of what can be described as algorithmic pedagogy, a condition in which data-driven systems do not merely support teaching but actively participate in determining what teachers teach, how they teach, and how learning is valued.

The expansion of algorithmic decision-making in education must be understood within the broader political economy of digital governance. Scholars such as Williamson (2017) and Selwyn (2019) have shown that education has become a central site for the application of data analytics, predictive modeling, and artificial intelligence, reflecting wider trends in public sector reform where governance is increasingly exercised through metrics and computational systems. In classrooms and institutions, algorithms now inform curriculum pacing, personalize instructional materials, automate assessment, and generate performance dashboards for teachers and administrators. These systems operate across contexts, from adaptive learning platforms in primary education to learning analytics infrastructures in higher education.

Empirical evidence indicates the rapid scale of this transformation. According to Holmes et al. (2019), more than sixty percent of higher education institutions in middle- and high-income countries report using some form of learning analytics to monitor student engagement and performance. In school education, adaptive platforms such as DreamBox, Knewton, and Byju's report serving millions of learners worldwide, with instructional decisions increasingly driven by

DOI: 10.4018/979-8-3373-8983-7.ch028

real-time data streams rather than teacher-designed lesson plans. In India, the National Education Policy 2020 explicitly promotes data-driven personalization and technology-enabled teaching, embedding algorithmic systems into the future vision of schooling and higher education (Ministry of Education, 2020).

While proponents argue that algorithmic pedagogy enables personalization, efficiency, and scalability, critical questions remain unresolved. Who exercises pedagogical authority when algorithms guide instructional decisions? To what extent do teachers retain autonomy over curriculum, assessment, and classroom practices? How do data-driven systems shape whose knowledge is valued and whose learning trajectories are prioritized? These questions are not merely technical but normative, as they concern the democratic and ethical foundations of education.

Research demonstrates that algorithms increasingly function as governing devices that structure educational possibilities by defining what counts as success, risk, and improvement. When predictive models identify students as at risk, or recommendation engines prioritize specific learning resources, pedagogical decisions are partially displaced from human judgment to computational inference. This shift does not eliminate human agency. Instead, it reconfigures the teacher's role as implementers and monitors of algorithmically generated pathways rather than primary decision-makers. The implications of this shift are particularly significant in contexts marked by inequality. Studies by Eubanks (2018) and Noble (2018) show that algorithmic systems often reproduce and intensify existing social hierarchies because they are trained on historical data reflecting unequal access, biased assessments, and exclusionary norms. When such systems are embedded in education, they risk reinforcing stratified learning pathways, narrowing curricular exposure for marginalized learners, and normalizing surveillance as a condition of participation in schooling.

This chapter situates algorithmic pedagogy at the intersection of educational technology, critical pedagogy, and data governance. It argues that algorithms should be understood not as neutral tools but as pedagogical actors that exercise power over knowledge production, instructional priorities, and professional identities. By synthesizing theoretical perspectives with empirical evidence from diverse educational systems, the chapter examines how algorithmic systems reshape teaching practices and what this means for equity, autonomy, and democratic education. The analysis proceeds by tracing the datafication of teaching, examining the role of algorithms as pedagogical agents, and articulating principles for reclaiming pedagogy in human-centered ways.

Datafication and the Changing Nature of Teaching

The rise of algorithmic pedagogy is inseparable from the broader process of datafication in education, a process through which complex social and pedagogical practices are translated into quantifiable data points. Teaching has historically relied on tacit knowledge, professional experience, and relational judgment, elements that are difficult to formalize or measure. However, as educational systems have increasingly emphasized accountability and performance measurement, these qualitative dimensions have been progressively overshadowed by metrics that render teaching legible to administrative and computational systems.

The accountability turn in education marked a critical shift in how teaching quality and student learning were defined. Standardized testing regimes, learning outcomes frameworks, and performance indicators reframed education as a system of measurable outputs. Teachers became accountable not only to students and communities but also to data infrastructures that compare classrooms, institutions, and nations. International assessments such as the Programme for International Student Assessment have played a significant role in this transformation. Analyses by Breakspear (2012) show that PISA results have influenced curriculum reforms in more than seventy countries, encouraging alignment with competencies that are easily assessed and compared across contexts. As accountability regimes expanded, digital technologies provided the infrastructure necessary to intensify data collection. Learning management systems, classroom apps, and educational platforms now generate continuous streams of data on attendance, assignment submissions, time spent on tasks, interaction patterns, and assessment outcomes.

For teachers, this datafication has altered the conditions under which pedagogical decisions are made. Rather than relying primarily on observational insights or dialogic feedback, teachers are increasingly encouraged or required to consult dashboards, alerts, and predictive scores. Studies by StatAnalytica (2025, June 4) demonstrate that teachers in data-intensive environments often adjust lesson pacing, assessment strategies, and student support based on algorithmically generated indicators. While such practices can support early intervention, they also shift the epistemic basis of teaching from situated judgment to statistical inference. The adoption of learning analytics in higher education provides a clear illustration. Long and Siemens (2011) originally framed learning analytics as a means of empowering educators through actionable insights. However, subsequent empirical research paints a more ambivalent picture. A large-scale study by Viberg et al. (2018), involving universities across Europe, found that while analytics systems improved monitoring of student progression, many instructors felt pressured to conform to data-driven norms that prioritized retention and completion over intellectual exploration. Teaching became aligned with indicators of engagement rather than broader educational goals.

In school education, adaptive learning platforms further intensify this dynamic. These systems continuously collect performance data and adjust content in real time, effectively outsourcing key pedagogical decisions to algorithms. Research by Pane et al. (2017) on personalized learning initiatives in the United States found modest gains in mathematics achievement but also noted significant variation in outcomes depending on students' socioeconomic background. Teachers reported that algorithmic pacing sometimes conflicted with their professional judgment, particularly when students required contextualized explanations or emotional support that the system could not recognize. Datafication also extends to the monitoring of teachers. Classroom observation tools, automated lesson planning software, and performance analytics increasingly quantify instructional practices. Studies by Williamson (2017) show that teacher evaluation systems in several countries now integrate student performance data and algorithmic scoring, contributing to a culture of surveillance. Teaching is rendered transparent to management systems but less responsive to local classroom dynamics.

The implications for professional identity are significant. When teaching is mediated through data, teachers are positioned simultaneously as data producers and data subjects. Their actions generate the data that feed algorithmic systems, while those same systems evaluate their effectiveness and guide future practice. Research by Selwyn (2019) suggests that this dual role can create tension, as teachers experience a loss of discretion alongside increased responsibility for outcomes defined by opaque metrics. Crucially, datafication does not affect all teachers and learners equally. In such contexts, algorithmic recommendations may narrow curricular exposure to test-aligned content, limiting opportunities for creative and critical learning. This raises concerns about equity and epistemic justice, as certain forms of knowledge and learning are systematically privileged over others.

In short, the datafication of teaching represents a structural transformation rather than a simple technological upgrade. It redefines what counts as evidence, how pedagogical success is measured, and who holds authority in the classroom. By translating teaching into data, educational systems create the conditions under which algorithmic pedagogy can flourish. Understanding this transformation is essential for assessing both the promises and the risks of allowing data-driven systems to decide what teachers teach. While datafication creates the conditions for algorithmic decision-making, it is through specific systems and tools that these transformations become operational in classrooms. The next section therefore examines how algorithms function as active pedagogical agents.

ALGORITHMS AS PEDAGOGICAL ACTORS

In education, algorithms are increasingly positioned not merely as background computational tools but as *active agents* that shape pedagogical processes. They inform, prioritise and in many instances automate decisions about what content students encounter, how learning pathways are sequenced, and which interventions are triggered in response to learner data. Empirical research in the field of Artificial Intelligence in Education (AIED) supports this reconceptualisation of algorithms as pedagogical actors whose outputs extend beyond administrative support into the core domain of instructional decision-making. A large systematic review by Wang and colleagues shows that across 2,223 AIED research articles, adaptive learning systems, personalized tutoring, learning analytics and predictive profiling constitute the primary algorithmic applications explored in educational settings, illustrating how embedded these systems have become within teaching and learning processes (Wang et al., 2024).

Algorithmic systems perform several pedagogically consequential functions. First, adaptive learning systems use machine learning to tailor instructional content and pacing in response to individual learners' performance and engagement patterns. Second, algorithms embedded in learning analytics systems function as pedagogical mediators by generating dashboards that visualise student engagement, performance trends and risk indicators for educators. Third, algorithms in intelligent tutoring systems (ITS) offer personalised guidance that approximates one-to-one support, often without direct teacher mediation. ITS draw on natural language processing and predictive models to interact with learners, provide tailored feedback and scaffold problem solving. Such systems redefine the locus of pedagogical action from teacher to machine, particularly in contexts where human resources are scarce. For example, in a Grade 6 mathematics classroom using an adaptive platform, a student struggling with fractions may automatically receive simpler practice problems and step-by-step hints, while another student progresses to more complex applications. In such cases, the teacher's role shifts from delivering uniform instruction to interpreting system recommendations and supporting students who need conceptual clarification beyond what the algorithm provides

Algorithmic mediation extends into predictive analytics, where historical and real-time data about learners are used to forecast future performance and identify students at risk of failure or disengagement. These predictions, in turn, trigger recommended interventions or prioritise students for support resources. The U.S. Department of Education's analysis (2023) of AI in educational settings underscores the prevalence of predictive models in early warning systems, while also noting the need to address inherent biases rooted in historical data that can unfairly disadvantage certain student groups.

Collectively, these algorithmic functions reconfigure traditional pedagogical roles. Rather than serving solely as tools to extend teacher capability, algorithms in contemporary education often define, influence and prioritise instructional decisions that were historically the domain of human educators. This shift has been characterised in recent sociological research as one where algorithmic systems "mediate teacher-student relationships, redistribute agency, and contribute to new forms of digital stratification," which extends implications for instructional authority and teacher autonomy (Bouakaz & Khalid, 2025).

The pedagogical actions performed by algorithms have both technical and social dimensions. On the technical side, algorithms rely on patterns learned from large datasets to infer learner needs and suggest actions. For example, adaptive learning systems may classify learners into proficiency clusters using clustering algorithms, and then deliver customised instructional sequences based on that classification. On the social side, these systems introduce new hierarchies of knowledge authority: algorithmic interpretations of student performance gain prominence alongside, or even above, professional teacher judgment. This shift implicates not only how instruction is delivered, but also what counts as valid evidence of learning.

Empirical investigations of adaptive and analytics systems provide measurable outcomes associated with algorithmic pedagogies. A systematic review of AI-driven adaptive learning in higher education reported academic performance improvements of 15 percent to 25 percent and learner engagement increases of up to 40 percent where these systems were implemented, albeit with persistent challenges related to infrastructure, faculty readiness, and ethical concerns such as data privacy and bias (Yuensook et al., 2025). Outcomes such as these highlight the potential of algorithmic actors to support learning gains, while the associated challenges underscore the complexity of integrating these systems equitably and ethically. Nevertheless, algorithmic mediation is not neutral in its influence. Algorithms are designed and trained under particular epistemic, cultural and institutional assumptions, which shape the priorities embedded within pedagogical decisions. For example, systems that optimise for retention and test performance may inadvertently deprioritize socio-emotional learning, creativity or collaborative problem-solving dimensions of teaching that are harder to quantify. As such, algorithmic pedagogies risk narrowing educational goals to what can be operationalised in data, reinforcing a focus on measurable performance at the expense of broader pedagogical values.

In summary, algorithms in education have moved beyond auxiliary support roles into functions that actively mediate instruction, personalise learning paths and recommend interventions. They act as pedagogical actors by participating in core decisions about content sequencing, learner grouping, feedback and intervention triggers. Empirical evidence from adaptive learning research and learning analytics studies confirms measurable impacts on learning outcomes and instructional practices. At the same time, this emergent role raises critical questions about authority, professional agency and the values encoded in algorithmic logic. Understanding these expanding roles requires a theoretical lens that explains how algorithmic systems reshape authority, knowledge, and learning. The following section outlines key theoretical frameworks that inform this analysis.

THEORETICAL FOUNDATIONS

Algorithmic pedagogy must be understood through key theoretical lenses that explain how technology interacts with teaching. Four perspectives are particularly useful: sociotechnical systems theory, critical pedagogy, data justice, and educational psychology. Rather than treating algorithms as neutral tools, these frameworks highlight how they reshape power, knowledge, and learning processes.

Sociotechnical systems theory emphasises that algorithms operate within networks of teachers, institutions, and policies. In education, this means algorithmic tools do not simply support teaching but actively reshape classroom practices and decision-making. A sociological analysis of AI in education using Actor-Network Theory illustrates that intelligent systems mediate relationships and redistribute agency among teachers, students and technologies, highlighting the sociotechnical nature of these interventions (Bouakaz & Khalid, 2025).

Sociotechnical systems thinking aligns with literature on human-centred learning analytics and AI, which argues that excluding educators and learners from the design and implementation of algorithmic tools can lead to misalignment between system logic and educational goals. A systematic review of human-centred learning analytics research found limited involvement of educational stakeholders in the design process, underscoring the need to balance human control with algorithmic automation to maintain trust and relevance in pedagogical contexts (Alfredo et al., 2024). This body of work situates algorithmic pedagogy within a network of actors whose interests, values and interpretations shape how technologies function in practice.

Critical pedagogy offers a complementary lens that interrogates power dynamics, ideological assumptions and the political dimensions of educational practices. Rooted in the work of Paulo Freire (2017) and subsequent scholars, critical pedagogy emphasises education as a site of power where dominant norms and values can be challenged or reproduced. Within the context of algorithmic systems, critical pedagogues argue that algorithmic infrastructures can reinforce existing hierarchies by encoding normative assumptions about who succeeds, what counts as legitimate knowledge and how learning should be measured. Conceptual work on critical algorithmic mediation argues for recognizing how algorithmic infrastructures mediate symbolic power in education, shaping students' visibility, opportunities and pedagogical attention. This approach problematises the seeming neutrality of data-driven systems and calls attention to whose interests they serve, highlighting the potential for algorithmic practices to entrench inequities unless critically examined and contested (Sánchez-Vera, 2025).

Critical pedagogy also draws attention to the potential erosion of teacher agency as algorithmic systems prescribe instructional paths and evaluate performance through metrics that may not align with broader educational aims centred on critical thinking, democratic engagement or socio-emotional development. This critique resonates with broader concerns in education technology research about the risk of technocratic dominance, where technological imperatives shape pedagogical priorities in ways that marginalise professional judgement and student voice.

Data justice and critical data studies extend these concerns by emphasising the ethical, political and distributional dimensions of data and algorithmic governance. Data justice frameworks highlight that data collection, algorithm training and analytical outputs are inherently value-laden processes that reflect power relations and can perpetuate inequalities unless actively mitigated. Within education, data justice theorists challenge data universalism - the assumption that data interpretations are neutral and universally applicable arguing that data practices must be contextualised with attention to local cultures, histories and social conditions. Algorithms trained on historical data risk perpetuating structural biases present in those data, with implications for students from marginalised groups who may be misclassified, overlooked or unfairly targeted by predictive systems.

Theoretical work on responsible AI frameworks in education further underscores the need for incorporating principles of fairness, transparency and accountability into algorithmic systems. A responsible AI framework tailored for learning analytics emphasises these principles, noting that without them, algorithmic systems may produce unequal support for minority students and undermine inclusive educational goals. Such frameworks anchor theoretical analysis in practical imperatives for equitable design and governance.

Educational psychology and learning theory contribute another layer of analysis by interrogating assumptions about how learning occurs and how it should be supported. Theories such as connectivism highlight that learning in the digital age is distributed across networks of information, technologies and social interactions, rather than residing solely within individual cognition. Connectivism posits that knowledge and learning emerge through the formation and recognition of patterns across networks, an insight that aligns with the data-driven principles of many algorithmic systems. However, it also cautions against conflating networked data generation with deeper forms of meaning-making and human interpretation.

Educational psychology also raises questions about the influence of algorithmic recommendations on learner motivation, self-regulated learning and socio-emotional development. While adaptive systems can enhance engagement by personalising content, there is limited evidence about their impact on skills such as critical reflection, collaborative problem solving and resilience, which are central to holistic educational aims.

Together, these theoretical lenses provide a multifaceted foundation for understanding algorithmic pedagogy. They emphasise that educational technologies are embedded within sociotechnical networks, are shaped by power and ideological dynamics, implicate questions of justice and equity, and intersect with fundamental assumptions about how learning is understood. These frameworks foreground the complexities and contested dimensions of algorithmic integration in education, moving beyond purely technical evaluations toward normative analyses of what educational systems ought to be in an age of data-driven decision making (see Figure 1).

Figure 1. Theoretical Framework

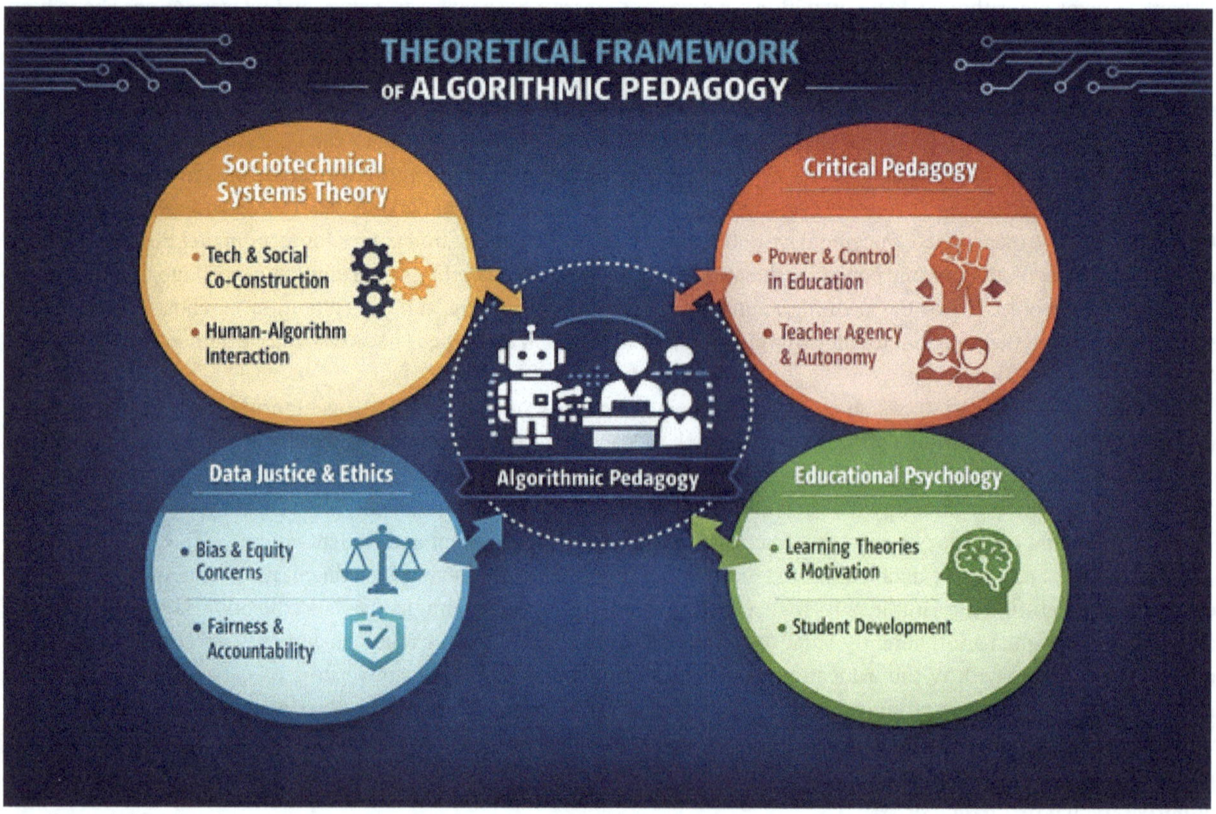

(Source: Author estimate)

The theoretical framework of this chapter positions *algorithmic pedagogy* within a network of intersecting theories that clarify how data-driven systems reshape educational practice. At its core, sociotechnical systems theory foregrounds that algorithms in education do not operate in isolation but are co-constituted with social actors, institutional norms and professional practices. Algorithms both respond to and reshape teaching work, implying that technological logic is inseparable from contextual human judgment. Critical pedagogy contributes by prompting interrogation of power relations embedded in algorithmic systems, foregrounding questions of whose knowledge is privileged when algorithmic recommendations influence curriculum sequencing or assessment. Data justice frameworks further expand this analysis by directing attention to fairness, bias and equity; algorithms trained on historical educational data can reproduce structural inequalities unless explicitly designed for fairness and interpretability. Finally, insights from educational psychology and learning theory highlight how algorithmic recommendations intersect with cognitive, motivational and socio-emotional processes of learning. Together, these theories depict algorithmic pedagogy not as a neutral enhancement of instruction but as a contested space where authority, values and outcomes are negotiated among teachers, learners, and data systems. This framework undergirds empirical analysis by clarifying conceptual anchors for interpreting case evidence.

The theoretical framework is particularly relevant to the Indian educational landscape, where algorithmic systems are being rapidly integrated into large-scale public education infrastructures. From a sociotechnical perspective, platforms such as DIKSHA, UDISE+, and the emerging National Digital Education Architecture illustrate how algorithms are embedded within state governance structures, institutional mandates, and teacher practices rather than operating as neutral instructional aids. These systems co-produce pedagogical decisions by linking classroom activity with national data repositories and performance indicators. Critical pedagogy sharpens this analysis by drawing attention to power asymmetries in India's data-driven reforms, where curricular sequencing, assessment feedback, and teacher performance are increasingly shaped by centrally designed platforms, often with limited teacher participation in system design. Data justice frameworks are essential in the Indian context given persistent structural inequalities related to language, region, caste, gender, and digital access. Algorithmic models trained on uneven datasets risk reinforcing these disparities if equity safeguards are not explicitly embedded. Educational psychology further clarifies how algorithmic personalization intersects with heterogeneous learner needs in India's linguistically and socioeconomically diverse classrooms. Together, these theoretical lenses position algorithmic pedagogy in India as a negotiated space where efficiency and scale coexist with concerns about autonomy, epistemic diversity, and democratic accountability.

EMPIRICAL EVIDENCE: CASE STUDIES AND GLOBAL EXPERIENCES WITH A FOCUS ON INDIA

India's Turn Toward Data-Driven Education

India represents one of the largest contemporary experiments in algorithmic and data-driven education. The scale of the system, with over 260 million school students and more than 9 million teachers, necessitates governance models that rely heavily on digital data infrastructures (Ministry of Education, 2022). Over the last decade, policy initiatives such as Digital India, Samagra Shiksha, and the National Education Policy 2020 have accelerated the adoption of learning analytics, adaptive platforms, and centralized data systems. These developments position algorithms not only as instructional supports but as instruments of pedagogical governance. The creation of UDISE+ marked a major shift in educational data practices. According to the Ministry of Education, UDISE+ now captures over 3 million data points annually across schools, including enrolment, attendance, infrastructure, and teacher deployment. These data increasingly inform funding decisions, teacher rationalisation, and curricular interventions, illustrating how datafication reshapes pedagogical priorities at systemic levels.

DIKSHA and Platform-Mediated Pedagogy

DIKSHA, India's national digital learning platform, is one of the most prominent examples of algorithmic mediation of teaching. As of 2023, DIKSHA reported over 190 million registered users, including teachers and students, with more than 7.4 billion learning sessions recorded (Ministry of Education, 2023). The platform uses metadata tagging, recommendation logic, and usage analytics to surface content aligned with grade level, subject, and curriculum standards. While this supported continuity of learning at scale, it also narrowed pedagogical discretion by privileging centrally curated content over locally developed materials. For instance at the classroom level, a teacher using DIKSHA may rely on recommended videos and worksheets aligned with a specific topic, such as 'photosynthesis' in a Grade 7 science class. While this reduces preparation time, it can also limit the inclusion of locally relevant examples, such as agricultural practices familiar to students.

Adaptive Learning and Personalised Instruction in Indian States

India has also witnessed the deployment of adaptive learning systems aimed at improving foundational literacy and numeracy. One of the most cited examples is the Personalized Adaptive Learning (PAL) programme in Andhra Pradesh. A large-scale evaluation covering more than 1,200 government schools found that students exposed to adaptive software demonstrated learning gains equivalent to 1.9 additional years of schooling over a 17-month period (World Bank, 2023). The system used continuous assessment data to adjust content difficulty and pacing, effectively acting as a pedagogical decision-maker. However, qualitative findings from the same evaluation indicate that teachers often followed algorithmic recommendations without fully understanding the underlying logic, raising concerns about deskilling and over-reliance on automated pathways. This highlights how algorithmic personalization can simultaneously enhance learning outcomes while reshaping teacher roles.

Learning Analytics and Teacher Monitoring

Learning analytics in India are increasingly linked to teacher accountability frameworks. Platforms integrated with state education management systems generate dashboards tracking student attendance, assessment performance, and teacher engagement with digital resources. In states such as Rajasthan and Gujarat, analytics dashboards are used to flag "low-performance" schools and teachers for intervention.

A policy evaluation by NITI Aayog reported that data-driven monitoring contributed to improvements in attendance and assessment completion rates but also created pressures for compliance with platform metrics rather than pedagogical innovation (NITI Aayog, 2021). Teachers interviewed in the study reported that algorithmic indicators increasingly shaped classroom priorities, often privileging test-aligned activities.

Predictive Analytics and Early Warning Systems

Predictive analytics are emerging in Indian higher education institutions. While effective in identifying risk patterns, these models rely heavily on historical performance data, which may reflect structural disadvantages faced by first-generation learners and rural students. Without contextual interpretation by educators, predictive outputs risk reinforcing deficit narratives.

Table 1. Comparative empirical data

Initiative	Algorithmic Function	Scale	Key Outcomes
DIKSHA	Content recommendation and usage analytics	190+ million users	Centralised content shaping pedagogy
UDISE+	System-level analytics	1.5 million schools	Data-driven funding and teacher deployment
PAL Andhra Pradesh	Adaptive learning	1,200+ schools	+1.9 learning years in 17 months
State dashboards	Teacher and student monitoring	Multi-state	Improved attendance and reporting
IGNOU analytics	Dropout prediction	Higher education	>80% prediction accuracy

Based on the following sources: Ministry of Education (2022 & 2023); World Bank (2023); NITI Aayog (2021); & Sharma et al. (2021)

The Indian evidence (see Table 1) demonstrates that algorithmic systems have produced measurable gains in access, continuity, and foundational learning outcomes, particularly at scale. Adaptive platforms show strong performance effects in early learning, while analytics systems enhance administrative visibility. However, these gains are accompanied by structural shifts in pedagogical authority. Algorithms increasingly mediate what content is taught, how learning is paced, and which students are prioritised for support. The reliance on centrally designed systems raises concerns about contextual responsiveness, linguistic diversity, and teacher autonomy in a highly heterogeneous education system.

Despite positive outcomes, several limitations persist. Digital access remains uneven; ASER (2022) reports that only 68 percent of rural households have access to smartphones suitable for learning. Teacher data literacy varies widely, limiting meaningful engagement with analytics. Most evaluations remain short-term and focus on test-based outcomes, with limited evidence on long-term impacts on critical thinking or socio-emotional learning.

In India, algorithmic pedagogy operates at an unprecedented scale, offering efficiency also centralising pedagogical authority within data infrastructures. Empirical evidence suggests that algorithmic systems can support learning gains when aligned with teacher capacity and governance safeguards. Without such alignment, they risk narrowing pedagogy to measurable outputs and undermining professional autonomy. Adaptive interventions in India, show tangible improvements in learning outcomes quantified as years of learning gains or additional months of progress especially in foundational reading and arithmetic. This evidence aligns with international research suggesting that adaptive systems can enhance engagement and personalised content pathways, though global studies often emphasise potential benefits without quantifying effects uniformly across contexts. India's multilingual adaptations (e.g., vernacular adaptive platforms on DIKSHA) address the unique equity challenge of linguistic diversity that is largely absent in global literature which predominantly reflects English-medium or high-resource settings. The ASER report 2024 (Pratham Education Foundation, 2024) shows persistent foundational learning gaps in India despite high enrolment, and recent data indicate that adaptive tools in local languages are part of strategies to narrow these gaps.

Globally, learning analytics dashboards are often introduced in higher education and blended learning contexts, with emphasis on supporting self-regulated learning and predictive insights rather than mandated national deployments. In India, these tools are woven into state and national systems for governance, teacher professional development, and classroom support, creating deeper entanglement with policy objectives but also a stronger imperative to address infrastructure and training gaps.

Challenges Across Contexts

Whether in India or other countries, adoption challenges persist. Research highlights the importance of teacher data literacy, ethical safeguards, and human-centred implementation for meaningful use of algorithmic systems. A systematic study of learning analytics emphasises that ethical design, pedagogical impact, and adoption readiness are co-dependent factors shaping real-world use.

The comparative analysis reveals that India is not merely following global trends but is implementing algorithmic pedagogy at a scale and with context-specific adaptations unique to its linguistic plurality and policy architecture. Indian evidence shows quantifiable gains in learning outcomes from adaptive systems deployed in government schools, while global research provides broader insight into algorithmic mechanisms and pedagogical effects across diverse environments. However, both contexts share common challenges in infrastructure, teacher readiness, and ethical integration. Placing India within global patterns helps highlight that algorithmic pedagogy's impact is shaped by governance frameworks, data environments, and equity priorities, not just by technological sophistication.

KNOWLEDGE, BIAS, AND EPISTEMIC JUSTICE IN ALGORITHMIC SYSTEMS

The integration of algorithmic systems into Indian education raises acute questions about knowledge representation, bias, and epistemic justice because of India's socio-cultural diversity, historical inequalities, and persistent digital divides. Algorithmic systems whether embedded in adaptive learning platforms, assessment engines, or analytics dashboards are trained on data that reflect existing social realities. Without careful attention to representation, fairness, and inclusivity, the very systems intended to support learning can unintentionally reinforce historically entrenched disadvantages.

Structural Inequalities Underpinning Algorithmic Bias

Algorithmic bias in India cannot be understood solely as a technical artifact. Research shows that bias is deeply rooted in India's socio-economic fabric, shaped by caste, class, gender, linguistic diversity, and geographic disparities. Algorithms trained on data that reflect unequal access to schooling, uneven internet connectivity, and unequal digital fluency risk reproducing exclusionary outcomes even when neutrality is assumed.

A concrete example comes from research examining student experiences with AI in Indian learning environments. A study involving 113 university students across linguistic and socio-economic backgrounds found that 53.1 percent of learners reported that AI systems failed to accurately recognize speech or language patterns linked to regional dialects, with tribal language speakers particularly disadvantaged. The study also documented that 60.16 percent of students reported discomfort with AI surveillance mechanisms during online proctoring, and students from historically marginalised groups (e.g., SC/ST categories) experienced significantly higher rates of misrecognition and misclassification by algorithmic systems (Begum et al., 2025) . Such findings illustrate epistemic harms that extend beyond mere metrics to affect dignity, participation, and identity.

Linguistic Marginalisation and Cultural Mismatch

Epistemic justice issues in India are acutely tied to language representation. National platforms like DIKSHA and analytics systems predominantly rely on content and metadata structured around English or major state languages, leaving speakers of minority and tribal languages underrepresented. The linguistic diversity of India where the Census of India identifies 22 scheduled languages and hundreds of local dialects creates an immediate challenge for systems that assume linguistic uniformity. Language models and speech recognition systems calibrated on non-Indian language corpora misinterpret learner input, leading to both technical errors and perceptions of exclusion.

A related critique of global AI fairness frameworks finds that Western-centric definitions of bias do not map cleanly onto the Indian context. Fairness measures that focus on gender and race, for example, do not capture caste-based or linguistic biases that operate in India's classrooms and assessment systems (Sambasivan et al., 2021). This mismatch underscores the need for context-specific frameworks of fairness rooted in Indian socio-historical realities.

Representation in Educational Datasets

Bias in education algorithms often stems from training data that fail to reflect the population's diversity. For example, large language models (LLMs) used in tutoring or assessment tools often encode stereotypes related to caste and religion when evaluated against an Indian-centric dataset, with probabilities of stereotypical outputs ranging between 63 percent and 79 percent for caste-related content (Khandelwal et al., 2023) . Although this study focuses on LLMs broadly, the implications for educational AI are immediate: if tutorial content, automated feedback, or assessment suggestions are shaped by biased patterns, they risk reproducing social stratification within learning environments.

The UDISE+ and Analytics Governance Conundrum

India's unified database UDISE+ collects administrative and performance data on millions of students and thousands of schools, enabling predictive analytics for dropout risk, resource allocation, and outcome monitoring. While improved data visibility can support targeted interventions, researchers and policy analysts caution that metrics drawn from UDISE+ may embed existing inequities because they reflect underlying disparities in access to quality instruction, connectivity and infrastructure. If predictive models trained on such data do not adjust for structural factors, the result can be unequal rationing of interventions, privileging students in better-resourced districts over those in marginalised areas.

Epistemic Justice and Pedagogical Knowledge

Epistemic justice in education refers to fair representation of diverse knowledge and learner identities within pedagogical systems. Algorithmic systems that prioritise metrics easily quantifiable such as multiple-choice performance or engagement clicks fail to recognise forms of knowledge that are contextually meaningful but less quantifiable, such as local cultural knowledge, oral traditions, and project-based reasoning. This narrow representation of intelligence undermines pedagogical breadth and contributes to epistemic injustice where certain forms of reasoning are systematically marginalised. Beyond representational justice, procedural justice how decisions are made and how transparent systems are is also critical. Studies on AI in Indian education highlight the need for transparency in recommendation logic, so that teachers can contest or interpret algorithmic outputs rather than accept them as unquestionable. Without such transparency, accountability resides with opaque systems rather than teachers or educational authorities, eroding professional judgement and community trust.

Mitigation Strategies for Bias and Epistemic Inclusion

Addressing bias and promoting epistemic justice requires multiple coordinated interventions:

1. Diversification of Data Sources: Datasets used for training educational AI must include diverse linguistic, socio-economic and regional variants reflective of Indian populations.
2. Algorithmic Audits: Independent evaluations of learning and assessment algorithms should be standard practice to identify systemic biases and assess predictive validity across student subpopulations.
3. Contextual Fairness Measures: Fairness metrics should extend beyond universalist measures to incorporate Indian context-specific indicators, such as caste-equity measures and multilingual effectiveness.
4. Teacher and Community Governance: Teachers should retain interpretive authority over algorithmic recommendations, and local communities should participate in governance to ensure cultural relevance and responsiveness.

In India, algorithmic systems are not only technical artefacts but also cultural and political instruments embedded within a complex socio-historical matrix of inequality. Unless policymakers, data scientists, and educators actively incorporate epistemic justice into the design, deployment and governance of algorithmic tools, these systems risk reinforcing the very disparities they aim to ameliorate. A nuanced understanding of bias including structural social factors and contextual interpretations of fairness is essential to ensure that educational AI supports inclusive learning rather than reproducing social exclusion.

DEMOCRATIC EDUCATION IN DATA-DRIVEN CLASSROOMS

Algorithmic systems in Indian classrooms reshape not only how students learn, but also how democratic values participation, voice, and shared decision-making are enacted in pedagogical spaces. Democratic education traditionally foregrounds student agency, teacher professionalism and participatory decision-making; data-driven classrooms introduce new actors, visibility mechanisms, and accountability structures that can both support and challenge democratic practices.

Democratic Education and Indian Policy Goals

The National Education Policy (NEP) 2020 underscores values that implicitly align with democratic education: holistic learning, critical thinking, equity, multilingualism, and learner agency. NEP articulates a vision where learners are co-creators of knowledge and teachers facilitate enquiry and exploration. Embedding algorithmic systems within this vision demands examination of whether data-driven tools reinforce or undermine democratic pedagogy. For example in practice, a teacher might use analytics dashboards to identify students with low engagement and initiate a classroom discussion about learning challenges, allowing students to explain their difficulties rather than being passively categorized by the system.

Technology, Surveillance, and Student Agency

Data-intensive tools provide teachers with unprecedented visibility into student behaviour and learning patterns, but this visibility is double-edged. Analytics dashboards, predictive scores and engagement trackers can be used to support personalised interventions, yet they also produce forms of surveillance that may constrain student autonomy. For instance, analytics flags for 'at-risk' students can trigger administrative interventions without sufficient student voice, potentially labeling learners before they are invited to reflect. Research in Indian contexts notes this tension: a survey of educators and students found that while teachers appreciated predictive insights, many expressed concern that data systems could foster transactional learning focused on metrics rather than inquiry and dialogue (Education for All in India, 2025) .

Inclusion and Participation in Data Interpretation

Democratic classrooms involve participatory interpretation of data rather than unilateral decision-making by authorities or opaque systems. In India, where classrooms are multilingual and socio-economically diverse, interpreting learner data solely through algorithmic outputs risks marginalising students whose performance does not fit dominant patterns. Democratic practice requires that teachers and students engage with data collaboratively with space to question algorithmic inferences so that interpretation is transparent, contextualised, and responsive to learner voice.

Governance of Algorithmic Tools

Democratic education extends beyond the classroom to governance structures that control the design and use of algorithmic systems. In India, platforms such as DIKSHA and UDISE+ are centrally governed, with limited direct participation from teachers and local communities in shaping system logic. Democratic governance would entail mechanisms for teacher representation in platform design, open review of algorithmic logic, and local adaptation, rather than top-down deployment. Without such governance, data systems risk becoming instruments of compliance rather than instruments of empowerment.

Resistance and Critical Engagement

Democratic classrooms encourage critical engagement with data rather than passive acceptance. Teachers in India are developing practices to contest or adapt algorithmic recommendations to local pedagogical goals. For example, educators negotiate around analytics dashboards, using data as a starting point for dialogue with students about goals, strategies and reflections rather than as definitive indicators of success or failure.

Equity, Voice, and Power Dynamics

Algorithmic systems can reinforce power imbalances in democratic spaces if they privilege categories that reflect existing hierarchies. For instance, risk scores may disproportionately flag students from rural or marginalised backgrounds not because of lower ability but because of structural disadvantages in access to resources. Democratic education demands that such scores be interpreted with contextual knowledge and corrective scaffolding rather than automated categorisation.

Assessments and Democratic Participation

Data-driven assessments automate aspects of evaluation, yet democratic education holds that assessment should be dialogical, reflective and participatory. Automated scoring systems can provide rapid feedback, but they may lack sensitivity to creative, culturally rooted or project-based learning, which are central to democratic classrooms. Incorporating student self-assessment, peer assessment and reflective portfolios complemented by algorithmic insights supports a more democratic assessment regime.

Ethical Data Practices as Democratic Imperatives

Democratic education requires ethical data practices that protect privacy, ensure consent and respect student agency. India's Digital Personal Data Protection Act (DPDP) 2023 provides a normative framework for data rights that includes informed consent and limitations on automated profiling. Ethical commitments like these must shape classroom practices, ensuring that data collection and use are transparent, consensual and oriented toward learner development rather than surveillance or punishment.

Student Engagement and Agency

Data-driven insights can support student agency when used as feedback for self-regulated learning. Democratic classrooms encourage students to reflect on their data, set goals, and negotiate strategies. In India's diverse classrooms, this means fostering data dialogues that respect linguistic and cultural contexts, ensuring that visualisations and feedback mechanisms are accessible across languages. Democratic education in data-driven classrooms is possible in India but requires intentional design and governance that foregrounds participation, voice, and contextual interpretation. Algorithmic tools can support democratic values when their outputs are transparent, contestable and situated within dialogic pedagogical practices. Ethical safeguards, teacher empowerment, and participatory governance are essential to prevent data systems from becoming instruments of compliance and surveillance. A democratic data culture in Indian classrooms must balance the efficiencies and insights of algorithmic systems with learner agency, equity, and shared decision-making.

RECLAIMING PEDAGOGY

Reclaiming pedagogy in the age of algorithmic systems requires a deliberate shift from technology-led optimization to human-centered educational AI that foregrounds pedagogical purpose, contextual knowledge, and democratic values. In the Indian context, this imperative is shaped by scale, diversity, and deep structural inequalities. Human-centered educational AI does not reject data or algorithms; rather, it repositions them as supportive instruments embedded within professional judgment, ethical governance, and culturally responsive teaching.

A first principle is pedagogical primacy. Educational AI must be designed to serve clearly articulated learning goals rather than allowing metrics to define pedagogy. In Indian classrooms, where curricular aims include multilingual competence, critical thinking, and social-emotional development as outlined in NEP 2020, algorithms should support diverse learning pathways without narrowing instructional focus to what is easily measurable. Human-centered systems therefore align analytics with curricular breadth, formative assessment, and holistic development rather than test-centric optimization.

A second principle is teacher interpretive authority. Teachers remain the central pedagogical agents who contextualize learner data, interpret algorithmic recommendations, and adapt instruction to local realities. In India's heterogeneous classrooms, algorithmic outputs cannot account for contextual factors such as language transition, first-generation learners, or infrastructural constraints. Human-centered AI systems must be designed to be contestable and interpretable, allowing teachers to question, override, and annotate algorithmic suggestions. Professional development in data literacy is essential so teachers can engage critically with analytics rather than comply with them.

A third principle concerns equity-by-design. Human-centered AI requires proactive measures to mitigate bias through inclusive data practices, multilingual interfaces, and fairness audits tailored to Indian social categories, including caste, region, and language. Equity-by-design moves beyond post hoc corrections by embedding representational diversity into datasets and model evaluation. In practice, this means prioritizing regional language corpora, disaggregated performance analysis, and safeguards against disproportionate profiling of students from marginalized communities.

A fourth principle is transparency and explainability. Black-box systems undermine trust and accountability, particularly in public education systems. Human-centered educational AI should provide explanations that are pedagogically meaningful to teachers and learners, clarifying why certain recommendations or predictions are made. Explainability supports reflective practice, enabling teachers and students to engage in dialogue about learning strategies rather than treating algorithmic outputs as authoritative judgments.

A fifth principle emphasizes student agency and participatory learning. Human-centered AI supports self-regulated learning by making data accessible and interpretable to students, encouraging reflection, goal-setting, and metacognition. In India, where democratic education is tied to empowerment and inclusion, algorithmic feedback should be framed as formative guidance rather than surveillance. Consent, awareness, and choice in data use are essential to preserving learner dignity and autonomy.

A sixth principle is ethical and democratic governance. Educational AI systems operate within institutional and policy frameworks that must ensure accountability, privacy protection, and participatory oversight. India's Digital Personal Data Protection Act provides a baseline for lawful data use, but human-centered pedagogy requires governance mechanisms that include teacher representation, local adaptation, and public scrutiny of system design. Democratic governance ensures that algorithmic systems remain aligned with educational values rather than administrative expediency.

Human-centered educational AI requires continuous evaluation and reflexivity. Pedagogical impacts should be assessed not only through efficiency metrics but also through qualitative indicators such as learner engagement, inclusion, and professional satisfaction. Reflexive evaluation acknowledges that educational contexts evolve and that algorithmic systems must be periodically reassessed to prevent mission drift. Reclaiming pedagogy is therefore not a return to pre-digital teaching but a reassertion of human judgment, ethical responsibility, and democratic purpose within data-rich environments. In India's education system, where scale magnifies both opportunity and risk, human-centered principles provide a normative framework for integrating AI without surrendering pedagogical autonomy.

CONCLUSION

This chapter has examined the emergence of algorithmic pedagogy as a defining feature of contemporary education and its implications for teaching, knowledge production, and democratic practice, with particular attention to the Indian context. As data-driven systems increasingly influence curriculum sequencing, assessment, and instructional decision-making, pedagogy is no longer shaped solely by human deliberation but by sociotechnical assemblages in which algorithms act as powerful pedagogical actors. The analysis demonstrates that algorithmic pedagogy offers tangible benefits, including personalization, scalability, and predictive insights that can support large and diverse education systems such as India's. Empirical evidence from national initiatives and adaptive learning platforms shows measurable learning gains, particularly in foundational skills, and highlights the potential of data-driven tools to address long-standing access and quality challenges. However, these gains are accompanied by significant risks related to teacher autonomy, surveillance, bias, and epistemic exclusion. The chapter argues that algorithmic systems are not neutral instruments but are embedded within social, political, and historical contexts. In India, these contexts include linguistic plurality, caste-based inequality, uneven digital infrastructure, and centralized governance structures. Without intentional safeguards, algorithmic pedagogy risks reinforcing existing hierarchies by privileging quantifiable forms of knowledge, marginalizing local epistemologies, and constraining professional judgment through opaque decision-making processes.

Through engagement with critical pedagogy, sociotechnical systems theory, and debates on epistemic justice, the chapter underscores the need to reframe educational AI as a supportive, accountable, and contestable partner in teaching rather than an authoritative substitute for pedagogical expertise. Democratic education in data-driven classrooms depends on participatory interpretation of data, ethical governance, and the preservation of student and teacher agency. The concluding argument is that the future of education in India will be shaped not by whether algorithms are used, but by how they are designed, governed, and integrated into pedagogical practice. Human-centered educational AI offers a pathway to reconcile innovation with equity, efficiency with ethics, and data-driven insight with democratic values. Reclaiming pedagogy in this manner is essential to ensuring that educational transformation advances learning as a public good rather than reducing it to an exercise in optimization.

REFERENCES

Aayog, N. I. T. I., & the Development Monitoring and Evaluation Office (DMEO). (2021). *Evaluation of Centrally Sponsored Schemes: Best Practices Compendium – Jobs & Skills Sector*. Government of India. Retrieved from https://nitiforstates.gov.in/public-assets/Best_Practices/Compendiums/Best%20Practices%20Compendium_%20Jobs%20_%20Skills%20Sector.pdf

Alfredo, R., Echeverria, V., Jin, Y., Yan, L., Swiecki, Z., Gašević, D., & Martinez-Maldonado, R. (2024). Human-centred learning analytics and AI in education: A systematic literature review. *Computers in Human Behavior*, *152*, 107123.

Begum, S., & Singh, A. K. (2025). *AI as a teacher's ally: Transforming classroom management for the 21st century. The Academic, 3*(7), 819–827. Assam University, Silchar. DOI: 10.5281/zenodo.16793475

Bouakaz, L., & Khalid, S. (2025). AI in education: A sociological exploration of technology in learning environments. *Frontiers in Education*, *10*, 1700876. Advance online publication. DOI: 10.3389/feduc.2025.1700876

Breakspear, S. (2012). The policy impact of PISA: An exploration of the normative effects of international benchmarking in school system performance. *OECD Education Working Papers*, No. 71, OECD Publishing. Retrieved from https://www.oecd.org/en/publications/the-policy-impact-of-pisa_5k9fdfqffr28-en.html

Eubanks, V. (2018). *Automating inequality: How high-tech tools profile, police, and punish the poor*. St. Martin's Press.

Freire, P. (2017). *Pedagogy of the oppressed*. Penguin Classics.

Holmes, W., Fadel, C., & Bialik, M. (2019). *Artificial intelligence in education: Promise and implications for teaching and learning*. Vicasa. Retrieved from https://vicasa.org/wp-content/uploads/2024/05/ArtificialIntelligenceinEducation.PromiseandImplicationsforTeachingandLearning.pdf

Khandelwal, K., Tonneau, M., & Andre, Q. (2023). *IBED: A dataset for measuring India-centric biases in large language models*. arXiv preprint arXiv:2309.08573. Retrieved January 20, 2026, from https://arxiv.org/pdf/2309.08573

Long, P., & Siemens, G. (2011). Penetrating the fog: Analytics in learning and education. *EDUCAUSE Review*, *46*(5), 31–40.

Ministry of Education. (2020). *National Education Policy 2020*. Government of India. Retrieved from https://www.education.gov.in/sites/upload_files/mhrd/files/NEP_Final_English_0.pdf

Ministry of Education. (2022). *Unified District Information System for Education (UDISE+): National data system*. Government of India. Retrieved from https://udiseplus.gov.in

Ministry of Education. (2023). *Annual report 2023–24*. Government of India. Retrieved from https://www.education.gov.in/sites/upload_files/mhrd/files/document-reports/AR_2023-24_en.pdf

Noble, S. U. (2018). *Algorithms of oppression: How search engines reinforce racism*. New York University Press. DOI: 10.18574/nyu/9781479833641.001.0001

Pane, J. F., Steiner, E. D., Baird, M. D., Hamilton, L. S., & Pane, J. D. (2017). *Informing progress: Insights on personalized learning implementation and effects*. RAND Corporation. Retrieved from https://www.rand.org/pubs/research_reports/RR2042.html

Pratham Education Foundation. (2024). *Annual Status of Education Report (ASER) 2024*. ASER Centre. Retrieved from ASER 2024 - ASER: Annual Status of Education Report

Sambasivan, N., Arnesen, E., Hutchinson, B., Doshi, T., & Prabhakaran, V. (2021). Re-imagining algorithmic fairness in India and beyond. *Proceedings of the 2021 ACM Conference on Fairness, Accountability, and Transparency (FAccT '21)*, 747–757. ACM. DOI: 10.1145/3442188.3445896

Sánchez-Vera, F. (2025). Critical algorithmic mediation: Rethinking cultural transmission and education in the age of artificial intelligence. *Societies, 15*(7), 198. MDPI. DOI: 10.3390/soc15070198

Selwyn, N. (2019). What's the problem with learning analytics? *Journal of Learning Analytics*, *6*(3), 11–19. DOI: 10.18608/jla.2019.63.3

StatAnalytica. (2025, June 4). *How data analytics in education is transforming learning*. StatAnalytica Blog. Retrieved from https://statanalytica.com/blog/data-analytics-in-education/

U.S. Department of Education, Office of Educational Technology. (2023, May). *Artificial Intelligence and the Future of Teaching and Learning: Insights and Recommendations*. Washington. Retrieved from https://www.ed.gov/sites/ed/files/documents/ai-report/ai-report.pdf?

Viberg, O., Hatakka, M., & Mavroudi, A. (2018). The current landscape of learning analytics in higher education. *Computers in Human Behavior*, *89*, 98–110. DOI: 10.1016/j.chb.2018.07.027

Wang, S., Wang, F., Zhu, Z., Wang, J., Tran, T., & Du, Z. (2024). Artificial intelligence in education: A systematic literature review. *Expert Systems with Applications*, *252*, 124167. https://www.sciencedirect.com/science/article/pii/S0957417424010339. DOI: 10.1016/j.eswa.2024.124167

Williamson, B. (2017). Big data in education: The digital future of learning, policy and practice. *Sage (Atlanta, Ga.)*. Advance online publication. DOI: 10.4135/9781529714920

World Bank. (2023). *India: Supporting Andhra's Learning Transformation (SALT) Operation Program-for-Results Project*. Washington, DC: World Bank. Retrieved January 20, 2026, from https://documents1.worldbank.org/curated/en/149391624240914510/pdf/India-Supporting-Andhras-Learning-Transformation-Operation-Program-for-Results-Project.pdf

Yuensook, T., Jantakoon, T., & Limpinan, P. (2025). AI-driven adaptive learning systems in higher education: A systematic review. *Journal of Education and Learning*, *15*(2), 45–62. DOI: 10.5539/jel.v15n2p117

Chapter 29
Future Directions in Education

Thomas C. De Bello
http://orcid.org/0009-0007-4235-1174
SUNY Buffalo State University, USA

ABSTRACT

Society and education are changing significantly due to increased global migration and diversity in student populations. Educational systems must accommodate these diverse learners, making cross-cultural collaboration crucial for fostering productive societies. Institutions must commit to inclusive education that addresses the needs of pluralistic societies. Technological advancements add complexity, as varying cultural values influence the ethical implications of technologies like artificial intelligence in education. Schools must promote technological literacy, ensure access to digital resources, and prepare students for a tech-driven workforce while addressing the digital divide faced by marginalized communities. To adapt, teachers will need greater cultural competency and professional development, and schools should focus on attracting a diverse staff and engaging communities to ensure equal access for all learners.

FUTURIST PERSPECTIVES

Throughout time, humans have been interested in determining the future. The more unsettled the times, the more people want to know what the future holds in store for them. Whether through astrology, palm reading, casting lots, or, more recently, statistical analysis of trends, computer modeling, or algorithms, people have put their faith in projections of what the future will be like. I suspect that no matter how sophisticated the tools are, we will always be at a disadvantage. Social, environmental, technological, economic, and, yes, political influences provide us with such variables that predictions, based on such considerations, are at best short-range and limited by the speed at which change is apt to occur. Be that as it may, planning requires some sense of the future, and no matter how technologically sophisticated we may become, humans will and must be at the core of all decisions.

Leading futurists like Gerd Leonhard remind us that, "Although climate change is surely the biggest threat we are facing, the externalities and unintended consequences of exponential technological progress are not far behind" (Leonhard, 2021, p. 147). Clearly, we are at least to consider our role in shaping it. He reminds us of Apple CEO Tim Cook's remarks, "Technology is capable of doing great things. But it does not want to do great things. It doesn't want anything" (Cook, 2018), and Leonhard further cautions us that while we are concerned with issues like identity theft, and how stored data could be used, we need to think more about how we have become machine reliant and readable subjects, controlled by algorithms. Specifically, "In my view, the biggest risk today is not that AI will steal our jobs or take over, let alone kill us. The greatest danger really lies in us becoming too much like them" (Leonhard, 2021, p. 147).

The American futurist, James Canton, CEO of Institute for Global Futures, while also recognizing the need for sustainable practices and technological innovations to diminish the impact of climate change, calls for a greater awareness of the implications of quickly developing technologies, including artificial intelligence, biotechnology, and the Internet of Things, focusing on how they can transform societies and economies, for better or worse. He takes it even a step further

DOI: 10.4018/979-8-3373-8983-7.ch029

by linking AI and sustainability. In cautioning corporations, he states, "It is a pitfall to think of AI and sustainability as two separate developments. According to their significant societal importance, firms must understand and leverage the interdependencies between AI and sustainability to manage risk and create competitive advantage" (Canton, 2019, p. 381). There is a distinct caution for us as educators not to think of AI strictly as an independent classroom tool, but to consider its overall implications for the society and culture in which we live and work.

Futurists' approaches to their topic are as varied as the futurists themselves. For example, Brian Solis, in his book *Mindshift* (Solis, 2013), begins by accepting a future of radical change, aided, if not driven, by AI technological advances. What he offers is not a roadmap or a prediction of the future, but an understanding of the importance of developing a growth mindset to adapt to the disruptions that such advances produce. In an online interview, section entitled, Generative AI and the Path to Artificial General Intelligence (AGI), Solis stated, "I work with leaders to identify tasks AI can automate, allowing teams to focus on creativity, strategy, and empathy-driven roles that machines cannot replicate" (Corsetti, 2025, para.4). That, within the context of assisting businesses to adapt beyond automation, recognizes the cultural and operational shifts that AI will make necessary.

Noted Futurist Audrey Watters, in a fascinating address delivered at Ryerson University's Chang School Talks, discussed the history of the future of education (Watters, 2015). In that address, she talks about an "amnesia" that has crept from technology into education and education technology. In an attempt to tell the future of education, she states that the rich and fascinating past of education is forgotten and erased. She points out that educational technology existed well before Silicon Valley, and erasing that history leads to a faulty premise for future studies. Watters reminds us that in early images and writings about the future, humans were often depicted as conquering the sea and sky, with labor performed by machines.

> It is worth noting that quite often (but not always) the labor we imagine being replaced by machines is the labor that society does not value highly. It is menial labor. It is emotional labor. … So it is interesting, don't you think, when we see these pictures and predictions that suggest that machines will do more and more teaching. Do we value the labor of teaching? Moreover, do we value the labor of learning? (Watters, 2015, para. 8)

Watters further illustrates her point with an example of Henry Ford's prediction that, in the future, movies will replace schoolbooks because they are more "efficient." She concludes that from those remarks, efficiency is the unstated goal of education. "Efficiency. What does that even mean? Because unexamined, this prediction, this goal for education has become an undercurrent of so many predictions of teaching and learning as enhanced by technology." I understand this to be a warning: there is no going back, and there is much to be gained through the use of new technologies, but beware of the assumptions underlying their use and the implied statement regarding the value of the teaching profession.

There are three key ideas to consider when examining futurists and their approaches. The first is that change does not happen in a vacuum. Instead, there are essential drivers such as technological advances, demographic shifts, and environmental and social movements. To understand these factors, futurists adopt an interdisciplinary approach, integrating insights from various fields to maintain a long-term focus. Secondly, while we may approach the future with the aim of resolving a specific education-related issue or problem, we need to be aware of and sensitive to other specific implications, such as sociological, environmental, economic, health, equity, or other issues that may be affected, or in turn may impact how we proceed. Finally, and in my view most significantly, how can the role of the teacher be understood and valued as we proceed into a future that will inevitably include increased use of technological innovations?

Add this to the previously discussed issues of futurists and technology, and we can begin to understand the scope of concerns that committed educators are facing on an international scale. Are we prepared? How will we meet those challenges? With this in mind, let us look at some global visions for the future of education.

VISIONS FOR THE FUTURE FROM DIVERSE EDUCATORS

Whether it is major international organizations, educational institutions, or committed individual teachers, all who consider the future of education realize that current conditions significantly impact how we view our future needs. Since 1971, the World Economic Forum has been a collaboration of private and public organizations, composed of business, political, academic, and societal leaders whose aim is to improve the world through understanding and collaboration. One aspect of their work involves education at various levels.

Bernal's Six-Prong Approach

While recognizing the issues arising from serious global changes, Raquel Bernal, president of the University of the Andes, Bogota, Colombia, in conjunction with the World Economic Forum, has focused on concerns particular to the Global South, where inequities, unemployment, and the lack of opportunities for youth affect how academic leaders view the future of education. Assuring access to quality education, technology, and economic opportunities should be a goal of educational programs. Addressing these disparities requires educational models that not only bridge gaps but also empower learners with the skills and resilience to thrive in the face of uncertain futures" (Bernal, 2025). That, in Bernal's vision, requires redefining education, which proposes a six-prong approach.

In Bernal's view, redefining education is an imperative and must begin with an understanding that education systems must become more flexible, adaptable, and personalized. That first major point includes reimagining programs that meet students' needs in ways beyond what traditional programs have done. Specifically, she refers to Stackable Credentials, which universities like Stanford and Harvard have introduced, allowing students to earn higher certifications and skills that help them work toward higher qualifications, such as associate degrees or master's degrees. They may be seen as faster, lower-cost alternatives to traditional education pathways.

According to Stanford University's Stanford Online, students can choose to focus on individual graduate courses to gain experience in new subject areas. If they become interested in the area, they can then include that course in a multi-course graduate credential issued by Stanford. That certificate, along with other coursework accumulated, can then be incorporated into a program of study or an advanced degree (Stanford Online, 2026). This, along with modular programs, provides flexibility and personalization that meet students' needs by adapting to their circumstances. While these program adaptations may seem a boon to traditional students, their real value, to me, seems to be providing access to licensed and certified careers for people who would otherwise be closed out of the process.

While thinking about Bernal's second major point, the role of technology in transforming education, I was reminded of an incident that took place thirty years ago, when I visited an international school in Maputo, Mozambique. I was shown a classroom where approximately ten students sat silently, laboring studiously at workbooks, occasionally checking what appeared to be well-worn dictionaries on their desks. A teacher sat disengaged at the front desk. It was explained to me that these motivated students were taking a certified correspondence course in third-level Italian. The adult in the room was there to facilitate issues beyond the lesson material since she did not teach or speak Italian. The "teacher" collected materials that were mailed off to a center where they were graded and returned. The process could take a couple of weeks. The students' commitment was evident, but how many others, despite their desire to learn, could not learn in this single-modality approach? Reflection on that experience has caused me to have a profound appreciation for the potential of technological advances in education.

That second point Bernal makes regarding the transformative role of technology is one that educators globally are continually grappling with. Her approach is reasoned and focuses on the personalized and adaptive possibilities that AI potentially offers individuals, as well as on the ability of digital online platforms to break barriers to educational access. Online and virtual classrooms have the potential to "connect learners across borders, providing opportunities for those previously excluded from traditional education" (Bernal, 2026, para. 8). Surely, those students would have benefited from more immediate feedback and from interactions with a teacher as well as a program adapted to various learner characteristics. However, it is not just to be a high-tech version of correspondence schools of old; incorporated into the process must be a sense of digital awareness, not just hitting the keyboard or pointing the mouse, but giving students a way to use technology effectively and, in the process, to better understand its implications. Education needs to equip learners with the skills to navigate the intricacies of a digital world responsibly, including data privacy and the ethical dilemmas posed by AI.

A third critical point made is that learners must be equipped with future-ready skills. By doing so, Bernal (2026) highlights the development of key competencies in areas such as critical thinking and creativity, collaboration and communication, and ethical and global awareness. Having the technical knowledge and skills must be balanced with a mindset that is grounded in a critical socio-humanistic education that contributes to a "just and empathetic society." Schools and universities are increasingly building these abilities into their programs through hands-on learning, research projects, collaborations with employers, and community-based activities to solve real-life problems.

The fourth point made is the importance of research and local impact. High standards of academic rigor are key, but research also needs to be closely tied to the specific circumstances of the communities that universities serve, encouraging joint work and co-design with local stakeholders so that it remains meaningful and effective. By aligning research agendas with the needs of their regions and seeking opportunities for global-scale-up, innovative, grounded solutions can be achieved that potentially lead to transformative outcomes (Bernal, 2025).

The fifth point in this vision is the necessity of addressing equity and inclusion. Referring to the Global South, in particular, Latin America, regions where inequality continues to pose a major challenge, education must center on inclusion. This entails not just broadening access but also designing learning environments that recognize and uphold diverse perspectives. Targeted programs for marginalized groups, scholarships for students with limited financial resources, and partnerships with community organizations are essential for advancing equity.

In this context, Bernal uses the term "NEETs" (not in education, employment, or training), especially when referring to young people, and emphasizes that this demographic needs targeted interventions, such as high-quality vocational education. This approach is consistent with her position that research should be deeply rooted in the communities that universities serve.

The last component of Bernal's vision for the future includes financial and institutional sustainability through a transformation of education systems. In her view, reforming education systems must also take into account their long-term financial and institutional sustainability. Expanding revenue sources - such as corporate collaborations, philanthropic funding, and innovative business approaches - is crucial. By entering lifelong learning markets or developing digital platforms that generate income, institutions can decrease their reliance on traditional tuition. Public support for research, technology, and financial aid remains vital, particularly in the Global South, where funding is often constrained.

This comprehensive vision encompasses an understanding of current educational issues in the context of global economic interests. It is a realistic assessment of the challenges facing societies today, which offers a clear, systematic approach to addressing them at various levels. Like many of the futurists reviewed previously, Bernal places those concerns within the broader context of environmental and societal concerns. But what does it say about her belief in the purpose of education? What is clear from the outset is that she does not see education as a distinct appendage to society, but as an integral and integrated part of how any society grows and adapts to its needs. Her focus on the need for education to be responsive to learners, highlighting adaptability, flexibility, and personalization, underscores a holistic approach. Additionally, her cautions regarding the transformative role of technology and its potential for marginalized communities highlight humanist values. That being said, some might emphasize the more utilitarian aspects of Bernal's six-prong approach to education as a tool for economic advancement rather than personal development. Given the state of worldwide education, the priority, if it exists, may be justified.

Giannini's Three Main Transitions

In *Reimagining the futures of education*, Stefania Giannini (2025) relies heavily on UNESCO's 2021 report, *Reimagining our futures together*, and as such, addresses the essential changes required in education to create inclusive, collaborative, and equitable systems for a sustainable future. Giannini highlights three main transitions, specifically: From exclusion to inclusion; From competition to cooperation; From elitism to solidarity.

In her initial phase, from exclusion to inclusion, Giannini recognizes the progress that has been made in global educational access. . However, significant disparities remain, specifically, with over 270 million children and youth out of school and 739 million adults lacking basic literacy, two-thirds of whom are women. Additionally, children with disabilities and those from low-income countries still face major obstacles to learning. Moreover, while the Global North is still recovering from academic losses due to the COVID-19 pandemic, the rest of the world faces the fact that 70% of children in low-income nations cannot read a simple text by age 10 (World Bank et al., 2022). While these figures appear to be disheartening, Giannini remains positive, "Is it a lost battle? I do not think so, but to succeed, we need to redouble our efforts in investment and innovation and commit to placing inclusion at the heart of education transformation (2025, p. 300).

From competition to cooperation

There are a few of us who cannot recall a time, especially in elementary school, when we were pitted against our classmates in a "spelling bee" or a math challenge. Who will spell the most words correctly? Who can answer the most questions correctly in the least amount of time? Certainly, it was fun for some, but also misery for many. Education systems frequently focus on individual success and competition, whether in classrooms, school districts, states, or national statistics; there is a great emphasis on competition. In some US states, scores from statewide exams are published in local newspapers, and realtors rank communities' education services based on reported scores, with little regard to other contributing factors. Despite the claims of accountability, competition is fostered, even if it is on unequal playing fields. That emphasis creates values that, in Giannini's words, "have shaped the way learning is structured, often reinforcing competitive models that prioritize ranking and comparison over collaboration and shared progress" (2025, p. 301).

The problems we face today - climate change, armed conflicts, food insecurity, digital revolution, and migration - all transcend borders. Their effects are felt worldwide, emphasizing the need for a unified approach, awareness of our interconnections, and a collective strategy to tackle these problems. For example, climate change and the ecological disasters that accompany it are causing population displacement and impacting education systems. And yet competition for resources and infrastructure exists within and between nations to the detriment of ordinary citizens. Failure to educate our population about the causes of climate change leads to piecemeal band-aid efforts to address its consequences.

This situation is sadly best illustrated in the United States, where such competition between states has impacted education on a couple of levels. Rather than a collaborative funding system, states compete for funds that affect the environment and safety of their residents. In one example, an article appearing in the Washington Post titled *States siphoned millions in infrastructure law climate, emissions funds* describes how states maneuver and compete to direct federal infrastructure and climate-related funds, including transfers and reallocation decisions (Duncan, 2023). Additionally, in a government publication, the US Department of Commerce's *Regional Competitiveness Fact Sheet* states that "regional competitions were oversubscribed by as much as 27 times the available funds" (U.S. Department of Commerce, 2025). Such competitiveness, even within a nation, has direct consequences, especially now that reports of extreme weather conditions, such as record-breaking flooding, extreme heat, or record low temperatures, have become the norm.

Nostalgically, schoolchildren in the Northeastern US looked forward to snow days as free time off, a rare winter break from studies. Today, those extended snow days have become more frequent and have prompted schools to employ online learning to compensate for lost classroom time. However, what happens when there is a power failure, or if students lack the necessary technology? Alternatively, in the South, the disastrous floods that hit western North Carolina devastated entire mountain communities that are still recovering. And on the West Coast of the US, the fires and landslides in California left communities destroyed, many homeless, and wrecked infrastructure. Collaboration in addressing natural disasters resulting from climate change is one area that needs improvement, but identifying the underlying causes and man's role in creating them is an issue that goes beyond borders. That level of collaboration is crucial to future survival, and education has a particular role to play.

On another level, Giannini reports that a UNESCO (2023b) review of 100 national curriculum frameworks indicated that only 50% included a reference to climate change. Concurrently, over 70% of young people reported that they cannot fully explain climate change, and that only 23% of teachers feel equipped to teach it (Giannini, 2025)! The UN has worked since 2022 on the Greening Education Partnership, recognizing that no significant climate action can take root without international cooperation and the transformative power of education.

From elitism to solidarity

Education has always been a way for people to find opportunities and hope to improve their situation. Today, higher education has become essential for full participation in society's socioeconomic life. But critical roadblocks remain. Giannini recounts that, "Low-income students, migrant and refugee populations, people with disabilities, those in rural areas, and women in many contexts continue to face systemic obstacles in accessing education—especially higher education" (Giannini, 2025, p.302). In fact, she reports that in a number of middle-income countries, the gap in college enrollment between the wealthiest and poorest is greater than 60% (Giannini, 2025)! Today, this takes on greater urgency. The impact of violence and displacement has extended beyond physical borders and has even been enlarged through social media.

Giannini further states that the updated 2023 UNESCO Recommendation on Education for Peace, Human Rights, and Sustainable Development emphasizes that education goes beyond imparting knowledge; it also involves fostering the values, skills, and attitudes necessary to establish, safeguard, and maintain peace (UNESCO, 2023a). With that approach, education clearly has the potential to promote peace, lessen inequalities, and bridge societal divides.

But what will it take to transform education?

Giannini sets forth action steps for societies based on the three main transitions outlined above, offering a challenging roadmap for the future. First, that "shared vision, strong cooperation, and a sustained political will" (Giannini, 2025, p. 304) must precede everything if change is to be realized. That change cannot exist only at the national level but must be from the grassroots up through the national and international education systems, with cooperation and a commitment to valuing education by placing it at the center of national development initiatives.

Secondly, all that cannot be achieved without proper funding for educational initiatives. Such funding should be aimed at closing the gap between lower-income and lower-middle-income countries. Decreasing competition and increasing solidarity, as Giannini would put it, might promote an atmosphere in which wealthier countries would feel a duty to support lower-income countries - whether through financial aid, tax reform support, or funneling debt relief toward investment in educational institutions or programs.

Third, Giannini reminds us that confronting educational challenges requires addressing the fundamental causes of poverty, exclusion, and inequality. Inequities present outside of education directly contribute to exclusion within the educational system. Bridging learning gaps and guaranteeing equal access involves more than just policy reforms in schools; it requires coordinated actions across sectors to tackle the root causes of poverty and discrimination (Giannini, 2025).

THE SIGNIFICANCE OF EDUCATION'S ROLE

Like Bernal, Giannini makes us aware of the interrelatedness of societies and the fact that education is at the core of all initiatives, whether social or economic in focus. As my colleague Natela Doghonadze is likely to say, "Education is the mother of all disciplines." Without education, there are no other disciplines. Clearly, these writers represent the overlapping perspectives of the World Economic Forum and the United Nations Educational, Scientific, and Cultural Organization and, in a different way, reiterate Doghonadze's perspective on the primacy of education.

Perhaps it is not a surprise that while most educators internationally are calling for a more globalized approach to education, one that emphasizes collaboration and shared problem-solving, with a plan to address the inequality and injustice of the current systems, political backlash can occur. Michael McAlister, writing on the State of Global Education (McAlister, 2025), discussed the impact of cultural pressures and distortions. Frankly stating, "In some countries, history is rewritten to suit nationalist agendas. In others, science education is under attack from ideological forces. …the global classroom is not immune to the same polarization and tribalism that grips the US political systems." McAlister emphasizes the need for education to develop a perspective grounded in reality that accounts for cultural context. It involves learning to think critically instead of merely accepting and repeating what has been communicated to a specific group. Conscious of respecting individual cultures, he also warns against giving in to extremes. "When systems give in to either distortion - whether through censorship, misinformation, or neglect - they deny a citizenry and its students the tools needed to meet the world and its challenges with maturity and sobriety. This immaturity and conspiratorial intoxication then leads to alienation, and alienation leads to fear, which leads to hate, among other things" (McAlister, 2025, para. 12). That sobering view is a caution as we look towards the future. For that educator, the way forward is to resist the notion of quick fixes and to focus on equity, addressing the vulnerable first. Support teachers through proper training and with salaries and respect that are commensurate with the importance of their work.

In many regards, McAlister agrees with Bernal and Giannini, especially in his support for critical and contextual thinking, as well as for a more global perspective that recognizes interconnected challenges such as climate change, migration, and AI disruption. But his words, "Our goal should be to create good 'thinkers', and good 'citizens' rather than good 'workers' who pay their taxes," (McAlister, 2025) especially resonated with me. It is a matter of emphasis, more than semantics, for me. If we focus on developing critical thinking, especially in the age of AI disruption and media distortion, balance STEM with literature and the arts as expressions of our culture, and practice equality and justice as democratic essentials, then, in the process, we will be preparing workers, who will be able to pay their taxes, taxes that should go to fund school systems that nurtures their continuous development. The only thing more expensive than education is ignorance; is a sentiment that seems appropriate to reiterate at this point.

THE IMPORTANCE OF CROSS-CULTURAL COLLABORATION IN EDUCATION

When studying the futurists and anyone interested in the future of education, it becomes apparent that, for a variety of reasons, cross-cultural collaboration has a firm place in that future. But what exactly does it mean, and how can we begin to conceptualize it?

My good friend, Larry Hohler, taught social studies for 30 years in New York before retiring. As a youngster in Ohio, his third-grade teacher introduced her class to the idea of "Pen Pals." She no doubt thought that it would improve their writing skills by encouraging students to write to others their age overseas. The details of exactly how that was arranged are lost to history, but the impact on at least one of her students was lifelong. Larry somehow wound up with two pen pals, one in Australia and another in Poland! Not only was he scrupulous in writing to each of them and returning their letters, but he also maintained those connections well into adulthood. Visiting them in their homelands and hosting them when they visited the United States. Before ever having the ability to travel internationally, for the price of an airmail stamp, that youngster from middle America developed roots in two countries on opposite sides of the world! Those connections and the links that followed influenced Larry's life and teaching in ways that are difficult to classify, but ultimately led to his global perspectives, particularly in education. Larry's story does not end there.

After 10 years of teaching, Larry was awarded a sabbatical leave, which he chose to spend in Kenya; he had never been to Africa. A chance meeting with a young student eventually led to a lifelong collaboration and the establishment of a school and orphanage, with former residents now with the opportunity to graduate from college, enter careers, and lead lives no longer defined by poverty and abandonment (Desjeunes, 2022). Larry's story illustrates the strength of cross-cultural connections, but more so, the influence of a teacher. How much more powerful and influential cross-cultural collaborations in a digital age have the potential to be?

In the previous section, we heard about challenges to global society that transcend borders. If those plans to work collaboratively are to succeed, mutual respect and trust must first be in place. The idea of such collaborations has been successfully implemented in various ways over the years, beyond pen-pals, through programs sponsored by governments or private organizations. For example, Erasmus+ is a program of the European Union (EU) that promotes cross-cultural education and learning opportunities among students and educators across Europe and beyond. It supports student exchanges, collaborative projects, and partnerships between educational institutions (Feyen & Krzaklewska, 2012). Additionally, the USA-sponsored Fulbright Program offers international educational and cultural exchange opportunities for students, scholars, and professionals to study, teach, and conduct research in over 140 countries, promoting mutual understanding between the United States and other nations (Vogel, 1978). Both programs have been in existence for many years, supporting greater understanding and cross-cultural collaboration.

But not everyone can win a Fulbright Scholarship or receive an Erasmus+ grant; however, more and more students, especially at the university level, have benefited from the growing number of online courses. Whether through totally online courses, hybrid courses, or massive open online courses (MOOCs), college education has been revolutionized. Additionally, the global pandemic necessitated the establishment and efficacy of online education, and within that context, cross-cultural online education (CCOE) began to flourish (Mohiyeddini, 2024). Creating online classrooms where all students are welcome and let to feel respected requires careful planning and, of course, familiarity with online platforms. Mohiyeddini recommends that strategies such as collaborative projects, interactive discussions, and technology integration can make learning more active and engaging. Employing differentiated instruction, culturally responsive teaching practices, and creating a supportive classroom environment that values diversity is no less important in online classrooms than in traditional classrooms.

Alex Kumi-Yeboah's findings indicated that instructors teaching online should consider instructional strategies that cater to diverse students' needs and encourage intercultural interactions (Kumi-Yeboah, 2018). Observations from online teaching and interviews revealed that integrating local and international examples into the online curriculum helps students connect with course materials and construct knowledge. This approach offers valuable insights into student learning in online settings.

Moreover, his findings highlight the need for instructors to create cross-cultural, collaborative online frameworks that enhance student interaction. It is essential for instructors to be accessible in large-scale online courses, allowing students to ask questions and engage in group work and collaborative learning. Such availability fosters a strong sense of community, motivating students to actively participate and build knowledge (Kumi-Yeboah, 2018).

It appears that, as in much of teaching, the management of the process of learning, though by its nature different from that in traditional classrooms, is critical to success. Lim's research highlights Kumi-Yeboah's (2018) conclusions and takes them a step further: "The weakest aspect of online instruction has been said to be the lack of instructor-student relationship through 'eye-to-eye' communication that creates emotional involvement of online learners in the learning process" (Lim, 2004, p.868). Lim, therefore, proposes direct interaction between students and instructors using alternative communication tools such as chat, discussion boards, and audio/video conferencing to promote a more direct interaction between teacher and student.

Technological advances will facilitate CCOE, but like Larry and his third-grade teacher, it will still take the knowledge and skill of a caring teacher to make the process live up to its potential.

RECOMMENDATIONS FOR POLICY AND PRACTICE

Imagining the future of education from various perspectives while challenging assumptions highlighted the potential for great achievements ahead, but it also indicated possible missteps along the way. None of the writers we have looked at purports to be like the soothsayers of old, with cryptic chimeras of the future. All have presented carefully reasoned and thoughtfully considered positions, although from different perspectives. They overlap in their concern for climate change, the environment, and global education toward an equitable and just society. Also, no one doubts the economic divide that holds back the educational futures of many, nor the impact of AI disruption in society in general and education in particular. If we are to succeed and meet the educational challenges ahead, we need to stay focused on our actions. Alfred Montapert is often attributed with saying, "Do not confuse motion and progress. A rocking horse keeps moving but does not make any progress" (Wright, 2022) Sometimes we see a lot of movement in education, switching reading or math programs every few years, but often there is little progress to show for it. With that in mind, based on our previous discussion and shared experience, I propose the following recommendations.

Teacher training and professional development

Practice what you preach

When I was sixteen years old, like many of my friends at school, I went to get my driving permit. I was eager to get behind the wheel and experience the freedom of the open road. My father was a diesel engineer by training. He had that kind of mindset that said no one, especially a child of his, should get behind the wheel of a 600-horsepower engine and not be able to explain the workings of the internal combustion engine, change the oil and spark plugs, or fix a flat. Dare I say it, but I did not get my driver's license until two months after I started my first teaching job in the US, 9 years later! I admit, I learned to change the oil, and fix a flat, and if needed, I could change or clean the spark plug heads, but the intricacies of fuel injection escaped me entirely.

My point is this: teacher education programs need to be reimagined, with lessons taught using strategies consistent with the instructional design being emphasized. Simply use the strategy to teach the strategy. Driving skills cannot be taught to most people through an analysis of the engine, any more than lessons in syntax alone can produce another Tolstoy, Dickens, or Hemingway. Learning is more lasting if it takes place in context. An effective example of that is *Micro Teaching*, a teacher training technique developed by Dwight Allen at Stanford University in the 1960s (Allen & Ryan, 1969). As a personal product of Dr. Allen's technique back then, I can attest to the insights and concrete help it provides. Also, the structure of the process is geared to promoting self-reflection. A number of universities use this technique today. I was heartened to read the positive effects reported by Koross (2016) in Kenya, specifically, "Majority of them cited that micro teaching improved their speaking skills, confidence, questioning and reinforcement skills, and planning skills." (Koross, 2016, p. 296)

Additionally, practices such as peer coaching, co-teaching, critical friends' peer review, and professional learning communities, to name just a few, have demonstrated effectiveness in promoting a collaborative approach to teaching. If we ever hope to move education from competitive to collaborative, we must avoid creating new teachers in competitive models. Research supporting futurists' assertions of the need to address problems collaboratively, whether within or across cultures, is imperative. How can our efforts be taken seriously if we cannot implement the process ourselves?

Competition to collaboration

Two quotes from earlier teacher narratives in this publication stand out in my memory and illustrate two conditions that foster the environment necessary to make the classroom collaborative. "I was lucky to witness exceptional educators working together, creating a culture in which leadership, wellbeing, classroom management, careers, and community all aligned." There just cannot be collaboration if it is not modeled by teachers in their own interactions and collegial lives. Sometimes, while extolling collaboration, the system itself sabotages it. For example, the question of merit pay, which pits teachers against teachers. By awarding bonuses or salary increases based on teacher effectiveness, typically measured by student test scores, it undermines collegiality. It is Pavlovian in its inception; merit pay is the "carrot." But teachers forget that the second part of the equation is the "stick."

The other quote that stayed with me is "Their students respected them without being afraid. There was structure, but also warmth and authenticity. They did not raise their voices, yet they were listened to." No need to shout, "Teacher! Teacher!" for attention. Attention is not a commodity to be rationed out to the most vocal or insistent in a collaborative environment; everyone understands they will be listened to!

Parental and community involvement

"The connections between home and school are often strongest at this level. Families play a key role and need to be supported to help children thrive and enhance their physical, socio-emotional, and cognitive development" (UNESCO, 2021, p.57). Undergraduate education majors may encounter phrases like the previous one throughout their undergraduate careers, but how often do schools of education offer courses directed at engaging parents and the community in education? Such courses could include specific strategies for encouraging parental involvement beyond bake sales. They might even bring in community representatives to talk with prospective teachers, giving them insights into how the public views their roles. While such courses are more common at the graduate level, especially in administration programs, early education of fledgling teachers would help prevent the sink-or-swim mentality often associated with beginning teachers. Where they are lacking, teaching standards should include building positive relationships with family and community.

Friend or foe, know the difference

We have discussed AI disruption at great length, and we recognize that it is here to stay. In March 2026 (The White House, 2026), the first lady of the United States hosted an international panel of first ladies on the future of education. She entered the gathering, accompanied by a robot resembling a *Star Wars* prop. She then announced, without any embarrassment, that they had witnessed the future of teaching!

Teacher education must acknowledge the significance of digital culture and not be intimidated by it or by those who propose to use it to destroy education. Technology has a significant role in shaping how knowledge is created and shared, as well as the changes it brings to human life and the environment. Although technology should not be seen as a solution to all problems, digital media should be incorporated not just as a resource for blended and online professional development, but also as an area of academic focus. Additionally, it is important to conduct research to investigate the advantages, teaching effects, epistemological and ethical considerations, and the limitations and drawbacks of digital media and platforms. Hold fast when challenged and remember Lim's research about "eye to eye" contact (Lim, 2004).

Teachers as teacher educators

Janet Perrin was a colleague and friend who collaborated with me in the design and implementation of a summer program for at-risk primary school children. The cornerstone of the program was an integrated three-prong approach: reading, the arts, and social work. We developed the program using a thematic approach that incorporated input from each of the three areas literature at the base was always linked to social issues and some aspects of art or music. Funding, of course, was on a shoestring, but we managed. What always amazed me was how Janet could explain to the teachers exactly how she envisioned a lesson, all the knowledge of a cordon bleu chef, but with the ease of a grandmother showing a favorite recipe. Teachers know how to do it!

I thought of Janet as I read Smith's (2014) chapter in *Teacher Educators and Teachers as Learners.* His description of the Teacher Educator's skill set reminded me of my friend, and other teachers I have worked with by describing "effective Teacher Educators are able to deconstruct learning and teaching and as 'experts' can demystify and make the art of learning and teaching look and feel easy through a range of sequential problem-solving activities. His expert craft includes what is referred to as 'explicit modelling'" (Smith, 2014, p. 24).

Teachers have skills to share and experiences to relate, but sometimes we do not give them the opportunity or platform to do that in ways that are productive and rewarding. I became the principal of a large elementary school with an established staff and two unique programs that attracted students from throughout the school district. There were many talented and experienced teachers, but there was also an air of thinly veiled competition between them. Logically, there was no reason for competition; they all excelled in various ways, and I felt fortunate to be among them and learn from them. However, I also felt responsible for trying to do something about it. The school was popular among colleges to locate their student teachers. I noticed during my first year that many came and went to different places. For taking student teachers, each college rewards teachers with a voucher for a free course. Many of the senior teachers had already completed advanced degrees and certifications, so these vouchers meant little to them, and yet they continued to take student teachers.

I had met a professor from one of the colleges and discussed a plan with him to establish the school as a Professional Development School. By that, I meant we would only take students from his college, the teachers who became master teachers would still receive a free course as a gratuity, but instead of a college professor who appeared a few times during the semester and another professor who taught a weekly seminar that included student teachers from different schools, the teachers from my school would perform those roles. He agreed to approach the dean, and I would approach my staff. I held an after-school informal meeting with a vague reference to student teaching, and about 10 teachers showed up. I pitched the idea to them. I proposed it as levels of participation. Some semesters, if they had the time, they would take a student teacher; at other times, they could volunteer to share the supervising teacher role; and still other times, they could share the seminar leader role.

Supervising teachers would be trained in observation techniques, consistent with the model used by administrators in the school district. Moreover, they would share the salary. Same for the teachers who ran the seminar. We would be given a preparation day at the university, where we would meet with the dean and have a presentation by a professor on a topic of mutual interest. Student teachers would be treated as a cohort group, developing a team mentality among them as well as all the teachers involved, whether master teachers, who opened their classrooms, supervising teachers, who evaluated student teachers, or seminar leaders, all worked to have a successful cohort group! Teachers organized the seminars themselves, choosing the weekly topics and deciding among themselves who was best at which topic. Sometimes a topic would be chosen, such as integrating language arts with social studies and art, and two collaborating teachers would present together. Sometimes the same strategy might be illustrated by a primary teacher in collaboration with an intermediate-level teacher to illustrate its adaptability. It was not unusual for student teachers to be told which other faculty members were doing a particular lesson that week on the topic or strategy in the week ahead. Using a sign-up process, those teachers would open their doors to x number of student teachers to observe. Their master teachers would release them from their duties at that time, so that the student teacher could observe a colleague. In that way, even faculty who were not directly involved with student teachers felt welcome to participate.

All aspects of teaching were covered in creative ways throughout the semester, and it usually culminated in a session on applying for and interviewing for a teaching position. For each semester's final session, administrators from across the district were invited to conduct 10-minute mock interviews with the student teachers. Each student was given two opportunities to interview, and after each session, there was a debriefing. This allowed them to take a recommendation from the first interview and try it out immediately on the second!

No project is ever perfect; we had our snags as we learned the process and adjusted as we went along. Pretty soon, we were turning away student teachers; we had become so popular among the college's students. Word spread! But something also happened to the teachers themselves. A spirit of collaboration began to spread among them. Administrators from other buildings who had sat in on mock interviews were impressed by the professional demeanor of the student teachers during those events, and that came back to the teachers who had worked with them in the classroom, as teacher educators, and as supervising teachers.

As teachers understood that others recognized and appreciated their skills, they were more likely to recognize the same in others. That direct peer validation is priceless to boost morale and self-esteem. In the chapter *Emotional and Material Support Needed by Teachers* Velmurugan et al. (in this volume) discuss various ways leadership can encourage and support teachers, and, in relation to this specific experience, the importance they place on teamwork in schools. Although a generation apart from my experience, I feel that such collaborative programs continue to be supported by research (Āboltiņa et al., 2024).

Aside from the individual components of this project, the significance to me for future student teaching, if not teacher training in general, is the mutual respect that the partnership between the classroom teachers and university teachers engenders. Recalling Bernal's exhortation to universities to research within their communities and Giannini's emphasis on the importance of collaboration over competition, a uniquely formatted, cross-institutional approach could be a way forward.

There is so much potential left untapped in all our schools; it just takes a different way of looking at things, and, most of all, respect for teaching as well as for teachers. Now think about it, can some AI creation in a mechanical form do all that?

Improve salaries and financial support

In the United States, school districts are configured in different ways. Some states have districts that are regional by counties, others by townships, and most have separate districts in cities. In any given situation, teachers tend to make up the largest percentage of "public employees" in nearly any area. Think about it. Unless it is a large urban area, police departments or even fire departments will not have as many employees as in a typical school district. So, it is the rite of every budget season to see teachers' salaries as the item that gets the most blame for governments needing to cover the significant wage costs of employing a large number of teachers, and raising salaries would limit their capacity to invest in other policy priorities.

The following is taken from a recent publication of the Organization for Economic Cooperation and Development:

> While a 10% increase in teacher salaries would have significant budgetary implications, it remains unclear what such an increase would achieve in practice. According to OECD's TALIS 2018 data, 61% of teachers reported being unsatisfied with their salaries, yet the vast majority – 90% – reported being "all in all, satisfied with their job" (OECD, 2020). This suggests that salary dissatisfaction does not necessarily translate into overall job dissatisfaction. Therefore, beyond increasing financial compensation, it is important to make the teaching profession more intellectually stimulating and fulfilling – for example, by enhancing professional development, fostering collaboration, creating clearer career pathways, and differentiating salaries to promote instructional quality and equitable teacher allocation. OECD (2025)

Recognizing that teachers' salaries are below those of other similar education workers, the data have been presented in a way that seems to justify not paying teachers an increase. "Why should we pay them more? They are satisfied with their work, so that must equal satisfaction with their salary?"

In a recent CNN Business article, Matt Egan reports that US teachers are working two jobs and barely getting by. Sure, they love their jobs; that is why they became teachers, and many take years to pay off their college loans! More than that, Eagan noted, "The majority of public school teachers (71%) hold at least one side job, according to a survey released Monday by Gallup in partnership with the Bipartisan Policy Center and the Walton Family Foundation" (Egan, 2026).

While teachers have some "perks" that other workers may not have, like pension plans and healthcare plans, these date back to a time when it was cheaper for municipalities to pay insurance premiums than pay teachers cash directly. Times have changed, and plans have begun to cost more; teachers have had to renegotiate contracts to maintain the benefits they received in the past, rather than receive salary increases.

What if we explored creative solutions, such as student loan forgiveness for teachers? Many educators carry the weight of student loan debt for years, all while earning salaries that are not competitive with other professions. Although some programs exist in the United States, the amount of debt relief offered is often minimal compared to the rising costs of education.

As it becomes increasingly challenging to attract qualified teachers, broader access to debt forgiveness could serve as a significant incentive for educators both in this country and around the globe. In the context of the national economy, such measures might not seem substantial, but for individuals trying to support a family amid rising inflation, this relief could make a meaningful difference.

As public employees, why not consider offering special mortgage rates for teachers? While some programs exist in various states, they are not consistently available across the United States or in many other countries. Implementing such a program would be particularly beneficial for first-time homeowners. It could encourage teachers to establish roots in the communities where they work, fostering stability and commitment to their chosen profession.

Government-backed mortgages have already been successfully utilized for groups like veterans, and similar initiatives could be extended to teachers. This approach could significantly alleviate long-term debt without imposing additional burdens on local taxpayers. Additionally, international banks could collaborate to develop specialized mortgage rates, making it more feasible for educators to afford to remain in the profession for which they are trained and passionate.

Strengthening parental involvement and community engagement

In *Reimagining our futures together: A new social contract for education*, we are reminded of the scope of the role of parents and the community must have in shaping the future of education. "Local leaders, elders, authorities, communities, and families all have crucial roles to play" (UNESCO, 2021, p. 82). That is infused throughout the document, but those of us who have worked in schools understand that, especially today, defining the roles of non-staff is not always easy.

Talk to teachers about parental roles, and I suppose the first things that come to their minds are how they can support instruction. In fact, according to the Pew Research Center survey, these are the three top views teachers hold of parental involvement: 1) Holding their children accountable if they misbehave in school (79%); 2) Helping their children with their schoolwork (68%); 3) Ensuring their children's attendance in school (63%) (Lin et al., 2024, p. 36). That same study indicates that parents in high-poverty areas are less likely to assist their children with schoolwork. What is most telling is that it may mean teachers see parental participation as action in support of classroom instruction, failing to recognize the potential for a larger role.

On another positive note, the National Education Association (NEA) noted that, according to the National Association for Family, School, and Community Engagement (NAFSCE) research, 84 percent of educators would choose a school with more engaged parents over one offering a higher salary. Additionally, 61 percent say that state teaching standards do not address building relationships and trust with families, underscoring the need to address parent and community involvement in teacher education programs (Long, 2023).

Long also reported that 73 percent of the participating teachers identify engaging with parents and the community as challenging. That is especially true today in the US, where public education has become far more politically charged, particularly around what is taught and how marginalized groups are represented. Conservative campaigns to restrict classroom discussions of race, gender, and sexuality have grown more common, echoing earlier efforts to shape schooling to fit specific ideological agendas (Birman, 2025).

The COVID-19 pandemic further pulled public health disputes into schools, sparking intense arguments over masking, vaccines, and online learning. These clashes weakened confidence in education officials and left unresolved debates about the extent of authority schools should have.

Across the country, book bans have further reduced access to works addressing race, gender, and sexuality. By targeting these titles, conservative groups have narrowed the range of viewpoints available in school libraries and classrooms, posing a direct threat to intellectual freedom. At the same time, new "advocacy" organizations have moved aggressively to shape district policy, often through school board races (Birman, 2025). It seems to me that the role envisioned by the authors of *Reimagining Our Futures Together: A New Social Contract for Education* was more of collaboration than censorship, mutual trust rather than suspicion, and collegiality rather than intimidation. I have every belief that true partnership can work effectively to the benefit of students.

Sometimes teachers walk a thin line between community pressure and following their conscience. A sixth-grade social studies teacher in Iowa was told to remove a poster she had put up at the start of school for the past few years. It reads, "Everyone is welcome here," and displays a series of hands reaching up with hearts in their palms. Each hand is a different color, ranging from white to black, with various shades of brown in between. When she first posted about the opening of the school year, the point was to make all her students feel welcome. However, the principal and vice principal came to her classroom to inform her that two posters on her walls were controversial and needed to be removed. Today show reporter Portée stated the district's comment, "This policy is designed to maintain consistency across all classrooms while ensuring that no one group is targeted or offended by the display of certain items." (Portée, 2025, para. 31) But who could be offended by the statement that all are welcome? The teacher's comment, "There's no way I would be able to allow myself to take it down and roll over to what I feel like they're asking me to do" (Portée, 2025, para.35).

American teachers, and I suspect others, are challenged by conflicting pressures from parents and the community. Whether it is curriculum issues, book banning, art displays, etc., controversy abounds. Respecting individual rights and freedoms, whether in the workplace or in broader society, is critical to a just and equitable future.

CONCLUSION

It is important to have high goals and aspirations, and the futurists we have seen have pointed us in directions that remind me of what a former superintendent used to tell us, beginning teachers: "Shoot for the stars but settle for the moon." He meant always set ambitious goals, knowing that even if you fall short, you can still achieve something impressive and worthwhile, but if we lower expectations, we will never achieve anything worthwhile.

If the teachers' narratives have taught us one thing, it's that we are a determined, resilient, and hardworking bunch. Many of us have overcome economic or socio-cultural issues that have defeated others. Don't think any less of them; instead, help them and their children see a path to a better future. Most of all, research and common sense tell us to connect with others; collaboration, not competition, will help us meet the challenges of education for all in the future.

There are many serious issues facing educators today, but it is clear that solutions that exist will not be in isolation, but will be through combined efforts, some internationally, and some originating locally, but always shared collaboratively. Where do we go from here? We have heard the voices of teachers across continents. We have seen their common concerns. We have looked at research from different perspectives that has tried to shed more light on the future of the profession that we all love. And, if you have gotten this far, you realize that your concerns are not in isolation.

I remember the afternoon so clearly, my mom and two of her sisters were talking about their high school teachers. Miss Fritz and Mr. Sauer. Miss Fitz taught history, and she could draw maps on the board from memory, using different colored chalk for the countries. She was so pretty and so friendly to all her students. Mr. Sauer taught physical education. Aunt Julie said, "Don't forget, he was very handsome; all the girls had a crush on him." He would wait for Miss Fitz after school and walk with her to the bus stop. "Do you think they ever got married?" my mom asked. And the conversation went on. Mom was 87 at the time, one sister was 85, and the other was 93! The time they were talking about is a little over 100 years ago, but thanks to their memories, Mr. Sauer and Miss Fitz live on. Students remember teachers, not just for the life changing incidents, but how we live our lives on a day-to-day basis. It is hard to imagine a job that touches so many and can mean so much to others.

Many of the teacher narratives in this book involve teachers who made a difference in someone's life. I encourage you to be that teacher over and over again for your students. Who knows? Maybe someday, 100 years from now, a person you have never met will be talking about you!

REFERENCES

Allen, D. W., & Ryan, K. A. (1969). *Microteaching*. Addison-Wesley.

Bernal, R. (2025, January 17). *How education can adapt to prepare learners for tomorrow's demands.* World Economic Forum. Retrieved from https://www.weforum.org/stories/2025/01/future-of-education-and-skills/

Birman, S. (2025, May 12). *Public schools under siege: How politics are shaping education.* The Science Survey. https://thesciencesurvey.com/editorial/2025/05/12/public-schools-under-siege-how-politics-are-shaping-education/

Canton, J. (2019). Why every CEO needs to be future smart: From AI to sustainability. In Wunder, T. (Ed.), *Rethinking strategic management: Sustainable strategizing for positive impact* (pp. 377–394). Springer Nature Switzerland., DOI: 10.1007/978-3-030-06014-5_18

Cook, T. [@tim_cook]. (2018, October 27). *Twitter post.* Twitter. Retrieved from https://twitter.com/tim_cook/status/1055035552037253121

Corsetti, C. (2025, February 26). Brian Solis of ServiceNow on how leaders are preparing for the innovations, disruptions, and strategies that will define tomorrow: An interview with Cynthia Corsetti. *Medium.* Retrieved from https://medium.com/authority-magazine/the-future-is-faster-than-you-think-brian-solis-of-servicenow-on-how-leaders-are-preparing-for-the-7fe1f3473bce

Desjeunes, M. M. (2022, June 10). *Larry Hohler: Honoring his service. Hope Children's Fund.* Retrieved from https://hopechildrensfund.org/2022/06/10/larry-hohler-honoring-his-service/

Duncan, I. (2023, July 27). States siphoned away $750 million in infrastructure law climate funds. *The Washington Post.* Retrieved from https://www.washingtonpost.com/transportation/2023/07/27/infrastructure-law-climate-change-money/?utm_source=openai

Egan, M. (2026, March 2). *America's teachers are working two jobs and barely getting by.* CNN Business. Retrieved from https://www.cnn.com/2026/03/02/business/jobs-teachers-salary-prices?cid=ios_app

Feyen, B., & Krzaklewska, E. (2012). *The ERASMUS programme and the 'Generation ERASMUS': A short overview.* Deutsche Nationalbibliothek. Retrieved from https://www.google.com/books/edition/The_ERASMUS_Phenomenon_Symbol_of_a_New_E/1lpyAwAAQBAJ?hl=en&gbpv=1&dq=articles+about+erasmus%2B+program&pg=PA9&printsec=frontcover

Giannini, S. (2025). Reimagining the futures of education. *Prospects, 55*(3-4), 299–307. DOI: 10.1007/s11125-025-09740-0

Koross, R. (2016). Micro teaching an efficient technique for learning effective teaching skills: Pre-service teachers' perspective. *IRA-International Journal of Education & Multidisciplinary Studies, 4*(2), 289–299. DOI: 10.21013/irajems.v4.n2.p7

Kumi-Yeboah, A. (2018). Designing a cross-cultural collaborative online learning framework for online instructors. *Online Learning : the Official Journal of the Online Learning Consortium, 22*(4), 181–201.

Leonhard, G. (2021). The next 10 years: How Europe can shape and create a 'good future' (pp. 143-150). In A. Nestoras (Ed.). *EU Policy Review* (Vol. 1). European Liberal Forum.

Lim, C. P. (2004). Engaging learners in online learning environments. *TechTrends, 48*(4), 16–23. DOI: 10.1007/BF02763440

Lin, L., Parker, K., & Horowitz, J. (2024, April 4). *What's it like to be a teacher in America today?* Pew Research Center.

Long, C. (2023, April 5). Advocating for parent involvement in education. *NEA Today.* Retrieved from https://www.nea.org/nea-today/all-news-articles/advocating-parent-involvement-education

McAlister, M. (2025, October 3). The current state of global education. *Medium.* Retrieved from https://medium.com/@drmgmcalister/the-current-state-of-global-education-a5d7a37777fa

Mohiyeddini, C. (2024). Cross-cultural online education: Benefits, challenges, and solutions. [OLER]. *Online Learning in Educational Research, 4*(2), 157–166. DOI: 10.58524/oler.v4i2.456

OECD (2020). *TALIS 2018 Results (Volume II): Teachers and school leaders as valued professionals.* TALIS, OECD Publishing. .DOI: 10.1787/19cf08df-en

OECD. (2025, July 31). How are countries balancing teaching staff compensation with broader education investment? *Education Indicators in Focus.* DOI: 10.1787/22267077

Portée, A. (2025, March 14). Teacher ordered to remove signs from classroom, including one saying "Everyone is welcome here". *Today.* Retrieved from https://www.today.com/parents/teacher-remove-everyone-is-welcome-here-sign-rcna196282

Smith, H. (2014). Teacher education in Scotland: The challenges facing teachers and teacher educators within a rapidly changing education landscape. In P. Boyd, A., Szplit, & Z. Zbrog (eds). *Teacher educators and teachers as learners: International perspectives*, pp. 7-21. University of the West of Scotland.

Solis, B. (2013). *Mindshift: Break through the noise to take back your focus and create the future.* Wiley.

Stanford Online. (2026). *Stack your skills: Advance your career with power stackable credentials.* Retrieved from https://online.stanford.edu/stack-your-skills-advance-your-career-power-stackable-credentials

The White House. (2026, March 24). *First Lady Melania Trump launches fostering the future together, 45 Member Nations attend the Inaugural Coalition Summit.* Retrieved from https://www.whitehouse.gov/briefings-statements/2026/03/first-lady-melania-trump-launches-fostering-the-future-together-45-member-nations-attend-the-inaugural-coalition-summit/

UNESCO. (2021). *Reimagining our futures together: A new social contract for education.* DOI: 10.54675/ASRB4722

UNESCO. (2023a). *Recommendation on education for peace and human rights, international understanding, cooperation, fundamental freedoms, global citizenship and sustainable development.* Retrieved from https://unesdoc.unesco.org/ark:/48223/pf0000391686_eng/PDF/391686eng.pdf.multi.page=3

UNESCO. (2023b). *SDG 4 mid-term progress review: Progress since 2015 has been far too slow.* Retrieved from https://unesdoc.unesco.org/ark:/48223/pf0000386852

U.S. Department of Commerce. (2025). *Regional competitiveness fact sheet.* Retrieved from https://www.commerce.gov/sites/default/files/2025-01/Regional-Competitiveness-Fact-Sheet.pdf

Vogel, R. H. (1978). The making of the Fulbright program. *The Annals of the American Academy of Political and Social Science, 491*(1), 10–27. DOI: 10.1177/000271627849100010

Watters, A. (2015, February 19). *The history of the future of education.* Medium. https://medium.com/the-history-of-the-future-of-education/the-history-of-the-future-of-education-b30925fc6963

World Bank. UNESCO, UNICEF, USAID, FCDO, & Bill & Melinda Gates Foundation. (2022). *The state of global learning poverty: 2022 update.* Retrieved from https://documents.worldbank.org/en/doc/e52f55322528903b27f1b7e61238e416-0200022022/original/Learning-poverty-report-2022-06-21-final-V7-0-conference-edition.pdf

Wright, C. (2022, July 19). *Avoiding the rocking horse of regret.* Medium. https://medium.com/new-writers-welcome/avoiding-the-rocking-horse-of-regret-9c4ed0f6d936

Conclusion

SUMMARY OF KEY INSIGHTS AND TAKEAWAYS

My wife and I went to dinner with another couple the other night. We commented to the waitress about the crowded dining room. She reminded us that the local university was holding a graduation the following day and added that her daughter was among the graduates. After four years in the military, her daughter decided to earn a degree in mathematics and become a teacher. The waitress then said that she is a social worker in a school for the disabled. There, a few short comments encapsulated much of what this book is about. People find their way into teaching through various experiences in their lives, and, as our global narratives confirm, they do so with a sense of mission, often bucking the trends that make teaching seem neither prestigious nor popular. Despite reported factors such as overload, stress, and burnout; lack of support/security; pressure from parents/administration/students; poor student discipline/motivation; and low pay, committed individuals enter the profession and continue to see their work as a mission and a meaningful contribution to society.

The global narratives describe an almost sacred responsibility for students' safety, along with humanizing education through personal connections, fostering cognitive development and intellectual growth, promoting student autonomy and resilience. They illustrate the lives of teachers who see their role as contributing actively to society by nurturing future generations. It has been fascinating to see the similarities in classroom experiences, despite the cultural and societal differences. Moreover, to paraphrase Marvin Espinoza in Chapter 5, reflecting on practitioner experiences promotes epistemic justice by validating the knowledge of educators who are often marginalized within educational structures. By integrating teachers' narratives into peer-reviewed research, we contribute to a more inclusive knowledge base that can effectively inform policy and drive institutional reform. This approach also creates space for exploring contradictions and tensions within the teaching profession, fostering a richer understanding of the complexities educators face.

Using qualitative and/or quantitative approaches, our authors have identified and analyzed key insights into global education.

Inequality and Socio-Economic Barriers: Whether discussing the differences between the Global South and Global North, or recognizing that many countries face persistent, generational gaps in educational access and equality, it becomes clear that poverty, conflict, and resource scarcity play a major role in these divides. Socio-economic differences among students lead to unequal opportunities and outcomes. International organizations have attempted to provide standards and guidance, but as long as core causes remain unaddressed, these inequalities will be difficult to overcome. In the rush to be at the vanguard of algorithmic pedagogy, Lata's study in Chapter 12 provides educators, policy makers, and parents with a clear warning. Democratic practices require participatory data interpretation, transparency, and ethical data use, warning, among other things, that algorithmic models trained on uneven datasets risk reinforcing disparities if equity safeguards are not explicitly embedded.

Teacher Quality, Status, and Shortage: The number and qualifications of teachers are often insufficient. The conditions of teacher overload, burnout, as well as the an increasing aging workforce are widespread, with fewer young people entering the profession. In some countries, teachers may lack the required degrees; in others, their skills may be outdated. Velmurugan et al., in Chapter 6, remind us that teacher well-being is central to educational effectiveness and requires multifaceted interventions that address individual and systemic factors. It becomes imperative to improve teacher working conditions and professional development if we are ever to increase teacher status and strengthen long-term educational systems.

Curriculum Relevance and Overload: There is a need to integrate life skills, critical thinking, and adaptability, but curricula are often overloaded, leaving little room for a deeper understanding of practical application. Utilizing effective curriculum-abandonment strategies not only reduces content but also refocuses attention on more holistic, personalized learning approaches that value empathy and understanding.

Inclusivity and Cultural Sensitivity: Globalization and migration have increased classroom diversity, posing challenges for fostering inclusivity and mutual respect. Issues such as cultural tolerance, language barriers, and differing norms require staff development focusing on sensitivity. Schools are challenged to develop curriculum and instructional designs that foster inclusion. Respecting diversity while promoting shared values is not automatic; it requires patience and a willingness to live in an inclusive society.

Student Motivation, Discipline, and Well-being: Problems of student motivation and discipline are often linked to previous negative educational experiences, societal instability, and a lack of engaging teaching methods. Aggression, bullying, and mental health issues are rising, reflecting broader social tensions. Positive behavioral interventions and social-emotional learning are two approaches that have gained widespread use. In Chapter 11, Asrifan and Furwana explore changes in teachers' roles. Specifically, teachers are no longer just transmitters of knowledge but are expected to be facilitators, mentors, digital guides, ethical leaders, and agents of change. This evolution is driven by global, technological, and social shifts requiring continuous professional development and a renewed sense of mission focused on adaptability, inclusivity, and lifelong learning.

Parental Involvement and School Community Relations: Relationships with parents can be strained, with some parents disengaged, and others overly interventionist. Despite those distinct, polar-opposite situations, effective communication and partnerships between schools and families are essential for student success. Honoring the commitment of parents while respecting the role of the teacher can be a balancing act among the adults, but should always be undertaken with the goal of providing a successful learning environment for the student.

Commercialization and Equity in Higher Education: The commercialization of higher education, including teacher training, can undermine quality and equity. Admission policies may favor privileged groups, limiting opportunities for underrepresented or enthusiastic candidates. It is necessary to provide better training tied to practice, material and moral support, positive media representation, recognition events, and accessible, continuous professional development. The university's commitment need not stop with the conferring of a degree.

Globalization and Standardization Pressures: International reforms often impose Western standards without considering local contexts, leading to resistance and potential conflicts. The push for standardization can also devalue local knowledge and reduce educational autonomy. If we understand teachers' broad societal role, we should then be aware that cultural differences must be considered.

Balancing Innovation with Stability: Continuous reforms and rapid societal changes create instability for educators, who may not have time or support to adapt. There is a need for balanced, supported innovation that considers teachers' capacity and well-being. In that regard, it is necessary to recognize teaching as a way of life while avoiding overloading teachers, so they have time for professional and personal growth.

Adapting to Technological Change: Rapid technological advancements outpace many schools' ability to keep up. While technology can enhance learning, it also brings challenges such as unequal access, cyberbullying, distraction, and overdependence. Teachers and students often lack training to use technology effectively and safely. To counter the arguments around the use of AI, some of our authors posed critical points that raise questions about, if not challenge, AI's wholesale adoption. In Chapter 7, Guclu and Kavak, among other issues, point out that AI must be seen as a tool to support instruction, not for values education or moral guidance, highlighting that AI lacks emotional depth, cultural sensitivity, and the ability to assume responsibility for its consequences. Ashrafuzzaman, in Chapter 8, cautions us to prioritize human-centered AI that supplements rather than replaces teachers, protecting teacher autonomy, socio-emotional work, and ethical governance through participatory design and hybrid human–AI models. Lata, in Chapter 10, echoes that coming from a slightly different perspective. The central argument of this chapter is that the irreplaceability of teachers lies not in their mastery of information but in their moral and relational capacities. Machine-based learning environments, despite their adaptability, cannot replicate the subtle cues and empathic responses that constitute elements of classroom life.

While I have listed key insights and takeaways in a manner that might suggest they are discrete concerns, I want to emphasize that these challenges are interconnected and require coordinated efforts from educators, policy makers, communities, and international organizations. It is only through collaboration and integration of efforts that we can hope to ensure equitable, relevant, and high-quality educational opportunities for all students.

CALL TO ACTION FOR EDUCATORS, POLICYMAKERS, AND COMMUNITIES

My colleague and collaborator, Natela Doghonadze, in her introduction, stated, "The editors, authors, and contributors of this book express the desire for teachers to be heard and supported in their efforts. If the book can help foster a positive attitude towards and care for teaching jobs at least a little, their goal will be reached." To assist in achieving that goal, we are called to take action, action that is grounded in and consistent with the views expressed by the international contributors to this book.

1. Prioritize and professionalize teaching: invest in competitive, equitable compensation, career pathways, workload limits, and wellbeing supports (loan forgiveness, housing/mortgage incentives, protected planning time) to recruit and retain mission-driven educators globally.
2. Reimagine teacher preparation and continuous learning: require practice-based teacher education (micro-teaching, co-teaching, peer coaching), mandatory coursework on family/community engagement and digital pedagogy, and funded, accessible professional development tied to classroom practice.
3. Center equity and contextualized curricula: reform to reduce overload, embed life skills, critical thinking, and culturally responsive content, and target resources to address socio-economic and post-conflict gaps so all learners have a genuine opportunity.
4. Adopt human-centered, ethical tech and AI governance: mandate participatory design with teachers, transparency and fairness safeguards, hybrid human–AI models that protect teacher autonomy and socio-emotional work, and ongoing research into pedagogical and ethical impacts.
5. Strengthen family and community partnerships regionally and locally: build training and structures for meaningful parental and community engagement, protect academic freedom and inclusive values, and create formal channels for community voices to co-design and support schooling.
6. Communicate with policymakers and the general public to promote a positive image of teachers, which is of critical importance. Utilize media, especially technology-driven outlets, to get the message across. While we need scholarship and research, and the journals published for the profession, we also need outlets to share information with the general public in reliable, valid, and relatable ways. Through podcasts, social media, Instagram, TikTok, Facebook, and other platforms, teachers and their organizations have current, useful options for reaching the public.

Through greater involvement in our schools, professional organizations, communities, and governmental agencies, teachers can and should let our voices be heard.

FINAL THOUGHTS ON THE ROLE OF EDUCATORS IN SHAPING RESILIENT EDUCATIONAL SYSTEMS

Teachers, like any profession, have good days and bad days, but we go back because we find hope in our students' success, and that becomes our mission. We have all faced times when we have used up all of our instructional skills with our students, and we are left with only our role as their cheerleaders, edging them through one more successfully completed academic unit. Our commitment and responsibility have been confirmed through the narratives and research that we have reported. But what is also clear is that society does not always value our profession, and this weighs on us and makes us question its future. We need, at times, to become our own cheerleaders.

Each of us has a role to play in assuring that the next generation of educators can grow and benefit from our experience and work. We must use the skills we possess in organizing, planning, assessing, and self-reflection to promote our own cause. We have tasks before us that compel us to advocate individually and collectively for the growth and development of our profession. Also, we should lead in school governance by taking every opportunity to protect planning time and have meaningful input into curriculum and assessment decisions.

If we build and share evidence through action research, presentations, and publications, our experience and that of our colleagues will serve as testaments to the work we do for the children of your communities. By creating and maintaining positive relationships with universities, we can support our higher-ed colleagues in developing pre-service training and meaningful, practice-based professional development. Be proactive in engaging your communities and policymakers by inviting stakeholders into schools for meaningful discussions. Those relationships can help ensure that teachers are represented in all decisions on education reform and AI governance.

If we as teachers take an active role and speak with an informed, united voice, the profession's status, conditions, and influence will rise. We owe it to ourselves, as well as to that newly minted math teacher and all the others like her, who see teaching as a mission and responsibility capable of shaping a more just and compassionate society.

Thomas C. De Bello
State University of New York at Buffalo State, USA

Glossary

Academic integrity: issues dealing with honesty and respect in academic studies. It includes confidentiality and anonymity policies dealing with research participants' personal data, also citing /referencing the works by other authors used in the publication, as well as presenting true results of true studies.

Accountability theory: As explained by Vance, Lowry and Eggett (2015), it explains how the perceived need to justify one's behaviors to another party causes one to consider and feel accountable for the process by which decisions and judgments have been reached.

Accreditation: legal/official assessment (of an institution or a program) and recognition.

Activity theory: it is a conceptual framework originating from the socio-cultural tradition in psychology. The foundational concept of the framework is "activity", which is understood as purposeful, transformative, and developing interaction between actors ("subjects") and the world ("objects").

Adjunct: an Adjunct Professor is a professor who teaches on a limited-term contract and is ineligible for tenure.

ADHD: see attention deficit hyperactivity disorder.

Affect: emotion (affective – emotional, dealing with emotoin).

Alma mater: the mother of your soul: school or university one graduated from.

Algorithm: a process or set of rules to be followed in calculations or other problem-solving operations, especially by a computer.

Andragogy: pedagogy of adults.

Artificial intelligence (AI): the application of computer software able to perform tasks or produce output normally requiring human intelligence, especially by applying machine learning techniques to large collections of data.

Assessment vs. **evaluation and testing:** while assessment includes observation, providing feedback, giving grades, in order to see how well the learning process is going on, evaluation includes these plus decision-making (e.g., transferring to the next grade, being admitted to a school/college/university). Testing is the procedure of assessment, mostly written, the result includes a grade (but no decision may be taken based on a single testing).

At-risk: students at-risk are those who often fail to learn, many of them come from families at-risk – extremely poor, single-parent, alcoholic or drug-addicted, criminal.

Attention deficit hyperactivity disorder (ADHD): a developmental disorder characterized by one or more of the following symptoms: having difficulty paying/concentrating attention, keeping on task, or staying organized. Children with the disorder cannot sit calmly, they need to move all the time. Some people believe it is connected with mental retardation, in fact, it is not.

Attrition: a reduction or decrease in numbers, size, or strength.

Authenticity/authentic: teaching in a way that is real life-like.

Authorisation: document giving official permission.

Autism/Autism Spectrum Disorder/ASD: a developmental disability that can cause significant social, communication, and behavioral challenges. It is a condition related to brain development which makes it difficult if possible at all to communicate with other people. Early signs of autism include limited eye contact and body language and repetitive motions or speech.

Autonomous learning – learner's ability to acquire/develop knowledge independently, mostly without a teacher's help.

Baccalaureate: see **International Baccalaureate.**

Batch: students enrolled and/or graduating at the same time, for example, a group of students studying the same Program together will be called a student batch. See also Cohort.

BEd: Bachelor of Education

Bifocal: characterized by two foci, paying great attention to two things

Bloom's taxonomy: a framework for categorising educational goals, developed by a committee of educators chaired by Benjamin Bloom in 1956. It comprises three learning domains: the cognitive, affective, and psychomotor, and assigns to each of these domains a hierarchy that corresponds to different levels of learning: I. Knowledge. Remembering information. II. Comprehension. Understanding and explaining the meaning of information. III. Application. Using abstractions in concrete situations. IV. Analysis. Breaking down a whole into component parts. V. Synthesis. Putting parts together to form a new and integrated whole. VI. Evaluation. VII. Creation. Producing new or original work.

Bologna process: an intergovernmental higher education reform process launched in 1999 that includes 48 European countries and a number of European organisations. It aims at the increase of European higher education prestige, introduction of European Credit Transfer System (1 ECTS credit equals 25-30 hours of contact and independent study), recognition of each other's degrees and stimulating student, academic staff and specialists' international mobility.

Burnout: being very tired, disappointed, unmotivated as result of too heavy load and/or negative experiences.

Cluster sampling: a population is divided into smaller groups known as clusters, mostly geographically spread.

Cognitive skills: as opposed to motor (movement) skills, they deal with people's mind. Cognitive skills enable people think, learn, memorise, and solve problems.

Cohort: a group of people who are around the same age, like a cohort of college students who have similar experiences and concerns (See also Batch).

Collaborative learning: a method which involves group participation and collective problem-solving, while **cooperative learning** involves dividing tasks among group members to achieve a common goal.

Competence/competency: knowledge and skills developed on a high level that bring the person to success at job (compare to knowledge, skills).

Complexity science: it defines a worldview that no longer sees the world as mechanistic, linear, and predictable. Rather it sees the world as interconnected. The interactions between elements being nonlinear make the behaviour of complex systems unpredictable.

Concept-based learning/teaching: it is structured through inquiry and looks through a conceptual lens. It encourages learning within, between and across subjects and disciplines

Constructivism: a learning theory states students learn new information by building on top of a foundation of what they've already learned, knowledge, according to this theory, is rather co-constructed by teacher and students than just transferred by the teacher.

Content: normally, by content the subject/syllabus/curriculum topics are meant.

Continuous learning/education: Continuous education starts when formal education is over, it is primarily aimed at improving skills and knowledge relevant to a specific work or career.

Convenience sampling: a type of non-probability sampling that involves the sample being drawn from that part of the population that is close at hand, e.g., lecturers from one's faculty.

Cooperative learning: see Collaborative learning.

Corona virus: see COVID-19.

Corporal punishment: bodily punishment, such as beating, putting on knees and/or in the corner.

COVID - Coronavirus disease 2019 (COVID-19) is a contagious disease caused by the coronavirus SARS-CoV-2. In January 2020, the disease spread worldwide. Education was cancelled and then went online for months. Thousands of people died.

Critical thinking: the ability to objectively analyse and evaluate an issue in order to form a judgment (pay attention: it does not necessarily imply criticizing).

Curriculum as practice: it centers on what students and teachers actually do – how curriculum is enacted and experienced in real settings.

Curriculum vs. **educational program and syllabus:** a curriculum is an orderly set of subjects, their goals, major requirements, teaching methods, etc. While a curriculum deals with the design, organisation and planning of learning activities, a programme refers to the implementation of these activities. E.g.: The curriculum was approved at the faculty board. Peter studies at the program of Educational Psychology. A syllabus is a plan for teaching a particular subject: topics, educational materials, objectives, assessment methods, etc.

Decentralisation in education: shift from traditional centralized systems toward more localized (schools, districts, and communities) decision-making and governance.

Decision theory: or the theory of rational choice is a branch of probability, economics, and analytic philosophy that uses expected utility and probability. It is concerned with the reasoning underlying an agent's choices, whether this is a mundane choice between taking the bus or getting a taxi, or a more far-reaching choice made by a powerful agent about whether to pursue significant social change

Deliberate practice: Defined by the psychologist Anders Ericsson and colleagues, Deliberate Practice is the individualized training activities specially designed by a coach or teacher to improve specific aspects of an individual's performance through repetition and successive refinement.

Digital skills/literacy: the ability to find, evaluate, create, and communicate information using contemporary technologies.

Direct instruction: the explicit/open teaching using lectures or demonstrations of the material to students; it provides readymade knowledge.

Discernment: an ability to judge well

Discovery learning: active student engagement in learning, analising the offered materials and making conclusions, under a greater or lesser degree of teacher involvement.

Disparity: unequality, unfairness.

Diversity: see Student diversity.

Dyslexia: a learning disability that makes reading and language-related tasks harder. A person, for example, may be unable to build up meaningful sentences or memorise words.

Early years foundation stage (EYFS): The standards that school and childcare providers must meet for the learning, development and care of children from birth to 5.

Ecosystem: see Educational ecosystem.

Edtech: educational technology

Educational ecosystem: it is a network or framework that provides all students with what they need to succeed throughout their educational journey. At the center of the ecosystem is the school district. It connects school, home, and community. Every school within the district is a learning hub within the ecosystem. The educational eco-system means that all levels of education (macro-, meso- and micro) are working towards the same goals. The stakeholders from these levels cooperate, work together, and share experiences and knowledge to achieve the common vision. At the macro-level, curriculum includes societal and educational policies. The meso-level comprises the institutional context and organizing structures. The micro-level involves classroom activities and teacher-student interactions.

Educational program vs. **curriculum and syllabus:** see Curriculum vs. educational program and syllabus.

EFL (English as a foreign language): English learned in classrooms, not in natural environment, e.g., English learned in Georgia is EFL, as it is not spoken by the locals for their communication. See ESL.

Elementary school: in some countries called primary school (depending on the country) first 4-6 years of school education, where the basics are taught, first of all, reading, writing and counting.

Emotional intelligence: according to Howard Gardner, learners may be especially successful in various spheres, such as linguistic/verbal (dealing with language), mathematical-logical, visual/spatial (dealing with space), bodily-kinesthetic (dealing with movement), interpersonal (dealing with abilities to communicate) and intrapersonal (dealing with ability to observe oneself), musical/rhythmic, naturalistic, and emotional (ability to understand and manage one's own and other people's emotions).

Empathy: the ability to understand and share another person's emotions.

Empirical: based on, concerned with, or verifiable by observation or experience rather than theory or pure logic.

Empowerment in education: refers to the process of enabling the powerless (women, students, the poor, etc.) have more agency over their learning experiences, develop critical thinking skills, and become more independent learners. Empower the powerless was Paolo Freire's central idea.

Epistemic: relating to knowledge or to the degree of its validation (epistemology is the theory of knowledge – its degree of being objectively verified).

Epistemic integrity: staying honest about how we know what we know. It means making sure our beliefs and decisions are based on solid evidence, clear reasoning, and a willingness to question assumptions.

Equality vs. equity: see Equity.

Equity: While equality means each individual or group of people is given the same rights or opportunities, equity recognizes that each person has different circumstances and allocates the exact resources and opportunities needed to reach an equal outcome. Women are mostly given equal rights with men in contemporary society, however, the need to care for children makes it more difficult than for men to get higher education, to provide equity, it is necessary to have free-of-charge kindergartens, flexible timetable at work, etc.

Erasmus+ teaching mobility program: A European program that supports/finances teaching periods at higher education institutions abroad, at an institution in an Erasmus+ Programme or Partner country.

ESL (English as a second language): English learned in a natural environment, e.g., when English is learned both in the classroom and natural environment in the UK or the US.

Evaluation vs. assessment and testing: see in Assessment vs. evaluation and testing.

Exclusion: opposite to inclusion. Not letting/enabling to participate.

Experiential learning: it is the process of learning by doing. By engaging students in hands-on experiences and reflection, they are better able to connect theories and knowledge learned in the classroom to real-world situations.

Extracurricular: beyond the educational program, e.g., reader and sports clubs, holiday parties, excursions.

Extrinsic motivation: motivation dealing from outside, such as rewards, punishment, grades, certificates, etc.

Facilitator vs. **knowledge provider:** in the past, teachers were viewed only as knowledge providers (see also Teaching vs. sharing knowledge), today, we speak about helping (facilitating) knowledge creating. Facilitators guide students to develop their own knowledge.

Feedback: information about reactions to a person's performance of a task, which is used as a basis for improvement; teacher feedback: feedback provided by the teacher; students' feedback: feedback received directly or elicited from students.

Flipped classroom: the order of material presentation and practice is flipped: students gain necessary knowledge before class (via studying the offered electronic materials by themselves), and instructors guide students to actively and interactively clarify and apply that knowledge during class.

Framing Theory: it explores how groups create and utilize meaning to mobilize individuals toward collective action.

Freirean: dealing with Paolo Freire (1921-1997), Brazilian educator and philosopher. In his *Pedagogy of the Oppressed* he requires inclusion and equity for ethnic minorities and the poor.

Graduate: programme awarding a Master's or a doctoral degree.

HEI - higher education institution

Hermeneutic: a method or theory of interpretation

Hiatus: pause, break.

Holistic, or whole-child education: a multisided, balanced approach to teaching in which educators do their best to address the emotional, social, ethical, and academic needs of students in an integrated learning format.

Impaired: limited by a physical or mental condition (e.g., hearing or speaking-impaired).

Implicit: hidden, not visible, but mean/expected, e.g., implicit curriculum – not stated in any official document, but characterising a particular teacher/program/school, which the learner may 'calculate' through experience.

Inclusive education: all children in the same classrooms, in the same schools. It means real learning opportunities for groups who have traditionally been excluded – not only children with disabilities, but speakers of minority languages too.

Indigenous: native, inhabiting or existing in a land from the earliest times or from before the arrival of colonists.

Inquiry-based learning: classroom practices that promote student learning through guided and, increasingly, independent investigation of complex questions and problems.

In-service: in the process of work, e.g., in-service training – a training conducted during work hours in the institution where the teacher works.

International Baccalaureate (IB) is a global leader in international education; their school certificates are recognized in 150 countries/territories.

Intrinsic motivation: motivation that the person him/herself feels, such as interest in the topic/subject. Compare: Extrinsic motivation.

Job design theory: it deals with the process of establishing employees' roles and responsibilities. Its main purpose is to optimise work processes to create value and maximise performance. But, it's also a key element in creating good quality jobs which benefit both workers and employers.

Kinesthetic (or kinaesthetic): dealing with movement.

Knowledge: awareness or understanding, especially of an act, a fact, or the truth; we keep in memory what we know. Compare with skills, competence/competency.

Kolb's cycle of learning - Kolb's experiential learning theory works on two levels: a four-stage learning cycle and four separate learning styles: concrete experience, reflective observation, abstract conceptualization, and active experimentation.

Legitimacy theory: a business concept relating to the behaviors and perceptions of businesses, other organizations, and larger social institutions within a society. This theory involves the idea of a social contract linking people with organizations and institutions.

Lifelong learning: ongoing, voluntary, and self-motivated pursuit of learning for either personal or professional reasons, it includes professional development and personal interests like hobbies, as well as just reading books, visiting museums, etc. Also see continuous learning.

Life skills, also soft/transversal/transferable skills, 21st-century skills, power skills: skills that can be used in a wide variety of situations in life and in work. They are to be taught both at school and universities. Life skills are not directly related to the subject/course we teach, they may be applied in connection with any academic subject or any field of work, such as leadership, communication, information technology skills, etc.

Likert scale: A Likert scale is a rating scale used to measure survey participants' opinions, attitudes, motivations, and more. It often is a 5-point scale, with assessment growing from 1 (totally disagree) to 5 (completely agree). Sometimes a 4-point (without the neutral answer) scale is used.

Literacy: 1) the ability to read, write, and count 2) basic skills in an important area, such as computer literacy.

Longitudinal: longitudinal studies are carried out for a long period of time, normally several years.

MEd: Master of Education

Mediation: arbitration, helping two parties of a conflict fund mutual understanding.

Metacognition: awareness and understanding of one's own thought/learning processes. Metacognitive strategies are those that help explain how the person learns.

Miaeutic method: see Socratic method.

Micro-credential: a series of courses that culminate in a digital badge from an accredited university.

Mindfulness: a way of cultivating a learning environment that encourages students to become more aware of their internal and external experiences, promoting a sense of calm and focus.

Montessori Kindergarten: Child-Led/Independent Learning. The classroom is designed to facilitate independent learning and provide opportunities for children to explore with hands-on activities, interact with other students, and move between activities as they choose. Named after Maria Montessori (1870-1952) - an Italian physician and educator best known for her philosophy of education and her writing on scientific pedagogy.

Motivation: the drive that stimulated people to do something.

Motor skills: ability to produce/control movements.

NGO – non-governmental organization.

Non-coercive deliberation: it defines a communicative setting where participants discuss issues freely, without pressure, manipulation, or domination by authority or powerful interests.

Nurture (v.): care for; in the phrase nature or nurture 'nurture' stands for education/upbringing, while 'nature' for genetics.

OECD: organization for economic cooperation and development.

Paradigm: a typical example, pattern, model; paradigmatic: serving as a typical example of something, e.g., his biography is paradigmatic of the experiences of this generation. In linguistics: of or denoting the relationship between a set of linguistic items that form mutually exclusive choices in particular syntactic roles.

Path dependence: the dependence of future societal decision processes and/or socio-ecological outcomes on those that have occurred in the past.

Peer: an equal (by age, position, education) person; peer assessment: (usually) informal assessment of colleagues/students by each other.

Phenomenology: the study of phenomena as they manifest in our experience, of the way we perceive and understand phenomena, and of the meaning phenomena have in our subjective experience.

PIRLS: the Progress in International Reading Literacy Study (PIRLS) is an international assessment and research project designed to measure reading achievement at the fourth-grade level, as well as school and teacher practices related to instruction.

PISA-The Program for International Student Assessment: an international assessment that measures 15-year-old students' reading, mathematics, and science literacy.

Popularity: the state of being liked, enjoyed, accepted, chosen, or done by a large number of people.

Population (in research): the entire group of individuals that share a common characteristic and are the focus of the study, e.g., primary school teachers in the USA.

Positionality: a person's standing or identity in relation to others, especially with reference to issues of culture, ethnicity, or gender.

Positive psychology: it is an umbrella term for the scientific study of the various contributors to a healthy and thriving life for the self and others (e.g., positive emotions, life meaning, engaging work, and close relationships). It is the study of strengths, assets, and positive attributes. Its five building blocks are Positive Emotion, Engagement, Relationships, Meaning and Mattering, and Accomplishment (PERMA).

Postgraduate: a programme awarding a Master's or a doctoral degree. Often "graduate" and "postgraduate" are used interchangeably, however, sometimes, 'graduate' stands for Master's and postgraduate for doctorate programmes.

Practice theory: the term refers to a cluster of social science approaches that focus on what people physically do rather than on mental processes that go on in their heads.

Pragmatism: is an educational philosophy that says that education should be about life and growth. That is, teachers should be teaching students things that are practical for life and encourage them to grow into better people

Prescriptive: giving exact rules, directions, or instructions about how something should be done.

Pre-service teacher (also **teacher candidate**): the term describes students in teacher education program working towards teacher certification.

Prestige: value, respect and admiration given to someone or something, usually because of a reputation for high quality, success, or social influence.

Primary school: see elementary school.

Professional development: reading up, participating in conferences, training sessions, research projects, sharing one's experiences with other teachers, writing reflective diaries, etc.. Professional development is needed to update one's knowledge and skills in the profession.

Proxy: representation, especially, numeric representation

Psyche: from Greek 'soul'. Here is where the word 'psychology' comes from – study of the soul (of course, it studies much more, but...).

Purposive sampling: a non-probability sampling technique where researchers intentionally select participants based on specific characteristics relevant to their study, e.g., only female students.

Rapport: close relationship, based on mutual understanding and support.

Reflection: analysing one's teaching, thinking over it to find the possibilities to improve it. Reflective teaching is, therefore, teaching accompanied by critical self-analysis (via reflective diaries, mutual peer observation, and discussion with colleagues.

Relational pedagogy: it draws on the relationships, interactions, communication and interconnection of people, places and things in children's sociocultural contexts to enhance and extend children's learning and development. Relational pedagogy fosters empathy, compassion and care by creating meaningful connections, both between students and teachers, and between peers.

Replicate: reproduce, copy, imitate, and repeat.

Resilience: the capacity to withstand or to recover quickly from difficulties.

Rote memorisation: memorising through multiple repetitions, without giving much thought to it.

Sabbatical leave: it is a break from work, allowing employees to pursue interests such as traveling, writing, research, or volunteering. During this period, employees remain part of their organization but are exempt from regular duties.

Sample (in research): a group of people selected from a larger population. There are two major types of sampling: probabilistic (random or chance selection; is viewed as representative of the population) and non-probabilistic (based on arbitrary criteria rather than random selection, leading to a sample that may not accurately represent the larger population).

Self-determination theory: a motivation theory by Ryan and Deci suggesting that people feel more motivated when they can make their own choices.

Scaffolding: Vygotsky's scaffolding is a method of teaching that helps learners understand educational content by working with an educator or someone who has a better understanding of the material ('More knowledgeable Others").

Sharing knowledge vs. **teaching:** see Teaching vs. sharing knowledge.

Situated learning: situated learning theory is a concept that emphasizes the role of context in the learning process. It emphasizes the social and contextual nature of knowledge acquisition. It emphasizes the importance of social interaction and participation in learning, where individuals learn through engagement with information sources and practices within a specific social setting.

Skill: the ability to do something automatically, without much thinking, e.g., walking normally is a skill. Compare with knowledge, competence/competency.

Snowball sampling: a non-probability sampling method where new units are recruited by other units to form part of the sample.

Social cohesion: a measure of how well groups stay together and complete their tasks.

Social/sociocultural constructivism: a theory by Vygotsky (see) based on a collaborative learning approach that emphasizes student involvement, discussion, and knowledge exchange. Knowledge is co-constructed by teacher and his/her students through cooperation. Such factors as gender, ethnicity, race, and social class are built within a structure of social relations; they impact learning. Language, as one of the central factors of culture, has a great impact on leaning.

Socratic teaching/method: the Socratic method, also can be known as maieutics, method of elenchus, elenctic method, or Socratic debate, is a form of cooperative argumentative dialogue between individuals, based on asking and answering questions to stimulate critical thinking and to draw out ideas and underlying presumptions.

Special education: education of students with special needs (see).

Stakeholder: Anybody who participates in, influences and is influenced by the process (of education).

Standardised testing: a method of evaluating student performance through uniform assessments that allow for comparison among individuals with similar characteristics, such as grade levels. Standardised tests are developed by teams of experts: the person who makes it up, the experts who assess it. They are usually piloted – applied with participants who are maximally similar to those test-takers who will use it for evaluation, and ambiguous, too easy and too difficult items are removed.

STEM: science, technology, engineering, and mathematics, disciplines that drive innovation and address global challenges.

Stratified sampling: the population is divided into subgroups called strata based on characteristics that they share (age, gender, education level, etc.).

Student-centered vs. teacher-centered: the student-centered approach includes more time for students (compared to teachers) to speak, selecting activities and topics (sub-topics) together with students, providing teaching beneficial for various learning styles to fit all students in the classroom, involving students in self-assessment and peer-assessment, etc. Some educators say teaching has always been student-centered, well, yes and no. Of course, what teachers did was for their students (at least, the way teachers understood it), however, it was teacher alone who made all decisions – planning, selecting materials and activities, explaining, and assessing. In student-centered teaching, students have a say in all these.

Student diversity: recognizing that all students are unique in their own ways, with differences in reading levels, mental and physical abilities, learning styles, cultural backgrounds, beliefs, and more. Contrary to the views in the past (that student diversity is one of the major challenges for educators) nowadays it is recognized that student diversity enriches education.

Students with special needs: students who different from the 'mainstream'/majority of students. They are either exceptionally talented/gifted, and need special treatment to support the development of their talents, or experience some physical or mental challenges, which also requires that they get some special attention.

Substantive teacher: a temporary position with an option of a permanent at some point, normally substantive post is being issued or advertised if the teacher has passed away, retired early, or is ill for a long time.

Syllabus: see Curriculum vs. educational program and syllabus.

Symbolic capital: In sociology and anthropology, it can be referred to as the resources available to an individual on the basis of honor, prestige or recognition, and serves as value that one holds within a culture.

System dynamics: it is defined as a methodology for studying and managing complex feedback systems, integrating qualitative and quantitative analysis to understand their behavior over time, particularly in the context of nonlinear interactions and feedback loops.

Tangible: which can be touched, tangible rewards, for example, are chocolates or some other prizes.

Taxonomy: classification

Teacher candidate: see pre-service teacher.

Teachers vs. **educators:** teachers deliver classes, educators are people who work in the system of education: administrators, materials developers, and teachers.

Teaching vs. **sharing knowledge**: by 'teaching' providing what you know or what books tell to those who are expected not to know it, while sharing knowledge is a cooperative process, you don't impose your knowledge which is 'the only correct one' on your students, you discuss it, and knowledge is built cooperatively (together with your learners), knowledge is co-created, students learn from you, and you learn from students.

Teaching reception: the first year in primary school which welcomes children between four and five years. Teaching reception usually involves imparting numeracy and literacy skills to children to prepare them for primary education.

Tenure: a safeguard that protects good teachers from unfair firing. Once a teacher is granted tenure - a right that must be earned after three years or more of service, oversight and evaluation - a teacher cannot be fired without a fair hearing.

Tertiary education: the education obtained after the secondary (school) education, includes learning at colleges, vocational schools/colleges, or universities.

Testing vs. **assessment and evaluation**: see Assessment vs. evaluation and testing.

Triage: diagnosing, understanding the of the need of treatment

Triangulation: it refers to the use of multiple methods or data sources in research to develop a comprehensive understanding of phenomena and to get more reliable results

Top-down: used about decisions made 'on-top' (by leaders/bosses) – authoritarian approach. Cf: bottom-up: decisions made democratically.

TTOCs or teachers teaching on call are certificated and qualified individuals who replace a regular classroom teacher for the purpose of continuing the instructional program, maintaining discipline, and generally promoting the educational welfare of the students. Being a teacher on call is a great way to experience different classroom environments within a flexible work schedule.

Uncoerced deliberation: see Non-coercive deliberation

Undergraduate: a programme that awards a Bachelor's degree. See graduate & postgraduate.

Valorisation: the process of preserving or enhancing the value of something, most commonly done with the help of the government or an organization.

Virtual: imaginary, not physically existing as such but made by software to appear to do so, e.g., "virtual images".

Vocational education and training (VET): the training in skills and teaching of knowledge related to a specific trade or occupation in which the student wishes to participate.

Vigostkyan: dealing with Lev Vygostky (1896-1934) who was a Russian and Soviet psychologist, best known for his work on psychological development in children and creating the framework known as Sociocultural Theory of Cognitive Development.

Zone of Proximal Development (ZPD): a term introduced by Vygostky (see), it stands for knowledge zone that reasonably exceeds what learners already know; teaching by ZPD makes learning viable for the majority of students.

About the Contributors

Natela Doghonadze is a Doctor of Education Sciences, Professor at the International Black Sea University, Tbilisi, Georgia, at the School of Education, Humanities and Social Sciences. She defended her Candidate of Sciences (Soviet equivalent to PhD) in 1983 in Ilya State University (then Sulkhan-Saba Tbilisi State Pedagogical University) on the methods of teaching English vocabulary at school. She defended her Doctor of Sciences dissertation (equivalent to postdoctoral) in 1998 Ilya State University (then Sulkhan-Saba Tbilisi State Pedagogical University) on the methods of developing a coursebook in English for adult students. She authors more than 200 publications, almost 100 of them in English. Her most cited article is The Degree of Readiness to Total Distance learning in the Face of COVID-19 - Teachers' view (Case of Azerbaijan, Georgia, Iraq, Nigeria, UK, and Ukraine) (2020) (149 references, according to Google Scholar). Another recognized publication is Critical Analysis of Open-Book Exam for University Students (2013), cited 5 times on WoS. WoS ID is F-5493-2018 and Scopus ID is 57216149010. She was the scientific advisor of 44 defended PhD dissertations. She initiated and authored 4 programs at her University: BA in English Philology, 60-credit one-year teacher certification program, MA in Higher Education Administration, and PhD in Education Sciences and coordinated them for years. She initiated the Journal of Education in Black Sea Region (JEBS) and was the editor-in-chief for years, now she is on the editorial board. She founded the International Research Conference on Education, English Language and literature Teaching (IRCEELT), and is the honorary President of the conference.

Thomas C. De Bello holds a Doctor of Education degree and was recently an adjunct associate professor in the International Graduate Program for Educators at the State University of New York at Buffalo State. He earned his EdD in Administration and Supervision from St. John's University in New York City. His Doctoral dissertation is titled A Critical Analysis of the Achievement and Attitude Effects of Administrative Assignments to Social Studies Writing Instruction Based on Identified Eighth Grade Students' Preferences for Learning Alone, with Peers, or with Teachers. He attended the State University of New York at Stony Brook, where he received a Master of Arts in Liberal Studies (1971) and a Master of Arts in Sociology (1974). He also holds professional licenses, including Permanent New York State Administrator's Certification as a School District Administrator and School Administrator and Supervisor, as well as Permanent New York State Teacher's Certification for Secondary English and Social Studies. Thomas C. De Bello is a former social studies teacher, principal, consultant, and professor, and has mentored numerous doctoral students. He has authored or co-authored 18 publications and is known for his work on Learning Styles. His most popular article that still gets hits is De Bello, T. and Guez, R. (Nov. 1996). Parents' Perceptions of Their Child's Learning Style.

***

Lanja Abdulrazzaq Shehabaddin Dabbagh is an Assistant Professor at the Department of English, College of Languages, Salahaddin University in Iraqi Kurdistan. Her area of specialization is Discourse Analysis, with particular focus on literary and dramatic discourse. She earned her BA, followed by an MA in English Language and Linguistics/Psycholinguistics in 2001, specializing in Language Acquisition. In 2009, she completed her PhD in English Language and Linguistics/Literary Discourse Analysis in 2009, with her doctoral research centered on Dramatic Discourse Analysis. Dr. Dabbagh began her professional career in 1993, working as a translator at the College of Medicine for four years. In 2001, she joined the College of Arts as a faculty member, where she contributed extensively to teaching and research. She has also served as the Head of the German Department for six years and two years as the Acting Head of the English

Department. Thus, she was the Head of the Scientific Committee in both the German and English Departments. Also, the head of the Quality Assurance Committee for both departments. Lanja participated as a researcher in many conferences (national and international), published over 70 papers in different (national and international) journals, and many MA and PhD Vivas. As from current academic year 2025-2026, she works as a teacher and supervisor for MA and PhD programs at the English Department, working on several linguistic and literary research.

Gulhayat Abdullayeva - With over 40 years of teaching experience, she is a highly skilled and enthusiastic English instructor. She currently teaches at Azerbaijan State Pedagogical University and has taught English at various academic levels, from universities to middle and high schools. She is well-known for her captivating teaching methods and deep knowledge of both classic and modern literature, inspiring thousands of students to appreciate the power and diversity of the English language. Gulhayat Abdullayeva gained a reputation for her academic integrity, compassion, and dedication to student growth. She has developed and taught courses in literary analysis, public speaking, writing, grammar, and creative expression, while also mentoring new teachers, delivering professional development seminars, and contributing to curriculum development. She is actively involved in extracurricular activities such as debate clubs, school publications, and literary organizations, many of her former students have pursued careers in literature, teaching, and the arts, often crediting her guidance.

Laila Addasi was born in Los Angeles and raised in Ottawa, Canada, where her passion for learning and service began early. After leading her high school's Cancer Drive Night and raising $36,000 in four hours, she dedicated herself to empowering others. Laila earned her Bachelor of Science (Honors) in Human Kinetics, Summa Cum Laude, and a Master's in Multidisciplinary Studies in Education from the State University of New York at Buffalo. In her early twenties, she began teaching in Kuwait, where her dedication and leadership led her from classroom teacher to Head of Science, and eventually to Vice Principal. She later contributed to TELUS's National Youth Engagement Strategy after volunteering with the United Way Ottawa Youth Board. Recipient of the Canadian Governor General's Caring Canadian Award, the Canadian Association of Fundraising Professionals' Outstanding Youth Award, and Ottawa's Spirit of the Capital Global Citizenship Award, Laila remains grateful for every opportunity to serve, learn, and help others grow.

Eseoghene Elsie Adeniji is the Head Teacher of Doyens School, a graduate of University of Ibadan Nigeria, with professional experience in teaching, school leadership, and academic writing.

Abdulsalam Adeyemi Ahmed is the Head Master of NTIC Kano Nursery and Primary School. He has taught Biology, Integrated Science and Agricultural Science.

Aysel Aghamaliyeva is a PhD student in Linguistics at Azerbaijan University of Languages in Baku, specializing in linguistic theory. Her research investigates the typology of qualitative word modifers across languages, seeking to map the universal constraints and variations in how languages express qualitative word modifiers. With 18 years of experience in English language teaching at school, she is particularly interested in the implications of the theoretical work for pedagogy, especially in the teaching of vocabulary and descriptive language. Her scholarly approach is enriched by a passion for travel and literature, which provides cross-cultural and narrative context to her formal linguistic analysis

Ashraf Alam is an Assistant Professor in the Department of Education at NIT Calicut, Kerala, India. He has been recognised among the *World's Top 2% Scientists* by Stanford University and Elsevier. He earned his Ph.D. from IIT Kharagpur, where his research engaged with foundational concerns in educational policy, curriculum design, educational technology, philosophy of education, innovation in education, educational administration, governance, and pedagogical transformation. His academic contributions include more than 95 Scopus-indexed publications and over 100 conference presentations delivered at national and international academic forums. His work has appeared in reputed research publication platforms including Elsevier, Springer, Taylor & Francis, CRC Press, Routledge, Atlantis Press, Springer Nature, Palgrave Macmillan, and IEEE. His work is grounded in a transdisciplinary orientation that draws from educational sciences, digital pedagogy, curriculum theory, learning analytics, sustainability education, instructional design, artificial intelligence, ethics of technology, and socio-technical studies. Dr. Ashraf's scholarship strives to interrogate and expand the boundaries of educational thought by examining the epistemological, ethical, and social dimensions of digital and post-digital pedagogies. His work critically engages with the changing nature of knowledge production, learner agency, pedagogical mediation, and institutional transformation in technologically saturated educational environments. He is particularly invested in advancing inclusive digital learning, gamified instructional strategies, AI-mediated educational ecosystems, and ethically governed technology integration in education. His research agenda is animated by the pursuit of design-oriented, ethically attuned, and contextually responsive frameworks that can support meaningful educational reform. Through his work, he seeks to contribute to the development of pedagogical models that are not only technologically innovative but also socially just, epistemically inclusive, developmentally sensitive, and aligned with the broader goals of sustainable and human-centred education.

Sara Al-Essa is a Life Skills teacher and school administrator at Al-Ruya Bilingual School in Kuwait, with 19 years of experience in the field of education. She holds a Bachelor's degree in Civil Engineering, followed by a Diploma in Effective Teaching, and later completed a Master's degree in Multidisciplinary Science from Buffalo State University. She teaches at the secondary (high school) level. Her professional interests focus on human-centered education, inclusive teaching practices, the role of emotion in effective learning, and educational equity.

Huda Abdullah Abdulateef Al-Hassani is a Lecturer in the Department of English at the University of Mosul, specializing in Contemporary Literature, Culture, and Literary Criticism. She earned her M.A. in Contemporary Literature and Culture from Brunel University, UK, in 2011, following a Bachelor's degree in English Language from the University of Basra in 2004. With a professional academic career spanning over a decade, she attained the title of Assistant Lecturer in 2013 and was promoted to Lecturer in 2018. Beyond her academic role, she is an active literary writer and director. Her extensive teaching portfolio includes Literary Criticism, British and American Literature, Novel, and Drama, as well as Teaching English as a Foreign Language (TEFL) across various departments and the Universal Education Centre. Her scholarly work is recognized through her contributions to Research Gate, Google Scholar, and ORCID.

Aydin Aliyev is an education leader and researcher with expertise in Educational Leadership, English Language Teaching (ELT), and Educational Technologies. He currently serves as the Dean of the School of English-Taught Programs at Odlar Yurdu University in Baku, Azerbaijan, where he oversees English-medium academic programs and works to enhance institutional quality, foster international collaboration, and support student and faculty success. He earned his Bachelor's degree in English Language Teaching from Dokuz Eylül University (Türkiye) and completed his PhD in Education Sciences at the International Black Sea University (Georgia). With more than fourteen years of academic and administrative experience, he has contributed extensively to curriculum development, postgraduate supervision, and the improvement of teaching and learning systems. He also serves as an academic supervisor for master's and PhD students at multiple universities, supporting research and academic development across institutions. Since 2019, he has worked with the British Council Azerbaijan as a trainer and teacher, providing professional training for schoolteachers and delivering English courses for professionals from diverse sectors and leadership positions, both in Azerbaijan and internationally.

Ruth Allen has over 30 years of professional experience in education, including more than 20 years working in Colombia in international and bilingual school contexts. Her career includes teaching and leadership roles, with experience in curriculum development, school culture, and educational innovation. She holds a Doctorate in Education (EdD) from the University of Bath, UK, an MSc in Educational Science from the State University of New York at Buffalo, US and an MA in Language Studies from the University of Lancaster UK.

Mary Josephine Amimo holds a Certificate in Primary Teacher Education. She is a loving, passionate and committed teacher from Kenya with over five years' experience in teaching. She has a strong background in classroom management, delivering and engaging lessons, assessing learner progress and creating supportive learning environment that promotes academic and personal growth. Mary and is skilled in curriculum implementation and learner teaching methods. Throughout the five years, she has been a classroom and subject teacher. She is committed to nurturing and mentoring young minds by fostering discipline, nurturing talents and encouraging critical thinking. Mary continues to strive to positively impact the lives of learners and the school community in general.

Md. Ashrafuzzaman is an Assistant Professor in the Department of Educational Technology and Engineering (EdTE) at the University of Frontier Technology, Bangladesh. He has been working for about sixteen years in the field of education and educational research with different organizations. In 2014, he received an MPhil degree in English Language Education from the Institute of Education and Research (IER), University of Dhaka (DU). He has also completed his BEd (Hons.) and MEd from IER, DU. He has published research articles and book chapters in national and international journals. His primary areas of research and training focus on teacher education, curriculum design and development, underprivileged children's education (Rohingya, sex workers, and transgender children), language education, classroom practice, teaching methods and techniques, assessment and feedback practice, blended learning, ICT in education, educational technology and AI in Education.

Andi Asrifan, S.Pd., M.Pd. is a senior lecturer in the Doctoral Program in English Language Education at the Graduate School of Universitas Negeri Makassar (UNM), Indonesia. With a Doctor of Education in English Language Education, he has demonstrated a consistent commitment to advancing research in English as a Foreign Language (EFL), digital pedagogy, and the integration of artificial intelligence (AI) in language instruction. Dr. Asrifan previously served as Head of the Institute for Cooperation and International Affairs at Universitas Muhammadiyah Sidenreng Rappang and continues to collaborate across academic institutions, both nationally and internationally, actively. Over the past two years, Dr. Asrifan has led several research initiatives focused on AI-driven curriculum development, bilingual education in Southeast Asia, and digital parenting in urban Indonesia. He is frequently invited as a keynote speaker at international conferences and serves as a reviewer and editorial board member for various Scopus-indexed journals. His publications have appeared in high-impact outlets and span the disciplines of education, linguistics, and cultural studies.

Sudhanshu Bhushan is a hospitality professional and academic with over 15 years of experience in food and beverage operations, restaurant management, and hospitality training. He has worked with leading hotel brands including Taj, Ramada, Ibis, Holiday Inn, Park Plaza, and Golden Tulip, gaining deep insight into hotel operations and service quality. He currently works in higher education, where he focuses on practical learning, industry-oriented teaching, and preparing students for real-world hospitality careers. His writing reflects his belief that hospitality education should be simple, practical, and closely connected to industry needs.

Eric Bird has over 25 years of educational experience, both in and out of the classroom, working with children from kindergarten through high school as a teacher and teacher assistant. He is experienced working with students with diverse learning, language, and social-emotional needs. With a certificate of International School Counseling from the Principal Training Center, and a recently completed Master of Arts Counselling Psychology (MACP) degree from Yorkville University, he believes that concept-based inquiry and differentiation are the keys to meeting the needs of diverse classrooms. He excels in providing scaffolded, learner-centered learning programs incorporating a wide range of classroom management and motivational strategies. With experience in Special Education, working with both EFL and English Language Learners, teaching Drama to middle-year students, and supporting high schoolers in their after-school theatre endeavours. Eric has been an asset to the many schools he has worked in. Beginning his career in Victoria BC, Eric spread his wings and taught English in Furukawa, Japan and Taichung, Taiwan. Jakarta, Indonesia, and Manila, Philippines, were his next ports of call, where he received PYP training, taught grade 5, and served as the grade-level coordinator for many years. He returned to Canada in 2019, where he taught briefly in Vancouver and has since returned home to Vancouver Island and the Victoria School District. He is currently working as a teacher on call (TTOC) and hopes to launch his school counselling career in the very near future.

Maria Alice da Silva Brandão is a private English teacher for adults and teenagers, and a book editor. She has 18 years of teaching experience. She holds a Bachelor's degree in Pedagogy from UNIJUÍ (Regional University of

Northwestern Rio Grande do Sul State, Brazil), with international experience in Canada with CELTA (Certificate in Teaching English to Speakers of Other Languages) from Cambridge.

Riyam Chaar holds a doctorate degree in Education Sciences, a master's degree in Educational Management and Leadership, and a bachelor's degree in English Language and Literature. She is licensed to identify and carry out programs for gifted students through certifications from Germany and Connecticut University. With over 20 years of experience in education, she teaches master's level Educational Leadership students at Arkansas State University in Doha and serves as Vice Principal at Heritage International Academy, Qatar. She is also Community Education Manager at Global Studies Institute in Qatar. Her professional work includes accreditation, policy development, teacher training, and community partnerships. She is also the author of several educational book series and an active member of regional and international professional organizations.

Rusudan Chachanidze has been a public school English leader teacher from 2012 year and civic education leader teacher from 2018. She is a head of department of foreign languages at state school Zvare in Kharagauli district, Georgia. In 2007 she gained Bachelor's degree with distinction in Law at Ilia State University. In 2017 she obtained an MA degree in Education specialized in Methods in English language teaching. In 2012 she became a certified English language teacher by passing national exams in English teaching and pedagogy. In 2017 she started her PhD study in Education. In 2018 she became a certified teacher in civic education by passing the relevant national exam. In 2019 she got the status of a teacher leader in English and Civic Education by assessment of the Georgian Teachers National House. In 2019 and 2020 she worked in Teachers' National House of Georgia as an assessor of English Mentor teachers for Imereti Region. Currently, she is a head of foreign language department in a public school.

Gladys Jebet Cheserem is a Kenyan, teacher by profession, with a BED Arts History/CRE option, with a 6 years teaching experience, 3 years in Secondary School and 3 years in Junior Secondary School,(has experienced the transition of Kenyan education from 8-4-4 to the CBE model)she is an activist under the Kenyan Peasants League Movement(KPL) advocating for Agroecology and Food Sovereignity, Peasants Rights and general rights of citizens(I get self fulfillment when the scales of justice balance to the oppressed:in Kenya and globally)A social media influencer through social media platforms(Find me as Gladys Cheserem or Cheserem Gladys in all my platforms) and an upcoming artist(Gospel: to tell the beautiful story of Jesus)

Marvin Espinoza, Ed.D., is an educational leader, scholar, and nonprofit executive with more than 25 years of experience in higher education and community-based organizations. He serves as Assistant Professor at East Los Angeles College, where he has taught for approximately two decades in both in-person and online modalities. In addition, he is the Chief Operating Officer of the Girls Club of Los Angeles, a nonprofit organization serving children, youth, and families in South Los Angeles, where he oversees strategic operations aligned with mission-driven community impact. Dr. Espinoza earned his Doctor of Education in Educational Leadership with a specialization in community college and higher education from California State University, San Bernardino, where he received the Outstanding Doctoral Award. His dissertation, Legacy of Learning: The Journey of Males of Color and the Sustaining Power of Community Cultural Wealth, examines how first-generation African American and Latino/Latinx males navigate educational pathways by drawing on forms of community cultural wealth. He also holds a Master of Arts in Education, a Bachelor of Arts in Liberal Studies and Child Development from California State University, Dominguez Hills, and an Associate of Arts in Child Development from Los Angeles Southwest College. His scholarship and professional work focus on educational equity, community cultural wealth, youth development, strategic planning, and systemic change in community college and nonprofit contexts. Dr. Espinoza's leadership has been recognized by the City and County of Los Angeles and the Los Angeles Unified School District. His research and practice are centered on advancing equitable educational access and strengthening institutional capacity to support historically underserved communities.

Arooj Farooqi is a seasoned educator, teacher trainer, and language assessment professional with extensive experience across English as a Second Language (ESL), English for Academic Purposes (EAP/EAL), Language Instruction for Newcomers to Canada (LINC), IELTS, CELPIP, IESOL, and secondary education in Canada and international contexts. She holds the Ontario Certified English Language Teacher (OCELT) designation from TESL Ontario, along with the International Certificate in Teaching English as an Additional Language (ICTEAL) and Post TESL Certificate Training (PTCT), reflecting advanced expertise in adult English teaching and instruction. Her professional qualifications are further supported by CELTA and specialised training in CELPIP and CAEL instruction. She also holds certification in Avenue Stages 3 and 4, demonstrating expertise in online instructional delivery and curriculum design within the LINC framework. She has also acquired the Advanced Avenue Learning Leadership course and received PTCT for the same. Arooj holds a Master of Education in Educational Leadership & Policy, and a Master of Arts in Applied Linguistics and English Literature, alongside a Postgraduate Diploma in TEFL and Advanced TESL qualifications. She is working as a University Pathway Instructor with iLAC, Toronto, in a permanent position for the past five years. Arooj has recently returned from China, where she was employed by Dalhousie University, Canada, as a Quality Assurance and Academic Integrity Officer for the English Department and an EAP Instructor for Architecture students. She is also an IESOL Examiner/Moderator in the UK. Her experience also includes leadership roles in Program Directors, Director of English Programs, Program development, teacher training, curriculum design, and project management across institutions in Canada Arooj contributes to the sector through leadership and governance. She serves as Vice Chair of the Board of Directors for a respected language school in Canada, contributing strategic leadership and governance to advance excellence in adult English language education across Canada, and is an active presenter at post-secondary institutions in Canada, conferences and webinars in Canada and around the globe. Her professional practice integrates assessment literacy, digital pedagogy, and teacher development, reflecting a strong commitment to quality, equity, and innovation in language education.

Dewi Furwana is a lecturer in the English Education Study Program at the Faculty of Tarbiyah and Teacher Training, UIN Palopo, Indonesia. She specializes in teaching listening, grammar, vocabulary, and English for Specific Purposes (ESP), with a strong commitment to improving students' communicative competence and academic performance. Her research interests include English Language Teaching (ELT), instructional materials development, digital learning, and ESP. She has actively participated in various research projects funded by institutional grants and has published her work in reputable national and international journals. Her scholarly contributions also extend to several books and book chapters that address contemporary issues in language education. In addition to her academic and research activities, she regularly participates in international conferences and community engagement programs. She is also an active member of professional organizations related to English language teaching, contributing to the advancement of the field.

Tatiana Gkatsa is a member of the teaching and laboratory staff at the Department of Primary Education, University of Ioannina, Greece, specializing in School Psychology. Her academic and research interests focus on mental health, psychosocial resilience, school bullying, and educational interventions for children and adolescents. She has contributed extensively to the field through books, academic book chapters, and numerous peer-reviewed journal articles. She also serves as an International Doctoral Supervisor at the University of the Black Sea, is an external scientific collaborator at the European University of Cyprus and the Hellenic Open University, and is a research associate at a research institute in the United States.

Ruhan Güçlü is an associate professor at the Department of English Language and Literature, Gaziantep University, Türkiye. She holds a BA, an MA, and a PhD in English Linguistics from Hacettepe University. Her research interests include stylistics, discourse analysis, metadiscourse, cognitive linguistics, and sociolinguistics. She has published several papers on discourse-oriented approaches to literary and non-literary texts.

Richard Guez is a Mathematics and Science teacher at Gelinas Middle School in New York. He teaches 6th-grade students (11–12 year-olds). Richard holds a Bachelor of Education from St. Joseph's University, a master's degree from SUNY Stony Brook, and a diploma from GreenTree, an extensive ecology program. He has taught for the Three Village Central School District in Setauket, NY, for 31 years. He co-authored a published study on Learning Styles and Parent Perceptions. He has been involved in the arts, from lighting and sound to stage crew at the Middle School (20 years) and the elementary school (15 years). He has developed and administered professional learning courses including generating teacher-led parent presentations. He has volunteered on the board of the TKO Strong Foundation for eleven years; a grassroots charity that funds international research into a rare childhood disease. Richard is an NYSUT and NYSTRS-elected representative for teachers in his union and also serves as its Grievance Chairperson (27 yrs.). Additionally, he has served on his district's Budget Advisory, Curriculum Development, Technology, and Professional Relations Committees.

Huda Fadhil Ismaeel is an Assistant Professor of English Language and Linguistics at the University of Mosul, where she has been a dedicated faculty member since 1993. Specializing in Discourse Analysis and Pragmatics, her diverse research interests include Semiotics, Ecolinguistics, and Language Teaching, with a prolific publication record spanning topics from visual discourse in Iraqi graffiti to environmental awareness in children's drawings and distance learning during COVID-19. She holds both a Ph.D. (2008) and a Master's degree (1998) from the University of Mosul, achieving high academic standing in her focus areas of semantics and pragmatics. As an expert in her field, she actively supervises MA and PhD candidates, serves as a linguistic evaluator for dissertations, and acts as a reviewer for Scopus-indexed journals. A frequent participant in international research conferences, such as IRCEELT in Georgia, her recent 2024 and 2025 contributions to the Journal of Ecohumanism and the International Journal of Arabic-English Studies highlight her ongoing commitment to advancing multimodal and socio-linguistic scholarship.

Konstantinos Haskis is a school principal and classical philologist with extensive academic and professional experience in both secondary education and classical studies. He completed his undergraduate studies at the University of Ioannina, Greece – Philology of Ioannina, Department of Classics -, and pursued postgraduate studies in Ancient Comedy at Royal Holloway, University of London. He earned his PhD at the University of Ioannina, Department of Classical Philology, with a dissertation entitled 'Mythical Fragments: Myth in the Minor Tragedians of the 5th and 4th centuries BC', addressing both mythological reconstruction and philological challenges. He is presently conducting postdoctoral research at the National and Kapodistrian University of Athens, undertaking a comparative philological study of comic and tragic fragments. He has served as a teacher and is currently leading a secondary school as principal, where he is committed to fostering inclusive learning environments, advancing pedagogical innovation, and promoting the intellectual and personal development of students. His work seeks to integrate rigorous scholarship with practical educational leadership, bridging research and classroom practice.

Kerry Huke has worked in Victorian Government schools since 2009. Holding a Bachelor's Degree in Fine Arts, a Postgraduate Certificate in Careers Education, and a Graduate Diploma of Secondary Education, she has gained experience across both special education settings and mainstream secondary schools. Kerry is dedicated to supporting students in achieving their individual goals—whether their aspirations lie in classroom learning, pursuing further study, or engaging in more vocational pathways.

Vildan İnci Kavak is an assistant professor at Gaziantep Islam Science and Technology University in Türkiye and a visiting scholar at Khoja Akhmet Yassawi International Kazakh-Turkish University. She is the former managing director of the School of Foreign Languages. She received her BA and MA degrees in ELT from Muğla Sıtkı Koçman University and completed her PhD in ELT at Çukurova University. She studied for the Cambridge DELTA at Leeds Metropolitan University (Beckett) in England. She published articles in many prestigious journals and authored many book chapters for international publishers. Her research interests include bilingualism, Conversation Analysis, translanguaging theory, teacher professional development, first and second language acquisition, and teaching English to young learners.

Hanul Jang is an elementary school teacher in South Korea and a doctoral candidate in Practical Arts Education at Korea National University of Education. She earned her master's degree in Practical Arts Education and has conducted research on digital literacy, educational technology, and teacher professionalism. Her academic interests focus on AI education, digital literacy, practical arts education. She is currently teaching at Seoseon Elementary School and has also served as an instructor for the regional English Gifted Class at Andong Songhyeon Elementary School (2021–2025). Her dedication to innovative teaching has been recognized with several awards, including the Superintendent's

Commendation for Excellence in Online Teaching (2021), the Grand Prize at the Hellomaple Research Association Teaching Contest (2024), the Best Award at the 14th Creative Teaching Practices Contest (2024), and others. Her publications include research papers and books such as Development of Experiential Task Activities in Practical Arts Education and Educational Needs of Elementary Teachers, Understanding and Practice of Experiential Practical Arts Education, The Effects of an Invention Education Program Using 3D Modeling on Elementary Students' Technical Creativity and Interest, and Learning Artificial Intelligence (AI) with RoboMaster EP/EP CORE.

Yeonjung Kim is an elementary school teacher in South Korea and hold a Ph.D. in Practical Arts Education from Korea National University of Education. She earned her doctoral degree with a focus on Practical Arts Education and conducted research on elementary school food and clothing education as well as teacher agency. Her academic interests include Practical Arts Education, teacher agency, teacher education, home economics education, and multicultural education.

Fabiana Diniz Kurtz is a Professor at the Universidade Regional do Noroeste do Estado do Rio Grande do Sul (Regional University of Northwestern Rio Grande do Sul State - UNIJUÍ), Brazil. She holds a Ph.D. in Education in Sciences from UNIJUÍ, with a doctoral internship at the University of Lisbon (Ph.D. Program in ICT in Education, Coordination for the Improvement of Higher Education Personnel – CAPES - scholarship), and a Postdoctoral Fellowship in Scientific and Technological Education at URI Santo Ângelo. In 2024, she completed a Teaching Mobility at Liepaja University, Latvia, through the Erasmus+ Program, and she is currently a Fulbright Visiting Researcher (2025–2026). She coordinates the PIBID English Program and the research group Mongaba: Education, Languages, and Technology. Her academic work focuses on teacher education, curriculum and digital technologies, Applied Linguistics, English for Academic Purposes, and the integration of AI and computational thinking in education.

Manal Mostapha is an English language teacher and Coordinator at Heritage International Academy, Qatar. Manal graduated from Beirut Arab University in 2005. Manal began her professional career in 2005, at Omar Primary 2 School for Boys. Manal is a dedicated, well-organized teacher. She is committed to fostering student academic and social growth. Manal believes that every student can succeed through personalized, and engaging instructions. Manal has taught different levels, from grade 3 to 12 and has an over 20 years of experience. For Manal, teaching is a learning and self-discovery career.

Lori Nichols is a Visual and Performing arts teacher at Sunbury and Macedon Ranges Specialist School. She teaches students from age 5 through to 18 years. Lori has a Bachelor of Education from Australian Catholic University, a Diploma in Auslan from Kangan Batman Tafe and a Diploma of Interpreting from RMIT (Royal Melbourne Institute of Technology. She has been involved in the arts from the age 3, performing on stage as a dancer and actor, worked as an extra on a few TV sows and features in the Documentary "This is Going To Be Big" directed by Thomas Charles Hyland, produced by Truce Films, ABC, Screen Vic, Screen Australia and Netflix.

Sylwia Niewczas, Ph.D. employed at the Department of Applied Linguistics, John Paul II Catholic University of Lublin (KUL). She has been teaching English Philology and Linguistics courses at KUL since 2022. She has over fourteen years of experience as an English language instructor at various educational levels in Poland and abroad. Her research interests include English language teaching to adults and older learners, the role of positive psychology in education, bilingualism, and teaching neurodivergent students.

Sibhekinkosi Anna Nkomo is a lecturer in the Foundation Phase Division in the School of Education, University of the Witwatersrand, South Africa. She is an early literacy specialist and an advocate of quality education, particularly with respect to children in disadvantaged communities, as a way of addressing the existing educational inequalities through implementing reading interventions. Her research interests broadly include literacy, emergent literacy development in third spaces, bi/multilingual education, multiculturalism, multi-literacies, and multi-modality, as she views language and literacy as a social practice. She has published several research articles, book chapters, and research reports in these research areas. She has a best publication award (2018) from the Reading and Writing journal for her research article titled Grade 3 learners' imagined identities as readers revealed through their drawings. She is also a recipient of the W.K. Kellogg Foundation Southern African Scholarship and a member of the South African Human Rights Commission Section 11 committee on the Right to Read and Write.

Izabela Olszak, Ph.D., is an Assistant Professor at the Department of Applied Linguistics, John Paul II Catholic University of Lublin (KUL), Poland. Academic expertise includes Computer-Assisted Language Learning (CALL), EFL didactics, bilingual and trilingual education, inclusive language teaching, and intercultural communication. Research interests focus on second language acquisition, learning strategies, and the psychological and sociological dimensions of language education. Author and co-author of scholarly publications, including "AI, will you help?" How learners use Artificial Intelligence when writing (XLinguae), Artificial Intelligence Tools in Academic Writing Instruction (Roczniki Humanistyczne, KUL), and On Reading in Trilingual Learners (Peter Lang). Member of the review team for the journal Humanities and Social Sciences and the International Research Group "English as a Foreign Language for Deaf and Hard-of-Hearing Persons (EFL DHH)", with active involvement in inclusive language education research.

Muazu Omeji is a Doctor of Physical Education, Human Relations Manager at Nigerian Tulip International College (NTIC), Abuja, Nigeria. He worked as Examinations Officer at Nigerian Tulip International Colleges in Abuja from February to September 2005, as Vice Principal of Nigerian Turkish International College (NTIC) between 2008 and 2016, Principal at the same college between 2016 and 2020. His qualifications include: Bachelor of Science in Education (Mathematics) in 1999, MSc. In 2005, and PhD in Mathematics Education in 2025. He has been teaching in various schools for 24 years.

Akhilesh Pandey is a distinguished academic and researcher in the field of hospitality and tourism management. Currently serving as Professor at School of Hospitality Management & Tourism in Galgotias University, Dr. Pandey has over 18 years of teaching, research, and consulting experience in hospitality operations, sustainable tourism, and service innovation. Dr. Pandey has published extensively in peer-reviewed journals, contributed chapters to edited volumes, and presented at international conferences organized by leading bodies. Their research interests include sustainable tourism development, digital transformation in hospitality, customer experience management, and the integration of emerging technologies such as AI and blockchain into service delivery. In addition to academic contributions, Dr. Pandey has collaborated with industry stakeholders on projects related to eco-tourism, destination branding, and post-pandemic recovery strategies. They have served as a reviewer and editorial board member for several international journals, demonstrating strong editorial expertise. Through this proposed volume, Dr. Pandey aims to bring together global perspectives and innovative practices to advance scholarship and industry knowledge in hospitality and tourism.

Panagiota Papanikolaou is a primary education teacher with over 22 years of classroom teaching experience. Since 2024, she has been serving as the Principal of a public primary school. She holds a PhD in Philosophy of Education and a Master's Degree in Social Sciences and Education. Additionally, she has earned a second degree from the Department of Philosophy, Pedagogy, and Psychology, specializing in Psychology. She actively participates in innovative educational programs and European initiatives such as Erasmus+, Teachers4Europe (T4E), and the Role Models program of the State Scholarships Foundation (IKY). She also serves as a speaker at conferences and seminars on topics related to literature, educational activities outside the school environment, and the prevention of school bullying. She is proficient in English and French and has received training in the use of new technologies in education. She collaborates with the Institute of Educational Policy (IEP) on the evaluation of the Multiple Textbook Program.

Linda Parish has been a lecturer and researcher in mathematics education at Australian Catholic University (ACU) for the past 18 years. She has a background in Primary (Elementary) School teaching and teaching General Education: Literacy and Numeracy to "at-risk" youth at TAFE (an Australian government-run system that provides vocational education beyond compulsory Secondary School). Her passion is for students who don't fit mainstream expectations – both those who struggle to learn, and those who learn quicker than most. Her PhD focused on identifying and understanding the specific learning needs of mathematically gifted students and how and why classroom teachers need to support these students.

Harman Qarani is a Sociology and AP Psychology instructor at RISE (Ronaki International School, Erbil, Iraqi Kurdistan). He is currently pursuing a Master's degree in applied linguistics. Over the past eight years at RISE, he has demonstrated a strong commitment to teaching and professional growth, completing multiple accredited pedagogy and professional development programs. His academic background includes a Bachelor's degree in English Language Teaching from the Faculty of Education at Tishk University, Iraqi Kurdistan.

R. Bhuvaneswari working as an Assistant Professor of English at Dr.Mahalingam College of Engineering and Technology, Pollachi. To her credit she completed 10 NPTEL / SWAYAM and published few articles in Scopus indexed journals.

R. Velmurugan is presently working as a Professor in the Department of Commerce at Karpagam Academy of Higher Education, Coimbatore. He began his career as a Project Fellow under a UGC-sponsored Major Research Project at NGM College, Pollachi. He has 19 years of teaching experience and 15 years of research experience. To his credit, he has successfully supervised 25 Ph.D. scholars and 5 M.Phil. scholars. At present, two scholars have submitted their theses, and six Ph.D. scholars are pursuing their research under his guidance. He has published 168 research articles in various international journals, of which 137 are in Scopus-indexed journals, 15 in Web of Science journals, and 76 in edited volumes. He has also participated in and presented 27 papers in international seminars/conferences and 154 papers in national seminars/conferences. He has served as an external examiner for numerous M.Phil. and Ph.D. viva voce examinations. He has been a Vice-Chancellor's nominee for Doctoral Committee meetings at Bharathiar University, Coimbatore, and Periyar University, Salem. He has also served as Chairperson at various national-level conferences. Furthermore, he has contributed as an expert in Syllabus Scrutiny Committees, Question Paper Scrutiny Committees, and Boards of Studies at several reputed colleges. In recognition of his meritorious contributions, he has received awards such as Best Paper Presenter, Best Research Supervisor, and Best Faculty Award from various research foundations and councils. He has also served as a resource person for 27 guest lectures, 30 workshops, and 10 faculty development programmes.

S. Senthilkumar working as an Associate Professor, Department of Finance and Management Skyline University, Nigeria. To his credit he produced more Ph.D. Research scholars and published more number of articles in national and international journals.

Schavana Suelin Schreiber is a professor and coordinator at erviço Nacional de Aprendizagem Comercial - SENAC RS, Brazil, working in the field of languages education. She holds a Bachelor's degree in Portuguese and English Languages from the Regional University of Northwestern Rio Grande do Sul State (UNIJUÍ) and a postgraduate degree in School Management and Neuropsychopedagogy. She has international experience in Canada, where she studied English as a Second Language, and in Poland, where she participated in an academic exchange program at Maria Curie-Skłodowska University (UMCS). Her professional background reflects a strong commitment to education, intercultural communication, and innovative teaching practices. She teaches English Language and Portuguese as a Foreign Language to students ranging from early childhood to older adults, fostering meaningful learning experiences through creativity, and a learner-centered approach.

Himanshu Sharma is a Professor in the School of Hospitality Management at Galgotias University, Greater Noida, Uttar Pradesh, India. He holds a Master's degree in Tourism Management and is currently pursuing a Ph.D. in Management. With over two decades of academic and industry experience, his expertise includes hospitality operations, tourism management, personality development, and service quality. He has published book chapters and research papers in reputed edited volumes and actively contributes to curriculum development, faculty training, and academic mentoring in hospitality and tourism education.

Jonathan Shaw is an educational developer in the Studio for Teaching and Learning at Saint Mary's University in Halifax, Canada, and a part-time instructor in the Faculty of Education at the same university. He is also a doctoral student in Education Sciences at the International Black Sea University in Tbilisi, Georgia. He studied at Saint Mary's University, University of King's College, and Mount Saint Vincent University. His doctoral research investigates the teaching of critical thinking in university classrooms and the extent to which it is hampered by a failure to address foundational epistemological and teleological questions. His other research interests include the metastasis of ideological dogma and pedagogical trends among educators, which he argues occur when we fail to give critical thinking (meaning goal-directed, rational, and evidence-based belief formation, judgement, and decision-making) a superordinate position within our hierarchy of educational goals.

J. Sudarvel working as an Assistant Professor of Management at Karpagam Academy of Higher Education. He produced five Ph.D. Scholars and four Ph.D. Scholars are under his guidance. Further, to his credit he published 51 articles in Scopus indexed journals and published more than 50 articles in international journals. He is acting as a Subject Experts in Board of studies of various autonomous colleges.

Shamal Taher is a dedicated educator and linguistics professional based in Duhok, within the Kurdistan Region of Iraq (KRI). He holds a Master of Arts in Linguistics, a credential that provides him with a deep theoretical understanding of language structure and acquisition. Currently, Shamal applies his expertise as an English teacher at Trba Spi Primary School, where he helps young learners build a strong foundational command of the language. His academic background allows him to bridge the gap between complex linguistic theories and practical classroom instruction tailored for children.

Małgorzata Tetiurka is a specialist in foreign language education at the Lubelskie Samorządowe Centrum Doskonalenia Nauczycieli (LSCDN) in Lublin, Poland. She supports language teachers through professional development programs, workshops, and conferences, providing practical resources and guidance for teaching English and other foreign languages. Małgorzata has contributed to various educational publications and initiatives aimed at enhancing teaching practices and promoting continuous learning for educators in the region

Eka Tkavashvili is a Doctor in Education, an Associate Professor at the Faculty of Business, Technology and Education at Ilia State University, Tbilisi, Georgia. Her academic interests include general school and higher education pedagogy, English language didactics, intercultural dialogue, and teacher professional development. She graduated with honors from the Tbilisi Ilia Chavchavadze Pedagogical Institute of Foreign Languages in 1991, majoring in English and qualifying as an English teacher. In 1996, she completed a postgraduate program at the Tbilisi Ilia Chavchavadze State Institute of Western Languages and Cultures, specializing in English didactics. In 2022, she earned a Doctor of Philosophy in Education. Dr. Tkavashvili has received research grants from universities in Germany, Austria, Israel, and Estonia and has been affiliated with the Innovative Education Research Center of Ilia State University since 2019. She is the author of several scientific articles and methodological manuals for English language teachers, including a methodological manual developed under the supervision of the British Council Georgia, and wrote all ELT modules for the Teacher Certification Program at Ilia State University. She also serves as a trainer-consultant for the National Center for Teacher Professional Development and as an evaluator for the National Center for Evaluation and Examinations. A recipient of the Hornby Scholarship, she studied in Cambridge and obtained the Certificate of Trainer of Trainers of English Language Teachers.

Caroline Tomossian holds a bachelor's degree in English literature and is a dedicated teacher and coordinator with over 10 years of experience in the field of education at a private school in Qatar. Throughout her teaching journey, she has worked with students of various age groups and diverse learning needs, helping them develop strong communication skills with a focus on speaking and writing. Her approach includes engaging lessons, interactive activities, and simplified tasks to support all students' needs in reaching their full potential. Believing that every student is capable of success, she is committed to creating an inclusive and supportive learning environment where each learner feels valued. She is an EpoC certified in identifying gifted students and has led different school clubs, support classes, and public speaking sessions, as well as directed school plays to enhance students' confidence. Beyond the classroom, she enjoys reading and continuously seeking opportunities for personal and professional growth.

Alejandra Villa has over 15 years of professional experience in education, having worked in private, bilingual school contexts in a range of roles including substitute teacher, teaching assistant, homeroom teacher, team leader, and teacher librarian. She holds an MSc in Educational Science from the State University of New York at Buffalo, US a Bachelor's degree in Education, and university studies in advertising and merchandising, bringing an interdisciplinary perspective to her professional practice.

Omar Wardere is a dedicated science educator whose teaching career began shortly after completing his Bachelor of Science in Microbiology in 2009. That same year, he accepted his first teaching position at Centennial College HP Campus, where he taught microbiology labs from 2009 to 2012. This early experience revealed his passion for teaching and the joy he found in helping students connect with science. In 2014, Omar took his first overseas teaching position at Al Ruya Bilingual School in Kuwait. Over the next four years (2014–2018), he taught a wide range of science courses from early middle school up to grade 12, gaining valuable experience across multiple age groups and curriculum levels. In 2018, he joined Hayat Universal Bilingual School, where he taught middle school science until 2024 and further refined his instructional practice and classroom leadership. During his career, Omar continued to advance professionally, earning his master's degree in Educational Leadership from SUNY Buffalo in 2018 and his teaching license from Moreland University in 2024. He is currently an MYP science teacher at the American International School of Kuwait, an IB school that aligns with his passion for inquiry-driven, holistic, and student-centered learning. With over a decade of teaching experience across diverse educational settings, Omar remains committed to inspiring curiosity, critical thinking, and a love of science in every student he teaches.

Martin Yahuma is a dedicated educator with a profound passion for shaping young minds. Holding a Bachelor's degree in Education Arts, with a focus on English and Literature, he has honed his craft over a decade of teaching experience. As a mentor to young men at Kabarnet High School in Baringo County, Martin's impact extends beyond the classroom. He employs a personalized approach, leveraging his "He methodology" to cater to individual learners' needs, fostering a nurturing environment where students thrive. Beyond academics, Martin is the driving force behind the school's handball team, coaching with enthusiasm and expertise. His commitment to holistic development has earned him a revered place among students and peers alike. Through his work, Martin embodies a dedication to empowering the next generation, making a lasting impact on the lives of those he touches.

Reginald O. York, PhD, is Adjunct Professor in the School of Social Work at the University of North Carolina Wilmington. Previously, he served on the social work faculties of East Carolina University and the University of North Carolina Chapel Hill. He is the author of Human Service Planning (The University of North Carolina Press, 1982), Building Basic Competencies in Social Work Research (Allyn and Bacon, 1997), Conducting Social Work Research (Allyn and Bacon, 1998), Evaluating Social Work Practice (Pearson, 2009), and Statistics for Human Service Evaluation (Sage Publications, 2017). Prior to his entry into academia, he served as a foster care social worker, a child protective services supervisor, and the director of two human service organizations. His research interests include evidence-based practice, social work education, and human service management.

Bhekuyise Zungu is a lecturer in the School of Education at the University of the Witwatersrand (Wits), Johannesburg. He completed his undergraduate studies in the United States, where he also earned two master's degrees before returning to South Africa to join Wits as a lecturer. While teaching and engaging in student-affairs initiatives, he pursued and completed his PhD at the same institution. Dr Zungu's educational journey reflects both resilience and a global perspective. Having experienced the transformative impact of mentorship and opportunity, he is committed to inspiring young people, particularly those from under-resourced or township backgrounds, to dream boldly and strive for academic and personal excellence. Dr Zungu contributes to both the academic and developmental growth of students.

His teaching and mentorship are grounded in a philosophy of empowerment, emphasizing the importance of self-belief, discipline, and community engagement. Beyond the classroom, he plays an active role in student affairs.

Andres Julian Zuñiga has over 20 years of dedicated experience within the Colombian private education sector. His professional journey has been defined by a multidisciplinary approach to learning and innovation. Holding a Master's in Multidisciplinary Studies and a background as an Electronic Engineer, he has navigated a diverse range of roles, from classroom instruction in Mathematics, Computer Science, and Technology to strategic leadership in curriculum design and Maker spaces. Currently serving as an Ed Tech leader and the Lead Mentor for Robotics at the high school level, Andres Julian combines his technical roots with pedagogical expertise to inspire the next generation of creators, shaping the future of digital literacy and hands-on engineering in the classroom.

Index

Symbols

A

B

C

D

E

F

G

H

I

J

L

M

N

O

P

U

V

W

www.ingramcontent.com/pod-product-compliance
Lightning Source LLC
LaVergne TN
LVHW081252011026
849162LV00007BA/1573